Painting by W. J. Aylward

THE "CHESAPEAKE'S" MIZZENTOP DURING THE BATTLE

HARPER'S ENCYCLOPAEDIA OF UNITED STATES HISTORY

FROM 458 A.D. TO 1915

NEW EDITION. ENTIRELY REVISED AND ENLARGED

BASED UPON THE PLAN OF

BENSON JOHN LOSSING, LL.D.

SOMETIME EDITOR OF "THE AMERICAN HISTORICAL RECORD" AND AUTHOR OF "THE PICTORIAL FIELD-BOOK OF THE REVOLUTION" "THE PICTORIAL FIELD-BOOK OF THE WAR OF 1812" ETC.

WITH SPECIAL CONTRIBUTIONS
COVERING EVERY PHASE OF AMERICAN HISTORY AND DEVELOPMENT
BY EMINENT AUTHORITIES, INCLUDING

JOHN FISKE
THE AMERICAN HISTORIAN

WOODROW WILSON, Ph.D., LL.D.
FORMER PRESIDENT OF PRINCETON UNIVERSITY

WM. R. HARPER, Ph.D., LL.D., D.D.
PRESIDENT OF THE UNIV. OF CHICAGO

GOLDWIN SMITH, D.C.L., LL.D.
PROF. OF HISTORY UNIV. OF TORONTO

ALBERT BUSHNELL HART, Ph.D.
PROF. OF HISTORY AT HARVARD

MOSES COIT TYLER, LL.D.
PROF. OF HISTORY AT CORNELL

ALFRED T. MAHAN, D.C.L., LL.D.
ADMIRAL UNITED STATES NAVY

EDWARD G. BOURNE, Ph.D.
PROF. OF HISTORY AT YALE

JOHN FRYER, A.M., LL.D.
PROF. OF LIT. AT UNIV. OF CALIF.

R. J. H. GOTTHEIL, Ph.D.
PROF. SEMITIC LANGUAGES, COLUMBIA

WM. T. HARRIS, Ph.D., LL.D.
U. S. COMMISSIONER OF EDUCATION

JOHN B. MOORE
PROF INTERN'L LAW, COLUMBIA

ETC., ETC., ETC.

WITH A PREFACE ON THE STUDY OF AMERICAN HISTORY BY

WOODROW WILSON, PH.D., LL.D.

AUTHOR OF
"A HISTORY OF THE AMERICAN PEOPLE" ETC.

SIXTEEN ILLUSTRATIONS IN COLOR. ORIGINAL
DOCUMENTS, PORTRAITS, MAPS, PLANS, ETC.
COMPLETE IN TEN VOLUMES.

VOL II.

HARPER & BROTHERS PUBLISHERS
NEW YORK AND LONDON

Republished by Gale Research Company, Book Tower, Detroit, 1974

Library of Congress Cataloging in Publication Data

Lossing, Benson John, 1813-1891.
Harper's encyclopedia of United States history; from 458 A.D. to 1915.

Reprint of the 1915 ed.
1. United States--History--Dictionaries. I. Wilson, Woodrow, Pres. U.S., 1856-1924. II. Title. III. Title: Encyclopedia of United States History.
E174.L92 1974 917.3'03'03 73-22093
ISBN 0-8103-3954-4

LIST OF PLATES

MAPS IN COLOR

Copyright by C. M. Bell

Grover Cleveland

HARPERS' ENCYCLOPÆDIA
OF
UNITED STATES HISTORY

C.

Cabell, James Laurence, sanitarian; born in Nelson county, Va., Aug. 26, 1813; graduated at the University of Virginia in 1833; studied medicine in Baltimore, Philadelphia, and Paris; and became Professor of Anatomy and Surgery in the University of Virginia. He was in charge of the Confederate military hospitals during the Civil War. When yellow fever broke out at Memphis he was appointed chairman of the National Sanitary Conference, and devised the plan which checked the spread of the epidemic. From 1879 till the time of his death, which occurred in Overton, Va., Aug. 13, 1889, he was president of the National Board of Health.

Cabell, Samuel Jordan, military officer; born in Amherst county, Va., Dec. 15, 1756; was educated at William and Mary College. In 1775 he recruited a company of riflemen for the American service, which is said to have opened the action at Saratoga. During the siege of Charleston he was captured, and not being able to procure an exchange remained inactive till peace was concluded. He was a Representative in Congress in 1785–1803, and in 1788, as a member of the constitutional convention, voted against the adoption of the proposed national Constitution. He died Aug. 4, 1818.

Cabell, William, statesman; born in Licking Hole, Va., March 13, 1730; was a commissioner to arrange military claims in 1758. During the trouble between the American colonies and Great Britain, prior to the Revolutionary War, he was a delegate to all the conventions for securing independence; was also a member of the committee which drew up the famous "declaration of rights." On Jan. 7, 1789, he was one of the Presidential electors who voted for Washington as the first President of the United States. He died in Union Hill, March 23, 1798.

Cabet, Etienne, communist; born in Dijon, France, in 1788; studied law, but applied himself to literature and politics. In 1840 he attracted much attention through his social romance, *Voyage en Icarie,* in which he described a communistic Utopia. In 1848 he sent an Icarian colony to the Red River in Texas, but the colony did not thrive; and in 1850, as the leader of another colony, he settled in Nauvoo, Ill., whence the Mormons had been expelled. This colony likewise failed to prosper, and was abandoned in 1857 He died in St. Louis, Mo., Nov. 9, 1856.

CABEZA DE VACA, ALVAR NUÑEZ

Cabeza de Vaca, Alvar Nuñez, Spanish official and author; born in Jerez de la Frontera, Spain, probably in 1490. In 1528 he accompanied the expedition of Narvaez to Florida in the capacity of comptroller and royal treasurer, and he and three others were all of a party who escaped from shipwreck and the natives. These four lived for several years among the Indians, and, escaping, made their way to the Spanish settlements in northern Mexico in the spring of 1536. In the following year Cabeza de Vaca returned to Spain; in 1540 was appointed governor of Paraguay; in 1543 explored the upper Paraguay River, and in 1544 was deposed by the colonists and afterwards imprisoned and sent to Spain. After trial he was sentenced to be banished to Africa, but was subsequently recalled, granted many favors by the King, and was made judge of the Supreme Court of Seville. He published two works, one relating to his experiences in Florida, and the other to his administration in Paraguay, both of which are of considerable historical value, and have been published in various languages. He died in Seville about 1560.

The Journey Through New Mexico.—The following is his narrative of his journey through New Mexico in 1535–36, from his *Relation:*

We told these people that we desired to go where the sun sets; and they said inhabitants in that direction were remote. We commanded them to send and make known our coming; but they strove to excuse themselves the best they could, the people being their enemies, and they did not wish to go to them. Not daring to disobey, however, they sent two women, one of their own, the other a captive from that people; for the women can negotiate even though there be war. We followed them, and stopped at a place where we agreed to wait. They tarried five days; and the Indians said they could not have found anybody.

We told them to conduct us towards the north; and they answered, as before, that except afar off there were no people in that direction, and nothing to eat, nor could water be found. Notwithstanding all this, we persisted, and said we desired to go in that course. They still tried to excuse themselves in the best manner possible. At this we became offended, and one night I went out to sleep in the woods apart from them; but directly they came to where I was, and remained all night without sleep, talking to me in great fear, telling me how terrified they were, beseeching us to be no longer angry, and said that they would lead us in the direction it was our wish to go, though they knew they should die on the way.

Whilst we still feigned to be displeased lest their fright should leave them, a remarkable circumstance happened, which was that on the same day many of the Indians became ill, and the next day eight men died. Abroad in the country, wheresoever this became known, there was such dread that it seemed as if the inhabitants would die of fear at sight of us. They besought us not to remain angered, nor require that more of them should die. They believed we caused their death by only willing it, when in truth it gave us so much pain that it could not be greater; for, beyond their loss, we feared they might all die, or abandon us of fright, and that other people thenceforward would do the same, seeing what had come to these. We prayed to God, our Lord, to relieve them; and from that time the sick began to get better.

We witnessed one thing with great admiration, that the parents, brothers, and wives of those who died had great sympathy for them in their suffering; but, when dead, they showed no feeling, neither did they weep nor speak among themselves, make any signs, nor dare approach the bodies until we commanded these to be taken to burial.

While we were among these people, which was more than fifteen days, we saw no one speak to another, nor did we see an infant smile: the only one that cried they took off to a distance, and with the sharp teeth of a rat they scratched it from the shoulders down nearly to the end of the legs. Seeing this cruelty, and offended at it, I asked why they did so: they said for chastisement, because the child had wept in my presence. These terrors they imparted to all those who had lately come to know us, that they might give us whatever they had; for they knew we kept nothing, and would relinquish all to them. This people were the most obedient we had found in all the land, the best conditioned, and, in general, comely.

The sick having recovered, and three days having passed since we came to the place, the women whom we sent away returned, and said they had found very few people; nearly all had gone for cattle, being then in the season. We ordered the convalescent to remain and the well to go with us, and that at the end of two days' journey those women should go with two of our number to fetch up the people, and bring them on the road to receive us. Consequently, the next morning the most robust started with us.

At the end of three days' travel we stopped, and the next day Alonzo del Castillo set out with Estevanico, the negro, taking the two women as guides. She that was the captive led them to the river which ran between some ridges, where was a town at which her father lived; and these habitations were the first seen, having the appearance and structure of houses.

Here Castillo and Estevanico arrived, and, after talking with the Indians, Castillo returned at the end of three days to the spot where he had left us, and brought five or six of the peopie. He told us he had found fixed dwellings of civilization, that the inhabitants lived on beans and pumpkins, and that he had seen maize. This news the most of anything delighted us, and for it we gave infinite thanks to our Lord. Castillo told us the negro was coming with all the population to wait for us in the road not far off. Accordingly we left, and, having travelled a league and a half, we met the negro and the people coming to receive us. They gave us beans, many pumpkins, calabashes, blankets of cowhide, and other things. As this people and those who came with us were enemies, and spoke not each other's language, we discharged the latter, giving them what we received, and we departed with the others. Six leagues from there, as the night set in we arrived at the houses, where great festivities were made over us. We remained one day, and the next set out with these Indians. They took us to the settled habitations of others, who lived upon the same food.

From that place onward was another usage. Those who knew of our approach did not come out to receive us on the road as the others had done, but we found them in their houses, and they had made others for our reception. They were all seated with their faces turned to the wall, their heads down, the hair brought before their eyes, and their property placed in a heap in the middle of the house. From this place they began to give us many blankets of skin; and they had nothing they did not bestow. They have the finest persons of any people we saw, of the greatest activity and strength, who best understood us and intelligently answered our inquiries. We called them the Cow nation, because most of the cattle killed are slaughtered in their neighborhood, and along up that river for over 50 leagues they destroy great numbers.

They go entirely naked after the manner of the first we saw. The women are dressed with deer skin, and some few men, mostly the aged, who are incapable of fighting. The country is very populous. We asked how it was they did not plant maize. They answered it was that they might not lose what they should put in the ground; that the rains had failed for two years in succession, and the seasons were so dry the seed had everywhere been taken by the moles, and they could not venture to plant again until after water had fallen copiously. They begged us to tell the sky to rain, and to pray for it, and we said we would do so. We also desired to know whence they got the maize, and they told us from where the sun goes down; there it grew throughout the region, and the nearest was by that path. Since they did not wish to go thither, we asked by what direction we might best proceed, and bade them inform us concerning the way; they said the path was along up by that river towards the north, for otherwise in a journey of seventeen days we should find nothing to eat, except a fruit they call chacan, that is ground between stones, and even then it could with difficulty be eaten for its dryness and pungency — which was true. They showed it to us there, and we could not eat it. They informed us also that, whilst we travelled by the river upward, we should all the way pass through a people that were their enemies, who spoke their tongue, and, though they had nothing to give us to eat, they would receive us with the best good-will, and present us with mantles of cotton, hides, and other articles of their wealth.

Still it appeared to them we ought by no means to take that course.

Doubting what it would be best to do, and which way we should choose for suitableness and support, we remained two days with these Indians, who gave us beans and pumpkins for our subsistence. Their method of cooking is so new that for its strangeness I desire to speak of it; thus it may be seen and remarked how curious and diversified are the contrivances and ingenuity of the human family. Not having discovered the use of pipkins, to boil what they would eat, they fill the half of a large calabash with water, and throw on the fire many stones of such as are most convenient and readily take the heat. When hot, they are taken up with tongs of sticks and dropped into the calabash until the water in it boils from the fervor of the stones. Then whatever is to be cooked is put in, and until it is done they continue taking out cooled stones and throwing in hot ones. Thus they boil their food.

Two days being spent while we tarried, we resolved to go in search of the maize. We did not wish to follow the path leading to where the cattle are, because it is towards the north, and for us very circuitous, since we ever held it certain that going towards the sunset we must find what we desired.

Thus we took our way, and traversed all the country until coming out at the South sea. Nor was the dread we had of the sharp hunger through which we should have to pass (as in verity we did, throughout the seventeen days' journey of which the natives spoke) sufficient to hinder us. During all that time, in ascending by the river, they gave us many coverings of cow-hide; but we did not eat of the fruit. Our sustenance each day was about a handful of deer-suet, which we had a long time been used to saving for such trials. Thus we passed the entire journey of seventeen days, and at the close we crossed the river and travelled other seventeen days.

As the sun went down, upon some plains that lie between chains of very great mountains, we found a people who for the third part of the year eat nothing but the powder of straw, and, that being the season when we passed, we also had to eat of it, until reaching permanent habitations, where was abundance of maize brought together. They gave us a large quantity in grain and flour, pumpkins, beans, and shawls of cotton. With all these we loaded our guides, who went back the happiest creatures on earth. We gave thanks to God, our Lord, for having brought us where we had found so much food.

Some houses are of earth, the rest all of cane mats. From this point we marched through more than a hundred leagues of country, and continually found settled domiciles, with plenty of maize and beans. The people gave us many deer and cotton shawls better than those of New Spain, many beads and certain corals found on the South sea, and fine turquoises that come from the North. Indeed, they gave us everything they had. To me they gave five emeralds made into arrow-heads, which they use at their singing and dancing. They appeared to be very precious. I asked whence they got these; and they said the stones were brought from some lofty mountains that stand towards the north, where were populous towns and very large houses, and that they were purchased with plumes and the feathers of parrots.

Among this people the women are treated with more decorum than in any part of the Indias we had visited. They wear a shirt of cotton that falls as low as the knee, and over it half sleeves with skirts reaching to the ground, made of dressed deer skin. It opens in front and is brought close with straps of leather. They soap this with a certain root that cleanses well, by which they are enabled to keep it becomingly. Shoes are worn. The people all came to us that we should touch and bless them, they being very urgent, which we could accomplish only with great labor, for sick and well all wished to go with a benediction.

These Indians ever accompanied us until they delivered us to others; and all held full faith in our coming from heaven. While travelling, we went without food all day until night, and we ate so little as to astonish them. We never felt exhaustion, neither were we in fact at all weary, so inured were we to hardship. We possessed great influence and authority: to preserve both, we seldom talked with them. The negro was in constant conversation; he informed himself about the ways we wished to take, of the towns there were, and the matters we desired to know.

We passed through many and dissimilar tongues. Our Lord granted us favor with the people who spoke them, for they always understood us, and we them. We questioned them, and received their answers by signs, just as if they spoke our language and we theirs; for, although we knew six languages, we could not everywhere avail ourselves of them, there being a thousand differences.

Throughout all these countries the people who were at war immediately made friends, that they might come to meet us, and bring what they possessed. In this way we left all the land at peace, and we taught all the inhabitants by signs, which they understood, that in heaven was a Man we called God, who had created the sky and the earth; him we worshipped and had for our master; that we did what he commanded and from his hand came all good; and would they do as we did, all would be well with them. So ready of apprehension we found them that, could we have had the use of language by which to make ourselves perfectly understood, we should have left them all Christians. Thus much we gave them to understand the best we could. And afterward, when the sun rose, they opened their hands together with loud shouting towards the heavens, and then drew them down all over their bodies. They did the same again when the sun went down. They are a people of good condition and substance, capable in any pursuit.

In the town where the emeralds were presented to us the people gave Dorantes over six hundred open hearts of deer. They ever keep a good supply of them for food, and we called the place Pueblo de los Corazones. It is the entrance into many provinces on the South sea. They who go to look for them, and do not enter there, will be lost. On the coast is no maize: the inhabitants eat the powder of rush and of straw, and fish that is caught in the sea from rafts, not having canoes. With grass and straw the women cover their nudity. They are a timid and dejected people.

We think that near the coast by way of those towns through which we came are more than a thousand leagues of inhabited country, plentiful of subsistence. Three times the year it is planted with maize and beans. Deer are of three kinds; one the size of the young steer of Spain. There are innumerable houses, such as are called bahíos. They have poison from a certain tree the size of the apple. For effect no more is necessary than to pluck the fruit and moisten the arrow with it, or, if there be no fruit, to break a twig and with the milk do the like. The tree is abundant and so deadly that, if the leaves be bruised and steeped in some neighboring water, the deer and other animals drinking it soon burst.

We were in this town three days. A day's journey farther was another town, at which the rain fell heavily while we were there, and the river became so swollen we could not cross it, which detained us fifteen days. In this time Castillo saw the buckle of a sword-belt on the neck of an Indian and stitched to it the nail of a horseshoe. He took them, and we asked the native what they were: he answered that they came from heaven. We questioned him further, as to who had brought them thence: they all responded that certain men who wore beards like us had come from heaven and arrived at that river, bringing horses, lances, and swords, and that they had lanced two Indians. In a manner of the utmost indifference we could feign, we asked them what had become of those men. They answered us that they had gone to sea, putting their lances beneath the water, and going themselves also under the water; afterwards that they were seen on the surface going towards the sunset. For this we gave many thanks to God our Lord. We had before despaired of ever hearing more of Christians. Even yet we were left in great doubt and anxiety, thinking those people were merely persons who had come by sea on discoveries. However, as we had now such exact information, we made greater speed, and, as we advanced on our way, the news of the Christians continually grew. We told the natives that we were going in search of that people, to order them not to kill nor make slaves of them, nor take them from their lands, nor do other injustice. Of this the Indians were very glad.

We passed through many territories and found them all vacant: their inhabitants wandered fleeing among the mountains, without daring to have houses or till the earth for fear of Christians. The sight was one of infinite pain to us, a land very fertile and beautiful, abounding in springs and streams, the hamlets deserted and burned, the people thin and weak, all fleeing or in concealment. As they did not plant, they appeased their keen hunger by eating roots and the bark of trees. We bore a share in the famine along the whole way; for poorly could these unfortunates provide for us, themselves being so reduced they looked as though they would willingly die. They brought shawls of those they had concealed because of the Christians, presenting them to us; and they related how the Christians at other times had come through the land, destroying and burning the towns, carrying away half the men, and all the women and the boys, while those who had been able to escape were wandering about fugitives. We found them so alarmed they dared not remain anywhere. They would not nor could they till the earth, but preferred to die rather than live in dread of such cruel usage as they received. Although these showed themselves greatly delighted with us, we feared that on our arrival among those who held the frontier, and fought against the Christians, they would treat us badly, and revenge upon us the conduct of their enemies; but, when God our Lord was pleased to bring us there, they began to dread and respect us as the others had done, and even somewhat more, at which we no little wondered. Thence it may at once be seen that, to bring all these people to be Christians and to the obedience of the Imperial Majesty, they must be won by kindness, which is a way certain, and no other is.

They took us to a town on the edge of a range of mountains, to which the ascent is over difficult crags. We found many people there collected out of fear of the Christians. They received us well, and presented us all they had. They gave us more than two thousand back-loads of maize, which we gave to the distressed and hungered beings who guided us to that place. The next day we despatched four messengers through the country, as we were accustomed to do, that they should call together all the rest of the Indians at a town distant three days' march. We set out the day after with all the people. The tracks of the Christians and marks where they slept were continually seen. At mid-day we met our messengers, who told us they had found no Indians, that they were roving and hiding in the forests, fleeing that the Christians might not kill nor make them slaves; the night before they had observed the Christians from behind trees, and discovered what they were about, carrying away many people in chains.

Those who came with us were alarmed at this intelligence; some returned to spread the news over the land that the Christians were coming; and many more would have followed, had we not forbidden it and told them to cast aside their fear, when they reassured themselves and were well content. At the time we had Indians with us belonging 100 leagues behind, and we were in no condition to discharge them, that they might return to their homes. To encourage them, we stayed there that night; the day after we marched and slept on the road. The following day those whom we had sent forward as messengers guided us to the place where they had seen Christians. We arrived in the afternoon, and saw at once that they told the truth. We perceived that the persons were mounted, by the stakes to which the horses had been tied.

From this spot, called the river Petutan, to the river to which Diego de Guzman came, we heard of Christians, may be as many as 80 leagues; thence to the town where the rains overtook us, 12 leagues, and that is 12 leagues from the South sea. Throughout this region, wheresoever the mountains extend, we saw clear traces of gold and lead, iron, copper, and other metals. Where the settled habitations are, the climate is hot; even in January the weather is very warm. Thence toward the meridian, the country unoccupied to the North sea is unhappy and sterile. There we underwent great and incredible hunger. Those who inhabit and wander over it are a race of evil inclination and most cruel customs. The people of the fixed residences and those beyond regard silver and gold with indifference, nor can they conceive of any use for them.

When we saw sure signs of Christians, and heard how near we were to them, we gave thanks to God our Lord for having chosen to bring us out of a captivity so melancholy and wretched. The delight we felt let each one conjecture, when he shall remember the length of time we were in that country, the suffering and perils we underwent. That night I entreated my companions that one of them should go back three days' journey after the Christians who were moving about over the country, where we had given assurance of protection. Neither of them received this proposal well, excusing themselves because of weariness and exhaustion; and although either might have done better than I, being more youthful and athletic, yet seeing their unwillingness, the next morning I took the negro with eleven Indians, and, following the Christians by their trail, I travelled 10 leagues, passing three villages, at which they had slept.

The day after I overtook four of them on horseback, who were astonished at the sight of me, so strangely habited as I was, and in company with Indians. They stood staring at me a length of time, so confounded that they neither hailed me nor drew near to make an inquiry. I bade them take me to their chief: accordingly we went together half a league to the place where was Diego de Alcaraz, their captain.

After we had conversed, he stated to me that he was completely undone; he had not been able in a long time to take any Indians; he knew not which way to turn, and his men had well begun to experience hunger and fatigue. I told him of Castillo and Dorantes, who were behind, 10 leagues off, with a multitude that conducted us. He thereupon sent three cavalry to them, with fifty of the Indians who accompanied him. The negro returned to guide them, while I remained. I asked the Christians to give me a certificate of the year, month, and day I arrived there, and of the manner of my coming, which they accordingly did. From this river to the town of the Christians, named San Miguel, within the government of the province called New Galicia, are 30 leagues.

Five days having elapsed, Andrés Dorantes and Alonzo del Castillo arrived with those who had been sent after them. They brought more than six hundred persons of that community, whom the Christians had driven into the forests, and who had wandered in concealment over the land. Those who accompanied us so far had drawn them out, and given them to the Christians, who thereupon dismissed all the others they had brought with them. Upon their coming to where I was, Alcaraz begged that we would summon the people of the towns on the margin of the river, who straggled about under cover of the woods, and order them to fetch us something to eat. This last was unnecessary, the Indians being ever diligent to bring us all they could. Directly we sent our messengers to call them, when there came six hundred souls, bringing us all the maize in their possession. They fetched it in certain pots, closed with clay, which they had concealed in the earth. They brought us whatever else they had; but we, wishing only to have the provision, gave the rest to the Christians, that they might divide among themselves. After this we had many high words with them; for they wished to make slaves of the Indians we brought.

In consequence of the dispute, we left at our departure many bows of Turkish shape we had along with us and many pouches. The five arrows with the points of emerald were forgotten among others, and we lost them. We gave the Christians a store of robes of cowhide and other things we brought. We found it difficult to induce the Indians to return to their dwellings, to feel no apprehension and plant maize. They were willing to do nothing until they had gone with us and delivered us into the hands of other Indians, as had been the custom; for, if they returned without doing so, they were afraid they should die, and, going with us, they feared neither Christians nor lances. Our countrymen became jealous at this, and caused their interpreter to tell the Indians that we were of them, and for a long time we had been lost; that they were the lords of the land who must be obeyed and served, while we were persons of mean condition and small force. The Indians cared little or nothing for what was told them; and conversing among themselves said the Christians lied: that we had come whence the sun rises, and they whence it goes down; we healed the sick, they killed the sound; that we had come naked and barefooted, while they had arrived in clothing and on horses with lances; that we were not covetous of anything, but all that was given to us we directly turned to give, remaining with nothing; that the others had the only purpose to rob whomsoever they found, bestowing nothing on any one.

In this way they spoke of all matters respecting us, which they enhanced by contrast with matters concerning the others, delivering their response through the interpreter of the Spaniards. To other Indians they made this known by means of one among them through whom they understood us. Those who speak that tongue we discriminately call Primahaitu, which is like saying Vasconyados. We found it in use over more than 400 leagues of our travel, without another over that whole extent. Even to the last, I could not convince the Indians that we were of the Christians; and only with great effort and solicitation we got them to go back to their residences. We ordered them to put away apprehension, establish their towns, plant and cultivate the soil.

From abandonment the country had already grown up thickly in trees. It is, no doubt, the best in all these Indias, the most prolific and plenteous in provisions. Three times in the year it is planted. It produces great variety of fruit, has beautiful rivers, with many other good waters. There are ores with clear traces of gold and silver. The people are well disposed: they serve such Christians as are their friends, with great good will. They are comely, much more so than the Mexicans. Indeed, the land needs no circumstance to make it blessed.

The Indians, at taking their leave, told us they would do what we commanded, and would build their towns, if the Christians would suffer them; and this I say and affirm most positively, that, if they have not done so, it is the fault of the Christians.

After we had dismissed the Indians in peace, and thanked them for the toil they had supported with us, the Christians with subtlety sent us on our way under charge of Zeburos, an Alcalde, attended by two men. They took us through forests and solitudes, to hinder us from intercourse with the natives, that we might neither witness nor have knowledge of the act they would commit. It is but an instance of how frequently men are mistaken in their aims; we set about to preserve the liberty of the Indians and thought we had secured it, but the contrary appeared; for the Christians had arranged to go and spring upon those we had sent away in peace and confidence. They executed their plan as they had designed, taking us through the woods, wherein for two days we were lost, without water and without way. Seven of our men died of thirst, and we all thought to have perished. Many friendly to the Christians in their company were unable to reach the place where we got water the second night, until the noon of next day. We travelled 25 leagues, little more or less, and reached a town of friendly Indians. The Alcalde left us there, and went on 3 leagues farther to a town called Culiaçan where was Melchior Diaz, principal Alcalde and Captain of the Province.

The Alcalde Mayor knew of the expedition, and, hearing of our return, he immediately left that night and came to where we were. He wept with us, giving praises to God our Lord for having extended over us so great care. He comforted and entertained us hospitably. In behalf of the governor, Nuño de Guzmân and himself, he tendered all that he had, and the service in his power. He showed much regret for the seizure, and the injustice we had received from Alcaraz and others. We were sure, had he been present, what was done to the Indians and to us would never have occurred.

The night being passed, we set out the next day for Anhacan. The chief Alcalde besought us to tarry there, since by so doing we could be of eminent service to God and your Majesty; the deserted land was without tillage and everywhere badly wasted, the Indians were fleeing and concealing themselves in the thickets, unwilling to occupy their towns; we were to send and call them, commanding them in behalf of God and the King, to return to live in the vales and cultivate the soil.

To us this appeared difficult to effect. We had brought no native of our own, nor of those who accompanied us according to custom, intelligent in these affairs. At last we made the attempt with two captives, brought from that country, who were with the Christians we first overtook. They had seen the people who conducted us, and learned from them the great authority and command we carried and exercised throughout those parts, the wonders we had worked, the sick we had cured, and the many things besides we had done. We ordered that they, with others of the town, should go together to summon the hostile natives among the mountains and of the river Petachan, where we had found the Christians, and say to them they must come to us, that we wished to speak with them. For the protection of the messengers, and as a token to the others of our will, we gave them a gourd of those we were accustomed to bear in our hands, which had been our principal insignia and evidence of rank, and with this they went away.

The Indians were gone seven days, and returned with three chiefs of those revolted among the ridges, who brought with them fifteen men, and presented us beads, turquoises, and feathers. The messengers said they had not found the people of the river where we appeared, the Christians having again made them run away into the mountains. Melchior Diaz told the interpreter to speak to the natives for us; to say to them we came in the name of God, who is in heaven; that we had travelled about the world many years, telling all the people we found that they should believe in God and serve him; for he was the master of all things on the earth, benefiting and rewarding the virtuous, and to the bad giving perpetual punishment of fire; that, when the good die, he takes them to heaven, where none ever die, nor feel cold, nor hunger, nor thirst, nor any inconvenience whatsoever, but the greatest enjoyment possible to conceive; that those who will not believe in him, nor obey his commands, he casts beneath the earth into the company of demons, and into a great fire which is never to go out, but always torment; that, over this, if they desired to be Christians and serve God in the way we required, the Christians would cherish them as brothers and behave towards them very kindly; that we would command they give no offence nor take them from their territories, but be their great friends. If the Indians did not do this, the Christians would treat them very hardly, carrying them away as slaves into other lands.

They answered through the interpreter that they would be true Christians and serve God. Being asked to whom they sacrifice and offer worship, from whom they ask rain for their corn-fields and health for themselves, they answered of a man that is in heaven. We inquired of them his name, and they told us Aguar; and they believed he created the whole world, and the things in it. We returned to question them as to how they knew this; they answered their fathers and grandfathers had told them, that from distant time had come their knowledge, and they knew the rain and all good things were sent to them by him. We told them that the name of him of whom they spoke we called Dios; and if they would call him so, and would worship him as we directed, they would find their welfare. They responded that they well understood, and would do as we said. We ordered them to come down from the mountains in confidence and peace, inhabit the whole country and construct their houses: among these they should build one for God, at its entrance place a cross like that which we had there present; and, when Christians came among them, they should go out to receive them with crosses in their hands, without bows or any arms, and take them to their dwellings, giving of what they have to eat, and the Christians would do them no injury, but be their friends; and the Indians told us they would do as we had commanded.

The Captain having given them shawls and entertained them, they returned, taking the two captives who had been used as emissaries. This occurrence took place before the Notary, in the presence of many witnesses.

As soon as these Indians went back, all those of that province who were friendly to the Christians, and had heard of us, came to visit us, bringing beads and feathers. We commanded them to build churches and put crosses in them: to that time none had been raised; and we made them bring their principal men to be baptized.

Then the Captain made a covenant with God, not to invade nor consent to invasion, nor to enslave any of that country and people, to whom we had guaranteed safety; that this he would enforce and defend until your Majesty and the Governor Nuño de Guzmán, or the Viceroy in your name, should direct what would be most for the service of God and your Highness.

When the children had been baptized, we departed for the town of San Miguel. So soon as we arrived, April 1, 1536, came Indians, who told us many people had come down from the mountains and were living in the vales; that they had made churches and crosses, doing all we had required. Each day we heard how these things were advancing to a full improvement.

Fifteen days of our residence having passed, Alcaraz got back with the Christians from the incursion, and they related to the Captain the manner in which the Indians had come down and peopled the plain; that the towns were inhabited which had been tenantless and deserted, the residents, coming out to receive them with crosses in their hands, had taken them to their houses, giving of what they had, and the Christians had slept among them overnight. They were surprised at a thing so novel; but, as the natives said they had been assured of safety, it was ordered that they should not be harmed, and the Christians took friendly leave of them.

CABINET, PRESIDENT'S

Cabinet, PRESIDENT'S, a body of executive advisers authorized by Congress in the absence of a constitutional provision, and appointed by the President at the beginning of his administration. Unless death, personal considerations, or other circumstances prevent, cabinet officers hold their places throughout the administration. Each cabinet officer is at the head of a department comprising a number of executive bureaus. The chief of the Department of Justice is the Attorney-General of the United States; the chiefs of all other departments are officially called secretaries of the departments. The cabinet of a President of the United States is somewhat similar in its functions to the ministry of a monarchical government; but there are notable differences. As a general thing, members of a ministry have the right to urge or defend any public measure before the supreme legislature of their country, a privilege with which the American cabinet officer has never been invested. While cabinet officers hold their places through an administration or at the pleasure of themselves or the President, and are in no wise affected by any legislation in Congress to which they may be officially opposed, the members of a ministry almost invariably tender their resignations when the supreme legislative body acts adversely to any measure on which the ministry has decided. In the cabinet no one member takes precedence of another, and when the members are assembled in formal conference the President presides. In a ministry the spokesman is the president of the council, and usually the minister for foreign affairs is officially known either as the prime minister or premier. The various cabinet officers receive a salary of $12,000 per annum.

The following is a summary of the organization and the functions of the ten executive departments as they existed in 1912 to 1915:

The Secretary of State has charge of what is known as the State Department. This was created by act of Congress, July 27, 1789, having been in existence, however, at that time for some months, under the name of the Department of Foreign Affairs. The first to fill the office was Thomas Jefferson. The Secretary of State has in his charge all business between our own and other governments. The department conducts the correspondence with our ministers and other agents in foreign countries, and with the representatives of other countries here. All communications

SEAL OF THE STATE DEPARTMENT.

respecting boundary and other treaties are also under the direction of this department. This department also files all acts and proceedings of Congress, and attends to the publication of the same and their distribution throughout the country. No regular annual report is made to Congress concerning the work of this department, but special information is given whenever any unusual event or complication in our foreign relations occurs.

The first Secretary of the Treasury was Alexander Hamilton, who was appointed upon the organization of the department, Sept. 2, 1789. This department has charge of all moneys paid into the Treasury of the United States, also of all disbursements, the auditing of accounts, and

SEAL OF THE TREASURY DEPARTMENT.

the collection of revenue. It also supervises the construction of public buildings and the coinage and printing of money. The marine hospitals of the government are also under its direction, and it controls the regulation and appointments of all custom-houses. The Secretary is obliged to make a full report to Congress, at the opening of each regular session, of the business done by the department during the year, and the existing financial condition of the government. The department has an important bureau of statistics dealing with the foreign and domestic trade of the country. It also supervises the life-saving, revenue-cutter, and the public health and marine hospital branches of the public service.

The War Department dates from Aug. 7,

SEAL OF THE WAR DEPARTMENT.

1789. John Knox was its first Secretary. It has in charge all business growing out of the military affairs of the government, attends to the paying of troops, and furnishing all army supplies; also supervises the erection of forts, and all work of military engineering. The department is divided into a number of important bureaus, the chief officers of which are known as the chief of staff, the adjutant-general, the quartermaster-general, the paymaster-general, the commissary-general, the surgeon-general, the chief engineer, the chief of ordnance, and the chief of insular affairs. The signal service is under the control of this department. It is made the duty of the Secretary of War to report annually to Congress concerning the state of the army, the expenditures of the military appropriations in detail, and

SEAL OF THE DEPARTMENT OF JUSTICE.

all matters concerning the bureaus over which the department has special supervision. This department has also in charge the publication of the official records of the Civil War, an enormous work. All the archives captured from or surrendered by the Confederate government are also in charge of this bureau of records.

The first Attorney-General of the United States, Edmund Randolph, of Virginia, was appointed under act of Congress of Sept. 24, 1789. The Attorney - General is required to act as attorney for the United States in all suits in the Supreme Court; he is also the legal adviser of the President and the heads of departments, and also of the Solicitor of the Treasury. He is further charged with the superintendence of all United States district attorneys and marshals, with the examination of all applications to the President for pardons, and with the transfer of all land purchased by the United States for government buildings, etc. The name, "Department of Justice," by which this division of the cabinet is now largely known, was given to it about 1872.

The Navy Department (1789) was at first included in the War Department, but in 1798 the two branches of the service were separated. Aug. 21, 1842, this department was organized into five bureaus —the bureau of navy-yards and docks; of construction, equipment, and repair; of provisions and clothing; of ordnance and hydrography; of medicine and surgery.

SEAL OF THE DEPARTMENT OF THE INTERIOR.

SEAL OF THE NAVY DEPARTMENT.

To these have since been added bureaus of navigation and of steam engineering. The commandant of the Marine Corps is responsible to the Secretary of the Navy. The department also keeps a library of war records. The Secretary of the Navy has charge of everything connected with the naval service of the government, and the execution of the laws concerning it, and makes annual reports to Congress of the conditions of the department. All instructions to subordinate officers of the navy and to all chiefs of the bureaus emanate from him, while the department supervises the building and repairs of all vessels, docks, and wharves, and enlistment and discipline of sailors, together with all supplies needed by them. The first Secretary of the Navy was Benjamin Stoddert, of Maryland.

The Department of the Interior was created by act of Congress, March 3, 1849. The business of the department is conducted by eight bureaus—viz., bureau of the public lands, pensions, Indian affairs, patents, education, reclamation service, and the geological survey. These different bureaus have charge, under the Secretary, of all matters relating to the sale and survey of the public lands; the adjudication and payment of pensions; the treaties with the Indian tribes of the West; the issue of letters patent to inventors; the collection of statistics on the progress of education, etc. The Secretary of the Interior has also charge of the mining interests of the government, and of the receiving and arranging of printed journals of Congress, and other books printed and purchased for the use of the government. The first to fill this office was Thomas Ewing, of Ohio.

It has been suggested that the bureau of education be made the basis of a separate "Department of Education and the Fine Arts."

The Post-Office Department was established May 8, 1794. It has the supervision of all the post-offices of the country, their names, the establishment and discontinuance of post-offices, the modes of carrying the mails, the issue of stamps, the receipt of the revenue of the office, and all other matters connected with the management and transportation of the mails. Samuel Osgood, of Massachusetts, was the first to fill this office.

The Department of Agriculture was at first a bureau of the Interior Department;

SEAL OF THE POST-OFFICE DEPARTMENT.

SEAL OF THE DEPARTMENT OF AGRICULTURE.

but in 1889, by act of Congress, it was made independent, and its chief, the Secretary of Agriculture, became a member of the President's cabinet. This department embraces numerous divisions and sections, such as the botanical division, the section of vegetable pathology, the pomological division, the forestry division, the chemical division, the division of entomology, the seed division, the silk section, the ornithological division, the bureau of animal industry, etc. On July 1, 1891, the weather bureau, which had hitherto been a branch of the signal service of the War Department, was transferred, by act of Congress, to this department.

SEAL OF THE DEPARTMENT OF COMMERCE AND LABOR.

The Department of Commerce and Labor was created by act of Congress in February, 1903. It comprised the bureau of corporations, bureau of manufactures, bureau of labor, bureau of fisheries, the light-house board, the light-house establishment, the steamboat-inspection service, the bureau of standards, the coast and geodetic survey, the bureau of immigration and naturalization, the bureau of statistics, the bureau of navigation, the bureau of foreign commerce, the census bureau, and the divisions of naturalization, publications, and supplies. Under the act of March 4, 1913, the above offices were divided between a newly created Department of Labor and the reorganized Department of Commerce.

CABINET, PRESIDENT'S

The following is a list of all members of Presidential cabinets since the organization of the federal government:

SECRETARIES OF STATE.

Name.	*Appointed.*
Thomas Jefferson	Sept. 26, 1789
Edmund Randolph	Jan. 2, 1794
Timothy Pickering	Dec. 10, 1795
John Marshall	May 13, 1800
James Madison	March 5, 1801
Robert Smith	March 6, 1809
James Monroe	April 2, 1811
John Quincy Adams	March 5, 1817
Henry Clay	March 7, 1825
Martin Van Buren	March 6, 1829
Edward Livingston	May 24, 1831
Louis McLane	May 29, 1833
John Forsyth	June 27, 1834
Daniel Webster	March 5, 1841
Hugh S. Legare	May 9, 1843
Abel P. Upshur	July 24, 1843
John C. Calhoun	March 6, 1844
James Buchanan	March 6, 1845
John M. Clayton	March 7, 1849
Daniel Webster	July 22, 1850
Edward Everett	Nov. 6, 1852
William L. Marcy	March 7, 1853
Lewis Cass	March 6, 1857
Jeremiah S. Black	Dec. 17, 1860
William H. Seward	March 5, 1861
Elihu B. Washburne	March 5, 1869
Hamilton Fish	March 11, 1869
William M. Evarts	March 12, 1877
James G. Blaine	March 5, 1881
F. T. Frelinghuysen	Dec. 12, 1881
Thomas F. Bayard	March 6, 1885
James G. Blaine	March 5, 1889
John W. Foster	June 29, 1892
Walter Q. Gresham	March 6, 1893
Richard Olney	June 7, 1895
John Sherman	March 5, 1897
William R. Day	April 26, 1898
John Hay	Sept. 20, 1898
Elihu Root	July 6, 1905
Philander C. Knox	March 5, 1909

SECRETARIES OF THE TREASURY.

Name.	*Appointed.*
Alexander Hamilton	Sept. 11, 1789
Oliver Wolcott	Feb. 2, 1795
Samuel Dexter	Jan. 1, 1801
Albert Gallatin	May 14, 1801
George W. Campbell	Feb. 9, 1814
Alexander J. Dallas	Oct. 6, 1814
William H. Crawford	Oct. 22, 1816
Richard Rush	March 7, 1825
Samuel D. Ingham	March 6, 1829
Louis McLane	Aug. 2, 1831
William J. Duane	May 29, 1833
Roger B. Taney	Sept. 23, 1833
Levi Woodbury	June 27, 1834
Thomas Ewing	March 5, 1841
Walter Forward	Sept. 13, 1841
John C. Spencer	March 3, 1843
George M. Bibb	June 15, 1844
Robert J. Walker	March 6, 1845
William M. Meredith	March 8, 1849
Thomas Corwin	July 23, 1850
James Guthrie	March 7, 1853
Howell Cobb	March 6, 1857
Philip F. Thomas	Dec. 12, 1860
John A. Dix	Jan. 11, 1861
Salmon P. Chase	March 7, 1861
William Pitt Fessenden	July 1, 1864
Hugh McCulloch	March 7, 1865
George S. Boutwell	March 11, 1869
William A. Richardson	March 17, 1873
Benjamin H. Bristow	June 4, 1874
Lot M. Morrill	July 7, 1876
John Sherman	March 8, 1877
William Windom	March 5, 1881
Charles J. Folger	Oct. 27, 1881
Walter Q. Gresham	Sept. 24, 1884
Hugh McCulloch	Oct. 28, 1884
Daniel Manning	March 6, 1886
Charles S. Fairchild	April 1, 1887
William Windom	March 5, 1889
Charles Foster	Feb. 21, 1891
John G. Carlisle	March 6, 1893
Lyman J. Gage	March 5, 1897
Leslie M. Shaw	Jan. 8, 1902
George B. Cortelyou	March 4, 1907
Franklin MacVeagh	March 5, 1909

SECRETARIES OF WAR.

Name.	*Appointed.*
Henry Knox	Sept. 12, 1789
Timothy Pickering	Jan. 2, 1795
James McHenry	Jan. 27, 1796
Samuel Dexter	May 13, 1800
Roger Griswold	Feb. 3, 1801
Henry Dearborn	March 5, 1801
William Eustis	March 7, 1809
John Armstrong	Jan. 13, 1813
James Monroe	Sept. 27, 1814
William H. Crawford	Aug. 1, 1815
George Graham	*Ad interim*
John C. Calhoun	Oct. 8, 1817
James Barbour	March 7, 1825
Peter B. Porter	May 26, 1828
John H. Eaton	March 9, 1829
Lewis Cass	Aug. 1, 1831
Joel R. Poinsett	March 7, 1837
John Bell	March 5, 1841
John C. Spencer	Oct. 12, 1841
James M. Porter	March 8, 1843
William Wilkins	Feb. 15, 1844
William L. Marcy	March 6, 1845
George W. Crawford	March 8, 1849
Charles M. Conrad	Aug. 15, 1850
Jefferson Davis	March 5, 1853
John B. Floyd	March 6, 1857
Joseph Holt	Jan. 18, 1861
Simon Cameron	March 5, 1861
Edwin M. Stanton	Jan. 15, 1862
Ulysses S. Grant, *ad interim*	Aug. 12, 1868
Lorenzo Thomas, *ad interim*	Feb. 21, 1868
John M. Schofield	May 28, 1868
John A. Rawlins	March 11, 1869
William W. Belknap	Oct. 25, 1869
Alphonso Taft	March 8, 1876
James D. Cameron	May 22, 1876

CABINET, PRESIDENT'S

Name.	*Appointed.*
George W. McCrary	March 12, 1877
Alexander Ramsey	Dec. 10, 1879
Robert T. Lincoln	March 5, 1881
William C. Endicott	March 6, 1885
Redfield Proctor	March 5, 1889
Stephen B. Elkins	Dec. 17, 1891
Daniel S. Lamont	March 6, 1893
Russell A. Alger	March 5, 1897
Elihu Root	Aug. 1, 1899
William H. Taft	Aug. 25, 1903
Luke E. Wright	July 1, 1908
Jacob M. Dickinson	March 4, 1909
Henry L. Stimson	May 12, 1911

SECRETARIES OF THE NAVY.

Name	Appointed
Benjamin Stoddert	May 21, 1798
Robert Smith	July 15, 1801
J. Crowninshield	March 3, 1805
Paul Hamilton	March 7, 1809
William Jones	Jan. 12, 1813
B. W. Crowninshield	Dec. 19, 1814
Smith Thompson	Nov. 9, 1818
Samuel L. Southard	Sept. 16, 1823
John Branch	March 9, 1829
Levi Woodbury	May 23, 1831
Mahlon Dickerson	June 30, 1834
James K. Paulding	June 25, 1838
George E. Badger	March 5, 1841
Abel P. Upshur	Sept. 13, 1841
David Henshaw	July 24, 1843
Thomas W. Gilmer	Feb. 15, 1844
John Y. Mason	March 14, 1844
George Bancroft	March 10, 1845
John Y. Mason	Sept. 9, 1846
William B. Preston	March 8, 1849
William A. Graham	July 22, 1850
John P. Kennedy	July 22, 1852
James C. Dobbin	March 7, 1853
Isaac Toucey	March 6, 1857
Gideon Welles	March 5, 1861
Adolph E. Borie	March 5, 1869
George M. Robeson	June 25, 1869
Richard W. Thompson	March 12, 1877
Nathan Goff, Jr.	Jan. 6, 1881
William H. Hunt	March 5, 1881
William E. Chandler	April 1, 1882
William C. Whitney	March 6, 1885
Benjamin F. Tracy	March 5, 1889
Hilary A. Herbert	March 6, 1893
John D. Long	March 5, 1897
William H. Moody	May 1, 1902
Paul Morton	June 24, 1904
Charles J. Bonaparte	July 1, 1905
Victor H. Metcalf	Dec. 17, 1906
Truman H. Newberry	Dec. 1, 1908
George L. von Meyer	March 6, 1909

SECRETARIES OF THE INTERIOR.

Name.	*Appointed.*
Thomas Ewing	March 8, 1849
Alexander H. H. Stewart	Sept. 12, 1850
Robert McClelland	March 7, 1853
Jacob Thompson	March 6, 1857
Caleb B. Smith	March 5, 1861
John P. Usher	Jan. 8, 1863
James Harlan	May 15, 1865
Orville H. Browning	July 27, 1866
Jacob D. Cox	March 5, 1869
Columbus Delano	Nov. 1, 1870
Zachariah Chandler	Oct. 19, 1875
Carl Schurz	March 12, 1877
Samuel J. Kirkwood	March 5, 1881
Henry M. Teller	April 6, 1882
L. Q. C. Lamar	March 6, 1885
William F. Vilas	Jan. 16, 1888
John W. Noble	March 5, 1889
Hoke Smith	March 6, 1897
David R. Francis	Aug. 24, 1896
Cornelius N. Bliss	March 5, 1897
Ethan A. Hitchcock	Dec. 21, 1898
James R. Garfield	March 4, 1907
Richard A. Ballinger	March 5, 1909
Walter Lowrie Fisher	March 7, 1911

POSTMASTERS-GENERAL.

Name	Appointed
Samuel Osgood	Sept. 26, 1789
Timothy Pickering	Aug. 12, 1791
Joseph Habersham	Feb. 25, 1795
Gideon Granger	Nov. 28, 1801
Return J. Meigs, Jr.	March 17, 1814
John McLean	June 26, 1823
William T. Barry	March 9, 1829
Amos Kendall	May 1, 1835
John M. Niles	May 25, 1840
Francis Granger	March 6, 1841
Charles A. Wickliffe	Sept. 13, 1841
Cave Johnson	March 6, 1845
Jacob Collamer	March 8, 1849
Nathan K. Hall	July 23, 1850
Samuel D. Hubbard	Aug. 31, 1852
James Campbell	March 5, 1853
Aaron V. Brown	March 6, 1857
Joseph Holt	March 14, 1859
Horatio King	Feb. 12, 1861
Montgomery Blair	March 5, 1861
William Dennison	Sept. 24, 1864
Alexander W. Randall	July 25, 1866
John A. J. Creswell	March 5, 1869
Marshall Jewell	Aug. 24, 1874
James N. Tyner	July 12, 1876
David McK. Key	March 12, 1877
Horace Maynard	June 2, 1880
Thomas L. James	March 5, 1881
Timothy O. Howe	Dec. 20, 1881
Walter Q. Gresham	April 3, 1883
Frank Hatton	Oct. 14, 1884
William F. Vilas	March 6, 1885
Don M. Dickinson	Jan. 16, 1888
John Wanamaker	March 5, 1889
Wilson S. Bissell	March 6, 1893
William L. Wilson	Feb. 28, 1895
James A. Gary	March 5, 1897
Charles E. Smith	April 21, 1898
Henry C. Payne	Jan. 8, 1902
Robert J. Wynne	Oct. 10, 1904

Name.	*Appointed.*
George B. Cortelyou	March 7, 1905
George L. von Meyer	March 4, 1907
Frank H. Hitchcock	March 5, 1909

ATTORNEYS-GENERAL.

Name	Appointed
Edmund Randolph	Sept. 26, 1789
William Bradford	Jan. 27, 1794
Charles Lee	Dec. 10, 1795
Theophilus Parsons	Feb. 20, 1801
Levi Lincoln	March 5, 1801
Robert Smith	March 3, 1805
John Breckinridge	Aug. 7, 1805
Cæsar A. Rodney	Jan. 28, 1807
William Pinkney	Dec. 11, 1811
Richard Rush	Feb. 10, 1814
William Wirt	Nov. 13, 1817
John M. Berrien	March 9, 1829
Roger B. Taney	July 20, 1831
Benjamin F. Butler	Nov. 15, 1833
Felix Grundy	July 5, 1838
Henry D. Gilpin	Jan. 11, 1840
John J. Crittenden	March 5, 1841
Hugh S. Legare	Sept. 13, 1841
John Nelson	July 1, 1843
John Y. Mason	March 6, 1845
Nathan Clifford	Oct. 17, 1846
Isaac Toucey	June 21, 1848
Reverdy Johnson	March 8, 1849
John J. Crittenden	July 22, 1850
Caleb Cushing	March 7, 1853
Jeremiah S. Black	March 6, 1857
Edwin M. Stanton	Dec. 20, 1860
Edward Bates	March 5, 1861
Titian J. Coffey *ad interim*	June 22, 1863
James Speed	Dec. 2, 1864
Henry Stanbery	July 23, 1866
William M. Evarts	July 15, 1868
E. Rockwood Hoar	March 5, 1869
Amos T. Ackerman	June 23, 1870
George H. Williams	Dec. 14, 1871
Edwards Pierrepont	April 26, 1875
Alphonso Taft	May 22, 1876
Charles Devens	March 12, 1877
Wayne MacVeagh	March 5, 1881
Benjamin H. Brewster	Dec. 19, 1881
Augustus H. Garland	March 6, 1885
W. H. H. Miller	March 5, 1889
Richard Olney	March 6, 1893
Judson Harmon	June 7, 1895
Joseph McKenna	March 5, 1897
John W. Griggs	Jan. 25, 1898
Philander C. Knox	April 5, 1901
William H. Moody	July 1, 1904
Charles J. Bonaparte	Dec. 18, 1906
George W. Wickersham	March 5, 1909

SECRETARIES OF AGRICULTURE.

Name.	*Appointed.*
Norman J. Coleman	Feb. 13, 1889
Jeremiah M. Rusk	March 4, 1889
J. Sterling Morton	March 6, 1893
James Wilson	March 5, 1897

SECRETARIES OF COMMERCE AND LABOR.

Name	Appointed
George B. Cortelyou	Feb. 16, 1903
Victor H. Metcalf	July 1, 1904
Oscar S. Straus	Dec. 17, 1906
Charles Nagel	March 5, 1909

Cabinet Council. See CABINET, PRESIDENT'S.

Cabinet, THE KITCHEN. See KITCHEN CABINET.

Cable, ATLANTIC. See ATLANTIC TELEGRAPH.

Cables, OCEAN. The first permanent Atlantic cable was laid in July, 1866, from Valentia Bay, Ireland, to Trinity Bay, Newfoundland. In September of the same year a cable lost by an unsuccessful attempt in 1865 was recovered, and its laying completed, thus making two lines between the two points named (see ATLANTIC TELEGRAPH). These lines constituted what was known as the Anglo-American Cable, managed by a company of the same name. In 1868 the French Atlantic Telegraph Company was formed, and the following year it laid a line from Brest, France, to Duxbury, Mass. The fourth Atlantic telegraph cable was laid from Valentia, Ireland, to Heart's Content, Trinity Bay, Newfoundland, in the summer of 1873, and a few months later the Brazilian telegraph cable was laid from Rio de Janeiro, Brazil, to a bay on the coast of Portugal. In 1874 the Direct United States Cable Company was formed and laid a line from Ballinskelligs Bay, Ireland, to Rye, N. H., *via* Nova Scotia. The same year a sixth line across the Atlantic was laid from Ireland to Newfoundland. Another French line was laid from Brest to St. Pierre, an island in the Gulf of St. Lawrence, in 1880. The companies owning all these lines having formed a combination and pooled their receipts, to keep up rates on the transmission of messages, a competing company was formed by James Gordon Bennett and John W. Mackay. This laid in 1884–85 two lines from Ireland to Nova Scotia, having also a connecting line from Ireland to France. A Pacific cable, extending from San Francisco to Honolulu, thence to Wake Island, Guam Island, and Manila, all United States possessions, was formally opened July 4, 1903.

The following table shows the various submarine cables in which the United States has a direct interest. It owns the 13 cables in and to Alaska, 2,145 miles in length.

COMPANIES.	Number of Cables.	Length of Cables in Nautical Miles.
Anglo-American Telegraph Co..	13	9,554
Transatlantic System—Valentia (Ireland) to Heart's Content (Newfoundland).		
Commercial Cable Co..	12	15,498
Transatlantic System—Waterville (Ireland) to Canso (Nova Scotia).		
Canso, N. S., to New York.		
Canso, N. S., to Rockport, Mass.		
Commercial Pacific Cable Co...	6	10,010
San Francisco to Manila.		
Manila to Shanghai.		
De l'Ils de Peel (Bonins) à Guam.		
Commercial Cable Co. of Cuba.	1	1,285
Coney Island (New York) to Havana (Cuba).		
Direct United States Cable Co..	2	3,112
Ballinskellig's Bay (Ireland) to Halifax (Nova Scotia).		
Halifax, N. S., to Rye Beach, N. H.		
Western Union Telegraph Co...	12	7,357
Transatlantic System — Sennen Cove, near Penzance, England, to Dover Bay, Dover Bay, N. S., to New York, near Canso, N. S.		
Compagnie Française des Câbles Télégraphiques	24	11,430
Brest (France) to Cape Cod, Mass.		
Brest (France) to St. Pierre-Miq.		
St. Pierre to Cape Cod, Mass.		
Cape Cod, Mass., to New York		
Cuba Submarine Telegraph Co.	10	1,143
Direct Spanish Telegraph Co...	4	711
Compagnie Allemande des Câbles Transatlantiques	5	9,556
Borkum Island to Azores to Coney Island, N. Y.		
Deutsch-Niederlandische Telegraphen gesellschaft	3	3,415
Menado (Célebes) — Japan (Caroline); Guam (Mariannes); Shanghai.		
Mexican Telegraph Co.........	5	2,821
United States and Haiti Telegraph and Cable Co.........	1	1,391

THE FARADAY LAYING THE ATLANTIC CABLE.

Cable, GEORGE WASHINGTON, author; born in New Orleans, Oct. 12, 1844. In 1863–65 he served in the Confederate army. In 1879 he gave himself up wholly to literature, making a specialty of describing Creole life in Louisiana. In 1887 he established the House-Culture Clubs, a system of small clubs for the purpose of promoting more cordial relations among the different classes of society. His writings include *Old Creole Days; The Grandissimes; Madame Delphine; The Silent South; The Creoles of Louisiana; The Negro Question; Strange True Stories of Louisiana; John March, Southerner.*

SEBASTIAN CABOT.
(From an old print.)

Cabot, the name of a family of explorers intimately connected with the history of America. JOHN is supposed to have been born in Genoa, although some historians have claimed Venice as his birthplace. There is evidence that for fifteen years prior to 1476 he resided in Venice, and in that year formally became a citizen. Subsequently he removed to Bristol, England, and engaged in the mercantile business. With a view of finding a shorter route to India, he determined to attempt a northwest passage. To further his undertaking he secured from Henry VII. a patent for the discovery of any unknown lands lying in either the eastern, western, or northern seas.

SEBASTIAN, the second son of John, was

HUDSON BAY WHERE CABOT SOUGHT A NORTHWEST PASSAGE.

born in Bristol, England, in 1477. As his name appears in the petition of his father to Henry VII. for the patent above mentioned, it is believed that he accompanied his father in the voyage described below. Sebastian died in London in 1557.

The latest evidence shows that John and probably his son Sebastian sailed from Bristol, May, 1497, discovered in June what was supposed to be the Chinese coast, and returned in July. In April, 1498, they most to lat. 60°, when the ice again barred his way. Then he sailed southward, and discovered a large island, which he called New Found Land (Newfoundland), and perceived the immense number of codfish in the waters surrounding it. Leaving that island, he coasted as far as the shores of Maine, and, some writers think, as far south as the Carolinas. On his return Cabot revealed the secret of the codfish at New Found Land, and within five or

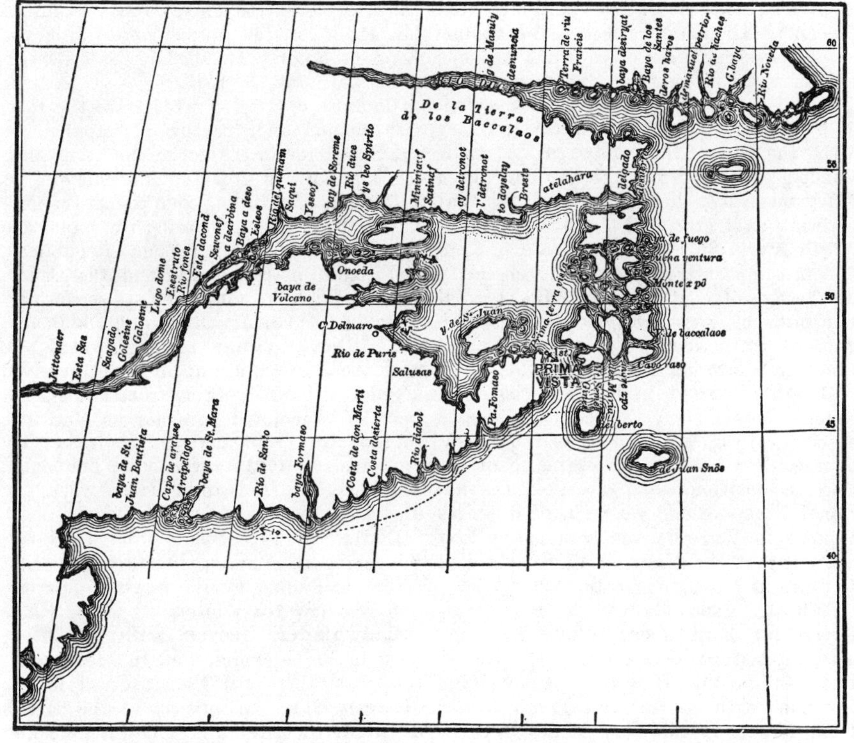

MAP OF THE GULF OF ST. LAWRENCE, AFTER CHARTS MADE BY SEBASTIAN CABOT.

sailed again from Bristol; on *this* voyage JOHN died and Sebastian succeeded to the command. The place of the landfall is uncertain; probably Labrador and Prince Edward Island were reached. A common account is that he was stopped by the ice-pack in Davis Strait. Then he sailed southwest, and discovered the shores of Labrador, or, possibly, the northern shore of Newfoundland. Turning northward, he traversed the coast of the continent almost to lat. 60°... six years thereafter fishermen from England, Brittany, and Normandy were gathering treasures there. As Cabot did not bring back gold from America, King Henry paid no more attention to him; and in 1512 he went to Spain, by invitation of King Ferdinand, and enjoyed honors and emoluments until that monarch's death in 1516, when, annoyed by the jealousies of the Spanish nobility, he returned to England. Henry VIII.

furnished Cabot with a vessel, in 1517, to seek for a northwest passage to India; but he unsuccessfully fought the ice-pack at Hudson Bay and was foiled. The successor of Ferdinand invited Cabot to Spain and made him chief pilot of the realm. He was employed by Spanish merchants to command an expedition to the Spice Islands by way of the then newly discovered Strait of Magellan; but circumstances prevented his going farther than the southeast coast of South America, where he discovered the rivers De la Plata and Paraguay. His employers were disappointed, and, resigning his office into the hands of the Spanish monarch, he returned to England in his old age, and was pensioned by the King. After the death of Henry VIII. the "boy King," Edward VI., made Cabot grand pilot of England; but Queen Mary neglected him, and allowed that eminent navigator and discoverer of the North American continent to die in London in comparative poverty and obscurity at the age of eighty years. His cheerful temperament was manifested by his dancing at an assembly of young seamen the year before his death.

Cabot, GEORGE, statesman; born in Salem, Mass., Dec. 3, 1751; educated at Harvard College; member of the Massachusetts Provincial Congress; also of the State convention which accepted the national Constitution; was a United States Senator in 1791–96; and became the first Secretary of the Navy in 1798. He died in Boston, Mass., April 18, 1823.

Cabral, PEDRO ALVAREZ, Portuguese navigator; born about 1460. In 1499, after VASCO DA GAMA (*q. v.*) returned from India, Cabral was sent by King Emanuel, with thirteen ships, on a voyage from Lisbon to the East Indies, for the purpose of following up Gama's discoveries. He left Lisbon on March 9, 1500. In order to avoid the calms on the Guinea shore, he went so far westward as to discover land on the coast of Brazil at lat. 10° S. He erected a cross, and named the country "The Land of the Holy Cross." It was afterwards called Brazil, from *brasil*, a dyewood that abounded there. Cabral took possession of the country in the name of the King. After it was ascertained that it was a part of the American continent, a controversy arose between the crowns of Spain and Portugal, but it was settled amicably—Portugal to possess the portion of the continent discovered by Cabral—that is, from the River Amazon to the Plate. This discovery led Emmanuel to send out another expedition (three ships) under AMERICUS VESPUCIUS (*q. v.*), in May, 1501. They touched Brazil at lat. 5° S., and returned home after a voyage of sixteen months. Cabral died about 1526.

Cabrilla, JUAN RODRIGUEZ, Portuguese navigator; born late in the fifteenth century; explored the Pacific coast as far as lat. 44° N., in 1542, under orders from the King of Spain. He died at San Bernardino, Cal., Jan. 3, 1543.

Cacique, a word derived from the Haytien tongue and inaccurately applied by the Spaniards to the native nobles of Mexico, and also to great Indian chiefs.

Caddoan Indians, comprising the Arikari tribe in North Dakota; the four Pawnee villages, Grand, Tapage, Republican, and Skidi. in Oklahoma, and the Caddo, Kichai, Wichita, and other tribes, formerly in Louisiana, Arkansas, and Oklahoma.

Cadillac, ANTOINE DE LA MOTHE, pioneer; born in France about 1660; received a grant of land in Maine from Louis XIV. in 1688; appointed governor of Mackinac in 1694 by Frontenac; founded the city of Detroit in 1701; governor of Louisiana, 1712–17; returned to France, where he died Oct. 18, 1730.

Cadiz. In 1495 Spain ordered all vessels going to America to start from and return to Cadiz. Seville received this monopoly a few years later.

Cadwalader, GEORGE, military officer; born in Philadelphia, Pa., in 1804; practised law there till 1846; served in the Mexican War; was present at the battles of Molino del Rey and Chapultepec; and for bravery in the latter was brevetted major-general. In 1861, he was appointed major-general, and placed in command of Baltimore, and in 1862 he was made a member of a board to revise the United States military laws and regulations. He published *Services in the Mexican Campaign.* He died in Philadelphia, Pa., Feb. 3, 1879.

Cadwalader, JOHN, military officer; born in Philadelphia, Pa., Jan. 10, 1742. He was colonel of one of the city battalions; later as brigadier-general he was placed in command of the Pennsylvania militia, co-operating with Washington in the attack on Trenton, and participating in the battle of Princeton. He was in the battles of Brandywine, Germantown, and Monmouth. He challenged Gen. Thomas Conway to fight a duel because of offensive words the latter used towards Wash-

JOHN CADWALADER.

ington. They fought, and Conway was badly wounded. After the war Cadwalader lived in Maryland, and was in its legislature. He died in Shrewsbury, Pa., Feb. 11, 1786.

Cagayan, an island of the Philippine group; the largest of fourteen islands known as the Cagayan-Sulu group. The chief products are tobacco and sugar. There are pearl and shell fisheries. Cagayan was sold by Spain to the United States, with Sibutu, in 1900, upon payment of $100,000, having been inadvertently excluded from the terms of the treaty of peace. The province of Cagayan had a population of 156,239 in 1903, of whom 13,500 were classed as wild.

Cahenslyism, a movement among Roman Catholic immigrants in the United States to secure separate ecclesiastical organization for each nationality or language, and in particular for Germans; named after Peter Paul Cahensly, Austro-Hungarian envoy to the Vatican, and a leader of the St. Raphael Society in Germany and Austria for promoting Roman Catholic interests among emigrants. In 1886 German priests petitioned that German Catholics be obliged to join German-speaking churches, and be forbidden to attend those speaking English. They secured the co-operation of many German bishops and priests in the United States, and especially of Archbishop Katzer, of Milwaukee; but were opposed by many others, especially by Cardinal Gibbons, of Baltimore, who at the installation of Archbishop Katzer in 1891 denounced the movement as unpatriotic and disloyal. It was overshadowed later by the predominance of more liberal views, and Archbishop Corrigan publicly declared it a dead issue and condemned by the Pope.

Cahokia, village in St. Clair county, Ill., on the Mississippi River, four miles southeast of East St. Louis; was settled by the French in 1682, and has near-by interesting relics of the ancient mound-builders.

Caimanera, a town on the Bay of Guantanamo, province of Oriente, Cuba, about 35 miles east of the entrance of the harbor of Santiago. At the beginning of the war with Spain in 1898 the town and vicinity were the scene of important military and naval operations. On June 10 the bay was seized for a base of supplies by Captain McCalla, with the *Marblehead*, *Yankee*, and *St. Louis*, and the last vessel, supported by the others, cut the cable at Caimanera, which was connected with Santiago. The town was garrisoned by 3,000 Spanish soldiers, and protected by several gunboats and a fort. When the American vessels opened fire at 800 yards, forcing the Spaniards to withdraw from the block-house and the town, the *Alfonso Pinzon* appeared at the entrance of the bay and at a range of 4,000 yards fired on the American vessels. The latter soon found the range, but the Spanish vessel refused to withdraw until the *Marblehead* gave chase, when she retired behind the fort, still keeping up her firing. On June 11 a battalion of 600 marines, the first United States troops to set foot upon Cuban soil, were landed under Lieutenant-Colonel Huntington from the troop-ship *Panther* and the men-of-war. They established themselves at the entrance of the bay, little expecting that the Spanish soldiers, who had been driven in panic to the mountains, would return during the night. Consequently, when their pickets were fired upon, there was considerable surprise. On the night of June 12 the Spaniards appeared in greater numbers, and charging up to the camp killed Surgeon John B. Gibbs and two marines. The attack lasted until morning, when the assailants were forced to retire under the fire of the American field-guns. During the night of June 13 the Spaniards again attacked the camp, and kept up such a continuous fire that the Americans had no rest. The next night, however, the same plan did not work, as a force of Cubans under Colonel La Borda, who had hastened to the camp, were sent out on skirmish duty. On the following day a company of marines, with the Cubans, drove the Spanish away. The American losses were six killed and three wounded, while more than forty of the Spanish were killed. See GUANTANAMO BAY.

Cairo, a city at the confluence of the Ohio and Mississippi rivers, 150 miles s. e. of St. Louis; is the trade centre of Southern Illinois, and has freight and passenger steamer communications with all river ports, and important manufactures. Population (1900), 12,566; (1910), 14,548. It is of great importance as the key to a vast extent of navigable waters, and to it National troops were sent at an early period in the Civil War. Both the national government and Governor Yates, of Illinois, had been apprised of the intention of the Confederates to secure that position, hoping thereby to control the navigation of the Mississippi to St. Louis, and of the Ohio to Cincinnati and beyond. They also hoped that the absolute control of the Mississippi below would cause the Northwestern States to join hands with the Confederates rather than lose these great trade advantages. The scheme was foiled. Governor Yates, under the direction of the Secretary of War, sent Illinois troops at an early day to take possession of and occupy Cairo. By the middle of May there were not less than 5,000 Union volunteers there, under the command of Gen. B. M. Prentiss, who occupied the extreme point of the peninsula, where they cast up fortifications and gave the post the name of Camp Defiance. Before the close of May it was considered impregnable against any force the Confederates might send. It soon became a post of great importance to the Union cause as the place where some of the land and naval expeditions in the valley of the Mississippi were fitted out.

Caldwell, JAMES, clergyman; born in Charlotte county, Va., in April, 1734. Graduating at Princeton in 1759, he became pastor of the Presbyterian Church at Elizabethtown in 1762. Zealously espousing the revolutionary cause, he was much disliked by the Tories. Appointed chaplain of a New Jersey brigade, he was for a time in the Mohawk Valley. In 1780 his church and residence were burned by a party of British and Tories; and the same year a British incursion from Staten Island pillaged the village of Connecticut Farms, where his family were temporarily residing. A soldier shot his wife through a window while she was sitting on a bed with her babe. At that time Mr. Caldwell was in Washington's camp at Morristown. In the successful defence of Springfield, N. J., June 23, 1780, when the wadding for the soldiers' guns gave out, he brought the hymn-books from the neighboring church and shouted, "Now put Watts into them, boys." In an altercation at Elizabethtown Point with an American sentinel, he was killed by the latter, Nov. 24, 1781. The murderer was afterwards hanged.

Calef, ROBERT, author; place and date of birth uncertain; became a merchant in Boston; and is noted for his controversy with Cotton Mather concerning the witchcraft delusion in New England. Mather had published a work entitled *Wonders of the Invisible World,* and Calef attacked the book, the author, and the subject in a publication entitled *More Wonders of the Invisible World.* Calef's book was published in London in 1700, and in Salem the same year. About this time the people and magistrates had come to their senses, persecutions had ceased, and the folly of the belief in witchcraft was broadly apparent. Mather, however, continued to write in favor of it, and to give instances of the doings of witches in their midst. "Flashy people," wrote Mather, "may burlesque these things, but when hundreds of the most sober people, in a country where they have as much mother-wit certainly as the rest of mankind, know them to be true, nothing but the absurd and froward spirit of Sadducism [disbelief in spirits] can question them." Calef first attacked Mather in a series of letters, which were subsequently published in book form, as above stated. In these letters he exposed Mather's credulity, and greatly irritated that really good man. Mather retorted by calling Calef a "weaver turned minister." Calef tormented Mather more by other letters in the same vein, when the former, becoming wearied by the fight, called the latter "a coal from hell," and prosecuted him for slander. When these letters of Calef were published in book form, Increase Mather, President of Harvard College, caused copies of the work to be publicly burned on the college green. Calef died about 1723.

Calendar. Our present calendar is the creation of Julius Cæsar, based on a slight error which in the course of 1,600 years amounted to ten days. Pope Gregory XIII. rectified the calendar in 1582. The Gregorian calendar was accepted ultimately by all civilized nations, with the exception of Russia, which still continues the use of the Julian Calendar.

CALHOUN, JOHN CALDWELL

Calhoun, John Caldwell, statesman; born in Abbeville District, S. C., March 18, 1782. His father was a native of Ireland; his mother, formerly Miss Caldwell, was of Scotch-Irish descent. The son was graduated, with all the honors, at Yale College, in 1804, and studied law in the famous law-school in Litchfield, Conn. In 1807 he began the practice of the profession in his native district. Thoughtful, ardent, and persevering, he soon took high rank in his profession, and gained a very lucrative practice. Fond of politics, he early entered its arena, and in 1808–10 was a member of the State legislature. He was sent to Congress in 1811, where he remained, by successive elections, until 1817. Mr. Calhoun was very influential in pressing Madison to make a declaration of war with Great Britain in 1812. President Monroe called him to his cabinet as Secretary of War (Dec. 16, 1817), and he served as such during the President's double term of office. In 1824 he was chosen Vice-President of the United States, and was re-elected with Andrew Jackson in 1828. In 1831 he was elected United States Senator by the legislature of South Carolina. He was Secretary of State in 1844–45, and from 1845 till 1850 he was again a member of the United States Senate. The doctrine of State sovereignty and supremacy, and that the Union was a compact of States that might be dissolved by the secession of any one of them, independent of all action on the part of others, was held by Mr. Calhoun nearly all his life. His influence in his own State was very great; and his political tenets, practically carried out by acts of nullification, brought South Carolina to the verge of civil war in 1832; and it made that State foremost and most conspicuous in inaugurating the Civil War. He died in Washington, D. C., March 31, 1850. His remains

JOHN CALDWELL CALHOUN.

lie under a neat monument in St. Philip's church-yard at Charleston, S. C. His writings and a biography have been published in 6 volumes. See Webster, Daniel.

Government of the United States.—The following is Senator Calhoun's conception

of the national government, from his discourse on "The Constitution":

Ours is a system of government, compounded of the separate governments of the several States composing the Union, and of one common government of all its members, called the government of the United States. The former preceded the latter, which was created by their agency. Each was framed by written constitutions; those of the several States by the people of each, acting separately, and in their sovereign character; and that of the United States, by the same, acting in the same character, but jointly instead of separately. All were formed on the same model. They all divide the powers of government into legislative, executive, and judicial; and are founded on the great principle of the responsibility of the rulers to the ruled. The entire powers of government are divided between the two; those of a more general character being specifically delegated to the United States; and all others not delegated, being reserved to the several States in their separate character. Each, within its appropriate sphere, possesses all the attributes, and performs all the functions of government. Neither is perfect without the other. The two combined, form one entire and perfect government. With these preliminary remarks, I shall proceed to the consideration of the immediate subject of this discourse.

The government of the United States was formed by the Constitution of the United States; and ours is a democratic, federal republic.

It is democratic, in contradistinction to aristocracy and monarchy. It excludes classes, orders, and all artificial distinctions. To guard against their introduction, the Constitution prohibits the granting of any title of nobility by the United States, or by any State. The whole system is, indeed, democratic throughout. It has for its fundamental principle, the great cardinal maxim, that the people are the source of all power; that the governments of the several States and of the United States were created by them, and for them; that the powers conferred on them are not surrendered, but delegated; and, as such, are held in trust, and not absolutely; and can be rightfully exercised only in furtherance of the objects for which they were delegated.

It is federal as well as democratic. *Federal,* on the one hand, in contradistinction to *national,* and, on the other, to a *confederacy.* In showing this, I shall begin with the former.

It is federal, because it is the government of States united in a political union, in contradistinction to a government of individuals socially united—that is, by what is usually called, a social compact. To express it more concisely, it is federal and not national, because it is the government of a community of States, and not the government of a single State or nation.

That it is federal and not national. we have the high authority of the convention which framed it. General Washington, as its organ, in his letter submitting the plan to the consideration of the Congress of the then confederacy, calls it in one place "the general government of the Union," and in another "the federal government of these States." Taken together, the plain meaning is, that the government proposed would be, if adopted, the government of the States adopting it, in their united character as members of a common Union; and, as such, would be a federal government. These expressions were not used without due consideration, and an accurate and full knowledge of their true import. The subject was not a novel one. The convention was familiar with it. It was much agitated in their deliberations. They divided, in reference to it, in the early stages of their proceedings. At first, one party was in favor of a national and the other of a federal government. The former, in the beginning, prevailed; and in the plans which they proposed, the constitution and government are styled "national." But, finally, the latter gained the ascendency, when the term "national" was superseded, and *United States* substituted in its place. The Constitution was accordingly styled, *The Constitution of the United States of America;* and the government, *The government of the United States,* leaving out "America" for the sake of brevity. It cannot admit of a doubt, that the Convention, by the expression, "United States," meant the

States united in a federal Union; for in no other sense could they, with propriety, call the government *the federal government of these States*, and *the general government of the Union*, as they did in the letter referred to. It is thus clear, that the Convention regarded the different expressions, "the federal government of the United States"; "the general government of the Union," and "government of the United States" as meaning the same thing—a federal, in contradistinction to a national government.

Assuming it, then, as established, that they are the same thing, it is only necessary, in order to ascertain with precision what they meant by *federal government*, to ascertain what they meant by *the government of the United States*. For this purpose it will be necessary to trace the expression to its origin.

It was at that time, as our history shows, an old and familiar phrase, having a known and well-defined meaning. Its use commenced with the political birth of these States; and it has been applied to them, in all the forms of government through which they have passed, without alteration. The style of the present Constitution and government is precisely the style by which the confederacy that existed when it was adopted, and which it superseded, was designated. The instrument that formed the latter was called, *Articles of Confederation and Perpetual Union*. Its first article declares that the style of this confederacy shall be, "The United States of America"; and the second, in order to leave no doubt as to the relation in which the States should stand to each other in the confederacy about to be formed, declared—"Each State retains its sovereignty, freedom, and independence; and every power, jurisdiction, and right, which is not, by this confederation, expressly delegated to the United States in Congress assembled." If we go one step further back, the style of the confederacy will be found to be the same with that of the revolutionary government, which existed when it was adopted, and which it superseded. It dates its origin with the Declaration of Independence. That act is styled—"The unanimous Declaration of the thirteen United States of America." And here again, that there might be no doubt how these States would stand to each other in the new condition in which they were about to be placed, it concluded by declaring—"that these United Colonies are, and of right ought to be, free and independent States"; "and that, as free and independent States, they have full power to levy war, conclude peace, contract alliances, and to do all other acts and things which independent States may of right do." The "United States" is, then, the baptismal name of these States—received at their birth—by which they have ever since continued to call themselves; by which they have characterized their constitution, government, and laws, and by which they are known to the rest of the world.

The retention of the same style, throughout every stage of their existence, affords strong, if not conclusive evidence that the political relation between these States, under their present constitution and government, is substantially the same as under the confederacy and revolutionary government; and what that relation was, we are not left to doubt; as they are declared expressly to be *free, independent*, and *sovereign* States. They, then, are now united, and have been, throughout, simply as confederated States. If it had been intended by the members of the convention which framed the present Constitution and government, to make any essential change, either in the relation of the States to each other, or the basis of their union, they would, by retaining the style which designated them under the preceding governments, have practised a deception, utterly unworthy of their character, as sincere and honest men and patriots. It may, therefore, be fairly inferred, that, retaining the same style, they intended to attach to the expression, "the United States," the same meaning, substantially, which it previously had; and, of course, in calling the present government "the federal government of these States" they meant by "federal" that they stood in the same relation to each other—that their union rested, without material change, on the same basis—as under the confederacy and the revolutionary government; and that federal and confederated States meant substantially the same thing. It follows, also, that the changes made by the present Constitution were not in the foundation, but in the superstructure of the system. We accordingly find, in confirmation of this conclusion, that the convention, in their letter to Congress, stating the reasons for the changes that had been made, refer only to the necessity which required a different *organization* of the government, without making any allusion whatever to any change in the relations of the States towards each other, or the basis of the system. They state that "the friends of our country have long seen and desired that the power of making war, peace, and treaties; that of levying money and regulating commerce, and the correspondent executive and judicial authorities, should be fully and effectually vested in the government of the Union: but the impropriety of delegating such extensive trusts to one body of men is evident; hence results the necessity of a *different organization.*" Comment is unnecessary.

We thus have the authority of the convention itself for asserting that the expression, "United States," has essentially the same meaning, when applied to the present Constitution and government, as it had previously; and, of course, that the States have retained their separate existence, as independent and sovereign communities, in all the forms of political existence through which they have passed. Such, indeed, is the literal import of the expression, "the United States," and the sense in which it is ever used, when it is applied politically—I say, *politically*—because it is often applied, *geographically*, to designate the portion of this continent occupied by the States composing the Union, including Territories belonging to them. This application arose from the fact, that there was no appropriate term for that portion of this continent; and thus, not unnaturally, the name by which these States are politically designated, was employed to designate the region they occupy and possess. The distinction is important, and cannot be overlooked in discussing questions involving the character and nature of the government, without causing great confusion and dangerous misconceptions.

But as conclusive as these reasons are to prove that the government of the United States is federal, in contradistinction to national, it would seem, that they have not been sufficient to prevent the opposite opinion from being entertained. Indeed, this last seems to have become the prevailing one; if we may judge from the general use of the term "national," and the almost entire disuse of that of "federal." National is now commonly applied to the "general government of the Union"—and "the federal government of these States"—and all that appertains to them or to the Union. It seems to be forgotten that the term was repudiated by the convention, after full consideration; and that it was carefully excluded from the Constitution, and the letter laying it before Congress. Even those who know all this—and, of course, how falsely the term is applied—have, for the most part, slided into its use without reflection. But there are not a few who so apply it, because they believe it to be a national government in fact; and among these are men of distinguished talents and standing, who have put forth all their powers of reason and eloquence, in support of the theory. The question involved is one of the first magnitude, and deserves to be investigated thoroughly in all its aspects. With this impression, I deem it proper—clear and conclusive as I regard the reasons already assigned to prove its federal character—to confirm them by historical references; and to repel the arguments adduced to prove it to be a national government. I shall begin with the formation and ratification of the Constitution.

That the States, when they formed and ratified the Constitution, were distinct, independent, and sovereign communities, has already been established. That the people of the several States, acting in their separate, independent, and sovereign character, adopted their separate State constitutions, is a fact uncontested and incontestable; but it is not more certain than that, acting in the same character, they ratified and adopted the Constitution of the United States; with this difference only, that in making and adopting the one, they acted without concert or agreement; but, in the other, with concert in making, and mutual agreement in adopting it. That the delegates who constituted the convention which framed the Constitution, were appointed by the several States, each on its own authority; that they voted in the convention by States; and that their votes were counted by States, are recorded and unquestionable facts. So, also, the facts that the Constitution, when framed, was submitted to the people of the several States for their respective ratification; that it was ratified by them, each for itself; and that it was binding on each, only in consequence of its being so ratified by it. Until then, it was but the plan of a Constitution, without any binding force. It was the act of ratification which established it as a Constitution between the States ratifying it; and only between *them*, on the condition that not less than nine of the then thirteen States should concur in the ratification—as is expressly provided by its seventh and last article. It is in the following words: "The ratification of the conventions of nine States shall be sufficient for the establishment of this Constitution between the States so ratifying the same." If additional proof be needed to show that it was only binding between the States that ratified it, it may be found in the fact that two States—North Carolina and Rhode Island—refused, at first, to ratify; and were, in consequence, regarded in the interval as foreign States, without obligation, on their parts, to respect it, or, on the part of their citizens, to obey it. Thus far, there can be no difference of opinion. The facts are too recent and too well established, and the provision of the Constitution too explicit, to admit of doubt.

That the States, then, retained, after the ratification of the Constitution, the distinct, independent, and sovereign character in which they formed and ratified it, is certain; unless they divested themselves of it by the act of ratification, or by some provision of the Constitution. If they have not, the Constitution must be federal, and not national; for it would have, in that case, every attribute necessary to constitute it federal, and not one to make it national. On the other hand, if they have divested themselves, then it would necessarily lose its federal character, and become national. Whether, then, the government is federal or national, is reduced to a single question; whether the act of ratification, of itself, or the Constitution, by some one, or all of its provisions, did, or did not, divest the several States of their character of separate, independent, and sovereign communities, and merge them all in one great community or nation, called the American people.

Before entering on the consideration of this important question, it is proper to remark, that, on its decision, the character of the government, as well as the Constitution, depends. The former must, necessarily, partake of the character of the latter, as it is but its agent, created by it, to carry its powers into effect. Accordingly, then, as the Constitution is federal or national, so must the government be; and I shall, therefore, use them indiscriminately in discussing the subject.

Of all the questions which can arise under our system of government, this is by far the most important. It involves many others of great magnitude; and among them, that of the allegiance of the citizen; or, in other words, the question to whom allegiance and obedience are ultimately due. What is the true relation between the two governments—that of the United States, and those of the several States? and what is the relation between the individuals respectively composing them? For it is clear, if the States still retain their sovereignty as separate and independent communities, the allegiance and obedience of the citizens of each would be due to their respective States; and that the government of the United States and those of the several States would stand as equals and co-ordinates in their respective spheres; and, instead of being united socially, their citizens would be politically connected through their respective States. On the contrary, if they have, by ratifying the Constitution, divested themselves of their individuality and sovereignty, and merged themselves into one great community or nation, it is equally clear that the sovereignty would reside in the whole—or what is called the American people; and that allegiance and obedience would be due to them. Nor is it less so, that the government of the several States would, in such case, stand to that of the United States, in the relation of inferior and subordinate, to superior and paramount; and that the individuals of the several States, thus fused, as it were, into one general mass, would be united *socially*, and not *politically*. So great a change of condition would have involved a thorough and radical revolution, both socially and politically—a revolution much more radical, indeed, than that which followed the Declaration of Independence.

They who maintain that the ratification of the Constitution effected so mighty a change, are bound to establish it by the most demonstrative proof. The presumption is strongly opposed to it. It has already been shown that the authority of the convention which formed the Constitution is clearly against it; and that the history of its ratification, instead of supplying evidence in its favor, furnishes strong testimony in opposition to it. To these, others may be added; and, among them, the presumption drawn from the history of these States, in all the stages of their existence down to the time of the ratification of the Constitution. In all, they formed separate, and, as it respects each other, independent communities, and were ever remarkable for the tenacity with which they adhered to their rights as such. It constituted, during the whole period, one of the most striking traits in their character,—as a very brief sketch will show.

During their colonial condition, they formed distinct communities,—each with its separate charter and government,—and in no way connected with each other, except as dependent members of a common empire. Their first union amongst themselves was, in resistance to the encroachments of the parent country on their chartered rights,—when they adopted the title of,—" the United Colonies." Under that name they acted, until they declared their independence; — always, in their joint councils, voting and acting as separate and distinct communities;—and not in the aggregate, as composing one community or nation. They acted in the same character in declaring independence; by which act they passed from their dependent, colonial condition, into that of free and sovereign States. The declaration was made by delegates appointed by the several colonies, each for itself, and on its own authority. The vote making the declaration was taken by delegations, each counting one. The declaration was announced to be unanimous, not because every delegate voted for it, but because the majority of each delegation did; showing clearly that the body itself, regarded it as the united act of the several colonies, and not the act of the whole as one community. To leave no doubt on a point so important, and in reference to which the several colonies were so tenacious, the declaration was made in the name and by the authority of the people of the colonies, represented in Congress; and that was followed by declaring them to be " free and independent States." The act was, in fact, but a formal and solemn annunciation to the world that the colonies had ceased to be dependent communities, and had become free and independent States, without involving any other change in their relations with each other than those necessarily incident to a separation from the parent country. So far were they from supposing, or intending that it should have the effect of merging their existence, as separate communities, into one nation, that they had appointed a committee—which was actually sitting, while the declaration was under discussion—to prepare a plan of a confederacy of the States, preparatory to entering into their new condition. In fulfilment of their appointment, this committee prepared the draft of the articles of confederation and perpetual union, which afterwards was adopted by the governments of the several States. That it instituted a mere confederacy and union of the States had already been shown. That, in forming and assenting to it, the States were exceedingly jealous and watchful in delegating power, even to a confederacy; that they granted the powers delegated most reluctantly and sparingly; that several of them long stood out, under all the pressure of the Revolutionary War, before they acceded to it; and that, during the interval which elapsed between its adoption and that of the present Constitution, they evinced, under the most urgent necessity, the same reluctance and jealousy, in delegating power—are facts which cannot be disputed.

To this may be added another circumstance of no little weight, drawn from the preliminary steps taken for the ratification of the Constitution. The plan was laid, by the convention, before the Congress of the confederacy, for its consideration and action, as has been stated. It was the sole organ and representative of these States in their confederated character. By submitting it, the convention recognized and acknowledged its authority over it, as the organ of distinct, independent, and sovereign States. It had the right to dispose of it as it pleased; and, if it had thought proper, it might have defeated the plan by simply omitting to act on it. But it thought proper to act, and to adopt the course recommended by the convention, which was, to submit it "to a convention of delegates, chosen in each State, by the people thereof, for their assent and adoption." All this was in strict accord with the federal character of the Constitution, but wholly repugnant to the idea of its being national. It received the assent of the States in all the possible modes in which it could be obtained: first, in their confederated character, through its only appropriate organ, the Congress; next, in their individual character, as separate States, through their respective State governments, to which the Congress referred it; and finally, in their high character of independent and sovereign communities, through a convention of the people, called in each State, by the authority of its government. The States acting in these various capacities might, at every stage, have defeated it or not, at their option, by giving or withholding their consent.

With this weight of presumptive evidence, to use no stronger expression, in favor of its federal, in contradistinction to its national character, I shall next proceed to show that the ratification of the Constitution, instead of furnishing proof against, contains additional and conclusive evidence in its favor.

We are not left to conjecture as to what was meant by the ratification of the Constitution, or its effects. The expressions used by the conventions of the States, in ratifying it, and those used by the Constitution in connection with it, afford ample means of ascertaining with accuracy, both its meaning and effect. The usual form of expression used for the former is: "We, the delegates of the State" (naming the State), "do, in behalf of the people of the State, assent to, and ratify the said Constitution." All use "ratify," and all, except North Carolina, use "assent to." The delegates of that State use "adopt" instead of "assent to," a variance merely in the form of expression, without, in any degree, affecting the meaning. Ratification was, then, the act of the several States in their separate capacity. It was performed by delegates appointed expressly for the purpose. Each appointed its own delegates; and the delegates of each acted in the name of, and for the State appointing them. Their act consisted in "assenting to," or, what is the same thing, "adopting and ratifying" the Constitution.

By turning to the seventh article of the Constitution, and to the preamble, it will be found what was the effect of ratifying. The article expressly provides that, "the ratification of the conventions of nine States shall be sufficient for the establishment of this Constitution, between the States so ratifying the same." The preamble of the Constitution is in the following words: "We, the people of the United States, in order to form a more perfect union, establish justice, insure domestic tranquillity, provide for the common defence, promote the general welfare, and secure the blessings of liberty to ourselves and our posterity, do ordain and establish this Constitution for the United States of America." The effect, then, of its ratification was, to ordain and establish the Constitution, and thereby to make, what was before but a plan, "The Constitution of the United States of America." All this is clear.

It remains now to show *by whom* it was ordained and established; *for whom* it was ordained and established; *for what* it was ordained and established; and *over whom* it was ordained and established. These will be considered in the order in which they stand.

Nothing more is necessary, in order to show by whom it was ordained and established, than to ascertain who are meant by "We, the people of the United States"; for, by their authority, it was done. To this there can be but one answer: it meant the people who ratified the instrument; for it was the act of ratification which ordained and established it. Who they were, admits of no doubt. The process preparatory to ratification, and the acts by which it was done, prove, beyond the possibility of a doubt, that it was ratified by the several States, through conventions of delegates, chosen in each State by the people thereof; and acting, each in the name and by the authority of its State: and, as all the States ratified it, "We, the people of the United States," mean We, the people of the several States of the Union. The inference is irresistible. And when it is considered that the States of the Union were then members of the confederacy, and that, by the express provision of one of its articles, "each State retains its sovereignty, freedom, and independence," the proof is demonstrative, that "We, the people of the United States of America," mean the people of the several States of the Union, acting as free, independent, and sovereign States. This strikingly confirms what has been already stated—to wit, that the convention which formed the Constitution meant the same thing by the terms "United States" and "federal," when applied to the Constitution or government; and that the former, when used politically, always mean these States united as independent and sovereign communities.

Having shown *by whom* it was ordained, there will be no difficulty in determining *for whom* it was ordained. The preamble is explicit—it was ordained and established for "The United States of America," adding "America," in comformity to the style of the then confederacy, and the Declaration of Independence. Assuming, then, that the "United States" bears the same meaning in the conclusion of the preamble as it does in its commencement (and no reason can be assigned why it should not), it follows, necessarily, that the Constitution was ordained and established *for* the people of the several States, *by* whom it was ordained and established.

Nor will there be any difficulty in showing *for what* it was ordained and established. The preamble enumerates the objects. They are—"to form a more perfect union, to establish justice, insure domestic tranquillity, provide for the common defence, promote the general welfare, and secure the blessings of liberty to ourselves and our posterity." To effect these objects, they ordained and established, to use their own language, "the Constitution for the United States of America," clearly meaning by "for" that it was intended to be *their* Constitution; and that the objects of ordaining and establishing it were to perfect *their* union, to establish justice among *them;* to insure *their* domestic tranquillity, to provide for *their* common defence and general welfare, and to secure the blessings of liberty to *them* and *their* posterity. Taken all together, it follows, from what has been stated, that the Constitution was ordained and established *by* the several States, as *distinct, sovereign communities;* and that it was ordained and established by them for *themselves*—for their common welfare and safety, as *distinct and sovereign communities.*

It remains to be shown *over whom* it was ordained and established. That it was not over *the several States* is settled by the seventh article beyond controversy. It declares that the ratification by nine States shall be sufficient to establish the Constitution between the States so ratifying. "Between" necessarily excludes *over*—as that which is *between* States cannot be *over* them. Reason itself, if the Constitution had been silent, would have led, with equal certainty, to the same conclusion. For it was the several States, or, what is the same thing, their people, in their sovereign capacity, who ordained and established the Constitution. But the authority which ordains and establishes is higher than that which is ordained and established; and, of course, the latter must be subordinate to the former, and cannot, therefore, be *over* it. "Between" always means more than over, and implies in this case that the authority which ordained and established the Constitution was the joint and united authority of the States ratifying it; and that, among the effects of their ratification, it became a contract between them; and, *as a compact*, binding on them; but only as such. In that sense the term "between" is appropriately applied. In no other can it be. It was, doubtless, used in that sense in this instance; but the question still remains, *over whom* was it ordained and established? After what has been stated, the answer may be readily given. It was *over the government* which it created, and all its functionaries in their official character, and the individuals composing and inhabiting the several States, as far as they might come within the sphere of the powers delegated to the United States.

I have now shown, conclusively, by arguments drawn from the act of ratification, and the Constitution itself, that the several States of the Union, acting in their confederated character, ordained and established the Constitution; that they ordained and established it for themselves, in the same character; that they ordained and established it for their welfare and safety, in the like character; that they established it as a compact *between* them, and not as a Constitution *over* them; and that, as a compact, they are parties to it, in the same character. I have thus established, conclusively, that these States, in ratifying the Constitution, did not lose the confederated character which they possessed when they ratified it, as well as in all the preceding stages of their existence; but, on the contrary, still retained it to the full.

Those who oppose this conclusion, and maintain the national character of the government, rely, in support of their views, mainly on the expressions, "We, the people of the United States," used in the first part of the preamble; and "do ordain and establish this Constitution for the United States of America," used in its conclusion. Taken together, they insist, in the first place, that "we, the people," mean the people in their individual character, as forming a single community; and that "the United States of America" designates them in their aggregate character as the American people. In maintaining this construction, they rely on the omission to enumerate the States by name, after the word "people" (so as to make it read, "We, the people of New Hampshire, Massachusetts, &c.," as was done in the articles of the confederation, and, also, in signing the Declaration of Independence); and, instead of this, the simple use of the general term "United States."

However plausible this may appear, an explanation perfectly satisfactory may be given, why the expression, as it now stands, was used by the framers of the Constitution, and why it should not receive the meaning attempted to be placed upon it. It is conceded that, if the enumeration of the States after the word, "people," had been made, the expression would have been freed from all ambiguity, and the inference and argument founded on the failure to do so left without pretext or support. The omission is certainly striking, but it can be readily explained. It was made intentionally, and solely from the necessity of the case. The first draft of the Constitution contained an enumeration of the States, by name, after the word "people"; but it became impossible to retain it after the adoption of the seventh and last article, which provided, that the ratification by nine States should be sufficient to establish the Constitution as between *them;* and for the plain reason, that it was impossible to determine whether all the States would ratify; or, if any failed, which, and how many of the number; or, if nine should ratify, how to designate them. No alternative was thus left but to omit the enumeration, and to insert the "United States of America" in its place. And yet, an omission, so readily and so satisfactorily explained, has been seized on, as furnishing strong proof that the government was ordained and established by the American people, in the aggregate, and is therefore national.

But the omission, of itself, would have caused no difficulty, had there not been connected with it a twofold ambiguity in the expression as it now stands. The term "United States," which always means, in Constitutional language, the several States in their confederated character, means also, as has been shown, when applied geographically, the country occupied and possessed by them. While the term, "people," has, in the English language, no plural, and is necessarily used in the singular number, even when applied to many communities or States confederated in a common union, as is the case with the United States. Availing themselves of this double ambiguity, and the omission to enumerate the States by name, the advocates of the national theory of the government, assuming that *we, the people,* meant individuals generally, and not people as forming States; and that *United States* was used in a geographical and not a political sense, made out an argument of some plausibility, in favor of the conclusion that "we, the people of the United States of America," meant the aggregate population of the States regarded *en masse*, and not in their distinctive character as forming separate political communities. But in this gratuitous assumption, and the conclusion drawn from it, they overlooked the stubborn fact, that the very people who ordained and established the constitution, are identically the same who ratified it; for it was by the act of ratification alone that it was ordained and established, as has been conclusively shown. This fact, of itself, sweeps away every vestige of the argument drawn from the ambiguity of those terms, as used in the preamble.

They next rely, in support of their theory, on the expression, "ordained and established this Constitution." They admit that the Constitution, in its incipient state, assumed the form of a compact; but contend that "ordained and established," as applied to the Constitution and government, are incompatible with the idea of compact; that, consequently, the instrument or plan lost its federative character when it was ordained and established as a Constitution; and, thus, the States ceased to be parties to a compact, and members of a confederated union, and became fused into one common community, or nation, as subordinate and dependent divisions or corporations.

I do not deem it necessary to discuss the question whether there is any compatibility between the terms "ordained and established" and that of "compact," on which the whole argument rests; although it would be no difficult task to show that it is a gratuitous assumption, without any foundation whatever for its support. It is sufficient for my purpose to show that the assumption is wholly inconsistent with the Constitution itself—as much so, as the conclusion drawn from it has been shown to be inconsistent with the opinion of the convention which formed it. Very little will be required, after what has been already stated, to establish what I propose.

That the Constitution regards itself in the light of a compact, still existing between the States, after it was ordained and established; that it regards the union, then existing, as still existing; and the several States, of course, still members of it, in their original character of confederated States, is clear. Its seventh article, so often referred to, in connection with the arguments drawn from the preamble, sufficiently establishes all these points, without adducing others; except that which relates to the continuance of the union. To establish this, it will not be necessary to travel out of the preamble and the letter of the convention, laying the plan of the Constitution before the Congress of the confederation. In enumerating the objects for which the Constitution was ordained and established, the preamble places at the head of the rest, as its leading object—"to form a more perfect union." So far, then, are the terms "ordained and established" from being incompatible with the union, or having the effect of destroying it, the Constitution itself declares that it was intended "to form a more perfect union." This, of itself, is sufficient to refute the assertion of their incompatibility. But it is proper here to remark that it could not have been intended, by the expression in the preamble, "to form a more perfect union," to declare that the old was abolished, and a new and more perfect union established in its place: for we have the authority of the convention which formed the Constitution, to prove that their object was to continue the then existing union. In their letter, laying it before Congress, they say, "In all our deliberations on this subject, we kept steadily in our view that which appears to us the greatest interest of every true American, the consolidation of our union." "Our union" can refer to no other than the then existing union, the old union of the confederacy, and of the revolutionary government which preceded it, of which these States were confederated members. This must, of course, have been the union to which the framers referred in the preamble. It was this, accordingly, which the Constitution intended to make more perfect; just as the confederacy made more perfect that of the revolutionary government. Nor is there anything in the term "consolidation," used by the convention, calculated to weaken the conclusion. It is a strong expression; but as strong as it is, it certainly was not intended to imply the destruction of the union, as it is supposed to do by the advocates of a national government; for that would have been incompatible with the context, as well as with the continuance of the union, which the sentence and the entire letter imply. Interpreted, then, in conjunction with the expression used in the preamble, "to form a more perfect union," although it may more strongly intimate closeness of connection, it can imply nothing incompatible with the professed object of perfecting the union, still less a meaning and effect wholly inconsistent with the nature of a confederated community. For to adopt the interpretation contended for, to its full extent, would be to *destroy* the union, and not to consolidate and perfect it.

If we turn from the preamble and the ratifications, to the body of the Constitution, we shall find that it furnishes most conclusive proof that the government is federal, and not national. I can discover nothing, in any portion of it, which gives the least countenance to the opposite conclusion. On the contrary, the instrument, in all its parts, repels it. It is, throughout, federal. It everywhere recognizes the existence of the States, and invokes their aid to carry its powers into execution. In one of the two Houses of Congress the members are elected by the legislatures of their respective States; and in the other by the people of the several States, not as composing mere districts of one great community, but as distinct and independent communities. General Washington vetoed the first act apportioning the members of the House of Representatives among the several States, under the first census, expressly on the ground that the act assumed, as its basis, the former and not the latter construction. The President and Vice-President are chosen by electors, appointed by their respective States; and, finally, the judges are appointed by the President and the Senate; and, of course, as these are elected by the States, they are appointed through their agency.

But however strong be the proofs of its federal character derived from this source, that portion which provides for the amendment of the Constitution, furnishes, if possible, still stronger. It shows, conclusively, that the people of the several States still retain that supreme ultimate power called sovereignty—the power by which they ordained and established the Constitution; and which can rightfully create, modify, amend, or abolish it, at its pleasure. Wherever this power resides, there the sovereignty is to be found. That it still continues to exist in the several States, in a modified form, is clearly shown by the fifth article of the Constitution, which provides for its amendment. By its provisions, Congress may propose amendments, on its own authority, by the vote of two-thirds of both Houses; or it may be compelled to call a convention to propose them, by two-thirds of the legislatures of the several States: but, in either case, they remain, when thus made, mere proposals of no validity, until adopted by three-fourths of the States, through their respective legislatures; or by conventions, called by them for the purpose. Thus far, the several States, in ordaining and establishing the Constitution, agreed, for their mutual convenience and advantage, to modify, by compact, their high sovereign power of creating and establishing constitutions, as far as it related to the Constitution and government of the United States. I say, for their mutual convenience and advantage; for without the modification, it would have required the separate consent of all the States of the Union to alter or amend their constitutional compact; in like manner as it required the consent of all to establish it between them; and to obviate the almost insuperable difficulty of making such amendments as time and experience might prove to be necessary, by the unanimous consent of all, they agreed to make the modification. But that they did not intend, by this, to divest themselves of the high sovereign right (a right which they still retain, notwithstanding the modification) to change or abolish the present Constitution and government at their pleasure, cannot be doubted. It is an acknowledged principle, that sovereigns may, by compact, modify or qualify the exercise of their power, without impairing their sovereignty; of which the confederacy existing at the time furnishes a striking illustration. It must reside, unimpaired and in its plentitude, somewhere. And if it do not reside in the people of the several States, in their confederated character, where—so far as it relates to the Constitution and government of the United States—can it be found? Not, certainly, in the government; for, according to our theory, sovereignty resides in the people, and not in the government. That it cannot be found in the people, taken in the aggregate, as forming one community or nation, is equally certain. But as certain as it cannot, just so certain is it that it must reside in the people of the several States; and if it reside in them at all, it must reside in them as separate and distinct communities; for it has been shown that it does not reside in them in the aggregate, as forming one community or nation. These are the only aspects under which it is possible to regard the people; and, just as certain as it resides in them, in that character, so certain is it that ours is a federal and not a national government.

CALIFORNIA

California (name applied by Cortez to the bay and region, which he believed to be an island; derived from that of an island in an old Spanish romance abounding in precious stones), a State in the Pacific division of the North American Union; bounded on the n. by Oregon, e. by Nevada and Arizona, s. by the Lower California territory of Mexico, and w. by the Pacific Ocean; area, 158,297 square miles, of which 2,205 are water surface; extreme breadth, e. to w., 375 miles, extreme length, n. to s., 770 miles; number of counties, 57; capital, Sacramento; popular name, "the Golden State"; State flower, the poppy; State motto, "Eureka" ("I have found it"); admitted into the Union as the thirty-first State, Sept. 9, 1850; population (1910), 2,377,549.

General Statistics.—California is particularly noted for its production of petroleum, gold, copper, fruits (especially grapes, oranges, and lemons), and beet sugar; its world-wide commerce; and the extent and variety of its manufactures. Its mineral productions reached their maximum output in 1909, with a total value of $82,972,209, petroleum yielding $32,398,187; gold, $20,237,870; and copper, $8,478,424. The total output in the twenty-three years then ended was valued at $757,508,849. There are over 87,000 farms, having 27,880,000 acres, nearly one-half of which is improved; value of farm lands, buildings, and implements, $1,484,950,000; value of ordinary farm crops, $65,500,000 (barley predominating); value of live-stock, $122,395,000. Vineyards, total, 342,520 acres, of which 160,573 are in wine grapes, 128,217 in raisin grapes, and 53,730 in table grapes; and orchards have in bearing over 34,355,000 deciduous and citrus fruit and nut trees. In 1910 California gained first rank in the production of beet sugar, with an output of 144,746 tons, nearly thirty per cent. of the total of the country. The value of all products of the soil was $495,288,466.

Manufacturing industries have over 7,650 factory-system establishments, with $537,134,000 capital and $529,760,000 in value of annual products, the most important being the canning and preserving of fruits and vegetables, slaughtering and meat-packing, lumber products, and wines and liquors. California has rapidly expanding commercial relations with the Philippines, China, Japan, Asiatic Russia, Alaska, Hawaii, Mexico, and South American ports. Humboldt, Los Angeles, San Diego, and San Francisco are ports of delivery and seats of customs districts. During the calendar year 1910 the aggregate value of the imports of merchandise at all ports was $53,782,277; of exports, $38,638,550; imports of gold and silver ore, bullion, and coin (San Francisco), $6,452,607; exports, $9,457,967—total foreign trade, $108,331,401.

Business interests are promoted by national, State, and savings banks, having combined capital, $177,668,790; individual deposits, $666,000,000; and resources exceeding $993,500,000; exchanges

A CALIFORNIA VINEYARD.

at clearing houses at San Francisco, Los Angeles, Oakland, San José, Sacramento, San Diego, Stockton, Fresno, and Pasadena have amounted to $3,440,731,900 in a single year.

Religious interests are represented by 2,897 organizations, having 2,521 church edifices, 611,464 communicants or members, 243,672 Sunday-school scholars, and church property valued at $28,065,261, the strongest denominations being the Roman Catholic, Methodist, Presbyterian, Baptist, Congregational, Protestant Episcopal, and Disciples. The Roman Catholic Church has an archbishop at San Francisco, and bishops there, at Los Angeles, and Sacramento; the Protestant Episcopal has bishops at San Francisco, Sacramento, San Joaquin, and Los Angeles; and the Methodist Episcopal has a bishop resident at San Francisco. The public-school age is 5–17; enrollment, 352,278; average daily attendance, 272,252; value of public-school property, $38,651,800; total revenue, $12,835,500; total expenditure, $15,985,000. For the higher education of men and women there are the State University, with agricultural and mechanical college, at Berkeley; Pomona College (Cong.), Claremont; Occidental College (Presb.), Los Angeles; University of Southern California (M. E.), Los Angeles; St. Mary's College (R. C.), Oakland; Throop Polytechnic Institute (non-sect.), Pasadena; St. Ignatius College (R. C.), San Francisco; University of the Pacific (M. E.), San José; Santa Clara College (R. C.), Santa Clara; and Leland Stanford, Jr., University (non-sect.), Stanford University Station. Mills College (non-sect.), at San Francisco, is for women on... There are State normal schools at C... Los Angeles, San Diego, and San Jos...

Government.—The executive au... is vested in a governor (annual... $10,000), lieutenant-governor, ... of state, treasurer, comptroller... general, attorney-general, su... of education, and commissio... rance and agriculture—offic... years. The legislature co... ate of forty members and... resentatives of eighty ... Senators, four years; ... two years; salary ... term; sessions, bie... members draw pa... The chief judicia...

Court, comprising a chief justice and six associate justices. The section of the constitution relating to the bonding of counties, cities, towns, districts, etc., was amended in 1891 to render it more rigid; a new law regulating indebtedness for municipal improvements was enacted in 1901; an amendment exempting various bonds issued in the State from taxation was favorably voted on in 1902; and eight additional amendments, relating to the issue of bonds for the Panama-Pacific International Exposition (1915) and other financial interests, were favorably voted on in 1910. An Australian ballot law became effective in 1891; pure food, anti-trust, and child labor laws in 1907; a direct primary law in 1910; and woman suffrage in 1911. The assessed property valuations aggregate over $2,471,505,000. The total bonded debt (1911) was $4,881,500, and the treasury held $5,929,915 in cash.

California ranked twenty-ninth in population among the States and Territories under the census of 1850; twenty-sixth in 1860; twenty-fourth in 1870 and 1880; twenty-second in 1890; twenty-first in 1900; and twelfth in 1910.

...NISH GOVERNORS OF CALIFORNIA.

...me.	Term.
....	1767 to 1771
....	1771 " 1774
...	1774 " 1782
	1782 " 1790
	1790 " 1792
	...92 " 1794
	" 1800
	" 1814
	" 1815
	" 1822

...3
...5

CALIFORNIA REPUBLIC GOVERNOR.

Name.	Term.
John C. Frémont..........	1846

PROVISIONAL OR MILITARY GOVERNORS.

Name.	Term.
Com. John D. Sloat........	1847
Com. Robert F. Stockton....	1847
John C. Frémont..........	1847
Gen. Stephen W. Kearny...	1847
Richard B. Mason.........	1847 to 1849
Gen. Persifer F. Smith.....	1849
Bennett Riley	1849

STATE GOVERNORS.

Name.	Term.
Peter H. Burnett	1849 to 1851
John McDougall............	1851 " 1852
John Bigler................	1852 " 1856
J. Neely Johnson..........	1856 " 1858
John B. Weller............	1858 " 1860
Milton S. Latham..........	1860
John G. Downey...........	1860 to 1862
Leland Stanford...........	1862 " 1863
Frederick F. Low..........	1863 " 1867
Henry H. Haight..........	1867 " 1871
Newton Booth.............	1871 " 1875
Romnaldo Pacheco..........	1875
William Irwin.............	1875 to 1880
George C. Perkins..........	1880 " 1883
George Stoneman..........	1883 " 1887
Washington Bartlett........	1887
Robert W. Waterman........	1887 to 1891
Henry H. Markham........	1891 " 1895
J. H. Budd................	1895 " 1899
Henry T. Gage............	1899 " 1903
George C. Pardee	1903 " 1907
James N. Gillett...........	1907 " 1911
Hiram W. Johnson.........	1911 " 1915

UNITED STATES SENATORS.

Name.	No. of Congress.	Term.
John C. Frémont.	31st	1849 to 1851
William M. Gwin .	31st to 36th	1849 " 1861
John B. Weller ..	32d " 34th	1851 " 1857
David C. Broderick.	35th " 36th	1857 " 1859
Henry P. Hann....	36th	1859
Milton S. Latham.	36th to 37th	1860 " 1863
James A. McDougall	37th " 39th	1861 " 1867
John Conners.....	38th " 40th	1863 " 1869
Cornelius Cole....	40th " 42d	1867 " 1873
Eugene Casserly...	41st " 42d	1869 " 1873
John S. Hager.....	43d	1874
Aaron A. Sargent.	43d to 45th	1873 to 1879
Newton Booth.....	44th " 46th	1875 " 1881
James T. Farley...	46th " 48th	1879 " 1885
John F. Miller....	47th " 49th	1881 " 1887
Leland Stanford...	49th " 53d	1885 " 1893
George Hearst.....	50th " 51st	1887 " 1891
Charles N. Felton.	52d " 53d	1891 " 1893
Stephen M. White..	53d " 56th	1893 " 1899
George C. Perkins.	53d " —	1893 " —
Thomas R. Bard...	56th " 58th	1899 " 1904
Frank P. Flint....	59th " 61st	1905 " 1911
John D. Works....	62d " —	1911 " —

In the apportionment of representation in Congress, California was given two members under the censuses of 1840 and 1850; three under 1860; four under 1870; six under 1880; seven under 1890; eight under 1900; and eleven under 1910.

History: Early Period.—In 1534 HERNANDO CORTEZ (*q. v.*) sent Hernando de Grijalva on an errand of discovery to the Pacific coast, who probably saw the peninsula of California. Twenty-five years before the Spanish leader discovered the country, a romance was published in Spain in which are described the doings of a pagan queen of Amazons, who brought from the "right hand of the Indies" her allies, to assist the infidels in their attack upon Constantinople. The romance was entitled *Las Sergus de Esplandian,* the name of an imaginary Greek emperor living in Stamboul, the Turkish name of Constantinople. The Amazonian queen was named Calafia, whose kingdom, rich in gold, diamonds, and pearls, was called California. The author probably derived the name from Calif, the title of a successor of Mohammed. The author says: "Know that on the right hand of the Indies there is an island, called California, very close to the Terrestrial Paradise, and it was peopled by black women without any man among them, for they lived in the fashion of the Amazonia. They were of strong and hardy bodies, of ardent courage, and of great force. Their island was the strongest in all the world, with its steep cliffs and rocky shore. Their arms were all of gold, and so was the harness of the wild beasts which they tamed and rode. For in the whole island there was no metal but gold. They lived in caves wrought out of the rocks with much labor. They had many ships with which they sailed out to other countries to obtain booty." Both Cortez and Grijalva believed, as everybody then believed, that they were in the neighborhood of the coast of Asia; and, as the aspect of the country corresponded with the description in the romance, they named the peninsula California. In the Gulf of California were found pearls; so the description of the country of the black Amazons—a country filled with gold and pearls—suited the actual condition of the region explored.

Although parts of the present territory of the State are believed to have been discovered about 1534, settlements in Old or Lower California were first made in 1683 by Jesuit missionaries. New or Upper California was discovered later, and the first mission there (San Diego) was planted in 1768. For many years the government of California, temporal and spiritual, was under the control of monks of the Order of St. Francis. It was not until about 1770 that the Bay of San Francisco was discovered, and in 1776 a mission was established there. At the beginning of the nineteenth century eighteen missions had been established in California, with over 15,000 converts. In 1812, the Russians, coming from what was then Russian America, founded in the n. part of the coast a small colony, which remained till 1841. In 1822, Mexican in-

CATHEDRAL ROCKS, YOSEMITE VALLEY.

dependence was proclaimed in California, and the first provincial legislature was chosen; but throughout the whole succeeding period the subjection of the province to the Mexican government was often not much more than nominal. The Californians showed themselves jealous of all Mexican interference, quarrelled with the Mexican governors, and in 1836 by revolution put themselves in a position of virtual independence, under a Californian governor, Alvarado. By 1840 the white population of the "department" had increased to 5,780. The rest of the political history of California, to the time of the conquest by the Americans, is one of petty quarrel and intrigue. In 1843–46 many thousand emigrants from the United States settled in California; and when the war with Mexico broke out in 1846, the struggle for the mastery in that Pacific coast province speedily ended in victory for the Americans in 1847. By the treaty of peace at GUADALUPE HIDALGO (*q. v.*), California and other territory were ceded to the United States.

United States Territory.—In the month of February, 1848, gold was discovered in California, on the Sacramento River, by John W. Marshall, who was working for JOHN A. SUTTER (*q. v.*), and as the news spread abroad thousands of enterprising and energetic men flocked thither, not only from the United States, but from South America, Europe, and China, to secure the precious metal. Very soon there was a mixed population of all sorts of characters in California of at least 250,000 persons. The military governor called a convention to meet at Monterey, Sept. 1, 1849, to frame a State constitution. One was formed by which slavery was to be excluded from the new State; and this document revived in Congress, in great intensity, debates on the subject of slavery in 1849–50. See KEARNY, STEPHEN WATTS; STOCKTON; ROBERT FIELD.

Prior to the assembly of the constitutional convention the people of California, in convention at San Francisco, had voted against the admission of the slave-labor system in that country. The constitution adopted at Monterey also had a provision to exclude slavery from the State. Thus came into political form the crude

BIG TREES OF CALIFORNIA.

elements of a State, the birth and maturity of which seems like a strange dream. All had been accomplished within twenty months from the time when gold was discovered at Sutter's Mill. Under this constitution JOHN CHARLES FRÉMONT (*q. v.*) and WILLIAM M. GWIN (*q. v.*) were chosen by the State legislature United States Senators. Edward Gilbert and G. H. Wright were elected to the House of Representatives. When Frémont and Gwin went to Washington, they took the State constitution with them, and presented a petition (February, 1850) asking for the admission of California into the Union as a free and independent State. The article in its constitution which excluded slavery became a cause of violent debate in Congress and of bitter feeling in the South against the people of the North. The Union, so strong in the hearts of the people, was shaken to its centre. Mr. Clay again appeared as a compromiser for the sake of peace and union. It seemed that some compromise was needed to avoid serious difficulty, for already the representatives of the slave interest had taken action, and the Southern members in Congress boldly declared their intention to break up the Union if California should be admitted under such a constitution. A joint resolution was adopted to appoint a committee of thirteen (six Northern and six Southern members, who should choose the thirteenth) to consider the subject of a Territorial government for California, New Mexico, and Utah, with instructions to report a plan of compromise embracing all the questions thus arising out of the subject of slavery. Henry Clay was made chairman of that committee. He had already presented (Jan. 25, 1850) a plan of compromise to the South, and spoke eloquently in favor of it (Feb. 5); and on May 8 he reported a plan of compromise in a series of bills, intended to be a pacification. This was called the OMNIBUS BILL (*q. v.*). It made large concessions to the slave-holders, and yet it was not satisfactory to them. For months a violent discussion of the compromise act was carried on throughout the country, and it was denounced upon diametrically opposite grounds. It finally became a law, and on Sept. 9, 1850, California was admitted to the Union as a State.

California in Statehood.—So lawless were a large class of the population at this time that only the "Vigilance Committees" could control them and preserve social order. The first vigilance committee of San Francisco was organized in 1851. Finally, these committees assumed the functions and powers of judges and executives, which guaranteed all accused persons a fair trial. Dangerous men of every kind were arrested, tried, hanged, or transported. In 1856 the vigilance committee surrendered its powers to the regularly constituted civil authority. No quota of troops was assigned to California in the Civil War, but 16,000 men entered the National service and served on the coast. In addition, some 500 men enlisted in California were incorporated into the 2d Massachusetts U. S. C. V. The Pacific Railroad was completed May 12, 1869, thus connecting California with the Atlantic seaboard. The progress of the State was phenomenal up to the earthquake of April 18, 1906. The destruction of San Francisco by fire and the damage to the smaller cities simply stimulated the energies of the people.

The first capital of California was Los Angeles, founded in 1781, and made a city and the capital in 1835. For several years, under the Mexican rule, that city and Monterey alternated as the seat of administration. In 1854 Sacramento became the permanent capital of the State. The present constitution was adopted in 1879, and has been amended many times, the most recent changes being noted under *Government*. California was conspicuous in a short-lived international excitement in 1906–07, caused by an attempt to segregate Japanese youth in the public schools of San Francisco. Further details of the share of the State in the general history of the United States will be found under CHINESE EXCLUSION ACTS; KEARNEY, DENIS; MEXICO, WAR WITH; NATIONAL MONUMENTS; SAN FRANCISCO. See also DYNAMITE OUTRAGES.

Callahan, JAMES MORTON, historian; born in Bedford, Ind., Nov. 4, 1864; was graduated at the University of Indiana in 1894; acting professor of American history and constitutional law at Hamilton College in 1897–98; lecturer on American diplomatic history at the Johns Hopkins University in 1898–1902; director of Bureau of Historical Research in 1900–02; chief of department of history and political science at the University of West Virginia from 1902. His publications include *Neutrality of the American Lakes; Cuba and International Relations; American Relations in the Pacific and the Far East; Confederate Diplomacy; The American Expansion Policy; The Monroe Doctrine and Inter-American Relations; Evolution of Seward's Mexican Policy; History of West Virginia*, etc.; editor *West Virginia University Studies in American History*, etc.

Callava, Spanish governor of Florida, was arrested by Andrew Jackson in September, 1821, because he refused to deliver the Spanish archives. After obtaining the papers Jackson released Callava. The treaty of 1819 with Spain for the purchase of the Floridas was ratified Feb. 22, 1821, but the transfer was delayed.

Callender, JAMES THOMPSON, editor and author; born in Scotland. He published in Edinburgh, in 1792, a book called *Political Progress of Great Britain,* which so offended the authorities that he was banished from the kingdom, and went to Philadelphia, where he published the *Political Register* in 1794–95, and the *American Annual Register* for 1796–97. He was a violent and unscrupulous opponent of Washington's administration, and delighted in abusing Hamilton and other Federalist leaders. For a season he enjoyed the friendship of Jefferson. The latter became disgusted with Callender when the former, becoming Jefferson's enemy, calumniated him fearfully. He published the Richmond *Recorder,* in which he made fierce attacks upon the characters of Washington and Adams, and also wrote *Sketches of the History of America,* and *The Prospect Before Us.* He was drowned near Richmond, Va., in July, 1813.

Callender, JOHN, historian; born in Boston, Mass., in 1706; graduated at Harvard College in 1723; pastor of the First Baptist Church in Newport, R. I., in 1731–48. On March 24, 1738, he delivered a public address entitled *An Historical Discourse on the Civil and Religious Affairs of the Colony of Rhode Island and Providence Plantations, from the First Settlement to the end of the First Century.* For more than 100 years this was the only history of Rhode Island. He also collected a number of papers treating of the history of the Baptists in America. He died in Newport, R. I., Jan. 26, 1748.

Callis, JOHN B., military officer; born in Fayetteville, N. C., Jan. 3, 1828; went to Wisconsin in 1840; entered the army as captain in the 7th Wisconsin Volunteers when the Civil War broke out; brevetted brigadier-general in March, 1864; sent to Huntsville, Ala., as assistant commissioner of the Freedmen's Bureau; resigned and elected to Congress in 1868. During his term of office he presented the resolution on which the KU-KLUX KLAN (*q. v.*) bill was passed. He died in Lancaster, Wis., Sept. 23, 1898.

Calumet, a kind of pipe for smoking used by the North American Indians. The bowl is generally of stone, and the stem is ornamented with feathers, etc. The calumet is the emblem of peace and hospitality. To refuse the offer of it is to make a proclamation of enmity or war, and to accept it is a sign of peace and friendship.

Calvert, the family name of the Lords Baltimore—George, Cecilius, Charles 1st, Benedict Leonard, Charles 2d, and Frederick. See BALTIMORE, LORDS.

Calvert, LEONARD, son of the first Lord Baltimore, and first governor of Maryland; born about 1606. Having been appointed governor of the new colony by his brother Cecil, he sailed from Cowes, Isle of Wight, for Chesapeake Bay, Nov. 22, 1633, with two vessels (*Ark* and *Dove*), and over 300 emigrants. The *Ark* was a ship of 300 tons, and the *Dove* a pinnace of 50 tons. Among the company were two Jesuit priests, Andrew White and John Altham. At religious ceremonies performed at the time of departure, the expedition was committed "to the protection of God especially, and of His most Holy Mother, and St. Ignatius, and all the guardian angels of Maryland." The two vessels were convoyed beyond danger from Turkish corsairs. Separated by a furious tempest that swept the sea three days, ending with a hurricane which split the sails of the *Ark,* unshipped her rudder, and left her at the mercy of the waves, the voyagers were in despair, and doubted not the little *Dove* had gone to the bottom of the ocean. Delightful weather ensued, and at Barbadoes the *Dove* joined the Ark after a separation of six weeks. Sailing northward, they touched at Point Comfort, at the entrance to the Chesapeake, and then went up to Jamestown, with royal letters borne by Calvert, and received there a kind reception from Governor Harvey. They tarried nine days, and then entered the Potomac River, which delighted them. The colonists sailed up the river to the Heron Islands, and, at a little past the middle of March, landed on one of them, which they named

St. Clement's. On the 25th they offered the sacrifice of the mass, set up a huge cross hewn from a tree, and knelt in solemn devotion around it. Going farther up, they entered a river which they called St. George; and on the right bank founded the capital of the new province with military and religious ceremonies, and called it St. Mary's. That scene occurred March 27, 1634. It remained the capital of Maryland until near the close of the century, when it speedily became a ruined town, and now scarcely a trace of it remains. They found the natives friendly, and awed into reverence for the white men by the flash and roar of cannon, which they regarded as lightning and thunder. The successful medical services of Father White in curing a sick Indian king gained the profound respect of these children of the forest. He and his queen and three daughters were baptized by Father White, and became members of the Christian Church. William Claiborne, an earlier settler on Kent Island, in the Chesapeake, gave Calvert much trouble, and was abetted in his course by the Virginia authorities, who regarded the Maryland colonists as intruders. He was driven away, and his property was confiscated. But he was a "thorn in the side" of the proprietor for a long time. Governor Calvert tried to carry out the grand design of the proprietor to establish a feudal nobility with hereditary titles and privileges, the domain for the purpose being divided into manorial estates of 2,000 and 3,000 acres each, but the provisions of the charter fortunately prevented such a consummation of Lord Baltimore's order. Governor Calvert went to England in 1643, and during his absence for nearly a year much trouble ensued in the colony, for Claiborne, with Capt. Richard Ingle, harassed the settlement at St. Mary's. Civil war ensued (1645), and Governor Calvert was expelled from Maryland, and took refuge in Virginia. Finally, Calvert returned from Virginia with a military force, took possession of Kent Island, and re-established proprietary rights over all the province of Maryland. He died June 9, 1647. See BALTIMORE, LORDS.

Cambon, JULES MARTIN, diplomatist; born in Paris, France, April 5, 1845; French ambassador to the United States in 1897–1902; then to Spain. After the destruction of the fleets in Manila Bay and off Santiago, the surrender of the army at the city of Santiago, and the failure of the Spanish government to secure the intervention of the European powers, the Spanish authorities undertook direct negotiations for peace. As diplomatic relations with the United States had been broken off, M. Cambon was appointed the special representative of the Spanish government to arrange for a cessation of hostilities as well as the preliminaries of peace. He executed this mission in a manner that won the appreciation of both governments concerned, and after the ratification of peace he was selected by the two governments to make the formal exchange of certified copies of the act.

JULES MARTIN CAMBON.

Cambridge, city, and one of the county seats of Middlesex county, Mass., separated from Boston by the Charles River; was founded in 1631 under the name of Newtown; and is noted as the place where Washington took command of the Continental army on July 2, 1775; as the seat of HARVARD UNIVERSITY (*q. v.*); and as the place where the sons of Alvan Clark carry on the manufacture of astronomical instruments which have a world-wide reputation. In 1910 the city had a total assessed valuation of taxable property of $110,796,735, and the net city and water debt was $8,036,600. The population in 1900 was 91,886; in 1910, 104,839.

The second synod of Massachusetts met at Cambridge in 1646, and was not dissolved until 1648. The synod composed and adopted a system of church discipline called "The Cambridge Platform," and recommended it, together with the Westminster Confession of Faith, to the general court and to the churches. The latter, in New England, generally complied with the recommendation, and "The Cambridge Platform," with the ecclesiastical laws, formed the theological constitution of the New England colonies.

The seeming apathy of Congress in respect to the army besieging Boston greatly perplexed Washington. The cool season was approaching, and not only powder and artillery were wanting, but fuel, shelter, clothing, provisions, and the wages of the soldiers. Washington, wearied by ineffectual remonstrances, at length wrote a letter to Congress, implying his sense that the neglect of that body had brought matters in his army to a crisis. He submitted to their consideration the wants of the army, a mutinous spirit prevailing among them, and the danger that, when the terms of enlistment of all the troops excepting the regulars should expire in December, it would be difficult to re-enlist them or get new recruits. Congress had really no power to provide an adequate remedy for this state of things; therefore it appointed a committee (Sept. 30, 1775), consisting of Dr. Franklin, Lynch, and Harrison, to repair to the camp, and, with the New England colonies and Washington, devise a plan for renovating the army. They arrived at Cambridge, Oct. 15. With such a representative of Congress as Franklin and such a military leader as Washington, the New England commissioners worked harmoniously; and they devised a scheme for forming, governing, and supplying a new army of about 23,000 men, whom the general was authorized to enlist without delay. See ARMY; WASHINGTON, GEORGE.

Cambridge Platform. See CAMBRIDGE, MASS.

Camden, a village in South Carolina, where, on Aug. 16, 1780, about 3,600 Americans, commanded by General Gates, were defeated by from 2,000 to 2,500 British under Lord Cornwallis, losing 700 men, among them Baron de Kalb, mortally wounded, and nearly all their luggage and artillery.

Cameron, HENRY CLAY, educator; born in Shepherdstown, Va., Sept. 1, 1827; graduated at Princeton College in 1847; in 1855 became professor of Greek at Princeton; in 1877, of Greek language and literature. His publications include *The History of the American Whig Society; Old Princeton: Its Battles, Its Cannon*, etc. He died in Princeton, N. J., Oct. 26, 1906.

Cameron, JAMES DONALD, statesman; born in Middletown, Pa., May 14, 1833; graduated at Princeton in 1852; Secretary of War, 1876–77; United States Senator, 1877–97. He was chairman of the national Republican committee in 1880.

Cameron, SIR RODERICK WILLIAM, capitalist; born in Williamstown, Ontario, Canada, July 25, 1825; entered mercantile life in New York and acquired a large fortune as an exporter and importer; was knighted in 1883; became prominent in Canadian-American diplomacy. He died in London, England, Oct. 19, 1900.

Cameron, SIMON, statesman; born in Lancaster county, Pa., March 18, 1799; elected to the United States Senate in 1845; resigned from the Senate to become Secretary of War in 1861; resigned this office, Jan. 11, 1862, to become minister to Russia; re-elected to the United States Senate in 1866, and again re-elected, but resigned in 1877 in favor of his son. He practically dictated the policy of the Republican party in Pennsylvania for many years. He died June 26, 1889.

Camillus. *Nom-de-plume* of Alexander Hamilton, used in a series of papers entitled *Defence of the Treaty,* published in 1795.

Camorra, a thoroughly organized and wide-spread secret criminal society, believed to have been founded in Naples, Italy, and to have had its strongholds there and in Calabria and Sicily. The Mafia and Black Hand bands that in recent years have committed outrages and murders in various parts of the United States are supposed to be branches of the organization in Italy. The Camorristi have seemed to be all-powerful in their own country, levying a kind of blackmail at all markets, fairs, and public gatherings, claiming the right of deciding disputes, hiring themselves out for any criminal service from the passing of contraband goods to assassination. Many efforts have been made by public authorities and influential Italians in the United States to break up the operations of the desperadoes, and within the last few years quite a number of the leaders have been captured and sentenced to considerable imprisonment. On the night of March 12, 1909, Lieut. Joseph Petrosino, chief of the Italian squad of the New York City Detective Bureau, was murdered in Palermo, Sicily, whither he had gone in search of information concerning the leaders of the Italian criminal bands in the United States. The Italian authorities offered a reward for the arrest of his assassins; the secret council of the Mafia warned all members against giving any information; and, as no clues were discovered, it was generally believed that the main and allied societies were too powerful for the Italian authorities to proceed against with vigor. Early in 1911, however, the authorities captured a number of alleged Camorristi, charged with murder, and their trial at Viterbo was one of the most sensational cases on record and developed astounding revelations of nearly all manner of crimes.

Campbell, ALEXANDER, clergyman; born in County Antrim, Ireland, in June, 1786; educated at the University of Glasgow; came to the United States in 1809, and became pastor of the Presbyterian church in Washington county, Pa. In 1810 with his father he left the Presbyterian Church and founded in 1827 the sect which he named THE DISCIPLES OF CHRIST (*q. v.*), and which is now known as the Campbellites. Mr. Campbell established Bethany College in 1840–41, and was its first president. He died in Bethany, W. Va., March 4, 1866.

Campbell, ALEXANDER, legislator; born in Concord, Pa., Oct. 4, 1814; member of the State legislature in 1858–59; and member of Congress in 1875–77. He obtained wide repute as the "Father of the Greenbacks." He died in La Salle, Ill., Aug. 9, 1898.

Campbell, ALLAN, civil engineer; born in Albany, N. Y., in 1815; laid out the route of the New York & Harlem Railroad; built a railroad from Callao to Lima, Peru; became engineer of the harbor defences of New York in the early part of the Civil War; was chief engineer in the construction of the Union Pacific Railroad; and commissioner of public works in New York. He died in New York City, March 18, 1894.

Campbell, CHARLES, historian; born in Petersburg, Va., May 1, 1807; graduated at Princeton College in 1825, and became a teacher. He was a member of the Virginia Historical Society, and a contributor to the *Historical Register.* He edited the *Orderly Book* of Gen. Andrew Lewis in 1776, and published *An Introduction to the History of the Colony and Ancient Dominion of Virginia; Genealogy of the Spotswood Family.* He died in Staunton, Va., July 11, 1876.

Campbell, CHARLES THOMAS, military officer; born in Franklin county, Pa., Aug. 10, 1823; was educated at Marshall College; served in the war with Mexico; promoted captain in August, 1847. When the Civil War broke out he entered the army, and in December, 1861, was commissioned colonel of the 57th Pennsylvania Infantry. Later he and his regiment were captured, but they escaped and brought into the Union lines more than 200 Confederate captives. On March 13, 1863, he was promoted brigadier-general.

Campbell, CLEVELAND J., military officer; born in New York City, in July, 1836; graduated at the University of Göttingen; enlisted in the 44th New York Regiment early in the Civil War; and was brevetted brigadier-general of volunteers March 13, 1865. During the engagement of Petersburg he was colonel of the 23d Regiment of colored troops, and while leading his command into the thickest of this fight the famous mine exploded, killing and wounding nearly 400 of his troops. He also received injuries which caused his death in Castleton, N. Y., June 13, 1865.

Campbell, DONALD, military officer; born in Scotland about 1735; entered the British army, and on Jan. 4, 1756, became a lieutenant in the "Royal American" Regiment; promoted captain of the same, Aug. 29, 1759; was acting commandant of Fort Detroit when that place was besieged by Pontiac. He was captured by Pontiac and tortured to death in 1763.

Campbell, DOUGLAS, author; born in Cooperstown, N. Y., July 13, 1840; practised law in New York, 1865–90; wrote *The Puritan in Holland, England, and America,* considered an authoritative work. He died in Schenectady, N. Y., March 7, 1893.

Campbell, GEORGE WASHINGTON, statesman; born in Tennesse in 1768; graduated at Princeton in 1794; member of Congress, 1803–9; United States Senator, 1811–14, 1815–18; Secretary of the Treasury, 1814; minister to Russia, 1818–20. He died in Nashville, Tenn., Feb. 17, 1898.

Campbell, JAMES, jurist; born in Philadelphia in 1813; admitted to the bar in 1834; Postmaster-General, 1853–57. He died in Philadelphia, Jan. 27, 1893.

Campbell, JOHN, author; born in Edinburgh, Scotland, March 8, 1708. His publications relating to the United States include *Concise History of Spanish America; Voyages and Travels from Columbus to Anson.* He died Dec. 28, 1775.

Campbell, JOHN, military officer; born in Strachur, Scotland; joined the British army in 1745; participated in the attack on Fort Ticonderoga in 1758. When the Revolutionary War broke out he commanded the British forces in west Florida until surrendered to the Spanish, May 10, 1781. He died in 1806.

Campbell, JOHN ARCHIBALD, jurist; born in Washington, Ga., June 24, 1811; justice of the United States Supreme Court, 1853–61, when he resigned to become assistant Secretary of War of the Confederate States. He died in Baltimore, Md., March 12, 1889.

Campbell, JOHN TEN BROOK, scientist; born near Montezuma, Ind., May 21, 1833; enlisted as a private at the outbreak of the Civil War, and rose to the rank of captain; studied engineering and physical science; and perfected many surveying implements; author of *National Finances,* and pamphlets on mathematical science and astro-physics.

Campbell, LEWIS DAVIS, diplomatist; born in Franklin, O., Aug. 9, 1811; member of Congress in 1849–58; colonel of an Ohio regiment in 1861–62; appointed minister to Mexico in December, 1865. He returned to the United States in 1868, and held a seat in Congress in 1871–73. He died Nov. 26, 1882.

Campbell, LOOMIS J., philologist; born in Oneonta, N. Y., in 1831; author of a *United States History,* also of the popular *Franklin Series* of school-books. He died in Oneonta, Nov. 6, 1896.

Campbell, RICHARD, military officer; born in Virginia; was made a captain in 1776; served with Gibson in Pittsburg, and with McIntosh against the Ohio Indians in 1778; promoted lieutenant-colonel; and while leading the charge at Eutaw Springs which forced the British to retreat received a wound from which he died, Sept. 8, 1781. A few hours after the battle, on hearing that the British were defeated, he exclaimed, "I die contented."

Campbell, SIR ARCHIBALD, military officer; born in Inverary, Scotland, in 1739; entered the British army in 1758; became a lieutenant-colonel in 1775; with a part of his command was captured in Boston Harbor early in the Revolutionary War, and was cruelly treated in retaliation for treatment of American officers captured by the British. On Dec. 29, 1778, he captured Savannah, Ga., and gave orders to his officers to show leniency to the people. On Jan. 29, 1779, he took Augusta, but on Feb. 13, he was forced to evacuate that city. He died in London, England, March 31, 1791.

Campbell's Station, a village in Knox county, Tenn., 12 miles southwest of Knoxville, where, on Nov. 16, 1863, the National army under General Burnside was attacked by a Confederate force under General Longstreet. The engagement lasted from noon till dark, and resulted in the defeat of the Confederates. The National force comprised portions of the 9th and 23d Corps, with cavalry.

Campbell, WILLIAM, military officer; born in Augusta county, Va., in 1745; was in the battle of Point Pleasant, in 1774, and was captain of a Virginia regiment in 1775. Being colonel of Washington county militia in 1780, he marched, with his regiment, 200 miles to the attack of Major Ferguson at KING'S MOUNTAIN (*q. v.*), where his services gained for him great distinction. So, also, were his prowess and skill conspicuous in the BATTLE AT GUILFORD (*q. v.*), and he was made a brigadier-general. He assisted Lafayette in opposing Cornwallis in Virginia, and received the command of the light infantry and riflemen, but died a few weeks before the surrender of the British at Yorktown, Aug. 22, 1781.

Campbell, WILLIAM, LORD, royal governor; younger brother of the fifth Duke of Argyll; became a captain in the British navy in August, 1762; was in Parliament in 1764; governor of Nova Scotia 1766–73; and was appointed governor of South Carolina, where he had acquired large possessions by his marriage to an American lady, in 1774. He arrived at Charleston in July, 1775; was received with courtesy; and soon summoned a meeting of the Assembly. They came, declined to do business, and adjourned on their own authority. The Committee of Safety proceeded in their preparations for resistance without regard to the presence of the governor. Lord Campbell professed great love for the people. His sincerity was suspected, and the hollowness of his professions was soon proved. Early in September Colonel Moultrie, by order of the Committee of Safety, proceeded to take possession of a small post on Sullivan's Island, in Charleston Harbor. The small garrison fled to the British sloops-of-war *Tamar* and *Cherokee*, lying near. Lord Campbell, seeing the storm of popular indignation against him daily increasing, particularly after it was discovered that he had attempted to incite the Indians to make war for the King, and had tampered with the Tories of the interior of the province, also fled to one of these vessels for shelter, and never returned. He died Sept 5, 1778.

Campbell, WILLIAM W., historian; born in Cherry Valley, N. Y., in 1806; became a judge of the New York State Supreme Court; wrote *Annals of Tryon County* (reissued as *Border Warfare*); *Life and Writings of De Witt Clinton; Sketches of Robin Hood and Captain Kidd*, etc. He died in Cherry Valley, Sept. 7, 1881.

Campbellites. See CAMPBELL, ALEXANDER; DISCIPLES OF CHRIST.

Camp Meetings, gatherings of devout persons, held usually in thinly populated districts, and continued for several days at a time, with a view of securing prolonged and uninterrupted religious exercises. Assemblies of a like kind have been more or less usual at various periods in the history of the Christian Church; but it was in connection with Methodism in the United States that such meetings became especially prominent.

Campos, ARSENIO MARTINEZ. See MARTINEZ-CAMPOS.

Camp Wild-cat. The invasion of Kentucky by Zollicoffer from Tennessee, in the early part of the Civil War, aroused the loyalists of eastern Kentucky, and they flew to arms. Some of them were organized under Colonel Garrard, a loyal Kentuckian, and among the Rock Castle hills they established Camp Wild-cat. There they were attacked (Oct. 21, 1861), by Zollicoffer. When he appeared, Garrard had only about 600 men, but was joined by some Indiana and Ohio troops, and some Kentucky cavalry under Colonel Woolford. With the latter came General Schoepf, who took the chief command. Zollicoffer, with his Tennesseans and some Mississippi "Tigers" fell upon them in the morning, and were twice repulsed. The last was in the afternoon. After a sharp battle, Zollicoffer withdrew. Garrard had been reinforced in the afternoon by a portion of Colonel Steadman's Ohio regiment. General Schoepf, deceived by false reports that a force was coming from General Buckner's camp at Bowling Green, fell back hastily towards the Ohio River, by means of forced marches. See KENTUCKY.

CANADA

Canada (name derived from the Iroquois Indian word *Kan-na-ta*, a "village" or "cluster of cabins"), the largest of all British possessions; occupying the upper part of the North American continent excepting Alaska; bounded on the n. by the Arctic Ocean, e. by the Atlantic Ocean, Davis Strait, and Baffin Bay, s. by the United States, and w. by the Pacific Ocean and Alaska; area, 3,729,665 square miles, of which 125,765, exclusive of the territorial seas and the Gulf of

St. Lawrence, are water surface; politically divided into nine provinces, a vast region known as the Northwest Territories, the Territory of Yukon, and the Colony of Newfoundland and Labrador, all, excepting Newfoundland and Labrador, federated under the name of the Dominion of Canada; capital, Ottawa; population (1911), 7,081,869.

General Statistics.—Agriculture is the main industry of the Dominion, and in Manitoba and the northwest the wheat-growing as well as general farming capabilities are practically immeasurable. Of 65,000,000 acres of occupied land more than half are under crop. In value of all field crops, the banner year was 1909, when the aggregate reached $532,992,000, and in value of live-stock the banner year was 1910 — $593,768,000. The mineral output exceeds $105,000,000, about forty-seven per cent. of which is credited to metallic products, chiefly gold, silver, copper, lead, and nickel. The fisheries have nearly $18,000,000 invested in boats and apparatus, and yield an average annual catch valued at over $30,000,000. Official estimates give a forest area of about 535,000,000 acres, and the exports of various forest products, including wood-pulp, in 1910, were valued at $47,517,000, the largest on record, of which $31,835,000 went to the United States. Manufactures, according to a special census report in 1906, had a capital investment of $846,585,000, and $718,353,000 in productive output.

The customs tariff of the Dominion is protective, but there is a preferential tariff in favor of the United Kingdom and most of the colonies. The foreign trade in 1910, exclusive of coin and bullion, amounted to $740,024,880, of which $383,173,805 was with the United States. The total railway mileage is nearly 30,000, and the capital invested in the railways exceeds $1,410,298,000. Chartered banks have a paid-up capital of over $98,788,000 and assets of $1,211,452,000, and the post-office savings banks have received as much as $12,293,274 in deposits on 165,691 open accounts in a single year. During the fiscal year ending March 31, 1911, the revenue of the Dominion on the consolidated fund account reached $117,780,409, the highest annual amount on record, and the expenditures, $87,773,998, giving a surplus of $30,006,411. The total debt was $470,663,046; assets, $134,394,500; net debt, $336,268,546.

Canada has no state church. The Church of England is represented by two archbishops, nineteen bishops, and about 1,000 clergy; the Roman Catholic Church by one cardinal, seven archbishops, twenty-three bishops, and 1,500 clergy; the Presbyterian by about 1,400 clergy and 2,358 churches and stations; the Methodist by 1,950 clergy; and the Baptist by 500. The total church membership exceeds 5,371,000, the Roman Catholic, Methodist, Presbyterian, and Anglican denominations predominating in the order given. Each province has one or more universities (eighteen in all, with about 500 professors and teachers, and 9,000 students) and several colleges. There are in all twenty degree-conferring bodies, with about forty colleges, having an estimated attendance of 25,000. In Ontario, Quebec, Alberta, and Saskatchewan, there are separate schools for Roman Catholic students; in all other provinces the schools are unsectarian.

Government.—The constitution is modelled on the general laws of the mother-country. The supreme authority is the British sovereign, represented by a governor-general (annual salary, $50,000), appointed by the crown, who is assisted by a privy council chosen from time to time by the governor-general. The ministry or cabinet is composed of fifteen members, each of whom holding a portfolio receives an annual salary of $7,000, excepting the premier, who receives $12,000, and the leader of the opposition is given $7,000 per annum. The Parliament consists of a Senate of eighty-seven members and a House of Commons of 221 members; compensation of each member $2,500 per session; of the speaker of each House, $4,000 per annum. Senators are appointed by the crown on the nomination of the governor-general; members of the House of Commons are elected under provincial franchises. The Dominion is represented in London by a high commissioner, who has an annual salary of $10,000. Each province has a lieutenant-governor, appointed by the Federal government for a term of five years, and a legislature chosen by popular vote. The judiciary comprises a Supreme Court, with a chief justice (annual salary, $10,000) and five associate justices (salary, $9,000 each), an Exchequer Court for hearing causes connected with the revenue, and supreme and county courts in the several provinces. In many respects the provinces are similar to the States in the American Union. The territories and districts are under the jurisdiction of commissioners.

GOVERNORS-GENERAL OF CANADA.

Name.	Date of Appointment.
The Right Hon. Viscount Monck, G.C.M.G.	June 1, 1867
The Right Hon. Lord Lisgar, G.C.M.G. (Sir John Young)	Dec. 29, 1868
The Right Hon. the Earl of Dufferin, K.P., K.C.B., G.C.M.G.	May 22, 1872
The Most Hon. the Marquis of Lorne, K.T., G.C.M.G.	Oct. 5, 1878
The Most Hon. the Marquis of Lansdowne, G.C.M.G.	Aug. 18, 1883
The Right Hon. Lord Stanley of Preston, G.C.B.	May 1, 1888
The Right Hon. the Earl of Aberdeen, K.T., G.C.M.G	May 22, 1893
The Right Hon. the Earl of Minto, G.C.M.G.	July 30, 1898
The Right Hon. the Earl Grey, G.C.M.G.	Sept. 26, 1904
H. R. H. Prince Arthur, Duke of Connaught	—— — 1911

Political Divisions.—The following shows the provincial, territorial, and district divisions of the Dominion, with their areas, seats of government, and population by census of 1901, the first nine being provinces:

Provinces.	Area Square Miles.	Population. 1911.	Seats of Government.
Alberta	253,540	374,663	Edmonton
British Columbia	357,600	392,480	Victoria
Manitoba	73,732	455,614	Winnipeg
New Brunswick	27,985	351,889	Fredericton
Nova Scotia	21,428	492,338	Halifax
Ontario	260,862	2,523,208	Toronto
Prince Edward Island	2,184	93,728	Charlottetown
Quebec	351,873	2,002,712	Quebec
Saskatchewan	250,650	492,432	Regina
Mackenzie, Ungava, and Franklin, N.W.T. Keewatin, N. W. Territory	1,922,735	16,951	Ottawa
Yukon Territory	207,076	8,512	Dawson
Total	3,729,665	7,024,527	

History: Early Period.—Canada originally comprised an extensive range of country reaching, under the French, as far even as the Mississippi, away beyond the boundary lakes. It was subsequently limited to a region chiefly in the basin of the St. Lawrence—including in that term the lakes with the river. The district was divided in 1791 into two provinces—Ontario and Quebec, or Upper and Lower Canada; but these two, after being politically reunited (1840) were again disassociated only to enter together as separate members of the Confederation—the Dominion of Canada—on July 1, 1867, when an act of the imperial parliament (passed March 29) came into effect, uniting the separate provinces into one federation.

On June 24, 1497, Cabot discovered the eastern coast of North America; in the following year he discovered Hudson Strait; in 1500 Gaspar Cortereal entered the Gulf of St. Lawrence; in 1524 Verrazano explored the Atlantic coast of Nova

Scotia; on June 21, 1534, Jacques Cartier made the first landing on Canadian soil, at Eskimo Bay; in July–August, 1535, Cartier made a second visit, and anchored in a small bay at the mouth of St. John River, which in honor of the day (August 10, he named after St. Lawrence, which name was afterwards extended to the gulf and river; in 1585 John Davis discovered Davis Strait; and in 1608, on the occasion of his second visit to this region, Samuel de Champlain founded Quebec, the first permanent settlement in New France.

Champlain established a semi-military and semi-religious colony at Quebec, and from it Jesuit and other missions spread over the Lake regions. Then came the civil power of France to lay the foundations of an empire, fighting one nation of Indians and making allies of another, and establishing a feudal system of government, the great land-holders being called *seigneurs*, who were compelled to cede the lands granted to them, when demanded by settlers, on fixed conditions. They were not absolute proprietors of the soil, but had certain valuable privileges, coupled with prescribed duties, such as building mills, etc. David Kertk, or Kirk, a Huguenot refugee, received a royal commission from King Charles I. to seize the French forts in ACADIA (*q. v.*) and on the river St. Lawrence. With a dozen ships he overcame the small French force at Port Royal, and took possession of Acadia in 1629. Later in the summer he entered the St. Lawrence, burned the hamlet of Tadousac, at the mouth of the Saguenay, and sent a summons for the surrender of Quebec. It was refused, and Kirk resolved to starve out the garrison. He cruised in the Gulf of St. Lawrence, and captured the transports conveying winter provisions for Quebec. The sufferings there were intense, but they endured them until August the next year, when, English ships-of-war, under a brother of Admiral Kirk, appearing before Quebec, instead of the expected supply-ships, the place was surrendered, and the inhabitants, not more than 100 in all, were saved from starvation. By a treaty, Canada was restored to the French in 1632.

In the early history of the colony, the governors, in connection with the intendant, held the military and civil administration in their hands. Jesuit and other priests became conspicuous in the public service. Finally, when a bishop was appointed for Quebec, violent dissensions occurred between the civil and ecclesiastical authorities. Until the treaty of Utrecht (1713), Canada included all of present British America, and more. At that time Hudson Bay and vicinity was restored to England by Louis XIV. Newfoundland and Acadia (Nova Scotia) were ceded to the English, and all right to the Iroquois country (New York) was renounced, reserving to France only the valleys of the St. Lawrence and the Mississippi.

British Conquest.—The easy capture of Louisburg revived a hope that Canada might be conquered. Governor Shirley proposed to have the task performed by a colonial army alone. They would not comply, for the colonists, thus perceiving their own strength, might claim Canada by right of conquest, and become too independent; so they authorized an expedition for the purpose after the old plan of attacking that province by land and sea. An English fleet was prepared to go against Quebec; a land force, composed of troops from Connecticut, New York, and colonies farther south, gathered at Albany, to march against Montreal. Governor Clinton assumed the chief command of the land expedition. His unpopularity thwarted his plans. The corporation of Albany refused to furnish quarters for his troops, and his drafts on the British treasury could not purchase provisions. Meanwhile, Massachusetts and Rhode Island had raised nearly 4,000 troops, and were waiting for an English squadron. Instead of a British armament, a French fleet of forty war vessels, with 3,000 veteran troops, was coming over the sea. New England was greatly alarmed. It was D'Anville's armament, and it was dispersed by storms. Ten thousand troops gathered at Boston for its defence; the fort on Castle Island was made very strong, and the land expedition against Montreal was abandoned.

When Quebec fell, in the autumn of 1759, the French held Montreal, and were not dismayed. In the spring of 1760, Vaudreuil, the governor-general of Canada, sent M. Levi, the successor of Montcalm, to recover Quebec. He descended the St. Lawrence with six frigates and a powerful land force. The English, under General Murray, marched out of Quebec, and met him at Sillery, three miles above the city; and there was fought (April 4) one of the most sanguinary battles of the war. Murray was defeated. He lost about 1,000 men and all his artillery, but succeeded in retreating to the city with the remainder of his army. Levi laid siege to Quebec, and Murray's condition was becoming critical, when an English squadron appeared (May 9) with reinforcements and provisions. Supposing it to be the whole British fleet, Levi raised the siege (May 10), and fled to Montreal, after losing most of his shipping. Now came the final struggle. Three armies were soon in motion towards Montreal, where Vaudreuil had gathered all his forces. Amherst, with 10,000 English and provincial troops, and 1,000 Indians of the Six Nations, led by Johnson, embarked at Oswego, went down Lake Ontario and the St. Lawrence to Montreal, where he met Murray (Sept. 6), who had come up from Quebec with 4,000 men. The next day, Colonel Haviland arrived with 3,000 troops from Crown Point, having taken possession of Isle aux Noix on the way. Resistance to such a crushing force would have been in vain, and, on Sept. 8, 1760, Vaudreuil signed a capitulation surrendering Montreal and all French posts in Canada and on the border of the Lakes to the English. General Gage was made military governor of Montreal, and General Murray, with 4,000 men, garrisoned Quebec. The conquest of Canada was now completed, and by the Treaty of Paris in 1763, the French dominions in America were given up to England.

ISLE AUX NOIX, IN THE SOREL.

First American Invasion.—When news of the surrender of TICONDEROGA (*q. v.*) reached Governor Carleton, of Canada, he issued a proclamation (June 9, 1775) in which he declared the captors to be a band of rebellious traitors; established martial law; summoned the French peasantry to serve under the old colonial nobility; and instigated the Indian tribes to take up the hatchet against the people of New York and New England. This proclamation neutralized the effects of the address of Congress to the Canadians. The Quebec Act had soothed the French nobility and Roman Catholic clergy. The English residents were offended by it, and these, with the Canadian peasantry, were disposed to take sides with the Americans. They denied the right of the French nobility, as magistrates or the seigneurs, to command their military services. They welcomed invasion, but had not the courage to join the invaders. At the same time, the French peasantry did not obey the order of the Roman Catholic bishop, which was sent to the several parishes, and read by the local clergy, to come out in defence of the British government. It was known that the bishop was a stipendiary of the crown.

There was a decided war spirit visible in the second Continental Congress, yet it was cautious and prudent. Immediately after the seizure of Ticonderoga and Crown Point (May 10–12, 1775), the Congress was urged to authorize the invasion and seizure of Canada. That body hoped to gain a greater victory by making the Canadians their friends and allies. To this end they sent a loving address to them, and resolved, on June 1, "that no expedition or incursion ought to be undertaken or made by any colony or body of colonists against or into Canada." The Provincial Congress of New York had expressly disclaimed any intention to make war on Canada. But Gage's proclamation (June 10), that all Americans in arms were rebels and traitors, and especially the battle of Bunker (Breed's) Hill, made a radical change in the feelings of the people and in Congress. It was also ascertained that Governor Carleton had received a commission to muster and arm the people of the province, and to march them into any province in America to arrest and put to death, or spare, "rebels" and other offenders. Here was a menace that could not go unheeded. Cols. Ethan Allen, Benedict Arnold, and others renewed their efforts to induce the Congress to send an expedition into Canada. The latter perceived the importance of securing Canada either by alliance or by conquest. At length the Congress prepared for an invasion of Canada. Maj.-Gen. Philip Schuyler had been appointed to the command of the Northern Department, which included the whole province of New York. Gen. Richard Montgomery was his chief lieutenant. The regiments raised by the province of New York were put in motion, and General Wooster, with Connecticut troops, who were stationed at Harlem, was ordered to Albany. The New-Yorkers were joined by "Green Mountain Boys." Schuyler sent into Canada an address to the inhabitants, in the French language, informing them that "the only views of Congress were to restore to them those rights which every subject of the British empire, of whatever religious sentiments he may be, is entitled to"; and that, in the execution of these trusts, he had received the most positive orders to "cherish every Canadian, and every friend to the cause of liberty, and sacredly to guard their property." It was now too late. Had the Congress listened to Allen and Arnold at the middle of May, and moved upon Canada, its conquest would have been easy, for there were very few troops there. When, near the close of August, an expedition against Canada, under Schuyler, was ready to move, preparations had been made to thwart it. The clergy and seigneurs of Canada, satisfied with the Quebec Act, were disposed to stand by the British government. The invading army first occupied Isle aux Noix, in the Sorel River; but the expedition made little advance beyond until November. Colonel Allen had attempted to take Montreal, without orders, and was made a prisoner and sent to England. A detachment of Schuyler's army captured Fort Chambly, 12 miles from St. Johns, on the Sorel (Nov. 3), and, on the same day, the fort at the latter, which Montgomery had besieged for some time, cut off from supplies, also surrendered. Montreal fell before the patriots on the 13th, and Montgomery, leaving a garrison at both places, prepared to move on Quebec. Meanwhile Colonel Arnold had led an expedition by way of the Kennebec and Chaudière rivers, through a terrible wilderness, to the banks of the St. Lawrence (Nov. 9) opposite Quebec. He crossed the river, ascended to the Plains of Abraham (Nov. 13), and, at the head of only 750 half-naked men with not more than 400 muskets, demanded the surrender of the city. Intelligence of an intended sortie caused Arnold to move 20 miles farther up the river, where he was soon joined by Montgomery. The combined forces returned to Quebec, and began a siege. At the close of the year (1775), in an attempt to take the city by storm, the invaders were repulsed and Montgomery was killed. Arnold took the command, and was relieved by General Wooster, in April (1776). A month later General Thomas took command, and, hearing of the approach of a large armament, land and naval, to Quebec, he retreated up the river. Driven from one post to another, the Americans were finally expelled from Canada, the wretched remnant of the army, reduced by disease, arriving at Crown Point in June, 1776.

The American Board of War, General Gates president, arranged a plan, late in 1777, for a winter campaign against Canada, and appointed Lafayette to the command. The Marquis was cordially received at Albany by General Schuyler, then out of the military service. General Conway, who had been appointed inspector-general of the army, was there before him. Lafayette was utterly disappointed and disgusted by the lack of preparation and the delusive statements of Gates. "I do not believe," he wrote to Washington, "I can find 1,200 men fit for duty—and the quarter part of these are naked—even for a summer campaign." The Marquis soon found the whole affair to be only a trick of Gates to detach him from Washington. General Schuyler, in a long letter to Congress (Nov. 4, 1777), had recommended a winter campaign against Canada, but it was passed unnoticed by the Congress, and Gates appropriated the thoughts as his own in forming the plan, on paper, which he never meant to carry out.

BARRACKS AT SANDWICH.

Another campaign for liberating Canada from British rule was conceived late in 1778. From Boston, D'Estaing, in the name of Louis XVI., had summoned the Canadians to throw off British rule. Lafayette exhorted (December) the barbarians of Canada to look upon the English as their enemies. The Congress became inflamed with zeal for the projected measure, formed a plan, without consulting a single military officer, for the "emancipation of Canada," in co-operation with an army from France. One American detachment from Pittsburg was to capture Detroit; another from Wyoming was to seize Niagara; a third from the Mohawk Valley was to capture Oswego; a fourth from New England was to enter Montreal by way of the St. Francis; a fifth to guard the approaches from Quebec; while to France was assigned the task of reducing Halifax and Quebec. Lafayette offered to use his influence at the French Court in furtherance of this grand scheme; but the cooler judgment and strong common-sense of Washington interposed the objection that the part which the United States had to perform in the scheme was far beyond its resources. It was abandoned, as was another scheme for a like result, early in the following year.

Second American Invasion.—The first important military movement in 1812 was the invasion of Canada by an attack on its western border on the Detroit River. It then consisted of two provinces—Lower Canada, with a population of 300,000, mostly of French origin, and Upper Canada, with a population of 100,000, composed largely of American loyalists and their descendants. The regular military force in both provinces did not exceed 2,000 men, scattered over a space of 1,200 miles from Quebec to the foot of Lake Superior. Sir George Prevost was then governor general, with his residence at Montreal. To enter the province from the States, a water-barrier had to be crossed, while the American frontier was destitute of roads, infected with summer fevers, and sparsely settled. William Hull, a soldier of the Revolution, then governor of Michigan Territory, was consulted about an invasion of Canada while on a visit at Washington. He insisted that before such an enterprise should be undertaken a naval control of Lake Erie should be acquired, and not less than 3,000 troops should be provided for the invasion. He accepted the commission of brigadier-general with the special object in view of protecting his territory from the Indian allies of the British; yet, by orders of the government, he prepared to invade Canada. Governor Meigs, of Ohio, called for troops to assemble at Dayton, and volunteers flocked thither in considerable numbers. There General Hull took command of them (May 25, 1812), and they started off in good spirits for their march through the wilderness. It was a perilous and most fatiguing journey. On the broad morasses of the summit lands of Ohio, Hull received a despatch from the War Department urging him to press on speedily to Detroit, and there await further orders. When he reached the navigable waters of the Maumee, his beasts of burden were so worn down by fatigue that he despatched for Detroit, in a schooner, his own baggage and that of most of his officers; also all of his hospital stores, intrenching tools, and a trunk containing his most valuable military papers. The wives of three of his officers, with thirty soldiers to protect the schooner, also embarked in her. In a smaller vessel the invalids of the army were conveyed. Both vessels arrived at the site of Toledo on the evening of July 1. The next day, when near Frenchtown (afterwards Monroe), Hull received a note from the postmaster at Cleveland announcing the declaration of war. It was the first intimation he had received of that important event. In fact, the British at Fort Malden (now Amherstburg) heard of the declaration before Hull did, and captured his schooner, with all its precious freight. The commander at Malden had been informed of it, by express, as early as June 30—two days before it reached Hull. The latter pressed forward, and encamped near Detroit on July 5. The British were then casting up intrenchments at Sandwich on the opposite side of the Detroit River. There Hull awaited further orders from his government. His troops, impatient to invade Canada, had evinced a mutinous spirit, when he received orders to "commence operations immediately," and, if possible, take possession of Fort Malden. At dawn on the morning of July 12, the greater part of his troops had crossed the Detroit River, and were on Canadian soil. Hull issued a proclamation to the Canadians, assuring them of protection in case they remained quiet. Many of the Canadian militia deserted the British standard. Hull advanced towards Malden (July 13). After a successful encounter with British and Indians he fell back to Sandwich, without attacking Malden. His troops were disappointed and mutinous. Then information came of the capture of MACKINAW (*q. v.*) by the British. News also came that General Proctor, of the British army, had arrived at Malden with reinforcements. This was followed by an intercepted despatch from the northwest announcing that 1,200 white men and several hundred Indians were coming down to assist in the defence of Canada. General Brock was approaching from the east, with a force gathered on his way. These events, and other causes, impelled Hull to recross the river to Detroit with his army, and take shelter in the fort there (Aug. 8, 1812). The British congregated in force at Sandwich, and from that point opened a cannonade upon the fort at Detroit. On Sunday morning, the 16th, the British crossed the river to a point below Detroit, and moved upon the fort. Very little effort was made to defend it, and on that day Hull surrendered the fort, army, and Territory of Michigan into the hands of the British. See DETROIT; HULL, WILLIAM.

On Oct. 17, 1813, General Harrison, of the United States army, and Commodore Perry, commander of the fleet on Lake Erie, issued a proclamation stating that, by the combined operations of the land and naval forces of the United States, British power had been destroyed within the upper districts of Canada, which was in quiet possession of United States troops. They therefore proclaimed that the rights and privileges of the inhabitants and the laws and customs of the country, which were in force before the arrival of the conquerors, should continue to prevail, and that all magistrates and other civil officers might resume their functions, after taking an oath of fidelity to the United States government so long as the troops should remain in possession of the country.

Third American Invasion.—In 1814, the third year of the second war for independence, a favorite project with the United States was the conquest of Canada. The principal forces in Upper Canada were under Lieutenant-General Drummond. When the Army of the North, commanded by Major-General Brown, reached the Niagara frontier, Drummond's headquarters were at Burlington Heights, at the western end of Lake Ontario. General Riall was on the Niagara River, at Fort George and Queenstown; but when he heard of the arrival of the Americans at Buffalo, under General Scott, he advanced to Chippewa and established a fortified camp. At the close of June, General Brown arrived at Buffalo, and assumed chief command, and, believing his army to be strong enough, he proceeded to invade Canada. His army consisted of two brigades, commanded respectively by Generals Scott and Ripley, to each of which was attached a train of artillery, commanded by Capt. N. Towson and Maj. J. Hindman. He had also a small corps of cavalry, under Capt. S. D. Harris. These regulars were well disciplined and in high spirits. There were also volunteers from Pennsylvania and New York, 100 of them mounted, and nearly 600 Seneca Indians—almost the entire military force of the Six Nations remaining in the United States. These had been stirred to action by the venerable Red Jacket, the great Seneca orator. The volunteers and Indians were under the chief command of Gen. Peter B. Porter, then quartermaster-general of the New York militia. Major McRee, of North Carolina, was chief-engineer, assisted by Maj. E. D. Wood. On the Canada shore, nearly opposite Buffalo, stood Fort Erie, then garrisoned by 170 men, under the command of Major Buck. On July 1 Brown received orders to cross the Niagara, capture Fort Erie, march on Chippewa, menace Fort George, and, if he could have the co-operation of Chauncey's fleet, to seize and fortify Burlington Heights. Accordingly, Brown arranged for General Scott and his brigade to cross on boats and land a mile below the fort, while Ripley, with his brigade, should be landed a mile above it. This accomplished, the boats were to return and carry the remainder of the army, with its ordnance and stores, to the Canada shore. The order for this movement was given on July 2. It was promptly obeyed by Scott, and tardily by Ripley, on the 3d. When Scott had pressed forward to invest the fort, he found Ripley had not crossed, and no time was lost in crossing the ordnance and selecting positions for batteries These preparations alarmed the garrison, and the fort, which was in a weak condition, was surrendered. Nearly 200 men, including officers, became prisoners of war, and were sent across the river. The Treaty of Ghent (Dec. 24, 1814) terminated the second war between the United States and Great Britain and American operations in Canada. For further details of American movements in Canada during the war of 1812–15, see CHRYSLER'S FIELD, BATTLE OF; ERIE, FORT; ERIE, LAKE, BATTLE ON; and LUNDY'S LANE, BATTLE OF, in addition to previous references.

Rebellion of 1837–38.—By an act of the Imperial Parliament, in 1791, Canada was divided into two provinces, Upper Canada and Lower Canada, and each had a parliament or legislature of its own. An imperial act was passed in 1840 to unite the two provinces under one administration and one legislature. Antecedent political struggles had taken place, which culminated in open insurrection in 1837–38. A movement for a separation of the Canadas from the crown of Great Britain, and their political independence, was begun simultaneously in Upper and Lower Canada in 1837. In the former province the most conspicuous leader was William Lyon McKenzie, a Scotchman, a journalist of rare ability and a great political agitator; in the lower province, the chief leader was Joseph Papineau, a large land-owner and a very influential man among the French inhabitants. Both leaders were republican in sentiment. The movements of the revolutionary party were well planned, but local jealousies prevented unity of action, and the effort failed. It was esteemed highly patriotic, and elicited the warmest sympathy of the American people, especially of those of the Northern States. Banded companies and individuals joined the "rebels," as they were called by the British government, and "patriots" by their friends; and so general became the active sympathy on the northern frontier that peaceful relations between the United States and Great Britain were endangered. President Van Buren issued a proclamation, calling upon all persons engaged in the schemes of invasion of the Canadian territory to abandon the design, and warning them to beware of the penalties that must assuredly follow such infringement of international laws.

In December 1837, a party of sympathizing Americans took possession of Navy Island, belonging to Canada, in the Niagara River about two miles above the falls. They mustered about 700 men, well provisioned and provided with twenty pieces of cannon. They had a small steamboat named the *Caroline* to ply between the island and Schlosser, on the American side. On a dark night a party of Canadian royalists crossed the river, cut the *Caroline* loose from her moorings, and set her on fire. She went down the current and over the great cataract in full blaze. It is supposed some persons were on board of her. Gen. Winfield Scott was finally sent to the northern frontier to preserve order, and was assisted by a proclamation by the governor of New York. Yet secret associations, known as "Hunters' Lodges," continued quite active for some time. Against the members of these lodges, President Tyler issued an admonitory proclamation, which prevented further aggressive movements. For four years this ominous cloud hung upon our horizon. It disappeared in 1842, when the leaders of the movement were either dead or in exile.

Later Events.—The first United Parliament was opened at Kingston, June 13, 1841; boundary line between Canada and the United States settled by the Webster-Ashburton Treaty (see ASHBURTON, ALEXANDER BARING, LORD), Aug. 9, 1842; Oregon boundary treaty with the United States negotiated, 1846; reciprocity treaty with the United States signed, June 5, 1854 (terminated May 17, 1866); gold discovered in British Columbia, April, 1858; Prince of Wales (afterward King Edward VII.) arrived in Quebec, Aug. 8, 1860; first meeting of Parliament in new buildings at Ottawa, June 8, 1866; Fenian invasion from the United States, May 25, 1870; Imperial Act respecting establishment of provinces in Canada passed, June 28, 1871; British evacuate island of San Juan on its being awarded to the United States by the Emperor of Germany, Nov. 7, 1873; all British possessions on North American continent (excepting Newfoundland) annexed to Canada, Sept. 1, 1880; rebellion in the Northwest broke out at Duke Lake, March 26, 1885; Riel surrendered, May 16, 1885; rebellion suppressed, July 2, 1885; convention signed with the United States for survey of Alaska and Passamaquoddy Bay boundaries, 1892; Bering Sea arbitrators awarded Canadian sealers $464,000, Dec. 22, 1897; British preferential tariff act passed, 1897; Joint High Commission met at Quebec, Aug. 23, 1898; Canada contributed liberally to aid the mother-country in the Boer War, 1899–1902; Alaska boundary dispute settled, 1903; Alberta and Saskatchewan created provinces, 1905; British troops withdrawn from Canada, and Dominion assumed maintenance of garrisons and fortifications at Halifax and Esquimalt, 1905; the Duke of Connaught, uncle of King George V., named as new governor-general, June 9, 1910; Parliament dissolved and new elections ordered to settle the question of the proposed reciprocity agreement with the United States, July 29, 1911. Many of the events above briefly summarized will be found treated at appropriate length under readily suggestive titles.

Reciprocity with the United States.—Doubtless the most important event in the later history of Canada was the reciprocity agreement with the United States, negotiated in 1910, passed by both Houses of Congress (House, April 27; Senate, July 22), and approved by President Taft, July 26, 1911. While the measure was pending in the Canadian Parliament, that body was dissolved (July 29), and new elections were ordered to settle the fate of the agreement. These were held Sept 21, and resulted in the defeat of the Liberal party and, temporarily, it was believed, of the reciprocity agreement. Sir Wilfred Laurier retired as Premier and was succeeded by Robert L. Borden, the Conservative leader, as a result of the election. The preliminary steps in the United States were taken in 1909, in negotiations over the maximum and minimum clause of the Aldrich-Payne tariff bill, and formal negotiations with Canada were undertaken in March, 1910, when President Taft had a conference with W. S. Fielding, Canadian Minister of Finance, and William Patterson, Canadian Minister of Customs. The agreement was submitted to Congress in a special message by the President, Jan. 26, 1911. While many of the most influential members of the Canadian as well as the British government gave hearty approval to the proposition, there was a considerable opposition, based on a fear lest the agreement should prove an entering wedge for the annexation of Canada to the United States, a fear that President Taft, Premier Laurier, and Earl Grey, the British Secretary of State for Foreign Affairs, took prompt personal measures to allay, all declaring that naught but friendly trade betterments was contemplated. In the United States the strongest opposition sprang from a conviction that the agreement would lessen the prices of farm and other commodities through the introduction of cheaper corresponding articles from Canada. The bill as it passed the United States Senate differed from the one originally introduced in the House only in regard to the wood pulp and print-paper amendments. This amendment made the entry of wood pulp and print paper from Canadian provinces which maintain no discrimination against the United States free as soon as the treaty goes into effect. Under the legislation as originally drafted pulp wood and print paper would not go on the free list until the Canadian provinces had removed all restrictions against the exportation of wood pulp and pulp wood from Canada into the United States.

Generally speaking, the agreement opens the markets of the United States to Canada's leading agricultural products, notably wheat and other grains, and also to her dairy products, eggs and poultry, fish, sheep, cattle and other live animals. Her rough lumber also is admitted duty free to the United States. In return for these concessions Canada takes down the bars altogether on cottonseed oil and American fruits and some other products and grants reduced duties on agricultural implements and other manufactured articles.

The total value of dutiable articles which the United States made free under the agreement was $39,811,000, or 76.4 per cent. of the total dutiable exportations of Canada into the United States in the fiscal year 1910. The total value of dutiable articles which Canada made free, on the other hand, was only $21,858,000, which was 16.5 per cent. of all the dutiable imports into Canada from the United States in the same year.

The total amount of duties to be remitted by the United States under the agreement was $4,850,000, as compared with $2,560,000 with Canada. The United States, however, gained a decided advantage in Canadian reductions on agricultural implements, manufactured articles, and other dutiable imports which were not put on the free list, but on which reductions were made. The total value of Canada's dutiable articles in this class was $25,870,000, or 19.5 per cent. of the dutiable imports into Canada from the United States in 1910. The value of such imports passing from Canada to the United States in 1910, on the other hand, was only $7,521,000, or 14.4 per cent. of the total dutiable imports for that year.

Here are some of the more important items placed on the reciprocal free list by the agreement.

Live animals, cattle, horses, mules, swine, sheep and lambs, poultry; wheat, rye, oats, barley, buckwheat, corn, or maize; hay and straw, fresh vegetables, including potatoes; fresh and dried fruits, dairy products, eggs, honey, cottonseed oil, fish of all kinds, seal, herring, whale and other fish oil, salt mineral waters, timber (hewn, sided or squared otherwise than by sawing); sawed boards, planks and other lumber, mica, feldspar, asbestos, glycerine, salt, sulphate of soda, extracts of hemlock bark, brass in bars and rods, rolled iron or steel, sheets, crucible cast steel, wire, galvanized iron or steel wire; type-casting and type-setting machines, barb fencing wire, coke, pulp wood and print paper.

Under the terms of the agreement mutually reciprocal reductions are made wherever possible on secondary food products. Fresh meats, on which the United States placed a duty of 1½ cents a pound under the Payne-Aldrich law, are admitted under the proposed legislation at 1¼ cents a pound. The duty on bacon and hams, which is 4 cents a pound under the present law, is reduced to 1¼ cents a pound. Corresponding reductions have been made in the duties on smoked and canned meats and on lard.

Canada grants a reduction on ploughs,

harvesters, harrows, reapers, mowers, threshing-machines, and other agricultural implements; on sanitary fixtures, clocks, and watches. The mutually reduced manufactured commodities include motor vehicles, cutlery, leather goods, plate glass and printing ink. Particular stress has been laid by the American negotiators upon concessions obtained for American automobiles and motor vehicles. The Canadian tariff on these was 35 per cent., and under the agreement is reduced to 30 per cent. Canada reduces her duty on bituminous coal from 53 to 45 cents a ton, which is regarded as one of the important concessions in the treaty. She also reduces her duty on cement from 12½ to 11 cents per 100 pounds. The United States, on the other hand, reduces the duty on iron ore from 15 to 10 cents per 100 pounds.

The two decisive factors in the Canadian election of 1911 which resulted in the overthrow of Laurier and the Liberal Party were the use made by the Opposition in quoting President Taft's remark that "Canada stood at the parting of the ways," and Champ Clark's statement that "Reciprocity was the first step to annexation." The result was a Liberal majority of 50 was changed to a Conservative majority of 50. President Taft, in speaking at Battle Creek, said: "The treaty was nothing but a trade agreement, through which there was not even a remote possibility of annexation of the Dominion by the United States. The accusation that this government had resorted to trickery or had played unfairly in order to gain reciprocity was without foundation.

"I know that some irresponsible newspapers say I in some way deceived or played unfairly with the ministers of Canada to secure the treaty. Well, I am not conscious of it, and I do not believe they are.

"They say we want to annex Canada. Gentlemen, my experience in this government has taught me that we have territory enough without enlarging our borders. Canada is our good neighbor, and along her border-line of 4,000 miles there is not a gun or a fort or a battleship worthy of the name. They have their troubles; we have our own. I can say for one that the talk of those on the other side who say that the trade treaty was to facilitate annexation is 'bosh.'

"I want to prophesy that in eighteen months—and that will be about the time of the next general election—the effect of reciprocity, so far as the business of the farmer is concerned, will be so slight that it will form no part at all of the issues."

The President said that he favored the abolition of all custom-houses on the border-line of Canada and wished that we had absolute free trade with the Dominion.

Canada Company. In 1621 James I. granted to Sir William Alexander and others the whole of Canada and a large part of the United States. The company failed and dissolved.

Canals. Gen. Philip Schuyler may justly be regarded as the father of the United States canal system. As early as 1761, when he was in England, he visited the famous canal which the Duke of Bridgewater had just completed. On his return he urged the matter upon the attention of his countrymen. Meanwhile ELKANAH WATSON (*q. v.*) in 1785 visited Mount Vernon, where he found Washington planning the connection of the waters of the Potomac with those west of the Alleghany Mountains. He and General Schuyler projected canals between the Hudson River and Lakes Champlain and Ontario, and in 1792 the legislature of New York chartered two companies known respectively as the "Western Inland Lock Navigation Company" and "Northern Inland Lock Navigation Company," of both of which Schuyler was made president, and to his death, in 1804, he was actively engaged in the promotion of both projects. The Western canal was never completed, according to its original conception, but was supplemented by the great Erie Canal, suggested by Gouverneur Morris about 1801. In a letter to David Parish, of Philadelphia, that year, he distinctly foreshadowed that great work. As early as 1774 Washington favored the passage of a law by the legislature of Virginia for the construction of works—canals and good wagon-roads—by which the Potomac and Ohio rivers might be connected by a chain of commerce. After the Revolution, the States of Virginia and Maryland took measures which resulted in the formation of the famous Potomac Company, to carry out Washington's project. In 1784 Washington revived a project for making a canal through the Dismal Swamp, not only for drainage, but for navigation between the Elizabeth River and Albemarle Sound. The oldest work of the kind in the United States is a canal, begun in 1792, five miles in extent, for passing the falls of the Connecticut River at South Hadley. The earliest completed and most important of the great canals of our country is the Erie, connecting the waters of Lake Erie with those of the Hudson River. A committee appointed by Congress during Jefferson's administration reported in favor of this canal, and a survey was directed to be made. Commissioners were appointed in 1810, who reported to Congress in March, 1811. In consequence of the War of 1812, the project languished until 1817. In that year ground was broken for the Erie Canal on July 4, under the authority of New York State, and on Oct. 26, 1825, the canal was completed. It was built by the State of New York at an original cost of $9,000,000, from the operation of which untold wealth has been derived by the city and State of New York. It was completely and formally opened by Governor De Witt Clinton, its great advocate, in 1825, and has been enlarged at great expense since. The canal changed the whole aspect of commercial affairs in the Lake region. The total area of these five great inland seas is about 90,000 square miles, and their inlets drain a region of 336,000 square miles.

The Harlem River Ship Canal, connecting the Hudson River and Long Island Sound by way of Spuyten Duyvil Creek and the Harlem River at the northern extremity of Manhattan Island, was completed in 1895 at a cost of about $2,700,000. In 1911 the Erie, Oswego, and Champlain canals were being enlarged to accommodate barges of 2,500 tons each, at a cost of $101,000,000; the Cayuga and Seneca Canal was being similarly enlarged at a cost of $7,000,000; and there were under construction the Cape Cod sea-level ship canal, about 12 miles long, to connect Massachusetts and Buzzard's bays, and the Beaufort Canal, extending from Beaufort, N. C., to the Neuse River. Of the various larger canals that have been constructed in the United States, the following were the only ones (excepting the Harlem River Ship Canal) in commercial operation in 1911, and several of these were proposed to be abandoned.

CANALS IN THE UNITED STATES AND CANADA.

NAME.	Cost.	Completed.	Length in miles.	LOCATION.
Albemarle and Chesapeake	$1,641,363	1860	44	Norfolk, Va., to Currituck Sound, N. C.
Augusta	1,500,000	1847	9	Savannah River, Ga., to Augusta, Ga.
Black River	3,581,954	1849	35	Rome, N. Y., to Lyons Falls, N. Y.
Cayuga and Seneca	2,232,632	1839	25	To Cayuga and Seneca Lakes, N. Y.
Champlain	4,044,000	1822	81	Whitehall, N. Y., to Waterford, N. Y.
Chesapeake and Delaware	3,730,230	1829	14	Chesapeake City, Md., to Delaware City, Del.
Chesapeake and Ohio	11,290,327	1850	184	Cumberland, Md., to Washington, D. C.
Chicago Drainage. See next page.				
Companys	90,000	1847	22	Mississippi River, La., to Bayou Black, La.
Delaware and Raritan	4,888,749	1838	66	New Brunswick, N. J., to Trenton, N. J.
Delaware Division	2,433,350	1830	60	Easton, Pa., to Bristol, Pa.
Des Moines Rapids	4,582,009	1877	7½	To Mississippi River.
Dismal Swamp	2,800,000	1822	22	Connects Chesapeake Bay with Albemarle Sd.
Erie	52,540,800	1825	381	Albany, N. Y., to Buffalo, N. Y.
Fairfield	....	....	4½	Alligator River to Lake Mattimuskeet, N. C.
Galveston and Brazos	340,000	1851	38	Galveston to Brazos River, Tex.
Hocking	975,481	1843	42	Carroll, O., to Nelsonville, O.
Illinois and Michigan	7,357,787	1848	102	Chicago, Ill., to La Salle, Ill.
Illinois and Mississippi	568,643	1895	4½	Around rapids of Rock River, Ill.
Lake Drummond	2,800,000	1899	22	Connects Chesapeake Bay with Albemarle Sd.
Lehigh Coal and Navigation Co.	4,455,000	1821	108	Coalport, Pa., to Easton, Pa.
Miami and Erie	8,062,680	1835	274	Cincinnati, O., to Toledo, O.
Morris	6,000,000	1836	103	Easton, Pa., to Jersey City, N. J.
Muscle Shoals and Elk River Shoals	3,156,919	1889	16	Big Muscle to Elk River Shoals, Tenn.
Ogeechee	407,818	1840	16	Savannah River, Ga., to Ogeechee River, Ga.
Ohio	4,695,204	1835	317	Cleveland, O., to Portsmouth, O.
Oswego	5,239,526	1828	38	Oswego, N. Y., to Syracuse, N. Y.
Portage Lake and Lake Superior	528,892	1873	25	From Keweenaw Bay to Lake Superior.
Port Arthur	....	1899	7	Port Arthur, Tex., to Gulf of Mexico.
Santa Fé	70,000	1880	10	Waldo, Fla., to Melrose, Fla.
Sault Ste. Marie	4,000,000	1895	3	Connects Lakes Superior and Huron.
Schuylkill Navigation Co.	12,461,600	1826	108	Mill Creek, Pa., to Philadelphia, Pa.
Walhonding	607,269	1843	25	Rochester, O., to Roscoe, O.
Welland (in Canada)	23,796,353	....	26¾	Connects Lake Ontario and Lake Erie.

Chicago Drainage Canal, a canal intended chiefly for carrying off the sewage of Chicago, but which may be used for commercial purposes; begun in September, 1892; completed in January, 1900. The main channel is 29 miles long, extending from Chicago to Locksport on the Illinois River, into which strean it discharges. About 9 miles of the channel is cut through solid rock, with a minimum depth of 22 feet and a width of 160 feet on the bottom in rock, which makes it the largest artificial channel in the world. The length of the waterway from the mouth of the Chicago River to its terminus south of Joliet is about 42 miles. The cost of the canal was estimated at about $45,000,000.

Canby, EDWARD RICHARD SPRIGG, military officer; born in Kentucky in 1819; graduated at West Point in 1839; served in the SEMINOLE WAR (*q. v.*) and the war with Mexico. He was twice brevetted for eminent services in the latter

EDWARD R. S. CANBY.

war. He was promoted to major in 1855, and colonel in 1861. In 1861 he was in command in New Mexico until late in 1862, and in March of that year was made brigadier-general of volunteers. He was promoted to major-general of volunteers in May, 1864, and took command of the Department of West Mississippi. He captured Mobile, April 12, 1865, and afterwards received the surrender of the Confederate armies of Generals Taylor and E. Kirby Smith. On July 28, 1866, he was commissioned a brigadier-general in the regular army, and in 1869 took command of the Department of the Columbia, on the Pacific coast. He devoted himself to the settlement of difficulties with the MODOC INDIANS (*q. v.*), and, while so doing, was treacherously murdered by Captain Jack, their leader, in northern California, April 11, 1873.

Cancer, LUIS, missionary; born in Saragossa, Spain; became a member of the Dominican Order. With two companions and Magdalena, a converted Indian woman, whom he had brought from Havana as an interpreter, landed in Florida in 1549. By presents he gained the friendship of the Indians, but a few days later was killed by the Indians.

Cane River, BATTLE OF. See RED RIVER EXPEDITION.

Cane Sugar. See SUGAR.

Canning, GEORGE, statesman; born in London, April 11, 1770; British Secretary for Foreign Affairs, 1807–09, 1822–27; approved the ORDERS IN COUNCIL (*q. v.*), and defended the War of 1812; accepted the Monroe Doctrine. He died Aug. 8, 1827.

Canning, STRATFORD DE REDCLIFFE, VISCOUNT, statesman; born in London, Nov. 4, 1786; minister to the United States, 1820–24. He died Aug. 14, 1880.

Cannon, in the United States, were cast at Lynn, Mass., by Henry Leonard, in 1647, and at Orr's foundry, Bridgewater, 1648. In 1735 the Hope Furnace was established in Rhode Island, where six heavy cannon, ordered by the State, were cast in 1775. The heaviest guns used at this time were 18-pounders.

William Denning makes wrought-iron cannon of staves bound together with wrought-iron bands, and boxed and breeched, 1790.

Colonel Bomford, of the United States ordnance department, invents a cannon called the columbiad, a long-chambered piece for projecting solid shot and shell with a heavy charge of powder, 1812.

West Point foundry established under special patronage of the government, 1817.

First contract of Gouverneur Kemble, president, for the West Point Foundry Association, for thirty-two 42-pounders, long guns, July 11, 1820.

First gun rifled in America at the

South Boston Iron Company's foundry, 1834.

Cyrus Alger patents and makes the first malleable iron guns cast and converted in an oven, 1836.

Earliest piece of heavy ordnance cast at the South Boston foundry, a 10-in. columbiad, under the supervision of Colonel Bomford; weight, 14,500 lbs.; shot, 130 lbs.; shell, 90 lbs.; charge of powder, 18 lbs., Sept. 6, 1839.

Character of "gun iron" definitely fixed by the "metallo-dynamoter," a testing-machine invented by Major Wade, 1840.

First 12-in. columbiad; weight, 25,510 lbs.; extreme range, 5,761 yds.; weight of shell, 172 lbs.; charge of powder, 20 lbs.; cast at the South Boston foundry, July 8, 1846.

Dahlgren gun, of iron, cast solid and cooled from the exterior, very thick at breech and diminishing to muzzle; first cast, May, 1850.

Rodman gun, a columbiad model, smooth-bore, made by the Rodman process of hollow casting, cooled from the interior; adopted by the United States for all sea-coast cannon, 1860.

First 10-lb. Parrot gun, of iron, cast hollow, cooled from the inside and strengthened by an exterior tube made of wrought-iron bars spirally coiled and shrunk on; made at the West Point foundry, 1860.

15-in. Rodman gun, weighing 49,000 lbs., cast by the South Boston Iron Company, 1860.

Parrott gun first put to test of active warfare in the battle of Bull Run, July 21, 1861.

Gatling rapid-firing gun, from five to ten barrels around one common axis; ten-barrel Gatling discharges 1,200 shots a minute; range, 3,000 yds.; invented in 1861.

S. B. Dean, of South Boston Iron Company, patents a process of rough boring bronze guns and forcibly expanding the bore to its finished size by means of mandrels, 1869.

Pneumatic dynamite torpedo-gun built and mounted at Fort Lafayette (founded on invention of D. M. Mefford, of Ohio), 1885.

Congress makes an appropriation for the establishment of a plant for gun-making at the Watervliet arsenal, West Troy, 1889.

Manufacture of heavy ordnance begun at the Washington navy-yard, 1890.

Hotchkiss gun, English make, five barrels, revolving around a common axis, placed upon block weighing about 386 tons, fires thirty rounds a minute; adopted by the United States in 1891.

Automatic rapid-firing gun, invented by John and Matthew Browning, of Ogden, Utah; firing 400 shots in one minute and forty-nine seconds; adopted by the United States in 1896.

Zalinski's dynamite gun, calibre 15 ins.; throws 500 lbs. of explosive gelatine 2,100 yds.; also discharges smaller shells. Three of the guns of this class were used with tremendous effect by the United States dynamite cruiser *Vesuvius* at the bombardment of Santiago de Cuba in 1898, and larger ones have been installed at Fort Warren, Boston; Fort Schuyler, N. Y.; Fort Hancock, N. J., and at San Francisco.

Graydon dynamite gun, calibre 15 ins.; using 3,000 lbs. of compressed air to the square inch; throws 600 lbs. of dynamite 3 miles.

Armstrong gun, calibre 6 ins.; weight of shot, 69.7 lbs.; of powder, 34 lbs.; pressure per square inch, 31,000 lbs.

Hurst, double-charge gun, same principles apply as in the Armstrong and Haskell guns.

Brown wire-wound gun, made in segments; kind authorized by Congress, 37½ ft. long; weight, 30,000 lbs.

Maxim-Nordenfeldt quick-firing gun; lowest weight, 25 lbs.; maximum firing ability, 650 rounds a minute.

Cannon, George Q., Mormon leader; born in Liverpool, England, Jan. 11, 1827; came to the United States in 1844; brought up in the Mormon faith; was driven out of Nauvoo, Ill., with the other Mormons in 1846, and settled in Utah in 1847. In 1857 he was chosen an apostle; in 1872-82 represented the Territory of Utah in Congress; and during this period his right to a seat in that body was many times hotly contested. He became the object of public scorn and suffered much personal calumniation both in Congress and in the press, but held his seat till absolutely forced to retire. When Utah was seeking admission to the Union he was one of the chief promoters of the movement. He died in Monterey, Cal., April 12, 1901.

Cannon, JOSEPH GREENLEAF, legislator; born in Guilford, N. C., May 7, 1836. He removed to Illinois, and was admitted to the bar there. He was State attorney in 1861–68; was elected to the 43d Congress (1873–75) as a Republican, and, with the exception of the session of 1891–93, has held the seat by re-elections. He was Speaker of the House in 1903–11, and

JOSEPH GREENLEAF CANNON.

the loss of control of the House in the elections of 1910 was charged in a large measure to his arbitrary actions as Speaker; but in the elections of 1914 he regained his seat.

Cannon, NEWTON, military officer; born in Guilford county, N. C., about 1781; received a common-school education; was colonel of the Tennessee Mounted Rifles in 1813; was a representative in Congress in 1814–17 and in 1819–23; and governor of Tennessee in 1835–39. He died in Harpeth, Tenn., Sept. 29, 1842.

Cannon, WILLIAM, patriot; born in Bridgeville, Del., in 1809; was a member of the Peace Congress in 1861, and it was said that he was "the firm friend of the Crittenden Compromise and of an unbroken Union." In 1864 he became governor of Delaware, and during his incumbency was opposed by the legislature. He died in Philadelphia, Pa., March 1, 1865.

Canonicus, Indian chief; king of the Narragansets; born about 1565. He was at first unwilling to be friendly with the Pilgrims at New Plymouth. To show his contempt and defiance of the English he sent a message to Governor Bradford with a bundle of arrows in a rattlesnake's skin. That was at the dead of winter, 1622. It was a challenge to engage in war in the spring. Like the venomous serpent that wore the skin, the symbol of hostility gave warning before the blow should be struck—a virtue seldom exercised by the Indians. Bradford acted wisely. He accepted the challenge by sending the significant quiver back filled with gunpowder and shot. "What can these things be?" inquired the ignorant and curious savage mind, as the ammunition was carried from village to village, in superstitious awe, as objects of evil omen. They had heard of the great guns at the seaside, and they dared not keep the mysterious symbols of the governor's anger, but sent them back to Plymouth as tokens of peace. The chief and his associates honorably sued for the friendship of the white people. Canonicus became the firm friend of the English, especially of Roger Williams, who found a retreat in his dominions. Before Williams's arrival there had been war between the Narragansets and Pequods concerning the ownership of lands, in which a son of Canonicus was slain. In his grief the king burned his own house and all his goods in it. Roger Williams, who often experienced his kindness, spoke of Canonicus as "a wise and peaceable prince." He was uncle of MIANTONOMOH (*q. v.*), who succeeded him as sachem of the Narragansets in 1638. Canonicus died June 4, 1647.

Canteen, a regimental establishment managed by a commitee of officers, in barracks or forts, for the sale of liquors, tobacco, groceries, etc., to the soldiers at reasonable prices. The profits are employed for the benefit of the soldiers themselves. The question of the abolition of the canteen in the army of the United States has provoked a large amount of discussion pro and con.

Cantilever. See BRIDGES.

Cap, LIBERTY. See LIBERTY CAP.

Cape Ann, original name of the present city of Gloucester, Mass., noted for more than 250 years for its extensive fishery interests. It was chosen as a place of settlement for a fishing colony by Rev. John White (a long time rector of Trinity Church, Dorchester, England) and several other influential persons. Through the exertions of Mr. White a joint-stock association was formed, called the "Dorchester Adventurers," with a capital of about $14,000. Cape Ann was purchased, and fourteen persons, with live-stock, were sent out in 1623, who built a house and made preparations for curing fish. Affairs were not prosperous there. Roger Conant was chosen governor in 1625, but the Adventurers became discouraged and concluded on dissolving the colony. Through the encouragement of Mr. White some of the colonists remained, but, not liking their seat, they went to Naumkeag, now Salem, where a permanent colony was settled. Population in 1890, 24,651; in 1900, 26,121; in 1910, 24,398.

Cape Breton, a large island at the entrance of the Gulf of St. Lawrence, and separated from Nova Scotia by the narrow Strait of Sanso; discovered by Cabot, 1497. The French fortress LOUISBURG (*q. v.*) was situated on this island. This was taken by the New England troops in 1745. Island ceded to England, Feb. 10, 1763; incorporated with Nova Scotia, 1819. Population, 1901, 97,605.

Cape Cod, a peninsula on the s. side of Massachusetts Bay; 65 miles long and from one to twenty broad. It is mostly sandy and barren, but populous. The navigation around the cape is peculiarly hazardous, and the saving to commerce and human life which would result from a short-cut waterway would be immense. A proposition to cut a canal from Buzzard's Bay to Barnstable Bay dates from the early part of the seventeenth century, a charter was granted in 1878, and, after many delays, a canal built with private capital, at a cost of $12,000,000, was opened to commerce, July 29, 1914.

Cape Fear, ACTION AT. Gen. Braxton Bragg was in command of the Confederates in the Cape Fear region at the time of the fall of Fort Fisher, and General Hoke was his most efficient leader. He held Fort Anderson, a large earthwork about halfway between Fort Fisher and Wilmington. Gen. Alfred Terry did not think it prudent to advance on Wilmington until he should be reinforced. To effect this General Grant ordered Schofield from Tennessee to the coast of North Carolina, where he arrived with the 23d Corps on Feb. 9, 1865, and swelled Terry's force of 8,000 to 20,000. Schofield, outranking Terry, took the chief command. The Department of North Carolina had just been created, and he was made its commander. The chief object now was to occupy Goldsboro, in aid of Sherman's march to that place. Terry was pushed forward towards Hoke's right, and, with gunboats, attacked Fort Anderson (Feb. 18) and drove the Confederates from it. The fleeing garrison was pursued, struck, and dispersed, with a loss of 375 men and two guns. The National troops pressed up both sides of the Cape Fear River, pushed Hoke back, while gunboats secured torpedoes in the stream and erected batteries on both banks. Hoke abandoned Wilmington Feb. 22, 1865, after destroying all the steamers and naval stores there. Among the former were the Confederate privateers *Chickamauga* and *Tallahassee.* Wilmington was occupied by National troops, and the Confederates abandoned the Cape Fear region.

Cape Girardeau, a city in Cape Girardeau county, Mo., on the Mississippi River, 150 miles below St. Louis; is in a farming, paint clay, limestone, and kaolin region; seat of a State normal school, St. Vincent's College and Convent, and Convent of the Sisters of Loretto; was a base of supplies for General Grant's army; and was unsuccessfully attacked by the Confederates under General Marmaduke, April 26, 1863. Population (1900), 4,815; (1910), 8,475.

Capen, NAHUM, historian; born at Canton, Mass., April 1, 1804; postmaster of Boston, Mass., 1857–61; introduced street letter-box colections; wrote *The Republic of the United States; History of Democracy*, etc. He died in Dorchester, Mass., Jan. 4, 1886.

Cape Nome, a cape extending from the southern part of the western peninsula of Alaska, which lies between Kotzebue Sound on the north and Bering Sea on the south. It is about 2,500 miles northwest of Seattle, and 175 miles southeast of Siberia. In September, 1898, gold was first discovered here by a party of Swedes. Since then it has become the centre of a rich gold-mining region, which lies about the lower course of the Snake River, a winding stream emerging from a range of mountains not exceeding from 700 to 1,200 feet in altitude. In October, 1899, Nome City had a population of 5,000 inhabitants living in tents. It is believed that the rapid growth of this town has never been equalled. Early prospecting indicated that the Nome district would compare for richness with the celebrated KLONDIKE (*q. v.*) region. In the short season of 1899 the yield in gold from this section alone was estimated at $1,500,000. Its early promise, however, soon gave out; other fields opened up better prospects, and by 1910 the population had decreased to 2,600 from 12,488 in 1900.

Capital. A politico-economical term. J. B. Say, the French economist, defines it as "in the broadest sense an accumulation of values withdrawn from unproductive consumption." Another definition is, "a product saved and intended for reproduction." Land, climate, or the instruments of production provided by nature are not considered as capital, as they are the gifts of nature.

Capital, NATIONAL. Owing to the shifting scenes of important military operations, the seat of government of the United States had no fixed abiding-place for many years. The early seat of government was the place where the Continental Congress found it safe and convenient to hold its sessions, and any chosen place was subject to change on sudden notice. The cities that had the honor of thus being the seat of government were: Philadelphia, Sept. 5, 1774, May 10, 1775, March 4, 1777, and July 2, 1778; Baltimore, Dec. 20, 1776; Lancaster, Pa., Sept. 27, 1777; York, Pa., Sept. 30, 1777; Princeton, N. J., June 30, 1783; Annapolis, Md., Nov. 26, 1783; Trenton, N. J., Nov. 1, 1784; and New York from Jan. 11, 1785 till the adoption of the Constitution, Sept. 28, 1787. The seat of government of the United States was permanently settled in the city of Washington, D. C., in the summer of 1800. It seemed like transferring it to a wilderness. Only the north wing of the Capitol was finished, and that was fitted up to accommodate both Houses of Congress. The President's house was finished externally, but much had to be done on the inside. There was only one good tavern, and that was insufficient to accommodate half the Congressmen. There was only a path through an alder swamp along the line of Pennsylvania Avenue from the President's house to the Capitol. Mrs. Adams wrote concerning the President's house that it was superb in design, but then dreary beyond endurance. "I could content myself almost anywhere for three months," she said, "but surrounded with forests, can you believe that wood is not to be had, because people cannot be found to cut and cart it! . . . We have, indeed, come into a new country." The public offices had hardly been established in the city when the War Office, a wooden structure, took fire and was burned, with many valuable papers.

From time to time there have been movements in favor of removing the seat of government from Washington, D. C. The first of this kind was in 1808. The really miserable situation and condition of the city at that time rendered a removal desirable to most of the members of Congress, and the city of Philadelphia, anxious to win it back to the banks of the Delaware, offered to furnish every accommodation to Congress and the public offices at its own expense. The new Hall of Representatives, by its ill adaptation whether for speakers or hearers, occasioned great dissatisfaction. A motion for removal occasioned much discussion in Congress and great excitement in the District of Columbia, especially among land-owners. The Southern members objected to Philadelphia because they would there be continually pestered

WASHINGTON IN 1800

by anti-slavery politicians and other annoyances connected with the subject. A resolution for removal came within a very few votes of passing. It is believed that it would have been carried but for the opposition of the Southern men to Philadelphia. In more recent years there have been agitations favoring removal to St. Louis or some other Western city, on the ground of having it in a more central location geographically.

In 1816 Congress, by joint resolution, authorized the President of the United States to procure, for the ornamenting of the new Capitol, then building, four large paintings of Revolutionary scenes from the hand of John Trumbull, a worthy pupil of Benjamin West. He possessed a large number of portraits of the prominent actors in the events of the Revolution, painted by himself, and these he used in his compositions. These pictures are now in the rotunda of the Capitol, under the magnificent dome, and are of peculiar historic value, as they perpetuate correct likenesses of the men whom Americans delight to honor. These paintings represent the *Signers of the Declaration of Independence*, the *Surrender of Burgoyne* at Saratoga, the *Surrender of Cornwallis* at Yorktown, and the *Resignation of Washington's Commission* at Annapolis. To these have since been added others, of the same general size—namely, the *Landing of Columbus*, by John Vanderlyn; the *Burial of De Soto*, by George Powell; the *Baptism of Pocahontas*, by J. G. Chapman; the *Embarkation of the Pilgrims*, by Robert W. Weir; *President Lincoln Signing the Emancipation Proclamation*, by Frank B. Carpenter, etc. The old Hall of Representatives is now used for a national Hall of Statuary, to which each State has been asked to contribute statues of two of its most distinguished citizens. The Capitol has already become the permanent depository of a large collection of grand paintings and statuary illustrative of the progress of the nation.

The Capitol was made a vast citadel on the arrival of troops there after the close of April, 1861. Its halls and committee-rooms were used as barracks for the soldiers; its basement galleries were converted into store-rooms for barrels of pork, beef, and other provisions for the army; and the vaults under the broad terrace on the western front of the Capitol were converted into bakeries, where 16,000 loaves of bread were baked every day. The chimneys of the ovens pierced the terrace, and there for three months dense volumes of black smoke poured forth.

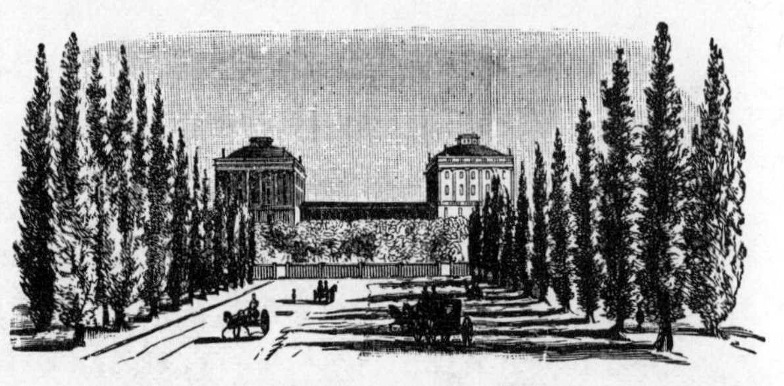

CAPITOL AT WASHINGTON, 1814.

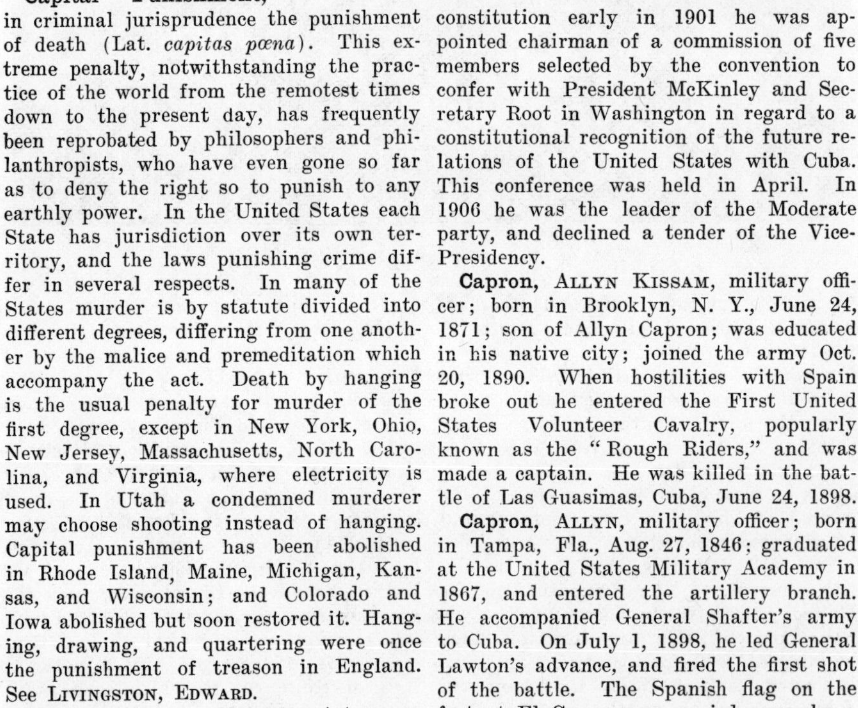

Capital Punishment, in criminal jurisprudence the punishment of death (Lat. *capitas pœna*). This extreme penalty, notwithstanding the practice of the world from the remotest times down to the present day, has frequently been reprobated by philosophers and philanthropists, who have even gone so far as to deny the right so to punish to any earthly power. In the United States each State has jurisdiction over its own territory, and the laws punishing crime differ in several respects. In many of the States murder is by statute divided into different degrees, differing from one another by the malice and premeditation which accompany the act. Death by hanging is the usual penalty for murder of the first degree, except in New York, Ohio, New Jersey, Massachusetts, North Carolina, and Virginia, where electricity is used. In Utah a condemned murderer may choose shooting instead of hanging. Capital punishment has been abolished in Rhode Island, Maine, Michigan, Kansas, and Wisconsin; and Colorado and Iowa abolished but soon restored it. Hanging, drawing, and quartering were once the punishment of treason in England. See LIVINGSTON, EDWARD.

Capote, DOMINGO MENDEZ, statesman; born in Cardenas, Cuba, in 1863; received his education at the University of Havana, where he later served as a professor of law for many years. In December, 1895, he abandoned his practice to join the Cuban forces under Gen. Maximo Gomez. Afterwards he reached the rank of brigadier-general, and also served as civil governor of Matanzas and of Las Villas. In November, 1897, he was elected vice-president of the republic of Cuba. After the adoption in convention of the new Cuban constitution early in 1901 he was appointed chairman of a commission of five members selected by the convention to confer with President McKinley and Secretary Root in Washington in regard to a constitutional recognition of the future relations of the United States with Cuba. This conference was held in April. In 1906 he was the leader of the Moderate party, and declined a tender of the Vice-Presidency.

Capron, ALLYN KISSAM, military officer; born in Brooklyn, N. Y., June 24, 1871; son of Allyn Capron; was educated in his native city; joined the army Oct. 20, 1890. When hostilities with Spain broke out he entered the First United States Volunteer Cavalry, popularly known as the "Rough Riders," and was made a captain. He was killed in the battle of Las Guasimas, Cuba, June 24, 1898.

Capron, ALLYN, military officer; born in Tampa, Fla., Aug. 27, 1846; graduated at the United States Military Academy in 1867, and entered the artillery branch. He accompanied General Shafter's army to Cuba. On July 1, 1898, he led General Lawton's advance, and fired the first shot of the battle. The Spanish flag on the fort at El Caney was carried away by a shot from his battery. His exposure in the Santiago campaign resulted in a fever, from which he died near Fort Myer, Va., Sept. 18, 1898.

Caravel, a small sea-going vessel of about 100 tons' burden, built somewhat like a galley, formerly used by the Spanish and Portuguese; two of the vessels of Columbus on his first voyage to America were caravels.

THE CAPITOL, WASHINGTON

Card-cloth. The manufacture of cards for carding wool by hand was quite an important industry in America before the Revolution, and was carried on successfully during that war. In 1787 Oliver Evans, the pioneer American inventor, engaged in making card-teeth by hand, invented a machine that produced 300 a minute. Already Mr. Crittendon, of New Haven, Conn., had invented a machine (1784) which produced 86,000 card-teeth, cut and bent, in an hour. These inventions led to the contrivance of machines for making card-cloth, for the purpose of carding and arranging the fibres preparatory to spinning. A machine for making the card-cloth was invented by Eleazar Smith, of Walpole, Mass., near the close of the eighteenth century, for which invention Amos Whittemore received the credit. (See WHITTEMORE, AMOS.) About 1836 William B. Earle made improvements, which were modified in 1843.

Cardenas, a seaport in the province of Matanzas, Cuba, about 90 miles east of Havana. It was here, on May 11, 1898, that the *Wilmington*, a United States gunboat, engaged the fortifications and Spanish gunboats, and rescued the *Hudson* and *Winslow*. Three Spanish gunboats which lay under the fortifications had been challenged by the torpedo-boat *Winslow* and other United States vessels, but they refused to leave the protection of the batteries. When the *Wilmington* arrived the *Hudson* and *Winslow* steamed into the inner harbor to attack the Spanish vessels. They did not, however, suspect that there was a strong battery near the water's edge until a sudden fire was opened upon them. The first shot crippled the steering-gear of the *Winslow*, and another wrecked her boiler, wounding her commander, Lieut. John B. Bernadon, and killing Ensign WORTH BAGLEY (*q. v.*) and four men. During this action the *Wilmington* sailed within 1,800 yards of the shore, and, after sending 376 shells into the batteries and the town, silenced the Spanish fire. In the meantime, amid a storm of shots, the *Hudson* ran alongside the *Winslow* and drew her out of danger. Population (1907), 28,576.

Cardiff Giant, name given to a rude statue, 10½ feet high, dug up in 1869 at Cardiff, N. Y., and exhibited for months as a petrifaction. The persons who thus deluded the public at last confessed that the "Giant" had been cut from a block of gypsum quarried at Fort Dodge, Ia., sculptured at Chicago, conveyed to Cardiff, and there buried and "accidentally discovered."

Cardinal, a prince in the Church of Rome, the council of the Pope, and the conclave or "sacred college," at first was the principal priest or incumbent of the parishes in Rome, and said to have been called *cardinale* in 853. The cardinals claimed the exclusive power of electing the Pope about 1179. In the United States the first cardinal was John McCloskey, Archbishop of New York, created 1875; the second, James Gibbons, Archbishop of Baltimore, created 1886; the third, Sebastian Martinelli, Papal Ablegate to the United States, created 1901. In 1911 Archbishop Farley of New York, Archbishop O'Connell of Boston, and Diomedes Falconio, Apostolic Delegate to the United States, were created cardinals.

Carey, HENRY CHARLES, political economist; born in Philadelphia, Dec. 15, 1793; retired from the book trade in 1835 and devoted himself to the study of political economy, publishing many important books on the subject. Free trade, in his opinion, while the ideal condition, could be reached only through protection. His publications include *Essay on the Rate of Wages; The Principles of Political Economy; The Credit System in France, Great Britain, and the United States; the Principles of Social Science*, etc. He died in Philadelphia, Oct. 13, 1879.

Carey, MATTHEW, publicist; born in Dublin, Ireland, Jan. 28, 1760; learned the business of printer and bookseller. He was compelled to fly to Paris in consequence of a charge of sedition, but returned to Ireland in the course of a year, where, in 1783, he edited the *Freeman's Journal*, and established the *Volunteer's Journal*. Because of a violent attack on Parliament he was confined in Newgate prison, and after his release he sailed for the United States, arriving in Philadelphia Nov. 15, 1784. There he started the *Pennsylvania Herald*. While the War of 1812–15 was kindling he wrote much on political subjects, and in 1814 his *Olive*

Branch appeared, in which he attempted to harmonize the contending parties in the United States. It passed through ten editions. In 1819 appeared his vindication of his countrymen, entitled *Vindicæ Hiberniæ.* In 1820 he published his *New Olive Branch,* which was followed by a series of tracts, the object being to demonstrate the necessity of a protective system. His writings on political economy were widely circulated. His advocacy of internal improvements led to the construction of the Pennsylvania canals. He published Bibles, etc., which were sold by book agents. He died in Philadelphia, Pa., Sept. 16, 1839.

Carey's Rebellion. See NORTH CAROLINA, 1706-11.

Caricature in American History, one form of the liberty of the press, appealing especially to people who cannot, or will not, read. During the anti-Tweed campaign in New York City it was reported that Tweed had said that he cared nothing for the articles in the newspapers, the pamphlets, and books written in antagonism to the Tweed ring, but he did feel bitterly that the caricatures by Thomas Nast in *Harper's Weekly* angered him more than all other forms of opposition combined. As he graphically put it, "I do not care what they write; my constituents do not read, but they can all understand these pictures by Thomas Nast." Caricature has always been a favorite method of political agitation. There can be no question but that these caricatures in *Harper's Weekly* were a powerful instrument in overthrowing the Tweed ring. After Tweed escaped from prison he took refuge in Spain, and was recognized there by the Nast caricatures. He was extradited and imprisoned.

Carleton, SIR GUY, LORD DORCHESTER, civil and military officer; born in Strabane, Ireland, Sept. 3, 1724; entered the Guards at an early age, and became a lieutenant-colonel in 1748. He was aide to the Duke of Cumberland in the German campaign of 1757; was with Amherst in the siege of Louisburg in 1758; with Wolfe at Quebec (1759), and was a brigadier-general at the siege of Belle Isle, where he was wounded. He was also quartermaster-general in the expedition against Havana in 1762, and in 1767 he was made lieutenant-governor of Quebec. The next year he was appointed governor. In 1772 he was promoted to major-general, and in 1774 he was made governor-general of the Province of Quebec. In an expedition against the forts on Lake Champlain in 1775 he narrowly escaped capture; and at the close of the year he successfully resisted a siege of Quebec by Montgomery.

GUY CARLETON.

The next spring and summer he drove the Americans out of Canada, and totally defeated the American flotilla in an engagement on Lake Champlain in October.

Sir John Burgoyne had been in England during the earlier part of 1777, and managed, by the help of Sir Jeffrey Amherst, to obtain a commission to take command of all the British forces in Canada. When Sir John arrived at Quebec (May 6, 1777), Carleton was ordered, "for the speedy quelling of the rebellion," to make over to Burgoyne, his inferior officer, the command of the Canadian army.

Governor Carleton was a strict disciplinarian and always obeyed instructions to the letter. When Burgoyne, after the capture of Ticonderoga (July, 1777), pushing on towards the valley of the Hudson, desired Carleton to hold that post with the 3,000 troops which had been left in Canada, the governor refused, pleading his instructions, which confined him to his own province. This unexpected refusal was the first of the embarrassments Burgoyne endured after leaving Lake Champlain. He was compelled, he said, to "drain the life-blood of his army" to garrison Ticonderoga and hold Lake George. No doubt this weakening of his army at that time was one of the principal causes of his defeat near Saratoga. Carleton was made lieutenant-general in 1778; was appointed commander-in-chief of the British forces in America in 1781; and sailed for England Nov. 25, 1783. In 1786 he was created Baron Dorchester, and from that year until 1796 he was governor of British North America. He died Nov. 10, 1808.

Carleton, James Henry, military officer; born in Maine in 1814. He served in the Mexican War, and when the Civil War broke out was ordered to southern California as major of the 6th United States Cavalry. In April, 1862, he relieved General Canby in the command of the Department of New Mexico. He was brevetted major-general, U. S. A. He was the author of *The Battle of Buena Vista, with the Operations of the Army of Occupation for one Month.* He died in San Antonio, Tex., Jan. 7, 1873.

Carleton, Thomas, military officer; born in England in 1736; joined the British army and came to America in 1755 as an ensign in Wolfe's command; was promoted lieutenant-general in 1798, and general in 1803. During the Revolutionary War he received a wound in the naval battle with Arnold on Lake Champlain in 1776. He died in Ramsgate, England, Feb. 2, 1817.

Carleton, Will, author; born in Hudson, Mich., Oct. 21, 1845; graduated at Hillsdale College; journalist, lecturer, reader, and poet. Editor of *Everywhere.* Author of *Farm Ballads, Legends, and Festivals; City Ballads, Legends, and Festivals; Young Folks' Centennial Rhymes* (1876); *Rhymes of Our Planet,* etc. He died Dec. 18, 1912.

Carlin, William Passmore, military officer; born in Greene county, Ill., Nov. 24, 1829; was graduated at West Point in 1850, and was in the Sioux expeditions under General Harney in 1855, and under General Sumner against the Cheyennes in 1857. He was in the Utah expedition in 1858; and did efficient service in Missouri for the Union in the early part of the Civil War, where he commanded a district until March, 1862. He commanded a brigade under Generals Steele and Pope, which bore a prominent part in the battle of Stone River (*q. v.*). In the operations in northern Georgia late in 1863, and in the Atlanta campaign the next year, he was very active. In the famous march to the sea he commanded a division in the 14th Corps; and was with Sherman in his progress through the Carolinas, fighting at Bentonville. He was brevetted major-general, U. S. A. in 1893; retired Nov. 24 of that year; and died in Livingstone, Mont., Oct. 4, 1903.

Carlisle, Frederick Howard, fifth Earl of, royal commissioner; born in May, 1748; was one of the three commissioners sent on a conciliatory errand to America in 1788; and was lord-lieutenant of Ireland in 1780–82. He died Sept. 4, 1825.

Carlisle, John Griffin, statesman; born in Campbell (now Kenton) county, Ky., Sept. 5, 1835; was admitted to the bar in 1858. He rapidly acquired a reputation both as a lawyer and politician. Having gained experience in both houses of the Kentucky legislature and served as lieutenant-governor from 1871 to 1875, he entered the national House of Representatives in 1877 as Democratic member from his native State. In Congress he became rapidly one of the most notable and influential figures, especially on financial and commercial matters. He was a member of the Ways and Means Committee, and was recognized as one of the ablest debaters and leaders in the movement for revenue reform. When his party obtained control of the House in 1883, Carlisle, as the candidate of the revenue-reform wing of the Democrats, received the nomination and election to the office of Speaker. He was twice re-elected, serving until 1889. From 1890 to 1893 he was United States Senator. On March 4, 1893, he entered Cleveland's second cabinet as Secretary of the Treasury, and on retiring therefrom engaged in the practice of law in New York City, where he died July 31, 1910.

Carmichael, William, diplomatist; born in Maryland, date uncertain; was a man of fortune. He was in Europe in

1776, and assisted Silas Deane in his political and commercial operations in France. He also assisted the American commissioners in Paris. In 1778–80 he was in Congress, and was secretary of legation to Jay's mission to Spain. When the latter left Europe (1782) Carmichael remained as *chargé d'affaires*, and retained the office for several years. In 1792 he was associated with William Short on a commission to negotiate with Spain a treaty concerning the navigation of the Mississippi. Sparks's *Diplomatic Correspondence* contains many of his letters. He died in February, 1795.

Carnegie, ANDREW, philanthropist; born in Dunfermline, Scotland, Nov. 25, 1837; was brought to the United States by his parents, who settled in Pittsburg in 1848. He became successively a telegraph messenger boy, operator, employe of the Pennsylvania Railroad Company, and superintendent of the Pittsburg division of that system. In 1868 he went to England, where the Bessemer system of making steel rails had recently been perfected; acquired all possible information concerning the new process, and on his return entered the steel-making business; was enabled to buy out his strongest rivals, and by 1888 controlled seven large plants, all within five miles of Pittsburg, which were subsequently merged into the Carnegie Steel Company, and this later became the chief holding of the United States Steel Corporation. In 1901 he received a large amount of money from the giant corporation for his interest, retired from active business, and thereafter gave himself up to the distribution of his enormous wealth for the benefit of the world's general public. By 1911 the total amount of his benefactions was estimated at over $200,000,000. His most noteworthy gifts were $50,000,000 for public libraries in the United States; $16,000,000 for the Carnegie Institution in Pittsburg, Pa.; $15,000,000 for college professors' pensions; $22,000,000 for the Carnegie Institution in Washington, D. C.; $10,000,000 for libraries in foreign countries; $10,000,000 for a Peace Fund; $10,000,000 for Scotch universities; $5,000,000 for a Hero Fund in the United States; $5,000,000 for Carnegie Steel Company's employes; $5,000,000 for Dunfermline (Scotland) endowment; $4,000,000 for Carnegie Technical Institute at Pittsburg; $1,750,000 for Temple of Peace at The Hague; $1,500,000 for the Allied Engineers' Societies in New York; $850,000 for a building for the Bureau of American Republics in Washington, D. C.; $20,000,000 to colleges in the United States; $20,000,000 in miscellaneous gifts in the United States; and $3,500,000 in the same in Europe. His largest gift was $125,000,000 to the Carnegie Corporation of New York, the body which was incorporated by the legislature on June 9, 1911, for the purpose of taking over Mr. Carnegie's work in connection with educational institutions, libraries, and hero funds. The gift was in the form of 5 per cent. first-mortgage bonds of the United States Steel Corporation, the bonds being given as at par. The bonds were worth 102⅝, so that this munificent benefaction represented a much larger amount than the face value of the bonds, and insured to the incorporators a splendid annual amount to continue his work. The gift was announced at a meeting of the incorporators in Mr. Carnegie's home.

On May 5, 1911, he was presented with a gold medal by twenty-one American republics. His publications include *Triumphant Democracy; The Gospel of Wealth; The Empire of Business; Problems of To-day; The Life of James Watt;* and many magazine articles.

Carnegie Endowment for International Peace. On Dec. 14, 1910, Andrew Carnegie transferred to a board of trustees $10,000,000 in 5 per cent. first-mortgage bonds, the revenue of which will be used to "hasten the abolition of international war" and to establish lasting world peace. The formal transfer was made at a meeting in the rooms of the Carnegie Research Foundation. The trustees organized by choosing as president United States Senator Elihu Root, permanent representative of the United States at The Hague Tribunal. President Taft consented to be honorary president of the foundation.

The method by which the annual income of $500,000 shall be expended is left by Mr. Carnegie entirely to the trustees. The foundation is to be perpetual, and when the establishment of universal peace

ANDREW CARNEGIE

is attained the donor provides that the revenue shall be devoted to the banishment of the "next most degrading of evils," the suppression of which would "most advance the progress, elevation, and happiness of men."

The informal trust deed presented by Mr. Carnegie to the trustees reads in part as follows:

"Gentlemen: I have transferred to you as trustees of the Carnegie peace fund $10,000,000 5 per cent. first-mortgage bonds, value $11,500,000, the revenue of which is to be administered by you to hasten the abolition of international war, the foulest blot upon our civilization. Although we no longer eat our fellow men or torture prisoners, or sack cities, killing their inhabitants, we still kill each other in war like barbarians. Only wild beasts are excusable for doing that in this the twentieth century of the Christian era, for the crime of war is inherent, since it decides not in favor of the right but always of the strong. The nation is criminal which refuses arbitration and drives its adversary to a tribunal which knows nothing of righteous judgment."

At the opening of the seventeenth annual meeting of the Lake Mohonk Conference on International Arbitration, May 24, 1911, President Nicholas Murray Butler of Columbia University, presiding officer of the Conference, for the first time made public, "with authority," the plans of the trustees of the endowment, as follows:

The trustees of the endowment have taken a broad and statesmanlike view of its aims and purposes. While they do not overlook the value of the work of the propaganda, and intend to aid in carrying it on, they believe that the time has come when the resources of modern scientific method be brought to bear upon the problem of international relations.

It has been determined by the trustees of the Carnegie Endowment to organize the undertaking committed to their charge as a great institution for research and public education and to carry on its work in three parts or divisions—a division of international law, a division of economics and history, and a division of intercourse and education. Otherwise stated, these three divisions will represent the juristic, the economic, and, broadly speaking, the educational aspect of the problem before the trustees, which is to hasten the abolition of international war by the erection of an international judicial system competent to hear and to determine all questions of difference arising between nations.

The division of international law will be under the direction of Professor James Brown Scott, whose services in the Department of State, at the second Hague Conference, and in connection with the American Society and *Journal of International Law* are too well known to need specific enumeration. This division will promote the development of international law, and by study, by conferences, by aiding negotiations, and by publication will assist in bringing about such a progressive development of the rules of international law as will enable them to meet with constantly growing adequacy the needs of the nations of the world in their juristic relations towards each other. Furthermore, this division of the endowment will aim constantly to inculcate the belief that intercourse between nations should be based upon a correct and definite idea of international justice. To the perfecting and clarifying of the fundamental conception of international justice this division will assiduously devote itself.

All this study and activity have for their object to hasten the day when the principles and rules of international law will be so clearly apprehended and so satisfactory that the settlement of international differences and disputes in accordance with their terms will become the unvarying practice of civilized nations.

For this purpose the endowment will associate with Dr. Scott a consultative board composed of some of the most distinguished international lawyers in the world. The point of view of each great nation will be represented in its council, and the results to be arrived at will be the joint work of jurists of every school and of every language. We need, first, an agreement as to the fundamental principles which should regulate the rights and duties of nations in their mutual intercourse, which principles would then form the substantive law of nations.

The Hague Conference has solemnly declared that the maintenance of peace is the supreme duty of nations. For the execution of this supreme duty adequate means must be provided. If they are at hand they should be strengthened; if they are not at hand, they must be brought into existence. This whole process is one of legal evolution.

The second division of the work of the Carnegie Endowment will be the Division of Economics and History. It will be under the direction of Professor John Bates Clark, of Columbia University, whose foremost place among English-speaking economists is gladly recognized everywhere. The Division of Economics and History will aim at the education of public opinion and at the formulation of conclusions that may serve for the guidance of governmental policy. With Professor Clark will be associated a score of the world's leading economists. England, Germany, France, Italy, Austria-Hungary, Switzerland, Holland, Denmark, Japan, the Argentine Republic, and other nations will have a voice and a part in formulating the problems to whose solution this division will address itself, and in working out the solutions of those problems.

It will be the business of this division to study the economic causes and effects of war, the effect upon the public opinion of nations and upon international goodwill of retaliatory, discriminatory and preferential tariffs; the economic aspects of the present huge expenditures for military purposes; and the relation between military expenditures and international well-being and the world-wide programme for social improvement and reform which is held in waiting through lack of means for its execution.

There remains a third and important division of the work of endowment—the Division of Intercourse and Education—the director for which has not yet been announced. It will be the function of this division to supplement the work of the two divisions, which may be called, perhaps, the scientific ones, by carrying forward vigorously, and in co-operation with existing agencies, the educational work of propaganda, of international hospitality, and of promoting international friendship.

Among the tasks of this division will be to diffuse information and to educate public opinions regarding the causes, nature, and effects of war, and the means for its prevention and avoidance; to establish a better understanding of international rights and duties and a more perfect sense of international justice among the inhabitants of civilized nations; to cultivate friendly feelings among the inhabitants of different countries, and to increase the knowledge and understanding of each other of the several nations; to promote a general acceptance of peaceable methods in the settlement of international disputes, and to maintain, promote, and assist such establishments, organizations, associations, and agencies as shall be deemed necessary or useful in the accomplishment of the purposes for which the endowment exists. In other words, this division will make practical application of the teachings and findings of the divisions of international law and economics and history.

It can hardly be doubted that the men at the head of these three important divisions of the work of the endowment, with their immediate associates and colleagues in this and other countries, will speedily come to form a veritable faculty of peace, and that the world will look to them more and more for instruction and for inspiration alike.

The government of the United States has been at work, through appropriate diplomatic channels, upon the problem of bringing about the establishment of the International Court of Arbitral Justice, and it is with no small satisfaction that I am enabled to say, with the knowledge and approval of the Secretary of State, that the progress made during the last year has been so marked that in all likelihood such a court, created by general agreement, will be erected at The Hague even earlier than seemed probable a year ago.

Carnegie Hero Funds. April 15, 1904, Andrew Carnegie placed in the hands of a commission the sum of $5,000,000 to be known as "the Hero Fund." Its purpose is to reward with medals and money the men and women who perform heroic deeds, or, in case they lose their lives, to care for those dependent upon them. Widows are given support until they remarry, and children are given allowances until they are 16 years of age. Only such as follow peaceful vocations on sea or land in the United States and Canada are eligible to become beneficiaries of the fund. The first awards of medals and money were made in May, and others in October, 1905. Up to Jan. 31, 1910, the commissioners had made 336 awards. These included 13 gold medals, 148 silver medals, and 175 bronze medals. A total of 4,621 cases had been considered. The sum of $248,406.54 had been paid to heroes and their dependents, the amounts paid on pension allowances being included. Besides this $124,462.06 had been given to funds for the relief of sufferers in the Grover factory disaster at Brockton, Mass., the California earthquake disaster, the Monongah mine disaster, the Dorr mine disaster, and the Lick Branch mine disaster.

Since establishing the above fund, Mr. Carnegie gave $1,250,000 for one in Great Britain in 1908; $1,000,000 for one in France in 1909; $1,250,000 for one in Germany in 1910; $100,000 for one in Denmark, $230,000 for one in Sweden, and $125,000 for one in Norway, all in 1911.

Carnegie Institution, an educational body in Washington, D. C., founded by Andrew Carnegie with a first gift of $10,000,000 (to which he subsequently added $15,000,000), and incorporated Jan. 4, 1902, by John Hay, Secretary of State; Edwin D. White, Justice of the Supreme Court; Daniel C. Gilman, ex-president of Johns Hopkins University; Charles D. Walcott, superintendent of the United States Geological Survey; Dr. John S. Billings, Director of the New York Public Library; and Carroll D. Wright, United States Commissioner of Labor. The aims of the institution, as expressed by the founder, are: (1) To increase the efficiency of the universities and other institutions of learning throughout the country by utilizing and adding to their existing facilities, and by aiding teachers in the various institutions for the experimental and other work in these institutions as far as may be advisable. (2) To discover the exceptional man in every department of study, whenever and wherever found, to enable him by financial aid to make the work for which he seems especially designed his life work. (3) To promote original research, paying great attention thereto as being one of the chief purposes of this institution. (4) To increase the facilities for higher education. (5) To enable such students as may find Washington the best point for their special studies to avail themselves of such advantages as may be open to them in the museums, libraries, laboratories, observatory, meteorological, piscicultural, and forestry schools, and kindred institutions of the several departments of the government. (6) To insure the prompt publication and distribution of the results of scientific investigation, a field considered to be highly important.

By an act of Congress, approved April 28, 1904, the institution was placed under the control of a board of twenty-four trustees, all of whom had been members of the original board. The trustees meet annually, and during the intervals between such meetings the affairs of the Institution are conducted by an executive committee, chosen by and from the board of trustees, acting through the president of the Institution as chief executive officer.

Carnegie Teachers' Retiring Fund. In April, 1905, Andrew Carnegie transferred to a board of trustees $10,000,000 in United States Steel Corporation fifty-year bonds bearing 5 per cent. interest, the purpose of the trust fund thus created being to provide retiring allowances or annuities to teachers in the higher institutions of learning in the United States, Canada, and Newfoundland under such regulations as the trustees might decide to be wise. Schools below the rank of college and institutions directly under the control of religious denominations are excluded from the benefits of the fund. State universities were also originally excluded from the benefits of the fund, but March 31, 1908, Mr. Carnegie, at the request of the National Association of State Universities, admitted them and at the same time added to the foundation $5,000,000 in 5 per cent. bonds, making the fund $15,000,000 in all.

The policy of the Board has been to confer the retiring allowances through the institutions themselves rather than to individual teachers, on the principle that the annuity must come as a right and not as a charity. The professors in the accepted institutions receive retired pay in due course and under established rules. Allowances are granted on the basis of age, service, and disability. Any person 65 years of age who has had not less than fifteen years of service as professor or not less than twenty-five years of service as instructor or as instructor and professor, and who is at the time a professor or an instructor in an accepted institution, shall be entitled to an annual retiring allowance, computed as follows:

(a) For an active pay of $1,200 or less an allowance of $1,000, provided no retiring allowance shall exceed 90 per cent. of the active pay.

(b) For an active pay greater than $1,200 the retiring allowance shall equal $1,000, increased by $50 for each $100 of active pay in excess of $1,200.

(c) No retiring allowance shall exceed $4,000.

Any person who has had twenty-five years of service as a professor or thirty years of service as professor and instructor, and who is at the time either a professor or an instructor in an accepted institution, shall, in the case of disability unfitting him for the work of a teacher, as proved by medical examination, be entitled to a retiring allowance computed as follows:

(a) For an active pay of $1,200 or less a retiring allowance of $800, provided that no retiring allowance shall exceed 80 per cent. of the active pay.

(b) For an active pay greater than $1,200 the retiring allowance shall equal $800, increased by $40 for each $100 in excess of $1,200.

(c) For each additional year of service above twenty-five for a professor or thirty for an instructor the retiring allowance shall be increased by 1 per cent. of the active pay.

(d) No retiring allowance shall exceed $4,000.

At the beginning of 1910 the foundation was paying 318 pensions, the cost being $466,000. The professors receiving these pensions came from 139 colleges, distributed over forty-three States of the Union and provinces of Canada.

Carnifex Ferry, BATTLE AT. The Confederate troops left by Garnett and Pegram in western Virginia in the summer of 1861 were placed in charge of Gen. Robert E. Lee. At the beginning of August he was at the head of 16,000 fighting men. John B. Floyd, the late Secretary of War, was placed in command of the Confederates in the region of the Gauley River. From him much was expected, for he promised much. He was to drive General Cox out of the Kanawha Valley, while Lee should disperse the army of 10,000 men under Rosecrans at Clarksburg, on the Baltimore and Ohio Railroad, and so open a way for an invading force of Confederates into Maryland, Pennsylvania, and Ohio. Early in September Rosecrans marched southward in search of Floyd. He scaled the Gauley Mountains, and on the 10th found Floyd at Carnifex Ferry, on the Gauley River, eight miles from Summersville, the capital of Nicholas county, Va. Already a detachment of Floyd's men had surprised and dispersed (Aug. 26, 1861) some Nationals, under Col. E. B. Taylor, not far from Summersville. At the summit of Gauley Mountain Rosecrans encountered Floyd's scouts and drove them before him; and on Sept. 10, Floyd's camp having been reconnoitered by General Benham, Rosecrans fell upon him with his whole force (chiefly Ohio troops), and for three hours a desperate battle raged. It ceased only when the darkness of night came on. Rosecrans intended to renew it in the morning, and his troops lay on their arms that night. Under cover of darkness, Floyd stole away, and did not halt in his flight until he reached the Big Sewell Mountain, near New River, thirty miles distant. The battle at Carnifex Ferry was regarded as a substantial victory for the Nationals. The latter lost fifteen killed and seventy wounded; the Confederates lost one killed and ten wounded.

Carnochan, JOHN MURRAY, surgeon; born in Savannah, Ga., July 4, 1817; began practice in New York City in 1847. In 1851 he became professor of surgery at the New York Medical College, and surgeon-in-chief to the State Immigrant Hospital. At one time he cured neuralgia by exercising the whole trunk of the second branch of the fifth pair of nerves. In 1852 he tied the femoral artery to cure exaggerated nutrition. He also tied the primitive carotid artery on both sides, to cure elephantiasis of the neck. In 1853 he exsected the entire radius, in 1854 the entire ulna. He published several technical treatises. He died in New York, Oct. 28, 1887.

Carolinas. See NORTH CAROLINA; SOUTH CAROLINA.

Caroline Affair. Navy Island, on the Canadian side of the Niagara, in 1839, was occupied by a body of Canadian insurgents, under the leadership of W. L. Mackenzie and Louis J. Papineau, and their sympathizers from the United States. The *Caroline* was a steamer which, for the sake of greater profit, was used as a ferryboat to carry armed men and munitions of war to Navy Island. On the night of December 29, while in New York waters, the steamer was attacked by volunteers from Canada. One of the crew, a citizen of the United States, was killed, and the *Caroline* was set on fire and drifted over the falls.

The attack on the *Caroline* was approved by both the Canadian and British governments, and Colonel McNab, the officer who had ordered the attack, was knighted. Secretary of State Forsyth at once made complaint to the British minister of the "extraordinary outrage committed . . . on the persons and property of citizens of the United States within the jurisdiction of the State of New York." The Canadian government took the responsibility for the destruction of the "piratical craft"; and, January 8, 1838, Van Buren asked for appropriations to back up his demands for redress, and called upon New York and Vermont for militia to defend the frontier. The filibusters evacuated Navy Island, and the vigilance of the United States authorities prevented the organization of any effective invasion of Canada; but there was strong local sympathy for the insurgents, which manifested itself in efforts to aid them, including the destruction of the Canadian steamer *Sir Robert Peel* in the St. Lawrence River.

In November, 1840, Alexander McLeod, who had been deputy sheriff in Canada, came over to New York and boasted that he was a member of the party that attacked the *Caroline*, and that it was he who killed a member of her crew; whereupon he was arrested and indicted for murder. The British government reasserted its responsibility, and demanded the release of McLeod, which the United States doubtless would have accorded, but the State of New York was not so easy to satisfy. The situation was perilous, for New York was aroused, and a conviction would have been in effect a challenge to Great Britain by that State. Fortunately the defence was able to prove McLeod only a vain boaster, by establishing an alibi; and on Oct. 12, 1841, he was acquitted.

Caroline Islands, a group in the South Pacific, said to have been discovered by the Portuguese, 1525; also by the Spaniard Lopez de Villalobos, 1545; and named after Charles II. of Spain, 1686. These islands were virtually given up to Spain in 1876. The Germans occupying some of the islands, Spain protested in August, 1885. Spanish vessels arrived at the island of Yop, Aug. 21; the Germans landed and set up their flag, Aug. 24; dispute referred to the Pope; the sovereignty awarded to Spain, with commercial concessions to Germany and Great Britain; agreement signed, Nov. 25; confirmed at Rome, Dec. 17, 1885; natives subdued, Spaniards in full possession, 1891; sold by Spain to Germany in 1899.

The chief American interest in the Caroline Islands lies in the facts that American missionaries in 1852 were believed to have been the first white people to occupy that island; that the missionaries were ultimately expelled by the Spaniards from the islands. The United States government secured the payment of an indemnity by Spain of $17,500 in 1894.

Carpenter, CHARLES CARROLL, naval officer; born in Greenfield, Mass., Feb. 27, 1834; promoted rear-admiral, Nov. 11, 1894; was commander-in-chief of the United States Asiatic squadron in 1894–95; retired Feb. 28, 1896. During the summer of 1895 he rendered invaluable service in China in protecting American missionaries and in co-operating with United States Minister Charles Denby and the British and Chinese authorities to preserve peace, particularly after the Kucheng massacre. He died in Boston, Mass., April 1, 1899.

Carpenter, FRANK BICKNELL, painter and author; born in Homer, N. Y., in 1830; was mostly self-educated in art; settled in New York in 1851, and became an associate of the National Academy of Design in 1852. He painted numerous portraits of Presidents, statesmen, and other noted persons. His best-known works are the historical painting of *President Lincoln Signing the Emancipation Proclamation*, now in the Capitol in Washington, and *Arbitration*, a view of the British and American commissioners on the *Alabama* claims in session in Washington in 1871, presented to Queen Victoria in 1892. He wrote *Six Months in the White House with Abraham Lincoln.* He died May 23, 1900.

Carpenter, MATTHEW HALE, lawyer; born in Moretown, Vt., Dec. 22, 1824; was admitted to the Vermont bar in 1847; settled in Wisconsin in the following year, and later in Milwaukee. During the Civil War he was a stanch Union man. In March, 1868, with Lyman Trumbull, he represented the government in the famous McCardle trial, which involved the validity of the reconstruction act of Congress of March 7, 1867. Up to that time this was the most important cause ever argued before the United States Supreme Court, and Carpenter and Trumbull won. He was a member of the United States Senate in 1869–75 and 1879–81. He was counsel for Samuel J. Tilden before the electoral commission in 1877. His greatest speeches in the Senate include his defence of President Grant against the attack of Charles Sumner, and on the Ku-klux act, Johnson's amnesty proclamation, and the iron-clad oath. He died in Washington, D. C., Feb. 24, 1881.

Carpenter, STEPHEN CUTTER, journalist; born in England. Came to the United States in 1803, and settled in Charleston, S. C., where he founded and published, with John Bristed, the *Monthly Register Magazine and Review of the United States.* Later he was editor of the *Mirror of Taste and Dramatic Censor*, in which appeared some clever sketches of American actors. His works include: *Memoirs of Jefferson, Containing a Concise History of the United States from the Acknowledgment of Their Independence, with a View of the Rise and Progress of French Influence and French Principles in that Country; Select American Speeches, Forensic and Parliamentary, with Prefatory Remarks;* and under the pen-name of "Donald Campbell," *Letter on the Present Times.* He died about 1820.

Carpenter's Hall, Philadelphia. The first and second Continental Congresses held their sessions in this hall.

Carpet-bag Governments. During the period between the ending of the Civil War and the restoration of all rights, many of the Southern States were controlled by unscrupulous white men (see CARPET-BAGGERS) and negro majorities. Enormous State debts were incurred and frauds of all kinds perpetrated.

Carpet-baggers, a name of reproach given by the South to citizens of the North who went South after the Civil War. Many went there with the best intentions; some in hope of political advancement by the aid of negro votes. These latter were eliminated by 1877.

Carr, EUGENE ASA, military officer; born in Concord, N. Y., March 20, 1830; graduated at West Point in 1850. As a member of mounted rifles he was engaged in Indian warfare in New Mexico, Texas, and the West; and in 1861 served under Lyon in Missouri, as colonel of Illinois cavalry. He commanded a division in the BATTLE OF PEA RIDGE (*q. v.*), and was severely wounded. He was made a brigadier-general of volunteers in 1862. He commanded a division in the BATTLE OF PORT GIBSON (*q. v.*) and others preceding the capture of Vicksburg; also in the assaults on that place. He assisted in the capture of Little Rock, Ark., and the defences of Mobile. He was retired as brevet major-general U. S. A. in 1893; died in Washington, D. C., Dec. 2, 1910.

Carr, LUCIEN, archæologist; born in Lincoln county, Mo., in 1829. Received a collegiate education; from 1876 to 1894 was assistant curator in the Peabody Museum; author of *Mounds of the Mississippi Valley; Missouri, a Bone of Contention;* and *Prehistoric Remains of Kentucky* (with Prof. N. S. Shaler), etc.

Carr, SIR ROBERT, commissioner; born in Northumberland, England. In 1664 he was appointed, with SIR RICHARD NICOLLS (*q. v.*) and others, on a commission to regulate the affairs of New England, and to take possession of NEW NETHERLAND (*q. v.*). The commission came on a fleet which had been fitted out to operate against the Dutch settlers on the Hudson. Carr and Nicolls gained possession of New Netherland Aug. 27,

1664, and named it New York in honor of the Duke of York. On Sept. 24 of the same year Fort Orange surrendered to the English, and was renamed Albany. In February, 1665, Carr and his associates went to Boston, but the colonists there declined to recognize them, as did also the towns in New Hampshire. In Maine, however, the commissioners were well received, and a new government was established in that colony, which lasted from 1666 to 1668. He died in Bristol, England, June 1, 1667.

Carranza, VENUSTIANO, Mexican Constitutional leader, born in Cuatro Ciencgas, Coahuila, of Spanish-Indian stock, about 1858; acquired a liberal education; studied law; and gained considerable wealth as a wheat-grower, cattle-breeder, and rubber-producer. He served several years in the senate and as governor; opposed the Diaz régime; aided the Madero party, and took the field against VICTORIANO HUERTA (*q. v.*), as supreme chief of the Constitutionalist faction. On Aug. 14, 1914, he assumed the government of Mexico as Provisional President, but the warfare continued.

Carrington, EDWARD, military officer; born in Charlotte county, Va., Feb. 11, 1749; became lieutenant-colonel of a Virginia artillery regiment in 1776; was sent to the South; and was made a prisoner at Charleston in 1780. He was Gates's quartermaster-general in his brief Southern campaign. Carrington prepared the way for Greene to cross the Dan, and was an active and efficient officer in that officer's famous retreat. He commanded the artillery at Hobkirk's Hill, and also at Yorktown. Colonel Carrington was foreman of the jury in the trial of AARON BURR (*q. v*). He died in Richmond, Va., Oct. 28, 1810. His brother PAUL, born Feb. 24, 1733, became an eminent lawyer; was a member of the House of Burgesses, and voted against Henry's Stamp Act resolutions; but was patriotic, and helped along the cause of independence in an efficient manner. He died in Charlotte county, Va., June 22, 1818.

Carrington, HENRY BEEBEE, military officer; born in Wallingford, Conn., March 2, 1824; graduated at Yale College in 1845. When the first call for troops was issued at the beginning of the Civil War he raised nine regiments of militia in western Virginia for three-months' volunteers; was promoted brigadier-general of volunteers in November, 1862; and served throughout the war with distinction. In 1870–73 he held the chair of Military Science and Tactics at Wabash College, Ind. His publications include *Battles of the American Revolution; Battle Maps and Charts of the American Revolution; Beacon Lights of Patriotism; Washington, the Soldier;* etc. He died in Boston, Mass., Oct. 26, 1912.

Carrington, PAUL, statesman; born in Charlotte county, Va., Feb. 24, 1733; was a member of various conventions during the Revolution, and of the Committee of Safety; opposed the Stamp-Act resolutions of Patrick Henry; became a member of the Court of Appeals, and in the Virginia convention voted for the adoption of the Federal Constitution. He died in Charlotte county, Va., June 22, 1818.

Carroll, CHARLES, OF CARROLLTON, signer of the Declaration of Independence; born in Annapolis, Md., Sept. 20, 1737. His family were wealthy Roman Catholics, the first appearing in America at the close of the seventeenth century. He studied law in France and London; returned to America in 1764, and became a writer on the side of the liberties of the people. He inherited a vast estate, and was considered one of the richest men in the colonies. Mr. Carroll was a member

CHARLES CARROLL.

of one of the first vigilance committees established at Annapolis, and a member of the Provincial Convention. Early in 1776 he was one of a committee appointed by Congress to visit Canada to persuade the Canadians to join the other colonies in resistance to the measures of Parliament. His colleagues were Dr. Franklin and Samuel Chase. The committee was accompanied by Rev. John Carroll. The mission was fruitless; and when, in June, the committee returned to Philadelphia, it found the subject of independence under consideration in Congress. Carroll and Chase induced Maryland to change its attitude. Carroll was the last survivor of that band of fifty-six patriots who signed the Declaration of Independence. Mr. Carroll served his State in its Assembly, in the national Congress, and in other responsible offices, with fidelity and ability. At the age of over ninety years (July 4, 1828) he laid the corner-stone of the Baltimore & Ohio Railway, attended by an imposing civic procession. The story that he appended "of Carrollton" to his name defiantly, to enable the British crown to identify him, is a fiction. He was accustomed to sign it so to prevent confusion, as there was another Charles Carroll. He died in Baltimore, Md., Nov. 14, 1832. His great-grandson, John Lee Carroll, of Baltimore, Md., is the general president of the Society of the Sons of the Revolution.

Carroll, GEORGE W., philanthropist and business man; born in Mansfield, La., in 1854; removed to Texas in 1873; was the Prohibition party's candidate for governor of Texas in 1902, receiving four times the largest Prohibition vote ever before cast in Texas. In 1904 he was nominated for Vice-President of the United States on the Prohibition ticket.

Carroll, HOWARD, journalist; born in Albany, N. Y., in 1854; travelling and special correspondent of the New York *Times* for several years, when he resigned to enter business. He subsequently declined the post of United States minister to Belgium. Among his works are *Twelve Americans: Their Lives and Times; A Mississippi Incident*, etc.

Carroll, JOHN, clergyman; born in Upper Marlboro, Md., Jan. 8, 1735; was educated at St. Omer's, Liege, and Bruges; ordained a priest in 1769, and entered the order of Jesuits soon afterwards. He travelled through Europe with young Lord Staunton in 1770 as private tutor, and in 1773 became a professor in the college at Bruges. In 1775 he returned to Maryland, and the next year, by desire of Congress, he accompanied a committee of that body on a mission to Canada. That committee was composed of Dr. Franklin, Charles Carroll of Carrollton, and Samuel Chase. He was appointed the papal vicar-general for the United States in 1786. In 1790 he became the first Roman Catholic bishop in the United States. A few years before his death, in Georgetown, D. C., Dec. 3, 1815, he was made archbishop.

Carson, CHRISTOPHER, popularly known as "Kit Carson," military officer; born in Madison county, Ky., Dec. 24, 1809; began a life of adventure when seventeen years old; was a trapper on the plains for sixteen years. He became acquainted with JOHN C. FRÉMONT (*q. v.*), who employed him as a guide on his later explorations. His extensive familiarity with the habits and language of the various Indian tribes in the Western country, and his possession of their confidence, made him exceptionally effective in promoting the settlement of that region. In 1847 he was appointed a second lieutenant in the United States Mounted Rifles; in 1853 drove 6,500 sheep across the mountains into California, and on his return was made Indian agent in New Mexico. During the Civil War he rendered important service in Colorado, New Mexico, and the Indian Territory, for which he was brevetted a brigadier-general of volunteers. At the close of the war he again became an Indian agent. He died in Fort Lynn, Col., May 23, 1868.

Carson, HAMPTON LAWRENCE, lawyer; born in Philadelphia, Pa., Feb. 21, 1852; admitted to the bar in 1874; professor of law, University of Pennsylvania, 1895–1901; attorney-general of Pennsylvania, 1903–07; author of *Law of Criminal Conspiracies as Found in American Cases; History of the One Hundredth Anniversary of the Promulgation of the Constitution of the United States; History of the Supreme Court of the United States*, etc.

Carter, SAMUEL POWHATAN, naval and military officer; born in Elizabethtown,

Tenn., Aug. 6, 1819; was educated at Princeton College; entered the navy in February, 1840, and became assistant instructor of seamanship at the Naval Academy in 1857. He served in the army through the war, and on March 13, 1865, received the brevet of major-general. He then re-entered the navy; in 1869–72 was commandant of the Naval Academy; retired Aug. 6, 1881; and was promoted rear-admiral May 16, 1882. He died in Washington, May 26, 1891.

Carter, William Harding, military officer; born in Nashville, Tenn., Nov. 19, 1851; was graduated at West Point in 1873; became a major-general, 1909; was awarded a Congressional Medal of Honor for distinguished bravery in action against the Apache Indians (Aug. 30, 1881); commanded the army mobilized along the Rio Grande in Texas in 1911 on account of the revolution in Mexico. He wrote *Horses, Saddles, and Bridles; From Yorktown to Santiago with the Sixth Cavalry; Old Army Sketches; Giles Carter of Virginia*, etc.

Carteret, Sir George, English naval officer; born in St. Ouen, Jersey, in 1599. Charles I. appointed him governor of the Island of Jersey. In 1645 he was created a baronet, and returned to his government of Jersey, where he received and sheltered the Prince of Wales (afterwards Charles II.) when the royal cause was ruined in England. Other refugees of distinction were there, and he defended the island gallantly against the forces of Cromwell. Being a personal friend of James, Duke of York, to whom Charles II. granted New Netherland, Carteret and Berkeley obtained a grant of territory between the Hudson and Delaware rivers, which, in gratitude for his services in the Island of Jersey, was called New Jersey. Sir George was one of the grantees of the Carolinas, and a portion of that domain was called Carteret colony. Governor Andros, of New York, claimed political jurisdiction, in the name of the Duke of York, over all New Jersey. Philip Carteret, governor of east Jersey, denied it, and the two governors were in open opposition. A friendly meeting of the two magistrates, on Staten Island, was proposed. Carteret declined it; and Andros warned him to forbear exercising any jurisdiction in east Jersey, and announced that he should erect a fort to aid him (Andros) in the exercise of his authority. Carteret defied him; and when, a month later, Andros went to New Jersey, seeking a peaceful conference, Carteret met him with a military force. As Andros came without troops, he was permitted to land. The conference was fruitless. A few weeks later Carteret was taken from his bed, in his house at Elizabethtown, at night, by New York soldiers, and carried to that city and placed in the hands of the sheriff. He was tried in May (1678), and though Andros sent his jurors out three times, with instructions to bring in a verdict of guilty, he was acquitted. But he was compelled to give security that he would not again assume political authority in New Jersey. The Assembly of New Jersey were asked to accept the duke's laws, but they preferred their own. At the same time they accepted the government of Andros, but with reluctance. Carteret went to England with complaints, and the case was laid before the duke by his widow after his death. The Friends, of west Jersey, had already presented their complaints against Andros, and the case was referred to the duke's commissioners. These, advised by Sir William Jones, decided that James's grant reserved no jurisdiction, and that none could be rightly claimed. This decided the matter for east Jersey also, and in August and October, 1680, the duke signed documents relinquishing all rights over east and west Jersey.

Carthage, Battle of. In the summer of 1861 General Lyon sent Col. Franz Sigel in pursuit of the Confederates under General Price in southwestern Missouri. His force consisted of nearly 1,000 loyal Missourians (of his own and Salomon's regiments) with two batteries of artillery of four field-pieces each—in all about 1,500 men. Though the Confederates were reported to be more than 4,000 in number, Sigel diligently sought them. On the morning of July 5, 1861, he encountered large numbers of mounted riflemen, who seemed to be scouting, and a few miles from Carthage, the capital of Jasper county, he came upon the main body, under Governor Jackson, who was assisted by General Rains and three other brigadier-generals. They were drawn up in battle order on the crown of a gentle hill. A battle commenced at a little past ten o'clock, by Sigel's field-pieces, and lasted about three hours, when, seeing his baggage in danger and his troops in peril of being outflanked, Sigel fell back and retreated, in perfect order, to the heights near Carthage, having been engaged in a running fight nearly all the way. The Confederates pressed him sorely, and he continued the retreat (being outnumbered three to one) to Springfield, where he was joined by General Lyon (July 13), who took the chief command of the combined forces. This junction was timely, for the combined forces of Generals McCulloch, Rains, and others had joined those of Price, making the number of Confederates in that region about 20,000.

Carthagena, a city in the United States of Colombia, founded in 1533 by the Spaniards. In 1544 it was taken by the French; in 1585 it was captured by Sir Francis Drake; and in 1697 it was pillaged by the buccaneers. In 1741 a powerful fleet, under Admiral Vernon, with a large body of soldiers, mostly from the English colonies in America, attacked the city. There were 29 ships and 12,000 land troops. The expedition was unsuccessful, as most of the soldiers fell ill with the fever and thousands of them died.

Cartier, Jacques, French navigator; born at St. Malo, France, Dec. 31, 1494; was commissioned by Francis I., King of France, to command an expedition to explore the Western Continent. After a prosperous voyage of twenty days, he arrived at Newfoundland. Sailing northward, he entered the Strait of Belle Isle, and, touching the coast of Labrador, he formally took possession of the country in the name of his King. He followed the west coast of Newfoundland to Cape Race. Then he explored the Bay of Chaleurs, landed in Gaspé Bay, held friendly intercourse with the natives, and induced a chief to allow two of his sons to go with him to France. Sailing across the Gulf of St. Lawrence, he entered the St. Lawrence River north of Anticosti Island. Unconscious of having discovered a magnificent river, he turned and sailed for France and arrived at St. Malo on Sept. 5, 1534, reporting to the King.

JACQUES CARTIER.

Encouraged by the success of this voyage, the King placed Cartier in command of three ships, which left St. Malo at the middle of May, 1535. They reached the Strait of Belle Isle in July, and sailed up the St. Lawrence to the mouth of a river (now the St. Charles) at the site of Quebec, which they reached on Sept. 14th. His squadron consisted of the *Great Hermine*, 120 tons; *Little Hermine*, 60 tons; *L'Emérillon*, a small craft. On the day after their arrival, they were visited by Donnaconna,

JACQUES CARTIER SETTING UP A CROSS AT GASPÉ.

"King of Canada," who received them with the greatest kindness, and, through the two young men whom Cartier had brought back, they were enabled to converse. Mooring the larger vessels in the St. Croix (as Cartier named the St. Charles), he went up the river in the smaller one, with two or three volunteers, and, with a small boat, they reached the Huron village called Hochelaga, on the site of Montreal. He called the mountain back of it Mont Réal (Royal Mountain), hence the name of Montreal. There he enjoyed the kindest hospitality, and bore away with him a pretty little girl, eight years old, daughter of one of the chiefs, who lent her to him to take to France. Returning to Stadacona (now Quebec) early in October, the Frenchmen spent a severe winter there, during which twenty-five of them died of scurvy. Nearly every one of them had the disease. When Cartier was prepared to leave for France, in the spring, the *Little Hermine* was found to be rotten and unseaworthy, and, as the other two vessels could carry his reduced company, she was abandoned. He formally took possession of the country in the name of his King, and, just before his departure (May 9, 1536), he invited Donnaconna and eight chiefs on board the flagship to a feast. They came, and Cartier treacherously sailed away with them to France as captives, where they all died of grief. Cartier reached St. Malo July 16.

There was now a pause in this enterprise, but finally Francis de la Roque, Lord of Roberval, Picardy, prevailed upon the King to appoint him viceroy and lieutenant-general of the new territory, and Cartier captain-general and chief pilot of the royal ships. Five vessels were fitted out, and Cartier, with two of them, sailed from St. Malo in May, 1541. Late in August these reached Stadacona. The people there eagerly pressed to the ships to welcome their monarch, whom Cartier had promised to bring back. They shook their heads incredulously when he told them Donnaconna was dead. They grew more sullen every hour, and became positively hostile. After visiting Hochelaga, Cartier returned to Stadacona, and caused a fort to be built for protection through the ensuing winter, where he waited patiently for the viceroy, but he came not. Towards the end of May the ice moved out of the St. Lawrence, and Cartier departed for France. He ran into the harbor of St. Johns, Newfoundland, where he found De la Roque on his way to the St. Lawrence. Cartier tried to induce him to turn back by giving him most discouraging accounts of the country, but he ordered the navigator to go back with him to the great river. Cartier disobeyed and sailed for France. The viceroy went above the site of Quebec, where he built a fort and spent the next winter in great suffering, returning to France in the autumn of 1534. Cartier had arrived the previous summer, and did not make another voyage. He died in 1555.

Cartwright, John, author; born in Marnham, England, Sept. 28, 1740; became widely known as an advocate of the freedom of the American colonies; and issued a pamphlet entitled *American Independence the Glory and Interest of Great Britain,* in 1775. In this he pleaded for a union between England and the colonies, but with separate legislative bodies. This tract, supplemented by his refusal to accept a commission in the British army on American soil, destroyed the friendship between Lord Howe and himself. On April 2, 1777, he recommended the King to use his power to establish peace with the colonies on the basis suggested in his pamphlet. He died in London, Sept. 23, 1824.

Carver, John, first governor of New Plymouth; born in England, between 1575 and 1590; spent a considerable estate in forwarding the scheme of the "Pilgrims" for emigrating to America, and accompanied them in the *Mayflower.* He was a deacon or elder in Robinson's church at Leyden, and was one of the committee sent to London to effect a treaty with the Virginia Company concerning colonization in America. When the written instrument for the government of the colony was subscribed on board the *Mayflower* Mr. Carver was chosen to be governor. His wife died during the succeeding winter. Governor Carver's chair (the first throne of a chief magistrate set up in New England) is preserved by the Massachusetts Historical Society. He died in New Plymouth, Mass., April 5, 1621.

Carver, Jonathan, traveller, born in Stillwater, Conn., in 1732; served in the French and Indian War, and afterwards attempted to explore the vast region in America which the English had acquired from the French. He penetrated the country to Lake Superior and its shores and tributaries, and after travelling about 7,000 miles he returned to Boston, whence he departed in 1766, and sailed for England, to communicate his discoveries to the government and to petition the King for a reimbursement of his expenses. His *Travels* were published in 1778. He was badly used in England, and, by utter neglect, was reduced to a state of extreme destitution. He died in London, Jan. 31, 1780.

Cary, Lott, negro slave; born in Virginia in 1780; educated himself; became a Baptist minister; purchased the freedom of himself and his two children for $850, and joined the colony sent in 1822 to Liberia, where he performed inestimable services in behalf of the new republic. He was accidentally killed while making cartridges for defence against the slave-traders, in Monrovia, Nov. 8, 1828.

Cary, Samuel Fenton, legislator; born in Cincinnati, O., Feb. 18, 1814; member of Congress, 1867–69; was the only Republican in the House who voted against the impeachment of President Johnson. In 1876 he was nominated by the Independent party for Vice-President on the ticket with Peter Cooper. He died in 1900.

Casa de Mata. See El Molino del Rey.

Casas, Bartolomé. See Las Casas, Bartolomé de.

Case, Augustus Ludlow, naval officer; born in Newburg, N. Y., Feb. 3, 1813; joined the navy in 1828; served in the Gulf of Mexico during the Mexican

War, and took part in the engagements of Vera Cruz, Alvarado, and Tabasco. In 1861–63 he was fleet-captain of the North Atlantic blockading squadron, and was present at the capture of Forts Clark and Hatteras. Early in 1863 he was assigned to the *Iroquois*, and in that year directed the blockade of New Inlet, N. C. He became rear-admiral May 24, 1872. During the *Virginius* trouble with Spain in 1874 he was commander of the combined North Atlantic, South Atlantic, and European fleets at Key West. He died Feb. 17, 1893.

Casey, SILAS, military officer; born in East Greenwich, R. I., July 12, 1807; was graduated at West Point in 1826; served with Worth in Florida (1837–41) and under Scott in the war with Mexico (1847–48); was also in the operations against the Indians on the Pacific coast in 1856. Early in the Civil War he was made brigadier-general of volunteers, and organized and disciplined the volunteers at and near Washington. He was made major-general of volunteers in May, 1862, and commanded a division in General Keyes's corps on the Peninsula, and received the first attack of the Confederates in the battle of FAIR OAKS (*q. v.*). General Casey was brevetted major-general U. S. A. in March, 1865, for "meritorious service during the rebellion," and the legislature of Rhode Island gave him a vote of thanks in 1867. He was author of a *System of Infantry Tactics* (1861) and *Infantry Tactics for Colored Troops* (1863). He died in Brooklyn, N. Y., Jan. 22, 1882.

Cass, LEWIS, statesman; born in Exeter, N. H., Oct. 9, 1782; entered upon the practice of law about 1802, in Zanesville, O., and at the age of twenty-five was a member of the legislature. He was colonel of an Ohio regiment, under General Hull, in 1812, and was with the troops surrendered at DETROIT (*q. v.*). In March, 1813, he was made a brigadier-general, and was volunteer aide to General Harrison at the battle of the THAMES (*q. v.*), when he was appointed governor of Michigan Territory. As superintendent of Indian affairs in that region, he negotiated nineteen treaties with the Indians. In 1829 he organized a scientific expedition to explore the upper Mississippi. In 1831 he resigned the governorship and became Secretary of War, under President Jackson. From 1836 to 1842 he was United States minister to France, and from 1845 to 1848 United States Senator. He received the Democratic nomination

LEWIS CASS.

for President in 1848, but was defeated, and was again in the United States Senate from 1851 to 1857, when President Buchanan called him to his cabinet as Secretary of State; but when the President refused to reinforce the garrison at Fort Sumter, he resigned. General Cass favored the compromise of 1850, and also favored a compromise with the disunionists until they became Confederates, when he favored the supporters of the Union. He was author of a work entitled *France: Its King, Court, and Government.* He died in Detroit, Mich., June 17, 1866.

Castine, CAPTURE OF. A British fleet, consisting of four 74-gun ships, two frigates, two sloops of war, and one schooner, with ten transports, the latter bearing almost 4,000 troops, sailed from Halifax Aug. 26, 1814, under the command of Lieut.-Gen. Sir John Cope Sherbrooke, governor of Nova Scotia, assisted by Maj.-Gen. Gerard Gosselin. The fleet was in command of Rear-Admiral Edward Griffith. The destination of the armament was the Penobscot River, with a design to take possession of the country between that river and Passamaquoddy Bay. Sherbrooke intended to stop and take possession of Machias, but, learning that the corvette *John Adams*, 24 guns, had entered the Penobscot, he hastened to overtake her. On the morning of Sept. 1 they arrived in the harbor of Castine. There was a small American force there, under Lieutenant Lewis, occupying a little battery. Lewis, finding resistance would be in vain, spiked the guns, blew up the battery, and fled. About 600 British troops landed and took quiet possession of the place. The *John Adams* had just returned from a long cruise, much crippled by striking on a rock on entering the bay. It was with difficulty that she was kept afloat until she reached Hampden, far up the river, to which she fled. The British immediately detached a land and naval force to seize or destroy her. Sherbrooke and Griffith issued a joint proclamation assuring the inhabitants of their intention to take possession of the country between the Penobscot and Passamaquoddy Bay, and offering them protection on condition of their acquiescence. All persons taken in arms were to be punished, and all who should supply the British with provisions were to be paid and protected. General Gosselin was appointed military governor. See HAMPDEN, ACTION AT.

Castine, VINCENT, BARON DE, military officer; born in Orleans, France; a scion of a noble family. At the age of seventeen years, he was colonel of the King's body-guard, and when the regiment to which he belonged was sent to Canada (1665) he went with it and remained after it was disbanded. In 1667 he established a trading-post and built a fort at or near the mouth of the Penobscot River, and married the daughter of a Penobscot chief. By him Christianity was first introduced among the natives of that region. In 1696, with 200 Indians, he assisted Iberville in the capture of the Fort at Pemaquid. In 1706–07 he assisted in the defence of Port Royal, and was wounded. He lived in America thirty years, when he returned to France, leaving his domain to his half-breed son. The young baron was really a friend to the English, but, suspected of being an enemy, he was surprised and captured in 1721, taken to Boston, and imprisoned several months.

REMAINS OF FORT CASTINE.

Castle Garden. In the early days of New York City the place was a small fortified island; later it became a public hall. Here Jenny Lind made her American début. The island was incorporated with the Battery by filling the intervening space with earth and rock, and the place was devoted to the purpose of landing steerage immigrants. In 1890 it was turned over to the city of New York. The old fort is now used as a public aquarium.

Castle William, a defensive work on the northwest point of Governor's Island, New York Harbor; completed in 1811; and now used chiefly as a military prison. It is the most conspicuous building on the island, and from it is fired the regulation gun signal at sunrise and sunset. As a defensive work Castle William is now of no importance whatever.

Castle Thunder. See CONFEDERATE PRISONS.

Castries, ARMAND CHARLES AUGUSTIN, DUC DE, military officer; born in France, in April, 1756; came to America in the early part of the Revolutionary War; was an officer under Rochambeau; and was promoted brigadier-general in 1782. He died in France in 1842.

Castro, CIPRIANO, military officer; born of peasant parents near Capacho, Venezuela, in 1855; became a coffee grower and politician; organized a successful insurrection against President Andrade in 1899; declared himself provisional president in 1900; and was elected president by Congress in 1901 for a term of six years from Feb. 20, 1902. He embroiled his country with almost every civilized Power; was especially arrogant towards the United States, and in 1908 fled the country and was deposed.

Caswell, RICHARD, military officer; born in Maryland, Aug. 3, 1729; went to North Carolina in 1746, and practised law there, serving in the Assembly from 1754 to 1771, and being Speaker in 1770. In the battle of the Allamance he commanded Tryon's right wing, but soon afterwards identified himself with the cause of the patriots, and was a member of the Continental Congress (1774–75). For three years he was president of the Provincial Congress of North Carolina, and was governor of the State from 1777 to 1779. In February, 1776, he was in command of the patriot troops in the battle of Moore's Creek Bridge, and received the thanks of Congress and the commission of major-general for the victory there achieved. He led the State troops in the battle near Camden (August, 1780); and was controller-general in 1782. He was again governor in 1784–86; and a member of the convention that framed the national Constitution. While presiding as Speaker in the North Carolina Assembly he was stricken with paralysis, and died in Fayetteville, N. C., Nov. 20, 1789.

Catawba Indians, one of the eight Indian nations of North America. They occupied the region between the Yadkin and Catawba rivers. They were southward of the Tuscaroras, and were generally on good terms with them. They were brave, but not warlike, and generally acted on the defensive. In 1672 they expelled the fugitive Shawnees; but their country was desolated by bands of the Five Nations in 1701. They assisted the Carolinians against the Tuscaroras and their confederates in 1711; but four years afterwards they joined the powerful league of the southern Indians in endeavors to extirpate the white people. A long and virulent war was carried on between them and the Iroquois. The English endeavored to bring peace between them, and succeeded. When, in 1751, William Bull, commissioner for South Carolina, attended a convention at Albany he was attended by the chief sachem of the Catawbas and several chiefs. The hatred between the two nations was so bitter that the English commissioners deemed it prudent to keep the Catawbas alone in a chamber until the opening of the convention to prevent violence. In the convention, after a speech by Mr. Bull, attended by the usual presents of wampum, the Catawba "king" and his chiefs approached the grand council, singing a song of peace. A seat was prepared for them at the right hand of the English company. The singers continued their song, half fronting the old sachems to whom their words were addressed, while their "king" was preparing and lighting the calumet, or pipe of peace. The king first smoked, and then presented the pipe to King Hendrick, of the Mohawks, who gracefully accepted and smoked it. The Catawbas were the active allies of the Carolinians in 1760. In the Revolution they joined the Americans, though few in numbers. They have occupied a reservation only a few miles square upon the Catawba River, and are now nearly extinct.

Cathay, the old name of China, so called by the Venetian traveller Marco Polo, who, in the employ of the Khan of Tartary, visited it early in the thirteenth century. It was the land Columbus expected to find by sailing westward from Spain.

Cathcart, WILLIAM SCHAW, EARL, military officer; born in Petersham, England, Sept. 17, 1755; joined the British army in June, 1777, and came to the United States; later was aide to Gen. Spencer Wilson and General Clinton, and participated in the siege of Forts Montgomery and Clinton, and in the battles of Brandywine and Monmouth. In May, 1778, during the reception given in honor of Lord Howe, in Philadelphia, he led one section of the "knights" at the celebrated MISCHIANZA (*q. v.*). Later he recruited and commanded the Caledonian Volunteers, which subsequently was called Tarleton's Legion. He returned to England in 1801. He died in Cartside, Scotland, June 16, 1843.

Catholic Benevolent Union, an organization of Roman Catholics in the United States, founded in 1881 as a fraternal and protective order; has six State councils, 363 subordinate councils, and over 16,500 members, and has disbursed over $21,000,000 in benefits.

Catholic Knights of America, an organization of Roman Catholics in the United States, founded in 1887 as a fraternal and protective order; has over 600 subordinate councils and 20,000 members, and has disbursed nearly $17,000,000 in benefits.

Catholicism in the United States. See ROMAN CATHOLICISM.

Cat Island, or GUANAHANI, an island of the Bahama group for centuries supposed to be identical with the San Salvador of Columbus, a surmise now disproved. Length, 36 miles; breadth, 3 to 7 miles.

Catlin, GEORGE, artist; born in Wilkesbarre, Pa., in 1796. In 1832 he went to the Far West, where he lived for several years among the Indians. His paintings, illustrative of Indian life and customs, numbered in all more than 500. His publications include *Manners, Customs, and Condition of the North American Indians; O-kee-pa: A Religious Ceremony, and Other Customs of the Mandans,* etc. He died in Jersey City, N. J., Dec. 23, 1872.

Caton, JOHN DEAN, lawyer; born at Monroe, N. Y., March 19, 1812; was Chief Justice of Illinois, 1855-64; wrote *The Last of the Illinois, and a Sketch of the Pottawatomies, The Antelope and Deer of America,* etc. He died in 1895.

Catron, JOHN, jurist; born in Wythe county, Va., in 1788; justice of the United States Supreme Court, 1837–65. He died in Nashville, Tenn., May 30, 1865.

Catskill Mountains, a group of the Appalachian range on the west bank of the Hudson River in New York State. Highest point, Round Top, 3,804 feet.

Catt, CARRIE CHAPMAN; born in Ripan, Wisconsin; studied law; teacher in public schools of Mason City, Iowa; president of the International Woman Suffrage Alliance.

Cattell, JAMES MCKEEN, educator; born in eastern Pennsylvania, May 25, 1860; studied in Germany; member of many learned societies; editor of *Science, Popular Science Monthly, Library of Philosophy,* etc.

Cattle. The live stock on the farms and ranches of the United States exceeds in value $5,138,486,000, and of this total dairy cows and other cattle represent $1,697,761,000. According to a report of the Department of Agriculture in 1910 there were 21,801,000 dairy cows, valued at $780,308,000, and 47,279,000 other cattle valued at $917,453,000. Of cattle other than dairy cows Texas led, with 7,131,000, and was followed by Iowa, 3,611,000; Kansas, 3,260,000; Nebraska, 3,040,000; Missouri, 2,165,000; Illinois, 1,974,000; Oklahoma, 1,637,000; Colorado, 1,425,000; South Dakota, 1,341,000; Minnesota, 1,228,000; California, 1,120,000; Wisconsin, 1,081,000; and Indiana, 1,020,000—all other States having less than 1,000,000. The allied industry of wholesale slaughtering and meat packing had a capital investment of $219,818,627, and an annual output valued at $801,757,137, and that of wholesale slaughtering without meat packing had $17,896,063 capital and $112,157,487 in value of output. The tanning, currying and finishing of leather, exclusive of manufactures, had capital, $242,584,254, and value of output, $252,620,986. For the other great allied industry, see DAIRY PRODUCTS.

Catubig, a town in the island of Samar, Philippine Islands, noted as the place where a small body of United States troops withstood an attack by 600 insurgents in June, 1900; one of the most stirring incidents of the war in the islands. Pop. (1903), 9,563.

Caucus, a word in the vocabulary of the politics of the United States, probably a corruption of the word *calkers*—men who drive oakum or old ropes untwisted into the seams of vessels. These men naturally associated much with ropemakers in seaports. In Boston the calkers had formed an association of which the father of Samuel Adams, and Samuel Adams himself afterwards, were members. After the Boston Massacre this society at their meetings, in speeches and resolutions, took strong grounds against the

British government, its acts, and its instruments in America, and planned schemes for relieving their country of oppression. The Tories, in derision, called these assemblies "*calkers'* meetings," which became corrupted to "caucus meetings"—gatherings at which politicians of the same creed meet, consult, and lay plans for political action.

The word first appears in the *Diary* of John Adams, under the date of February, 1763: "This day find that the Caucus Club meets at certain times in the garret of Tom Dowes, the adjutant of the Boston militia regiment." He adds that the town officials and representatives were first chosen in this club before they were elected in the town meeting. In 1796 the Republican members of Congress agreed to support Jefferson and Burr; the Federalist members, Adams and Pinkney. From 1800 to 1824, inclusive, Presidential candidates were practically all nominated by caucus. In 1824, in consequence of the extinction of the Federal party, party lines had disappeared. In addition the State legislatures had instructed their Senators and Representatives not to attend a caucus if one should be called. Of the Congressional caucus 68 only were present. Of these 64 voted for Crawford, and Albert Gallatin received 57 votes for Vice-President.

In 1828 the candidates were made by the State legislatures, but in 1832 the present system of nominating conventions was introduced, as a result of which electors, provided for by the United States Constitution, were practically deprived of any power. Only of late years the successful candidates for the United States Senate have been elected by a caucus of the party in power. This has resulted in an uneasiness on the part of the general body of electors, as a result of which Senators will probably be more and more elected by the people, not directly, but indirectly, in the same way as the President is elected through the nominal action of the electoral body. See NOMINATING CONVENTIONS; DIRECT ELECTION OF SENATORS.

Caughnawagas, Canadian Indians allied with the Mohawks.

Caulkins, FRANCES MAINWARIN, author; born in New London, Conn., in 1796; was highly educated; and was the author of *A History of Norwich, Conn.; A History of New London, Conn.*, etc. She died in New London, Conn., Feb. 3, 1869.

Cavaliers, adherents of the fortunes of the Stuarts—the nobility, and the bitter opposers of the Puritans. On the death of Charles I. (1649), they fled to Virginia by hundreds, where only, in America, their Church and their King were respected. They made an undesirable addition to the population, excepting their introduction of more refinement of manner than the ordinary colonist possessed. They were idle, inclined to luxurious living, and haughty in their deportment towards the "common people." It was they who rallied around Berkeley in his struggles with Bacon (see BACON, NATHANIEL), and gave him all his strength in the Assembly. They were extremely social among their class, and gatherings and feastings and wine-drinking were much indulged in until poverty pinched them. They gave a stimulus to the slave-trade, for, unwilling to work themselves, they desired servile tillers of their broad acres; and so were planted the seeds of a landed oligarchy in Virginia that ruled the colony until the Revolution in 1775, and in a measure until the close of the Civil War in 1865.

Cavalry. See ARMY.

Cavité, a former Spanish military post on a narrow peninsula jutting out from the mainland of Luzon Island, Philippines, into Manila Bay, about eight miles southwest of the city of Manila. On the night of April 30, 1898, Commodore Dewey, in command of the Pacific squadron, sailed boldly past the batteries on Corregidor Island, into Manila Bay, and on the morning of May 1 attacked the Spanish fleet which had hastily formed in battle-line under the protection of the guns of the Cavité fort. When the American vessels neared the fort they had to sustain both its fire and that of the Spanish ships. But Commodore Dewey so manœuvred his fleet as to keep in an advantageous position in the strong currents of the bay and to avoid the fire of the Spaniards. Some of the American ships engaged the fleet and others directed their fire against the batteries. The water battery at Cavité was shelled until a magazine exploded, killing forty men, when the commander raised a white flag as a sign of a truce. Later the forts of Cavité and Corregidor surrendered, and the six batteries at the entrance of the bay were destroyed. After the destruction of Admiral Montijo's fleet the Americans established a hospital at Cavité, where 250 Spanish wounded and sick were cared for. In 1900 the United States authorities converted Cavité into a stronger protective post than it had ever been. See DEWEY, GEORGE; MANILA; MANILA BAY, BATTLE OF.

Cayuga Indians, one of the four nations of the IROQUOIS CONFEDERACY (*q. v.*), calling themselves *Goiogwen*, or "Men of the Woods." Tradition says hat at the formation of the confederacy, *Hi-a-wat-ha* said to the Cayugas: "You, Cayugas, a people whose habitation is the 'Dark Forest,' and whose home is everywhere, shall be the fourth nation, because of your superior cunning in hunting." They inhabited the country about Cayuga Lake in central New York, and numbered about 300 warriors when first discovered by the French at the middle of the seventeenth century. The nation was composed of the families of the Turtle, Bear, and Wolf, like the other cantons, and also those of the Beaver, Snipe, Heron, and Hawk. They were represented in the congress of the league by ten sachems. Through Jesuit missionaries the French made fruitless attempts to Christianize the Cayugas and win them over to the French interest, but found them uniformly enemies. During the Revolutionary War the Cayugas were against the colonists. They fought the Virginians at Point Pleasant in 1774. They hung upon the flank and rear of the army under Sullivan that invaded the territory of the Senecas in 1779; but they soon had their own villages destroyed, which greatly annoyed them. After the war they ceded their lands to the State of New York, excepting a small reservation. In 1800 some of them joined the Senecas, some went to the Grand River in Canada, and some to Sandusky, O., whence they were removed to the INDIAN TERRITORY (*q. v.*). In 1899 there were only 161 left at the New York agency.

Cebu, one of the Philippine Islands, lying between Luzon and Mindanao, 135 mile long, with an extreme width of 30 miles. Sugar cultivation and the manufacture of abaca are the chief industries. Population, 320,000.—The town of CEBU, on the eastern coast of the island, the oldest Spanish settlement in the Philippines, is a place of considerable trade, and has a cathedral and several churches. It is about 360 miles from Manila, and has a population of 40,000. There are valuable and extensive coal deposits near the town. The China Steam Navigation Company began in 1900 to run a regular steamer from Hong-Kong to the port of Cebu. Hemp was exported in 1899 to the value of $3,151,910; sugar, $770,503; copra, $241,953. Imports in 1899 were valued at $1,055,285. The population in 1903 (special United States census) was 653,727, all classified as civilized.

Cedar Creek, BATTLE AT. In October, 1864, the National army, commanded by General Wright, in the temporary absence of Sheridan at Washington, were so strongly posted behind Cedar Creek that they had no expectation of an attack. They were mistaken. Early felt keenly his misfortune, and, having been reinforced by Kershaw's division and 600 cavalry sent by Lee, he determined to make a bold movement, swiftly and stealthily, against the Nationals. He secretly gathered his forces at Fisher's Hill behind a mask of thick woods, and formed them in two columns to make a simultaneous attack upon both flanks of the Nationals. He moved soon after midnight (Oct. 19, 1864), with horse, foot, and artillery, along rugged paths over the hills, for he shunned the highways for fear of discovery. The divisions of Gordon, Ramseur, and Pegram formed his right column; his left was composed of the divisions of Kershaw and Wharton. At dawn these moving columns fell upon the right, left, and rear of the Nationals. It was a surprise. So furious was the assault before the Nationals had time to take battle order, that in fifteen minutes Crook's corps, that held a position in front, and had heard mysterious sounds like the dull, heavy tramp of an army, was broken into fragments, and sent flying back in disorder upon the corps of Emory and Wright. Crook left 700 men as prisoners, with many cannon, small-arms, and munitions of war in the hands of the Confederates. Emory tried in vain to stop the fugitives, but very soon his own corps gave way, leaving several guns behind. These, with Crook's, eighteen in all, were turned upon the fugitives with fearful effect, while Early's right column, led by Gordon, continued their flanking advance with vigor, turning the Nationals out of every position where they attempted to make a stand.

VIEW AT CEDAR CREEK BATTLE-GROUND.

Seeing the peril of his army, Wright ordered a general retreat, which was covered by the 6th Corps, under the command of Ricketts, which remained unbroken. The whole army retreated to Middletown, a little village 5 miles north of Strasburg, where Wright rallied his broken columns, and, falling back a mile or more, left Early in possession of Middletown. The Nationals had lost since daybreak (it was now ten o'clock) 1,200 men made captive, besides a large number killed and wounded; also camp equipage, lines of defence, and twenty-four cannon. There being a lull in the pursuit, Wright had reformed his troops and changed his front, intending to attack or retreat to Winchester as circumstances might dictate.

At that critical moment Sheridan appeared on the field. He had returned from Washington, and had slept at Winchester. Early in the morning he heard the booming of cannon up the valley, and supposed it to be only a reconnoissance. After breakfast he mounted his horse—a powerful black charger—and moved leisurely out of the city southward. He soon met the van of fugitives, who told a dreadful tale of disaster. He immediately ordered the retreating artillery to be parked on each side of the turnpike. Then, ordering his escort to follow, he put his horse on a swinging gallop, and at that pace rode nearly 12 miles to the front. The fugitives became thicker and thicker every moment. He did not stop to chide or coax, but, waving his hat as his horse thundered on over the magnificent stone road, he shouted to the cheering crowds, "Face the other way, boys! face the other way! We are going back to our camp. We are going to lick them out of their boots!" Instantly the tide of retreating troops turned and followed after the young general. As he dashed along the lines and rode in front of forming regiments, he gave a word of cheer to all. He declared they should have all those camps and cannon back again. They believed the prophecy, and fought fiercely for its fulfilment. The reformed army advanced in full force. Already (10 A.M.) General Emory had quickly repulsed an attack, which inspirited the whole corps. A general and severe struggle ensued. The whole

Confederate army were soon in full and tumultuous retreat up the valley towards Fisher's Hill, leaving guns, trains, and other hindrances to flight behind. Early's army was virtually destroyed; and, with the exception of two or three skirmishes between cavalry, there was no more fighting in the Shenandoah Valley. That night the Nationals occupied their old position at Cedar Creek. The promise of Sheridan, "We will have all the camps and cannon back again," was fulfilled. Sheridan was rewarded by the commission of a major-general in the regular army, dated Nov. 4, 1864. "Sheridan's Ride" was made the theme of poetry and painting.

Cedar Mountain, Battle of. Pope's main army was near Culpeper Court-house, and "Stonewall" Jackson was at Gordonsville, with a heavy force, at the close of July, 1862. Pope had taken command on June 28, and assumed control in the field on July 29. Both armies advanced early in August. Jackson, reinforced, had thrown his army across the Rapidan River on the morning of the 8th, and driven the National cavalry back on Culpeper Court-house. Gen. S. W. Crawford was sent with his brigade to assist the latter in retarding Jackson's march, and to ascertain his real intentions, if possible. The movements of the Confederates were so mysterious that it was difficult to guess where they intended to strike. On the morning of Aug. 9 Pope sent General Banks forward with about 8,000 men to join Crawford near Culpeper Court-house, and Sigel was ordered to advance from Sperryville at the same time to the support of Banks. Jackson had now gained the commanding heights of Cedar Mountain, and he sent forward General Ewell under the thick mask of the forest. Early's brigade of that division was thrown upon the Culpeper road. The Confederates planted batteries and opened fire upon Crawford's batteries. Before Crawford and Banks were about 20,000 veteran soldiers in line of battle. Against these Banks moved towards evening, and almost simultaneously fell upon Jackson's right and left. The attacking force was composed of the division of General Auger (the advance led by General Geary) and the division of General Williams, of which Crawford's brigade was a part. The Nationals, outnumbered, were pushed back after much loss by both parties. At dusk Rickett's division came upon the field, and checked the pursuit. Sigel's corps soon arrived, and these reinforcements kept Jackson in check. On the night of the 11th, alarmed for the safety of his communications with Richmond, he crossed the Rapidan, leaving a part of his dead unburied.

Cedars, Affair at the. In 1776 there was a small American party posted at the Cedar Rapids of the St. Lawrence River, under Colonel Bedel, of New Hampshire. While the colonel was sick at Lachine, Captain Foster, with some regulars, Canadians, and 500 Mohawks, under Brant, came down the river, capturing this post without resistance. Arnold went out from Montreal with a force to attack the captors; but, to prevent the Indians murdering the prisoners, he consented to a compromise for an exchange.

Cellulose. Corn-pith cellulose is used as a packing in warships to protect them from sinking when pierced by shot or shell. This packing is placed like a belt three feet in thickness, inside the steel hull along the water line. The *Kearsarge*, *Alabama*, *Kentucky*, and *Illinois* were thus protected. As soon as the water reaches the cellulose, it begins to swell and completely fills up the hole made by the shot.

Céloron de Bienville, French explorer; born about 1715. The treaty of peace at Aix-la-Chapelle in 1748 did not fix the boundaries between the French and English colonies. The Ohio Company was formed partly for the purpose of planting English settlements in the disputed territory. The French determined to counteract the movement by preoccupation; and in 1749 the governor of Canada, the Marquis de la Galissonière, sent Céloron, with subordinate officers, cadets, twenty soldiers, 180 Canadians, thirty Iroquois, and twenty-five Abenakes, with instructions to go down the Ohio River and take formal possession of the surrounding country in the name of the King of France, accompanied by Contrecœur, who later on commanded Fort Duquesne. Céloron was provided with a number of leaden tablets, properly inscribed, to bury at different places as a record of pre-occupation by the French. The expedition left Lachine on June 15, ascended the St. Lawrence, crossed Lake Ontario, arrived at Niagara, July 6, coasted some distance along the southern shores of Lake Erie, and then made an overland journey to the head-waters of the Alleghany River. Following that stream to its junction with the Monongahela, they went down the Ohio to the mouth of the Great Miami, below Cincinnati, proclaiming French sovereignty, and burying six leaden tablets at as many different places. From the mouth of the Miami they made an overland journey to Lake Erie, and reached Fort Niagara, Oct. 19, 1749. The place and date of Céloron's death are uncertain.

Cemeteries, in the United States. By an act of the legislature of New York State, April 27, 1847, land devoted to cemeteries is exempt from taxation. Other States followed this act.

Cemeteries, NATIONAL. National cemeteries for soldiers and sailors may be said to have originated in 1850, the army appropriation bill of that year providing money for a cemetery near the city of Mexico, for the interment of the remains of soldiers who fell in the Mexican War. The remains of Federal soldiers and sailors who fell in the Civil War have been buried in seventy-eight cemeteries, exclusive of those interred elsewhere, a far greater number. In the subjoined list are given the names and locations of the national cemeteries, with the number therein buried, known and unknown:

	Known.	*Unknown.*
Cypress Hills, N. Y.	3,710	76
Woodlawn, Elmira, N. Y.	3,074	16
Beverley, N. J.	145	7
Finn's Point, N. J.	....	2,644
Gettysburg, Pa.	1,967	1,608
Philadelphia, Pa.	1,881	28
Annapolis, Md.	2,285	204
Antietam, Md.	2,853	1,818
London Park, Baltimore, Md.	1,637	166
Laurel, Baltimore, Md.	232	6
Soldiers' Home, D. C.	5,314	288
Battle, D. C.	43	.....
Grafton, W. Va.	634	620
Arlington, Va.	11,915	4,349
Alexandria, Va.	3,402	124
Ball's Bluff, Va.	1	24
Cold Harbor, Va.	673	1,281
City Point, Va.	3,778	1,374
Culpeper, Va.	456	911
Danville, Va.	1,172	155
Fredericksburg, Va.	2,487	12,770
Fort Harrison, Va.	236	575
Glendale, Va.	234	961
Hampton, Va.	4,930	494
Poplar Grove, Va.	2,197	3,993
Richmond, Va.	842	5,700
Seven Pines, Va.	150	1,208
Staunton, Va.	233	520
Winchester, Va.	2,094	2,365
Yorktown, Va.	748	1,434
Newbern, N. C.	2,177	1,077
Raleigh, N. C.	619	562
Salisbury, N. C.	94	12,032
Wilmington, N. C.	710	1,398
Beaufort, S. C.	4,748	4,493
Florence, S. C.	199	2,799
Andersonville, Ga.	12,793	921
Marietta, Ga.	7,188	2,963
Barrancas, Fla.	798	657
Mobile, Ala.	756	113
Corinth, Miss.	1,789	3,927
Natchez, Miss.	308	2,780
Vicksburg, Miss.	3,896	12,704
Alexandria, La.	534	772
Baton Rouge, La.	2,469	495
Chalmette, La.	6,837	5,674
Port Hudson, La.	596	3,223
Brownsville, Tex.	1,417	1,379
San Antonio, Tex.	324	167
Fayetteville, Ark.	431	781
Fort Smith, Ark.	711	1,152
Little Rock, Ark.	3,265	2,337
Chattanooga, Tenn.	7,999	4,963
Fort Donaldson, Tenn.	158	511
Knoxville, Tenn.	2,090	1,046
Memphis, Tenn.	5,160	8,817
Nashville, Tenn.	11,825	4,701
Pittsburg Landing, Tenn.	1,229	2,361
Stone River, Tenn.	3,821	2,324
Camp Nelson, Ky.	2,477	1,165
Cave Hill, Louisville, Ky.	3,344	583
Danville, Ky.	335	8
Lebanon, Ky.	591	277
Lexington, Ky.	805	108
Logan's, Ky.	345	366
Crown Hill, Indianapolis, Ind.	681	32
New Albany, Ind.	2,139	676
Camp Butler, Ill.	1,007	355
Mound City, Ill.	2,505	2,721
Rock Island, Ill.	277	19
Jefferson Barracks, Mo.	8,584	2,906
Jefferson City, Mo.	349	412
Springfield, Mo.	845	713
Fort Leavenworth, Kan.	835	928
Fort Scott, Kan.	390	161
Keokuk, Iowa	612	33
Fort Gibson, Ore.	215	2,212
Fort McPherson, Neb.	152	291
City of Mexico, Mexico	284	750
Total	171,302	147,568

Censors. The Constitution of Pennsylvania (1776–90) and that of Vermont (1776–1870) provided for the election of a Board of Censors whose duties were to investigate all departments of the government, to see that the Constitution had not been violated.

Censures. Where impeachment is impossible, one of the branches of Congress has at various times tried to inflict an extra-judicial condemnation of the President. In 1834 the Senate by a vote of 26 to 20 resolved "that the President, in the late executive protest in relation to the public revenue, has assumed upon himself authority and power not conferred by the Constitution and laws." President Jackson protested against this resolution on the ground that it accused him of perjury, without an opportunity to defend himself. The Senate refused to receive the President's protest, or to record it upon the *Journal.* Three years later the resolution of censure was marked on the *Journal* by a broad black line with the notation "Expunged by order of the Senate, this 16th day of January, 1837." In 1842 President Tyler vetoed a tariff bill. The Whigs, though in a majority in both Houses, were unable to command a sufficient number of votes to either impeach the President or to pass the measure over his veto. They therefore, referred the President's veto message to a committee, whose report censured the President for his improper use of his power of veto. The President protested, but he having voted against the reception of President Jackson's protest in 1834 when a member of the United States Senate, the House of Representatives sent him a copy of the Senate resolution on that occasion. See IMPEACHMENT.

CENSUS

Census, UNITED STATES. The following table gives the total and the urban population of the United States at each decade, together with the percentage of increase, the balance of sexes, and the population to each square mile, the figures for 1910 being for continental United States:

GENERAL TABLE 1790–1910

Date.	Total Population.	Per Cent. of Increase.	Population per Square Mile.	Sexes per 1,000 Population.		Urban Population.	Per Cent. of Urban Population to Total.
				Male.	Female.		
1790....	3,929,214	......	4.75	509	491	131,472	3.35
1800....	5,308,483	35.1	6.41	512	488	210,873	3.97
1810....	7,239,881	36.4	3.62	510	490	356,920	4.93
1820....	9,638,453	33.5	4.82	508	492	475,135	4.93
1830....	12,866,020	33.5	6.25	508	492	864,509	6.72
1840....	17,069,453	32.7	8.29	509	491	1,453,994	8.52
1850....	23,191,876	35.9	7.78	511	489	2,897,586	12.49
1860....	31,443,321	35.6	10.39	511	489	5,072,256	16.13
1870....	38,558,371	22.6	10.70	507	493	8,071,875	20.93
1880....	50,155,783	30.1	13.92	510	490	11,318,547	22.57
1890....	62,947,714	25.5	21.2	511	489	18,235,670	29.12
1900....	75,994,575	20.7	25.6	512	488	31,587,542	40.5
1910....	91,972,266	21	30.9			42,623,383	46.30

Previous to 1790 there were no definite figures of population; everything was estimated. During the life of the Continental Congress the taxation apportionment, as well as the calls for troops from the colonies, was made on meagre information, and that often of a purely conjectural character. Mr. DeBow, who edited the census returns in 1850, gave the following estimates of colonial population:

1707....................	262,000
1749....................	1,046,000
1775....................	2,803,000

Mr. Bancroft gives the estimates of the Board of Trade, which had its agents in the colonies, as follows:

1714....................	434,600
1727....................	580,000
1754....................	1,485,634

The Constitution of the United States provides for a census every ten years. The first act of Congress for the taking of the census was dated March 1, 1790; the enumeration was to begin the first Monday of August, and close within nine months thereafter. The free persons were to be distinguished from others, males and females, and Indians not taxed were to be omitted from the enumeration. Free males of sixteen years and over were to be distinguished from those under that age. By that census there were 3,929,214 persons in the United States, of whom 697,681 were slaves and 59,527 were free colored persons. In 1810 the act provided for an enumeration of the inhabitants, distinguishing between races, sexes, and ages. In 1820 another step forward was taken, in that it was required of the enumerators that their reports show the number of persons engaged in agriculture, manufactures, and commerce.

In 1830 there was required an enumeration of the deaf, dumb, and blind, but there were no statistics of agriculture, manufactures, or commerce. In 1838 preparations were made for taking the sixth census, and the act is very comprehensive, embracing the enumeration of the population, with classification, according to age, sex, and color, the deaf, dumb, and blind, insane, idiots, free and slave colored; number of persons drawing pensions from the United States, with their names and ages; also statistical tables of mines, agriculture, commerce, manufactures, and schools. The returns made show the product of mines, manufactures, number of bushels of grain of every kind, of potatoes, tons of hay and hemp, pounds of tobacco and cotton and sugar, the value of dairy products, etc. The census of 1850 was placed under the charge of the newly created Department of the Interior. The first superintendent was Joseph C. G. Kennedy, of Pennsylvania.

In the taking of the ninth census (1870) the act of 1850 was substantially followed, and Gen. Francis A. Walker was the superintendent. There were the volumes of statistics, of population, agriculture, and manufactures, and, besides, a compendium was issued Nov. 1, 1872, in which were well-prepared summaries of the more important reports. The tenth census act directed the establishment of a census office in the Department of the Interior. Additions were made to the previous acts, such as the indebtedness of cities, counties, and incorporated villages; reports were provided for from railways, to ascertain their condition, business, etc.; also, similar information was asked for in regard to express and telegraph companies; experts were employed in place of the enumerators to collect social and manufacturing statistics. General Walker was appointed superintendent of the census April 1, 1879; resigned Nov. 3, 1881; and was succeeded by Charles W. Seaton, who died before the work was completed. The office of superintendent of the census was abolished in 1885, and was reestablished by the act of March 1, 1889. Robert P. Porter was appointed superintendent of the eleventh census; served till 1893; and was succeeded by Carroll D. Wright. The twelfth census (1900) was taken under the directorship of William R. Merriam, who was succeeded in 1903 by Simon U. D. North. He began planning the taking of the thirteenth census (1910), but was superseded in 1909 by Edward Dana Durand, who completed it. This census, taken as of April 15, 1910, was restricted by the authorizing act of Congress (July 2, 1909) to population, agriculture, manufactures, and mines and quarries, and the results were ordered to be completed within three years from July 1, 1909. The Director of the Bureau of the Census (which had now become a permanent branch of the Department of Commerce and Labor) was assisted by 300 district supervisors, about 70,000 enumerators, and 3,500 clerks. The combination and tabulation of the figures as gathered by the enumerators were performed entirely by means of ingenious automatic electrical machinery. Congress made an initial appropriation of $10,000,000 for taking the census, and it was estimated that the ultimate cost would exceed $13,000,000. In the authorizing act Congress also directed that in 1915, and once in every ten years thereafter a census of agriculture and live stock should be taken.

The following table shows the population of the United States by States, Territories, and other possessions, exclusive of the Philippines, Guam, Tutuila, and Wake islands, in 1900 and 1910, with the changes between those dates:

CENSUS, UNITED STATES

States, etc.	1910	1900	Increase
Alabama	2,138,093	1,828,697	309,396
Arizona	204,354	122,931	81,423
Arkansas	1,574,419	1,311,564	262,885
California	2,377,549	1,485,053	892,496
Colorado	799,024	539,700	259,324
Connecticut	1,114,756	908,420	206,336
Delaware	202,322	184,735	17,587
Dist. of Columbia	331,069	278,718	52,351
Florida	751,139	528,542	222,597
Georgia	2,609,121	2,216,331	392,799
Idaho	325,594	161,772	163,822
Illinois	5,638,591	4,821,550	817,041
Indiana	2,700,876	2,516,462	184,414
Iowa	2,224,771	2,231,853	Dec. 7,082
Kansas	1,690,949	1,470,495	220,454
Kentucky	2,289,905	2,147,174	142,731
Louisiana	1,656,388	1,381,625	274,763
Maine	742,371	694,466	47,905
Maryland	1,295,346	1,188,044	107,302
Massachusetts	3,366,416	2,805,346	561,070
Michigan	2,810,173	2,420,982	389,191
Minnesota	2,075,708	1,751,394	324,314
Mississippi	1,797,114	1,551,270	245,844
Missouri	3,293,335	3,106,665	186,670
Montana	376,053	243,329	132,724
Nebraska	1,192,214	1,066,300	125,914
Nevada	81,875	42,335	39,540
New Hampshire	430,572	411,588	18,984
New Jersey	2,537,167	1,883,669	653,498
New Mexico	327,301	195,310	131,991
New York	9,113,279	7,268,894	1,844,385
North Carolina	2,206,287	1,893,810	312,477
North Dakota	577,056	319,146	257,910
Ohio	4,767,121	4,157,545	609,576
Oklahoma	1,657,155	790,391	866,764
Oregon	672,765	413,536	259,229
Pennsylvania	7,635,111	6,302,115	1,362,996
Rhode Island	542,610	428,556	114,054
South Carolina	1,515,400	1,340,316	175,084
South Dakota	583,888	401,570	182,318
Tennessee	2,184,789	2,020,616	164,173
Texas	3,896,542	3,048,710	847,832
Utah	373,351	276,749	96,602
Vermont	355,956	343,641	12,315
Virginia	2,061,612	1,854,184	207,428
Washington	1,141,990	518,103	623,887
West Virginia	1,221,119	958,800	262,319
Wisconsin	2,333,860	2,069,042	264,818
Wyoming	145,965	92,531	53,434
Continental U. S.	91.972,267	75,994,575	15,977,692
Alaska	64,356	63,592	764
Hawaii	191,909	154,001	37,908
Porto Rico	1,118,012	953,243	
Military and naval service	55,607	91,219	
Total U. S.	93,402,151	77,256,630	16,145,521

COMPARATIVE RANK OF STATES AND TERRITORIES, 1790–1910.

States, etc.	First Census.	1790	1800	1810	1820	1830	1840	1850	1860	1870	1880	1890	1900	1910
Alabama	127,901	..	..	..	19	15	12	12	13	16	17	17	18	18
Alaska	......	..	..	..	..	..	..	..	..	..	..	..	51	52
Arizona	9,658	..	..	..	..	..	..	..	..	46	44	48	49	46
Arkansas	14,273	..	..	..	26	28	25	26	25	26	25	24	25	25
California	92,597	..	..	..	..	..	..	29	26	24	24	22	21	12
Colorado	34,277	..	..	..	..	..	..	..	38	41	35	31	31	32
Connecticut	237,946	8	8	9	14	16	20	21	24	25	28	29	29	31
Delaware	59,096	16	17	19	22	24	26	30	32	35	38	42	46	47
District of Columbia	14,093	..	19	22	25	25	28	33	35	34	36	39	42	43
Florida	34,730	..	..	..	..	26	27	31	31	33	34	32	32	33
Georgia	82,548	13	12	11	11	10	9	9	11	12	13	12	11	10
Hawaii	......	..	..	..	..	..	..	..	..	..	..	..	48	50
Idaho	14,999	..	..	..	..	..	..	..	..	44	46	45	47	45
Illinois	12,282	..	..	24	24	20	14	11	4	4	4	3	3	3
Indiana	5,641	..	21	21	18	13	10	7	6	6	6	8	8	9
Indian Territory	....	..	..	..	..	..	..	..	..	..	..	..	39	..
Iowa	41,112	..	..	..	..	..	29	27	20	11	10	10	10	15
Kansas	107,206	..	..	..	..	..	..	..	33	29	20	19	22	22
Kentucky	73,677	14	9	7	6	6	6	8	9	8	8	11	12	14
Louisiana	76,556	..	..	18	17	19	19	18	17	21	22	25	23	24
Maine	96,540	11	14	14	12	12	13	16	22	23	27	30	30	34
Maryland	319,728	6	7	8	10	11	15	17	19	20	23	27	26	27
Massachusetts	378,787	4	5	5	7	8	8	6	7	7	7	6	7	6
Michigan	4,762	..	..	25	27	27	23	20	16	13	9	9	9	8
Minnesota	6,077	..	..	..	..	..	..	36	30	28	26	20	19	19
Mississippi	8,850	..	20	20	21	22	17	15	14	18	18	21	20	21
Missouri	20,845	..	..	23	23	21	16	13	8	5	5	5	5	7
Montana	20,595	..	..	..	..	..	..	..	..	43	45	44	44	40
Nebraska	28,841	..	..	..	..	..	..	..	39	36	30	26	27	29
Nevada	6,857	..	..	..	..	..	..	..	41	40	43	49	52	51
New Hampshire	141,885	10	11	16	15	18	22	22	27	31	31	33	36	39
New Jersey	184,139	9	10	12	13	14	18	19	21	17	19	18	16	11
New Mexico	61,547	..	..	..	..	..	..	32	34	37	41	43	45	44
New York	340,120	5	3	2	1	1	1	1	1	1	1	1	1	1
North Carolina	393,751	3	4	4	4	5	7	10	12	14	15	16	15	16
North Dakota }	4,837	..	..	..	..	..	..	..	42	45	40	{ 41	41	37
South Dakota }												{ 37	37	36
Ohio	45,365	..	18	13	5	4	1	1	1	3	3	4	4	4
Oklahoma	....	..	..	..	..	..	..	..	..	..	..	46	38	23
Oregon	13,294	..	..	..	..	..	..	34	36	38	37	38	35	35
Pennsylvania	434,373	2	2	3	3	2	2	2	2	2	2	2	2	2
Rhode Island	68,825	15	16	17	20	23	24	28	29	32	33	35	34	38
South Carolina	249,073	7	6	6	8	9	11	14	18	22	21	23	24	26
Tennessee	35,691	17	15	10	9	7	5	5	10	9	12	13	14	17
Texas	212,592	..	..	..	..	..	..	25	23	19	11	7	6	5
Utah	11,380	..	..	..	..	..	..	35	37	39	39	40	43	41
Vermont	85,425	12	13	15	16	17	21	23	28	30	32	36	40	42
Virginia	747,610	1	1	1	2	3	4	4	5	10	14	15	17	20
Washington	11,594	..	..	..	..	..	..	..	40	42	42	34	33	30
West Virginia	442,014	..	..	..	..	..	..	..	..	27	29	28	28	28
Wisconsin	30,945	..	..	..	..	..	30	24	15	15	16	14	13	13
Wyoming	9,118	..	..	..	..	..	..	..	..	47	47	47	50	49

CENSUS, UNITED STATES

The following table shows the population of all cities naving 25,000 and upwards inhabitants in the census years 1900 and 1910 with the changes between those dates:

CITIES WITH POPULATION EXCEEDING 25,000 IN 1910.

Cities.	Population 1910	Population 1900	Increase since 1900
New York, N. Y.	4,766,883	3,437,202	1,329,681
Chicago, Ill.	2,185,283	1,689,575	486,708
Philadelphia, Pa.	1,549,008	1,293,697	255,311
St. Louis, Mo.	687,029	575,238	111,791
Boston, Mass.	670,585	560,892	109,693
Cleveland, Ohio	560,663	381,768	178,895
Baltimore, Md	558,485	508,957	49,528
Pittsburg, Pa.	533,905	a451,512	82,393
Detroit, Mich.	465,766	285,704	180,062
Buffalo, N. Y.	423,715	352,387	71,328
San Francisco, Cal.	416,912	342,782	74,130
Milwaukee, Wis.	373,857	285,315	88,542
Cincinnati, Ohio	364,463	325,902	38,561
Newark, N. J.	347,469	246,070	101,399
New Orleans, La.	339,075	287,104	51,971
Washington, D. C.	331,069	278,718	52,351
Los Angeles, Cal.	319,198	102,497	216,719
Minneapolis, Minn.	301,408	202,718	98,690
Jersey City, N. J.	267,779	206,433	61,346
Kansas City, Mo.	248,381	163,752	84,629
Seattle, Wash.	237,194	80,671	156,523
Indianapolis, Ind.	233,650	169,164	64,486
Providence, R. I.	224,326	175,597	48,729
Louisville, Ky.	223,928	204,731	19,197
Rochester, N. Y.	218,149	162,608	55,541
St. Paul, Minn.	214,744	163,065	51,679
Denver, Col.	213,381	133,859	79,522
Portland, Ore	207,214	90,426	116,788
Columbus, Ohio	181,548	125,560	55,988
Toledo, Ohio	168,497	131,822	36,675
Atlanta, Ga.	154,839	89,872	64,967
Oakland, Cal.	150,174	66,960	83,214
Worcester, Mass.	145,986	118,421	27,565
Syracuse, N. Y.	137,249	108,374	28,875
New Haven, Conn.	133,605	108,027	25,578
Birmingham, Ala.	132,685	38,415	94,270
Memphis, Tenn.	131,105	102,320	28,785
Scranton, Pa.	129,867	102,026	27,841
Richmond, Va.	127,628	85,050	42,578
Paterson, N. J.	125,600	105,171	20,429
Omaha, Neb.	124,096	102,555	21,541
Fall River, Mass.	119,295	104,863	14,432
Dayton, Ohio	116,577	85,333	31,244
Grand Rapids, Mich.	112,571	87,565	25,006
Nashville, Tenn.	110,364	80,865	29,499
Lowell, Mass.	106,294	94,969	11,325
Cambridge, Mass.	104,839	91,886	12,953
Spokane, Wash.	104,402	38,848	67,554
Bridgeport, Conn,	102,054	70,996	31,058
Albany, N. Y.	100,253	94,151	6,102
Hartford, Conn.	98,915	79,850	19,065
Trenton, N. J.	96,815	73,307	23,508
New Bedford, Mass.	96,652	62,442	34,210
San Antonio, Tex.	96,614	53,321	43,293
Reading, Pa.	96,071	78,961	17,110
Camden, N. J.	94,538	75,935	18,603
Salt Lake City, Utah	92,777	53,531	39,246
Dallas, Texas	92,104	42,638	49,466
Lynn, Mass.	89,336	68,513	20,823
Springfield, Mass.	88,926	62,059	26,867
Wilmington, Del.	87,411	76,508	10,903
Des Moines, Iowa	86,368	62,139	24,229
Lawrence, Mass.	85,892	62,559	23,333
Tacoma, Wash.	83,743	37,714	46,029
Kansas City, Kan.	82,331	51,418	30,913
Yonkers, N. Y.	79,803	47,931	31,872
Youngstown, Ohio	79,066	44,885	34,181
Houston, Tex.	78,800	44,633	34,167
Duluth, Minn.	78,466	52,969	25,497
St. Joseph, Mo.	77,403	102,979	b25,576
Somerville, Mass.	77,236	61,643	15,593
Troy, N. Y.	76,813	60,651	16,162

CITIES WITH POPULATION EXCEEDING 25,000 IN 1910.

Cities.	Population 1910	Population 1900	Increase since 1900
Utica, N. Y.	74,419	56,383	18,036
Elizabeth, N. J.	73,409	52,130	21,279
Fort Worth, Tex.	73,312	26,688	46,623
Waterbury, Conn.	73,141	45,859	27,282
Schenectady, N. Y.	72,826	31,682	41,144
Hoboken, N. J.	70,324	59,361	10,964
Manchester, N. H.	70,063	56,987	13,076
Evansville, Ind.	69,647	59,007	10,640
Akron, Ohio	69,067	42,728	26,339
Spokane, Wash.	67,554	36,848	67,554
Norfolk, Va.	67,452	46,624	20,828
Wilkesbarre, Pa.	67,105	51,721	15,384
Peoria, Ill.	66,950	56,100	10,850
Erie, Pa.	66,525	52,733	13,792
Savannah, Ga.	65,064	54,244	10,820
Oklahoma City, Okla.	64,205	32,452	31,753
Harrisburg, Pa.	64,186	50,167	14,019
Fort Wayne, Ind.	63,933	45,115	18,818
Charleston, S. C.	58,833	55,807	3,026
Portland, Me.	58,571	50,145	8,426
East St. Louis, Ill.	58,547	29,655	28,892
Terre Haute, Ind.	58,157	36,673	21,484
Holyoke, Mass.	57,730	45,712	12,018
Jacksonville, Fla.	57,699	28,429	29,270
Brockton, Mass.	56,878	40,063	16,815
Bayonne, N. J.	55,545	32,722	22,823
Johnstown, Pa.	55,482	35,936	10,546
Passaic, N. J.	54,773	27,777	26,996
South Bend, Ind.	53,843	35,999	17,685
Covington, Ky.	53,270	42,938	10,332
Wichita, Kan.	52,450	24,671	27,779
Honolulu, Hawaii	52,183	39,306	12,877
Altoona, Pa.	52,127	38,973	13,154
Allentown, Pa.	51,913	35,416	16,497
Springfield, Ill.	51,678	34,159	17,519
Pawtucket, R. I.	51,622	39,231	12,391
Mobile, Ala.	51,521	38,469	13,052
Saginaw, Mich.	50,510	42,315	8,165
Canton, Ohio	50,217	30,667	19,550
San Juan, Porto Rico	48,716	32,048	16,668
Binghamton, N. Y.	48,443	39,647	8,796
Sioux City, Iowa	47,828	33,111	14,717
Lancaster, Pa.	47,227	41,459	5,768
Springfield, Ohio	46,921	38,253	8,668
Atlantic City, N. J.	46,150	27,838	18,312
Little Rock, Ark.	45,941	38,307	7,634
Rockford Ill.	45,401	31,051	14,350
Bay City, Mich.	45,166	27,628	17,538
York, Pa.	44,750	33,708	11,042
Sacramento, Cal.	44,696	29,282	15,414
Chattanooga, Tenn.	44,604	30,154	14,450
Malden, Mass.	44,404	33,664	10,740
Pueblo, Col.	44,395	28,157	16,238
Haverhill, Mass.	44,115	37,175	6,940
Lincoln, Neb.	43,973	40,169	3,804
New Britain, Conn.	43,916	25,998	17,914
Salem, Mass.	43,697	35,956	7,741
Topeka, Kan.	43,684	33,608	10,076
Davenport, Ia.	43,028	35,254	7,774
McKeesport, Pa.	42,694	34,227	8,467
Wheeling, W. Va.	41,641	38,878	2,763
Augusta, Ga.	41,040	39,411	1,629
Macon, Ga.	40,665	23,272	17,393
Berkeley, Cal.	40,434	13,214	27,220
Superior, Wis.	40 384	31,091	9,293
Newton, Mass.	39,806	33,587	6,219
San Diego, Cal.	39,578	17,700	21,878
Kalamazoo, Mich.	39,437	24,404	15,033
El Paso, Tex.	39,279	15,906	23,373
Butte, Mont.	39,165	30,470	8,695
Flint, Mich.	38,550	13,103	25,447
Chester, Pa.	38,537	33,988	4,549
Dubuque, Ia.	38,494	36,297	2,197
Montgomery, Ala.	38,136	30,346	7,790
Woonsocket, R. I.	38,125	28,204	9,921
Racine, Wis.	38,002	29,102	8,900
Fitchburg, Mass.	37,826	31,531	6,295
Tampa, Fla.	37,782	15,839	21,943
Elmira, N. Y	37,176	35,672	1,504
Galveston, Tex.	36,981	37,789	b808
Quincy, Ill.	36,587	36,252	335
Knoxville, Tenn.	36,346	32,637	3,709
Newcastle, Pa.	36,280	28,339	7,941
West Hoboken, N. J.	35,403	23,094	12,309

CENSUS, UNITED STATES

CITIES WITH POPULATION EXCEEDING 25,000 IN 1910.

Cities.	Population.		Increase since 1900.
	1910.	1900.	
Hamilton, Ohio	35,279	23,914	11,365
Springfield, Mo.	35,201	23,267	11,934
Lexington, Ky.	35,099	26,369	8,730
Ponce, Porto Rico	35,027	27,952	7,075
Roanoke, Va.	34,874	21,495	13,379
Joliet, Ill.	34,670	29,353	5,317
Auburn, N. Y.	34,668	30,345	4,323
East Orange, N. J.	34,371	21,506	12,865
Taunton, Mass.	34,259	31,036	3,223
Charlotte, N. C.	34,014	18,091	15,923
Everett, Mass.	33,484	24,336	9,148
Portsmouth, Va.	33,190	17,427	15,763
Oshkosh, Wis.	33,002	28,284	4,778
Cedar Rapids, Ia.	32,811	25,656	7,155
Quincy, Mass.	32,642	23,899	8,743
Chelsea, Mass.	32,452	34,072	*b*1,620
Perth Amboy, N. J.	32,121	17,699	14,422
Pittsfield, Mass.	32,121	21,766	10,355
Joplin, Mo.	32,073	26,023	6,050
Williamsport, Pa.	31,860	28,757	3,103
Jackson, Mich.	31,433	25,180	6,253
Jamestown, N. Y.	31,297	22,892	8,405
Amsterdam, N. Y.	31,267	20,929	10,338
Lansing, Mich.	31,229	16,485	14,744
Huntington, W. Va.	31,161	11,923	19,238
Decatur, Ill	31,140	20,754	10,386
Mount Vernon, N. Y.	30,919	21,228	9,691
Lima, Ohio	30,508	21,723	8,785
Niagara Falls, N. Y.	30,445	19,457	10,988
La Crosse, Wis.	30,417	28,895	1,522
Newport, Ky.	30,309	28,301	2,008
Pasadena, Cal.	30,291	9,117	21,174
Austin, Tex.	29,860	22,258	7,602
Aurora, Ill.	29,807	24,147	5,660
Orange, N. J.	29,630	24,141	5,489
Lynchburg, Va.	29,491	18,891	10,603
Council Bluffs, Ia.	29,292	25,802	3,490
Colorado Springs, Col.	29,078	21,085	7,993
San José, Cal.	28,946	21,500	7,449
Lorain, Ohio	28,883	16,028	12,855
New Rochelle, N. Y.	28,867	14,720	14,147
Easton, Pa.	28,523	25,238	3,285
Zanesville, Ohio	28,026	23,538	4,488
Shreveport, La.	28,015	16,013	12,002
Poughkeepsie, N. Y.	27,936	24,029	3,907
Norristown, Pa.	27,875	22,265	5,610
Danville, Ill.	27,871	16,354	11,517
Waltham, Mass.	27,834	23,481	4,353
Newburg, N. Y.	27,805	24,943	2,862
Brookline, Mass.	27,792	19,935	7,857
Meriden, Conn.	27,265	24,296	2,969
Newport, R. I.	27,149	22,441	4,708
Watertown, N. Y.	26,730	21,696	5,034
Waterloo, Ia.	26,693	12,580	14,113
Waco, Tex.	26,425	20,686	5,739
Sheboygan, Wis.	26,398	22,962	3,436
Columbia, S. C.	26,319	21,108	5,211
South Omaha, Neb.	26,259	26,001	258
Lewiston, Me.	26,247	23,761	2,486
Nashua, N. H.	26,005	23,898	2,107
Elgin, Ill.	25,976	22,433	3,543
Kingston, N. Y.	25,908	24,535	1,373
Shenandoah, Pa.	25,774	20,321	5,453
Bloomington, Ill.	25,768	23,286	2,482
Wilmington, N. C.	25,748	20,976	4,772
Ogden, Utah	25,580	16,313	9,267
Clinton, Ia.	25,577	22,698	2,879
Madison, Wis.	25,531	19,164	6,367
Hazleton, Pa.	25,452	14,230	11,222
Newark, Ohio	25,404	18,157	7,247
Chicopee, Mass.	25,401	19,167	6,234
Muskogee, Okla.	25,278	14,418	10,860
New Albany, Ind.	25,275	20,628	4,647
Battle Creek, Mich.	25,267	18,563	6,704
Green Bay, Wis.	25,236	18,684	6,552
Stamford, Conn.	25,138	15,997	9,141

a Pittsburg and Allegheny. *b* Decrease. *c* 1899.

A table showing the centre of population from 1790 to 1910 will be found under **Centre of Population.**

The total rural population in 1910 was 49,348,883; the total urban was 42,623,363, divided as follows:

In Cities of	No. of Cities	Population
1,000,000 or more	3	8,501,174
500,000 to 1,000,000	5	3,010,667
250,000 to 500,000	11	3,949,839
100,000 to 250,000	31	4,840,458
50,000 to 100,000	59	4,178,915
25,000 to 50,000	120	4,062,763
10,000 to 25,000	374	5,609,208
5,000 to 10,000	629	4,364,703
2,500 to 5,000	1,173	4,105,656

POPULATION PER SQUARE MILE, BY STATES: 1910, 1900, AND 1890.

State.	Population per Square Mile.		
	1910.	1900.	1890.
Continental U. S.	30.9	25.6	21.2
Rhode Island	508.5	400.7	323.8
Massachusetts	418.8	349.0	278.5
New Jersey	337.7	250.7	192.3
Connecticut	231.3	188.5	154.8
New York	191.2	152.5	126.0
Pennsylvania	171.0	140.6	117.3
Maryland	130.3	119.5	104.9
Ohio	117.0	102.1	90.1
Delaware	103.0	94.0	85.8
Illinois	100.7	86.1	68.3
Indiana	75.3	70.1	61.1
Kentucky	57.0	53.4	46.3
Tennessee	52.4	48.5	42.4
Virginia	51.2	46.1	41.1
West Virginia	50.8	40.0	31.8
South Carolina	49.7	44.0	37.8
Michigan	48.9	42.1	36.4
Missouri	47.9	45.2	39.0
New Hampshire	47.7	45.6	41.7
North Carolina	45.3	38.9	33.2
Georgia	44.4	37.7	31.3
Wisconsin	42.2	37.4	30.7
Alabama	41.7	35.7	29.5
Iowa	40.0	40.2	34.4
Vermont	39.0	37.7	36.4
Mississippi	38.8	33.5	27.8
Louisiana	36.5	30.4	24.6
Arkansas	30.0	25.0	21.5
Minnesota	25.7	21.7	16.2
Maine	24.8	23.2	22.1
Oklahoma	23.9	11.4	3.7
Kansas	20.7	18.0	17.5
Washington	17.1	7.8	5.3
Nebraska	15.5	13.9	13.8
California	15.2	9.5	7.8
Texas	14.8	11.6	8.5
Florida	13.7	9.6	7.1
North Dakota	8.2	4.6	2.7
Colorado	7.7	5.2	4.0
South Dakota	7.6	5.2	4.5
Oregon	7.0	4.3	3.3
Utah	4.5	3.4	2.6
Idaho	3.9	1.9	1.1
New Mexico	2.7	1.6	1.3
Montana	2.6	1.7	1.0
Arizona	1.8	1.1	0.8
Wyoming	1.5	1.0	0.6
Nevada	0.7	0.4	0.4
District of Columbia	5,517.8	4,645.3	3,839.9

Centennial Exhibition, the "World's Fair," held in Philadelphia in 1876, commemorating the centennial of the political existence of the North American Republic. On June 1, 1872, Congress passed an act providing for a Centennial Board of Finance. The members of this board were authorized to procure subscriptions to a capital stock not exceeding $10,000,000, in shares of $10 each. John Welsh, of Philadelphia, was chosen president of this board. William Sellers and John S. Barbour were appointed vice-presidents, and Frederick Fraley treasurer. An official seal was adopted, simple in design. The words UNITED STATES CENTENNIAL COMMISSION were placed in concentric circles around the edge of the seal. In the centre was a view of the old State-house in Philadelphia; and beneath the building were the words (cast on the State-house bell ten years before the Revolution), "PROCLAIM LIBERTY THROUGHOUT THE LAND, UNTO ALL THE INHABITANTS THEREOF." It was soon decided to make the affair international, instead of national—an exhibition of the products of all nations.

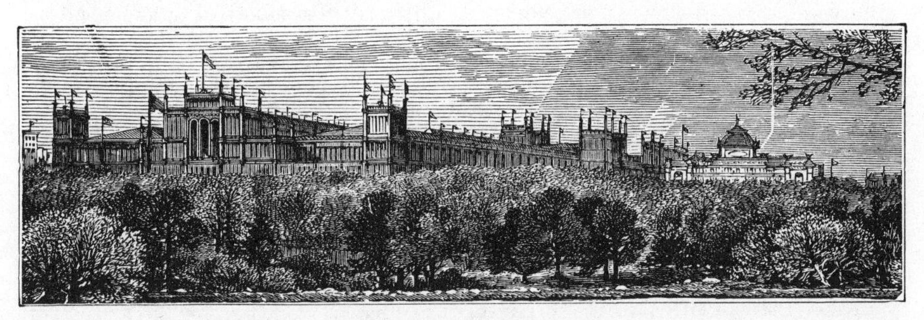

CENTENNIAL EXHIBITION BUILDINGS.

Fairmount Park, Philadelphia, an ideal site for the purpose, was chosen as the place to hold the great fair. Suitable buildings were erected, five in number — namely, Main Exhibition Building, Memorial Hall (or Art Gallery), Machinery Hall, Horticultural Hall, and Agricultural Hall. The aggregate cost of these buildings was about $4,444,000. The space occupied by them was about 49 acres of ground, and their annexes covered 26 acres more, making a total of 75 acres. The main building alone covered over 21 acres. The national government issued invitations to all foreign nations having diplomatic relations with the United States to participate in the exhibition by sending the products of their industries. There was a generous response, and thirty-three nations, besides the United States, were represented — namely, Argentine Republic, Austria, Belgium, Brazil, Canada, Chili, China, Denmark, Egypt, France, Germany, Great Britain and Ireland, India and British colonies, Hawaiian Islands, Hungary, Italy, Japan, Liberia, Luxemburg Grand Duchy, Mexico, Netherlands, Norway, Orange Free State, Peru, Portugal, Russia, Santo Domingo, Spain and Spanish colonies, Siam, Sweden, Switzerland, Tunis, Turkey, and Venezuela. A "Woman's Executive Committee" was formed, composed of Philadelphians, who raised money sufficient among the women of the Union for the erection of a building for the exhibition exclusively of women's work—sculpture, painting, engraving, lithography, literature, telegraphy, needlework of all kinds, etc.—at a cost of $30,000. The building was called the "Women's Pavilion." In it were exhibited beautiful needlework from England and etchings from the hand of Queen Victoria.

The women of the republic also contributed to the general fund of the Centennial Commission more than $100,000. The great exhibition was opened May 10. The opening ceremonies were grand and imposing. Representatives of many nations were present. The late Dom Pedro II., then Emperor of Brazil (with his empress), was the only crowned head present. The American Congress and the foreign diplomats were largely represented. The President of the United States (General Grant), in the presence of fully 100,000 people, appeared upon the great platform erected for the occasion, accompanied by his wife, when the "Grand Centennial March," composed by Richard Wagner, the great German musical composer, was performed by the orchestra of Theodore Thomas. Then Bishop Simpson, of the Methodist Episcopal Church, uttered a prayer, and was followed by a thousand voices chanting an impressive "Centennial Hymn," composed by John Greenleaf Whittier, accompanied by a grand organ and the whole orchestra. When the chanting was ended the chairman of the Centennial Board of Finance formally presented the building to the United States Centennial Commission. After a cantata, composed by Sidney Lanier, of Georgia, was sung, General Hawley, president of the Commission, presented the exhibition to the President of the United States, after which the latter made a brief response. The American flag was then unfurled over the Main Building, which gave notice to the multitude that the Centennial Exhibition was opened. The government of the United States, separate States, foreign governments, different industries, corporations, and individuals erected buildings on the grounds, making the whole number of structures 190. The exhibition was open for pay admissions 159 days, the pay-gates being closed on Sundays. The total number of cash admissions at fifty cents each was 7,250,620; and at twenty-five cents, 753,654. The number of free admissions was 1,906,692, making the grand total of admissions 9,910,966. The largest number of admissions in a full month was in October, when it reached 2,663,911. The largest number admitted in a single day—"Pennsylvania Day"—was 274,919. The total amount of cash receipts was $3,813,725.50. The exhibition closed, with imposing ceremonies, on Nov. 10. In all respects it was the grandest and most comprehensive international exposition that had then been held. See COLUMBIAN EXPOSITION, WORLD'S.

Centennial Oration. See WINTHROP, ROBERT CHARLES.

Central America, a large expanse of territory connecting North and South America, and comprising in 1901 the republics of Guatemala, Honduras, Salvador, Nicaragua, and Costa Rica. The region was discovered by Columbus, in his fourth voyage, in 1502. He found the bay of Honduras, where he landed; then proceeded along the main shore to Cape Gracias a Dios; and thence to the Isthmus of Darien, hoping, but in vain, to obtain a passage to the Pacific Ocean. At the

SANDSTONE ROCK, RIO ABAJO, TEGUCIGALPA, CENTRAL AMERICA.

isthmus he found a harbor, and, on account of its beauty and security, he called it Porto Bello. At another place in that country, on the Dureka River, he began a settlement with sixty-eight men; but they were driven off by a warlike tribe of Indians—the first repulse the Spaniards had ever met with. But for this occurrence, caused by the rapacity and cruelty of the Spaniards, Columbus might have had the honor of planting the first European colony on the continent of America. In 1509 Alonzo de Ojeda, with 300 soldiers, began a settlement on the east side of the Gulf of Darien. At the same time Diego Nicuessa, with six vessels and 780 men, began another settlement on the west side. Both were broken up by the fierce natives; and thus the Spaniards, for the first time, were taught to dread the dusky people of the New World. This was the first attempt of Europeans to make a permanent lodgment on the *continent* of America. Many attempts have been made in recent years to bring about a federation of the five republics, the latest in 1895, when the Greater Republic of Central America was formed, and in 1898, when, by treaty, Honduras, Salvador, and Nicaragua formed the United States of Central America, Guatemala and Costa Rica declining to enter the compact. Local revolutions and mutual jealousies have so far prevented a permanent union.

Centre of Population, the centre of gravity of the population of a country, each individual being assumed to have the same weight. The centre of population in the United States has clung to the parallel of 39° lat. and has moved in a westward direction during the last 110 years. The following table shows the movement of the centre of population since 1790:

Census Year.	North Latitude.	West Longitude.	Approximate Location by Important Town.
1790	39° 15′ 5″	76° 11′ 2″	Twenty three miles east of Baltimore, Md.
1800	39° 16′ 1″	76° 56′ 5″	Eighteen miles west of Baltimore, Md.
1810	39° 11′ 5″	77° 37′ 2″	Forty miles northwest by west of Washington, D. C.
1820	39° 5′ 7″	78° 33′ 0″	Sixteen miles north of Woodstock, Va.
1830	38° 57′ 9″	79° 16′ 9″	Nineteen miles west-southwest of Moorefield, W. Va.
1840	39° 2′ 0″	80° 18′ 0″	Sixteen miles south of Clarksburg, W. Va.
1850	38° 59′ 0″	81° 19′ 0″	Twenty-three miles southeast of Parkersburg, W Va.
1860	39° 0′ 4″	82° 48′ 8″	Twenty miles south of Chillicothe, O.
1870	39° 12′ 0″	83° 35′ 7″	Forty-eight miles east by north of Cincinnati, O.
1880	39° 4′ 1″	84° 39′ 7″	Eight miles west by south of Cincinnati, O.
1890	39° 11′ 9″	85° 32′ 9″	Twenty miles east of Columbus, Ind.
1900	39° 9′ 36″	85° 48′ 54″	Six miles southeast of Columbus, Ind.
1910	39°	86° 23′ 20″	Western part of Bloomington, Ind.

Cerro Gordo, BATTLE OF. Cerro Gordo is a difficult mountain pass, at the foot of the eastern slope of the Cordilleras, on the great national road from Vera Cruz to the city of Mexico. Santa Ana, by extraordinary efforts after the battle of BUENA VISTA (*q. v.*), had gathered a force of about 12,000 men from among the sierras of Orizaba, concentrated them upon the heights of Cerro Gordo, and strongly fortified the position. When the capture of VERA CRUZ (*q. v.*) was completed, General Scott prepared to march upon the Mexican capital, along the national road. He left General Worth as temporary governor of Vera Cruz, with a sufficient garrison for the Castle of San Juan de Ulloa, and moved forward (April 8, 1847) with about 8,000 men, the division of Gen. D. A. Twiggs in advance. Twiggs approached Cerro Gordo on the 13th, and found Santa Ana in his path. Scott arrived the next morning and prepared to attack the stronghold. On the 17th he issued a remarkable general order, directing, in detail, the movements of the army in the coming battle. These directions followed, secured a victory. That order appeared almost prophetic. On the 18th the attack commenced, and very severe was the struggle. It was fought in a wild place in the mountains. On one side was a deep, dark river; on the other was a frowning declivity of rock 1,000 feet in height, bristling with batteries; while above all arose the strong fortress of Cerro Gordo. The place had to be taken by storm; and the party chosen to do the work was composed of the regulars of Twiggs's division, led by Colonel Harney. Victory followed the efforts of skill and bravery, and strong Cerro Gordo fell. Velasquez, the commander of the fortress, was killed; and the Mexican standard was hauled down by Serg. Thomas Henry. Santa Ana, with Almonte and other generals, and 8,000 troops, escaped; the remainder were made prisoners. Santa Ana attempted to fly with his carriage, which contained a large amount of specie; but it was overturned, when, mounting a mule taken from the carriage harness, he fled to the mountains, leaving behind him his wooden leg—a substitute for the real one which was amputated after a wound received in the defence of Vera Cruz in 1837. In the vehicle were found his papers, clothing, and a pair of woman's satin slippers. The victory of the Americans was complete and decisive. The trophies were 3,000 prisoners (who were paroled), forty-three pieces of bronze artillery (cast in Seville, Spain), 5,000 stand of arms (which were destroyed), and a large quantity of munitions of war. The fugitives were pursued towards Jalapa with vigor. In that battle the Americans lost 431 men. The loss of the Mexicans was about 1,200 killed and wounded.

Cervera y Topeto, PASCUAL DE, CONDE DE JEREZ, MARQUIS DE SANTA ANA, naval officer; born in the province of Jerez, Spain, in 1833; was graduated at the San Fernando Naval Academy in 1851. He participated in the expeditions to Morocco

ADMIRAL CERVERA.

in 1859 and Cochin-China in 1862, and in the blockade of Cuba against filibusters in 1870; and later became secretary of the navy. He was promoted admiral in 1888. In the war with the United States in 1898 he was given command of the fleet sent to operate in Cuban waters. After Hobson and his companions, who sunk the collier at the entrance of Santiago Harbor, were captured by the Spaniards, they were handsomely treated by Admiral Cervera till regularly exchanged. When the admiral received orders to attempt an escape from the harbor of Santiago he saw and reported the hopelessness of such an undertaking, yet when peremptory orders were received he did not hesitate to act upon them. The result was one of the most thrilling naval encounters in history, ending in the destruction of all his ships, on July 3. After his surrender his dignified bearing and high qualities as a naval officer, together with the remembrance of his kind treatment of Hobson and his companions, prompted marks of exceptional consideration from the United States authorities between the time of his surrender and departure for Spain. He died April 3, 1909. See CUBA; SAMPSON, WILLIAM THOMAS; SANTIAGO DE CUBA; SCHLEY, WINFIELD SCOTT.

Cesnola, LUIGI PALMA DI, archæologist; born near Turin, Italy, June 29, 1832; attended the Royal Military Academy; came to the United States in 1860; and entered the army as colonel of the 4th New York Cavalry; was wounded and captured in the battle of Aldie, in June, 1862. While United States consul at Cyprus he made archæological explorations, securing a collection of antiquities which were placed in the Metropolitan Museum of Art in New York City in 1873. He became director of the museum in 1878, and died in New York City, Nov. 20, 1904.

Chabert, JOSEPH BERNARD, MARQUIS DE, naval officer; born in Toulon, France, Feb. 28, 1724; joined the navy in 1741; came to America, and fought with the French in the Revolutionary War, winning much distinction. Later he planned and finished maps of the shores of North America. He was author of *Voyages sur les cotés de l'Amérique septentrionale.* He died in Paris, Dec. 1, 1805.

Chadd's Ford, a town in Delaware county, Pa., on Brandywine Creek, 30 miles southwest of Philadelphia. The battle of Brandywine was fought here, Sept. 11, 1777.

Chaffee, ADNA ROMANZA, military officer; born in Orwell, O., April 14, 1842; entered the regular army as a private in the 6th Cavalry, July 22, 1861; soon afterwards was made first sergeant of his troop; March 13, 1863, was promoted to second lieutenant; Feb. 22, 1865, to first lieutenant, and Oct. 12, 1867, to cap-

ADNA ROMANZA CHAFFEE.

tain. For several years his regiment was employed in almost continuous service against the Indians in the Southwest, where he proved himself a brave and stubborn fighter. For his gallantry in various actions he was, in March, 1868, brevetted major, and Feb. 27, 1890, lieutenant-colonel. Meanwhile, on July 7, 1888, he had been promoted to major, and assigned to the 9th Cavalry, one of the two regiments of regular cavalry composed of colored men. Major Chaffee was instructor in cavalry tactics at the Fort Leavenworth school for officers in 1894–96. On June 1, 1897, he was promoted to lieutenant-colonel of the 3d Cavalry, and made commandant of the Cavalry School of Instruction at Fort Riley, which post he held at the opening of the war with Spain, in 1898. He was appointed a brigadier-general of volunteers, May 4, 1898; promoted to major-general, July 8, following; honorably discharged from the volunteer service and reappointed a brigadier-general, April 13, 1899. From December, 1898, he served as chief-of-staff to the governor-general of Cuba. He had command of the troops which captured El Caney, and practically closed the Santiago campaign. On May 8, 1899, he was promoted to colonel of the 8th Cavalry, and July 19, 1900, was assigned to command the American troops with the allied armies in China, with the rank of major-general of volunteers. He took an active part in the capture of Peking and in the establishment of order. In 1901 he commanded the military division of the Philippines; in 1904–06 was lieutenant-general and chief of staff, retiring in the latter year. He died in Los Angeles, Nov. 1, 1914.

Chafin, Eugene Wilder, Presidential Prohibition nominee in 1908 and 1912, was born in East Troy, Wis., Nov. 1, 1852; was graduated from the University of Wisconsin, practised law in Waukesha, Wis., for nearly twenty years, and later for seven years in Chicago. Author of *Voters' Handbook; Lives of the Presidents; Lincoln, the Man of Sorrow; Washington as a Statesman.*

Chaillé-Long, Charles, diplomatist; born in Princess Anne, Md., July 2, 1842; served in the 11th Maryland Volunteers, 1862–65; entered the Egyptian army, 1869; chief-of-staff to General Gordon, governor-general, Egyptian Soudan, 1874–77; discovered Lake Ibrahim, determining the source of the Nile, 1874; promoted to colonel and bey, 1874; retired, 1877. He was acting United States consul at Alexandria and made the consulate a general refuge after the bombardment of 1882; secretary of legation and consul-general to Korea, 1887–89; secretary Universal Postal Congress, Washington, 1897; and secretary United States Special Commission to the Paris Exposition, 1897–1900. He received many honors for his services to science in Central Africa and Egypt, and published numerous works on Egyptian and African subjects.

Chain, The Great, across the Hudson. See Clinton, Fort.

Chalmers, George, historian; born in Fochabers, Scotland, in 1742; studied law; came to America in 1763, and practised in Baltimore. Being opposed to the Revolutionary War he returned to England. His publications relating to the United States include *Political Annals of the Present United Colonies; Opinions on In-*

teresting Subjects arising from American Independence; and *Life of Thomas Paine.* He died in London, May 21, 1825.

Chalmette Plantation, La., a few miles below New Orleans on the Mississippi River, where General Jackson repulsed an advance of the British, Dec. 28, 1814. See JACKSON, ANDREW; NEW ORLEANS.

Chamberlain, DANIEL HENRY, lawyer; born in West Brookfield, Mass., June 23, 1835; was graduated at Yale College in 1862, and at Harvard Law School in 1864; entered the Union army as an officer in the 5th Massachusetts Colored Cavalry; after the war settled in South Carolina, of which he was (Republican) governor in 1874–76. He died at Charlottesville, Va., April 13, 1907.

Chamberlain, JOSEPH, statesman; born in London, England, in 1836; was educated at the University College School, in London; and was mayor of Birmingham

JOSEPH CHAMBERLAIN.

in 1870–75. He was elected to Parliament from Birmingham as a Liberal Unionist in 1875, and has since held his seat; was president of the Board of Trade in 1880–85; president of the Local Government Board in 1886; one of the British commissioners to settle the North American fisheries dispute in 1887, and lord rector of Glasgow University. In 1895–1903 he was Secretary of State for the Colonies. He also served as chancellor of the University of Birmingham. During 1898, and especially when the international troubles concerning China were thickening, he made several notable speeches, voicing a widespread sentiment in Great Britain that there should be a closer understanding between the United States and Great Britain touching their various commercial interests. In 1888 he married Mary, daughter of William C. Endicott, former U. S. Secretary of War. He died in London, July 2, 1914.

Chamberlain, JOSHUA LAWRENCE, military officer and educator; born in Bangor, Me., Sept. 8, 1828; was graduated at Bowdoin College in 1852. He attended a military academy in his boyhood. He was a professor in his *alma mater* from 1855 to 1862, when he was appointed lieutenant-colonel of a Maine regiment, and rose to brigadier-general of volunteers in the summer of 1864. He was severely wounded in the siege of Petersburg, and again at Quaker Road in March, 1865. In the final operations ending in Lee's surrender he commanded a division of the 5th Corps. General Chamberlain was a most active and efficient officer, and was in twenty-four pitched battles. He was six times wounded—three times severely. He was designated to receive the formal surrender of the weapons and colors of Lee's army, and was brevetted major-general in 1865. He resumed his professional duties in the college in 1865; was governor of Maine in 1866–71; president of Bowdoin College in 1871–83; and afterwards engaged in writing and lecturing. His works include *The People, the State, and the Nation; Gettysburg; Five Forks; Appomattox; Maine, Her Place in History; American Ideals; Ethics and Politics of the Spanish War; The New Nation; De Monts and Acadia; Ruling Powers in History,* etc. He died Feb. 24, 1914.

Chambers, B. J., of Texas, was nominated by the Greenback Party in June, 1880, as their candidate for Vice-President of the United States, at the convention held in Chicago. The platform demanded that all money should be issued by the United States and not through banks, that legal-tender currency should be substituted for bank-notes, and that an unlimited coinage of silver as well as gold should be established by law. It also declaimed against convict labor, child labor, and "Chinese serfs," who tended to brutalize and degrade American labor. See GREENBACK PARTY.

Chambers, WILLIAM, author; born in

Peebles, Scotland, in 1800; was author of *Things as they are in America;* and *Slavery and Color in America;* and compiler of a *Hand-book of American Literature.* He died in Edinburgh, May 20, 1883.

Chambersburg, borough and capital of Franklin county, Pa., on the Conecocheague and Falling Creeks; 52 miles w. s. w. of Harrisburg. In Early's raid in the Civil War General McCausland entered Chambersburg with Confederate cavalry, July 30, 1864, and demanded a tribute of $200,000 gold; this not being paid, the place was set on fire and two-thirds of it burned, causing a loss of $1,000,000. It was soon rebuilt, chiefly of brick or stone. Pop. (1900), 8,864; (1910) 11,-800. See also PENNSYLVANIA.

Chambers of Commerce, bodies of merchants and traders associated for the purpose of promoting the interests of their own members, of the city to which the society belongs, and of the community generally, in so far as these have reference to trade and merchandise. Of the means by which these objects are sought to be accomplished the following may be mentioned as the most prominent: (1) by representing and urging on the legislature the views of their members in mercantile affairs; (2) by aiding in the preparation of legislative measures having reference to trade; (3) by collecting statistics bearing upon the staple trade of the city; (4) in some places by acting as a sort of court of arbitration in mercantile questions; (5) by attaining by combination advantages in trade which might be beyond the reach of individual enterprise. The first institution of the kind in the United States, the New York Chamber of Commerce, was organized in 1768 and incorporated by royal charter from King George III. in 1770. There are similar bodies in every city and town of consequence in the United States.

The extension of the functions of chambers of commerce in the United States has been considerable since 1890. The movement had its origin in Germany and grew out of organized efforts to foster the world commerce of the empire. The chambers of commerce in leading cities like Berlin and Hamburg undertook the commercial training of young men, with a view to their future advancement in mercantile life and the consular service. The result was the securing of a higher order of talent in such pursuits. The hint thus thrown out was promptly taken up in the United States. The New York Chamber of Commerce, in 1899, voted a fund for the endowment of a lecture course on commerce at Columbia University; in Chicago a chair of commerce was established by that city's chamber at the University of Chicago, and in 1900 a School of Commerce, Accounts and Finance was established by the University of New York. Students were assured in the event of a satisfactory course of study, that they would be given posts in leading commercial establishments or appointed to consular offices so far as influence could attain that result.

Chambly, FORT, CAPTURE OF. In 1775 it was supposed by General Carleton that the fort at Chambly, 12 miles below St. John, at the rapids of the Sorel, the outlet of Lake Champlain, could not be reached by the Republicans so long as the British held the post above and kept only a feeble garrison there. Informed of this by Canadian scouts, Montgomery, besieging St. John, sent Colonel Bedel, of New Hampshire, with troops to capture the post. He was assisted by Majors Brown and Livingston. The attack was planned by Canadians familiar with the place. Artillery was placed in bateaux, and, during a dark night, was conveyed past the fort at St. John to the head of Chambly Rapids, where the guns were mounted and taken to the place of attack. The garrison surrendered after making slight resistnace. The spoils were a large quantity of provisions and military stores; also the colors of the 7th Regiment of British regulars, which were sent to the Continental Congress, and were the first trophies of war received by that body. This disaster hastened the downfall of St. John. See ST. JOHN, SIEGE OF.

Champe, JOHN, patriot; born in Loudon county, Va., in 1752; was sent to New York as a spy after the treason of Arnold, at the request of Washington. As it was also rumored that another American officer (supposed to be General Gates) was a traitor, Champe was instructed to discover the second traitor, and, if possible, to take Arnold. He left the American camp at Tappan at night, in the character of a deserter, was pursued, but reached Paulus Hook, where the British vessels were anchored. After he had been examined by Sir Henry Clinton, he was sent to Arnold, who appointed him a sergeant-major in a force which he was recruiting. He found evidence which proved that the suspected general was innocent, and forwarded the same to Washington. He learned also that Arnold was accustomed to walk in his garden every night, and conceived a plan for his capture. With a comrade he was to seize and gag him, and convey him as a drunken soldier to a boat in waiting, which would immediately cross to the New Jersey shore, where a number of horsemen were to be in waiting. Unfortunately, on the night set, Arnold changed his quarters, and the command of which Champe was a member was ordered to Virginia. Later he escaped and joined the army of Greene in North Carolina. He died in Kentucky, about 1798.

FORT CHAMBLY.

Champion Hills, BATTLE OF. Grant, at JACKSON (*q. v.*), hearing of the arrival of Johnston and his order for Pemberton to strike his rear, perceived the reason for the sudden evacuation of their post by the troops at the capital. No doubt they had been sent to join Pemberton that the latter might crush Grant by the weight of superior numbers. The latter comprehended his peril, and instantly took measures to meet Pemberton before such junction could take place. He ordered a concentration of his forces at Edwards's Station, 2 miles from the railway bridge over the Big Black River. While Sherman tarried in Jackson long enough to destroy the railways, military factories, arsenal, bridges, cotton factories, stores, and other public property, the remainder of the army turned their faces towards Vicksburg. Pemberton was at or near Edwards's Station, with about 25,000 troops and ten batteries of artillery. Blair moved towards the station, followed by McClernand and Osterhaus; while McPherson, on another road, kept up communication with McClernand. Pemberton had advanced to Champion Hills, when a note from Johnston caused him to send his trains back to the Big Black River; and he was about to follow with his troops, when Grant, close upon him, compelled him to remain and fight (May 16, 1863). General Hovey's division now held the advance directly in front of Pemberton. At eleven o'clock a battle began, Hovey's division bearing the brunt, and, after a severe contest of an hour and a half, his infantry were compelled to fall back half a mile to the position of his artillery. Reinforced, he renewed the battle with great energy. Finally Pemberton's left began to bend under Logan's severe pressure, and, at five o'clock, gave way. The rest of his army became so confused and disheartened that they began to fly. Seeing this, Pemberton ordered his whole army to retreat towards the Big Black River; when Grant ordered the fresh brigades of Osterhaus and Carr to follow with all speed, and cross the river, if possible. In the retreat Pemberton lost many of his troops, made prisoners. This battle was fought mainly by Hovey's division of McClernand's corps and Logan's and Quinby's divisions (the latter commanded by Crocker) of McPherson's corps. The National loss was 2,457, of whom 426 were killed. The loss of the Confederates was estimated to have been quite equal to that of the Nationals in killed and wounded, besides almost 2,000 prisoners, eighteen guns, and a large quantity of small-arms. Among the killed was General Tilghman, who was captured at Fort Henry the year before.

Champlain, Samuel de, French navigator; born in Brouage, France, in 1567. His family had many fishermen and mariners, and he was carefully educated for a navigator. In early life he was in the cavalry of Brittany, and was with his uncle, pilot-general of the fleets of Spain, when that officer conducted back to that country the troops who had served in France. In 1599 he commanded a vessel of the Spanish fleet that sailed to Mexico, and he drew up a faithful account of the voyage. On his return he received a pension from Henry IV. of France; and he was induced by M. de Chastes, governor of Dieppe, to explore and prepare the way for a French colony in America. Chastes had received a charter from the King to found settlements in New France, and the monarch commissioned Champlain lieutenant-general of Canada. With this authority, he sailed from Honfleur on March 5, 1603, with a single vessel, commanded by Pont-Grevé, a skilful navigator. In May they ascended the St. Lawrence and landed near the site of Quebec, from which place Pont-Grevé and five men ascended the river in a canoe to Lachine Rapids, above Montreal. The Indians at Stadacona yet remembered Cartier's perfidy (see Cartier, Jacques), but were placable.

SAMUEL DE CHAMPLAIN.

Champlain, on his return to France in the autumn, found Chastes dead and his concessions transferred by the King to Pierre de Gast, the Sieur de Monts, a wealthy Huguenot, who had received the commission of viceroy of New France. The latter made a new arrangement with Champlain, and in March, 1604, he sailed with the navigator from France with four vessels. They landed in Nova Scotia, and remained there some time planting a settlement and exploring the neighboring regions; and when de Monts returned to France, he left Champlain to explore the New England coast. He went as far south as Cape Cod, and in 1607 returned to France. Having suggested to De

Monts that a point on the St. Lawrence would be a more eligible site for the seat of the projected new empire, Champlain was sent to the river in 1608 with Pont-Grevé, and, at Stadacona, founded Quebec, the Indian name for "the narrows," and pronounced *Kebec.* There the colonists built cabins and prepared to plant. In 1609 Champlain, who had made the Montagnais Indians on the St. Lawrence his friends, marched with them against their enemies, the Iroquois. They were joined by a party of Hurons and Algonquins, and ascended the Sorel to the Chambly Rapids, whence Champlain proceeded in a canoe and discovered a great lake, and gave it his own name. On its borders he fought and defeated the Iroquois, who fled in terror before the fire of his arquebuses. He returned to France, but went back in 1610, and the same year was wounded by an arrow in a fight with the Iroquois. Again returning to France, he, at the age of forty-four years, married a girl of twelve; and in 1612 he went back to Canada, with the title and powers of lieutenant-governor, under the Prince of Condé, who had succeeded De Soissons, the successor to De Monts, as viceroy.

In 1815 he started on his famous expedition to the Onondaga Indians. He followed Father Le Caron and his party to Lake Huron, to which he gave the name of Mer Douce. Returning across the great forests, he sailed with several hundred canoes down a stream into the Bay of Quinté, and entered the broad Lake Ontario, which he named Lac St. Louis. With a considerable war party, chiefly Hurons, he crossed the lake into the country of the Iroquois, in (present) New York. Hiding their canoes in the forest, they pressed onward to the Indian post on the shore of Onondaga Lake. It was at the time of the maize harvest, and the Iroquois were attacked in the fields. They retired to their town, which was fortified with four rows of palisades. On the inside of these were galleries furnished with stones and other missiles, and a supply of water to extinguish a fire if kindled beneath these wooden walls. The Hurons were rather insubordinate, and the attack was ineffectual. Champlain had constructed a wooden tower, which was dragged

CHAMPLAIN'S FORTIFIED RESIDENCE AT QUEBEC.

near the palisades, and from the top of which his marksmen swept the galleries filled with naked Iroquois. But he could not control the great body of the Hurons, and, in their furious and tumultuous assault upon the palisades, they were thrown back in confusion, and could not be induced to repeat the onset, but resolved to retreat. Champlain, wounded in the leg, was compelled to acquiesce, and he made his way back to Quebec (1616), after a year's absence. The same year he went to France and organized a fur-trading company.

On his return to Canada he took with him some Recollet priests to minister to the colonists and the pagans. The colony languished until 1620, when a more energetic viceroy gave it a start. Champlain got permission to fortify it, and he returned with the title and power of governor, taking with him his child-wife. Jesuit priests were sent to Canada as missionaries, and Champlain worked energetically for the cause of religion and the expansion of French dominion. In 1628 Sir David Kertk appeared with an English fleet before Quebec and demanded its surrender. Champlain's bold refusal made Kertk retire, but on his way down the St. Lawrence he captured the French supply-ships. This produced great distress in Quebec; and in July of next year Champlain was compelled to surrender to Kertk's brothers, and was carried to England. By a treaty in 1632, Canada was restored to the French. Champlain was reinstated as governor, and sailed for the St. Lawrence in 1633. He did not long survive, but worked energetically and faithfully until the last. His wife survived him. She was a Protestant when she was married, but died an Ursuline nun. Champlain's zeal for the propagation of Christianity was intense. A college was established at Quebec, in which the children of the savages were taught and trained in the habits of civilization. In 1603 Champlain published an account of his first voyage, and, in 1613 and 1619, a continuation of his narrative. In 1632 they were included in a work of his then published, which comprised a history of New France from the time of Verrazani's discoveries to 1631, entitled *Les Voyages à la Nouvelle France Occidentale et Canada*. He died in Quebec, Dec. 25, 1635. In 1870 a complete collection of his works, including his voyage to Mexico, with facsimiles of his maps, was published in Quebec, edited by Abbés Laverdière and Casgrain.

Champlain, LAKE, OPERATIONS ON. After the Americans left Canada in sad plight in June, 1776, Carleton, the governor of Canada and general of the forces there, appeared at the foot of Lake Champlain with a well-appointed force of 13,000 men. Only on the bosom of the lake could they advance, for there was no road on either shore. To prevent this invasion, it was important that the Americans should hold command of its waters. A flotilla of small armed vessels was constructed at Crown Point, and Benedict Arnold was placed in command of them as commodore. A schooner called the *Royal Savage* was his flag-ship. Carleton, meanwhile, had used great diligence in fitting out an armed flotilla at St. John for the recovery of Crown Point and Ticonderoga. Towards the close of August, Arnold went down the lake with his fleet and watched the foe until early in October, when he fell back to Valcour Island and formed his flotilla for action without skill. Carleton advanced, with Edward Pringle as commodore, and, on the morning of Oct. 11, gained an advantageous position near Arnold's vessels. A very severe battle ensued, in which the *Royal Savage* was first crippled and afterwards destroyed. Arnold behaved with the greatest bravery during a fight of four or five hours, until it was closed by the falling of night. In the darkness Arnold escaped with his vessels from surrounding dangers and pushed up the lake, but was overtaken on the 13th. One of the vessels, the *Washington*, was run on shore and burned, while Arnold, in the schooner *Congress*, with four gondolas, kept up a running fight for five hours, suffering great loss. When the *Congress* was almost a wreck, Arnold ran the vessels into a creek about 10 miles from Crown Point, on the eastern shore, and burned them. Then he and his little force made their way through the woods to a place opposite Crown Point, just avoiding an Indian ambush, and escaped to the port whence he started in safety. At Crown Point he found two schooners, two galleys, one sloop, and one gondola—all that remained of his proud little fleet. In the two actions the Americans lost about ninety men; the British not half that number. General Carleton took possession of Crown Point on Oct. 14, but abandoned it in twenty days and returned to Canada.

When the War of 1812–15 was declared, the whole American naval force on Lake Champlain consisted of only two boats that lay in a harbor on the Vermont shore. The British had two or three gunboats, or armed galleys, on the Richelieu, or Sorel, River, the outlet of Lake Champlain. Some small vessels were hastily fitted up and armed, and Lieut. Thomas McDonough was sent to the lake to superintend the construction of some naval vessels there. In the spring of 1813 he put two vessels afloat—the sloops-of-war *Growler* and *Eagle*. Early in June, 1813, some small American vessels were attacked near Rouse's Point by British gunboats. McDonough sent the *Growler* and *Eagle*, manned by 112 men, under Lieut. Joseph Smith, to look after the matter. They went down the Sorel, chased three British gunboats some distance down the river, and were in turn pursued by three armed row-galleys, which opened upon the flying sloops with long 24-pounders. At the same time a land force, sent out on each side of the river, poured volleys of musketry upon the American vessels, which were answered by grape and canister. For four hours a running fight was kept up, when a heavy shot tore off a plank from the *Eagle* below water, and she sank immediately. The *Growler* was disabled and run ashore, and the people of both vessels were made prisoners. The loss of the Americans in killed and wounded was twenty; that of the British almost 100. The captured sloops were refitted, and named, respectively, *Finch* and *Chubb*. They were engaged in the battle off Plattsburg the next year, when McDonough recaptured them. For a while the British were masters of Lake Champlain. This loss stimulated McDonough to greater exertions. By Aug. 6 he had fitted out and armed three sloops and six gunboats. At the close of July a British armament, under Col. J. Murray, attacked defenceless Plattsburg. It was composed of soldiers, sailors, and marines, conveyed in two sloops-of-war, three gunboats, and forty-seven long-boats. They landed on Saturday afternoon, and continued a work of destruction until ten o'clock the next day. General Hampton, who was then at Bur-

THE ROYAL SAVAGE.*

* This engraving was made from a drawing in water-colors, of the *Royal Savage*, found by the late Benson J. Lossing among the papers of General Schuyler, and gave the first positive information as to the design and appearance of the "UNION FLAG" (*q. v.*), displayed by the Americans at Cambridge on Jan. 1, 1776. The drawing exhibited, in proper colors, the thirteen stripes, alternate red and white, with the British union (the crosses of St. George and St. Andrew) on a blue field in the dexter corner.

lington, only 20 miles distant, with 4,000 troops, made no attempt to oppose the invaders. The block-house, arsenal, armory, and hospital at Plattsburg were destroyed also private store-houses. The 300th anniversary of the discovery of Lake Champlain was celebrated in July, 1909, under the auspices of the United States Government. In May, 1912, the French government presented to the United States the Rodin bust, *La France*, to be affixed to the Champlain Memorial Light-house at Crown Point.

SCENE OF ARNOLD'S NAVAL BATTLE.*

Champlin, STEPHEN, naval officer; born in South Kingston, R. I., Nov. 17, 1789; went to sea when sixteen years old, and commanded a ship at twenty-two. In May, 1812, he was appointed sailing-master in the navy, and was first in command of a gunboat under Perry, at Newport, R. I., and was in service on Lake Ontario in the attacks on Little York (Toronto) and Fort George, in 1813. He joined Perry on Lake Erie, and commanded the sloop-of-war *Scorpion* in the battle on Sept. 10, 1813, firing the first and last gun in that action. He was the last surviving officer of that engagement. In the following spring, while blockading Mackinaw with the *Tigress*, he was attacked in the night by an overwhelming force, severely wounded, and made prisoner. His wound troubled him until his death, and he was disabled for any active service forever afterwards. He died in Buffalo, N. Y., Feb. 20, 1870.

Chancellorsville, BATTLE OF. Early in April, 1863, Hooker, in command of the Army of the Potomac, became impatient, and resolved to put it in motion towards Richmond, notwithstanding his ranks were not full. Cavalry under Stoneman were sent to destroy railways in Lee's rear, but were foiled by the high water in the streams. After a pause, Hooker determined to attempt to turn Lee's flank, and, for that purpose, sent 10,000 mounted men to raid in his rear. Then he moved 36,000 of the troops of his right wing across the Rappahannock, with orders to halt and intrench at Chancellorsville, between the Confederate army near Fredericksburg and Richmond. This movement was so masked by a demonstration on Lee's front by Hooker's left wing, under General Sedgwick, that the right was well advanced before Lee was aware of his peril. These troops reached Chancellorsville, in a region known as "The Wilderness," on the evening of April 30, 1863, when Hooker expected to see Lee, conscious of danger, fly towards Richmond. He did no such thing, but proceeded to strike the National army a heavy blow, for the twofold purpose of seizing the communications between the two parts of that army and compelling its commander to fight at a disadvantage, with only a part of his troops in hand. Hooker had made his headquarters in the spacious brick house of Mr. Chancellor, and sent out Pleasonton's cavalry to reconnoitre. A part of these encountered the Confederate cavalry, under Stuart, and were defeated.

Lee had called "Stonewall" Jackson's large force to come up when he perceived Sedgwick's movements. Lee left General Early with 9,000 men and thirty cannon to hold his fortified position at Fredericksburg against Sedgwick, and, at a little past midnight (May 1, 1863), he put Jackson's column in motion towards Chancellorsville. It joined another force under General Anderson at eight o'clock in the morning, and he, in person, led the Con-

* This scene is between Port Kent and Plattsburg, on Lake Champlain, western shore. On the left is seen a point of the mainland; on the right a part of Valcour Island. Between these Arnold formed his little fleet for action.

federates to attack the Nationals. Hooker had also disposed the latter in battle order. Aware of the peril of fighting with the Wilderness at his back, he had so disposed his army as to fight in the open country, with a communication open with the Rappahannock towards Fredericksburg. At eleven o'clock the divisions of Griffin and Humphreys, of Meade's corps, pushed out to the left, in the direction of Banks's Ford, while Sykes's division of the same corps, supported by Hancock's division, and forming the centre column, moved along a turnpike. Slocum's entire corps, with Howard's, and its batteries, massed in its rear, comprising the right column, marched along a plank road. The battle was begun about a mile in advance of the National works at Chancellorsville, by the van of the centre column and Confederate cavalry. Sykes brought up his entire column, with artillery, and, after a severe struggle with McLaws, he gained an advantageous position, at noon, on one of the ridges back of Fredericksburg. Banks's Ford, which Lee had strenuously sought to cover, was now virtually in possession of the Nationals, and the distance between Sedgwick, opposite Fredericksburg, and the army at Chancellorsville was shortened at least 12 miles.

Meanwhile, Slocum and Jackson had met and struggled fiercely on the plank road. Perceiving Jackson endeavoring to flank Slocum, and his strong column overlapping Sykes's flank, Hooker, fearing his army might be beaten in detail before he could successfully resist the furious onslaught of Jackson, ordered its withdrawal behind his works at Chancellorsville, the Confederates following close in the rear of the retreating troops. So ended the movements of the day. Hooker's position was a strong one. The National line extended from the Rappahannock to the Wilderness church, 2 miles west of Chancellorsville. Meade's corps, with Couch's, formed his left; Slocum's, and a division of Sickles's, his centre, and Howard's his right, with Pleasonton's cavalry near. Lee's forces had the Virginia cavalry of Owen and Wickham on the right, and Stuart's and a part of Fitzhugh Lee's on the left. McLaws's forces occupied the bridge on the east of the Big Meadow Swamp, and Anderson's continued the line to the left of McLaws. Such was the general disposition of the opposing armies on the morning of May 2.

Lee was unwilling to risk a direct attack on Hooker, and Jackson advised a secret flank movement with his entire corps, so as to fall on Hooker's rear. Lee hesitated, but so much did he lean on Jackson as adviser and executor that he consented. With 25,000 men Jackson made the perilous movement, marching swiftly and steadily through the thick woods, with Stuart's cavalry between his forces and those of the Nationals. But the movement was early discovered; the Nationals, however, believing it to be a retreat of the Confederates towards Richmond. Sickles pushed forward Birney's division to reconnoitre, followed by two brigades of Howard's corps. Birney charged upon the passing column, and captured a Georgia regiment, 500 strong, but was checked by Confederate artillery. The Nationals now held the road over which Jackson was moving. Disposition was made to pursue the supposed fugitives, when Jackson made a quick and startling movement towards Chancellorsville, concealed by the thick woods, at six o'clock in the evening, suddenly burst forth from the thickets with his whole force, like an unexpected and terrible tornado, and fell with full force upon Howard's corps (the 11th), with tremendous yells, just as they were preparing for supper and repose. Devens's division, on the extreme right, received the first blow, and almost instantly the surprised troops, panic-stricken, fled to the rear, communicating their alarm to the other divisions of the corps. The Confederates captured men and guns and a commanding position, while the fugitives, in evident confusion, rushed towards Chancellorsville, upon the position of General Schurz, whose division had already retreated. The tide of affrighted men rolled back upon General Steinwehr.

While the divisions of Devens and Schurz were reforming, Steinwehr quickly changed front, threw his men behind some works, rallied some of Schurz's men, and checked the pursuit for a brief space. But the overwhelming number of the Confederates speedily captured the works. These disasters on the right were partially relieved by Hooker, who sent forward troops at the double-quick, under Generals Berry and French, and also a courier to apprise Sickles, who had pushed some distance beyond the National lines, of the disaster to the 11th Corps and his own peril. He was directed to fall back and attack Jackson's left flank. He was in a critical situation, but Pleasonton saved him by a quick and skilful movement, greatly assisting in checking the pursuit. This was done long enough for Pleasonton to bring his own horse-artillery and more than twenty of Sickles's guns to bear upon the Confederates, and to pour into their ranks a destructive storm of grape and canister shot. Generals Warren and Sickles soon came to Pleasonton's assistance, when there was a severe struggle for the possession of cannon. Meanwhile Lee was making a strong artillery attack upon Hooker's left and centre. Soon a great misfortune befell the Confederate commander, in the loss of "Stonewall" Jackson, the strong right arm of his power. Jackson had sent for Hill, and was anxious to follow up the advantage he had gained by extending his lines to the left and cutting off Hooker's communication with the United States Ford. While waiting for Hill, he pushed forward with his staff, on a personal reconnoissance, and, when returning, in the gloom of evening, his men, mistaking them for National cavalry, fired upon them and mortally wounded the great leader.

RUINS OF CHANCELLORSVILLE.

No more fighting occurred in that part of the field. Birney's division drove back the Confederates at midnight, recovered some lost ground, and brought back some abandoned guns and caissons. During the night a new line of intrenchments was thrown up by the Nationals; but Hooker's forces were in a very perilous position on Sunday morning, May 3. When he heard of the movement of Jackson on Saturday morning, he had called from Sedgwick Reynolds's corps, 20,000 strong, and it arrived the same evening. Hooker's force was now 60,000 strong, and Lee's 40,000. The former ordered Sedgwick to cross the river and seize and hold Fredericksburg and the heights behind it, and then, pushing along the roads leading to Chancellorsville, crush every impediment and join the main army. Each army made disposition for a battle on Sunday morning. Stuart advanced to the attack with Lee's left wing, and when he came in sight of the Nationals he shouted, "Charge, and remember Jackson!" With thirty pieces of artillery presently in position on an elevation, his men made a desperate charge under cover of their fire, and were soon struggling with Sickles's corps and four other divisions. These were pushed back, and a fierce battle ensued, the tide of success ebbing and flowing for more than an hour. During this struggle Hooker had been prostrated, and Couch took command of the army. Almost the whole National army became engaged in the battle, at different points, excepting the troops under Meade and Reynolds. Couch fell back towards the Rappahannock, and, at noon, Hooker, having recovered, resumed chief command.

Lee's army was now united, but Hooker's was divided. Sedgwick had seriously menaced Lee's flank, but had not joined Hooker. After a hard conflict and the loss of 1,000 men, Sedgwick had captured the Confederate works on the heights back of Fredericksburg, and sent Early, their defender, flying southward with his shattered columns. Intelligence of these events made Lee extremely cautious. Sedgwick, leaving Gibbon in command at Fredericksburg, marched for Chancellorsville, when Lee was compelled to divide his army to meet this new peril. He sent McLaws with four brigades to meet Sedgwick. At Salem church they had a sanguinary conflict. The Confederates won, and the losses of Sedgwick, added to those sustained in the morning, amounted to about 5,000 men. Hooker, at the same time, seemed paralyzed in his new position, for his army appeared being beaten in detail. On the following morning, perceiving that Hooker's army had been much strengthened, Lee thought it necessary to drive Sedgwick across the Rappahannock before again attacking the main body. Early was sent to retake the Heights of Fredericksburg, and he cut Sedgwick off from the city. Early was reinforced by Anderson, by which Sedgwick was enclosed on three sides. At six o'clock in the evening the Confederates attacked him. His forces gave way and retreated to Banks's Ford, and before morning the remains of Sedgwick's corps had crossed the Rappahannock over pontoon bridges. Gibbon also withdrew from Fredericksburg to Falmouth that night, and, on Tuesday, Lee had only Hooker to contend with. He concentrated his forces to strike Hooker a crushing blow before night, but a heavy rain-storm prevented. Hooker prepared to retreat, and did so on the night of May 5 and morning of the 6th, crossing the Rappahannock and returning to the old quarters of the army opposite Fredericksburg. The losses of each army had been very heavy. That of the Confederates was reported at 12,277, including 2,000 prisoners, and that of the Nationals was 17,197, including about 5,000 prisoners. The latter also lost thirteen heavy guns, about 20,000 small-arms, seventeen colors, and a large amount of ammunition. The Union Generals Berry and Whipple were killed.

Chancery Jurisdiction. In all the crown colonies, excepting New Hampshire, the chancery court had been introduced, in spite of the colonists, who dreaded its prolix proceedings and heavy fees. Wherever it had been introduced, it was retained in the State governments after the Revolution. In New Jersey and South Carolina the governor was made chancellor, as in colonial times. In New York and Maryland a separate officer was appointed with that title. In Virginia there were several distinct chancellors. In North Carolina and Georgia the administration both of law and equity was intrusted to the same tribunals. In Pennsylvania a limited chancery power was conferred upon the Supreme Court. In Connecticut the Assembly vested the judicial courts with chancery powers in smaller cases, reserving to itself the decision in matters of more importance. In New England there was such a strong prejudice against chancery practice that for many years there was a restriction to the system of common-law remedies.

Chandler, John, legislator; born in Epping, N. H., in 1760. His business was that of blacksmith, and he became wealthy. With much native talent, he rose to the places of councillor and Senator (1803–5); member of Congress (1805–8); and, in July, 1812, was commissioned a brigadier-general. Wounded and made prisoner in the battle at Stony Creek, in Canada, he was soon afterwards exchanged. From 1820 to 1829 he was United States Senator fom Maine, one of the first appointed from that new State. From 1829 to 1837 he was collector of the port of Portland. He became a major-general of militia, and held several civil local offices. He died in Augusta, Me., Sept. 25, 1841.

Chandler, William Eaton; born in Concord, N. H., Dec. 28, 1835; graduated at the Harvard Law School, and admitted to the bar in 1855; appointed reporter of the New Hampshire Supreme Court in 1859; was a member of the New Hampshire House of Representatives in 1862–1864, being twice elected speaker. In 1865 President Lincoln appointed him judge-advocate-general of the navy, and soon afterwards he was made Assistant Secretary of the Treasury. He resigned in 1867, and began practising law in New Hampshire. During the Presidential campaigns of 1868, 1872, and 1876 he rendered effective work for the Republican party as secretary of the National Republican Committee. After the campaign of 1876 he was active in the investigation of the electoral counting in Florida and South Carolina; and in 1878–79 was an important witness in the cipher despatch investigation. He was appointed solicitor-general of the United States, March 23, 1881, but his nomination was rejected by the Senate; and in 1882–85 was Secretary of the Navy. In 1887, 1889, and 1895 he was elected United States Senator; in 1900 was defeated; in 1901–07 president of the Spanish Treaty Claims Commission.

Chandler, ZACHARIAH, legislator; born in Bedford, N. H., Dec. 10, 1813; settled in Detroit, Mich., in 1833. In 1857 he was elected United States Senator, and held the seat until 1874, when he was appointed Secretary of the Interior; and in 1879 was again elected to the Senate. He was active in the organization of the Republican party; and sent a famous letter to Governor Blair, of Michigan, on Feb. 11, 1861, in which he used the words, "Without a little blood-letting this Union will not, in my estimation, be worth a rush." He died in Chicago, Ill., Nov. 1, 1879.

Channing, EDWARD, historian; born in Dorchester, Mass., June 15, 1856; was graduated at Harvard College in 1878; professor of history there from 1897. His publications include *The United States, 1765–1865; A Student's History of the United States; Town and County Government in the English Colonies of North America; Narragansett Planters; Companions of Columbus,* in Justin Winsor's *Narrative and Critical History of America; Guide to the Study of American History* (with Albert B. Hart); *English History for Americans* (with Thomas W. Higginson); *Narrative and Critical History of America* (with Justin Winsor); *The Planting of a Nation in the New World; A Century of Colonial History,* etc.

Channing, WILLIAM ELLERY, clergyman; born in Newport, R. I., April 7, 1780; graduated at Harvard in 1798. In 1802 he studied theology, and became pastor of the Federal Street Church in Boston, June 1, 1803. All through his laborious life he suffered from ill-health. In 1822 he sought physical improvement by a voyage to Europe, and in 1830 he went to St. Croix,

WILLIAM ELLERY CHANNING

W. I., for the same purpose. With a colleague he occasionally officiated in the pulpit until 1840, when he resigned. In August, 1842, he delivered his last public address at Lenox, Mass., in commemoration of the abolition of slavery in the West Indies. Mr. Channing contributed much towards stimulating anti-slavery feeling. He died in Bennington, Vt., Oct. 2, 1842.

Chantilly, BATTLE OF. On the morning after the second battle at Bull Run Pope was joined at Centreville by the corps of Franklin and Sumner. The next day (Sept. 1, 1862), Lee, not disposed to make a direct attack upon the Nationals, sent Jackson on another flanking movement, the latter taking with him his own and Ewell's division. With instructions to assail and turn Pope's right, he crossed Bull Run at Sudley Ford, and, after a while, turning to the right, turned down the Little River pike, and marched towards Fairfax Court-house. Pope had prepared to meet this movement. Heintzelman and Hooker were ordered to different points, and just before sunset Reno met Jackson's advance (Ewell and Hill) near Chantilly. A cold and drenching rain was falling, but it did not prevent an immediate engagement. Very soon McDowell, Hooker, and Kearny came to Reno's assistance. A very severe battle raged for some time, when Gen. Isaac J. Stevens, leading Reno's second division in person, was shot dead. His command fell back in disorder. Seeing this, Gen. Philip Kearny advanced with his division and renewed the action, sending Birney's brigade to the front. A furious thunderstorm was then raging, which made the use of ammunition very difficult. Unheeding this, Kearny brought forward a battery and planted it in position himself. Then, perceiving a gap caused by the retirement of Stevens's men, he pushed forward to reconnoitre, and was shot dead a little within the Confederate lines, just at sunset, and the command of his division devolved on Birney, who instantly made a bayonet charge with his own brigade of New York troops, led by Colonel Eagan. The Confederates were pushed back some distance. Birney held the field that night, and the broken and demoralized army was withdrawn within the lines at Washington the next day. See KEARNY, PHILIP.

After the battle at Chantilly, the Army of Virginia was merged into the Army of the Potomac, and General Pope returned to service in the West. The loss of Pope's army, from Cedar Mountain to Chantilly, in killed, wounded, prisoners, and missing, was estimated at 30,000. Lee's losses during the same time amounted to about 15,000. He claimed to have taken 7,000 prisoners, with 2,000 sick and wounded, thirty pieces of artillery, and 20,000 small-arms. Of the 91,000 veteran troops from the Peninsula, lying near, Pope reported that only 20,500 men had joined him in confronting Lee.

Chapelle, PLACIDE LOUIS, clergyman; born in Mende, France, Aug. 28, 1842. He came to the United States in 1859; and was graduated at St. Mary's College, and ordained a Roman Catholic priest in 1865. For five years he was a missionary, and from 1870 to 1891 held pastorates in Baltimore and Washington. He was made coadjutor archbishop of Santa Fé in 1891; archbishop in 1894; and archbishop of New Orleans in 1897. In 1898 he was Apostolic Delegate to Cuba, Porto Rico, and the Philippines, and rendered valuable service in the establishment of American civil government. He died in New Orleans, La., Aug. 9, 1905.

Chaplain, originally a clergyman who performed divine service in a chapel, for a prince or nobleman. In the United States one who holds divine service in the army or navy or for any public body.

Chaplin's Hills, BATTLE OF. See PERRYVILLE.

Chapultepec, BATTLE OF. The city of Mexico stands on a slight swell of ground, near the centre of an irregular basin, and encircled by a broad and deep navigable canal. The approaches to the city are over elevated causeways, flanked by ditches. From these the capital is entered by arched gateways; and these, when the victorious Americans approached the city (August, 1847), were strongly fortified. When El Molino del Rey and Casa de Mata had been captured (Sept. 8, 1847), the castle of Chapultepec alone remained as a defence for the city—this and its outworks. The hill, steep and rocky, rises 150 feet above the surrounding country. The castle was built of heavy stone masonry. The whole fortress was 900 feet in length, and the *terreplein* and main buildings 600 feet. The castle was about 100 feet in height, and presented a splendid specimen of military architecture. A dome, rising about 20 feet above the walls, gave it a grand appearance. Two strongly built walls surrounded the whole structure, 10 feet apart and 12 or 15 feet high. The works were thoroughly armed, and the garrison, among whom were some expert French gunners, was commanded by General Bravo. The whole hill was spotted with forts and outworks.

To carry this strong post with the least loss of men, Scott determined to batter it with heavy cannon. Accordingly, on the night of Sept. 11, four batteries of heavy cannon were erected on a hill between Tucabaya and Chapultepec, commanded respectively by Captains Drew, Haynes, and Brooks, and Lieutenant Stone. They were placed in position by the engineer officers Huger and Lee (the latter afterwards commander-in-chief of the Confederate army). On the morning of the 12th these batteries opened fire, every ball crashing through the castle, and every shell tearing up the ramparts. The fire of the Mexicans was not less severe, and this duel of great guns was kept up all day. The next morning

(13th) troops moved to assail the works, at their weakest point, in two columns, one led by General Pillow and the other by General Quitman. Pillow marched to assail the works on the west side, while Quitman made a demonstration on the easterly part. Both columns were preceded by a strong party—that of Pillow by 250 of Worth's division, commanded by Captain McKenzie; and that of Quitman by the same number, commanded by Captain Carey. Each storming party was furnished with scaling-ladders. While the troops were advancing the American batteries kept up a continuous fire over their heads upon the works to prevent reinforcements reaching the Mexicans. Pillow's column bore the brunt of the battle. It first carried a redoubt, and drove the Mexicans from shelter to shelter. At length the ditch and the wall of the main work were reached; the scaling-ladders and fascines were brought up and planted by the storming parties; and the work was soon taken and the American flag unfurled over the ramparts amid prolonged cheers.

CASTLE OF CHAPULTEPEC.

Meanwhile Quitman's column had moved along a causeway, captured two batteries, and joined Pillow's column in time to share in the work of accomplishing a final victory. Together they took the strong castle of Chapultepec, and scattered its defenders in every direction. It was literally torn in pieces; and within, a crowd of prisoners of all grades were seized, among them fifty general officers. There were also 100 cadets of the Military College, the latter "pretty little boys," wrote an American officer, "from ten to sixteen years of age." Several of their little companions had been killed, "fighting like demons." The fugitives fled to the city, along an aqueduct, pursued by General Quitman to the very gates engaged all the way in a running fight, which was sometimes severe. See Lee, Robert Edward; Mexico, War with; Pillow, Gideon Johnson; Quitman, John Anthony; Worth, William Jenkins.

Charles I., King of England; second son of James I.; was born at Dunfermline, Scotland, Nov. 19, 1600. The death of his elder brother, Henry, in 1612, made him heir-apparent to the throne, which he ascended as King in 1625. He sought the hand of the infanta of Spain, but finally married (1625) Henrietta Maria, daughter of Henry IV. of France. She was a Roman Catholic, and had been procured for Charles by the infamous Duke of

Buckingham, whose influence over the young King was disastrous to England and to the monarch himself.

Charles was naturally a good man, but his education, especially concerning the doctrine of the divine right of kings and the sanctity of the royal prerogative, led to an outbreak in England which cost him his life. Civil war began in 1641, and ended with his execution at the beginning of 1649. His reign was at first succeeded by the rule of the "Long Parliament," and then by Cromwell—a half-monarch, called the "Protector." After various vicissitudes during the civil war, Charles was captured, and imprisoned in Carisbrooke Castle, in the Isle of Wight, from whence he was taken to London at the close of 1648. He was brought to trial before a special high court in Westminster Hall on Jan. 20, 1649, on the 27th was condemned to death, and on the 30th was beheaded on a scaffold in front of the banqueting-house at Whitehall.

Charles had eight children by his queen, Henrietta, six of whom survived him. His family was driven into exile; but a little more than eleven years after his death his eldest son, Charles, ascended the throne as King of Great Britain. The son held much more intimate relations, as monarch, with the English-American colonies than the father.

Charles II., King of England; son and successor of Charles I.; born in London, May 29, 1630. His mother was Henrietta

CHARLES II.

Maria, daughter of Henry IV. of France, and sister of the then reigning King of that realm. As the fortunes of his father waned, his mother returned to France, where the son joined her; and, at the Hague, he heard of the death of his parent by the axe, when he assumed the title of King, and was proclaimed such at Edinburgh, Feb. 3, 1649. He was crowned at Scone, Scotland, Jan. 1, 1651. After an unsuccessful warfare with Cromwell for the throne, he fled to Paris; and finally he became a resident of Breda, in Belgium, whence he was called to England by a vote of Parliament, and restored to the

Charles R

throne, May 8, 1660. He was a very profligate monarch—indolent, amiable, and unscrupulous. He misgoverned England twenty-five years in an arbitrary manner, and disgraced the nation. He became a Roman Catholic, although professing to be a Protestant; and, when dying from a stroke of apoplexy, Feb. 6, 1685, he confessed to a Roman Catholic priest, and received extreme unction. The throne descended to his brother James, an avowed Roman Catholic. See JAMES II.

In March, 1663, Charles II. granted to several of his courtiers the vast domain of the Carolinas in America. They were men, most of them past middle life in years, and possessed of the "easy virtues" which distinguished the reign of that profligate monarch. They begged the domain under pretence of a "pious zeal for the propagation of the Gospel among the heathen," while their real object was to rob the "heathen" of these valuable lands, and to accumulate riches and honors for themselves. It is said that when these petitioners appeared before Charles in the gardens at Hampton Court, and presented their memorial so full of pious pretensions, the monarch, after looking each man in the face for a moment, with a merry twinkle in his eyes, burst into loud laughter, in which his audience joined involuntarily. Then taking up a little shaggy spaniel, with large meek eyes, and holding it at arm's-length before them, he said, "Good friends, here is a model of piety and sincerity which it might be wholesome for you to copy." Then, tossing the little pet to Clarendon, he said, "There, Hyde, is a worthy prelate; make him archbishop of the domain I shall give you." With grim satire, Charles introduced into the preamble of their charter that the petitioners, "excited with a laudable and pious zeal for the propagation of the Gospel, have begged a certain country in the parts of America not yet cultivated and planted, and only inhabited by some barbarous people who have no knowledge of God." See NORTH CAROLINA; SOUTH CAROLINA.

Charles City Cross Roads, BATTLE OF. See GLENDALE.

Charleston, commercial metropolis of South Carolina; on a peninsula between the Cooper and Ashley rivers, with an admirable harbor. The city was founded in 1680 by an English colony; was occupied by the British in 1780–82; and was the State capital till 1790. It has been the scene of many stirring and historical events. The Democratic National Convention of 1860 was opened here, and after the split among the delegates an adjourned session was held in Baltimore. It was the birthplace, the same year, of the Secession movement; the first act of hostility to the National Government occurred here (see SUMTER, FORT; BEAUREGARD, PIERRE GUSTAVE TOUTANT); was besieged during the last two years of the war; and was evacuated by the Confederates on Feb. 17, 1865. On Aug. 31, 1886, a large part of the city was destroyed by an earthquake, in which many lives were lost.

In the calendar year 1910 the foreign merchandise trade of the port was: Imports, $5,707,661; exports, $7,494,296. In 1909 the assessed valuation of all taxable property was $18,824,978. The population in 1900 was 55,807; in 1910, 58,833.

History.—Provoked by the attack on St. Augustine by the South Carolinians in 1706, the Spaniards fitted out an expedition to retaliate. It consisted of five vessels of war, under the command of the French Admiral Le Feboure, bearing a large body of troops from Havana. It was proposed to conquer the province of South Carolina and attach it to Spanish territory in Florida. The squadron crossed Charleston Bar (May, 1706), and about 800 troops were landed at different points. Then the commander made a peremptory demand for the surrender of the city, threatening to take it by storm in case of refusal. Governor Moore, apprised of the expedition, was prepared for it. When the flag arrived with the demand for a surrender, he had so disposed the provincial militia and a host of Indian warriors that it gave an exaggerated idea of the strength of the Carolinians. Before the messenger had made any extended observations he was dismissed with the defiant reply that the people were ready to meet the promised attack. That night was passed in quiet; but at dawn a strong party of Carolinians on the shore, led by the governor and Colonel Rhett, made a furious assault upon the invaders; killed many, captured more, and drove the remnant back to their ships. Meanwhile the little provincial navy, lying in the harbor, prepared to attack the invading squadron, when the French admiral, amazed by this display of valor, hoisted his anchors and fled to sea. A French war-ship, uninformed of these events, soon afterwards sailed into the harbor with troops, and was captured. The victory was complete, and the Spaniards became circumspect.

In the Revolutionary War.—In the spring of 1776 a considerable fleet, under Admiral Sir Peter Parker, sailed from England with troops, under Earl Cornwallis, to operate against the coasts of the Southern provinces. This armament joined that of Sir Henry Clinton at Cape Fear. After some marauding operations in that region, the united forces proceeded to Charleston Harbor, to make a combined attack by land and water upon Fort Sullivan, on Sullivan's Island, and then to seize the city and province. The Southern patriots had cheerfully responded to the call of Governor Rutledge to come to the defence of Charleston, and about 6,000 armed men were in the vicinity when the enemy appeared. The city and eligible points near had been fortified. Fort Sullivan was composed of palmetto logs and earth, armed with twenty-six cannon, and garrisoned by about 500 men, chiefly militia, under Col. William Moultrie. It commanded the channel leading to the town. Gen. Charles Lee, who had been ordered by Washington to watch the movements of Clinton, had made his way southward, and arrived at Charleston on June 4, but was of no service whatever. Late in the month Clinton had landed troops on Long Island, which was separated from Sullivan's Island by a shallow creek. There he erected batteries to confront those on Sullivan's Island, and awaited the signal for attack by Parker. It was given on the morning of June 28, and a terrible storm of shot and shell was poured upon the fort, with very little effect, for the spongy palmetto logs would not fracture, and the balls were embedded in them. The conflict raged for almost ten hours between the fort and the fleet, and the latter was terribly shattered.

Meanwhile Clinton had endeavored to pass over to Sullivan's Island with 2,000 men, but was kept back by the determined troops under Colonel Thompson with two cannon and deadly rifles. The fire from the fleet slackened at sunset, and ceased at nine o'clock. The admiral's flag-ship, *Bristol*, and another were nearly a wreck. The flag-ship was pierced by not less than seventy balls. All but two of the vessels (which were destroyed) withdrew. The British lost in the engagement 225 men killed and wounded, while the Americans lost but two killed and twenty-one wounded. Three days afterwards the British all departed for New York; and the fort, so gallantly defended, was called Fort Moultrie in honor of its commander.

Sir Henry Clinton sailed from New York on Christmas Day, 1779, for the purpose of invading South Carolina. He took with him the main body of his army, leaving General Knyphausen in command in New York. The troops were borne by a British fleet, commanded by Admiral Arbuthnot, who had 2,000 marines. They encountered heavy storms off Cape Hatteras, which scattered the fleet. One vessel, laden with heavy battery-cannon, went to the bottom. Another, bearing Hessian troops, was driven across the Atlantic, and dashed on the shore of England. The troops landed on islands below Charleston, and it was late in February before the scattered British forces appeared on St. John's Island, in sight of the wealthy city, containing a population of 15,000 inhabitants, white and black. The city was then defended by less than 2,000 effective troops, under General Lincoln, who cast up intrenchments across Charleston Neck. Commodore Whipple had sunk some of his armed vessels in the channels of the harbor, after transferring the cannon and seamen to the land fortifications. Fort Moultrie was well garrisoned. The invading troops appeared before the defences of Charleston March 29, and the fleet entered the harbor, unmolested, April 9.

On the following day Clinton and Arbuthnot demanded the surrender of the city, which was promptly refused, and a siege began. On the 13th Lincoln and a council of officers considered the propriety of evacuating the city to save it from destruction, for the American troops were too few to hope for a successful defence. It was then too late, for cavalry, sent out to keep open communications with the country, had been dispersed by the British troopers. The arrival of Cornwallis (April 19) with 3,000 fresh troops rendered an evacuation impossible. The siege continued about a month. Fort Moultrie surrendered on May 6, when a third demand for the surrender of the city was made and refused. Late on the succeeding evening a severe cannonade was opened upon it from land and water. All night long the thunder of 200 heavy guns shook the city, and fiery bombshells were rained upon it, setting the town on fire in different places.

At two o'clock on the morning of the 12th Lincoln proposed to yield, and on that day the city and garrison were surrendered, and the latter, as well as the adult citizens, became prisoners of war. The latter were paroled; and by this extraordinary proceeding Clinton could boast of over 5,000 captives. The city was given up to pillage by the British and Hessian troops. When the whole amount of plunder was appraised for distribution, it aggregated in value $1,500,000. Clinton and his major-generals each received about $20,000. Houses were rifled of plate, and slaves were seized, driven on board the ships, and sent to the West Indies to be sold, so as to swell the money-gains of the conquerors. Over 2,000 men and women, without regard to the separation of families, were sent at one embarkation; and only upon the promise of unconditional loyalty to the crown was British protection offered to citizens. In utter violation of the terms of surrender, a large number of the leading men of Charleston were taken from their beds (August) by armed men, and thrust on board filthy prison-ships, under the false accusation of being concerned in a conspiracy to burn the town and murder the loyal inhabitants.

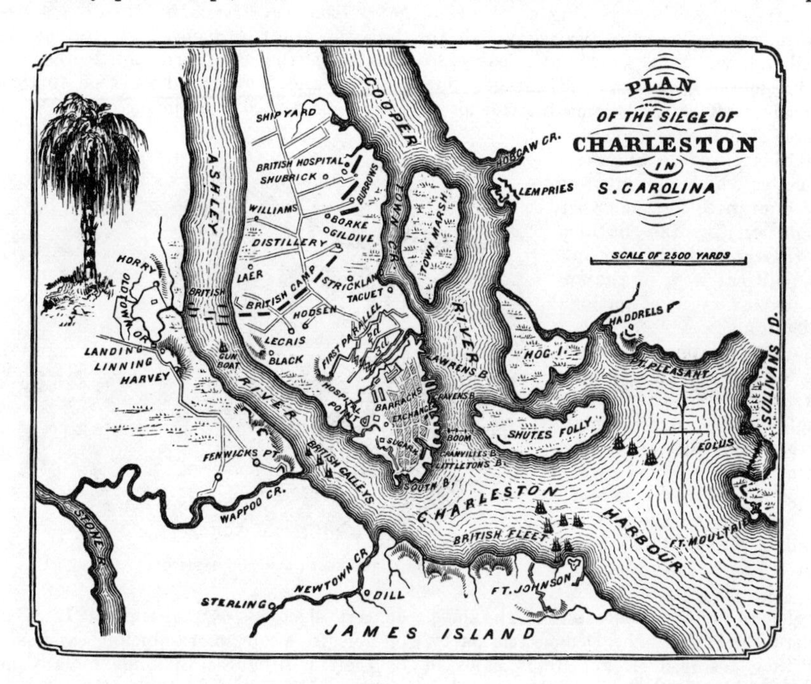

The evacuation of the city took place on Dec. 14, 1782. GEN. ALEXANDER LESLIE (*q. v.*) had levelled the fortifications around the city, and demolished Fort Johnson, on St. John's Island, near by, on the morning of the 13th. The American army slowly approached the city that day, and at dawn the next morning the British marched to Gadsden's wharf and embarked. An American detachment took formal possession of the town. At 3 P.M. General Greene escorted Governor Mathews and other civil officers to the town-hall, the troops greeted on their way by cheers from windows and balconies, and even from house-tops. Handkerchiefs waved, and thousands of voices exclaimed, "God bless you, gentlemen! Welcome! welcome!" Before night the British squadron (about 300 vessels) crossed the bar, and the last sail was seen like a white speck just as the sun went down.

The Democratic Convention.—On April 23, 1860, about 600 representatives of the Democratic party assembled in convention in the hall of the South Carolina Institute in Charleston, and chose CALEB CUSHING (*q. v.*), of Massachusetts, their chairman. From the first hour of the session knowing ones discovered omens of an impending tempest, which might topple from its foundations their political organization. Mr. Cushing's opening address to the convention pleased them. In it he declared it to be the mission of the Democratic party "to reconcile popular freedom with constituted order," and to maintain "the sacred reserved rights of the sovereign States." He charged the Republicans with "laboring to overthrow the Constitution." He declared that the Republicans were aiming to produce "a perpetual sectional conspiracy," which would "hurry the country on to civil war," and that it was "the high and noble part of the Democratic party of the Union to withstand—to strike down and conquer—these banded enemies of the Constitution."

This speech was applauded by all but the extreme pro-slavery wing of the convention, who, it is said, desired rather to "strike down" the Democratic party, to obtain more important advantages for themselves. They had come instructed to demand from the convention a candidate and an avowal of principles which should promise a guarantee for the speedy recognition by the national government and the people, in a political way, of the system of slavery as a national institution.

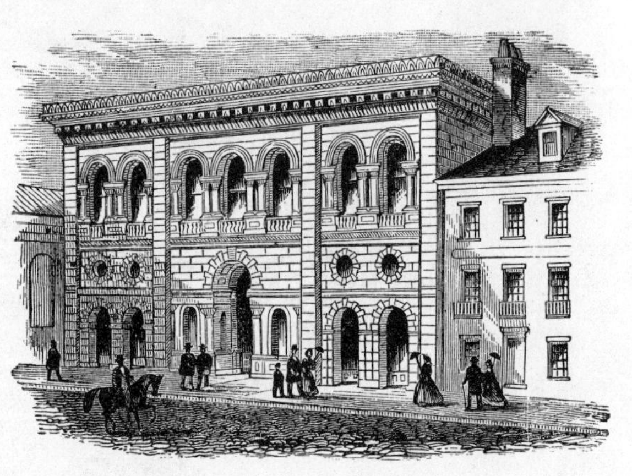

THE SOUTH CAROLINA INSTITUTE.

The most prominent candidate for the Presidency in the convention was Stephen A. Douglas, who was committed to an opposite policy concerning slavery, and whose friends would never vote for the demands of the extreme pro-slavery men. This the latter well knew. They also knew that the rejection of Mr. Douglas by the representatives of the slave-holders would split the Democratic party, and they resolved to act, it is said, in accordance with their convictions. They held the dissevering wedge in their own hands, and they determined to use it with effect. A committee of one delegate from each State was appointed to prepare a platform of principles for the action of the convention. BENJAMIN F. BUTLER (*q. v.*) of Massachusetts, proposed in that committee to adopt the doctrine of the right of the people in any State or Territory to decide whether slavery should or should not exist within its borders. This was rejected by seventeen States (only two of them free-labor States) against fifteen. This was the entering of the dissevering wedge. The majority now offered to accept that doctrine, with an additional resolution declaring that, in the spirit of Judge Taney's opinion (see DRED SCOTT CASE), neither Congress nor any other legislative body had a right to interfere with slavery anywhere, or to impair or destroy the right of property in slaves by any legislation. This was a demand for the Democratic party to recognize slavery as a sacred, permanent, and national institution.

The minority, composed wholly of delegates from the free-labor States, resolved that the limit of concession to the demands of the Southern politicians was reached, and they would yield no further. They represented a majority of the Presidential electors—172 against 127. They offered to adopt a resolution expressive of their willingness to abide by any decision of the Supreme Court of the United States. To this concession Butler objected, and three reports from the committee went into the convention—a majority and a minority report, and one from Mr. Butler. A warm debate ensued, and Avery, from North Carolina, declared that the doctrine of popular sovereignty—the authority of the people concerning slavery—was as dangerous as that of congressional interference with the institution. The debate continued until the 29th, and the next morning a vote was taken.

The minority report, in favor of popular sovereignty, was adopted by a decided majority, when Walker, of Alabama, afterwards the Confederate Secretary of War, announced that the delegates from his State would secede from the convention. The movement was preconcerted.

This delegation was followed by those of other slave-labor States, and the seceders assembled in St. Andrew's Hall, to prepare for an independent political organization. The disruption of the Democratic party, as represented in the convention, was now complete. When D. C. Glenn, of Mississippi, announced the secession of the delegation from his State, he said: "I tell Southern members, and for them I tell the North, that in less than sixty days you will find a united South standing side by side with us."

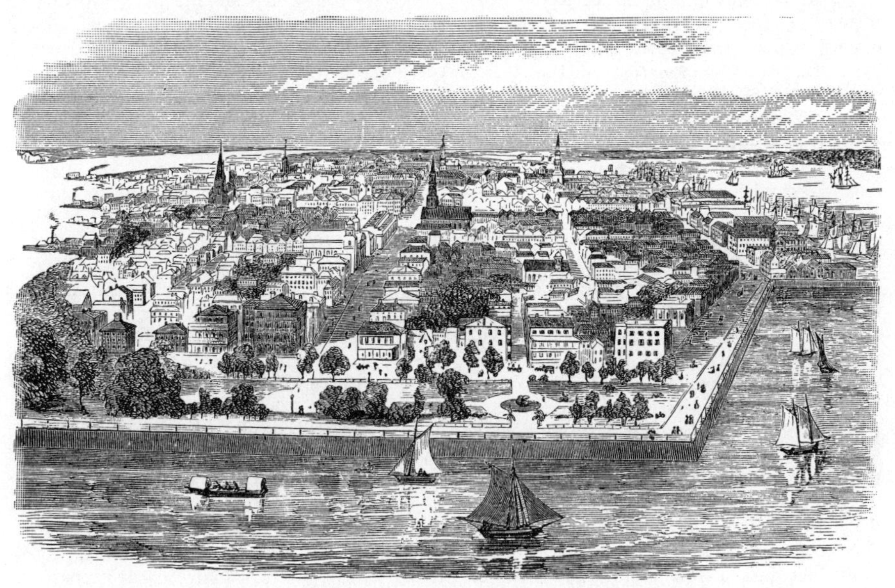

CHARLESTON DURING THE CIVIL WAR.

There was great rejoicing in Charleston that night because of this secession, for the politicians were aware that the scheme for disunion was ripe for execution. The seceders organized a "Constitutional Convention," with James A. Bayard, of Delaware, as chairman. They called the body they had left the "Rump Convention." On May 3 they adjourned, to meet in Richmond, Va., in June. The regular convention also adjourned, to meet in Baltimore June 18. See BALTIMORE.

In the Civil War.—Although Charleston had become a comparatively unimportant point in the grand theatre of war at the beginning of 1863, its possession was coveted by the national government because of the salutary moral effect which such a conquest would produce. A strong effort to accomplish that end was made in the spring of 1863. On April 6 Admiral Dupont crossed Charleston Bar with nine "monitors," or turreted iron vessels, leaving five gunboats outside as a reserve, and proceeded to attack FORT SUMTER (*q. v.*)—the most formidable object in the way to the city. At the same time, a land force near at hand, 4,000 strong, under Gen. Truman Seymour, took a masked position on Folly Island, ready to coöperate, if necessary. The military works that defended Charleston were numerous and formidable. Between Forts Sumter and Moultrie the sea was strewn with torpedoes, and there were other formidable obstructions. On Morris Island, abreast of Fort Sumter, was a strong work, called Fort Wagner. Dupont's squadron lay quietly within the bar until noon of April 7, when it advanced directly upon Sumter, intending not to reply to any attack from Fort Wagner. The *Weehawken* led. Dupont was ignorant of the torpedoes, but the discovery of these soon explained the ominous silence of Sumter and Fort Wagner as he advanced. Suddenly, when the *Weehawken* had become entangled in a net-work of cables, the barbette guns of Sumter opened upon her with plunging shot. Then the other "monsters of the deep" commanded by Dupont came forward and delivered tremendous discharges of heavy metal on Sumter, and at the same time that fortress, Fort Wagner, and other batteries, with an aggregate of nearly 300 guns, poured heavy shot and shell upon the squadron—then within the focus of their concentric fire—at the rate of 160 a minute. A greater portion of these missiles glanced off harmlessly from the mailed "monitors." The weaker *Keokuk* was nearly destroyed; all of the other vessels were more or less injured. The flag-ship was in peril, and Fort Sumter was but slightly hurt, when Dupont, after a terrible fight of forty minutes, signalled the squadron to withdraw. In that time it was estimated that the Confederates fired 3,500 shells and shots. The attack was a failure, but not a disaster. Dupont lost but a few men, and only one vessel.

Second Attack on Fort Sumter.— It was now seen that a land force on Morris Island to keep Fort Wagner employed was necessary to secure a successful attack on Sumter. After this attack Dupont watched the Confederates on Morris Island, and did not allow them to erect any more works on it. Gen. Quincy A. Gillmore was assigned to the command of the Department of the South June 2, 1863. The government determined to renew the attack on Fort Sumter by a land and naval force. Gillmore was at the head of 18,000 men, with a generous supply of great guns, small-arms, and ordnance stores. He determined to seize Morris Island preliminary to an attack on Sumter and Charleston. That island and the military works in his possession, he might batter down Fort Sumter from Fort Wagner, with the aid of the navy, and lay Charleston in ashes by firing shells, if it should not be surrendered.

As Dupont did not approve this plan, Admiral Dahlgren took his place in July. Gillmore had batteries constructed, under the direction of General Vogdes, on the northern end of Folly Island. This work was completely masked by a pine forest. When all was in readiness, Gen. Alfred H. Terry was sent, with nearly 4,000 troops, up the Stono River, to make a demonstration against James Island to mask Gillmore's real intentions, and Col. T. W. Higginson, with some negro troops, went up the Edisto to cut the railway communication between Charleston and Savannah.

Thirty hours after Terry's departure Gen. George C. Strong silently embarked 2,000 men in small boats and crossed over to Morris Island before dawn (July 13), unsuspected by the Confederates. At that hour Vogdes's masked batteries opened a tremendous cannonade, and Dahlgren's four "monitors," at tne same time, opened a cross-fire upon the Confederates, who saw the amazing apparition of a strong National force ready to attack them. After a sharp battle, Strong gained possession of the powerful Confederate works on the southern end of Morris Island, with eleven guns. The occupants were driven away, and took shelter in Fort Wagner, the garrison of which had been kept quiet by Dahlgren's guns.

BOMB AND SPLINTER PROOF, FORT WAGNER.

Meanwhile, Terry had fought and repulsed Confederate assailants at Secessionville, on James Island, in which he lost about 100 men, and his adversary 200.

He then hastened to Morris Island to join in the attack on Fort Wagner. Five batteries were speedily erected across the island to confront Wagner, and at noon (July 13) Gillmore opened a bombardment of that fort. Dahlgren, at the same time, moved his "monitors" nearer to it, and poured a continuous stream of shells upon it. From noon until sunset 100 guns were continually assailing the fort, which replied with only two guns at long intervals.

When night fell, a tremendous thunderstorm swept over the harbor and the islands, when General Strong, with a heavy assaulting party, moved upon the fort. It was composed of a Massachusetts regiment of colored troops, under Col. R. G. Shaw, and one regiment each from Connecticut, New Hampshire, New York, and Pennsylvania. The storming party advanced against a shower of shot and shell from Wagner, Sumter, and Battery Gregg.

When at the fort they were met by a furious tempest of musketry, while howitzers swept the ditch where the assailants were crossing. Hand-grenades were also thrown upon the Unionists. Colonel Shaw was shot dead, and fell among the slain of his dusky followers. General Strong, and also Colonel Chatfield, of the Connecticut regiment, were mortally wounded. The Nationals were repulsed, when another brigade pushed forward to the assault, led by Col. H. L. Putnam. It was composed of Ohio and New York troops. Some of Putnam's men actually got into the fort, but were expelled. Finally their leader was killed, and the second storming party was repulsed. The loss on the part of the Nationals was fearful. The Confederates said they buried 600 of them in front of the fort. Among the bodies of the slain so buried was that of Colonel Shaw, who was cast into a trench, and upon it were piled those of his slain colored troops. He was hated by the Confederates because he commanded negro troops.

Siege of Fort Sumter.—Gillmore now abandoned the idea of assaults, and began a regular siege. He planted batteries of heavy siege and breaching guns at different points, and mounted a 200-pounder Parrott gun upon a battery constructed of timber in a marsh between Morris and James islands, which might hurl shell upon the city, or, at least, upon the shipping and wharves of Charleston. This gun was named "The Swamp Angel." It was about 5 miles from Charleston. On the morning of Aug. 17 Gillmore, having completed his arrangements for attack, opened the guns from twelve batteries and from Dahlgren's naval force on Forts Sumter and Wagner and Battery Gregg. Fort Sumter, 2 miles distant, was the chief object of attack—to make it powerless as an assistant of Fort Wagner. This was continued until the 24th, when Gillmore telegraphed to Washington, "Fort Sumter is to-day a shapeless and harmless mass of ruins." "The Swamp Angel" sent some 150-℔. shells that fell in Charleston—one penetrating St. Michael's Church—and greatly alarmed the people.

On the fall of Sumter, the attack centred on Fort Wagner; and at two o'clock on the morning of Sept. 7 General Terry, with 3,000 troops, in three columns, was about to advance to assail that strong fortification, when it was found that the Confederates had evacuated it and Battery Gregg before midnight. During forty hours no less than 120,000 pounds of iron had been rained upon the fort. Dahlgren, believing the channel to be strewn with torpedoes, did not venture to pass the silent forts with his vessels and appear before Charleston.

Indeed, Sumter was not dead, but slumbering. On the night of Sept. 8 a portion of the men of the squadron went in thirty row-boats to take possession of Sumter. They scaled the ruins, where, as they supposed, the decimated garrison were sleeping, but were met by determined men, and repulsed. They were assailed not only by the garrison, but by neighboring batteries, a gunboat, and a "ram," and lost 200 men, four boats, and three colors.

Finally, on Oct. 26, perceiving the garrison mounting cannon on the southeast face of Sumter, to command Fort Wagner, Gillmore opened heavy rifled cannon on the former, which soon reduced it to an utterly untenable ruin. From that time until near the close of the year Gillmore kept up an irregular fire on Charleston, when, seeing no prospect of the fleet entering the harbor, he kept silent.

When Hardee, in command of the Confederate troops at Charleston, heard of the fall of COLUMBIA (*q. v.*), he perceived the necessity for his immediate flight by the only railway then left open for his use, and of endeavoring to join Beauregard, with the remnant of Hood's army, then making their way into North Carolina, where Johnston was gathering all of his available forces in Sherman's path. Hardee at once fired every building, warehouse, or shed in Charleston stored with cotton, and destroyed as much other property that might be useful to the Nationals as possible. The few remaining inhabitants of the city were filled with consternation, for the flames spread through the town. An explosion of gunpowder shook the city to its foundations and killed fully 200 persons. Four whole squares of buildings were consumed.

That night (Feb. 17, 1865) the last of Hardee's troops left Charleston. On the following morning Major Hennessey, sent from Morris Island, raised the National flag over ruined Fort Sumter. The mayor surrendered the city, and some National troops, with negroes in Charleston, soon extinguished the flames that threatened to devour the whole town. On that day (Feb. 18, 1865) the city of Charleston was "repossessed" by the national government, with over 450 pieces of artillery, a large amount of gunpowder, and eight locomotives and other rolling-stock of a railway. General Gillmore took possession of the city, and appointed Lieut.-Col. Stewart L. Woodford military governor.

Charlestown, a former city and seaport in Middlesex county, Mass.; settled June 4, 1629; boundary between it and Boston established July 8, 1635; burned by the British on the day of the battle of Bunker Hill, June 17, 1775; given a city charter in 1847; annexed to Boston Oct. 7, 1873.

Charlestown, a town in West Virginia, where on Dec. 2, 1859, John Brown was hanged, and on the 16th, Green, Copeland, Cook, and Coppo, and on March 16, 1860, Stephens and Hazlett. See BROWN, JOHN.

Charlevoix, PIERRE FRANCOIS XAVIER DE, traveller; born in Saint-Quentin, France, Oct. 29, 1682. He was sent as a Jesuit missionary to Quebec in 1705; later returned to France; and in 1720 again went to Canada. On his second visit he ascended the St.Lawrence River; travelled through Illinois; and sailed down the Mississippi to New Orleans; and returned to France in 1722. His publications include *Histoire de la Nouvelle France.* He died in La Fleche, France, Feb. 1, 1761. See JESUIT MISSIONS.

Charlotte, city and capital of Mecklenburg county, N. C.; the center of the Southern cotton mill industry, having 100 mills within a radius of 200 miles. The Mecklenburg Declaration of Independence was adopted here in 1775, and the place was occupied by the British in 1780. Pop. (1910), 34,014. See DECLARATION OF INDEPENDENCE, MECKLENBURG.

Charter Oak, THE, a famous oak-tree that stood upon the northern slope of the Wyllys Hill, in Hartford. The trunk was 25 feet in circumference near the roots. A large cavity, about two feet from the ground, was the place of concealment of the original charter of Connecticut from the summer of 1687 until the spring of 1689, when it was brought forth, and under it Connecticut resumed its charter government.

This tree was blown down by a heavy gale on Aug. 21, 1856. The Wyllys Hill has been graded to a terrace, called Charter Oak Place, fronting on old Charter Oak Street, running east from Main Street, and now called Charter Oak Avenue. On the terrace, a few feet from the entrance to Charter Oak Place, a white-marble slab marks the exact spot where the famous tree stood.

THE CHARTER OAK.

Charters, granted to corporate towns to protect their manufactures by Henry I. in 1132; modified by Charles II. in 1683; the ancient charters restored in 1698. Alterations were made by the Municipal Reform act in 1835. Ancient Anglo-Saxon charters are printed in Kemble's *Codex Diplomaticus,* 1829. For colonial charters in the United States, see different State articles.

Chase, ANN, patriot; born in Ireland, in 1809; came to the United States in 1818; settled in New Orleans in 1832, and in Tampico, Mexico, in 1833, where she married Franklin Chase, United States consul, in 1836. During the war with Mexico she held possession of the consulate, in the absence of her husband, to protect the American records. A mob attempted to remove the American flag which floated over the consulate, but she protected it with drawn revolver, exclaiming that her flag would not be touched except over her dead body. Later, through her efforts, the city of Tampico was captured without the loss of life or treasure. She died in Brooklyn, N. Y., Dec. 24, 1874.

Chase, SALMON PORTLAND, statesman; born in Cornish, N. H., Jan. 13, 1808. When twelve years of age he was placed in charge of his uncle, Bishop Chase, in Ohio, who superintended his tuition. He entered Cincinnati College; and after a year there returned to New Hampshire and entered Dartmouth College, where he graduated in 1826. He taught school and studied law in Washington, D. C., and was admitted to the bar there in 1829. The next year he went to Cincinnati to practise, where he became eminent. He prepared an edition of the *Statutes of Ohio,* with copious notes, which soon superseded all others. In 1834 he became solicitor of the Bank of the United States in Cincinnati. Acting as counsel for a colored woman who was claimed as a slave (1837), he controverted the authority of Congress to impose any duties or confer any powers, in fugitive-slave cases, on State magistrates. The same year, in his defence of J. G. BIRNEY (*q. v.*), prosecuted under a State law for harboring a fugitive slave, Mr. Chase asserted the doctrine that slavery was local, and dependent upon State law for existence, and that the alleged slave, being in Ohio, where slavery did not exist, was free. From that time he was regarded as the great legal champion of the principles of the anti-slavery party.

He entered the political field in 1841, on organizing the LIBERTY PARTY (*q. v.*) in

SALMON PORTLAND CHASE.

Ohio, and was ever afterwards active in its conventions, as well as in the ranks of the opposers of slavery. The Democrats of the Ohio legislature elected him (1849) to a seat in the United States Senate, where he opposed the Fugitive Slave Bill and other compromise measures, and, on the nomination of Mr. Pierce for the Presidency, he separated from the Democratic party. He opposed the KANSAS-NEBRASKA BILL (*q. v.*), and in 1855 was elected governor of Ohio.

He was one of the founders of the Republican party in 1856, and was governor until 1859. In 1861 he became Secretary of the Treasury of the United States, under President Lincoln, and managed the finances of the nation with great ability until October, 1864, when he was appointed Chief-Justice of the United States in place of Judge Taney, deceased. In that capacity he presided at the trial of President Johnson in the spring of 1868. Being dissatisfied with the action of the Republican majority in Congress, Mr. Chase was proposed, in 1868, as the Democratic nominee for President. He was willing to accept the nomination, but received only four out of 663 votes in the convention.

He then withdrew from the political field, but in 1872 he opposed the re-election of General Grant to the Presidency. He died in New York City, May 7, 1873.

Chase, SAMUEL, jurist; born in Somerset county, Md., April 17, 1741; admitted to the bar in 1761; entered on practice at Annapolis, and soon rose to distinction. He was twenty years a member of the colonial legislature; was a strong opposer of the Stamp Act; a member of the Committee of Correspondence; and a delegate to the Continental Congress (1774–79). In 1776 he was a fellow-commissioner of Franklin and Carroll to seek an alliance with the Canadians, and was efficient in changing the sentiments of Maryland in favor of independence, so as to authorize him and his colleagues to vote for the Declaration, which he signed. In 1783 Mr. Chase was sent to England, as agent for Maryland, to redeem a large sum of money intrusted to the Bank of England, $650,000 of which was finally recovered. From 1791 to 1796 he was chief-justice of his State, and was a warm supporter of the administrations of Washington and Adams.

In the session of Congress in the early part of 1804, it was determined by the leaders of the dominant, or Democratic, party to impeach Judge Chase, then associate-justice of the Supreme Court of the United States. He was an ardent Federalist, and warmly attached to the principles of Washington's administration. At the instance of John Randolph, of Virginia, Democratic leader of the House of Representatives, he was impeached for his conduct during the trial of Callender and Fries, solely on political grounds. Eight articles of impeachment were agreed to, most of them by a strict party vote. One was founded on his conduct at the trial of Fries (see FRIES), five on the trial of Callender (see CALLENDER, J. T.), and two on a late charge to a Maryland grand jury. Having been summoned by the Senate to appear for trial, he did so (Jan. 2, 1805), and asked for a delay until the next session. The boon was refused, and he was given a month to prepare for trial. His case excited much sympathy and indignation, even among the better members of the administration party. His age, his Revolutionary services, and his pure judicial character all pleaded in his favor, and not in vain, for he was acquitted. He died June 19, 1811.

Chastellux, FRANÇOIS JEAN, CHEVALIER DE, historian; born in Paris, France, in 1734; served in the American Revolution under Rochambeau as a major-general. His amiability gained him the friendship of Washington. He was the author of *Voyage dans l'Amérique septentrionale dans les années 1780–82*, etc. He also translated into French Humphrey's *Address to the Army of the United States.* He died in Paris, Oct. 28, 1788.

Chateaugay, N. Y., BATTLE OF, Oct. 26, 1813. Gen. Wade Hampton, with 3,500 men, while guarding the ford on the Chateaugay River, was attacked by the British under De Salaberry with a thousand men. By a clever stratagem, Salaberry led Hampton to believe himself surrounded. He immediately ordered a retreat, and was followed by the Canadian militia. The whole affair was a disgrace to the American arms. The Americans lost fifteen killed and twenty-three wounded, while the British had five killed, sixteen wounded, and four missing. See CHRYSLER'S FIELD, BATTLE OF.

Chatham, EARL OF. See PITT, WILLIAM.

Chatham Island, one of the Galapagos Archipelago, in the Pacific Ocean, 600 miles west of Ecuador, to which it belongs. It is of volcanic origin, the fifth in size of the Galapagos. It has several times been the subject of negotiation between the United States and Ecuador, the former desiring it as a coaling station and as a protection for the Panama Canal. The United States renewed negotiations for the purchase of the group in 1910, but the Ecuador government refused consent.

Chattahoochee, PASSAGE OF THE. On July 3, 1864, General Johnston's Confederate army passed through Marietta, Ga., closely followed by Sherman with the National army, who hoped to strike his antagonist a heavy blow while he was crossing that stream. By quick and skilful movements, Johnston passed the Chattahoochee without much molestation and made a stand behind intrenchments on its left bank. Again Sherman made a successful flanking movement. Howard laid a pontoon bridge 2 miles above the ferry where the Confederates crossed. Demonstrations by the rest of the Nationals made Johnston abandon his position and retreat to another that covered Atlanta. The left of the Confederates rested on the Chattahoochee, and their right on Peach-tree Creek. There the two armies rested some time. On July 10, or sixty-five days after Sherman put his army in motion southward, he was master of the country north and west of the river on the banks of which he was reposing—nearly one-half of Georgia—and had accomplished the chief object of his campaign—namely, the advancement of the National lines from the Tennessee to the Chattahoochee.

Chattanooga, city and capital of Hamilton county, Tenn.; on the Tennessee River, with railroad and steamship communications with all Southern ports; is situated on high grounds, at the foot of Lookout Mountain, and in the midst of picturesque scenery. It is the site of a National Soldiers' Cemetery, with over 13,000 graves, and the Chickamauga and Chattanooga National Park. Pop. (1900) 32,490; (1910) 44,604.

History.—Chattanooga was settled in 1836, and was originally called Ross's Landing. It was incorporated in 1851, and in 1863 was occupied and nearly destroyed by the Union forces. It was the scene of three of the greatest battles of the Civil War: Chickamauga, Missionary Ridge, and Lookout Mountain.

In 1863 the Army of the Cumberland, under Rosecrans, after crossing the Cumberland Mountains in pursuit of the Confederates under Bragg, was stretched along the Tennessee River from a point above Chattanooga 100 miles westward. Rosecrans determined to cross that stream at different points, and, closing around Chattanooga, attempted to crush or starve the Confederate army there. General Hazen was near Harrison's, above Chattanooga (Aug. 20). He had made slow marches, displaying camp-fires at different points, and causing the fifteen regiments of his command to appear like the advance of an immense army.

On the morning of Aug. 21, National artillery under Wilder, planted on the mountain-side across the river, opposite Chattanooga, sent screaming shells over that town and among Bragg's troops. The latter was startled by a sense of immediate danger; and when, soon afterwards, Generals Thomas and McCook crossed the Tennessee with their corps and took possession of the passes of Lookout Mountain on Bragg's flank, and Crittenden took post at Wauhatchie, in Lookout Valley, nearer the river, the Confederates abandoned Chattanooga, passed through the gaps of Missionary Ridge, and encamped on Chickamauga Creek, near Lafayette in northern Georgia, there to meet expected National forces when pressing through the gaps of Lookout Mountain and threatening their communications with Dalton and Resaca. From the lofty summit of Lookout Mountain Crittenden had seen the retreat of Bragg. He immediately led his forces into the Chattanooga Valley and encamped at Ross's Gap, in Missionary Ridge, within three miles of the town. See CHICKAMAUGA, BATTLE OF; CHICKAMAUGA AND CHATTANOOGA NATIONAL PARK.

Chattanooga Campaign. The campaign of Chattanooga, following closely that of CHICKAMAUGA (*q. v.*), may properly be termed a continuation of it, with a change of commanders, a new formation of the army corps, and an increase of the army by reinforcements. The following is a chronological narrative of this famous campaign:

Immediately after the battle of Chickamauga the Army of the Cumberland falls back to Chattanooga ....21–22 Sept. 1863

[The Confederate army follows at once, and occupies the strong positions of Missionary Ridge and Lookout Mountain. Chattanooga is thus practically invested, the Federal army having but one route whereby it can obtain its supplies, and that over the Cumberland mountains by an obscure wagon road maintained with difficulty.]

The 11th and 12 Corps, under command of Maj.-Gen. Hooker, ordered from the Army of the Potomac to aid the Army of the Cumberland ....23 Sept. "

Maj.-Gen. Grant is placed in command of the military division of the Mississippi, including the armies and departments of the Tennessee, Cumberland, and the Ohio. Maj.-Gen. Rosecrans is relieved of command of the Army of the Cumberland, and Maj.-Gen. George

H. Thomas placed in command by general order No. 337, War Dept. ....16 Oct. 1863

This order relieving Gen. Rosecrans left optional with Gen. Grant. Gen. Rosecrans is relieved. 19 Oct. "

Gen. Grant reaching Chattanooga takes command ....23 Oct. "

He orders Gen. Sherman at once from Corinth, Miss., to Chattanooga ....24 Oct. "

Gen. Hooker, now at Bridgeport, Ala., with the 11th and 12th corps, is ordered to cross the Tennessee at that place and reach the Wauhatchie Valley by.........27 Oct. "

To support this movement and open another route for supplies, Gen. Grant decides on a pontoon bridge across the Tennessee at Brown's Ferry, a few miles below Chattanooga. It is placed by Brig.-Gen. W. F. Smith on the night of 27 Oct. "

On the morning of the 28th a sufficient force has passed over and intrenched to hold the position. During the day Gen. Hooker moves down the Wauhatchie Valley to within a mile of the United States force at Brown's ferry. The Confederates, watching Hooker's advance from Lookout Mountain, plan a night attack on him. It begins about 1 A.M., and at 4 they retire, repulsed. This battle is known as that of Wauhatchie. Gen. Hooker loses nearly 500 killed and wounded. This occupation of the Wauhatchie Valley opens an excellent route for supplies, removing all danger of famine, and prepares the way for Gen. Sherman's advance from Bridgeport. Grant, before further attack on the besieging forces, awaits Sherman, who is hastening from Corinth, while Bragg detaches from his army some 16,000 men under Longstreet to move against Burnside, at Knoxville, 4 Nov. Sherman's advance arrives at Bridgeport, 13 Nov., but as the position assigned his command on the extreme left necessitates moving his forces above Chattanooga, they are not in position with facilities for crossing the Tennessee until the afternoon of ....23 Nov "

Gen. Thomas advances his centre and occupies "Orchard Knob," a slight eminence midway between the defences of Chattanooga and the foot of Missionary Ridge ......23 Nov. "

To cover Sherman's crossing, Grant orders Gen. Hooker, 24 Nov., to make a diversion by attacking the Confederates on the slope of Lookout Mountain towards the Wauhatchie Valley. Gen. Hooker, with about 10,000 men, by 4 o'clock P.M. has driven the Confederates from the Wauhatchie Valley around the slope of Lookout Mountain into the Chattanooga Valley, and connected with Gen. Thomas in Chattanooga on his left. This is called the battle of Lookout Mountain. Gen. Sherman crosses the Tennessee and intrenches on the morning of ....24 Nov. 1863

Battle of Chattanooga or Missionary Ridge the decisive battle of the campaign ....25 Nov. "

Gen. Sherman is ordered to turn the Confederate right at the extreme north end of Missionary Ridge. at early dawn, Nov. 5, he attacks the strong position of the Confederates, but up to 3 P.M. has made no decided advance. Gen. Hooker meanwhile advances from the foot of Lookout Mountain towards Rossville against the Confederate left. Up to 3 P.M. the Confederate line on the ridge remains intact, when Gen. Thomas advances the division of Baird, of the 14th Corps, and Wood's, Sheridan's, and Johnson's, of the 4th Corps, on the Confederate centre occupying the heights of the ridge, well defended by rifle-pits at the foot and on the slope. The intrenchments at the foot of the ridge are carried, and the troops continue, without orders, to ascend and carry the heights, breaking the Confederate centre. The pursuit ceases because of darkness. The Confederate loss is over 9,000 (of which 6,000 are prisoners), 40 pieces of artillery, and 7,000 stands of small-arms. The Federal loss is between 5,000 and 6.000. Gen. Grant detaches Gen. Sherman's command with the 4th Corps of the Army of the Cumberland to relieve KNOXVILLE (*q. v.*) ....28 Nov. "

[Gen. Bragg was beaten by his inaction, and by detaching Longstreet's command in the midst of an aggressive movement of the Federals. The Federal forces in the final battle were about 65,000; the Confederates about 45,000 (in a position almost impregnable)].

Chauncey, ISAAC, naval officer; born in Black Rock, Conn., Feb. 20, 1772; in early life was in the merchant service, and commanded a ship at the age of nineteen years. He made several voyages to the East Indies in the ships of John Jacob Astor. In 1798 he was made a lieutenant of the navy, and was acting captain of the *Chesapeake* in 1802. He became master in May, 1804, and captain in 1806. During the War of 1812–15 he was in command of the American naval force on Lake Ontario, where he performed efficient service. After that war he commanded the Mediterranean squadron, and, with Consul Shaler, negotiated a treaty with Algiers. In 1820 he was naval commissioner in Washington, D. C., and again from 1833 until his death, in that city, Jan. 27, 1840. Commodore Chauncey's remains were interred in the Congressional Cemetery in Washington, and at the head of his grave stands a fine white-marble monument, suitably inscribed.

ISAAC CHAUNCEY.

Chautauqua System of Education, an enterprise established in 1878 at Chautauqua, N. Y., in connection with the Chautauqua Assembly, which had been organized in 1874, by the joint efforts of Lewis Miller and the Rev. John H. Vincent, for the purpose of holding annual courses of instruction in languages, science, literature, etc., at Chautauqua, in July and August annually. The aim of the Chautauqua Literary and Scientific Circle, organized in 1878, is to continue the work of the assembly throughout the year in all parts of the country. Since that year more than 260,000 students have enrolled their names for the various courses. The circle aims to promote habits of reading and study in literature, history, art, and science, without interfering with the regular routine of life. The complete course covers four years, and aims to give "the college outlook" on life and the world. The books for study include specified works approved by the counsellors; a membership book, with review outlines; a monthly magazine, with additional readings and notes; and other aids. Local circles can be formed with three or four members. One hour each day for nine months is the time annually required. All who complete the course receive certificates, and in case any have pursued collateral and advanced reading seals are affixed to the certificate.

Chauvin Grant. In 1600, Henry IV., King of France, granted a royal monopoly of the fur trade in Canada to his friends Chauvin and Pierre du Guast, both Calvinists, and François Grave, the Sieur du Pont, commonly called Pontgrave.

CHAUNCEY'S MONUMENT.

Cheatham, Benjamin Franklin, military officer; born in Nashville, Tenn., Oct. 20, 1820. He entered the Mexican War as captain in the 1st Tennessee Regiment; distinguished himself in the battles of Monterey, Medelin, and Cerro Gordo, and became colonel of the 3d Tennessee Regiment. At the conclusion of the war he was appointed major-general of the Tennessee militia. When the Civil War broke out he organized the whole supply department for the Western Army of the Confederacy—a work in which he was employed when he was appointed brigadier-general (September, 1861). He participated in the battles of Belmont and Shiloh and accompanied Bragg on his expedition into Kentucky in September, 1862. Later he was promoted to major-general, and was engaged at Chickamauga, Chattanooga, Nashville, and other places. After the war he applied himself chiefly to agriculture. In October, 1885, he was made postmaster of Nashville. He died in Nashville, Sept. 4, 1886.

Cheat River, Battle of. See Carricksford, Battle of.

Checkley, John. One of the most dramatic incidents in the long-drawn-out struggle between Puritans and Anglicans in New England was the libel case of John Checkley, an Anglican bookseller in Boston, who in 1724 was tried by the superior court of Masachusetts, convicted of seditious libel, and sentenced to pay a heavy fine for an argumentative publication asserting the exclusive Episcopal authority as against Congregational ordination. This seems to have been the last attempt to check dissenting publications by legal process.

Checks and Balances, the equilibrium which should be established between the different powers of the State by means of the constitutional definition of their rights and limitations, for the purpose of conducting different affairs properly and preserving the liberty of the citizens.

Cheese. See Dairy Industry.

Cheeshahteaumuck, Caleb, Indian; born in Massachusetts in 1646; graduated at Harvard College in 1665, being the only Indian who received a degree from that institution. He died in Charlestown, Mass., in 1666.

Cheever, George Barrell, clergyman; born in Hallowell, Me., April 17, 1807; was editor of the New York *Evangelist* from 1845 to 1846, and at different times connected with the New York *Observer* and *Independent*. Among his publications are: *God's Hand in America; Poets of America; God Against Slavery, and the Freedom and Duty of the Pulpit to Rebuke It*. He died in Englewood, N. J., Oct. 1, 1890.

Chemung, a village and town in the county and on a river of the same name, N. Y.; 13 miles southeast of Elmira. Here, on Aug. 29, 1779, a force of Tories under Sir John Johnson, and of Indians under Brant, attacked General Sullivan while on a march, but were defeated with considerable loss.

Cheney, Charles Edward, clergyman; born in Canandaigua, N. Y., Feb. 12, 1836; ordained in the Protestant Episcopal Church in 1858. Becoming rector of Christ Church, Chicago, he incurred censure for heterodoxy and was tried on that charge and deposed from the priesthood. He at once became a leader in the Reformed Episcopal movement, and was consecrated bishop of the new denomination in 1873, a post he held in connection with the rectorship of Christ Church. His publications include *What Do Reformed Episcopalians Believe?*

Cheney, Theseus Apoleon, historian; born in Leon, N. Y., March 16, 1830; educated at Oberlin. When the Republican party was forming he suggested its name in an address at Conewango, N. Y., Aug. 20, 1854. His publications include *Report on the Ancient Monuments of Western New York; Historical Sketch of Chemung Valley; Historical Sketch of Eighteen Counties of Central and Southern New York; Relations of Government to Science;* and *Antiquarian Researches*. He died in Starkey, N. Y., Aug. 2, 1878.

Cherokee Indians, a nation formerly inhabiting the hilly regions of Georgia, western Carolina, and northern Alabama, and called the Mountaineers of the South. They were among high hills and fertile valleys, and have ever been more susceptible of civilization than any of the other Indian tribes within the domain of the United States. They were the determined foes of the Shawnees, and, after many conflicts, drove those fugitives back to the

Ohio. They united with the Carolinians and Catawbas against the Tuscaroras in 1711, but joined the great Indian league against the Carolinians in 1715.

When, early in 1721, Gov. Francis Nicholson arrived in South Carolina, he tried to cultivate the good-will of the Spaniards and Indians in Florida. He held a conference with the chiefs of the Cherokees. He gave them presents, and marked the boundaries of the lands between them and the English settlers. He then concluded a treaty of commerce and peace with the Creeks.

About 1730 the projects of the French for uniting Canada and Louisiana by a cordon of posts through the Ohio and Mississippi valleys began to be developed. To counteract this scheme, the British wished to convert the Indians on the frontiers into allies or subjects. The British government accordingly sent out Sir Alexander Cumming to conclude a treaty with the Cherokees, who could then put 6,000 warriors in the field. In April, 1730, Sir Alexander met the chief warriors of all the Cherokee towns in council, and made a treaty with them.

For a long time the Cherokees and the Five Nations had bloody contests; but the English effected a reconciliation between them about 1750, when the Cherokees became the allies of the British, and allowed them to build forts on their domain. They were now at the height of

CHEROKEE INDIANS.

their power, inhabiting sixty-four villages; but soon afterwards nearly one-half the population were swept off by the small-pox. The Cherokees assisted in the capture of Fort Duquesne in 1758. On their return through Virginia and the Carolinas, they quarrelled with the settlers, and several white men and Indians were killed. Some Cherokee chiefs, sent to Charleston to arrange the dispute, were treated almost with contempt by the governor. This was soon followed by an invasion of the Cherokee country by Governor Littleton (October, 1759) with 1,500 men, contributed by Virginia and the Carolinas. He found the Cherokees ready for war, and was glad to make the insubordination of his soldiers and the prevalence of small-pox among them an excuse for leaving the country. He accepted twenty-two Indian hostages as security for peace and the future delivery of the murderers, and retired in haste and confusion (June, 1760). These hostages were placed in Fort St. George, at the head of the Savannah River. The Cherokees attempted their rescue as soon as Littleton and his army had gone. A soldier was wounded, when his companions, in fiery anger, put all the hostages to death.

The Cherokee nation was aroused by the outrage. They beleaguered the fort, and war-parties scourged the frontiers. The Assembly of South Carolina voted 1,000 men and offered £25 for every Indian scalp. North Carolina voted a similar provision, and authorized the holding of Indian captives as slaves. General Amherst detached 1,200 men, under Colonel Montgomery, to chastise the Cherokees. Montgomery left Charleston early in April, with regular and provincial troops, and laid waste a portion of the Cherokee country. They were not subdued. The next year Colonel Grant led a stronger force against them, burned their towns, and killed many of their warriors. Then the Indians sued for peace (June, 1761).

In 1776 the Cherokees seriously threatened the frontier. Georgia, North Carolina, and Virginia joined in the defence of South Carolina. Col. Andrew Williamson led an expedition into the Cherokee country, and destroyed all their settlements eastward of the Appalachian Mountains. This conquest was effected between July 15 and Oct. 11, 1776. Fort Rutledge was erected in the Cherokee country.

In 1781 the Cherokees, having made a hostile incursion into District Ninety-six, in South Carolina, murdered some families and burned several houses. Gen. Andrew Pickens, at the head of about 400 mounted militia, in fourteen days burned thirteen villages, killed more than forty Indians, and took a number of prisoners, without losing a man.

By a treaty concluded at Hopewell, on the Keowee, the Cherokees submitted to the protection of the United States, and the boundaries of their hunting-grounds were settled.

These Indians were friends of the United States in the War of 1812, and helped to subjugate the Creeks. Civilization took root among them and produced contention. They were so divided that in 1818 a portion of the nation emigrated to land assigned to them west of the Mississippi. The Cherokees had ceded large portions of their lands, and their domain was mostly confined to northern Georgia. The Georgians coveted their lands, but the Cherokees were yet powerful in numbers, and disposed to defend their rights against encroachments.

President Jackson favored the Georgians, and the white people then proceeded to take possession of the lands of the Cherokees. The United States troops had been withdrawn from Georgia, and the national government offered no obstacle to the forcible seizure of the Indian territory by the Georgians. The Cherokees then numbered 15,000 east of the Mississippi. The dispute was adjudicated by the Supreme Court of the United States, and on March 30, 1832, that tribunal decided against the claims of the Georgians. An amicable settlement was finally reached, and in 1838 the Cherokees left Georgia and went to the Indian territory.

In 1861, John Ross, the renowned principal chief of the Cherokees, who had led them wisely for almost forty years, took a decided stand against the Confederates. But he and his loyal associates among the Cherokees and Creeks were overborne by the tide of secession. The chief men of the Cherokees held a mass-meeting at Tahlequah in August, when, with great unanimity, they declared their allegiance to the "Confederate States." Ross still held out, but was finally compelled to yield. At a council held on Aug. 20 he recommended the severance of the connection with the national government.

During the Civil War the Cherokees suffered much. The Confederates would not trust Ross, for his Union feelings were very apparent. When, in 1862, they were about to arrest him, he and his family escaped to the North.

In 1902 there were officially reported 28,016 persons of Cherokee blood in the Cherokee Nation, Indian Territory, and about 2,000 in North Carolina.

Cherry Valley, Massacre at. During a heavy storm of sleet on Nov. 11, 1778, a band of Indians and Tories—the former led by Brant, and the latter by Walter N. Butler, son of Col. John Butler—fell upon Cherry Valley, Otsego co., N. Y., and murdered thirty-two of the inhabitants, mostly women and children, with sixteen soldiers of a little garrison there. Nearly forty men, women, and children were carried away captive. Butler was the arch-fiend on this occasion, and would listen to no appeals from Brant for mercy on the innocent and helpless. The captives were led away in the darkness and a cold storm; and when they rested they were huddled together, half naked, with no resting-place but the wet ground.

Cherubusco.. See CHURUBUSCO.

Chesapeake, the name of a famous United States frigate that will always be memorable because of her interest-absorbing career. In the spring of 1807 a small British squadron lay (as they had lately) in American waters, near the mouth of Chesapeake Bay, watching some French frigates blockaded at Annapolis. Three of the crew of one of the British vessels, *Melampus,* and one of another, *Halifax,* had deserted, and enlisted on board the *Chesapeake,* lying at the Washington navy-yard. The British minister made a formal demand for their surrender. The United States government refused compliance, because it was ascertained that two of them (colored) were natives of the United States, and there was strong presumptive evidence that the third one was, likewise. The commodore of the British squadron took the matter into his own hands. The *Chesapeake,* going to sea on the morning of June 22, 1807, bearing the pennant of Commodore Barron, was intercepted by the British frigate *Leopard,* whose commander, hailing, informed the commodore that he had a despatch for him. A British boat bearing a lieutenant came alongside the *Chesapeake.* The officer was politely received by Barron, in his cabin, when the former presented a demand from the captain of the *Leopard* to allow the bearer to muster the crew of the *Chesapeake,* that he might select and carry away the alleged deserters. The demand was authorized by instructions received from Vice-Admiral Berkeley, at Halifax.

Barron refused compliance, the lieutenant withdrew, and the *Chesapeake* moved on. The *Leopard* followed, and her commander called out through his trumpet, "Commodore Barron must be aware that the vice-admiral's commands must be obeyed." This insolent announcement was repeated. The *Chesapeake* moved on, and the *Leopard* sent two shots athwart her bow. These were followed by the remainder of the broadside, poured into the hull of the *Chesapeake.* Though Barron, suspecting mischief, had hastily tried to prepare his ship for action, he was unable to return the shots, for his guns had no priming-powder. After being severely injured by repeated broadsides, the *Chesapeake* struck her colors. The vice-admiral's command was obeyed. The crew of the *Chesapeake* were mustered by British officers, and the deserters were carried away; one of them, who was a British subject, was hanged at Halifax, and the lives of the Americans were spared only on condition that they should re-enter the British service.

This outrage caused fiery indignation throughout the United States. The President issued a proclamation, at the beginning of July, ordering all British armed vessels to leave the waters of the United States, and forbidding any to enter until ample satisfaction should be given. A British envoy extraordinary was sent to Washington to settle the difficulty. Instructed to do nothing until the President's proclamation should be withdrawn, the matter was left open more than four years. In 1811 the British government disavowed the act. Barron, found guilty of neglect of duty in not being prepared for the attack, was suspended from the service for five years, without pay or emolument.

While the *Hornet,* Captain Lawrence, was on her homeward-bound voyage with her large number of prisoners, the *Chesapeake* was out on a long cruise to the Cape de Verde Islands, and the coast of South America. She accomplished nothing except the capture of four British merchant vessels; and as she entered Boston Harbor, in the spring of 1813, in a gale, her topmast was carried away, and with it several men who were aloft, three of whom were drowned. Among the superstitious sailors she acquired the character of an "unlucky" ship, and they were loath to embark in her. Evans was compelled to leave her on account of the loss of the sight of one of his eyes; and

Lawrence, who had been promoted to captain for his bravery, was put in command of her, with the *Hornet*, Captain Biddle, as her consort.

At the close of May the British frigate *Shannon*, thirty-eight guns, Capt. Philip Bowes Vere Broke, appeared off Boston Harbor, in the attitude of a challenger. She then carried fifty-two guns. He wrote to Lawrence, requesting the *Chesapeake* to meet the *Shannon*, "ship to ship, to try the fortunes of their respective flags." He assured Lawrence that the *Chesapeake* could not leave Boston without the risk of being "crushed by the superior force of the British squadron," then abroad, and proposed that they should meet in single combat, without the interference of other vessels.

Lawrence accepted the challenge, and, with Lieut. Augustus Ludlow as second in command, he sailed out of Boston Harbor to meet the *Shannon*, at mid-day, June 1, 1813. The same evening, between five and six o'clock, they engaged in a close conflict. After fighting twelve minutes, the *Shannon* so injured the spars and rigging of the *Chesapeake* that she became unma ageable. This misfortune occurred at the moment when the latter was about to take the wind out of the sails of her antagonist, shoot ahead, lay across her bow, rake her, and probably secure a victory.

THE SHANNON AND CHESAPEAKE ENTERING THE HARBOR OF HALIFAX.

Her mizzen rigging was entangled in the fore-chains of the *Shannon*, in which position the decks of the *Chesapeake* were swept with terrible effect by the balls of her antagonist. Lawrence ordered his boarders to be called up. There was some delay, when a musket-ball mortally wounded the gallant young commander, and he was carried below. As he left the deck he said, "Tell the men to fire faster, and not to give up the ship; fight her till she sinks." These words of the dying hero slightly paraphrased to "Don't give up the ship," became the battle-cry of the Americans, and the formula of an encouraging maxim in morals for those who are struggling in life's contests.

Broke's boarders now swarmed upon the deck of the *Chesapeake*, and Lieutenant Ludlow, the second in command, was mortally wounded by a sabre cut. After a severe struggle, in which the Americans lost, in killed and wounded, 146 men, victory remained with the *Shannon*. The British lost eighty-four men. Broke sailed immediately for Halifax with his prize, and the day before his arrival there (June 7) Lawrence expired, wrapped in the flag of the *Chesapeake*.

England rang with shouts of exultation because of this victory. An American writer remarked: "Never did any victory—not even of Wellington in Spain, nor those of Nelson—call forth such expressions of joy on the part of the British"; a proof that our naval character had risen in their estimation. Lawrence fought under great disadvantages. He had been in command of the ship only about ten days and was unacquainted with the abilities of her officers and men; some of the former were sick or absent. His crew were almost mutinous because of disputes concerning prize-money, and many of them had only recently enlisted; besides, the feeling among the sailors that she was an "unlucky" ship was disheartening.

The remains of Lawrence and Ludlow were conveyed to Salem, Mass., and thence to New York, and were deposited (Sept. 16) in Trinity churchyard. The vestry of Trinity Church erected a handsome mausoleum of brown freestone (1847) in commemoration of both Lawrence and Ludlow. Captain Lawrence's coat, chapeau and sword are now in possession of the New Jersey Historical Society.

The freedom of the city of London and a sword were given to Captain Broke by the corporation, and the Prince Regent knighted him, and the inhabitants of his native county (Suffolk) presented him with a gorgeous piece of silver as a testimonial of their sense of his eminent service. The *Chesapeake* was taken to England and sold to the government for about $66,000, and in 1814 was put in commission. In 1820 she was sold to a private gentleman for a very small sum, who broke her up and sold her timbers for building purposes, much of it for making houses in Portsmouth, and a considerable portion for the erection of a mill at Wickham.

Chesapeake Bay. At the mouth of this bay a contest took place between the British admiral Graves and the French admiral de Grasse, aiding the American colonies against Great Britain; the former was obliged to retire Sept. 5, 1781. The Chesapeake and Delaware were blockaded by the British fleet in the War of 1812, and the bay was at that period the scene of hostilities, with various results. See MARYLAND; VIRGINIA.

Chesney, CHARLES CORNWALLIS, military writer; born in England, Sept. 29, 1826; entered the British army, and was professor at Sandhurst Military College. His publications relating to the United States include *Military View of Recent Campaigns in Virginia* (1863-65), and *Military Biographies* (1873), in which is included several American military officers. He died in England, March 19, 1876.

Chester, city on the Delaware River, 15 miles s. of Philadelphia. It is the oldest city in the State, having been settled by Swedes in 1643, under the name of Upland; was incorporated in 1866; and is noted as the site of one of the largest ship-building plants in the world, founded by John Roach in 1872, where many naval and commercial vessels have been built. Pop. (1900), 33,988; (1910) 38,537.

Chester, JOSEPH LEMUEL (pen name JULIAN CRAMOR), antiquarian; born in Norwich, Conn., April 30, 1821; removed to London, England, in 1858, and devoted himself to the history and genealogy of the early settlers in New England. His publications include *Educational Laws of Virginia; The Personal Narrative of Mrs. Margaret Douglas; John Rogers* (with a genealogy of the family), etc. He died in London, England, May 28, 1882.

Chestnut, JAMES, JR., Senator; born near Camden, S. C., in 1815; graduated at Princeton College in 1835; elected United States Senator from South Carolina, Jan. 5, 1859. He resigned his seat, but his resignation was not accepted, and on July 11, 1861, he was expelled. He was a member of the Confederate Provisional Congress; became aide to Jefferson Davis; and was promoted brigadier-general in 1864. He died in Camden, S. C., Feb. 1, 1885.

Chestnut Hill, a present part of Philadelphia where a severe skirmish occurred between the British under Haine and Americans under Irvine, Dec. 4, 1777. The Americans were defeated, and Irvine was left wounded in the hands of the British.

Chevalier, MICHEL, political economist; born in Limoges, France, Jan. 13, 1806; educated in a polytechnic school; came to the United States to examine its canals and railroads. His publications include *Lettres sur l'Amérique du Nord; Introduction aux rapports du jury international; Histoire et description des voies de communication aux États-Unis et des travaux qui en dépendent; Cours d'économie; L'Isthme de Panama; La liberté aux États-Unis; L'expédition du Mexique; Le Mexique ancien et moderne,* etc. He died Nov. 28, 1879.

Cheves, LANGDON, statesman; born in Abbeville District, S. C., Sept. 17, 1776. Admitted to the bar in 1800, he soon became eminent as a lawyer and as a leader in the State legislature, which he entered in 1808. He was attorney-general of the State, and was a member of Congress from 1811 to 1816, zealously supporting all war measures introduced. When, in 1814, Henry Clay was sent to negotiate a treaty of peace with Great Britain, he succeeded the Kentuckian as speaker of the House, which place he held for a year, his casting vote defeating a bill for the rechartering of the United States Bank. The bank was rechartered in 1816; and when in trouble in 1819 Cheves was appointed president of its directors, and by his great energy and keen judgment it was saved from dissolution. He became chief commissioner under the treaty of Ghent for settling some of its provisions. He was a public advocate of disunion as early as the year 1830, but opposed NULLIFICATION (*q. v.*). He died in Columbia, S. C., June 25, 1857.

Chew, BENJAMIN, jurist; born in West River, Md., Nov. 29, 1722; settled in Philadelphia in 1745; was recorder in 1755–72; and became chief-justice of Pennsylvania in 1774. During the Revolutionary War he sided with the royalist party, and in 1777 he was imprisoned in Fredericksburg, Va., because he had refused to give a parole. On Oct. 4, 1777, during the battle of Germantown, a British outpost took refuge in his large stone mansion, and the Americans, in order to drive them out, fired on the building with muskets and cannon. The building, however, was too strongly built to be demolished by the 3 and 6 pounder field-pieces of that time. A brigade commanded by Maxwell was left to surround the house, while the main American force pushed on. This incident gave the British time to prepare for the American attack. From 1790 to 1806, when the High Court of Errors and Appeals was abandoned, he was president of that court. He died Jan. 20, 1810. See GERMANTOWN, BATTLE OF.

Cheyenne Indians, one of the most westerly tribes of the Algonquian nation. They were seated on the Cheyenne, a branch of the Red River of the North. Driven by the Sioux, they retreated beyond the Missouri. Near the close of the eighteenth century they were driven to or near the Black Hills (now in the Dakotas and Wyoming), where Lewis and Clarke found them in 1804, when they possessed horses and made plundering raids as far as New Mexico. See CLARKE, GEORGE ROGERS; LEWIS, MERIWETHER.

About 1825, when they were at peace with the Sioux, and making war upon the Pawnees, Kansas, and other tribes, a feud occurred in the family. A part of them remained with the Sioux, and the others went south to the Arkansas River and joined the Arapahoes. Many treaties were made with them by agents of the United States, but broken; and, finally, losing all confidence in the honor of the white race, they began hostilities in 1861. This was the first time that the Cheyennes were at war with the white people. While negotiations for peace and friendship were on foot, Colonel Chivington, of Colorado, fell upon a Cheyenne village (Nov. 29, 1864) and massacred about 100 men, women, and children. The whole tribe was fired with a desire for revenge, and a fierce war ensued, in which the United States lost many gallant soldiers and spent between $30,000,000 and $40,000,000.

The ill-feeling of the Indians towards the white people remained unabated. Some treaties were made and imperfectly carried out; and, after General Hancock burned one of their villages in 1867, they again made war, and slew 300 United States soldiers and settlers. General Custer defeated them on the Washita, killing their chief, thirty-seven warriors, and two-thirds of their women and children. The northern band of the Cheyennes remained peaceable, refusing to join the Sioux in 1865.

The Northern Cheyennes, 1,409 in number, are now in Montana. The Southern Cheyennes, 1,903 in number, had their lands allotted in severalty, and are now American citizens.

CHICAGO

Chicago, city, port of entry, county-seat of Cook county, Ill., commercial metropolis of the West, and second city in the United States in population (1910), and in national bank clearings (1910); popularly known as the "Garden City." Population, 1850, 28,269; 1860, 109,206; 1870, 306,605; 1880, 503,185; 1890, 1,099,-850; 1900, 1,698,575; 1910, 2,185,283. See CENSUS.

Location, Area, etc.—It is situated on the southwestern shore of Lake Michigan, about eighteen miles north of its southern extremity; has a water frontage by the Chicago River and its branches of fifty-eight miles and by the lake of twenty-two miles; extends about twenty-six miles north and south along the lake, with an extreme width of about fifteen miles; and has an area of 191 square miles. The Calumet and Chicago rivers flow into the lake within the city limits, and the Chicago River, sweeping to the west, divides into the north and south branches a short distance north of the court-house, these running about two miles in each direction nearly parallel with the lake. The south branch is connected with the Illinois & Michigan Canal, which extends to the Illinois River at La Salle, and affords communication for boats of 140 tons with the Mississippi and its tributaries during three-quarters of the year, and with Chicago's great drainage canal, which has its southern terminus in the Desplaines River at Lockport.

The location of a commanding commercial centre could not possess greater advantages, the city being at the head of navigation of the four lower lakes, thus having direct communication with all important Canadian ports and an entrance into the Atlantic Ocean through the Gulf of St. Lawrence, and another by way of the Erie Canal and Hudson River at New York; and being also on the line of twenty-eight trunk railroads operating more than 93,934 miles of direct track, and reaching with their connections every city and port of consequence on the continent.

Those exceptional facilities for domestic and foreign communication have promoted commercial, industrial, and financial interests till they have reached a volume which has prompted the statement by many competent authorities on the drift of monetary and commercial affairs in the country that the city is rapidly becoming

CHICAGO ART INSTITUTE.

KINZIE MANSION AND FORT DEARBORN.

the financial centre of the nation. It has been pointed out that on Nov. 10, 1904, the banks west of the Mississippi had more than $700,000,000 of loans and discounts, and nearly $800,000,000 in individual deposits. These figures showed a gain of 133 per cent. in loans and discounts and of 139 per cent. in deposits since 1898, while the national banks in all the rest of the country gained only 65 per cent. in loans and 72 per cent. in deposits. The explanation is to be found in the fact that the country west of the Mississippi in 1904 produced 70 per cent. of all the wheat, 50 per cent. of all the corn, 43 per cent. of all the oats, and 80 per cent. of all the barley and flax grown in the United States.

Topography. — Originally the surface rose gradually towards the west from the water's edge on the lake till it reached a height of about twenty-eight feet, and then merged into a prairie extending for hundreds of miles to the south and west; but since 1856 the ground in what is now the business section has been raised to a height of fourteen feet above the lake. The natural drainage, though slow, was sufficient for many years, the sewage passing through the river into the lake. In 1866–

MEDAL GIVEN TO BLACK PARTRIDGE BY THE AMERICANS.

1870, when the city deepened the Illinois & Michigan Canal it also dredged the river channel to a depth sufficient to allow the water of the lake to flow through it, thus forcing the sewage towards the Illinois River and keeping the Chicago River imperfectly cleansed. Subsequently, with the increase of industrial plants, domiciles, and population, a more extensive system became imperative, and a great canal, whose main channel is twenty-eight miles long, was constructed in 1892–1900, at a cost of about $45,000,000, primarily to carry off the sewage, but with an ultimate purpose of transforming it into a ship-canal.

THE LAST VESTIGE OF FORT DEARBORN.

The Chicago River and its two branches divide the city into three sections, known as the North, South, and West sides. The North and South, and the South and West sides, are each connected by tunnels under the river, and the three divisions are bound together by a large number of bridges. The city is laid out methodically, with streets intersecting at right angles. Under an Act of the Legislature of February, 1869, about eighty parks have been laid out, having a total area of 3,180 acres.

The mouth of the Chicago River has been improved by deepening and the construction of piers extending into the lake on either side, by the building of long breakwaters by the national government, forming an outer harbor with sixteen feet of water and an area of over 450 acres; and by an exterior breakwater, 5,436 feet long. A second though smaller harbor has been formed at the mouth of the Calumet River, by the construction of long piers, 300 feet apart.

Government.—In 1906 the municipal government was in a transition state. A new section to Article IV. (Section 34) of the State Constitution, proposed in the Legislature of 1903, was ratified by the voters of the State at the general election on Nov. 8, 1904. This amendment permitted the Legislature to form a new charter for the local government of the city of Chicago; authorized the consolidation in the new municipal government of the powers previously vested in the city, board of education, township, park, and other local governments; limited to five per cent. of the full value of the taxable property the indebtedness of the city, including the existing debt, the debt of all municipal corporations lying wholly in the city, and also the city's proportion of the debt of the county and sanitary district; and required that new bond issues under the amendment should be submitted to the voters for approval. Steps were taken immediately after the ratification of the foregoing amendment to give it vitality, and the following were appointed a committee to have charge of the framing of the new charter: Chairman, John P. Wilson; Judge M. F. Tuley, Judge Francis Adams, John S. Miller, B. A. Eckhart, B. E. Sunny, and Mayor Carter H. Harrison. On Sept. 17, 1907, however, the proposition for a new city charter was defeated at the polls.

On April 5, 1904, the city voted in favor of the municipal ownership of the street railways, and on April 6, 1905, Judge Edward F. Dunne, the Democratic candidate for mayor, was elected, by a majority of approximately 25,000, over John M. Harlan, Republican; both candidates stood on a municipal ownership platform, Judge Dunne representing the demand for immediate ownership, and Mr. Harlan that for a tentative arrangement with the traction companies providing for ultimate ownership.

Under the redistricting ordinance of Jan. 7, 1901, the city was divided into thirty-five wards for administrative purposes, and in 1911 its affairs were conducted by a mayor, elected for two years, with salary of $18,000 per annum; a Board of Aldermen, comprising two members from each ward, annual salary of each $3,000; the usual municipal executive departments and their bureaus; justices of the peace are appointed by the governor for terms of four years; and police magistrates, selected from the list of justices of the peace, are appointed by the mayor.

Under the provisions of the constitutional amendment, adopted in 1903, the new Municipal Court thus constituted, consisting of one chief justice, salary $7,500 a year; twenty-seven associate justices, $6,000 each; one chief clerk, $6,000; and one chief bailiff, $6,000, was created for the purpose of rapidly disposing of small litigation, and was given as great powers as any of the *nisi prius* courts. It entirely supplanted the courts formerly presided over by justices of the peace and police magistrates, and abolished the constabulary system. The first election for municipal court officers was held Nov. 6, 1906.

Financial Interests.—According to municipal reports of 1910 the city owns buildings and real estate to the value of $129,094,933, including the water-works plant, which cost $51,098,617, and the electric-lighting system. The assessed valuations of taxable property in 1909 as equalized were: Real estate, $586,253,655; personal property, $246,897,242, including railroad property, $37,354,520, and capital stock, $34,322,841—total, $833,150,897. The tax rate for city purposes only was $13.08 per $1,000; for all purposes, $49.-10. The annual cost of maintaining the city government exceeds $22,000,000, of which the public schools cost over $9,000,-000, the fire department, $3,000,000; the police department, $5,750,000; removal of ashes and garbage, $1,070,000; street cleaning, $825,000; and street lighting, by gas $300,000 and electricity $550,000. On Oct. 1, 1910, the total bonded debt was $29,800,500, including $3,541,500 in outstanding water bonds, and excluding $4,293,000 in World's Fair bonds; and the sinking funds aggregated $5,543,684, including water sinking funds of $1,010,305.

The city has 2,880 miles of streets and alleys, of which 1,542 miles are paved. There are 1,838 miles of sewer mains and laterals; water-works plant with ten pumping-stations, daily capacity of 676,-000,000 gallons; daily consumption, 479,-440,000 gallons; 2,229 miles of mains; and land and lake water tunnels having a total length of thirty-eight miles; a police department of 4,250 men; a fire department of 1,839 men; and a public-school system with 301,170 pupils and 6,390 teachers.

Commerce.—Reference has already been made to the extraordinary facilities for carrying on a large domestic and foreign trade. The domestic trade is enormous, but its great volume cannot be measured with any degree of accuracy because of the conditions imposed on the city as a distributing centre. So, too, with the foreign trade, which has this additional feature, that large quantities of merchandise shipped to and from Chicago pass through Atlantic or lake ports and are credited to them, the city being thus deprived of the showing to which it is entitled. With this disadvantage in mind an approximate estimate may be made of the extent of the foreign trade by considering the official reports for the year 1910.

In the calendar year 1910 the imports of merchandise had a value of $27,700,-664, and the exports $4,511,878 ($7,371,-406 in 1909). The net tonnage movement in the foreign trade was: Entrances: American sail, 19,919; American steam, 181,049; foreign sail, none; foreign steam, 31,308—total sail and steam, 232,276; clearances: American sail, 19,936; American steam, 286,062; foreign sail, none; foreign steam, 26,370—total sail and steam, 332,368. During the year the arrivals of vessels engaged in the coastwise trade numbered 6,345, of 8,391,115 net tons; and the departures, 6,186, of 8,320,-115 tons.

Manufactures.—Not only is Chicago the greatest railroad, grain, lumber, furniture, agricultural-implement, and live and dressed meat centre in the world, but it has attained high rank in general industrial activities. According to a tentative Federal census summary, covering 1909, the city had 9,663 manufacturing and industrial establishments operated under the factory-system classification (excluding small shops and hand trades), which employed $971,990,000 capital and 293,992 wage-earners; paid $240,056,000 for salaries and wages, $123,037,000 for miscellaneous expenses, and $793,571,000 for materials used in manufacturing; and had aggregate products valued at $1,281,313,000.

The principal industries, by the census of 1905, in the order of value of output, were: Slaughtering and meat-packing, wholesale, $262,586,609; men's clothing, $53,230,436; foundry and machine-shop products, $51,774,095; printing and publishing, book and job, $26,200,564; iron and steel, in steel works and rolling mills, $24,839,623; steam railroad cars, $23,798,-900; printing and publishing, newspapers and periodicals, $21,597,388; bread and bakery products, $20,653,538; furniture, $17,488,257; malt liquors, $16,983,421; electrical machinery and supplies, $16,-291,546; coffee and spice, roasting and grinding, $15,563,301; planing-mill products, $13,855,883; soap, $13,769,946; women's clothing, $11,636,818; and steam-railroad shop constructions, $11,171,554—all others under $10,000,000. In the tentative census summary for 1909, the slaughtering and meat-packing industry was credited with $115,311,628 capital and products valued at $325,061,657.

With a value of products much larger than that reported individually by a majority of the States, the manufacturing industries of Chicago are almost as varied as those of Illinois. The city has experienced a marvelous growth both in population and manufactures, having attained in a remarkably short time a position second only to New York City. Ideally situated near the southern end of Lake Michigan, with an extensive water-front and a deep-water harbor, the city has water communication with all the parts of the Great Lakes, and even with the world. There is no other city in the world that has the railroad advantages of Chicago. Moreover, the city is the natural market of an enormous stretch of country in all directions. In 1905 Chicago had 54.7 per cent. of all the manufacturing establishments in the State; 65.4 per cent of all the capital invested therein; 63.8 per cent. of all wage-earners; 65.5 per cent. of all wages paid; and 67.7 per cent of the value of all products.

Banking.—The report of the Comptroller of the Currency for the banking year ending Sept. 1, 1910, credited Chicago with eleven national banks, having an aggregate capital of $41,400,000; surplus, $22,-188,000; circulation, $17,205,382; individual deposits $191,663,540; loans and discounts, $288,656,931; specie, $47,722,-993; legal-tender notes, $34,310,944; and assets and liabilities balancing at $501,-265,804. The clearing-house here ranked second to New York in the volume of annual exchanges. These, in the year ending Sept. 30, 1910, aggregated $14,031,-258,900, an increase in a year of $617,-285,800. Comparing the foregoing with the similar report for the year ending Sept. 5, 1900, it is found that in the latter year there were fourteen national banks, with a total capital of $19,250,000; surplus, $9,180,000; circulation, $4,897,410; individual deposits, $102,942,776; loans and discounts, $142,067,182; specie, $26,-939,053; legal-tender notes, $20,237,906; and assets and liabilities, $275,749,135. The city then ranked third in clearing-house operations, having total exchanges of $6,811,052,828, an increase in a year of $442,106,514. In 1910 the national, State, and private banks aggregated 109 in number.

Social Transit.—In 1910 the street railways had a total mileage of 1,350; capital of four operating companies, $98,529,977; value of properties as stated by Traction Commission, $55,775,000; aggregate assets and liabilities, $102,053,154; city's proportion of profits in 1909, $1,274,916; companies' proportion, $1,016,371. Ordinances were passed by the City Council and accepted by the companies for the elevation of roadbeds and tracks between May 23, 1892 and Nov. 1, 1910, calling for the elevation of 155.89 miles of main track and 935.55 miles of all tracks, and the construction of 795 subways, at an estimated cost of $76,700,000; and by Jan. 1, 1911, there had been 143.74 miles of main track and 883.52 miles of all tracks elevated and 598 subways constructed, at a cost of $63,662,000. There are three tunnels under the Chicago River, at Washington, La Salle, and Van Buren streets, all used for street-railway purposes. They cost originally $2,083,000; were built in 1867–92; and were rebuilt in 1909–11.

At the election of April 6, 1905, the following questions were submitted to popular vote: (1) "Shall the city council pass the ordinance reported by the local transportation committee to the city council of August 24, 1904, granting a franchise to the Chicago City Railroad Company?" (2) "Shall the city council pass any ordinance granting a franchise to the Chicago City Railroad Company?" (3) "Shall the city council pass any ordinance granting a franchise to any street-railroad company?" The result was: The first proposition received 64,391 affirmative and 157,785 negative votes; the second, 60,020 affirmative and 151,974 negative votes; and the third, 59,013 affirmative and 152,135 negative votes. The extension, or tentative, ordinance was placed on file by the city council in accordance with the dictates of the foregoing vote. The city authorities had contended that the franchises of the traction companies had expired July 1, 1903, and the case was carried to the United States Supreme Court, which tribunal decided, March 12, 1906, that the city was right. A year after the election of Mayor Dunne municipal ownership again was made an issue in the aldermanic campaign, and on April 3, 1906, Chicago voted on these questions: (1) "Shall the city proceed to operate street railways?" (2) "Shall the ordinance making provision for the issue of street-railway certificates not to exceed in amount $75,000,000, as authorized by the Mueller enabling act passed by the legislature in May, 1903, be approved?" (3) "Shall the city council proceed without delay to secure municipal ownership and operation of all street railways in Chicago under the Mueller law?" The result of this vote was: First question, yeas, 121,916; nays, 110,323; second question, yeas, 110,225; nays, 106,859; third question, yeas, 111,955; nays, 108,087. On the question of municipal operation, while the affirmative vote was 11,593 in excess of the negative, the principle of operation was defeated, because under the Mueller law, a 60-per-cent. instead of a majority vote was required on this issue. On June 7, 1906, a bill was filed to test the validity of the Mueller-law railway certificates. On Sept. 16, 1906, a decision was rendered in the Cook County Circuit Court upholding the constitutionality of the Mueller law and the validity of the certificates. The case was then taken to the Supreme Court, and by a decision handed down April 18, 1907, the certificates were declared invalid. At the election in the latter month ordinances granting franchises to the existing street railways were ratified. The Federal government, by ordering the old street-railway tunnels under the Chicago River removed because of the serious obstruction they offered to navigation, forced the city to issue permits allowing the traction companies to adopt the trolley system instead of the cables.

A unique feature of the local-traffic system is the underground, narrow-gauge railway connected with many down-town business establishments, which handles the merchandise of the stores, the coal for heating, etc. The plan of tracks underlies all of the down-town streets, with switches at every corner, thus forming a loop around every city block. The motive power is the third-rail electric system, and the total mileage under the original scheme is about twenty-one miles.

Parks and Boulevards, etc.—In 1869 the legislature provided for the creation of a public-park system that now comprises a total area of 4,388.30 acres. Prior to that date about sixty "lungs" were established by the city, less than a dozen being parks proper, the remainder being small patches, mostly triangles, at street intersections. The commissions authorized by the legislature proceeded systematically to establish the present chain of connected parks, which includes Lincoln, Humboldt, Garfield, Douglas, Washington, Jackson, McKinley, and Gage, with their connecting boulevards. Subsequently the city council appointed a special park commission to consider the feasibility of creating breathing-spots in the most congested sections, and as a result there are over fifty improved small parks and squares, and fifteen unimproved, sixteen playgrounds, and two bathing beaches.

The chain of principal parks contains numerous statues, monuments, and fountains. Lincoln Park has the following monuments: Andersen, Beethoven, Franklin, Garibaldi, Goethe, Grant, La Salle, Lincoln, Linne, Schiller, Shakespeare, "Signal of Peace," "The Alarm," and Kennison, and also the Electric Fountain of Columbian World's Fair celebrity; Humboldt Park has memorials of Humboldt, Leif Ericsson, Reuter, and Kosciusko; Union Park has the Haymarket Monument; and Garfield Park, Victoria. There are also monuments to Logan in Lake Front Park; Douglas, at foot of Thirty-fifth Street; and Washington, on the Grand Boulevard and Fifty-first Street; a Confederate monument in Oakwoods Cemetery; and a commemoration of the Fort Dearborn Massacre, on Calumet Avenue and Eighteenth Street. The public fountains include the Drake, on La Salle Street; the Drexel, on Drexel Boulevard; and the Rosenberg, at the south end of Lake Front Park.

Notable Buildings.—The mother of the sky-scraper, Chicago has an array of extraordinarily tall buildings that cannot be surpassed—if equalled—by any city in the world. Chief among these structures are the Masonic Temple, on State and Randolph streets (cost $3,500,000), twenty stories high; the Great Northern Hotel, and the Manhattan and Monadnock (cost, $2,500,000) buildings, each seventeen stories; the Woman's Temple, built by the Woman's Christian Temperance Union (cost $1,500,000), sixteen stories; the First National Bank, American Trust and Savings Bank, and the Commercial National Bank buildings, each eighteen stories; the Marshall Field group of buildings, forming the largest retail store in the world; the Young Men's Christian Association, Stock Exchange, Chamber of Commerce, Railway Exchange, Fine Arts, Medinah Temple, Pullman, and Rookery buildings; the Chicago, Union League, University, Chicago Athletic, Illinois Athletic, Union, and Germania Club buildings; the Post-office and Federal building; and scores of commercial buildings of the sky-scraper type, reaching the legal-height limit of 260 feet. The county buildings include a court-house, criminal-court building and jail, hospital, morgue, detention hospital, and several institutions at Dunning. The City Hall is an imposing structure that cost $2,000,000; and a new county building and court-house, of steel and granite construction, has recently been completed at a cost of $5,000,000. The Auditorium is one of the most remarkable non-civic buildings in the world. It contains a theatre with 7,000 seats, a large concert-hall, a hotel occupying ten floors, and nearly 150 offices and storerooms. Connected with the Auditorium are the Annex and Annex Apartments, the three buildings together forming the largest hotel in the world.

One of the most striking buildings of a public character is the Field Museum of Natural History, the Art Palace of the great Columbian World's Exposition of 1893, containing many choice exhibits of that event, and named in honor of Marshall Field, who gave it $1,000,000. The museum was opened to the public in 1894, in what was then considered only a temporary structure; and in 1911 work was begun on the erection of a permanent building in Jackson Park, estimated to cost $5,000,000 and to house treasures worth $10,000,000. Other notable buildings are the Public Library, on Michigan Avenue and Randolph and Washington streets, one of the most attractive buildings of its character in the country, containing over 405,000 bound volumes, and having fourteen circulating branches, fifteen branch reading-rooms, and forty-four delivery stations; the Art Institute, on the Lake Front, a granite and marble structure, costing $800,000, and containing an art museum with modern and old-master paintings, Greek vases and antiquities, ivory carvings, and other valuable art objects, an art school, and a hall

MARSHALL FIELD.

for loan exhibitions; the Chicago Historical Museum; the Newberry Library; the Hammond Library; the Blackstone Library; and the North Side Water-works, comprising a stone water-tower 160 feet high, from which a cylindrical brick tunnel extends a distance of two miles beneath the lake, six other large tunnels, great intake, and numerous cribs and pumping-stations. The second largest terminal in the world used by only one railroad, erected by the Chicago and Northwestern Railroad, was completed in 1911, at a cost of $12,190,000 for building and $11,560,000 for ground.

The Union stock-yards occupy an area of 400 acres, with thirty-two miles of drainage, twenty miles of streets and alleys, and 2,300 gates, and represent an outlay of more than $4,000,000. They have a capacity for 25,000 cattle, 120,000 hogs, 15,000 sheep, and 1,200 horses. Connected with the stock-yards are great slaughtering and packing houses, hotels, banks, churches, schools, post-office, telegraph-offices, and a board of trade.

Churches.—According to a special census report on *Religious Bodies* (2 vols., 1910) Chicago ranked second among the cities of the United States in the number of church communicants or members, reporting a total of 833,441, of whom 28.5 per cent. were Protestants and 68.2 per cent. Roman Catholics. All denominations reported 1,058 organizations; 899 church edifices; 108 halls used for religious purposes; value of church property of 839 organizations, $27,016,248; and 939 Sunday-schools, with 17,167 officers and teachers and 210,899 scholars. Protestant bodies had a membership of 237,220; the Roman Catholic Church (all members of families), 568,764.

Chicago is the seat of a Roman Catholic archbishop and of two bishops, of a Protestant Episcopal bishop, and of two Reformed Episcopal bishops, and the official residence of a Methodist Episcopal bishop, and of two African Methodist Episcopal bishops. The Roman Catholic Cathedral is a fine building on the North Side. The Church of the Holy Family is a type of Gothic architecture. The First Church of Christ, Scientist, is a striking building, having a seating capacity of 1,600. Grace Episcopal Church is a Gothic stone edifice; and St. James's, also Episcopal, is very massive, with a square tower. The peculiar spire of the Second Baptist Church gives attractiveness to an otherwise plain Italian structure; and the very tall spire of the Union Park Congregational Church, on Ashland Avenue and Washington Street, renders it a marked building in its class. Unity Church (Unitarian) and Immanuel Baptist Church, on Michigan Avenue, are both Gothic. St. James's Methodist Episcopal Church is the most noticeable church of that denomination.

Schools and Colleges.—In 1910 the school population was over 647,000, of whom about 301,000 were enrolled in the public schools and about 103,000 in private and parochial schools. There were 263 public elementary and 20 high schools, with a total of 6,390 teachers. The receipts from all sources were $14,348,929; expenditures for all purposes, $11,969,934. With the erection of five new buildings and additions to six others in 1910, it was claimed that every child of school age could attend school every day and have a seat. Much attention is being given to manual and industrial training, for which there are two schools; also the Chicago Manual Training School, Chicago Sloyd School, Jewish Training School, Lewis Institute, and the Richard T. Crane Manual Training School. Normal training was provided by the Chicago Normal School, the University of Chicago, and St. Ignatius College, and private secondary instruction by the Academy of Our Lady, Academy of the Sacred Heart, Lake View Institute, Ascham Hall, Dearborn Seminary, Harvard School, Kenwood Institute, Kirkland School, Loring School, St. Francis School (boys), St. Francis Xavier School (girls), Starrett's School for Girls, and the preparatory department of Zion College.

At the head of the institutions for higher education is the University of Chicago, a coeducational, non-sectarian institution, founded in 1890, and taking the name of an earlier school which, from financial difficulties, was closed in 1886. The present university was opened in 1892. John D. Rockefeller subscribed $7,000,000 towards its establishment, and has since given it several millions more; citizens of Chicago have given more than $7,000,000, and in 1903 were credited with the erection of all but three of the twenty-nine buildings on the campus; and the late Charles T. Yerkes, another citizen, gave $500,000 for a telescope for the university's observatory, located at Lake Geneva, Wis. Through the later munificence of Mr. Rockefeller the Rush Medical College has become a part of the university. In addition to the regular academic courses there are departments of law, medicine, theology, civil, mechanical, and electrical engineering, pedagogy, music, etc. The university has upward of 4,500 students in all departments, 360 professors and instructors, over 400,000 volumes in its various libraries, grounds and buildings valued at upward of $8,500,000, and productive funds exceeding $10,000,000.

The Armour Institute of Technology was founded by the late Philip D. Armour in 1893 on an initial gift of $1,500,000, to which he added $750,000 in 1899. The Armour Institute, Armour Mission, and Armour Flats form a group of closely related interests that together cost the donor nearly $5,000,000; the first two receive a considerable part of the annual income from the rentals of the last. St. Ignatius College, opened in 1869, and St. Stanislaus, opened in 1890, are both Roman Catholic institutions of high grade and reputation. Professional schools include the Chicago Lutheran Theological Seminary (Evangelical Lutheran), opened in 1891; Chicago Theological Seminary (Congregational), 1858; McCormick Theological Seminary (Presbyterian), 1830; Divinity School of the University of Chicago (Baptist), 1866; and the Western Theological Seminary (Protestant Episcopal), 1885; College of Law of Lake Forest University, 1888; Chicago Law School, 1896; Illinois College of Law, 1898; John Marshall Law School, 1899; and the School of Law of Northwestern University, 1859; American Medical Missionary College, 1895; College of Physicians and Surgeons of the University of Chicago, 1882; Harvey Medical College, 1891; Illinois Medical College, 1894; Jenner Medical College, 1893; Medical School of Northwestern University, 1859; and the Rush Medical College of the University of Chicago, 1867; dental schools of Lake Forest University, Northwestern University, and the University of Chicago; three schools of pharmacy, one of veterinary surgery, and twenty-three training-schools for nurses, all connected with local hospitals.

Chicago has over eighty libraries of all grades besides the Public Library, of which mention has already been made, belonging largely to schools, colleges, hospitals, and public institutions. Of these, three deserve a special word. That of the Chicago Historical Society contains about 40,000 bound volumes and 75,000 pamphlets, many of the latter being of priceless value; the library established under the will of John Crerar, and bearing his name, excludes all sensational novels and sceptical works, cost for building, books, and endowment. $2,500,000, and contains over 265,000 volumes, chiefly scientific; and the Newberry Library, with an endowment of $3,000,000, is general in character, contains over 259,000 volumes, and is widely known for possessing what is probably the largest collection of musical publications in the country.

Humane Activities.—For the relief of human suffering and misfortune Chicago has a great heart, as befits a city whose every impulse, effort, and achievement are on a grand scale. Besides the United States Marine Hospital, at Lake View, beyond Lincoln Park, one of the largest and costliest in the country, and the Cook County Hospital, on Harrison and Wood streets, there are twenty-three hospitals, municipal, denominational, and memorial, and all doing such excellent work that it is quite delicate to individualize. The Mercy, Michael Reese, German, Hahnemann, Woman's, Chicago, St. Joseph's, Alexian Brothers, Augustana, St. Luke's, and Wesley may be mentioned, however, as containing the largest number of beds for patients.

The asylums, homes, retreats, and reformatories number over seventy. Noticeable among them are the Home for the Friendless, on Fifty-first Street, fronting on Washington Park; Protestant Orphan Asylum, on Michigan Avenue and Twenty-second Street; St. Joseph's (male) and St. Mary's (female) orphan asylums on North State Street, both under charge of the Sisters of Mercy; Jewish Orphan Asylum, Drexel Boulevard and Sixty-first Street; Old People's Home, on Indiana Avenue; Foundlings' Home, on Wood Street, near Madison; Newsboys' Home, the Washington Home for Inebriates, and the Armour Mission, previously mentioned, which contains an assembly hall, crèche, library, kindergarten, and free dispensary.

The charitable organizations include the Associated Jewish Charities of Chicago, Austro-Hungarian Benevolent Association, Chicago Bureau of Charities, Chicago Bureau of Justice, Chicago *Daily News* Fresh Air Fund, Chicago Medical Mission and Allied Charities, Chicago Relief and Aid Society, Chicago Woman's Aid Society, Hungarian Charity Society, Illinois Charitable Relief Corps, Illinois Children's Home and Aid Society, Société Française de Bienfaisance de l'Illinois, Société Française de Secours Mutuals, United Hebrew Charities, Visitation and Aid Society, and the Woman's Benevolent Association of Chicago.

History.—The site of Chicago was first visited by Louis Joliet and Jacques Marquette, French missionaries and explorers, in 1673, and the name is first mentioned in Hennepin's account of the building of a new fort on the Illinois River in 1680, as Che-caw-gou. This fort when completed was commanded by an officer in the Canadian service, and before the end of the seventeenth century the Jesuits made it a mission post. Permanent settlement was retarded by Indian hostilities, and it was not till 1803 that the United States Government deemed it advisable to take possession of the place as a possible strategic point of importance. In July of that year a company of soldiers under command of Captain John Whistler arrived at the Chicago River, and at once began the erection of Fort Dearborn on the south side of the river. John Kinzie, the "Father of Chicago," emigrated from Michigan and bought some property here in 1804, and in the same year a United States Indian agency was established, and the first white child, Ellen Marion Kinzie, was born.

The garrison of Fort Dearborn and the family of Mr. Kinzie, living near by, maintained friendly relations with the surrounding Indians till the spring of 1812, when hostile feelings created by British emissaries began to be manifested. A scalping party of Winnebagoes made a raid on a settlement near Chicago in April, and during the early part of the ensuing summer the inhabitants saw with alarm a continued gathering of Indians. On Aug. 7, a friendly Pottawottamie chief arrived at the fort with a letter to Captain Nathan Heald, the commandant, from General Hull, giving notice of the declaration of war against England and the fall of Mackinaw, and advising the evacuation of the fort. On Aug. 12, Captain Heald called a council of the

Indians, and, under General Hull's instructions, told them to come to the fort and receive and distribute among themselves the United States property there, and accepted their offer to escort the white people through the wilderness to Fort Wayne.

On Aug. 15, the day fixed for the evacuation, the whites became convinced that the Indians intended to murder the whole party, but it was then too late to plan resistance. They had gone but a short distance from the gate of the fort when their savage escort, 500 strong, fell upon them suddenly, and in the fight that ensued twelve children, all the male civilians excepting Mr. Kinzie and his sons, three officers, and twenty-six privates were killed. Only the surrender of the remainder of the party saved them from a similar fate. The fort was burned by the Indians on the following day; the government rebuilt it in 1816; and it was garrisoned till 1837. The site of Fort Dearborn is near the present junction of Michigan Avenue and River Street. The last vestige of the fort—a blockhouse—was preserved till 1856.

A town was surveyed and platted by James Thompson near the fort in 1830, with an area of about three-eighths of a square mile; in the following year the settlement contained twelve families besides the garrison, and was made the county-seat of Cook county; and on Aug. 10, 1833, it was incorporated as a town, with a population of about 150. The first regular school had been opened in 1816; the first sermon preached in English in 1825; the first post-office established in 1831; the first frame business structures erected in 1832; and the first improvement of the harbor begun in 1833. Domestic commerce had its beginning in 1834, when the first steamboat to enter the river below Dearborn Street, the *Michigan*, made its appearance, followed a month later by the *Illinois*, the first lake schooner, from Sackett's Harbor, N. Y., which sailed up to Wolf Point. The town was incorporated as a city on March 4, 1837, and its first mayor was William B. Ogden.

The free public-school system was established in 1840. The water-works system, using wooden pipes, dates from 1842, and the first propeller built on Lake Michigan was launched at Averell's ship-yard the same year. The slaughtering and meat-packing industry had its birth in 1844–5, when a quantity of beef was packed and shipped to England; the first permanent public-school building was erected on Madison Street at a cost of $7,500 in 1845; and a great River and Harbor Convention held in July, 1847, gave Chicago its first celebrity as a "Convention City." The success of the first shipment of packed or dressed meat to England led to the opening of the first cattle-yards, known as the "Bull's Head," in the vicinity of Ashland Avenue and Madison Street, in 1848. That year is memorable also because the first boat locked through the Illinois & Michigan Canal, the *General Frye*, arrived at Lake Michigan, a pleasing feature of the formal opening of this important waterway, April 16, and because the Chicago & Galena Union Railroad completed ten miles to the Des Plaines River and opened that section to passenger and freight traffic.

The first disasters of note visited the city in 1849, when there were a great flood in the Illinois River in March and an epidemic of cholera in July and August. Gas was first used for lighting the streets in 1850; an improved water service was established, the Chicago & Rock Island Railroad was completed to Chicago, and the city had another epidemic of cholera, all in 1854.

The foregoing "firsts" have a large interest, not only to the citizens of Chicago, but to students of municipal development and political economy, as they illustrate the formative processes which made the city the great financial, commercial, and industrial metropolis of the West; and in its later history the city has been the scene of several events of far-reaching influence and importance. Here, in May, 1860, the Republican National Convention put Abraham Lincoln in nomination for the Presidency. Here, on Oct. 8–9, 1871, occurred the most destructive conflagration ever known, the fire breaking out in a barn on De Koven Street at about 8.45 P.M. on the 8th (Sunday), burning over about three and a half square miles of territory, destroying 17,450 buildings, causing the death of 200 persons, rendering 98,500 persons homeless, and involving a loss of over $200,000,000. The city was rapidly recovering from this disaster when, in 1874, another fire broke out, consuming eighteen blocks with over 600 buildings, and caused a loss of more than $4,000,000. In May, 1886, there was an anarchist outbreak, resulting in rioting at the Haymarket, during which six police officers were killed and several others wounded. Eight of the rioters were convicted, of whom four were executed.

Chicago secured the World's Columbian Exposition, and from May 1 till Oct. 30, 1893, entertained more than 17,000,000 people in her "White City." (See COLUMBIAN EXPOSITION.) The noteworthy political events of 1904-05 have already been detailed. During 1910 nearly $96,000,000 was expended on new buildings in the city, more than $38,500,000 being for residences.

Chickahominy, a river in Virginia. As it lay between the Union armies and Richmond, on and near it occurred many of the most important events of McClellan's Peninsula campaign in 1862, including the battles of Williamsburg, Hanover Court-House, Fair Oaks, Mechanicsville, Cold Harbor, Savage's Station, Frazier's Farm and Malvern Hill. For details of these battles see PENINSULAR CAMPAIGN.

Chickamauga, BATTLE OF. Rosecrans, erroneously supposing Bragg had begun a retreat towards Rome when he abandoned CHATTANOOGA (*q. v.*) and marched southward through the gaps of Missionary Ridge, pushed his forces through the mountain passes and was surprised to find his antagonist attacking instead of retreating. Rosecrans proceeded at once to concentrate his own forces; and very soon the two armies were confronting each other on each side of Chickamauga Creek, in the vicinity of Crawfish Spring, each line extending towards the slope of Missionary Ridge. Rosecrans did not know that Lee had sent troops from Virginia, under Longstreet, to reinforce Bragg, who was then making his way up from Atlanta to swell the Confederate forces to the number of fully 70,000. Johnston, in Mississippi, also sent thousands of prisoners, paroled at Vicksburg and Port Hudson, to still further reinforce Bragg.

In battle order on Chickamauga Creek (Sept. 19, 1863), the Confederate right was commanded by General Polk, and the left by General Hood until Longstreet should arrive. During the previous night nearly two-thirds of the Confederates had crossed to the west side of the creek, and held the fords from Lee and Gordon's mills far towards Missionary Ridge. Rosecrans's concentrated army did not then number more than 55,000 men.

Gen. George H. Thomas, who was on the extreme left of the National line, on the slopes of Missionary Ridge, by a movement to capture an isolated Confederate brigade brought on a battle with great fierceness until dark, when the Nationals seemed to have the advantage. It had been begun by Croxton's brigade of Brannan's division, which struggled sharply with Forrest's cavalry. Thomas sent Baird's division to assist Croxton, when other Confederates became engaged, making the odds against the Nationals, and the latter, having driven the Confederates, were in turn pushed back. The pursuers dashed through the lines of United States regulars and captured a Michigan battery and about 500 men.

At that moment a heavy force of Nationals came up and joined in the battle. They now outnumbered and outflanked the Confederates, and, attacking them furiously, drove them back in disorder for a mile and a half on their reserves. The lost battery was recovered, and Brannan and Baird were enabled to reform their shattered columns. There was a lull, but at five o'clock the Confederates renewed the battle and were pressing the National line heavily, when Hazen, who was in charge of a park of artillery—twenty guns—hastened to put them in position, with such infantry supports as he could gather, and brought them to bear upon the Confederates at short range as they dashed into the road in pursuit of the Nationals. The pursuers recoiled in disorder, and thereby the day was saved on the left. Night closed the combat.

There had been some lively artillery work on the National right during the day; and at three o'clock in the afternoon Hood threw two of his divisions upon General Davis's division of McCook's corps, pushing it back and capturing a battery. Davis fought with great pertinacity until near sunset, when a brigade of Sheridan's division came to his aid. Then a successful countercharge was made; the Confederates were driven back, the battery was retaken, and a number of Confederates were made prisoners. That night General Hindman came to the Confederates with his division, and Longstreet arrived with two brigades of McLaws's veterans from Virginia, and took command of the left of Bragg's army.

BATTLE OF CHICKAMAUGA.
(From a contemporaneous sketch.)

Preparations were made for a renewal of the struggle in the morning. It was begun (Sept. 20), after a dense fog had risen from the earth, between eight and nine o'clock. The conflict was to have been opened by Polk at daylight on the National left, but he failed. Meanwhile, under cover of the fog, Thomas received reinforcements, until nearly one-half of the Army of the Cumberland present were under his command, and had erected breastworks of logs, rails, and earth. The battle was begun by an attack by Breckinridge. The intention was to interpose an overwhelming force between Rosecrans and Chattanooga, which Thomas had prevented the previous day. An exceedingly fierce struggle ensued, with varying fortunes for the combatants. The carnage on both sides was frightful. Attempts to turn the National flank were not successful, for Thomas and his veterans stood like a wall in the way. The conflict for a while was equally severe at the centre; and the blunder of an incompetent staff officer, sent with orders to General Wood, produced disaster on the National right. A gap was left in the National line, when Hood, with Stewart, charged furiously, while Buckner advanced to their support. The charge, in which Davis and Brannan and Sheridan were struck simultaneously, isolated five brigades, which lost forty per cent. of their number. By this charge the National right wing was so shattered that it began crumbling, and was soon seen flying in disorder towards Chattanooga, leaving thousands behind, killed, wounded, or prisoners.

The tide carried with it the troops led by Rosecrans, Crittenden, and McCook; and the commanding general, unable to join Thomas, and believing the whole army would speedily be hurrying pell-mell to Chattanooga, hastened to that place to provide for rallying them there. Thomas, meanwhile, ignorant of the disaster on the right, was maintaining his position firmly.

Sheridan and Davis, who had been driven over to the Dry Valley road, rallying their shattered columns, reformed them by the way, and, with McCook, halted and changed front at Rossville, with a determination to defend the pass at all hazards against the pursuers. Thomas finally withdrew from his breastworks and concentrated his troops, and formed his line on a slope of Missionary Ridge. Wood and Brannan had barely time to dispose their troops properly, when they were furiously attacked, the Confederates throwing in fresh troops continually. General Granger, commanding reserves at Rossville, hastened to the assistance of Thomas with Steedman's division. The latter fought his way to the crest of a hill, and then turning his artillery upon his assailants, drove them down the southern slope of the ridge with great slaughter. They returned to the attack with an overwhelming force, determined to drive the Nationals from the ridge, and pressed Thomas most severely.

Finally, when they were moving along a ridge and in a gorge, to assail his right flank and rear, Granger formed two brigades (Whittaker's and Mitchell's) into a charging party, and hurled them against the Confederates led by Hindman. Steedman led the charging party, with a regimental flag in his hand, and soon won a victory. In the space of twenty minutes the Confederates disappeared, and the Nationals held both the ridge and gorge.

Very soon a greater portion of the Confederate army were swarming around the foot of the ridge, on which stood Thomas with the remnant of seven divisions of the Army of the Cumberland. The Confederates were led by Longstreet. There seemed no hope for the Nationals. But Thomas stood like a rock, and his men repulsed assault after assault until the sun went down, when he began the withdrawal of his troops to Rossville, for his ammunition was almost exhausted. General Garfield, Rosecrans's chief of staff, had arrived with orders for Thomas to take the command of all the forces, and, with McCook and Crittenden, to take a strong position at Rossville. It was then that Thomas had the first reliable information of disaster on the right. Confederates seeking to obstruct the movement were driven back, with a loss of 200 men made prisoners. So ended the battle of Chickamauga.

The National loss was reported at 16,326, of whom 1,687 were killed. The total loss of officers was 974. It is probable the entire Union loss, including the missing, was 19,000. The Confederate loss was reported at 20,500, of whom 2,673 were killed. Rosecrans took 2,003 prisoners, thirty-six guns, twenty caissons, and 8,450 small-arms, and lost, as prisoners, 7,500. Bragg claimed to have captured over 8,000 prisoners (including the wounded), fifty-one guns, and 15,000 small-arms.

The Confederates were victors on the field, but their triumph was not decisive. On the evening of the 20th the whole National army withdrew in good order to a position in front of Chattanooga, and on the following day Bragg advanced and took possession of Lookout Mountain and the whole of Missionary Ridge.

Chickamauga and Chattanooga National Park, established by Congress in 1890, in the southeastern part of Tennessee and northwestern part of Georgia; embraces the famous battle-fields of Chickamauga and of the scenes which occurred around Chattanooga. Both Tennessee and Georgia ceded to the United States jurisdiction over the historic fields as well as the approaching roads. The roads, buildings, and conditions existing at the time of the battles are gradually being restored. A road 20 miles in extent has been constructed along the crest of Missionary Ridge where occurred some of the heaviest actions. The headquarters of the general officers and the positions of participating organizations, batteries, regiments and detached forces of both armies, are marked with inscribed tablets. The erection of monuments to commemorate the smaller organizations has been left to the States and veterans' societies. The park is designed to create a "comprehensive and extended military object-lesson."

Chickasaw Bayou, BATTLE OF. When Gen. W. T. Sherman came down from Memphis to engage in the siege of Vicksburg, late in 1862, with about 20,000 men and some heavy siege guns, he was joined by troops from Helena, Ark., and was met by a gunboat fleet, under Admiral Porter, at the mouth of the Yazoo River, just above the city (Dec. 25). The two commanders arranged a plan for attacking Vicksburg in the rear. They went up the Yazoo to capture some batteries at Chickasaw Bayou and other points. The Yazoo sweeps round in a great bend within a few miles of Vicksburg. The range of hills on which Vicksburg stands extends to the Yazoo, about 12 miles above the city, where they terminate in Haines's Bluff.

There is a deep natural ditch extending from the Yazoo below Haines's Bluff to the Mississippi, called Chickasaw Bayou, passing near the bluffs, which were fortified, and along their bases were rifle-pits for sharp-shooters. This bayou lay in the path of Sherman's march up the bluffs, which must be carried to gain the rear of Vicksburg. His troops moved in four columns, commanded respectively by Generals Morgan, A. J. Smith, Morgan L. Smith, and F. Steele. They moved on Dec. 27, bivouacked without fire that night, and proceeded to the attack the next morning. The Nationals drove the Confederate pickets across the bayou, and everywhere the ground was so soft that causeways of logs had to be built for the passage of troops and artillery. The Nationals were seriously enfiladed by the Confederate batteries, and sharp-shooters. The right of the Union troops was commanded by Gen. F. P. Blair, who led the way across the bayou over a bridge his men had built, captured two lines of rifle-pits, and fought desperately to gain the crest of the hill before him. Others followed, and a severe battle ensued. Pemberton, the Confederate chief, had arrived, and so active were the Confederates on the bluffs that the Nationals were repulsed with heavy loss. Blair lost one-third of his brigade. Darkness closed the struggle, when Sherman had lost about 2,000 men, and his antagonists only 207.

Chickasaw Indians, a tribe of the Creek confederacy that formerly inhabited the country along the Mississippi from the borders of the Choctaw domain to the Ohio River, and eastward beyond the Tennessee to the lands of the Cherokees

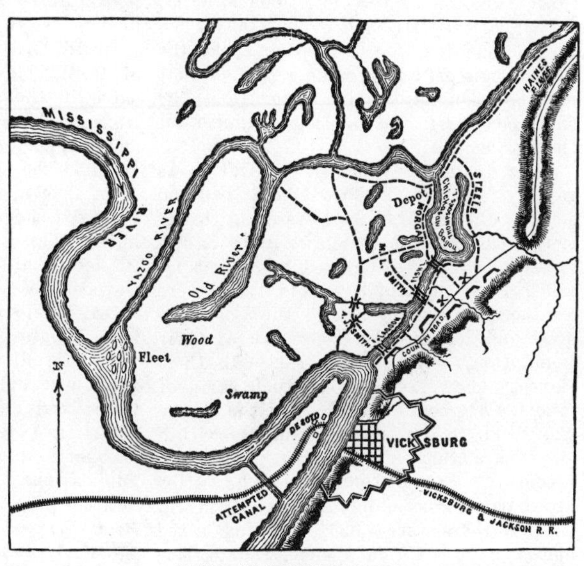

BATTLE OF CHICKASAW BAYOU.

and Shawnees. They were warlike, and were the early friends of the English and the inveterate foes of the French, who twice (1736 and 1740) invaded their country under Bienville and De Noailles. The Chickasaws said they came from west of the Mississippi, under the guardianship of a great dog, with a pole for a guide. At night they stuck the pole in the ground, and went the way it leaned every morning. Their dog was drowned in crossing the Mississippi, and after a while their pole, in the interior of Alabama, remained upright, and there they settled. De Soto passed a winter among them (1540–41), when they numbered 10,000 warriors. These were reduced to 450 when the French seated themselves in Louisiana.

Wars with the new-comers and surrounding tribes occurred until the middle of the eighteenth century. They favored the English in the Revolution, when they had about 1,000 warriors. They joined the white people against the Creeks in

1795, and always remained the friends of the pale faces; and, in 1818, they had ceded all their lands north of the State of Mississippi. Some of the tribe had already emigrated to Arkansas. In 1834 they ceded all their lands to the United States, amounting to over 6,400,000 acres, for which they received $3,646,000. Then they joined the Choctaws, who spoke the same language, and became a part of that nation. During their emigration the small-pox destroyed a large number of their tribe.

They did not advance in civilization as rapidly as the Choctaws, and had no schools until 1851. They were politically separated from the Choctaws in 1855, and have since been recognized as a distinct tribe. Led by their agents, who were Southern men, they joined the Confederates, and lost nearly one-fourth of their population, much stock, and all their slaves. They gave up 7,000,000 acres of land for 4½ cents an acre, and the money was to go to the freedmen, unless within two years they allowed the negroes to become a part of the tribe. The latter alternative was adopted, Jan. 10, 1873. In 1904 there were 4,826, including mixed bloods, at the Union agency, Indian Territory. See CHOCTAW INDIANS.

Chickering, JESSE, political economist; born in Dover, N. H., Aug. 31, 1797; graduated at Harvard College in 1818; later studied medicine and practised in Boston, Mass. His publications include *Statistical View of the Population of Massachusetts from 1765–1840; Emigration into the United States; Reports on the Census of Boston;* and a *Letter Addressed to the President of the United States on Slavery, considered in Relation to the Principles of Constitutional Government in Great Britain and in the United States.* He died in West Roxbury, Mass., May 29, 1855.

Child, DAVID LEE, abolitionist; born in West Boylston, Mass., July 8, 1794; graduated at Harvard College in 1817; was later admitted to the bar. In 1830 he was editor of the *Massachusetts Journal,* and while holding a seat in the legislature opposed the annexation of Texas; afterwards he issued a tract on the subject entitled *Naboth's Vineyard.* In 1836 he published ten articles on the subject of slavery, and in the following year, while in Paris, addressed a memoir to the *Société pour l'abolition d'esclavage.* He also forwarded a pamphlet on the same subject to the *Eclectic Review* in London. In 1843–44 he edited (with his wife) the *Anti-Slavery Standard* in New York. He died in Wayland, Mass., Sept. 18, 1874.

Child, LYDIA MARIA, author; born in Medford, Mass., Feb. 11, 1802; educated in the common schools; began her literary career in 1819; and was noted as a supporter of the abolition movement. In 1859 she sent a letter of sympathy to John Brown, who was then imprisoned at Harper's Ferry, offering to become his nurse. This offer he declined, but requested her to aid his family, which she did. Governor Wise, of Virginia, politely rebuked her in a letter, and another epistle from Senator Mason's wife threatened her with eternal punishment. These letters with her replies were subsequently published and reached a circulation of 300,000. In 1840–43 she was editor of the *National Anti-Slavery Standard.* Her publications include *The Rebels; The First Settlers of New England; Freedman's Book; Appeal for that Class of Americans called Africans,* etc. She died in Wayland, Mass., Oct. 20, 1880.

Children, DEPENDENT. See DEPENDENT CHILDREN, CARE OF.

Children's Day, or FLORAL SUNDAY, a Sunday set apart annually in June by most of the Protestant evangelical churches in the United States, when the Sunday-school children are given charge of one or both church services.

Childs, GEORGE WILLIAM, publisher; born in Baltimore, Md., May 12, 1829; book publisher, 1850–63; editor of the Philadelphia *Public Ledger* (purchased in conjunction with A. J. Drexel), 1864–94. He died in Philadelphia, Pa., Feb. 3. 1894.

Chile. Towards the close of 1890 a revolution occurred in Chile, South America. It was the result of certain abuses of power on the part of the President of that republic, and the conflict was carried on with great bitterness between his adherents and the revolutionary party, with the Chilean Congress at its head. Early in the course of the war almost the entire Chilean navy deserted the cause of the President and espoused that of the revolutionists. Among the vessels employed by the latter was the *Itata*. In the spring of 1891 this vessel put in at the harbor of San Diego, Cal., for the purpose of securing a cargo of arms and ammunition for the revolutionists. She was seized by the United States authorities.

Soon afterwards, on the night of May 6, the *Itata*, disregarding this action of the United States, sailed away from San Diego with the American officer on board. The latter, however, was landed a few miles south of San Diego. The *Itata* then took on board, from the American schooner *Robert and Minnie*, a cargo of arms and ammunition and sailed for Chile. On May 9 the United States war-ship *Charleston* was ordered in pursuit, with instructions to take her at all hazards. The chase lasted twenty-five days. The *Charleston* reached the bay of Iquique first. A few days later, upon arriving at Iquique, the *Itata* was promptly given over to the United States officers. She was manned with an American crew, and sent back to the harbor of San Diego.

The Chilean war, however, was brought to a close by the complete success of the revolutionary forces, and the case against the *Itata* was allowed to drop.

About the same time another complication arose between Chile and the United States. While the United States cruiser *Baltimore* was in the harbor of Valparaiso, a party of her sailors became involved in a riot with the Chileans, Oct. 16, 1891. Several sailors were wounded, two died; thirty-six were arrested by the authorities. On Oct. 23 President Harrison despatched a message to United States Minister Egan at Santiago, demanding reparation, and two war-ships were sent to the country. On Dec. 11, the Chilean minister of foreign affairs, Matta, sent an offensive communication, which became known as the "Matta Note." The President despatched a protest to the Chilean government, and on Jan. 25 sent a message to Congress. Meantime at Valparaiso an inquiry was held on the riot, and three Chileans were sentenced to penal servitude. President Montt withdrew the "Matta Note" and Chile paid an indemnity of $75,000.

During 1893 and 1894 Chile was shaken by several domestic revolutions, during which much American property was destroyed. In November, 1895, Señor Barros, a liberal, formed a cabinet and paid to the United States $250,000 for damage done during the revolutions. In 1896 Chile concluded peace treaties with all her neighbors.

Chilkat, name of a village at the head of the Lynn Canal, Alaska, on the peninsula between Chilkat and Chilkoot inlets; also a pass, known as the DALTON TRAIL; altitude, 3,100 feet; traversed by miners in reaching the Klondike gold-fields.

Chilkoot, name of (1) an inlet of Alaska; the e. arm of the Lynn Canal; also known as the TAYA and DYEA INLET; receives the Skagway and Taya rivers; has the towns of Skagway and Dyea at its upper extremity; to the n. are White and Chilkoot passes, leading to the Yukon and Klondike regions; (2) a notable pass in Alaska; altitude, 3,500 feet; is the old trail used by the Indians, and for many years the only one taken by miners to reach the interior. It is the shortest route to the Yukon. The difficulties and dangers attending this route formerly were many, proving fatal in numerous instances to those unaccustomed to endure hardships, but the route has lost much of its importance since the completion of an aerial railway across the pass and of a railroad across the neighboring White Pass.

Chillicothe, city and capital of Ross county, O.; on the Sciolo River, 51 miles s. of Columbus; in a farming and iron and coal mining region; founded in 1796 by immigrants from Virginia; State capital, 1800–10. Pop. (1900) 12,976; (1910) 14,508.

CHINA

China. From time to time during the latter part of 1899 and the early part of 1900 came disturbing reports, from missionaries and the representatives of the United States and the European powers stationed in the northern provinces of China, of the rapid spread and threatening attitude of the Boxers, a secret organization having for its purpose the extermination of all foreigners and the abolition of all foreign influence from Chinese territory. The native name of this society is *I-ho-ch'uan*, "Combination of Righteous Harmony Fists"; it had for its leader Prince Tuan, the father of the heir-presumptive to the Chinese throne; and had its origin in the intense anti-foreign sentiment excited by the occupation by the European powers of Chinese territory under various cessions in the years immediately following the Chino-Japanese War (1895), the superstitions of the ignorant classes, and the hatred, in certain districts, of the missionaries, who, in their zeal for converts, had entered under treaty rights into every part of the empire.

Conditions grew more critical and the threatening of the missionaries increased in extent and intensity until, on May 19, 1900, the Christian village of Lai-Shun, 70 miles from Peking, was destroyed, and seventy-three native converts massacred. The representatives of the foreign powers, on May 21, addressed a joint note to the Tsung-li-Yamen, the foreign office of the Chinese government, calling for the suppression of the Boxers, and the restoration of order. This and all further attempts on the part of the ministers met with little or no response, the Court itself openly encouraging the anti-foreign sentiment, and the young Emperor, Kwang-Su, being entirely under the influence of the Empress Dowager, notorious for her hatred of and opposition to the reformation policy. Upon the report of United States MINISTER EDWIN H. CONGER (*q. v.*), that the Boxers were operating within a few miles of Peking, and of the great danger to the property and lives of the Americans in that part of the world, the United States government ordered REAR-ADMIRAL LOUIS KEMPFF (*q. v.*) to proceed at once with the flag-ship *Newark* to Taku, at the mouth of the Peiho River, the harbor for Tientsin and Peking. Here gathered, within a few days, the available war-ships of Great Britain, Russia, France, Germany, and Italy. Captain McCalla, with 100 men from the *Newark*, landed and proceeded to Tientsin, and on May 31, a small international force, including seven officers and fifty-six men of the American marine corps, were despatched to Peking, as a guard for the legations, and were admitted to the city.

On June 2, Mr. H. V. Norman, an English missionary, was murdered by the Boxers at Yung Ching, a few miles from Peking, and during the following days the rioting and destruction of property seemed to break out on every side with renewed violence. The imperial decrees against the rioters were only half-hearted, and it was responsibly reported that, in spite of the representations of the Chinese government of heavy engagements in their efforts to put down the uprising, a large number of the imperial forces were fighting with the Boxers. Fifty miles of the Luban Railway had been destroyed by the anti-foreign mob, with many stores and supplies for the new lines then under construction. Chapels and mission settlements in Shantung and Pechili provinces were looted and burned and hundreds of native Christians massacred. Finally the railway from Tientsin to Peking was cut.

On June 10, the British Admiral Seymour, with 2,000 men, drawn from the international forces in Tientsin, set out to repair the railway, and found it so badly damaged that in two days he had advanced only 35 miles. Then came the news that he had been surrounded by countless hordes of Chinese, imperial soldiers and Boxers, and that all communication with Tientsin and Peking was closed. Not until June 26 was he able, after receiving reinforcements, to cut his way back into Tientsin. He had lost 374 men, and had not been able to get within 25 miles of Peking, his whole command barely escaping annihilation. In this unfortunate advance and retreat, Captain McCalla, who was the leader of the American contingent, was highly commended for his bravery and resourcefulness.

On June 17, the Chinese forts at Taku opened fire upon the warships of the allied forces, and those of Germany, Russia, Great Britain, France, and Japan immediately returned the bombardment. The fortifications were finally captured at the point of the bayonet by soldiers landed at a point enabling them to assault in the rear. Over 100 Europeans were killed and wounded in this engagement; the Chinese loss was estimated at 700. The American Admiral Kempff did not participate in the attack, taking the ground that the United States was not at war with China, and that such hostile action would merely serve to unite the Chinese against the foreigners.

On June 18, the United States government ordered the battle-ship *Oregon* and the gunboats *Yorktown*, *Nashville*, and *Monocacy*, and the 9th Regiment, 1,400 men, under Col. Emerson H. Liscum, from Manila to Taku, and other United States forces were held in readiness fo service in China. While on the way, June 28, the *Oregon* ran aground in the Gulf of Pechili, in a fog. One week later she was floated, without having suffered serious damage, and through the courtesy of the Japanese government sent to the national docks at Kure for repairs. On June 24, REAR-ADMIRAL GEORGE C. REMEY (*q. v.*) proceeded with the flag-ship *Brooklyn* from Manila to succeed Admiral Kempff in the command of the American fleet. On June 26, GEN. ADNA R. CHAFFEE (*q. v.*) was appointed to the command of the American army in China, and 6,300 troops, infantry and cavalry, intended for the Philippines, proceeded to China, and the United States government announced that it would, if necessary, increase the American army of occupation to 16,000. On July 4, Secretary of State John Hay, in a note to the European powers, declared the attitude of the United States towards the Chinese troubles.

AMERICAN TROOPS ENTERING PEKING.

On June 21–23 the allies had forced their way, by the aid of fire from the fleet, into the foreign quarter at Tientsin, and had united with the Europeans there besieged by the Chinese Boxers and imperial soldiers; for many days hard fighting was carried on against this enemy, sheltered in the native portion of the city and on the walls. On July 2, the women and children, at great risk, were sent down the Peiho to Taku, and for the following ten days the Chinese bombarded the foreign city. On June 9, 11, and 13, attempts were made by the allies to capture the native city. On the 13th Colonel Liscum was killed while leading his men. On July 14, the forts were captured, and the Chinese driven out with great loss. The casualties of the allies were 875, of whom 215 were Americans.

The temporary success of the Chinese at Tientsin, the siege of the legations in Peking, and the murder, June 12, of the Japanese chancellor of legation, and, June 20, of Baron von Ketteler, the German minister, seemed to inspire them with new fury, and the Boxer craze spread with fearful rapidity over all the northern districts, while in the south much uneasiness was shown. On July 15, a Chinese force invaded Russia, and the latter government immediately declared the Amur district in a state of war. July 23, President McKinley, in answer to the request of the Chinese Emperor for the good offices of the United States in bringing about peace, demanded that the imperial government should first make known to the world whether the representatives of the foreign powers in Peking were alive; and that it co-operate with the allied army gathering for their relief. On July 20, a message, purporting to have been sent by Minister Conger, dated July 18, was received through Minister Wu at Washington, and was accepted as authentic by the United States government, and subsequently by the European powers, Minister Wu having personally guaranteed to get a message to and from Mr. Conger.

By the latter part of July the international force numbered 30,000 men, and on Aug. 4, a relief column 16,000 strong left Tientsin and met its first determined resistance at Peitsang, Aug. 5, which it captured after a hard fight, with a loss of about 200 killed and wounded. With a considerable loss, Yangtsun, Aug. 7, and Tung Chow, Aug. 12, were occupied, and on Aug. 14, the relief forces entered Peking. The Emperor and the Empress Dowager had fled and the Chinese troops were surrounded in the inner city. Fighting in the streets continued till Aug. 28, when the allied troops marched in force through the Forbidden City.

The relief of the besieged foreigners was most timely. For forty-five days, 3,000 souls, including 2,200 native converts, had been shut up in the compound of the British Legation, subjected to the artillery and rifle fire of 50,000 troops under Prince Tuan. With the exception of a truce of twelve days after the fall of Tientsin, July 17, the bombardment scarcely ceased day or night. Provisions and ammunition were very short, and the exposure and constant labor were telling severely on the besieged. Many efforts were made on the part of the Chinese to induce the besieged to proceed to Tientsin under promise of safe escort, but were promptly refused. The missionaries were in many cases less fortunate. A few made their way into Peking, one party escaped across the Gobi Desert, and some succeeded in making their way to the more tolerant southern provinces; but in the inland cities many perished at their posts. At Pao-ting-fu, 80 miles southwest of Peking, fourteen persons, including women and children, were butchered by order of the authorities.

Military operations ceased with the occupation of Peking, with the exception of punitive expeditions sent to Pao-ting-fu and the more disturbed districts. On Aug. 10, Count von Waldersee, field-marshal of the German army, was unanimously approved as commander of the allied forces. He arrived in Shanghai Sept. 21. On Oct. 3, the withdrawal of the United States troops was begun. Oct. 1, Li Hung Chang reached Peking, and the Chinese Peace Commission, consisting of Li Hung Chang, Yung Lu, Hsu Tung, and Prince Ching, was announced. Negotiations were begun at once, and on Dec. 22 the allied forces came to an agreement as to the demands upon China, which was accepted by the Chinese Emperor on Dec. 30.

This agreement provided: 1. The sending of an Imperial prince to Berlin on an expiatory mission. 2. Punishment of those designated by the powers. 3. Reparation to Japan for the murder of Mr. Sujyama. 4. An expiatory monument in all the desecrated foreign cemeteries. 5. Importation of arms and ammunition to cease. 6. Indemnity to each and every individual or society for loss incurred through Chinese. 7. Right to maintain guards in foreign legations. 8. Destruction of Tientsin forts. 9. Right to military occupation of certain points. 10. Imperial decree to be issued prohibiting, under penalty of death, membership in any anti-foreign society, and holding viceroys responsible for maintenance of order. 11. New commercial treaties to be negotiated. 12. Reform of the Chinese foreign office. Occupation of Peking until the agreement is carried out. Prince Tuan and Duke Lan were banished to Turkestan, General Tung Fu Siang was degraded, Prince Chuang Ying Niew and Chao Su Kiam were ordered to commit suicide, Hsu Cheng Yu, Yu Hsieu, and Kih Sin were beheaded.

The Chinese court made their formal re-entry into Peking on Jan. 7, 1902. An Anglo-Japanese agreement for maintaining the independence and territorial integrity of China and Korea was signed Jan. 30, 1902, and a convention between China and Russia on April 8, in which Russia recognized Manchuria as an integral part of China, and agreed to reduce the period of Russian occupation from three years to eighteen months. A treaty with Great Britain was signed Sept. 5, in which China agreed to abolish the likin and kindred taxes for adequate considerations, on Jan. 1, 1904, provided the other powers entered into a similar engagement. China also agreed to open four new treaty ports; and, in a treaty with the United States, guaranteed to make Mukden and Antung open ports also. In 1903 Japan and Russia engaged in negotiations concerning paramount interests in Korea and the status of Manchuria. On Feb. 6, 1904, Japan severed diplomatic relations with Russia, and on the 8th began war against her, Manchuria becoming the field of action.

China and the Powers. A clear exposition of the Chinese situation in 1900 is given in the following article written by Lord Charles Beresford:

Observation of recent events teaches us that, if we continue to leave China to herself without recuperative power from within, or firm and determined assistance from without, her ultimate disintegration is only a question of time. The reforms which are urgently required in China, both for the benefit of that empire and its people, and for the development of the trade of friendly nations, may be shortly summarized as follows:

1. The appointment of a foreign financial adviser to direct the administration and collection of internal revenue.

2. The reform of currency, so as to afford a more stable exchange.

3. The establishment and centralization of mints.

4. The abolition of the present *octroi* and likin charges on goods which have already paid duty at the ports. In return for this, China should be allowed to increase her present tariff. Trade would not be damaged so much by slightly increased taxation, as it is injured and hindered by the delays and uncertainties of the present fiscal system.

5. The rearrangement of the salt monopoly, and general administrative reform.

6. The establishment and maintenance of a proper military and police, capable of affording that protection to which the foreign merchant is entitled for himself or his goods.

7. The opening up of the country and its resources, by giving greater facilities to native or foreign capital in the development of the minerals of the country, and improvements in the lines of communication, including postal and telegraphic reforms.

8. The right of residence in the interior to be conceded to foreigners.

9. The promotion of all reforms and the introduction of all changes which are likely to promote the cause of civilization and the well-being of the Chinese people.

A coalition of the four great trading powers—England, Germany, Russia, and the United States—could obtain these reforms with advantage to themselves and benefit to China, and, indeed, the trading world.

In a very few years, with this assistance loyally rendered, China would have an army capable of protecting herself, as long as she retained the foreign officers. The idea that the Chinese are not good soldiers is a great mistake. I was permitted to inspect most of the armies, and all of the forts and arsenals of China, as will be seen by the detailed account in my report, and I am convinced that, properly armed, disciplined, and led, there could be no better material than the Chinese soldier. I leave it to the commercial classes of the United States to say whether it is not worth their while to incur such slight risks for such great profit, and for so good an object.

On sound business lines this policy appeals to the American nation; but, in addition to that, are we going to let this opportunity slip of drawing the two Anglo-Saxon nations together for the cause of civilized progress, and the benefit of the world at large? Great nations have great responsibilities, to which they must be true, and when those responsibilities and self-interest go hand in hand, it would be unwise to miss the opportunity.

Events are moving very rapidly in the Far East. A decision must be arrived at, and action of some sort taken very soon. It is the duty of Great Britain to lead, and I believe that the United States will not refuse to follow, but that both nations will combine to hoist aloft the banner of civilization and industrial progress, for the benefit of their own people, as well as for the benefit of China, and of the world.

Chinese-American Reciprocity. Wu Ting Fang, former Chinese minister to the United States, wrote as follows:

Confucius was once asked for a single word which might serve as a guiding principle through life. "Is not reciprocity such a word?" answered the great sage. "What you do not want done to yourself, do not do to others." This is the "Golden Rule" which should govern the relations of man to man. It is the foundation of society. It lies at the bottom of every system of morality, and every system of law. Therefore, if permanent relations are to be established between two nations, reciprocity must be the key-note of every arrangement entered into between them.

Having recognized this great principle of international intercourse, how shall we apply it to the case of China and the United States in such a manner as to result in mutual helpfulness? Assuredly, the first thing to do is to take a general survey of the situation and see what are the needs of each country. Then we shall perceive clearly how each may help the other to a higher plane of material development and prosperity.

The United States now has its industrial machinery perfectly adjusted to the production of wealth on a scale of unprecedented magnitude. Of land, the first of the three agents of production enumerated by economists, the United States is fortunately blessed with an almost unlimited amount. Its territory stretches from ocean to ocean, and from the snows of the Arctic Circle to the broiling sun of the tropics. Within these limits are found all the products of soil, forest, and mine that are useful to man. With respect to labor, the second agent of production, the United States at first naturally suffered the disadvantage common to all new countries. But here the genius of the people came into play to relieve the situation. That necessity which is "the mother of invention" substituted the sewing-machine for women's fingers, the reaper for farm-hands, the cotton-gin for slaves. The efficiency of labor was thereby multiplied, in many cases, a hundredfold. The ingenious manner in which capital, the third agent of production, is put to a profitable use is equally characteristic of America. Since competition reduces profits, the formation of industrial combinations, commonly called trusts, is for the capitalist the logical solution of the difficulty. These enable the vast amount of capital in the country to secure the best results with the greatest economy. Whether they secure "the greatest good to the greatest number" is another matter.

The development of the resources of the United States by the use of machinery and by the combination of capital has now reached a point which may be termed critical. The productive power of the country increases so much faster than its capacity for consumption that the demand of a population of 75,000,000 is no sooner felt than supplied. There is constant danger of over-production, with all its attendant consequences. Under these circumstances, it is imperative for the farmers and manufacturers of the United States to seek an outlet for their products and goods in foreign markets. But whither shall they turn?

On the other side of the Pacific lies the vast empire of China, which in extent of territory and density of population exceeds the whole of Europe. To be more particular, the province of Szechuen can muster more able-bodied men than the German Empire. The province of Shantung can boast of as many native-born sons as France. Scatter all the inhabitants of Costa Rica or Nicaragua in Canton, and they would be completely lost in that city's surging throngs. Transport all the people of Chile into China and they would fill only a city of the first class. Further comparisons are needless. Suffice it to say that China has her teeming millions to feed and to clothe. Many of the supplies come from outside. The share furnished by the United States might be greatly increased. According to the statistics published by the United States government, China in 1899 took American goods to the value of $14,437,422, of which amount $9,844,565 was paid for cotton goods. All the European countries combined bought only $1,484,363 worth of American cotton manufactures during the same period. The amount of similar purchases made by the Central American states was $739,259; by all the South American countries $2,713,967. It thus appears that China is the largest buyer of American cotton goods. British America comes next in the list with purchases amounting to $2,759,164. Cotton cloth has a wide range of uses in all parts of the Chinese Empire, and it is almost impossible for the supply to equal the demand.

Up to the year 1898 cotton goods and kerosene were the only articles imported from the United States in large enough quantities to have a value of over $1,000,000. But I noticed in the statistics published by the United States government for the year 1899 that manufactures of iron and steel have also passed that mark. This is due to the fact that China has now begun in real earnest the work of building railroads. The demand for construction materials is great. The value of locomotives imported in 1899 from the United States was $732,212.

Besides the articles mentioned, there are many others of American origin which do not figure in the customs returns as such. These find their way into China through adjacent countries, especially Hong-Kong. At least three-fourths of the imports of Hong-Kong, notably wheat, flour, and canned goods, are destined for consumption in the Chinese mainland.

Such is the present condition of trade between the United States and China. That trade can be greatly extended. Let the products of American farms, mills, and workshops once catch the Chinese fancy, and America need look no farther for a market. The present popularity of American kerosene illustrates the readiness of the Chinese to accept any article that fills a long-felt want. They have recognized in kerosene a cheap and good illuminant, much superior to their own nut-oil, and it has consequently found its way into distant and outlying parts of the empire where the very name of America is unknown. Stores in the interior now send their agents to the treaty-ports for it. I would suggest that American farmers and manufacturers might find it to their advantage to study the wants and habits of the Chinese and the conditions of trade in China.

Thus we see that China can give the United States a much-needed market. What, on the other hand, can the United States do for China? Let us consider China's stock of the three requisites for the production of wealth—land, labor, and capital.

The Chinese Empire embraces a continuous territory which stretches over sixty degrees of longitude and thirty-four degrees of latitude. Nature has endowed this immense region with every variety of soil and climate, but has, however, scattered her bounties over it with an uneven hand. That portion which comprises the eighteen provinces of China proper, extending from the Great Wall to the China Sea, and from the Tibetan plateau to the Pacific Ocean, is more highly favored than the rest. Whenever China is mentioned, it is generally this particular portion of the empire that is meant. On this land hundreds of generations of men have lived and died without exhausting its richness and fertility. There remains for generations to come untold wealth of nature lying hidden within the bowels of the earth. The mines of Yunnan, though they have for centuries supplied the government mints with copper for the coining of those pieces of money commonly known as cash, only await the introduction of modern methods of extraction to yield an annual output as large as that of the famous Calumet and Hecla mines. The sands of the Yangtsze, washed down from the highlands of Tibet, contain so much gold that that part of its course as it enters the province of Szechuen is called the River of Golden Sand. Much more important than these, however, are the deposits of coal which underlie the surface formation of every province. All varieties of coal are found, from the softest lignite to the hardest anthracite, and in such quantities that, according to the careful estimate of Baron Richtofen, the famous German traveller and geologist, the province of Shansi alone can supply the whole world, at the present rate of consumption, for 3,000 years. In most cases beds of iron-ore lie in close proximity to those of coal, and can hence be easily worked and smelted. In short, the natural resources of China, in both variety and quantity, are so great that she stands second to no other nation in potential wealth. To reduce this potentiality to actuality is for her the most important question of the hour. For this purpose she has an almost unlimited supply of labor at her command.

Every village can count its thousands of laborers, every city its tens of thousands. Experience proves that the Chinese as all-round laborers can easily distance all competitors. They are industrious, intelligent, and orderly. They can work under conditions that would kill a man of a less hardy race, in heat that would suit a salamander or in cold that would please a polar bear, sustaining their energies through long hours of unremitting toil with only a few bowls of rice.

But have the Chinese sufficient capital to carry on their industrial operations? They are a nation of shopkeepers. What capital they have is usually invested in small business ventures. It is their instinct to avoid large enterprises. Thus the capital in the country, though undoubtedly large, may be likened to a pile of sand on the beach. It has great extent, but is so utterly lacking in cohesion that out of it no lofty structure can be built. Before China can be really on the high road to prosperity, it must find means of fully utilizing every economic advantage that it has. Modern methods are its greatest need. Here is America's opportunity.

Of all public works, China has most pressing need of railroads. Only a few years ago it would have been difficult to convince one man in ten of the immediate necessity for the introduction of railroads into all the provinces of the empire. To-day at least nine out of every ten believe that railroads ought to be built as fast as possible. This complete change of public opinion within so short a time shows perhaps better than anything else how fast China is getting into the swing of the world's forward movement. There are at present only about 400 miles of railroad open to traffic throughout the whole country, and all the lines building and projected foot up to 5,000 or 6,000 miles more. China proper covers about as many square miles as the States east of the Mississippi. Those States, with a population of 50,000,000, require 100,000 miles of railroad to do their business. China, with a population eight times as large, would naturally be supposed to need at least about an equal mileage of roads for her purposes. It would not be strange if the activity in railroad construction in the United States soon after the Civil War should find a parallel in China in coming years.

The building of railroads in China does not partake of the speculative character which attended the building of some of the American roads. There are no wild regions to be opened up for settlement, no new towns to be built along the route. Here is a case of the railroad following the population, and not that of the population following the railroad. A road built through populous cities and famous marts has not long to wait for traffic. It would pay from the beginning.

The first railroad in China was built for the transportation of coal from the Kaiping mines to the port of Taku. The line, though in an out-of-the-way corner of the empire, proved so profitable from the very start that it was soon extended to Tientsin and Peking in one direction, and to Shanhaikwan, the eastern terminus of the Great Wall, in the other. Not long ago it was thought advisable to build a branch beyond Shanhaikwan to the treaty-port of Newchwang. The era of railroad building in China may be said to have just dawned. China desires nothing better than to have Americans lend a hand in this great work.

It gave me great pleasure two years ago to obtain for an American company a concession to build a railroad between Hankow, the great distributing centre of central China, and Canton, the great distributing centre of south China. The line is to connect with the Lu-Han line on the north and with the Kowloon line on the south, and throughout its whole length of more than 900 miles will run through opulent cities, fertile valleys, and cultivated plains. The construction of such a line by Americans through the heart of China cannot fail to bring the people of the two countries into closer relations.

Besides railroads, there are other public works which China must undertake sooner or later. Among them are river and harbor improvements, city water supplies, street lighting, and street railways. Owing to the traditional friendship between the two countries, our people are well disposed towards Americans. They are willing to follow their lead in these new enterprises, where they might spurn the assistance of other people with whom they have been on less friendly terms in the past.

Now, reciprocity demands the "open door." China long ago adopted that policy in her foreign intercourse. She has treaty relations with all the European powers, together with the United States, Brazil, Peru, Mexico, Japan, and Korea. All these are equally "favored nations" in every sense of the term. The Swede and the Dane enjoy the same rights, privileges, immunities, and exemptions, with respect to commerce, navigation, travel, and residence throughout the length and breadth of the empire as are accorded to the Russian or the Englishman. Any favor that may be granted to Japan, for instance, at once inures to the benefit of the United States. Indeed, China, in her treatment of strangers within her gates, has in a great many respects gone even beyond what is required of international usage. According to the usual practice of nations, no country is expected to accord to foreigners rights which are not enjoyed by its own subjects or citizens. But China has been so long accustomed to indemnify foreigners who have fallen victims to mob violence that she is looked upon in a sense as an insurer of the lives and property of all foreigners residing within her borders. To such an extent is this idea current among foreigners in China that some years ago an American missionary in the province of Shantung, who happened to have some articles stolen from his house in the night, estimated his loss at $60, and actually sent the bill through the American minister at Peking to the Foreign Office for payment. The Chinese tariff also favors foreigners resident in China much more than it does the Chinese themselves. Most articles imported for the use of foreigners are on the free-list. Such is the treatment which Americans, in common with the subjects and citizens of other foreign powers, receive in China.

Justice would seem to demand equal consideration for the Chinese on the part of the United States. China does not ask for special favors. All she wants is enjoyment of the same privileges accorded other nationalities. Instead, she is singled out for discrimination and made the subject of hostile legislation. Her door is wide open to the people of the United States, but their door is slammed in the face of her people. I am not so biased as to advocate any policy that might be detrimental to the best interests of the people of the United States. If they think it desirable to keep out the objectionable class of Chinese, by all means let them do so. Let them make their immigration laws as strict as possible, but let them be applicable to all foreigners. Would it not be fairer to exclude the illiterate and degenerate classes of all nations rather than to make an arbitrary ruling against the Chinese alone? Would it not be wiser to set up some specific test of fitness, such as ability to read intelligently the American Constitution? That would give the Chinese a chance along with the rest of the world, and yet effectually restrict their immigration.

Since the law and the treaty forbid the coming of Chinese laborers, I must do all I can to restrict their immigration. I should, however, like to call attention to the fact that the Chinese Exclusion Act, as enforced, scarcely accomplishes the purpose for which it was passed. It aimed to provide for the exclusion of Chinese laborers only, while freely admitting all others. As a matter of fact, the respectable merchant, who would be an irreproachable addition to the population of any country, has been frequently turned back, whereas the Chinese highbinders, the riffraff and scum of the nation, fugitives from justice and adventurers of all types, have too often effected an entrance without much difficulty. This is because the American officials at the entrance ports are ignorant of Chinese character and dialects and cannot always discriminate between the worthy and the unworthy. Rascals succeed in deceiving them, while the respectable but guileless Chinese are often unjustly suspected, inconveniently detained, or even sent back to China. A number of such cases have been brought to my attention. It must not be supposed, however, that I blame any official. In view of their limited knowledge of Chinese affairs, it is not strange that the officials sometimes make mistakes. The Americans judge us wrongly, just as we often misjudge them. This unpleasant state of things is to be deplored, and I would suggest that difficulties might be avoided if the regular officials, in passing on immigrant Chinamen, could have the assistance of Chinese consuls, or people fitted by training and experience in China for the discharge of such duties.

Great misunderstanding exists in the United States in regard to Chinese questions. There is a current fear that if all restrictions on Chinese immigration were removed, the United States would be flooded with my countrymen. Inasmuch as China contains some 400,000,000 inhabitants, a wholesale emigration would certainly be a serious matter for the people of the country to which they removed. But there is no danger of such a calamity befalling the United States. One of the most striking features of the conservatism of the Chinese is their absolute horror of travel, especially by sea. They regard any necessity for it as an unmitigated evil.

How, then, is the presence of so many Chinese in America explained? By the fact that some forty years ago, when the Pacific Railway was building, there was great scarcity of laborers. Agents went to China and induced a considerable number of Chinese to come to this country and assist in the construction of the railroad. After their work was done most of them returned home, taking their earnings with them. They told their relatives of the exceptional opportunities for making money in this country, and they in turn decided to seek their fortunes here. Were it not for this circumstance, there would be no more Chinese in this country than there are in Europe, where wages are also much higher than in China. As it is, all who are in the United States are from the province of Canton, and they come from two or three places only of that one province.

It has been said that the rules of international intercourse as observed by Western nations among themselves are not applicable to intercourse with Eastern nations. True it is that the people of the East speak different languages and have different customs, manners, religions, and ways of thinking from the people of the West. But the rule of contraries is by no means a safe guide through the intricacies of social observances. By disregarding the common civilities of life, which are considered very important in China, and by assuming a lofty air of superiority, foreigners frequently make themselves unpopular in China. Americans have the reputation there of being abrupt, English dictatorial. In recent years competition in trade with people of other nationalities has reduced their profits and forced them, for the sake of obtaining custom, to be more suave in their manners. Foreigners are sometimes guilty, also, of practising all sorts of tricks upon the unsuspecting natives. It should be remembered that the Chinese standard of business honesty is very high. The "yea, yea" of a Chinese merchant is as good as gold. Not a scrap of paper is necessary to bind him to his word.

I believe that the Western nations want to treat the people of the Orient fairly. It is gratifying to see that Japan has been able to revise her ex-territorial treaties, and it speaks well for the fair-mindedness of England and other countries that they have thrown no obstacles in her way. I hope that the day will soon come when China may follow in her footsteps.

In the mean time, China observes with interest that the planting of the Stars and Stripes in the Philippine Islands will make the United States her neighbor in the future, as she has been her friend in the past. It is her earnest hope that the United States will make no attempt to bar Asiatics from her new shores, but that she will seize this opportunity to strengthen friendly relations of mutual helpfulness between the two countries. No other nation has a stronger claim to the confidence of China than has the United States. More than once the United States government has used its good offices to promote Chinese interests and welfare. Nations, like individuals, appreciate favors, and, like them also, resent indignities. The sentiment of good-will entertained by the government and people of China towards the goverment and people of the United States is strong and profound because of the long, unblemished past, but underneath it all there is, I am sorry to say, a natural feeling of disappointment and irritation that the people of the United States deal less liberally with the Chinese than with the rest of the world. China does not ask for much. She has no thought of territorial aggrandizement, of self-glorification in any form.

See WU TING-FANG.

Chinese Exclusion Acts. In 1881 a treaty was effected and ratified between the United States and China, which provided that the government of the former should have power to limit, suspend, or regulate, but not prohibit, the importation of Chinese laborers. Chinese merchants, travellers and their servants, teachers, and students in this country were to enjoy the same rights as those vouchsafed to the citizens of the most favored nations.

On May 6, 1882, however, Congress passed an act suspending Chinese immigration for a period of ten years. To enforce this law a heavy fine was ordered to be imposed upon any captain or shipowner who should bring Chinese laborers to any part of the United States, and each laborer so coming was liable to imprisonment for a period not exceeding twelve months. Other Chinese persons—as students, travellers, merchants, scientists, diplomatists, etc.—were to be provided with an official certificate or passport from their home government.

Notwithstanding this exclusion act, many Chinamen still found entrance into the United States by first landing in British Columbia, whence they were systematically smuggled across the border. It was estimated that the number of laborers thus surreptitiously introduced into the United States averaged not less than 1,500 per year for several years after the passage of the law.

The feeling against the Chinese was especially strong on the Pacific slope. A bill promoted by Representative Geary, of California, and known as the Geary Act, became law May 5, 1892. By this measure the previous exclusion acts of 1882, 1884, and 1888 were re-enacted for ten years. Only about 12,000 out of 100,000 complied with the law. The question of its constitutionally was settled by a decision of the U. S. Supreme Court, May 15, 1893.

Chinese Exclusion Bill, VETO OF. See ARTHUR, CHESTER ALAN.

Chinese Indemnity, approved May 25, 1908, returned to China $13,655,492.69 remitted by the U. S. as a friendly act.

Chinese Loans. In 1904 the American minister at Pekin, Edwin H. Conger, concluded an agreement with the Chinese government by which, in issues of loans for the Szcheuen railway, the United States should have the privilege of subscribing. In March, 1909, the Chinese government contracted for a loan of $27,500,000 for the building of this railway, the lenders being England, France, and Germany, the United States not being included. While the protocol for the loan had been signed it had not been officially approved by the authorities in Pekin and the American State Department requested that the matter be reopened and bankers in this country be given an opportunity to participate in the loan. Secretary Knox made urgent representations to the Pekin government on the subject and succeeded in having the terms of the loan rearranged to the entire satisfaction of this government, in spite of the opposition of the foreign bankers, who held that it was too late for the United States to intervene after the protocol had been signed. May 24, 1910, the railway loan agreement was signed in Paris, France, by the representatives of financial groups in the United States, France, Great Britain, and Germany. The amount of the loan was fixed at $30,000,000, and it was announced that the basis of the agreement was absolute equality among the four groups, both as to the loan itself and as to the tender of supplies. On April 15, 1911, one of the most important achievements of recent years in the field of Far Eastern diplomacy was consummated by the action of the Chinese government in signing and ratifying, by imperial edict, the contract for the loan of $50,000,000 from the group of American, British, German, and French banking interests. This loan was entirely distinct from the $30,000,000 railway loan.

Chinese Revolution of 1911. A popular revolt against the Manchu dynasty broke out in the summer of 1911 and spread rapidly over the most populous provinces, causing much concern in the United States, especially as to the safety of American missionaries and their charges. By the middle of November, United States Minister Calhoun felt constrained to order all Americans in the interior to remove at once to the nearest ports; preparations were completed to send troops from Manila whenever Minister Calhoun deemed them necessary; and nineteen American war-ships had been assembled in Chinese waters.

All the missionaries of the American Baptist Foreign Mission Society in Western China made their way in safety to Shanghai. At Fuchau there were fifty-five missionaries under the American Board and the Episcopal and Methodist Churches, separate colleges for males and females, a general hospital, and a special hospital for women, but at the time of writing neither the missionaries nor the property had been molested. At Hsian-fu, the capital of the province of Shen-shi, however, Mrs. Beckman, Mr. Vatna, and five mission children were murdered.

Both the imperialists and the revolutionists soon ran short of money; the large foreign loan, negotiated early in the year, was held up; and the United States instructed Minister Calhoun to refuse sanction to any new loan unless it was ratified by both the Republican and the Monarchist parties. A republic was proclaimed in several provinces, and Mongolia and Manchuria, where there are large American commercial interests, declared their independence. Dr. Wu Ting-fang, former Chinese minister to the United States, became Secretary of Foreign Affairs in the provisional government established at Shanghai, issued numerous appeals for foreign recognition, and made a special plea to the United States to use its influence to secure the abdication of the Prince Regent and the entire Manchu *regime.*

Owing to the financial stress, it was believed that the government funds for the education of Chinese youth in the United States, pledged when the American government remitted a large part of its share in the Boxer indemnity, would be cut off, but such a possibility was officially denied.

On Dec. 6, Prince Chun, the regent and father of the baby emperor, formally abdicated; Shih-Hsu, former president of the National Assembly, and Hsu-Shih-chang, vice-president of the Privy Council, became guardians of the throne; and Yuan Shih-kai was made premier, and on Feb. 15, 1912, was elected President of the Chinese Republic.

Chinook Indians, a former distinct and interesting nation in the Northwest. They once inhabited the country on each side of the Columbia River from the Grand Dalles to its mouth. The Chinooks proper were on the north side of that stream, and the other division, called Clatsops, were on the south side and along the Pacific coast. Broken into roving bands, they began fading away, and the nation and their language have become almost extinct.

Chippewa, BATTLE OF. General Brown took prompt measures to secure the advantages derived from the capture of Fort Erie (see CANADA), for it was known that General Riall, who was then in chief command on the Niagara frontier, was moving towards Fort Erie. Early in the morning of July 3, 1814, he had sent forward some of the Royal Scots to reinforce the garrison. At Chippewa, at the mouth of Chippewa Creek, they heard of the surrender of the fort, when Riall determined to make an immediate attack upon the Americans on Canadian soil. Hearing that reinforcements were coming from York, he deferred the attack until the next morning. To meet this force, General Brown sent forward General Scott with his brigade, accompanied by Towson's artillery, on the morning of the 4th. Ripley was ordered in the same direction with his brigade, but was not ready to move until the afternoon. Scott went down the Canada side of the Niagara River, skirmishing nearly all the way to Street's Creek, driving back a British advanced detachment.

The main portions of Brown's army reached Scott's encampment on the south side of Street's Creek that night, and on the morning of the 5th the opposing armies were only two miles apart. At about noon Scott was joined by General Porter, with his volunteers and Indians. The British had also been reinforced.

The two armies were feeling each other for some time, when preliminary skirmishing was begun by Porter with marked success. The Indians behaved gallantly under the leadership of Captain Pollard and the famous Red Jacket. The British advanced corps, severely smitten, fled back in affright towards Chippewa. Porter pursued, and found himself within a few yards of the entire British force, advancing in battle order. A desperate struggle ensued. Finally the British made a furious charge with bayonets. Hearing nothing from Scott, Porter ordered a retreat. It became a tumultuous rout.

It was now towards evening. Brown had been watching Porter's movements with great anxiety, and had ordered Scott to cross Street's Creek, when Porter's flying troops were observed. Riall had sent forward some Royal Scots, part of another regiment of regulars, a regiment of Lincoln militia, and about 300 Indians. These composed the force that fought Porter. Scott crossed Street's Creek in the face of a heavy cannonade, and very soon the battle raged with fury along the entire line of both armies. Several times the British line was broken and closed up again.

Finally a flank movement and a furious charge were made by Major McNeill with Colonel Campbell's 11th regiment, and a terrific fire from a corps under Major Jesup in the centre made the British line give way. It broke and fled in haste to the intrenchments below Chippewa Creek. The fugitives tore up the bridge over the creek behind them, leaving an impassable chasm between themselves and the Americans. The battle-field (opposite Navy Island) was strewn with the dead and dying. The Americans lost, in killed, wounded, and missing, 355 men; the British lost, by the same casualties, 604 men, of whom 236 were killed.

On that hot July evening a gentle shower of rain descended, which mitigated the horrors of the battle-field. Scott was eager to pursue, but was compelled to wait for the tardy Ripley, who did not arrive in time to participate in the battle or to join in an instant pursuit. The immediate results of the battle were important. The Indian allies of the British were disheartened, and nearly all of them left the army and returned to their homes. The Americans were greatly inspirited.

Chippewa Indians, also known as OJIBWAYS, an Algonquian family, living in scattered bands on the shores and islands of the upper Lakes, first discovered by the French in 1640 at the Sault Ste. Marie, when they numbered about 2,000. They were then at war with the Iroquois, the Foxes, and the Sioux; and they drove the latter from the head-waters of the Mississippi and from the Red River of the North. The French established missionaries among them, and the Chippewas were the firm friends of these Europeans until the conquest of Canada ended French dominion in America. In 1712 they aided the French in repelling an attack of the Foxes on Detroit.

In Pontiac's conspiracy (see PONTIAC) they were his confederates; and they sided with the British in the war of the Revolution and of 1812. Joining the Miamis, they fought Wayne and were defeated, and subscribed to the treaty at Greenville in 1795. In 1816 they took part in the pacification of the Northwestern tribes, and in 1817 they gave up all their lands in Ohio. At that time they occupied a vast and undefined territory from Mackinaw along the line of Lake Superior to the Mississippi River. The limits of this territory were defined by a treaty in 1825, after which they gradually ceded their lands to the United States for equivalent annuities. All but a few bands had gone west of the Mississippi in 1851; and in 1866 the scattered bands in Canada, Michigan, on the borders of Lake Superior, and beyond the Mississippi numbered more than 15,000.

Their religion is simply a belief in a good and evil spirit, and the deification of the powers of nature. Various denominations have missionaries among the Chippewas.

In 1905 it was estimated that the Chippewa Indians numbered between 30,000 and 32,000, of whom about 15,000 were in British America and 14,144 in the United States, exclusive of about 3,000 in Michigan. All of the Chippewas have adopted civilization.

Chisolm, William Wallace, jurist; born in Morgan county, Ga., Dec. 6, 1830; settled in Kemper county, Miss., in 1847. In 1858 he was made chief-justice of the peace; in 1860–67 was probate judge; and subsequently was sheriff for several terms. During the Civil War he was a strong Unionist, and this fact made him an object of suspicion to the Confederate authorities. Early in 1877, John W. Gully, a Democrat, was murdered near Judge Chisolm's house, and Judge Chisolm and several of his Republican friends were arrested. Later the jail was broken into by a mob, one of whom shot Judge Chisolm's young son John. Thereupon the judge immediately killed the assassin with a gun that had been left by a faithless guard. The cry was now raised, "Burn them out." Believing that the jail had been set on fire Judge Chisolm descended the stairs with his family, who had accompanied him to the jail. As soon as he appeared the crowd opened fire upon him, and he fell mortally wounded. His daughter also, a girl eighteen years old, received several wounds. The father died, May 13, 1877, and two days later his daughter succumbed to her injuries. Though the leaders of the crowd were indicted, not one of them was ever punished. In December, 1877, the real murderer of Gully, Walter Riley, a negro, confessed that he was guilty of the crime, and also declared that neither Judge Chisolm nor any of his friends had tried to influence him.

Chittenden, Thomas, first governor of Vermont; born in East Guilford, Conn., Jan. 6, 1730. He held local offices in his native State before 1774, when he emigrated to the New Hampshire Grants, and settled at Williston. During the Revolution he was an active participant in the councils of his State, and was a leader in the convention which (Jan. 16, 1777) declared Vermont an independent State. He was also a leader in the convention (July, 1777) which formed a constitution for that State, and president of the council of safety vested with governmental powers. He was elected governor of Vermont in 1778, and, with the exception of one year, filled that office until his death, during which time the controversy between New York and Vermont was settled and the latter admitted as a State of the Union. He died in Williston, Vt., Aug. 24, 1797.

Choate, Joseph Hodges, diplomatist; born in Salem, Mass., Jan. 24, 1832;

JOSEPH HODGES CHOATE.

graduated at Harvard University in 1852; admitted to the bar in 1855, and settled in New York to practise. He was employed in many famous lawsuits; was one of the committee of seventy which broke up the Tweed ring, and was instrumental in having Gen. Fitz-John Porter reinstated in the army. In 1894 he was president of the New York Constitutional Convention; in 1899–1905 was United States ambassador to England; and in 1907 was a delegate to the International Peace Conference at The Hague. He is an entertaining public and after-dinner speaker, and author of *Addresses* on Abraham Lincoln, Admiral Farragut, Rufus Choate, etc.

Choate, RUFUS, lawyer; born in Essex, Mass., Oct. 1, 1799; studied at the Cambridge Law School, and, with William Wirt, became one of the most eminent lawyers and orators of his time. He began the practice of law at Danvers, Mass., in 1824. He was a distinguished member of both branches of his State legislature, a member of the Lower House of Congress, and United States Senator, succeeding Daniel Webster in 1841. In 1853 he was attorney-general of Massachusetts. After the death of Webster, Mr. Choate was the acknowledged leader of the Massachusetts bar. Impaired health compelled him to retire from public life in 1858. He died in Halifax, N. S., July 13, 1859.

Choctaw Indians, a tribe mostly Mobilians, and a peaceful agricultural people. Their domain comprised southern Mississippi and western Alabama. De Soto fought them in 1540. They became allies of the French in Louisiana, where they numbered about 2,500 warriors, and formed forty villages. In the Revolution they were mostly with the English, but were granted peaceable possession of their lands by the United States government.

On Jan. 3, 1786, a treaty was made with the leaders of the nation, of the same purport and upon the same terms as that made with the Cherokees the previous year. As early as 1800 numbers of them went beyond the Mississippi, and in 1803 it was estimated that 500 families had emigrated. They served with the United States troops in the second war with England and in that with the Creeks, and in 1820 they ceded a part of their lands for a domain in what is now the Indian Territory.

In 1830 they ceded the rest of their lands and joined their brethren west of the Mississippi, where the Chickasaws joined them.

In 1861 they had a population of 25,000, with 5,000 negro slaves. They were seduced into an alliance with the Confederates in the Civil War, and disaster befell them. They lost an immense amount of property, and their numbers, including the Chickasaws, were reduced to 17,000. Slavery was abolished, and part of their lands was forfeited for the benefit of the freedmen. In 1904 they numbered 17,805, exclusive of 4,722 Choctaw freedmen (negroes), at the Union agency, then in Indian Territory, besides a few in Mississippi and Louisiana.

Choiseul, ÉTIENNE FRANCOIS, DUC DE, French statesman; born June 28, 1719; became a lieutenant-general in the army in 1759; and was at the head of the French ministry when, in 1761, cabinet changes in England threatened to diminish the power of that government. He was minister of foreign affairs, and in January, 1761, became minister of war, and annexed those departments to the marine. Like Pitt, he was a statesman of consummate ability. He was of high rank and very wealthy, and was virtually sole minister of France.

When the British had despoiled France of her American possessions Choiseul eagerly watched for an opportunity to inflict a retaliatory blow; and he was delighted when he perceived that a rising quarrel between Great Britain and her American colonies foreshadowed a dismemberment of the British Empire. Choiseul determined to foster the quarrel as fas as possible. He sent the Baron de Kalb to America in the disguise of a traveller, but really as a French emissary, to ascertain the temper of the people towards the mother country. The report of the baron did not warrant the hope of an immediate rupture.

But Choiseul waited and watched, and in the summer of 1768 he saw reasons for expecting an almost immediate outbreak of rebellion in America. He wrote to the French minister in London that facts and not theories must shape French action at that crisis. He proposed to make a commercial treaty with the discontented colonies, both of importation and exportation, at the moment of rupture, the advantages of which might cause them at once to detach themselves from the British government. He believed the separation must come sooner or later and wished to hasten the hoped-for event. He said to the minister, "I firmly believe and hope this government will so conduct itself as to widen the breach"; and he was sanguine that his plans would result in gratifying the wishes of every Frenchman. But Choiseul had to wait seven years before these wishes were gratified, and then he was dismissed from office by the successor of the old King (Louis XV.) whom he had ruled so long. He died in Paris, May 7, 1785.

Choisi, CLAUDE GABRIEL DE, military officer; born in France; entered the French army June 16, 1741; came to America in 1780; was given command of a brigade with which, in conjunction with Lauzun's cavalry, he defeated Tarleton, Oct. 3, 1781. During the Reign of Terror in France, through his friendship for the King, he was imprisoned and, it is supposed, died there.

Cholera, ASIATIC, described by Garcia del Huerto, a physician of Goa, about 1560, appeared in India in 1774, and became endemic in Lower Bengal, 1817; gradually spread till it reached Russia, 1830; Germany, 1831; carrying off more than 900,000 persons on the Continent in 1829–30; in England and Wales in 1848–49, 53,293 persons; in 1854, 20,097. First death by cholera in North America, June 8, 1832, in Quebec. In New York, June 22, 1832. Cincinnati to New Orleans, October, 1832 (very severe throughout the United States). Again in the United States in 1834, slightly in 1849, severely in 1855, and again slightly in 1866–67. By the prompt and energetic enforcement of quarantine it was prevented from entering the United States in 1892. The German steamship *Moravia* reached New York Harbor Aug. 31, having had twenty-two deaths from cholera during the voyage. The President ordered twenty days' quarantine for all immigrant vessels from cholera-infected districts, Sept. 1. On Sept. 3 the *Normannia* and *Rugia,* from Hamburg, were put in quarantine. On Sept. 10 the *Scandia* arrived with more cholera cases. The Surf Hotel property on Fire Island was bought by Governor Flower for quarantine purposes.

Chouteau, PIERRE, trader; born in New Orleans in 1749; ascended the Mississippi River and founded the city of St. Louis, Mo. He died in St. Louis, Mo., July 9, 1849.

Christ, DISCIPLES OF. See DISCIPLES OF CHRIST.

Christian Associations, YOUNG MEN'S, societies organized for the purpose of providing for the social, physical, intellectual, and spiritual advancement of young men. The first association of this character was established in London, in 1841, by George Williams. The first societies in the United States were established in Boston in 1851 and in New York City in 1852. Since then similar societies have sprung up throughout the civilized world. In 1910 there were 8,098 associations in the world, of which 2,017 were in North America, principally in the United States. The total membership of the North American societies was 496,591, with 696 buildings, valued at $50,919,915. They had 567 libraries, containing 424,507 volumes; employed 2,687 general secretaries and other paid officials; and expended for all purposes $8,297,689. See YOUNG MEN'S CHRISTIAN ASSOCIATIONS.

Christian Associations, YOUNG WOMEN'S, societies established for work by and among women. The members aim (1) to develop women physically, by systematic training in the gymnasium and holiday outings; (2) socially, by receptions, helpful companionships, musical and literary entertainments, boarding clubs, employment bureaus, etc.; (3) intellectually, by reading-rooms and libraries, lecture courses, educational classes, concerts, art clubs, etc.; (4) spiritually, by Gospel meetings, evangelistic meetings, Bible training classes, and personal work. The World's Young Women's Christian Association was established in 1894, and holds biennial conventions. A supreme body was formed in December, 1906, the object being stated thus: "To unite in one body the Young Women's Christian Associations of the United States; to establish, develop, and unify such associations; to advance the physical, social, intellectual, moral, and spiritual interests of young women." 189 city associations, 639 student associations, and 9 industrial and rural associations are members of the national organization.

Christiana Case. In 1851 a number of citizens of Maryland attempted to seize a fugitive slave in Christiana, Penn. The leader of the party, Edward Gorsuch, was killed. A Quaker, Castner Hanway, was charged with treason because he refused to help the United States marshal in quelling the disturbance. Elijah Lewis, another Quaker, was charged with riot and bloodshed. No indictments were found.

Christian Commission, UNITED STATES, an organization that had its origin in the Young Men's Christian Association, in New York City, and was first suggested by VINCENT COLYER (*q. v.*), who, with Frank W. Ballard and Mrs. Dr. Harris, who represented the Ladies' Aid Society, of Philadelphia, went to Washington immediately after the battle of Bull Run (July, 1861) to do Christian work in the camps and hospitals there. Mr. Colyer distributed Bibles and tracts and hymnbooks among the soldiers, and held prayer-meetings. In August he suggested the combination of all the Young Men's Christian Associations of the land in the formation of a society similar to that of the United States Sanitary Commission. The suggestion was acted upon, and at a meeting of the Young Men's Christian Association, held in New York, Sept. 23, 1861, a committee was appointed to conduct the correspondence and make arrangements for holding a national convention of such associations.

A convention was called, and assembled in New York, Nov. 14, 1861, when the United States Christian Commission was organized, with George H. Stuart, of Philadelphia, as president. Its specific work was to be chiefly for the moral and religious welfare of the soldiers and sailors, conducted by oral instruction, and the circulation of the Bible and other proper books, with pamphlets, newspapers, etc., among the men in hospitals, camps, and ships.

The commission worked on the same general plan pursued by the United States Sanitary Commission. Its labors were not confined wholly to spiritual and intellectual ministrations, but also to the distribution of a vast amount of food, hospital stores, delicacies, and clothing. It, too, followed the great armies, and was like a twin angel of mercy with the Sanitary Commission. It co-operated most efficiently with the army and navy chaplains, and in various ways cast about the soldier a salutary hedge of Christian influence. The money collected for the use of the commission was chiefly gathered by the women of various religious denominations. The entire receipts of the commission amounted to over $6,000,000. See SANITARY COMMISSION, UNITED STATES.

Christian Connection. See CHRISTIANS.

Christian Endeavor, YOUNG PEOPLE'S SOCIETY OF, a religious society organized by the REV. FRANCIS CLARK (*q. v.*) in the Williston Congregational Church, in Portland, Me., on Feb. 2, 1881. He called the young people of his church together after a period of religious interest, and read to them substantially the same constitution which governs all the societies now organized throughout the world. The society is strictly a religious body, having for its main purpose the forwarding of the church's interests. Each society is in some local church, and in no sense outside. It exists simply to make the young people loyal and efficient members of the Church of Christ. It is the Church training the young. Its motto is, "For Christ and the Church." In 1912 there were about 75,000 societies, with a membership of nearly 4,000,000, chiefly in the United States and Canada, and in Australia, Great Britain, China, India, Japan, and in all missionary lands. It is found in about the same proportions in all the great evangelical denominations and in all their subdivisions.

Christian Psychology. See WORCESTER, ELLWOOD.

Christians, a religious body organized from several independent movements. In 1792 James O'Kelly and twenty or thirty ministers, and about 1,000 members, left the Methodist Episcopal Church in North Carolina and Virginia. On Aug. 4, 1794, they agreed to be known as "Christians, and should acknowledge no head over the church but Christ, and should have no creed or discipline but the Bible." Abner Jones, M.D., left the Baptists in New England, and preached similar principles. He established the first churches to have no name but Christian at Lyndon, Vt., in 1800; at Bradford, Vt., in 1802; at Piermont, N. H., and at Haverhill, Mass., in 1803. In April, 1801, a religious excitement, called "the falling exercise," began in southern Kentucky. It soon spread northward to the Presbyterian churches at Cane Ridge and Concord, over which Rev. Barton W. Stone was pastor. His usual "May meeting" was attended by 2,500 persons, many of whom were from other States. This revival lasted for several years, and spread over several States.

The enthusiasm going beyond the denominational conservatism of those days, there were many trials for heresy, and finally a new presbytery was organized. But on June 28, 1804, they disbanded and published a document called *The Last Will and Testament of the Springfield Presbytery*, in which they ignored all doctrinal standards and denominational names. In 1802 Elias Smith, a Baptist minister at Portsmouth, N. H., met Abner Jones, and became converted to his views, and subsequently led his church over to the new movement. On Sept. 1, 1808, at Portsmouth, N. H., Smith started the publication of the *Herald of Gospel Liberty*, which is now issued at Dayton, O., and is the oldest religious periodical in the United States. At first the Christians had no separate ecclesiastical organization, but ultimately circumstances became such that that they were compelled to organize. According to the special report of the Bureau of the Census on *Religious Bodies* (1910), this denomination had 1,379 organizations in 70 conferences in 30 States, Ohio and Indiana leading; 110,117 communicants or members; 1,253 church edifices and 85 halls used for religious purposes; church property valued at $2,740,322; 1,011 ministers; and 1,149 Sunday-schools, with 10,510 officers and teachers and 72,963 scholars.

Christian Science. The Church of Christ, Scientist, was founded by Mrs. Mary Baker Glover Eddy (born in Bow, N. H., July 16, 1821; died in Boston, Mass., Dec. 3, 1910; bequeathed to the church the bulk of an estate estimated at $2,750,000). As early as 1862 she had written and given to friends certain conclusions derived from the study of the Scriptures, while in 1867 she began her first school of Christian Science mind healing, in Lynn, Mass. Three years later she copyrighted her first pamphlet on Christian Science, which, however, did not appear in print until 1876, a year after the publication of the Christian Science text-book, *Science and Health with Key to the Scriptures*, also written by her. The Church of Christ, Scientist, organized by twenty-six students of Mrs. Eddy, was chartered in 1879. In 1881 Mrs. Eddy became the pastor of the First Church of Christ, and in the same year she opened the Massachusets Metaphysical College in Boston under a State charter. Subsequently she founded or instituted every department of the work of the denomination, including a committee on publication, reading-rooms, and a board of lectureship. A reorganization of the church in Boston was effected in 1892 under the name of the First Church of Christ, Scientist. It is but proper to state here, in view of the various publications denying the accuracy of Mrs. Eddy's statements concerning the origin of Christian Science, that the foregoing is an official exposition of its history.

There are many institutes for teaching Christian Science, and upward of 4,000 practitioners of Christian Science mind-healing. Organizations can now be found in almost every city in the United States, and there are branches in Canada, Nova Scotia, British Columbia, Mexico, the Bahamas, British West Indies, the Hawaiian Islands, Cuba, Philippine Islands, Sandwich Islands, British Isles, France, Germany, Norway, Switzerland, Italy, Australia, New South Wales, India, China, South Africa, South America, and many other countries.

All Christian Science Churches other than the Mother Church in Boston are branches of that Church. In all of these the Sunday services are uniform, and consist of correlative passages read from the Bible and the Christian Science text-book. On Wednesday evening a meeting is held in every church of this denomination.

Mrs. Eddy says in her book, *Retrospection and Introspection*: "I claim for healing scientifically the following advantages: 1. It does away with all material medicines and recognizes the antidote for all sickness, as well as sin, in the immortal mind, and mortal mind as the source of all the ills which befall mortals. 2. It is more effectual than drugs, and cures when they fail or only relieve, thus proving the superiority of metaphysics over physics. 3. A person healed by Christian Science is not only healed of his disease, but he is advanced morally and spiritually. The mortal body being but the objective state of the mortal mind, this mind must be renovated to improve the body." The absence of creed and dogma in the Christian Science Church, its freedom from materialism, mysticism and superstition, also the simplicity, uniformity, and impersonality of its form of worship and organization, are among the distinguishing features which characterize this modern religious movement. Hypnotism, mesmerism, spiritualism, theosophy, faith cure and kindred systems are foreign to true Christian Science. Those practising these beliefs are denied admission to the Christian Science Church.

What is known among Christian Scientists as "the scientific statement of being," is thus summarized: "There is no life, truth, intelligence nor substance in matter. All is infinite mind and its infinite manifestation, for God is All-in-all. Spirit is immortal Truth; matter is mortal error. Spirit is the real and eternal; matter is the unreal and temporal. Spirit is God, and man is His image and likeness. Therefore man is not material; he is spiritual."

Christmas Ship. Popular name given to the United States naval auxiliary *Jason*, which was sent to Europe in November, 1914, with a cargo of more than 6,000,000 packages, each representing a Christmas gift, for the children of war sufferers. Thousands of dolls, toys, and other playthings were included.

Chrysler's Field, BATTLE OF. When Wilkinson's expedition down the St. Lawrence River against Montreal, composed of land troops borne by a flotilla of boats, arrived at a point 4 miles below Ogdensburg, information reached the commander of the expedition that the opposite shore of the river was lined with posts of musketry and artillery, and that a large reinforcement of British troops under Lieutenant-Colonel Morrison had arrived at Prescott. Wilkinson had already ordered Col. Alexander Macomb, with 1,200 of the best troops of the army, to cross the river to oppose the British detachments on the Canadian side (Nov. 7, 1813), and these were soon followed by riflemen under Lieutenant-Colonel Forsythe, who did excellent service in the rear of Macomb.

When news was received of the arrival of reinforcements at Prescott, Wilkinson called a council of war (Nov. 8), and it was decided "to proceed with all possible rapidity to the attack of Montreal." General Brown was at once ordered to cross the river with his brigade and some dragoons. Morrison's troops, fully 1,000 strong, had come down to Prescott in armed schooners, with several gunboats and bateaux under Captain Mulcaster, and were joined by provincial infantry and dragoons under Lieutenant-Colonel Pearson. They pushed forward, and on the morning of the 9th were close upon Wilkinson, and the land troops were debarked to pursue the Americans—2,000 men, including cavalry.

General Boyd and his brigade were now detached to reinforce Brown, with orders to cover his march, to attack the pursuing enemy if necessary, and to co-operate with the other commanders. Wilkinson now found himself in a perilous position, for the British armed vessels were close upon his flotilla, and the British land troops were hanging upon the rear of Brown and Boyd. The latter also encountered detachments coming up from below.

The British gunboats attacked the flotilla, but Wilkinson made such disposition of his cannon in battery on the shore that they were repulsed, and fled up the river. Brown had captured a British post at the foot of the rapids, and Wilkinson had just issued orders for the flotilla to proceed down these rapids, and Boyd to resume his march, when a British column attacked the rear of the latter. Boyd turned upon his antagonist, and a sharp battle ensued. General Swartwout was detached with his brigade to assail the British vanguard, and General Covington took position at supporting distance from him. Their antagonists were driven back out of the woods on the main line in the open fields of John Chrysler, a British militia captain then in the service.

That line was covered by Mulcaster's gunboats, and protected in part by deep ravines.

Then General Covington led his brigade against the British left, near the river, and the battle became general. By charge after charge the British were forced back nearly a mile, and the American cannon, under the direction of Col. J. G. Swift, did excellent execution. At length Covington fell, seriously wounded, and the ammunition of the Americans began to fail. It was soon exhausted, and Swartwout's brigade, hard pushed, slowly fell back, followed by others.

CHRYSLER'S IN 1855.

The British perceived this retrograde movement, followed up the advantage gained with great vigor, and were endeavoring by a flank movement to capture Boyd's cannon, when a gallant charge of cavalry, led by Adjutant-General Walbach, whom Armstrong had permitted to accompany the expedition, drove them back and saved the pieces. The effort was renewed. Lieutenant Smith, who commanded one of the cannon, was mortally wounded, and the piece was seized by the British.

For five hours the conflict had been carried on in the midst of sleet and snow, and victory had swayed between the belligerents like a pendulum. It would doubtless have rested with the Americans had their ammunition held out. Their retreat was promising to be a rout, when the fugitives were met by 600 troops under Colonel Upham and Major Malcolm, whom Wilkinson had sent up to the support of Boyd. These checked the flight, drove back the British, and saved the American army.

Meanwhile Boyd had reformed a portion of the army, and then awaited another attack. It was not made. The Americans, under cover of darkness, retired to their boats unmolested. Neither party had gained a victory, but the advantage lay with the British, who held the field. The British army on that occasion was slightly superior in numbers, counting its Indian allies. The Americans lost in the battle, in killed and wounded, 339; the British lost 187.

On the morning after the battle, the flotilla, with the gunboats and troops, passed safely down the rapids, and 3 miles above Cornwall they formed a junction with the forces under General Brown. There Wilkinson was informed that Hampton, whom he had invited in Armstrong's name to meet him at St. Regis, had refused to join him. A council of war (Nov.

12, 1813) decided that it was best to abandon the expedition against Montreal, although it was said there were not more than 600 troops there, and put the army into winter quarters at French Mills, on the Salmon River, which was done. Thus ended in disaster and disgrace an expedition which in its inception promised salutary results. In preparing their representation for the pageant at the coronation of King George V. (June 22, 1911) the Canadian authorities decided to have a tableau showing the defeat of the Americans at this point, called by them Chateauguay, under the belief that the result of this battle saved Canada to the empire. Subsequently the committee having the representation in charge decided to omit the tableau, some said because of unwillingness to offend the Americans, others because the scene did not represent Canadian life or development; but later it was restored. See CANADA; MACOMB, ALEXANDER; MONTREAL; PRESCOTT; WILKINSON, JAMES.

Church, BENJAMIN, military officer; born in Plymouth, Mass., in 1639; was a leader in King Philip's War; commanded the party by whom Philip was slain (August, 1676); and with his own sword cut off the head of the dusky monarch. While Phipps was operating against Quebec in 1690, Colonel Church was sent on an expedition against the eastern Indians. He went up the Androscoggin River to the site of Lewiston, Me., where he, "for example," put to death a number of men, women, and children whom he had captured. The Indians retaliated fearfully.

In May, 1704, Governor Dudley sent from Boston an expedition to the eastern bounds of New England. It consisted of 550 soldiers, under Church. The campaign then undertaken against the French and Indians continued all summer, and Church inflicted much damage to the allies at Penobscot and Passamaquoddy. He is represented by his contemporaries as distinguished as much for his integrity, justice, and purity as for his military exploits. He is the author of *Entertaining Passages Relating to Philip's War*. He died in Little Compton, R. I., Jan. 17, 1718.

Church, BENJAMIN, surgeon; born in Newport, R. I., Aug. 24, 1734; son of Col. Benjamin Church; was graduated at Harvard College; studied medicine in London, and became eminent as a surgeon. He lived a bachelor, extravagantly and licentiously, in a fine mansion which he built at Raynham, Mass., in 1768. For several years preceding the Revolution he was conspicuous among the leading Whigs. Of the Massachusetts Provincial Congress he was an active member. At the same time, while he was trusted as an ardent patriot, Church was evidently the secret enemy of the Republicans. As early as 1774 he wrote parodies of his own popular songs in favor of liberty for the Tory newspapers; and in September, 1775, an intercepted letter written by him in cipher to Major Cain in Boston, which had passed through the hands of the mistress of Church, was deciphered, and the woman confessed that he was the author. The case was laid before the Continental Congress, and he was dismissed from his post of chief director of the general hospital. He was arrested and tried by a court-martial at Cambridge on a charge of "holding a criminal correspondence with the enemy." He was convicted (Oct. 3) and imprisoned at Cambridge.

On Nov. 7 the Congress ordered him to be "close confined, without the use of pen, ink, or paper; and that no person be allowed to converse with him except in the presence and hearing of a magistrate of the town or the sheriff of the county where he shall be confined, and in the English language, until further orders from this or a future Congress." He was so confined in the jail at Norwich, Conn. In May, 1776, he was released on account of failing health, and sailed for the West Indies in a merchant vessel. He and the vessel were never heard of afterwards. Benjamin Church was the first traitor to the republican cause in America. He was well educated, and a writer in prose and verse of considerable ability.

Church, FREDERICK EDWIN, landscape painter; born in Hartford, Conn., May 4, 1826; pupil of Thomas Cole; earliest productions, views of the Catskill Mountains, among which he resided, and a view of East Rock, near New Haven. Other works include: *View of Niagara Falls from the Canadian Shore*, regarded by many as the most successful representation of the great cataract; *Under Niagara; Sunrise on Mount Desert Island*, etc. He died in New York City, April 7, 1900.

Church, SANFORD ELIAS, jurist; born in Milford, N. Y., April 18, 1815; member of the State legislature in 1842; district attorney, 1846-51; lieutenant-governor, 1851-55; State comptroller, 1858-59; delegate to the Constitutional Convention in 1867; chief justice of the Court of Appeals, 1870 till his death at Albin, N. Y., May 14, 1880.

Church, WILLIAM CONANT, journalist; born in Rochester, N. Y., Aug. 11, 1836; was war correspondent of the New York *Times* (1861-62); in conjunction with his brother Francis established the *Army and Navy Journal* (1863); author of a notable biography of General Grant.

Church, a word commonly applied to the whole body of Christians; the place of Christian worship; the clergy; and a sect or denomination of Christians. For history and statistics of the church in the first of these applications, see the articles on the different denominations.

Church and State in America. The relations between church and state in the colonies differed in many respects from those in force in Europe. There it was the rule that either the church governed the state—a theocracy—or the church and state limited each other by common consent, as embodied in concordats. The United States's contribution to the science of politics is absolute religious liberty. In Article VI of the Constitution it is declared that "no religious test shall ever be required as a qualification to any office or public trust," and the first amendment is that "Congress shall make no law respecting an establishment of religion or prohibiting the free exercise thereof."

The various State constitutions are equally emphatic as to the entire separation of the civil and religious organizations.

The conditions for the creation of a new type of church in America were from the first favorable. The Protestant Reformation in Europe involved three of the countries—England, Holland, and Sweden—which were to plant colonies in the New World; and a narrow Protestantism developed in the English colonies, especially in New England, planted by radicals who had long been a thorn in the side of the English Church. The cardinal principle of these Puritans was an appeal to an authority higher and more subtle than that of all other churches. They disclaimed the venerable doctrine that "The Church" by the majesty of its tradition could establish religious truth. They objected, likewise, to any form of government under which a presbytery of churches in association could lay down rules for their guidance.

Instead, they based their ideals on the authority of Scripture, and no Protestants have ever been so zealous in the reading of that book. Though they insisted on the right of private judgment in the interpretation of the Scriptures, they were much influenced by the expositions of their clergy, and especially by the religious system of John Calvin, whose rigorous logic and relentless spirit they admired.

In New Netherland the Dutch Protestants, in their Reformed churches, followed substantially the Presbyterian polity, which after the English conquest was organized in all the Middle colonies by Scotch and English Presbyterians. Into New Jersey and Pennsylvania came also early representatives of the extremest English sect, the Friends, commonly called Quakers, a people who applied literally the doctrines of peace and good-will to men. The Middle colonies, with their variety of population, from the first practised a toleration, which was not felt farther south, where existed an established church, nominally a part of the national church of England: its ministry was ordained in England, sent out from England, and under the direction of the English government was supported from local taxes.

Church of Jesus Christ of Latter Day Saints, the largest of the two bodies constituting what is popularly known as "the Mormon Church," the other being officially designated as the REORGANIZED CHURCH OF JESUS CHRIST OF LATTER DAY SAINTS (*q. v.*). For a history of the inception and vicissitudes of the largest and original body the reader is referred to the article on MORMONS, the present one being confined to a summary of the general statistics of the original body as given in a special report of the United States Bureau of the Census on *Religious Bodies* (2 vols., 1910). According to this report this body had 683 organizations, 624 church edifices, 824 officers of various distinctions, 215,796 members, church property valued at $2,645,363, and 766 Sunday-schools, with 14,765 officers and teachers and 113,139 scholars.

Church-membership Suffrage. From 1631 to 1691 the suffrage was denied by the colony of Massachusetts to any individual who was not a member of some church.

Churchill, SYLVESTER, military officer; born in Woodstock, Vt., August, 1783; received a common-school education; served through the War of 1812–15, and especially distinguished himself on Burlington Heights in defending the fleet of Macdonough when it was attacked while being repaired. In 1835 he was promoted major, and took part in the Creek Indian War; in 1836–41 was acting inspector-general of the Creeks in Florida; then became inspector-general; served in the Mexican War, and for his gallantry at Buena Vista was brevetted brigadier-general in February, 1847; retired in September, 1861. He died in Washington, D. C., Dec. 7, 1862.

Churubusco, BATTLE OF. After the victory at Contreras, Mexico, the Americans proceeded to attack the fortresses of San Antonio and Churubusco. The latter was a small village six miles south of the city of Mexico, and connected with it by a spacious causeway. At the head of the causeway, near the village, was erected a strong redoubt, mounted with batteries and heavily garrisoned. This was in front of the bridge over the Churubusco River.

The convent-church of San Pablo, with its massive stone walls, on an eminence, was converted into a fort. All of the stores and artillery saved from the wreck of Contreras were gathered at Churubusco, with much sent from the city, for Santa Ana had resolved to make a stand at this place. He was at the city with 12,000 troops. When the Americans began to move forward the garrison of Antonio, perceiving themselves in great danger of being cut off, abandoned the fort and fled towards Churubusco, attacked and divided on the way.

The retreat of the Mexicans from San Antonio and the general march of all the Americans upon Churubusco began the grand movements of the day. The divisions of Twiggs and Pillow were advancing on the west, and on a causeway south the division of Worth was rapidly advancing to storm the redoubt at the bridge. General Scott, at a mile distant from Churubusco, was directing all the movements. The redoubt at the bridge was carried at the point of the bayonet. At the same time Twiggs was assailing the fortified church and hamlet, where a fierce battle raged for some time. There the able Mexican General Rinçon commanded, and there three masses of Santa Ana's men opposed General Shields. The veterans of Gen. Persifer F. Smith, who had captured Contreras, were conspicuous in this fearful contest. The most desperate defence at the church was made by deserters from the American army, led by Thomas Riley. The alarmed Mexicans several times hoisted a white flag, in token of surrender, when these Americans with halters about their necks as often tore it down. The battle raged for three hours, when the church and the other defences of Churubusco were captured.

Meanwhile Generals Shields and Pierce (afterwards President of the United States) were battling furiously with Santa Ana's men, partly in the rear of the defences of Churubusco. The Mexicans were there 7,000 strong—4,000 infantry and 3,000 cavalry—but victory again crowned the Americans.

This was the *fifth* victory won on that memorable 20th of August, 1847—Contreras, San Antonio, the redoubt at the bridge, the Church of San Pablo, and with Santa Ana's troops. In fact, the combined events of that day formed one great contest over a considerable extent of territory, and might properly be known in history as the "Battle of the Valley of Mexico." The number engaged on that day was 9,000 effective American soldiers and 32,000 Mexicans. The result was the capture by the former of the exterior line of Mexican defences, opening the causeway to the city and leaving it no other resources but its fortified gates and the

Castle of Chapultepec. Fully 4,000 Mexicans had been killed or wounded that day; 3,000 were made prisoners. Thirty-seven pieces of fine artillery had been captured, with a vast amount of munitions of war. The Americans lost, in killed and wounded, about 1,100 men. See MEXICO, WAR WITH; PIERCE, FRANKLIN; PILLOW, GIDEON JOHNSON; SANTA ANA, ANTONIO; SCOTT, WINFIELD; SMITH, PERSIFER FRAZER; WORTH, WILLIAM JENKINS.

Cibitu, or CIBUTU (Philippines). See SIBUTU.

Cibola, SEVEN CITIES OF. Fabulous accounts of seven wonderfully rich cities in the New World led to many expeditions. They were supposed to be located in Florida or west of the Mississippi River.

Cilley, JONATHAN, lawyer; born in Nottingham, N. H., July 2, 1802; graduated at Bowdoin College in 1825; elected to Congress as a Democrat in 1837, and served until Feb. 24, 1838, when he was fatally wounded in a duel with William J. Graves, a Representative from Kentucky. When the affair became known in Congress, a committee was appointed, which reported that Mr. Graves should be censured by the House for his conduct. See BLADENSBURG DUELLING FIELD.

Cilley, JONATHAN PRINCE, military officer; born in Thomaston, Me., Dec. 29, 1835; son of the preceding; graduated at Bowdoin College in 1858, and became a lawyer. When the Civil War broke out he was commissioned a captain in the 1st Maine Cavalry. On May 24, 1862, when General Banks retreated from the Shenandoah Valley, Captain Cilley was wounded and taken prisoner. In recognition of his services at Five Forks, Farmville, and Appomattox Court-House he was brevetted brigadier-general at the close of the war. He is the author of a genealogy of the Cilley family.

Cilley, JOSEPH, military officer; born in Nottingham, N. H., in 1735; took part in the dismantling of the fort at Portsmouth in 1774; led a company of volunteers into Boston after the battle of Lexington; made colonel of the 1st New Hampshire Regiment in 1777; took part in the attack on Ticonderoga and in the actions at Bemis's Heights, Monmouth, and Stony Point. He died in Nottingham, N. H., Aug. 25, 1799.

CINCINNATI

Cincinnati, city, port of delivery, and county-seat of Hamilton county, Ohio; second city in the State and thirteenth in the United States in population, according to the Federal census of 1910, popularly known as the "Queen City of the West." Population (1890) 296,908; (1900) 325,902; (1910) 364,463.

Location, Area, etc.—It is situated in an amphitheatre of great natural beauty, on the north bank of the Ohio River and opposite the mouth of the Licking River, and geographically possesses many of the distinctive features of a Northern and a Southern city. Its long river frontage faces the apex of Kentucky, and makes the city the centre of large interstate interests shared by Covington, Newport, Bellevue, Dayton, Ludlow, and Bromley, all belonging to the Southland. Two terraces, one about 60 feet above the level of the river, the other about 112 feet, on which the city has been built, enhance the beauty of a spot already exceedingly picturesque by reason of the hills that nearly surround it.

Topographically, the city is divided into three sections. The lowest ground, or river bottoms, is mainly devoted to manufacturing and wholesale trade; the northeastern part, separated from the rest of the city by the Miami & Erie Canal, is locally called "Over the Rhine," because of its large German population; and the west end is the handsomest residential portion. By the annexation in 1895 and 1903 of a number of suburban villages, the city has attained an area of about forty square miles.

Public Interests.—In 1902 the legislature provided in the new municipal code what is practically a new charter, the change being necessitated by the declaration of the Supreme Court that the existing classification of the cities of the State was unconstitutional. Under the new code the Board of Legislation, consisting of thirty-one members, was succeeded by a City Council, composed of one member from each of the twenty-four wards into which the city was redistricted. Avondale, Clifton, Linwood, Riverside, and Westwood had been annexed in 1895, and in 1903, when the new code went into effect, Hyde Park, Evanston, Bond Hill, and Winton Place were absorbed, increasing the area of the city to 43½ square miles. The village of Delhi was annexed in 1909, and in 1910 College Hill, Sayler Park, Carthage, Madisonville, Mt. Airy, and Mt. Washington also voted for annexation.

In 1910 there were 763 miles of streets, of which 497 were paved; 326 miles of sewers; a police department of 627 men; a fire department of 626 men; and a water-works system owned by the city that had 540 miles of mains, and cost $18,000,000. The assessed valuations of taxable property (1909) were $250,283,550; the general bonded debt was $51,335,304; sinking-fund holdings, $8,276,255; net debt, $43,059,049. The city owns the Cincinnati Southern Railroad, leased till Oct. 12, 1966, at annual rentals running for specific periods from $1,050,000 to $1,200,000, the lessee to pay interest on $2,500,000 bonds for terminal improvements and an annual sum for a sinking-fund. The water-works system pays the interest on all water-bonds and is creating a sinking-fund for their redemption.

The city has an extensive domestic trade, promoted by twenty-five railroads that radiate from it, by several bridges to the Kentucky shore, and by invaluable water communications, comprising the Ohio River, navigable from Pittsburgh to the Mississippi, and the Miami & Erie Canal, connecting Cincinnati with Lake Erie. As an interior port of delivery the city received foreign merchandise to the value of $2,893,534 in the calendar year 1910.

Notable Buildings.—The United States Government Building, on the square bounded by Main, Walnut, Fifth, and Patterson streets, built of granite in the Renaissance style, 354 feet long, 164 feet deep, and six stories high, is considered the handsomest structure in this city of handsome buildings. It cost about $5,000,000. The new County Court-House, on Main Street, is Romanesque in style. In its rear, occupying an entire square, is the County Jail. The Municipal Buildings, on the square bounded by Plum, Eighth, and Ninth streets and Central Avenue, are built of red sandstone, and cost over $1,600,000. Springer Music Hall, in modified Gothic, is a grand edifice, 178 feet wide, 293 feet deep, and 150 feet high from sidewalk to gable pinnacle, has extremely rich interior decorations, and contains one of the largest organs in the world. The Public Library is of stone and brick, Romanesque in style, with shelf-room for 300,000 volumes, and now containing over 225,000. Byzantine in style, the Masonic Temple arrests the sweep of the eye from a distance by reason of its two towers and its spire 180 feet high. Other notable society buildings are the Cathedral of the Masonic Scottish Rite on Broadway, and Odd Fellows' Hall on Elm Street.

On Elm Street, fronting Washington Park, are the Exposition Buildings, covering three and a half acres and having an exhibiting space of seven acres. Pike's Building, the widely famed Rookwood Pottery, the Emery Arcade, the Board of Trade, the College of Music, and the magnificent building of the Cincinnati Museum in Eden Park, amply repay close inspection. The Tyler-Davidson Fountain, on Fifth Street between Vine and Walnut, is a beautiful classic in bronze, embellished with statuary and supporting a female figure of more than heroic size. The fountain was cast in Munich, and cost over $200,000. Eden Park is the principal public reservation; others are Burnet Woods, Lincoln Park, Washington Park, Hopkins Park, and Chester Park. Among the noteworthy monuments in the city are those to Presidents William Henry Harrison and James A. Garfield, and to Colonels R. L. McCook and Frederick Hecker.

Manufactures.—According to the tentative Federal census of 1909, the city had 2,184 manufacturing and industrial establishments operated under the factory-system classification (excluding small shops and hand trades), which employed $150,254,000 capital and 60,192 wage-earners; paid $43,860,000 for salaries and wages, and $28,995,000 for miscellaneous expenses, and $101,932,000 for materials used in manufacturing; and had aggregate products valued at $193,788,000. The principal industries, in the order of value of output, were: Men's clothing; foundry and machine-shop products; slaughtering and meat-packing, wholesale; boots and shoes; distilled liquors; malt liquors; carriages and wagons—all others under $5,000,000.

Banks.—The report of the Comptroller of the Currency for the banking year ending Sept. 1, 1910, credited Cincinnati with eight national banks, having an aggregate capital of $13,900,000; surplus, $7,250,000; circulation, $7,617,095; individual deposits, $43,687,376; loans and discounts, $61,862,210; specie, $6,360,944; and assets and liabilities balancing at $109,582,237. The clearing-house here ranked ninth among those of the country in the volume of annual exchanges. These, in the year ending Sept. 30, 1910, aggregated $1,277,996,900, a decrease in a year of $48,716,400. In 1900 there were thirteen national banks, with capital, $7,700,000; circulation, $12,371,587; individual deposits, $27,141,271; and total resources, $67,332,885; and the clearing-house exchanges were $792,434,950, an increase in a year of $82,915,050.

Schools and Colleges.—The city has over 47,500 pupils in daily attendance in its public schools, with 1,225 teachers, and spends annually for public education more than $1,825,000. The estimated attendance at private and parochial schools is about 20,000. Public secondary schools include the Hughes, Norwood, Walnut Hills, and Woodward high schools, and private ones, the Bartholomew-Clifton, Butler, Collegiate, Franklin, Fredin, and Lupton schools, Academy of the Sacred Heart, St. Francis Seraphim's College, St. Mary's Educational Institute, Ursuline Academy, and Ohio Military Institute. Technical instruction is furnished by the Ohio Mechanic's Institute and the Cincinnati Technical School; and training-schools for nurses are maintained by the Bethesda, Christ's, Cincinnati, Jewish, and the Ohio Women's and Children's hospitals.

The University of Cincinnati, founded and endowed by Charles McMicken, and occupying with its cluster of substantial buildings a tract of forty acres in Burnet Woods Park, has grounds and buildings valued at over $1,500,000, scientific and other apparatus valued at $185,000, productive funds aggregating $1,500,000, and a library of about 115,000 volumes. The former Cincinnati Law School and the Medical College of Ohio are now departments of the university. St. Xavier College (Roman Catholic) was opened in 1831, and occupies a building in the Romanesque style on Sycamore Street.

Professional schools include the Hebrew Union College, opened in 1875, and the Lane Theological Seminary (Presbyterian), 1829; Law Department, University of Cincinnati, and Law School of McDonald Institute; and the Medical Department, University of Cincinnati, Laura Memorial Woman's Medical College, Miami Medical College, Cincinnati College of Medicine and Surgery, and the Pulte and Eclectic colleges.

Churches.—Cincinnati is the seat of a Roman Catholic archbishop and of a Protestant Episcopal bishop, and the official residence of a Methodist Episcopal bishop. According to a special census report on *Religious Bodies* (1910), the city had 255 religious organizations, 159,663 communicants or members (including 51,520 Protestants and 106,211 Roman Catholics), 247 church edifices, 15 halls used for religious purposes, church property of 234 organizations valued at $8,681,987, and 284 Sunday-schools, with 3,823 officers and teachers, and 47,505 scholars.

Charities.—Occupying a square of four acres on Twelfth Street, between Central Avenue and Plum Street, is the Cincinnati Hospital, a group of buildings around a central court with connecting corridors, that is claimed to be the largest and most thoroughly appointed institution of its kind in the country. The Good Samaritan Hospital is on Sixth and Lock streets; St. Mary's, on Baymiller and Betts streets; St. Francis's, on Queen City Avenue; Jewish, on Burnet Avenue; and the Longview Asylum for the Insane is at Carthage, ten miles north of the city, a brick building in the Italian style, and noticeable for the absence of grated windows and other former features of such institutions.

There are a House of Refuge on Colerain Avenue; a City Workhouse near by; the Cincinnati Orphan Asylum on Mount Auburn; and a Widows' and Old Men's Home on Ashland Avenue; besides a large number of helpful associations connected with the various churches, societies, and business interests.

History.—Cincinnati was originally known as Losantiville, from L = Licking, os=mouth, anti=against, ville=town—*i. e.*, "the town opposite the mouth" of the Licking—because Israel Ludlow crossed the Ohio from the mouth of the Licking River and settled here, on Dec. 28, 1788. The site of the city is believed to have been visited first by white men about eight years previously. The site was probably selected as being on the Indian trail between Detroit, the Great Lakes, and Lexington, Ky., where the trail crossed the Ohio River. The ground on which the city stands was purchased by Matthias Denman, who associated with himself Robert Patterson and John Filson. The latter was killed by Indians while on a visit to the site of the proposed settlement, and Ludlow took his place in the enterprise. The next year, 1789, Major Doughty, with about 140 men, left Fort Harmar on the Muskingum River, and built Fort Washington on the line of the present Third Street, between Broadway and Lawrence. A village soon sprang up around this fort, which was a cluster of strongly built log-cabins, a story and a half high, arranged for soldiers' barracks, and occupying a hollow square enclosing about an acre of ground. At the suggestion of General St. Clair, the place was renamed Cincinnati, in honor of the Society of the Cincinnati, with which he and the principal officers of the Revolutionary War were connected.

CINCINNATI IN 1812.

The first post-office was established in 1793; the legislature passed a bill to remove the seat of government from Chillicothe to Cincinnati in 1801; the town was incorporated in 1802; and the United States reservation around Fort Washington was sold in 1808. In 1816 the shipbuilding industry was introduced and a steamboat completed, and in 1819 the town was incorporated as a city. In 1819 Col. Samuel W. Davis began supplying water through wooden pipes. Seven years afterwards the Cincinnati Water Company was incorporated. Public education was established in 1831; the first city bonds were issued and the locks on the Miami & Erie Canal here were completed, both in 1834; and the Little Miami Railroad was built in 1840. From this period till 1862 the history of the city was one of wholesome growth.

On Sept. 2, 1862, a Confederate force under command of Gen. E. Kirby Smith, which had invaded Kentucky and pushed on towards the Ohio for the purpose of capturing Cincinnati, was unexpectedly confronted by a Union force under Gen. Lew Wallace, who had been ordered by General Wright to provide for the defence of this city. Martial law was proclaimed, and in a few hours General Wallace had a force of 40,000 workers and fighters at his service. This force crossed the river on a pontoon bridge, and within three days built a line of intrenchments ten miles long on the hills of Covington. When the Confederates discovered the barrier against them they retreated in great haste, and made no further attempt to occupy or injure either city.

The National Democratic Convention which nominated Buchanan met here in 1856; the Liberal Republican which nominated Greeley, in 1872; the Republican which nominated Hayes, in 1876; and the Democratic which nominated Hancock, in 1880. The most serious local trouble the city has experienced was in March, 1884, when a riot broke out because of a verdict of manslaughter in the Berner and Palmer murder trial after both had confessed to murder, and while there were about twenty untried murderers in the city jail. A mob, incensed at what was generally considered a miscarriage of justice, fired the court-house; the militia were called out; and in an attack on the mob 45 persons were killed and 138 wounded.

Cincinnati, SOCIETY OF THE. A few weeks before the disbanding of the Continental army (June, 1783) a tie of friendship had been formed among the officers, at the suggestion of General Knox, by the organization, at the headquarters of Baron von Steuben, near Fishkill Landing, N. Y., of an association known as the "Society of the Cincinnati." Its chief objects were to promote a cordial friendship and indissoluble union among themselves, and to extend benevolent aid to such of its members as might need assistance. Washington was chosen the first president of the society, and remained president-general until his death. Gen. Henry Knox was its first secretary-general. State societies were formed, auxiliary to the general society. To perpetuate the association, it was provided in the constitution of the society that the eldest masculine descendant of an original member should be entitled to wear the order and enjoy the privileges of the society. The *order*, or badge, of the society consists of a golden eagle, with enamelling, suspended upon a ribbon. On the breast of the eagle is a medallion, with a device representing Cincinnatus at his plough receiving the Roman senators who came to offer him the chief magistracy of Rome. The members' certificate is eighteen and a half inches in breadth and twenty inches in length. The general Society of the Cincinnati is still in existence, and also State societies. The president-general from 1854 till his death in 1893 was Hamilton Fish, son of Col. Nicholas Fish, one of the original members. In 1900 William Wayne, of Pennsylvania, held the office. The order worn by the president-general at the meetings of the society is a beautifully jewelled one. It was presented to Washington by the French officers. The society met with much jealous opposition from the earnest

ORDER OF THE CINCINNATI.

republicans of the day. Among the most powerful of these opponents was Judge Aedanus Burke, of Charleston, S. C., who, in an able dissertation, undertook to prove that the society created two distinct orders among the Americans—first, a race of hereditary nobles founded on the military, together with the most influen-

Be it known that Robert Wilson an Ensign in the First New York Reg. in late War is a Member of the Society of the Cincinnati instituted by the Officers of the American Army, at the Period of its Dissolution, as well to commemorate the great Event which gave Independence to North America, as for the laudable Purpose of inculcating the Duty of laying down in Peace Arms assumed for public Defence, and of uniting in Acts of brotherly Affection, and Bonds of perpetual Friendship the Members constituting the same.

IN TESTIMONY whereof I, the President of the said Society, have hereunto set my Hand at Mont Vernon in the State of Virginia this Tenth Day of December in the Year of our Lord One Thousand Seven Hundred and Eighty Five and in the Tenth Year of the Independence of the United States

By order,

H Knox Secretary

G. Washington President.

SOCIETY OF THE CINCINNATI—MEMBER'S CERTIFICATE.

tial families and men in the State; and, second, the people, or plebeians. These suspicions were natural, but were not justified.

Cinque, African chief and slave. See AMISTAD, CASE OF THE.

Cipher Despatches. The result of the Presidential election of 1876 in the United States depended upon the electoral votes of Louisiana, South Carolina, and Florida, long in dispute. Mr. Hayes needed all three States, while any one of them would have elected Mr. Tilden. Pending the result, many despatches in cipher passed between Mr. Tilden's friends and persons in the South, which, when translated and published in the New York *Tribune*, 1877, suggested attempted bribery. A great scandal arose, and Mr. Tilden publicly disclaimed all knowledge of the despatches.

Ciquard, FRANÇOIS, missionary; born in Clermont, France, about 1760; entered the Sulpitian order; came to the United States in 1792, and settled in Old Town, Me., where he labored among the Penobscot and Passamaquoddy Indians, for whom he prepared a code of laws, but had great difficulty in inducing them to adopt a civilized life. He died in Canada.

Circuit Courts. See FEDERAL GOVERNMENT.

Circular Letter. On. Feb. 11, 1768, Massachusetts sent a circular letter to all the American colonies asking them to co-operate with Massachusetts in obtaining redress of grievances.

This letter was laid before the English cabinet, which resolved,

1. That the Massachusetts assembly should rescind the letter, and

2. That the other colonial legislatures before whom it had been laid should reject the letter.

The legislature of Massachusetts by a vote of 92 to 17 refused to do the first, and the other legislatures refused the second later in December.

Circulation, MONETARY. The population of the continental United States in 1910 was 91,972,266, and the amount of money in circulation on April 1, 1912, was equal to $34.45 for every man, woman, and child in the country. The following table shows the amount of gold and silver coin and certificates, United States notes and national bank notes in circulation and in the treasury on that date:

AMOUNT OF CURRENCY IN CIRCULATION AND IN TREASURY, APRIL 1, 1912.

KIND OF MONEY.	General Stock of Money in the United States.	Held in Treasury as Assests of Government.	Money in Circulation.
	Dollars.	*Dollars.*	*Dollars.*
Gold coin (including bullion in Treasury)....	†1,798,389,525	172,841,816	597,115,340
Gold certificates ‡..........................	....	81,295,114	947,137,255
Standard silver dollars....................	565,269,367	7,577,904	70,528,463
Silver certificates..........................	....	12,307,624	474,855,376
Subsidiary silver	¶165,073,658	24,306,074	140,767,584
Treasury notes of 1890.....................	3,010,000	11,004	2,998,996
United States notes........................	346,681,016	8,880,271	337,800,745
National bank notes........................	744,871,283	34,887,276	709,784,007
Total	3,623,294,849	342,107,083	3,281,187,766

* This statement of money held in the Treasury as assets of the Government does not include deposits of public money in National bank depositories to the credit of the Treasurer of the United States, amounting to $33,836,839,48.

† A revised estimate by the Director of the Mint of the stock of gold coin was adopted in the statement for August 1, 1907. There was a reduction of $135,000,000.

‡ For redemption of outstanding certificates an exact equivalent in amount of the appropriate kinds of money is held in the Treasury, and is not included in the account of money held as assets of the Government.

¶ A revised estimate by the Director of the Mint of the stock of subsidiary silver coin was adopted in the statement of September 1, 1910. There was a reduction of $9,700,000.

See COINAGE, UNITED STATES; CURRENCY, NATIONAL; MONETARY REFORM.

Cisneros, SALVADOR, MARQUIS DE SANTA LUCIA, statesman; born in Cuba, in 1831. In 1868, the year that the Ten Years' War broke out, he renounced all allegiance to Spain and his right to a noble title, declaring himself henceforth a republican. He was a man of large wealth, but when his affiliation with the Cuban cause became known in Spain his property was confiscated. Upon the organization of the first Cuban government he was elected president of the House of Representatives, and in 1895 he became chief executive of the Cuban Republic.—His niece, EVANGELINA COSIO CISNEROS, was imprisoned by the Spaniards for aiding the insurgents during the insurrection in 1896–97, and made a sensational escape, coming to the United States, where she became a protégé of Mrs. Gen. John A. Logan.

Cist, CHARLES, printer; born in St. Petersburg, Russia, Aug. 15, 1783; graduated at Halle; came to America in 1773; and lived in Philadelphia, where he founded a printing and publishing business with Melchior Steiner. Later he became sole proprietor and publisher of *The American Herald* and the *Columbian Magazine.* He introduced anthracite coal into general use in the United States. During the Revolutionary War he endorsed Continental currency to a large amount, which he was afterwards compelled to redeem.

Cist, HENRY MARTIN, military officer; born in Cincinnati, O., Feb. 20, 1839; graduated at Belmont College in 1858; in April, 1861, enlisted in the 6th Ohio Regiment, and at the time of his resignation had attained the rank of brigadier-general. He was the author of *The Army of the Cumberland,* and editor of the *Reports of the Society of the Army of the Cumberland.* He died in Rome, Italy, Dec. 17, 1902.

Cities, TOWNS, VILLAGES, DISTRICTS. The census of 1790 showed 13 cities with more than 5,000 inhabitants. The largest of these was much less than 50,000. The percentage of inhabitants at that time living in cities of more than 8,000 inhabitants was .3 per cent. Each succeeding census for the next 120 years showed a gradually increasing percentage of urban population. Under the census of 1910, the urban population was 42,623,383, or 46.3 per cent. of the whole, and the rural population, 49,348,883, or 53.7 per cent. of the whole. See CENSUS.

Citizen. By a change in the political character of the English-American colonies, the word "citizen" took the place of "subject," and was as comprehensive in its application to the inhabitants of the territories included in the United States of America. All persons born or naturalized in the United States and subject to the jurisdiction thereof are citizens of the United States and of the State wherein they reside.

All persons born in the United States and not subject to any foreign power, excluding Indians not taxed, are declared to be citizens of the United States.

All children heretofore born or hereafter born out of the limits and jurisdiction of the United States, whose fathers were or may be, at the time of their birth, citizens thereof, are declared to be citizens of the United States; but the rights of citizenship shall not descend to children whose fathers never resided in the United States.

Any woman who is now or may hereafter be married to a citizen of the United States and who might herself be lawfully naturalized shall be deemed a citizen. (See 1995, U. S. Revised Statutes.)

Children born in the United States of alien parents are citizens of the United States.

When any alien who has formally declared his intention of becoming a citizen of the United States dies before he is actually naturalized, the widow and children of such aliens are citizens.

Children of Chinese parents who are themselves aliens and incapable of becoming naturalized are citizens of the United States.

Children born in the United States of persons engaged in the diplomatic service of foreign governments are not citizens of the United States.

Children born of alien parents on a vessel of a foreign country while within the waters of the United States are not citizens of the United States, but of the country to which the vessel belongs.

Children born of alien parents in the United States have the right to make an election of nationality when they reach their majority.

Minors and children are citizens within the meaning of the term as used in the Constitution.

Deserters from the military or naval service of the United States are liable to loss of citizenship.

Any alien being a free white person, an alien of African nativity or of African descent may become an American citizen by complying with the naturalization laws.

"Hereafter no State court or court of the United States shall admit Chinese to citizenship; and all laws in conflict with this act are repealed." (Sec. 14, act of May 6, 1882.)

The courts have held that neither Chinese, Japanese, Hawaiians, Burmese nor Indians can be naturalized.

The naturalization laws apply to women as well as men. An alien woman who marries a citizen, native or naturalized, becomes a naturalized citizen of the United States.

Aliens may become citizens of the United States by treaties with foreign powers, by conquest or by special acts of Congress.

In an act approved March 2, 1907, it is provided that any American citizen shall have expatriated himself when he has been naturalized in any foreign state in conformity with its laws, or when he has taken an oath of allegiance to any foreign state.

When any naturalized citizen shall have resided for two years in the foreign state from which he came, or five years in any other foreign state, it shall be presumed that he has ceased to be an American citizen, and the place of his general abode shall be deemed his place of residence during said years; provided, however, that such presumption may be overcome on the presentation of satisfactory evidence to a diplomatic or consular officer of the United States, under such rules and regulations as the department of state may prescribe; and, provided, also, that no American citizen shall be allowed to expatriate himself when this country is at war.

Any American woman who marries a foreigner shall take the nationality of her husband. At the termination of the marital relation she may resume her American citizenship, if abroad, by registering as an American citizen within one year with a consul of the United States, or by returning to reside in the United States, or, if residing in the United States at the termination of the marital relation, by continuing to reside therein.

Any foreign woman who acquires American citizenship by marriage to an American citizen shall be assumed to retain the same after the termination of the marital relation if she continue to reside in the United States, unless she makes formal renunciation thereof before a court having jurisdiction to naturalize aliens, or, if she resides abroad, she may retain her citizenship by registering as such before a United States consul within one year after the termination of such marital relation.

A child born without the United States, of alien parents, shall be deemed a citizen of the United States by virtue of the naturalization of or resumption of American citizenship of the parent; provided that such naturalization or resumption takes place during the minority of such child; and, provided further, that the citizenship of such minor child shall begin at the time such minor child begins to reside permanently in the United States.

All children born outside the limits of the United States, who are citizens thereof in accordance with the provisions of section 1993 of the Revised Statutes of the United States, and who continue to reside outside of the United States, shall, in order to receive the protection of the government, be required, upon reaching the age of 18 years, to record at an American consulate their intention to become residents and remain citizens of the United States and shall further be required to take the oath of allegiance to the United States upon attaining their majority. See NATURALIZATION; ELECTIVE FRANCHISE.

Citronelle, a village in Mobile county, Ala., where General Canby defeated the Confederates under General Taylor. When the news of Johnston's surrender was received all the Confederate forces east of the Mississippi were surrendered to General Canby, May 4, 1865.

City of Brotherly Love. The popular name of Philadelphia.

City of Churches, a name formerly applied to the city of Brooklyn, N. Y., because it contained a larger number of churches in proportion to its size and population than any other American city.

City of Charities, Utica, N. Y., so called because of its large number of benevolent institutions.

City of Elms, New Haven, Conn., whose streets are shaded by many of these noble trees.

City of Homes, Philadelphia, Pa.; so named on account of the large number of private dwellings it contains, and the almost total absence of "tenement" houses.

City of Notions, a popular name given to the city of Boston, Mass.

City of Rocks, Nashville, Tenn. Quarries of fine limestone abound in the immediate vicinity, which enters largely into the construction of its buildings.

City of Smoke, Pittsburg, Pa.; also known as the Iron City.

City of Spindles, a popular name given to the city of Lowell, Mass.

City of the Strait, the popular name of Detroit (the French word for "strait"), situated upon the strait between Lakes St. Clair and Erie.

City Planning, a recent feature of municipal improvement in the United States, intended to increase the attractiveness of a city, and involving in general the concentration of municipal and other public buildings at a civic centre, with broad avenues radiating therefrom into the suburbs, interspersed with ornamental plazas, squares, parks, playgrounds, and other "breathing" spots. The "city beautiful" is a creation of slow progress because of the great cost, the crooked thoroughfares that have to be straightened or closed, and the antiquated and unsightly buildings that have to be removed; but the spirit of the innovation is widespread, and in many cities recent local improvements have been made on plans leading ultimately to a complete transformation.

At the International Town Planning Conference and Exhibition, held in the Royal Academy, London, in October, 1910, the exhibits from the United States occupied the largest gallery, and comprised maps, plans, diagrams, sketches, photographs, and models from Washington, New York, Boston, Philadelphia, St. Louis, Savannah, and other cities, where municipal reconstruction has been attempted or planned to beautify the city, alleviate the congestion of certain sections, and provide better housing for the ever-increasing industrial populace. The universality of the movement is attested by the fact that nearly every large city in the world was represented by plans at the conference.

City Point, on the James River at the mouth of the Appomattox, near Petersburg, Va. In May, 1864, General Butler seized this place, which became the principal base of supplies for the army operating against Richmond under Grant.

Civic Association, AMERICAN, an organization formed by merger of the American League for Civic Improvement and the American Park and Outdoor Art Association, June 10, 1904. The Association seeks to combine and make efficient the country-wide effort for civic betterment. It has led in the effort to prevent the destruction of Niagara Falls for power purposes; it advocates rational forest treatment; it is inaugurating a campaign for the restraint and reduction of objectionable outdoor advertising as a defacement of nature, and it urges community beauty. It fosters parks, playgrounds, and outdoor recreation; it arouses communities, and leads them toward betterment; it conducts a city-planning department, and directs a national crusade against the "typhoid" fly. A lantern-slide service is maintained, and many bulletins are issued.

Civic Federation. See NATIONAL CIVIC FEDERATION.

Civil Death. The extinction of a man's civil rights and capacities. In some States imprisonment for life is civil death.

Civil Rights Bill, an important measure introduced in the United States Senate on Jan. 29, 1866; adopted there Feb. 2 by a vote of 33 to 12, and passed in the House on March 13 by a vote of 111 to 38. The bill was vetoed March 27 by President Johnson, but was passed over the veto, in the Senate on April 6, and in the House on April 9. While the bill was passing through these stages a number of amendments were proposed for the purpose of nullifying the decision in the Dred Scott case; and on April 30 Thaddeus Stevens, of Pennsylvania, in the House, reported from a joint committee the measure that became the Fourteenth Amendment to the CONSTITUTION (*q. v.*).

The original civil rights bill comprised in brief the following provisions:

1. All persons born in the United States and not subject to any foreign power, excluding Indians not taxed, were therein declared to be citizens of the United States, having the same rights as white citizens in every State and Territory to sue and to be sued, make and enforce contracts, take and convey property, and enjoy all civil rights whatever. 2. Any person who, under color of any State law, deprived any such citizen of any civil rights secured by this act was made guilty of a misdemeanor. 3. Cognizance of offences against the act was entirely taken away from State courts and given to federal courts. 4. Officers of the United States Courts or of the Freedmen's Bureau, and special executive agents, were charged with the execution of the act. 5. If such officers refused to execute the act, they were made subject to fine. 6. Resistance to the officers subjected the offender to fine and imprisonment. 7. This section related to fees. 8. The President was empowered to send officers to any district where offences against the act were likely to be committed. 9. The President was authorized to use the services of special agents, of the army and navy, or of the militia, to enforce the act. 10. An appeal was permitted to the Supreme Court. The federal courts had exclusive jurisdiction.

Charles Sumner, the distinguished Senator from Massachusetts, was exceedingly anxious to secure the adoption of an amendment to the original bill, which, among other things, should prevent common carriers, inn-keepers, theatre-managers, and officers or teachers of schools from distinguishing blacks from whites; should prevent the exclusion of negroes from juries; and should give federal courts exclusive cognizance of offences against it. In 1872 he offered a bill covering these grounds as an amendment to the amnesty act, but it failed of passage by a single vote. Later in the same year it was introduced in the House. On April 30, 1874, the measure was adopted in the Senate, but rejected in the House, and in February, 1875, it was adopted in both Houses, becoming a law March 1. On Oct. 25, 1883, the Supreme Court of the United States, through Justice Bradley, decided that the supplementary civil rights bill (Sumner's) was unconstitutional.

Civil Service Reform. The civil service is a name applied to the duties rendered to the government other than naval and military service. That is, all persons employed by the government outside of the army and navy are in the civil service. By civil service reform is meant the doing away with many objectionable customs and abuses that had found their way, through the influence of politicians, into the civil service. Away back in President Jackson's time the custom was introduced of making appointments to this service a reward for party effort, and not in consequence of any particular fitness for the positions. The change of the political character of an administration would, of course, under this plan, cause an entire change in the civil service, no faithful performance of tasks assigned or acquired experience counting as of any value in competition with party service. It can readily be seen how a system like this would demoralize most branches of the public service, how patronage, or the control of offices, would come to be a mere matter of traffic, and how it would lead to a condition of wastefulness and inefficiency in many instances. The matter was made even worse by a system of levying a tax or assessment, at each election, on all office-holders to bear party expenses, the understanding being that the payment of this tax was a condition of the retention of the office.

The first attempt to call the attention of Congress to the need of reform in the civil service was made in 1867. On Feb. 2 of that year, Mr. Jenckes, of Rhode Island, a Republican, brought forward a bill for the investigation and reorganization of that service. The bill was referred to a committee, but the report of the committee when received was tabled, and nothing further was done about it. In 1870 Mr. Jenckes tried to get a bill passed for the introduction of a system of competitive examination in the civil service, but this also failed. President Grant gave it the weight of his influence, and really made legislation in that regard possible. In his message to Congress, Dec. 5, 1870, the President thus referred to the measure: "Always favoring practical reform, I respectfully call your attention to one abuse of long standing which I would like to see remedied by this Congress. It is a reform in the civil service of the country. I would have it go beyond the mere fixing of the tenure of office of clerks and employés who do not require the advice and consent of the Senate to make their appointments complete. I would have it govern, not the tenure, but the manner of making all appointments. There is no duty which so much embarrasses the executive and heads of departments as that of appointments; nor is there any such arduous and thankless labor for Senators and Representatives as that of finding places for constituents. The present system does not secure the best men, and often not even fit men, for public place. The elevation and purification of the civil service of the government will be hailed with approval by the whole people of the United States."

Following this was a bill called the civil service bill, which carried out the spirit of President Grant's recommendation. The first civil service commission consisted of G. W. Curtis, of New York; Joseph Medill, of Chicago; A. J. Cattell, of New Jersey; D. A. Walker, of Pennsylvania; S. B. Elliott, and J. H. Blackfair. A second commission was appointed March 1, 1883, consisting of Dorman B. Eaton, of New York; Leroy D. Thoman, of Ohio; and Dr. John B. Gregory, of Illinois. In 1912 the commission consisted of John C. Black, John A. McIlhenny and William S. Washburn. At the end of that year the number of persons in the classified civil service of the national government was over 367,800. See address on the "Spoils System," under CURTIS, GEORGE WILLIAM.

Civil Service, United States Colonial. Prof. Edward Gaylor Bourne, Professor of History in Yale University, writes as follows concerning the civil service for our new possessions:

Our previous annexations of territory, with the possible exception of Alaska, have never involved questions of administration essentially different from those with which our public men have been familiar; for, from the first settlement of the colonies, the occupation of new land and the organization of new communities have been the special task and most noteworthy achievement of the American people. Acquisitions, like the Louisiana and Mexican cessions, merely afforded room for the natural overflow of our people, and the new possessions soon became more distinctively American than the mother States. The wonderful results of this spontaneous process are accepted by too many of our people as a demonstration that we can cope equally well with the extremely difficult and complicated task of governing large masses of alien and unwilling subjects. Yet a moment's reflection must show every one that the simple form of growth which has expanded the United States from the Alleghanies to the Pacific cannot be extended to our recent acquisitions.

Neither Cuba nor Porto Rico is likely ever to be populated by English-speaking Americans. Our ideas, no doubt, will pervade these islands to some extent, but that their civilization will cease to be Spanish is highly improbable. Their inhabitants are a civilized people, heirs, like ourselves, of a European culture, possessing a noble language, a splendid literature, and a highly developed jurisprudence. This inheritance they will never voluntarily give up, nor can they be forced to sacrifice it without tyrannical oppression. Those who think differently should study the case of French Canada, or, even better, the case of Louisiana. It would have been natural to expect, in 1803, that the inflowing tide of American immigration would soon absorb or overwhelm the scattered little settlements of French creoles, numbering in all, masters and slaves, within the bounds of the present State of Louisiana, not more than 30,000. On the contrary, French life and manners still survive, the civil law has never been displaced by the English common law, and after nearly a century, over one-sixth of the native whites of the State cannot speak the English language. In view of this experience how remote is the possibility that the dense population of Porto Rico will ever lose its Spanish character!

Turning to the Philippines we find a task still more widely different from any that we have ever undertaken, and far more complicated. This archipelago is nothing less than an ethnological museum. Its population of 6,000,000 or 7,000,000 ranges from the Negrito head-hunters to the civilized Tagals and Visayas, who had a written language before the Spaniards came among them, to say nothing of the Chinese, the Chinese-Malay, and Spanish-Malay mixtures who constitute the enterprising element in the towns. Furthermore, although hitherto beyond our horizon, these islands are not in a remote corner of the earth like Alaska, where failure would be hidden or unnoticed, but they lie at the very meeting-place of nations, and all that we do there will be under a white light of publicity. The most energetic and ambitious powers of Europe will be our neighbors and critics.

To expect that the problem of the Philippines or of Cuba and Porto Rico can be dealt with by our ordinary methods of administration and of appointment to office is to live in a fool's paradise. Only a blind national pride can believe for a moment that the average American politician or office-seeker can deal with the situation any better than the Spanish political heelers have done. In fact, the American, with his ignorance of the language and customs and his contempt for "dagoes" and "niggers," will be even less qualified for the task. A repetition in the West Indies of the mistake of Jefferson, who committed the French and Spanish population of Louisiana to the government of Claiborne and Wilkinson, men grossly ignorant of their language, customs, institutions, and history, will make our rule less tolerable than that of Spain. A repetition in the Philippines of the government of Alaska or of South Carolina in 1869, would be a world-wide scandal, and bring more disgrace on the American name than all the fraud, stealing, and murder of the entire Reconstruction period.

As a civilized, progressive, and conscientious people, we must either not attempt the work which has fallen upon our hands, or we must intrust it to the best administrative ability that the country possesses, to men not inferior in natural powers and special training to our leading army and navy officers, who will, like these officers, enjoy permanence of tenure, the social distinction of an honored profession, and the privilege of retiring after their term of service on an allowance adequate to their comfortable support.

The nucleus for such a body of officials will naturally be found in the regular army, and for the transition work of establishing order and restoring confidence they are fitted by their professional experience and discipline. But a permanent military government is alien to our ideas and should be established only as a final resort. The education of a soldier does not prepare him for civil administration. The military mind is arbitrary and unconciliatory; it is disposed to crush rather than to win; it holds life cheap. In brief, its ideals and standards are those engendered by war and its necessities.

What, then, should be the nature of the special training required of candidates for administrative positions in our dependencies? In thoroughness and extent, it should not be less than that demanded of our own lawyers and physicians. This means two or three years of distinctively professional training resting on the solid foundation of a regular course of study in a college or scientific school. Starting from the same general level of preparation as the student of law or medicine, the colonial civil service candidate should devote himself to the following groups of studies: Geography and ethnology, history, economics and law, languages, religions, and folk psychology.

The work in geography should cover the physical features, climate, plants, and economic resources of our dependencies, and the principles of tropical hygiene. Under the head of ethnology, the elements of the comparative study of the races of man would be followed by a more thorough examination of the peoples of eastern Asia and Polynesia. The next group would deal with the history of the relations of Europeans with the East, and, in particular, with the history of the colonial systems of England, France, Holland, and Spain; with the tariffs and financial systems; and, finally, with the principles of administration, including the study of the civil law as developed in the Spanish codes, Mohammedan law, and the legal customs of the native tribes. Between customs and religions the dividing line is really invisible, and this branch of the work may just as well be included under the general head of folk psychology. By this somewhat unfamiliar name we mean the study of the outfit of ideas, moral, religious, social, and philosophical, which any well-differentiated human group inherits from its ancestors and passes over to its posterity. Into this mental world in which they live he must enter who wishes to stand on common ground with any alien race. In no other way can suspicion and hatred be made to give place to sympathy and confidence. The entrance to this strange world, vastly more remote and inaccessible to the average man than the Philippines, is to be found only through the study of language and with the help of a trained scientific imagination. Translations and interpreters, at the best, leave one still outside and merely peering in through a dense and highly refracting medium.

Does all this seem impracticable and Utopian? In proportion as it does, the reader may be sure that he falls short of realizing what we have really undertaken to do. It is no more than England, Holland, France, and Germany are doing for their colonial and diplomatic service. If we do less, we shall take heavy risks that European colonial authorities will have the same contempt for our management that we now have for Spain's. Mr. John Foreman, after an experience in Spain and the Philippines of nearly a quarter of a century, writes: "Of the hundreds of officials that I have known, not one had the most elementary notions of Tagalog or Visaya (the native languages of the Philippine Islands) at the time of their appointment, and not one in fifty took the trouble to learn either language afterwards." In not one of the Spanish universities is there taught a modern Oriental language, except Arabic, nor was there in 1898 a single chair devoted to colonial problems, nor in the university of Manila was there any opportunity to study the languages and customs of the Philippines. The civil service in the Spanish colonies, like that of the mother-country, was purely a spoils system. No examinations of any kind were required. Offices were the reward of fidelity to the political "*caciques*" (bosses), and the dangers and discomforts of colonial service were compensated for by the abundant opportunities for "*chocolate*" (boodle). Not least among the causes of the final collapse of Spain's colonial power was the blight of spoils.

In marked contrast to Spain stands little Holland, with substantially the same problems in the East. Whatever have been the dark sides of the Dutch colonial system, incapacity and venality have not been among them. For the last fifty years the Dutch government has required a definite standard of proficiency for the various grades of the colonial service, to be proved by passing the colonial service examinations or by the attainment of a degree in law. The candidate for the colonial service finds in Holland extensive provision for his instruction. At the University of Leyden there are professors of colonial and Mohammedan law, the Japanese and Chinese languages, of ethnography, and lecturers on the Sunda languages, on Malayan, Persian, and Turkish, on Mohammedan civilization, and religious history. Designed especially for training men for the colonial service is the Indisches Institut at Delft, where there are courses in the administrative and constitutional law of the Netherlands, Indies, the Malayan and Sunda languages, Japanese, ethnology, geography, religious legislation and customary law, the law and institutions of the Dutch Indies, and the Bata, Bali, and Madura languages. This systematic training has borne abundant fruit in the indefatigable activity of the Dutch officials, travellers, and scientific men in the collection of material and the diffusion of knowledge relating to every aspect of their colonial domain, to an extent of which the average American can have no idea. In 1895 a clerk in the Dutch colonial office published a bibliography of the literature of the Netherlands East Indies, covering only the twenty-seven years 1866–1893. This simple list of titles and references fills 400 octavo pages.

Turning to England, France, or Germany, we find, as we might expect, a highly trained colonial service, and university courses of study designed to supply such a training. At Oxford, there are teachers of Hindustani, Persian, Tamil, Telugu, Marathi, Bengalese, Turkish, and Chinese, Indian law and Indian history. In Cambridge, nine courses of a practical character are provided for the candidates for the Indian civil service. In London, University College has professors and lecturers on Arabic, Persian, Pali, Hindustani, Bengali, Hindi, Gujarati, Marathi, Tamil, and Telugu, and Indian law. Still further provision is made by King's College joining with the University in establishing a separate school of modern Oriental languages in which instruction is given in Burmese, Arabic, Japanese, modern Greek, Chinese, Persian, Russian, Turkish, Armenian, and Swahili. Candidates for the Indian service in their final examination must be examined in the Indian penal code, the language of the province in which they seek appointment, the Indian Evidence Act and the Indian Contract Act, and in any two of the following: Civil procedure, Hindu and Mohammedan law, Sanscrit, Arabic, Persian, and the history of India.

France is not behind England in the effort to obtain highly qualified men to take up the responsibilities of administration in Africa and Asia. In Paris the École Libre des Sciences Politiques, founded in 1874, is designed especially to prepare students for foreign diplomatic service. Its corps of teachers is recruited from the most eminent scholars in France within and without the regular faculties, and the courses embrace administrative law, political economy, finance, commercial geography, commercial law, history, and modern languages. On "colonial questions" alone there are six lecturers. Side by side with this school of politics is the school of modern Oriental languages, a list of whose graduates is annually communicated to the ministers of war, marine, commerce, and foreign affairs. In this institution the course of study extends over three years, and instruction is provided in Arabic, written and colloquial, Persian, Russian, Turkish, Armenian, modern Greek, Chinese, Japanese, Hindustani, Roumanian, Annamese, Malayan, and Malagasy, in the geography, history and legislation of the Far East and of the Mohammedan countries.

Germany, although a late competitor in the field of colonial and commercial expansion, has realized as fully as England and France the importance of trained men in the public service, and the seminary for the study of modern Oriental languages at Berlin is one of the most systematically equipped in the world. The teaching force is made up both of Germans and of Orientals, who teach their native tongues, and includes instructors in Arabic (2), Chinese (2), Japanese (2), Gujarati, Persian, Hindustani, Syrian Arabic, Maroccan Arabic, Egyptian Arabic, Turkish (2), Swahili (2), Hausa (2), Russian and modern Greek, in the technique of the natural sciences, the hygiene of the tropics, and tropical botany. The unequalled opportunities in both Berlin and Paris for studying anthropology, ethnology, comparative religions, and all branches of geographical science need not be set forth here.

This brief review of what Holland, England, France, and Germany are doing to obtain trained men for the diplomatic and colonial service cannot fail to impress every thinking reader with the simple fact that we have entered the race for the control and development of the East far behind our rivals and critics in preparation for the work. Vastly superior to Spain in wealth and energy and progressiveness of spirit, and actuated in some measure by philanthropic impulses, we take up our task under a fearful handicap. We lack not only trained men, but the belief that training is necessary. The most ominous feature of the situation is that the controlling element among the advocates of expansion look upon a trained civil service with hostility and contempt. Yet, if our colonial service is sacrificed to party interests as spoils, nothing can be more certain than that we shall take up Spain's work with her methods, and that with such discredited methods we shall fall far short in our colonial administration of the disciplined and intelligent efficiency of the English and Dutch services. The consequence will be humiliation for ourselves and irritation and discontent among our dependents.

Yet, supposing that the seriousness and perplexity of the problems of government in our new dependencies should convince our authorities of the need of highly trained men, where can they be found? Pending the organization of a regular system of preparation, the first resort should be to men of successful diplomatic experience in Spanish-speaking countries and in the Orient. A knowledge of Spanish should be insisted upon at the earliest practicable moment for every official in the West Indies and the Philippines. The events of 1898 have already given such an impulse to the study of Spanish at our colleges that before long this requirement will be as practicable as it is reasonable. For service in the Philippines a certain number of men of the highest character and thorough knowledge, and familiar with Oriental life and thought, could be recruited from the ranks of our missionaries in Asia. Suitable instruction for candidates for a colonial service in such subjects as Oriental history, colonial problems, administrative law, civil law, comparative religions, ethnology, anthropology, and folk psychology could be supplied to-day in no small degree at several of our universities. The facilities at these institutions and at others would be enlarged and adjusted in prompt response to a specific demand. In fact, in a surprisingly short time it would be entirely practicable for our government to have as candidates for appointment for the colonial service men as thoroughly equipped for intelligent and efficient administration as those at the disposal of England, France, Holland, and Germany. As I have just said, the most serious difficulty will not be to get the right kind of men, but to educate public opinion to demand trained men for such work. This will require resolute, persistent, and intelligent agitation, and the energetic diffusion of knowledge in regard to the nature of our task and the ways of dealing with it. In this direction a good beginning has already been made in the despatch of the Philippine Commission, and in the appointment of committees by the American Historical Association and the American Economic Association to collect information. Much may be hoped from both these committees in the way of extending our knowledge of every phase of the expansion of Europe in the nineteenth century. In the light of this knowledge, an intelligent and well-directed public opinion may guide and control the expansion of America in the twentieth century.

Civil War in the United States. This great struggle was actually begun when, after the attack on Fort Sumter, in Charleston Harbor, in April, 1861, President Lincoln, recognizing the fact that a part of the people in the Union were in a state of rebellion, called for 75,000 men (April 15, 1861) to suppress the insurrection. Then an immediate arming and other preparations for the impending struggle began in all parts of the republic, and very soon hostile armies came in contact. The first overt act of war was committed by the Confederates in Charleston Harbor at the beginning of 1861 (see STAR OF THE WEST). The last struggle of the war occurred in Texas, near the battle-ground of Palo Alto, on May 13, 1865, between Confederates and the 63d United States regiment of colored troops, who fired the last volley. The last man wounded in the Civil War was Sergeant Crockett, a colored soldier. The whole number of men called into the military service of the government in the army and navy during the war was 2,656,553. Of this number about 1,490,000 men were in actual service. Of the latter, nearly 60,000 were killed in the field and about 35,000 were mortally wounded. Diseases in camp and hospitals slew 184,000. It is estimated that at least 300,000 Union soldiers perished during the war. Fully that number of Confederate soldiers lost their lives, while the aggregate number of men, including both armies, who were crippled or permanently disabled by disease, was estimated at 400,000. The actual loss to the country of able-bodied men caused by the rebellion was fully 1,000,000.

The total cost of the war has been moderately estimated at $8,000,000,000. This sum includes the debt which on Aug. 31, 1865, had reached $2,845,907,626.56; the estimated value of the slaves was $2,000,000,000; in addition about $800,000,000 were spent during the war by the government, mainly in war expenses, and large outlays were made by States; one estimate of the total pension bill raises this item to $1,500,000,000. The property destroyed is beyond computation. The harmony of action in the several States which first adopted ordinances of secession seemed marvellous. It was explained in a communication published in the *National Intelligencer*, written by a "distinguished citizen of the South, who formerly represented his State in the popular branch of Congress," and was then temporarily residing in Washington. He said a caucus of the senators of seven cotton-producing States (naming them) had been held on the preceding Saturday night, in that city, at which it was resolved, in effect, to assume to themselves political power at the South, and to control all political and military operations for the time; that they telegraphed directions to complete the seizures of forts, arsenals, customhouses, and all other public property, and advised conventions then in session, or soon to assemble, to pass ordinances for immediate secession. They agreed that it would be proper for the representatives of "seceded States" to remain in Congress, in order to prevent the adoption of measures by the national government for its own security. They also advised, ordered, or directed the assembling of a convention at Montgomery, Ala., on Feb. 15. "This can," said the writer, "of course, only be done by the revolutionary conventions usurping the power of the people, and sending delegates over whom they will lose all control in the establishment of a provisional government, which is the plan of the dictators." This was actually done within thirty days afterwards. They resolved, he said, to use every means in their power to force the legislatures of Tennessee, Kentucky, Missouri, Arkansas, Texas, Virginia, and Maryland into the adoption of revolutionary measures. They had already possessed themselves of the telegraph, the press, and wide control of the postmasters in the South; and they relied upon a general defection of the Southern-born members of the army and navy.

Of the 11,000,000 inhabitants in the slave-labor States at the beginning of the Civil War, the ruling class in the South—those in whom resided in a remarkable degree the political power of those States—numbered about 1,000,000. Of these the large land and slave holders, whose influence in the body of 1,000,000 was almost supreme, numbered less than 200,000. In all the Southern States, in 1850, less than 170,000 held 2,800,000 out of 3,300,000 slaves. The production of the great staple, cotton, which was regarded as king of kings, in an earthly sense, was in the hands of less than 100,000 men. The 11,000,000 inhabitants in the slave-labor States in 1860 consisted of 6,000,000 small slave-holders, and non-slave-holders, mechanics, and laboring-men; 4,000,000 negro slaves, and 1,000,000 known in those regions by the common name of "poor white trash," a degraded population scattered over the whole surface of those States. These figures are round numbers, approximately exact according to published statistics.

Chronology of the War.—The following is a brief record of the most important of the minor events of the war, the greater ones being treated more at length under readily suggestive titles:

1860.—Nov. 18. The Georgia Legislature voted $100,000 for the purpose of arming the State, and ordered an election for a State convention.—29. The legislature of Vermont refused, by a vote of 125 to 58, to repeal the Personal Liberty Bill. The legislature of Mississippi voted to send commissioners to confer with the authorities of the other slave-labor States.—Dec. 6. In Maryland, a Democratic State Convention deplored the hasty action of South Carolina.—10. The legislature of Louisiana voted $500,000 to arm the State. —22. The Crittenden Compromise voted down in the United States Senate.—24. The South Carolina delegation in Congress offered their resignation, but it was not recognized by the speaker, and their names were called regularly through the session. —31. The Senate committee of thirteen reported that they could not agree upon any plan of adjustment of existing difficulties, and their journal was laid before the Senate.

1861.—Jan. 2. The authorities of Georgia seized the public property of the United States within its borders.—4. Governor Pickens, having duly proclaimed the "sovereign nation of South Carolina," assumed the office of chief magistrate of the new empire, and appointed the following cabinet ministers: A. G. Magrath, Secretary of State; D. F. Jamison, Secretary of War; C. G. Memminger, Secretary of the Treasury; A. C. Garlington, Secretary of the Interior; and W. W. Harllee, Postmaster-General.—7. The United States House of Representatives, by a vote, commended the course of Major Anderson in Charleston Harbor.—12. The five representatives of Mississippi withdrew from Congress.—14. The Ohio legislature, by a vote of 58 to 31, refused to repeal the Personal Liberty Bill.—21. Jefferson Davis, of Mississippi; Benjamin Fitzpatrick and C. C. Clay, of Alabama, and David L. Yulee and Stephen R. Mallory, of Florida, finally withdrew from the United States Senate. Representatives from Alabama withdrew from Congress.—23. Representatives from Georgia, excepting Joshua Hill, withdrew from Congress. Hill refused to go with them, but resigned.—24. The Anti-Slavery Society of Massachusetts, at its annual session, broken up by a mob.—25. Rhode Island repealed its Personal Liberty Bill by act of its legislature.—Feb. 5. John Slidell and J. P. Benjamin, of Louisiana, withdrew from the United States Senate, the representatives in the Lower House also withdrew, excepting Bouligny, under instructions from the Louisiana State Convention. Bouligny declared he would not obey the instructions of that illegal body.—11. The House of Representatives "Resolved, that neither the Congress nor the people or governments of the non-slave-holding States have a constitutional right to legislate upon or interfere with slavery in any slave-holding State of the Union."—28. Jefferson Davis, President of the Southern Confederacy, vetoed a bill for legalizing the African slave-trade.—March 16. A convention at Mesilla, Ariz., passed an ordinance of secession, and subsequently the Confederate Congress erected a territorial government there. — April 17. Governor Letcher, of Virginia, recognized the Confederate government. — 20. Property valued at $25,000,000, belonging to the United States government, lost at the Gosport navy-yard, Va. Eleven vessels, carrying 602 guns, were scuttled.—21. The Philadelphia, Wilmington, and Baltimore Railway taken possession of by the United States government.—23. The first South Carolina Confederate regiment started for the Potomac.—28. Virginia proclaimed a member of the Confederacy by its governor.—30. The legislature of Virginia, by act, established a State navy.—May 3. The legislature of Connecticut voted $2,000,000 for the public defence.—4. The governors of Pennsylvania, Ohio, Wisconsin, Michigan, Indiana, Illinois, and other States met at Cleveland, O., to devise plans for the defence of the Western States.—7. The governor of Tennessee announced a military league between the State and the Confederacy.—10. The President of the United States proclaimed martial law on the islands of Key West, the Tortugas, and Santa Rosa.—11. The blockade of Charleston, S. C., established.—13. The blockade of the Mississippi River at Cairo established.—15. The legislature of Massachusetts offered to loan the United States government $7,000,000. — 20. All mail-steamships on the coast, and running in connection with the Confederates, were stopped.—21. The Confederate Congress, at Montgomery, adjourn to meet at Richmond, July 20. — 26. New Orleans blockaded by sloop-of-war *Brooklyn.*—27. The ports of Mobile and Savannah blockaded.—June 1. The postal system in the Confederacy put into operation.—10. Forty-eight locomotives, valued at $400,000, belonging to the Baltimore and Ohio Railroad, were destroyed by the Confederates at Martinsburg, Va.—July 11. The United States Senate expelled from that body James M. Mason, R. M. T. Hunter, T. L. Clingman, Thomas Bragg, Louis T. Wigfall, J. A. Hemphill, Charles B. Mitchell, W. K. Sebastian, and A. O. P. Nicholson, charged with treasonable acts.—25. The governor of New York called for 25,000 more troops.—Aug. 16. Several newspapers in New York presented by the grand jury for hostility to the government.—19. Secretary of State ordered that all persons leaving or entering the United States shall possess a passport. Major Berrett, of Washington, D. C., arrested on a charge of treason, and conveyed to Fort Lafayette, in the Narrows, at the entrance of New York Harbor.—24. Transmission of Confederate journals through the mails prohibited.—Sept. 12. Col. John A. Washington, formerly of Mount Vernon, aide of Gen. Robert E. Lee, killed while reconnoitring in western Virginia.—18. Bank of New Orleans suspended specie payments.—21. John C. Breckinridge fled from Frankfort, Ky., and openly joined the Confederates.—24. Count de Paris and Duc de Chartres entered the United States service as aides to General McClellan.—Oct. 11. Marshal Kane, of Baltimore, sent to Fort Lafayette.—15. Three steamers despatched from New York after the Confederate steamer *Nashville,* which escaped from Charleston on the 11th.—23. The privilege of the writ of *habeas corpus* suspended in the District of Columbia.—30. All the state-prisoners (143) in Fort Lafayette transferred to Fort Warren, Boston Harbor.—Nov. 3. Rising of Union men in eastern Tennessee, who destroy railroad bridges.—Dec. 1. Loyal legislature of Virginia meet at Wheeling.—3. Henry C. Burnett, representative from Kentucky, and John W. Reid, representative from Missouri, expelled from the House of Representatives because of alleged treacherous acts. Fortifications at Bolivar Point, Galveston Harbor, Tex., destroyed by the United States frigate *Santee.* — 9. The Confederate Congress passed a bill admitting Kentucky into the Southern Confederacy. — 20. Confederates destroyed about 100 miles of the North Missouri Railroad, with its stations, bridges, ties, fuel, water-tanks, and telegraph-poles.—30. The banks of New York, Albany, Philadelphia, and Boston suspend specie payments.

1862.—Jan. 10. Waldo P. Johnson and Trusten Polk, of Missouri, expelled from the United States Senate.—11. Bridges of the Louisville and Nashville Railroad burned by the Confederates.—16. The Ohio legislature authorized the banks of that State to suspend specie payments.—17. Cedar Keys, Fla., captured by Union troops. — 30. The *Monitor* launched.—Feb. 3. Confederate steamer *Nashville* ordered to leave Southampton (England) Harbor; the United States gunboat *Tuscarora,* starting in pursuit, stopped by the British frigate *Shannon.*—5. Jesse D. Bright, of Indiana, expelled from the United States Senate. British schooner *Mars* captured off Florida.—8. General Hunter declared martial law throughout Kansas.—9-13. The House Treasury-note Bill, with legal-tender clause, passed the United States Senate. Chesapeake and Albemarle Canal destroyed by Union forces.—17. Confederates defeated at Sugar Creek, Ark. First regular Congress of the

Confederates assembled at Richmond.—10. Confederate government ordered all Union prisoners to be released.—20. Fully 4,000 Confederates, sent to reinforce Fort Donelson, captured on the Cumberland River.—21. First execution of a slave-trader under the laws of the United States took place at New York, in the case of N. P. Gordon.—22. Martial law proclaimed over western Tennessee.—24. Fayetteville, Ark., captured by the Union troops, but burned by the Confederates on leaving it.—25. Telegraph lines taken possession of by government, and army news not to be published until authorized.—26. Legal tender bill approved by the President.—28. Confederate steamer *Nashville* ran the blockade at Beaufort, N. C. Fast Day in the Confederacy.—March 1. John Minor Botts arrested at Richmond, Va., for treason to the Confederate States. Schooner *British Queen* captured while trying to run the blockade at Wilmington, N. C.—2. Brunswick, Ga., captured by Union troops.—6. President Lincoln asks Congress to declare that the United States ought to co-operate with any States which may adopt a gradual abolition of slavery, giving to such State pecuniary indemnity.—8. Fort Clinch, St. Mary, Ga., and Fernandina, Fla., taken by Dupont's expedition.—10. Confederate troops from Texas occupy Santa Fé, N. M.—11. General McClellan relieved of the supreme command of the army, and made commander of the Army of the Potomac. Resolution recommending gradual emancipation adopted by the House of Representatives.—13. Point Pleasant, Mo., captured by Pope.—18. Name of Fort Calhoun, at the Rip Raps, Hampton Roads, changed to Fort Wool.—21. Washington, N. C., occupied by Union troops. Departments of the "Gulf" and "South" created.—26. Skirmish near Denver City, Col., and fifty Confederate cavalry captured.—31. Baltimore and Ohio Railroad reopened, after being closed nearly a year. Confederate camp at Union City, Tenn., captured, with a large amount of spoils.—April 1. General Banks drove the Confederates from Woodstock, Va. Battle at Putnam's Ferry, Ark., and Confederate stores captured.—2. The emancipation and compensation resolution passed the United States Senate. Appalachicola, Fla., surrendered to Union troops.—4. Departments of the Shenandoah and Rappahannock created. Pass Christian, on the Gulf coast, taken by National troops.—8. National tax bill passed the House of Representatives.—11. Bill for the abolition of slavery in the District of Columbia passed the House of Representatives.—12. General Hunter declares all the slaves in Fort Pulaski and on Cockspur Island free. Engagement at Martinsburg, Va.—15. Confederates cut the levee on the Arkansas side of the Mississippi, near Fort Wright, causing an immense destruction of property.—16. President Lincoln signed the bill for the abolition of slavery in the District of Columbia. Battle of Lee's Mills, near Yorktown.—17. Skirmish on Edisto Island.—19. Battle of Camden, or South Mills, N. C.—21. Santa Fé evacuated by the Texans. Confederate Congress at Richmond broken up and dispersed.—24. Destruction of the Dismal Swamp Canal completed.—May 1. Skirmish at Pulaski, Tenn., and 200 Union troops captured. — 3. Skirmish near Monterey, Tenn., and Union victory. Skirmish near Farmington, Miss., and Union victory. — 4. British steamer *Circassian* captured near Havana, Cuba. Skirmish at Lebanon, Tenn.; the Confederates defeated, with the loss of 105 men, their guns, and horses. The Confederates burn their gunboats on the York River. Battle of West Point, Va., and Union victory.—8. Union cavalry surprised and captured near Corinth, Miss.—9. Attack on Sewell's Point by the *Monitor*. Confederates evacuate Pensacola. Skirmish at Slater's Mills, Va. Bombardment of Fort Darling, on James River.—10. Craney Island abandoned by the Confederates. General Butler seized $800,000 in gold in the office of the Netherlands Consulate, New Orleans, when all the foreign consuls uttered a protest.—11. Pensacola occupied by Union troops; the navy-yard and public buildings, excepting the custom-house, had been burned by the Confederates.—12. President Lincoln proclaimed that the ports of Beaufort, N. C., Port Royal, S. C., and New Orleans should be open to commerce after June 1.—13. Natchez, Miss., surrendered to Union gunboats.—17. Naval expedition up the Pamunkey River, and Confederate vessels

THE FIGHT BETWEEN THE "MERRIMAC" AND THE "MONITOR"

burned.—18. Suffolk, 17 miles below Norfolk, occupied by National troops.—19. May, recorder and chief of police of New Orleans, arrested and sent to Fort Jackson.—22. The United States Senate organized as a High Court of Impeachment for the trial of W. H. Humphreys, a United States district judge, for treason.—23. Confederates defeated at Lewisburg, Va.—26. The government, by proclamation, took possession of all railroads for the transportation of troops and munitions of war. Confiscation bill passed the United States House of Representatives. Hanover Court-House, Va., captured by National troops.—29. Skirmish at Pocotaligo, S. C.—June 2. General Wool transferred to the Department of Maryland, and General Dix ordered to Fortress Monroe.—3. National troops landed on James Island, S. C.—4. Battle near Trentor's Creek, N. C. Skirmish on James Island, S. C.—5. Artillery battle at New Bridge, near Richmond; Confederates defeated.—6. Tax bill passed United States Senate. Battle of Union Church, near Harrisonburg, Va.—14. A severe battle on James Island, S. C.—17. Battle between Union gunboats and Confederate batteries at St. Charles, on the White River, Ark., the batteries being carried.—18. Confederate works at Cumberland Gap, Tenn., occupied by National troops.—19. An act confiscating the slaves of Confederates passed the United States House of Representatives. — 20. Commodore Porter arrived before Vicksburg with ten mortar-boats. Free territory act signed by President Lincoln.—26. High Court of Impeachment ordered Judge Humphreys to be removed from office and disqualified. Confederates destroy their gunboats on the Yazoo River.—27. Vicksburg bombarded.—28. The governors of eighteen loyal States petition the President of the United States to call out additional troops.—30. Battle of Charles City Cross-roads.—July 1. Defeat of Confederates at Booneville, Mo. Brunswick, Ga., established as a port of entry. Skirmish at Turkey Bend, on the James River. President Lincoln calls for 600,000 additional volunteers.—6. Engagement at Duval's Bluff.—7. Battle of Bayou de Cachi, Ark.; the Confederates defeated. Engagement 10 miles above Duval's Bluff; all the camp-equipage and provisions of the Confederates captured.—8. Union expedition up Roanoke River started from Plymouth, N. C.—9. Confederate batteries at Hamilton, on the Roanoke River, with steamers, schooners, and supplies, captured.—11. Gen. H. W. Halleck appointed commander of all the land forces of the republic.—13. National troops at Murfreesboro, Tenn., captured by Confederate cavalry.—14. Battle of Fayetteville, Ark.; the Confederates defeated. — 15. Confederate "ram" *Arkansas* ran past the Union flotilla, and reached the batteries at Vicksburg.—17. Congress authorized the use of postage and other stamps as currency, to supply a deficiency of small change, and made it a misdemeanor for any individual to issue a fractional paper currency, or "shin-plasters." National troops defeated at Cynthiana, Ky.—20. National cavalry struck a guerilla band between Mount Sterling and Owensville, Ky., and scattered them, taking their cannon and horses.—22. The President issued an order for the seizure of supplies in all the States wherein insurrection prevailed; directed that persons of African descent should be employed as laborers, giving them wages; also that foreigners should not be required to take the oath of allegiance.—23. General Pope ordered to arrest all disloyal citizens within the lines under his command. National troops victors in a sharp engagement near Carmel Church.—25. The Confederates notified by the President of the provisions of the confiscation act. — 22. Skirmish at Bollinger's Mills, Mo.—29. Confederates driven from Mount Sterling, Ky., by "Home Guards." Confederate guerillas defeated at Moore's Mills, near Fulton, Mo.—30. Skirmish at Paris, Ky., when a part of a Pennsylvania regiment drove Morgan's guerillas from the town.—Aug. 1. Retaliatory order issued by the Confederate government, and General Pope and his officers declared not to be entitled to the consideration of prisoners of war. Confederates attacked Newark, Mo., and captured seventy Union troops; the next day the Unionists recovered everything.—2. Orange Court-House, Va., taken by Pope's troops. A draft of the militia to serve nine months was ordered by the President.—5. Malvern Hills occupied by National troops.—6. Battle near Kirksville, Mo.; the Union troops victorious.—8. Battle near Fort Fillmore, N. M.; Unionists victorious. The privilege of the writ of *habeas corpus,* in respect to all persons arrested under it, suspended; also for the arrest and imprisonment of persons who by act, speech, or writing discourage volunteer enlistments.—11. Skirmishes near Williamsport, Tenn., and also at Kinderhook, Tenn.; Confederates defeated. Independence, Mo., surrendered to the Confederates.—12. Gallatin, Tenn., surrendered to Morgan's guerillas. Battle at Yellow Creek, Clinton co., Tenn.; Confederates defeated.—18. Confederate Congress reassembled at Richmond.—19. Department of the Ohio formed of the States of Ohio, Michigan, Indiana, Illinois, Missouri, and Kentucky east of the Tennessee River, and including Cumberland Gap. Cavalry expedition to Charleston, Mo.—20. Clarkesville, on the Cumberland, Tenn., surrendered to the Confederates.—21. Gallatin, Tenn., surrendered to the Confederates.—22. Catlett's Station, Va., captured by Stuart's cavalry.—24. Battle between Bloomfield and Cape Girardeau, Mo.; the Confederates were defeated.—25. Skirmish at Waterloo Bridge, Va. Combined military and naval expedition under General Curtis and Commander Davis returned to Helena, Ark., having captured the Confederate steamer *Fair Play,* containing a large quantity of small-arms and ammunition, also four field-guns, and another laden with tents and baggage, and, proceeding up the Yazoo River, captured a Confederate battery of four guns, with a large quantity of powder, shot, shells, and grape.—27. Skirmish near Rienzi, Miss. Confederates routed by General Hooker at Kettle Run, near Manassas, Va.—28. Battle near Centreville, Va., by Nationals under McDowell and Sigel, and Confederates under Jackson, when the latter were defeated with a loss of 1,000 made prisoners and many arms. Skirmish near Woodbury, Tenn.; Confederates defeated.—29. City Point, on the James River, shelled and destroyed by Union gunboats.—30. Buckhannon, Va., entered and occupied by Confederates. Battle of Bolivar, Tenn.; Confederates routed.—31. Skirmish at Weldon, Va.; Confederates defeated.—Sept. 1. The legislature of Kentucky, alarmed by Confederate raids, adjourned from Frankfort to Louisville. Battle at Britton's Lane, near Estanaula, Tenn.; Confederates defeated. Skirmish near Jackson, Tenn.; Confederates defeated. — 2. General McClellan placed in command of the defences of, and troops for the defence of, Washington, D. C. Martial law declared in Cincinnati. Fighting between Fairfax Court-House and Washington.—3. Centreville, Va., evacuated by the Union forces.—4. Confederate steamer *Oreto* ran the blockade into Mobile Harbor.—6. Confederate cavalry attacked the Union outposts at Martinsburg, Va., and were repulsed.—8. General Pope relieved of the command of the Army of Virginia, and assigned to that of the Northwest. General Lee issued a proclamation to the people of Maryland. Skirmish near Cochran's Cross Roads, Miss. Restrictions on travel rescinded, and arrests for disloyalty forbidden except by direction of the judge-advocate at Washington.—9. Confederate cavalry attacked a Union force at Williamsburg, Va., and were repulsed.—10. Governor Curtin, of Pennsylvania, issued an order calling on all able-bodied men in the State to organize immediately for its defence. Confederates attacked Union troops near Gauley, Va.; the latter burned all the government property and fled. Skirmish near Covington, Ky.—11. Maysville, Ky., taken by the Confederates. Bloomfield, Mo., captured by the Confederates, and recaptured by the Unionists the next day.—12. Eureka, Mo., captured by the Nationals.—13. Confederates attacked Harper's Ferry, and the next night the National cavalry escaped from that post, and it was surrendered on the 15th.—17. Cumberland Gap, Tenn., evacuated by the Union forces. Confederate soldiers captured at Glasgow, Ky.—18. A day of fasting and prayer held by the Confederates. Prentiss, Miss., shelled and burned. — 19. Confederates evacuated Harper's Ferry. Confederates attacked Owensboro, Ky., and were repulsed.—21. Sharp skirmish on the Virginia side of the Potomac near Shepherdstown, Va., and the Nationals forced back across the river with considerable loss. Cavalry fight near Lebanon Junction, Ky.—22. President Lincoln's preliminary Proclamation of Emancipation for the slaves issued.—24. Convention of the governors of the loyal States at Altoona, Pa. President Lincoln suspended the privilege of the writ of *habeas corpus* in respect to all persons arrested and imprisoned in any fort, camp, arsenal, military prison, or other place by any military authority, or by sentence of court-martial. Engagement at Donaldsonville, La.—25. Commodore Wilkes's squadron arrived at Bermuda, and he was ordered to leave in twenty-four hours.—27. Augusta, Ky., attacked by Confederates, who captured the garrison and destroyed the town.—29. General Buell ordered to turn over the command of his troops to General Thomas. Warrenton, Va., taken by the Nationals.—30. Retaliatory resolutions introduced into the Confederate Congress on account of the Emancipation Proclamation.—Oct. 1. General Halleck sent to McClellan, urging him to cross the Potomac and attack the Confederates. National soldiers crossed at Shepherdstown and drove the Confederates to Martinsburg. The Western gunboat fleet transferred from the War to the Navy Department. National naval and military expedition sailed from Hilton Head for St. John's River, Fla., opened fire on the Confederate fortifications at St. John's Bluff on the 2d, and reduced the works on the 3d.—3. The Confederates drove in the Union pickets at Corinth, Miss., and on the 4th a severe battle was fought there.—5. Galveston, Tex., occupied by National troops.—6. Battle of La Vergne, Tenn.; the Confederates were defeated.—7. Expedition to destroy the salt-works on the coast of Florida. Confederates evacuate Lexington, Ky.—9. Stuart's cavalry start on their famous expedition into Pennsylvania; reached Chambersburg on the 10th, and on the 11th destroyed much property there.—11. General Wool arrived at Harrisburg and assumed command of the troops for the defence of the State of Pennsylvania. Battle between Harrodsburg and Danville, Ky., in which the Confederates were defeated.—13. The Confederate Congress adjourned, to meet again early in January, 1863.—14. In the State elections held in Pennsylvania, Ohio, and Indiana, the Republicans were defeated.—15. Severe battle between Lexington and Richmond, in which 45,000 Confederates were repulsed by 18,000 Nationals. There was heavy loss on both sides.—18. The guerilla chief Morgan dashed into Lexington, Ky., and took 125 prisoners.—20. In the early hours of the morning a small Confederate force destroyed a National train of wagons near Bardstown, Ky., and at daylight they captured another train there.—21. Confederates near Nashville attacked and dispersed.—22. The governor of Kentucky called on the people of Louisville to defend the menaced city.—24. General Rosecrans succeeded General Buell in command of the army in Kentucky. Skirmish at Morgantown, Ky.—27. Confederates attacked and defeated at Putnam's Ferry, Mo.—28. Battle near Fayetteville, Ark., where the Confederates were defeated and chased to the Boston Mountains. Skirmish at Snicker's Gap, Va. — Nov. 1. Artillery fight at Philomont, Va., lasting five hours. The Confederates pursued towards Bloomfield, where another skirmish ensued, lasting four hours.—4. Maj. Reid Sanders, a Confederate agent, captured on the coast of Virginia while endeavoring to escape with Confederate despatches. National troops destroy salt-works at Kingsbury, Ga.—5. The Confederates attacked Nashville and were repulsed. General Burnside superseded General McClellan in command of the Army of the Potomac.—9. Town of St. Mary, Ga., shelled and destroyed by Union gunboats.—10. Great Union demonstration in Memphis.—15. Army of the Potomac began its march from Warrenton towards Fredericksburg.—17. Artillery engagement near Fredericksburg. Jefferson Davis ordered retaliation for the execution of ten Confederates in Missouri.—18. Confederate cruiser *Alabama* escaped the *San Jacinto* at Martinique.—19. First general convention of "The Protestant Episcopal Church of the Confederate States of America" met at Augusta, Ga.—25. Confederate raid into Poolesville, Md. A body of 4,000 Confederates attacked Newbern, but were forced to retreat in disorder.—27. Nearly all the political prisoners released from forts and government prisons. Confederates defeated near Frankfort, Va.—28. General Grant's army marched towards Holly Springs, Miss. Confederates crossed the Potomac and captured nearly two companies of Pennsylvania cavalry near

Hartwood.—29. General Stahl fights and routs a Confederate force near Berryville. —Dec. 2. King George Court-House, Va., captured by National cavalry. Expedition went out from Suffolk, Va., and recaptured a Pittsburg battery.—4. General Banks and a part of his expedition sailed from New York for New Orleans.—5. Skirmish near Coffeeville, Miss.—6. Confederates repulsed at Cane Hill, Ark.—7. California steamer *Ariel* captured by the *Alabama*.—9. Concordia, on the Mississippi, burned by Union troops.—10. National gunboats shell and destroy most of the town of Front Royal, Va.—11. Skirmish on the Blackwater, Va., and National troops pushed back to Suffolk.—12. National gunboat *Cairo* blown up by a torpedo on the Yazoo.—13. National troops surprise and capture Confederates at Tuscumbia, Ala.—14. Gen. N. P. Banks succeeded General Butler in command of the Department of the Gulf. Plymouth, N. C., destroyed by Confederates.—15. Confederate salt-works at Yellville, Ark., destroyed.—21. A body of Union cavalry destroyed important railroad bridges in eastern Tennessee, with locomotives, and captured 500 prisoners and 700 stand of arms.—23. Jefferson Davis issued a proclamation directing retaliatory measures to be taken because of the course of General Butler in New Orleans, and dooming him and his officers to death by hanging when caught. He ordered that no commanding officer should be released or paroled before exchanged until General Butler should be punished.—24. Heavy skirmish at Dumfries, Va., when the Confederates were repulsed.—27. A company of Union cavalry were surprised and captured at Occoquan, Va.—31. The *Monitor* sunk at sea south of Cape Hatteras.

1863.—Jan. 1. General Sullivan fought Forrest near Lexington, Tenn. Emancipation jubilee of the negroes at Hilton Head, S. C.—2. Gold at New York, 133¼ @ 133⅞.—3. Department of the East created, and General Wool assigned to its command.—4. Confederates defeated at Moorefield, W. Va. The Confederate General Magruder declares the port of Galveston, Tex., opened to the commerce of the world. Clarkesville, Tenn., surrenders to the Union forces.—5. An "indignation meeting" of the opposition was held at Springfield, Ill., to protest against the President's Emancipation Proclamation.—8. Confederates drive Union forces out of Springfield, Miss.—9. Exchange of 20,000 prisoners effected. — 10. Cavalry skirmish at Catlett's Station. Bombardment of Galveston. The National gunboat *Hatteras* sunk by the *Alabama* on the coast of Texas.—11. General Weitzel destroyed the Confederate gunboat *Cotton* on the Bayou Teché.—12. Jefferson Davis recommends the Confederate Congress to adopt retaliatory measures against the operation of the Emancipation Proclamation. — 13. Peace resolutions introduced into the New Jersey legislature. Several boats carrying wounded Union soldiers destroyed by the Confederates at Harpeth Shoals, on the Cumberland River. Confederate steamer *Oreto* (afterwards the *Florida*) runs the blockade at Mobile.—15. National gunboat *Columbia*, stranded at Masonboro Inlet, N. C., burned by the Confederates. Mound City, Ark., burned by National troops.—17. Confederate cruiser *Oreto* destroyed the brig *Estelle*. Congress resolved to issue $100,000,000 in United States notes.—20. General Hunter assumes command of the Department of the South.—22. Gen. Fitz-John Porter dismissed from the National service.—24. General Burnside, at his own request, relieved from the command of the Army of the Potomac.—25. First regiment of negro Union soldiers organized at Port Royal, S. C.—26. Peace resolutions offered in the Confederate Congress by Mr. Foote. Engagement at Woodbury, Tenn.—27. Fort McAllister, on the Ogeechee River, Ga., bombarded by the *Montauk*.—30. Union gunboat *Isaac Smith* captured in Stono River, S. C.—31. Blockading squadron off Charleston Harbor attacked by Confederate iron-clad gunboats, and the harbor proclaimed opened by Beauregard and the Confederate Secretary of State. Skirmish near Nashville, Tenn., and the Confederates defeated.—Feb. 1. National troops occupy Franklin, Tenn. — 2. United States House of Representatives passed a bill providing for the employment of negro soldiers.—3. Fort Donelson invested by Confederate troops, who were repulsed.—4. Skirmish near Lake Providence, La. — 5. Second attack on

Fort Donelson by Confederates repulsed.—6. The Emancipation Proclamation published in Louisiana.—7. Mutiny of the 100th Illinois Regiment. Confederates declare the blockade at Galveston and Sabine Pass opened.—8. Circulation of the Chicago *Times* suppressed.—10. Official denial that the blockade at Charleston had been raised.—11. Confederates attempt to assassinate General Banks on his way to the Opera-house in New Orleans.—12. National currency bill passes the Senate. The *Jacob Bell,* from China, with a cargo of tea worth $1,000,000, captured and burned by the Confederate cruiser *Florida.*—14. National cavalry defeated at Annandale, Va.—15. Confederates defeated at Arkadelphia, Ark. — 16. Conscription bill passed the United States Senate.—20. National currency bill passed the United States House of Representatives. — 23. United States Senate authorized the suspension of the privilege of *habeas corpus.*—25. English-Confederate steamer *Peterhoff* captured by the *Vanderbilt.* National currency act approved by the President.—26. Cherokee national council repeal the ordinance of secession.—28. Confederate steamer *Nashville* destroyed by the *Montauk* in Ageechee River.—March 4. Palmyra, Mo., burned by Union gunboats. — 6. General Hunter ordered the drafting of negroes in the Department of the South. Confederates capture Franklin, Tenn.—8. Brigadier-General Stoughton captured by Moseby's cavalry at Fairfax Court-House, Va. Twenty-three Confederate steamers captured on the Yazoo River.—11. Governor Cannon, of Delaware, declared the national authority supreme.—18. House of Representatives of New Jersey pass peace resolutions.—19. Mount Sterling, Ky., taken by Confederates, and retaken by Nationals on the 23d. English-Confederate steamer *Georgia,* laden with arms, destroyed near Charleston.—25. Impressment of private property in the Confederacy authorized.—31. General Herron appointed to the command of the Army of the Frontier. Jacksonville, Fla., burned by Union colored troops and evacuated.—April 1. Cavalry fight near Drainesville, Va.—2. Farragut's fleet ravaged in Red River. Serious bread-riot in Richmond; the mob mostly women.—3. Arrest of Knights of the Golden Circle at Reading, Pa.—4. Town of Palmyra, on the Cumberland, destroyed by National gunboats.—5. Confederate vessels detained at Liverpool by order of the British government.—6. President Lincoln and family visited the Army of the Potomac.—7. Combined attack of iron-clad vessels on Fort Sumter; five out of seven National vessels disabled. Emperor of the French intimates his abandonment of the European intervention policy in our national affairs.—8. Raid of Nationals through Loudon county, Va.—14. Engagement at Kelly's Ford, on the Rappahannock.—20. Great mass-meeting at Union Square, New York, in commemoration of the uprising of the loyal people in 1861.—24. National forces defeated at Beverly, Va. Confederates defeated on the Iron Mountain Railroad near St. Louis. National forces rout the Confederates at Tuscumbia, Ala.—26. Destructive Union raid on Deer Creek, Miss. Confederates defeated at Rowlesburg, Va.—27. Confederate "Texan Legion" captured near Franklin, Ky.—28. Cavalry engagement at Sand Mountain, Ga.; Confederates defeated.—29. Fairmount, Va., captured by Confederates.—30. Fast Day in the United States. Artillery engagement at Chancellorsville, Va. Confederates defeated at Williamsburg, Va.—May 1. Battle at Monticello, Ky.; Confederates defeated.—3. Mosby's guerillas routed at Warrenton Junction.—4. Admiral Porter takes possession of Fort de Russy, on Red River.—6. Confederates put to flight near Tupelo, Miss. Battle near Clinton, Miss.—15. Corbin and Grau hung at Sandusky for recruiting within the Union lines.—18. Democratic convention in New York City expresses sympathy with Vallandigham.—22–23. Battle of Gum Swamp, N.C.,—28. First negro regiment from the North left Boston.—June 1. Democratic convention in Philadelphia sympathized with Vallandigham.—3. Peace party meeting in New York, under the lead of Fernando Wood.—8. Departments of Monongahela and Susquehanna created.—12. Darien, Ga., destroyed by National forces. Governor Curtin, of Pennsylvania, calls out the militia and asks for troops from New York to repel threatened Confederate invasion. General Gillmore in command of the Department of the South.—14.

The consuls of England and Austria dismissed from the Confederacy.—15. President Lincoln calls for 100,000 men to repel invasion.—19. Confederate invasion of Indiana.—21. Confederate cavalry defeated at Aldie Gap, Va.—28. General Meade succeeded General Hooker in the command of the Army of the Potomac. Bridge over the Susquehanna burned. The authorities of the city of Philadelphia petition the President to relieve General McClellan of command.—30. Martial law proclaimed in Baltimore.—July 1. Battle at Carlisle, Pa.—10. Martial law proclaimed at Louisville, Ky. Cavalry engagement on the Antietam battle-field.—11. Conscription under the draft begins in New York City.—12. Martial law proclaimed in Cincinnati.—13. Yazoo City, Miss., captured by the Nationals.—14. Draft riots in Boston.—15. Riots in Boston, Brooklyn, Jersey City, Staten Island, and other places. —23. Engagement at Manassas Gap; 300 Confederates killed or wounded, and ninety captured.—30. President Lincoln proclaims a retaliating policy in favor of negro soldiers. Defeat of Confederates at Winchester, Ky.—Aug. 1. Heavy cavalry fight at Kelly's Ford, Va., and Confederates defeated.—3. Governor Seymour, of New York, remonstrated against the enforcement of the draft, because of alleged unfair enrolment. On the 7th President Lincoln replied and intimated that the draft should be carried out.—6. National Thanksgiving Day observed.—12. Gen. Robert Toombs exposes the bankruptcy of the Confederacy. —15. The Common Council of New York City voted $3,000,000 for conscripts.—21. National batteries opened on Charleston. —22. Beauregard protests against shelling Charleston.—25. Many regiments in the squares of New York City to enforce the draft; removed Sept. 5.—28. The Supervisors of New York county appropriate $2,000,000 for the relief of conscripts.—Sept. 4. Bread-riot at Mobile, Ala.—11. One-half of James Island, Charleston Harbor, captured by National troops.—13. Brilliant cavalry engagement at Culpeper Court-House, Va.—21. Sharp cavalry fight and National victory at Madison Court-House, Va.—24. Port of Alexandria. Va., officially declared to be open to trade. —Oct. 5. Confederates under Bragg bombarded Chattanooga, Tenn., from Lookout Mountain. — 7. The British government seized the Confederate "rams" building in the Mersey, and forbid their departure.—10. Confederates defeated at Blue Springs, Tenn.—17. The President orders a levy of 300,000 men, announcing that if not furnished by Jan. 1, 1864, a draft for the deficiency would be made. —30. Union meeting at Little Rock, Ark. —31. Battle of Shell Mound, Tenn.; Confederates defeated.—Nov. 1. Plot to liberate Confederate prisoners in Ohio discovered.—2. Landing of General Banks's army in Texas.—3. Confederate cavalry defeated near Columbia, and at Colliersville, Tenn. Battle of Bayou Coteau, La.—4. Banks takes possession of Brownsville on the Rio Grande.—9. Gen. Robert Toombs denounces the course of the Confederate government in a speech in Georgia.—11. Lord Lyons, the British minister, officially informed the United States government of a contemplated Confederate raid from Canada, to destroy Buffalo, and liberate Confederate prisoners on Johnson's Island, near Sandusky. A fleet of French steamers arrived off Brazos, Tex.—15. Corpus Christi Pass, Tex., captured by National troops.—18. Mustang Island, Tex., captured by the Nationals.—19. Gettysburg battle-field consecrated as a national cemetery for Union soldiers who fell in the July battles.—26. National Thanksgiving Day observed.—Dec. 8. President Lincoln issued a proclamation of amnesty. Congress thanked General Grant and his army, and ordered a gold medal to be struck in honor of the general.—12. Notice given that the Confederate authorities refused to receive more supplies for the starving Union prisoners in Richmond, Va.

1864.—Jan. 11. General Banks issued a proclamation for an election in Louisiana, Feb. 22. A provisional free-State government inaugurated at Little Rock, Ark.— 25. Congress thanked Cornelius Vanderbilt for the gift to the government of the steamer *Vanderbilt*, worth $800,000.—26. The United States Circuit Court at Louisville, Ky., decided that guerillas were "common enemies," and that carriers could not recover at law goods stolen by such.—27. Ladies' Loyal League, New York, sent a petition for general emancipation, bearing

100,000 signatures. Confederate cavalry defeated at Sevierville, Tenn. Three hundred Confederate salt-kettles destroyed at St. Andrew's Bay, Fla.—28. Battle at Fair Garden, Tenn.; Confederates defeated.—Feb. 1. The President ordered a draft, on March 10, for 500,000 men, for three years or the war.—4. Colonel Mulligan drove Early out of Moorefield, W. Va. —13. Governor Bramlette, of Kentucky, proclaims protection to slaves from claims by Confederate owners.—22. Michael Hahn elected governor of Louisiana by the loyal vote. Moseby defeats Union cavalry at Drainesville.—23. Admiral Farragut began a six days' bombardment of Fort Powell, below Mobile.—March 2. Ulysses S. Grant made lieutenant-general.—6. Confederates hung twenty-three Union prisoners of war (one a drummer-boy aged fifteen) at Kinston, N. C.—7. Vallandigham advises forcible resistance to United States authority.—8. New York State voted by over 30,000 majority for the soldiers' voting law.—9. Colored troops under Colonel Cole captured Suffolk, Va.—15. President Lincoln calls for 200,000 men in addition to the 500,000 called for Feb. 1. —16. Governor of Kentucky remonstrates against employing slaves in the army. Arkansas votes to become a free-labor State.—17. General Grant assumes command of all the armies of the republic. Fort de Russy blown up by the National forces.—28. Louisiana State Constitutional Convention met at New Orleans.—31. Longstreet's army, after wintering in eastern Tennessee, retired to Virginia.—April 10. Confederates seized and blew up Cape Lookout light-house, N. C.—13. New York Senate passes the soldiers' voting bill by a unanimous vote.—16. Ohio Superior Court decides the soldiers' voting law constitutional. Surprise and defeat of Confederates at Half Mountain, Ky., by Colonel Gallup.—17. Women's bread-riot in Savannah, Ga.—21. Nationals destroy the State salt-works near Wilmington, N. C., worth $100,000.—25. The offer of 85,000 100-days' men by the governors of Ohio, Indiana, Illinois, Wisconsin, and Iowa accepted by the President.—May 2. Ohio National Guard, 38,000 strong, report for duty.—4. Colonel Spear, 11th Pennsylvania Cavalry, departed on a raid from Portsmouth, Va., captured a Confederate camp on the Weldon road, and destroyed $500,000 worth of property at Jarratt's Station.—7. To this date, one lieutenant-general, five major-generals, twenty-five brigadiers, 186 colonels, 146 lieutenant-colonels, 214 majors, 2,497 captains, 5,811 lieutenants, 10,563 non-commissioned officers, 121,156 privates of the Confederate army, and 5,800 Confederate citizens had been made prisoners by National troops. General Crook defeated the Confederates at Cloyd's Mountain, W. Va., and fought an artillery duel on the 10th. —16. Sortie from Fort Darling upon General Butler's besieging force.—18. General Howard defeats a Confederate force at Adairsville, Ga. Nationals defeat Confederates at Yellow Bayou, La., the latter led by Prince Polignac. A forged Presidential proclamation, calling for 400,000 more troops, was published for the purpose of gold speculation. The perpetrators (Howard and Mallison) were sent to Fort Lafayette.—26. Major-General Foster takes command of the Department of the South. Louisiana State Constitutional Convention adopts a clause abolishing slavery.—27. Eight steamers and other shipping burned at New Orleans by incendiaries.—30. McPherson had a sharp encounter at the railroad near Marietta, Ga., taking 400 prisoners, with a railroad train of sick and wounded Confederates.—June 1. To this date the Nationals had taken from the Confederates as naval prizes, 232 steamers, 627 schooners, 159 sloops, twenty-nine barks, thirty-two brigs, fifteen ships, and 133 yachts and small craft; in all, 1,227 vessels, worth $17,000,000.—2. Heavy artillery firing and skirmishing at Bermuda Hundred. United States gunboat *Water Witch* surprised and captured in Ossabaw Sound, Ga.—6. General Hunter occupied Staunton, Va.—9. Blockade-runner *Pervensey* run ashore by the supply-steamer *Newbern*, and taken; worth, with cargo, $1,000,000.—13. The United States House of Representatives repealed the Fugitive Slave law.—17. Near Atlanta 600 Confederate conscripts fled to the Union lines.—22. Battle of Culp's Farm, Ga.—24. Maryland Constitutional Convention passed an emancipation clause.—25. General Pillow, with 3,000 Confederates, repulsed at Lafayette, Tenn. —27. General Carr defeated the Confederates near St. Charles, Mo.—30. Secretary Chase, of the Treasury, resigned his office.—July 1. General Sherman captured 3,000 prisoners near Marietta, Ga.—3. General Sherman occupied Kenesaw Mountain at daylight.—4. A national salute of double-shotted cannon fired into Petersburg, Va.—5. The Confederates in Jackson flanked and driven out by General Slocum. Gen. Bradley Johnson, with 3,000 Confederate troops, crossed the Potomac into Maryland.—9. Governor Brown, of Georgia, called out the reserve militia, from fifteen to fifty-five years of age. A mass-meeting in Geneva, Switzerland, adopted resolutions of sympathy with the United States and approved the emancipation measure. President Lincoln, in a proclamation, put forth his plan for reorganizing the disorganized States.—12. Confederates approached within 5 miles of the Patent Office at Washington and were repulsed with heavy loss.—13–14. Gen. A. J. Smith defeated the Confederates under Forrest, Lee, and Walker, in five different engagements, in Mississippi, killing and wounding over 2,000.—15. Six steamers burned at St. Louis by incendiaries.—16. Gold in New York rose to 284. General Rousseau burned four store-houses and their contents of provisions at Youngsville, Ala.—17. General Slocum defeated the Confederates at Grand Gulf, Miss.—18. Rousseau sent out raiders on the Atlantic and Montgomery Railway, who destroyed a large section of it, defeated 1,500 Confederates in a battle, and captured 400 conscripts. The President called for 300,000 volunteers within fifty days, the deficiency to be made up by drafts.—20. General Asboth captured a Confederate camp for conscripts in Florida.—21. Henderson, Ky., attacked by 700 guerillas.—22. General Rousseau reached Sherman's lines near Atlanta, having in fifteen days traversed 450 miles, taken and paroled 2,000 prisoners, killed and wounded 200, captured 800 horses and mules, and 800 negroes, destroyed 31 miles of railroad, thirteen depots, some cars and engines, and a great quantity of cotton, provisions, and stores. Louisiana State Convention adopted a constitution abolishing slavery.—26. A gunboat expedition on Grand Lake, La., destroyed many boats of the Confederates, and on the 27th destroyed saw-mills worth $40,000.—29. General Canby enrolled all citizens in the Department of the Gulf, and expelled the families of Confederate soldiers.—Aug. 1. Confederates defeated by General Kelly at Cumberland, Md.—2. General Banks enrolled into the service all the negroes in the Department of the Gulf between eighteen and forty years of age.—9. An ordnance-boat, laden with ammunition, was blown up at City Point, James River, killing fifty persons, wounding 120, and destroying many buildings.—15. Commodore Craven, on the *Niagara*, seized the Confederate cruiser *Georgia*, near Lisbon.—18. The Confederate cruiser *Tallahassee*, after great depredations on the sea, gets into Halifax, N. S.; but, having secured some coal, was ordered out of the harbor and ran the blockade into Wilmington.—23. Nearly all the 5th Illinois Volunteers captured near Duval's Bluff by Shelby.—29. General Hunter superseded in command of the Department of western Virginia by General Crook.—Sept. 7. Confederates defeated at Reedyville, Tenn., by Colonel Jourdan, with about 250 Pennsylvania cavalry.—8. The Confederate General Price crossed the Arkansas River at Dardanelles, on his way to Missouri.—14. Governor Brown, by proclamation, withdrew the Georgia militia, 15,000 strong, from the Confederate army at Atlanta.—19. Confederate passengers seized the steamers *Island Queen* and *Parsons* on Lake Erie, with the intention of capturing the United States gunboat *Michigan;* but the latter captured the whole party; the *Queen* was sunk and the *Parsons* was abandoned. A Confederate force of 1,500 captured a train worth $1,000,000 at Cabin Creek, Kan.—26. The Confederate governor (Allen) of Louisiana wrote to the Confederate Secretary of War that the time had arrived for them to "put into the army every able-bodied negro as a soldier."—29. The United States steam-packet *Roanoke*, just after passing out of Havana, Cuba, admitted on board three boat-loads of men claiming to be passengers, who seized the vessel, put the passengers on board another vessel, went to Bermuda, burned the steamer there, and went ashore.—30. The Confederate General Vaughan driven out of his works at Carroll Station, Tenn., by General Gillem.—Oct. 3. John B. Meigs, Sheridan's chief engineer in the Shenandoah Valley, having been brutally murdered by some guerillas, all the houses within a radius of 5 miles were burned in retaliation.—6. A Richmond paper advocated the employment of slaves as soldiers.—7. Commander Collins, in the gunboat *Wachusett*, ran down and captured in the harbor of Bahia, Brazil, the Confederate cruiser *Florida*.—10. Maryland adopted a new constitution which abolished slavery.—12. It was announced that all the regimental flags taken from the Nationals in the Department of Arkansas and the Gulf had been retaken while on their way to Richmond.—13. Some of the negro Union soldiers, prisoners of war, having been set at work in the trenches by the Confederates, General Butler put eighty-seven Confederate prisoners of war at work, under the fire of Confederate shells, at Dutch Gap.—17. The governors of Virginia, North Carolina, South Carolina, Georgia, Alabama, and Missouri held a conference at Augusta, Ga., and resolved to strengthen the Confederate army with white men and negroes.—18. Some of the feminine nobility of England and Confederate women opened a fair in Liverpool for the benefit of the Confederate cause.—22. General Auger, about this time, put in practice an effective way of defending National army trains on the Manassas Gap Railway from guerillas, by placing in each train, in conspicuous positions, eminent Confederates residing within the Union lines.—25. General Pleasonton, in pursuit of Price in Missouri, attacked him near the Little Osage River; captured Generals Marmaduke and Cabell, and 1,000 men, and sent the remainder flying southward. — 28. General Gillem defeated the Confederates at Morristown, Tenn., taking 500 prisoners and thirteen guns.—31. Plymouth, N. C., taken by Commander Macomb.—Nov. 5. Forrest, with artillery, at Johnsville, Tenn., destroyed three "tin-clad" gunboats and seven transports belonging to the Nationals.—8. Gen. George B. McClellan resigns his commission in the National army. A flag-of-truce fleet of eighteen steamers departed from Hampton Roads for the Savannah River, to effect an exchange of 10,000 prisoners. The exchange began Nov. 12 by Colonel Mulford near Fort Pulaski.—13. General Gillem defeated by General Breckinridge, near Bull's Gap, Tenn., who took all his artillery, trains, and baggage.—16. Confederates surprised and captured Butler's picket-line at Bermuda Hundred.—19. The President, by proclamation, raised the blockade at Norfolk, Va., and Pensacola and Fernandina, Fla.—22. Hood advances from near Florence, Ala., towards Nashville, with 40,000 Confederate troops. — 24. Thanksgiving Day observed in the Army of the Potomac, when 59,000 lbs. of turkeys, sent from the North, were consumed. About 36,000 lbs. were sent to Sheridan's army in the Shenandoah Valley.—25. An attempt was made by Confederate agents to burn the city of New York by lighting fires in rooms hired by the incendiaries in fifteen of the principal hotels. General Dix, in the morning, ordered all persons from the Confederate States to register themselves at the provost-marshal's office, and declared the incendiaries to be spies, who, if caught, would be immediately executed.—29. General Foster co-operated with General Sherman as he approached the sea from Atlanta.—Dec. 2. The Pope declined to commit himself to the Confederate cause. Up to this time sixty-five blockade-running steamers had been taken or destroyed in attempts to reach Wilmington, N. C., the vessels and cargoes being worth $13,000,000.—6. Milroy defeated the Confederates near Murfreesboro, Tenn.—8. Confederate plot to burn Detroit discovered.—15. Rousseau, at Murfreesboro, defeated Forrest, who lost 1,500 men.—17. To keep out improper persons from Canada, the Secretary of State issued an order that all persons entering the United States from a foreign country must have passports, excepting emigrants coming direct from sea to our ports.—19. The President issued a call for 300,000 volunteers, any deficiency to be made up by a draft on Feb. 5, 1865. Colonel Mulford reached Fortress Monroe with the last of the 12,000 Union prisoners he was able to obtain by exchange.—21. Admiral Farragut made vice-admiral.—27. Completion of the destruction of the Mobile and Ohio Railroad from Corinth to below Okolona, by a raiding force sent out by General Dana.

1865.—Jan. 6. A fleet of transports and 9,000 troops, under General Terry, sailed from Fort Monroe for an attack on Fort Fisher.—10. Meeting in Philadelphia to give charitable aid to Confederates in Savannah. On the 14th two vessels left New York with supplies for the suffering citizens of Savannah.—15. Confederate post at Pocotaligo Bridge, S. C., taken by the Nationals, and the (railroad) bridge saved.—16. Magazine in captured Fort Fisher exploded and killed or wounded about 300 National troops. Another vessel left New York laden with provisions for the suffering citizens of Savannah. The policy of Jefferson Davis unsparingly assailed in the Confederate Congress at Richmond.—17. The monitor *Patapsco* blown up by a torpedo at Charleston and sunk, with seven officers and sixty-five men.—18. Three fine blockade-runners went into the Cape Fear River, ignorant of the fall of Fort Fisher, and were captured.—23. The main ship-channel at Savannah was opened.—25. Jefferson Davis proclaimed March 10 a day for a public fast.—26. This day was observed as a festival in Louisiana, by proclamation of Governor Hahn, in honor of the emancipation acts in Missouri and Tennessee.—Feb. 1. The legislature of Illinois ratified the emancipation amendment to the national Constitution; the first to do so. John S. Rock, a negro of pure blood, admitted to practise as a lawyer in the Supreme Court of the United States; the first.—2. Gen. Robert E. Lee made commander-in-chief of the Confederate forces.—4. Lieutenant-Commander Cushing, with fifty-one men, in four boats, destroyed cotton valued at $15,000 at All Saints, N. C.—5. Harry Gilmor's camp broken up and himself captured at Moorefield, W. Va., by Lieutenant-Colonel Whittaker, who marched over mountains and across streams filled with floating ice—140 miles in forty-eight hours—with 300 picked cavalry for the purpose.—6. A number of soldiers in Early's army send a petition to Jefferson Davis to stop the war.—7. The Confederate Senate rejected the plan to raise 200,000 negro soldiers. Of 500 Confederate prisoners at Camp Chase, Ohio, ordered for exchange, 260 voted to remain prisoners, preferring their good treatment there.—13. Superintendent Conway, in charge of free labor in Louisiana, reported that, during the year 1864, 14,000 freedmen had been supported by the national government, at a cost of $113,500; and that 50,000 freedmen were at work under him, and 15,000 others under military rule.—16. By permission of the Confederate authorities, vessels were allowed to take cotton from Savannah to New York to purchase blankets for Confederate prisoners; the first two vessels of the fleet arrived at New York with cargoes valued at $6,000,000. Confederate iron-works in the Shenandoah Valley destroyed by National troops.—18. General Lee wrote a letter to a Confederate Congressman declaring that the white people could not carry on the war, and recommending the employment of negroes as soldiers.—21. Generals Crook and Kelly seized in their beds at Cumberland, Md., and carried away prisoners by Confederate guerillas.—22. The divisions of Terry and Cox enter Wilmington, N. C., evacuated by the Confederates. —24. John Y. Beall, of Virginia, hanged as a spy at Fort Lafayette, N. Y., He was one of the pirates who tried to seize the *Michigan* on Lake Erie.—25. Gen. Joseph E. Johnston supersedes Beauregard in command of the Confederate forces in North Carolina.—March 1. Admiral Dahlgren's flag-ship *Harvest Moon* blown up by a torpedo and sunk; only one life lost. New Jersey rejects the emancipation amendment to the national Constitution.—2. The Confederates at Mobile fire twenty-four shots at a flag-of-truce steamer. A secret council of Confederate leaders in Europe ended at Paris this day.—8. Battle near Jackson's Mills, N. C., in which the Confederates captured 1,500 Nationals and three guns.—10. Up to this day Sherman's march through the Carolinas has resulted in the capture of fourteen cities, the destruction of hundreds of miles of railroad and thousands of bales of cotton, the taking of eighty-five guns, 4,000 prisoners, and 25,000 animals, and the freeing of 15,000 white and black refugees; also the destruction of an immense quantity of machinery and other property. —18. The Confederate Congress adjourned *sine die.* It was their final session. One of their latest acts was to authorize the raising of a negro military force.—25. R. C. Kennedy hanged at Fort Lafayette for having been concerned in the attempt to burn the city of New York.—27. General

Steele encounters and defeats 800 Confederates at Mitchell's Fork.—28. Monitor *Milwaukee* blown up and sunk by a torpedo in Mobile Bay; only one man injured. The monitor *Osage* blown up and sunk the next day by a torpedo in Mobile Bay. Of her crew, four were killed and six wounded. The *Milwaukee,* having sunk in shallow water, kept up her firing. —30. The amount of cotton taken at Savannah reported at 38,500 bales, of which 6,000 bales were Sea Island.—31. The transport *General Lyon* burned off Cape Hatteras, and about 500 soldiers perished. —April 1. Newbern, N. C., fired in several places by incendiaries; little harm done. Battle of Big Mulberry Creek, Ala.; Confederates defeated by Wilson.—2. The Confederates at Richmond blow up their forts and "rams" preparatory to evacuating the city.—3. Rejoicing throughout the loyal States because of the evacuation of Richmond by the Confederate troops and flight of the Confederate government. National troops enter Petersburg at 3 A.M. —4. President Lincoln sent a despatch dated "Jefferson Davis's late residence in Richmond," and held a reception in that mansion.—8. The last of the state-prisoners in Fort Lafayette discharged. First review of Union troops in Richmond took place.—9. Secretary Stanton ordered a salute of 200 guns at West Point, and at each United States post, arsenal, and department and army headquarters, for Lee's surrender.—10. The American consul at Havana hoisted the American flag, when the Confederate sympathizers there threatened to mob him, but were prevented by the authorities.—11. A proclamation was issued to the effect that hereafter all foreign vessels in American ports were to have exactly the same treatment that ours have in foreign ports.—13. An order from the War Department announced that it would stop all drafting and recruiting in the loyal States, curtail military expenses, and discontinue restrictions on commerce and trade as soon as possible. Raleigh, N. C., occupied by National cavalry. — 14. The colored men of eastern Tennessee presented a petition in the State Senate for equality before the law and the elective franchise. Four National vessels—two gunboats, a tug, and a transport — blown up by torpedoes in Mobile Bay.—15. General Saxton called a mass-meeting at Charleston, and William Lloyd Garrison addressed it. — 18. The Confederate prisoners at Point Lookout, 22,000 in number, express, by resolutions, their abhorrence of the assassination of President Lincoln.—22. General Hancock reported that nearly all of the command of Moseby, the guerilla chief, had surrendered, and some of his men were hunting for him to obtain the $2,000 reward offered for him.—26. Booth, the murderer of President Lincoln, found in a barn belonging to one Garnett, in Virgina, 3 miles from Port Royal, with Harrold, an accomplice, and refused to surrender. The barn was set on fire, and Booth, while trying to shoot one of his pursuers, was mortally wounded by a shot in the head, fired by Sergeant Corbett, and died in about four hours.—27. General Howard issued an order to the citizens along the line of march of Sherman's army to the national capital to the effect that they were to

FORT LAFAYETTE.*

* Fort Lafayette was built in the narrow strait between Long Island and Staten Island, known as "The Narrows," at the entrance to the harbor of New York. During the Civil War it was used as a prison for persons disaffected towards the national government. On Dec. 1, 1868, the fort was partially destroyed by fire, and the place has since been used for the storage of ordnance supplies.

keep at home; that foraging was stopped; that supplies were to be bought; and all marauders punished.—28. The steamer *Sultana,* with 2,106 persons on board, mostly United States soldiers, blew up, took fire, and was burned at Memphis. Only about 700 of the people were saved. —29. President Johnson removed all restrictions on commerce not foreign in all territory east of the Mississippi, with specified exceptions.

Civilized Tribes, THE FIVE, the official designation of the Cherokee, Chickasaw, Choctaw, Creek, and Seminole nations of Indians, all now located in the State of Oklahoma. For details, see their respective titles.

Claiborne, JOHN FRANCIS HAMTRAMCK, lawyer; born in Natchez, Miss., April 24, 1809; admitted to the Virginia bar; and represented Mississippi in Congress in 1835–38. He published *Life and Correspondence of Gen. John A. Quitman; Life and Times of Gen. Sam. Dale;* and *Mississippi as a Province, a Territory, and a State.* He died in Natchez, Miss., May 17, 1884.

Claiborne, or **Clayborne,** WILLIAM, colonial politician; born in Westmoreland, England, about 1589; appointed surveyor of the Virginia plantations under the London company in 1621. In 1627 the governor of Virginia gave him authority to explore the head of Chesapeake Bay; and in 1631 Charles I. gave him a license to make discoveries and trade with the Indians in that region. With this authority, he established a trading-post on Kent Island, in Chesapeake Bay, not far from the site of Annapolis. When Lord Baltimore claimed jurisdiction over Kent and other islands in the bay, Claiborne refused to acknowledge his title, having, as he alleged, an earlier one from the King. Baltimore ordered the arrest of Claiborne. Two vessels were sent for the purpose, when a battle ensued between them and one owned by Claiborne. The Marylanders were repulsed, and one of their number was killed. Claiborne was indicted for and found guilty of constructive murder and other high crimes, and fled to Virginia. Kent Island was seized and confiscated by the Maryland authorities. Sir John Harvey, governor of Virginia, refused to surrender Claiborne, and he went to England to seek redress. After the King heard his story he severely reprimanded Lord Baltimore for violating royal commands in driving Claiborne from Kent Island. In the spring of 1635 Claiborne despatched a vessel for trading, prepared to meet resistance. The Marylanders sent out two armed vessels under Cornwallis, their commissioner, or councillor, to watch for any illegal traders within the bounds of their province. On April 23 they seized Claiborne's vessel. The latter sent an armed boat, under the command of Ratcliffe Warren, a Virginian, to recapture the vessel. Cornwallis met Warren with one of his vessels in a harbor (May 10), and captured it after a sharp fight, in which Warren and two of his men were killed; also one of Cornwallis's crew. This event caused intense excitement. The first Maryland Assembly, which had convened just before the event, decreed "that offenders in all murders and felonies shall suffer the same pains and forfeitures as for the same crimes in England." A requisition was made upon Governor Harvey for the delivery of Claiborne. That functionary decided that Claiborne might go to England to justify his conduct before the home government. A court of inquiry—held three years afterwards to investigate the matter—resulted in a formal indictment of Claiborne, and a bill of attainder passed against him. Thomas Smith, next in rank to Warren, was hanged. Claiborne, who was now treasurer of Virginia, retaliated against Maryland by stirring up civil war there, and, expelling Gov. Leonard Calvert (1645), assumed the reins of government. In 1651 Claiborne was appointed, by the council of state in England, one of the commissioners for reducing Virginia to obedience to the commonwealth ruled by Parliament; and he also took part in governing Maryland by a commission. He was soon afterwards made secretary of the colony of Virginia, and held the office until after the restoration of monarchy (1660) in England. Claiborne was one of the court that tried the captured followers of NATHANIEL BACON (*q. v.*). He resided in New Kent county, Va., until his death, about 1676.

Claiborne, WILLIAM CHARLES COLE, jurist; born in Sussex county, Va., in

1775; became a lawyer, and settled in Tennessee, where he was appointed a Territorial judge. In 1796 he assisted in framing a State constitution, and was a member of Congress from 1797 to 1801. In 1802 he was appointed governor of the Mississippi Territory, and was a commissioner, with Wilkinson, to take possession of Louisiana when it was purchased from France. On the establishment of a new government in 1804, he was appointed governor; and when the State of Louisiana was organized he was elected governor, serving from 1812 to 1816. In the latter year he became United States Senator, but was prevented from taking his seat on account of sickness. He died in New Orleans, La., Nov. 23, 1817.

WILLIAM C. C. CLAIBORNE.

Clap, Roger, pioneer; born in Salcomb, England, April, 1609; settled in Dorchester, Mass., with Maverick and others in 1630; was representative of the town in 1652–66, and also held a number of military and civil offices. In 1685–86 he was captain of Castle William. He wrote a memorial of the New England worthies, and other *Memoirs*, which were first published in 1731 by Rev. Thomas Prince, and later republished by the Historical Society of Dorchester. He died in Boston, Mass., Feb. 2, 1691.

Clarendon, Edward Hyde, Earl of, English statesman; born Feb. 18, 1608; was one of eight persons to whom Charles II. granted the territory extending w. from the Atlantic Ocean between lat. 31° and 36°, which they named Carolina, March 20, 1663; was also one of the committee to settle the government of New England; became Lord High Chancellor; chief publication, *History of the Rebellion*, considered inaccurate and misleading. He died in Rouen, France, Dec. 9, 1674.

Clark, Abraham, signer of the Declaration of Independence; born in Elizabethtown, N. J., Feb. 15, 1726. He taught himself mathematics and a knowledge of law. Mr. Clark was appointed (June 21, 1776), one of the five representatives of New Jersey in the Continental Congress, where he voted for and signed the Declaration of Independence. He served in Congress (excepting a single session) until near the close of 1783. He was one of the commissioners of New Jersey who met at Annapolis in 1786 for the purpose of arranging national commercial intercourse, which meeting led to the formation of the national Constitution the following year, in which labor he was chosen to be a participant; but ill health compelled him to decline. In 1790 he was made a member of the second national Congress, and retained his seat until a short time before his death in Rahway, N. J., Sept. 15, 1794.

Clark, Alvan, optician; born at Ashfield, Mass., March 8, 1804. In 1835 he relinquished engraving and set up a studio for painting in Boston. He was over forty years of age before he became practically interested in telescope-making. Owing to the extraordinary acuteness of his vision, his touch, and his unlimited patience, he was specially skilful in grinding lenses of enormous size. Just before the Civil War he produced object-glasses equal, if not superior, to any others ever made. One 18 inches in diameter, then the largest ever made, went to Chicago. With his sons Mr. Clark established a manufactory of telescopes at Cambridge. They have produced some of extraordinary power. In 1883 they completed a telescope for the Russian government which had a clear aperture of 30 inches and a magnifying power of 2,000 diameters. It was the largest in the world, for which they were paid $33,000. At the time of his death, in Cambridge, Mass., Aug. 19, 1887, Mr. Clark was engaged in making a telescope for the Lick Observatory, California, having a lens 36 inches in diameter. After his death the business was carried on by his sons.

Clark, CHAMP, legislator; born in Anderson county, Ky., March 7, 1850; received a university education; was president of Marshall College (W. Va.) in 1873–74; admitted to the bar in 1875; member of Missouri House of Representatives in 1889–91; member of Congress in 1893–95 and

CHAMP CLARK.

from 1897; minority (Democratic) leader in Congress in 1909–11; and was elected Speaker at the special session of the 62d Congress, April 4, 1911. He was a member of the Congressional Committee on Ways and Means, and permanent chairman of the Democratic National Convention at St. Louis in 1904.

On his election to the Speakership he outlined the policy of the Democratic majority in the national House of Representatives as follows:

"My Democratic brethren, coupled with the joy of once more seeing a House, a large majority of which is of my own political faith, is a keen sense of our responsibility to our country and our kind. It is an old adage worthy of acceptation that where much is given much is required.

"After sixteen years of exclusion from power in the House and fourteen years of exclusion from power in every department of government, we are restored to power in the House of Representatives and in that alone. We are this day put upon trial, and the duty devolves upon us to demonstrate not so much by fine phrases as by good works that we are worthy of the confidence reposed in us by the voters of the land, and that we are worthy of their wider confidence.

"We could not if we would and we would not if we could escape this severe test. We will not shirk our duty. We shrink not from the responsibility. That we will prove equal to the emergency in which we find ourselves placed through our own efforts and through our own desires there can be no doubt, and the way to accomplish that is to fulfil with courage, intelligence, and patriotism the promises made before the election in order to win the election.

"By discharging our duty thoroughly and well, subordinating personal desires to principle and personal ambition to an exalted love of country, we will not only receive the endorsement of the people, but, what is far better, we will deserve their endorsement. Chief among these promises were:

"1. An honest, intelligent revision of the tariff downwards in order to give every American citizen an equal chance in the race of life, and to pamper none unduly by special favor or privilege; to reduce the cost of living by eradicating the enormities and cruelties of the present tariff bill, and to raise the necessary revenue to support the government.

"2. The passage of a resolution submitting to the States for ratification a constitutional amendment providing for the election of United States Senators by the popular vote.

"3. Such changes in the rules of the House as are necessary for the thorough and intelligent consideration of measures for the public good, several of which changes are accomplished facts. If other changes are deemed wise they will be promptly made.

"I congratulate the House and the country, and particularly do I congratulate the members of the Committee on Ways and Means, upon the success of the important and far-reaching experiment of selecting committees through the instrumentality of a committee, an experiment touching which dire predictions were made and concerning the operation of which grave doubts were entertained, even by some honest reformers.

"4. Economy in the public expense, that labor may be lightly burdened. The literal fulfilment of that promise which so nearly affects the comfort and happiness of millions we have begun—and we began at the proper place—by cutting down the running expenses of the House by more than $188,000 per annum. Economy, like charity, should begin at home. That's where we began. We cannot with straight faces and clear consciences reform expenses elsewhere unless we reform them here at the fountainhead.

"5. The publication of campaign contributions and disbursements before the election.

"6. The admission of both Arizona and New Mexico as States. I violate no confidence in stating that, so far as the House is concerned, they will be speedily admitted together.

"These are a few of the things which we promised. We are not only going to fulfil them. We have already begun the great task. What we have done is only an earnest of what we will do. We this day report progress to the American people. The rest will follow.

"No man is fit to be a lawgiver for a great people who yields to the demands and solicitations of the few having access to his ear, but is forgetful of that vast multitude who may never hear his voice or look into his face.

"I suggest to my fellow-members on both sides of the Big Aisle—which is the line of demarcation betwixt us as political partisans, but not as American citizens or American representatives—that he serves his party best who serves his country best."

A few days later, in replying to comment on his failure to allude to Canadian reciprocity in his speech on his election to the Speakership, Mr. Clark said that his position in favor of reciprocity with Canada was too well known to need expansion, and that he had confined his remarks to the promises made by the Democrats before the preceding elections.

The history of the negotiations with Canada was stated by Mr. Clark as follows: "In 1854 a Democratic administration negotiated a reciprocity agreement with Canada. In 1867 a Republican administration abrogated it. In 1911 a Republican President negotiated another one, and a bill was introduced to carry it out. All the Democrats in the House except five voted for it. The President could not muster even a majority of the House Republicans for it. The next day he wrote a letter to Representative McCall, of Massachusetts, thanking him for getting it through the House. Then it was sent to a Republican Senate, and they would not even consider the matter. The Democrats have demonstrated over and over that they are in favor of reciprocity. Individually, I have been advocating reciprocity, not only with Canada, but with all of the civilized nations of the earth."

Clark, CHARLES EDGAR, naval officer; born in Bradford, Vt., Aug. 10, 1843; was

CHARLES EDGAR CLARK.

trained in the naval academy in 1860–63, becoming ensign in the latter year. In

1863–65 he served on the sloop *Ossipee*, and participated in the battle of Mobile Bay, Aug. 5, 1864, and the bombardment of Fort Morgan, Aug. 23. He was promoted lieutenant in 1867; lieutenant-commander in 1868; commander in 1881, and captain, June 21, 1896, and was given command of the *Monterey*. He held this post till March, 1898, when he was given command of the battle-ship *Oregon*, then at San Francisco, under orders to hurry her around Cape Horn to the vicinity of Cuba. He made the now famous run of 14,000 miles to Key West in sixty-five days, arriving at his destination on May 26. This was the longest and quickest trip of any battle-ship afloat. Despite her long voyage, the *Oregon* immediately joined Admiral Sampson's squadron. Captain Clark's excellent discipline was evident in the effective work against the Spanish fleet at Santiago. In company with the *Brooklyn*, he gave chase to the *Vizcaya*, the *Colon*, and the flag-ship of Admiral Cervera, the *Maria Teresa*, and aided in the destruction of each. In 1902 he was promoted rear-admiral; in 1904–05 was president of the Naval Examining and Retiring Board; in 1905 was retired.

Clark, CLARENCE DON, Senator; born in Sandy Creek, N. Y., April 16, 1851; admitted to the bar, 1874; member of Congress from Wyoming, 1890–92; United States Senator, 1895–1911.

Clark, EDWARD, architect; born in Philadelphia in 1824; studied under and appointed assistant to Thomas W. Walker, architect of the Capitol at Washington; appointed architect of the Capitol in 1864, when Walker resigned. He died in Washington in 1902.

Clark, EMMONS, military officer; born in Huron, N. Y., Oct. 14, 1827; graduated at Hamilton College, 1847; enlisted in the Seventh Regiment, N. G. S. N. Y., 1857; captain in the United States army, 1861–63; colonel of the Seventh Regiment, 1864–89. He died in New York City in 1905.

Clark, FRANCIS EDWARD, clergyman; born of New England parents in Aylmer, Quebec, Sept. 12, 1851; studied at Kimball Union Academy, in Meriden, Conn.; graduated at Dartmouth College in 1873, and studied theology at the Andover Seminary; and became pastor of the Williston Congregational Church, Portland, Me., Oct. 19, 1876. In this church, on Feb. 2, 1881, he founded the Society of Christian Endeavor, which has spread throughout the world. In 1883 he became pastor of the Phillips Congregational Church in South Boston, but in 1887 he resigned that charge to become president of the United Society of Christian Endeavor, and editor of the *Golden Rule*, the official organ of the society. He is the author of *World-Wide Endeavor; Our Journey Around the World; The Great Secret; A New Way Around an Old World; Christian Endeavor in All Lands; The Continent of Opportunity; the Gospel in Latin Lands* (with Mrs. Clark), etc. See CHRISTIAN ENDEAVOR, YOUNG PEOPLE'S SOCIETY OF.

Clark, GEORGE HARLOW, naturalist; born in Hyde Park, Mass., Feb. 21, 1871; with Lookout Mountain Exploration Party, 1890; naturalist of Peary's Arctic Expedition, 1893; commander of North Alaska Expedition, 1898–1900; member of expedition to explore the interior of Labrador, 1902. He was also the leader of several minor exploration expeditions in the arctics.

CLARK, GEORGE ROGERS

Clark, or **Clarke,** GEORGE ROGERS, military officer; born near Monticello, Albemarle county, Va., Nov. 19, 1752; was a land surveyor, and commanded a company in Dunmore's war against the Indians in 1774. He went to Kentucky in 1775, and took command of the armed settlers there. It was ascertained in the spring of 1778 that the English governor of Detroit (Hamilton) was inciting the Western Indians to make war on the American frontiers. Under the authority of the State of Virginia, and with some aid from it in money and supplies, Clark enlisted 200 men for three months, with whom he embarked at Pittsburg, and descended to the site of Louisville, where thirteen families, following in his train, located on an island in the Ohio (June, 1778). There Clark was joined by some Kentuckians, and, descending the river some distance farther, hid his boats and marched to attack Kaskaskia (now in Illinois), one of the old French settlements near the Mississippi. The expeditionists were nearly

GEORGE ROGERS CLARK.

starved when they reached the town. Taken entirely by surprise, the inhabitants submitted (July 4, 1778) without resistance. Cahokia and two other posts near also submitted. In the possession of the commandant of Kaskaskia were found letters directing him to stimulate the Indians to hostilities. Clark established friendly relations with the Spanish commander at St. Louis, across the Mississippi. The French inhabitants in that region, being told of the alliance between France and the United States, became friendly to the Americans. The Kaskaskians, and also those of Vincennes, on the Wabash, took an oath of allegiance to Virginia, and Clark built a fort at the Falls of the Ohio, the germ of Louisville. The Virginia Assembly erected the conquered country, embracing all the territory north of the Ohio claimed as within their limits, into the country of Illinois, and ordered 500 men to be raised for its defence. Commissioned a colonel, Clark successfully labored for the pacification of the Indian tribes. Learning that Governor Hamilton, of Detroit, had captured Vincennes, Clark led an expedition against him (February, 1779), and recaptured it (Feb. 20). He also intercepted a convoy of goods worth $10,000, and afterwards built Fort Jefferson, on the west side of the Mississippi. The Indians from north of the Ohio, with some British, raided in Kentucky in June, 1780, when Clark led a force against the Shawnees on the Grand Miami, and defeated them with heavy loss at Pickaway. He served in Virginia during its invasion by Arnold and Cornwallis; and in 1782 he led 1,000 mounted riflemen from the mouth of the Licking, and invaded the Scioto Valley, burning five Indian villages and laying waste their plantations. The savages were so awed that no formidable war-party ever afterwards appeared in Kentucky. Clark made an unsuccessful expedition against the Indians on the Wabash with 1,000 men in 1786. His great services to his country in making the frontiers a safe dwelling-place were overlooked by his countrymen, and he died in poverty and obscurity, near Louisville, Ky., Feb. 18, 1818. See JEFFERSON, THOMAS.

Capture of Vincennes.—The story of the capture of Vincennes by the "Hannibal of the West" is thus told in his *Memoirs:*

Everything being ready, on Feb. 5, after receiving a lecture and absolution from the priest, we crossed the Kaskaskia River with 170 men, marched about 3 miles and encamped, where we lay until the [7th], and set out. The weather wet (but fortunately not cold for the season) and a great part of the plains under water several inches deep. It was difficult and very fatiguing marching. My object was now to keep the men in spirits. I suffered them to shoot game on all occasions, and feast on it like Indian war-dancers, each company by turns inviting the others to their feasts, which was the case every night, as the company that was to give the feast was always supplied with horses to lay up a sufficient store of wild meat in the course of the day, myself and principal officers putting on the woodsmen, shouting now and then, and running as much through the mud and water as any of them. Thus, insensibly, without a murmur, were those men led on to the banks of the Little Wabash, which we reached on the 13th, through incredible difficulties, far surpassing anything that any of us had ever experienced. Frequently the diversions of the night wore off the thoughts of the preceding day. We formed a camp on a height which we found on the bank of the river, and suffered our troops to amuse themselves. I viewed this sheet of water for some time with distrust; but, accusing myself of doubting, I immediately set to work, without holding any consultation about it, or suffering anybody else to do so in my presence; ordered a pirogue to be built immediately, and acted as though crossing the water would be only a piece of diversion. As but few could work at the pirogue at a time, pains were taken to find diversion for the rest to keep them in high spirits. . . . In the evening of the 14th our vessel was finished, manned, and sent to explore the drowned lands on the opposite side of the Little Wabash, with private instructions what report to make, and, if possible, to find some spot of dry land. They found about half an acre, and marked the trees from thence back to the camp, and made a very favorable report.

Fortunately, the 15th happened to be a warm, moist day for the season. The channel of the river where we lay was about 30 yards wide. A scaffold was built on the opposite shore (which was about 3 feet under water), and our baggage ferried across and put on it. Our horses swam across, and received their loads at the scaffold, by which time the troops were also brought across, and we began our march through the water. . . .

By evening we found ourselves encamped on a pretty height, in high spirits, each party laughing at the other, in consequence of something that had happened in the course of this ferrying business, as they called it. A little antic drummer afforded them great diversion by floating on his drum, etc. All this was greatly encouraged; and they really began to think themselves superior to other men, and that neither the rivers nor the seasons could stop their progress. Their whole conversation now was concerning what they would do when they got about the enemy. They now began to view the main Wabash as a creek, and made no doubt but such men as they were could find a way to cross it. They wound themselves up to such a pitch that they soon took Post Vincennes, divided the spoil, and before bedtime were far advanced on their route to Detroit. All this was, no doubt, pleasing to those of us who had more serious thoughts. . . . We were now convinced that the whole of the low country on the Wabash was drowned, and that the enemy could easily get to us, if they discovered us, and wished to risk an action; if they did not, we made no doubt of crossing the river by some means or other. Even if Captain Rogers, with our galley, did not get to his station agreeable to his appointment, we flattered ourselves that all would be well, and marched on in high spirits. . . .

The last day's march through the water was far superior to anything the Frenchmen had an idea of. They were backward in speaking; said that the nearest land to us was a small league called the Sugar Camp, on the bank of the [river?]. A canoe was sent off, and returned without finding that we could pass. I went in her myself, and sounded the water; found it deep as to my neck. I returned with a design to have the men transported on board the canoes to the Sugar Camp, which I knew would spend the whole day and ensuing night, as the vessels would pass slowly through the bushes. The loss of so much time, to men half-starved, was a matter of consequence. I would have given now a great deal for a day's provisions or for one of our horses. I returned but slowly to the troops, giving myself time to think. On our arrival, all ran to hear what was the report. Every eye was fixed on me. I unfortunately spoke in a serious manner to one of the officers. The whole were alarmed without knowing what I said. I viewed their confusion for about one minute, whispered to those near me to do as I did: immediately put some water in my hand, poured on powder, blackened my face, gave the war-whoop, and marched into the water without saying a word. The party gazed, and fell in, one after another, without saying a word, like a flock of sheep. I ordered those near me to begin a favorite song of theirs. It soon passed through the line, and the whole went on cheerfully. I now intended to have them transported across the deepest part of the water; but, when about waist deep, one of the men informed me that he thought he felt a path. We examined, and found it so, and concluded that it kept on the highest ground, which it did; and, by taking pains to follow it, we got to the Sugar Camp without the least difficulty, where there was about half an acre of dry ground, at least, not under water, where we took up our lodging. The Frenchmen that we had taken on the river appeared to be uneasy at our situation. They begged that they might be permitted to go in the two canoes to town in the night. They said that they would bring from their own houses provisions, without a possibility of any persons knowing it; that some of our men should go with them as a surety of their good conduct: that it was impossible we could march from that place till the water fell, for the plain was too deep to march. Some of the [officers?] believed that it might be done. I would not suffer it. I never could well account for this piece of obstinacy, and give satisfactory reasons to myself or anybody else why I denied a proposition apparently so easy to execute and of so much advantage; but something seemed to tell me that it should not be done, and it was not done.

The most of the weather that we had on this march was moist and warm for the season. This was the coldest night we had. The ice, in the morning, was from one-half to three-quarters of an inch thick near the shores and in still water. The morning was the finest we had on our march. A little after sunrise I lectured the whole. What I said to them I forget, but it may be easily imagined by a person that could possess my affections for them at that time. I concluded by informing them that passing the plain that was then in full view and reaching the opposite woods would put an end to their fatigue, that in a few hours they would have a sight of their long-wished-for object, and immediately stepped into the water without waiting for any reply. A huzza took place. As we generally marched through the water in a line, before the third entered I halted, and called to Major Bowman, ordering him to fall in the rear with twenty-five men, and put to death any man who refused to march, as we wished to have no such person among us. The whole gave a cry of approbation, and on we went. This was the most trying of all the difficulties we had experienced. I generally kept fifteen or twenty of the strongest men next myself, and judged from my own feelings what must be that of others. Getting about the middle of the plain, the water about mid-deep, I found myself sensibly failing; and, as there were no trees nor bushes for the men to support themselves by, I feared that many of the most weak would be drowned. I ordered the canoes to make the land, discharge their loading, and play backward and forward with all diligence, and pick up the men; and, to encourage the party, sent some of the strongest men forward, with orders, when they got to a certain distance, to pass the word back that the water was getting shallow, and when getting near the woods to cry out, "Land!" This stratagem had its desired effect. The men, encouraged by it, exerted themselves almost beyond their ability; the weak holding by the stronger. . . . The water never got shallower, but continued deepening. Getting to the woods, where the men expected land, the water was up to my shoulders; but gaining the woods was of great consequence. All the low men and the weakly hung to the trees, and floated on the old logs until they were taken off by the canoes. The strong and tall got ashore and built fires. Many would reach the shore, and fall with their bodies half in the water, not being able to support themselves without it.

This was a delightful dry spot of ground of about ten acres. We soon found that the fires answered no purpose, but that two strong men taking a weaker one by the arms was the only way to recover him; and, being a delightful day, it soon did. But, fortunately, as if designed by Providence, a canoe of Indian squaws and children was coming up to town, and took through part of this plain as a nigh way. It was discovered by our canoes as they were out after the men. They gave chase, and took the Indian canoe on board of which was near half a quarter of a buffalo, some corn, tallow, kettles, etc. This was a grand prize, and was invaluable. Broth was immediately made, and served out to the most weakly with great care. Most of the whole got a little; but a great many gave their part to the weakly, jocosely saying something cheering to their comrades. This little refreshment and fine weather by the afternoon gave new life to the whole. Crossing a narrow, deep lake in the canoes, and marching some distance, we came to a copse of timber called the Warrior's Island. We were now in full view of the fort and town, not a shrub between us, at about 2 miles' distance. Every man now feasted his eyes, and forgot that he had suffered anything, saying that all that had passed was owing to good policy and nothing but what a man could bear; and that a soldier had no right to think, etc.—passing from one extreme to another, which is common in such cases. It was now we had to display our abilities. The plain between us and the town was not a perfect level. The sunken grounds were covered with water full of ducks. We observed several men out on horseback, shooting them, within a half-mile of us, and sent out as many of our active young Frenchmen to decoy and take one of these men prisoner in such a manner as not to alarm the others, which they did. The information we got from this person was similar to that which we got from those we took on the river, except that of the British having that evening completed the wall of the fort, and that there were a good many Indians in town.

Our situation was now truly critical—no possibility of retreating in case of defeat, and in full view of a town that had, at this time, upward of 600 men in it—troops, inhabitants, and Indians. The crew of the galley, though not fifty men, would have been now a reinforcement of immense magnitude to our little army (if I may so call it), but we would not think of them. We were now in the situation that I had labored to get ourselves in. The idea of being made prisoner was foreign to almost every man, as they expected nothing but torture from the savages, if they fell into their hands. Our fate was now to be determined, probably in a few hours. We knew that nothing but the most daring conduct would insure success. I knew that a number of the inhabitants wished us well, that many were lukewarm to the interest of either, and I also learned that the grand chief, the Tobacco's son, had but a few days before openly declared, in council with the British, that he was a brother and friend to the Big Knives. These were favorable circumstances; and, as there was but little probability of our remaining until dark undiscovered, I determined to begin the career immediately, and wrote the following placard to the inhabitants:

"To the Inhabitants of Post Vincennes:

"Gentlemen,—Being now within 2 miles of your village with my army, determined to take your fort this night, and not being willing to surprise you, I take this method to request such of you as are true citizens and willing to enjoy the liberty I bring you to remain still in your houses; and those, if any there be, that are friends to the King will instantly repair to the fort, and join the hair-buyer general, and fight like men. And if any such as do not go to the fort shall be discovered afterwards, they may depend on severe punishment. On the contrary, those who are true friends to liberty may depend on being well treated; and I once more request them to keep out of the streets. For every one I find in arms on my arrival I shall treat him as an enemy.

"(Signed) G. R. Clark."

I had various ideas on the supposed results of this letter. I knew that it could do us no damage, but that it would cause the lukewarm to be decided, encourage our friends, and astonish our enemies. . . . We anxiously viewed this messenger until he entered the town, and in a few minutes could discover by our glasses some stir in every street that we could penetrate into, and great numbers running or riding out into the commons, we supposed, to view us, which was the case. But what surprised us was that nothing had yet happened that had the appearance of the garrison being alarmed—no drum nor gun. We began to suppose that the information we got from our prisoners was false, and that the enemy already knew of us, and were prepared. . . . A little before sunset we moved, and displayed ourselves in full view of the town, crowds gazing at us. We were plunging ourselves into certain destruction or success. There was no midway thought of. We had but little to say to our men, except inculcating an idea of the necessity of obedience, etc. We knew they did not want encouraging, and that anything might be attempted with them that was possible for such a number—perfectly cool, under proper subordination, pleased with the prospect before them, and much attached to their officers. They all declared that they were convinced that an implicit obedience to orders was the only thing that would insure success, and hoped that no mercy would be shown the person that should violate them. Such language as this from soldiers to persons in our station must have been exceedingly agreeable. We moved on slowly in full view of the town; but, as it was a point of some consequence to us to make ourselves appear as formidable, we, in leaving the covert that we were in, marched and countermarched in such a manner that we appeared numerous. In raising volunteers in the Illinois, every person that set about the business had a set of colors given him, which they brought with them to the amount of ten or twelve pairs. These were displayed to the best advantage; and, as the low plain we marched through was not a perfect level, but had frequent risings in it 7 or 8 feet higher than the common level (which was covered with water), and as these risings generally ran in an oblique direction to the town, we took the advantage of one of them, marching through the water under it, which completely prevented our being numbered. But our colors showed considerably above the heights, as they were fixed on long poles procured for the purpose, and at a distance made no despicable appearance; and, as our young Frenchmen had, while we lay on the Warrior's Island, decoyed and taken several fowlers with their horses, officers were mounted on these horses, and rode about, more completely to deceive the enemy. In this manner we moved, and directed our march in such a way as to suffer it to be dark before we had advanced more than half-way to the town. We then suddenly altered our direction, and crossed ponds where they could not have suspected us, and at about eight o'clock gained the heights back of the town. As there was yet no hostile appearance, we were impatient to have the cause unriddled. Lieutenant Bayley was ordered, with fourteen men, to march and fire on the fort. The main body moved in a different direction, and took possession of the strongest part of the town.

The firing now commenced on the fort, but they did not believe it was an enemy until one of their men was shot down through a port, as drunken Indians frequently saluted the fort after night. The drums now sounded, and the business fairly commenced on both sides. Reinforcements were sent to the attack of the garrison, while other arrangements were making in town. . . . We now found that the garrison had known nothing of us; that, having finished the fort that evening, they had amused themselves at different games, and had just retired before my letter arrived, as it was near roll-call. The placard being made public, many of the inhabitants were afraid to show themselves out of the houses for fear of giving offence, and not one dare give information. Our friends flew to the commons and other convenient places to view the pleasing sight. This was observed from the garrison, and the reason asked, but a satisfactory excuse was given; and, as a part of the town lay between our line of march and the garrison, we could not be seen by the sentinels on the walls. Capt. W. Shannon and another being some time before taken prisoners by one of their [scouting parties], and that evening brought in, the party had discovered at the Sugar Camp some signs of us. They supposed it to be a party of observation that intended to land on the height some distance below the town. Captain Lamotte was sent to intercept them. It was at him the people said they were looking, when they were asked the reason of their unusual stir. Several suspected persons had been taken to the garrison; among them was Mr. Moses Henry. Mrs. Henry went, under the pretence of carrying him provisions, and whispered him the news and what she had seen. Mr. Henry conveyed it to the rest of his fellow-prisoners, which gave them much pleasure, particularly Captain Helm, who amused himself very much during the siege, and, I believe, did much damage.

Ammunition was scarce with us, as the most of our stores had been put on board of the galley. Though her crew was but few, such a reinforcement to us at this time would have been invaluable in many instances. But, fortunately, at the time of its being reported that the whole of the goods in the town were to be taken for the King's use (for which the owners were to receive bills), Colonel Legras, Major Bosseron, and others had buried the greatest part of their powder and ball. This was immediately produced, and we found ourselves well supplied by those gentlemen.

The Tobacco's son, being in town with a number of warriors, immediately mustered them, and let us know that he wished to join us, saying that by the morning he would have 100 men. He received for answer that we thanked him for his friendly disposition; and, as we were sufficiently strong ourselves, we wished him to desist, and that we would counsel on the subject in the morning; and, as we knew that there were a number of Indans in and near the town that were our enemies, some confusion might happen if our men should mix in the dark, but hoped that we might be favored with his counsel and company during the night, which was agreeable to him.

The garrison was soon completely surrounded, and the firing continued without intermission (except about fifteen minutes a little before day) until about nine o'clock the following morning. It was kept up by the whole of the troops, joined by a few of the young men of the town, who got permission, except fifty men kept as a reserve. . . . I had made myself fully acquainted with the situation of the fort and town and the parts relative to each. The cannon of the garrison was on the upper floors of strong block-houses at each angle of the fort, 11 feet above the surface, and the ports so badly cut that many of our troops lay under the fire of them within 20 or 30 yards of the walls. They did no damage, except to the buildings of the town, some of which they much shattered; and their musketry, in the dark, employed against woodsmen covered by houses, palings, ditches, the banks of the river, etc., was but of little avail, and did no injury to us except wounding a man or two. As we could not afford to lose men, great care was taken to preserve them sufficiently covered, and to keep up a hot fire in order to intimidate the enemy as well as to destroy them. The embrasures of their cannon were frequently shut, for our riflemen, finding the true direction of them, would pour in such volleys when they were opened that the men could not stand to the guns. Seven or eight of them in a short time got cut down. Our troops would frequently abuse the enemy, in order to aggravate them to open their ports and fire their cannon, that they might have the pleasure of cutting them down with their rifles, fifty of which, perhaps, would be levelled the moment the port flew open; and I believe that if they had stood at their artillery, the greater part of them would have been destroyed in the course of the night, as the greater part of our men lay within 30 yards of the walls, and in a few hours were covered equally to those within the walls, and much more experienced in that mode of fighting. . . . Sometimes an irregular fire, as hot as possible, was kept up from different directions for a few minutes, and then only a continual scattering fire at the ports as usual; and a great noise and laughter immediately commenced in different parts of the town, by the reserved parties, as if they had only fired on the fort a few minutes for amusement, and as if those continually firing at the fort were only regularly relieved. Conduct similar to this kept the garrison constantly alarmed. They did not know what moment they might be stormed or [blown up?], as they could plainly discover that we had flung up some intrenchments across the streets, and appeared to be frequently very busy under the bank of the river, which was within 30 feet of the walls. The situation of the magazine we knew well. Captain Bowman began some works in order to blow it up, in case our artillery should arrive; but, as we knew that we were daily liable to be overpowered by the numerous bands of Indians on the river, in case they had again joined the enemy (the certainty of which we were unacquainted with), we resolved to lose no time, but to get the fort in our possession as soon as possible. If the vessel did not arrive before the ensuing night, we resolved to undermine the fort, and fixed on the spot and plan of executing this work, which we intended to commence the next day.

The Indians of different tribes that were inimical had left the town and neighborhood. Captain Lamotte continued to hover about it, in order, if possible, to make his way good into the fort. Parties attempted in vain to surprise him. A few of his party were taken, one of which was Maisonville, a famous Indian partisan. Two lads that captured him tied him to a post in the street, and fought from behind him as a breastwork, supposing that the enemy would not fire at them for fear of killing him, as he would alarm them by his voice. The lads were ordered, by an officer who discovered them at their amusement, to untie their prisoner, and take him off to the guard, which they did, but were so inhuman as to take part of his scalp on the way. There happened to him no other damage. As almost the whole of the persons who were most active in the department of Detroit were either in the fort or with Captain Lamotte, I got extremely uneasy for fear that he would not fall into our power, knowing that he would go off, if he could not get into the fort in the course of the night. Finding that, without some unforeseen accident, the fort must inevitably be ours, and that a reinforcement of twenty men, although considerable to them, would not be of great moment to us in the present situation of affairs, and knowing that we had weakened them by killing or wounding many of their gunners, after some deliberation, we concluded to risk the reinforcement in preference of his going again among the Indians. The garrison had at least a month's provisions; and, if they could hold out, in the course of that time he might do us much damage. A little before day the troops were withdrawn from their positions about the fort, except a few parties of observation, and the firing totally ceased. Orders were given, in case of Lamotte's approach, not to alarm or fire on him without a certainty of killing or taking the whole. In less than a quarter of an hour, he passed within 10 feet of an officer and a party that lay concealed. Ladders were flung over to them; and, as they mounted them, our party shouted. Many of them fell from the top of the walls—some within, and others back; but, as they were not fired on, they all got over, much to the joy of their friends. But, on considering the matter, they must have been convinced that it was a scheme of ours to let them in, and that we were so strong as to care but little about them or the manner of their getting into the garrison.... The firing immediately commenced on both sides with double vigor; and I believe that more noise could not have been made by the same number of men. Their shouts could not be heard for the fire-arms; but a continual blaze was kept around the garrison, without much being done, until about daybreak, when our troops were drawn off to posts prepared for them, about 60 or 70 yards from the fort. A loop-hole then could scarcely be darkened but a rifle-ball would pass through it. To have stood to their cannon would have destroyed their men, without a probability of doing much service. Our situation was nearly similar. It would have been imprudent in either party to have wasted their men, without some decisive stroke required it.

Thus the attack continued until about nine o'clock on the morning of the 24th. Learning that the two prisoners they had brought in the day before had a considerable number of letters with them, I supposed it an express that we expected about this time, which I knew to be of the greatest moment to us, as we had not received one since our arrival in the country; and, not being fully acquainted with the character of our enemy, we were doubtful that those papers might be destroyed, to prevent which I sent a flag [with a letter] demanding the garrison.

The following is a copy of the letter which was addressed by Colonel Clark to Lieutenant-Governor Hamilton on this occasion:

"SIR,—In order to save yourself from the impending storm that now threatens you, I order you immediately to surrender yourself, with all your garrison, stores, etc. For, if I am obliged to storm, you may depend on such treatment as is justly due to a murderer. Beware of destroying stores of any kind or any papers or letters that are in your possession, or hurting one house in town; for, by Heavens! if you do, there shall be no mercy shown you.
"(Signed) G. R. CLARK."

The British commandant immediately returned the following answer:

"Lieutenant-Governor Hamilton begs leave to acquaint Colonel Clark that he and his garrison are not disposed to be awed into any action unworthy British subjects."

The firing then—says Clark—commenced warmly for a considerable time; and we were obliged to be careful in preventing our men from exposing themselves too much, as they were now much animated, having been refreshed during the flag. They frequently mentioned their wishes to storm the place, and put an end to the business at once. . . . The firing was heavy through every crack that could be discovered in any part of the fort. Several of the garrison got wounded, and no possibility of standing near the embrasures. Towards the evening a flag appeared with the following proposals:

"Lieutenant-Governor Hamilton proposes to Colonel Clark a truce for three days, during which time he promises there shall be no defensive works carried on in the garrison, on condition that Colonel Clark shall observe, on his part, a like cessation of any defensive work—that is, he wishes to confer with Colonel Clark as soon as can be, and promises that whatever may pass between them two and another person mutually agreed upon to be present shall remain secret till matters be finished, as he wishes that, whatever the result of the conference may be, it may tend to the honor and credit of each party. If Colonel Clark makes a difficulty of coming into the fort, Lieutenant-Governor Hamilton will speak to him by the gate.

"(Signed) HENRY HAMILTON.

"*February 24th, 1779.*"

I was at a great loss to conceive what reason Lieutenant-Governor Hamilton could have for wishing a truce of three days on such terms as he proposed. Numbers said it was a scheme to get me into their possession. I had a different opinion and no idea of his possessing such sentiments, as an act of that kind would infallibly ruin him. Although we had the greatest reason to expect a reinforcement in less than three days, that would at once put an end to the siege, I yet did not think it prudent to agree to the proposals, and sent the following answer:

"Colonel Clark's compliments to Lieutenant-Governor Hamilton, and begs leave to inform him that he will not agree to any terms other than Mr. Hamilton's surrendering himself and garrison prisoners at discretion. If Mr. Hamilton is desirous of a conference with Colonel Clark, he will meet him at the church with Captain Helm.

"(Signed) G. R. C.

"*February 24th, 1779.*"

We met at the church, about 80 yards from the fort, Lieutenant-Governor Hamilton, Major Hay, superintendent of Indian affairs, Captain Helm, their prisoner, Major Bowman, and myself. The conference began. Hamilton produced terms of capitulation, signed, that contained various articles, one of which was that the garrison should be surrendered on their being permitted to go to Pensacola on parole. After deliberating on every article, I rejected the whole. He then wished that I would make some proposition. I told him that I had no other to make than what I had already made—that of his surrendering as prisoners at discretion. I said that his troops had behaved with spirit; that they could not suppose that they would be worse treated in consequence of it; that, if he chose to comply with the demand, though hard, perhaps the sooner the better; that it was in vain to make any proposition to me; that he, by this time, must be sensible that the garrison would fall; that both of us must [view?] all blood spilt for the future by the garrison as murder; that my troops were already impatient, and called aloud for permission to tear down and storm the fort. If such a step was taken, many, of course, would be cut down; and the result of an enraged body of woodsmen breaking in must be obvious to him. It would be out of the power of an American officer to save a single man. Various altercation took place for a considerable time. Captain Helm attempted to moderate our fixed determination. I told him he was a British prisoner; and it was doubtful whether or not he could, with propriety, speak on the subject. Hamilton then said that Captain Helm was from that moment liberated, and might use his pleasure. I informed the captain that I would not receive him on such terms; that he must return to the garrison, and await his fate. I then told Lieutenant-Governor Hamilton that hostilities should not commence until five minutes after the drums gave the alarm. We took our leave, and parted but a few steps, when Hamilton stopped, and politely asked me if I would be so kind as to give him my reasons for refusing the garrison any other terms than those I had offered. I told him I had no objections in giving him my real reasons, which were simply these: that I knew the greater part of the principal Indian partisans of Detroit were with him; that I wanted an excuse to put them to death or otherwise treat them as I thought proper; that the cries of the widows and the fatherless on the frontiers, which they had occasioned, now required their blood from my hand; and that I did not choose to be so timorous as to disobey the absolute commands of their authority, which I looked upon to be next to divine; that I would rather lose fifty men than not to empower myself to execute this piece of business with propriety; that, if he chose to risk the massacre of his garrison for their sakes, it was his own pleasure; and that I might, perhaps, take it into my head to send for some of those widows to see it executed. Major Hay paying great attention, I had observed a kind of distrust in his countenance, which in a great measure influenced my conversation during this time. On my concluding, "Pray, sir," said he, "who is it that you call Indian partisans?" "Sir," I replied, "I take Major Hay to be one of the principal." I never saw a man in the moment of execution so struck as he appeared to be, pale and trembling, scarcely able to stand. Hamilton blushed, and, I observed, was much affected at his behavior. Major Bowman's countenance sufficiently explained his disdain for the one and his sorrow for the other. . . . Some moments elapsed without a word passing on either side. From that moment my resolutions changed respecting Hamilton's situation. I told him that we would return to our respective posts; that I would reconsider the matter, and let him know the result. No offensive measures should be taken in the mean time. Agreed to; and we parted. What had passed being made known to our officers, it was agreed that we should moderate our resolutions.

In the course of the afternoon of the 24th the following articles were signed, and the garrison capitulated:

"I. Lieutenant-Governor Hamilton engages to deliver to Colonel Clark Fort Sackville, as it is at present, with all the stores, etc.

"II. The garrison are to deliver themselves as prisoners of war, and march out with their arms and accoutrements, etc.

"III. The garrison to be delivered up at ten o'clock to-morrow.

"IV. Three days' time to be allowed the garrison to settle their accounts with the inhabitants and traders of this place.

"V. The officers of the garrison to be allowed their necessary baggage, etc.

"Signed at Post St. Vincent [Vincennes], 24th of February, 1779.

"Agreed for the following reasons: the remoteness from succor; the state and quantity of provisions, etc.; unanimity of officers and men in its expediency; the honorable terms allowed; and, lastly, the confidence in a generous enemy.

"(Signed) HENRY HAMILTON,
"*Lieut.-Gov. and Superintendent.*"

The business being now nearly at an end, troops were posted in several strong houses around the garrison and patrolled during the night to prevent any deception that might be attempted. The remainder on duty lay on their arms, and for the first time for many days past got some rest. . . . During the siege, I got only one man wounded. Not being able to lose many, I made them secure themselves well. Seven were badly wounded in the fort through ports. . . . Almost every man had conceived a favorable opinion of Lieutenant-Governor Hamilton—I believe what affected myself made some impression on the whole; and I was happy to find that he never deviated, while he stayed with us, from that dignity of conduct that became an officer in his situation. The morning of the 25th approaching, arrangements were made for receiving the garrison [which consisted of seventy-nine men], and about ten o'clock it was delivered in form; and everything was immediately arranged to the best advantage.

Clark, JOHN BATES, economist; born in Providence, R. I., Jan. 26, 1847; professor of political economy and history, Carleton College, 1877–81; of history and political science, Smith College, 1882–93; of political economy, Amherst, 1892–95, and Columbia from 1895; author of *The Philosophy of Wealth; The Distribution of Wealth; The Control of Trusts; The Problem of Monopoly; Essentials to Economic Theory; Wages; Capital and Its Earnings,* and numerous articles in Economical reviews.

Clark, JOHN BULLOCK, military officer; born in Madison county, Ky., April 17, 1802; went to Missouri in 1818; admitted to the bar in 1824; commanded a regiment in the Black Hawk War in 1832; and subsequently led the force which drove the Mormons out of Missouri. In 1857–61 he was a Democratic member of Congress. At the beginning of the Civil War he joined the Confederate army; was made a brigadier-general; and commanded the Missouri troops till seriously wounded in August, 1861. During the remainder of the war he was a member of the Confederate Congress, and at the conclusion of hostilities resumed law practice at Fayette, Mo., where he died, Oct. 29, 1885.

Clark, JONAS GILMAN, philanthropist; born in Hubbardston, Mass., Feb. 1, 1815; began life as a carriage-maker and acquired a fortune in business and real estate investments; founded Clark University at Worcester, Mass., with $2,000,000, in 1887. He died in Worcester, Mass., May 23, 1900, having bequeathed $200,000 to Clark University outright and $1,000,000 and the residue of his estate conditionally.

Clark, LEWIS GAYLORD, editor; born in Otis county, N. Y., 1810; editor of *The Knickerbocker Magazine*, which ceased in 1859. This periodical contained contributions by Irving, Bryant, Longfellow, and most of the other prominent American writers of the day. He died at Piermont, N. Y., Nov. 3, 1873.

Clark, LEWIS GEORGE, lecturer; born about 1811; was reared a slave, but, escaping, lectured for emancipation in 1841-50; claimed to be the original of Uncle Tom in Mrs. Stowe's novel, which the authoress denied. He died in Lexington, Ky., Dec. 16, 1897.

Clark, THOMAS, author; born in Lancaster, Pa., in 1787; educated at St. Mary's College, in Baltimore; made an assistant topographical engineer, with the rank of captain, April 1, 1813; served in the War of 1812–15 in building defences on the Delaware River, and after the war devoted himself to literature. His publications include *Naval History of the United States from the Commencement of the Revolutionary War*, and *Sketches of the Naval History of the United States*. He died in Philadelphia, Pa., in 1860.

Clark, THOMAS, born in England in 1599; he was mate of the *Mayflower*; he received this position because he had made two voyages to Virginia. He died in Plymouth, England, March 24, 1697.

Clark, WALTER, jurist; born in Halifax, N. C., Aug. 19, 1846; graduated at the University of North Carolina in 1864; became judge of the Superior Court of that State in 1885, of the Supreme Court in 1889, and its chief-justice in 1903. He compiled and edited *North Carolina State Records* (16 vols.); *Histories of North Carolina Regiments, 1861–65* (5 vols.), etc.

Clark, WILLIAM, military officer; born in Virginia, Aug. 1, 1770; removed to what is now Louisville, Ky., in 1784. He was appointed an ensign in the army in 1788; promoted lieutenant of infantry in 1792; and appointed a member of Captain Lewis's expedition to the mouth of the Columbia River in 1804. The success of the expedition was largely due to his knowledge of Indian habits. Afterwards he was made brigadier-general for the Territory of Upper Louisiana; in 1813–21 was governor of the Mississippi Territory; and in 1822–38 superintendent of Indian affairs in St. Louis. He died in St. Louis, Mo., Sept. 1, 1838. See CLARK, GEORGE ROGERS; LEWIS, MERIWETHER.

Clark, WILLIS GAYLORD, poet, twin brother of Lewis Gaylord Clark; contributor to the *Knickerbocker Magazine;* he was also editor of the *Philadelphia Gazette*. He died in Philadelphia, June 12, 1841.

Clark University, Worcester, Mass., founded by JONAS GILMAN CLARK (*q. v.*). It is devoted exclusively to post-graduate work.

Clarke, SIR ALURED, military officer; born in 1745; joined the British army in 1765; came to America, and during the Revolutionary War was lieutenant-colonel of the Seventh Foot. When the British took Savannah, Ga., he was placed in command of the city, and by the strict discipline of his troops and his courtesy to the inhabitants won their good will. He died in September, 1832.

Clarke, SIR CASPAR PURDON, art director; born in London, England, Dec. 21, 1846; became director of the South Kensington (London) Art Museum; resigned on being called to the same post in the Metropolitan Museum of Art, New York, in 1905; resigned on account of ill health,

1910; died in London, England, March 29, 1911.

Clarke, ELIJAH, military officer; born in North Carolina; went to Georgia in 1774, where he became a captain in 1776, and fought both British and Indians on the frontiers. He was an active leader in the War for Independence, and was largely instrumental in the capture of Augusta, Ga., in 1781. He fought many battles and made several treaties with the Indians; but in 1794 he was accused of a design to establish an independent government among the Creeks, where he had settled in violation of law. He died in Wilkes county, Ga., Dec. 15, 1799.

Clarke, GEORGE, colonial governor; born in England; came to America during the reign of Queen Anne, and settled in New York. When Governor Crosby died he was proclaimed governor *pro tem.* by the council, and later was commissioned lieutenant-governor by the British government. He died in Chester, England, in 1763.

Clarke, JAMES FREEMAN, author-clergyman; born in Hanover, N. H., April 4, 1810; graduated at Harvard College in 1829, and at Cambridge Divinity School in 1833; settled in Louisville, Ky., as pastor, 1833–40; pastor of the Church of the Disciple in Boston, Mass., 1841–88. His publications relating to the United States include *History of the Campaign of 1812, and Defence of General William Hull for the Surrender of Detroit;* and *Anti-Slavery Days.* He died in Jamaica Plains, Mass., June 8, 1888.

Clarke, or **Clerke,** JEREMY, one of the settlers of Newport, R. I., in 1639; became constable of the new plantation in 1640, and treasurer in 1647. He was elected as an assistant to the president in 1648, and when the president-elect, William Coddington, failed to enter upon his office and to answer certain accusations brought against him Clarke, who was a republican, was chosen by the assembly as president-regent, and served as such till the following May.

Clarke, JOHN, clergyman; born in Bedfordshire, England, Oct. 8, 1609; emigrated to Boston in 1637, but, espousing the cause of ANNE HUTCHINSON (*q. v.*), and claiming full toleration in religious belief, he was obliged to flee. He was welcomed to Providence by Roger Williams. He was one of the company who gained Rhode Island from the Indians, and began a settlement at Pocasset in 1638. A preacher of the Gospel, he founded at Newport (1664) the second Baptist church in America. He was treasurer of the colony in 1649. Mr. Clarke was persecuted while visiting friends in Massachusetts and driven out of the colony. He accompanied Williams to England in 1651 as agent for the colony, where he remained nearly twelve years, and returned (1663) with a second charter for Rhode Island. He resumed his pastorate at Newport, where for three successive years he was deputy-governor of the colony. His publications include *Ill News from New England; or a Narrative of New England's Persecution.* He died in Newport, R. I., April 20, 1676.

Clarke, RICHARD HENRY, lawyer; born in Washington, D. C., July 3, 1827; graduated at Georgetown College, 1847; admitted to the bar in 1848. He is the author of an illustrated *History of the Catholic Church in the United States; Lives of the American Catholic Bishops; Old and New Lights on Columbus; Life of Pope Leo XIII.,* etc. He died at White Hall, Ky., July 22, 1903.

Clarke, ROBERT, publisher; born in Scotland, May 1, 1829; settled in Cincinnati, O., in 1840. He edited *Col. George Rogers Clarke's Campaign in the Illinois in 1778–79; Captain James Smith's Captivity,* and *Pioneer Biographies.* He is the author of *The Prehistoric Remains which were found on the Site of the City of Cincinnati, with a Vindication of the Cincinnati Tablet.* He died in Cincinnati, Aug. 6, 1899.

Clarke, SAMUEL, clergyman; born in Warwickshire, England, in 1599. He was the author of *A True and Faithful Account of the Four Chiefest Plantations of the English in America;* and *New Description of the World,* etc. He died in 1682.

Clarke, THOMAS CURTIS, engineer; born in Newton, Mass., in 1827; graduated at Harvard in 1848; specialist in bridge and railroad engineering. He died in New York City, June 15, 1901.

Clarke, WALTER, colonial governor; deputy-governor of Rhode Island in 1675–76; governor in 1676–79; deputy in

1679-86; and then governor again. In 1687 he was compelled to surrender the government into the hands of the royal governor who had been commissioned in England; and in 1688 became a member of the governor's council under the new commission. In 1696, eight years after the overthrow of the royal governor, he was again elected governor, but after two years resigned.

Clarkson, THOMAS, philanthropist; born at Wissbeach, England, March 28, 1760. He was one of the members of an anti-slavery committee, and with William Wilberforce helped to pass the first act to abolish the slave trade in England, March 25, 1807. He died at Ipswich, England, Sept. 26, 1846.

Claxton, PHILANDER PRIESTLEY, educator; born in Bedford county, Tenn., Sept. 28, 1862; was graduated at the University of Tennessee in 1882; studied educational methods in the principal countries of Europe, 1885–86 and 1897; professor of pedagogy and director of Practice School, North Carolina Normal College, 1896–1902; professor of education, University of Tennesee, 1902–11; succeeded Dr. ELMER E. BROWN (*q. v.*) as United States Commissioner of Education, June 29, 1911.

Clay, CASSIUS MARCELLUS, diplomatist; born in Madison county, Ky., Oct. 19, 1810; son of Green Clay; was graduated at Yale College in 1832. He became a lawyer; was a member of the Kentucky legislature in 1835, 1837, and 1840. In June, 1845, he issued at Lexington, Ky., the first number of the *True American*, a weekly anti-slavery paper. In August his press was seized by a mob, after which it was printed in Cincinnati and published at Lexington, and afterwards at Louisville. Mr. Clay was a captain in the war with Mexico, and was made prisoner in January, 1847. In 1862 he was appointed major-general, and was United States minister to Russia from 1863 to 1869. Mr. Clay was sent to Russia, as Carl Schurz was to Spain; Geo. B. Marsh to Italy; William L. Dayton to France; and Charles Francis Adams to England, for the purpose of awakening sympathy with the North. They met in Europe a commission headed by William L. Yamcey, which was sent to awaken sympathy with the South. The representatives of neither section found a cordial reception. The European powers were bewildered and doubtful, and no one of them would take decided ground. He died in White Hall, Ky., July 22, 1903.

Clay, CLEMENT CLAIBORNE, lawyer; born in Huntsville, Ala., in 1819; graduated at the University of Alabama in 1835; admitted to the bar in 1840; elected United States Senator in 1853 and 1859; was expelled in 1861; and elected to the Confederate Senate. In 1864 he was a secret Confederate agent to Canada, and participated in laying the plans for the raids on the northern border. At the close of the war, hearing that a reward was offered for his capture, he surrendered himself, and was a prisoner with Jefferson Davis in Fort Monroe; was released in 1866. He practiced at Huntsville, Ala., where he died Jan. 3, 1882.

Clay, GREEN, military officer; born in Powhatan county, Va., Aug. 14, 1757.

GREEN CLAY.

Before he was twenty years old he emigrated to Kentucky, where he became a surgeon, and laid the foundation of a fortune. He represented the Kentucky district in the Virginia legislature, and was a member of the Virginia convention that ratified the national Constitution. He also assisted in framing the Kentucky constitution in 1799. Mr. Clay served long in the Kentucky legislature. In the spring of 1813 he led 3,000 Kentucky volunteers to the relief of FORT MEIGS (*q. v.*); and, being left in command of that post, he defended it against an attack by British and Indians under General Proctor and Tecumseh. He died in Kentucky, Oct. 31, 1826.

CLAY, HENRY

Clay, HENRY, statesman; born in Hanover county, Va., April 12, 1777; received the rudiments of education in a log-cabin school-house; labored on a farm until he was fifteen years of age, when he entered the office of the High Court of Chancery, in Richmond, at which time his mother, who had married a second time, emigrated to Kentucky. He studied law under the direction of Chancellor Wythe and was admitted to the bar in 1797, when he opened a law-office in Lexington, Ky., where he obtained an extensive practice. In 1803 he was elected to the Kentucky legislature, and was speaker in 1807–8. He became United States Senator in 1808, and member of Congress and Speaker in 1811–14. In 1814 he was a commissioner to treat for peace with Great Britain, and afterwards, in Congress, was five times elected Speaker of the House of Representatives. Mr. Clay was Secretary of State in the cabinet of John Quincy Adams (1825–29), and again a member of the United States Senate from 1831 till 1842. He was twice defeated as a candidate for the Presidency (1832 and 1844); and was in the Senate for the last time from 1849 till 1852, taking a leading part in the compromise measures of 1850, as he did in those of 1832. Mr. Clay did much by his eloquence to arouse a war spirit against Great Britain in 1812; and his efforts were effective in securing an acknowledgment of the independence of the Spanish colonies in South America. He always advocated the thoroughly American policy of President Monroe in excluding European influence on this continent. He died in Washington, D. C., June 29, 1852.

HENRY CLAY AT 40.

The secret history of Clay's Compromise Bill in 1832, which quieted rampant nullification, seems to be as follows: Mr. Calhoun, as leader of the nullifiers, had proceeded to the verge of treason in his opposition to the national government, and President Jackson had threatened him with arrest if he moved another step forward. Knowing the firmness and decision of the President, he dared not take the fatal step. He could not recede, or even stand still, without compromising his character with his political friends. In this extremity a mutual friend arranged with Clay to propose a measure which would satisfy both sides and save the neck and reputation of Calhoun. In discussing the matter in the Senate, the latter earnestly disclaimed any hostile feelings towards the Union on the part of South Carolina. He declared that the State authorities looked only to a judicial verdict on the question, until the concentration of United States troops at Charleston and Augusta (by order of the President) compelled them to make provision to defend themselves. Clay's compromise only postponed civil war a little less than thirty years.

The Consequences of Secession.—On Feb. 5, 1850, Senator Clay delivered the following speech in the Senate chamber:

Sir, this Union is threatened with subversion. I want, Mr. President, to take a very rapid glance at the course of public measures in this Union presently. I want, however, before I do that, to ask the Senate to look back upon the career which this country has run since the adoption of this Constitution down to the present day. Was there ever a nation upon which the sun of heaven has shone that has exhibited so much of prosperity? At the commencement of this government our population amounted to about 4,000,000; it has now reached upward of 20,000,000. Our territory was limited chiefly and principally to the border upon the Atlantic Ocean, and that which includes the southern shores of the interior lakes of our country.

CLAY'S MONUMENT AT LEXINGTON, KY.

Our country now extends from the northern provinces of Great Britain to the Rio Grande and the Gulf of Mexico on one side, and from the Atlantic Ocean to the Pacific on the other side—the largest extent of territory under any government that exists on the face of the earth, with only two solitary exceptions. Our tonnage, from being nothing, has risen in magnitude and amount so as to rival that of the nation who has been proudly characterized "the mistress of the ocean." We have gone through many wars—wars, too, with the very nation from whom we broke off in 1776, as weak and feeble colonies, and asserted our independence as a member of the family of nations. And, sir, we came out of that struggle, unequal as it was—armed as she was at all points, in consequence of the habits and nature of our country and its institutions—we came, I say, out of that war without any loss of honor whatever — we emerged from it gloriously.

In every Indian war—and we have been engaged in many of them—our armies have triumphed; and, without speaking at all as to the causes of the recent war with Mexico, whether it was right or wrong, and abstaining from any expression of opinion as to the justice or propriety of the war, when once commenced all must admit that, with respect to the gallantry of our armies, the glory of our triumphs, there is no page or pages of history which records more brilliant successes. With respect to one commander of an important portion of our army, I need say nothing here; no praise is necessary in behalf of one who has been elevated by the voice of his country to the highest station she could place him in, mainly on account of his glorious military career. And of another, less fortunate in many respects than some other military commanders, I must take the opportunity of saying that, for skill, for science, for strategy, for ability and daring fighting, for chivalry of individuals and of masses, that portion of the American army which was conducted by the gallant Scott, as the chief commander, stands unrivalled either by the deeds of Cortez himself, or of those of any other commander in ancient or modern times.

Sir, our prosperity is unbounded—nay, Mr. President, I sometimes fear that it is in the wantonness of that prosperity that many of the threatening ills of the moment have arisen. Wild and erratic schemes have sprung up throughout the whole country, some of which have even found their way into legislative halls; and there is a restlessness existing among us which I fear will require the chastisement of Heaven to bring us back to a sense of the immeasurable benefits and blessings which have been bestowed upon us by Providence. At this moment—with the exception of here and there a particular department in the manufacturing business of the country—all is prosperity and peace, and the nation is rich and powerful. Our country has grown to a magnitude, to a power and greatness, such as to command the respect, if it does not awe the apprehensions, of the powers of the earth with whom we come in contact.

Sir, do I depict with colors too lively the prosperity which has resulted to us from the operations of this Union? Have I exaggerated in any particular her power, her prosperity, or her greatness? And now, sir, let me go a little into detail with respect to sway in the councils of the nation, whether from the North or the South, during the sixty years of unparalleled prosperity that we have enjoyed. During the first twelve years of the administration of the government Northern counsels rather prevailed; and out of them sprang the Bank of the United States, the assumption of the State debts, bounties to the fisheries, protection to our domestic manufactures—I allude to the act of 1789—neutrality in the wars of Europe; Jay's treaty, the alien and sedition laws, and war with France. I do not say, sir, that these, the leading and prominent measures which were adopted during the administrations of Washington and the elder Adams, were carried exclusively by Northern counsels—they could not have been—but mainly by the ascendency which Northern counsels had obtained in the affairs of the nation. So, sir, of the later period—for the last fifty years.

I do not mean to say that Southern counsels alone have carried the measures which I am about to enumerate. I know they could not have exclusively carried them, but I say that they have been carried by their preponderating influence, with the co-operation, it is true—the large co-operation, in some instances—of the Northern section of the Union. And what are those measures? During that fifty years, or nearly that period, in which Southern counsels have preponderated the embargo and commercial restrictions of non-intercourse and non-importation were imposed, war with Great Britain, the Bank of the United States overthrown, protection enlarged and extended to domestic manufactures—I allude to the passage of the act of 1815 or 1816—the Bank of the United States re-established, the same bank put down, re-established by Southern counsels and put down by Southern counsels, Louisiana acquired, Florida bought, Texas annexed, war with Mexico, California and other territories acquired from Mexico by conquest and purchase, protection superseded and free trade established, Indians removed west of the Mississippi, and fifteen new States admitted into the Union. It is very possible, sir, that in this enumeration I may have omitted some of the important measures which have been adopted during this later period of time—the last fifty years—but these I believe to be the most prominent ones.

Now, sir, I do not deduce from the enumeration of the measures adopted by the one side or the other any just cause of reproach either upon one side or the other; though one side or the other has predominated in the two periods to which I have referred. These measures were, to say the least, the joint work of both parties, and neither of them have any just cause to reproach the other. But, sir, I must say, in all kindness and sincerity, that least of all ought the South to reproach the North, when we look at the long list of measures which, under her sway in the counsels of the nation, have been adopted; when we reflect that even opposite doctrines have been from time to time advanced by her; that the establishment of the Bank of the United States, which was done under the administration of Mr. Madison, met with the cooperation of the South—I do not say the whole South—I do not, when I speak of the South or the North, speak of the entire South or the entire North; I speak of the prominent and larger proportions of Southern and Northern men. It was during Mr. Madison's administration that the Bank of the United States was established. My friend, whose sickness—which I very much deplore—prevents us from having his attendance upon this occasion (Mr. Calhoun), was the chairman of the committee, and carried the measure through Congress. I voted for it with all my heart. Although I had been instrumental with other Southern votes in putting down the Bank of the United States, I changed my opinion and cooperated in the establishment of the bank of 1816. The same bank was again put down by the Southern counsels, with General Jackson at their head, at a later period. Again, with respect to the policy of protection. The South in 1815—I mean the prominent Southern men, the lamented Lowndes, Mr. Calhoun, and others—united in extending a certain measure of protection to domestic manufactures as well as the North.

We find a few years afterwards the South interposing most serious objection to this policy, and one member of the South threatening on that occasion a dissolution of the Union or separation. Now, sir, let us take another view of the question—and I would remark that all these views are brought forward not in a spirit of reproach but of conciliation—not to provoke, or exasperate, but to quiet, to produce harmony and repose if possible. What have been the territorial acquisitions made by this country, and to what interests have they conduced? Florida where slavery exists, has been introduced; Louisiana, or all the most valuable part of that State—for although there is a large extent of territory north of the line 36° 30′, in point of intrinsic value and importance, I would not give the single State of Louisiana for the whole of it—all Louisiana, I say, with the exception of that which lies north of 36° 30′, including Oregon, to which we obtain title mainly on the ground of its being a part of the acquisition of Louisiana; all Texas; all the territories which have been acquired by the government of the United States during its sixty years' operation, have been slave territories, the theatre of slavery with the exception that I have mentioned of that lying north of the line 36° 30′.

And here, in the case of a war made essentially by the South—growing out of the annexation of Texas, which was a measure proposed by the South in the councils of the country, and which led to the war with Mexico—I do not say all of the South, but the major portion of the South pressed the annexation of Texas upon the country—that measure, as I have said, led to the war with Mexico, and the war with Mexico led to the acquisition of those territories which now constitute the bone of contention between the different members of the confederacy. And now, sir, for the first time after the three great acquisitions of Texas, Florida, and Louisiana have been made and have redounded to the benefit of the South—now, for the first time, when these territories are attempted to be introduced without the institution of slavery, I put it to the hearts of my countrymen of the South, if it is right to press matters to the disastrous consequences which have been indicated no longer ago than this very morning, on the occasion of the presentation of certain resolutions even extending to a dissolution of the Union. Mr. President, I cannot believe it.

Such is the Union and such are the glorious fruits which are now threatened with subversion and destruction. Well, sir, the first question which naturally arises, is, supposing the Union to be dissolved for any of the causes or grievances which are complained of, how far will dissolution furnish a remedy for those grievances which are complained of, how far will dissolution furnish a remedy for these grievances? If the Union is to be dissolved for any existing cause, it will be because slavery is interdicted or not allowed to be introduced into the ceded territories; or because slavery is threatened to be abolished in the District of Columbia; or because fugitive slaves are not restored, as in my opinion they ought to be, to their masters. These, I believe, would be the causes, if there be any causes which lead to the dreadful event to which I have referred. Let us suppose the Union dissolved; what remedy does it, in a severed state, furnish for the grievances complained of in its united condition? Will you be able at the South to push slavery into the ceded territory? How are you to do it, supposing the North, or all the States north of the Potomac, in possession of the navy and army of the United States? Can you expect, I say, under these circumstances, that if there is a dissolution of the Union you can carry slavery into California and New Mexico? Sir, you cannot dream of such an occurrence.

If it were abolished in the District of Columbia and the Union were dissolved, would the dissolution of the Union restore slavery in the District of Columbia? Is your chance for the recovery of your fugitive slaves safer in a state of dissolution or of severance of the Union than when in the Union itself? Why, sir, what is the state of the fact? In the Union you lose some slaves and recover others; but here let me revert to a fact which I ought to have noticed before, because it is highly creditable to the courts and judges of the free States. In every instance, as far as my information extends, in which an appeal has been made to the courts of justice to recover penalties from those who have assisted in decoying slaves from their masters—in every instance, as far as I have heard, the court has asserted the rights of the owner, and the jury has promptly returned an adequate verdict on his behalf. Well, sir, there is then some remedy while you are a part of the Union for the recovery of your slaves, and some indemnification for their loss. What would you have if the Union was severed? Why, the several parts would be independent of each other—foreign countries — and slaves escaping from the United States to Canada. There would be no right of extradition, no right to demand your slaves; no right to appeal to the courts of justice to indemnify you for the loss of your slaves. Where one slave escapes now by running away from his master, hundreds and thousands would escape if the Union were dissevered—I care not how or where you run the line, or whether independent sovereignties be established. Well, sir, finally, will you, in case of a dissolution of the Union, be safer with your slaves within the separated portions of the States than you are now? Mr. President, that they will escape much more frequently from the border States no one will deny.

And, sir, I must take occasion here to say that, in my opinion, there is no right on the part of any one or more of the States to secede from the Union. War and dissolution of the Union are identical and inevitable, in my opinion. There can be a dissolution of the Union only by consent or by war. Consent no one can anticipate, from any existing state of things, is likely to be given, and war is the only alternative by which a dissolution could be accomplished. If consent were given—if it were possible that we were to be separated by one great line—in less than sixty days after such consent was given war would break out between the slave-holding and non-slave-holding portions of this Union—between the two independent parts into which it would be erected in virtue of the act of separation. In less than sixty days, I believe, our slaves from Kentucky, flocking over in numbers to the other side of the river, would be pursued by their owners. Our hot and ardent spirits would be restrained by no sense of the right which appertains to the independence of the other side of the river, should that be the line of separation. They would pursue their slaves into the adjacent free States; they would be repelled, and the consequences would be that, in less than sixty days, war would be blazing in every part of this now happy and peaceful land.

And, sir, how are you going to separate the States of this confederacy? In my humble opinion, Mr. President, we should begin with at least three separate confederacies. There would be a confederacy of the North, a confederacy of the Southern Atlantic slave-holding States, and a confederacy of the valley of the Mississippi. My life upon it, that the vast population which has already concentrated and will concentrate on the head-waters and the tributaries of the Mississippi will never give their consent that the mouth of that river shall be held subject to the power of any foreign state or community whatever. Such, I believe, would be the consequences of a dissolution of the Union, immediately ensuing; but other confederacies would spring up from time to time, as dissatisfaction and discontent were disseminated throughout the country—the confederacy of the Lakes; perhaps the confederacy of New England, or of the Middle States. Ah, sir, the veil which covers those sad and disastrous events that lie beyond it is too thick to be penetrated or lifted by any mortal eye or hand.

Mr. President, I am directly opposed to any purpose of secession or separation. I am for staying within the Union, and defying any portion of this confederacy to expel me or drive me out of the Union. I am for staying within the Union and fighting for my rights, if necessary, with the sword, within the bounds and under the safeguard of the Union. I am for vindicating those rights, not by being driven out of the Union harshly and unceremoniously by any portion of this confederacy. Here I am within it, and here I mean to stand and die, as far as my individual wishes or purposes can go—within it to protect my property and defend myself, defying all the power on earth to expel or drive me from the situation in which I am placed. And would there not be more safety in fighting within the Union than out of it? Suppose our rights to be violated, suppose wrong to be done to you, aggressions to be perpetrated upon you, can you not better vindicate them—if you have occasion to resort to the last necessity, the sword, for a restoration of those rights—within, and with the sympathies of a large portion of the population of the Union, than when a large portion of the population have sympathies adverse to your own? You can vindicate your rights within the Union better than if expelled from the Union, and driven from it without ceremony and without authority.

Sir, I have said that I thought there was no right on the part of one or more States to secede from the Union. I think so. The Constitution of the United States was made not merely for the generation that then existed, but for posterity—unlimited, undefined, endless, perpetual posterity. And every State that then came into the Union, and every State that has since come into the Union, came into it binding itself, by indissoluble bands, to remain within the Union itself, and to remain within it by its posterity forever. Like another of the sacred connections in private life, it is a marriage which no human authority can dissolve or divorce the parties from. And if I may be allowed to refer to some examples in private life, let me say to the North and the South, what husband and wife say to each other: We have mutual faults; neither of us is perfect; nothing in the form of humanity is perfect; let us, then, be kind to each other—forbearing, forgiving each other's faults—and, above all, let us live in happiness and peace together.

Mr. President, I have said, what I solemnly believe, that dissolution of the Union and war are identical and inevitable; that they are convertible terms; and such a war as it would be following a dissolution of the Union! Sir, we may search the pages of history, and none so ferocious, so bloody, so implacable, so exterminating—not even the wars of Greece, including those of the Commoners of England and the revolutions of France—none, none of them all would rage with such violence, or be characterized with such bloodshed and enormities, as would the war which must succeed, if that event ever happens, the dissolution of the Union. And what would be its termination? Standing armies and navies, to an extent stretching the revenue of each portion of the dissevered members, would take place. An exterminating war would follow—not, sir, a war of two or three years' duration, but a war of interminable duration—and exterminating wars would ensue until, after the struggles and exhaustion of both parties, some Philip or Alexander, some

Cæsar or Napoleon, would arise and cut the Gordian knot, solve the problem of the capacity of man for self-government, and crush the liberties of both the severed portions of this common empire. Can you doubt it?

Look at all history—consult her pages, ancient or modern—look at human nature; look at the contest in which you would be engaged in the supposition of war following upon the dissolution of the Union, such as I have suggested; and I ask you if it is possible for you to doubt that the final disposition of the whole would be some despot treading down the liberties of the people—the final result would be the extinction of this last and glorious light which is leading all mankind, who are gazing upon it, in the hope and anxious expectation that the liberty that prevails here will sooner or later be diffused throughout the whole of the civilized world. Sir, can you lightly contemplate these consequences? Can you yield yourself to the tyranny of passion, amid dangers which I have depicted in colors far too tame, of what the result would be if that direful event to which I have referred should ever occur? Sir, I implore gentlemen, I adjure them, whether from the South or the North, by all that they hold dear in this world—by all their love of liberty—by all their veneration for their ancestors—by all their regard for posterity—by all their gratitude to Him who has bestowed on them such unnumbered and countless blessings—by all the duties which they owe to mankind—and by all the duties which they owe to themselves, to pause, solemnly to pause, at the edge of the precipice, before the fearful and dangerous leap is taken into the yawning abyss below, from which none who have ever taken it shall return in safety.

Finally, Mr. President, and in conclusion, I implore, as the best blessing which Heaven can bestow upon me, upon earth, that if the direful event of the dissolution of this Union is to happen, I shall not survive to behold the sad and heartrending spectacle.

Claypoole, James, settler; born in England in 1634; a Quaker, and a close friend of William Penn; was a witness of the signing of the Charter of Privileges granted to the settlers in 1682; came with his family to Pennsylvania in 1683, and held important offices.

Clayton, John Middleton, jurist; born in Dagsboro, Sussex co., Del., July 24, 1796; graduated at Yale College in 1815, and at the famous Litchfield Law School; began practice in 1818; and, after serving in the State legislature, and as Secretary of State, was elected to the United States Senate in 1829 and 1835. In 1837 he resigned to become chief-justice of Delaware; from 1845 till 1849 was again in the United States Senate; in the latter year became Secretary of State under President Taylor; and from 1851 till his death was again in the United States Senate. It was during his service as Secretary of State that he negotiated with the British government what has since become known as the Clayton-Bulwer Treaty (*q. v.*). He died in Dover, Del., Nov. 9, 1856.

Clayton, Powell, diplomatist; born in Bethel, Pa., Aug. 7, 1833; received an academical education; removed to Kansas. At the beginning of the Civil War he joined the Union army; in May, 1863, he scattered a band of guerillas and captured Confederate stores at White River, Ark.; figured in other important actions; and was promoted brigadier-general in August, 1864. After the war he removed to Arkansas, where he was elected governor in 1868. He was a United States Senator in 1871–77; minister to Mexico in 1897; raised to rank of ambassador in 1899–1905.

Clayton-Bulwer Treaty, was negotiated in April, 1850, by Secretary of State Clayton, on the part of the United States, and Sir William Henry Bulwer, on the part of Great Britain, for the purpose of preventing dissensions on the subject of proposed canals and railways across the American isthmus. It has special reference to the Nicaragua route, which at that time had been proposed for a canal; but as it declared that its purpose was "not only to accomplish a particular object, but to establish a general principle," it must be taken to apply to all routes. By this treaty the two governments jointly declared that "neither the one nor the other will ever obtain or maintain for itself exclusive control over the projected ship canal"; that "neither will ever erect or maintain fortifications commanding the same or in the vicinity thereof," nor "fortify, or colonize, or assume any dominion over any part of Central America." Further, the treaty pledged that in case of war between Great Britain and the United States all vessels of both countries should, in going through the canal, be exempt from detention and capture. Further, the contracting parties engaged to protect and guarantee the neutrality of the canal, and to invite other states to do likewise, "to the end that all states may share in the honor or advantage" of assisting in so important a work. Now, previous to the adoption of this treaty Great Britain had held possessions in Central America. She had owned Balize, or British Honduras, since 1783, and had later acquired a protectorate over the Mosquito coast and over the Bay Islands, a group near Honduras. The question, therefore, arose whether by the pledge not to occupy any part of Central America in the future she was bound to surrender possessions held in the present. There was considerable debate over the matter for some years, and it seemed at one time doubtful whether an understanding satisfactory to both sides could be reached. However, on Great Britain's giving up the Bay Islands and signing a treaty with Nicaragua, yielding all claims on the Mosquito coast, the American Secretary of State, in 1860, in behalf of the government, consented to the continued occupation of Balize, and President Buchanan, in his next message, declared that all disputes under the Clayton-Bulwer treaty "had been satisfactorily adjusted."

This treaty then was accepted as settled and binding on both parties until November, 1881, when Mr. Blaine wrote to Mr. Lowell, the American minister to Great Britain, urging the abrogation of the treaty on the ground that it was formed thirty years before under circumstances that no longer existed; that the development of the Pacific coast had enormously increased the interest of the United States in the canal, and that the well-being of this country demanded a modification of the treaty. To this letter Lord Granville made reply in January, stating Great Britain's reasons for regarding the treaty as still in force; but as meanwhile Mr. Blaine had left the State Department there was no further diplomatic discussion on the subject until the publication of a proposed treaty with Nicaragua. This treaty was in direct violation of the Clayton-Bulwer treaty, for its object was to provide for the construction of a canal across Central America, at the expense of the United States, and to be controlled when completed by this country. The treaty was not accepted by Congress, so that the question of the abrogation of the Clayton-Bulwer treaty remained open.

The war between the United States and Spain created a new interest in the subject of an interoceanic canal as a new necessity was developed for having a speedy means of sending vessels from one ocean to the other. (See CLARK, CHARLES EDGAR). A new bill was introduced into Congress for the construction of a canal on the Nicaragua route, and this, after various vicissitudes and being amended materially, was adopted in the Senate on Jan. 21, 1899, by a vote of forty-eight to six. The chief provisions of this bill were: the issue of 1,000,000 shares of stock at $100 each, the United States to take 945,000 shares; the canal to be completed in six years; to be ample to accommodate the largest sea-vessels; and to cost not over $115,000,000. In case of failure in negotiating with Nicaragua or Costa Rica for the route the President was empowered to negotiate for another one. The bill guaranteed the neutrality of the canal. The most important feature of the bill in the present connection was the authority given to the President to open negotiations with the British government for the abrogation of the Clayton-Bulwer treaty. Under the last provision a convention was signed in February, 1900, by Secretary Hay, on the part of the United States, and by Lord Pauncefote on the part of Great Britain, in which the Clayton-Bulwer compact for the joint control of any canal which might be built across the isthmus was annulled, and the United States given an exclusive, unconditional right to build and manage such a water-way. The convention committed both nations to a declaration guaranteeing the neutrality of such a canal, and the United States was pledged to refrain from fortifying its approaches or entrances, and otherwise restricting open access to it on the part of the world's commerce. On Dec. 20, 1900, the United States Senate ratified this convention by a vote of 55 to 18, modifying it in three essential points, and a certified copy of the amended treaty was delivered to Lord Pauncefote for transmission to his government.

The British government did not see its way clear to accept the Senate amendment, but negotiations were resumed, and a new treaty was signed Nov. 16 (ratified by the Senate Dec. 16, 1902), substantially in accordance with the views of the United States. See BULWER, WILLIAM HENRY LYTTON EARLE, etc.

The United States of America and his Majesty, Edward the VII. of the United Kingdom of Great Britain and Ireland and of the British dominions beyond the seas, King, and Emperor of India, being desirous to facilitate the construction of a ship-canal to connect the Atlantic and Pacific oceans, by whatever route may be considered expedient, and to that end to remove any objection which may arise out of the convention of the 19th of April, 1850, commonly called the Clayton-Bulwer treaty, to the construction of such canal under the auspices of the government of the United States without impairing the "general principle" of neutralization established in article viii. of that convention, have for that purpose appointed as their plenipotentiaries: The President of the United States, John Hay, Secretary of State of the United States of America, and his Majesty, Edward the VII. of the United Kingdom of Great Britain and Ireland and of the British dominions beyond the seas, King, and Emperor of India, the Right Hon. Lord Pauncefote, G.C.B., G.C.M.G., his Majesty's ambassador extraordinary and plenipotentiary to the United States; who, having communicated to each other their full powers, which were found to be in due and proper form, have agreed upon the following articles:

Article I.—The high contracting parties agree that the present treaty shall supersede the aforementioned convention of the 19th April, 1850.

Article II.—It is agreed that the canal may be constructed under the auspices of the government of the United States, either directly at its own cost, or by gift or loan of money to individuals or corporations, or through subscription to or purchase of stock or shares, and that, subject to the provisions of the present treaty, the said government shall have and enjoy all the rights incident to such construction, as well as the exclusive right of providing for the regulation and management of the canal.

Article III.—The United States adopts as the basis of the neutralization of such ship-canal the following rules, substantially as embodied in the convention of Constantinople, signed the 28th October, 1888, for the free navigation of the Suez Canal, that is to say:

1. The canal shall be free and open to the vessels of commerce and of war of all nations observing these rules, on terms of entire equality, so that there shall be no discrimination against any such nation or its citizens or subjects, in respect of the conditions or charges of traffic or otherwise. Such conditions and charges of traffic shall be just and equitable.

2. The canal shall never be blockaded, nor shall any right of war be exercised nor any act of hostility be committed within it. The United States, however, shall be at liberty to maintain such military police along the canal as may be necessary to protect it against lawlessness and disorder.

3. Vessels of war of a belligerent shall not revictual nor take any stores in the canal except so far as may be strictly necessary, and the transit of such vessels through the canal shall be effected with the least possible delay in accordance with the regulations in force, and with only such intermission as may result from the necessities of the service. Prizes shall be in all respects subject to the same rules as vessels of war of the belligerents.

4. No belligerent shall embark or disembark troops, munitions of war, or warlike materials in the canal except in case of accidental hinderance of the transit, and in such case the transit shall be resumed with all possible despatch.

5. The provisions of this article shall

apply to waters adjacent to the canal, within three marine miles of either end. Vessels of war of a belligerent shall not remain in such waters longer than twenty-four hours at any one time, except in case of distress, and in such case shall depart as soon as possible, but a vessel of war of one belligerent shall not depart within twenty-four hours from the departure of a vessel of war of the other belligerent.

6. The plant, establishments, buildings, and all works necessary to the construction, maintenance, and operation of the canal shall be deemed to be parts thereof for the purposes of this treaty, and in time of war, as in time of peace, shall enjoy complete immunity from attack or injury by belligerents, and from acts calculated to impair their usefulness as part of the canal.

Article IV.—It is agreed that no change of territorial sovereignty or of international relations of the country or countries traversed by the before-mentioned canal shall affect the general principle of neutralization or the obligation of the high contracting parties under the present treaty.

Article V.—The present treaty shall be ratified by the President of the United States by and with the advice and consent of the Senate thereof, and by his Britannic Majesty; and the ratifications shall be exchanged at Washington or at London at the earliest possible time within six months from the date hereof.

In faith whereof the respective plenipotentiaries have signed this treaty and hereunto affixed their seals. Done in duplicate at Washington the 18th day of November in the year of our Lord one thousand nine hundred and one.

John Hay (Seal).
Pauncefote (Seal).

Clearing-houses, institutions established in the United States about 1853, for the convenience and economy of banking institutions in large cities. The system originated in London. By it the banks of a city become, in certain operations, as an individual in work; for it dispenses with the individual clerical labor of each bank associated, in the matter of the exchange of checks and drafts and bills coming in from abroad. Formerly each bank employed a man to go around every day and collect all checks and drafts drawn upon it by other banks in the city. Now, at the clearing-house, a messenger and a clerk from each bank appear every morning, each clerk taking a seat at the desk of his designated bank, arranged in the form of a hollow ellipse. Each messenger brings with him from his bank a sealed package for every other bank, properly marked with the amount enclosed, containing all the checks or drafts on each bank. The messengers take their places near the desks of their respective banks, with tabular statements of the amount sent to each bank and the aggregates. These are exhibited to the respective clerks and noted by them on blank forms. At a prescribed hour the manager of the clearing-house calls to order and gives the word for proceeding, when all the messengers move forward from left to right of the desks, handing in to them the packages addressed to their respective banks, and taking receipts for them on their statements. These clerks make a mutual exchange of all claims, and the balances, if any, are struck, each bank paying in cash the amount of such balance. This operation occupies about one hour. The balances due to the several banks are paid into the clearing-house within another hour.

The extent of the system and the enormous saving of time through its operations are clearly detailed in the report of the comptroller of the currency. In 1910 there were 137 clearing-houses in the United States, and in the year ending Sept. 30 the aggregate of exchanges was $169,025,172,600, as compared with 84, with aggregate exchanges of $84,546,685,-444, in the corresponding period of 1900. The principal clearing-houses, with amount of exchanges in 1910, were: New York, $102,553,959,100; Chicago, $14,031,258,-900; Boston, $8,414,461,900; Philadelphia, $7,760,336,900; St. Louis, $3,704,263,700; Pittsburg, $2,604,069,500; and San Francisco, $2,268,678,600.

Cleaveland, Moses, pioneer; born in Canterbury, Conn., Jan. 29, 1754; graduated at Yale College in 1777; admitted to the bar; made a brigadier-general in 1796; and the same year was selected by a land company, of which he was a shareholder, to survey the tract which had been purchased in northeastern Ohio. He set out with fifty emigrants from Schenectady, N. Y.; reached the mouth of the Cuyahoga on July 22; and finding it a favorable site for a town decided to settle there. His employers called the place Cleaveland in his honor. When the first newspaper, the *Cleveland Advertiser*, was established the head-line was found to be too long for the form and the editor cut out the letter "a," which revision was accepted by the public. General Cleaveland died in Canterbury, Conn., Nov. 16, 1806.

Cleburne, Patrick Ronayne, military officer; born in County Cork, Ireland, March 17, 1828; came to the United States and settled at Helena, Ark., where he later practised law. When the Civil War broke out he entered the Confederate army; in March, 1861, planned the capture of the United States arsenal in Arkansas; in 1862 was promoted brigadier-general; took part in many important engagements in the war, and in recognition of his defence of Ringgold Gap received the thanks of the Confederate Congress. He originated the Order of the Southern Cross, and was known as "the Stonewall of the West." He was killed in the battle of Franklin, Tenn., Nov. 30, 1864.

Clem, John L., military officer; born in Newark, O., Aug. 13, 1851. In May, 1861, he tried to enlist as a drummer-boy in the 3d Ohio Volunteers, but was rejected on account of his size and age. Subsequently he accompanied the 22d Michigan Volunteers to the field, and in the summer of 1862 was regularly enlisted as a drummer in that regiment. He displayed a fearless spirit in the battle of Shiloh, where his drum was destroyed by a piece of shell. At the battle of Chickamauga he served as a marker, carried a musket instead of a drum, and especially distinguished himself. He had been in the thickest of the fight, and three bullets had passed through his hat, when, separated from his companions, he was seen running, with a musket in his hand, by a mounted Confederate colonel, who called out, "Stop! you little Yankee devil!" The boy halted and brought his musket to an order, when the colonel rode up to make him a prisoner. With a swift movement young Clem brought his gun up and fired, killing the colonel instantly. He escaped, and for this exploit on the battle-field he was made a sergeant and placed on the Roll of Honor. In 1871 he was appointed a second lieutenant in the army; in 1875 was graduated at the Artillery School; in 1903 became colonel and assistant quartermaster-general.

JOHN L. CLEM.
(*From a print published in* 1862.)

Clemens, Jeremiah, statesman; born in Huntsville, Ala., Dec. 28, 1814; graduated at the Alabama University in 1833; took a company of riflemen to Texas in 1842; United States Senator, 1849–53; opposed secession, but accepted office under the Confederacy. He wrote several historical works. He died in Huntsville, Ala., May 21, 1865.

Clemens, Samuel Langhorne (pen-name, Mark Twain), author; born in Florida, Mo., Nov. 20, 1835; educated at Hannibal, Mo.; learned the printer's trade, served as a Mississippi river pilot, and became Territorial secretary of Nevada. He spent several years in mining and newspaper work. In 1884 he established the publishing house of C. L. Webster &

Co. in New York. The failure of this firm, after it had published General Grant's *Personal Memoirs* and paid over $250,000 to his widow, involved Mr. Clemens in heavy losses, but by 1900 he had paid off all obligations by the proceeds of his books and lectures. He travelled extensively in Europe, Australia, and other places. His books include *The Jumping Frog; The Innocents Abroad; Roughing It; Adventures of Tom Sawyer; The Adventures of Huckleberry Finn; The Prince and the Pauper; A Tramp Abroad; Life on the Mississippi; A Yankee at King Arthur's Court; Tom Sawyer Abroad; Pudd'nhead Wilson; Joan of Arc; The American Claimant; Following the Equator; Christian Science; Eve's Diary; Captain Stormfield's Visit to Heaven; Autobiography of Mark Twain,* etc. He died in Redding, Conn., April 21, 1910.

SAMUEL LANGHORNE CLEMENS.

Cleopatra's Needle. See GORRINGE, HENRY HONEYCHURCH.

CLEVELAND

Cleveland, city, port of entry (Cuyahoga), and county-seat of Cuyahoga county, Ohio; first city in the State and sixth in the United States in populotion, according to the Federal census of 1910; popularly known as the "Forest City." Pop. (1890), 261,353; (1900) 381,768; (1910) 560,663.

Location, Area, etc.—It is on the southeast shore of Lake Erie, on both sides of the mouth of the Cuyahoga River, at the lake terminus of the Ohio Canal, and on several lines of trunk and other great railroads; 244 miles northeast of Cincinnati; area, forty-one square miles. It has an excellent harbor, commodious, safe, and of sufficient depth to accommodate the largest ships afloat, formed by enormous breakwaters constructed by the national government. In addition to its lake frontage, the irregular course of the Cuyahoga River within its limits affords it more than twenty miles of docking facilities.

The city is considered the most beautiful one on the Great Lakes. Built on a bluff about one hundred feet above the lake, it is so embowered with trees that but little can be seen from the water excepting its church spires. It is laid out with much taste and regularity, its wide streets forming attractive squares and displaying an abundance of shade trees, principally elms. The surface is a gravelly plateau cut by the valley of the river, which is spanned by a great stone viaduct over 3,000 feet long, a remarkable piece of engineering work, completed in 1878 at a cost of $2,500,000, and by four minor viaducts, all of which form a belt elevated roadway connecting the several topographical divisions of the city.

The most important business thoroughfares are Superior, Ontario, Water, Bank, Seneca, St. Clair, Merwin, and River streets and a part of Euclid Avenue, on the east side, and Detroit, Pearl, and Lorain streets on the west side. The wholesale trade is largely on Merwin and River streets, on the eastern plateau; the retail trade on Superior, Ontario, Cedar, Central, Woodland, Broadway, Pearl, Lorain and Detroit streets; and the ore, coal, and lumber trades in the commodious slips along the winding river.

Public Interests.—A new city charter, which went into effect in April, 1891, modified the forms of municipal and school government after the federal plan. In 1902 the legislature provided a new code for the cities of the State, the former scheme of government having been declared unconstitutional, and under this the city is divided into twenty-six wards, with one councilman from each, and six more from the city at large.

Cleveland has over 660 miles of streets, of which about two-thirds are paved; 530 miles of sewers; a police department of 620 men; a fire department of 540 men; and a water-works system owned by the city, having 770 miles of mains, and an average daily consumption of 66,000,000 gallons, and costing $12,000,000. The valuation of property assessed for taxation for 1909 was $269,655,535 (assessment about 40 per cent. of actual value); tax rate fixed for 1910, $34.80 per $1,000. The total debt on Oct. 2, 1910 (including a water debt of $5,938,300) was $30,014,660, and sinking funds held $1,793,283, making the net debt $28,221,377. The annual cost of maintaining the city government is about $6,000,000. In the calendar year 1910 its receipts included 12,118,004 bushels of grain, 775,612 barrels of flour, 6,356,762 long tons of iron ore, 9,871 long tons of pig iron, 2,936 short tons of copper, and 77,557 m. feet of lumber; and its shipments, 2,685,406 bushels of grain, 64,951 barrels of flour, 7,660 long tons of pig iron, 217,087 short tons of iron manufactures, and 2,952,855 short tons of soft coal.

The city has an extensive trade by rail and water, particularly in ore, coal, grain, and lumber. Its foreign commercial interests are almost wholly with Canada.

Manufactures.—According to the tentative Federal census for 1909, the city had 2,148 manufacturing and industrial establishments operated under the factory-system classification (excluding small shops and hand trades), which employed $227,397,000 capital and 84,728 wage-earners; paid $63,646,000 for salaries and wages; $26,917,000 for miscellaneous expenses, and $153,801,000 for materials used in manufacturing; and had aggregate products valued at $271,961,000. The principal industries, in the order of value of output, were: Iron and steel, in steel works and rolling-mills; foundry and machine-shop products; slaughtering and meat-packing, wholesale; women's clothing; iron and steel, in blast furnaces; automobiles—all others under $4,000,000.

Banking.—The report of the Comptroller of the Currency for the banking year ending Sept. 1, 1910, credited Cleveland with seven national banks, having an aggregate capital of $9,350,000; surplus, $4,050,000; circulation, $5,721,795; individual deposits, $38,161,655; loans and discounts, $56,419,544; specie, $6,455,410; and total resources, $96,232,317. The clearing-house here ranked twelfth among those of the country in the volume of annual exchanges. These, in the year ending Sept. 30, 1910, aggregated $992,803,500, an increase in a year of $167,557,800. In 1900 there were fifteen national banks, with capital, $10,400,000; circulation, $3,103,140; deposits, $32,873,320; and resources, $68,200,572; and the clearing-house exchanges were $417,838,383, an increase in a year of $41,463,103.

Schools and Colleges.—Cleveland is credited with having built in 1846 the first public high school in the United States. It has over 75,000 pupils in average daily attendance in the public schools, and over 27,000 in private and parochial schools. Public-school teachers number about 2,000; and the annual cost of maintaining the public schools is about $3,000,000. There are the Central, East, Lincoln, South, and West high schools; Hathaway Brown School for Girls, Laurel Institute, Mittleberger School for Girls, University School, and Ursuline Academy; Jewish Orphan Asylum and Working Home for Young Women, both for manual and industrial training; the Cleveland Normal Training School; and training schools for nurses connected with the Cleveland City, Cleveland General, Huron Street, Lakeside, and St. Vincent's charity hospitals.

The institutions for higher education comprise the Western Reserve University (non-sectarian), opened in 1826, and St. Ignatius College (Roman Catholic), opened in 1886. The former is an outgrowth of Adelbert College, founded at Hudson under the name of the Western Reserve College, and removed to Cleveland in 1882, when its name was changed as at present, under conditions imposed by Amasa Stone, who gave it $500,000. The Case School of Applied Science is a technical school of high and wide repute, established in 1881, on an endowment of $1,250,000 by the late Leonard Case. Professional instruction is given in theology at St. Mary's Theological Seminary (Roman

Catholic), opened in 1848; in law, at the Law School of Baldwin University and at Western Reserve University; in medicine, at the Cleveland College of Physicians and Surgeons (Ohio Wesleyan University) and the Medical College of Western Reserve University; in pharmacy, at the Cleveland School of Pharmacy; and in dentistry, at the Dental College of Western Reserve University.

Churches.—Cleveland is the seat of a Protestant Episcopal and a Roman Catholic bishop. According to a special census report on *Religious Bodies* (1910), the city had 314 religious organizations, 146,338 communicants or members (including 76,174 Protestants and 66,432 Roman Catholics), 332 church edifices, 27 halls used for religious purposes, church property of 279 organizations valued at $10,877,070, and 321 Sunday schools, with 5,344 officers and teachers and 67,479 scholars. Of the Protestant bodies, the Lutheran and Methodist Episcopal Churches had the largest membership. The Roman Catholic Cathedral is a large and handsome building. The Episcopal churches include Trinity, in the Gothic style of architecture, and St. Paul's, on Case and Euclid avenues; the Presbyterian, Woodland Avenue, Old Stone, First, Second, Third, and Calvary; the Methodist, the First; the Congregational, the First and Plymouth; and the Baptist, the Euclid Avenue. The Young Men's Christian Association and the Young Women's Christian Association are large and influential organizations, handsomely supported, and carrying on a number of excellent works.

Charities.—The public charities comprise the Middle House or Home for the Aged Poor, the City, Children's, and Detention hospitals (the last a tuberculosis sanitarium), Home for the Insane, House of Correction, Boys' Home, and Bureau of Outdoor Relief. The Charity Hospital was established partly by the city and partly by private subscriptions, and is in charge of the Sisters of Charity. On the lake shore is an extensive group of buildings comprising the United States Marine Hospital. Other institutions of this character have already been mentioned. The Roman Catholic Church supports several hospitals, a House of the Good Shepherd, a House of Maternity, separate male and female orphan asylums, and other benevolent institutions. The Goodrich House is a model settlement centre, with an $80,000 building. The various charitable institutions represent a property value of over $3,500,000.

Notable Buildings.—The United States Government Building, fronting on Monumental Park, accommodates the customhouse, post-office, and federal courts. The City Hall, on Superior Street, is a six-story building, measuring 200 by 100 feet on the ground; Case Hall, belonging to the Case Library, is a beautiful structure near Monumental Park. The Euclid Avenue Opera House, Lyceum, Cleveland, Star, Bohemian, and German theatres are the principal places for dramatic entertainments. The water-works near the lake, whence pure water is taken by tunnels; the reservoirs; the great viaduct; the breakwater, just west of the river's mouth, which encloses 180 acres of water surface, and cost $1,200,000; and the Union Railroad Station, with its cluster of keystone portraits and symbolical designs, are all deserving of mention and a visit.

Park System.—Cleveland has a system of public parks and boulevards of which it is justly proud, acquired partly by purchase under the direction of the Park Commission and partly by gift of citizens. The work of enlarging (where possible), connecting, and beautifying these pleasure-grounds, and the acquisition of others, is still in progress. The most conspicuous park, by reason of its location, is the Monumental, at the intersection of Ontario and Superior streets, which divide its area of ten acres into four smaller squares. It contains a monument to the soldiers of Cuyahoga county, a bronze statue of Moses Cleaveland, the founder of the city, a handsome fountain, and a pool and cascade.

Other parks are the Gordon; Wade, containing a zoological collection, trout-pond, and a statue to Commodore Perry; Rockefeller, where public entertainments are given in season to immense gatherings; Shaker Heights, with the Ambler Parkway and the Giddings and Doan brooks; Woodland Hills, largely devoted to athletic games; Garfield; Lake View, with baseball diamonds, athletic-grounds, and recreation-fields; and Clinton, Sterling, Washington, Lincoln, Fairview (children's summer play-grounds in last three), Franklin, Edgewater, and Brookside.

History.—According to Professor Parkman, the Indian chief, Pontiac, met Major Rogers and his band of Rangers at the mouth of the Cuyahoga River, the site of Cleveland, on Nov. 7, 1760. No practical attempt at settlement seems to have been made until Sept. 16, 1796, when GENERAL MOSES CLEAVELAND (*q. v.*) began surveying. The first white child in Cuyahoga county was born to Mr. and Mrs. Stiles in 1797, and in the same year a second surveying party arrived, and Edward Paine opened a general store.

The first permanent frame house was built in 1802. The ship-building industry was started in 1808; Cleveland became the county-seat in 1809; the Ohio Canal was opened to Akron in 1827; and Cleveland was incorporated as a city March 5, 1836.

On July 22, 1896, the city celebrated the centennial of its settlement; in 1899 it was the scene of serious rioting, following a strike of street-railway operatives; and on Sept. 1, 1901, it was visited by a disastrous flood that spent its rage on the fashionable section. In the fourteen years ending with 1905, the city had three different forms of government; first, that of boards, illegally authorized by the legislature; second, that based on the federal plan, provided in 1891, and subsequently declared unconstitutional; and third, that by the new municipal code, enacted in 1902.

Cleveland, BENJAMIN, military officer, born in Prince William county, Va., May 26, 1738; removed to North Carolina in 1769; entered the American army in 1775; led a company in the campaign of Rutherford against the Cherokee Indians in 1776; greatly distinguished himself at KING'S MOUNTAIN (*q. v.*); and later settled in South Carolina, where he became a judge. He died in October, 1806.

Cleveland, CYNTHIA ELOISE; born in Canton, N. Y., Aug. 13, 1845; admitted to practise law in Dakota in 1883; author of several novels of Washington political life, and of United States army life; political speaker, etc.

Cleveland, FREDERICK ALBERT, economist; born in Sterling, Ill., March 17, 1865; graduated at De Pauw University in 1891; instructor in University of Chicago and University of Pennsylvania; director of the Bureau of Municipal Research, New York City, from 1907; author of *Growth of Democracy in the United States; Railroad Promotion and Capitalization; Chapters in Municipal Administration and Accounting,* etc.

CLEVELAND, GROVER

Cleveland, GROVER, twenty-second and twenty-fourth President of the United States, from 1885 to 1889, and from 1893 to 1897; Democrat; born in Caldwell, Essex county, N. J., March 18, 1837. After some experience as a clerk and some labor on the compilation of the *American Herd Book,* he became a bank clerk in Buffalo, and was admitted to the bar in 1859. From 1863 to 1865 he was assistant district-attorney, and in 1870 he was elected sheriff of Erie county and served three years. Elected mayor of Buffalo in 1881, he attracted during the first few months of his term more than local notice, and was the Democratic candidate for governor of New York in 1882. One of the successful nominees in this "tidal wave" Democratic year, Mr. Cleveland received the phenomenal majority of 192,000, and entered office in January, 1883. His administration of affairs at Albany secured the presentation of his name to the Democratic National Convention in 1884. He was nominated; and elected, after a close and exciting struggle, over James G. Blaine, and was inaugurated March 4, 1885 (see CABINET, PRESIDENT'S). President Cleveland, in his famous message to Congress on the surplus and the tariff in December, 1887, forced the fighting on the revenue-reform issue. He was the candidate of his party in 1888, but was defeated by Benjamin Harrison, and retired in 1889. He settled in New York, and resumed the practice of law. In 1892 he received for the third time the Democratic nomination. In the election he received 277 electoral and 5,556,533 popular votes, while Harrison (renominated) had 145 electoral and 5,175,577 popular votes. He was inaugurated March 4, 1893. He took up the practice of law again in 1897 at Princeton, N. J. For several years thereafter he delivered two lectures annually at Princeton University. Subsequently he became a trustee of the Equitable Life Assurance Society, and from 1907 till his death, in Princeton, N. J., June 24, 1908, he was chairman and counsel of the Association of Life Insurance Presidents.

Tariff Message of 1887.—Towards the close of 1887 he deemed the condition of the national finances so important as to justify a special expression of his views thereon, and accordingly he devoted his entire message of Dec. 6 to a consideration of the subject. The following is the text:

WASHINGTON, *Dec. 6, 1887.*

To the Congress of the United States,—You are confronted at the threshold of your legislative duties with a condition of the national finances which imperatively demands immediate and careful consideration.

The amount of money annually exacted, through the operation of present laws, from the industries and necessities of the people largely exceeds the sum necessary to meet the expenses of the government.

When we consider that the theory of our institutions guarantees to every citizen the full enjoyment of all the fruits of his industry and enterprise, with only such deduction as may be his share towards the careful and economical maintenance of the government which protects him, it is plain that the exaction of more than this is indefensible extortion and a culpable betrayal of American fairness and justice. This wrong inflicted upon those who bear the burden of national taxation, like other wrongs, multiplies a brood of evil consequences. The public Treasury, which should only exist as a conduit conveying the people's tribute to its legitimate objects of expenditure, becomes a hoarding-place for money needlessly withdrawn from trade and the people's use, thus crippling our national energies, suspending our country's development, preventing investment in productive enterprise, threatening financial disturbance, and inviting schemes of public plunder.

This condition of our Treasury is not altogether new, and it has more than once of late been submitted to the people's representatives in the Congress, who alone can apply a remedy. And yet the situation still continues, with aggravated incidents, more than ever presaging financial convulsion and widespread disaster.

It will not do to neglect this situation because its dangers are not now palpably imminent and apparent. They exist none the less certainly, and await the unforeseen and unexpected occasion, when suddenly they will be precipitated upon us.

On June 30, 1885, the excess of revenues over public expenditures, after complying with the annual requirement of the Sinking-fund Act, was $17,859,735.84; during the year ended June 30, 1886, such excess amounted to $49,405,545.20; and during the year ended June 30, 1887, it reached the sum of $55,567,849.54.

The annual contributions to the sinking-fund during the three years above specified, amounting in the aggregate to $138,058,320.94, and deducted from the surplus as stated, were made by calling in for that purpose outstanding 3 per cent. bonds of the government. During the six months prior to June 30, 1887, the surplus revenue had grown so large by repeated accumulations, and it was feared the withdrawal of this great sum of money needed by the people would so affect the business of the country that the sum of $79,864,100 of such surplus was applied to the payment of the principal and interest of the 3 per cent. bonds still outstanding, and which were then payable at the option of the government. The precarious condition of financial affairs among the people still needing relief, immediately after June 30, 1887, the remainder of the 3 per cent. bonds then outstanding, amounting with principal and interest to the sum of $18,877,500, were called in and applied to the sinking-fund contribution for the current fiscal year. Notwithstanding these operations of the Treasury Department, representations of distress in business circles not only continued, but increased, and absolute peril seemed at hand. In these circumstances the contribution to the sinking-fund for the current fiscal year was at once completed by the expenditure of $27,684,283.55 in the purchase of government bonds not yet due, bearing 4 and 4½ per cent. interest, the premium paid thereon averaging about 24 per cent. for the former and 8 per cent. for the latter. In addition to this, the interest accruing during the current year upon the outstanding bonded indebtedness of the government was to some extent anticipated, and banks selected as depositaries of public money were permitted to somewhat increase their deposits.

While the expedients thus employed to release to the people the money lying idle in the Treasury served to avert immediate danger, our surplus revenues have continued to accumulate, the excess for the present year amounting on Dec. 1 to $55,258,701.19, and estimated to reach the sum of $113,000,000 on June 30 next, at which date it is expected that this sum, added to prior accumulations, will swell the surplus in the Treasury to $140,000,000.

There seems to be no assurance that, with such a withdrawal from use of the people's circulating medium, our business community may not in the near future be subjected to the same distress which was quite lately produced from the same cause. And while the functions of our national Treasury should be few and simple, and while its best condition would be reached, I believe, by its entire disconnection with private business interests, yet when, by a perversion of its purposes, it idly holds money uselessly subtracted from the channels of trade, there seems to be reason for the claim that some legitimate means should be devised by the government to restore, in an emergency, without waste or extravagance, such money to its place among the people.

If such an emergency arises, there now exists no clear and undoubted executive power of relief. Heretofore the redemption of 3 per cent. bonds, which were payable at the option of the government, has afforded a means for the disbursement of the excess of our revenues; but these bonds have all been retired, and there are no bonds outstanding the payment of which we have a right to insist upon. The contribution to the sinking-fund which furnishes the occasion for expenditure in the purchase of bonds has been already made for the current year, so that there is no outlet in that direction.

In the present state of legislation the only pretence of any existing executive power to restore at this time any part of our surplus revenues to the people by its expenditure consists in the supposition that the Secretary of the Treasury may enter the market and purchase the bonds of the government not yet due, at a rate of premium to be agreed upon. The only provision of law from which such a power could be derived is found in an appropriation bill passed a number of years ago, and it is subject to the suspicion that it was intended as temporary and limited in its application, instead of conferring a continuing discretion and authority. No condition ought to exist which would justify the grant of power to a single official, upon his judgment of its necessity, to withhold from or release to the business of the people, in an unusual manner, money held in the Treasury, and thus affect at his will the financial situation of the country; and, if it is deemed wise to lodge in the Secretary of the Treasury the authority in the present juncture to purchase bonds, it should be plainly vested, and provided, as far as possible, with such checks and limitations as will define this official's right and discretion and at the same time relieve him from undue responsibility.

In considering the question of purchasing bonds as a means of restoring to circulation the surplus money accumulating in the Treasury, it should be borne in mind that premiums must of course be paid upon such purchase, that there may be a large part of these bonds held as investments which cannot be purchased at any price, and that combinations among holders who are willing to sell may reasonably enhance the cost of such bonds to the government.

It has been suggested that the present bonded debt might be refunded at a less rate of interest, and the difference between the old and new security paid in cash, thus finding use for the surplus in the Treasury. The success of this plan, it is apparent, must depend upon the volition of the holders of the present bonds; and it is not entirely certain that the inducement which must be offered them would result in more financial benefit to the government than the purchase of bonds, while the latter proposition would reduce the principal of the debt by actual payment instead of extending it.

The proposition to deposit the money held by the government in banks throughout the country for use by the people is, it seems to me, exceedingly objectionable in principle, as establishing too close a relation between the operations of the government Treasury and the business of the country, and too extensive a commingling of their money, thus fostering an unnatural reliance in private business upon public funds. If this scheme should be adopted, it should only be done as a temporary expedient to meet an urgent necessity. Legislative and executive effort should generally be in the opposite direction, and should have a tendency to divorce, as much and as fast as can be safely done, the Treasury Department from private enterprise.

Of course, it is not expected that unnecessary and extravagant appropriations will be made for the purpose of avoiding the accumulation of an excess of revenue. Such expenditure, besides the demoralization of all just conceptions of public duty which it entails, stimulates a habit of reckless improvidence not in the least consistent with the mission of our people, or the high and beneficent purposes of our government.

I have deemed it my duty to thus bring to the knowledge of my countrymen, as well as to the attention of their representatives charged with the responsibility of legislative relief, the gravity of our financial situation. The failure of the Congress heretofore to provide against the dangers which it was quite evident the very nature of the difficulty must necessarily produce caused a condition of financial distress and apprehension since your last adjournment which taxed to the utmost all the authority and expedients within executive control; and these appear now to be exhausted. If disaster results from the continued inaction of Congress, the responsibility must rest where it belongs.

Though the situation thus far considered is fraught with danger which should be fully realized, and though it presents features of wrong to the people as well as peril to the country, it is but a result growing out of a perfectly palpable and apparent cause, constantly reproducing the same alarming circumstances—a congested national Treasury and a depleted monetary condition in the business of the country. It need hardly be stated that while the present situation demands a remedy, we can only be saved from a like predicament in the future by the removal of its cause.

Our scheme of taxation, by means of which this needless surplus is taken from the people and put into the public Treasury, consists of a tariff or duty levied upon importations from abroad and internal-revenue taxes levied upon the consumption of tobacco and spirituous and malt liquors. It must be conceded that none of the things subjected to internal-revenue taxation are, strictly speaking, necessaries. There appears to be no just complaint of this taxation by the consumers of these articles, and there seems to be nothing so well able to bear the burden without hardship to any portion of the people.

But our present tariff laws, the vicious, inequitable, and illogical source of unnecessary taxation, ought to be at once revised and amended. These laws, as their primary and plain effect, raise the price to consumers of all articles imported and subject to duty by precisely the sum paid for such duties. Thus the amount of the duty measures the tax paid by those who purchase for use these imported articles. Many of these things, however, are raised or manufactured in our own country, and the duties now levied upon foreign goods and products are called protection to these home manufactures, because they render it possible for those of our people who are manufacturers to make these taxed articles and sell them for a price equal to that demanded for the imported goods that have paid customs duty. So it happens that, while comparatively a few use the imported articles, millions of our people, who never used and never saw any of the foreign products, purchase and use things of the same kind made in this country, and pay therefor nearly or quite the same enhanced price which the duty adds to the imported articles. Those who buy imports pay the duty charged thereon into the public Treasury, but the great majority of our citizens, who buy domestic articles of the same class, pay a sum at least approximately equal to this duty to the home manufacturer. This reference to the operation of our tariff laws is not made by way of instruction, but in order that we may be constantly reminded of the manner in which they impose a burden upon those who consume domestic products, as well as those who consume imported articles, and thus create a tax upon all our people.

It is not proposed to entirely relieve the country of this taxation. It must be extensively continued as the source of the government's income; and in a readjustment of our tariff the interests of American labor engaged in manufacture should be carefully considered, as well as the preservation of our manufacturers. It may be called protection or by any other name, but relief from the hardships and dangers of our present tariff laws should be devised with especial precaution against imperilling the existence of our manufacturing interests. But this existence should not mean a condition which, without regard to the public welfare or a national exigency, must always insure the realization of immense profits instead of moderately profitable returns. As the volume and diversity of our national activities increase, new recruits are added to those who desire a continuation of the advantages which they conceive the present system of tariff taxation directly affords them. So stubbornly have all efforts to reform the present condition been resisted by those of our fellow-citizens thus engaged that they can hardly complain of the suspicion, entertained to a certain extent, that there exists an organized combination all along the line to maintain their advantage.

We are in the midst of centennial celebrations, and with becoming pride we rejoice in American skill and ingenuity, in American energy and enterprise, and in the wonderful natural advantages and resources developed by a century's national growth. Yet, when an attempt is made to justify a scheme which permits a tax to be laid upon every consumer in the land for the benefit of our manufacturers, quite beyond a reasonable demand for governmental regard, it suits the purposes of advocacy to call our manufactures infant industries still needing the highest and greatest degree of favor and fostering care that can be wrung from federal legislation.

It is also said that the increase in the price of domestic manufactures resulting from the present tariff is necessary in order that higher wages may be paid to our working-men employed in manufactories than are paid for what is called the pauper labor of Europe. All will acknowledge the force of an argument which involves the welfare and liberal compensation of our laboring people. Our labor is honorable in the eyes of every American citizen; and as it lies at the foundation of our development and progress, it is entitled, without affectation or hypocrisy, to the utmost regard. The standard of our laborers' life should not be measured by that of any other country less favored, and they are entitled to their full share of all our advantages.

By the last census it is made to appear that, of the 17,392,000 of our population engaged in all kinds of industries, 7,670,493 are employed in agriculture, 4,074,238 in professional and personal service (2,934,876 of whom are domestic servants and laborers), while 1,810,256 are employed in trade and transportation, and 3,837,112 are classed as employed in manufacturing and mining.

For present purposes, however, the last number given should be considerably reduced. Without attempting to enumerate all, it will be conceded that there should be deducted from those which it includes 375,143 carpenters and joiners, 285,401 milliners, dressmakers, and seamstresses, 172,726 blacksmiths, 133,756 tailors and tailoresses, 102,473 masons, 76,241 butchers, 41,309 bakers, 22,083 plasterers, and 4,891 engaged in manufacturing agricultural implements, amounting in the aggregate to 1,214,023, leaving 2,623,089 persons employed in such manufacturing industries as are claimed to be benefited by a high tariff.

To these the appeal is made to save

their employment and maintain their wages by resisting a change. There should be no disposition to answer such suggestions by the allegation that they are in a minority among those who labor, and therefore should forego an advantage in the interest of low prices for the majority. Their compensation, as it may be affected by the operation of tariff laws, should at all times be scrupulously kept in view; and yet, with slight reflection, they will not overlook the fact that they are consumers with the rest; that they, too, have their own wants and those of their families to supply from their earnings, and that the price of the necessaries of life, as well as the amount of their wages, will regulate the measure of their welfare and comfort.

But the reduction of taxation demanded should be so measured as not to necessitate or justify either the loss of employment by the working-man or the lessening of his wages; and the profits still remaining to the manufacturer after a necessary readjustment should furnish no excuse for the sacrifice of the interests of his employés, either in their opportunity to work or in the diminution of their compensation. Nor can the worker in manufactures fail to understand that while a high tariff is claimed to be necessary to allow the payment of remunerative wages, it certainly results in a very large increase in the price of nearly all sorts of manufactures, which, in almost countless forms, he needs for the use of himself and his family. He receives at the desk of his employer his wages, and perhaps before he reaches his home is obliged, in a purchase for family use of an article which embraces his own labor, to return, in the payment of the increase in price which the tariff permits, the hard-earned compensation of many days of toil.

The farmer and the agriculturist, who manufacture nothing, but who pay the increased price which the tariff imposes upon every agricultural implement, upon all he wears, and upon all he uses and owns, except the increase of his flocks and herds and such things as his husbandry produces from the soil, is invited to aid in maintaining the present situation; and he is told that a high duty on imported wool is necessary for the benefit of those who have sheep to shear, in order that the price of their wool may be increased. They, of course, are not reminded that the farmer who has no sheep is by this scheme obliged, in his purchases of clothing and woollen goods, to pay a tribute to his fellow-farmer as well as to the manufacturer and merchant, nor is any mention made of the fact that the sheep-owners themselves and their households must wear clothing and use other articles manufactured from the wool they sell at tariff prices, and thus, as consumers, must return their share of this increased price to the tradesman.

I think it may be fairly assumed that a large proportion of the sheep owned by the farmers throughout the country are found in small flocks, numbering from twenty-five to fifty. The duty on the grade of imported wool which these sheep yield is 10 cents each pound if of the value of 30 cents or less, and 12 cents if of the value of more than 30 cents. If the liberal estimate of 6 ℔. be allowed for each fleece, the duty thereon would be 60 or 72 cents; and this may be taken as the utmost enhancement of its price to the farmer by reason of this duty. Eighteen dollars would thus represent the increased price of the wool from twenty-five sheep, and $36 that from the wool of fifty sheep; and at present values this addition would amount to about one-third of its price. If upon its sale the farmer receives this or a less tariff profit, the wool leaves his hands charged with precisely that sum, which in all its changes will adhere to it until it reaches the consumer. When manufactured into cloth and other goods and material for use, its cost is not only increased to the extent of the farmer's tariff profit, but a further sum has been added for the benefit of the manufacturer under the operation of other tariff laws. In the mean time the day arrives when the farmer finds it necessary to purchase woollen goods and materials to clothe himself and family for the winter. When he faces the tradesman for that purpose, he discovers that he is obliged not only to return in the way of increased prices his tariff profit on the wool he sold, and which then perhaps lies before him in unmanufactured form, but that he must add a considerable sum thereto to meet a further increase in cost caused by a tariff duty on the manufacture. Thus, in the end, he is aroused to the fact that he has paid upon a moderate purchase, as a result of the tariff scheme, which when he sold his wool seemed so profitable, an increase in price more than sufficient to sweep away all the tariff profit he received upon the wool he produced and sold.

When the number of farmers engaged in wool-raising is compared with all the farmers in the country, and the small proportion they bear to our population is considered; when it is made apparent that in the case of a large part of those who own sheep the benefit of the present tariff on wool is illusory; and, above all, when it must be conceded that the increase of the cost of living caused by such tariff becomes a burden upon those with moderate means and the poor, the employed and unemployed, the sick and well, and the young and old, and that it constitutes a tax which with relentless grasp is fastened upon the clothing of every man, woman, and child in the land, reasons are suggested why the removal or reduction of this duty should be included in a revision of our tariff laws.

In speaking of the increased cost to the consumer of our home manufactures resulting from a duty laid upon imported articles of the same description, the fact is not overlooked that competition among our domestic producers sometimes has the effect of keeping the price of their products below the highest limit allowed by such duty. But it is notorious that this competition is too often strangled by combinations quite prevalent at this time, and frequently called trusts, which have for their object the regulation of the supply and price of commodities made and sold by members of the combination. The people can hardly hope for any consideration in the operation of these selfish schemes.

If, however, in the absence of such combination, a healthy and free competition reduces the price of any particular dutiable article of home production below the limit which it might otherwise reach under our tariff laws, and if with such reduced price its manufacture continues to thrive, it is entirely evident that one thing has been discovered which should be carefully scrutinized in an effort to reduce taxation.

The necessity of combination to maintain the price of any commodity to the tariff point furnishes proof that some one is willing to accept lower prices for such commodity, and that such prices are remunerative; and lower prices produced by competition prove the same thing. Thus, where either of these conditions exists, a case would seem to be presented for an easy reduction of taxation.

The considerations which have been presented touching our tariff laws are intended only to enforce an earnest recommendation that the surplus revenues of the government be prevented by the reduction of our customs duties, and at the same time to emphasize a suggestion that in accomplishing this purpose we may discharge a double duty to our people by granting to them a measure of relief from tariff taxation in quarters where it is most needed, and from sources where it can be most fairly and justly accorded.

Nor can the presentation made of such considerations be with any degree of fairness regarded as evidence of unfriendliness towards our manufacturing interests or of any lack of appreciation of their value and importance.

These interests constitute a leading and most substantial element of our national greatness and furnish the proud proof of our country's progress. But if in the emergency that presses upon us our manufacturers are asked to surrender something for the public good and to avert disaster, their patriotism, as well as a grateful recognition of advantages already afforded, should lead them to willing co-operation. No demand is made that they should forego all the benefits of governmental regard; but they cannot fail to be admonished of their duty, as well as their enlightened self-interest and safety, when they are reminded of the fact that financial panic and collapse, to which the present condition tends, affords no greater shelter or protection to our manufactures than to other important enterprises. Opportunity for safe, careful, and deliberate reform is now afforded; and none of us should be unmindful of a time when an abused and irritated people, heedless of those who have resisted timely and reasonable relief, may insist upon a radical and sweeping rectification of their wrongs.

The difficulty attending a wise and fair revision of our tariff laws is not underestimated. It will require on the part of the Congress great labor and care, and especially a broad and national contemplation of the subject and a patriotic disregard of such local and selfish claims as are unreasonable and reckless of the welfare of the entire country.

Under our present laws more than 4,000 articles are subject to duty. Many of these do not in any way compete with our own manufactures, and many are hardly worth attention as subjects of revenue. A considerable reduction can be made in the aggregate by adding them to the free list. The taxation of luxuries presents no features of hardship; but the necessaries of life used and consumed by all the people, the duty upon which adds to the cost of living in every home, should be greatly cheapened.

The radical reduction of the duties imposed upon raw material used in manufactures, or its free importation, is of course an important factor in any effort to reduce the price of these necessaries. It would not only relieve them from the increased cost caused by the tariff on such material, but, the manufactured product being thus cheapened, that part of the tariff now laid upon such product, as a compensation to our manufacturers for the present price of raw material, could be accordingly modified. Such reduction or free importation would serve besides to largely reduce the revenue. It is not apparent how such a change can have any injurious effect upon our manufacturers. On the contrary, it would appear to give them a better chance in foreign markets with the manufacturers of other countries, who cheapen their wares by free material. Thus our own people might have the opportunity of extending their sales beyond the limits of home consumption, saving them from the depression, interruption in business, and loss caused by a glutted domestic market, and affording their employés more certain and steady labor, with its resulting quiet and contentment.

The question thus imperatively presented for solution should be approached in a spirit higher than partisanship, and considered in the light of that regard for patriotic duty which should characterize the action of those intrusted with the weal of a confiding people. But the obligation to declared party policy and principle is not wanting to urge prompt and effective action. Both of the great political parties now represented in the government have, by repeated and authoritative declarations, condemned the condition of our laws which permits the collection from the people of unnecessary revenue, and have in the most solemn manner promised its correction; and neither as citizens nor partisans are our countrymen in a mood to condone the deliberate violation of these pledges.

Our progress towards a wise conclusion will not be improved by dwelling upon the theories of protection and free-trade. This savors too much of bandying epithets. It is a *condition* which confronts us, not a theory. Relief from this condition may involve a slight reduction of the advantages which we award our home productions, but the entire withdrawal of such advantages should not be contemplated. The question of free-trade is absolutely irrelevant, and the persistent claim made in certain quarters that all the efforts to relieve the people from unjust and unnecessary taxation are schemes of so-called free-traders is mischievous and far removed from any consideration for the public good.

The simple and plain duty which we owe the people is to reduce taxation to the necessary expenses of an economical operation of the government and to restore to the business of the country the money which we hold in the Treasury through the perversion of governmental powers. These things can and should be done with safety to all our industries, without danger to the opportunity for remunerative labor which our working-men need, and with benefit to them and all our people by cheapening their means of subsistence and increasing the measure of their comforts.

The Constitution provides that the President "shall from time to time, give to the Congress information of the state of the Union." It has been the custom of the executive, in compliance with this provision, to annually exhibit to the Congress, at the opening of its session, the general condition of the country, and to detail with some particularity the operations of the different executive departments. It would be especially agreeable to follow this course at the present time, and to call attention to the valuable accomplishments of these departments during the last fiscal year; but I am so much impressed with the paramount importance of the subject to which this communication has thus far been devoted that I shall forego the addition of any other topic, and only urge upon your immediate consideration the "state of the Union" as shown in the present condition of our Treasury and our general fiscal situation, upon which every element of our safety and prosperity depends.

The reports of the heads of departments, which will be submitted, contain full and explicit information touching the transaction of the business intrusted to them, and such recommendations relating to legislation in the public interest as they deem advisable. I ask for these reports and recommendations the deliberate examination and action of the legislative branch of the government.

There are other subjects not embraced in the departmental reports demanding legislative consideration, and which I should be glad to submit. Some of them, however, have been earnestly presented in previous messages, and as to them I beg leave to repeat prior recommendations.

As the law makes no provision for any report from the Department of State, a brief history of the transactions of that important department, together with other matters which it may hereafter be deemed essential to commend to the attention of the Congress, may furnish the occasion for a future communication.

The Venezuela Boundary.—On Dec. 17, 1895, President Cleveland sent the following message to Congress concerning the dispute between Great Britain and Venezuela on the boundary question and its relation to the Monroe Doctrine:

To the Congress,—In my annual message addressed to the Congress on the 3d inst., I called attention to the pending boundary controversy between Great Britain and the republic of Venezuela, and recited the substance of a representation made by this government to her Britannic Majesty's government suggesting reasons why such dispute should be submitted to arbitration for settlement, and inquiring whether it would be so submitted.

The answer of the British government, which was then awaited, has since been received, and, together with the despatch to which it is a reply, is hereto appended.

Such reply is embodied in two communications addressed by the British prime minister to Sir Julian Pauncefote, the British ambassador at this capital. It will be seen that one of these communications is devoted exclusively to observations upon the Monroe Doctrine, and claims that in the present instance a new and strange extension and development of this doctrine is insisted on by the United States, that the reasons justifying an appeal to the doctrine enunciated by President Monroe are generally inapplicable "to the state of things in which we live at the present day," and especially inapplicable to a controversy involving the boundary-line between Great Britain and Venezuela.

Without attempting extended argument in reply to these positions, it may not be amiss to suggest that the doctrine upon which we stand is strong and sound because its enforcement is important to our peace and safety as a nation, and is essential to the integrity of our free institutions and the tranquil maintenance of our distinctive form of government. It is intended to apply to every stage of our national life, and cannot become obsolete while our republic endures. If the balance of power is justly a cause for jealous anxiety among the governments of the Old World and a subject for our absolute non-interference, none the less is an observance of the Monroe Doctrine of vital concern to our people and their government.

Assuming, therefore, that we may properly insist upon this doctrine without regard to "the state of things in which we live," or any changed conditions here or elsewhere, it is not apparent why its changed application may not be invoked in the present controversy.

If a European power, by an extension of its boundaries, takes possession of the territory of one of our neighboring republics against its will and in derogation of its rights, it is difficult to see why, to that extent, such European power does not thereby attempt to extend its system of government to that portion of this continent which is thus taken. This is the precise action which President Monroe declared to be "dangerous to our peace and our safety," and it can make no difference whether the European system is extended by an advance of frontier or otherwise.

It is also suggested in the British reply that we should not seek to apply the Monroe Doctrine to the pending dispute because it does not embody any principle of international law which "is founded on the general consent of nations," and that "no statesman, however eminent, and no nation, however powerful, are competent to insert into the code of international law a novel principle which was never recognized before, and which has not since been accepted by the government of any other country."

Practically, the principle for which we contend has peculiar, if not exclusive, relation to the United States. It may not have been admitted in so many words to the code of international law, but since in international councils every nation is entitled to the rights belonging to it, if the enforcement of the Monroe Doctrine is something we may justly claim, it has its place in the code of international law as certainly and as securely as if it were specifically mentioned, and when the United States is a suitor before the high tribunal that administers international law the question to be determined is whether or not we present claims which the justice of that code of law can find to be right and valid.

The Monroe Doctrine finds its recognition in those principles of international law which are based upon the theory that every nation shall have its rights protected and its just claims enforced.

Of course this government is entirely confident that under the sanction of this doctrine we have clear rights and undoubted claims. Nor is this ignored in the British reply. The prime minister, while not admitting that the Monroe Doctrine is applicable to present conditions, states: "In declaring that the United States would resist any such enterprise if it were contemplated, President Monroe adopted a policy which received the entire sympathy of the English government of that date." He further declares: "Though the language of President Monroe is directed to the attainment of objects which most Englishmen would agree to be salutary, it is impossible to admit that they have been inscribed by any adequate authority in the code of international law."

Again he says: "They (her Majesty's government) fully concur with the view which President Monroe apparently entertained, that any disturbance of the existing territorial distribution in that hemisphere by any fresh acquisitions on the part of any European state would be a highly inexpedient change."

In the belief that the doctrine for which we contend was clear and definite, that it was founded upon substantial considerations and involved our safety and welfare, that it was fully applicable to our present conditions and to the state of the world's progress, and that it was directly related to the pending controversy, and without any conviction as to the final merits of the dispute, but anxious to learn in a satisfactory and conclusive manner whether Great Britain sought, under a claim of boundary, to extend her possessions on this continent without right, or whether she merely sought possession of territory fairly included within her lines of ownership, this government proposed to the government of Great Britain a resort to arbitration as the proper means of settling the question, to the end that a vexatious boundary dispute between the two contestants might be determined and our exact standing and relation in respect to the controversy might be made clear.

It will be seen from the correspondence herewith submitted that this proposition has been declined by the British government, upon grounds which, in the circumstances, seem to me to be far from satisfactory. It is deeply disappointing that such an appeal, actuated by the most friendly feelings towards both nations directly concerned, addressed to the sense of justice and to the magnanimity of one of the great powers of the world and touching its relations to one comparatively weak and small, should have produced no better results.

The course to be pursued by this government, in view of the present condition, does not appear to admit of serious doubt. Having labored faithfully for many years to induce Great Britain to submit this dispute to impartial arbitration, and having been now finally apprised of her refusal to do so, nothing remains but to accept the situation, to recognize its plain requirements, and deal with it accordingly. Great Britain's present proposition has never thus far been regarded as admissible by Venezuela, though any adjustment of the boundary which that country may deem for her advantage and may enter into of her own free will cannot of course be objected to by the United States.

Assuming, however, that the attitude of Venezuela will remain unchanged the dispute has reached such a stage as to make it now incumbent upon the United States to take measures to determine with sufficient certainty for its justification what is the true divisional line between the republic of Venezuela and British Guiana. The inquiry to that end should of course be conducted carefully and judiciously, and due weight should be given to all available evidence, records, and facts in support of the claims of both parties.

In order that such an examination should be prosecuted in a thorough and satisfactory manner, I suggest that the Congress make an adequate appropriation for the expenses of a commission, to be appointed by the executive, who shall make the necessary investigation and report upon the matter with the least possible delay. When such report is made and accepted it will, in my opinion, be the duty of the United States to resist, by every means in its power, as a wilful aggression upon its rights and interests, the appropriation by Great Britain of any lands or the exercise of governmental jurisdiction over any territory which, after investigation, we have determined of right belongs to Venezuela.

In making these recommendations I am fully alive to the responsibility incurred, and keenly realize all the consequences that may follow.

I am, nevertheless, firm in my conviction that while it is a grievous thing to contemplate the two great English-speaking peoples of the world as being otherwise than friendly competitors in the onward march of civilization and strenuous and worthy rivals in all the arts of peace, there is no calamity which a great nation can invite which equals that which follows a supine submission to wrong and injustice and the consequent loss of national self-respect and honor, beneath which are shielded and defended a people's safety and greatness.

For the results of this message see VENEZUELA.

Cliff Dwellers, a race of Indians who lived in the cliffs bordering on the valleys of the Rio Grande and Rio Colorado. Their homes were built at a height of several hundred feet from the ground, and at the present time seemingly inaccessible. These dwellings consisted of many rooms, hewn in the rock. How the inhabitants subsisted is not known. The Pueblo Indians are probably descendants of the Cliff Dwellers.

Clifford, NATHAN, jurist; born in Rumney, N. H., Aug. 18, 1803; was graduated at the Hampton Literary Institution; admitted to the bar; member of Congress in 1839–43; attorney-general of the United States in 1846; went to Mexico in 1848 as United States commissioner to arrange terms for the cession of California to the United States. In 1858 was appointed an associate justice of the United States Supreme Court, and in 1877 was president of the ELECTORAL COMMISSION (*q. v.*). Died in Cornish, Me., July 25, 1881.

Clingman, THOMAS LANIER, legislator; born in Huntsville, N. C., July 27, 1812; was graduated at the University of North Carolina in 1832; settled in Asheville, N. C.; United States Senator from 1858 till 1861, when he resigned, with other members from the Southern States. He joined the Confederate army, and was made a brigadier-general in May, 1862. He died in Morgantown, N. C., Nov. 3, 1897.

Clinton, CHARLES, immigrant; born in Longford, Ireland, in 1690. With a number of relatives and friends, he sailed from Ireland for America in May, 1729. His destination was Philadelphia; but the captain of the vessel, with a view to their destruction by starvation, so as to obtain their property, landed them on barren Cape Cod, after receiving large sums of money as commutation for their lives. Clinton and his family and friends made their way to Ulster county, about 60 miles up the Hudson and 8 miles from it, in 1731, and there formed a settlement, he pursuing the occupation of farmer and land-surveyor. Subsequently he became a justice of the peace, county judge, and lieutenant-colonel of the Ulster County militia. Two of his four sons were generals in the war for independence, and his youngest (George) was governor of the State of New York and Vice-President of the United States. He died in Ulster (now Orange) county, N. Y., Nov. 19, 1773.

Clinton, DE WITT, statesman; born in Little Britain, Orange co., N. Y., March 2, 1769; graduated at Columbia College in 1786; studied law, and was admitted to the bar in 1788, but practised very little. He was private secretary to his uncle George, governor of New York, in 1790–95, in favor of whose administration he wrote much in the newspapers. He was in the Assembly of his State in 1797, and from 1798 to 1802 was a Democratic leader in the State Senate. He was mayor of New York City in 1803–7, 1809–10, and 1811–14. He was an earnest promoter of the establishment of the New York Historical Society and the American Academy of Fine Arts. Opposed to the War of 1812–15, he was the Peace candidate for the Presidency in 1812, but was defeated by James Madison. Mr. Clinton was one of the most efficient promoters of the construction of the Erie Canal. In 1817–22 and in 1824–27 he was governor of New York. He was the most conspicuous actor in the imposing ceremonies at the opening of the Erie Canal in the fall of 1825, when, outside the Narrows, he poured a vessel of water from Lake Erie into the Atlantic Ocean, as significant of their wedding. He was author of *Antiquities of Western New York; Natural History and Internal Revenues of New York, etc.* He died in Albany, N. Y., Feb. 11, 1828.

DE WITT CLINTON.

Clinton, GEORGE, naval officer and colonial governor; youngest son of Francis, sixth Earl of Lincoln, and rose to distinction in the British navy. In 1732 he was commissioned a commodore and governor of Newfoundland. In September, 1743, he was appointed governor of the colony of New York, and retained that office ten years. His administration was a tumultuous one, for his temperament and want of skill in the management of civil affairs unfitted him for the duties. He was unlettered; and being closely connected with the Dukes of Newcastle and Bedford, he was sent to New York to mend his fortune. In his controversies with the Assembly he was ably assisted by the pen of Dr. Cadwallader Colden, afterwards lieutenant-governor of the province. His chief opponent was Daniel Horsmanden, at one time chief-justice of the colony. After violent quarrels with all the political factions in New York, he abandoned the government in disgust, and returned home in 1753. He became governor of Greenwich Hospital—a sinecure. In 1745 he was vice-admiral of the red, and in 1757 admiral of the fleet. He died while governor of Newfoundland, July 10, 1761.

Clinton, GEORGE, Vice-President of the United States from 1805 to 1812; Republican; born in Little Britain, Ulster co., N. Y., July 26, 1739; was carefully educated by his father and a Scotch clergyman, a graduate of the University of Aberdeen. In early youth George made a successful cruise in a privateer in the French and Indian War, and soon afterwards joined a militia company, as lieutenant, under his brother James, in the expedition against Fort Frontenac in 1758. He chose the profession of law, studied it with William Smith, and became distinguished in it in his native county. In 1768 he was elected a member of the Provincial Assembly, wherein he soon became the head of a Whig minority. In 1775 he was elected to the Continental Congress, and voted for the resolution for independence in 1776; but the invasion of New York by the British from the sea called him home, and he did not sign the Declaration of Independence. He was appointed a brigadier-general, and as such performed good service in his State. On the organization of the State of New York, in 1777, he was elected the first governor, and held the office, by successive elections, eighteen years. He was very energetic, both in civil and military affairs, until the end of the war; and was chiefly instrumental in preventing the consummation of the British plan for separating New England from the rest of the Union by the occupation of a line of military posts, through the Hudson and

GEORGE CLINTON.

Champlain valleys, from New York to the St. Lawrence. In 1788 Governor Clinton presided over the convention held at Poughkeepsie to consider the new national Constitution. To that instrument he was opposed, because it would be destructive of State supremacy. In 1801 he was again elected governor of New York,

CLINTON'S MONUMENT.

and in 1804 was chosen Vice-President of the United States. In 1808 he was a prominent candidate for the Presidency, but was beaten by Madison, and was reelected Vice-President. By his casting-vote in the Senate of the United States, the renewal of the charter of the Bank of the United States was refused. While in the performance of his official duties at Washington, he died, April 20, 1812. His remains were transferred from the Congressional Cemetery at Washington to Kingston, N. Y., May 30, 1908.

Clinton, Sir Henry, military officer; born in 1738; was a son of George Clinton, colonial governor of New York. He entered the army when quite young, and had risen to the rank of major-general in 1775, when he was sent to America with Howe and Burgoyne. He participated in the battle of Bunker Hill (June 17, 1775), and was thereafter active in service against the oppressed colonists until June, 1782, when he returned to England. He

SIR HENRY CLINTON.

succeeded General Howe as commander-in-chief of the British forces in America in January, 1778.

In October, 1777, Sir Henry undertook a diversion in favor of General Burgoyne, then making his way towards Albany from Canada, in accordance with the British plan of conquest. Clinton, with a strong land and naval force, had captured Forts Clinton and Montgomery, in the Hudson Highlands (Oct. 6), and sent forces of both arms of the service up the river on a marauding excursion, hoping to draw Gates from Burgoyne's front to protect the country below. On the day after the capture of the forts Sir Henry wrote on a piece of tissue-paper the following despatch to Burgoyne: "*Nous y voici* [here we are], and nothing between us and Gates. I sincerely hope this little success of ours may facilitate your operations. In answer to your letter of the 28th September by C. C., I shall only say I cannot presume to order, or even advise, for reasons obvious. I heartily wish you success. Faithfully yours, H. CLINTON." This despatch was enclosed in an elliptical silver bullet, made so as to separate at the centre, and of a size (as delineated in the engraving) small enough to be swallowed by a man, if necessary. He intrusted it to a messenger who made his way north on the west side of the river, and, being suspected when in the camp of George Clinton back of New Windsor, was arrested. When brought before General Clinton, he was seen to cast something into his mouth. An emetic was administered to him, which brought the silver bullet from his stomach. The despatch was found in it, and the prisoner was executed as a spy at Hurley, a few miles from Kingston, while that village was in flames lighted by the British marauders. Sir Henry died in Gibraltar, Spain, Dec. 23, 1795.

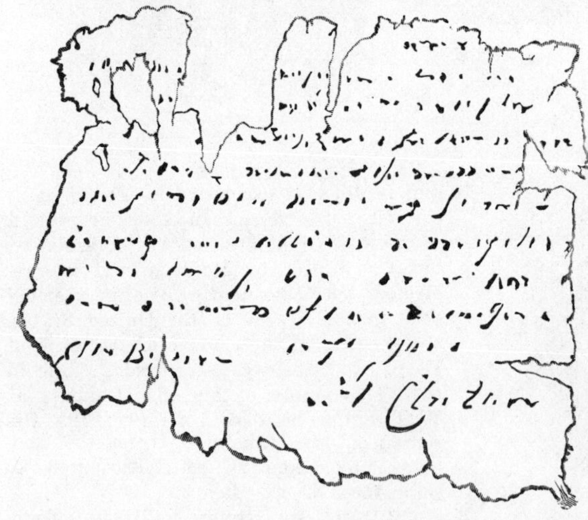

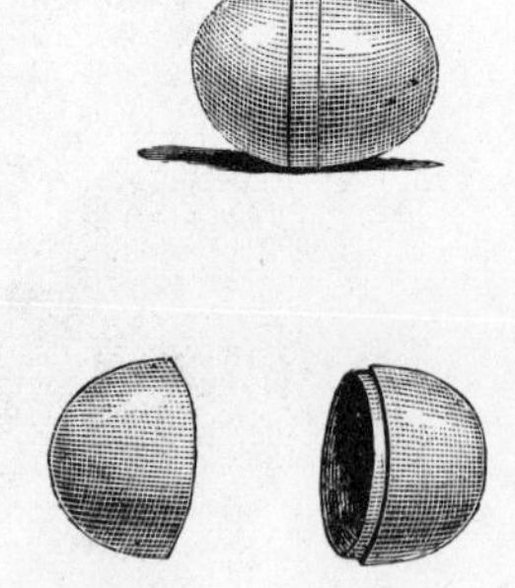

CLINTON'S DESPATCH AND BULLET.

Clinton, JAMES, military officer; born in Ulster (now Orange) county, N. Y., Aug. 9, 1736; son of Charles Clinton; was well educated, but he had a strong inclination for military life. Before the beginning of the Revolutionary War he was lieutenant-colonel of the militia of Ulster county. He was a captain under Bradstreet in the capture of Fort Frontenac in 1758; and he afterwards was placed in command of four regiments for the protection of the frontiers of Ulster and Orange counties—a position of difficulty and danger. When the war for independence broke out, he was appointed colonel of the 3d New York Regiment (June 30, 1775), and accompanied Montgomery to Quebec. Made a brigadier-general in August, 1776, he was active in the service; and was in command of Fort Clinton, in the Hudson Highlands, when it was attacked in October, 1777.

JAMES CLINTON.

In 1779 he joined Sullivan's expedition against the Senecas with 1,500 men. He was stationed at Albany during a great part of the war; but he was present at the surrender of Cornwallis. General Clinton was a commissioner to adjust the boundary-line between New York and Pennsylvania; and was a member of both the Assembly and Senate of the State of New York. He died in Little Britain, N. Y., Dec. 22, 1812.

Clinton, FORT, CAPTURE OF. While Burgoyne was contending with Gates on the upper Hudson, in 1777, Sir Henry Clinton was attempting to make his way up the river, to join him or to make a diversion in his favor. Among the Hudson Highlands were three forts of considerable strength, but with feeble garrisons—Fort Constitution, opposite West Point, and Forts Clinton and Montgomery, on the west side of the river at the lower entrance to the Highlands, standing on opposite sides of a creek, with high, rocky shores. From Fort Montgomery, on the northern side of the stream, to Anthony's Nose, opposite, the Americans had stretched a boom and chain across the river to prevent the passage of hostile vessels up that stream. Forts Clinton and Montgomery were under the immediate command of Gov. George Clinton, and his brother Gen. James Clinton. Tories had informed Sir Henry Clinton of the weakness of the garrisons, and as soon as expected reinforcements from Europe had arrived, he prepared transports to ascend the river. He sailed (Oct. 4, 1777) with more than 3,000 troops, in many armed and unarmed vessels, commanded by Commodore Hotham, and landed them at Verplanck's Point, a few miles below Peekskill, then the headquarters of General Putnam, commander of the Highland posts. He deceived Putnam by a feigned attack on Peekskill, but the more sagacious Governor Clinton believed he designed to attack the Highland forts. Under cover of a dense fog, on the morning of the 6th, Sir Henry re-embarked 2,000 troops, crossed the river, and landed them on Stony Point, making a circuitous march around the Dunderberg to fall upon the Highland forts. At the same time, his armed vessels were ordered to anchor within point-blank-shot distance of these forts, to beat off any American vessels that might appear above the boom and chain. Sir Henry divided his forces. One party, led by General Vaughan, and accompanied by the baronet (about 200 strong), went through a defile west of the Dunderberg, to strike Fort Clinton, while another party (900 strong), led by Colonel Campbell, made a longer march, back of Bear Mountain, to fall on Fort Montgomery at the same time. Vaughan had a severe skirmish with troops sent out from Fort Clinton, on the borders of Lake Sinnipink, near it; at the same time the governor sent a messenger to Putnam for aid. The messenger, instead, deserted to the British.

Campbell and his men appeared before Fort Montgomery at 5 P.M. and demanded the surrender of both forts. It was refused, when a simultaneous attack

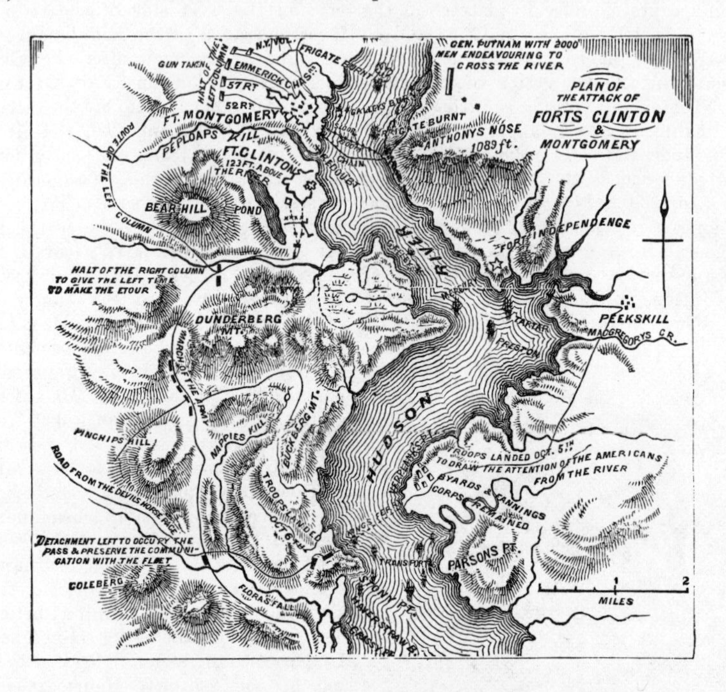

by both divisions and by the vessels in the river was made. The garrison (chiefly militia) made a gallant defence until dark, when they were overpowered and sought safety in a scattered retreat to the adjacent mountains. The governor fled across the river, and at midnight was in the camp of Putnam, planning future operations. His brother, badly wounded, made his way over the mountains to his home at New Windsor. Some American vessels lying above the boom, unable to escape, were burned by their crews. By the light of this conflagration the fugitive garrisons found their way through the mountains to settlements beyond.

Clitz, HENRY BOYNTON, military officer; born in Sackett's Harbor, N. Y., July 4, 1824; graduated at the United States Military Academy in 1845; served in the Mexican War, and for bravery at Cerro Gordo received the brevet of first lieutenant. During the Civil War he was wounded twice in the battle at Gaines's Mills; and after passing a month in Libby prison was exchanged and appointed commandant at West Point; brevetted brigadier-general in March, 1865; retired July 1, 1885; was last seen alive at Niagara Falls, Oct. 30, 1888.

Closure, a method of terminating debates; adopted by the British Parliament on Feb. 9, 1881, but not used until Feb. 24, 1884. Since then it has been frequently called into use. It is also freely used in the French Senate and Chamber of Deputies. In the United States House of Representatives a debate can be closed by adopting the previous question, but in the United States Senate there can be no closure under the present rules. Debates there are brought to a close by general consent, which is sometimes forced through physical exhaustion of those opposing a vote.

Clôture. See CLOSURE.

Clubs, originally a few persons of kindred tastes and pursuits, meeting at stated times for social intercourse. They may be political, literary, scientific, fine arts, business or commercial, athletic, etc.; and clubs of these classes are established in all of the principal cities of the United States. Political clubs often exert great influence in public affairs. The oldest club in the United States is the Wistar Club, established in Philadelphia in 1833, and the next, the Union Club, of New York City, established in 1836.

In the early part of the Civil War, Union League clubs were established in all the cities and towns in the Northern States, and exerted a powerful influence in maintaining patriotic sentiments in their communities. They partook somewhat of the character of secret and fraternal organizations. A few of the largest and wealthiest ones are still in existence, the others having gradually disbanded a few years after the close of the war. A striking feature of modern club-life in the United States is found in the large and constantly growing number of clubs organized by and for women exclusively. Of these the most conspicuous example is the Sorosis, of New York City, founded in 1868, and claiming to be the first distinctively women's club in the country. The growth of these clubs reached an extent in 1892 which warranted the organization of the Central Federation of Women's Clubs, which has in affiliation with it over 2,700 women's clubs, representing a membership of 200,000.

Cluseret, GUSTAVE PAUL, military officer; born in Paris, France, June 13, 1823; came to the United States in January, 1862; enlisted in the Union army and was made aide-de-camp to General McClellan, and received the brevet of brigadier-general of volunteers in 1862 for bravery in the battle of Cross Keys. On March 2, 1863, he resigned from the army, and the next year became editor of the *New Nation*, a weekly published in New York City. In this paper he strongly opposed the renomination of Lincoln and favored Frémont. He was the author of a number of articles on *The Situation in the United States*, which were published in the *Courier Français*. He returned to France in 1867; died Aug. 23, 1900.

Clymer, GEORGE, signer of the Declaration of Independence; born in Philadelphia in 1739; was an active patriot during the war for independence, and a member of the council of safety in Philadelphia. In July, 1775, he was made joint treasurer of Pennsylvania with Mr. Hillegas; and when, in December, 1776, Congress fled to Baltimore, Clymer was one of the commissioners left in Philadelphia to attend to the public interests. In 1777 he was a commissioner to treat with the Indians at Fort Pitt; and in 1780 he assisted in organizing the Bank of North America. At the close of the war he made his residence at Princeton, N. J.; and in 1784 was a member of the Pennsylvania legislature. In 1787 he was a member of the convention that framed the national Constitution, and was a member of the first Congress under it. A collector of the excise duties in 1791 which led to the WHISKEY INSURRECTION (*q. v.*), and serving on a commission to treat with Southern Indians, Mr. Clymer, after concluding a treaty (in June, 1796), withdrew from public life. He was one of the founders of the Pennsylvania Agricultural Society, the Pennsylvania Academy of Fine Arts, and the Pennsylvania Bank. He died in Morrisville, Pa., Jan. 23, 1813.

Coal. The business of coal-mining in the United States for commercial purposes has entirely grown up since 1825. It was known before the Revolution that coal existed in Pennsylvania. As early as 1769, a blacksmith, Obadiah Gore, in the Wyoming Valley, used coal found lying on the surface of the ground. Forty years afterwards he tried the successful experiment of burning it in a grate for fuel. During the Revolution anthracite coal was used in the armory at Carlisle, Pa., for blacksmiths' fires. In 1790 an old hunter, Philip Gintner, in the Lehigh Valley, discovered coal near the present Mauch Chunk. In 1792 the Lehigh Coal-Mining Company was formed for mining it, but it did little more than purchase lands. In 1806 200 or 300 bushels were taken to Philadelphia. but experiments to use it for ordinary fuel failed. In 1812 Col. George Shoemaker took nine wagon-loads to Philadelphia, but could not sell it. It was soon afterwards used with success in rolling-mills in Delaware county, and it soon found purchasers elsewhere. But it was not until 1825 that the coal-trade began to assume notable proportions, when anthracite was used in factories and in private houses for fuel. The whole amount of anthracite sent to market in 1820 was 365 tons.

In 1907, when the maximum output of both anthracite and bituminous coal in the United States was recorded, the total production amounted to 480,363,424 short tons, valued at $614,798,898, of which 85,604,312 short tons, valued at $163,584,-056, were Pennsylvania anthracite, and 394,759,112 short tons, valued at $451,-214,842, were bituminous, semi-bituminous, and lignite, with scattered lots of anthracite and semi-anthracite. The production was in 30 States and Territories; the various mines gave employment to 680,492 men; and the machine-mined product was 35.71 per cent. of the total output in States where machines were employed. Practically the entire output of both anthracite and bituminous coal in the United States is consumed within the country, and in a period of forty years the percentage of the world's total production contributed by the United States increased from less than 15 per cent. to nearly 40 per cent. (in 1907). The world's production in 1907 aggregated 1,218,337,677 short tons, the chief countries, in the order of output, being: United States, 480,-363,424 short tons; Great Britain, 299,-970,677; Germany, 226,773,605; Austria-Hungary, 53,109,750; France, 40,708,215; Russia 28,685,532; Belgium, 26,261,745, and Japan, 15,361,600.

A map of the coal-fields of the United States, with a statement covering the character and geologic age of the coals, was published in the report of the United States Geological Survey on *Mineral Resources of the United States* in 1907, and from a revision of that statement in 1908 it appeared that the total original coal supply of the country was 3,076,204,000,-000 short tons, of which 1,992,979,000,000 were considered to be easily accessible, and 1,153,225,000,000 accessible with difficulty. Up to the close of 1908 the total production was 7,280,940,265 short tons, which, including the waste involved in the mining and preparation, left as the apparent supply still available 99.6 per cent. of the original supply; in other words, up to the beginning of 1909 only 0.4 per cent. of the original supply of coal had been exhausted. So far as the natural supply is concerned, there need be no fear of a coal famine in this country for many years to come. An account of the great coal miners' strike of 1902 will be found under STRIKES. For the first time in the history of the United States the coal-mines of the country were credited in 1910 with an output exceeding half a billion short tons (501,596,378), having a spot value of $629,557,021. Of this output 84,-485,236 tons were Pennsylvania anthracite, and 417,111,142 bituminous and lignite.

Coan, TITUS, missionary; born in Killingsworth, Conn., Feb. 1, 1801; was graduated at Auburn Theological Seminary in 1833. With his wife and six others he sailed for Hawaii, Dec. 5, 1834, and reached Honolulu in July, 1835. His labors met with great success. In 1838–40 he made over 7,000 converts, and his subsequent efforts increased this number to 13,000. His publications include *Life in Hawaii*, etc. He died in Hilo, Hawaii, Dec. 1, 1882.

Coan, TITUS MUNSON, writer; born in Hilo, Hawaii, Sept. 27, 1836; graduated at Williams College, 1859; graduated at the College of Physicians and Surgeons, New York, 1861. He served throughout the Civil War in the military hospitals and navy as a surgeon. Author of *Ounces of Prevention; Hawaiian Ethnography*, etc.

Coast and Geodetic Survey, UNITED STATES, a national undertaking for the security of the vast commerce upon the very extended and often dangerous coasts of the United States. It is believed that to Professor Patterson, of Philadelphia, is due the honor of having first suggested to President Jefferson the idea of a geodetic survey of the coast. Mr. Gallatin was then Secretary of the Treasury, and warmly approved the measure. The first attempt to organize a national coast survey, "for the purpose of making complete charts of our coasts, with the adjacent shoals and soundings," was made in 1807. Congress authorized such a survey, and appropriated $50,000 for the purpose. Mr. Gallatin, with great assiduity, gathered information for scientific uses. A plan proposed by F. R. HASSLER (*q. v.*) was adopted, but, on account of political disturbances in Europe and America, nothing was done in the matter until 1811, when Mr. Hassler was sent to Europe for instruments and standards of measure. The War of 1812-15 detained him abroad. On his return, in 1815, he was formally appointed superintendent, and entered upon the duties in 1816, near the city of New York; but in less than two years it was discontinued. Mr. Hassler resumed it in 1832, and the work has been carried on continually ever since. Mr. Hassler died in 1842, and was succeeded by ALEXANDER DALLAS BACHE (*q. v.*). On his death, in 1867, PROF. BENJAMIN PEIRCE (*q. v.*) was made superintendent. Professor Bache greatly extended the scope of the survey, including an investigation of the Gulf Stream, the laws of tides, and their ebb and flow in harbors and rivers, so that navigators might have complete information concerning tide-waters of the United States. The observations and investigations also include meteorological charts—changes in the weather in different seasons at various points, and the laws of storms. During the Civil War the work ceased on the Southern coasts, for the Confederates captured some of the vessels employed in the survey; and officers and pilots engaged in the work were transferred to service in the navy, and, with their minute knowledge of the coasts, greatly assisted in the National operations there. Professor Peirce still further extended the survey, so as to constitute a great national triangulation—a geodetic survey intended to embrace the shores of the Atlantic and Pacific oceans within its limits. The Atlantic, Pacific, and Gulf coasts are divided into sections, each having its triangulation, astronomical, topographical, and hydrographical parties, all working independently, but upon the same system, so that the whole will form a connected survey from Maine to Texas and from San Diego to the 94th parallel on the Pacific. The coast of ALASKA (*q. v.*), since its acquisition, has been added to the field of operations, and a very large amount has been done and projected there. The whole work is under the control of the Treasury Department, while a superintendent (Otto H. Tittmann, since 1900) directs all the details of the work, governs the movements of the parties, and controls the expenditures. An annual report of the work of the Coast and Geodetic Survey is published annually by order of Congress.

Coasting Trade, a term used to indicate the trade carried on by sea between two or more ports or places in the same country. In England any vessel, British or foreign, can carry goods or persons between one port and another of the United Kingdom since 1894. In the United States this trade is restricted to registered vessels carrying the United States flag. This applies even to the trade between the Atlantic and Pacific coasts, although such ships are obliged to sail around Cape Horn.

Cobb, ANDREW JACKSON, jurist; born at Athens, Ga., April 12, 1857; was graduated at University of Georgia in 1876 and appointed professor of law in the university, 1884-93. He drew up the Athens, Ga., Dispensary Law, the first legally established dispensary law for sale of liquors in the United States.

Cobb, COLLIER, educator; born in Wayne county, N. C., March 21, 1862; was graduated at Harvard, 1889; connected with the United States Geological Survey, Harvard University, Massachusetts Institute of Technology, etc. Published a map of North Carolina in 1899, and assisted in preparing the colonial records of North Carolina, etc.

Cobb, CYRUS, artist; born in Malden, Mass., Aug. 6, 1834; graduated at Boston University Law School, 1873; resumed his art in 1879. He made the Soldiers' Monument at Cambridge, Mass., and many other busts and groups of prominent Americans. He served in the 44th Massachusetts Volunteers during the Civil War, and he also painted many historic scenes and portraits. He died in 1903.

Cobb, DARIUS, artist; twin brother of Cyrus Cobb; born Aug. 6, 1834; served throughout the Civil War in the 44th Massachusetts Regiment; sometime art critic of the *Boston Traveller*; well-known for his portraits and his pictures of historic scenes.

Cobb, DAVID, military officer; born in Attleboro, Mass., Sept. 14, 1748; was graduated at Harvard College in 1766; became a physician; member of the Provincial Congress in 1775; aide-de-camp to Washington for a number of years; and brevetted brigadier-general at the close of the Revolutionary War. Washington assigned him the duty of providing entertainment for the French officers, and of making terms for the evacuation of New York. He was a member of Congress in 1793–95; lieutenant-governor of Massachusetts in 1809. He died in Taunton, Mass., April 17, 1839.

Cobb, HOWELL, statesman; born in Cherry Hill, Jefferson co., Ga., Sept. 7, 1815; was a lawyer by profession, and was solicitor-general of the Western circuit of Georgia from 1837 to 1841; a member of Congress from 1843 to 1851; speaker of the 31st Congress; and governor of Georgia from 1851 to 1853. He was again elected to Congress in 1855,

HOWELL COBB.

and was Secretary of the Treasury under President Buchanan from 1857 to 1860. He was a zealous promoter of the Confederate cause in 1860–61, and was chosen president of the convention at Montgomery, Ala., that organized the Confederate government Feb. 4, 1861. He became a brigadier-general in the Confederate army; and at the close of the war he opposed the reconstruction measures of the national government. He died in New York City, Oct. 9, 1868.

Cobb, JONATHAN HOLMES, manufacturer; born in Sharon, Mass., July 8, 1799; graduated at Harvard College in 1817; and was one of the first to introduce the manufacture of silk in the United States. In 1831 he published *Manual of the Mulberry-Tree and the Culture of Silk.* Two years later Congress ordered 2,000 copies of this work for public distribution to promote the cultivation of mulberry-trees. In 1835 Mr. Cobb became superintendent of the first silk-manufacturing company organized in New England. He died in Dedham, Mass., March 12, 1882.

Cobb, JOSEPH BECKHAM, author; born in Oglethorpe county, Ga., April 11, 1819; educated at Franklin College, Ga., settled in Noxubee county, Miss., in 1838. His publications include *The Creole, or the Siege of New Orleans* (a novel); *Mississippi Scenes, or Sketches of Southern and Western Life and Adventure,* etc. He died in Columbus, Ga., Sept. 15, 1858.

Cobb, THOMAS R. R., lawyer; born in Cherry Hill, Ga., April 10, 1823; graduated at the University of Georgia in 1841; member of the Confederate Congress; general in the Confederate army. His publications include *Digest of the Laws of Georgia; Inquiry into the Law of Negro Slavery in the United States;* and *Historical Sketch of Slavery, from the Earliest Periods.* He was killed in the battle of Fredericksburg, Va., Dec. 13, 1862.

Cobbett, WILLIAM, journalist; born in Farnham, Surrey, England, March 9, 1762; was the self-educated son of a farmer, and in early manhood was eight years in the army, rising to the rank of sergeant-major. He obtained his discharge in 1791, married, and came to America in 1792, when he became a pamphleteer, bookseller, and journalist, having established *Peter Porcupine's Gazette* in 1794. He attacked Dr. Rush, of Philadelphia, because of his treatment of yellow-fever cases, especially of his blood-letting. Rush prosecuted him for libel, and obtained a verdict for $5,000 damages. That suit had been brought to a trial on the day of Washington's death (Dec. 14, 1799), and Cobbett remarked that it was a singular coincidence that while the great patriot was dying in consequence of the too free use of the lancet, he should be mulcted in a verdict of $5,000 for exposing and ridiculing the dangerous practice in yellow fever. In anticipation of the verdict, Cobbett stopped the publication of his paper and removed to New York, where he was threatened with imprisonment, but procured bail. There he issued a series of vigorous pamphlets, called *Rush Lights*, in which he exhibited in vivid colors the various phases of character of all engaged in his prosecution. Then he went back to England, and issued *Porcupine's Works*, in 12 octavo volumes, which sold largely on both sides of the Atlantic. In these he exhibited such pictures of his American enemies that he tasted the sweets of revenge. In 1802 he began his famous *Weekly Political Register*, which he conducted with ability about thirty years, but which caused him to incur fines and imprisonment because of his libellous utterances. He again came to the United States in 1817, but returned to England in 1819, taking with him the bones of Thomas Paine. He continued the business of writing and publishing, and many of his books, written in vigorous Anglo-Saxon, are very useful. He entered Parliament in 1832, and was a member three years. He died in Farnham, June 18, 1835.

Cobden Club, a club instituted in London for the purpose of putting into practical application the principles of Richard Cobden. Its first annual dinner was held July 21, 1866, with William E. Gladstone in the chair. Its active membership includes many of the best-known statesmen of Great Britain, and among its honorary members are quite a number of well-known Americans, several of whom have been subjected to severe political criticism because of their conection with the club.

Cochran, JOHN, surgeon; born in Sudsbury, Pa., Sept. 1, 1730; was a surgeon's mate in the French and Indian War; appointed surgeon-general in the army in 1776; and commissioned director-general of hospitals by Congress in 1781. When peace was concluded he settled in New York, and was appointed commissioner of loans for that State. He died in Palatine, N. Y., April 6, 1807.

Cochrane, SIR ALEXANDER FORESTER INGLIS, British naval officer; born April 22, 1758; won great distinction in the wars with the United States and France, but most particularly in an unequal engagement with five French ships in Chesapeake Bay. In the War of 1812-15 he was commander of the American station. In August, 1814, he participated with the land forces in capturing Washington, and later aided in the attack on NEW ORLEANS (*q. v.*). He was made admiral of the blue in 1819. He died in Paris, France, Jan. 26, 1832.

Cockburn, SIR ALEXANDER JAMES EDMUND, jurist; born in Langton, England, Dec. 24, 1802; became Lord Chief Justice in 1859; represented Great Britain at the arbitration of the *Alabama* claims at Geneva in 1872, and afterwards published an elaborate protest against the indirect claims of the United States government which had been brought before the arbitrators, under the title of *Reasons for Dissenting from the Decision of the Tribunal of Arbitration*, to which CALEB CUSHING (*q. v.*) replied in his book, *The Treaty of Washington*. He died in London, England, Nov. 21, 1880.

Cockburn, SIR GEORGE, naval officer; born in London, England, April 22, 1772; entered the royal navy in 1783, and was rear-admiral in 1812. During the spring and summer of 1813 a most distressing warfare was carried on upon land and water by a British squadron, under his command, along the coasts between Delaware Bay and Charleston Harbor. It was marked by many acts of cruelty. "Chastise the Americans into submission" was the substance of the order given to Cockburn by the British cabinet. An Order in Council issued on Dec. 20, 1812, declared the ports and harbors of much of the American coast in a state of blockade. Cockburn entered between the capes of Virginia early in February, 1813, with a squadron, of which his flag-ship was the *Marlborough*, seventy-four guns. This squadron bore a land force of about 1,800 men, a part of them captive Frenchmen who preferred active life in the British service to indefinite confinement in jails. The appearance of this force alarmed all lower Virginia, and the militia of the Peninsula and about Norfolk were soon in motion. At the same time the frigate *Constellation*, thirty-eight guns, lying at Norfolk, was making ready to attack the British vessels. A part of the British squadron went into Delaware Bay and attacked the village of Lewiston.

On April 3, 1813, a flotilla of a dozen boats filled with armed men from the British fleet, under Lieutenant Polkingthorne, of the *St. Domingo*, seventy-four guns, entered the Rappahannock River and attacked the Baltimore privateer *Dolphin,* ten guns, Captain Stafford, and three armed schooners prepared to sail for France. The three smaller vessels were soon taken, but the struggle with the *Dolphin* was severe. She was boarded, and for fifteen minutes a contest raged fearfully on her deck, when the *Dolphin* struck her colors. Cockburn now went up the Chesapeake with the brigs *Fantome* and *Mohawk,* and the tenders *Dolphin, Racer,* and *Highflyer,* and proceeded to destroy Frenchtown, a hamlet of about a dozen houses on the west coast of Delaware. Cockburn made the *Fantome* his flag-ship. The only defenders of the hamlet were a few militia who came down from Elkton, and some drivers of stages and transportation - wagons. The former garrisoned a redoubt which had just been erected, upon which lay four iron cannon. They were vanquished and retired. The storehouses were plundered and burned, but the women and children were well treated. Property on land worth $25,000 was destroyed, and on the water five trading-vessels were consumed. Thence Cockburn went up the bay to HAVRE DE GRACE (*q. v.*), at the mouth of the Susquehanna, which he plundered and burned. Afterwards he attacked the villages of Fredericktown and Georgetown (May 6, 1813), on the Sassafras River. They contained from forty to fifty houses each. He first visited Fredericktown, on the north shore. The militia, under Colonel Veazy, made a stout resistance, but were compelled to retire. The village was laid in ashes, and the storehouses were plundered and burned. The marauders then crossed over to Georgetown, and served it in the same way. Having deprived three villages on the Chesapeake of property worth at least $70,000, Cockburn returned to the fleet.

Early in July, 1813, Admiral Cockburn, with a part of his marauding fleet, went southward from Hampton Roads to plunder and destroy. His vessels were the *Sceptre,* seventy - four guns (flag - ship), *Romulus, Fox,* and *Nemesis.* Off Ocracoke Inlet, he despatched (July 12, 1813) about 800 armed men in barges to the waters of Pamlico Sound. There they attacked the *Anaconda* and *Atlas*, two American privateers, and captured both. The crew of one escaped, and gave the alarm at Newbern. The British boats proceeded to attack that place, but found it too well prepared to warrant their doing so. They captured Portsmouth, and plundered the country around. They decamped in haste (July 16), carrying with them cattle and other property, and many slaves, to whom they falsely promised their freedom. These, and others obtained the same way, Cockburn sold in the West Indies on his private account.

Leaving Pamlico Sound, the marauders went down the coast, stopping at and plundering Dewees's and Capers's islands, and filling the whole region of the lower Santee with terror. Informed of these outrages, the citizens of Charleston prepared for the reception of the marauders. Fort Moultrie and other fortifications were strengthened, breast-works were thrown up at exposed places, and a body of militia was gathered at Point Pleasant. In anticipation of the coming of an army of liberation, as they were falsely informed Cockburn's men were, the negroes were prepared to rise and strike for freedom. Cockburn did not venture into Charleston Harbor, but went down to Hilton Head, from which he carried off slaves and cattle. Then he visited the Georgia coast, and at Dungenness House, the fine estate of Gen. Nathaniel Greene, on Cumberland Island, he made his headquarters for the winter, sending his marauders out in all directions to plunder the plantations on the neighboring coast. He was concerned in the sack of Washington in 1814, and in an unsuccessful attempt to capture Baltimore in the same year. He was knighted in 1815; made a major-general of marines in 1821; and died in London, Aug. 19, 1853.

Cocke, PHILIP ST. GEORGE, military officer; born in Virginia in 1808; graduated at the United States Military Academy in 1832; brigadier-general in the Confederate army in 1861; and was commander of the 5th Brigade in the first engagement of Bull Run. After eight months' service he returned to his home in Powhatan county, Va., where he died, Dec. 26 1861.

Cockran, WILLIAM BOURKE, lawyer; born in Ireland, Feb. 28, 1854; became prominent in New York politics as an adherent of Tammany Hall; member of Congress in 1887-89, 1891-95, and 1904-09; spoke for McKinley and the gold standard in 1896, and for Bryan, from opposition to imperialism, in 1900.

Cockrell, Francis Marion, statesman; born in Johnson county, Mo., Oct. 1, 1834; graduated at Chapel Hill College in 1853; admitted to the bar in 1855; practised in Warrensburg, Mo., served in the Confederate army, rising from the rank of captain to that of brigadier-general; captured at Fort Blakeley, Ala., April 9, 1865; paroled, May 14 following; resumed practice of law; United States Senator in 1875–1905; member of the Interstate Commerce Commission in 1905–11; appointed a civilian member of the Board of Ordnance and Fortifications in 1913.

Cod, Cape. See Cape Cod.

Cod Fisheries. At Fortune bay, United States fishers set nets on Sunday, Jan. 13, 1878, contrary to local regulations; they were forcibly removed; controversy ensued. Mr. Evarts, for the United States, sent despatch Aug. 24. Marquis of Salisbury refused compensation, but Earl Granville granted it; £15,000 awarded by arbitration May 28, 1881.

Coddington, William, founder of Rhode Island; born in Lincolnshire, England, in 1601; came to America in 1630 as a magistrate of Massachusetts. He was a prosperous merchant in Boston, but, taking the part of Anne Hutchinson (*q. v.*) he was so persecuted that, with eighteen others, he removed to the island of Aquidneck (now Rhode Island), where he was appointed judge. In March, 1640, Coddington was elected governor, and held office seven years. He went to England in 1651, and in 1674–75 he was again governor. He adopted the tenets of the Quakers. He died Nov. 1, 1678.

Coddes, in general terms a colection of laws, the most notable of which in modern times is the *Code Napoléon*, which was promulgated between 1803 and 1810. In the United States the most notable codes are those prepared by Judge Stephen J. Field (*q. v.*) for use in California at the time of its admission into the Union, and the *Codes of Civil and Criminal Procedure* prepared by his brother, David Dudley Field (*q. v.*), for the State of New York. The latter, after completing the above-mentioned work, was appointed by the legislature chairman of a commission to prepare a political code, a penal code, and a civil code, which, with the codes of procedure alluded to, were designed to take the place of the common law and to cover the entire range of American law. A number of the States have adopted in whole or in part this last class of codes. Mr. Field also actively urged the preparation of a code of international law, and personally prepared *Outlines of an International Code*, which was highly commended by jurists and statesmen in all countries. One of Mr. Field's principal objects in his projected international code was to secure a general adoption of the principal of arbitration in international disputes, an end approximately reached in the international agreement at the Peace Conference at The Hague in 1899. See Arbitration, International Court of.

Codman, John, author; born in Dorchester, Mass., Oct. 16, 1814; educated at Amherst College; followed the sea in 1834–64, and in the Civil War was captain of the *Quaker City*, which carried provisions to Port Royal. His publications relating to the United States include *Restoration of the American Carrying Trade* and *The Mormon Country*. He died in Boston, Mass., April 6, 1900.

Cody, William Frederick, scout; born in Scott county, Ia., Feb. 26, 1846. In 1857–58 he was under contract to supply the Kansas Pacific Railroad with all the buffalo meat needed during its construction, and in eighteen months he killed 4,280 buffaloes, on account of which he received his widely known sobriquet of "Buffalo Bill." He was a guide and scout for the national government for many years, and in the action at Indian Creek, in a personal encounter, killed Yellow Hand, the Cheyenne chief. Latterly he managed a circus known as "The Wild West Show." He is co-author of *The Great Salt Lake Trail*.

Coeur d'Alene, an Indian tribe, which were subjugated by Colonel Wright in 1858. They were placed on reservations in 1867 and 1872.

Coffee, John, surveyor; born in Nottaway county, Va., in 1772. In December, 1812, he was colonel of Tennessee volunteers under Jackson, and was with him in all his wars with the Creek Indians. He was with him also in his expedition to PENSACOLA (*q. v.*), and in the defence of New Orleans. In 1817 he was surveyor of public lands. He died near Florence, Ala., July 7, 1833.

Coffin, CHARLES CARLETON (pen-name CARLETON), author; born in Boscawen, N. H., July 26, 1823; during the Civil War was war correspondent of the Boston *Journal.* His publications include *Days and Nights on the Battle-field; Following the Flag; Story of Liberty; Old Times in the Colonies; Boys of '76; Life of Garfield; Building of the Nation; Drumbeat of the Nation; Marching to Victory; Freedom Triumphant*, etc. He died in Brookline, Mass., March 2, 1896.

Coffin, SIR ISAAC, naval officer; born in Boston May 16, 1759; was the son of a collector of customs in Boston, who was a zealous loyalist. He entered the British navy in 1773, became a lieutenant in 1776, and was active on the American coast at different times during the War for Independence. He served under Rodney, was made post-captain in 1790, and rear-admiral of the blue in 1804, in which year he was knighted. In June, 1814, he was created admiral of the blue, and in 1820 admiral of the white. He was a member of Parliament in 1818. Having a real attachment for his native country, he endowed the "Coffin School" in Nantucket, where many of his relatives lived, and gave for its support $12,500. He died in Cheltenham, England, July 23, 1839.

Coffin, JOHN, loyalist; born in Boston, Mass., in 1756; took part in the battle of Bunker Hill; later recruited 400 men in New York, who were afterwards called the Orange Rangers; was promoted major and received a handsome sword from Cornwallis in recognition of his bravery and skill in many important actions. Later he was promoted major-general. He died in King's county, N. B., in 1838.

Coffin, JOSHUA, antiquarian; born in Newbury, Mass., Oct. 12, 1792; graduated at Dartmouth College in 1817; an earnest abolitionist; helped to establish the New England Anti-Slavery Society in 1832; published *The History of Ancient Newbury.* He died in Newbury, Mass., June 24, 1864.

Coffin, LEVI, philanthropist; born near New Garden, N. C., Oct. 28, 1798; early became interested in the welfare of the slaves in the South; financially aided on their way to Canada thousands of fugitive slaves, including Eliza Harris, who later became widely known through *Uncle Tom's Cabin.* In April, 1847, he went to Cincinnati, O., and opened a "free-labor goods" store, which he operated successfully for many years. For thirty years he was president of the secret society known as the "underground railroad," the purpose of which was to aid slaves in their escape by passing them on from member to member. He died in Avondale, O., Sept. 16, 1877.

Coggeshall, GEORGE, author; born in Connecticut in 1784; during the War of 1812-15 commanded two privateers. His publications relating to the United States include *History of American Privateers and Letters of Marque during our War with England, 1812-13-14;* and *Historical Sketch of Commerce and Navigation from the Birth of Our Saviour down to the Present Date.* He died in 1861.

Coghlan, JOSEPH BULLOCK, naval officer; born in Frankfort, Ky., Dec. 9, 1844; was appointed to the navy from Illinois in 1860; became a rear-admiral, April 11, 1902. He commanded the *Raleigh* in the battle of Manila Bay, May 1, 1898, and subsequent expeditions to reduce all Spanish batteries at the mouth of the bay and the one which captured Isla Grande, Luzon; commanded the North Atlantic Station in 1902-03, and the New York Naval Station in 1904-07; retired Dec. 9, 1906. The *Raleigh* was the first vessel of Dewey's fleet to return to the United States, and at a reception of her officers by the Union League Club of New York her commander recited the verses entitled *Hoch der Kaiser*, thereby giving offense to Germany, but the incident was smoothed over by President McKinley. He died near New Rochelle, N. Y., Dec. 5, 1908.

Coinage, CONFEDERATE STATES. When Louisiana seceded and seized the United States mint at New Orleans there were thousands of dollars' worth of gold and silver bullion in store. The State issued jointly with the Confederate government a gold coinage of $254,820 in double eagles, and a silver coinage of $1,101,316.50 in half-dollars, using the United States dies of 1861, the dies of 1860 having been destroyed. The bullion, when nearly exhausted, was transferred to the Confederate government, May, 1861, and all the United States dies were destroyed, the Confederate government ordering a new die for its use. When completed it was of such high relief as to be useless in the press. As there was but little if any bullion to coin, no attempt was made to engrave another. Four pieces, however, half-dollars, were struck, which formed the entire coinage of the Confederate States. The coin shows—*Obverse:* A goddess of liberty within an arc of thirteen stars. Exergue, 1861. *Reverse:* An American shield beneath a liberty-cap, the upper part of the shield containing seven stars, the whole surrounded by a wreath: to the left, cotton in bloom; to the right, sugar-cane. *Legend:* Confederate States of American. *Exergue:* Half Dol. Boarders, milled; edge, serrated.

Coinage, UNITED STATES. Wampum depreciated in value as currency in consequence of over-production, and a final blow was given to it as a circulating medium in New England by an order from the authorities of Massachusetts not to receive it in payment of taxes. As fast as coin came to the colony of Massachusetts by trade with the West Indies, it was sent to England to pay for goods purchased there. To stop this drain of specie Massachusetts set up a mint, and coined silver threepences, sixpences, and shillings, each bearing the figure of a pine-tree on one side, and the words "New England" on the other. The silver was alloyed a quarter below the English standard, with the expectation that the debasement would prevent the coin leaving the country. Thus the pound currency of New England came to be one-fourth less than the pound sterling of Great Britain; and this standard was afterwards adopted by the British Parliament for all the English American colonies. The "mint-house" in Boston existed about thirty-four years. All the coins issued from it bore the dates 1652 or 1662, the same dies being used, probably, throughout the thirty-four years of coining. Some coins had been made in Bermuda for the use of the Virginia colony as early as 1644.

Copper coins bearing the figure of an elephant were struck in England for the Carolinas and New England in 1694. Coins were also struck for Maryland, bearing the effigy of Lord Baltimore. In 1722–23, William Wood obtained a royal patent for coining small money for the "English plantations in America." He made it of pinchbeck—an alloy of copper and tin. One side of the coin bore the image of George I., and on the other was a large double rose, with the legend "*Rosa Americana utile dulci.*" In the coinage of 1724 the rose was crowned. This base coin was vehemently opposed in the colonies. A writer of the day, speaking of the speculation, said Wood had "the conscience to make thirteen shillings out of a pound of brass." The power of coinage was exercised by several of the independent States from 1778 until the adoption of the national Constitution. A mint was established at Rupert, Vt., by legislative authority in 1785, whence copper cents were issued, bearing on one side a plough and a sun rising from behind hills, and on the other a radiated eye surrounded by thirteen stars. Some half-cents also were issued by the Vermont mint. In the same year the legislature of Connecticut authorized the establishment of a mint at New Haven, whence copper coins were issued having on one side the figure of a human head, and on the other that of a young woman holding an olive-branch. This mint continued in operation about three years. In 1786 parties obtained authority from the legislature of New Jersey to coin money, and they established two mints in that State: one not far from Morristown, and the other at Elizabethtown. On one side of this coinage was the head of a horse, with a plough beneath; and on the reverse a shield. The head of a horse and three ploughs now form the chief device of the great seal of New Jersey.

Cents and half-cents were issued in Massachusetts in 1788, exhibiting on one side an eagle with a bundle of arrows in the right talon, an olive-branch in the left, and a shield on its breast bearing the word "cent." That device was, and is now, the chief on the great seal of the United States. On the other side of the Massachusetts cent was the figure of an Indian holding a bow and arrow; also a single star. As early as the adoption of the "Articles of Confederation" (1781) the subject of national coinage occupied the attention of statesmen. In 1782, Robert Morris, superintendent of finance, submitted to the Continental Congress a plan for a metallic currency for the United States, arranged by Gouverneur Morris, who attempted to harmonize all the moneys of the States. He found that the 1440th part of the Spanish dollar was a common divisor of all the various currencies. Starting with that fraction as a unit, he proposed the following table of moneys: Ten units to be equal to one penny, ten pence to one bill, ten bills to one dollar (about seventy-five cents of our present currency), and ten dollars to one crown. The superintendent reported the plan to Congress in February, 1782, and employed Benjamin Dudley, of Boston, to construct machinery for a mint. The subject was debated from time to time, and on April 22, 1783, some coins were submitted to Congress as patterns. Nothing further was done in the matter (and Mr. Dudley was discharged) until 1784, when Mr. Jefferson, chairman of a committee appointed for the purpose, submitted a report, disagreeing with that of Morris because of the diminutive size of its unit. He proposed to strike four coins upon the basis of the Spanish milled dollar as follows: A golden piece of the value of ten dollars, a dollar in silver, a tenth of a dollar in silver, and a hundredth of a dollar in copper.

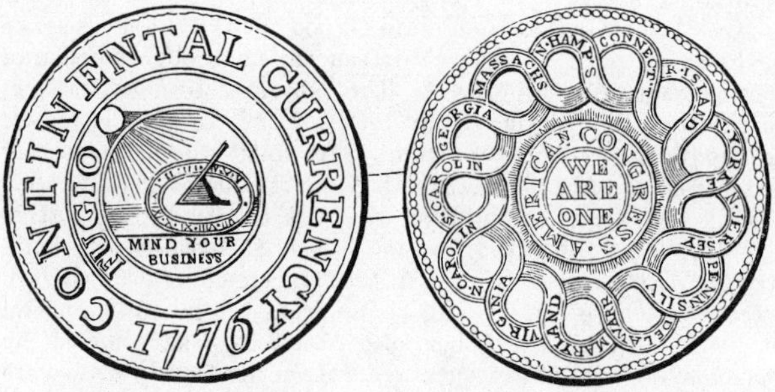

FACSIMILE OF THE FIRST MONEY COINED BY THE UNITED STATES.

This report was adopted by Congress in 1785, and was the origin of our copper cent, silver dime and dollar, and golden eagle. The following year Congress framed an ordinance for the establishment of a mint, but nothing further was done until 1787, when the board of treasury, by authority of Congress, contracted with James Jarvis for 300 tons of copper coins of the prescribed standard, which were coined at a mint in New Haven, Conn. They bore the following devices: On one side thirteen circles linked together; a small circle in the middle, with the words "American Congress" within it, and, in the centre, the sentence "We are one." On the other side a sun-dial, with the sun above it, and the word "*Fugio*"; and around the whole, "Continental Currency, 1776." Below the dial, "Mind your business." A few of these pieces, it is said, were struck in a mint at Rupert, Vt. The national Constitution vested the right of coinage exclusively in the national government. The establishment of a mint was authorized by act of Congress in April, 1792, but it did not go into full operation until 1795.

During the interval of about three years its operations were chiefly experimental, and hence the variety of silver and copper coins which appeared between 1792 and 1795, now so much sought after by coin-collectors. The most noted of these is the "Washington cent," or "Liberty-cap cent," so called because it has the profile of Washington on one side and a liberty-cap on the other. The subject of a device for the national coin caused much and sometimes warm debate in Congress. The bill for the establishment of the mint originated in the Senate, and provided for an eagle on one side of the gold and silver coins. To this there was no objection. The bill proposed for the reverse a representation of the head of the President of the United States for the time being, with his name and order of succession to the Presidency and the date of the coin-

LIBERTY-CAP CENT.

age. To this it was objected that the President might not always be satisfactory to the people, who would be disturbed by the effigy of an unpopular or unworthy one. Besides, the head of the President might be viewed as a stamp of royalty on the coins, and would wound the feelings of many. The House, after much debate, did not agree with the Senate, and the bill was sent back. Then it was proposed to substitute a head or figure of Liberty. This was finally agreed to, but an attempt was afterwards made to substitute the head of Columbus. At last the eagle, in the place of the head of Liberty, was chosen for the golden coins.

David Rittenhouse, of Philadelphia, was chosen the first director of the mint. At that city (being the seat of government) it was established, and was never moved from it. It was the sole mint until 1835, when Congress created several branches. The dies used in coinage in all the mints in the United States are under the supervision of the engraver of the mint at Philadelphia. By the act of 1792 the golden eagle of 10 dollars was to weigh 270 grains, the parts in the same proportion; all of the fineness of 22 carats. The silver dollar, of 100 cents, was to weigh 416 grains, the fractions in proportion; the fineness, 892.4 thousandths. The copper cent was to weigh 264 grains; the half-cent in proportion. In 1793 the weight of the cent was reduced to 208 grains, and the half-cent in the same proportion.

Assay offices were established at New York in 1854; at Denver, Col., in 1864; and at Boisé City, Ida., in 1872. In 1873 Congress made the mint and assay offices a bureau of the Treasury Department, the title of the chief officer of which is Superintendent of the Mint. An act was passed in June, 1834, changing the weight and fineness of the gold coin, and the relative value of gold and silver. The weight of the eagle was reduced to 258 grains, and the parts in proportion, of which 232 grains must be pure gold, making the fineness 21 carats. The silver coinage was not then changed, but in January, 1837, Congress reduced the weight of the silver dollar to 412½ grains, and the parts in proportion. By act of March 3, 1849, there were added to the series of gold coins the double eagle and the dollar; and in February, 1853, a 3-dollar piece. On March, 3, 1851, there was added to the silver coins a 3-cent piece (a legal tender for sums not exceeding 30 cents), and this piece continued to be coined until April 1, 1853, when its fineness was raised and its weight reduced. By act of Feb. 21, 1853, gold alone was made a legal tender, and the weight of the half-dollar was reduced to 206 grains, and smaller coins in proportion. Silver was made a legal tender only to the amount of 5 dollars. The silver dollar was not included in the change, but remained a legal tender. The copper cent and half-cent were discontinued in 1857, and a new cent of copper and nickel was coined. In 1864 the coinage of the bronze cent was authorized; also 2-cent pieces. By act of March 3, 1865, a 3-cent piece was authorized, of three-fourths copper and one-fourth nickel. May 16, 1866, a coinage of 5-cent pieces, three-fourths copper and one-fourth nickel, was authorized. The coinage act of 1873 prescribed the fineness of all gold and silver coins to be .900. The gold coins were of the same denomination as before; the silver coins were a "trade-dollar," weighing 420 grains; a half-dollar, or 50-cent piece; a quarter-dollar, and a dime. There were also 5-cent and 3-cent silver coins issued. The issuing of coins other than those enumerated in the act is prohibited. It was provided that upon the coins of the United States there shall be the following devices and legends: Upon one side an emblem of Liberty, with the word "Liberty" and the year of the coinage; and upon the reverse the figure of an eagle, with the inscriptions "United States of America" and "*E pluribus unum.*" The following table shows the coinage of the mints from their organization in 1792 to June 30, 1910.

DENOMINATION.	Pieces.	Values.
GOLD.		
Double eagles	112,807,169	$2,256,143,380.00
Eagles	48,177,301	481,773,010.00
Half eagles	70,986,884	354,933,376.00
Three-dollar pieces (coinage discontinued under act of September 6, 1890)	539,792	1,619,376.00
Quarter eagles	13,971,659	34,929,147.50
Dollars (coinage discontinued under act of September 26, 1890)	19,499,337	19,499,337.00
Dollars, Louisiana Purchase Exposition (act of June 28, 1902)	250,000	250,000.00
Dollars, Lewis Clark Exposition	60,000	60,000.00
Total gold	266,291,942	$3,149,207,670.50
SILVER.		
Dollars (coinage discontinued, act of Feb. 12, 1873, resumed act of Feb. 28, 1878)	578,303,848	$578,303,848.00
Trade dollars (discontinued, act of Feb. 19, 1887)	35,965,924	35,965,924.00
Dollars (Lafayette souvenir, act of March 3, 1899)	50,000	50,000.00
Half dollars	366,731,221	183,365,610.00
Half dollars (Columbian souvenir)	5,000,000	2,500,000.00
Quarter dollars	385,922,401	96,480,600.25
Quarter dollars (Columbian souvenir)	40,000	10,000.00
Twenty-cent pieces (coinage discontinued, act of May 2, 1878)	1,355,000	271,000.00
Dimes	602,967,986	60,296,798.60
Half dimes (coinage discontinued, act of February 12, 1873)	97,604,388	4,880,219.40
Three-cent pieces (coinage discontinued, act of Feb. 12, 1878)	42,736,240	1,282,087.20
Total silver	2,116,677,008	$963,406,087.95
MINOR.		
Five-cent pieces, nickel	642,501,287	$32,125,064.35
Three-cent pieces, nickel (discontinued, Sept. 26, 1890)	31,378,316	941,349.48
Two-cent pieces, bronze (discontinued, Sept. 26, 1890)	45,601,000	912,020.00
One-cent pieces, copper (discontinued, Feb. 21, 1857)	156,288,744	1,562,887.44
One-cent pieces, nickel (discontinued, April 22, 1864)	200,772,000	2,007,720.00
One-cent pieces, bronze	1,859,536,529	18,595,365.29
Half-cent pieces, copper (coinage discontinued, act of Feb. 21, 1857)	7,985,222	39,926.11
Total minor	2,944,063,098	$56,184,332.67
Total coinage	5,327,032,048	$4,168,798,091.12

Silver-dollar coinage under acts of April 2, 1792, $8,031,238; February 28, 1878, $378,166,793; July 14, 1890, $187,027,345; March 3, 1891, $5,078,472—total, $578,303,848.00.

See BIMETALLISM; CIRCULATION, MONETARY; CURRENCY, NATIONAL; MONETARY REFORM; UNITED STATES MINT.

Early Coinage of the United States.—The following is a chronology of early coinage in the United States.

Earliest coinage for America (for the Virginia company)..........about 1612-15
[The coin was used in the Bermudas, and is known as the "Hogge money," a hog being shown on it. It was issued in shillings and sixpences. But two of the shillings are known to exist, and but one sixpence.]

General Court of Massachusetts passes an act establishing at Boston the first mint in the U. S., 27 May, 1652, John Hull, mint-master. Denominations, shilling, sixpence, and threepence. This is known as the "Pine-tree money." Coining discontinued on the death of the mint-master........1 Oct., 1683

Maryland has shillings, sixpences, and pennies coined in England for her use, by Lord Baltimore..May, 1661

William Wood, of Wolverhampton, England, obtains a monopoly for coining "tokens" for currency in America 1722
[These tokens were made of a mixed metal resembling brass. (It was also coined for Ireland.) This is known as the "Rosa Americana" coinage or "Wood's money," and obtained quite a circulation.]

Connecticut had in circulation a private or unauthorized coinage, issued by John Higley, of Granby, known as the "Granby" or Higley token 1737

Copper coin, one cent, issued by Vermont 1785

Copper coined in New Jersey by act of legislature.............1 June, 1786

A Law of Massachusetts establishes a mint to coin gold, silver, and copper.................16 Oct., "
[No gold or silver ever coined in this mint.]

Coinage discontinued.......21 Jan., 1789

Following coins were decided upon by Congress: Gold: eagle, half eagle, and quarter eagle. Silver: dollar, half dollar, quarter dollar, dime and half dime. Copper: cent and half cent 1786

First U. S. mint established..2 April, 1792

First U. S. coinage.................. 1793

No gold coined in the years 1816 and 1817

No minor coinage in the years 1815 and 1823

First steam-power press in the U. S. mint 1836

Rare coins of the U. S. are the double eagles of the issue of..... 1849
[But one is known: in the cabinet of the U. S. mint; this is the rarest U. S. coin.]

Half eagles of the issue of........ 1815
[But seven of this date are known.]

Silver dollars of.................. 1794

Silver dollars of.................. 1804

Half dollars of 1796-97

Quarter dollars of 1827

The following table illustrates the monetary system of the United States in its relation to the national coinage.

Coinage of Confederate States.—When Louisiana seceded and seized the United States mint at New Orleans, there were thousands of dollars' worth of gold and silver bullion in store. The State issued jointly with the Confederate government a gold coinage of $254,820 in double eagles, and a silver coinage of $1,101,316.-50 in half dollars, using the United States dies of 1861, the dies of 1860 having been destroyed. The bullion, when nearly exhausted, was transferred to the Confederate government, May, 1861, and all the United States dies were destroyed, the Confederate government ordering a new die for its use. When completed it was of such high relief as to be useless in the press. As there was but little if any bullion to coin, no attempt was made to engrave another. Four pieces, however, half dollars, were struck, which formed the entire coinage of the Confederate States. The coin shows—*obverse:* A goddess of liberty within an arc of 13 stars. Exergue, 1861. *Reverse:* An American shield beneath a liberty-cap, the upper part of the shield containing 7 stars, the whole surrounded by a wreath: to the left, cotton in bloom; to the right, sugar-cane. *Legend:* Confederate States of America, Exergue, Half Dol. Borders, milled; edge, serrated.

	Gold Coin.	Standard Silver Dollars	Subsidiary Silver Coin.	Minor Coin.
Weight........	25.8 grains to the dollar.	412.5 grains.	385.8 grains to the dollar.	5c. piece: 77.16 grains, 75 p. c. copper, 25 p. c. nickel. 1c. piece: 48 grains, 95 p. c. copper, 5 p. c. tin and zinc.
Fineness.......	900-1000.	900-1000.	900-1000.	
Ratio to gold ..	....	15.988 to 1.	14.953 to 1.	
Limit of issue ..	Unlimited.	Coinage ceased in 1905.	Needs of the people.	Needs of the people.
Denominations	$20, $10, $5, $2½.	$1.	50 cents, 25 cents, 10 cents.	5 cents, 1 cent.
Legal tender...	Unlimited.	Unlimited, unless otherwise contracted.	Not to exceed $10.	Not to exceed 25 cents.
Receivable	For all public dues.	For all public dues.	For all dues up to $10.	For all dues up to 25 cents.
Exchangeable..	For gold certificates, as below, and subsidiary and minor coin.	For silver certificates and smaller coin.	For minor coin.	......
Redeemable....	....	....	In "lawful money" at the Treasury in sums or multiples of $20.	In "lawful money" at the Treasury in sums or multiples of $20.

	Gold Certificates.	Silver Certificates.	United States Notes.	Treasury Notes of 1890.	National Bank Notes.
Limit of issue..	Unlimited for gold coin unless gold reserve falls below $100,000,-000.	Quantity of silver dollars coined, $562,173,530.	$346,681,016.	No further issues, volume steadily diminishing by redemption with silver dollars.	Not to exceed capital and surplus of banks
Denominations.	$10,000, $5,000, $1,000, $500, $100, $50, $20, $10.	$100, $50, $20, $10, $5, $2, $1.	$1,000, $500, $100, $50, $20, $10, $5, $2, $1.	$1,000, $100, $50, $20, $10, $5, $2, $1.	$1,000, $500, $100, $50, $20, $10, $5.
Legal tender...	Not a tender.	Not a tender.	For all debts, public and private, except customs and interest on public debt.	Unlimited, unless otherwise contracted.	Not a tender.
Receivable	For all public dues	For all public dues	For all public dues	For all public dues	For all public dues except customs.
Exchangeable..	For subsidiary and minor coin.	For silver and minor coin.	For subsidiary and minor coin.	For silver and minor coin.	For subsidiary silver and minor coin.
Redeemable ...	In gold coin at the Treasury.	In silver dollars at the Treasury.	In gold at the Treasury.	In gold at the Treasury.	In "lawful money" at the Treasury, or at bank of issue.

Coke, Sir Edward, jurist; born at Mileham, Norfolk, England, Feb. 1, 1552. Passing through different grades of judicial office, he became lord chief-justice of England, opposed in his whole course by a powerful rival, Francis Bacon. Coke was a violent and unscrupulous man, and carried his points by sheer audacity, helped by tremendous intellectual force. He was in Parliament in 1621 when the question of monopolies by royal grants was brought before the House in the case of the council of Plymouth and the New England fisheries. Coke took ground against the validity of the patent, and so directly assailed the prerogative of the King. In other cases he took a similar course, and when the King censured the House of Commons as composed of "fiery, popular, and turbulent spirits" Coke, Speaker of the House, invited that body to an assertion of its rights, independent of the King, in the form of a protest entered on its minutes. The angry monarch sent for the book, tore out the record of the protest with his own hands, dissolved Parliament, and caused the arrest and the imprisonment of Coke, Pym, and other members for several months in the Tower. After that he was a thorn in the side of James and his successor. In 1628 Coke retired from public life, and died in Stoke Pogis, Sept. 3, 1634.

Colburn, ZERAH, mathematical prodigy; born in Cabot, Vt., Sept. 1, 1804; displayed such remarkable powers of calculation that in 1810 his father began exhibiting him in Europe. At this period he answered correctly such questions as "How many hours in 1811 years?" in twenty seconds, and a few years later much more complicated problems were solved with equal rapidity. In 1824 he returned to the United States, where he served as a Methodist preacher, and from 1835 was professor of languages in Norwich University, Vt., where he died, March 2, 1840.

CADWALLADER COLDEN.

Colden, CADWALLADER, physician; born in Dunse, Scotland, Feb. 17, 1688; graduated at the University of Edinburgh in 1705, and became a physician and mathematician. In 1780 he emigrated to Pennsylvania, and returned to his native country in 1712. He came again to America in 1716, and in 1718 made his abode in New York, where he was made first surveyor-general of the colony, became a master in chancery, and in 1720 obtained a seat in Governor Burnet's council. He received a patent for lands in Orange county, N. Y., and there he went to reside in 1755. He became president of the council in 1760, and was made lieutenant-governor in 1761, which station he held until his death, being repeatedly placed at the head of affairs by the absence or death of governors. During the Stamp Act excitement the populace burned his coach. After the return of Governor Tryon in 1775 he retired to his seat on Long Island. Dr. Colden wrote a *History of the Five Indian Nations of Canada* in 1727. He died on Long Island, N. Y., Sept. 28, 1776.

Cold Harbor, BATTLE OF. In 1864 the Army of the Potomac and a large part of the Army of the James formed a junction near Cold Harbor, the old battleground of McClellan and Lee in June, 1862. Gen. W. F. Smith and 16,000 men of the Army of the James had been taken in transports from Bermuda Hundred around to White House, whence they had marched towards the Chickahominy. Sheridan had seized the point at Cold Harbor, and the Nationals took a position extending from beyond Hanover Road to Elder Swamp Creek. Burnside's corps composed the right of the line, Warren's and Wright's the centre, and Hancock's the left. The Confederate line, reinforced by troops under Breckinridge, occupied a line in front of the Nationals—Ewell's corps on the left, Longstreet's in the centre, and A. P. Hill's on the right. On the morning of June 1, 1864, Hoke's division attempted to retake Cold Harbor. It was repulsed, but was reinforced by McLaws's division. Wright's 6th Corps came up in time to meet this new danger; and Smith's troops from the Army of the James, after a march of 25 miles, came up and took post on the right of the 6th Corps, then in front of Cold Harbor. Between the two armies was a broad, open, undulating field and a thin line of woods. Over this field the Nationals advanced to the attack at 4 P.M. The veterans of

Smith soon captured the first line of rifle-pits and 600 men. Their attack on the second line was a failure, and with darkness the struggle ceased, the Nationals having lost 2,000 men. They held the ground, and bivouacked on the battle-field.

During the night the Confederates made desperate but unsuccessful efforts to retake the rifle-pits. General Grant had ordered a redisposition of his army, making Hancock form the right, to the right of Wright's corps. Burnside was withdrawn entirely from the front and placed on the right and rear of Warren, who connected with Smith. Having made these dispositions on the 2d, it was determined to force the passage of the Chickahominy the next morning, and compel Lee to seek safety in the fortifications around Richmond. The Nationals moved at four o'clock on the morning of the 3d. Wilson's cavalry was on the right flank, and Sheridan's held the lower crossings of the river, and covered the roads to the White House. Orders had been given for a general assault along the whole line. At half-past four, or a little later, the signal for the advance was given, and then opened one of the most sanguinary battles of the war. It was begun on the right by the divisions of Barlow and Gibbon, of Hancock's corps, supported by Birney's. Barlow drove the Confederates from a strong position in front of their works, and captured several hundred men and three guns, when the Confederates rallied and retook the position. General Gibbon, who charged at the same time, was checked by a marsh of the Chickahominy which partly separated and weakened his command, and part of them gained the Confederate works, but could not hold them. There was a severe struggle, and in the assaults Hancock lost 3,000 men. The other divisions of the army were hotly engaged at the same time. The battle was "sharp, quick, and decisive." The Nationals were repulsed at nearly every point with great slaughter. It was estimated that within the space of twenty minutes after the struggle began 10,000 Union soldiers lay dead or wounded on the field, while the Confederates, sheltered by their works, had not lost more than 1,000. And so, at one o'clock in the afternoon of June 3, 1864, the battle of Cold Harbor ended.

BATTLE OF COLD HARBOR.

It was one of the most sanguinary struggles of the great Civil War. The Nationals had a fearful loss of life, but firmly held their position, with all their munitions of war. Their loss in this engagement, and in the immediate vicinity of Cold Harbor, was reported at 13,153, of whom 1,705 were killed and 2,406 were missing. Immediately after the battle Sheridan was sent to destroy the railways in Lee's rear, and so make Washington more secure. This task he effectually performed, fighting much of the time. Grant then resolved to transfer his army to the south side of the James River.

Cole, THOMAS, painter; born in Bolton-le-Moor, Lancashire, England, Feb. 1, 1801, of American parents who had gone to England previous to his birth, and returned in 1819, settling in Philadelphia, where Thomas practised the art of wood-engraving. He began portrait-painting in Steubenville, O., in 1820, soon wandered as an itinerant in the profession, and finally became one of the most eminent of American landscape-painters. He established himself in New York in 1825. The charming scenery of the Hudson employed his pencil and brush, and orders for his landscapes soon came from all quarters. From 1829 to 1832 he was in Europe, and on his return he made his home in Catskill, N. Y., where he resided until his death, Feb. 11, 1847. His two great finished works are *The Course of Empire* and *The Voyage of Life*, the former consisting of a series of five, and the latter of four, pictures. He produced many other fine compositions in landscape and figures, which gave him a place at the head of his profession. Mr. Cole left unfinished at his death a series entitled *The Cross and the World*, and was also the author of a dramatic poem and works of fiction.

Cole, NELSON, military officer; born in Dutchess county, New York, Nov. 18, 1833; subsequently settled in St. Louis, Mo. When the Civil War broke out he entered the Union army and served with conspicuous ability in numerous engagements. Early in 1865, at the head of 1,500 men, he led a successful expedition against the hostile Sioux, Arapahoe, and Cheyenne Indians at the sources of the Yellowstone River. He was made a brigadier-general of volunteers on May 28, 1898, and given command of the 3d Brigade, 2d Division, at Camp Alger. The unwholesome conditions of the camp caused his resignation, and his death, in St. Louis, Mo., July 31, 1899.

Coleman, WILLIAM T., pioneer; born in Cynthiana, Ky., Feb. 29, 1824; removed to San Francisco in 1849; became known through his affiliation with a secret organization for the suppression of crime in that city, called the Vigilance Committee. In the course of a few months this committee executed four notorious characters, and either drove out of California or terrified into concealment large numbers of others. In 1856 public indignation was again aroused by the murder of a well-known editor, James King. The Vigilance Committee again became active, and Mr. Coleman became chairman of the executive committee. In this capacity he presided at the trials and had charge of the execution of four murderers, including Casey, the murderer of King. For many years this organization was the dominating power in municipal politics. He died in San Francisco, Cal., Nov., 22, 1893.

Coles, EDWARD, governor; born in Albemarle county, Va., Dec. 15, 1786; graduated at William and Mary College in 1807; went to Russia on a confidential diplomatic mission for the United States government in 1817. He removed to Edwardsville, Ill., in 1819, and freed all the slaves which he had inherited, giving to the head of each family 160 acres of land. He was governor of Illinois from 1823 to 1826, and during his term of office he prevented the slavery party from obtaining control of the State. Later he settled in Philadelphia, Pa., and in 1856 read a *History of the Ordinance of 1787* before the Pennsylvania Historical Society. He died in Philadelphia, Pa., July 7, 1868.

Colfax, SCHUYLER, statesman; born in New York City, March 23, 1823; was grandson of the last commander of Washington's life-guard; became a merchant's clerk, and then, with his family, he went to New Carlisle, St. Joseph co., Ind., where for five years he was a clerk in a country store. In 1841 his step-father,

SCHUYLER COLFAX.

Mr. Mathews, was elected county auditor, and he removed to South Bend and made Schuyler his deputy. There he studied law, and finally established a weekly newspaper. In 1850 he was a member of the Indiana State constitutional convention, and the next year was a candidate for Congress, but was not elected. In 1856 the newly formed Republican party elected him to Congress, and he was re-elected for six consecutive terms. In December, 1863, he was elected Speaker of the House of Representatives, and was re-elected in 1865 and 1867. In November, 1868, he was elected Vice-President, with General Grant as President. After his retirement to private life in 1873 he frequently lectured to large audiences upon men he had known and subjects connected with his long career in public life. His best lecture was undoubtedly that on Lincoln and Garfield. He died suddenly, in Mankato, Minn., Jan. 13, 1885.

Collamer, JACOB, born in Troy, N. Y., Jan. 8, 1791; graduated at the University of Vermont in 1810; admitted to the bar in 1813; elected a justice of the Vermont Supreme Court in 1833; served until his election to Congress in 1843; appointed Postmaster-General under President Taylor in March, 1849; elected United States Senator in 1854, and served until his death, in Woodstock, Vt., Nov. 9, 1865.

College Fraternities. The principal Greek-letter societies in the United States are as follows:

Name.	Greek Letters.	Where Founded.	Date.
Kappa Alpha	Κ Α	Union	1825
Delta Phi	Δ Φ	"	1827
Sigma Phi	Σ Φ	"	"
Alpha Delta Phi	Α Δ Φ	Hamilton	1832
Psi Upsilon	Ψ Υ	Union	1833
Delta Upsilon	Δ Υ	Williams	1834
Beta Theta Pi	Β Θ Π	Miami	1839
Chi Psi	Χ Ψ	Union	1841
Delta Kappa Epsilon	Δ Κ Ε	Yale	1844
Zeta Psi	Ζ Ψ	New York University	1846
Delta Psi	Δ Ψ	Columbia	1847
Theta Delta Chi	Θ Δ Χ	Union	"
Phi Delta Theta	Φ Δ Θ	Miami	1848
Phi Gamma Delta	Φ Γ Δ	Jefferson	"
Phi Kappa Sigma	Φ Κ Σ	University of Pennsylvania	1850
Phi Kappa Psi	Φ Κ Ψ	Jefferson	1852
Chi Phi	Χ Φ	Princeton	1854
Sigma Chi	Σ Χ	Miami	1855
Sigma Alpha Epsilon	Σ Α Ε	Alabama	1856
Delta Tau Delta	Δ Τ Δ	Bethany	1860
Alpha Tau Omega	Α Τ Ω	Virginia Military Institute	1865
Kappa Alpha (south)	Κ Α	Washington and Lee	1867
Kappa Sigma	Κ Σ	Virginia	"
Sigma Nu	Σ Ν	Virginia Military Institute	1869

College Influence. The American college has rendered a service of greater value to American life in training men than in promoting scholarship. It has affected society more generally and deeply through its graduates than through its contributions to the sciences. It has been rather a mother of men than a nurse of scientists.

College Settlements, a plan to elevate the degraded masses of large cities. It consists in the establishment in tenement localities of settlements or houses where educated people live either permanently or temporarily for the purpose of working among the poor. The first attempt of this kind was made in 1867 when Edward Denison, a graduate of Oxford University, went to live in the East End of London that he might study the grievances of the poor, and do educational work among them.

The first American settlement was the Neighborhood Guild, later the University Settlement, established in New York City, in August, 1886. Since 1890 the number has doubled every five years, and on the twenty-fifth birthday of the movement the total number in the United States was 413. Settlement work has been extended to include charitable, educational, and industrial betterments. See ADDAMS, JANE.

Colleges for Women. One of the most striking features of the development of higher education in the United States in the closing years of the nineteenth century was the opening of regular courses to women by a remarkably large number of colleges. At the close of the school year 1910 there were 602 universities, colleges, and technological schools in the United States that reported to the National Commissioner of Education. These institutions included 352 for both men and women, and 108 for women only. The latter had a total of 2,612 professors and instructors (648 men and 1,964 women), and 26,606 students in all departments. The institutions exclusively for women, organized on the general basis of college requirements, were divided into two classes. The first class had 996 professors and instructors, 9,082 students, thirty-seven fellowships, 789 scholarships, $16,-190,461 invested in grounds and buildings, $12,888,307 invested in productive funds, and $4,197,566 in total income. The second division, which comprised institutions under the corporate name of colleges, institutes, and seminaries and were largely under the control of the different religious organizations, numbered ninety-two, with 1,616 professors and instructors, 17,524 students, $12,294,123 invested in grounds and buildings, $1,158,143 invested in productive funds, and $3,007,936 in total income.

Colleges in the United States. There were nine higher institutions of learning in the English-American colonies before the breaking-out of the Revolutionary War—namely, Harvard, in Massachusetts; William and Mary, in Virginia; Yale, in Connecticut; King's, in New York; College of New Jersey and Queen's, in New Jersey; College of Rhode Island; Dartmouth, in New Hampshire; and University of Pennsylvania. Hampden-Sidney College was founded in 1775, just as the war broke out. In these colonial institutions many of the brightest statesmen of the eighteenth century and beginning of the nineteenth were educated. (See their respective titles.) At the close of the school year 1909–10 collegiate education in the United States was afforded by 602 reporting colleges, universities, and technological schools, of which 352 were coeducational, 142 for men only, and 108 for women only; 184 theological schools; 114 law schools; 135 medical schools; 53 dental schools; 79 pharmaceutical schools; 20 veterinary schools; 1,105 training-schools for nurses; and 68 agricultural and mechanical colleges. These institutions combined reported 47,229 professors and instructors and 481,670 students. The universities, colleges, and technological schools for men and for both sexes had 694 fellowships, 9,279 scholarships, $32,-747,424 invested in scientific apparatus, $259,376,878 in productive funds, and $80,-438,987 in total receipts. The 494 universities, colleges, and technological schools for men and for both sexes had a teaching force of 24,667 (men, 21,813; women, 2,854) for all departments; a total enrollment of 275,212 (men, 201,341; women, 73,871); property of an aggregate value of $603,102,969; libraries containing 14,059,180 volumes valued at $19,246,-218; scientific apparatus valued at $32,-747,424; grounds, $67,688,727; buildings, $211,440,008; live-stock, $760,246; productive funds, $259,376,878; and receipts from all sources, $80,438,987, of which $70,667,865 was a working income, available for current expenses, buildings, improvements, etc. Nearly all of the professional schools were connected with the large universities and colleges.

Colleton, JAMES, colonial governor; was made governor of South Carolina, and given 48,000 acres of land in 1686. It was his duty to exercise the authority of the proprietaries, and enforce the laws which were being violated by the colonists. Upon his arrival in the colony Colleton excluded from the legislative halls all the members of the Parliament who opposed these acts. Later the Assembly defied the proprietaries and the governor, imprisoned the secretary of the colony, and afterwards impeached, disfranchised, and drove Colleton out of the province.

Collier, SIR GEORGE, naval officer; entered the British navy in 1761; given command of the *Rainbow* in 1775, and cruised off the American coast. In 1777 he captured the American vessel *Hancock;* destroyed the stores at Machias, and thirty vessels on the northeast coast; and later he ravaged the coasts of Connecticut and Chesapeake Bay. On Aug. 14, 1779, he captured the fleet of Commodore Saltonstall on the Penobscot River. He died April 6, 1795.

Collins, JOHN, governor; born June 8, 1717; was an active patriot during the Revolutionary War; in 1776 was made a commissioner to arrange the accounts of Rhode Island with Congress; in 1778–83 was a member of the old Congress, and in 1786–89 governor of Rhode Island. He was then elected to the first Congress under the national Constitution, but did not take his seat. He died in Newport, R. I., March 8, 1795.

Collins, NAPOLEON, naval officer; born in Pennsylvania, May 4, 1814; joined the navy in 1834; served in the war with Mexico; and in the Civil War was placed in command of the steam-sloop *Wachusett,* in 1863, when that vessel was assigned to capture privateers. On Oct. 7, 1864, he followed the Confederate steamer *Florida* into the harbor of Bahia, Brazil, and captured her. Later, as Brazil had complained that her neutrality had not been respected, his act was disavowed. Collins was promoted rear-admiral in 1874, and given command of the South Pacific squadron. He died in Callao, Peru, Aug. 9, 1875.

Colman, NORMAN JAY, agriculturist; born near Richfield Springs, N. Y., in 1827; began the practice of law in New Albany, Ind., and the editing of an agricultural paper in St. Louis, Mo., in 1871; was elected lieutenant-governor as a Democrat in 1874; was the first United States Secretary of Agriculture (1885–89); and was a founder of the Missouri State Horticultural Society. He died in St. Louis, Mo., Nov. 3, 1911.

Colon, a seaport of the republic of Panama; at the Atlantic extremity of the Panama railway (1849–55), and of the Panama Canal Zone; on the island of Mánzanilla, in Limon Bay, 8 miles n. e. of the old Spanish port of Chagres, 47 miles n. w. of Panama by rail, and equidistant from the great trading capitals of Valparaiso and San Francisco. From its commanding position as a place of transit, Colon benefits by the traffic in both directions. The climate, formerly very unhealthy, has been greatly improved by sanitation. In 1870 the Empress Eugénie presented the town with a statue of Columbus, when its name was changed form Aspinwall to Colon. It was burned by insurgents in 1885. See PANAMA CANAL.

Colonial Civil Service. See CIVIL SERVICE, COLONIAL.

Colonial Commissions. The first of two notable royal commissions to what is now the United States was sent out in 1634. Morton of Merry Mount had made serious charges against the people of Massachusetts before the privy council. That body summoned the council for New England before them to answer the charges. They denied having had anything to do with the matters complained of, and added new and serious charges of their own, declaring themselves unable to redress their grievances. They referred the whole matter to the privy council. A commission of twelve persons was appointed, with Laud, Archbishop of Canterbury, at its head, to whom full power was given to revise the laws, to regulate the Church, and to revoke charters. The members of the Massachusetts Company in England were called upon to give up their patent, and Governor Cradock wrote for it to be sent over. Morton wrote to one of the old planters that a governor-general had been appointed. Orders were also issued to the seaport towns of England to have all vessels intended for America stopped. The colonists were alarmed. The magistrates and clergy met on an island at the entrance to the inner harbor of Boston, and, resolving to resist the commissioners, agreed to erect a fort on the island and to advance the means for the purpose themselves until the meeting of the general court. They sent letters of remonstrance to England, and refused to send over the charter before the meeting of the court. When that body met, in May, active measures for defence were adopted. They ordered a fort to be built in Boston. Military preparations were ordered, and three commissioners were appointed to conduct "any war that might befall for the space of a year next ensuing." The English government threatened, but did nothing. In September, 1635, a writ of *quo warranto* was issued against the Massachusetts Company; but everything went on in the colony as if no serious threats were impending. The political disorders in England were safeguards to the infant colony. It was after the appointment of this commission that Endicott cut the cross from the standard at Salem.

The second of these commissions was sent over in 1664. Territorial claims, rights of jurisdiction, boundaries, and other matters had created controversies in New England, which were continually referred to the crown, and in 1664 the King signified his intention to appoint a commission for hearing and determining all matters in dispute. This occasioned alarm in Massachusetts, which had been a narrow oppressor of other colonies, especially of Rhode Island, and against which serious complaints had been made. A large comet appearing at that time increased the general alarm, for it was regarded as portentous of evil, and a fast was ordered. Fearing a design to seize their charter might be contemplated, it was intrusted to a committee for safekeeping. The commission was appointed, consisting of Sir Richard Nicolls, Sir Robert Carr, Sir George Cartwright, and Samuel Maverick, of Massachusetts. They came with an armament to take possession of New Netherland. Touching at Boston, the commissioners asked for additional soldiers, but the request was coldly received. The magistrates said they could not grant it without the authority of the general court. That body soon met and voted 200 soldiers. In Connecticut the commissioners were cordially received, and Governor Winthrop accompanied the expedition against New Netherland. After the conquest, they proceeded to settle the boundary between New York and Connecticut. Leaving Nicolls at New York as governor, the other commissioners proceeded to Boston. Meanwhile the authorities of Massachusetts had sent a remonstrance to England against the appointment of the commissioners. It was unheeded. The Massachusetts authorities were unyielding, the commissioners were haughty and overbearing, and a bitter mutual dislike finally made their correspondence mere bickerings. The commissioners proceeded to settle the boundary between Plymouth and Rhode Island. More difficult was the settlement of the boundary between Rhode Island and Connecticut, because of opposing claims to jurisdiction over the Pequod country. The commissioners finally directed that the region in dispute should constitute a separate district, under the title of the "King's Province." Neither party was satisfied, and the boundary dispute continued fifty years longer.

The commissioners now proposed to sit as a court to hear complaints against Massachusetts, of which there were thirty. The general court, by public proclamation, forbade such a proceeding, and the commissioners went to New Hampshire and Maine, when they decided in favor of claims of the heirs of Mason and Gorges. In the latter province they organized a new government; and on their return to Boston the authorities complained that the commissioners had disturbed the peace of Maine, and asked for an interview. It was denied by the commissioners, who denounced the magistrates as traitors because they opposed the King's orders. The commissioners having violated a local law by a carousal at a tavern, a constable was sent to break up the party, when one of the commissioners and his servant beat the officer. Another constable was sent to arrest the commissioners. They had gone to the house of a merchant. The officer went there and reproved them, saying, "It is well you have changed quarters, or I would have arrested you." "What!" exclaimed Carr. "Arrest the King's commissioners?" "Yes, and the King himself, if he had been here." "Treason! treason!" cried Maverick. "Knave, you shall hang for this!" The commissioners sent an account of their proceedings to the King, and soon afterwards they were recalled (1666). Their acts were approved, and those of all the colonies except Massachusetts, which was ordered to "appoint five able and meet persons to make answer for refusing the jurisdiction of the King's commissioners." Although this order produced considerable alarm, the sturdy magistrates of Massachusetts maintained their positions with much adroitness, and the country being engaged in a foreign war, the nation left his Majesty to fight alone for the maintenance of the royal prerogative. Massachusetts was victorious, and soon after the departure of the commissioners a force was sent to re-establish the authority of that colony over Maine.

Colonial Lords of Manors, an order incorporated at Baltimore, Md., in 1910, Mrs. Hester Dorsey Richardson president. The New York branch has John Henry Livingston as president. The object of the order is to preserve the records of the uniquely interesting phase of feudal institutions which existed in several of the thirteen original colonies; to collect all that can be gleaned in public and private archives, manuscript or otherwise, relating to those who held manor lands with the rights and privileges of manors in England, such as the right to hold court-baron and court-leet; to prepare a list of manor houses still existing; to locate portraits of lords and ladies of manors and to secure photographic copies of the same, and thus to contribute an unwritten page to the history of the American colonies. The eligibility list includes lords of manors, landgraves, caciques, and seignorial grants, the holders of which constituted a titled aristocracy in American colonies. Membership is composed of men and women whose descent from a lord of a manor is established.

Colonial Governments. Of the thirteen colonies Massachusetts was a corporation up to 1684; after 1691 it was a royal colony with a charter.

Rhode Island was chartered in 1643 by Parliament under the title of "Incorporation of Providence Plantations in the Narragansett Bay in New England." In 1663, the charter not being considered valid as the King had not joined with Parliament in issuing the same, Charles II. granted a charter for "Rhode Island and Providence Plantations." This charter remained in force until 1842.

Connecticut was founded in 1636 under a commission from Massachusetts. In 1639 the constitution known as the "FUNDAMENTAL ORDERS" (*q. v.*) was adopted. This was the first written constitution in history creating a government. In 1662 Charles II. granted a royal charter, which was adopted as a constitution in 1776, and continued in force until 1818.

Maryland. In 1632 a patent was issued to Lord Baltimore by Charles I., the first permanent proprietary government in America. In 1691 Maryland became a royal province.

Pennsylvania. Charles II. granted a charter to William Penn in 1681 as payment for £16,000 which the King owed him. Penn established a proprietary government, which existed until 1776, when the State purchased all the proprietors' rights.

Delaware formed a part of NEW SWEDEN (*q. v.*), and was captured by the Dutch in 1655. In 1664 the English conquered New Amsterdam and Charles II. gave it to his brother, the Duke of York. Penn purchased Delaware from the Duke in 1682 and annexed it to Pennsylvania. In 1702 Penn granted Delaware a separate charter, which existed until 1776.

Virginia was divided into two parts in 1606; one part was given to the LONDON COMPANY (*q. v.*), the other to the PLYMOUTH COMPANY (*q. v.*). In 1609 a new charter was granted by QUEEN ELIZABETH (*q. v.*). In 1624 Virginia became a royal colony, until 1776, when the first constitution was adopted.

North Carolina. Charles II. granted a charter in 1663 and 1665 to eight of his favorites of all the land south of Virginia. In 1669 the "FUNDAMENTAL CONSTITUTION" (*q. v.*) was adopted, but was abandoned in 1693. In 1700 North and South Carolina were separated and from 1729 to 1776 North Carolina was a royal colony.

South Carolina was a royal colony from 1729 to 1776.

New Hampshire was granted to Ferdinando Gorges and George Mason in 1622. It was a part of Massachusetts from 1641 to 1679, when it became a royal colony. In 1685 it was again annexed to Massachusetts and remained a part of that colony until 1749, when it again became a royal colony.

New York was a Dutch colony until 1664, when Charles II. granted it to the Duke of York. In 1688 it became a royal colony. In 1777 the first constitution was adopted.

New Jersey was granted by the Duke of York in 1664 to Lord Berkeley and Sir George Carteret. In 1702 it became a royal colony under the jurisdiction of New York until 1738.

Georgia was granted to James Oglethorpe in 1732 for a term of twenty-one years. In 1752 it became a royal colony. The first constitution was adopted in 1777.

Colonial Settlements. Settlements were made, as productive germs of colonies, in the following order of time: St. Augustine, Fla., was settled by Spaniards, under Mendez, 1565, and is the oldest settlement by Europeans within the domain of the United States. It was permanently occupied by the Spaniards, excepting for a few years, until Florida passed from their control (see FLORIDA and ST. AUGUSTINE). Virginia was first settled by the English temporarily (see RALEIGH, SIR WALTER). The first permanent settlement was made by them in 1607, under the auspices of London merchants, who that year sent five ships, with a colony, to settle on Roanoke Island. Storms drove them into the entrance to Chesapeake Bay, when they ascended the Powhatan River 50 miles, landed, and built a hamlet, which they called Jamestown. The stream they named James River—both in compliment to their King. After various vicissitudes the settlement flourished, and in 1619 the first representative Assembly in Virginia was held at Jamestown. Then were laid the foundations of the State of Virginia (see VIRGINIA). Manhattan Island (now the borough of Manhattan, city of New York) was discovered by Henry Hudson in 1609, while employed by the Dutch East India Company. Dutch traders were soon afterwards seated there and on the site of Albany, 150 miles up the Hudson River. The government of Holland granted exclusive privilege to Amsterdam merchants to traffic with the Indians on the Hudson, and the country was called New Netherland. The Dutch West India Company was formed in 1621, with unrestricted control over New Netherland. They bought Manhattan Island of the Indians for about $24, paid chiefly in cheap trinkets, and in 1623 thirty families from Holland landed there and began a settlement. Then were laid the foundations of the State of New York, as New Netherland was called after it passed into the possession of the English. Late in 1620 a company of English Puritans (see PURITANS) who had fled from persecution to Holland crossed the Atlantic and landed on the shores of Massachusetts, by permission of the Plymouth Company (see PLYMOUTH COMPANY). They built a town and called it New Plymouth; they organized a civil government and called themselves "Pilgrims." Others came to the shores of Massachusetts soon afterwards, and the present foundations of the State of Massachusetts were laid at Plymouth in 1620 (see PILGRIMS). In 1622 the Plymouth Company granted to Mason and Gorges a tract of land bounded by the rivers Merrimac and Kennebec, the ocean, and the St. Lawrence River, and fishermen settled there soon afterwards. Mason and Gorges dissolved their partnership in 1629, when the former obtained a grant for the whole tract and laid the foundations for the commonwealth of NEW HAMPSHIRE (*q. v.*).

King James of England persecuted the Roman Catholics in his dominions, and George Calvert, who was a zealous royalist, sought a refuge for his brethren in America. King James favored his project, but died before anything of much consequence was accomplished. His son Charles I. granted a domain between North and South Virginia to Calvert (then created Lord Baltimore). Before the charter was completed Lord Baltimore died, but his son Cecil received it in 1632. The domain was called Maryland, and Cecil sent his brother Leonard, with colonists, to settle it (see BALTIMORE; BALTIMORE, LORDS; CALVERT, LEONARD). They arrived in the spring of 1634, and at a place called St. Mary they laid the foundations of the commonwealth of Maryland (see MARYLAND). The Dutch navigator ADRIAN BLOCK (*q. v.*), sailing east from Manhattan, explored a river some distance inland, which the Indians called Quon-eh-ti-cut, and in the valley watered by that river a number of Puritans from Plymouth began a settlement in 1633. The first permanent settlement made in the valley of the Connecticut was planted by Puritans from Massachusetts (near Boston), in 1636, on the site of Hartford. In 1638 another company from Massachusetts settled on the site of New Haven. The two settlements were afterwards politically united, and laid the foundations of the commonwealth of CONNECTICUT (*q. v.*), in 1639.

Meanwhile, elements were at work for the formation of a new settlement between Connecticut and Plymouth. Roger Williams, a minister, was banished from Massachusetts in 1636. He went into the Indian country at the head of Narragansett Bay, where he was joined by a few sympathizers, and they located themselves at a place which they called Providence. Others, men and women, joined them, and they formed a purely democratic government. Others, persecuted at Boston, fled to the Island of Aquiday, or Aquitneck (now Rhode Island), in 1638, and formed a settlement there. The two settlements were consolidated under one government, called the Providence and Rhode Island Plantation, for which a charter was given in 1644. So the commonwealth of RHODE ISLAND (*q. v.*) was founded. A small colony from Sweden made a settlement on the site of New Castle, Del., and called the country New Sweden. The Dutch claimed the territory as a part of New Netherland, and the governor of the latter proceeded against the Swedes in the summer of 1655, and brought them under subjection. It is difficult to draw the line of demarcation between the first settlements in Delaware, New Jersey, and Pennsylvania, owing to their early political situation. The (present) State of Delaware remained in possession of the Dutch, and afterwards of the English, until it was purchased by William Penn, in 1682, and annexed to PENNSYLVANIA (*q. v.*). So it remained until the Revolution as "the Territories," when it became the State of DELAWARE (*q. v.*). The first permanent settlement in NEW JERSEY (*q. v.*) was made at Elizabethtown in 1644. A province lying between New Jersey and Maryland was granted to William Penn, in 1681, for an asylum for his persecuted brethren, the Quakers, and settlements were immediately begun there, in addition to some already made by the Swedes within the domain. Unsuccessful attempts to settle in the region of the Carolinas had been made before the English landed on the shores of the James River. Some settlers went into North Carolina from Jamestown, between the years 1640 and 1650, and in 1663 a settlement in the northern part of North Carolina had an organized government, and the country was named Carolina, in honor of Charles II., of England. In 1668 the foundations of the commonwealth of NORTH CAROLINA (*q. v.*) were laid at Edenton. In 1670 some people from Barbadoes sailed into the harbor of Charleston and settled on the Ashley and Cooper rivers (see SOUTH CAROLINA). The benevolent General Oglethorpe, commiserating the condition of the prisoners for debt, in England, conceived the idea of founding a colony in America with them. The government approved the project, and, in 1732, he landed, with emigrants, on the site of the city of Savannah, and there planted the germ of the commonwealth of GEORGIA (*q. v.*).

The first English colony planted in America was the one sent over in 1585 by Sir Walter Raleigh, who despatched Sir Richard Grenville, with seven ships and many people, to form a colony in Virginia, with Ralph Lane as their governor. At Roanoke Island Grenville left 107 men under Lane to plant a colony, the first ever founded by Englishmen in America. This colony became much straitened for want of provisions next year, and, fortunately for them, Sir Francis Drake, sailing up the American coast with a squadron, visited the colony and found them in great distress. He generously proposed to furnish them with supplies, a ship, a pinnace, and small boats, with sufficient seamen to stay and make a further discovery of the country; or sufficient provisions to carry them to England, or to give them a passage home in his fleet. The first proposal was accepted; but a storm having shattered his vessels, the discouraged colonists concluded to take passage for home with Drake, which they did. The whole colony sailed from Virginia June 18, 1586, and arrived at Portsmouth, England, July 28. Madame de Guercheville, a pious lady in France, zealous for the conversion of the American Indians, persuaded De Monts to surrender his patent, and then obtained a charter for "all the lands of New France." She sent out missionaries in 1613. They sailed from Honfleur March 12, and arrived in ACADIA (*q. v.*), where the arms of Madame Guercheville were set up in token of possession. Her agent proceeded to Port Royal (now Annapolis), where he found only five persons, two of whom were Jesuit missionaries previously sent over. The Jesuits went with other persons to Mount Desert Island. Just as they had begun to provide themselves with comforts, they were attacked by SAMUEL ARGALL (*q. v.*), of Virginia. The French made some resistance, but were compelled to surrender to superior numbers. One of the Jesuits was killed, several were wounded, and the remainder made prisoners. Argall took fifteen of the Frenchmen, besides the Jesuits, to Virginia; the remainder sailed for France. This success induced the governor of Virginia to send an expedition to crush the power of the French in Acadia, under the pretext that they were encroaching upon the rights of the English. Argall sailed with three ships for the purpose. On his arrival he broke in pieces, at St. Saviour, a cross which the Jesuits had set up, and raised another, on which he inscribed the name of King James. He sailed to St. Croix and destroyed the remains of De Mont's settlement there; and then he went to Port Royal and laid that deserted town in ashes. The English government did not approve the act, nor did the French government resent it.

Though the revolution in England (1688) found its warmest friends among the Low Churchmen and Non-conformists there, who composed the English Whig party, the high ideas which William entertained of royal authority made him naturally coalesce with the Tories and the High Church party. As to the government of the colonies, he seems not to have abated any of the pretensions set up by his predecessors. The colonial assemblies had hastened to enact in behalf of the people the Bill of Rights of the Convention Parliament. To these William gave frequent and decided negatives. The provincial acts for establishing the writ of *habeas corpus* were also vetoed by the King. He also continued the order of James II. prohibiting printing in the colonies. Even men of liberal tendencies, like Locke, Somers, and Chief-Justice Holt, conceded prerogatives to the King in the colonies which they denied him at home. The most renowned jurists of the kingdom had not yet comprehended the true nature of the connective principle between the parent country and her colonies.

As early as 1696 a pamphlet appeared in England recommending Parliament to tax the English-American colonies. Two pamphlets appeared in reply, denying the right of Parliament to tax the colonies, because they had no representative in Parliament to give consent. From that day the subject of taxing the colonies was a question frequently discussed, but not attempted until seventy years afterwards. After the ratification of the treaty of Paris in 1763, the British government resolved to quarter troops in America at the expense of the colonies. The money was to be raised by a duty on foreign sugar and molasses, and by stamps on all legal and mercantile paper. It was determined to make the experiment of taxing the American colonists in a way which Walpole feared to undertake. A debate arose in the House of Commons on the right of Parliament to tax the Americans without allowing them to be represented in that body. The question was decided by an almost unanimous vote in the affirmative. "Until then no act, avowedly for the purpose of revenue, and with the ordinary title and recital taken together, is found on the statute-book of the realm," said Burke. "All before stood on commercial regulations and restraints." Then the House proceeded to consider the STAMP ACT (*q. v.*).

In 1697 the right of appeal from the colonial courts to the King in council was sustained by the highest legal authority. By this means, and the establishment of courts of admiralty, England at length acquired a judicial control over the colonies, and with it a power (afterwards imitated in our national Constitution) of bringing her supreme authority to bear not alone upon the colonies as political corporations, but, what was much more effectual, upon the colonists as individuals.

At the beginning of the French and Indian War (1754), the period when the American people "set up for themselves" in political and social life, there was no exact enumeration of the inhabitants; but from a careful examination of official records, Mr. Bancroft estimated the number as follows:

Colonies.	White.	Colored.
Massachusetts	207,000	3,000
New Hampshire	50,000	
Connecticut	133,000	3,500
Rhode Island	35,000	4,500
New York	85,000	11,000
New Jersey	73,000	5,000
Pennsylvania and Delaware	195,000	11,000
Maryland	104,000	44,000
Virginia	168,000	116,000
North Carolina	70,000	20,000
South Carolina	40,000	40,000
Georgia	5,000	2,000
Total	1,165,000	260,000

At this period the extent of the territorial possessions of England and France in America was well defined on maps published by Evans and Mitchell—that of the latter (a new edition) in 1754. The British North American colonies stretched coastwise along the Atlantic about 1,000 miles, but inland their extent was very limited. New France, as the French settlers called their claimed territory in America, extended over a vastly wider space, from Cape Breton, in a sort of crescent, to the mouth of the Mississippi River, but the population was mainly collected on the St. Lawrence, between Quebec and Montreal. The English colonies in America at that time had a population of 1,485,634, of whom 292,738 were negroes. The French were scarcely 100,000 in number, but were strong in Indian allies, who, stretching along the whole interior frontier of the English colonies, and disgusted with constant encroachments upon their territories, as well as ill-treatment by the English, were always ripe and ready for cruel warfare.

The war with the French and Indians, and the contests with royal authority in which the colonies had been engaged at its close, in 1763, revealed to the colonists their almost unsuspected innate strength. During these contests, disease and weapons had slain 30,000 of the colonists. They had also spent more than $16,000,000, of which $5,000,000 had been reimbursed by Parliament. Massachusetts alone had kept from 4,000 to 7,000 men in the field, besides garrisons and recruits to the regular regiments. They served but a few months in the year, and were fed at the cost of the British government. At the approach of winter they were usually disbanded, and for every campaign a new army was summoned. Yet that province alone spent $2,000,000 for this branch of the public service, exclusive of all parliamentary disbursements. Connecticut had spent fully $2,000,000 for the same service, and the outstanding debt of New York, in 1763, incurred largely for the public service, was about $1,000,000.

The Southern colonies, too, had been liberal in such public expenditures, according to their means. At that time Virginia had a debt of $8,000,000. Everywhere the English-American colonies felt the consciousness of puissant manhood, and were able to grapple in deadly conflict with every enemy of their inalienable rights. They demanded a position of political equality with their fellow-subjects in England, and were ready to maintain their rights at all hazards.

In Pitt's cabinet, as chancellor of the exchequer, was the brilliant Charles Townshend, loose in principles and bold in suggestions. He had voted for the Stamp Act, and voted for its repeal as expedient, not because it was just. In January, 1767, by virtue of his office, on which devolved the duty of suggesting ways and means for carrying on the government, he proposed taxation schemes which aroused the most vehement opposition in America. He introduced a bill imposing a duty on tea, paints, paper, glass, lead, and other articles of British manufacture imported into the colonies. It was passed June 29. The exportation of tea to America was encouraged by another act, passed July 2, allowing for five years a drawback of the whole duty payable on the importation. By another act, reorganizing the colonial custom-house system, a board of revenue commissioners for America was established, to have its seat at Boston. Connected with these bills were provisions very obnoxious to the Americans, all having relation to the main object—namely, raising a revenue in America. There was a provision in the first bill for the maintenance of a standing army in America and enabling the crown to establish a general civil list; fixing the salaries of governors, judges, and other officers in all the provinces, such salaries to be paid by the crown, making these officers independent of the people and fit instruments for government oppression. A scheme was also approved, but not acted upon, for transferring to the mother-country, and converting into a source of revenue, the issue of the colonial paper currency.

The narrow-minded Hillsborough, British secretary of state for the colonies wishing, if possible, to blot out the settlements west of the Appalachian Mountains, and to extend an unbroken line of Indian frontier from Georgia to Canada, had issued repeated instructions to that effect, in order to make an impassable obstruction of emigration westward. These instructions were renewed with emphasis in 1768, when John Stuart, an agent faithful to his trust, had already carried the frontier line to the northern limit of North Carolina. He was now ordered to continue it to the Ohio, at the mouth of the Kanawha. By such a line all Kentucky, as well as the entire territory northwest of the Ohio, would be severed from the jurisdiction of Virginia and confirmed to the Indians by treaties. Virginia strenuously opposed this measure; and, to thwart the negotiations of Stuart with the Indians, sent Thomas Walker as her commissioner to the congress of the Six Nations held at FORT STANWIX (*q. v.*) late in the autumn of 1768. There about 3,000 Indians were present, who were loaded with generous gifts. They complied with the wishes of the several agents present, and the western boundary-line was established at the mouth of the Kanawha to meet Stuart's line on the south. From the Kanawha northward it followed the Ohio and Alleghany rivers, a branch of the Susquehanna, and so on to the junction of Canada and Wood creeks, tributaries of the Mohawk River. Thus the Indian frontier was defined all the way from Florida almost to Lake Ontario; but SIR WILLIAM JOHNSON (*q. v.*), pretending to recognize a right of the Six Nations to a larger part of Kentucky, caused the line to be continued down the Ohio to the mouth of the Tennessee River, which stream was made to constitute the western boundary of Virginia.

In striking a balance of losses and gains in the matter of parliamentary taxation in America, it was found in 1772 that the expenses on account of the Stamp Act exceeded $60,000, while there had been received for revenue (almost entirely from Canada and the West India islands) only about $7,500. The operation of levying a tax on tea had been still more disastrous. The whole remittance from the colonies for the previous year for duties on teas and wines, and other articles taxed indirectly, amounted to no more than about $400, while ships and soldiers for the support of the collecting officers had cost about $500,000; and the East India Company had lost the sale of goods to the amount of $2,500,000 annually for four or five years.

After the proclamation of King George III., in 1775, Joseph Hawley, one of the stanch patriots of New England, wrote from Watertown to Samuel Adams, in Congress: "The eyes of all the continent are on your body to see whether you act with firmness and intrepidity—with the spirit and despatch which our situation calls for. It is time for your body to fix on periodical annual elections—nay, to form into a parliament of two houses." This was the first proposition for the establishment of an independent national government for the colonies.

On April 6, 1776, the Continental Congress, by resolution, threw open their ports to the commerce of the world "not subject to the King of Great Britain." This resolution was the broom that swept away the colonial system within the present bounds of the republic, and the flag of every nation save one was invited to our harbors. Absolute free-trade was established. The act was a virtual declaration of independence.

Colonial Wars, SOCIETY OF, a patriotic society established in 1892 to "perpetuate the memory of those events and of the men who, in military, naval, and civil offices of high trust and responsibility, by their acts or counsel assisted in the establishment, defence, and preservation of the American colonies, and were in truth the founders of the nation. With this end in view it seeks to collect and preserve manuscripts, rolls, and records; to provide suitable commemorations or memorials relating to the American colonial period, and to inspire in its members the paternal and patriotic spirit of their forefathers, and in the community of respect and reverence for those whose public services made our freedom and unity possible." Any adult male may become a member who is the descendant of an ancestor who fought in any colonial battle from the Jamestown settlement in Virginia, in 1607, to the battle of Lexington, in 1775, or who at any time was a governor, deputy-governor, lieutenant-governor, member of the council, or as a military, naval, or marine officer in behalf of the colonies, or under the flag of England, or during that period was distinguished in military, official, or legislative life. The officers in 1911 were: Governor-general, Arthur J. C. Sowdon; vice-governor-general, Howland Pell; secretary-general, Clarence Storm; treasurer-general, Wm. Macpherson Hornor; registrar-general, George Norbury Mackenzie; historian-general, T. J. Oakley; chaplain-general, Rev. Daniel S. Tuttle.

Colonies, GRIEVANCES OF THE AMERICAN. See HOPKINS, STEPHEN.

Colonies, VINDICATION OF THE. See FRANKLIN, BENJAMIN.

Colonists, RIGHTS OF. See ADAMS, SAMUEL.

Colonization Society, AMERICAN. The idea of restoring Africans in America to their native country occupied the minds of philanthropists at an early period. It seems to have been first suggested by Rev. Samuel Hopkins and Rev. Ezra Stiles, of Newport, R. I., where the African slave-trade was extensively carried on. They issued a circular on the subject in August, 1773, in which they invited subscriptions to a fund for founding a colony of free negroes from America on the western shore of Africa. A contribution was made by ladies of Newport in February, 1774, and aid was received from Massachusetts and Connecticut. After the Revolution the effort was renewed by Dr. Hopkins, and he endeavored to make arrangements by which free blacks from America might join the English colony at Sierra Leone, established in 1787, for a home for destitute Africans from different parts of the world, and for promoting African civilization. He failed. In 1793 he proposed a plan of colonization to be carried on by the several States and by the national government. He persevered in his unavailing efforts until his death, in 1803. The subject continued to be agitated from time to time, and in 1815 a company of thirty-eight colored persons emigrated to Sierra Leone from New Bedford.

Steps had been taken as early as 1811 for the organization of a colonization society, and on Dec. 23, 1816, the constitution of the American Colonization Society was adopted at a meeting at Washington, and the first officers were chosen Jan. 1, 1817. All reference to emancipation, present or future, was specially disclaimed by the society, and in the course of the current session of Congress, Henry Clay, John Randolph, Bushrod Washington, and other slave-holders took a leading part in the formation of the society. In March, 1819, Congress appropriated $100,000 for the purpose of sending back to Africa such slaves as should be surreptitiously imported. Provision was made for agents and emigrants to be sent out, and early in 1820 the society appointed an agent, put $30,000 at his disposal, and sent in a government vessel thirty-eight emigrants, who were to erect tents for the reception of at least 300 recaptured Africans. The agents of the United States were instructed not to exercise any authority over the colonists, and the government of the colony was assumed by the society.

A constitution for the colony (which was named Liberia) was adopted (Jan. 24, 1820), by which all the powers of the government were vested in the agent of the colonization society. In 1824 a plan for a civil government in Liberia was adopted, by which the society retained the privilege of ultimate decision. Another constitution was adopted in 1828, by which most of the civil power was secured to the colonists. In 1841 Joseph J. Roberts, a colored man, was appointed governor by the society. Import duties were levied on foreign goods, and out of this grew a temporary difficulty with the British government. British subjects violated the navigation law with impunity, and, when the British government was appealed to, the answer was that Liberia had no national existence. In this emergency the society surrendered such governmental power as it had retained, and recommended the colony to proclaim itself a sovereign and independent state. It was done, and such a declaration of independence was made July 26, 1847. The next year the independence of Liberia was acknowledged by the United States, Great Britain, and France. So the American Colonization Society became mainly instrumental in the foundation of Liberia, and in sustaining the colony until it became self-supporting.

After that consummation the society continued to send out emigrants, and to furnish them with provisions and temporary dwellings; and it materially aided the republic in the development of its commerce and agriculture. It also aided in the dissemination of Christianity in that region, and in the promotion of education and the general welfare of the country. The whole amount of receipts of the society from its foundation to 1875 was, in round numbers, $2,400,000, and those of the auxiliary societies a little more than $400,000. The whole number of emigrants that had been sent out to that date by the parent society was nearly 14,000, and the Maryland society had sent about 1,250; also 5,722 Africans recaptured by the United States government had been returned. The society had five presidents—namely, Bushrod Washington, Charles Carroll, James Madison, Henry Clay, and J. H. B. Latrobe—all of whom were slave-holders.

COLORADO

Colorado (name derived from a Spanish word, meaning "ruddy" or "blood red," hence "colored"), a State in the Mountain Division of the North American Union; bounded on the n. by Wyoming and Nebraska, e. by Nebraska and Kansas, s. by Oklahoma and New Mexico, and w. by Utah; area, 103,948 square miles, of which 290 are water surface; extreme breadth, e. to w., 390 miles; extreme length, n. to s., 270 miles; number of counties, 60; capital, Denver; popular name, "the Centennial State"; State flower, the columbine; State motto, *nil sine numine* ("Nothing without God"); organized as a Territory, Feb. 28, 1861; admitted into the Union as the thirty-eighth State, Aug. 1, 1876; population (1910), 799,024.

General Statistics.—Colorado is called the wonderland of the American continent, because of the wild beauty of its great mountain ranges and majestic peaks and the picturesque parks inclosed by the ranges. The highest peak is Mount Lincoln, 15,000 feet, and from it may be seen 200 peaks, nearly 13,000 feet high, and twenty-five of 14,000 feet and over, and the most noted are Pike's Peak (14,147), discovered by Capt. Zebulon M. Pike in 1806, and the Mountain of the Holy Cross, the subject of Thomas Moran's most famous painting. See also COLORADO SPRINGS. Colorado is further noted for its extensive mineral productions, in the aggregate value of which it ranked fifth among the States in the record year, 1907, and first in the output of gold and silver. The total value was $71,105,128, of which gold yielded $20,897,600; coal, $15,079,449; silver, $7,587,000; and lead, $5,180,856. There are over 45,800 farms containing 4,291,000 improved acres, and representing in land, buildings, and implements nearly $420,000,000. The leading crops with values are; Hay and forage, $17,282,000; wheat, $6,464,000; oats, $4,177,000; potatoes, $3,705,000; corn, $2,674,000; and barley, $1,100,000. Livestock on farms and ranches represents a value of $70,021,211, an increase of over 40 per cent. in ten years.

The manufacturing industries have over 2,000 factory-system establishments, with $162,668,000 capital and $130,044,000 in value of products, the most important being flour and grist, foundry and machine-shop products, steam-railroad cars, and slaughtered and packed meat. Business interests are promoted by 122 national banks, with capital $10,025,000, and resources $131,835,000. Exchanges at the clearing-houses at Denver, Pueblo, and Colorado Springs have reached nearly

$560,000,000 in a single year. Denver is an interior post of commercial delivery, with annual imports of merchandise exceeding $500,000 in value and very limited exports.

Religious interests are represented by 1,208 organizations, having 956 church edifices, 205,666 communicants or members, 96,919 Sunday-school scholars, and church property valued at $7,723,200, the strongest denominations being the Roman Catholic, Methodist, Presbyterian, Baptist, Congregational, Disciples, Protestant Episcopal, and Lutheran, in the order given. The Roman Catholic, Methodist Episcopal, and Protestant Episcopal churches have each a bishop in Denver, and the latter has a missionary bishop at Glenwood Springs. The public-school age is 6–21; enrollment, 162,660; average daily attendance, 103,157; value of public school property, $13,586,309; total revenue, $5,181,412; total expenditure, $5,143,504. For higher education there are the State University, Colorado College (non-sect.), College of the Sacred Heart (Roman Catholic), Colorado Agricultural College (State), State School of Mines, University of Denver (Methodist Episcopal), and Westminster University (Presbyterian); for women only, Colorado Woman's College (Baptist). There are separate State industrial schools for boys and girls, a Manual Training High School in Denver, an Indian Training School at Grand Junction, and a State Institution for the Deaf and Blind at Colorado Springs.

Government.—The executive authority is vested in a governor (annual salary, $5,000), lieutenant-governor, secretary of state, treasurer, auditor, attorney-general, superintendent of public instruction, and commissioner of insurance—official terms, two years. The legislature consists of a Senate of thirty-five members, and a House of Representatives of sixty-five members; terms of Senators, four years; of Representatives, two years; salary of each, $1,000 per term; sessions, biennial; limit, ninety days. The chief judicial authority is a Supreme Court, comprising a chief-justice and five associate justices. An Australian ballot law was passed in 1891. Women possess suffrage on equal terms with men at all elections, and four were elected to the legislature in 1910. The same year the legislature adopted an initiative and referendum law. In May, 1911, the joint assembly of the legislature, balloting for a United States Senator, was dissolved, leaving unbroken a dead-lock that had existed since January. As a result, Colorado, with practically a complete Democratic State administration and with an overwhelming Democratic majority in the legislature, was left for two years with a single representative in the United States Senate, and he a Republican. Under the Revenue Law of 1901 property is required to be assessed at its full value, and at the close of 1910 the total assessed valuation was $414,885,770, and the total debt, $4,207,116.

TERRITORIAL GOVERNORS.

Name.	Term.
William Gilpin	1861 to 1862
John Evans	1862 " 1865
Alexander Cummings	1865 " 1867
A. C. Hunt	1867 " 1869
Edward M. McCook	1869 " 1873
Samuel H. Elbert	1873 " 1874
Edward M. McCook	1874 " 1875
John L. Routt	1875 " 1876

STATE GOVERNORS.

Name.	Term.
John L. Routt	1876 to 1878
Fred. W. Pitkin	1879 " 1882
James B. Grant	1883 " 1885
Benj. H. Eaton	1885 " 1886
Alvah Adams	1887 " 1888
Job A. Cooper	1889 " 1890
John L. Routt	1891 " 1893
Davis H. Waite	1893 " 1895
A. W. McIntyre	1895 " 1897
Alvah Adams	1897 " 1899
Charles S. Thomas	1899 " 1901
James B. Orman	1901 " 1903
James H. Peabody	1903 " 1905
Alvah Adams (to March 16)	1905
J. F. McDonald (Peabody resigns March 17)	1905 to 1907
Henry A. Buchtel	1907 " 1909
John F. Shafroth	1909 " 1913

COLORADO

Colorado ranked thirty-eighth in population among the States and Territories under the census of 1860; forty-first in 1870; thirty-fifth in 1880; thirty-first in 1890 and 1900; and thirty-third in 1910.

UNITED STATES SENATORS.

Name.	No. of Congress	Term.
Jerome B. Chaffee ..	44th to 45th	1876 to 1879
Henry M. Teller	44th " 47th	1877 " 1883
Nathaniel P. Hill ...	46th " 48th	1879 " 1885
Thomas M. Bowen ..	48th " 50th	1883 " 1889
Henry M. Teller	49th " 60th	1885 " 1909
Edward O. Wolcott .	51st " 57th	1889 " 1901
Thomas M. Patterson	57th " 60th	1901 " 1907
Simon Guggenheim...	60th " —	1907 " —
Charles J. Hughes	61st " 62d	1909 " 1911

In the apportionment of representation in Congress, Colorado was given one member under the censuses of 1870 and 1880; two under 1890; three under 1900; and four under 1910.

History.—The portion of the present State north of the Arkansas River, and east of the Rocky Mountains, was included in the Louisiana purchase of 1803 and the remainder in the Mexican cession of 1848. Francis Vasquez de Coronado is believed to have been the first European explorer of this region in 1540. In 1806 President Jefferson sent an expedition, under Lieut. Z. M. Pike, to explore this region, and it nearly crossed the territory from north to south in the mountain region, and discovered the mountain known as Pike's Peak. In 1820 another expedition, under Col. S. H. Long, visited this region; and in 1842–44 Col. John C. Frémont crossed it in his famous passage over the Rocky Mountains. Before the beginning of the nineteenth century, it is believed that no white inhabitants lived in Colorado, excepting a few Mexicans and Spaniards in the southern portion. Gold was discovered there, near the mouth of Clear Creek, in 1852, by a Cherokee cattle-dealer. This and other discoveries of the precious metal brought about 400 persons to Colorado in 1858–59; and the first discovery of a gold-bearing lode was by John H. Gregory, May 6, 1859, in what is now known as the "Gregory Mining District," in Gilpin county. An attempt to organize government among the miners was made by the erection of Arapahoe county and the election of a representative to the Kansas legislature, Nov. 6, 1858. He was instructed to urge the separation of the district from Kansas and the organization of a new Territory. The first movement for a Territorial government was by a convention of 128 delegates held at Denver in the autumn of 1859, who decided to memorialize Congress on

STATE SEAL OF COLORADO.

the subject. The Territory was organized in 1861, and but for the veto of President Johnson Statehood would have been granted in 1867. A further attempt was made in 1873, but Congress refused to pass an enabling act. On March 3, 1875, however, Congress passed such an act. Under its provisions a convention assembled in Denver, and after a session of eighty-six days completed a State constitution, which was ratified by the people on July 1, 1876, whereupon President Grant issued a proclamation, Aug. 1, declaring Colorado to be a State of the Union. The first election for State officers under the constitution was held on Oct. 3, when a Republican administration was chosen, and the new government was inaugurated on Nov. 3. The first State governor was John L. Routt, and the first United States Senators were Jerome B. Chaffee and Henry M. Teller.

Colorado was long noted as a silver-producing State, but after the repeal of the silver-purchase clause of the BLAND SILVER BILL (*q. v.*) by the Sherman Act of 1890, the serious apprehensions of local mine-operators were proved groundless by the results of a general exploitation for gold, and within a few years Colorado passed from the status of a silver to that of a gold State.

The Gunnison Tunnel, in the Uncompahgre Valley, Montrose county, the first and the greatest irrigation project undertaken by the national government up to that time, was completed and formally opened by President Taft on Sept. 23, 1909. It is six miles long, cut through a mountain range 2,000 feet high, has an inside measurement of eleven by thirteen feet, and is lined throughout with cement. The main canal is thirty feet wide at the bottom and eighty-three feet wide at the top, and has an average depth of water of ten feet. The work was begun in 1905; cost, with distributing canals, about $5,-000,000; and irrigates 150,000 acres of land previously semi-arid, by diverting the waters of the Gunnison River into the valley. Three modern and progressive towns were located in the valley while the work was in progress—Montrose, Olathe, and Delta.

The present high state of development of Colorado furnishes a significant response to the official report made to Congress by Maj. Stephen H. Long in 1819, in which he said that all the country drained by the Missouri, Arkansas, and Platte rivers was unsuitable for cultivation and uninhabitable, and Bancroft declares that this report contributed to delay the settlement of the region till after both Oregon and California had been settled. Seven years after the discovery of gold near the mouth of Clear Creek, gold-seekers found silver, which for many years was the most prolific of the precious-metal productions, and more especially after the discovery of the Forest Queen lode near Crested Butte in 1879. The massacre of N. C. Meeker, Indian agent, and twelve others, by the Indians at the White River Agency, and the ambushing and investing of a body of United States troops by the Indians at Mill Creek, during which fourteen soldiers were killed and forty-three wounded, in September and October, 1879, were the most serious of Colorado's Indian troubles. There were political troubles, necessitating the use of soldiers in 1891 and 1894; mining strikes in 1896–97 and 1903–04; and Italian rioting at Lake City in 1899; but, considering the mixed character of its early population, the State has had a very uniform and prosperous existence.

Colorado Springs, city and capital of El Paso county, Col.; at the base of the Rock Mountains, near Pike's Peak; 6,000 feet above sea-level; 75 miles s. of Denver; is widely noted for its grand scenic attractions, which include the famous Garden of the Gods, Manitou and Monument Valley parks, and South Cheyenne Cañon; is the seat of Colorado College (non-sect.), the State Institution for the Deaf and Dumb, and the Childs-Drexel Home for Union Printers; and is chiefly engaged in mining and mercantile business. The city was founded by Gen. William J. Palmer (1836–1909), who, in 1907, presented it with a chain of picturesque parks and scenic driveways, valued at $1,000,000, and covering 1,500 acres, including the noted Monument Valley and Manitou parks; and in 1908 the heirs of Charles E. Perkins presented it with the still more noted Garden of the Gods. Pop. (1910), 29,078.

Colton, Gardner Quincy, scientist; born in Georgia, Vt., Feb. 7, 1814; received a common-school education; removed to New York in 1835, and took up the study of medicine and science in 1842. Lecturing on chemistry and physics a few years later, accident led him to a discovery of the anæsthetic properties of nitrous oxide, or "laughing gas," credit for which is also given to Dr. HORACE WELLS (*q. v.*). He perfected an electric motor in 1847, went to California in 1849, and resumed his scientific lectures in 1860. He died in Rotterdam, Holland, Aug. 11, 1898.

Colquitt, ALFRED HOLT, statesman; born in Walton county, Ga., April 20, 1824; graduated at Princeton in 1844; admitted to the bar in 1845; served throughout the Mexican War as staff officer; in 1852 was elected to Congress; in 1859 was a member of the State legislature. He favored the secession of Georgia and entered the Confederate army, in which he rose to the rank of major-general. In 1876 he was elected governor of the State, and in 1882 United States Senator. He died March 26, 1884.

Colt, SAMUEL, inventor; born in Hartford, Conn., July 19, 1814; patented Colt's revolver in 1835; laid the first submarine cable (between Coney Island and New York City) in 1843. He died in Hartford, Conn., Jan. 10, 1862.

Columbia, CAPTURE OF. See SOUTH CAROLINA.

Columbia, DISTRICT OF. See DISTRICT OF COLUMBIA; WASHINGTON (D. C.).

Columbia, town and county-seat of Maury county, Tenn.; on the Duck River and several railroads; 47 miles s. of Nashville. It has valuable phosphate rock, iron ore, building stone, live-stock, and cotton and woolen interests, and is the seat of a large United States arsenal. During the Civil War there were two encounters here between the National and Confederate forces; the first on Sept. 9, 1862, when the 42d Illinois Volunteers were engaged, and on Nov. 24–28, when a considerable part of General Thomas's army fought what is sometimes known as the battle of Duck Run. Pop. (1910), 5,754.

Columbia River. Discovered by the Spanish in 1775; explored by Captain Gray in 1792, and by Lewis and Clarke in 1805–06.

Columbia University, founded in 1746. Originally named King's College, afterwards Columbia College, and in 1896 Columbia University. Rev. Samuel Johnson, of Stratford, Conn., was invited, in 1753, to become president of the proposed institution, and a royal charter constituting King's College was granted Oct. 31, 1754. The organization was effected in May, 1755. The persons named in the charter as governors of the college were the Archbishop of Canterbury, the principal civil officers of the colony, the principal clergymen of the five denominations of Christians in the city of New York, and twenty private gentlemen. The college opened July 17, 1754, with a class of eight, under Dr. Johnson, sole instructor in the vestry-room of Trinity Church. The corner-stone of the college building was laid Aug. 23, 1756, on the block now bounded by Murray, Church, and Barclay streets and College Place. It faced the Hudson River and "was the most beautifully situated of any college in the world." The first commencement was on June 21, 1758, when about twenty students were graduated. In 1767 a grant was made in the New Hampshire Grants of 24,000 acres of land, but it was lost by the separation of that part of Vermont from New York. In 1762 Rev. Myles Cooper was sent over by the Archbishop of Canterbury to become a "fellow" of the college. He was a strong loyalist, and had a pamphlet controversy with young Alexander Hamilton, one of his pupils. Cooper became president of the college, and so obnoxious were his politics that the college was attacked by the "Sons of Liberty" and a mob in New York on the night of May 10, 1775, and he was obliged to flee for his life. Rev. Benjamin Moore (afterwards bishop of the diocese) succeeded him. The college was prepared for the reception of troops the next year, when the students were dispersed, the library and apparatus were stored in the City Hall, and mostly lost, and the building became a military hospital. About 600 of the volumes were recovered thirty years afterwards in a room in St. Paul's Chapel, when none but the sexton knew of their existence. In 1784 regents of a State University were appointed, who took charge of what property belonged to the institution and changed its name to Columbia College. There was no president for several years. In 1787 the original charter was confirmed by the State legislature, and the college was placed in charge of twenty-four trustees. On May 21, 1787, William Samuel Johnson, LL.D., son of the first president, was chosen to fill his father's place, and the college started on a prosperous career. A new charter was obtained in 1810. A medical and law school was established, and in 1828 the Hon. James Kent delivered a course of law lectures in the college that formed the basis of his famous *Commentaries.* The college occupied the original site until 1857, when it was removed to the square between Madison and Fourth avenues and Forty-ninth and Fiftieth streets.

In 1892, the institution having outgrown its accommodations, a tract of land was purchased on Morningside Heights, between Amsterdam Avenue, the Boulevard, and 116th and 120th streets, and the erection of the first of a group of new buildings, the observatory, was begun. Later on the blocks between 114th and 116th streets were added, together with other real estate, in anticipation of the growth expected in the future. The work of construction has steadily progressed, and prominent among its completions is the noble library building, erected by President Seth Low at a cost of over $1,000,000. The departments included: Columbia College (the School of Arts), School of Political Science, School of Philosophy, School of Journalism, School of Pure Science, School of Law, School of Medicine, School of Applied Science, Barnard College (for women), Teacher's College, Summer School, and Extension Work.

Sixteen million dollars in a decade is the record of money benefactions to Columbia from 1901 to 1911. Concerning the year ended June 30, 1911, President Butler states:

"It is fortunately possible, in reviewing the year 1910–11, to quote literally the words that were used in the annual report for 1910: 'The year has brought to the university benefactions quite without a precedent, both in number and in amount. These benefactions serve to indicate that the work and place and mission of the university are increasingly recognized by the public, as well as that they will command a steadily growing measure of support.' As shown in detail in the annual report of the treasurer, the gifts, legacies, and other receipts for designated purposes received by him during the year ending on June 30, 1911, amounted to $2,535,064.23. Of this great sum, $975,000 was in partial payment of the legacy of the late John Stewart Kennedy, the terms of which were fully described in the last annual report. A further sum of $693,333.33 was in partial payment of the legacy of the late George Crocker, the terms of which were also fully described in the same report. Towards the erection of the Philosophy building, $165,000 was received during the year from an anonymous donor, and towards the erection of the Avery Library building $55,000 was received. Other large and noteworthy gifts were those of anonymous donors to establish the John W. Burgess fund of $100,000; of friends of the late Richard Watson Gilder, to establish the Richard Watson Gilder fund for the promotion of good citizenship, $45,362.51; of friends of the late Dr. William T. Bull, to establish the William T. Bull Memorial Fund, $32,119.45; of Edward D. Adams, of New York, for the purchase and equipment of the Deutsches Haus, $30,000; of a legacy from the late Caroline Phelps Stokes, $20,000; and of Samuel P. Avery, to increase the endowment fund of the Avery Architectural Library, $20,000.

"Including the gifts to Barnard College and to Teachers' College, the sum total of benefactions received during the year falls but very little short of the enormous sum of $3,000,000."

A comparative financial statement of the university's affairs reads as follows:

	1901.	1911.
Property Owned		
1. Occupied for educational purposes....	$11,976,700.00	$20,699,843.86
2. Held for investment.	13,731,446.27	31,733,339.61
Totals............	$25,708,146.27	$52,433,183.47
Outstanding debt........	4,954,850.06	4,284,668.29
Annual Budget—		
1. For educational administration.....	1,322,214.83	2,895,301.29
2. For interest on debt.	110,159.47	147,970.00
Totals............	$1.432,374.40	$3,043,271.29
Income—		
From fees of students	640,015.30	1,341,561.52
From rents..........	397,594.26	942,8 0.87
From interest.........	69,847.68	425,099.32
From miscellaneous sources............	284,441.33	463,154.90
Totals............	$1,391,898.57	$3,172,686.61

In 1911 there were 7,858 students, and 2,846 extension and special students, 767 teachers, and $52,433,183.47 in property, which is 1,256 students, 22 teachers, and $2,932,655.79 more than the institution reported last year, making it the largest and richest university in the world.

Degrees granted during 1910–11 number 1,165; diplomas, 472.

Columbiad. See CANNON.

Columbian Exposition. Early in 1890 an act was passed by Congress providing for an exhibition of arts, industries, manufactures, and products of the soil, mines, and sea in 1892. This exhibition was designed to be a commemoration and celebration of the 400th anniversary of the discovery of America by Columbus, and hence was designated "The World's

Columbian Exposition." When the question of a site for the exposition came up for determination, the four cities, New York, Chicago, St. Louis, and Washington, were competitors, and on Feb. 24 Chicago, which had given a good guarantee of $10,000,000, was awarded that honor. Congress at once appropriated $1,500,000 towards providing for the successful management of the enterprise. A commission of two persons from each State and Territory was appointed by the President on the nomination of the governors, and also eight commissioners at large, and two from the District of Columbia, to constitute the World's Columbian Commission. It was directed that the buildings should be dedicated Oct. 12, 1892. The exposition was to be opened on May 1, 1893, and closed on the last Thursday of October in the same year. In connection with the exposition a naval review was directed to be held in New York Harbor in April, 1893, and the President was authorized to extend to foreign nations an invitation to send ships of war to join the United States navy at Hampton Roads and proceed thence to the review. The national commission being chosen, the President appointed ex-Senator Thomas W. Palmer, of Michigan, to be permanent chairman, and John T. Dickinson, of Texas, permanent secretary. Col. George R. Davis, of Illinois, was chosen director-general of the exposition. The ground selected in Chicago for the erection of the buildings included the commons known as Lake Front, consisting of 90 acres at the edge of the lake adjoining the business centre of the city, and Jackson Park, containing over 600 acres. All the great buildings, except the permanent art building, were to be erected in the park. The entire work of the exposition was divided into fifteen branches, each of which was placed under the control of a director of acknowledged ability and national fame. These branches included the Bureau of Agriculture, the Departments of Ethnology, Fish and Fisheries, Mines and Mining, Liberal Arts, Publicity and Promotion, Fine Arts, Machinery, Manufactures, Electricity, Horticulture, Floriculture and the Woman's Department, besides the Bureau of Transportation and the Department of Foreign Affairs. The total estimated expenditure for the fair was $26,000,000.

The imposing naval parade in New York Harbor proved to be an event of surpassing interest. The fair was opened by President Cleveland; a poem, *Prophecy*, by William A. Croffut, was read, and the usual initiatory exercises occurred, but several weeks elapsed before all the exhibits were in place. Some special features of interest were the various congresses which assembled at Chicago. Aside from religious and educational reunions, there was a literary congress in July, which discussed copyright and general literature; the Jews, Roman Catholics, negroes, and engineers held special "congresses." In the autumn a monster "parliament of religions" assembled, at which were present representatives of the leading Protestant denominations, as well as of the Roman Catholic and Greek Churches, Confucianism, Buddhism, the Brahmo Samaj, Judaism, Mohammedanism, Theosophy, and Shintoism.

The attendance, despite the business depression, was large from the United States, particularly from the West. The visit of Columbus's descendant, the Duke of Veragua, excited much popular interest, as did that of the Princess Eulalie of the Spanish royal family. Restorations of the caravels of Columbus followed his track across the Atlantic, and were conducted to Chicago by way of New York; another noteworthy restoration was the viking ship, which also made the journey to the fair. The question of the Sunday opening of the fair called forth considerable controversy, and reached the courts. As to the general character of the exposition proper, opinions have varied. No mention of the fair would be complete without a reference to several popular features—the gigantic Ferris wheel and the Midway Plaisance, with its various "villages," Cairo street, etc. Two great fires—one in January, the other in June, 1894—swept away the great buildings, excepting the Fine Arts Building, which has been converted into the Field Columbian Museum, now amply endowed.

Columbian Order. See TAMMANY, SOCIETY OF.

Columbus, BARTHOLOMEW, elder brother of Christopher Columbus; born in Genoa about 1432. In 1470, when Christopher went to Lisbon, Bartholomew was there engaged as a mariner and a constructor of maps and charts. It is believed that he visited the Cape of Good Hope with Bartholomew Diaz. Christopher sent him to England to seek the aid of Henry VII. in making a voyage of discovery. He was captured by pirates, and long retained a captive; and, on his return through France, he first heard of his brother's great discovery beyond the Atlantic, and that he had sailed on a second voyage. Bartholomew was cordially received at the Spanish Court, and Queen Isabella sent him in command of three store-ships for the colony in Hispaniola, or Santo Domingo. His brother received him with joy, and made him lieutenant-governor of the Indies. He was uncommonly brave and energetic, and, when his brother was sent to Spain in chains, Bartholomew shared his imprisonment, was released with him, and was made Lord of Mona—an island near Santo Domingo. He died in Santo Domingo, in May, 1515.

COLUMBUS, CHRISTOPHER

Columbus, CHRISTOPHER (Cristoforo Colombo), discoverer of America; born in or near Genoa about 1435. At the age of ten years he was placed in the University of Pavia, where he was instructed in the sciences which pertain to navigation. In 1450 he entered the marine service of Genoa, and remained in it twenty years. His brother BARTHOLOMEW (*q. v.*) was then in Lisbon, engaged in constructing maps and charts, and making an occasional voyage at sea. Thither Christopher went in 1470. Prince Henry of Portugal was then engaged in explorations of the west coast of Africa, seeking for a passage to India south of that continent. The merchants of western Europe were then debarred from participation in the rich commerce of the East by way of the Mediterranean Sea by their powerful and jealous rivals, the Italians, and this fact stimulated explorations for the circumnavigation of Africa. Prince Henry had persisted in his efforts in the face of opposition of priests and learned professors, and had already, by actual discovery by his navigators, exploded the erroneous belief that the equator was impassable because of the extreme heat of the air and water. Columbus hoped to find employment in the prince's service, but Henry died soon after the Genoese arrived in Lisbon.

In the chapel of the Convent of All Saints at Lisbon, Columbus became acquainted with Felipa, daughter of Palestrello, an Italian cavalier, then dead, who had been one of the most trusted of Prince Henry's navigators. Mutual love led to marriage. The bride's mother placed in the hands of Columbus the papers of her husband, which opened to his mind a new field of contemplation and ambition.

The desire for making explorations in the western waters was powerfully stimulated by stories of vegetable productions, timber handsomely carved, and the bodies of two men with dusky skins, which had been washed ashore at the Azores from some unknown land in the west. These had actually been seen by Pedro Correo, a brother of the wife of Columbus. These things confirmed Columbus in his belief that the earth was a sphere, and that Asia might be reached by sailing westward from Europe. He laid plans for explorations, and, in 1474, communicated them to the learned Florentine cosmographer, Paul Toscanelli, who gave him an encouraging answer, and sent him a map constructed partly from Ptolemy's and partly from descriptions of Farther India by Marco Polo, a Venetian traveller who told of Cathay (China) and Zipango (Japan) in the twelfth century. In 1477, Columbus sailed northwest from Portugal beyond Iceland to lat. 73°, when pack-ice turned him back; and it is believed that he went southward as far as the coast of Guinea. Unable to fit out a vessel for himself, it is stated that he first applied for aid, but in vain, to the Genoese. With like ill-success he applied to King John of Portugal, who favored his suit, but priests and professors interposed controlling objections. The King, however, sent a caravel ostensibly with provisions for the Cape Verde Islands, but with secret instructions to the commander to pursue a course westward indicated by Columbus. The fears of the mariners caused them to turn back from the threatenings of the turbulent Atlantic.

CHRISTOPHER COLUMBUS.

Disgusted with this pitiful trick, reduced to poverty, and having lost his wife, he determined to leave Portugal and ask aid from elsewhere. With his son Diego, he left Lisbon for Spain secretly in 1484, while his brother Bartholomew prepared to go to England to ask aid for the projected enterprise from Henry VII. Genoa again declined to help him; so also did Venice; and he applied to the powerful and wealthy Spanish dukes of Medina-Sidonia and Medina-Celi. They declined, but the latter recommended the project to Queen Isabella, then with her Court at Cordova, who requested the navigator to be sent to her. In that city he became attached to Donna Beatrice Enriques, by whom he had a son, Ferdinand, born in 1487, who became the biographer of his father. It was an inauspicious moment for Columbus to lay his projects before the Spanish monarchs, for their courts were moving from place to place, in troublous times, surrounded by the din and pageantry of war. But at Salamanca he was introduced to King Ferdinand by Mendoza, Archbishop of Toledo and Grand Cardinal of Spain.

A council of astronomers and cosmographers was assembled at Salamanca to consider the project. They decided that the scheme was visionary, unscriptural, and irreligious, and the navigator was in danger of arraignment before the tribunal of the Inquisition. For seven years longer the patient navigator waited, while the Spanish monarchs were engaged with the Moors in Granada, during which time Columbus served in the army as a volunteer. Meanwhile the King of Portugal had invited him (1488) to return, and Henry VII. had also invited him by letter to come to the Court of England, giving him encouraging promises of aid. But Ferdinand and Isabella treated him kindly, and he remained in Spain until 1491, when he set out to lay his projects before Charles VIII. of France.

On his way, at the close of a beautiful October day, he stopped at the gate of the Franciscan monastery of Santa Maria de Rabida, near the port of Palos, in Andalusia, and asked for refreshment for his boy, Diego. The prior of the convent, Juan Perez de Marchena, became interested in the conversation of the stranger, and he invited him to remain as his guest. To him Columbus unfolded his plans. Alonzo Pinzon and other eminent navigators at Palos, with scientific men, were invited to the convent to confer with Columbus, and Pinzon offered to furnish and command a ship for explorations. Marchena, who had been Queen Isabella's confessor, wrote to her, asking an interview with her for Columbus. It was granted. Marchena rode to the camp of the monarchs at Santa Fé, when the Queen sent a little more than $200 to Columbus to enable him to appear decently at Court. He explained his project to the sovereigns. He had already, by the operations of a poetic temperament, regarded himself as a preordained gospel-bearer to the heathen of unknown lands. His name implied it—"Christ-bearer"—and hearing that the Sultan of Egypt intended to destroy the sepulchre of Jesus, he recorded a vow that he would devote the proceeds of his explorations to the rescue of that holy place from destruction. He urged his suit with eloquence, but the Queen's confessor opposed the demands of Columbus, and he left Granada—just conquered from the Moors—for France.

A more enlightened civil officer at Court remonstrated, and the Queen sent for him to return. Ferdinand said their wars had so exhausted the treasury that money could not be spared for the enterprise. The Queen declared that she would pledge her crown jewels, if necessary, to supply the money, and would undertake the enterprise for her own crown of Castile. An agreement was signed by their Majesties and Columbus at Santa Fé, April 17, 1492, by which he and his heirs should forever have the office of admiral over all lands he might discover, with honors equal to those of Grand Admiral of Castile; that he should be viceroy and governor-general over the same; that he should receive one-tenth of all mineral and other products that might be obtained; that he and his lieutenants should be the sole judges in all disputes that might arise between his jurisdiction and Spain, and that he might advance one-eighth in any venture, and receive a corresponding share of the profits. He was also authorized to enjoy the title of Don, or noble.

The monarchs fitted out two small vessels—caravels, or undecked ships—and one larger vessel. Leaving Diego as page to Prince Juan, the heir apparent, Columbus sailed from Palos in the decked vessel *Santa Maria*, with Martin Alonzo Pinzon as commander of the *Pinta*, and his brother, Vincent Yañez Pinzon, as commander of the *Nina*, the two caravels. They left the port with a complement of officers and crews on Friday morning, Aug. 3, 1492, and after a voyage marked by tempests—the crew in mortal fear most of the time, and at last mutinous—some indications of land were discovered late in the night of Oct. 11. Many times they had been deceived by presages of land, and what they thought were actual discoveries of it. The crown had offered a little more than $100 to the man who should first discover land, and to this Columbus added the prize of a silken doublet. All eyes were continually on the alert. At ten o'clock on the night of the 11th, Columbus was on his deck, eagerly watching for signs of land, when he discovered a light on the verge of the horizon.

Early the next morning, Rodrigo Tricena, a sailor of the *Pinta*, first saw land; but the award was given to Columbus, who saw the light on the land. At dawn a wooded shore lay before them; and, after a perilous voyage of seventy-one days, the commander, with the banner of the expedition in his hand, leading his followers, landed, as they supposed, on the shores of Farther India. Columbus, clad in scarlet and gold, first touched the beach. A group of naked natives, with skins of a copper hue, watched their movements with awe, and regarded the strangers as gods. Believing he was in India, Columbus called the inhabitants "Indians." Columbus took possession of the land in the name of the crown of Castile. He soon discovered it to be an island—one of the Bahamas—which he named San Salvador. Sailing southward, he discovered Cuba, Haiti, and other islands, and these were denominated the West Indies. He called Haiti Hispaniola, or Little Spain. On its northern shores the *Santa Maria* was wrecked. With her timbers he built a fort, and leaving thirty-nine men there to defend it and the interests of Castile, he sailed in the *Nina* for Spain in January, 1493, taking with him several natives of both sexes. On the voyage he encountered a fearful tempest, but he arrived safely in the Tagus early in March, where the King of Portugal kindly received him. On the 15th he reached Palos, and hastened to the Court at Barcelona, with his natives, specimens of precious metals, beautiful birds, and other products of the newly found regions.

There he was received with great honors; all his dignities were reaffirmed, and on Sept. 25, 1493, he sailed from Cadiz with a fleet of seventeen ships and 1,500 men. Most of these were merely adventurers, and by quarrels and mutinies gave the admiral a great deal of trouble. After discovering the Windward Islands, Jamaica and Porto Rico, founding a colony on Hispaniola, and leaving his brother Bartholomew lieutenant-governor of the island, he returned to Spain, reaching Cadiz, July 11, 1494. Jealousy had promulgated many slanders concerning him; these were all swept away in his presence. The nobles were jealous of him, and used every means in their power to thwart his grand purposes and to bring him into disrepute. He calmly met their opposition by reason, and often confused them by simple illustrations. He had already, by his success, silenced the clamor of the ignorant and superstitious priesthood about the "unscriptural" and "irreligious" character of his proposition, and finally, on May 30, 1498, Columbus sailed from San Lucar de Barrameda, with six ships, on his third voyage of discovery.

He took a more southerly course, and discovered the continent of South America on Aug. 1, at the mouth of the river Orinoco, which he supposed to be one of the rivers flowing out of Eden. Having discovered several islands and the coast of Pará, he finally went to Hispaniola to recruit his enfeebled health. The colony was in great disorder, and his efforts to restore order caused him to be made the victim of jealousy and malice. He was misrepresented at the Spanish Court, and Francisco de Bobadilla was sent from Spain to inquire into the matter. He was ambitious and unscrupulous, and he sent Columbus and his brother to Spain in chains, usurping the government of the island. The commander of the ship that conveyed him across the sea offered to liberate him while on board. "No," he proudly replied, "the chains have been put on by command of their Majesties, and I will wear them until they shall order them to be taken off. I will preserve them afterwards as relics and memorials of the reward of my services."

The monarchs and the people of Spain were indignant at this treatment of the

THE VISION OF COLUMBUS (From an old print).

great discoverer. He was released and Bobadilla was recalled, but, through the influence of the jealous Spanish nobles, Nicolas Ovando was appointed by the King governor of Hispaniola, instead of Columbus. The great Admiral was neglected for a while, when the earnest Queen Isabella caused an expedition to be fitted out for him, and on May 9, 1502, he sailed from Cadiz, with a small fleet, mostly caravels. He was not allowed to refit at his own colony of Hispaniola or Santo Domingo, and he sailed to the western verge of the Gulf of Mexico in search of a passage through what he always believed to be Zipango (Japan) to Cathay, or China. After great sufferings, he returned to Spain in November, 1504, old and infirm, to find the good Queen dead, and to experience the bitterness of neglect from Ferdinand, her husband. His claims were rejected by the ungrateful monarch, and he lived in poverty and obscurity in Valladolid until May 20, 1506, when he died. In a touching letter to a friend just before his death he wrote, "I have no place to repair to except an inn, and am often with nothing to pay for my sustenance." For seven years his remains lay unnoticed in a convent at Valladolid, when the ashamed Ferdinand had them removed to a monastery in Seville, and erected a monument to his memory on which were inscribed the words, "*A Castilla y a Leon Nuevo Mundo Dio Colon*"—"To Castile and Leon Columbus gave a New World." He died in the belief that the continent he had discovered was Asia. His remains were conveyed, in 1536, to Santo Domingo, where they were deposited in the cathedral, and there they yet remain, despite a comparatively recent declaration by the Spanish government that his remains had been transferred to the cathedral in Havana. A noble monument to his memory has been erected in the city of Genoa, Italy. See AMERICA, DISCOVERY OF.

Columbus in Cuba.—The following is the narrative of the explorer's visit to Cuba during his first voyage (1492) from his *Journal*. The *Journal* was forwarded to the King and Queen, but is now lost. In his *Life of Columbus*, Ferdinand Columbus drew largely from the *Journal* (see AMERICA, DISCOVERY OF), and in the subjoined abstract we have parts of the *Journal* word for word, with many quotations by another chronicler concerning what Columbus did and said:

Sunday, Oct. 28—"I went thence in search of the island of Cuba on a south-southwest coast, making for the nearest point of it, and entered a very beautiful river without danger of sunken rocks or other impediments. All the coast was clear of dangers up to the shore. The mouth of the river was 12 *brazos* across, and it is wide enough for a vessel to beat in. I anchored about a lombard-shot inside." The Admiral says that "he never beheld such a beautiful place, with trees bordering the river, handsome, green, and different from ours, having fruits and flowers each one according to its nature. There are many birds, which sing very sweetly. There are a great number of palm-trees of a different kind from those in Guinea and from ours, of a middling height, the trunks without that covering, and the leaves very large, with which they thatch their houses. The country is very level." The Admiral jumped into his boat and went on shore. He came to two houses, which he believed to belong to fishermen who had fled from fear. In one of them he found a kind of dog that never barks, and in both there were nets of palm-fibre and cordage, as well as horn fish-hooks, bone harpoons, and other apparatus "for fishing, and several hearths. He believed that many people lived together in one house. He gave orders that nothing in the houses should be touched, and so it was done." The herbage was as thick as in Andalusia during April and May. He found much purslane and wild amaranth. He returned to the boat and went up the river for some distance, and he says it was great pleasure to see the bright verdure, and the birds, which he could not leave to go back. He says that this island is the most beautiful that eyes have seen, full of good harbors and deep rivers, and the sea appeared as if it never rose; for the herbage on the beach nearly reached the waves, which does not happen where the sea is rough. He says that the island is full of very beautiful mountains, although they are not very extensive as regards length, but high; and all the country is high like Sicily. It is abundantly supplied with water, as they gathered from the Indians they had taken with them from the island of Guanahani. These said by signs that there are ten great rivers, and that they cannot go round the island in twenty days. When they came near land with the ships, two canoes came out; and, when they saw the sailors get into a boat and row about to find the depth of the river where they could anchor, the canoes fled. The Indians say that in this island there are gold-mines and pearls, and the Admiral saw a likely place for them and mussel-shells, which are signs of them. He understood that large ships of the Gran Can came here, and that from here to the mainland was a voyage of ten days. The Admiral called this river and harbor San Salvador.

Monday, Oct. 29.—The Admiral weighed anchor from this port and sailed to the westward, to go to the city, where, as it seemed, the Indians said that there was a king. They doubled a point 6 leagues to the northwest, and then another point, then east 10 leagues. After another league he saw a river with no very large entrance, to which he gave the name of Rio de la Luna. He went on until the hour of vespers. He saw another river much larger than the others, as the Indians told him by signs, and near he saw goodly villages of houses. He called the river Rio de Mares. He sent two boats on shore to a village to communicate, and one of the Indians he had brought with him, for now they understood a little, and show themselves content with Christians. All the men, women, and children fled, abandoning their houses with all they contained. The Admiral gave orders that nothing should be touched. The houses were better than those he had seen before, and he believed that the houses would improve as he approached the mainland. They were made like booths, very large, and looking like tents in a camp without regular streets, but one here and another there. Within they were clean and well swept, with the furniture well made. All are of palm branches beautifully constructed. They found many images in the shape of women, and many heads like masks, very well carved. It was not known whether these were used as ornaments, or to be worshipped. They had dogs which never bark, and wild birds tamed in their houses. There was a wonderful supply of nets and other fishing implements, but nothing was touched. He believed that all the people on the coast were fishermen, who took the fish inland, for this island is very large, and so beautiful that he is never tired of praising it. He says that he found trees and fruits of very marvellous taste; and adds that they must have cows or other cattle, for he saw skulls which were like those of cows. The songs of the birds and the chirping of crickets throughout the night lulled every one to rest, while the air was soft and healthy, and the nights neither hot nor cold. On the voyage through the other islands there was great heat, but here it is tempered like the month of May. He attributed the heat of the other islands to their flatness, and to the wind coming from the east, which is hot. The water of the rivers was salt at the mouth, and they did not know whence the natives got their drinking-water, though they have sweet water in their houses. Ships are able to turn in this river, both entering and coming out, and there are very good leading-marks. He says that all this sea appears to be constantly smooth, like the river at Seville, and the water suitable for the growth of pearls. He found large shells unlike those of Spain. Remarking on the position of the river and port, to which he gave the name of San Salvador, he describes its mountains as lofty and beautiful, like the Peña de las Enamoradas, and one of them has another little hill on its summit, like a graceful mosque. The other river and port, in which he now was, has two round mountains to the southwest, and a fine low cape running out to the west-southwest.

THE NEW WORLD.

Tuesday, Oct. 30.—He left the Rio de Mares and steered northwest, seeing a cape covered with palm-trees, to which he gave the name of Cabo de Palmas, after having made good 15 leagues. The Indians on board the caravel *Pinta* said that beyond that cape there was a river, and that from the river to Cuba it was four days' journey. The captain of the *Pinta* reported that he understood from that, that this Cuba was a city, and that the land was a great continent trending far to the north. The king of that country, he gathered, was at war with the Gran Can, whom they called Cami, and his land or city Fava, with many other names. The Admiral resolved to proceed to that river, and to send a present, with the letter of the sovereigns, to the king of that land. For this service there was a sailor who had been to Guinea, and some of the Indians of Guanahani wished to go with him, and afterwards to return to their homes.

Wednesday, Oct. 31.—All Tuesday night he was beating to windward, and he saw a river, but could not enter it because the entrance was narrow. The Indians fancied that the ships could enter wherever their canoes could go. Navigating onward, he came to a cape running out very far, and surrounded by sunken rocks, and he saw a bay where small vessels might take shelter. He could not proceed, because the wind had come round to the north, and all the coast runs northwest and southeast. Another cape farther on ran out still more. For these reasons and because the sky showed signs of a gale, he had to return to the Rio de Mares.

Thursday, Nov. 1.—At sunrise the Admiral sent the boats on shore to the houses that were there, and they found that all the people had fled. After some time a man made his appearance. The Admiral ordered that he should be left to himself, and the sailors returned to the boats. After dinner, one of the Indians on board was sent on shore. He called out from a distance that there was nothing to fear, because the strangers were good people and would do no harm to any one, nor were they people of the Gran Can, but they had given away their things in many islands where they had been. The Indian then swam on shore, and two of the natives took him by the arms and brought him to a house, where they heard what he had to say. When they were certain that no harm would be done to them they were reassured, and presently more than sixteen canoes came to the ships with cotton thread and other trifles. The Admiral ordered that nothing should be taken from them, but that they might understand that he sought for nothing but gold, which they called *nucay*. Thus they went to and fro between the ships and the shore all day, and they came to the Christians on shore with confidence. The Admiral saw no gold whatever among them, but he says that he saw one of them with a piece of worked silver fastened to his nose. They said, by signs, that within three days many merchants from inland would come to buy the things brought by the Christians, and would give information respecting the king of that land. So far as could be understood from their signs, he resided at a distance of four days' journey. They had sent many messengers in all directions, with news of the arrival of the Admiral. "These people," says the Admiral, "are of the same appearance and have the same customs as those of the other islands, without any religion, so far as I know, for up to this day I have never seen the Indians on board say any prayer; though they repeat the *Salve* and *Ave Maria* with their hands raised to heaven, and they make the sign of the cross. The language is also the same, and they are all friends; but I believe that all these islands are at war with the Gran Can, whom they call Cavila, and his province Bafan. They all go naked like the others." This is what the Admiral says. "The river," he adds, "is very deep, and the ships can enter the mouth, going close to the shore. The sweet water does not come within a league of the mouth. It is certain," says the Admiral, "that this is the mainland, and that I am in front of Zayto and Guinsay, 100 leagues, a little more or less, distant the one from the other. It was very clear that no one before has been so far as this by sea. Yesterday, with wind from the northwest, I found it cold."

Friday, Nov. 2.—The Admiral decided upon sending two Spaniards, one named Rodrigo de Jerez, who lived in Ayamonte, and the other Luis de Torres, who had served in the household of the Adelantado of Murcia, and had been a Jew, knowing Hebrew, Chaldee, and even some Arabic. With these men he sent two Indians, one from among those he had brought from Guanahani, and another native of the houses by the river-side. He gave them specimens of spices, to see if any were to be found. Their instructions were to ask for the king of that land, and they were told what to say on the part of the sovereigns of Castile, how they had sent the Admiral with letters and a present, to inquire after his health and establish friendship, favoring him in what he might desire from them. They were to collect information respecting certain provinces, ports, and rivers of which the Admiral had notice.

This night the Admiral took an altitude with a quadrant, and found that the distance from the equinoctial line was 42 degrees. He says that, by his reckoning, he finds that he has gone over 1,142 leagues from the island of Hierro. He still believes that he has reached the mainland.

Saturday, Nov. 3.—In the morning the Admiral got into his boat, and, as the river is like a great lake at the mouth, forming a very excellent port, very deep, and clear of rocks, with a good beach for careening ships, and plenty of fuel, he explored it until he came to fresh water at a distance of 2 leagues from the mouth. He ascended a small mountain to obtain a view of the surrounding country, but could see nothing, owing to the dense foliage of the trees, which were very fresh and odoriferous, so that he felt no doubt that there were aromatic herbs among them. He said that all he saw was so beautiful that his eyes could never tire of gazing upon such loveliness, nor his ears of listening to the songs of birds. That day many canoes came to the ships, to barter with cotton threads and with the nets in which they sleep, called *hamacas.*

Sunday, Nov. 4.—At sunrise the Admiral again went away in the boat, and landed to hunt the birds he had seen the day before. After a time, Martin Alonzo Pinzon came to him with two pieces of cinnamon, and said that a Portuguese, who was one of his crew, had seen an Indian carrying two very large bundles of it; but he had not bartered for it, because of the penalty imposed by the Admiral on any one who bartered. He further said that this Indian carried some brown things like nutmegs. The master of the *Pinta* said that he had found the cinnamon-trees. The Admiral went to the place, and found that they were not cinnamon-trees. He showed the Indians gold and pearls, on which certain old men said that there was an infinite quantity in a place called Bohio; he further understood them to say that there were great ships and much merchandise, all to the

REARING THE CROSS.

southeast. He also understood that, far away, there were men with one eye, and others with dogs' noses who were cannibals, and that when they captured an enemy they beheaded him and drank his blood.

The Admiral then determined to return to the ship and wait for the return of the two men he had sent, intending to depart and seek for those lands, if his envoys brought some good news touching what he desired. The Admiral further says: "These people are very gentle and timid; they go naked, as I have said, without arms and without law. The country is very fertile. The people have plenty of roots called *zanahorias* (yams), with a smell like chestnuts; and they have beans of kinds very different from ours. They also have much cotton, which they do not sow, as it is wild in the mountains, and I believe they collect it throughout the year, because I saw pods empty, others full, and flowers all on one tree. There are a thousand other kinds of fruits which it is impossible for me to write about, and all must be profitable." All this the Admiral says.

Monday, Nov. 5.—This morning the Admiral ordered the ship to be careened, afterwards the other vessels, but not all at the same time. Two were always to be at the anchorage, as a precaution; although he says that these people were very safe, and that without fear all the vessels might have been careened at the same time. Things being in this state, the master of the *Niña* came to claim a reward from the Admiral because he had found mastic, but he did not bring the specimen, as he had dropped it. The Admiral promised him a reward, and sent Rodrigo Sanchez and master Diego to the trees. They collected some, which was kept to present to the sovereigns, as well as the tree. The Admiral says that he knew it was mastic, though it ought to be gathered at the proper season. There is enough in that district for a yield of 1,000 quintals every year. The Admiral also found here a great deal of the plant called aloe. He further says that the Puerto de Mares is the best in the world, with the finest climate and the most gentle people. As it has a high, rocky cape, a fortress might be built, so that, in the event of the place becoming rich and important, the merchants would be safe from any other nations. He adds: "The Lord, in whose hands are all victories, will ordain all things for his service. An Indian said by signs that the mastic was good for pains in the stomach."

Tuesday, Nov. 6.—"Yesterday, at night," says the Admiral, "the two men came back who had been sent to explore the interior. They said that after walking 12 leagues they came to a village of fifty houses, where there were 1,000 inhabitants, for many live in one house. These houses are like very large booths. They said that they were received with great solemnity, according to custom, and all, both men and women, came out to see them. They were lodged in the best houses, and the people touched them, kissing their hands and feet, marvelling and believing that they came from heaven, and so they gave them to understand. They gave them to eat of what they had. When they arrived, the chief people conducted them by the arms to the principal house, gave them two chairs on which to sit, and all the natives sat round them on the ground. The Indian who came with them described the manner of living of the Christians, and said that they were good people. Presently the men went out, and the women came sitting round them in the same way, kissing their hands and feet, and looking to see if they were of flesh and bones like themselves. They begged the Spaniards to remain with them at least five days." The Spaniards showed the natives specimens of cinnamon, pepper, and other spices which the Admiral had given them, and they said, by signs, that there was plenty at a short distance from thence to the southeast, but that there they did not know whether there was any. Finding that they had no information respecting cities, the Spaniards returned; and if they had desired to take those who wished to accompany them, more than 500 men and women would have come, because they thought the Spaniards were returning to heaven. There came, however, a principal man of the village and his son, with a servant. The Admiral conversed with them, and showed them much honor.

They made signs respecting many lands and islands in those parts. The Admiral thought of bringing them to the sovereigns. He says that he knew not what fancy took them; either from fear, or owing to the dark night, they wanted to land. The ship was at the time high and dry, but, not wishing to make them angry, he let them go on their way, saying that they would return at dawn, but they never came back.

The two Christians met with many people on the road going home, men and women with a half-burnt weed in their hands, being the herbs they are accustomed to smoke. They did not find villages on the road of more than five houses, all receiving them with the same reverence. They saw many kinds of trees, herbs, and sweet-smelling flowers; and birds of many different kinds, unlike those of Spain, except the partridges, geese, of which there are many, and singing nightingales. They saw no quadrupeds except the dogs that do not bark. The land is very fertile, and is cultivated with yams and several kinds of beans different from ours, as well as corn. There were great quantities of cotton gathered, spun, and worked up. In a single house they saw more than 500 arrobas, and as much as 4,000 quintals could be yielded every year. The Admiral said that "it did not appear to be cultivated, and that it bore all the year round. It is very fine, and has a large boll. All that was possessed by these people they gave at a very low price, and a great bundle of cotton was exchanged for the point of a needle or other trifle. They are a people," says the Admiral, "guileless and unwarlike. Men and women go as naked as when their mothers bore them. It is true that the women wear a very small rag of cotton cloth, and they are of very good appearance, not very dark, less so than the Canarians. I hold, most serene Princes, that if devout religious persons were here, knowing the language, they would all turn Christians. I trust in our Lord that your Highnesses will resolve upon this with much diligence, to bring so many great nations within the Church, and to convert them, as you have destroyed those who would not confess the Father, the Son, and the Holy Ghost. And after your days, all of us being mortal, may your kingdoms remain in peace, and free from heresy and evil, and may you be well received before the eternal Creator, to whom I pray that you may have long life and great increase of kingdoms and lordships, with the will and disposition to increase the holy Christian religion as you have done hitherto. Amen!

"To-day I got the ship afloat, and prepared to depart on Thursday, in the name of God, and to steer southeast in search of gold and spices, and to discover land."

These are the words of the Admiral, who intended to depart on Thursday, but, the wind being contrary, he could not go until Nov. 12.

Monday, Nov. 12.—The Admiral left the port and river of Mares before dawn to visit the island called Babeque, so much talked of by the Indians on board, where, according to their signs, the people gather the gold on the beach at night with candles, and afterwards beat it into bars with hammers. To go hither it was necessary to shape a course east by south. After having made 8 leagues along the coast, a river was sighted, and another 4 leagues brought them to another river, which appeared to be of great volume, and larger than any they had yet seen. The Admiral did not wish to stop nor to enter any of these rivers, for two reasons: the first and principal one being that wind and weather were favorable for going in search of the said island of Babeque; the other that, if there was a populous and famous city near the sea, it would be visible, while, to go up the rivers, small vessels are necessary, which those of the expedition were not. Much time would thus be lost; moreover, the exploration of such rivers is a separate enterprise. All that coast was peopled near the river, to which the name of Rio del Sol was given.

The Admiral says that, on the previous Sunday, Nov. 11, it seemed good to take some person from among those at Rio de Mares, to bring to the sovereigns, that they might learn our language, so as to be able to tell us what there is in their lands. Returning, they would be the mouthpieces of the Christians, and would adopt our customs and the things of the faith. "I saw and knew," says the Admiral, "that these people are without any religion, not idolaters, but very gentle, not knowing what is evil, nor the sins of murder and theft, being without arms, and so timid that 100 would fly before one Spaniard, although they joke with them. They, however, believe and know that there is a God in heaven, and say that we have come from heaven. At any prayer that we say, they repeat, and make the sign of the cross. Thus your Highnesses should resolve to make them Christians, for I believe that, if the work was begun, in a little time a multitude of nations would be converted to our faith, with the acquisition of great lordships, peoples, and riches for Spain. Without doubt, there is in these lands a vast quantity of gold, and the Indians I have on board do not speak without reason when they say that in these islands there are places where they dig out gold, and wear it on their necks, ears, arms, and legs, the rings being very large. There are also precious stones, pearls, and an infinity of spices. In this river of Mares, whence we departed to-night, there is undoubtedly a great quantity of mastic, and much more could be raised, because the trees may be planted, and will yield abundantly. The leaf and fruit are like the mastic, but the tree and leaf are larger. As Pliny describes it, I have seen it on the island of Chios in the Archipelago. I ordered many of these trees to be tapped, to see if any of them would yield resin; but, as it rained all the time I was in that river, I could not get any, except a very little, which I am bringing to your Highnesses. It may not be the right season for tapping, which is, I believe, when the trees come forth after winter and begin to flower. But when I was there the fruit was nearly ripe. Here also there is a great quantity of cotton, and I believe it would have a good sale here without sending it to Spain, but to the great cities of the Gran Can, which will be discovered without doubt, and many others ruled over by other lords, who will be pleased to serve your Highnesses, and whither will be brought other commodities of Spain and of the Eastern lands; but these are to the west as regards us. There is also here a great yield of aloes, though this is not a commodity that will yield great profit. The mastic, however, is important, for it is only obtained from the said island of Chios, and I believe the harvest is worth 50,000 ducats, if I remember right. There is here, in the mouth of the river, the best port I have seen up to this time, wide, deep, and clear of rocks. It is an excellent site for a town and fort, for any ship could come close up to the walls; the land is high, with a temperate climate, and very good water.

"Yesterday a canoe came alongside the ship, with six youths in it. Five came on board, and I ordered them to be detained. They are here now. I afterwards sent to a house on the western side of the river, and seized seven women, old and young, and three children. I did this because the men would behave better in Spain if they had women of their own land than without them. For on many occasions the men of Guinea have been brought to learn the language of Portugal, and afterwards, when they returned, and it was expected that they would be useful in their land, owing to the good company they had enjoyed and the gifts they had received, they never appeared after arriving. Others may not act thus. But, having women, they have the wish to perform what they are required to do; besides, the women would teach our people their language, which is the same in all these islands, so that those who make voyages in their canoes are understood everywhere. On the other hand, there are 1,000 different languages in Guinea, and one native does not understand another.

"The same night the husband of one of the women came alongside in a canoe, who was father of the three children—one boy and two girls. He asked me to let him come with them, and besought me much. They are now all consoled at being with one who is a relation of them all. He is a man of about forty-five years of age." All these are the words of the Admiral. He also says that he had felt some cold, and that it would not be wise to continue discoveries in a northerly direction in the winter. On this Monday, until sunset, he steered a course east by south, making 18 leagues, and reaching a cape, to which he gave the name of Cabo de Cuba.

Tuesday, Nov. 13. — This night the ships were on the bowline, as the sailors say, beating to windward without making any progress. At sunset they began to see an opening in the mountains, where two very high peaks were visible. It appeared that here was the division between the land of Cuba and that of Bohio, and this was affirmed by signs, by the Indians who were on board. As soon as the day had dawned, the Admiral made sail towards the land, passing a point which appeared at night to be distant 2 leagues. He then entered a large gulf, 5 leagues to the south-southeast, and there remained 5 more, to arrive at the point where, between two great mountains, there appeared to be an opening; but it could not be made out whether it was an inlet of the sea. As he desired to go to the island called Babeque, where, according to the information he had received, there was much gold; and as it bore east, and as no large town was in sight, the wind freshening more than ever, he resolved to put out to sea, and work to the east with a northerly wind. The ship made 8 miles an hour, and from ten in the forenoon, when that course was taken, until sunset, 56 miles, which is 14 leagues to the eastward from the Cabo de Cuba. The other land of Bohio was left to leeward. Commencing from the cape of the said gulf, he discovered, according to his reckoning, 80 miles, equal to 20 leagues, all that coast running east-southeast and west-northwest.

Wednesday, Nov. 14. — All last night the Admiral was beating to windward (he said that it would be unreasonable to navigate among those islands during the night, until they had been explored), for the Indians said yesterday that it would take three days to go from Rio de Mares to the island of Babeque, by which should be understood days' journeys in their canoes, equal to about 7 leagues. The wind fell, and, the course being east, she could not lay her course nearer than southeast, and, owing to other mischances, he was detained until the morning. At sunrise he determined to go in search of a port, because the wind had shifted from north to northeast, and, if a port could not be found, it would be necessary to go back to the ports in the island of Cuba, whence they came. The Admiral approached the shore, having gone over 28 miles east-southeast that night. He steered south . . . miles to the land, where he saw many islets and openings. As the wind was high and the sea rough, he did not dare to risk an attempt to enter, but ran along the coast west-northwest, looking out for a port, and saw many, but none very clear of rocks. After having proceeded for 64 miles, he found a very deep opening, a quarter of a mile wide, with a good port and river. He ran in with her head south-southwest, afterwards south to southeast. The port was spacious and very deep, and he saw so many islands that he could not count them all, with very high land covered with trees of many kinds, and an infinite number of palms. He was much astonished to see so many lofty islands; and assured the sovereigns that the mountains and isles he had seen since yesterday seemed to him to be second to none in the world; so high and clear of clouds and snow, with the sea at their bases so deep. He believes that these islands are those innumerable ones that are depicted on the maps of the world in the Far East.

He believed that they yielded very great riches in precious stones and spices, and that they extend much further to the south, widening out in all directions. He gave the name of La Mar de Nuestra Señora, and to the haven, which is near the mouth of the entrance to these islands, Puerto de Principe. He did not enter it, but examined it from outside, until another time, on Saturday of the next week, as will there appear. He speaks highly of the fertility, beauty, and height of the islands which he found in this gulf, and he tells the sovereigns not to wonder at his praise of them, for that he has not told them the hundredth part. Some of them seemed to reach to heaven, running up into peaks like diamonds. Others have a flat top like a table. At their bases the sea is of a great depth, with enough water for a very large carrack. All are covered with foliage and without rocks.

Thursday, Nov. 15. — The Admiral went to examine these islands in the ship's boats, and speaks marvels of them, how he found mastic and aloes without end. Some of them were cultivated with the roots of which the Indians make bread; and he found that fires had been lighted in several places. He saw no fresh water. There were some natives, but they fled. In all parts of the sea where the vessels were navigated he found a depth of 15 or 16 fathoms, and all *basa,* by which he means that the ground is sand, and not rocks; a thing much desired by sailors, for the rocks cut their anchor cables.

Friday, Nov. 16. — As in all parts whether islands or mainlands, that he visited, the Admiral always left a cross, so, on this occasion, he went in a boat to the entrance of these havens, and found two very large trees on a point of land, one longer than the other. One being placed over the other made a cross, and he said that a carpenter could not have made it better. He ordered a very large and high cross to be made out of these timbers. He found canes on the beach, and did not know where they had grown, but thought they must have been brought down by some river, and washed up on the beach (in which opinion he had reason). He went to a creek on the southeast side of the entrance to the port. Here, under a height of rock and stone like a cape, there was depth enough for the largest carrack in the world close in shore, and there was a corner where six ships might lie without anchors as in a room. It seemed to the Admiral that a fortress might be built here at small cost, if at any time any famous trade should arise in that sea of islands.

Returning to the ship, he found that the Indians who were on board had fished up very large shells found in those seas. He made the people examine them, to see if there was mother-o'-pearl, which is in the shells where pearls grow. They found a great deal, but no pearls, and their absence was attributed to its not being the season, which is May and June. The sailors found an animal which seemed to be a *taso,* or *taxo.* They also fished with nets, and, among many others, caught a fish which was exactly like a pig, not like a tunny, but all covered with a very hard shell, without a soft place except the eyes. It was ordered to be salted, to bring home for the sovereigns to see.

Saturday, Nov. 17.– The Admiral got into the boat, and went to visit the islands he had not yet seen to the southwest. He saw many more very fertile and pleasant islands, with a great depth between them. Some of them had springs of fresh water, and he believed that the water of those streams came from some sources at the summits of the mountains. He went on, and found a beach bordering on very sweet water, which was very cold. There was a beautiful meadow, and many very tall palms. They found a large nut of the kind belonging to India, great rats, and enormous crabs. He saw many birds, and there was a strong smell of musk, which made him think it must be there. This day the two eldest of the six youths, brought from the Rio de Mares, who were on board the caravel *Niña,* made their escape.

Sunday, Nov. 18. — The Admiral again went away with the boats, accompanied by many of the sailors, to set up the cross which he had ordered to be made out of the two large trees at the entrance to the Puerto del Principe, on a fair site cleared of trees, whence there was an extensive and very beautiful view. He says that there is a greater rise and fall there than in any other port he has seen, and that this is no marvel, considering the numerous islands. The tide is the reverse of ours, because here, when the moon is south-southwest, it is low water in the port. He did not get under way, because it was Sunday.

Monday, Nov. 19. — The Admiral got under way before sunrise, in a calm. In the afternoon there was some wind from the east, and he shaped a north-northeast course. At sunset the Puerto del Principe bore south-southwest 7 leagues. He saw the island of Babeque bearing due east about 60 miles. He steered northeast all that night, making 60 miles, and up to ten o'clock of Tuesday another dozen; altogether 18 leagues northeast by west.

Tuesday, Nov. 20.—They left Babeque, or the islands of Babeque, to the east-southeast, the wind being contrary; and, seeing that no progress was being made, and the sea was getting rough, the Admiral determined to return to the Puerto del Principe, whence he had started, which was 25 leagues distant. He did not wish to go to the island he had called Isabella, which was 12 leagues off, and where he might have anchored that night, for two reasons: one was that he had seen two islands to the south which he wished to explore; the other, because the Indians he brought with him, whom he had taken at the island of Guanahani, which he named San Salvador, 8 leagues from Isabella, might get away, and he said that he wanted them to take to Spain. They thought that, when the Admiral had found gold, he would let them return to their homes. He came near the Puerto del Principe, but could not reach it, because it was night, and because the current drifted them to the northwest. He turned her head to northeast with a light wind. At three o'clock in the morning the wind changed, and a course was shaped east-northeast, the wind being south-southwest, and changing at dawn to south and southeast. At sunset Puerto del Principe bore nearly southwest by west 48 miles, which are 12 leagues.

Wednesday, Nov. 21.—At sunrise the Admiral steered east, with a southerly wind, but made little progress, owing to a contrary sea. At vespers he had gone 24 miles. Afterwards the wind changed to east, and he steered south by east, at sunset having gone 12 miles. Here he found himself 42 degrees north of the equinoctial line, as in the port of Mares, but he says that he kept the result from the quadrant in suspense until he reached the shore, that it might be adjusted (as it would seem that he thought this distance was too great, and he had reason, it not being possible, as these islands are only in . . . degrees).

This day Martin Alonzo Pinzon parted company with the caravel *Pinta*, in disobedience to and against the wish of the Admiral, and out of avarice, thinking that an Indian who had been put on board his caravel could show him where there was much gold. So he parted company, not owing to bad weather, but because he chose. Here the Admiral says: "He had done and said many other things to me."

Thursday, Nov. 22. — On Wednesday night the Admiral steered south-southeast, with the wind east, but it was nearly calm. At three it began to blow from north-northeast; and he continued to steer south to see the land he had seen in that quarter. When the sun rose he was as far off as the day before, owing to adverse currents, the land being 40 miles off. This night Martin Alonzo shaped a course to the east, to go to the island of Babeque, where the Indians say there is much gold. He did this in sight of the Admiral, from whom he was distant 16 miles. The Admiral stood towards the land all night. He shortened sail, and showed a lantern, because Pinzon would thus have an opportunity of joining him, the night being very clear, and the wind fair to come, if he had wished to do so.

Friday, Nov. 23.—The Admiral stood towards the land all day, always steering south with little wind, but the current would never let them reach it, being as far off at sunset as in the morning. The wind was east-northeast, and they could shape a southerly course, but there was little of it. Beyond this cape there stretched out another land or cape, also trending east, which the Indians on board called Bohio. They said that it was very large, and that there were people in it who had one eye in their foreheads, and others who were cannibals, and of whom they were much afraid. When they saw that this course was taken, they said that they could not talk to these people because they would be eaten, and that they were very well armed. The Admiral says that he well believes that there were such people, and that if they are armed they must have some ability. He thought that they may have captured some of the Indians, and because they did not return to their homes, the others believed that they had been eaten. They thought the same of the Christians and of the Admiral when some of them first saw the strangers.

Saturday, Nov. 24. — They navigated all night, and at three they reached the island at the very same point they had come to the week before, when they started for the island of Babeque. At first the Admiral did not dare to approach the shore, because it seemed that there would be a great surf in that mountain-girded bay. Finally he reached the sea of Nuestra Señora, where there are many islands, and entered a port near the mouth of the opening to the islands. He says that if he had known of this port before he need not have occupied himself in exploring the islands, and it would not have been necessary to go back. He, however, considered that the time was well spent in examining the islands. On nearing the land he sent in the boat to sound; finding a good sandy bottom in 6 to 20 fathoms. He entered the haven, pointing the ship's head southwest, and then west, the flat island bearing north. This, with another island near it, forms a harbor which would hold all the ships of Spain safe from all winds. This entrance on the southwest side is passed by steering south-southwest, the outlet being to the west very deep and wide. Thus a vessel can pass amidst these islands, and he who approaches from the north, with a knowledge of them, can pass along the coast. These islands are at the foot of a great mountain-chain running east and west, which is longer and higher than any others on this coast, where there are many. A reef of rocks outside runs parallel with the said mountains, like a bench, extending to the entrance. On the side of the flat island, and also to the southeast, there is another small reef, but between them is great width and depth. Within the port, near the southeast side of the entrance, they saw a large and very fine river, with more volume than any they had yet met with, and fresh water could be taken from it as far as the sea. At the entrance there is a bar, but within it is very deep, 19 fathoms. The banks are lined with palms and many other trees.

Sunday, Nov 25.—Before sunrise the Admiral got into the boat, and went to see a cape or point of land to the southeast of the flat island, about a league and a half distant, because there appeared to be a good river there. Presently, near to the southeast side of the cape, at a distance of two cross-bow shots, he saw a large stream of beautiful water falling from the mountains above, with a loud noise. He went to it, and saw some stones shining in its bed like gold. He remembered that in the river Tejo, near its junction with the sea, there was gold; so it seemed to him that this should contain gold, and he ordered some of these stones to be collected, to be brought to the sovereigns. Just then the sailor-boys called out that they had found large pines. The Admiral looked up the hill, and saw that they were so wonderfully large that he could not exaggerate their height and straightness, like stout yet fine spindles. He perceived that here there was material for great store of planks and masts for the largest ships in Spain. He saw oaks and arbutus-trees, with a good river, and the means of making water-proof. The climate was temperate, owing to the height of the mountains. On the beach he saw many other stones of the color of iron, and others that some said were like silver ore, all brought down by the river. Here he obtained a new mast and yard for the mizzen of the caravel *Niña.* He came to the mouth of the river, and entered a creek which was deep and wide, at the foot of that southeast part of the cape, which would accommodate 100 ships without any anchor or hawsers. Eyes never beheld a better harbor. The mountains are very high, whence descend many limpid streams and all the hills are covered with pines, and an infinity of diverse and beautiful trees. Two or three other rivers were not visited.

The Admiral described all this, in much detail, to the sovereigns, and declared that he had derived unspeakable joy and pleasure at seeing it, more especially the pines, because they enable as many ships as is desired to be built here, bringing out the rigging, but finding here abundant supplies of wood and provisions. He affirms that he has not enumerated a hundredth part of what there is here, and that it pleased our Lord always to show him one thing better than another, as well on the ground and among the trees, herbs, fruits, and flowers, as in the people, and always something different in each place. It had been the same as regards the havens and the waters. Finally, he says that, if it caused him who saw it so much wonder, how much more will it affect those who hear about it; yet no one can believe until he sees it.

Monday, Nov. 26.—At sunrise the Admiral weighed the anchors in the haven of Santa Catalina, where he was behind the flat island, and steered along the coast in the direction of Cabo del Pico, which was southeast. He reached the cape late, because the wind failed, and then saw another cape, southeast by east 60 miles, which, when 20 miles off, was named Cabo de Campana, but it could not be reached that day. They made good 32 miles during the day, which is 8 leagues. During this time the Admiral noted nine remarkable ports, which all the sailors thought wonderfully good, and five large rivers; for they sailed close along the land, so as to see everything. All along the coast there are very high and beautiful mountains, not arid or rocky, but all accessible, and very lovely. The valleys, like the mountains, were full of tall and fine trees, so that it was a glory to look upon them, and there seemed to be many pines. Also, beyond the said Cabo de Pico to the southeast there are two islets, each about 2 leagues round, and inside them three excellent havens and two large rivers. Along the whole coast no inhabited places were visible from the sea. There may have been some, and there were indications of them, for, when the men landed, they found signs of people and numerous remains of fire. The Admiral conjectured that the land he saw to-day southeast of the Cabo de Campana was the island called by the Indians Bohio: it looked as if this cape was separated from the mainland.

The Admiral says that all the people he has hitherto met with have very great fear of those of Caniba or Canima. They affirm that they live in the island of Bohio, which must be very large, according to all accounts. The Admiral understood that those of Caniba come to take people from their homes, they being very cowardly, and without knowledge of arms. For this cause it appears that these Indians do not settle on the sea-coast, owing to being near the island of Caniba. When the natives who were on board saw a course shaped for that land, they feared to speak, thinking they were going to be eaten; nor could they rid themselves of their fear. They declared that the Canibas had only one eye and dogs' faces. The Admiral thought they lied, and was inclined to believe that it was people from the dominions of the Gran Can who took them into captivity.

Tuesday, Nov. 27.—Yesterday, at sunset, they arrived near a cape named Campana by the Admiral; and, as the sky was clear and the wind light, he did not wish to run in close to the land and anchor, although he had five or six singularly good havens under his lee. The Admiral was attracted on the one hand by the longing and delight he felt to gaze upon the beauty and freshness of those lands, and on the other by a desire to complete the work he had undertaken. For these reasons he remained close hauled, and stood off and on during the night. But, as the currents had set him more than 5 or 6 leagues to the southeast beyond where he had been at nightfall, passing the land of Campana, he came in sight of a great opening beyond that cape, which seemed to divide one land from another, leaving an island between them. He decided to go back, with the wind southeast, steering to the point where the opening had appeared, where he found that it was only a large bay; and at the end of it, on the southeast side, there was a point of land on which was a high and square-cut hill, which had looked like an island. A breeze sprang up from the north, and the Admiral continued on a southeast course, to explore the coast and discover all that was there. Presently he saw, at the foot of the Cabo de Campana, a wonderfully good port, and a large river, and, a quarter of league on, another river, and a third, and a fourth to a seventh at similar distances, from the furthest one to Cabo de Campana being 20 miles southeast. Most of these rivers have wide and deep mouths, with excellent havens for large ships, without sand-banks or sunken rocks. Proceeding onwards from the last of these rivers, on a southeast course, they came to the largest inhabited place they had yet seen, and a vast concourse of people came down to the beach with loud shouts, all naked, with their darts in their hands. The Admiral desired to have speech with them, so he furled sails and anchored. The boats of the ship and the caravel were sent on shore, with orders to do no harm whatever to the Indians, but to give them presents. The Indians made as if they would resist the landing, but, seeing that the boats of the Spaniards continued to advance without fear, they retired from the beach. Thinking that they would not be terrified if only two or three landed, three Christians were put on shore, who told them not to be afraid, in their own language, for they had been able to learn a little from the natives who were on board. But all ran away, neither great nor small remaining. The Christians went to the houses, which were of straw, and built like the others they had seen, but found no one in any of them. They returned to the ships, and made sail at noon in the direction of a fine cape to the eastward, about 8 leagues distant. Having gone about half a league, the Admiral saw, on the south side of the same bay, a very remarkable harbor and to the southeast some wonderfully beautiful country like a valley among the mountains, whence much smoke arose, indicating a large population, with signs of much cultivation. So he resolved to stop at this port, and see if he could have any speech or intercourse with the inhabitants. It was so that, if the Admiral had praised the other havens, he must praise this still more for its lands, climate, and people. He tells marvels of the beauty of the country and of the trees, there being palms and pine-trees; and also of the great valley, which is not flat, but diversified by hill and dale, the most lovely scenery in the world. Many streams flow from it, which fall from the mountains.

As soon as the ship was at anchor the Admiral jumped into the boat, to get soundings in the port, which is the shape of a hammer. When he was facing the entrance he found the mouth of a river on the south side of sufficient width for a galley to enter it, but so concealed that it is not visible until close to. Entering it for the length of the boat, there was a depth of from 5 to 8 fathoms. In passing up it the freshness and beauty of the trees, the clearness of the water, and the birds, made it all so delightful that he wished never to leave them. He said to the men who were with him that to give a true relation to the sovereigns of the things which they had seen, 1,000 tongues would not suffice, nor his hand to write it, for that it was like a scene of enchantment. He desired that many other prudent and credible witnesses might see it, and he was sure that they would be as unable to exaggerate the scene as he was.

The Admiral also says: "How great the benefit that is to be derived from this country would be, I cannot say. It is certain that where there are such lands there must be an infinite number of things that would be profitable. But I did not remain long in one port, because I wished to see as much of the country as possible, in order to make a report upon it to your Highnesses; and, besides, I do not know the language, and these people neither understand me nor any other in my company; while the Indians I have on board often misunderstand. Moreover, I have not been able to see much of the natives, because they often take to flight. But now, if our Lord pleases, I will see as much as possible, and will proceed by little and little, learning and comprehending; and I will make some of my followers learn the language. For I have perceived that there is only one language up to this point. After they understand the advantages, I shall labor to make all these people Christians. They will become so readily, because they have no religion nor idolatry, and your Highnesses will send orders to build a city and fortress, and to convert the people. I assure your Highnesses that it does not appear to me that there can be a more fertile country nor a better climate under the sun, with abundant supplies of water. This is not like the rivers of Guinea, which are all pestilential. I thank our Lord that, up to this time, there has not been a person of my company who has so much as had a headache, or been in bed from illness, except an old man who has suffered from the stone all his life, and he was well again in two days. I speak of all three vessels. If it will please God that your Highnesses should send learned men out here, they will see the truth of all I have said. I have related already how good a place Rio del Mares would be for a town and fortress, and this is perfectly true; but it bears no comparison with this place, nor with the Mar de Nuestra Señora. For here there must be a large population, and very valuable productions, which I hope to discover before I return to Castile. I say that, if Christendom will find profit among these people, how much more will Spain, to whom the whole country should be subject. Your Highnesses ought not to consent that any stranger should trade here, or put his foot in the country, except Catholic Christians, for this was the beginning and end of the undertaking; namely, the increase and glory of the Christian religion, and that no one should come to these parts who was not a good Christian."

All the above are the Admiral's words. He ascended the river for some distance, examined some branches of it, and, returning to the mouth, he found some pleasant groves of trees, like a delightful orchard. Here he came upon a canoe, dug out of one tree, as big as a galley of twelve benches, fastened under a boat-house made of wood, and thatched with palm-leaves, so that it could be neither injured by sun nor by the water. He says that here would be the proper site for a town and fort, by reason of the good port, good water, good land, and abundance of fuel.

Wednesday, Nov 28.—The Admiral remained during this day, in consequence of the rain and thick weather, though he might have run along the coast, the wind being southwest, but he did not weigh, because he was unacquainted with the coast beyond, and did not know what danger there might be for the vessels. The sailors of the two vessels went on shore to wash their clothes, and some of them walked inland for a short distance. They found indications of a large population. but the houses were all empty, every one having fled. They returned by the banks of another river, larger than that which they knew of, at the port.

Thursday, Nov. 29.—The rain and thick weather continuing, the Admiral did not get under way. Some of the Christians went to another village to the northwest, but found no one, and nothing in the houses. On the road they met an old man who could not run away, and caught him. They told him they did not wish to do him any harm, gave him a few presents, and let him go. The Admiral would have liked to have had speech with him, for he was exceedingly satisfied with the delights of that land, and wished that a settlement might be formed there, judging that it must support a large population. In one house they found a cake of wax, which was taken to the sovereigns, the Admiral saying that where there was wax there were also 1,000 other good things. The sailors also found, in one house, the head of a man in a basket, covered with another basket, and fastened to a post of the house. They found the same things in another village. The Admiral believed that they must be the heads of some founder, or principal ancestor of a lineage, for the houses are built to contain a great number of people in each; and these should be relations, and descendants of a common ancestor.

Friday, Nov. 30.—They could not get under way to-day because the wind was east, and dead against them. The Admiral sent eight men well armed, accompanied by two of the Indians he had on board, to examine the village inland, and get speech with the people. They came to many houses, but found no one and nothing, all having fled. They saw four youths who were digging in the fields, but, as soon as they saw the Christians, they ran away, and could not be overtaken. They marched a long distance, and saw many villages and a most fertile land, with much cultivation and many streams of water. Near one river they saw a canoe dug out of a single tree, 95 *palmos* long, and capable of carrying 150 persons.

Saturday, Dec. 1.—They did not depart, because there was still a foul wind, with much rain. The Admiral set up a cross at the entrance of this port, which he called Puerto Santo, on some bare rocks. The point is that which is on the southeast side of the entrance; but he who has to enter should make more over to the northwest; for at the foot of both, near the rock, there are 12 fathoms and a very clean bottom. At the entrance of the port, towards the southeast point, there is a reef of rocks above water, sufficiently far from the shore to be able to pass between if it is necessary; for both on the side of the rock and the shore there is a depth of 12 to 15 fathoms; and on entering, a ship's head should be turned southwest.

Sunday, Dec. 2.—The wind was still contrary, and they could not depart. Every night the wind blows on the land, but no vessel need be alarmed at all the gales in the world, for they cannot blow home by reason of a reef of rocks at the opening to the haven. A sailor-boy found, at the mouth of the river, some stones which looked as if they contained gold; so they were taken to be shown to the sovereigns.

The Admiral says that there are great rivers at the distance of a lombard-shot.

Monday, Dec. 3.—By reason of the continuance of an easterly wind the Admiral did not leave this port. He arranged to visit a very beautiful headland a quarter of a league to the southeast of the anchorage. He went with the boats and some armed men. At the foot of the cape there was the mouth of a fair river, and on entering it they found the width to be 100 paces, with a depth of 1 fathom. Inside they found 12, 5, 4, and 2 fathoms, so that it would hold all the ships there are in Spain. Leaving the river, they came to a cove in which were five very large canoes, so well constructed that it was a pleasure to look at them. They were under spreading trees, and a path led from them to a very well-built boat-house, so thatched that neither sun nor rain could do any harm. Within it there was another canoe made out of a single tree like the others, like a galley with seventeen benches. It was a pleasant sight to look upon such goodly work. The Admiral ascended a mountain, and afterwards found the country level, and cultivated with many things of that land, including such calabashes as it was a glory to look upon them. In the middle there was a large village, and they came upon the people suddenly; but, as soon as they were seen, men and women took to flight. The Indian from on board, who was with the Admiral, cried out to them that they need not be afraid, as the strangers were good people. The Admiral made him give them bells, copper ornaments, and glass beads, green and yellow, with which they were well content. He saw that they had no gold, nor any other precious thing, and that it would suffice to leave them in peace. The whole district was well peopled, the rest having fled from fear. The Admiral assures the sovereigns that 10,000 of these men would run from ten, so cowardly and timid are they. No arms are carried by them, except wands, on the point of which a short piece of wood is fixed, hardened by fire, and these they are very ready to exchange. Returning to where he had left the boats, he sent back some men up the hill, because he fancied he had seen a large apiary. Before those he had sent could return, they were joined by many Indians, and they went to the boats, where the Admiral was waiting with all his people. One of the natives advanced into the river near the stern of the boat, and made a long speech which the Admiral did not understand. At intervals the other Indians raised their hands to heaven, and shouted. The Admiral thought he was assuring him that he was pleased at his arrival; but he saw the Indian who came from the ship change the color of his face, and turn as yellow as wax, trembling much, and letting the Admiral know by signs that he should leave the river, as they were going to kill him. He pointed to a cross-bow which one of the Spaniards had, and showed it to the Indians, and the Admiral let it be understood that they would all be slain, because that cross-bow carried far and killed people. He also took a sword and drew it out of the sheath, showing it to them, and saying the same, which, when they had heard, they all took to flight; while the Indian from the ship still trembled from cowardice, though he was a tall, strong man. The Admiral did not want to leave the river, but pulled towards the place where the natives had assembled in great numbers, all painted, and as naked as when their mothers bore them. Some had tufts of feathers on their heads, and all had their bundles of darts.

The Admiral says: "I came to them, and gave them some mouthfuls of bread, asking for the darts, for which I gave in exchange copper ornaments, bells, and glass beads. This made them peaceable, so that they came to the boats again, and gave us what they had. The sailors had killed a turtle, and the shell was in the boat in pieces. The sailor-boys gave them some in exchange for a bundle of darts. These are like the other people we have seen, and with the same belief that we came from heaven. They are ready to give whatever thing they have in exchange for any trifle without saying it is little; and I believe they would do the same with gold and spices if they had any. I saw a fine house, not very large, and with two doors, as all the rest have. On entering, I saw a marvellous work, there being rooms made in a peculiar way, that I scarcely know how tc describe it. Shells and other things were fastened to the ceiling. I thought it was a temple, and I called them and asked, by signs, whether prayers were offered up there. They said that they were not, and one of them climbed up and offered me all the things that were there, of which I took some."

Tuesday, Dec. 4.—The Admiral made sail with little wind, and left that port, which he called Puerto Santo. After going 2 leagues, he saw the great river of which he spoke yesterday. Passing along the land, and beating to windward on southeast and west-northwest courses, they reached Cabo Lindo, which is east-southeast, 5 leagues from Cabo del Monte. A league and a half from Cabo del Monte there is an important but rather narrow river, which seemed to have a good entrance, and to be deep. Three-quarters of a league further on, the Admiral saw another very large river, and he thought it must have its source at a great distance. It had 100 paces at its mouth, and no bar, with a depth of 8 fathoms. The Admiral sent the boat in, to take soundings, and they found the water fresh until it enters the sea.

THE RETURN VOYAGE.

This river had great volume, and must have a large population on its banks. Beyond Cabo Lindo there is a great bay, which would be open for navigation to east-northeast and southeast and south-southwest.

Wednesday, Dec. 5.—All this night they were beating to windward off Cape Lindo, to reach the land to the east, and at sunrise the Admiral sighted another cape, 2½ leagues to the east. Having passed it, he saw that the land trended south and southwest, and presently saw a fine high cape in that direction, 7 leagues distant. He would have wished to go there, but his object was to reach the island of Babeque, which, according to the Indians, bore northeast; so he gave up the intention. He could not go to Babeque either, because the wind was northeast. Looking to the southeast, he saw land, which was a very large island, according to the information of the Indians, well peopled, and called by them Bohio. The Admiral says that the inhabitants of Cuba, or Juana, and of all the other islands, are much afraid of the inhabitants of Bohio, because they say that they eat people. The Indians relate other things, by signs, which are very wonderful; but the Admiral did not believe them. He only inferred that those of Bohio must have more cleverness and cunning to be able to capture the others, who, however, are very poor-spirited. The wind veered from north-east to north, so the Admiral determined to leave Cuba, or Juana, which, up to this time, he had supposed to be the mainland, on account of its size, having coasted along it for 120 leagues.

Memorial to Ferdinand and Isabella.—Subjoined is the text of the memorial, or report, of the second voyage of Columbus to the Indies, drawn up by him for their Highnesses King Ferdinand and Queen Isabella; and addressed to Antonio de Torres, from the city of Isabella, Jan. 30, 1494, with the reply of their Highnesses at the end of each item in italics:

The report which you, Antonio de Torres, captain of the ship *Marigalante*, and governor of the city of Isabella, have to make, on my behalf, to the king and queen, our sovereigns, is as follows:

Imprimis: after having delivered the credentials which you bear from me to their Highnesses, you will do homage in my name, and commend me to them as to my natural sovereigns, in whose service I desire to continue till death; and you will furthermore be able to lay before them all that you have yourself seen and known respecting me.

Their Highnesses accept and acknowledge the service.

Item. Although, by the letters which I have written to their Highnesses, as well as to Father Buil and to the Treasurer, a clear and comprehensive idea may be formed of all that has transpired since our arrival, you will, notwithstanding, inform their Highnesses, on my behalf, that God has been pleased to manifest such favor towards their service that not only has nothing hitherto occurred to diminish the importance of what I have formerly written or said to their Highnesses, but, on the contrary, I hope, by God's grace, shortly to prove it more clearly by facts, because we have found upon the seashore, without penetrating into the interior of the country, some spots showing so many indications of various spices as naturally to suggest the hope of the best results for the future. The same holds good with respect to the gold-mines; for two parties only, who were sent out in different directions to discover them, and who, because they had few people with them, remained out but a short time, found, nevertheless, a great number of rivers whose sands contained this precious metal in such quantity that each man took up a sample of it in his hand, so that our two messengers returned so joyous, and boasted so much of the abundance of gold, that I feel a hesitation in speaking and writing of it to their Highnesses. But as Gorbalan, who was one of the persons who went on the discovery, is returning to Spain, he will be able to relate all that he has seen and observed; although there remains here another individual—named Hojeda, formerly servant of the Duke of Medina Celi, and a very discreet and painstaking youth—who without doubt discovered, beyond all comparison, more than the other, judging by the account which he gave of the rivers he had seen; for he reported that each of them contained things that appeared incredible. It results from all this that their Highnesses ought to return thanks to God for the favor which He thus accords to all their Highnesses' enterprises.

Their Highnesses return thanks to God for all that is recorded, and regard as a very signal service all that the Admiral has already done, and is yet doing; for they are sensible that, under God, it is he who has procured for them their present and future possessions in these countries, and, as they are about to write to him on this subject more at length, they refer to their letter.

Item. You will repeat to their Highnesses what I have already written to them, that I should have ardently desired to have been able to send them, by this occasion, a larger quantity of gold than what they have any hope of our being able to collect, but that the greater part of the people we employed fell suddenly ill. Moreover, the departure of this present expedition could not be delayed any longer for two reasons, namely: on account of the heavy expense which their stay here occasioned; and because the weather was favorable for their departure, and for the return of those who should bring back the articles of which we stand in the most pressing need. If the former were to put off the time of their starting, and the latter were to delay their departure, they would not be able to reach here by the month of May. Besides, if I wished now to undertake a journey to the rivers with those who are well—whether with those who are at sea or those who are on land in the huts—I should experience great difficulties, and even dangers, because, in traversing 23 or 24 leagues, where there are bays and rivers to pass, we should be obliged to carry, as provision for so long a journey, and for the time necessary for collecting the gold, many articles of food, etc., which could not be carried on our backs; and there are no beasts of burden to be found, to afford the necessary assistance. Moreover, the roads and passes are not in such a condition as I should wish for travelling over; but they have already begun to make them passable. It would be also extremely inconvenient to leave the sick men here in the open air, or in huts, with such food and defences as they have on shore; although these Indians appear every day to be more simple and harmless to those who land for the purpose of making investigations. In short, although they come every day to visit us, it would nevertheless be imprudent to risk the loss of our men and our provisions, which might very easily happen if an Indian were only, with a lighted coal, to set fire to the huts, for they ramble about both night and day. For this reason, we keep sentinels constantly on the watch while the dwellings are exposed and undefended.

He has done well.

Further, as we have remarked that the greatest part of those who have gone out to make discoveries have fallen sick on their return, and that some have even been obliged to abandon the undertaking in the middle of their journey, and return, it was equally to be feared that the same would occur to those who were at the time enjoying good health, if they were also to go. There were two evils to fear—one the chance of falling ill in undertaking the same work, in a place where there were no houses nor any kind of protection, and of being exposed to the attacks of the cacique called Caonabo, who, by all accounts, is a badly disposed man, and extremely daring, who, if he were to find us in a dispirited condition and sick, might venture upon what he would not dare to do if we were well. The other evil consisted in the difficulty of carrying the gold; for either we should have to carry it in small quantities, and go and return every day, and thus daily expose ourselves to the chance of sickness, or we should have to send it under the escort of a party of our people, and equally run the risk of losing them.

He has done well.

These are the reasons, you will tell their Highnesses, why the departure of the expedition has not been delayed, and why only a sample of the gold is sent to them; but I trust in the mercy of God, who in all things and in every place has guided us hitherto, that all our men will be soon restored to health, as, indeed, they are already beginning to be, for they have but to try this country for a little time, and they speedily recover their health. One thing is certain, that, if they could have fresh meat, they would very quickly, by the help of God, be up and doing; and those who are most sickly would speedily recover. I hope that they may be restored. The small number of those who continue well are employed every day in barricading our dwelling, so as to put it in a state of defence, and in taking necessary measures for the safety of our ammunition, which will be finished now in a few days; for all our fortifications will consist simply of stone walls. These precautions will be sufficient, as the Indians are not a people to be much afraid of; and, unless they should find us asleep, they would not dare to undertake any hostile movement against us even if they should entertain the idea of so doing. The misfortune which happened to those who remained here must be attributed to their want of vigilance; for, however few they were in number, and however favorable the opportunities that the Indians may have had for doing what they did, they would never have ventured to do them any injury if they had only seen that they took proper precautions against an attack. As soon as this object is gained, I will undertake to go in search of these rivers, either proceeding hence by land, and looking out for the best expedients that may offer, or else by sea, rounding the island until we come to the place which is described as being only 6 or 7 leagues from where these rivers that I speak of are situated, so that we may collect the gold in safety, and put it in security against all attacks in some stronghold or tower, which may be quickly built for that purpose; and thus, when the two caravels shall return thither, the gold may be taken away, and finally sent home in safety at the first favorable season for making the voyage.

This is well and exactly as he should do.

Item. You will inform their Highnesses (as indeed has been already said) that the cause of the sickness so general among us is the change of air and water, for we find that all of us are affected, though few dangerously. Consequently, the preservation of the health of the people will depend, under God, on their being provided with the same food that they are accustomed to in Spain; neither those who are here now nor those that shall come will be in a position to be of service to their Highnesses unless they enjoy good health. We ought to have fresh supplies of provisions until the time that we may be able to gather a sufficient crop from what we shall have sown or planted here; I speak of wheat, barley, and grapes, towards the cultivation of which not much has been done this year, from our being unable earlier to choose a convenient settlement. When we had chosen it, the small number of laborers that were with us fell sick; and, even when they recovered, we had so few cattle, and those so lean and weak, that the utmost they could do was very little. However, they have sown a few plots of ground, for the sake of trying the soil, which seems excellent, in the hope of thereby obtaining some relief in our necessities. We are very confident, from what we can see, that wheat and grapes will grow very well in this country. We must, however, wait for the fruit; and, if it grows as quickly and well as the corn, in proportion to the number of vines that have been planted, we shall certainly not stand in need of Andalusia and Sicily here. There are also sugar-canes, of which the small quantity that we have planted has taken root. The beauty of the country in these islands—the mountains, the valleys, the streams, the fields watered by broad rivers—is such that there is no country on which the sun sheds his beams that can present a more charming appearance.

Since the land is so fertile, it is desirable to sow of all kinds as much as possible; and Don Juan de Fonseca is instructed to send over immediately everything requisite for that purpose.

Item. You will say that, as a large portion of the wine that we brought with us has run away, in consequence, as most of the men say, of the bad cooperage of the butts made at Seville, the article that we stand most in need of now, and shall stand in need of, is wine; and, although we have biscuit and corn for some time longer, it is nevertheless necessary that a reasonable quantity of these be sent to us, for the voyage is a long one, and it is impossible to make a calculation for every day. The same holds good with respect to pork and salt beef, which should be better than what we brought out with us on this voyage. Sheep and, still better, lambs and lambkins, more females than males, young calves and heifers also, are wanted, and should be sent by every caravel that may be despatched hither; and at the same time some asses, both male and female, and mares for labor and tillage, for here there are no beasts that a man can turn to any use. As I fear that their Highnesses may not be at Seville, and that their officers or ministers will not, without their express instructions, make any movement towards the carrying out of the necessary arrangements for the return voyage, and that, in the interval between the report and the reply, the favorable moment for the departure of the vessels which are to return hither (and which should be in all the month of May) may elapse, you will tell their Highnesses, as I charged and ordered you, that I have given strict orders that the gold that you carry with you be placed in the hands of some merchant in Seville, in order that he may therefrom disburse the sums necessary for loading the two caravels with wine, corn, and other articles detailed in this memorial; and this merchant shall convey or send the said gold to their Highnesses, that they may see it, receive it, and from it cause to be defrayed the expenses that may arise from the fitting-up and loading of the said two caravels. It is necessary, for the encouragement of the men who remain here, and for the support of their spirits, that an effort should be made to let the expedition arrive in the course of the month of May, so that before summer they may have the fresh provisions and other necessaries, especially against sickness. We particularly stand in need of raisins, sugar, almonds, honey, and rice, of which we ought to have a great quantity, but brought very little with us; and what we had is now consumed. The greater part of the medicines, also, that we brought from Spain are used up, so many of our number having been sick. For all these articles, both for those who are in good health and for the sick, you carry, as I have already said, memorials signed by my hand. You will execute my orders to the full if there be sufficient money wherewith to do so, or you will at least procure what is more immediately necessary, and which ought, consequently, to come as speedily as possible by the two vessels. As to the remainder, you will obtain their Highnesses' permission for their being sent by other vessels without loss of time.

Their Highnesses will give instructions to Don Juan de Fonseca to make immediate inquiry respecting the imposition in the matter of the casks, in order that those who supplied them shall at their own expense make good the loss occasioned by the waste of the wine, together with the costs. He will have to see that sugarcanes of good quality be sent, and will immediately look to the despatch of the other articles herein required.

Item. You will tell their Highnesses that, as we have no interpreter through whom we can make these people acquainted with our holy faith, as their Highnesses and ourselves desire, and as we will do so soon as we are able, we send by these two vessels some of these cannibal men and women, as well as some children, both male and female, whom their Highnesses might order to be placed under the care of the most competent persons to teach them the language. At the same time they might be employed in useful occupations, and by degrees, through somewhat more care being bestowed upon them than upon other slaves, they would learn one from the other. By not seeing or speaking to each other for a long time, they will learn much sooner in Spain than they will here, and become much better interpreters. We will, however, not fail to do what we can. It is true that, as there is but little communication between one of these islands and another, there is some difference in their mode of expressing themselves, which mainly depends on the distance between them. But, as among all these islands those inhabited by the cannibals are the largest and the most populous, it must be evident that nothing but good can come from sending to Spain men and women who may thus one day be led to abandon their barbarous custom of eating their fellow-creatures. By learning the Spanish language in Spain, they will much earlier receive baptism and advance the welfare of their souls. Moreover, we shall gain great credit with the Indians who do not practise the above-mentioned cruel customs, when they see that we have seized and led captive those who injure them, and whose very name alone fills them with horror. You will assure their Highnesses that our arrival in this country and the sight of so fine a fleet have produced the most imposing effect for the present, and promise great security hereafter; for all the inhabitants of this great island, and of the others, when they see the good treatment that we shall show to those who do well, and the punishment that we shall inflict on those who do wrong, will hasten to submit, so that we shall be able to lay our commands on them as vassals of their Highnesses. And as even now they not only readily comply with every wish that we express, but also of their own accord endeavor to do what they think will please us, I think that their Highnesses may feel assured that, on the other side, also, the arrival of this fleet has in many respects secured for them, both for the present and the future, a wide renown among all Christian princes; but they themselves will be able to form a much better judgment on this subject than it is in my power to give expression to.

Let him be informed of what has transpired respecting the cannibals that came over to Spain. He has done well, and let him do as he says; but let him endeavor by all possible means to convert them to our holy Catholic religion, and do the same with respect to the inhabitants of all the islands to which he may go.

Item. You will tell their Highnesses that the welfare of the souls of the said cannibals, and of the inhabitants of this island also, has suggested the thought that the greater the number that are sent over to Spain the better, and thus good service may result to their Highnesses in the following manner. Considering what great need we have of cattle and of beasts of burden, both for food and to assist the settlers in this and all these islands, both for peopling the land and cultivating the soil, their Highnesses might authorize a suitable number of caravels to come here every year to bring over the said cattle and provisions and other articles. These cattle, etc., might be sold at moderate prices for account of the bearers; and the latter might be paid with slaves, taken from among the Caribbees, who are a wild people fit for any work, well proportioned and very intelligent, and who, when they have got rid of the cruel habits to which they have become accustomed, will be better than any other kind of slaves. When they are out of their country, they will forget their cruel customs; and it will be easy to obtain plenty of these savages by means of rowboats that we propose to build. It is taken for granted that each of the caravels sent by their Highnesses will have on board a confidential man, who will take care that the vessels do not stop anywhere else than here, where they are to unload and reload their vessels. Their Highnesses might fix duties on the slaves that may be taken over, upon their arrival in Spain. You will ask for a reply upon this point, and bring it to me, in order that I may be able to take the necessary measures, should the proposition merit the approbation of their Highnesses.

The consideration of this subject has been suspended for a time, until fresh advices arrive from the other side: let the Admiral write what he thinks upon the subject.

Item. You will also tell their Highnesses that freighting the ships by the ton, as the French merchants do, will be more advantageous and less expensive than any other mode, and it is for this reason that I have given you instructions to freight in this manner the caravels that you have now to send off, and it will be well to adopt this plan with all the others that their Highnesses may send, provided it meets their approbation; but I do not mean to say that this measure should be applied to the vessels that shall come over licensed for the traffic of slaves.

Their Highnesses have given directions to Don Juan de Fonseca, to have the caravels freighted in the manner described, if it can be done.

Item. You will tell their Highnesses that, in order to save any extra expense, I have purchased the caravels mentioned in the memorial of which you are the bearer, in order to keep them here with the two vessels, the *Gallega* and the *Capitana*, of which, by advice of the pilot, its commander, I purchased the three-eighths for the price declared in the said memorial, signed by my hand. These vessels will not only give authority and great security to those who will have to remain on shore and whose duty it will be to make arrangements with the Indians for collecting the gold, but they will be also very useful to ward off any attack that may be made upon them by strangers. Moreover, the caravels will be required for the task of making the discovery of *terra firma*, and of the islands which lie scattered about in this vicinity. You will therefore beg their Highnesses to pay, at the term of credit arranged with the sellers, the sums which these vessels shall cost; for without doubt their Highnesses will be very soon reimbursed for what they may expend, at least such is my belief and hope in the mercy of God.

The Admiral has done well. You will tell him that the sum mentioned has been paid to the seller of the vessels, and that Don Juan de Fonseca has been ordered to pay the cost of the caravels purchased by the Admiral.

Item. You will speak to their Highnesses, and beseech them on my behalf, in the most humble manner possible, to be pleased to give mature reflection to the observations I may make, in letters or more detailed statements, with reference to the peacefulness, harmony, and good feeling of those who come hither, in order that for their Highnesses' service persons may be selected who will hold in view the purpose for which these men are sent rather than their own interest; and, since you yourself have seen and are acquainted with these matters, you will speak to their Highnesses upon this subject, and will tell them the truth on every point exactly as you have understood it. You will also take care that the orders which their Highnesses shall give on this point be put into effect, if possible, by the first vessels, in order that no further injury occur here in the matters that affect their service.

Their Highnesses are well informed of all that takes place, and will see to it that everything is done as it should be.

Item. You will describe to their Highnesses the position of this city, the beauty of the province in which it is situated, as you have seen it, and as you can honestly speak of it; and you can inform them that, in virtue of the powers which I have received from them, I have made you governor of the said city; and you will tell them also that I humbly beseech them, out of consideration for your services, to receive your nomination favorably, which I sincerely hope they may do.

Their Highnesses are pleased to sanction your appointment as governor.

Item. As Messire Pedro Margarite, an officer of the household to their Highnesses, has done good service, and will, I hope, continue to do so for the future in all matters which may be intrusted to him, I have felt great pleasure in his continuing his stay in this country; and I have been much pleased to find that Gaspar and Beltran also remain, and, as they are all three well known to their Highnesses as faithful servants, I shall place them in posts or employments of trust. You will beg their Highnesses especially to have regard to the situation of the said Messire Pedro Margarite, who is married and the father of a family, and beseech them to give him some vacant command in the order of Santiago, of which he is a knight, in order that his wife and children may thus have a competence to live upon. You will also make mention of Juan Aguado, a servant of their Highnesses. You will inform them of the zeal and activity with which he has served them in all matters that have been intrusted to him, and also that I beseech their Highnesses on his behalf, as well as on behalf of those above mentioned, not to forget my recommendation, but to give it full consideration.

Their Highnesses grant an annual pension of 30,000 maravedis to Messire Pedro Margarite, and pensions of 15,000 maravedis to Gaspard and Beltram, which will be reckoned from this day, Aug. 15, 1494. They give orders that the said pensions be paid by the Admiral out of the sums to be paid in the Indies, and by Don Juan de Fonseca out of the sums to be paid in Spain. With respect to the matter of Juan Aguado their Highnesses will not be forgetful.

Item. You will inform their Highnesses of the continual labor that Dr. Chanca has undergone, from the prodigious number of sick and the scarcity of provisions, and that, in spite of all this, he exhibits the greatest zeal and kindness in everything that relates to his profession. As their Highnesses have intrusted me with the charge of fixing the salary that is to be paid to him while out here (although it is certain that he neither receives nor can receive anything from any one, and does not receive anything from his position, equal to what he did and could still do in Spain, where he lived peaceably and at ease, in a very different style from what he does here, and although he declares that he earned more in Spain, exclusive of the pay which he received from their Highnesses), I have, nevertheless, not ventured to place to the credit of his account more than 50,000 maravedis per annum, as the sum which he is to receive for his yearly labor during the time of his stay in this country. I beg their Highnesses to give their sanction to this salary, exclusive of his maintenance while here; and I do so, because he asserts that all the medical men who attend their Highnesses in the royal yachts, or in any of their expeditions, are accustomed to receive by right the day's pay out of the annual salary of each individual. Let

BOBADILLA AND COLUMBUS.

this be as it may, I am informed for certain that, on whatever service they are engaged, it is the custom to give them a certain fixed sum, settled at the will and by order of their Highnesses, as compensation for the said day's pay. You will, therefore, beg their Highnesses to decide this matter, as well with respect to the annual pay as to the above-mentioned usage, so that the said doctor may be reasonably satisfied.

Their Highnesses acknowledge the justice of Dr. Chanca's observations, and it is their wish that the Admiral shall pay him the sum which he has allowed him, exclusive of his fixed annual salary. With respect to the day's pay allowed to medical men, it is not the custom to authorize them to receive it, except when they are in personal attendance upon our Lord the King.

Item. You will tell their Highnesses what great devotion Coronel has shown to the service in many respects, and what great proofs he has given of it in every important matter that has been trusted to him, and how much we feel his loss now that he is sick. You will represent to them how just it is that he should receive the recompense of such good and loyal services, not only in the favors which may hereafter be shown to him, but also in his present pay, in order that he and all those that are with us may see what profit will accrue to them from their zeal in the service, for the importance and difficulty of exploring the mines should call for great consideration towards those to whom such extensive interests are intrusted; and, as the talents of the said Coronel have made me determine upon appointing him principal constable of this portion of the Indies, and as his salary is left open, I beg their Highnesses to make it as liberal as may be in consideration of his services, and to confirm his nomination to the service which I have allotted to him by giving him an official appointment thereto.

Their Highnesses grant him, besides his salary, an annual pension of 15,000 maravedis, the same to be paid him at the same time as the said salary.

Item. You will at the same time tell their Highnesses that the bachelor, Gil Garcia, came out here in quality of principal alcalde, without having any salary fixed or allowed to him, that he is a good man, well informed, correct in his conduct, and very necessary to us; and that

I beg their Highnesses to be pleased to appoint him a salary sufficient for his support, and that it be remitted to him together with his pay from the other side.

Their Highnesses grant him an annual pension of 20,000 maravedis during his stay in the Indies, and that over and above his fixed appointments; and it is their order that this pension be paid to him at the same time as his salary.

Item. You will tell their Highnesses, as I have already told them in writing, that I think it will be impossible to go this year to make discoveries until arrangements have been made to work the two rivers in which the gold has been found in the most profitable manner for their Highnesses' interest; and this may be done more effectively hereafter, because it is not a thing that every one can do to my satisfaction or with advantage to their Highnesses' service, unless I be present; for whatever is to be done always turns out best under the eye of the party interested.

It is the most necessary thing possible that he should strive to find the way to this gold.

Item. You will tell their Highnesses that the horse-soldiers that came from Grenada to the review which took place at Seville offered good horses, but that at the time of their being sent on board they took advantage of my absence (for I was somewhat indisposed), and changed them for others, the best of which does not seem worth 2,000 maravedis, for they sold the first and bought these; and this deception on the part of the horse-soldiers is very like what I have known to occur to many gentlemen in Seville of my acquaintance. It seems that Juan de Soria, after the price was paid, for some private interest of his own put other horses in the place of those that I expected to find; and, when I came to see them, there were horses there that had never been offered to me for sale. In all this the greatest dishonesty has been shown, so that I do not know whether I ought to complain of him alone, since these horse-soldiers have been paid their expenses up to the present day, besides their salary and the hire of their horses; and, when they are ill, they will not allow their horses to be used, because they are not present. It is not their Highnesses' wish that these horses should be purchased for anything but their Highnesses' service; but these men think they are only to be employed on work which requires them to ride on horseback, which is not the case at present. All these considerations lead me to think that it would be more convenient to buy their horses, which are worth but little, and thus avoid being exposed daily to new disputes. Finally, their Highnesses will decide on what plan is best for their own interests.

Their Highnesses order Don Juan de Fonseca to make inquiries respecting the matter of the horses, and, if it be true that such a deception has been practised, to send up the culprits to be punished as they deserve; also to gain information respecting the other people that the Admiral speaks of, and to send the result of the information to their Highnesses. With respect to the horse-soldiers, it is their Highnesses' wish and command that they continue where they are, and remain in service, because they belong to the guards and to the class of their Highnesses' servants. Their Highnesses also command the said horse-soldiers to give up their horses into the charge of the Admiral on all occasions when they shall be required; and, if the use of the horses should occasion any loss, their Highnesses direct that compensation shall be made for the amount of the injury, through the medium of the Admiral.

Item. You will mention to their Highnesses that more than 200 persons have come here without fixed salaries, and that some of them are very useful to the service; and, in order to preserve system and uniformity, the others have been ordered to imitate them. For the first three years it is desirable that we should have here 1,000 men, in order to keep a safeguard upon the island and upon the rivers that supply the gold; and, even if we were able to mount 100 men on horseback, so far from being an evil, it will be a very necessary thing for us. But their Highnesses might pass by the question of the horsemen until gold shall be sent. In short, their Highnesses should give instructions as to whether the 200 people who have come over without pay should receive pay, like the others, if they do their work well; for we certainly have great need of them to commence our labors, as I have already shown.

It is their Highnesses' wish and command that the 200 persons without pay shall replace such of those who are paid as have failed, or as shall hereafter fail, in their duty, provided they are fit for the service and please the Admiral; and their Highnesses order the Accomptant to enter their names in the place of those who shall fail in their duty, as the Admiral shall determine.

THE COLUMBUS MONUMENT IN GENOA, ITALY.

Item. As there are means of diminishing the expenses that these people occasion, by employing them as other princes do, in industrial occupations, I think it would be well that all ships that come here should be ordered to bring, besides the ordinary stores and medicines, shoes, and leather for making shoes, shirts, both of common and superior quality, doublets, laces, some peasants' clothing, breeches, and cloth for making clothes, all at moderate prices. They might also bring other articles, such as conserves, which do not enter into the daily ration, yet are good for preserving health. The Spaniards that are here would always be happy to receive such articles as these in lieu of part of their pay; and, if they were purchased by men who were selected for their known loyalty, and who take an interest in the service of their Highnesses, considerable economy would result from this arrangement. Ascertain their Highnesses' pleasure on this head; and, if the plan be deemed expedient for the service, it should be put in practice at once.

This matter may rest for the present until the Admiral shall write more fully on the subject. Meanwhile Don Juan de Fonseca shall be ordered to instruct Don

Ximenes de Bribiesca to make the necessary arrangements for the execution of the proposed plans.

Item. You will tell their Highnesses that, in a review that was holden yesterday, it was remarked that a great number of the people were without arms, which I think must be attributed partly to the exchange made at Seville or in the harbor, when those who presented themselves armed were left for a while, and for a trifle exchanged their arms for others of an inferior quality. I think it would be desirable that 200 cuirasses, 100 arquebuses, 100 arblasts, and many other articles of defensive armor, should be sent over to us; for we have great need of them to arm those who are at present without them.

Don Juan de Fonseca has already been written to, to provide them.

Item. Inasmuch as many married persons have come over here, and are engaged in regular duties, such as masons and other tradesmen, who have left their wives in Spain, and wish that the pay that falls due to them may be paid to their wives, or whomsoever they may appoint, in order that they may purchase for them such articles as they may need, I therefore beseech their Highnesses to take such measures as they may deem expedient on this subject; for it is of importance to their interests that these people be well provided for.

Their Highnesses have already ordered Don Juan de Fonseca to attend to this matter.

Item. Besides the other articles which I have begged from their Highnesses in the memorial which you bear, signed by my hand, and which articles consist of provisions and other stores, both for those who are well and for those who are sick, it would be very serviceable that fifty pipes of molasses should be sent hither from the island of Madeira; for it is the most nutritious food in the world, and the most wholesome. A pipe of it does not ordinarily cost more than 2 ducats, exclusive of the casks; and, if their Highnesses would order one of the caravels to call at the said island on the return voyage, the purchase might be made, and they might at the same time buy ten casks of sugar, of which we stand greatly in need. It is the most favorable season of the year to obtain it at a cheap rate; that is to say, between this and the month of April. The necessary orders might be given if their Highnesses think proper, and yet the place of destination be carefully concealed.

Don Juan de Fonseca will see to it.

Item. You will tell their Highnesses that, although the rivers contain in their beds the quantity of gold described by those who have seen it, there is no doubt that the gold is produced not in the rivers, but the earth, and that the water, happening to come in contact with the mines, washes it away, mingled with the sand. And, as among the great number of rivers that have been already discovered there are some of considerable magnitude, there are also some so small that they might rather be called brooks than rivers, only two fingers' breadth deep, and very short in their course. There will, therefore, be some men wanted to wash the gold from the sand, and others to dig it out of the earth. This latter operation will be the principal and the most productive. It will be expedient, therefore, that their Highnesses send men, both for the washing and for the mining, from among those who are employed in Spain in the mines at Almaden, so that the work may be done in both manners. We shall not, however, wait for the arrival of these workmen, but hope, with the aid of God and with the washers, that we have here with us, when they shall be restored to health, to send a good quantity of gold by the first caravels that shall leave for Spain.

This shall be completely provided for in the next voyage out. Meanwhile Don Juan de Fonseca has their Highnesses' orders to send as many miners as he can find. Their Highnesses write also to Almaden, with instructions to select the greatest number that can be procured, and to send them up.

Item. You will beseech their Highnesses very humbly in my name to be pleased to pay regard to my strong recommendation of Villacorta, who, as their Highnesses are aware, has been extremely useful, and has shown the greatest possible zeal in this affair. As I know him to be a zealous man and well disposed to their

Highnesses' service, I shall take it as a favor if they will deign to grant him some post of trust adapted to his qualifications, and in which he might give proof of his industry and warm desire to serve their Highnesses; and you will manage that Villacorta shall have practical evidence that the work which he has done for me, and in which I found him needful to me, has been of some profit to him.

This shall be done as he wishes.

Item. That the said Messire Pedro, Gaspar, Beltran, and others remaining here came out in command of caravels which have now gone back, and are in receipt of no salary whatever; but, as these are people who should be employed in the most important and confidential positions, their pay has not been fixed, because it ought to be different from that of the rest. You will beg their Highnesses, therefore, on my behalf, to settle what ought to be given them, either yearly or monthly, for the advantage of their Highnesses' service.

Given in the city of Isabella, the thirtieth of January, in the year fourteen hundred and ninety-four.

This point has been already replied to above; but, as in the said clause he says that they should receive their pay, it is now their Highnesses' command that their salary shall be paid to them from the time that they gave up their command.

Columbus, Diego, navigator; son of Christopher; born in Lisbon about 1472. He accompanied his father to Spain, and was instructed, in his youth, at the Monastery of Santa Maria de Rabida, near Palos, under the care of Father Marchena, the prior of the establishment. He was afterwards nurtured in the bosom of the Spanish Court as an attendant upon Prince Juan, and developed, in young manhood, much of the indomitable spirit of his father. After the death of the latter he made unavailing efforts to procure from King Ferdinand the offices and rights secured to his father and his descendants by solemn contract. At the end of two years he sued the King before the Council of the Indies and obtained a decree in his favor and a confirmation of his title to the viceroyalty of the West Indies. In 1509 he sailed for Santo Domingo with his young wife, and superseded Nicholas Ovando as governor, who had been wrongfully put in that office by the King. The same year he planted a settlement in Jamaica; and in 1511 he sent Diego Velasquez, with a small number of troops, to conquer Cuba, and the victor was made captain-general of the island. He died in Montalvan, near Toledo, Spain, Feb. 23, 1526.

Columbus, Ferdinand. See America, Discovery of.

Columbus, Ky. See Henry, Fort.

Colwell, Stephen, author; born in Brooke county, Va., March 25, 1800; graduated at Jefferson College, Pennsylvania, in 1819; admitted to the bar of Virginia in 1821. After the Civil War he was appointed a commissioner to examine the national system of internal revenue. He gave much time to this work, and his conclusions largely determined the financial policy of the country. His publications include *Letter to Members of the Legislature of Pennsylvania on the Removal of Deposits from the Bank of the United States by Order of the President; The Relative Position in our Industry of Foreign Commerce, Domestic Production, and Internal Trade; Position of Christianity in the United States, in its Relation with our Political System and Religious Instruction in the Public Schools; The South: A Letter from a Friend in the North with Reference to the Effects of Disunion upon Slavery,* etc. He died in Philadelphia, Pa., Jan. 15, 1872.

Colyer, Vincent, painter, born in Bloomingdale, N. Y., in 1825; studied in New York with John R. Smith, and afterwards at the National Academy, of which he became an associate in 1849. During 1849–61, he applied himself to painting in New York. When the Civil War broke out he originated the United States Christian Commission. He accompanied General Burnside on the expedition to North Carolina for the purpose of ministering to the needs of the colored people. After the capture of Newbern, he was placed in charge of the helpless inhabitants. He there opened evening schools for the colored people and carried on other benevolent enterprises till May, 1862, when his work was stopped by Edward Stanley, who was appointed by the President military governor of North Carolina, and who declared that the laws of the State made it a "criminal offence to teach the blacks to read." At the conclusion of the war Mr. Colyer settled in Darien, Conn. His

VINCENT COLYER.

paintings include *Johnson Straits, British Columbia; Pueblo; Passing Showers; Home of the Yackamas, Oregon; Darien Shore, Connecticut; Rainy Day on Connecticut Shore; Spring Flowers; French Waiter;* and *Winter on Connecticut Shore.* He died on Contentment Island, Conn., July 12, 1888. See CHRISTIAN COMMISSION, UNITED STATES.

Comanche Indians, a roving and warlike tribe of North American Indians of the Shoshone family who, when first known, inhabited the region from the headwaters of the Brazos and Colorado rivers to those of the Arkansas and Missouri, some of their bands penetrating to Santa Fé, in New Mexico, and to Durango, in Mexico. The Spaniards and the tribes on the central plains, like the Pawnees, felt their power in war from an early period. They called themselves by a name signifying "live people," believed in one supreme Father, and claim to have come from towards the setting sun. The tribe is divided into several bands, and all are expert horsemen. The French in Louisiana first penetrated their country in 1718, buying horses from them, and in 1724 made a treaty with them. They were then numerous. One village visited by the French had 140 lodges, containing 1,500 women, 2,000 children, and 800 warriors. Until 1783, they had long and bloody wars with the Spaniards, when, their great war-chief being slain, a peace was established. They numbered 5,000 in 1780. In 1816 they lost 4,000 of their population by small-pox. As late as 1847 their number was estimated at 10,000, with over 2,000 warriors; in 1872, a little over 4,000. They have always been troublesome. In 1904 there were 1,400 at the Kiowa agency in Oklahoma.

Combs,, LESLIE, military officer; born near Boonesboro, Ky., Nov. 28, 1793. His father was an officer in the Revolution. Leslie was the youngest of twelve children, and was distinguished for energy and bravery in the War of 1812–15. He commanded a company of scouts, and did admirable service for the salvation of Fort Meigs. When General Harrison was about to be closely besieged in Fort Meigs (May, 1813), he sent Capt. William Oliver to urge GEN. CLAY GREEN (*q. v.*) to push forward rapidly with the Kentuckians he was then leading towards the Maumee Rapids. While Colonel Dudley, whom Clay had sent forward, was on his way down the

LESLIE COMBS.

Au Glaize River, Clay heard of the perilous condition of Fort Meigs, and resolved to send word to Harrison of his near approach. He called for a volunteer, when

Leslie Combs—then nineteen years of age—promptly responded. "When we reach Fort Defiance," said Combs, "if you will furnish me with a good canoe, I will carry your despatches to General Harrison and return with his orders. I shall only require four or five volunteers and one of my Indian guides to accompany me." Combs was properly equipped, and on May 1 he started on his perilous errand, accompanied by two brothers named Walker and two others (Paxton and Johnson); also by young Black Fish, a Shawnee warrior. They passed the rapids in safety, when the roar of the siege met their ears. Great peril was in their way. It was late in the morning. To remain where they were until night or to go on was equally hazardous. "We must go on," said the brave Combs. As they passed the last bend in the stream that kept the fort from view they were greatly rejoiced to see "the flag was still there," and that the garrison was holding out against a strong besieging force. Suddenly they were assailed by some Indians in the woods, and were compelled to turn their canoe towards the opposite shore, where they abandoned it. One of the party was killed and another badly wounded. Combs and his unhurt companions made their way back to Fort Defiance. Subsequently, being made prisoner, he was taken by the Indians, his captors, to Fort Miami, below, where he was compelled to run the gantlet, in which he was pretty severely wounded. His life was saved by the humanity of Tecumseh. Combs became a general of the militia, and was always a zealous politician and active citizen. He was a Union man during the Civil War. He died in Lexington, Ky., Aug. 21, 1881.

Commander-in-Chief, the title usually applied to the supreme officer in the army or navy of a country. In the United States the national Constitution makes the President commander-in-chief of the army and navy, and, in time of war, of such of the State militia as may be called into general service. State constitutions give the same title to their respective governors in time of peace. Under the general orders of May, 1901, the actual command-in-chief of the army was given to Lieutenant-General Miles. After the abolition of the grades of general and lieutenant-general, on the death of Generals Grant, Sherman, Sheridan, and Schofield, the actual command was invested in the senior major-general.

Commerce, CHAMBERS OF. See CHAMBERS OF COMMERCE.

Commerce and Labor, DEPARTMENTS OF. See CABINET, PRESIDENT'S.

Commerce Destroyers. See NAVY.

COMMERCE OF THE UNITED STATES

Commerce of the United States. In his annual review of the foreign commerce of the United States in the fiscal year ending June 30, 1904, Oscar P. Austin, chief of the Bureau of Statistics in the Department of Commerce and Labor, stated that the foreign commerce of that year was the largest in the history of the country. In one preceding year, 1903, the imports were greater than in 1904, and in one preceding year, 1901, the exports were greater than in 1904; but in no year was the aggregate of imports and exports as great as in 1904. The imports of the year were $991,087,371, a reduction of $34,631,866 as compared with 1903, but exceeding those of any other year except 1903. The exports were $1,460,827,271, a sum $26,937,720 below those of 1901, but exceeding those of any other year except 1901. The aggregate of imports and exports was $2,451,914,642, which exceeded by $6,053,726 that of 1903, in which the total foreign commerce had exceeded any earlier year. The total foreign commerce showed an increase in each successive year since 1894, and was in 1904 more than 50 per cent. in excess of that of 1894, in which the aggregate of imports and exports was $1,547,135,194. Comparing details of 1904 with those of a decade earlier, it may be said that exports of domestic products in 1904 exceeded those of 1894 by 66 per cent., and that the imports exceeded those of 1894 by 51 per cent. The excess of exports over imports was $469,739,900, and exceeded that of 1903 by $75,317,458, but was less than that of the years 1898 to 1902, though greatly in excess of any year previous to 1898.

Remarkable as these statements then were, official statistics prove 1910 to have been the banner calendar year in the history of the commerce of the United States. With the enormous total of almost $3,500,000,000, the total value of the foreign trade was greater than that of any year before, and left a balance in favor of the country of over $300,000,000. The imports and exports exceeded the former high record of 1907 by about $80,000,000. Besides this new record another record was broken during 1910 in the value of the imports from abroad. They amounted to $1,562,807,622, compared with $1,423,169,820 in 1907. The exports during the year were larger than in any year except those of 1907, the total being $1,864,411,270, compared with $1,923,426,892 in 1907.

In the single item of cotton the exports in 1910 aggregated $530,000,000 in value, exceeding by more than $60,000,000 the highest record ever heretofore made. This exportation of raw cotton exported represented approximately two-thirds of the production of the country, a comparison of the figures of production and exportation for a long term of years showing that about one-third of the crop is usually retained for domestic use; and this suggests a valuation of approximately $800,000,000 for the total raw cotton product of the year represented by these export figures. To this, however, must be added the value of the cotton seed, of which the exportations in the form of oil amounted to nearly $13,000,000 and those of oil cake about $10,000,000. The countries to which this $530,000,000 worth of cotton exported in 1910 went, stated in order of magnitude of their purchases are: The United Kingdom, approximately $243,000,000; Germany, $140,000,000; France, $62,000,000; Italy, $28,000,000; Spain, $16,000,000; Canada, $10,500,000, and Japan, $9,500,000. Compare these figures with those of 1810, just one hundred years ago. Then there was little export and the entire number of spindles in the United States was 87,000, averaging 45 pounds per spindle per annum.

The following summary of the imports and exports of merchandise in this phenomenal year will give a clearer idea of the character and volume of our foreign trade and also a unique exposition of the great industrial activities of the country.

FOREIGN COMMERCE OF THE UNITED STATES IN 1910.

GROUPS.	CALENDAR YEAR 1910.	
	Value.	Per Cent.
IMPORTS.		
FREE OF DUTY:		
Foodstuffs in crude condition, and food animals	$124,252,152	16.15
Foodstuffs partly or wholly manufactured	12,171,720	1.58
Crude materials for use in manufacturing	423,710,638	55.07
Manufactures for further use in manufacturing	134,332,391	17.46
Manufactures ready for consumption	66,404,348	8.63
Miscellaneous	8,555,549	1.11
Total free of duty	$769,426,798	100.00
DUTIABLE:		
Foodstuffs in crude condition, and food animals	$ 30,478,135	3.84
Foodstuffs partly or wholly manufactured	178,335,728	22.47
Crude materials for use in manufacturing	118,364,498	14.92
Manufactures for further use in manufacturing	151,619,525	19.11
Manufactures ready for consumption	310,585,238	39.14
Miscellaneous	4,114,329	.52
Total dutiable	$793,497,453	100.00

FOREIGN COMMERCE OF THE UNITED STATES IN 1910.—*Continued.*

GROUPS.	CALENDAR YEAR 1910.	
	Value.	Per Cent.
FREE AND DUTIABLE:		
Foodstuffs in crude condition, and food animals	$154,730,287	9.90
Foodstuffs partly or wholly manufactured	190,507,448	12.19
Crude materials for use in manufacturing	542,075,036	34.68
Manufactures for further use in manufacturing	285,951,916	18.30
Manufactures ready for consumption	376,989,586	24.12
Miscellaneous	12,669,878	.81
Total imports of merchandise	$1,562,924,251	100.00
Per cent of free	....	49.23
Duties collected from customs	$327,064,495	
Remaining in warehouse at the end of month	....	
EXPORTS.		
DOMESTIC:		
Foodstuffs in crude condition, and food animals	$ 90,479,992	4.95
Foodstuffs partly or wholly manufactured	254,733,306	13.94
Crude materials for use in manufacturing	646,414,659	35.38
Manufactures for further use in manufacturing	286,437,521	15.67
Manufactures ready for consumption	541,143,488	29.62
Miscellaneous	8,046,703	.44
Total domestic	$1,827,255,669	100.00
FOREIGN:		
Free of duty	$21,939,242	58.92
Dutiable	15,296,733	41.08
Total foreign	$37,235,975	100.00
Total exports	$1,864,491,644	
Excess of exports	$301,567,393	
Total imports and exports	$3,427,415,895	

The movement of gold and silver coin and bullion in the same year was summarized as follows:

GOLD AND SILVER COIN AND BULLION.

GOLD:	
Imports	$59,222,518
Exports	58,774,822
SILVER:	
Imports	45,878,168
Exports	57,360,973

The following table shows the movement of shipping engaged in the foreign trade by net tonnage of vessels entered and cleared at the various ports, and also the proportion of vessels flying the American flag:

TONNAGE MOVEMENT IN THE FOREIGN TRADE

CLASS.	Entered.	Cleared.	Total.
American sail	1,165,020	1,116,703	2,281,723
American steam	8,055,694	8,023,317	16,079,011
Foreign sail	1,286,858	1,353,513	2,640,371
Foreign steam	30,608,064	30,266,565	60,875,529
Total	41,116,536	40,760,098	81,876,634

The commerce between the United States and its non-contiguous territories is shown below. Customs collectors were not required prior to the act of April 29, 1902, to furnish statements of shipments of merchandise between the United States and its non-contiguous possessions. Hawaii was annexed to the United States by act of Congress of July 7, 1898, and was made a Territory and customs district by act of April 30, 1900, which took effect June 14, 1900. Porto Rico was taken possession of by the United States, Oct. 18, 1898, and was given a civil government and made a customs district by act of April 12, 1900, to take effect May 1, 1900. The figures of the commerce between the Philippine Islands and the United States, while at present included in the general tables of foreign commerce of the United States, are also presented herewith in conjunction with the other tables of this group.

No figures are given for Panama Canal Zone, as the shipments to this district are not, strictly speaking, commercial, being mainly supplies to the army of men engaged in building the Panama Canal. Figures for Guam, Samoan Islands, Wake Island, etc., are too small for enumeration.

SHIPMENTS OF DOMESTIC MERCHANDISE TO NON-CONTIGUOUS TERRITORIES.

Groups.	1910.	
	Value.	Per Cent.
TO ALASKA.		
Foodstuffs in crude condition, and food animals	$1,423,840	8.46
Foodstuffs partly or wholly manufactured	4,438,809	26.39
Crude materials for use in manufacturing	662,982	3.94
Manufactures for further use in manufacturing	2,096,935	12.46
Manufactures ready for consumption	8,155,016	48.48
Miscellaneous	45,150	.27
Total	$16,822,732	100.00
TO HAWAII.		
Foodstuffs in crude condition, and food animals	$1,461,833	6.76
Foodstuffs, partly or wholly manufactured	3,228,428	14.92
Crude materials for use in manufacturing	1,301,365	6.01
Manufactures for further use in manufacturing	2,509,711	11.60
Manufactures ready for consumption	12,935,216	59.78
Miscellaneous	201,198	.93
Total	$21,637,751	100.00
TO PORTO RICO.		
Foodstuffs in crude condition, and food animals	$4,444,229	14.54
Foodstuffs partly or wholly manufactured	7,236,685	23.69
Crude materials for use in manufacturing	675,206	2.21
Manufactures for further use in manufacturing	2,283,299	7.47
Manufactures ready for consumption	15,906,500	52.03
Miscellaneous	19,104	.06
Total	$30,565,023	100.00
TO PHILIPPINE ISLANDS.		
Foodstuffs in crude condition, and food animals	$801,203	4.04
Foodstuffs partly or wholly manufactured	2,583,926	13.01
Crude materials for use in manufacturing	464,697	2.34
Manufactures for further use in manufacturing	1,960,683	9.87
Manufactures ready for consumption	14,044,107	70.73
Miscellaneous	2,212	.01
Total	$19,856,828	100.00

SHIPMENTS OF MERCHANDISE FROM NON-CONTIGUOUS TERRITORIES.

NON-CONTIGUOUS TERRITORIES.		1910.
DOMESTIC AND FOREIGN MERCHANDISE.		
ALASKA.		
Domestic merchandise		$13,464,325
Foreign merchandise		235,269
Total		$13,699,594
HAWAII.		
Domestic merchandise		$44,189,260
Foreign merchandise		35,403
Total		$44,224,663
PORTO RICO.		
Domestic merchandise		$35,765,405
Foreign merchandise		624
Total		$35,766,029
PHILIPPINE ISLANDS.		
Domestic merchandise		$18,040,745
Foreign merchandise		
Total		$18,040,745
Total domestic		$111,459,735
Total foreign		271,296
Grand total		$111,731,031
GOLD AND SILVER.		
ALASKA	Domestic	$15,195,954
	Foreign	3,441,834
HAWAII	Domestic	513,627
	Foreign	4,795
PORTO RICO	Domestic	
	Foreign	11,038
Total		$19,167,248

From the foregoing it appears that the total commerce between the United States and its non-contiguous territories in the remarkable year 1910 had a value of $219,-780,613.

America's Twenty Best Customers.—The following table, prepared by Consular Assistant Charles Lyon Chandler, is arranged to show the 20 heaviest buyers of American goods, as indicated by the value of exports from the United States during the fiscal year of 1910–11:

To—	Value.
England	$536,591,730
Germany	287,495,814
Canada	269,806,013
France	135,271,648
Netherlands	96,103,376
Mexico	61,281,715
Cuba	60,709,062
Italy	60,580,766
Belgium	45,016,622
Argentina	$43,918,511
Australasia	37,524,586
Japan	36,721,409
Scotland	27,373,595
Brazil	27,240,346
Spain	25,064,916
Russia	23,524,267
Panama	20,867,919
China	20,223,077
Austria	19,514,787
Denmark	13,196,950

O. P. AUSTIN (*q.v.*), chief of the Bureau of Statistics, Department of Commerce and Labor, writes as follows:

A large part of the exports to England, Germany and the Netherlands are intended ultimately for other countries. Our exports to British South Africa, Norway, British West Indies, and the South American republics are constantly growing larger.

A Century of Commerce.—Among the wonderful developments of the nineteenth century, none is more marvellous than that of its commerce. Ever watchful, and ever willing to hazard expenditure for the sake of prospective gain, it has adapted to its own use every discovery and invention which ingenuity and science have brought to the front. From the exchange of a few articles of luxury it has expanded until it now interchanges the products of all lands and all climes, utilizing the railway train by land and the steamer by sea; and exchanges which occupied months at the opening of the century are now effected in days or weeks. Business messages then sent by carrier and sailing-vessels took a year to reach the Orient and obtain a reply, while now but a few minutes or hours suffice for a similar service. A transfer of cash or commodities in which weeks or months were consumed are now arranged by telegraph and banks in minutes or hours; while the transfer of the merchandise is a matter of hours or days. From the narrow frontage of land along the ocean, or along water-courses, the seaboard has been extended landward indefinitely by the railway, while the carrying capacity and speed of the ocean vessel have been correspondingly increased. Instead of the pack-animals which could carry but a few hundred pounds, or the wagon which could at the best transport a ton of merchandise, the railway car accepts as much as twenty teams could haul, and the engine hurries from twenty to thirty of these cars to the ocean, 1,000 miles away, where the steamship calmly swallows the loads of twenty or thirty of these trains and steams across the ocean at almost the same speed with which the merchandise was transported to the water's edge; while, before it has passed out of sight of land, the consignee on the other side of the globe has received notice of its departure, of the cargo it carries, and of the day and almost the hour at which he may expect its arrival.

Meanwhile, discovery and invention have multiplied the producing capacity of these greatly increased areas. The shuttle has supplied fabrics more cheaply than the cheapest hand-labor could produce. Machinery and agricultural science have increased the products of the soil and transformed into merchandise that which was formerly refuse. Science has explored the earth and brought forth the precious and industrial metals, while invention has vied with art in transforming these products into articles which have become necessities of life and which have, in turn, contributed to the productiveness of the human race in all climes and conditions, thus multiplying commerce as well as production.

Thus, all the great developments of the wonderful nineteenth century have combined to aid commerce, and articles which, at its beginning, were luxuries enjoyed only by the rich are now considered necessaries by the masses. The natural products of the tropics have become the necessities of the temperate zone, and the manufactures of the temperate zone are demanded for daily life in the tropics. The grain-producing areas of the newer countries contribute to the food supply of the Old World and take in exchange the products of its workshops; and the Orient yields its silks, teas, and spices in exchange for our food-stuffs, machinery, and manufactures. Meantime, Finance, with its consummate art of balancing commodity against commodity and exchange against exchange, sits aloft and with golden reins skilfully guides the transactions which steam and electricity thus make possible, balancing the sales of one country against the purchases of another, weighing the value of this and measuring the usefulness of that, bringing order out of what appears endless confusion and hopeless disorder, and by its skilful, complex, and silent machinery making possible this enormous exchange of commodities with the transfer of the smallest possible proportion of circulating medium.

To measure accurately the commerce of the world, even in this day of improved business conditions, when the gathering of statistics has become a science and measures of value are reduced to a common denominator (gold), is difficult. That such attempts must have been much more difficult a century ago is so apparent that the fact need scarcely be mentioned as an apology for the use of estimates in regard to some portion of the earlier commerce of the century. Indeed, the fact that this method is still necessary with reference to certain remote spots in the commercial world shows how large a proportion of the statements of the world's commerce in the earlier years of the century must have been estimates, in many cases even conjecture. Yet there is no better method of reaching conclusions with regard to the early commerce of the century than to accept the estimates made by thoughtful men who had given years—lifetimes indeed—to the study of the subject; and, in this attempt to contrast conditions at the close of the century with those at its beginning, these estimates have been accepted as the best and, in fact, the only means of approximating the movement of merchandise between nations and grand divisions in those days when governments and trade organizations and financial interests were but beginning to realize the importance of comprehensive and accurate statements upon this subject. The interchange of commodities throughout the commercial world at the beginning of the century is estimated at $1,500,000,000 in value, and at the end of the century fully $20,000,000,000. Meantime, the population, which is estimated by Malte-Brun at 640,000,000 in 1804, is now estimated in round terms at about 1,500,000,000, the increase in population having thus been 135 per cent., while the increase in commerce has been

1,233 per cent. While these statements of the commerce of the earlier years of the century are necessarily estimates in many cases, the fact that the Oriental countries had little commercial intercourse with the outside world, or even with one another, and that the chief commerce of the world was carried on by a few nations whose transactions in these lines could be measured with a fair degree of accuracy, seems to justify an acceptance of these statements as, probably, fairly accurate.

An attempt to trace the commerce of the century by decades is even more difficult, because the occasional and semi-occasional estimates, especially those made of population, do not in all cases fall upon the year ending a decade—a circumstance which creates the further necessity of making new estimates for the decennial periods based upon those actually made by experts at the years nearest to those dates. The estimates of population made during the century are those of Malte-Brun, Balbi, Michelet, Behm-Wagner, and Levasseur; and, accepting these authorities as presenting the best obtainable guide, and the estimates made by Kaier, Palgrave, Mulhall, and Keltie of the commerce by decades, it is practicable, at least, to approach the average commerce, *per capita,* of the world at decennial periods during the century. This calculation gives the average *per capita* commerce, combining imports and exports to obtain the total commerce, at $2.31 *per capita* in 1800, $2.34 in 1830, $3.76 in 1850, $6.01 in 1860, $8.14 in 1870, $10.26 in 1880, $11.84 in 1890, and $13.27 in 1899.

What has caused this wonderful increase in the world's interchange of commodities, by which the commerce for each individual in the world is now practically six times as much as it was 100 years ago, if we accept these estimates made by the most distinguished experts of the century? One need not go far to find an answer to this inquiry. Increased areas of production, increased facilities for transporting the products of different sections and climes, increased power of communication between men in various parts of the world, and, coupled with these, the great underlying principle of specialization of labor and products, have led to this wonderful development of interchange among nations and peoples, by which articles most readily produced in one part of the world are exchanged for those most readily produced in another part. The great fertile plains of North America, South America, Australia, and Russia have become the world's producers of grain and provisions, and are increasing their supplies of the textiles and their supplies of the food-stuffs required by all the world in manufacturing or for daily consumption; while the Orient stands ready with its silks and teas, and Africa tenders its gold and diamonds and ivory and native tropical products, all of which articles are required by the great manufacturing centres of the United States and Europe, which furnish in exchange their manufactures of cotton, wool, silk, wood, iron, and steel.

Thus commerce is constantly increasing its volume by its own activity. The machinery produced by the manufacturing section enables one man in the great grain-fields of America to produce as much as a dozen or a score could produce by old methods at the beginning of the century or even later. The machinery of the factory enables a single individual to multiply many times his power of producing the articles required by his fellow-men. Exploration, colonization, and investment of capital have greatly increased the producing area of the tropical section of the world. Added to all these, and making practicable the interchange of articles whose production is thus so enormously increased, is the increased power of transportation, communication, and financial adjustment which the second half of the century developed.

Five great causes enter into, and combine to create, the wonderful development of the century's commerce. They may be stated in five words: steam, electricity, invention, finance, peace. The effect upon commerce of the use of steam as a motive power can scarcely be realized, until the progress of its development is compared with the progress of commerce. Then it is seen that the marked advance in the interchange of commodities was simultaneous with the development of the steamship and railway, and that the growth of the one was coincident with that of the other. The application of steam to transportation of merchandise by rail began in England in 1825, and in the United States in 1830, the number of miles of railway in the world in 1830 being about 200. In that year, the world's commerce, according to the best estimates obtainable, was $1,981,000,000 as against $1,659,000,000 in 1820, an increase in the decade of barely 17 per cent., while in the preceding decades of the century the increase had been even less. By 1840, railways had increased to 5,420 miles, and commerce had increased to $2,789,000,000, an increase of 40 per cent. From 1840 to 1850, railways increased to 23,960 miles, and commerce had increased to $4,049,000,000, a gain of 45 per cent. By 1860, the railways had increased to 67,350 miles and commerce to $7,246,000,000, an increase of 79 per cent. By 1870, the railroads had increased to 139,860 miles and commerce to $10,663,000,000; by 1880, the railroads had increased to 224,900 miles and commerce to $14,761,000,000; by 1890, the lines of railroad amounted to 390,000 miles and commerce to $17,519,000,000; and, in 1898, the railroad lines aggregated 442,200 miles, and commerce $19,915,000,000. A single instance will indicate the development which the railroad gives to the commerce of a country. India, with 300,000,000 of population and 22,000 miles of railway, has seen her commerce increase nearly 60 per cent. in the past twenty-five years, while that of China, with 400,000,000 of people, but no railways, has increased about 30 per cent. in that time.

In the meanwhile steam had also revolutionized the carrying-trade on the ocean. The first steamship crossed the ocean in 1819, and the total steam tonnage afloat in 1820 is estimated at 20,000 tons, against 5,814,000 of sail tonnage. By 1840, steam tonnage had increased to 368,000, while sail has grown to 9,012,000; by 1860, steam had reached 1,710,000, while sail was 14,890,000; by 1870, steam tonnage was 3,040,000, and sail had dropped to 13,000,000; by 1880, steam had become 5,880,000, and sail 14,400,000; by 1890, steam had reached 9,040,000, and sail had dropped to 12,640,000; and, in 1898, the steam tonnage was estimated at 13,045,000, and the sail tonnage at 11,045,000. The rapidity of growth of steam transportation, however, can only be realized when it is remembered that the steam-vessel, by reason of its superior speed, size, and ability to cope with all kinds of weather, is able to make four times as many voyages in a year as a sailing-vessel, and that, in comparing the steam tonnage of the late decades with the sail tonnage of the earlier ones, the former must be multiplied by four to give it a proper comparison with the unit of sail tonnage. Reducing the steam tonnage to that of the standard of measurement at the beginning of the century, we find that the carrying power of vessels on the ocean had increased from 4,026,000 tons in 1800, to 10,482,000 in 1840; 21,730,000 in 1860; 37,900,000 in 1880; 48,800,000 in 1890; and 63,225,000 in 1898–99, of which last enormous total but 11,450,000 was sailing tonnage. Not only has greater carrying power come on land and sea, but with it increased speed and safety. A century ago the voyage to Europe occupied over a month, and was a cause for constant anxiety as to the life of those travelling and the cargo carried by the vessel; now it is a holiday excursion of five days, in which there is no more thought of danger than on the cycle-path or an elevated railway.

News of the West India hurricane in 1818 reached the United States fully thirty days after its occurrence, while Havana is to-day less than forty-eight hours from New York. The first vessel from New York to China occupied fifteen months on its round trip, and a voyage to the Orient, before the introduction of steam, occupied from eight to twelve months for the round trip, while now it can be accomplished both ways in a little over one month. Not only have recent years brought increased speed and facility in the moving of commerce, but, with that, increased safety, thus reducing the danger of loss of both life and property; while, in the matter of cost, the reduction has been enormous, many articles which then could not possibly bear the cost of transportation now forming an important part of the world's commerce. Even in sailing-vessels, which still perform about one-fourth of the world's sea transportation, steam is being utilized to perform many duties formerly accomplished by hand-power, such as the hoisting of heavy sails, the steering of the vessels, and the handling of cargoes; and thus, as the size of the sailing-vessels is increased, the number of men required to manage them is reduced.

Still another influence which steam has given to commerce is the resultant increase in the quantity of goods offered for transportation. The great areas far removed from water transportation could never have been able to contribute to the world's supply of bread-stuffs without the railway to transport their products to the water's edge, and the capacity of men for production of food-stuffs or manufactures, which form the bulk of the world's commerce, has been multiplied by the aid of steam in the workshop, and even on the great farms, where steam-ploughs, steam-wagons, and steam-threshers increase the producing power of man, and reduce the cost of the product which he sends around the world for daily consumption by millions who could not have afforded its use in the early years of the century.

Electricity, whose use in behalf of commerce was nearly contemporaneous with steam, has also performed an important part in increasing the activity and volume of commerce. The merchant who desired to send a cargo across the ocean or to the other side of the globe did so formerly at great risk as to prices, or else after long correspondence and vexatious delays. Now, not only the dealer in the cities, but the very farmer who grows the grain, or the workman who produces the iron and steel, knows this evening what was its price in the markets of London and other parts of the world this morning. The merchant who desires to sell in Europe may contract his goods before shipping, and those who would make purchases in the Orient or the tropics can give their orders to-day, with the confidence that the goods will start to-morrow and reach them at a fixed date in time for the markets at their most favorable season. The growth of the telegraph and ocean cable has, like that of the railway and steamship, being contemporaneous with the growth of commerce. The first telegraph for commercial purposes was constructed in 1844, and so quickly did its influence become apparent that several thousand miles were in existence by 1850, while by 1860 the total had reached nearly 100,000 miles, by 1870 280,000 miles, by 1880 440,000 miles, by 1890 768,000 miles, and by 1900 1,000,000 miles. Submarine cables, by which the international commerce is guided and multiplied, date from 1851, in which year 25 miles were put into operation across the English Channel. By 1860 the total length of successful lines was about 1,500 miles, though one cable laid across the Atlantic, and another through the Red and Arabian seas, meantime, had worked long enough to prove the practicability of the enterprise. By 1870 the submarine cables in operation amounted to about 15,000 miles, by 1880 to about 50,000 miles, by 1890 to 132,000 miles, and by 1898 to 170,000 miles, the number of messages transmitted on them being 6,000,000 a year, while those by the land telegraphs are estimated at 1,000,000 per day, the greater proportion of both being in the service of commerce.

Invention has also contributed largely to the development of commerce, both directly and indirectly. What share it has had in that wonderful growth can scarcely be estimated; but, when we consider to what an extent the development of manufactures, as well as of agriculture, has been the result of labor-saving machinery and ingenious devices of men, it is apparent that to invention is due much, very much, of the enormous increase of production, and consequently the increase of exchange from section to section and from continent to continent. The cotton-gin, which had but begun to make itself felt at the beginning of the century, the reaping and threshing machines, by which labor of grain producing is greatly reduced, the application of machinery to mining operations and the handling of the product of mines, the engines—those powerful and intricate machines—which transport the merchandise to the seaboard, and the railways on which they run, the steamships, the screw propeller, the iron and steel vessels, and the thousands of articles from the factory which form an important part of the cargoes which they carry—all these are the inventions of the century, and all have contributed greatly to the producing and transporting power of man, and consequently to the multiplication of the commodities which he produces and exchanges.

Finance and financiers have contributed enormously to the growth of the commerce of the century. The gold discoveries in California and Australia, and later in other parts of the world, have greatly increased the volume of the circulating medium and encouraged the creation of a single and well-defined standard of value, so that the merchant may make his sales and purchases with an assurance that payments will be made in a measure of value acceptable to the whole world, and losses and uncertainty of traffic thus avoided. The supply of this precious metal has increased enormously during the century. Chevalier estimated that the amount of gold in Europe in 1492 was but $60,000,000. From that time to the beginning of the century, the average gold production was about $8,000,000 a year; from 1800 to 1850, about $15,000,000 a year; and, since that date, it has ranged steadily upward, until it has reached over $300,000,000 a year, thus multiplying many times the stock of the standard metal of the world. The result of this is that 95 per cent. of the commerce of the world is now carried on between nations having a fixed and well-regulated currency, with gold as the standard. Add to this fact the developments of the financial and credit systems, by which sums due in one part of the world are balanced against those due in another part, and by the use of simple pieces of paper the transportation of any considerable sums of money from place to place and country to country avoided, and it will be seen that finance has had much to do with the century's commercial growth.

"Peace," it has been said, "hath her victories no less renowned than war," and peace has doubtless been an important factor in the wonderful development of the century's commerce. Nothing so quickly affects commerce as protracted warfare. This was particularly noticeable in the early part of the century, when the seizure of vessels, the impressment of seamen, and the general destruction of commerce—not only the commerce of the enemy, but, in many cases, that of any others against whom the slightest suspicion could be charged—practically suspended European commerce. In addition to this, the danger from pirates, which then constantly existed in certain parts of the ocean, was increased during war times. During the first fifteen years of the century, British, French, and finally all European vessels were practically prohibited from engaging in commerce by the Napoleonic wars, and the commerce of the world was largely thrown into the hands of our own shipping, until the War of 1812 and the events immediately preceding it. With the advance of the century, wars became less frequent, and of shorter duration when entered on; while piracy has been generally suppressed, international laws for the protection of shipping enacted, and regulations established for the protection of those engaging in commerce. Not only has the actual loss from these causes been materially reduced, but the increased safety and absence of danger from losses have encouraged the increase in shipping and in commerce itself.

Many other causes might be named as contributing largely to the wonderful increase in commerce during the century. The area under cultivation in Europe, America, and Australia is estimated to have increased from 360,000,000 to nearly 900,000,000 acres; the coal-mines have increased their output from 11,000,000 to 600,000,000 tons; pig-iron production has grown from 460,000 tons to 37,000,000; cotton production has increased from 520,000,000 to 5,900,000,000 pounds; while the value of manufactures has increased perhaps a thousandfold in the 100 years. But all these are the results in a greater or less degree of the five great causes named above. Another cause which is frequently urged as contributing largely to the increase of commerce in the middle part of the century, is the repeal of navigation laws and excessive tariffs. While this is, doubtless, entitled to consideration, it is difficult to measure the share which it had in the development of that period. Steam, electricity, and gold discoveries were at that moment combining to stimulate commerce, while the fact that the growth of international commerce has been continued in the face of the return to protective duties by most of the commercial nations except Great Britain, adds to the difficulty of determining how far these important occurrences were factors in the growth of international trade of that time.

The following table indicates the growth of the commerce of the world during ninety-eight years of the nineteenth century.

change of merchandise between nation and nation throughout the entire world, wherever records of such commerce are attainable. And while it is quite probable that the development of business and statistical methods throughout the world has made it practicable for the inquirer of to-day to bring into the grand total the commerce of some countries whose business could only be estimated in the earlier part of the period, it is also likely that the

THE WORLD'S COMMERCIAL DEVELOPMENT DURING THE NINETEENTH CENTURY.

		Commerce.		Shipping.		
Year.	Population.	Aggregate. Dollars.	Per Capita. Dollars.	Sail. Tons.	Steam. Tons.	Carrying Power. Tons.
1800	(a) 640,000,000	1,479,000,000	2.31	4,026,000	None	4,026,000
1820	(b) 780,000,000	1,659,000,000	2.13	5,814,000	20,000	5,894,000
1830	(b) 847,000,000	1,981,000,000	2.34	7,100,000	107,000	7,528,000
1840	(c) 950,000,000	2,789,000,000	2.93	9,012,000	368,000	10,482,000
1850	(c) 1,075,000,000	4,049,000,000	3.76	11,470,000	858,000	14,902,000
1860	(c) 1,205,000,000	7,246,000,000	6.01	14,890,000	1,710,000	21,730,000
1870	(d) 1,310,000,000	10,663,000,000	8.14	12,900,000	3,040,000	25,100,000
1880	(e) 1,439,000,000	14,761,000,000	10.26	14,400,000	5,880,000	37,900,000
1890	(f) 1,488,000,000	17,519,000,000	11.80	12,640,000	9,040,000	48,800,000
1898	1,500,000,000	19,519,000,000	13.27	11,045,000	13,045,000	63,200,000

Year.	Railways (g). Miles.	Telegraphs. Miles.	Cables. Miles.	Area Cultivated. Acres (g).
1800	None	None	None	360,000,000
1820	None	None	None	402,000,000
1830	210	None	None	....
1840	5,420	None	None	492,000,000
1850	23,960	5,000	25	....
1860	67,350	99,800	1,500	583,000,000
1870	139,860	281,000	15,000	....
1880	224,900	440,000	49,000	749,000,000
1890	390,000	767,800	132,000	807,000,000
1898	442,200	933,000	168,000	861,000,000

Year.	Cotton Production. Pounds (g).	Coal Production. Tons.	Pig Iron Production. Tons (g).	Gold Production of Decade ending with year (h). Dollars (h).
1800	520,000,000	11,600,000	460,000	128,464,000
1820	630,000,000	17,200,000	1,010,000	76,063,000
1830	820,000,000	25,100,000	1,585,000	94,419,000
1840	1,310,000,000	44,800,000	2,680,000	134,841,000
1850	1,435,000,000	81,400,000	4,422,000	363,928,000
1860	2,551,000,000	142,300,000	7,180,000	1,333,981,000
1870	2,775,000,000	213,400,000	11,910,000	1,263,015,000
1880	3,601,000,000	340,000,000	18,140,000	1,150,814,000
1890	5,600,000,000	466,000,000	25,160,000	1,060,052,000
1898	5,900,000,000	610,000,000	37,150,000	1,950,000,000

(a) Malte-Brun's estimate for 1804.
(b) Based on Balbi's estimate for 1828.
(c) Based on Michelet's estimate for 1845.
(d) Based on Behm-Wagner estimate for 1874.
(e) Levasseur's estimate for 1878.
(f) Royal Geographical Society estimate.
(g) Mulhall's estimates, except 1830, 1890, and 1898.
(h) Saetbeer's estimates prior to 1860.

To discuss the part which the various nations have had in this commerce, the relations of imports to exports, or the classes of articles exchanged between the great sections of the globe, would carry this study beyond reasonable limits. In all of the above statements, the term "commerce" has covered both exports and imports, and has included the ex-

reduction in prices of the merchandise whose value only is stated fully offsets any increase in the closeness with which the field has been gleaned, and that the figures represent with a fair degree of accuracy the relative quantity of merchandise moved at the various periods under discussion. While the fact that the exports of each nation always become the imports of some other nation would suggest that export and import ought to balance each other in the grand aggregate, it is found that they do not, since the freight, insurance, and brokerage are in the most cases added to the export price in naming the value of the goods where they become an import, thus making the stated value of the world's import usually from 5 to 10 per cent. in excess of the stated value of the exports.

The United States has performed well her part in the century's development of the world's commerce. While the total commerce of the world has grown from $1,479,000,000 to $19,915,000,000, that of the United States has increased from $162,000,000 to over $2,000,000,000, while the ratio of increase in exports of domestic merchandise is even much greater. Indeed, the figures of our commerce for the first year and decade of the century are quite misleading for comparative purposes, as they include large quantities of foreign goods brought to our ports by our vessels and merely declared as entries, while in fact they in many cases never left shipboard and only entered nominally into our commerce because of their being carried by our vessels. This was due to the fact that European nations which had very rigorous laws prohibiting the carrying by foreign vessels of commerce between their own ports and colonies were willing to suspend the action of these laws while the war prevented them from doing their own carrying trade. The result of this was that, during the first decade of the century, our reported exports of foreign goods amounted to as much as those of domestic products, and in some years actually exceeded them, while now they only amount to about 2 per cent. of our total exports. Comparing the commerce in domestic goods during 1899 with that of 1800, it is found that the percentage of increase is very much greater than that shown by the world's total commerce.

In general, it may be said of our commerce of 1900 that the imports are about ten times as much as in 1800, and the exports twenty times as much.

What of the twentieth century? Can its commerce, and all those conveniences of traffic and intercourse which go to stimulate and create commerce, show such a marvellous growth as that of the century just ended? It seems almost impossible, yet no more impossible than the growth which has actually occurred during the past century would have appeared had it been predicted at its beginning. Aerial navigation may, long before the end of the present century, aid in the transportation of men and mails and the lighter articles of commerce to areas not supplied with other means of transportation; a similar service may be performed between great distributing centres by huge pneumatic tubes, a mere development of the system which now prevails for shorter distances in great cities; wireless telegraphy will communicate with all sections of the world; electricity will transfer to convenient points the power created by countless waterfalls now inaccessible for manufacturing purposes; steamships will develop their carrying powers and multiply communications between continents and great trading centres; a ship canal will connect the waters of the Atlantic and the Pacific; and vessels circumnavigating the globe in the interests of commerce may take further advantage of currents of air and water which move ever westward as the earth revolves ever towards the east; other ship canals will connect our Great Lakes with the ocean, and steamships from Europe and the Mediterranean countries and the Orient will land their merchandise at the docks of Chicago and Duluth, and the other great commercial cities of our inland seas; a great railway system will stretch from South America to Bering Straits, thence down the eastern coast of Siberia, through China, Siam, Burmah, across India, Persia, Arabia, past the pyramids of Egypt to the westernment point of Africa, where only 1,600 miles of ocean will intervene to prevent the complete encircling of the earth with a belt of steel and facilitate the interchange of commodities between them.

Many of the problems outlined in the foregoing survey were solved wholly or in part in the first fifteen years of the twentieth century. The exports of merchandise alone increased from $1,394,483,082 in 1900 to $1,744,984,720 in 1910, and the imports from $849,941,184 in 1900 to $1,556,947,430 in 1910. Previous records were broken in 1907, with exports of $1,880,851,078 and imports of $1,434,421,425; and in 1913, with exports of $2,465,884,149 and imports of $1,813,-008,234. The balance of trade in favor of the United States was $544,541,898 in 1900, $446,429,653 in 1907, $188,037,-290 in 1910, and $652,875,915 in 1913.

The fiscal year ended June 30, 1914, showed total exports of merchandise of $2,364,579,148; total imports, $1,893,-925,657; balance of trade, $470,653,491. With the outbreak of the European war in July, 1914, the export trade of the United States assumed marvelous proportions, as the warring nations, paralyzed in all their productive activities, looked to the United States for the supplies required for their armies, navies, and non-combatant citizens. In less than nine months of the war the trade balance leaped to over $760,000,000.

Commerce, COURT OF. An act of Congress, approved June 18, 1910, created the United States Commerce Court, with jurisdiction over the following cases:

1. The enforcement of any order of the Interstate Commerce Commission other than for the payment of money.

2. Cases brought to enjoin, set aside, annul, or suspend any order of the Interstate Commerce Commission.

3. Cases under Section 3 of the Commerce Act of 1903, previously maintained in a United States Circuit Court.

4. Mandamus proceedings under Sections 20 or 23 of the Commerce Act of 1887.

This court was abolished Dec. 31, 1913.

Commercial Crises. See CRISES; PANICS.

Commission Government, a form of municipal government that originated in Galveston, Tex., soon after the devastating storm of 1900, and attained such widespread popularity that by 1912 no less than 250 cities and towns in the country were being operated under it or a modification of it, and many others were seeking legislative authority for its adoption. The scheme became known by the names of the cities that early adopted it, as the "Galveston Plan," the "Denver Plan," and the later and largely varied "Des Moines Plan." The basic purpose of the plan is the substitution of strict business methods for partisan control of municipalities, the attainment of more effective service through the largest popular selection, and the elimination of bossism, graft, and official corruption by placing only the most respectable citizens in office. Under it the whole conduct of municipal affairs is vested in a mayor and a small commission elected by the city at large for a given period, usually four years. The several executive departments are divided among the commissioners; all proposed franchises must be submitted to popular vote; no ordinance passed by the commissioners can go into effect until thirty days; and within that period ten per cent. of the voting population can secure a referendum to the entire voting body if that percentage should deem the proposed measure unwise. A vital feature of government by commission is the vesting in the public of the privilege of the INITIATIVE, REFERENDUM, AND RECALL (*q. v.*), the general principle of the last-named in some places being modified so as to exempt the judiciary from its application, and in others being omitted entirely. That government by commission is fulfilling its basic purpose is shown by the fact that in ten years there were only three instances of a city exercising the right of recall. In 1915 there were 355 cities in 41 states under this form of government.

Commerce Commission. See INTERSTATE COMMERCE COMMISSION.

Commissioners to Foreign Courts. Soon after the Declaration of Independence a plan of treaties with foreign governments was reported by a committee on that subject, and Franklin, Deane, and Jefferson were appointed (Sept. 26, 1776) commissioners to the French Court. Unwilling to leave his wife, whose health was declining, Jefferson refused the appointment, and Arthur Lee, then in London, was substituted for him; and after the loss of New York these commissioners were urged to press the subject of a treaty of alliance and commerce. Commissioners were also appointed to other European courts in 1777—Arthur Lee to that of Madrid; his brother William (lately one of the sheriffs of London) to Vienna and Berlin, and Ralph Izard, of South Carolina, to Florence. All but the French mission were failures. Arthur Lee was not allowed to enter Madrid, and went on a fruitless errand to Germany; Izard made no attempt to visit Florence, and William Lee visited Berlin without accomplishing anything. There his papers were stolen from him, through the contrivance, it was believed, of the British resident minister. See AMBASSADOR.

Committees, certain members of a parliamentary body combined to facilitate business by examination, discussion, testimony, etc., and to prepare resolutions or bills, and to report the same to the body of which they are members. The early Congress had very few committees, as the members in each House were few in number. The Senate has grown by the addition of two members for each new State admitted; the House of Representatives, despite the increase of the ratio of apportionment from one member to each 30,000 inhabitants to one member for each 194,182 members in 1903, or one member to each 211,877 inhabitants as proposed for the ratio, according to the census of 1910, increased from 65 members in 1789 to 391 members under the census of 1900, or 433 members as proposed for the new apportionment in 1913.

The examination of questions in preparation of bills, with the consequent debate upon the same, in a body of nearly 400 members, many of whom are ready to proceed to dilatory practices to prevent legislation, has been found to be almost impossible. Consequently the government of the United States has more and more become a government by means of committees. There are many such committees in both the House and the Senate, and there are a number of joint committees made up by a membership from both Houses of Congress.

Committees of Correspondence, committees of colonial legislatures, whose function was to keep up correspondence with the agents of the colonies in London. Pennsylvania had such a committee from 1744. In 1772 Samuel Adams, in the legislature of Massachusetts, moved a committee of correspondence, which aimed to state the rights of the colonies, and to correspond with the other colonies and towns of New England. In 1773 the Virginia legislature appointed a similar committee to correspond with all the American colonies. This system of committees, which worked in secret, fostered the germs of the American Revolution.

Committees of the Whole, a committee of all the individual members of a parliamentary body. When Congress considers a question "as in Committee of the Whole" the Speaker leaves the chair, after appointing a chairman to preside. When the committee rises the Speaker resumes the chair.

Committees of Safety, formed before and during the Revolutionary War, to keep watch of and act upon events pertaining to the public welfare, were really committees of vigilance. They were of incalculable service during that period in detecting conspiracies against the interests of the people and restraining evilly disposed persons. They were sometimes possessed of almost supreme executive power, delegated to them by the people. Massachusetts took the lead in the appointment of a committee of safety so early as the autumn of 1774, of which John Hancock was chairman. It was given power to call out the militia, provide means for defence—in a word, perform many of the duties of a provisional government. Other colonies appointed committees of safety. One was appointed in the city of New York, composed of the leading citizens. These committees were in constant communications with committees of correspondence.

Commodities Clause, a section of the Railroad Rate Act of Congress, approved June 29, 1906, which became the subject of much controversy and litigation and of two decisions by the United States Supreme Court. The following is the text of the clause: "From and after May 1, 1908, it shall be unlawful for any railroad company to transport from any State, Territory, or the District of Columbia, to any other State, Territory, or the District of Columbia, or to any foreign country, any article or commodity, other than timber and the manufactured products thereof, manufactured, mined, or produced by it or under its authority, or which it may own, in whole or in part, or in which it may have any interest, direct or indirect, except such articles or commodities as may be necessary and intended for its use in the conduct of its business as a common carrier."

COMMODITIES CLAUSE

Under this clause twelve injunction and mandamus cases were brought by the government against the Delaware & Hudson, the Erie, the Central of New Jersey, the Delaware, Lackawanna & Western, the Pennsylvania and the Lehigh Valley railroad companies. The cases came to the Supreme Court from the United States Circuit Court for the Eastern District of Pennsylvania, whose decision, announced by Judge George Gray in 1908, attracted much attention. They originated in the Circuit Court, and in its petition the government charged that the railroad companies in question were engaged in transporting in interstate commerce coal mined by themselves in their own mines in Pennsylvania.

The Circuit Court decided against the constitutionality of the provision because, as it was alleged, it deprived the corporations of their liberty and of property in a way prohibited by the Fifth Amendment to the Constitution. It also was held by that court that the clause "direct or indirect" works a practical confiscation of the property of the railroad, hence the law was held to be invalid and "in its nature and effect a discriminative prohibition."

Although the clause went into effect on May 1, 1908, its operation was postponed, by agreement between the Department of Justice and the railroads concerned, until its constitutionality had been passed upon by the Supreme Court. On May 3, 1909, that tribunal rendered its decision upholding the constitutionality of the clause, but greatly modifying its effect.

The purpose of Congress was to prevent railroads from carrying commodities which they produced from mines or other sources, with the exception of timber. Under the decision of the court a railroad owning a mine, for instance, can sell its coal at the mouth of the mine and then transport it as the property of the purchaser, or it can organize a subsidiary company to own the mine, and then hold stock in that company.

As construed, the sole object of the clause is to prevent carriers from being associated in interest with the commodities transported at the time of transportation, hence the law only prohibits the transportation of articles when they have been produced by a railroad company which has not in good faith parted with them; when the company owns or controls, in whole or in part, the commodity to be transported, and when the company has an interest, direct or indirect, in the commodity in a legal sense. It was especially held, however, that the prohibition does not apply to the ownership of stock in a producing company, but that a carrier may own stock in such a company and at the same time transport the product of that company.

Summed up, the act only compels companies to dissociate themselves from the products they carry, and the contention of the government that the law applies to ownership of stock and prohibits the transportation of commodities simply because they have been produced by a railroad company, regardless of the fact that the company has parted with them, is untenable and incapable of enforcement. This is clearly shown by the following extracts from the opinion:

"We hold that the act does none of the things, rightly construed, for which the government contends; that the act, when you rightly construe it, is a mere regulation for a dissociation from the products which are carried, and in no way connected with the vast and extensive prohibitions for which the government contends, and, therefore, in no way lends itself either to any of the arguments respecting inconvenience, suggested at bar, or any of the considerations which led the lower court to hold as it did."

On April 3, 1911, the Supreme Court gave a second interpretation of the clause, by a unanimous vote. Chief-Justice White summed up this decision as follows:

"It must be held that while the right of a railroad company as a stockholder to use its stock ownership for the purpose of a bona fide separate administration of the affairs of a corporation in which it has a stock interest may not be denied, the use of such stock ownership in substance for the purpose of destroying the entity of a producing, etc., corporation and of commingling its affairs in administration with the affairs of the railroad company so as to make the two corporations virtually one, brings the railroad company so voluntarily acting as to such producing, etc., corporation within the prohibition of the commodities clause. In other words, that by operation and effect of the commodities clause there is a duty cast upon a railroad company purposing to carry on interstate commerce a product of the producing, etc., corporation in which it has a stock interest, not to abuse such power so as virtually to do by indirection that which the commodities clause prohibits, a duty which plainly would be violated by the unnecessary commingling of the affairs of the producing company with its own so as to cause them to be one and inseparable."

Common Law. In the United States the term "common law" means the common law of England and of statutes passed by the English Parliament which were in force at the time of American independence (with the exception of Louisiana), and all those universal usages, and all those inferences from and applications of established law which courts in this country have recognized as having among us the face of law. (Theophilus Parsons.) It is the basis of the jurisprudence of all States in so far as it conforms to the circumstances and institutions of the country, and has not been modified by statutory provision. See CODES.

Common Schools. See EDUCATION.

Common Schools, EARLY. In 1649 provision was made in the Massachusetts code for the establishing of common schools in that province. By it every township was required to maintain a school for reading and writing; and every town of 100 householders, a grammar school, with a teacher qualified to "fit youths for the university" (Harvard). This school law was reenacted in Connecticut in the very same terms, and was adopted also by Plymouth and New Haven. The preamble to this law declared that, "it being one chief project of that old deluder, Sathan, to keep men from the knowledge of the Scriptures." See EDUCATION.

Commons. At first lands cultivated in common by the early colonists; later, certain lands held for the public use of the colonists. The system was adopted from English custom.

Common-sense Pamphlet. See PAINE, THOMAS.

Communists. See SOCIALISM.

Compagnie de l'Occident. A company chartered by Louis XIV. in 1717 to succeed Anthony Crozot's rights, and absorbed in turn by the Compagnie des Indes in 1719. See LAW, JOHN.

Competition. See TRUSTS.

Compromises. Agreements to settle differences by mutual concessions.

In the Constitutional Convention of 1787 Massachusetts, Pennsylvania, Virginia, North Carolina, South Carolina, and Georgia favored a national form of government. Connecticut, New York, New Jersey, Maryland, and Delaware preferred a federation. New Hampshire was not represented in the convention until July 23, 1787, and Rhode Island took no part at all. The National, or "Virginia," plan provided for representation in the Senate as well as the House proportionate to the population of each State; the House to be chosen by the people direct and the Senate by the representatives from a list of nominations made by the State legislature. The federal, or "New Jersey," plan provided for a single body with an equal value of each State, and that the executive (President) should be chosen by Congress. A compromise was effected by providing for a House of Representatives, with proportionate representation, chosen direct by the people; and a Senate with equal representation, chosen by the legislature of each State.

Massachusetts, New Hampshire, Connecticut, Rhode Island, and Pennsylvania had either abolished slavery in 1787 or provided for its gradual extinction. In the convention the slavery question was involved with the question of the control of commerce. It was finally agreed that three-fifths of the slaves were to be counted in the population of each State; that Congress should not prohibit the importation of slaves until after 1808; that Congress could tax such importations, where permitted by State laws, $10 per head. The conflicting interests of the commercial and the more largely agricultural States led to a third compromise, by which Congress was denied any power to tax exports, but was given complete control over interstate and national commerce.

Missouri Compromise, 1820.—When Louisiana was purchased slavery was legal both by French and Spanish law, and was not prohibited by any organizing act of Congress, or by the laws of Louisiana or Missouri Territories. When Missouri applied for admission into the Union as a State the South claimed that even if Congress prohibited slavery in a Territory any State could introduce or abolish slavery if it should so desire; that by the terms of the treaty with France the inhabitants of the Territory were to have all the rights of citizens of the United States as soon as possible; that the Constitution recognized slavery and provided for a three-fifths representation of slaves. The North contended that Congress had prohibited slavery in the Northwest Territory, and it had power to prohibit everywhere outside the borders of the original thirteen States. By the compromise it was agreed that slavery should be prohibited in the territory ceded by France north of the parallel 36° 30′, with the exception of the State of Missouri. Jefferson said of this compromise: "A geographical line, coinciding with a marked principle, moral and political, once conceived and held up to the angry passions of men, will never be obliterated, and every new irritation will mark it deeper and deeper."

Compromise of 1850.—The admission of Texas and the probable annexation of New Mexico and California again brought up the question of the extension of slavery. Texas was admitted with a clause prohibiting slavery north of 36° 30′. The WILMOT PROVISO (*q. v.*) was offered in Congress Aug. 8, 1846, prohibiting slavery in the new Territory. For more than three years it was opposed by the Southern members, who were constantly defeated in the House, but by the assistance of a few Northern Senators prevented its adoption. The discovery of gold brought over a hundred thousand men to California. They adopted a constitution forbidding slavery, and applied for admission as a State. The people of New Mexico also adopted a free State constitution May 15, 1850. The Southern States called a convention, which met at Nashville in June and in November, 1850. (See SOUTHERN CONVENTIONS.) By the Clay Compromise California and any new States formed from Texas were to be admitted with or without slavery, as the people of each State might decide; Utah and New Mexico to be formed into Territories without the Wilmot proviso; the abolition of the slave trade (but not slavery) in the District of Columbia; and the passage of a more effective fugitive slave law. See FUGITIVE SLAVE LAW.

Crittenden Compromise.—The Missouri Compromise prohibiting slavery was repealed May 30, 1854, when Kansas Territory and Nebraska Territory were organized. This precipitated a conflict between the Northern Free State men who settled in Kansas and the Southern settlers in the State, aided by "squatters" from Missouri. (See KANSAS.) In 1860 John J. Crittenden introduced a resolution re-establishing the line of 36° 30′, but it was defeated March 3, 1861, by a vote of 19 to 20.

Tariff Compromise, 1833.—See TARIFF LEGISLATION.

See also CLAY, HENRY; CRITTENDEN, JOHN JORDAN; MISSOURI COMPROMISE.

Compromise, THE MISSOURI. See MISSOURI COMPROMISE.

Compromise Measures of 1850. See CLAY, HENRY.

Compromise Tariff of 1833. See CLAY, HENRY.

Compulsory Circulation. An obligation imposed upon subjects or citizens to accept certain paper money issued by the State as the equivalent of coin money. (See CURRENCY, CONTINENTAL; NATIONAL FINANCES.)

Concession. A privilege granted by a government to an individual, or a body of individuals, to carry on a certain industry, or to undertake a certain work, such as railroads, mines, etc.

Conciliation Measures. In the midst of the hot debate in Parliament, in 1775, on the New England restraining bill, Lord North astonished the King, the ministry, and the nation by himself bringing forward a conciliatory proposition, not unlike that offered by Chatham just before (Feb. 1), which required the colonists to acknowledge the supremacy and superintending power of Parliament, but provided that no tax should ever be levied except by the consent of the colonial assemblies. It also contained a provision for a congress of the colonies to vote, at the time of making this acknowledgment, a free grant to the King of a certain perpetual revenue, to be placed at the disposal of Parliament. All the assemblies rejected the proposition. A committee of the Continental Congress, to which the proposition had been referred, made a report (July 31, 1775), in which the generally unsatisfactory character and the unsafe vagueness of the ministerial offer were fully exposed. The Congress accepted the report and published it to the world.

When Parliament reassembled after the Christmas holidays (January, 1778), the opposition exposed the losses, expenses, and hopelessness of the war with the colonists; and, to the surprise and disgust of some of his most ardent supporters, Lord North presented a second plan for reconciliation (Feb. 17), and declared he had always been in favor of peace, and opposed to taxing the Americans. He introduced two bills: one renouncing, on the part of the British Parliament, any intention to levy taxes in America—conceding, in substance, the whole original ground of dispute; the other authorizing the appointment of five commissioners, the commanders of the naval and military forces to be two, with ample powers to treat for the re-establishment of royal authority. Meanwhile David Hartley, an opponent of the war, was sent to Paris to open negotiations with the American commissioners there. The war had already (1775–78) cost Great Britain more than 20,000 men, $100,000,000 of public expenditure, and 550 British vessels, chiefly in the merchant service, captured by American cruisers, worth about $12,000,000, besides a loss of trade with America, suspension of American debts, and the confiscation of the property of American loyalists. Added to all was the danger of a war with France. Copies of these conciliatory bills arrived in America in the middle of April (1778), and the Congress took immediate action upon them, for the partisans of the crown were very active in circulating them among the people. A committee of that body criticised these bills very keenly, showing their deceptiveness. Fearing the effect of the bills upon the people, they were ordered to be printed in the newspapers, together with the report of the committee, which concluded with a resolution, unanimously adopted, denouncing as open and avowed enemies all who should attempt a separate treaty, and declaring that no conference should be held by any commissioners until the British armies should be first withdrawn, or the independence of the United States acknowledged.

The commissioners appointed under the act, after fair and unfair efforts to accomplish their ends, were completely discomfited, and before leaving for England issued an angry and threatening manifesto (Oct. 3), addressed not to Congress only, but to the State legislatures and the people, charging upon Congress the responsibility of continuing the war; offering to the assemblies separately the terms already proposed to Congress; reminding the soldiers that Great Britain had already conceded all points originally in dispute; suggesting to the clergy that the French were papists; appealing to all lovers of peace not to suffer a few ambitious men to subject the country to the miseries of unnecessary warfare; allowing forty days for submission, and threatening, if this offer should be rejected, the desolation of the country as a future leading object of the war. This manifesto Congress had printed, with comments calculated to neutralize the proclamation of the commissioners.

Conciliation with the Colonies. See Burke, Edmund.

Concord. See Lexington and Concord; Dustin, Hannah.

Conduct of the War, Committee on the. On Dec. 9, 1861, the Senate, by a vote of 33 yeas to 3 nays, adopted a resolution providing for the appointing of a joint committee of three from the Senate and four from the House to inquire into the conduct of the war, the committee to have power to send for persons and papers, and to sit through that session of Congress. The House concurred in the resolution on the following day, and on the 17th and 19th the committee was appointed, consisting of Senators Benjamin F. Wade, of Ohio; Zachariah Chandler, of Michigan, and Andrew Johnson, of Tennessee; and Representatives Daniel W. Gooch, of Massachusetts; John Covode, of

Pennsylvania; George W. Julian, of Indiana, and Moses F. Odell, of New York. On Dec. 20 the committee held its first session and chose Senator Wade as chairman. This committee became an important factor in the early movements of the National army and navy. During its existence there were frequent complaints from officers in the field that their freedom of action was seriously interfered with by this committee; and in other quarters it was asserted that many of the early campaigns of the war were planned by "civilians in Washington" without the advice of experienced military men.

CONFEDERATE STATES OF AMERICA

Confederate States of America. An organization of Southern States in an attempt to secede from the Union and establish an independent government. The following table gives the dates of legislative action for secession in the several States:

State.	Act of Secession.	Vote.
South Carolina	Dec. 20, 1860	Unanimous.
Mississippi	Jan. 9, 1861	84 yeas, 15 nays.
Florida	" 10, "	62 " 7 "
Alabama	" 11, "	61 " 39 "
Georgia	" 19, "	208 " 89 "
Louisiana	" 26, "	113 " 17 "
Texas	Feb. 1, "	166 " 7 "
Virginia	Apr. 17, "	88 " 55 "
Arkansas	May 6, "	69 " 1 "
North Carolina	" 21, "	Unanimous.
Tennessee	June 8, "	

Legislatures of Missouri, Kentucky, Maryland, and Delaware refused to pass an ordinance of secession, and declared themselves neutral.

The convention of South Carolina, after passing the ordinance of secession (for text, see SOUTHERN CONFEDERACY), issued a call, Dec. 27, 1860, for a convention at Montgomery, Ala., of such slave-holding States as should secede, Feb. 4, 1861. At that date the following delegates met:

South Carolina: R. B. Rhett, Jas. Chestnut, Jr., W. P. Miles, T. J. Withers, R. W. Barnwell, C. G. Memminger, L. M. Keitt, W. W. Boyce.

Georgia: Robert Toombs, Howell Cobb, Benj. H. Hill, Alex. H. Stephens, Frank S. Bartow, Martin J. Crawford, E. A. Nisbet, Augustus R. Wright, Thos. R. R. Cobb, Augustus Kenan.

Alabama: Richard W. Walker, Robert H. Smith, Colin J. McRae, John Gill Shorter, S. L. Hale, David P. Lewis, Thomas M. Fearn, J. L. M. Curry, W. P. Chilton, J. J. Hooper (secretary to convention).

Mississippi: Wiley P. Harris, Walker Brooke, A. M. Clayton, W. S. Barry, J. T. Harrison, J. A. P. Campbell, W. S. Wilson.

Louisiana: John Perkins, Jr., Duncan F. Kenner, C. M. Conrad, E. Sparrow, Henry Marshall, A. de Cluet.

Florida: Jackson Morton, J. Patton Anderson, Jas. B. Owens.

CONFEDERATE ROSETTE AND BADGE.

This convention, with Howell Cobb as permanent president, adopted, on Feb. 9, 1861, a provisional constitution for the Confederate States of America. On the same day, Jefferson Davis of Mississippi was elected President, Alexander H. Stephens of Georgia Vice-President, by a unanimous vote of the delegates, 42 in number. Davis was inaugurated Feb. 18, 1861, oath of office being administered by Howell Cobb. The delegates from the other States of the Confederacy took seats in the provisional Congress as follows:

Texas, 1st session, March 2, 1861: Louis T. Wigfall, John H. Reagan, John Hemphill, T. H. Waul, William B. Ochiltree, W. S. Oldham, John Gregg.

Arkansas, 2d session, May, 1861: Robert W. Johnson, Albert Rust, Augustus H. Garland, Wm. W. Watkins, Hugh F. Thomasson.

Virginia, 2d session, May, 1861: Jas. A. Seddon, Wm. Ballard Preston, Robt. M. T. Hunter, John Tyler, Sr., Wm. H. McFarland, Roger A. Pryor, Thos. S. Bocock, Wm. C. Rives, J. W. Brockenborough, Robert Johnson, James Mason, Walter Preston,

Charles W. Russell, Robert E. Scott, Walter R. Staples.

Tennessee, 2d session, May, 1861: John F. House, Geo. W. Jones, John D. C. Atkins, W. H. De Witt, Robert L. Caruthers, David M. Currin, James H. Thomas.

North Carolina, 3d session, July, 1861: Geo. Davis, Wm. W. Avery, Wm. N. H. Smith, Thos. Ruffin, Thos. D. McDowell, Abram W. Venable, John M. Morehead, Robt. C. Puryear, Burton Craige, Andrew T. Davidson.

Kentucky, 4th session, December, 1861: Henry C. Burnett, —— Thomas, Willis B. Machen, Thomas B. Munroe.

Missouri, 4th session, December, 1861: Wm. H. Cook, Thos. A. Harris, Casper W. Bell, A. H. Conrow, Geo. C. Vest, Thos. W. Freeman, Samuel Hyer.

The permanent constitution of the Confederate States (for text, see SOUTHERN CONFEDERACY) was submitted to the provisional Congress March 11, and unanimously adopted, and was ratified by the following States: Alabama, March 13, 1861; Georgia, March 16; Louisiana, March 21; Texas, March 23; South Carolina, April 3; Virginia, April 25; North Carolina, May 21.

The Confederate (provisional) Congress held four sessions: (1) Feb. 4, 1861, to March 16, 1861; (2) April 29, 1861, to May 22, 1861; (3) July 20, 1861, to Aug. 22, 1861; (4) Nov. 18, 1861, to Feb. 17, 1862.

The government was removed from Montgomery, Ala., to Richmond, Va., May 24, 1861, where the 3d session of its Congress opened, July 20, 1861, and remained until February, 1862.

The Great Seal of the Confederacy was provided for by the joint resolution approved April 30, 1863. It was made in England at a cost of $600, and was completed July, 1864, but did not reach Richmond until April, 1865, when the city was being evacuated. It is now in the office of the secretary of state of South Carolina.

CONFEDERATE STATES SEAL.

PERMANENT GOVERNMENT.

Was organized at Richmond, Va., Feb. 22, 1862. Jefferson Davis, President; Alexander H. Stephens, Vice-President. (For cabinet, see below.)

FIRST CONGRESS.

Session (1) Feb. 18, 1862, to April 22, 1862; (2) Aug. 12, 1862, to Oct. 13, 1862; (3) Jan. 12, 1863, to May 8, 1863; (4) Dec. 7, 1863, to Feb. 18, 1864.

SENATE.

Alexander H. Stephens, Vice-President.
R. M. T. Hunter, President *pro tem.*

Alabama: Clement C. Clay, William L. Yancey.
Arkansas: Robt. W. Johnson, Chas. B. Mitchell.
Florida: Jas. M. Baker, Augustus E. Maxwell.
Georgia: Benj. H. Hill, John W. Lewis.
Kentucky: Henry C. Burnett, Wm. E. Simms.
Louisiana: Thos. J. Semmes, Edward Sparrow.
Mississippi: Albert G. Brown, Jas. Phelan.
Missouri: John B. Clark, R. L. Y. Peyton.
North Carolina: Wm. T. Dortch, Geo. Davis.
South Carolina: Robt. W. Barnwell, Jas. L. Orr.
Tennessee: Gustavus A. Henry, Landon C Haynes.
Virginia: Robt. M. T. Hunter, Wm. Ballard Preston.
Texas: Louis T. Wigfall, Williamson S. Oldham.

HOUSE.

Thos. S. Bocock, Speaker.

Members: Alabama 9, Arkansas 4, Florida 2, Georgia 10, Kentucky 12, Louisiana 6, Mississippi 7, Missouri 6, North Carolina 10, South Carolina 6, Tennessee 11, Texas 7, Virginia 16—total, 106.

SECOND CONGRESS.

Session (1) May 2, 1864, to June 15, 1864; (2) Nov. 7, 1864, to March 18, 1865.

SENATE.

Alexander H. Stephens, Vice-President.
R. M. T. Hunter, President *pro tem.*

Alabama: Robt. Jennson, Jr., Richard W. Walker.

SENATE—*Continued*

Arkansas: Robt. W. Johnson, Augustus H. Garland.

Florida: Jas. M. Baker, Augustus E. Maxwell.

Georgia. Benj. H. Hill, Herschel V. Johnson.

Kentucky: Henry C. Burnett, Wm. E. Simms.

Louisiana: Edward Sparrow, Thos. J. Semmes.

Mississippi: J. W. C. Watson, Albert G. Brown.

Missouri: Waldo P. Johnson, L. M. Louis.

North Carolina: Wm. T. Dortch, Wm. A. Graham.

South Carolina: Robt. W. Barnwell, Jas. L. Orr.

Tennessee: Gustavus A. Henry, Landon C. Haynes.

Texas: Louis T. Wigfall, Williamson S. Oldham.

Virginia: Robert M. T. Hunter, Allen T. Caperton.

HOUSE.

Thos. S. Bocock, Speaker.

Members: Alabama 9, Arkansas 3, Florida 2, Georgia 10, Kentucky 12, Louisiana 5, Mississippi 7, Missouri 7, North Carolina 10, South Carolina 6, Tennessee 11, Texas 6, Virginia 16—total, 104.

Kentucky and Missouri were represented, though as States they never seceded. This government lasted four years, one month, and fourteen days.

CABINET OFFICERS.

SECRETARIES OF STATE.

Robert Toombs, of Georgia, Feb. 21, 1861, to July 25, 1861.

R. M. T. Hunter, of Virginia, July 25, 1861, to March 18, 1862.

Judah P. Benjamin, of Louisiana, March 18, 1862, to end of the war.

DEPARTMENT OF JUSTICE.

Judah P. Benjamin, of Louisiana, Feb. 25, 1861, to Sept. 17, 1861.

Thomas Bragg, of North Carolina, Nov. 21, 1861, to March 18, 1862.

T. N. Watts, of Alabama, March 18, 1862, to Jan. 1, 1864.

George Davis, of North Carolina, Jan. 2, 1864, to end of the war.

SECRETARIES OF THE TREASURY.

Christopher G. Memminger, of South Carolina, Feb. 21, 1861, to July 18, 1864.

George A. Trenholm, of South Carolina, July 18, 1864, to end of the war.

SECRETARIES OF WAR.

Le Roy Pope Walker, of Alabama, Feb. 21, 1861, to Sept. 17, 1861.

Judah P. Benjamin, of Louisiana, Sept. 17, 1861, to March 17, 1862.

George W. Randolph, of Virginia, March 18, 1862, to Nov. 17, 1862.

General Gustavus A. Smith, of Kentucky, Acting Secretary of War, March 18, 1862, to Nov. 17, 1862.

James A. Seddon, of Virginia, Nov. 21, 1862, to Feb. 6, 1865.

John C. Breckinridge, of Kentucky, Feb. 6, 1865, to end of the war.

SECRETARY OF THE NAVY

Stephen R. Mallory, of Florida, March 1, 1861, to end of the war.

POSTMASTERS-GENERAL.

Henry T. Ellet, of Mississippi, Feb. 25, 1861, to March 5, 1861.

John H. Reagan, of Texas, March 6, 1861, to end of the war.

Before the first year ended, in December, 1861, gold was worth 120 in Confederate notes; in December, 1862, 300; in December, 1863, 1,900; in December, 1864, 5,000; in March, 1865, 6,000.

CONFEDERATE TREASURY NOTE.

CONFEDERATE STATES OF AMERICA

CONFEDERATE ARMY.

There are no accurate records of the total number of men in the Confederate armies. The records existing are very incomplete. For instance, Alabama, with a population of 964,296, shows a total of 1,466 deaths in the Confederate army; while North Carolina, with a population of 992,667, shows 40,275 deaths. The figures as given by Gen. James B. Fry, U. S. A., of deaths in battle, by wounds and by disease, from such muster-rolls as are accessible, are as follows:

State.	Deaths.	Population in 1860.
Alabama	1,466	964,296
Arkansas	6,862	435,427
Florida	2,346	140,439
Georgia	10,974	1,057,329
Louisiana	6,545	709,290
Mississippi	15,265	791,396
North Carolina	40,275	992,667
South Carolina	17,682	703,812
Tennessee	6,414	1,109,847
Texas	3,849	602,432
Virginia	14,794	1,596,079
Regular C. S. Army	2,515	
Border States	4,834	
Total	133,297	

From a statistical account of organizations in the service of the Confederate States, published in La Bree's *The Confederate Soldier in the Civil War*, the following figures are taken:

Infantry, 529 regiments and 85 battalions.
Cavalry, 127 regiments and 47 battalions.
Rangers, 8 regiments and 1 battalion.
Heavy artillery, 5 regiments and 6 battalions.
Light artillery, 261 batteries.

These figures exclude all regiments which served a short time only, all disbanded or consolidated regiments, State militia, senior and junior reserves, home guards, local-defence regiments, separate companies, and miscellaneous organizations. The average enrolment is unknown. Twenty-two of the North Carolina regiments, incomplete as they are, show an average of over 1,500 men in each, some of them even 1,800. The Confederacy organized very few regiments after 1862; all conscripts and recruits were assigned to the old regiments so as to keep them up to an effective strength.

GENERAL OFFICERS OF THE CONFEDERATE ARMY, WITH DATES OF APPOINTMENT.

COMMANDER-IN-CHIEF.

Robert E. Lee, of Virginia.....Jan. 31, 1865

GENERALS.

Samuel Cooper, of Virginia....May 16, 1861
Albert Sidney Johnston, of Texas May 30, 1861
P. G. T. Beauregard, of Louisiana July 21, 1861
Joseph E. Johnston, of Virginia Aug. 13, 1861
Braxton Bragg, of Louisiana..April 12, 1862
E. Kirby Smith, of Florida....Feb. 19, 1864
John B. Hood, of Texas......July 18, 1864

LIEUTENANT-GENERALS.

James Longstreet, of Alabama..Oct. 9, 1862
Leonidas Polk, of Louisiana....Oct. 10, 1862
Thomas J. Jackson, of Virginia Oct. 10, 1862
William T. Hardee, of Georgia.Oct. 10, 1862
T. H. Holmes, of North Carolina Oct. 10, 1862
John C. Pemberton, of Virginia Oct. 10, 1862
Richard S. Ewell, of Virginia..May 23, 1863
Ambrose P. Hill, of Virginia...May 24, 1863
Daniel H. Hill, of North Carolina July 11, 1863
Richard Taylor, of Louisiana..April 8, 1864
Jubal A. Early, of Virginia...May 31, 1864
Richard H. Anderson, of South Carolina May 31, 1864
Stephen D. Lee, of South Carolina June 23, 1864
Alexander P. Stewart, of Tennessee June 23, 1864
Simon B. Buckner, of Kentucky Sept. 20, 1864
Wade Hampton, of South Carolina Feb. 14, 1865
Nathan B. Forrest, of Tennessee Feb. 28, 1865
Joseph Wheeler, of Alabama..Feb. 28, 1865
John B. Gordon, of Georgia...Feb. 28, 1865

MAJOR-GENERALS.

David E. Twiggs............May 22, 1861
Earl Van Dorn..............Sept. 19, 1861
Gustavus W. Smith..........Sept. 19, 1861
Benjamin Hager...............Oct. 7, 1861
John B. Magruder.............Oct. 7, 1861
Mansfield Lovell..............Oct. 7, 1861
George B. Crittenden..........Nov. 9, 1861
W. W. Loring................Feb. 15, 1862
Sterling Price..............March 6, 1862
Benj. F. Cheetham..........March 10, 1862
John P. McCown...........March 10, 1862
Jones M. Withers.............April 6, 1862
Thomas C. Hindman.........April 14, 1862
John C. Breckinridge.........April 14, 1862
Samuel Jones.................May 10, 1862
Lafayette McLaws............May 23, 1862
J. E. B. Stuart..............July 25, 1862
S. G. French...............Aug. 31, 1862
Carter L. Stevenson..........Oct. 10, 1862
George E. Pickett............Oct. 10, 1862
David R. Jones..............Oct. 11, 1862
John H. Forney.............Oct. 27, 1862
Dabney H. Maury.............Nov. 4, 1862
M. L. Smith..................Nov. 4, 1862
John G. Walker..............Nov. 8, 1862
Arnold Elzey.................Dec. 4, 1862
Franklin Gardner.............Dec. 13, 1862

MAJOR-GENERALS.—*Continued.*

Patrick R. Cleburne..........Dec. 13, 1862
Isaac R. Trimble............Jan. 17, 1863
Daniel S. Donelson............Jan. 17, 1863
W. H. C. Whiting............Feb. 28, 1863
Edward Johnson............Feb. 28, 1863
R. E. Rodes................May 23, 1863
W. H. T. Walker............May 23, 1863
Henry Heth.................May 24, 1863
John S. Bowen..............May 25, 1863
Robert Ransom, Jr...........May 26, 1863
W. D. Pender...............May 27, 1863
Cadmus M. Wilcox............Aug. 3, 1863
Fitz-Hugh Lee...............Aug. 3, 1863
J. F. Gilmer................Aug. 20, 1863
William Smith...............Aug. 30, 1863
Howell Cobb.................Sept. 9, 1863
John A. Wharton............Nov. 10, 1863
Will T. Martin..............Nov. 10, 1863
Charles W. Field............Feb. 12, 1864
J. Patton Anderson..........Feb. 17, 1864
William B. Bate.............Feb. 23, 1864
C. T. de Polignac............April 8, 1864
Samuel B. Maxey...........April 18, 1864
Robert F. Hoke.............April 20, 1864
W. H. F. Lee...............April 23, 1864
James F. Fagan.............April 24, 1864
James B. Gordon.............May 14, 1864
J. B. Kershaw...............May 18, 1864
Bushrod R. Johnson..........May 21, 1864
Stephen D. Ramseur..........June 1, 1864
Ed. C. Walthall..............June 6, 1864
N. D. Clayton................July 7, 1864
William Mahone..............July 30, 1864
John C. Brown...............Aug. 4, 1864
L. L. Lomax.................Aug. 10, 1864
Henry W. Allen.............Sept. 19, 1864
James L. Kemper............Sept. 19, 1864
M. C. Butler................Sept. 19, 1864
G. W. C. Lee................Oct. 20, 1864
Thomas L. Rosser............Nov. 1, 1864
A. R. Wright...............Nov. 26, 1864
John Pegram................Nov. 26, 1864
P. M. B. Young..............Dec. 30, 1864
William Preston..............Jan. 1, 1865
Wm. B. Talliaferro............Jan. 1, 1865
Bryan Grimes................Feb. 15, 1865
John S. Marmaduke.........March 17, 1865
W. W. Allen...............March 17, 1865
T. J. Churchill.............March 17, 1865
W. Y. C. Humes............March 17, 1865
Harry T. Hays..............April 9, 1865
E. M. Law..................April 9, 1865
M. W. Gary.................April 9, 1865
Matt. W. Ransom.............April 9, 1865

BRIGADIER-GENERALS, 362.

CONFEDERATE BATTLE-FLAG.

The Confederate battle-flag was designed by General Beauregard, accepted by Gen. Joseph E. Johnston after the battle of Bull Run, and afterwards adopted by the Confederate Congress.

CONFEDERATE FLAG.

The Congress at Montgomery discussed the subject of a national flag with much feeling. Several models had been offered. One, from some women of Charleston, was composed of a blue cross on a red field,

FIRST CONFEDERATE FLAG.

with seven stars—similar to the South Carolina flag; the other was from a gentleman of the same city. It was a cross, with fifteen stars. The committee to

CONFEDERATE NATIONAL FLAG—NO 2
(Adopted May 1, 1863.)

whom the matter had been referred recommended a red, white, and blue flag, but with three stripes only. This was adopted, and was first displayed over the State-house at Montgomery, March 4, 1861.

CONFEDERATE NATIONAL FLAG—NO. 3.
(Adopted March 4, 1865.)

As the stars and bars had a certain resemblance to the stars and stripes, it led to mistakes by both armies. The Confederate Congress adopted a new flag May 1, 1863. The second flag, when limp, frequently resembled a flag of truce. To avoid further misunderstanding a strip of red was added, March, 4, 1865.

CONFEDERATE NAVY.

Early in January, 1861, Governor Pickens, of South Carolina, seized the United States cutter *William Aiken*, then in Charleston Harbor, together with several tenders. As the various States seceded other United States vessels were seized by the State authorities in whose waters they were at the time. These were the *Fulton* (three guns), *McClellan* (five guns), and seven one-gun ships. They were turned over to the Confederate States when President Davis had been empowered to provide and maintain a navy (March 11, 1861). Nearly one-half of the officers in the United States navy were of Southern birth, and of these 321 had resigned by June 1, 1861, to take office under the Confederacy,

CONFEDERATE BATTLE-FLAG.

leaving 350 in the United States service. Among those who resigned were Captains Tatnall, Rousseau, Ingraham, Hollins, and Randolph, and Commanders Semmes, Hartsene, Farrand, and Brent. A large number of gunboats and cruisers were ordered to be built, and, where possible, river boats and merchant vessels were reconstructed.

The first vessel to break the blockade was the *Savannah*, fitted out in Charleston. She escaped June 2, captured a sugar-ship on the morning of June 3, and on the afternoon of the same day was captured by the United States brig *Perry* and taken to New York. The cruiser *Sumter*, constructed at New Orleans, ran the blockade, and reached the West India Islands in July, 1861, making many prizes of American vessels, soon becoming the terror of the American merchant marine. The *Sumter* successfully eluded the United States war vessels, crossed the Atlantic, and took refuge in the harbor of Gibraltar, where the *Tuscarora*, of the United States, found her, and blockaded her by waiting outside. Unable to escape, Captain Semmes sold the *Sumter* in 1862 and went to England. In her short career the *Sumter* had captured (and mostly destroyed) over twenty merchant vessels.

The cruiser *Nashville* (Lieutenant Pegram) sailed from Charleston Oct. 21, 1861, touched at Bermuda, and reached Southampton, England, Nov. 21, 1862. Early in February, 1862, the *Tuscarora* sailed from Southampton and lay in open waters awaiting the coming out of the *Nashville*. The British authorities decided that the *Tuscarora* was within British waters, and sent a man-of-war to detain her for twenty-four hours after the departure of the *Nashville*, which succeeded in running the blockade at Beaufort. One year later (Feb. 28, 1862) she was destroyed by the *Montauk* (Captain Worden) in the Ogeechee River. The *Jeff Davis* had a short career. She escaped from Charleston about the same time as the *Sumter*, captured several Federal merchant vessels, and was shipwrecked in August, 1861, off St. Augustine, Fla.

In addition to the above, about twenty smaller ships were fitted out in Southern ports (*Winslow, York, Chickamauga, Retribution, Calhoun, Sallie*, etc.) Although they succeeded in destroying a number of merchant vessels, the sum of their combined exploits was of minor importance.

A much more serious matter was the building of Confederate cruisers in England with the connivance of the British government. Mr. Laird, a ship-builder at Liverpool and a member of the British Parliament, contracted to build armed cruisers for the Confederacy. The first of these that went to sea was the *Oreto*. Mr. Adams, the American minister, called the attention of the British government to the matter (Feb. 18, 1862), but nothing was done. She went to a British port of the Bahamas, and ran the blockade at Mobile, under British colors, with a valuable cargo. Her name was changed to *Florida*, and she was placed in charge of a late officer of the United States navy (John Newland Maffit), and again went to sea in December. The *Florida* hovered most of the time off the American coast, closely watched, everywhere leaving a track of desolation behind her. She ran down to the coast of South America, and, alarmed at the presence of a National vessel of war, ran in among the Brazilian fleet in the harbor of Bahia. Captain Collins, of the *Wachusett*, ran in (Oct. 7, 1864), boarded the *Florida*, lashed her to his vessel, and bore her to Hampton Roads, Va., where she was sunk. The most famous of the Anglo-Confederate vessels was the *Alabama*, built by Laird and commanded by Raphael Semmes, who had been captain of the *Sumter*. Her career is elsewhere related (see ALABAMA). The career of the *Shenandoah*, another Anglo-Confederate privateer, was largely in the Indian, Southern, and Pacific oceans, plundering and destroying American vessels. On the borders of the Arctic Ocean, near Bering Strait, she attended a convention of American whaling-ships (June 28, 1865) without being suspected, as she bore the United States flag. Suddenly she revealed her character, and before evening she had made prizes of ten whalers, of which eight were burned in a group before midnight. It was the last act in the drama of the Civil War. Her commander, informed of the close of the war, sailed for England and gave up the vessel to a British war-ship as a prize. The *Shenandoah* was a Clyde-built steamer, long and rakish, of 790 tons' burden. Against the sending out of all these vessels Mr. Adams protested in vain.

PRIVATEER SHIP SUMTER.

The *Georgia*, built at Glasgow, began her career in 1863. After a short raid on United States commerce, she was sold to a Liverpool merchant, who ordered her to Lisbon. On the way she was captured by the *Niagara* (Captain Craven), who landed her crew at Dover, England. The *Tallahassee*, afterwards called the *Olushee*, was built at London, and at first used as a blockade-runner. She was bought by the Confederate government, fitted out as a cruiser, and sailed from Wilmington, Aug. 6, 1864. She captured and destroyed a large number of pilot-boats, fishing-schooners, and small traders. She was eventually seized by the British government, and turned over to the United States in 1866.

The *Stonewall*, originally built for the Danish government, was purchased by the Confederate States. Her career was short and inglorious. She was blockaded in Havana by Admiral Godon, was surrendered to Spain, and turned over to the United States in May, 1865.

The last report of the Navy Department of the Confederate States gave a list of officers, the most important of which were:

ADMIRAL.

Franklin Buchanan.

CAPTAINS.

Samuel Barran, Raphael Semmes, W. W. Hunter, E. Farland, J. K. Mitchell, J. R. Tucker, T. J. Page, R. F. Pinckney, J. W. Cooke.

COMMANDERS.

T. R. Rootes, T. T. Hunter, I. N. Browne, R. B. Pegram, W. L. Maury, J. N. Moffitt, J. N. Barney, W. A. Webb, G. T. Sinclair, G. W. Harrison, J. D. Johnston, John Kell, W. T. Glassell, H. Davidson.

CONFEDERATE PRISONS.

At the beginning of the Civil War informal exchanges of prisoners under flags of truce were customary until the establishment of a formal cartel on the basis of equal exchange. During this period over 125,000 prisoners were exchanged. President Davis, in his message, Jan. 14, 1863, declared his intention to deliver to the authorities of the several States all commissioned officers of the United States thereafter captured in any of the States embraced in President Lincoln's emancipation proclamation, to be punished as criminals engaged in exciting servile insurrection. This determination was supported by the Confederate Congress. A joint resolution was passed May 1, 1863, that the white officers of negro regiments who should be captured were to be "put to death or otherwise punished," etc. But the cartel remained in force until July, 1863, when the Confederate government refused to recognize captured negro soldiers in the United States service or officers of negro regiments as prisoners of war. No officer was shot, however, under these provisions.

President Lincoln issued a retaliatory proclamation July 30, that for every United States soldier, white or negro, executed or enslaved, a Confederate prisoner would be executed or placed at hard labor. No such act of retaliation occurred, however.

This action by the two governments brought exchanges to an end. Captured Northern officers were, as a rule, sent to Libby prison, Richmond; all others to Belle Isle, Castle Thunder (for civilians), and Danville, in Virginia; Salisbury, in North Carolina; Charleston, in South Carolina; and Andersonville and Millen, in Georgia.

The Andersonville prison records, kept by Confederate officers, show that the—

Total number of prisoners received at Andersonville was	49,485

CASTLE THUNDER.

Largest number in prison at one time, Aug. 9, 1864	33,006
Total number of deaths as shown by hospital register	12,462
Total number of deaths in hospital	8,735
Total number of deaths in a stockade near	3,727
Percentage of deaths to whole number received	26
Percentage of deaths to whole number admitted to hospital	69 12-17
Average number of deaths for each of the thirteen months	958
Largest number of deaths in one day, Aug. 23, 1864	97
Cases returned from hospital to stockade	3,469
Total number of escapes	328

THE PRISON AT MILLEN.

Henry Wirz, the superintendent of the Andersonville prison, was tried by Federal court-martial in the summer of 1865, was found guilty on numerous charges of cruelty, and was hanged in November. Reports on the conditions existing in Andersonville prison were made by Col. D. T. Chandler, C. S. A., Aug. 5, 1864, and by General Winder, C. S. A., on Salisbury and Florence prisons, Dec. 13, 1864. Both

ANDERSONVILLE PRISON.

these Confederate reports censured the management of the prisons. These and many other reports are found in H. R. 45, Fortieth Congress, second session.

Secretary Stanton submitted the following report, which is frequently referred to:

"*July 19, 1866.*

"SIR,—In compliance with a resolution of the House of Representatives, dated July 12, directing the Secretary of War to report the number of Union and rebel soldiers who died while held as prisoners of war, I have the honor to report that it appears by a report of the Commissary-General of Prisoners—

"1. That 26,436 deaths of rebel prisoners of war are reported.

"2. That 22,576 Union soldiers are reported as having died in Southern prisons.

"The reports show that 220,000 rebel prisoners were held in the North, and about 126,940 Union prisoners in the South.

"Your obedient servant,
"EDWIN M. STANTON,
"Secretary of War.
"Hon. SCHUYLER COLFAX, Speaker."

THE END OF THE CONFEDERATE GOVERNMENT.

While the inhabitants of Richmond, the Confederate capital, were at their respective places of worship (Sunday, April 2, 1865), the message from Lee, "My lines are broken in three places; Richmond must be evacuated this evening," reached the doomed city. President Davis was at St. Paul's (Episcopal) Church, when the message was put in his hands by Colonel Taylor Wood. He immediately left the church. There was a deep and painful silence for a moment, when the religious services were closed and the rector (Dr. Minnegerode) dismissed the congregation after giving notice that General Ewell, the commander in Richmond, desired the local forces to assemble at 3 P.M. The Secretary of State (Benjamin), being a Jew, was not at church; the Secretary of the Navy (Mallory), a Roman Catholic, was at mass, in St. Peter's Cathedral; the Secretary of the Treasury (Trenholm) was sick; the Postmaster-General (Reagan) was at Dr. Petrie's Baptist Church; and the Secretary of War (Breckinridge) was at Dr. Duncan's church. The inhabitants of the city were kept in the most painful suspense for hours, for rumor was busy. Towards evening wagons were loaded at the departments and driven to the stations of the Danville Railway, preparatory to the flight of the government officers. At eight o'clock in the evening President lature fled from the city. The Confederate Congress had already departed; and all that remained of the government in Richmond at midnight was the War Department, represented by Major Melton. The gold of the Louisiana banks that had been sent to Richmond for safe-keeping, and that of the Richmond banks, was sent away by the Danville Railway early in

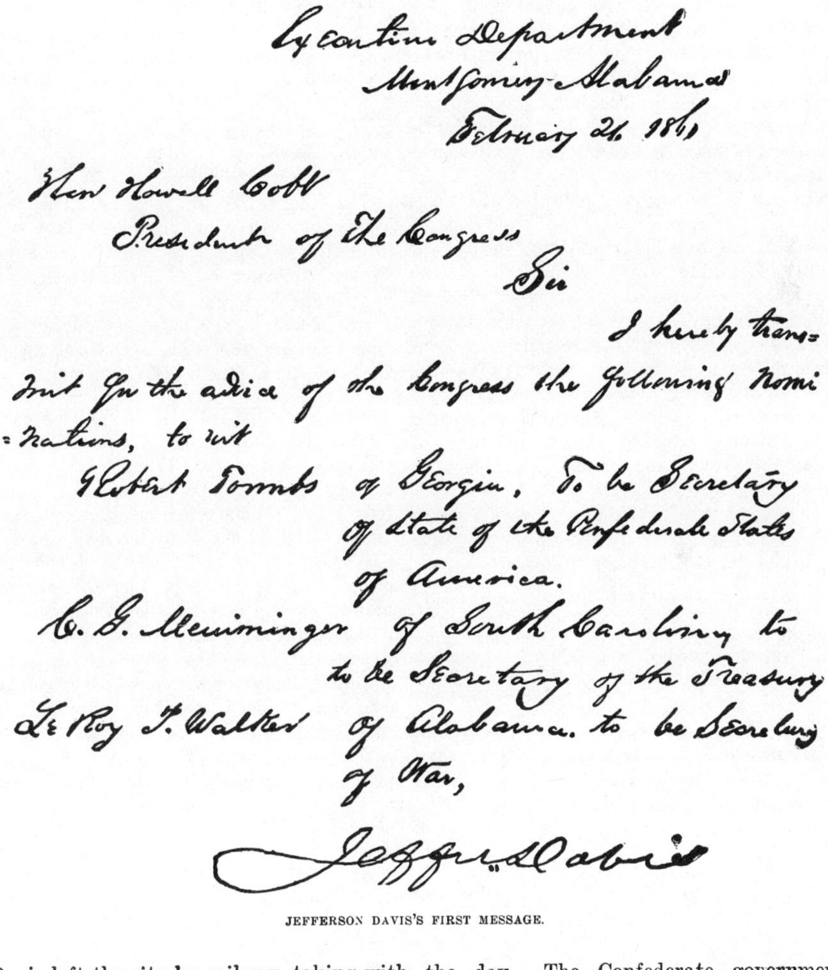

Executive Department
Montgomery Alabama
February 21. 1861

Hon Howell Cobb
President of The Congress
Sir

I hereby transmit for the advice of the Congress the following nominations, to wit

Robert Toombs of Georgia, To be Secretary of State of the Confederate States of America.

C. G. Memminger of South Carolina to to be Secretary of the Treasury

LeRoy P. Walker of Alabama. to be Secretary of War,

Jeffn. Davis

JEFFERSON DAVIS'S FIRST MESSAGE.

Davis left the city by railway, taking with him horses and carriages to use in case the road should be interrupted, declaring that he would not give up the struggle, but would make other efforts to sustain the cause. At nine o'clock the Virginia legis- the day. The Confederate government halted in its flight at Danville, where an attempt was made at reorganization, to continue the contest "so long as there was a man left in the Confederacy." On hearing of the surrender of Lee, they fled from Danville to Greensboro, N. C., and made their official residence in a railroad carriage, where they remained until the 15th, when, it being seen that the surrender of Johnston was inevitable, they again took flight on horses and in ambulances for Charlotte, for the railway was crippled. There Davis proposed to establish the future capital of the Confederacy, but the surrender of Johnston prevented. The fugitive leaders of the government now took flight again on horseback, escorted by 2,000 cavalry. At Charlotte, George Davis, the Confederate Attorney-General, resigned his office; Trenholm gave up the Secretaryship of the Treasury on the banks of the Catawba, where Postmaster-General Reagan took Trenholm's place. The flight continued, the escort constantly diminishing. At Washington, Ga., the rest of Davis's cabinet deserted him, only Reagan remaining faithful. Mallory, the Secretary of the Navy, fled, with Wigfall, to La Grange, where he met his family and was subsequently arrested; and Benjamin fled to England. Near Irwinsville, the county seat of Irwin county, Ga., 3 miles south of Macon, Davis was arrested by National cavalry on the morning of May 11, 1865, and taken a prisoner to Fort Monroe.

The last official signature of President Davis is said to be affixed to the appointment of M. H. Clark, as follows:

WASHINGTON, GA., *May 4, 1865.*

M. H. Clark, Esq., is hereby appointed acting treasurer of the Confederate States, and is authorized to act as such during the absence of the treasurer.

JEFFERSON DAVIS.

Forty thousand dollars had been left at Greensboro, N. C., in charge of the treasurer, John C. Hendren. The balance on hand turned over to Mr. Clark was $288,000 in coin and bullion. A further sum of $230,000 in coin, belonging to the Richmond banks, was also turned over to Mr. Clark at Washington, Ga. General Breckinridge ordered a part of the money to be distributed among the soldiers, who got about $25 apiece. The treasury funds were distributed as follows:

Payment of troops	$108,322 90
Quartermaster's Department	5,000 00
President's guard	1,472 00
To Major Fisher for troops	4,000 00
Judge Reagan for naval schools	1,500 00
J. F. Wheeless for naval affairs	1,500 00
Gen. Braxton Bragg for Trans-Mississippi Department	3,000 00
Major Moses for Commissaries Department	40,000 00
Navy Department	86,000 00
Col. John Taylor Wood	1,500 00
Col. William P. Johnston	1,500 00
Col. F. R. Lubbock	1,500 00
Col. C. E. Thorburn	1,500 00
Judge Reagan	3,500 00
And various smaller sums.	

The above was all in coin. The bonds and paper currency, having a face value of many millions of dollars, were burned in the presence of General Breckinridge and Judge Reagan.

For a list of military and naval operations during the war, see BATTLES and CIVIL WAR IN THE UNITED STATES.

UNITED CONFEDERATE VETERANS.

This association was organized at New Orleans, June 10, 1889. Its purpose is "to endeavor to unite in a general federation all associations of Confederate veterans, soldiers and sailors, now in existence or hereafter to be formed; to gather authentic data for an impartial history of the war between the States; to preserve relics or mementoes of the same; to cherish the ties of friendship that should exist among men who have shared common dangers, common sufferings, and privations; to care for the disabled and extend a helping hand to the needy; to protect the widows and orphans." State organizations are authorized, and are called divisions. The permanent headquarters of the association are at New Orleans, La. Number of camps, 1,750; number of members, according to last report, about 55,000

CONFEDERATION, ARTICLES OF

Confederation, ARTICLES OF. In July, 1775, Dr. Franklin submitted to the Continental Congress a plan of government for the colonies, to exist until the war then begun with Great Britain should cease. It was not acted upon. On July 12, 1776, a committee, appointed on June 11, reported, through John Dickinson, of

Pennsylvania, a draft of "Articles of Confederation." Almost daily debates upon it continued until Aug. 20, when the report was laid aside, and was not called up for consideration until April 8, 1777. Meanwhile several of the States had adopted constitutions for their respective governments, and the Congress was practically acknowledged the supreme head in all matters appertaining to war, public finances, etc., and was exercising the functions of sovereignty. From April 8 until Nov. 15 ensuing, the subject was debated two or three times a week, and several amendments were made. On Nov. 15, 1777, after a spirited debate, daily, for a fortnight, a plan of government, known as "Articles of Confederation," was adopted. Congress again assembled, in Philadelphia, on July 2, 1778, and on the 9th the "Articles of Confederation," engrossed on parchment, were signed by the delegates of eight States. A circular was sent to the other States, urging them "to conclude the glorious compact which was to unite the strength and councils of the whole." North Carolina acceded to the Confederation on July 21, Georgia on the 24th, and New Jersey on Nov. 26 following. On May 5, 1779, the delegates from Delaware agreed to the compact; but Maryland refused to assent unless the public lands northwest of the Ohio should first be recognized as the common property of all the States, and held as a common resource for the discharge of the debts contracted by Congress for the expense of the war. Maryland alone stood in the way of the consummation of the union at that time. This point was finally settled by the cession, by claiming States, to the United States, of all unsettled and unappropriated lands, for the benefit of the whole Union. This action having removed all objections, the delegates from Maryland signed the "Articles of Confederation" March 1, 1781, and the league of States was perfected.

The following is the text of this document:

To all to whom these Presents shall come, We, the undersigned Delegates of the States affixed to our names, send greeting: Whereas, the Delegates of the United States of America, in Congress assembled, did, on the 15th day of November, in the year of our Lord, 1777, and in the second year of the Independence of America, agree to certain Articles of Confederation and Perpetual Union between the States of New Hampshire, Massachusetts Bay, Rhode Island and Providence Plantations, Connecticut, New York, New Jersey, Pennsylvania, Delaware, Maryland, Virginia, North Carolina, South Carolina, and Georgia, in the words following, viz.:

Articles of Confederation and Perpetual Union between the States of New Hampshire, Massachusetts Bay, Rhode Island and Providence Plantations, Connecticut, New York, New Jersey, Pennsylvania, Delaware, Maryland, Virginia, North Carolina, South Carolina, and Georgia.

Article I. The style of this Confederacy shall be "The United States of America."

Article II. Each State retains its sovereignty, freedom, and independence, and every power, jurisdiction, and right which is not by this confederation expressly delegated to the United States in Congress assembled.

Article III. The said States hereby severally enter into a firm league of friendship with each other for their common defence, the security of their liberties, and their mutual and general welfare, binding themselves to assist each other against all force offered to or attacks made upon them, or any of them, on account of religion, sovereignty, trade, or any other pretence whatever.

Article IV. The better to secure and perpetuate mutual friendship and intercourse among the people of the different States in this Union, the free inhabitants of each of these States—paupers, vagabonds, and fugitives from justice excepted—shall be entitled to all privileges and immunities of free citizens in the several States; and the people of each State shall have free ingress and regress to and from any other State, and shall enjoy therein all the privileges of trade and commerce, subject to the same duties, imposition, and restriction as the inhabitants thereof respectively, provided that such restriction shall not extend so far as to prevent the removal of property, imported into any State, to any other State of which the owner is an inhabitant; provided, also, that no imposition, duties, or restriction shall be laid by any State on the property of the United States, or either of them.

If any person guilty of, or charged with, treason, felony, or other high misdemeanor in any State shall flee from justice, and be found in any of the United States, he shall, upon demand of the governor, or executive power of the State from which he fled, be delivered up and removed to the State having jurisdiction of his offence.

Full faith and credit shall be given in each of these States to the records, acts, and judicial proceedings of the courts and magistrates of every other State.

Article V. For the more convenient management of the general interest of the United States, delegates shall be annually appointed, in such manner as the legislature of each State shall direct, to meet in Congress on the first Monday in November, in every year, with a power reserved to each State to recall its delegates, or any of them, at any time within the year, and to send others in their stead for the remainder of the year.

No State shall be represented in Congress by less than two nor by more than seven members; and no person shall be capable of being a delegate for more than three years in any term of six years; nor shall any person, being a delegate, be capable of holding any office under the United States for which he, or another for his benefit, receives any salary, fees, or emolument of any kind.

Each State shall maintain its own delegates in any meeting of the States, and while they act as members of the committee of the States.

In determining questions in the United States in Congress assembled, each State shall have one vote.

Freedom of speech and debate in Congress shall not be impeached or questioned in any court or place out of Congress, and the members of Congress shall be protected in their persons from arrests and imprisonments during the time of their going to and from and attendance on Congress, except for treason, felony, or breach of the peace.

Article VI. No State, without the consent of the United States in Congress assembled, shall send an embassy to, or receive an embassy from, or enter into any conference, agreement, alliance, or treaty with any king, prince, or state; nor shall any person holding any office of profit or trust under the United States, or any of them, accept of any present, emolument, office, or title of any kind whatever from any king, prince, or foreign state; nor shall the United States in Congress assembled, or any of them, grant any title of nobility.

No two or more States shall enter into any treaty, confederation, or alliance whatever between them, without the consent of the United States in Congress assembled, specifying accurately the purposes for which the same is to be entered into and how long it shall continue.

No State shall lay any imposts or duties which may interfere with any stipulations in treaties entered into by the United States in Congress assembled with any king, prince, or state, in pursuance of any treaties already proposed by Congress to the courts of France and Spain.

No vessels of war shall be kept up in time of peace by any State, except such number only as shall be deemed necessary by the United States in Congress assembled for the defence of such State or its trade; or shall any body of forces be kept up by any State in time of peace, except such number only as, in the judgment of the United States in Congress assembled, shall be deemed requisite to garrison the forts necessary for the defence of such State; but every State shall always keep up a well-regulated and disciplined militia, sufficiently armed and accoutred, and shall provide and have constantly ready for use, in public stores, a due number of field-pieces and tents, and a proper quantity of arms, ammunition, and camp equipage.

No State shall engage in any war without the consent of the United States in Congress assembled, unless such State be actually invaded by enemies, or shall have received certain advice of a resolution being formed by some nation of Indians to invade such a State, and the danger is so imminent as not to admit of a delay till the United States in Congress assembled can be consulted; nor shall any State grant commissions to any ships or vessels of war, nor letters of marque or reprisal, except it be after a declaration of war by the United States in Congress assembled, and then only against the kingdom or state and the subjects thereof against which war has been so declared, and under such regulations as shall be established by the United States in Congress assembled, unless such State be infested by pirates, in which case vessels of war may be fitted out for that occasion and kept so long as the danger shall continue, or until the United States in Congress assembled shall determine otherwise.

Article VII. When land forces are raised by any State for the common defence, all officers of, or under, the rank of colonel shall be appointed by the legislature of each State respectively, by whom such forces shall be raised, or in such manner as such State shall direct, and all vacancies shall be filled up by the State which first made the appointment.

Article VIII. All charges of war, and all other expenses that shall be incurred for the common defence or general warfare, and allowed by the United States in Congress assembled, shall be defrayed out of a common treasury, which shall be supplied by the several States, in proportion to the value of all land within each State, granted to or surveyed for any person, as such land and the buildings and improvements thereon shall be estimated according to such mode as the United States in Congress assembled shall, from time to time, direct and appoint. The taxes for paying that proportion shall be laid and levied by the authority and direction of the legislatures of the several States within the time agreed upon by the United States in Congress assembled.

Article IX. The United States in Congress assembled shall have the sole and exclusive right and power of determining on peace and war, except in the cases mentioned in the sixth article—of sending and receiving ambassadors—entering into treaties and alliances, provided that no treaty of commerce shall be made whereby the legislative power of the respective States shall be restrained from imposing such imposts and duties on foreigners as their own people are subject to, or from prohibiting the exportation or importation of any species of goods or commodities whatsoever—of establishing rules for deciding in all cases what captures on land or water shall be legal, and in what manner prizes taken by land or naval forces in the service of the United States shall be divided or appropriated—of granting letters of marque and reprisal in times of peace—appointing courts for the trial of piracies and felonies committed on the high seas, and establishing courts for receiving and determining finally appeals in all cases of captures, provided that no member of Congress shall be appointed a judge of any of the said courts.

The United States in Congress assembled shall also be the last resort on appeal in all disputes and differences now subsisting, or that hereafter may arise, between two or more States concerning boundary, jurisdiction, or any other cause whatever; which authority shall always be exercised in the manner following: Whenever the legislative or executive authority or lawful agent of any State in controversy with another shall present a petition to Congress, stating the matter in question and praying for a hearing, notice thereof shall be given, by order of Congress, to the legislative or executive authority of the other State in controversy, and a day assigned for the appearance of the parties by their lawful agents, who shall then be directed to appoint, by joint consent, commissioners or judges to constitute a court for hearing and determining the matter in question; but if they cannot agree Congress shall name three persons out of each of the United States, and from the list of such persons each party shall alternately strike out one, the petitioners beginning, until the number shall be reduced to thirteen; and from that number not less than seven nor more than nine names, as Congress shall direct, shall in the presence of Congress be drawn out by lot; and the persons whose names shall be so drawn, or any five of them, shall be commissioners or judges, to hear and finally determine the controversy, so always as a major part of the judges who shall hear the cause shall agree in the determination; and if either party shall neglect to attend at the day appointed, without showing reasons which Congress shall judge sufficient, or, being present, shall refuse to strike, the Congress shall proceed to nominate three persons out of each State, and the secretary of Congress shall strike in behalf of such party absent or refusing; and the judgment and sentence of the court to be appointed, in the manner above prescribed, shall be final and conclusive; and if any of the parties shall refuse to submit to the authority of such court, or to appear or defend their claim or cause, the court shall nevertheless proceed to pronounce sentence or judgment, which shall in like manner be final and decisive, the judgment or sentence and other proceedings being in either case transmitted to Congress, and lodged among the acts of Congress for the security of the parties concerned; provided that every commissioner, before he sits in judgment, shall take an oath, to be administered by one of the judges of the Supreme or Superior Court of the State where the cause shall be tried, "well and truly to hear and determine the matter in question, according to the best of his judgment, without favor, affection, or hope of reward"; provided, also, that no State shall be deprived of territory for the benefit of the United States.

All controversies concerning the private right of soil claimed under different grants of two or more States, whose jurisdictions, as they may respect such lands, and the States which passed such grants, are adjusted; the said grants or either of them being at the same time claimed to have originated antecedent to such settlement of jurisdiction, shall, on the petition of either party to the Congress of the United States, be finally determined as near as may be in the same manner as is before prescribed for deciding disputes respecting territorial jurisdiction between different States.

The United States in Congress assembled shall also have the sole exclusive right and power of regulating the alloy and value of coin struck by their own authority, or by that of the respective States—fixing the standard of weights and measures throughout the United States—regulating the trade and managing all affairs with the Indians, not members of any of the States; provided that the legislative right of any State within its own limits be not infringed or violated—establishing or regulating post-offices from one State to another, throughout all the United States, and exacting such postage on the papers passing through the same as may be requisite to defray the expenses of the said office—appointing all officers of the land forces in the service of the United States, excepting regimental officers — appointing all the officers of the naval forces—and commissioning all officers whatever in the service of the United States — making rules for the government and regulation of the said land and naval forces, and directing their operations.

The United States in Congress assembled shall have authority to appoint a committee, to sit in the recess of Congress, to be denominated "A Committee of the State," and to consist of one delegate from each State; and to appoint such other committees and civil officers as may be necessary for managing the general affairs of the United States under their direction—to appoint one of their number to preside, provided that no person be allowed to serve in the office of president more than one year in any term of three years—to ascertain the necessary sums of money to be raised for the service of the United States, and to appropriate and apply the same for defraying the public expenses—to borrow money or emit bills on the credit of the United States, transmitting every half-year to the respective States an account of the sums of money so borrowed or emitted—to build and equip a navy—to agree upon the number of land forces, and to make requisitions from each State for its quota, in proportion to the number of white inhabitants in such States; which requisition shall be binding, and thereupon the legislatures of each State shall appoint the regimental officers, raise the men, and clothe, arm, and equip them in a soldier-like manner, at the expense of the United States; and the officers and men so clothed, armed, and equipped shall march to the place appointed, and within the time agreed on by the United States in Congress assembled; but if the United States in Congress assembled shall, on consideration of circumstances, judge proper that any State should not raise men, or should raise a smaller number than its quota, and that any other State should raise a larger number of men than the quota thereof, such extra number shall be raised, officered, clothed, armed, and equipped in the same manner as the quota of such State, unless the legislature of such State shall judge that such extra number cannot be safely spared out of the same; in which case they shall raise, officer, clothe, arm, and equip as many of such extra number as they judge can be safely spared. And the officers and men so clothed, armed, and equipped shall march to the place appointed, and within the time agreed on by the United States in Congress assembled.

The United States in Congress assembled shall never engage in a war, nor grant letters of marque and reprisal in time of peace, nor enter into any treaties or alliances, nor coin money, nor regulate the value thereof, nor ascertain the sums and expenses necessary for the defence and welfare of the United States, or any of them, nor emit bills, nor borrow money on the credit of the United States, nor appropriate money, nor agree upon the number of vessels of war to be built or purchased, or the number of land or sea forces to be raised, nor appoint a commander-in-chief of the army or navy, unless nine States assent to the same, nor shall a question on any other point, except for adjourning from day to day, be determined, unless by the votes of a majority of the United States in Congress assembled.

The Congress of the United States shall have power to adjourn to any time within the year, and to any place within the United States, so that no period of adjournment be for a longer duration than the space of six months, and shall publish the journal of their proceedings monthly, except such parts thereof relating to treaties, alliances, or military operations as in their judgment require secrecy; and the yeas and nays of the delegates of each State on any question shall be entered on the journal when it is desired by any delegate, and the delegates of a State, or any of them, at his or their request, shall be furnished with a transcript of the said journal, except such parts as are above excepted, to lay before the legislature of the several States.

Article X. The committee of the States, or any nine of them, shall be authorized to execute, in the recess of Congress, such of the powers of Congress as the United States in Congress assembled, by the consent of nine States, shall from time to time think expedient to vest them with, provided that no power be delegated to the said committee for the exercise of which, by the Articles of Confederation, the voice of nine States in the Congress of the United States assembled is requisite.

Article XI. Canada, according to this confederation, and joining in the measures of the United States, shall be admitted into, and entitled to, all the advantages of this Union; but no other colony shall be admitted into the same, unless such admission be agreed to by nine States.

Article XII. All bills of credit emitted, moneys borrowed, and debts contracted by or under the authority of Congress, before the assembling of the United States, in pursuance of the present confederation, shall be deemed and considered as a charge against the United States, for payment and satisfaction whereof the said United States and the public faith are hereby solemnly pledged.

Article XIII. Every State shall abide by the determinations of the United States in Congress assembled, on all questions which by this confederation are submitted to them. And the articles of this confederation shall be inviolably observed by every State, and the Union shall be perpetual; nor shall any alteration at any time hereafter be made in any of them, unless such alterations be agreed to in a Congress of the United States, and be afterwards confirmed by the legislatures of every State.

And whereas, It hath pleased the Great Governor of the World to incline the hearts of the legislatures we respectively represent in Congress to approve of, and to authorize us to ratify, the said Articles of Confederation and perpetual union. Know ye that we, the undersigned delegates, by virtue of the power and authority to us given for that purpose, do by these presents, in the name and in behalf of our respective constituents, fully and entirely ratify and confirm each and every one of the said Articles of Confederation and perpetual union, and all and singular the matters and things therein contained. And we do further solemnly plight and engage the faith of our respective constituents, that they shall abide by the determinations of the United States in Congress assembled, on all questions which by the said confederation are submitted to them. And that the articles thereof shall be inviolably observed by the States we respectively represent, and that the union shall be perpetual. In witness whereof we have hereunto set our hands in Congress. Done at Philadelphia, in the State of Pennsylvania, the 9th day of July, in the year of our Lord, 1778, and in the 3d year of the Independence of America.

Conference of Governors. See GOVERNORS, CONFERENCE OF.

Confirmation by the Senate. By the Constitution of the United States, the President "shall nominate, and by and with the consent of the Senate, shall appoint ambassadors and other public ministers and consuls, judges of the Supreme Court," etc. (See TENURE OF OFFICE.)

Confiscation. When the Southern ports were blockaded in 1861, Congress passed an act confiscating all property used against the National government. This policy was strictly enforced.

Conger, EDWIN HURD, diplomatist; born in Knox county, Ill., March 7, 1843; was graduated at Lombard University, Galesburg, Ill., in 1862; served in the 102d Illinois Regiment in the Civil War from 1862–65; and was brevetted major. After the war he entered the Albany Law School, where he graduated in 1866; practised law in Galesburg, Ill.; and after 1868 was engaged in banking and stock-raising in Iowa. He was State treasurer of Iowa in 1882–85; member of Congress in 1885–91; and minister to Brazil in 1891–95, being reappointed to the latter post in 1897. On Jan. 12, 1898, he was transferred to China, and served in Pekin during the critical days of the Boxer uprising in 1900, and the negotiations for the restoration of order. He died at Pasadena, Cal., May 18, 1907. See CHINA.

EDWIN HURD CONGER.

Congregational Church, a religious body believing in the principle of self-government in the local church, and the duty of churches to unite in fellowship with one another. The principal instrument of church union lies in ecclesiastical councils, whose functions are to give counsel and to express fellowship, but never to issue commands. It is in this feature that the Congregational Church in the United States differs from that in Great Britain.

According to a special report of the Federal Bureau of the Census on *Religious Bodies* (1910), the denomination had 5,713 organizations, in forty-five conferences, located in every State and Territory except Delaware, of which 5,666 reported 700,480 communicants or members; 5,792 church edifices; church property valued at $63,240,305; 5,802 ministers; and 5,741 Sunday schools (reported by 5,327 organizations), with 75,801 officers and teachers and 638,089 scholars. The first Congregational Church was founded at Plymouth, New England, in 1620, by the Pilgrims.

Congress, COLONIAL. Soon after the attack on Schenectady (1690), the government of Massachusetts addressed a circular letter to all the colonies as far south as Maryland, inviting them to send commissioners to New York, to agree upon some plan of operations for the defence of the whole. Delegates from Massachusetts, Connecticut, and New York met in the city of New York in May, 1690, and the campaign against Canada was planned. This was the first Colonial Congress.

Congress, CONFEDERATE. See CONFEDERATE STATES OF AMERICA.

Congress, CONTINENTAL. The first Continental Congress assembled in Carpenters' Hall, Philadelphia, Pa., on Sept. 5, 1774, when eleven of the English-American colonies were represented by forty-four delegates — namely, two from New Hampshire, four from Massachusetts, two from Rhode Island, three from Connecticut, five from New York, five from New Jersey, six from Pennsylvania, three from Delaware, three from Maryland, six from Virginia, and five from South Carolina. Three deputies from North Carolina appeared on the 14th. Peyton Randolph, of Virginia, was chosen president of the Congress, and Charles Thomson, of Pennsylvania, was appointed secretary. Other delegates appeared afterwards, making the whole number fifty-four. Each colony had appointed representatives without any rule as to number, and the grave question at once presented itself, How shall we vote? It was decided to vote by colonies, each colony to have one vote, for as yet there were no means for determining the relative population of each colony.

Patrick Henry, in a speech at the opening of the business of the Congress, struck the key-note of union by saying, "British oppression has effaced the boundaries of the several colonies; the distinction between Virginians, Pennsylvanians, and New-Englanders is no more. *I am not a Virginian, but an American.*" This was the text of every speech afterwards. It was voted that the session of the Congress should be opened every morning with prayer, and the Rev. Jacob Duché, of the Protestant Episcopal Church, was employed as chaplain. There was much difference of opinion concerning the duties and powers of the Congress, Henry contending that an entirely new government must be founded; Jay, that they had not assembled to form a new government, but as a continental committee of conference, to try to correct abuses in the old. The members were unanimous in their resolves to support Massachusetts in resistance to the unconstitutional change in her charter. They appointed a committee to state the rights of the colonists in general, the several instances in which those rights had been violated or infringed, and to suggest means for their restoration. Other committees for various duties were appointed, and at

CARPENTERS' HALL.

about the middle of September the Congress was a theatre of warm debates, which took a wide range. On Sept. 20 they adopted a request for the colonies to abstain from commercial intercourse with Great Britain. They tried to avoid the appearance of revolution while making bold propositions. Some were radical, some conservative, and some very timid. The tyranny of Gage in Boston produced much irritation in the Congress; and on Oct. 8, after a short but spicy debate, it passed the most important resolution of the session, in response to the Suffolk resolutions, as follows: "That this Congress approve the opposition of the inhabitants of Massachusetts Bay to the execution of the late acts of Parliament; and if the same shall be attempted to be carried into execution by force, in such case all Americans ought to support them in their opposition." Thus the united colonies cast down the gauntlet of defiance. On the 14th the Congress adopted a *Declaration of Colonial Rights.* This was followed on the 20th by the adoption of *The American Association,* or general non-importation league. An *Address to the People of Great Britain*, written by John Jay, and a memorial *To the Inhabitants of the Several British-American Colonies*, from the pen of Richard Henry Lee, were adopted on the 21st. On the 26th—the last day of the session—a *Petition to the King* and an *Address to the Inhabitants of the Province of Quebec, or Canada*, both drawn by John Dickinson, were agreed to. A vote of thanks to the friends of the colonists in Parliament was sent to the colonial agents, with the petition of the King. Having already recommended the holding of another Continental Congress at Philadelphia on May 10, 1775, this Congress adjourned in the afternoon of Oct. 26, 1774, and the next day the members started for home, impressed with the belief that war was inevitable. The actual sessions of the Congress occupied only thirty-one days. Their proceedings produced a profound sensation in both hemispheres. The state papers they put forth commanded the admiration of the leading statesmen of Europe. The King and his ministers were highly offended, and early in January Lord Dartmouth issued a circular letter to all the royal governors in America signifying his Majesty's pleasure that they should prevent the appointment of deputies to another Continental Congress within their respective governments, and exhort all persons to desist from such proceedings. The members of the first Continental Congress were cautious concerning the assumption of direct political authority. They had met as a continental committee of conference. Even the American Association, the nearest approach to it, was opposed by Galloway of Pennsylvania, Duane of New York, and all the South Carolina delegation but two.

ROOM IN WHICH CONGRESS MET IN CARPENTERS' HALL.

The Southern members of the first Continental Congress were disturbed by the clause in the American Association, then adopted, by which they determined "wholly to discontinue the slave-trade"; and the paragraph in the Declaration of Independence in which Jefferson denounced the slave-trade and slavery was rejected by the Congress of 1776, in deference to the people of South Carolina and Georgia. A few days after the amended declaration was adopted, in the first debates on a plan for a confederation of the States, there appeared much antagonism of feeling between the representatives of the Northern and Southern States, founded partially upon climate, pursuits, and systems of labor, but more largely on the latter. When members from the North spoke freely of the evils of slavery, a member from South Carolina declared that "if property in slaves should be questioned, there must be an end to the confederation." So, in the convention that framed the national Constitution, that instrument could not have received the sanction of a majority of the convention had the immediate abolition of the slave-trade been insisted upon. Soon after the arrival of Gerard, the first French minister, at Philadelphia, he wrote (1778) to Vergennes: "The States of the South and of the North, under existing subjects of estrangement and division, are two distinct parties, which, at present, count but few deserters. The division is attributed to moral and philosophical causes."

The sessions of the Continental Congress were opened at the following times and places: Sept. 5, 1774, Philadelphia; May 10, 1775, ditto; Dec. 20, 1776, Baltimore; March 4, 1777, Philadelphia; Sept. 27, 1777, Lancaster, Pa.; Sept. 30, 1777, York, Pa.; July 2, 1778, Philadelphia; June 30, 1783, Princeton, N. J.; Nov. 26, 1783, Annapolis, Md.; Nov. 1, 1784, Trenton, N. J.; Jan. 11, 1785, New York. This continued to be the place of meeting from that time until the adoption of the Constitution of the United States in 1788. From 1781 to 1788 Congress met annually on the first Monday in November, which time was fixed by the ARTICLES OF CONFEDERATION (*q. v.*). The presidents of the Continental Congress were:

Name.	Where From.	When Elected.
Peyton Randolph	Virginia	Sept. 5, 1774.
Henry Middleton	South Carolina	Oct. 2, 1774.
Peyton Randolph	Virginia	May 10, 1775.
John Hancock	Massachusetts	May 24, 1775.
Henry Laurens	South Carolina	Nov. 1, 1777.
John Jay	New York	Dec. 10, 1778.
Samuel Huntington	Connecticut	Sept. 28, 1779.
Thomas McKean	Delaware	July 10, 1781.
John Hanson	Maryland	Nov. 5, 1781.
Elias Boudinot	New Jersey	Nov. 4, 1782.
Thomas Mifflin	Pennsylvania	Nov. 3, 1783.
Richard Henry Lee	Virginia	Nov. 30, 1784.
Nathan Gorham	Massachusetts	June 6, 1786.
Arthur St. Clair	Pennsylvania	Feb. 2, 1787.
Cyrus Griffin	Virginia	Jan. 22, 1788.

The colonists had been compelled to take up arms in self-defence. To justify this act, Congress agreed to a manifesto (July 6, 1775), in which they set forth the causes and necessity of their taking up arms. After a temperate but spirited preamble, presenting an historical view of the origin, progress, and conduct of the colonies, and of the measures of the British government towards them since 1763, they specified the various acts of Parliaments which were oppressive to the colonies. Having reverted to their fruitless petition to the throne and remonstrances to Parliament; to the unprovoked attack of British troops on the inhabitants of Massachusetts at Lexington and Concord; to the proclamation declaring the people of the colonies to be in a state of rebellion; to the events at Breed's Hill and the burning of Charlestown, the manifesto proceeded: "Our cause is just. Our union is perfect. Our internal resources are great, and, if necessary, foreign assistance is undoubtedly attainable." After acknowledging the evidence of divine favor towards the colonists by not permitting them to be called into this controversy until they had grown strong and disciplined by experience to defend themselves, the manifesto most solemnly declared that the colonists, having been compelled by their enemies to take up arms, they would, in defiance of every hazard, "with unabating powers and perseverance, employ for the preservation of their liberties all the means at their command, being with one mind resolved to die freemen rather than live slaves." Disclaiming all intention of separating from Great Britain and establishing independent States, they declared that having been forced to take up arms, they should lay them down when hostilities should cease on the part of the aggressors, and all danger of their being made slaves should disappear. In that manifesto the united colonies cast at the feet of their blinded sovereign the gauntlet of defiance.

A petition to the King was adopted and signed by the members of the Congress present July 8, 1775, in which, after allusion to the oppression the colonists had been subjected to, they declared their loyalty to the throne. It was taken to England from Philadelphia by Richard Penn, who delivered it to Lord Dartmouth. Penn assured him the colonies had no designs for independence. On the strength of that testimony the Duke of Richmond moved in the House of Lords that the petition, which had been laid before Parliament, be made the basis of a conciliation with America. After a warm debate the motion was rejected, and no further notice was taken of the petition.

The second Continental Congress met in Philadelphia May 10, 1775. Peyton Randolph was chosen president; Charles Thomson, secretary; Andrew McNeare, door-keeper, and William Shed, messenger. To this Congress all eyes were anxiously turned. Randolph was soon called to Virginia to attend a session of the Assembly as speaker, when his seat was temporarily filled by Thomas Jefferson, and his place as president by John Hancock. On May 25 Georgia was represented in the Continental Congress for the first time, Lyman Hall having been elected special representative from the parish of St. Johns and admitted to a seat, but without a vote.

In committee of the whole the Congress considered the state of the colonies. A full account of recent events in Massachusetts was laid before them; also a letter from the Congress of that province, asking advice as to the form of government to be adopted there, and requesting the Continental Congress to assume control of the army at Cambridge. This second Congress was regarded by the colonists as no longer a committee of conference, but a provisional government. The first Congress claimed no political power, though their signatures to the American Association implied as much. The present Congress, strengthened by the public voice of the colonists, entered at once upon the exercise of comprehensive authority, in which the functions of supreme executive, legislative, and sometimes judicial powers were united. These powers had no fixed limits of action nor formal sanction, except the ready obedience of a large majority in all the colonies. The committee of the whole reported and the Congress resolved (May 26) that war had been commenced by Great Britain.

The Congress denied any intention of casting off their allegiance, and expressed an anxious desire for peace; at the same time voted that the colonies ought to be put in a position of defence against any attempt to force them to submit to parliamentary schemes of taxation. Another petition to the King was adopted; and it was resolved that no provisions ought to be furnished by the colonists to the British army or navy; that no bills of exchange drawn by British officers ought to be negotiated, and that no colonial ships ought to be employed in the transportation of British troops. Committees were appointed to prepare an address to the people of Great Britain and Ireland; also to the Assembly of Jamaica, and an appeal to the "oppressed inhabitants of Canada." They also issued a proclamation (June 9) for a day (July 20) of general solemn fasting and prayer. They resolved that no obedience was due to the late act of Parliament for subverting the charter of Massachusetts, and advised the Congress of that province to organize a government in as near conformity to the charter as circumstances would admit. The Congress adopted the army at Cambridge as a continental one; appointed a commander-in-chief (June 15), with four major-generals and eight brigadiers; arranged the rank and pay of officers, and perfected a preliminary organization of the army. They worked industriously in perfecting a national civil organization and for support of the military force, authorizing the issue of bills of credit to the amount of $2,000,000, at the same time taking pains not to give mortal offence to the British government. But the inefficiency of the executive powers of Congress was continually apparent. The sagacious Franklin, seeing the futility of attempting to carry on the inevitable war with such a feeble instrument, submitted a basis of a form of confederation, similar in some respects to the one he proposed in convention at ALBANY (*q. v.*) twenty-one years before. It was a virtual declaration of independence, but it was not acted upon at that time. The Congress also established a postal system (July 26, 1775) and appointed Dr. Franklin postmaster-general. It also established a general hospital, with Dr. Benjamin Church as chief director. The army before Boston and an expedition for the conquest of Canada engaged much of the attention of the Congress for the rest of the year.

Late in December, 1776, the Congress, which had fled from Philadelphia and reassembled at Baltimore, cast aside its hitherto temporizing policy. Up to this time the Congress had left on their journal the suggestion that a reunion with Great Britain might be the consequence of a delay in France to declare immediately and explicitly in their favor. Now they voted to "assure foreign courts that the Congress and people of America are determined to maintain their independence at all events." It was resolved to offer treaties of commerce to Prussia, Austria, and Tuscany, and to ask for the intervention of those powers to prevent Russian or German troops from serving against the United States. They also drew up a sketch for an offensive alliance with France and Spain against Great Britain. These measures delighted the more radical members in Congress and, with the victory at Trenton which immediately followed, inspirited the people.

The extent and intensity of the struggle of the Continental Congress during the fifteen years of its existence to maintain its financial credit and carry on the war may never be known. Enough is known to prove that it involved great personal sacrifices, much financial ability, unwearied patriotism, and abounding faith in the cause and its ultimate triumph. As that Congress approached its demise, it addressed itself to a final settlement of its financial accounts. Since the adoption of the peace establishment, commencing with 1784, the liabilities incurred by the general government, including two instalments of the French debt, amounted to a little more than $6,000,000, over one-half of which had been met. Only $1,800,000 of the balance had been paid in by the States; the remainder had been obtained by three Dutch loans, amounting in the whole to $1,600,000, a fragment of which remained unexpended. The arrearage of nearly $8,000,000 consisted of interest on the French debt, and two instalments of over-dues. This indebtedness was passed over to the new government. The accounts of the quartermaster, commissary, clothing, marine, and hospital departments were either settled or about to be settled. The accounts of many of the loan offices were unsettled. There seems to have been much laxity in their management. The papers of the first Virginia loan office were lost. In South Carolina and Georgia, the loan-office proceeds had been appropriated to State uses, and from only five States had returns been made. Out of more than $2,000,000 advanced to the secret committee for foreign affairs prior to August, 1777, a considerable part remained unaccounted for. The expenditure of full one-third of the money borrowed abroad remained unexplained.

The Congress was barely kept alive, for several months before it expired, by the occasional attendance of one or two members. Among the last entries in its journals by Charles Thomson, its permanent secretary, was one under date of "Tuesday, Oct. 21, 1788," as follows: "From the day above mentioned to the 1st of November there attended occasionally, from New Hampshire, et cetera, many persons from different States. From Nov. 3 to Jan. 1, 1789, only six persons attended altogether. On that day Reed, of Pennsylvania, and Bramwell, of South Carolina, were present; and after that only one delegate was present (each time a different one) on nine different days." The very last record was: "Monday, March 2. Mr. Philip Pell, from New York." The history of that Congress has no parallel. At first it was a spontaneous gathering of representative patriots from the different English-American colonies to consult upon the public good. They boldly snatched the sceptre of political rule from their oppressors, and, assuming imperial functions, created armies, issued bills of credit, declared the provinces to be independent States, made treaties with foreign nations, founded an empire, and compelled their king to acknowledge the States which they represented to be independent of the British crown. The brilliant achievements of that Congress astonished the world. Its career was as short as it was brilliant, and its decadence began long before the war for independence had closed. Its mighty efforts had exhausted its strength. It was smitten with poverty, and made almost powerless by a loss of its credit. Overwhelmed with debt, a pensioner on the bounty of France, unable to fulfil treaties it had made, insulted by mutineers, bearded, encroached upon, and scorned by the State authorities, the Continental Congress sank fast into decrepitude and contempt. With ungrateful pride, the recipients of its benefits seem not to have felt a pang of sorrow or uttered a word of regret when the once mighty and beneficent Continental Congress expired.

Congress, FIRST PRAYER IN. See DUCHÉ, JACOB.

Congress, Library of. See Library of Congress.

Congress, National. March 4, 1789, was appointed as the time, and the City Hall in New York, renovated and called "Federal Hall," was designated as the place, for the meeting of the First Congress under the new Constitution. There was great tardiness in assembling. Only eight Senators and thirteen Representatives appeared on the appointed day. On March 11 a circular letter was sent to the absentees, urging their prompt attendance; but it was the 30th before a quorum (thirty members) of the House was present. Frederick A. Mühlenberg, of Pennsylvania, was chosen speaker of the House, and John Langdon, of New Hampshire, was made (April 6) president of the Senate, "for the sole purpose of opening and counting the votes for President and Vice-President of the United States." Washington was chosen President by a unanimous vote (sixty-nine), and John Adams was elected Vice-President by a majority. He journeyed to New York when notified of his election, and was inaugurated April 21, 1789. Washington was inaugurated April 30.

The pay of members of Congress (House of Representatives) had been $6 a day until 1814, when, on account of the increased expense of living, they fixed it at an annual salary of $1,500, without regard to the length of the session. At the same time bills were introduced to increase the salaries of foreign ministers, but these failed to pass. This act of the members of Congress in voting themselves a higher salary produced great excitement throughout the country. It opposed the popular doctrine that all public officers and servants should be kept on short allowance; and so indignant were the frugal people that at the next election many of the offending Congressmen lost their election. Even the popular Henry Clay was driven to a close canvass. The act was repealed.

The meeting of the Thirty-sixth Congress, in its last session (December, 1860), was looked forward to with deep anxiety by all Americans. The annual message of President Buchanan disappointed the people. It was so timid and indecisive that the friends and foes of the Union spoke lightly of it. Senator Jefferson Davis spoke of it as having "the characteristics of a diplomatic paper, for diplomacy is said to abhor certainty, as nature abhors a vacuum, and it is not in the power of man to reach any conclusion from that message." Senator Hale, of New Hampshire, said that if he understood the message on the subject of secession, it was this: "South Carolina has just cause for seceding from the Union; that is the first proposition. The second is that she has no right to secede. The third is that we have no right to prevent her from seceding. He goes on to represent that this is a great and powerful country, and that a State has no right to secede from it; but the power of the country, if I understand the President, consists in what Dickens makes the English constitution to be—a power to do nothing at all. . . . He has failed to look the thing in the face. He has acted like the ostrich, which hides her head, and thereby thinks to avoid danger." With no finger-post to guide them to definite action, Congress opened the business of the session. The Attorney-General (Black, of Pennsylvania) had infused into the message the only portion that pleased the extreme Southern wing—namely, the assertion that the national government possessed no power to coerce a State into submission in case of rebellion. Patriotic men had watched with intense interest for a few weeks the gathering storm, and instinctively drew the marked line of distinction between Jackson and Buchanan under similar circumstances. See Buchanan, James.

In the House of Representatives open declarations of disunion sentiments were made at the beginning. In the Senate, also, Senator Clingman boldly avowed the intention of the slave-labor States to revolt. "I tell those gentlemen [his political opponents] in perfect frankness that, in my judgment, not only will a number of States secede in the next sixty days, but some of the other States are holding on merely to see if proper guarantees can be obtained. We have in North Carolina only two considerable parties—the absolute submissionists are too small to be called a party." After demanding "guarantees" and "concessions," he broadly intimated that no concessions would satisfy the South; that a dissolution of the Union was at hand. He was opposed to free debate on the subject, and said that a Senator from Texas had told him that a good many free debaters "were hanging up by the trees in that country." The venerable Senator Crittenden, of Kentucky, arose and rebuked Clingman, and said: "I rise here to express the hope, and that alone, that the bad example of the gentleman will not be followed." He also expressed the hope that there was not a Senator present who was not willing to yield and compromise much for the sake of the government and the Union. Mr. Crittenden's mild rebuke and earnest appeal to the patriotism of the Senate were met by more scornful words from other Senators, in which the speakers seemed to emulate each other in the utterance of seditious words. Senator Hale replied with stinging words to Clingman's remarks, which aroused the anger of the Southern members. He had said, "The plain, true way is to look this thing in the face—see where we are." The extremists thought so too, and cast off all disguise, especially Senator Iveson, of Georgia, and Wigfall, of Texas. The former answered that the slave-labor States intended to revolt. "We intend to go out of this Union," he said. "I speak what I believe, that, before the 4th of March, five of the Southern States will have declared their independence." He referred to the patriotic governor of Texas (Houston) as a hinderance to the secession of that State, and expressed a hope that "some Texan Brutus will arise to rid his country of the hoary-headed incubus that stands between the people and their sovereign will." He said that in the next twelve months there would be a confederacy of Southern States, with a government in operation, of "the greatest prosperity and power that the world has ever seen." He declared that if war should ensue the South would "welcome" the North "with bloody hands to hospitable graves." Wigfall uttered similar sentiments in a coarser manner, declaring that cotton was king. "You dare not make war on cotton," he exclaimed; "no power on earth dare make war on cotton." He said South Carolina was about to secede, and that she would send a minister plenipotentiary to the United States, and when his credentials should be denied she would "assert the sovereignty of her soil, and it will be maintained at the point of the bayonet."

In the House of Representatives the Southern members were equally bold. When Mr. Boteler, of Virginia, proposed by resolution to refer so much of the President's message as related to the great question before the House to a committee of one from each State (thirty-three), the members from the slave-labor States refused to vote. "I do not vote," said Singleton, of Mississippi, "because I have not been sent here to make any compromise or patch up existing difficulties. The subject will be decided by a convention of the people of my State." They all virtually avowed their determination to thwart all legislation in the direction of compromise or conciliation. The motion for the committee of thirty-three was adopted, and it became the recipient of a large number of suggestions, resolutions, and propositions offered in the House for amendments to the Constitution, most of them looking to concessions to the demands of the slave interest. There was such an earnest desire for peace that the people of the free-labor States were ready to make all reasonable sacrifices for its sake.

In the Senate a committee of thirteen was appointed to consider the condition of the country and report some plan, by amendments to the Constitution or otherwise, for its pacification. Senator Crittenden offered a series of amendments and joint resolutions. These did not meet with favor on either side. On receiving news of the passage of the ordinance of secession by South Carolina, her two remaining Representatives (Boyce and Ashmun) left the House of Representatives and returned home. Early in January the proceedings of a secret caucus of Southern members of Congress was revealed, which showed that they should remain in Congress until its close to prevent means being adopted by the government for its own security, and that the movements in the South were principally directed by secession members in Congress. These revelations astonished and alarmed the people, for the President, in a message on Jan. 8, 1861, had uttered a sort of cry of despair. The Southerners in Congress became more and more bold and defiant, Senator Toombs, of Georgia, declared himself "a rebel." The two great committees labored in vain. Towards the middle of January, Hunter, of Virginia, and Seward, of New York, in able speeches, foreshadowed the determination of the Secession party and the Unionists. During January the extreme Southern members of Congress began to withdraw, and early in February, 1861, the national Congress had heard the last unfriendly word spoken, for the Secession party had left. Thenceforward, to the end of the session (March 4, 1861), Union men were left free to act in Congress in the preparation of measures for the salvation of the republic. The proceedings of the Thirty-sixth Congress had revealed to the country its great peril, and action was taken accordingly.

On Thursday, July 4, 1861, the Thirty-seventh Congress assembled in extraordinary session, in compliance with the call of President Lincoln, April 15. In the Senate twenty-three States, and in the House of Representatives twenty-two States and one Territory were represented. There were 40 Senators and 154 Representatives. Ten States, in which the political leaders had adopted ordinances of secession, were not represented. In both Houses there was a large majority of Unionists. It was the first session of this Congress, and Galusha A. Grow, of Pennsylvania, was chosen speaker of the House. The President, in his message, confined his remarks to the special object for which the Congress had been called together. He recited the many and grave offences of the conspirators against the life of the nation, such as the seizure of public property, making preparations for war, and seeking the recognition of foreign powers as an independent nation. In the act of firing on Fort Sumter, "discarding all else," he said, "they have forced upon the country the distinct issue, 'immediate dissolution or blood.'" He reviewed the conduct of the Virginia politicians, condemned the policy of armed neutrality proposed in some of the border States, alluded to the call for soldiers, and the necessity of vindicating the power of the national government. "It is now recommended," he said, "that you give the legal means for making the contest a short and decisive one; that you place at the control of the government for the work at least 400,000 men and $400,000,000. . . . A right result at this time will be worth more to the world than ten times the men and ten times the money. . . . The people will save the government if the government itself will do its part only indifferently well." He alluded to the preponderance of Union sentiment among the *people* in the South, and stated the remarkable fact that, while large numbers of officers of the army and navy had proved themselves unfaithful, "not one common soldier or sailor is known to have deserted his flag. . . . This is the patriotic instinct of plain people. They understand, without an argument, that the destroying of the government which was made by Washington means no good to them." The President assured the people that the sole object of the exercise of war-power should be the maintenance of the national authority and the salvation of the life of the republic. After expressing a hope that the views of Congress were coincident with his own, the President said, "Having chosen our course witho guile and with pure motives, let us renew our trust in God and go forward without fear and with manly hearts." There were important reports from the departments accompanying the President's message. The Secretary of War (Mr. Cameron) recommended the enlistment of men for three years, with a bounty of $100, for the additional regiments of the regular army; also, that appropriations be made for the construction, equipment, and current expenses of railways and telegraphs for the use of the government; for the furnishing of a more liberal supply of approved arms for the militia, and an increase in the clerical force of his department. The Secretary of the Treasury (Mr. Chase) asked for $240,000,000 for war expenses, and $80,000,000 to meet the ordinary demands for the fiscal year. He proposed to raise the $80,000,000, in addition to the sum of nearly $66,000,000, by levying increased duties on specified articles, and also by certain internal revenues, or by the direct taxation of real and personal property. For war purposes, he proposed a national loan of not less than $100,000,000, to be issued in the form of treasury notes, bearing an annual interest of 7 3-10 per cent., or 1 cent a day on $50, in sums from $50 to $5,000. He proposed to issue bonds or certificates of debt, in the event of the national loan proving insufficient, to an amount not exceeding $100,000,000, to be made redeemable at the pleasure of the government after a period not exceeding thirty years, and bearing interest not exceeding 7 per cent. He also recommended the issue of another class of treasury notes, not to exceed in amount $50,000,000, bearing an interest of 3.65 per cent., and exchangeable, at the will of the holder, for treasury notes. The Secretary of the Navy asked Congress to sanction his acts, and recommended the appointment of an assistant secretary in his department.

Congress acted promptly on the suggestions of the President. It was found at the outset that there were a few members of Congress who were in thorough sympathy with the Secessionists; but while these prolonged the debates, the majority of loyal men was so overwhelming that the disloyal ones could not defeat the will of the people. On the first day of the session Senator Wilson, of Massachusetts, chairman of the military committee of the Upper House, gave notice that he should, the next day, submit six bills having for their object the suppression of the rebellion. These were all adopted afterwards. They were: 1. To ratify and confirm certain acts of the President for the suppression of insurrection and rebellion; 2. To authorize the employment of volunteers to aid in enforcing the laws and protecting public property; 3. To increase the present military establishment of the United States; 4. To provide for the better organization of the military establishment; 5. To promote the efficiency of the army; 6. For the organization of a volunteer militia force, to be called the National Guard of the United States. At an early day the Senate expelled the following ten Senators: James M. Mason and R. M. T. Hunter, of Virginia; Thomas L. Clingman and Thomas Bragg, of North Carolina; James Chestnut, Jr., of South Carolina; A. O. P. Nicholson, of Tennessee; W. K. Sebastian and Charles B. Mitchell, of Arkansas; and John Hemphill and Louis T. Wigfall, of Texas. On July 13 the places of Mason and Hunter were filled by John S. Carlisle and W. J. Willey, appointed by the legislature of "reorganized (West) Virginia." On the same day John B. Clark, of Missouri, was expelled from the House of Representatives. Every measure for the suppression of the rebellion proposed by the President and heads of departments was adopted. On the 19th the venerable J. J. Crittenden, who was then a member of the House of Representatives, offered a joint resolution, "That the present deplorable Civil War has been forced upon the country by the disunionists of the Southern States, now in revolt against the constitutional government and in arms around the capital; that in this national emergency, banishing all feelings of mere passion or resentment, we will recollect only our duty to our country; that this war is not waged, on our part, in any spirit of oppression, nor for any purpose of conquest or subjugation, nor for the purpose of overthrowing or interfering with the rights or established institutions of those States, but to defend and maintain the supremacy of the Constitution, and to preserve the Union, with all the dignity, equality, and rights of the several States, unimpaired; and that as soon as these objects are accomplished the war ought to cease." It was laid over until Monday. On Sunday (July 21) the battle of Bull Run was fought. Notwithstanding the capital was filled with fugitives from the shattered army, and it was believed by many that the seat of government was at the mercy of its enemies, Congress, with sublime faith, debated as calmly as before. By an almost unanimous vote, Mr. Crittenden's resolution was adopted, and a few days afterwards one identical with it passed the Senate by a vote almost as decisive. It was such a solemn refutation of the false charges of the Confederate leaders, that it was a war for subjugation and emancipation of the slaves, that it was not allowed to be published in the Confederacy. On the same day Congress resolved to spare nothing essential for the support of the government, and pledged "to the country and the world the employment of every resource, national and individual, for the suppression, overthrow, and punishment of rebels in arms." They passed a bill providing for the confiscation of property used for insurrectionary purposes, and that the master of a slave who should employ him in any naval or military service against the government of the United States should forfeit all right to his services thereafter. When Congress had finished the business for which it was called, and had made ample provision in men and means for the suppression of the rebellion, it adjourned (Aug. 6), after a session of thirty-three days. The product of its labors consisted in the passage of sixty-one public and seven private bills and five joint resolutions. On the day before its adjournment it requested the President to appoint a general fast-day.

The Sixty-second Congress.—The life of this Congress extends officially from April 4, 1911, to March 3, 1913. The Senate consisted, at the beginning of the first session, of 92 members, divided politically as follows: Republicans, 50; Democrats, 42. The House of Representatives consisted of 391 members, divided politically as follows: Democrats, 228; Republicans, 160; Socialist, 1; vacancies, 2. The ratio of representation in the House, based on the census of 1900, was 194,182; on the census of 1910, 211,877.

The practical work of the Senate was carried on in 1912 by 71 standing committees, and in the House of Representatives by 56, and there were also 10 joint committees and commissions. The most important committees of Congress are finance in the Senate, and ways and means in the House; appropriations in each; foreign relations in the Senate, and foreign affairs in the House; banking and currency in the House; coast defences in the Senate; commerce in the Senate, and interstate and foreign commerce in the House; immigration in both bodies; judiciary in both bodies; military and naval affairs in both bodies; pensions in both bodies; and post-offices and post-roads in both bodies. The Senate has always elected its committees, and in 1911 the House adopted the same method. See FEDERAL GOVERNMENT, etc., and for important acts of Congress, see readily suggestive titles or subjects of bills.

CONGRESS, SESSIONS OF

Cong.	Sess.	From	To
1	1	March 4, 1789	Sept. 29, 1789
	2	Jan. 4, 1790	Aug. 12, 1790
	3	Dec. 6, 1790	March 3, 1791
2	1	Oct. 24, 1791	May 8, 1792
	2	Nov. 5, 1792	March 2, 1793
3	1	Dec. 2, 1793	June 9, 1794
	2	Nov. 3, 1794	March 3, 1795
4	1	Dec. 7, 1795	June 1, 1796
	2	Dec. 5, 1796	March 3, 1797
5	1	May 15, 1797	July 10, 1797
	2	Nov. 18, 1797	July 16, 1798
	3	Dec. 3, 1798	March 3, 1799
6	1	Dec. 2, 1799	May 14, 1800
	2	Nov. 17, 1800	March 3, 1801
7	1	Dec. 7, 1801	May 3, 1802
	2	Dec. 6, 1802	March 3, 1803
8	1	Oct. 17, 1803	March 27, 1804
	2	Nov. 5, 1804	March 3, 1805
9	1	Dec. 2, 1805	April 21, 1806
	2	Dec. 1, 1806	March 3, 1807
10	1	Oct. 16, 1807	April 25, 1808
	2	Nov. 7, 1808	March 3, 1809
11	1	May 22, 1809	June 28, 1809
	2	Nov. 27, 1809	May 1, 1810
	3	Dec. 3, 1810	March 3, 1811
12	1	Nov. 4, 1811	July 6, 1812
	2	Nov. 2, 1812	March 3, 1813
13	1	May 24, 1813	Aug. 2, 1813
	2	Dec. 6, 1813	April 18, 1814
	3	Sept. 19, 1814	March 3, 1815
14	1	Dec. 4, 1815	April 30, 1816
	2	Dec. 2, 1816	March 3, 1817
15	1	Dec. 1, 1817	April 20, 1818
	2	Nov. 16, 1818	March 3, 1819
16	1	Dec. 6, 1819	May 15, 1820
	2	Nov. 18, 1820	March 3, 1821
17	1	Dec. 3, 1821	May 8, 1822
	2	Dec. 2, 1822	March 3, 1823
18	1	Dec. 1, 1823	May 27, 1824
	2	Dec. 6, 1824	March 3, 1825
19	1	Dec. 5, 1825	May 22, 1826
	2	Dec. 4, 1826	March 3, 1827
20	1	Dec. 3, 1827	May 26, 1828
	2	Dec. 1, 1828	March 3, 1829
21	1	Dec. 7, 1829	May 31, 1830
	2	Dec. 6, 1830	March 3, 1831
22	1	Dec. 5, 1831	July 16, 1832
	2	Dec. 3, 1832	March 3, 1833
23	1	Dec. 2, 1833	June 30, 1834
	2	Dec. 1, 1834	March 3, 1835
24	1	Dec. 7, 1835	July 4, 1836
	2	Dec. 5, 1836	March 3, 1837
25	1	Sept. 4, 1837	Oct. 16, 1837
	2	Dec. 4, 1837	July 9, 1838
	3	Dec. 3, 1838	March 3, 1839
26	1	Dec. 2, 1839	July 21, 1840
	2	Dec. 7, 1840	March 3, 1841
27	1	May 31, 1841	Sept. 13, 1841
	2	Dec. 6, 1841	Aug. 31, 1842
	3	Dec. 5, 1842	March 3, 1843
28	1	Dec. 4, 1843	June 17, 1844
	2	Dec. 2, 1844	March 3, 1845
29	1	Dec. 7, 1845	Aug. 10, 1846
	2	Dec. 7, 1846	March 3, 1847
30	1	Dec. 6, 1847	Aug. 14, 1848
	2	Dec. 4, 1848	March 3, 1849
31	1	Dec. 3, 1849	Sept. 30, 1850
	2	Dec. 2, 1850	March 3, 1851
32	1	Dec. 1, 1851	Aug. 31, 1852
	2	Dec. 6, 1852	March 3, 1853
33	1	Dec. 5, 1853	Aug. 7, 1854
	2	Dec. 4, 1854	March 3, 1855
34	1	Dec. 3, 1855	Aug. 18, 1856
	2	Aug. 21, 1856	Aug. 30, 1856
	3	Dec. 1, 1856	March 3, 1857
35	1	Dec. 7, 1857	June 14, 1858
	2	Dec. 6, 1858	March 3, 1859
36	1	Dec. 5, 1859	June 25, 1860
	2	Dec. 3, 1860	March 2, 1861

CONGRESS, SESSIONS OF—*Continued*

Cong.	Sess.	From	To
37	1	July 4, 1861	Aug. 6, 1861
	2	Dec. 2, 1861	July 17, 1862
	3	Dec. 1, 1862	March 3, 1863
38	1	Dec. 7, 1863	July 2, 1864
	2	Dec. 5, 1864	March 3, 1865
39	1	Dec. 4, 1865	July 28, 1866
	2	Dec. 3, 1866	March 2, 1867
40	1	March 4, 1867	March 30, 1867
		July 1, 1867	July 20, 1867
		Nov. 21, 1867	Dec. 2, 1867
	2	Dec. 2, 1867	July 27, 1868
		Sept. 21, 1868	
		Nov. 1, 1868	Nov. 10, 1868
	3	Dec. 7, 1868	March 3, 1869
41	1	March 4, 1869	April 22, 1869
	2	Dec. 6, 1869	July 15, 1870
	3	Dec. 5, 1870	March 3, 1871
42	1	March 4, 1871	May 27, 1871
	2	Dec. 4, 1871	June 10, 1872
	3	Dec. 2, 1872	March 3, 1873
43	1	Dec. 1, 1873	June 23, 1874
	2	Dec. 7, 1874	March 3, 1875
44	1	Dec. 6, 1875	Aug. 15, 1876
	2	Dec. 4, 1876	March 3, 1877
45	1	Oct. 15, 1877	Dec. 3, 1877
	2	Dec. 3, 1877	June 20, 1878
	3	Dec. 2, 1878	March 3, 1879
46	1	March 18, 1879	July 1, 1879
	2	Dec. 1, 1879	June 16, 1880
	3	Dec. 6, 1880	March 3, 1881
47	1	Dec. 5, 1881	Aug. 8, 1882
	2	Dec. 4, 1882	March 3, 1883
48	1	Dec. 3, 1883	July 7, 1884
	2	Dec. 1, 1884	March 3, 1885
49	1	Dec. 7, 1885	Aug. 5, 1886
	2	Dec. 6, 1886	March 3, 1887
50	1	Dec. 5, 1887	Oct. 20, 1888
	2	Dec. 3, 1888	March 2, 1889
51	1	Dec. 2, 1889	Oct. 1, 1890
	2	Dec. 1, 1890	March 3, 1891
52	1	Dec. 7, 1891	Aug. 5, 1892
	2	Dec. 5, 1892	March 3, 1893
53	1	Aug. 7, 1893	Nov. 3, 1893
	2	Dec. 4, 1893	Aug. 28, 1894
	3	Dec. 3, 1894	March 2, 1895
54	1	Dec. 2, 1895	June 11, 1896
	2	Dec. 7, 1896	March 3, 1897
55	1	March 15, 1897	July 24, 1897
	2	Dec. 6, 1897	July 8, 1898
	3	Dec. 5, 1898	March 3, 1899
56	1	Dec. 4, 1899	June 7, 1900
	2	Dec. 3, 1900	March 2, 1901
57	1	Dec. 2, 1901	July 1, 1902
	2	Dec. 1, 1902	March 3, 1903
58	1	Nov. 9, 1903	Dec. 7, 1903
	2	Dec. 7, 1903	April 28, 1904
	3	Dec. 5, 1904	March 3, 1905
59	1	Dec. 4, 1905	June 30, 1906
	2	Dec. 3, 1906	March 2, 1907
60	1	Dec. 2, 1907	May 30, 1908
	2	Dec. 7, 1908	March 3, 1909
61	1	March 15, 1909	Aug. 5, 1909
	2	Dec. 6, 1909	June 25, 1910
	3	Dec. 5, 1910	March 3, 1911
62	1	April 4, 1911	Aug. 22, 1911
	2	Dec. 4, 1911	....

Special Sessions of the Senate.—The Senate has been convened in special session for various purposes as follows: 1791, March 4; 1793, March 4; 1795, June 8-26; 1797, March 4; 1798, July 17-19; 1801, March 4-5; 1809, March 4-7; 1825, March 4-9; 1829, March 4-17; 1837, March 4-10; 1841, March 4-15; 1845, March 4-20; 1849, March 5-23; 1851, March 4-13; 1853, March 4–April 11; 1857, March 4-14; 1858, June 15-16; 1859, March 4-10; 1860, June 26-28; 1861, March 4-28; 1863, March 4-14; 1865, March 4-11; 1867, April 1-20; 1869, April 12-22; 1871, May 10-27; 1873, March 4-26; 1875, Mrach 5-24; 1877, March 5-17; 1881, March 4–May 20 and Oct. 10-29; 1885, March 4–April 2; 1889, March 4–April 2; 1893, March 4–April 14; 1897, March 4-10; 1901, March 4-9; 1903, March 5-19; 1905, March 4-18; 1909, March 4-6.

Senate as Impeachment Court.—The Senate has sat as a Court of Impeachment in the cases of the following accused officials, with the result stated and for the periods named: William Blount, a Senator of the United States from Tennessee; charges dismissed for want of jurisdiction, he having previously resigned; Dec. 17, 1798–Jan. 14, 1799. John Pickering, judge of the United States District Court for the District of New Hampshire; removed from office; March 3, 1803–March 12, 1804. Samuel Chase, associate justice, United States Supreme Court; acquitted; Nov. 30, 1804–March 1, 1805. James H. Peck, judge of the United States District Court for the District of Missouri; acquitted April 26, 1830–Jan. 31, 1831. West H. Humphreys, judge of the United States District Court for the Middle, Eastern, and Western Districts of Tennessee; removed from office; May 7–June 26, 1862. Andrew Johnson, President of the United States; acquitted; Feb. 25–May 26, 1868. William W. Belknap, Secretary of War; acquitted; March 3–Aug. 1, 1876. Charles Swayne, judge of the United States District Court for the Northern District of Florida; acquitted; Dec. 14, 1904–Feb. 27, 1905.

Note.—All records differ. The *Congressional Directories* have been used for these tables.

Congressional Apportionment. See APPORTIONMENT, CONGRESSIONAL.

Congressional District. See DISTRICT, CONGRESSIONAL.

Congressman-at-Large, in the United States, a member elected to the House of Representatives by the voters of the entire State instead of by districts. An act of Congress, 1872, provided that in each

State entitled under the apportionment to more than one representative the number to which such State might be entitled in the Forty-third and each subsequent Congress should be elected by districts composed of contiguous territory and containing as nearly as possible an equal number of inhabitants, etc.; but on the election of members to the Forty-third Congress in any State to which an increased number of representatives was given by reapportionment, the additional representative or representatives might be elected by the State at large. In the Sixty-second Congress (1911-13) there were representatives-at-large from Colorado, Connecticut, Delaware, Montana, Nevada, North Dakota, South Dakota, and Utah.

Conkling, ALFRED RONALD, lawyer; born in New York City, Sept 28, 1850; graduated at Yale, 1870; admitted to the bar, 1879. Member of New York legislature, 1892–96. Author of *Life of Roscoe Conkling; City Government in the United States; Handbook for Voters*, etc.

Conkling, ALFRED, jurist; born in Ammagansett, N. Y., Oct. 12, 1789; graduated at Union College, 1810; admitted to the bar, 1812; member of Congress, 1821–23; judge of the United States District Court, 1825–52; minister to Mexico, 1852–53. He was the father of Roscoe Conkling. He wrote *The Organization and Jurisdiction of the United States Courts; The Powers of the Executive Department of the United States; Young Citizen's Manual*, etc.

Conkling, JENNIE MARIA (DRINKWATER), author; born in Portland, Me., April 14, 1841; while in her teens won fame with her stories for children; in 1880 married Rev. Nathaniel Conkling; founded the "Shut-in Society," an organization of invalids for correspondence. She died in New Vernon, N. J., April 28, 1900.

Conkling, ROSCOE, statesman; born in Albany, N. Y., Oct. 30, 1829; received an academic education; studied law with his father, a judge in the United States District Court, and former minister to Mexico; admitted to the bar in 1850 in Utica; elected mayor in 1858, and also to Congress as a Republican; re-elected to Congress in 1860, 1864, and 1866; and in January, 1867, was chosen United States Senator and held his seat till 1881. During his service in the Senate he was active in the promotion of the reconstruction measures and in opposition to President Johnson's policy; was influential in securing the passage of the CIVIL RIGHTS BILL (*q. v.*) over President Johnson's veto; and was notably conspicuous in his support of President Grant.

ROSCOE CONKLING.

Senator Conkling was a member of the judiciary committee during the entire course of his senatorial career. He was a strong advocate of a third term for President Grant in 1880, and after the election of James A. Garfield, when an influential federal appointment was made in New York City, Senator Conkling and his associate, Senator Platt, claiming that they should have been consulted concerning such an appointment in their State, resigned. At the ensuing session of the State legislature, the two ex-Senators failed to secure re-election, after an extremely exciting canvass, and Mr. Conkling retired to the practice of law in New York City. He was appointed counsel to the New York Senate Committee to investigate the charges of frauds and bribery in the grant of the Broadway (N. Y. City) railroad franchise by the board of aldermen in 1884. His argument in this case led to the repeal of the franchise. He was offered by President Arthur a seat on the bench of the United

States Supreme Court in 1882, but declined. He died in New York City, April 18, 1888.

Renominating Grant.—The following is Senator Conkling's speech before the National Republican Convention, in Chicago, on June 6, 1880, nominating General Grant for a third Presidential term:

> "When asked what State he hails from,
> Our sole reply shall be,
> He came from Appomattox
> And its famous apple-tree."

In obedience to instruction I should never dare to disregard—expressing, also, my own firm convictions—I rise to propose a nomination with which the country and the Republican party can gladly win. The election before us is to be the Austerlitz of American politics. It will decide, for many years, whether the country shall be Republican or Cossack. The supreme need of the hour is not a candidate who can carry Michigan. All Republican candidates can do that. The need is not of a candidate who is popular in the Territories, because they have no vote. The need is of a candidate who can carry doubtful States. Not the doubtful States of the North alone, but doubtful States of the South, which we have heard, if I understand it aright, ought to take little or no part here, because the South has nothing to give, but everything to receive. No, gentlemen, the need that presses upon the conscience of this convention is a candidate who can carry doubtful States, both North and South. And believing that he, more surely than any other man, can carry New York against any opponent, and can carry not only the North, but several States of the South, New York is for Ulysses S. Grant. Never defeated in peace or in war, his name is the most illustrious borne by living man.

His services attest his greatness, and the country—nay, the world—knows them by heart. His fame was earned not alone in things written and said, but by the arduous greatness of things done. And perils and emergencies will search in vain in the future, as they have searched in vain in the past, for any other on whom the nation leans with such confidence and trust. Never having had a policy to enforce against the will of the people, he never betrayed a cause or a friend, and the people will never desert or betray him. Standing on the highest eminence of human distinction, modest, firm, simple, and self-poised, having filled all lands with his renown, he has seen not only the high-born and the titled, but the poor and the lowly in the uttermost ends of the earth, rise and uncover before him. He has studied the needs and the defects of many systems of government, and he has returned a better American than ever, with a wealth of knowledge and experience added to the hard common-sense which shone so conspicuously in all the fierce light that beat upon him during sixteen years, the most trying, the most portentous, the most perilous in the nation's history.

Vilified and reviled, ruthlessly aspersed by unnumbered presses, not in other lands, but in his own, assaults upon him have seasoned and strengthened his hold on the public heart. Calumny's ammunition has all been exploded; the powder has all been burned once; its force is spent; and the name of Grant will glitter a bright and imperishable star in the diadem of the republic when those who have tried to tarnish that name have mouldered in forgotten graves, and when their memories and their epitaphs have vanished utterly.

Never elated by success, never depressed by adversity, he has ever, in peace as in war, shown the genius of common-sense. The terms he prescribed for Lee's surrender foreshadowed the wisest prophecies and principles of true reconstruction. Victor in the greatest war of modern times, he quickly signalized his aversion to war and his love of peace by an arbitration of internal disputes which stands as the wisest, the most majestic example of its kind in the world's diplomacy. When inflation, at the height of its popularity and frenzy, had swept both Houses of Congress, it was the veto of Grant, which, single and alone, overthrew expansion and cleared the way for specie resumption. To him, immeasurably more than to any other man, is due the fact that every paper dollar is at last as good as gold.

With him as our leader we shall have no defensive campaign. No! We shall have nothing to explain away. We shall have no apologies to make. The shafts and the arrows have all been aimed at him, and they lie broken and harmless at his feet.

Life, liberty, and property will find a safeguard in him. When he said of the colored men in Florida, "Wherever I am, they may come also"—when he so said, he meant that, had he the power, the poor dwellers in the cabins of the South should no longer be driven in terror from the homes of their childhood and the graves of their murdered dead. When he refused to see Dennis Kearney in California, he meant that communism, lawlessness, and disorder, although it might stalk high-headed and dictate law to a whole city, would always find a foe in him. He meant that, popular or unpopular, he would hew to the line of right, let the chips fly where they may.

His integrity, his common-sense, his courage, his unequalled experience, are the qualities offered to his country. The only argument, the only one that the wit of man or the stress of politics has devised, is one which would dumfounder Solomon, because he thought there was nothing new under the sun. Having tried Grant twice and found him faithful, we are told that we must not, even after an interval of years, trust him again. My countrymen! my countrymen! what stultification does not such a fallacy involve! The American people exclude Jefferson Davis from public trust. Why? Why? Because he was the archtraitor and would-be destroyer; and now the same people are asked to ostracize Grant, and not to trust him. Why? Why? I repeat: because he was the archpreserver of his country, and because, not only in war, but twice as Civil Magistrate, he gave his highest, noblest efforts to the republic. Is this an electioneering juggle, or is it hypocrisy's masquerade? There is no field of human activity, responsibility, or reason in which rational beings object to an agent because he has been weighed in the balance and not found wanting. There is, I say, no department of human reason in which sane men reject an agent because he has had experience, making him exceptionally competent and fit. From the man who shoes your horse to the lawyer who tries your case, the officer who manages your railway or your mill, the doctor into whose hands you give your life, or the minister who seeks to save your soul, what man do you reject because by his works you have known him and found him faithful and fit? What makes the Presidential office an exception to all things else in the common-sense to be applied to selecting its incumbent? Who dares—who dares to put fetters on that free choice and judgment which is the birthright of the American people? Can it be said that Grant has used official power and place to perpetuate his term? He has no place, and official power has not been used for him. Without patronage and without emissaries, without committees, without bureaus, without telegraph wires running from his house to this convention, or running from his house anywhere else, this man is the candidate whose friends have never threatened to bolt unless this convention did as they said. He is a Republican who never wavers. He and his friends stand by the creed and the candidates of the Republican party. They hold the rightful rule of the majority as the very essence of their faith, and they mean to uphold that faith against not only the common enemy, but against the charlatans, jayhawkers, tramps, and guerillas —the men who deploy between the lines, and forage now on one side and then on the other. This convention is master of a supreme opportunity. It can name the next President. It can make sure of his election. It can make sure not only of his election, but of his certain and peaceful inauguration. More than all, it can break that power which dominates and mildews the South. It can overthrow an organization whose very existence is a standing protest against progress.

The purpose of the Democratic party is spoils. Its very hope of existence is a solid South. Its success is a menace to order and prosperity. I say this convention can overthrow that power. It can dissolve and emancipate a solid South. It can speed the nation in a career of grandeur eclipsing all past achievements.

Gentlemen, we have only to listen above the din and look beyond the dust of an hour to behold the Republican party advancing with its ensigns resplendent with illustrious achievements, marching to certain and lasting victory with its greatest marshal at its head.

Connecticut (name derived from the Indian *quonoktacut,* meaning "land of the long tidal river," or "the long river"), a State in the New England Division of the North American Union; one of the original thirteen; bounded on the n. by Massachusetts, e. by Rhode Island, s. by Long Island Sound, and w. by New York; area, 4,965 square miles, of which 145 are water surface; extreme breadth e. to w., 90 miles; extreme length n. to s., 75 miles; number of counties, 8; capital, Hartford; popular name, "The land of steady habits"; State flower, the mountain laurel; State motto, "*Qui translulit, sustinet*" ("He who transplanted, still sustains"); ratified the federal Constitution Jan. 9, 1788; population (1910), 1,114,756.

General Statistics.—Connecticut is noted for the diversity and value of its manufactures, its tobacco industry, and its vast life and fire insurance interests. The manufacturing industries have over 4,250 factory-system establishments, employing a capital of $517,547,000 and 210,790 wage-earners, paying $135,756,000 for salaries and wages and $257,259,000 for materials, and having a combined output valued at $490,272,000, the most important being cotton, woollen, silk, brass, and copper goods, hardware, foundry, and machine-shop products, felt hats, rubber and elastic goods, musical instruments, cutlery and edge tools, paper and wood-pulp, and clocks. There are over 26,400 farms, containing 984,000 improved acres, and representing in land, buildings, and implements nearly $143,500,000. The leading crops, with values, are: Hay and forage, $7,255,000; tobacco, $4,416,000; potatoes, $1,882,000; and corn, $1,694,000. Livestock on farms have a value of over $13,113,000. Mineral productions total over $3,565,000, lime leading.

Business interests are promoted by seventy-nine national banks, with capital $19,914,200 and resources $114,153,000, and exchanges at the clearing-houses at Hartford and New Haven have aggregated over $354,400,000 in a single year. Six life-insurance companies have combined assets exceeding $262,000,000; seven fire-insurance companies have capital $11,000,000, and surplus $18,000,000; sixteen mutual fire-insurance companies have aggregate surplus of over $2,250,000; and five miscellaneous companies, assets and surplus of over $6,075,000. Bridgeport, Hartford, New Haven, New London, and Stonington are commercial ports of delivery, and together have imported merchandise to the value of over $4,300,000 in a year.

Religious interests are represented by 1,384 organizations, having 1,414 church edifices, 502,560 communicants or members, 179,673 Sunday-school scholars, and church property valued at $29,196,000, the strongest denominations being the Roman Catholic, Congregational, Protestant Episcopal, Methodist Episcopal, Baptist, and Lutheran. The Roman Catholic and Protestant Episcopal churches have each a bishop in Hartford. The public-school age is 4–16; enrollment, 187,876; average daily attendance, 144,963; value of public-school property, $17,418,000; total revenue, $5,048,617; total expenditure, $5,023,152. For the higher education of men and women there are YALE UNIVERSITY (*q. v.*), Trinity College, WESLEYAN UNIVERSITY (*q. v.*), and the Connecticut Agricultural College; for professional education, divinity, law, and medical schools of Yale University, Hartford School of Religious Pedagogy (Cong.), Hartford Theological Seminary (Cong.), and Berkeley Divinity School (P. E.); for manual training, State schools at Danbury, New Britain, New Haven, and Willimantic; for manual and industrial training-schools at Bridgeport, Hartford, New London, Stamford, and Waterbury; State industrial schools at Meriden (boys), and Middletown (girls); and for the defective classes, Connecticut Institute for the Blind and American School for the Deaf, both of Hartford; Oral School for the Deaf, at Mystic; and Connecticut School for Imbeciles, at Lakeville.

Government.—Under the constitution adopted Oct. 12, 1818, and many times amended, as in force in 1911, the executive authority is vested in a governor (annual salary, $4,000), lieutenant-governor, secretary of state, treasurer, auditors, comptroller, attorney-general, commissioner of agriculture, superintendent of education, and commissioner of insurance—official term, two years. The General Assembly consists of a Senate of thirty-five members and a House of Representatives of 255 members; terms of each, two years; salary of each, $300 per annum; sessions, biennial; limit, none. The chief judicial authority is the Supreme Court, comprising a chief-justice and four associate justices. A constitutional amendment, practically the old constitution recast so as to incorporate in the body of the document the numerous amendments adopted from time to time, and increasing the compensation of members of the General Assembly from $300 to $500 per annum, was rejected by popular vote in 1907. The State election in 1910, resulting in the choice of the Democratic candidate for governor and the Republican candidates for all other State offices, following an unusually vigorous campaign, and one heightened in warmth by a personal controversy between Judge Simeon E. Baldwin, the Democratic nominee for governor, and former President Roosevelt. Another noteworthy feature of the campaign was the marked similarity in the platform declarations of the two leading parties—control of public utilities, abolition of the $5,000 death limit, employers' liability act, and a number of other questions of local concern. The Australian ballot was used for the first time at this general election.

GOVERNORS OF THE CONNECTICUT COLONY.

Name.	Date.
John Haynes	1639 to 1640
Edward Hopkins	1640 " 1641
John Haynes	1641 " 1642
George Wyllys	1642 " 1643
John Haynes / Edward Hopkins } alternately from	1643 " 1655
Thomas Welles	1655 " 1656
John Webster	1656 " 1657
John Winthrop	1657 " 1658
Thomas Welles	1658 " 1659
John Winthrop	1659 " 1665

Until this time no person could be elected to a second term immediately following the first.

GOVERNORS OF THE NEW HAVEN COLONY.

Name.	Date.
Theophilus Eaton	1639 to 1657
Francis Newman	1658 " 1660
William Leete	1661 " 1665

GOVERNORS OF CONNECTICUT.

Name.	Date.
John Winthrop	1665 to 1676
William Leete	1676 " 1683
Robert Treat	1683 " 1687
Edmund Andros	1687 " 1689
Robert Treat	1689 " 1698
Fitz John Winthrop	1698 " 1707
Gurdon Saltonstall	1707 " 1724
Joseph Talcott	1724 " 1741
Jonathan Law	1741 " 1750
Roger Wolcott	1750 " 1754
Thomas Fitch	1754 " 1766
William Pitkin	1766 " 1769
Jonathan Trumbull	1769 " 1784
Mathew Griswold	1784 " 1786
Samuel Huntington	1786 " 1796
Oliver Wolcott	1796 " 1798
Jonathan Trumbull	1798 " 1809
John Treadwell	1809 " 1811
Roger Griswold	1811 " 1813
John Cotton Smith	1813 " 1817
Oliver Wolcott	1817 " 1827
Gideon Tomlinson	1827 " 1831
John S. Peters	1831 " 1833
H. W. Edwards	1833 " 1834
Samuel A. Foote	1834 " 1835
H. W. Edwards	1835 " 1838
W. W. Ellsworth	1838 " 1842
C. F. Cleveland	1842 " 1844
Roger S. Baldwin	1844 " 1846
Clark Bissell	1846 " 1849
Joseph Trumbull	1849 " 1850
Thomas H. Seymour	1850 " 1853
Charles H. Pond	1853 " 1854
Henry Dutton	1854 " 1855
W. T. Minor	1855 " 1857
A. H. Holley	1857 " 1858
William A. Buckingham	1858 " 1866
Joseph R. Hawley	1866 " 1867
James E. English	1867 " 1869
Marshall Jewell	1869 " 1870
James E. English	1870 " 1871
Marshall Jewell	1871 " 1873
Charles R. Ingersoll	1873 " 1876
R. D. Hubbard	1876 " 1879
Charles B. Andrews	1879 " 1881
H. B. Bigelow	1881 " 1883
Thomas M. Waller	1883 " 1885
Henry B. Harrison	1885 " 1887
Phineas C. Lounsbury	1887 " 1889
Morgan G. Bulkeley	1889 " 1893
Luzon B. Morris	1893 " 1895
O. Vincent Coffin	1895 " 1897
Lorrin A. Cooke	1897 " 1899
George E. Lounsbury	1899 " 1901
George P. McLean	1901 " 1903
Abiram Chamberlain	1903 " 1905
Henry Roberts	1905 " 1907
Rollin S. Woodruff	1907 " 1909
Frank B. Weeks	1909 " 1911
Simeon E. Baldwin	1911 " 1913

Connecticut ranked eighth in population among the States and Territories under the censuses of 1790 and 1800; ninth in 1810; fourteenth in 1820; sixteenth in 1830; twentieth in 1840; twenty-first in 1850; twenty-fourth in 1860; twenty-fifth in 1870; twenty-eighth in 1880; twenty-ninth in 1890 and 1900; and thirty-second in 1910.

CONNECTICUT

UNITED STATES SENATORS.

Name.	No. of Congress.	Date.
Oliver Ellsworth	1st to 4th	1789 to 1797
William S. Johnson	1st	1789 " 1791
Roger Sherman	2d	1791 " 1793
Stephen Nix Mitchell	3d	1793 " 1795
James Hillhouse	4th to 11th	1796 " 1811
Jonathan Trumbull	4th	1795 " 1796
Uriah Tracy	4th to 9th	1796 " 1807
Chauncey Goodrich	10th " 12th	1807 " 1813
Samuel W. Dana	11th " 16th	1810 " 1821
David Daggett	13th " 15th	1813 " 1819
James Lanman	16th " 18th	1819 " 1825
Elijah Boardman	17th	1821 " 1823
Henry W. Edwards	18th to 19th	1823 " 1827
Calvin Willey	19th " 21st	1825 " 1831
Samuel A. Foote	20th " 22d	1827 " 1833
Gideon Tomlinson	22d " 24th	1831 " 1837
Nathan Smith	23d	1833 " 1835
John M. Niles	24th to 25th	1835 " 1839
Perry Smith	25th " 27th	1837 " 1843
Thaddeus Betts	26th	1839 " 1840
Jabez W. Huntington	26th to 29th	1840 " 1847
John M. Niles	28th " 30th	1843 " 1849
Roger S. Baldwin	30th " 31st	1847 " 1851
Truman Smith	31st " 33d	1849 " 1854
Isaac Toucey	32d " 34th	1852 " 1857
Francis Gillett	33d	1854 " 1855
Lafayette Foster	34th to 39th	1855 " 1867
James Dixon	35th " 40th	1857 " 1869
Orris S. Ferry	40th " 44th	1867 " 1875
Wm. A. Buckingham	41st " 43d	1869 " 1875
William W. Eaton	43d " 46th	1875 " 1881
James E. English	44th	1875 " 1877
William H. Barnum	44th to 45th	1875 " 1879
Orville H. Platt	46th " 59th	1879 " 1905
Joseph R. Hawley	47th " 59th	1881 " 1905
Morgan G. Bulkeley	59th " 62d	1905 " 1911
Frank B. Brandegee	59th " ——	1905 " ——
George P. McLean	62d " ——	1911 " ——

In the apportionment of representation in Congress, Connecticut was given five members under the federal Constitution and under the censuses of 1900 and 1910; seven under the censuses of 1790, 1800, and 1810; six under 1820 and 1830; and four under 1840, 1850, 1860, 1870, 1880, and 1890.

History, Early Period.—It is uncertain whether Connecticut was visited first by the English or by the Dutch. Both claimed to be the first explorers, and their rival claims to possession afterwards gave great annoyance to the settlers. The Dutch claimed the territory by reason of the reported discovery of the mouth of the Connecticut River by Adrian Block about 1613, and the earlier discoveries of Hendrik Hudson, though they made considerable purchases from the Indians; and the English claimed it by virtue of a patent granted by Robert, Earl of Warwick, to Lords Say and Seal, Lord Brook, Sir Richard Saltonstall, and others associated under the name of the "Plymouth Company" in 1631. The "Plymouth Council for the planting, ruling, and governing of New England, in America," was incorporated by King James I., 1620, and from it was derived the above patent and the numerous grants under which the early settlements were made. The Dutch further claimed that they had explored the river and sea-coast as early as 1615, and it is known that they established a colony at Hartford, Connecticut, in 1633, but soon afterwards sold it to the English. On the other hand, it is known that a sachem living on the river visited Plymouth and Boston, 1631, and solicited the governors of those settlements to send a colony to occupy the country. A small party went from Plymouth to the Connecticut River and selected a convenient spot for a trading-station in the present Windsor, near the mouth of the Farmington River, and Gov. Winslow and Mr. Bradford, of the Plymouth colony, proposed to Gov. Winthrop, of Massachusetts, and his council that they should join them in establishing such a house there to secure the country against the designs of the Dutch, who were reported to be about carrying a similar project into execution. In 1633 the Connecticut River was visited by several vessels from Plymouth, and on reaching the site of Hartford it was found that the Dutch had erected a small fort there. The party sailed past it, and on reaching Windsor built the trading-house and surrounded it with a palisade, the ground having been purchased by the Plymouth people from the Indians.

First Permanent Settlement.—The first systematic plan formed for the settlement of Connecticut was proposed to the general court of Massachusetts in 1634. Strenuous opposition was made to the removal of so many families as were interested in the project, and while awaiting the decision of the court five impatient men started from Watertown and proceeded to a place about four miles below the present Hartford, where they erected huts (1635) and spent the winter. The court consented to the removal of the petitioners in May, 1636, on condition that they would remain under the jurisdiction of

Massachusetts. The party was composed mainly of married men with their families, and included several religious congregations with their ministers, Messrs. Warham, Thomas Hooker, and Samuel Stone—the last two of whom had been ordained Oct. 11, 1633—church officers, and members. The five prospectors settled Hartford, 1635, and the colonists took possession in the following year. The first court assembled there April 26, 1636, and Messrs. Hooker and Stone had pastoral charge of the first church, 1636–47. The settlers of Windsor were from Dorchester, those of Hartford from Newtown (now Cambridge), Mass. Wethersfield was settled (1636) by people from Watertown, Mass.; the settlement of Springfield, Mass., was begun the same year, and buildings and fortifications were erected at Saybrook.

Second Permanent Settlement.—The second large settlement was made at New Haven, 1638, by a company which had left England in a body to form a settlement by themselves in the New World. They were under the spiritual leadership of the Rev. Mr. Davenport, and included a number of wealthy men. They spent their first Sabbath there April 18, and at the close of a subsequent day of fasting and prayer formed the "Plantation Covenant," in which they bound themselves "That, as in matters that concern the gathering and ordering of a church, so also in all public offices which concern civil order, as choice of magistrates and officers, making and repealing laws, dividing allotments of inheritance, and all things of like nature, they would, all of them, be ordered by the rules which the Scriptures held forth to them." The three settlements bore the names of the places whence the settlers came, but not long afterwards were changed by the court to their present names.

Constitution of 1639.—The first constitution of Connecticut was formed at Hartford at an assembly of the free planters of the towns, Jan. 14, 1639. The preamble stated that they formed one public State or commonwealth for the establishment of order and government, and that they confederated for themselves and their successors to maintain the liberty and purity of the gospel and the discipline of the churches according to its institutions. This document is noted for being the first example in history of a written constitution organizing a government and defining its powers; it formed the basis of the charter of 1662, and that was considered so amply wise and sufficient in all its provisions that it was allowed to continue unaltered as the constitution of the State till 1818, when the present one was adopted. The early constitution provided for two general courts or assemblies annually, declared all to be freemen who had been received as members of the towns and taken oath to the commonwealth, and required that the governor should be a member of a regular church. The first assembly under the constitution met at Hartford in May, 1639, and thence till 1701 the sessions were held in that town; after that date one session was held in Hartford and the second in New Haven till 1874, when the former city became the sole capital. It is worthy of note that the first law passed under the constitution was the "Bill of Rights," which ordained that unless by virtue of an express law of the colony sufficiently published, or in defect of such law, by some plain rule of God's Word, in which the whole court shall concur, no man shall lose his life or good name, be arrested, restrained, banished, dismembered, or in any way punished, deprived of wife, children, or property under color of authority." The colony of New Haven formed a constitution soon afterwards, but it was not adopted till the following year.

Under English Charter.—On the restoration of monarchy in England the Connecticut colonists had fears regarding their political future, for they had been stanch republicans during the interregnum. The General Assembly therefore resolved to make a formal acknowledgment of their allegiance to the King and ask him for a charter. A petition to that effect was signed in May, 1661, and Gov. Winthrop bore it to the monarch. He was at first coolly received, but by the gift to the King of a precious memento of the sovereign's dead father the heart of Charles was touched, and, turning to Lord Clarendon, who was present, he said: "Do you advise me to grant a charter to this good man and his people?" "I do, sire," answered Clarendon. "It shall be done," said Charles, and Winthrop was dismissed with a hearty shake of his hand and a blessing from the royal lips. A charter was issued May 1, 1662 (N. S.). It confirmed the popular constitution, and contained more liberal provisions than any that had yet been issued by royal hands. It defined the boundaries so as to include the New Haven colony and a part of Rhode Island on the east, and westward to the Pacific Ocean. The New Haven colony reluctantly gave its consent to the union in 1665, but Rhode Island refused. A dispute concerning the boundary-line between Connecticut and Rhode Island lasted more than sixty years.

The charter, engrossed on parchment and decorated with a finely executed miniature of Charles II. (done in India-ink by Samuel Cooper, it is supposed, who was an eminent London miniature painter of the time), was brought across the sea in a handsome mahogany box, in which it is still preserved in the State Department of Connecticut. It was of so general a character and conferred such large powers that when Connecticut became an independent State it was considered a good fundamental law for the commonwealth, and was not changed until 1818. It provided for the election of the governor of the colony and the magistrates by the people, substantially as under the previous constitution; allowed the free transportation of colonists and merchandise from England to the colony; guaranteed to the colonists the rights of English citizens; provided for the making of laws and the organization of courts by the General Assembly, and the appointment of all necessary officers for the public good; for the organization of a military force, and for the public defence.

Saving the Charter.—Determined to hold absolute rule over New England, King James II. made Andros a sort of viceroy, with instructions to take away the colonial charters. For the purpose of seizing that of Connecticut, whose General Assembly had refused to surrender it, Andros arrived at Hartford, where the Assembly was in session in their meeting-house, Oct. 31, 1687 (O. S.). He was received by the Assembly with the courtesy due to his rank when he appeared before them, with armed men at his back, and demanded the charter to be put into his hands. It was then near sunset. A debate upon some unimportant subject was continued until after the candles were lighted. Then the long box containing the charter was brought in and placed upon the table. A preconcerted plan to save it was now put into operation. Just as the usurper was about to grasp the box with the charter the candles were snuffed out. When they were relighted the charter was not there, and the members were seated in proper order. The charter had been carried out into the darkness by Captain Wadsworth and deposited in the trunk of a hollow oak-tree on the outskirts of the village (see CHARTER OAK). Andros was compelled to content himself with dissolving the Assembly, and writing in a bold hand "Finis" in the journal of that body. When the Revolution of 1688 swept the Stuarts from the English throne the charter was brought from its hiding-place, and under it the colonists of

STATE SEAL OF CONNECTICUT.

Connecticut flourished for 129 years afterwards.

Under the charter given by Charles II., in 1662, Connecticut, like Rhode Island, assumed independence in 1776, and did not frame a new constitution of government. Under that charter it was governed until 1818. In 1814 Hartford, Conn., became the theatre of a famous convention which attracted much anxious attention for a while (see HARTFORD CONVENTION). In 1818 a convention assembled at Hartford and framed a constitution, which was adopted by the people at an election on Oct. 5.

War Periods.—In the French, Indian, Revolutionary, 1812, Civil, and Spanish-American wars the State and her citizens rendered their full share of patriotic work. For a narrative of the State's part in early Indian warfare see PEQUOD WAR. In the Revolutionary struggle Col. Samuel H. Parsons and Benedict Arnold planned at Hartford the capture of Ticonderoga; the General Assembly voted $500,000 to equip eight regiments; ex-Governor Tryon destroyed Danbury, plundered New Haven, and burned Fairfield, Green's Farm, and Norwalk; Benedict Arnold plundered and burned New London; and Fort Griswold was the scene of the massacre of Colonel Ledyard and 73 of his garrison of 150 men after surrendering. During this war this little State furnished 31,959 troops, only Massachusetts having a larger record. In 1812 the people of the State opposed the war, and during its progress New London was blockaded by the British for twenty months and Stonington was bombarded.

During the Civil War the State furnished to the National army 54,882 soldiers, of whom 1,094 men and 97 officers were killed in action, 666 men and 48 officers died from wounds, and 3,246 men and 63 officers from disease; 389 men and 21 officers "missing."

Later Events.—The General Assembly ratified the Fourteenth Amendment to the federal Constitution June 30, 1866, and the Fifteenth, March 16, 1869; Hartford was made the sole and permanent capital Oct. 7, 1873; the new capitol was first occupied March 26, 1878; boundary dispute with New York, begun in 1856, settled 1880; amendment to constitution changed legislative sessions from annual to biennial, ratified Oct. 6, 1884; deadlock in legislature on the governorship settled in favor of Governor Bulkeley (Republican) by the Superior Court, June 24, 1891; both claimants to governorship take case to the Supreme Court, which decides in favor of Bulkeley, Jan. 5, 1892; bicentennial of Yale College celebrated Oct. 20–23, 1901; fire at Waterbury does $4,000,000 damage Feb. 2, 1902; legislature votes $4,500,000 for good roads and makes toll bridges free at the expense of the State, and 97 towns out of 168 voted "no license," 1907; notable stone bridge costing $3,000,000, and connecting Hartford and East Hartford, dedicated with three days' celebration Oct. 6–9, 1908; and steel bridge costing upwards of $500,000, connecting Old Saybrook and Lyme, and having more than State-wide interest as providing direct trolley and auto transit between New York and Boston, dedicated Aug. 24, 1911. See also MASSACHUSETTS; PENNSYLVANIA; PENNYMITE AND YANKEE WAR; PLYMOUTH COMPANY; SUSQUEHANNA SETTLERS; WESTERN RESERVE, THE.

The Fundamental Orders of Connecticut.—*Jan. 14, 1638 (O. S.). The first constitution of Connecticut—the first written constitution, in the modern sense of the term, as a permanent limitation on governmental power, known in history, and certainly the first American constitution of government to embody the democratic idea—was adopted by a general assembly, or popular convention, of the planters of the three towns, held at Hartford, Jan. 14, 1638. The common opinion is that democracy came into the American system through the compact made in the cabin of the Mayflower, though that instrument was based on no political principle whatever, and began with a formal acknowledgment of the King as the source of all authority. It was the power of the crown "by virtue" of which "equal laws" were to be enacted, and the "covenant" was merely a make-shift to meet a temporary emergency; it had not a particle of political significance, nor was democracy an impelling force in it. It must be admitted that the Plymouth system was accidentally democratic, but it was from the absence of any great need

* Until 1752, the legal year in England and America began March 25 (Lady Day), not January 1. All the days between January 1 and March 25 of the year which we now call 1639 were therefore then a part of the year 1638; so that the date of the constitution is given by its own terms as 1638, instead of 1639.

for government, or for care to preserve homogeneity in religion, not from political purpose, as in Connecticut. The text is as follows:

Forasmuch as it hath pleased the Allmighty God by the wise disposition of his diuyne pruidence so to Order and dispose of things that we the Inhabitants and Residents of Windsor, Harteford and Wethersfield are now cohabiting and dwelling in and vppon the River of Conectecotte and the Lands thereunto adioyneing; And well knowing where a people are gathered togather the word of God requires that to mayntayne the peace and vnion of such a people there should be an orderly and decent Gouerment established according to God, to order and dispose of the affayres of the people at all seasons as occation shall require; doe therefore assotiate and conioyne our selues to be as one Publike State or Comonwelth; and doe, for our selues and our Successors and such as shall be adioyned to vs att any tyme hereafter, enter into Combination and Confederation togather, to mayntayne and presearue the liberty and purity of the gospell of our Lord Jesus which we now professe, as also the disciplyne of the Churches, which according to the truth of the said gospell is now practised amongst vs; As also in our Ciuell Affaires to be guided and gouerned according to such Lawes, Rules, Orders, and decrees as shall be made, ordered and decreed, as followeth:

1. It is Ordered, sentenced, and decreed that there shall be yerely two generall Assemblies or Courts, the one on the second thursday in Aprill, the other the second thursday in September, following; the first shall be called the Courte of Election, wherein shall be yerely Chosen from tyme to tyme soe many Magestrats and other publike Officers as shall be found requisitte: Whereof one to be chosen Gouernour for the yeare ensueing and vntill another be chosen, and noe other Magestrate to be chosen for more than one yeare; prouided allwayes there be sixe chosen besids the Gouernour; which being chosen and sworne according to an Oath recorded for that purpose shall haue power to administer iustice according to the Lawes here established, and for want thereof according to the rule of the word of God; which choice shall be made by all that are admitted freemen and haue taken the Oath of Fidellity, and doe cohabitte within this Jurisdiction, (hauing beene admitted Inhabitants by the maior part of the Towne wherein they liue,) or the mayor parte of such as shall be then present.

2. It is ordered, sentensed and decreed, that the Election of the aforesaid Magestrats shall be on this manner: euery person present and quallified for choyse shall bring in (to the persons deputed to receaue them) one single paper with the name of him written in yt whom he desires to haue Gouernour, and he that hath the greatest nuber of papers shall be Gouernor for that yeare. And the rest of the Magestrats or publike Officers to be chosen in this manner: The Secretary for the tyme being shall first read the names of all that are to be put to choise and then shall seuerally nominate them distinctly, and euery one that would haue the person nominated to be chosen shall bring in one single paper written vppon, and he that would not haue him chosen shall bring in a blanke: and euery one that hath more written papers then blanks shall be a Magistrat for that yeare; which papers shall be receaued and told by one or more that shall be then chosen by the court and sworne to be faythfull therein; but in case there should not be sixe chosen as aforesaid, besids the Gouernor, out of those which are nominated, then he or they which haue the most written papers shall be a Magestrat or Magestrats for the ensueing yeare, to make vp the foresaid nuber.

3. It is Ordered, sentenced, and decreed, that the Secretary shall not nominate any person, nor shall any person be chosen newly into the Magestracy which was not propownded in some Generall Courte before, to be nominated the next Election; and to that end yt shall be lawfull for ech of the Townes aforesaid by their deputyes to nominate any two whō they conceaue fitte to be put to election; and the Courte may ad so many more as they iuge requisitt.

4. It is Ordered, sentenced, and decreed, that noe person be chosen Gouernor aboue once in two yeares, and that the Gouernor be always a mēber of some approved congregation, and formerly of the Magestracy within this Jurisdiction; and all

the Magestrats Freemen of this Comonwelth: and that no Magestrate or other publike officer shall execute any parte of his or their office before they are seuerally sworne, which shall be done in the face of the Courte if they be present, and in case of absence by some deputed for that purpose.

5. It is Ordered, sentenced, and decreed, that to the aforesaid Courte of Election the seueral Townes shall send their deputyes, and when the Elections are ended they may proceed in any publike searuice as at other Courts. Also the other Generall Courte in September shall be for makeing of lawes, and any other publike occation, which conserns the good of the Comonwelth.

6. It is Ordered, sentenced, and decreed, that the Gouernor shall, ether by himselfe or by the secretary, send out sumons to the Constables of euer Towne for the cauleing of these two standing Courts, on month at lest before their seueral tymes: And also if the Gouernor and the gretest parte of the Magestrats see cause vppon any spetiall occation to call a generall Courte, they may giue order to the secretary soe to doe within fowerteene dayes warneing; and if vrgent necessity so require, vppon a shorter notice, giueing sufficient grownds for yt to the deputyes when they meete, or els be questioned for the same; And if the Gouernor and Mayor parte of Magestrats shall ether neglect or refuse to call the two Generall standing Courts or ether of them, as also at other tymes when the occations of the Comonwelth require, the Freemen thereof, or the Mayor parte of them, shall petition to them soe to doe: if then yt be ether denyed or neglected the said Freemen or the Mayor parte of them shall haue power to giue order to the Constables of the seuerall Townes to doe the same, and so may meete togather, and chuse to themselues a Moderator, and may proceed to do any Acte of power, which any other Generall Courte may.

7. It is Ordered, sentenced, and decreed, that after there are warrants giuen out for any of the said Generall Courts, the Constable or Constables of ech Towne shall forthwith give notice distinctly to the inhabitants of the same, in some Publike Assembly or by goeing or sending frō howse to howse, that at a place and tyme by him or them lymited and sett, they meet and assemble thē selues togather to elect and chuse certen deputyes to be att the Generall Courte then following to agitate the afayres of the Comonwelth; which said Deputyes shall be chosen by all that are admitted Inhabitants in the seueral Townes and have taken the oath of fidellity; prouided that non be chosen a Deputy for any Generall Courte which is not a Freeman of this Comonwelth.

The foresaid deputyes shall be chosen in manner following: euery person that is present and quallified as before expressed, shall bring the names of such, written in seuerall papers, as they desire to haue chosen for that Imployment, and these 3 or 4, more or lesse, being the number agreed on to be chosen for that tyme, that haue greatest nuber of papers written for thē shall be deputyes for that Courte; whose names shall be endorsed on the backe side of the warrant and returned into the Courte, with the Constable or Constables hand vnto the same.

8. It is Ordered, sentenced, and decreed, that Wyndsor, Hartford, and Wethersfield shall haue power, ech Towne, to send fower of their freemen as deputies to euery Generall Courte; and whatsoeuer other Townes shall be hereafter added to this Jurisdiction, they shall send so many deputyes as the Courte shall judge meete, a resonable proportion to the nuber of Freemen that are in the said Townes being to be attended therein; which deputyes shall have the power of the whole Towne to giue their voats and alowance to all such lawes and orders as may be for the publike good, and unto which the said Townes are to be bownd.

9. It is ordered and decreed, that the deputyes thus chosen shall haue power and liberty to appoynt a tyme and a place of meeting togather before any Generall Courte to aduise and consult of all such things as may concerne the good of the publike, as also to examine their owne Elections, whether according to the order, and if they or the gretest parte of them find any election to be illegal they may seclud such for present from their meeting, and returne the same and their resons to the Courte; and if yt proue true, the Courte may fyne the party or partyes

so intruding and the Towne, if they see cause, and giue out a warrant to goe to a newe election in a legall way, either in parte or in whole. Also the said deputyes shall haue power to fyne any that shall be disorderly at their meetings, or for not coming in due tyme or place according to appoyntment; and they may returne the said fynes into the Courte if yt be refused to be paid, and the tresurer to take notice of yt, and to estreete or leuy the same as he doth other fynes.

10. It is Orderered, sentenced, and decreed, that euery Generall Courte, except such as through neglecte of the Gouernor and the gretest parte of Magestrats the Freeman them selues doe call, shall consist of the Gouernor, or some one chosen to moderate the Court, and 4 other Majestrats at lest, with the mayor parte of the deputyes of the seueral Townes legally chosen; and in case the Freemen or mayor parte of thē, through neglect or refusall of the Gouernor and mayor part of the majestrats, shall call a Courte, yt shall consist of the mayor parte of Freemen that are present or their deputyes, with a Moderator chosen by the: In which said Generall Courts shall consist the supreme power of the Comonwelth, and they only shall haue power to make laws or repeale thē to graunt leuyes, to admitt of Freemen, dispose of lands vndisposed of, to seuerall Townes or persons, and also shall haue power to call ether Courte or Magestrate or any other person whatsoeuer into question for any misdemeanour, and may for iust causes displace or deale otherwise according to the nature of the offence; and also may deale in any other matter that concerns the good of this Comonwelth, excepte election of Magestrats, which shall be done by the whole boddy of Freemen.

In which Courte the Gouernour or Moderator shall have power to order the Courte to giue liberty of speech, and silence vnceasonable and disorderly speakeings, to put all things to voate, and in case the vote be equall to have the casting voice. But non of these Courts shall be adiorned or dissolued without the consent of the maior parte of the Court.

11. It is ordered, sentenced, and decreed, that when any Generall Courte vppon the occations of the Comonwelth haue agreed vppon any sume or somes of money to be leuyed vppon the seuerall Townes within this Jurisdiction, that a Comittee be chosen to sett out and appoynt what shall be the proportion of euery Towne to pay of the said leuy, prouided the Comittees be made vp of an equall number out of each Towne.

14th January, 1638 the 11 Orders abousaid are voted.

THE OATH OF THE GOUERNOR, FOR THE [PRESENT.]

I, N. W. being now chosen to be Gouernor within this Jurisdiction, for the yeare ensueing, and vntil a new be chosen, doe sweare by the greate and dreadfull name of the everliueing God. to promote the publicke good and peace of the same, according to the best of my skill; as also will mayntayne all lawfull priuiledges of this Comonwelth; as also that all wholsome lawes that are or shall be made by lawfull authority here established, be duly executed; and will further the execution of Justice according to the rule of Gods word; so helpe me God, in the name of the Lo: Jesus Christ.

THE OATH OF A MAGESTRATE, FOR THE [PRESENT.]

I, N. W. being chosen a Magestrate within this Jurisdiction for the yeare ensueing, doe sweare by the great and dreadfull name of the euerliueing God, to promote the publike good and peace of the same, according to the best of my skill, and that I will mayntayne all the lawfull priuiledges thereof according to my vnderstanding, as also assist in the execution of all such wholsome lawes as are made or shall be made by lawfull authority heare established, and will further the execution of Justice for the tyme aforesaid according to the righteous rule of Gods word; so helpe me God, etc.

Connecticut Tract, THE. Grants by the English crown to New York and Massachusetts overlapped. In 1786 a convention of commissioners from the two colonies was held at Hartford, Conn.; Massachusetts ceded to the State of New York all that territory lying west of the present eastern boundary of New York, and New York ceded to Massachusetts a tract of territory running from the northern boundary of Pennsylvania due north through Seneca Lake to Lake Ontario, with the exception of a strip of land one mile wide on Niagara River—about 6,000,000 acres in all. Of this M. Gorham and O. Phelps bought the title of the Indians, and also the title of Massachusetts to 2,600,000 acres. Robert Morris purchased most of the remainder and sold a part of it to Sir William Pultney. He sold another large portion to the Holland Company and to the State of Connecticut.

Conner, DAVID, naval officer; born in Harrisburg, Pa., about 1792; entered the navy in January, 1809, and as acting-lieutenant was in the action between the *Hornet* and *Peacock*. He was made a lieutenant in 1813, and remained on the *Hornet*. In her action with the *Penguin*, Conner was dangerously wounded, and for his brave conduct was presented with a medal by Congress, and by the legislature of Pennsylvania with a sword. He was promoted to the rank of commander in March, 1825, and to captain in 1835. During the war with Mexico (1846–48) he commanded the American squadron on the Mexican coast, and assisted in the reduction of the fortress of San Juan de Ulloa in the spring of 1847. He captured Tampico in November, 1846. His last service was in command of the Philadelphia navy-yard. He died in Philadelphia, March 20, 1856.

Connor, PATRICK EDWARD, military officer; born in Ireland, March 17, 1820; came to the United States and was educated in New York City; served in the war with Mexico and then engaged in business in California. When the Civil War broke out he recruited a band of 200 men and was ordered to Utah to drive plundering Indians out of the overland routes of travel, and to check the threatened revolt among the Mormons. After marching 140 miles he fell upon a fortified camp of 300 Indians in Washington Territory and destroyed the whole band. At the close of the war he received the brevet of major-general. Later he commanded 2,000 cavalry to punish the Sioux and Arapahoe Indians for their robberies. He met and defeated the latter at Tongue River in August, 1865. He died in Salt Lake City, Utah, Dec. 18, 1891.

Conrad, CHARLES M., legislator; born in Winchester, Va., about 1804; admitted to the bar in 1828; and began practice in New Orleans. In 1842–43 he served out the unexpired term of Alexander Monton in the United States Senate; in 1848–50 was a representative in Congress; and in 1850–53 was Secretary of War. He was a leader in the Secession movement in 1860; a deputy from Louisiana in the Montgomery Provisional Congress in 1861; and a member of the Confederate Congress, and also a brigadier-general in the Confederate army in 1862–64. He died in New Orleans, La., Feb. 11, 1878.

Conrad, JOSEPH, military officer; born in Germany, May 17, 1830; settled in Missouri; and joined the National army at the beginning of the Civil War in the 3d Missouri Infantry. He was brevetted brigadier-general of volunteers; joined the regular army in 1866; retired with the rank of colonel in 1882. He died in Fort Randall, S. D., Dec. 4, 1891.

Conscience Whigs. Those Whigs who opposed the extension of slavery. They gradually joined the Free-Soil and later the Republican parties.

Conscriptions. In October, 1814, the acting Secretary of War (James Monroe) proposed vigorous measures for increasing the army and giving it material strength. Volunteering had ceased, and he proposed to raise, by conscription or draft, sufficient to fill the existing ranks of the army to the full amount of 62,448 men; also an additional regular force of 40,000 men, to be locally employed for the defence of the frontiers and sea-coast. Bills for this purpose were introduced into Congress (Oct. 27, 1814). The proposition to raise a large force by conscription brought matters to a crisis in New England. Radical and indiscreet men of the opposition proposed the secession of the New England States from the Union as a cure for existing evils. During the Civil War conscription was resorted to by both governments. The National armies, however, were less dependent on the measure, as large bounties brought them almost enough volunteers.

The first Confederate conscription law, April 16, 1862, annulled all contracts with volunteers for short terms, holding them for two additional years, and made every white male between eighteen and thirty-five liable to service at a moment's notice. On Sept. 27, 1862, the law was extended to all men between eighteen and forty-five.

In July, 1863, all between eighteen and forty-five were called into active service. In February, 1864, the law was extended to include all between seventeen and fifty. See HARTFORD CONVENTION; NEW YORK CITY (*The Draft Riots*).

Conservation of Natural Resources. See NATURAL RESOURCES, CONSERVATION OF.

Conservatives. The advocacy of an extensive specie currency, and the proposition for a sub-treasury, in 1837, alienated many of the Democratic party, and they formed a powerful faction known as "Conservatives." They finally joined the Whigs, and in 1840 assisted in electing General Harrison President.

Conservation. See ALASKA, BALLINGER-PINCHOT CONTROVERSY.

Conspiracy. See BOOTH, JOHN WILKES; BURR, AARON.

Constellation. See TRUXTON, THOMAS.

Constitution and Government of the United States. See CALHOUN, JOHN CALDWELL.

CONSTITUTION OF THE UNITED STATES

Constitution of the United States. Sagacious men perceived the utter inefficiency of the ARTICLES OF CONFEDERATION (*q. v.*) as a constitution of a national government as early as 1780, while their ratification by the States was pending. Alexander Hamilton, then only twenty-three years of age, in a long letter to James Duane, in Congress, dated "At the Liberty Pole," Sept. 3, gave an outline sketch of a national constitution, and suggested the calling of a convention to frame such a system of government. During the following year he published in the *New York Packet* (then published at Fishkill, N. Y.) a series of papers under the title of "The Constitutionalist," which were devoted chiefly to the discussion of the defects of the Articles of Confederation. In the summer of 1782 he succeeded in having the subject brought before the legislature of New York, then in session at Poughkeepsie, and that body, by a resolution drawn by Hamilton and presented by his father-in-law, General Schuyler, recommended (July 21, 1782) the assembling of a national convention to revise the Articles, "reserving the right of the respective legislatures to ratify their determinations." In the spring of 1783 Hamilton, in Congress, expressed an earnest desire for such a convention. Pelatiah Webster and Thomas Paine wrote in favor of it the same year, and in 1784 Noah Webster wrote a pamphlet on the subject which he carried in person to General Washington. In that pamphlet Webster proposed "a new system of government which should act, *not on the States, but directly on individuals*, and vest in Congress full power to carry its laws into effect." The plan deeply impressed the mind of Washington.

Events in North Carolina and Massachusetts made many leading men anxious about the future. They saw the weakness of the existing form of government. In the autumn of 1785 Washington, in a letter to James Warren, deplored that weakness, and the "illiberality, jealousy, and local policy of the States," that was likely to "sink the new nation in the eyes of Europe into contempt." Finally, after many grave discussions at Mount Vernon, Washington, acting upon the suggestions of Hamilton made five years before, proposed a convention of the several States to agree upon a plan of unity in a commercial arrangement, over which, by the existing Constitution, Congress had no control. Coming from such an exalted source, the suggestion was acted upon.

A convention of delegates from the several States was called at Annapolis, Md. Only five States (New York, New Jersey, Pennsylvania, Delaware, and Virginia) sent deputies. These met Sept. 11, 1786. There being only a minority of the States present, they deferred action, at the same time recommending another convention. On Feb. 21, 1787, the Congress, by resolution, strongly urged the several legislatures to send deputies to a convention to meet in Philadelphia in May following, "for the sole and express purpose of revising the Articles of Confederation." Delegates were appointed by all the States excepting Rhode Island. The convention assembled at the appointed time (May 14), but only one-half the States were then represented. The remainder did not all arrive before May 24. Washington, who was a delegate from Virginia, was chosen president of the convention, and William Jackson, one of his most intimate friends, was made secretary. Edmund Randolph, of Virginia, opened the proceedings by a carefully prepared speech, in which the defects of the existing Constitution were pointed out. At its conclusion he offered fifteen resolutions, in which were embodied the leading principles whereon to construct a new form of government. In these was the suggestion that "a *national* government ought to be established, consisting of a supreme legislature, executive, and judiciary."

Upon this broad idea the convention proceeded, and had not gone far when they perceived that the Articles of Confederation were too radically defective to form a basis for a stable government. Therefore they did not attempt to amend them, but proceeded to form an entirely new Constitution. For many weeks debates went on, when (Sept. 10, 1787) all plans and amendments adopted by the convention were referred to a committee for revision and arrangement. It consisted of James Madison, Alexander Hamilton, Thomas Johnson, Rufus King, and Gouverneur Morris. The latter put the document into proper literary form. It was signed by nearly all the members of the convention on the 17th. The convention ordered these proceedings to be laid before Congress, and recommended that body to submit the instrument to the *people* (not the *States*) and ask them, the *source of all sovereignty*, to ratify or reject it. It was done. The Constitution was violently assailed, especially by the extreme supporters of the doctrine of State sovereignty. The Constitution was ratified by Delaware, Dec. 7, 1787; Pennsylvania, Dec. 12; New Jersey, Dec. 18; Georgia, Jan. 2, 1788; Connecticut, Jan. 9; Massachusetts, Feb. 6; Maryland, April 28; South Carolina, May 23; New Hampshire, June 21; Virginia, June 25; New York, July 26; North Carolina, Nov. 21, 1789; Rhode Island, May 29, 1790. When nine States had ratified the Constitution it became operative. The new government began March 4, 1789.

The ratification of the national Constitution was celebrated at Philadelphia (July 4, 1788) with imposing ceremonies. The ten ratifying States were represented by as many ships moored at intervals in the Delaware, along the front of the city, each displaying at her mast-head a white flag bearing the name of the State represented in golden letters. All the river craft were embellished with flags and streamers. A large procession paraded the streets, in which several of the principal citizens personated in appropriate dresses some such event as "Independence," the "French Alliance," the "Definitive Treaty of Peace," "Washington," the "New Era," the "Federal Constitution," the "Ten Ratifying States." In a car in the form of an eagle, lofty and ornamental, sat Chief-Justice McKean and two of his bench associates, bearing a framed copy of the Constitution on a staff. The car and its contents personified the new Constitution. On the staff was a cap of Liberty, bearing in golden letters the legend "The People." A citizen and an Indian chief rode together, smoking a pipe of peace, personifying peace on the frontiers. Various trades were represented; also the shipping interest, and different associations in Philadelphia. Altogether there were about 5,000 in the procession, which ended at Union Square, where 17,000 persons were addressed by James Wilson, who took a conspicuous part in framing the Constitution. The oration was followed by a collation. About three weeks afterwards a similar celebration occurred in the city of New York where a large majority of the inhabitants were in favor of the Constitution. Greenleaf's *Political Register* —anti-Federal in its politics—contained a disparaging account of the celebration; and when, a night or two afterwards, news came of the ratification of the Constitution by the convention in session at Poughkeepsie, a mob attacked the print-

CONSTITUTION OF THE UNITED STATES

MEMBERS OF THE CONVENTION FRAMING THE CONSTITUTION, MAY 25–SEPTEMBER 17, 1787.

Elected.	Serving.	Signing.	Representing.
Baldwin, Abraham	Served	Signed	Georgia.
Bassett, Richard	"	"	Delaware.
Bedford, Gunning, Jr.	"	"	Delaware.
Blair, John	"	"	Virginia.
Blount, William	"	"	North Carolina.
Breasley, David	"	"	New Jersey.
Broom, Jacob	"	"	Delaware.
Butler, Pierce	"	"	South Carolina.
Carroll, Daniel	"	"	Maryland.
Caswell, Richard	No	Resigned	North Carolina.
Clark, Abraham	"	No	New Jersey.
Clymer, George	Served	Signed	Pennsylvania.
Dana, Francis	No	No	Massachusetts.
Davie, Wm. Richardson	Served	Sick	North Carolina.
Dayton, Jonathan	"	Signed	New Jersey.
Dickinson, John	"	"	Delaware.
Ellsworth, Oliver	"	Sick	Connecticut.
Few, William	"	Signed	Georgia.
Fitzsimons, Thomas	"	"	Pennsylvania.
Franklin, Benjamin	"	"	Pennsylvania.
Gerry, Elbridge	"	Refused	Massachusetts.
Gilman, Nicholas	"	Signed	New Hampshire.
Gorham, Nathaniel	"	"	Massachusetts.
Hamilton, Alexander	"	"	New York.
Henry, Patrick	No	No	Virginia.
Houston, W. Churchill	Served	"	New Jersey.
Houstoun, William	"	"	Georgia.
Ingersoll, Jared	"	Signed	Pennsylvania.
Jenifer, Daniel, of St. Thomas	"	"	Maryland.
Johnson, Wm. Samuel	"	"	Connecticut.
Jones, Willie	No	No	North Carolina.
King, Rufus	Served	Signed	Massachusetts.
Langdon, John	"	"	New Hampshire.
Lansing, John, Jr.	"	Refused	New York.
Livingston, William	"	Signed	New Jersey.
Madison, James	"	"	Virginia.
Martin, Alexander	"	No	North Carolina.
Martin, Luther	"	Refused	Maryland.
Mason, George	"	"	Virginia.
McClurg, James	"	Absent	Virginia.
McHenry, James	"	Signed	Maryland.
Mercer, John Francis	"	Refused	Maryland.
Mifflin, Thomas	"	Signed	Pennsylvania.
Morris, Gouverneur	"	"	Pennsylvania.
Morris, Robert	"	"	Pennsylvania.
Neilson, John	No	No	New Jersey.
Patterson, William	Served	Signed	New Jersey.
Pendleton, Nathaniel	No	No	Georgia.
Pickering, John	"	"	New Hampshire.
Pierce, William	Served	Absent	Georgia.
Pickney, Charles	"	Signed	South Carolina.
Pickney, C. Cotesworth	"	"	South Carolina.
Randolph, Edmund, Jr.	"	Refused	Virginia.
Read, George	"	Signed	Delaware.
Rutledge, John	"	"	South Carolina.
Sherman, Roger	"	"	Connecticut.
Spaight, Richard Dobbs	"	"	North Carolina.
Strong, Caleb	"	Absent	Massachusetts.
Walton, George	No	No	Georgia.
Washington, George	Served	Signed	Virginia.
West, Benjamir	No	No	New Hampshire.
Williamson, Hugh	Served	Signed	North Carolina.
Wilson, James	"	"	Pennsylvania.
Wythe, George	"	Absent	Virginia.
Yates, Robert	"	Refused	New York.

Rhode Island not represented.

ing-office, broke in the doors, and destroyed the type. The people of Providence, R. I., were in favor of the Constitution, and were preparing to celebrate its ratification on July 4, with other ceremonies appropriate to the day, when 1,000 men, some of them armed, headed by a judge of the Supreme Court, came in from the country, and compelled the citizens to omit in the celebration anything favorable to the Constitution. A more violent collision took place in Albany. The friends of the Constitution celebrated its ratification on July 3, the opponents at the same time burning it. Both parties united in celebrating the 4th, but dined at different places. After dinner the Federalists formed a new procession, and when they were passing the headquarters of the anti-Federal party a quarrel occurred, followed by a fight, in which clubs and stones, swords and bayonets, were freely used, to the injury of several persons. There was much asperity of feeling everywhere exhibited.

The following is the text of the national Constitution and of its several amendments:

CONSTITUTION OF THE UNITED STATES.

ARTICLE I.

SECTION 1. Legislative powers; in whom vested.

SEC. 2. House of Representatives, how and by whom chosen—Qualifications of a representative — Representatives and direct taxes, how apportioned—Census—Vacancies to be filled—Power of choosing officers, and of impeachment.

SEC. 3. Senators, how and by whom chosen—How classified—State Executive to make temporary appointments, in case, etc.—Qualifications of a senator—President of the Senate, his right to vote—President *pro tem.*, and other officers of Senate, how chosen—Power to try impeachment—When President is tried, chief-justice to preside—Sentence.

SEC. 4. Times, etc., of holding elections, how prescribed—One session in each year.

SEC. 5. Membership—Quorum—Adjournments—Rules—Power to punish or expel—Journal—Time of adjournments limited, unless, etc.

SEC. 6. Compensation—Privileges—Disqualification in certain cases.

SEC. 7. House to originate all revenue bills—Veto—Bill may be passed by two-thirds of each House notwithstanding, etc.—Bill not returned in ten days—Provision as to all orders, etc., except, etc.

SEC. 8. Powers of Congress.

SEC. 9. Provision as to migration or importation of certain persons — *Habeas Corpus* — Bills of attainder, etc. — Taxes, how apportioned — No export duty — No commercial preference—No money drawn from treasury, unless, etc.—No titular nobility—Officers not to receive presents, unless, etc.

SEC. 10. States prohibited from the exercise of certain powers.

ARTICLE II.

SECTION 1. President; his term of office—Electors of President; number and how appointed—Electors to vote on same day — Qualification of President — On whom his duties devolve in case of his removal, death, etc.—President's compensation—His oath.

SEC. 2. President to be commander-in-chief—He may require opinion of, etc., and may pardon—Treaty-making power—Nomination of certain officers—When President may fill vacancies.

SEC. 3. President shall communicate to Congress—He may convene and adjourn Congress, in case, etc.; shall receive ambassadors, execute laws, and commission officers.

SEC. 4. All civil offices forfeited for certain crimes.

ARTICLE III.

SECTION 1. Judicial power — Tenure — Compensation.

SEC. 2. Judicial power; to what cases it extends — Original jurisdiction of supreme court—Appellate—Trial by jury, except, etc.—Trial, where.

SEC. 3. Treason defined—Proof of—Punishment of.

ARTICLE IV.

SECTION 1. Each State to give credit to the public acts, etc., of every other State.

SEC. 2. Privileges of citizens of each State—Fugitives from justice to be delivered up—Persons held to service having escaped, to be delivered up.

SEC. 3. Admission of new States—Power of Congress over territory and other property.

SEC. 4. Republican form of government guaranteed—Each State to be protected.

ARTICLE V.

Constitution; how amended—Proviso.

ARTICLE VI.

Certain debts, etc., adopted—Supremacy of Constitution, treaties, and laws of the United States—Oath to support Constitution, by whom taken—No religious test.

ARTICLE VII.

What ratification shall establish Constitution.

ADMENDMENTS.

I. Religious establishment prohibited —Freedom of speech, of the press, and right to petition.
II. Right to keep and bear arms.
III. No soldier to be quartered in any house, unless, etc.
IV. Right of search and seizure regulated.
V. Provisions concerning prosecutions, trial, and punishment—Private property not to be taken for public use, without, etc.
VI. Further provisions respecting criminal prosecutions.
VII. Right of trial by jury secured.
VIII. Excessive bail or fines and cruel punishments prohibited.
IX. Rule of construction.
X. Same subject.
XI. Same subject.
XII. Manner of choosing President and Vice-President.
XIII. Slavery abolished.
XIV. Citizenship.
XV. Right of suffrage.

PREAMBLE.

WE, THE PEOPLE OF THE UNITED STATES, in order to form a more perfect union, establish justice, insure domestic tranquillity, provide for the common defence, promote the general welfare, and secure the blessings of liberty to ourselves and our posterity, do ordain and establish this constitution for the United States of America.

ARTICLE I.

SECTION 1.

1. All legislative powers herein granted shall be vested in a Congress of the United States, which shall consist of a Senate and House of Representatives.

SECTION 2.

1. The House of Representatives shall be composed of members chosen every second year by the people of the several States; and the electors in each State shall have the qualifications requisite for electors of the most numerous branch of the State legislature.

2. No person shall be a representative who shall not have attained to the age of twenty-five years, and been seven years a citizen of the United States, and who shall not, when elected, be an inhabitant of that State in which he shall be chosen.

3. Representatives and direct taxes shall be apportioned among the several States which may be included within this Union, according to their respective numbers, which shall be determined by adding to the whole number of free persons, including those bound to service for a term of years, and excluding Indians not taxed, three-fifths of all other persons. The actual renumeration shall be made within three years after the first meeting of the Congress of the United States, and within every subsequent term of ten years, in such manner as they shall by law direct. The number of representatives shall not exceed one for every thirty thousand, but each State shall have at least one representative; and until such enumeration shall be made, the State of New Hampshire shall be entitled to choose three; Massachusetts, eight; Rhode Island and Providence Plantations, one; Connecticut, five; New York, six; New Jersey, four; Pennsylvania, eight; Delaware, one; Maryland, six; Virginia, ten; North Carolina, five; South Carolina, five; and Georgia, three.

4. When vacancies happen in the representation from any State, the executive authority thereof shall issue writs of election to fill such vacancies.

5. The House of Representatives shall

choose their speaker and other officers, and shall have the sole power of impeachment.

SECTION 3.

1. The Senate of the United States shall be composed of two senators from each State, chosen by the legislature thereof, for six years, and each senator shall have one vote.

2. Immediately after they shall be assembled in consequence of the first election, they shall be divided as equally as may be into three classes. The seats of the senators of the first class shall be vacated at the expiration of the second year, of the second class at the expiration of the fourth year, and of the third class at the expiration of the sixth year, so that one-third may be chosen every second year; and if vacancies happen, by resignation or otherwise, during the recess of the legislature of any State, the executive thereof may make temporary appointments until the next meeting of the legislature, which shall then fill such vacancies.

3. No person shall be a senator who shall not have attained to the age of thirty years, and been nine years a citizen of the United States, and who shall not, when elected, be an inhabitant of that State for which he shall be chosen.

4. The Vice-President of the United States shall be President of the Senate, but shall have no vote unless they be equally divided.

5. The Senate shall choose their other officers, and also a president *pro tempore* in the absence of the Vice-President or when he shall exercise the office of President of the United States.

6. The Senate shall have the sole power to try all impeachments. When sitting for that purpose they shall be on oath or affirmation. When the President of the United States is tried, the chief-justice shall preside; and no person shall be convicted without the concurrence of two-thirds of the members present.

7. Judgment in cases of impeachment shall not extend further than to removal from office, and disqualification to hold and enjoy any office of honor, trust, or profit under the United States; but the party convicted shall, nevertheless, be liable and subject to indictment, trial, judgment, and punishment, according to law.

SECTION 4.

1. The times, places, and manner of holding elections for senators and representatives shall be prescribed in each State by the legislature thereof; but the Congress may at any time by law make or alter such regulations, except as to the places of choosing senators.

2. The Congress shall assemble at least once in every year; and such meeting shall be on the first Monday in December, unless they shall by law appoint a different day.

SECTION 5.

1. Each House shall be the judge of the elections, returns, and qualifications of its own members, and a majority of each shall constitute a quorum to do business; but a smaller number may adjourn from day to day, and may be authorized to compel the attendance of absent members, in such manner and under such penalties as each House may provide.

2. Each House may determine the rules of its proceedings, punish its members for disorderly behavior, and with the concurrence of two-thirds, expel a member.

3. Each House shall keep a journal of its proceedings, and from time to time publish the same, excepting such parts as may, in their judgment, require secrecy; and the yeas and nays of the members of either House on any question shall, at the desire of one-fifth of those present, be entered on the journal.

4. Neither House, during the session of Congress, shall, without the consent of the other, adjourn for more than three days, nor to any other place than that in which the two Houses shall be sitting.

SECTION 6.

1. The senators and representatives shall receive a compensation for their services, to be ascertained by law and paid out of the treasury of the United States. They shall, in all cases except treason, felony, and breach of the peace, be privileged from arrest during their attendance at the session of their respective Houses, and in going to and returning from the same; and for any speech

or debate in either House they shall not be questioned in any other place.

2. No senator or representative shall, during the time for which he was elected, be appointed to any civil office under the authority of the United States, which shall have been created, or the emoluments whereof shall have been increased, during such time; and no person holding any office under the United States shall be a member of either House during his continuance in office.

SECTION 7.

1. All bills for raising revenues shall originate in the House of Representatives; but the Senate may propose or concur with amendments as on other bills.

2. Every bill which shall have passed the House of Representatives and the Senate shall, before it become a law, be presented to the President of the United States; if he approve, he shall sign it; but if not, he shall return it, with his objections, to that House in which it shall have originated; who shall enter the objections at large on their journal, and proceed to reconsider it. If, after such reconsideration, two-thirds of that House shall agree to pass the bill, it shall be sent, together with the objections, to the other House, by which it shall likewise be reconsidered, and, if approved by two-thirds of that House, it shall become a law. But in all such cases, the votes of both Houses shall be determined by yeas and nays, and the names of the persons voting for and against the bill shall be entered on the journal of each House respectively. If any bill shall not be returned by the President within ten days (Sundays excepted) after it shall have been presented to him, the same shall be a law in like manner as if he had signed it, unless the Congress, by their adjournment, prevent its return, in which case it shall not be a law.

3. Every order, resolution or vote, to which the concurrence of the Senate and House of Representatives may be necessary (except on a question of adjournment), shall be presented to the President of the United States; and before the same shall take effect, shall be approved by him; or, being disapproved by him, shall be repassed by two-thirds of the Senate and House of Representatives, according to the rules and limitations prescribed in the case of a bill.

SECTION 8.

The Congress shall have power:

1. To lay and collect taxes, duties, imposts and excises; to pay the debts and provide for the common defence and general welfare of the United States· but all duties, imposts, and excises shall be uniform throughout the United States.

2. To borrow money on the credit of the United States.

3. To regulate commerce with foreign nations, and among the several States, and with the Indian tribes.

4. To establish an uniform rule of naturalization, and uniform laws on the subject of bankruptcies throughout the United States.

5. To coin money, regulate the value thereof, and of foreign coin, and fix the standard of weights and measures.

6. To provide for the punishment of counterfeiting the securities and current coin of the United States.

7. To establish post-offices and post-roads.

8. To promote the progress of science and useful arts, by securing for limited times, to authors and inventors, the exclusive right to their respective writings and discoveries.

9. To constitute tribunals inferior to the supreme court; to define and punish piracies and felonies committed on the high seas, and offences against the law of nations.

10. To declare war, grant letters of marque and reprisal, and make rules concerning captures on land and water.

11. To raise and support armies; but no appropriation of money to that use shall be for a longer term than two years.

12. To provide and maintain a navy.

13. To make rules for the government and regulation of the land and naval forces.

14. To provide for calling forth the militia to execute the laws of the Union, suppress insurrections, and repel invasions.

15. To provide for organizing, arming, and disciplining the militia, and for gov-

erning such part of them as may be employed in the service of the United States; reserving to the States respectively the appointment of the officers and the authority of training the militia according to the discipline prescribed by Congress.

16. To exercise exclusive legislation in all cases whatsoever, over such district (not exceeding ten miles square) as may, by cession of particular States, and the acceptance of Congress, become the seat of the government of the United States; and to exercise like authority over all places purchased, by the consent of the legislature of the State in which the same shall be, for the erection of forts, magazines, arsenals, dock-yards, and other needful buildings; and

17. To make all laws which shall be necessary and proper for carrying into execution the foregoing powers, and all other powers vested by this constitution in the government of the United States, or in any department or officer thereof.

Section 9.

1. The migration or importation of such persons as any of the States now existing shall think proper to admit, shall not be prohibited by the Congress prior to the year one thousand eight hundred and eight; but a tax or duty may be imposed on such importation not exceeding ten dollars for each person.

2. The privilege of the writ of *habeas corpus* shall not be suspended, unless when, in cases of rebellion or invasion, the public safety may require it.

3. No bill of attainder, or *ex post facto* law shall be passed.

4. No capitation or other direct tax shall be laid, unless in proportion to the census or enumeration hereinbefore directed to be taken.

5. No tax or duty shall be laid on articles exported from any State. No preference shall be given by any regulation of commerce or revenue to the ports of one State over those of another; nor shall vessels bound to or from one State be obliged to enter, clear, or pay duties in another.

6. No money shall be drawn from the treasury but in consequence of appropriations made by law; and a regular statement and account of the receipts and expenditures of all public money shall be published from time to time.

7. No title of nobility shall be granted by the United States; and no person holding any office of profit or trust under them shall, without the consent of the Congress, accept of any present, emolument, office, or title of any kind whatever, from any king, prince, or foreign State.

Section 10.

1. No State shall enter into any treaty, alliance or confederation; grant letters of marque and reprisal; coin money; emit bills of credit; make anything but gold and silver coin a tender in payment of debts; pass any bill of attainder, *ex post facto* law, or law impairing the obligation of contracts; or grant any title of nobility.

2. No State shall, without the consent of the Congress, lay any imposts or duties on imports or exports, except what may be absolutely necessary for executing its inspection laws, and the net produce of all duties and imposts laid by any State on imports or exports shall be for the use of the treasury of the United States, and all such laws shall be subject to the revision and control of the Congress. No State shall, without the consent of Congress, lay any duty of tonnage, keep troops or ships of war in time of peace, enter into any agreement or compact with another State, or with a foreign power, or engage in war, unless actually invaded, or in such imminent danger as will not admit of delay.

ARTICLE II.

Section 1.

1. The executive power shall be vested in a President of the United States of America. He shall hold his office during the term of four years; and, together with the Vice-President chosen for the same term, be elected as follows:

2. Each State shall appoint, in such manner as the legislature thereof may direct, a number of electors equal to the whole number of senators and representatives to which the State may be entitled in the Congress; but no senator or representative, or person holding an office of

trust or profit under the United States, shall be appointed an elector.

3. [The electors shall meet in their respective States, and vote by ballot for two persons, of whom one at least shall not be an inhabitant of the same State with themselves. And they shall make a list of all the persons voted for, and of the number of votes for each; which list they shall sign and certify, and transmit sealed to the seat of government of the United States, directed to the president of the Senate. The president of the Senate shall, in the presence of the Senate and House of Representatives, open all the certificates, and the votes shall then be counted. The person having the greatest number of votes shall be the President, if such number be a majority of the whole number of electors appointed; and if there be more than one who have such majority, and have an equal number of votes, then the House of Representatives shall immediately choose, by ballot, one of them for President; and if no person have a majority, then, from the five highest on the list, the said House shall, in like manner, choose the President. But in choosing the President, the vote shall be taken by States, the representation from each State having one vote; a quorum for this purpose shall consist of a member or members from two-thirds of the States, and a majority of all the States shall be necessary to a choice. In every case, after the choice of the President, the person having the greatest number of votes of the electors shall be the Vice-President. But if there should remain two or more who have equal votes, the Senate shall choose from them, by ballot, the Vice-President.]*

4. The Congress may determine the time of choosing the electors, and the day on which they shall give their votes, which day shall be the same throughout the United States.

5. No person, except a natural born citizen, or a citizen of the United States at the time of the adoption of this constitution, shall be eligible to the office of President; neither shall any person be eligible to that office who shall not have attained to the age of thirty-five years, and been fourteen years a resident within the United States.

6. In case of the removal of the President from office, or of his death, resignation, or inability to discharge the powers and duties of the said office, the same shall devolve on the Vice-President; and the Congress may, by law, provide for the case of removal, death, resignation or inability, both of the President and Vice-President, declaring what officer shall then act as President; and such officer shall act accordingly, until the disability be removed, or a President shall be elected.

7. The President shall, at stated times, receive for his services a compensation which shall neither be increased nor diminished during the period for which he shall have been elected; and he shall not receive within that period any other emolument from the United States, or any of them.

8. Before he enter on the execution of his office, he shall take the following oath or affirmation:

"I do solemnly swear (or affirm) that I will faithfully execute the office of President of the United States; and will, to the best of my ability, preserve, protect, and defend the Constitution of the United States."

SECTION 2.

1. The President shall be commander-in-chief of the army and navy of the United States, and of the militia of the several States, when called into the actual service of the United States. He may require the opinion, in writing, of the principal officer in each of the executive departments upon any subject relating to the duties of their respective offices; and he shall have power to grant reprieves and pardons for offences against the United States, except in cases of impeachment.

2. He shall have power, by and with the advice and consent of the Senate, to make treaties, provided two-thirds of the senators present concur; and he shall nominate, and by and with the advice and consent of the Senate shall appoint, ambassadors, other public ministers and consuls, judges of the supreme court,

* This paragraph has been superseded and annulled by the 12th amendment.

and all other officers of the United States whose appointments are not herein otherwise provided for, and which shall be established by law. But the Congress may, by law, vest the appointment of such inferior officers as they think proper in the President alone, in the courts of law, or in the heads of departments.

3. The President shall have power to fill up all vacancies that may happen during the recess of the Senate, by granting commissions which shall expire at the end of their next session.

SECTION 3.

1. He shall, from time to time, give to the Congress information of the state of the Union, and recommend to their consideration such measures as he shall judge necessary and expedient. He may, on extraordinary occasions, convene both Houses, or either of them; and in case of disagreement between them with respect to the time of adjournment, he may adjourn them to such time as he shall think proper. He shall receive ambassadors and other public ministers. He shall take care that the laws be faithfully executed; and shall commission all the officers of the United States.

SECTION 4.

1. The President, Vice-President, and all civil officers of the United States, shall be removed from office on impeachment for, and conviction of, treason, bribery, or other high crimes and misdemeanors.

ARTICLE III.

SECTION 1.

1. The judicial power of the United States shall be vested in one supreme court, and in such inferior courts as the Congress may, from time to time, ordain and establish. The judges, both of the supreme and inferior courts, shall hold their offices during good behavior; and shall, at stated times, receive for their services a compensation, which shall not be diminished during their continuance in office.

SECTION 2.

1. The judicial power shall extend to all cases in law and equity arising under this Constitution, the laws of the United States, and treaties made, or which shall be made, under their authority; to all cases affecting ambassadors, other public ministers, and consuls; to all cases of admiralty and maritime jurisdiction; to controversies to which the United States shall be a party; to controversies between two or more States; between a State and citizens of another State; between citizens of the same State claiming lands under grants of different States, and between a State, or the citizens thereof, and foreign states, citizens or subjects.

2. In all cases affecting ambassadors, other public ministers and consuls, and those in which a State shall be party, the supreme court shall have original jurisdiction. In all the other cases before mentioned, the supreme court shall have appellate jurisdiction, both as to law and fact, with such exceptions and under such regulations as the Congress shall make.

3. The trial of all crimes, except in cases of impeachment, shall be by jury, and such trial shall be held in the State where the said crimes shall have been committed; but when not committed within any State, the trial shall be at such place or places as the Congress may by law have directed.

SECTION 3.

1. Treason against the United States shall consist only in levying war against them or in adhering to their enemies, giving them aid and comfort. No person shall be convicted of treason, unless on the testimony of two witnesses to the same overt act, or on confession in open court.

2. The Congress shall have power to declare the punishment of treason; but no attainder of treason shall work corruption of blood, or forfeiture, except during the life of the person attainted.

ARTICLE IV.

SECTION 1.

1. Full faith and credit shall be given in each State to the public acts, records, and judicial proceedings of every other State; and the Congress may, by general laws, prescribe the manner in which such

acts, records, and proceedings shall be proved, and the effect thereof.

SECTION 2.

1. The citizens of each State shall be entitled to all privileges and immunities of citizens in the several States.

2. A person charged in any State with treason, felony, or other crime, who shall flee from justice, and be found in another State, shall, on demand of the executive authority of the State from which he fled, be delivered up, to be removed to the State having jurisdiction of the crime.

3. No person held to service or labor in one State under the laws thereof, escaping into another, shall, in consequence of any law or regulation therein, be discharged from such service or labor; but shall be delivered up on claim of the party to whom such service or labor may be due.

SECTION 3.

1. New States may be admitted by the Congress into this Union; but no new State shall be formed or erected within the jurisdiction of any other State, nor any State be formed by the junction of two or more States or parts of States, without the consent of the legislatures of the States concerned, as well as of the Congress.

2. The Congress shall have power to dispose of and make all needful rules and regulations respecting the territory or other property belonging to the United States; and nothing in this constitution shall be so construed as to prejudice any claims of the United States, or of any particular State.

SECTION 4.

1. The United States shall guarantee to every State in this Union a republican form of government, and shall protect each of them against invasion; and, on application of the legislature, or of the executive (when the legislature cannot be convened), against domestic violence.

ARTICLE V.

1. The Congress, whenever two-thirds of both Houses shall deem it necessary, shall propose amendments to this constitution; or, on the application of the legislatures of two-thirds of the several States, shall call a convention for proposing amendments which, in either case, shall be valid to all intents and purposes, as part of this constitution, when ratified by the legislatures of three-fourths of the several States, or by conventions in three-fourths thereof, as the one or the other mode of ratification may be proposed by the Congress; provided that no amendment which may be made prior to the year one thousand eight hundred and eight shall in any manner affect the first and fourth clauses in the ninth section of the first article; and that no State, without its consent, shall be deprived of its equal suffrage in the Senate.

ARTICLE VI.

1. All debts contracted and engagements entered into before the adoption of this constitution shall be as valid against the United States under this constitution, as under the confederation.

2. This constitution, and the laws of the United States which shall be made in pursuance thereof, and all treaties made, or which shall be made, under the authority of the United States, shall be the supreme law of the land; and the judges in every State shall be bound thereby, anything in the constitution or laws of any State to the contrary notwithstanding.

3. The senators and representatives before mentioned, and the members of the several State legislatures, and all executive and judicial officers, both of the United States and of the several States, shall be bound by oath or affirmation to support this constitution; but no religious test shall ever be required as a qualification to any office or public trust under the United States.

ARTICLE VII.

1. The ratification of the conventions of nine States shall be sufficient for the establishment of this constitution between the States so ratifying the same.

Done in convention by the unanimous consent of the States present, the seventeenth day of September, in the year of our Lord one thousand seven hundred and eighty-seven, and of the Independence of the United States of America the twelfth. In witness whereof we have hereunto subscribed our names.

G°: WASHINGTON,
Presidt, and Deputy from Virginia.

New Hampshire.

John Langdon, Nicholas Gilman.

Massachusetts.

Nathaniel Gorham, Rufus King.

Connecticut.

Wm. Saml. Johnson, Roger Sherman.

New York.

Alexander Hamilton.

New Jersey.

Wil: Livingston, David Brearley,
Wm. Paterson, Jona: Dayton.

Pennsylvania.

B. Franklin, Thomas Mifflin,
Robt. Morris, Geo. Clymer,
Thomas Fitzsimons, Jared Ingersoll,
James Wilson, Gouv. Morris.

Delaware.

Geo: Read, Jaco: Broom,
John Dickinson, Richard Bassett,
Gunning Bedford, Jun.

Maryland.

James McHenry, Danl. Carroll,
Dan of St. Thos. Jenifer.

Virginia.

John Blair, James Madison, Jr.

North Carolina.

Wm. Blount, Hu Williamson,
Richd. Dobbs Spaight.

South Carolina.

J. Rutledge, Charles Pinckney,
Charles Cotesworth Pinckney,
Pierce Butler.

Georgia.

William Few, Abr. Baldwin.

Attest:
William Jackson, Secretary.

AMENDMENTS

To the Constitution of the United States.

The following amendments were proposed at the first session of the First Congress of the United States, which was begun and held at the city of New York on the 4th of March, 1789, and were declared in force Dec. 15, 1791.

The following preamble and resolution preceded the original proposition of the amendments, and as they have been supposed to have an important bearing on the construction of those amendments, they are here inserted. They will be found in the journals of the first session of the First Congress.

CONGRESS OF THE UNITED STATES.

Begun and held at the city of New York, on Wednesday, the 4th day of March, 1789.

The conventions of a number of the States having, at the time of their adopting the Constitution, expressed a desire, in order to prevent misconstruction or abuse of its powers, that further declaratory and restrictive clauses should be added, and as extending the ground of public confidence in the government will best insure the beneficent ends of its institution:

Resolved, By the Senate and House of Representatives of the United States of America, in Congress assembled, two-thirds of both Houses concurring, that the following articles be proposed to the legislatures of the several States, as amendments to the constitution of the United States; all or any of which articles, when ratified by three-fourths of the said legislatures, to be valid to all intents and purposes, as part of the said constitution, namely:

ARTICLE I.

Congress shall make no law respecting an establishment of religion, or prohibiting the free exercise thereof; or abridging the freedom of speech or of the press; or the right of the people peaceably to assemble, and to petition the government for a redress of grievances.

ARTICLE II.

A well-regulated militia being necessary to the security of a free State, the right of the people to keep and bear arms shall not be infringed.

ARTICLE III.

No soldier shall, in time of peace, be quartered in any house without the consent of the owner, nor in time of war but in a manner to be prescribed by law.

ARTICLE IV.

The right of the people to be secure in their persons, houses, papers, and effects, against unreasonable searches and seizures, shall not be violated; and no warrants shall issue but upon probable cause, supported by oath or affirmation, and particularly describing the place to be searched, and the persons or things to be seized.

ARTICLE V.

No person shall be held to answer for a capital or otherwise infamous crime, unless on a presentment or indictment of a grand jury, except in cases arising in the land or naval forces, or in the militia, when in actual service in time of war or public danger; nor shall any person be subject for the same offence to be twice put in jeopardy of life or limb; nor shall be compelled in any criminal case, to be a witness against himself, nor be deprived of life, liberty, or property, without due process of law; nor shall private property be taken for public use without just compensation.

ARTICLE VI.

In all criminal prosecutions, the accused shall enjoy the right to a speedy and public trial, by an impartial jury of the State and district wherein the crime shall have been committed, which district shall have been previously ascertained by law; and to be informed of the nature and cause of the accusation; to be confronted with the witnesses against him; to have compulsory process for obtaining witnesses in his favor, and to have the assistance of counsel for his defence.

ARTICLE VII.

In suits at common law, where the value in controversy shall exceed twenty dollars, the right of trial by jury shall be preserved; and no fact tried by a jury shall be otherwise re-examined in any court of the United States, than according to the rules of the common law.*

* This affects only United States Courts.

ARTICLE VIII.

Excessive bail shall not be required, nor excessive fines imposed, nor cruel and unusual punishments inflicted.

ARTICLE IX.

The enumeration in the constitution of certain rights shall not be construed to deny or disparage others retained by the people.

ARTICLE X.

The powers not delegated to the United States by the constitution, nor prohibited by it to the States, are reserved to the States respectively, or to the people.

[The following amendment was proposed at the second session of the Third Congress. Declared in force Jan. 8, 1798.]

ARTICLE XI.

The judicial power of the United States shall not be construed to extend to any suit in law or equity, commenced or prosecuted against one of the United States by citizens of another State, or by citizens or subjects of any foreign state.

[The three following sections were proposed as amendments at the first session of the Eighth Congress. Declared in force Sept. 25, 1804.]

ARTICLE XII.

1. The electors shall meet in their respective States, and vote by ballot for President and Vice-President, one of whom at least shall not be an inhabitant of the same State with themselves. They shall name in their ballots the person voted for as President, and in distinct ballots the person voted for as Vice-President; and they shall make distinct lists of all persons voted for as President, and of all persons voted for as Vice-President, and of the number of votes for each; which lists they shall sign and certify, and transmit sealed to the seat of the government of the United States, directed to the president of the Senate. The president of the Senate shall, in the presence of the Senate and House of Representatives, open all the certificates, and the votes shall then be counted. The person having the greatest number of votes for President

shall be the President, if such number be a majority of the whole number of electors appointed; and if no person have such majority, then from the persons having the highest number, not exceeding three, on the list of those voted for as President, the House of Representatives shall choose immediately, by ballot, the President. But in choosing the President, the votes shall be taken by States, the representation from each State having one vote; a quorum for this purpose shall consist of a member or members from two-thirds of the States, and a majority of all the States shall be necessary to a choice. And if the House of Representatives shall not choose a President, whenever the right of choice shall devolve upon them, before the fourth day of March next following, then the Vice-President shall act as President as in the case of the death or other constitutional disability of the President.

2. The person having the greatest number of votes as Vice-President shall be the Vice-President, if such number be a majority of the whole number of electors appointed, and if no person have a majority, then from the two highest numbers on the list the Senate shall choose the Vice-President. A quorum for the purpose shall consist of two-thirds of the whole number of senators, and a majority of the whole number shall be necessary to a choice.

3. But no person constitutionally ineligible to the office of President shall be eligible to that of Vice-President of the United States.

ARTICLE XIII.*

SECTION 1.

Neither slavery nor involuntary servitude, except as a punishment for crime, whereof the party shall have been duly convicted, shall exist within the United States, or any place subject to their jurisdiction.

SECTION 2.

Congress shall have power to enforce this article by appropriate legislation.

* Proposed by Congress Feb. 1, 1865. Ratification announced by Secretary of State, Dec. 18, 1865.

ARTICLE XIV.*

SECTION 1.

All persons born or naturalized in the United States, and subject to the jurisdiction thereof, are citizens of the United States and of the State wherein they reside. No State shall make or enforce any law which shall abridge the privileges or immunities of citizens of the United States; nor shall any State deprive any person of life, liberty, or property, without due process of law, nor deny to any person within its jurisdiction the equal protection of the laws.

SECTION 2.

Representatives shall be apportioned among the several States according to their respective numbers, counting the whole number of persons in each State, excluding Indians not taxed. But when the right to vote at any election for the choice of electors for President and Vice-President of the United States, representatives in Congress, the executive and judicial officers of a State, or the members of the legislature thereof, is denied to any of the male inhabitants of such State, being twenty-one years of age, and citizens of the United States, or in any way abridged, except for participation in rebellion or other crime, the basis of representation therein shall be reduced in the proportion which the number of such male citizens shall bear to the whole number of male citizens twenty-one years of age in such State.

SECTION 3.

No person shall be a senator or representative in Congress, or elector of President and Vice-President, or hold any office, civil or military, under the United States, or under any State, who, having previously taken an oath as a member of Congress, or as an officer of the United States, or as a member of any State legislature, or as an executive or judicial officer of any State, to support the constitution of the United States, shall have en-

* Proposed by Congress June 16, 1866. Ratification announced by Secretary of State, July 28, 1868.

gaged in insurrection or rebellion against the same, or given aid or comfort to the enemies thereof. But Congress may, by a vote of two-thirds of each House, remove such disability.

SECTION 4.

The validity of the public debt of the United States authorized by law, including debts incurred for payment of pensions and bounties for services in suppressing insurrection or rebellion, shall not be questioned. But neither the United States nor any States shall assume or pay any debt or obligation incurred in aid of insurrection or rebellion against the United States, or any claim for the loss or emancipation of any slave; but all such debts, obligations, and claims shall be held illegal and void.

SECTION 5.

The Congress shall have power to enforce, by appropriate legislation, the provisions of this article.

ARTICLE XV.*

SECTION 1.

The right of citizens of the United States to vote shall not be denied or abridged by the United States or by any State on account of race, color, or previous condition of servitude.

SECTION 2.

The Congress shall have power to enforce this article by appropriate legislation.

Constitution, Construction of the.—There are two general divisions of opinion, one in favor of a strict and narrow construction; the other in favor of a broad or loose construction. No constitution can mean exactly the same thing in every point to any two individuals, or to any two generations of individuals. The ordinary development of the construction of the constitution results in a general equilibrium due to an infinite variety of opinions. See CENTRALIZATION and DECENTRALIZATION.

Amendments of the Constitution.—The ratification of New Hampshire brought into existence the Constitution of the United States. The last of the original thirteen colonics to adopt the constitution was Rhode Island in 1790.

The first ten amendments to the Constitution were made in consequence of the propositions by the various States as follows:

Massachusetts, 9 amendments; North Carolina, 26 amendments; New Hampshire, 12 amendments; South Carolina, 4 amendments; New York, 32 amendments; Pennsylvania minority, 14; Maryland minority, 28; Virginia, 20 amendments.

Many of these propositions were reproductions; all were brought before Congress in 1789. In place of them the House agreed upon 17 amendments; the Senate upon 12 amendments, which last were passed by two-thirds of both houses, Sept. 25, 1789.

Ten of the twelve amendments were ratified by the States, but the two (1) an amendment as to representation in House of Representatives (2) as to compensation for the services of Senators and Representatives, were rejected.

The Eleventh Amendment was passed by two-thirds of both Houses March 5, 1794, and declared in force Jan. 8, 1798.

The Twelfth Amendment was declared in force Sept. 25, 1804.

The Thirteenth Amendment was passed in 1865, was rejected by Delaware and Kentucky, not acted upon by Texas, conditionally ratified by Alabama and Mississippi, and accepted by the other States. The vote was 31 to 5, and the amendment was proclaimed in force Dec. 18, 1865.

The Fourteenth Amendment was passed in 1866, rejected by Delaware, Kentucky, and Maryland, not acted upon by California, ratified by a vote of 33 to 7. Amendment was declared in force July 28, 1868. New Jersey and Ohio had rescinded their ratifications, but Congress by resolutions declared the amendment lawfully adopted, and instructed the Secretary of State to proclaim the ratification, which he did on July 28, 1868. The subsequent ratification of three other States cleared away any doubt as to the existence of this amendment.

The Fifteenth Amendment was not acted upon by Tennessee. It was rejected by California, Delaware, Kentucky, Maryland, New Jersey, and Oregon. New York

* Proposed by Congress Feb. 27, 1869. Ratification announced by Secretary of State, March 30, 1870.

rejected its ratification, but the amendment was declared in force March 30, 1870.

ARTICLE XVI.

The Congress shall have power to lay and collect taxes on incomes from whatever source derived, without apportionment among the several States, and without regard to any census or enumeration.

[This amendment was declared in force Feb. 25, 1913.]

ARTICLE XVII.

1. The Senate of the United States shall be composed of two Senators from each state, elected by the people thereof, for six years; and each Senator shall have one vote. The electors in each State shall have the qualifications requisite for electors of the most numerous branch of the State legislatures.

2. When vacancies happen in the representation of any State in the Senate, the executive authority of such State shall issue writs of election to fill such vacancies: Provided that the legislature of any State may empower the executive thereof to make temporary appointment until the people fill the vacancies by election as the legislature may direct.

3. This amendment shall not be so construed as to affect the election or term of any Senator chosen before it becomes valid as a part of the Constitution.

[This amendment was declared in force May 31, 1913.]

CONSTITUTION, OR OLD IRONSIDES

Constitution, or **Old Ironsides,** the most renowned vessel of the United States navy; built in Boston in 1797; rated as a frigate of 1,576 tons, with an armament of forty-four guns, but actually carrying fifty-two. The frigate, then under command of Capt. Isaac Hull, had just returned from foreign service when the War of 1812–15 was declared. She sailed from Annapolis (July 12, 1812) on a cruise to the northward. On the 17th she fell in with a small squadron under Captain Broke, when one of the most remarkable naval retreats and pursuits ever recorded occurred. The *Constitution* could not cope with the whole squadron, and her safety depended on successful flight. There was almost a dead calm, and she floated almost independent of her helm. Her boats were launched, and manned by strong seamen with sweeps. A long 18-pounder was rigged as a stern chaser, and another of the same calibre was pointed off the forecastle. Out of her cabin windows, which by sawing were made large enough, two 24-pounders were run, and all the light canvas that would draw was set. A gentle breeze sprang up, and she was just getting under headway when a shot at long range was fired from the *Shannon*, Broke's flag-ship, but without effect. Calm and breeze succeeded each other, and kedging and sails kept the *Constitution* moving in a manner that puzzled her pursuers.

At length the British discovered the secret, and instantly the *Shannon* was urged onward by the same means, and slowly gained on the *Constitution.* The *Guerrière,* thirty-eight guns, Captain Dacres, another of the squadron, had now joined in the chase. All day and all night the pursuit continued; and at dawn of the second day of the chase the whole British squadron were in sight, bent on capturing the plucky American frigate. There were now five vessels in chase, clouded with canvas. Expert seamanship kept the space between the *Constitution* and her pursuers so wide that not a gun was fired. She was four miles ahead of the *Belvidere,* the nearest vessel of the squadron. At sunset (July 19) a squall struck the *Constitution* with great fury, but she was prepared for it. Wind, lightning, and rain made a terrific commotion on the sea for a short time, but the gallant ship outrode the tempest, and at twilight she was flying before her pursuers at the rate of eleven knots an hour. At midnight the British fired two guns, and the next morning gave up the chase, which had lasted sixty-four hours. The newspapers were filled with the praises

THE ENGAGEMENT BETWEEN THE "CONSTITUTION" AND THE "GUERRIÉRE"

of Hull and his good ship, and doggerel verse in songs and sonnets, like the following, abounded:

"'Neath Hull's command, with a taught band,
And naught beside to back her,
Upon a day, as log-books say,
A fleet bore down to thwack her.

"A fleet, you know, is odds or so
Against a single ship, sirs,
So 'cross the tide her legs she tried,
And gave the rogues the slip, sirs."

On Aug. 12 Captain Hull sailed from Boston and cruised eastward in search of British vessels. He was anxious to find the *Guerrière*, thirty-eight guns, Capt. James Richard Dacres. The British newspapers, sneering at the American navy, had spoken of the *Constitution* as a "bundle of pine boards sailing under a bit of striped bunting." They had also declared that "a few broadsides from England's wooden walls would drive the paltry striped bunting from the ocean." Hull was eager to pluck out the sting of these insults. He sailed as far as the Bay of Fundy, and then cruised eastward of Nova Scotia, where he captured a number of British merchant vessels on their way to the St. Lawrence. On the afternoon of Aug. 19 he fell in with the *Guerrière*, in lat. 41° 40′, long. 55° 48′. Some firing began at long range. Perceiving a willingness on the part of his antagonist to have a fair yard-arm to yard-arm fight, Hull pressed sail to get his vessel alongside the *Guerrière*. When the *Guerrière* began to pour shot into the *Constitution*, Lieutenant Morris, Hull's second in command, asked, "Shall I open fire?" Hull quietly replied, "Not yet." The question was repeated when the shots began to tell on the *Constitution*, and Hull again answered, "Not yet." When the vessels were very near each other, Hull, filled with intense excitement, bent himself twice to the deck and shouted, "Now, boys, pour it into them!" The command was instantly obeyed.

The guns of the *Constitution* were double-shotted with round and grape, and their execution was terrible. The vessels were within pistol-shot of each other. Fifteen minutes after the contest began the mizzen-mast of the *Guerrière* was shot away, her main-yard was in slings, and her hull, spars, sails, and rigging were torn to pieces. By a skilful movement the *Constitution* now fell foul of her foe, her bowsprit running into the larboard quarter of her antagonist. The cabin of the *Constitution* was set on fire by the explosion of the forward guns of the *Guerrière*, but the flames were soon extinguished. Both parties attempted to board, while the roar of the great guns was terrific. The sea was rolling heavily, and would not allow a safe passage from one vessel to the other. At length the *Constitution* became disentangled and shot ahead of the *Guerrière*, when the main-mast of the latter, shattered into weakness, fell into the sea. The *Guerrière*, shivered and shorn, rolled like a log in the trough of the sea, entirely at the mercy of the billows. Hull sent his compliments to Captain Dacres, and inquired whether he had struck his flag. Dacres, who was a "jolly tar," looking up and down and at the stumps of his masts, coolly and dryly replied, "Well, I don't know; our mizzen-mast is gone; our main-mast is gone; upon the whole, you may say we *have* struck our flag." Too much bruised to be saved, the *Guerrière* was set on fire and blown up after her people were removed. This exploit of Hull made him the theme of many toasts, songs, and sonnets. One rhymester wrote concerning the capture of the *Guerrière:*

"Isaac did so maul and rake her,
That the decks of Captain Dacre
Were in such a woful pickle,
As if Death, with scythe and sickle,
With his sling, or with his shaft,
Had cut his harvest fore and aft.
Thus, in thirty minutes, ended
Mischiefs that could not be mended;
Masts and yards and ship descended
All to Davy Jones's locker—
Such a ship, in such a pucker."

Hull had seven men killed and seven wounded. Dacres lost seventy men killed and wounded. The news of this victory was received with joy throughout the country. The people of Boston gave Hull and his officers a banquet, at which 600 citizens sat down. The authorities of New York gave him the freedom of the city in a gold box. Congress thanked him and awarded him a gold medal, and appropriated $50,000 to be distributed as prize-money among the officers and crew of the *Constitution*. The British public were amazed by the event. Their faith in the impregnability of the "wooden walls of Old England" was shaken. Its bearing on the future of the war was incalculable. The London *Times* regarded it as a serious blow to the British supremacy of the seas. "It is not merely that an English frigate has been taken," said that journal, "but that it has been taken by a *new enemy*—an enemy *unaccustomed to such triumphs*, and likely to be rendered *insolent* and *confident* by them."

After his decisive victory over the *Guerrière*, Captain Hull generously retired from the command of the *Constitution* to allow others to win honors with her. Capt. William Bainbridge was appointed his immediate successor, and was placed in command of a small squadron—the *Constitution*, *Essex*, thirty-two guns, and *Hornet*, eighteen. Bainbridge sailed from Boston late in October, 1812, with the *Constitution* and *Hornet*. The *Essex* was ordered to follow to designated ports, and, if the flag-ship was not found at any of them, to go on an independent cruise. After touching at these ports, Bainbridge was off Bahia or San Salvador, Brazil, where the *Hornet* blockaded an English sloop-of-war, and the *Constitution* continued down the coast. On Dec. 29 she fell in with the British frigate *Java*, forty-nine guns, Capt. Henry Lambert, one of the finest vessels in the royal navy. They were then about 30 miles from the shore, southeast of San Salvador. About two o'clock in the afternoon, after running upon the same tack with the *Constitution*, the *Java* bore down upon the latter with the intention of raking her. This calamity was avoided, and very soon a most furious battle at short range was begun. When it had raged about half an hour the wheel of the *Constitution* was shot away, and her antagonist, being the better sailer, had the advantage of her for a time.

Bainbridge managed his crippled ship with so much skill that she was first in coming to the wind on the next tack, and gave her antagonist a terrible raking fire. Both now ran free, with the wind on their quarter, and at three o'clock the *Java* attempted to close by running down the *Constitution's* quarter. She missed her aim, and lost her jib-boom and the head of her bowsprit by shots from the *Constitution*. In a few moments the latter poured a heavy raking broadside into the stem of the *Java*. Another followed, when the fore-mast of the *Java* went by the board, crushing in the forecastle and main-deck in its passage. At that moment the *Constitution* shot ahead, keeping away to avoid being raked, and finally, after manœuvring nearly an hour, she forereached her antagonist, wore, passed her, and luffed up under her quar-

HULL'S MEDAL.

ter. Then the two vessels lay broadside to broadside, engaged in deadly conflict yard-arm to yard-arm. Very soon the *Java's* mizzen-mast was shot away. The fire of the *Java* now ceased, and Bainbridge was under the impression that she had struck her colors. He had fought about two hours, and occupied an hour in repairing damages, when he saw an ensign fluttering over the *Java*. Bainbridge was preparing to renew the conflict, when the *Java's* colors were hauled down and she was surrendered. She was bearing as passenger to the East Indies Lieutenant-General Hyslop (just appointed governor-general of Bombay) and his staff, and more than 100 English officers and men destined for service in the East Indies. The *Java* was a wreck, and the *Constitution's* sails were very much riddled. The commander of the *Java* was mortally wounded. Her officers and crew numbered about 446. Some of the above-described passengers assisted in the contest. How many of the British were lost was never revealed. It was believed their loss was nearly 100 killed and 200 wounded. The *Constitution* lost nine killed and twenty-five wounded. Bainbridge, also, was wounded. After every living being had been transferred from the *Java* to the *Constitution*, the former was fired and blown up (Dec. 31, 1812). The prisoners were paroled at San Salvador. The news of the victory created great joy in the United States.

Bainbridge received honors of the most conspicuous kind—a banquet at Boston (March 2, 1813); thanks of legislatures; the freedom of the city of New York, in a gold box, by its authorities; the same by the authorities of the city of Albany; an elegant service of silver-plate by the citizens of Philadelphia; and the thanks of Congress, with a gold medal for himself and silver ones for his officers, besides $50,000 in money to Bainbridge and his companions-in-arms as compensation for their loss of prize-money. The conflict between the *Constitution* and the *Java* was the closing naval engagement of the first six months of the war. From this time the *Constitution* was ranked among the seamen as a "lucky ship," and she was called "Old Ironsides."

GOLD BOX PRESENTED TO BAINBRIDGE BY THE CITY OF NEW YORK.

When Bainbridge relinquished the command of the *Constitution*, in 1813, she was thoroughly repaired and placed in charge of Capt. Charles Stewart. She left Boston Harbor, for a cruise, on Dec. 30, 1813, and for seventeen days did not see a sail. At the beginning of February, 1814, she was on the coast of Surinam, and, on the 14th, captured the British war-schooner *Picton*, sixteen guns, together with a letter-of-marque which was under her convoy. On her way homeward she chased the British frigate *La Pique*, thirty-six guns, off Porto Rico, but she escaped under cover of the night. Early on Sunday morning, April 3, when off Cape Ann, she fell in with two heavy British frigates (the *Junon* and *La Nymphe*); and she was compelled to seek safety in the harbor of Marblehead. She was in great peril there from her pursuers. These were kept at bay by a quickly gathered force of militia, infantry, and artillery, and she was soon afterwards safely anchored in Salem Harbor. Thence she went to Boston,

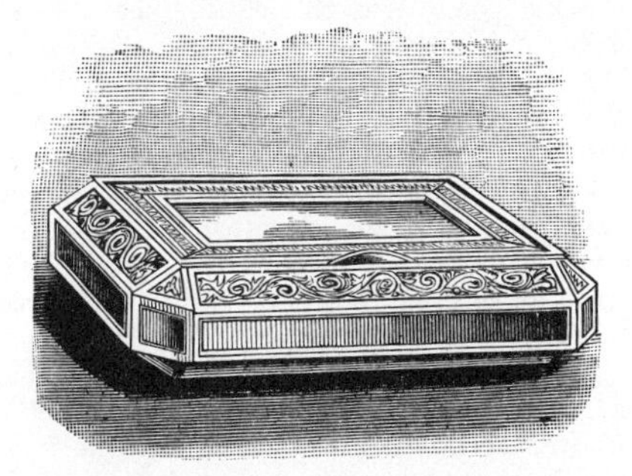

GOLD BOX PRESENTED TO BAINBRIDGE BY THE CITY OF ALBANY

where she remained until the close of the year.

At the end of December (1814) the *Constitution*, still under the command of Stewart, put to sea. Crossing the Atlantic, she put into the Bay of Biscay, and then cruised off the harbor of Lisbon. Stewart sailed southward towards Cape St. Vincent, and, on Feb. 20, 1815, he discovered two strange sails, which, towards evening, flung out the British flag. Then Stewart displayed the American flag. By skilful management he obtained an advantageous position, when he began an action with both of them; and, after a severe fight of about fifteen minutes in the moonlight, both vessels became silent, and, as the cloud of smoke cleared away, Stewart perceived that the leading ship of his assailants was under the lee-beam of his own vessel, while the sternmost was luffing up as with the intention of tacking and crossing the stem of the *Constitution*. The latter delivered a broadside into the ship abreast of her, and then, by skilful management of the sails, backed swiftly astern, compelling the foe to fill again to avoid being raked. For some time both vessels manœuvred admirably, pouring heavy shot into each other whenever opportunity offered, when, at a quarter before seven o'clock, the British struck her flag. She was the frigate *Cyane*, thirty-six guns, Captain Falcoln, manned by a crew of 180 men. Stewart now sought her consort, which had been forced out of the fight by the crippled condition of her running-gear. She was ignorant of the fate of the *Cyane*. About an hour after the latter had surrendered, she met the *Constitution* searching for her. Each delivered a broadside, and, for a while, there was a brisk running fight, the *Constitution* chasing, and her bow guns sending shot that ripped up the planks of her antagonist. The latter was soon compelled to surrender, and proved to be the *Levant*, eighteen guns, Captain Douglass. The *Constitution* was then equipped with fifty-two guns, and her complement of men and boys was about 470. The loss of the *Constitution* in this action was three killed and twelve wounded; of the two captured vessels, seventy-seven. The *Constitution* was so little damaged that three hours after the action she was again ready for conflict. That battle on a moonlit sea lasted only forty-five minutes.

STEWART'S MEDAL.

Placing Lieutenant Ballard in command of the *Levant*, and Lieutenant Hoffman of the *Cyane*, Stewart proceeded with his prizes to one of the Cape Verd Islands, where he arrived on March 10, 1815. The next day the *Constitution* and her prizes were in imminent peril by the appearance of English vessels of war coming portward in a thick fog. He knew they would have no respect for the neutrality of the port

(Porto Praya), and so he cut the cables of the *Constitution,* and, with his prizes, put to sea. They were chased by the strangers, which were the British frigate *Leander,* fifty guns, Sir George Collier; *Newcastle,* fifty guns, Lord George Stuart; and *Acasta,* forty guns, Captain Kerr. They pressed hard upon the fugitives. The *Cyane* was falling astern, and must soon have been overtaken. Stewart ordered her commander to tack. He obeyed, and she escaped in the fog, reaching New York in April. The three ships continued to chase the *Constitution,* the *Newcastle* firing her chase guns without effect. Meanwhile the *Levant* fell far in the rear. Stewart signalled her to tack, which she did, when the three vessels gave up the chase of the *Constitution,* and pursued the *Levant* into Porto Praya Harbor—a Portuguese port. Regardless of neutrality, 120 prisoners, whom Stewart had paroled there, seized a battery, and opened upon the *Levant,* which, receiving the fire of the pursuers at the same time, was compelled to surrender.

Stewart crossed the Atlantic, landed many of his prisoners in Brazil, and at Porto Rico heard of the proclamation of peace. Then he returned home, taking with him the news of the capture of the *Cyane* and *Levant.* The *Constitution* was hailed with delight, and Stewart received public honors. The Common Council of New York gave him the freedom of the city in a gold box, and a public dinner to him and his officers. The legislature of Pennsylvania voted him a gold-hilted sword; and Congress voted him and his men the thanks of the nation and directed a medal of gold, commemorative of the capture of the *Cyane* and *Levant,* to be presented to him.

The famous frigate is yet afloat. Many years ago the Navy Department concluded to break her up and sell her timbers, as she was thought to be a decided "invalid." The order had gone forth, when the execution of it was arrested by the opposition of public sentiment created and called forth largely by the following poetic protest by Dr. Oliver Wendell Holmes:

"Ay, tear her tattered ensign down!
Long has it waved on high,
And many an eye has danced to see
That banner in the sky.
Beneath it rang the battle-shout,
And burst the cannon's roar;
The meteor of the ocean air
Shall sweep the clouds no more.

"Her deck once red with heroes' blood,
Where knelt the vanquished foe,
When winds were hissing o'er the flood
And waves were white below,
No more shall feel the victor's tread,
Or know the conquered knee:
The harpies of the shore shall pluck
The Eagle of the Sea!

"Oh! better that her shattered hulk
Should sink beneath the wave;
Her thunders shook the mighty deep,
And there should be her grave.
Nail to the mast her holy flag,
Set every threadbare sail,
And give her to the God of Storms,
The lightning, and the gale!"

THE CONSTITUTION IN 1876.

"Old Ironsides" was saved and converted into a school-ship.

Constitutional Union Party, THE, a political party organized in 1860 by the Southern remnant of the old Whig party. In its convention, held at Baltimore, on May 9, 1860, there were delegates present from twenty States, who nominated JOHN BELL (*q. v.*) for President and EDWARD EVERETT (*q. v.*) for Vice-President. The platform consisted of a preamble antagonizing all platforms in general as tending to foster "geographical and sectional parties," and a resolution, a portion of which read: "That it is both the part of patriotism and of duty to recognize no political principle other than the Constitution of the country, the union of the States, and the enforcement of the laws." This party invited all patriotic voters to forsake the Republican party, which opposed, and the Democratic party, which favored, slavery, and unite in promoting a programme entirely ignoring slavery as a political issue. In the election of 1860 it carried Kentucky, Tennessee, and Virginia, and had a total popular vote of 589,581, and a total electoral vote of 39. The party was submerged in the first waves of the Civil War.

Constitutions, ORIGINAL STATES. The following is the record of the adoption of constitutions by the original thirteen States: New Hampshire, 1784; Massachusetts, 1780; Connecticut, 1818; Rhode Island, 1842; New York, 1777; Pennsylvania, 1777; New Jersey, 1776; Delaware, 1776; Maryland, 1776; Virginia, 1776; North Carolina, 1776; South Carolina, 1778; and Georgia, 1777.

CONSULAR SERVICE, THE

Consular Service, THE. The movement in favor of reform in the consular service has of late made noticeable strides in this country. People are beginning to realize that the present system of appointments and removals for political reasons is very prejudicial to our commercial interests, especially when those of other countries are in the hands of consuls whose training and experience give them every advantage over ours.

In Great Britain, Germany, France, and Austria, in particular, systematic efforts have been in progress for several years for the making of competent consular and commercial agents. A feature of this movement is the establishment of commercial schools usually supported (1) by the national government, (2) by municipal authorities, and (3) by large commercial organizations, such as chambers of commerce and boards of trade. Graduates are given the preference of employment over other applicants by the firms represented in the commercial bodies, and also constitute a body of young and specially trained men from which the national government makes selections for the minor commercial offices. Admitted to the consular and commercial bureaus, the future of the graduate becomes a matter of personal competence.

In the United States a beginning has been made on similar lines. In several universities there have been established either schools of commerce or lectureships on commercial practice, in several instances under the direct inspiration and support of local commercial bodies. The national government, too, has grown more exacting in its requirements (see closing part of this article).

Two views of the condition of the American consular service and of the great business need for reform therein are here presented, both of them by United States officials of large experience and of reputation commanding serious attention.

I.

BY HENRY WHITE,

SECRETARY OF EMBASSY AT LONDON.

We send out consuls, many of whom are not only ignorant of foreign languages, but often of everything which such officials should know; and in order to do this we remove others just as they are beginning to acquire the knowledge and experience indispensable to the position. The result is that the consular service of the United States is a very costly training-school, from which the country derives little or no benefit.

I refer to the system and not to individuals—certainly not to the efficient consuls whom I have known, especially in Great Britain. We usually send, however, men of ability and good standing to that country, where in any case their efficiency cannot be impaired by ignorance of the language.

The urgency for consular reform has of late been frequently brought to the attention of the public by a series of interesting magazine articles, each of which was extensively, and with very few exceptions favorably, commented upon by newspapers of both parties throughout the country. A forcible address was also delivered on the subject to the National Board of Trade by Hon. Theodore Roosevelt; and more recently Admiral Erben, whose opportunities have been frequent of observing the sorry figure often cut by our consuls in comparison with those of other countries, has expressed himself as strongly in favor of this reform, which is advocated by the National Board of Trade and other commercial bodies.

Between March 4 and Dec. 31, 1893, thirty out of thirty-five consuls-general and 133 out of 183 first-class consuls and commercial agents were changed, the numbers in the British Empire alone being seven consuls-general (the entire number), and sixty-two out of eighty-eight consuls and commercial agents. In Great Britain and Ireland the consul-general and eighteen consuls and commercial agents out of a total of twenty-four were changed, Manchester being the only first-class consulate omitted from this clean sweep.

It is impossible to suppose that such an upheaval was intended to benefit the consular service, or that it could have been otherwise than exceedingly detrimental to its efficiency. Nor is it a matter for surprise, when the numerous removals which have taken place afterwards are added to the above figures, that most people should agree with Mr. Theodore Roosevelt in the opinion that the present system is "undoubtedly directly responsible for immense damages to our trade and commercial relations, and costs our mercantile classes hundreds of thousands — in all probability, many millions — of dollars every year."

It is not my intention, however, to make out a "case" against the administration.

My object is (1) to show that the system under which it is possible for the President to dismiss consuls by the hundred, and to appoint in their stead men of whom no proof of fitness is required, is not only prejudicial to our commercial interests, but derogatory to our dignity as a nation; (2) to give a brief account of the manner in which the efficient consular services of Great Britain and France are recruited; and (3) to make a few suggestions as to the system, which should be adopted in the United States.

The numerous duties of a consul have been so fully set forth of late by others that it would be superfluous for me to repeat them. Suffice it to say that the most important of them all are: (1) the increase of our national revenue by detecting frauds in invoices on which articles to be imported to the United States are entered at less than their value; and (2) the promotion of our foreign trade by obtaining and sending home such information as is likely to be of assistance to our merchants in its maintenance and development.

There is, unfortunately, no means of estimating accurately the immense annual loss incurred through failure on the part of consuls to keep our merchants promptly and accurately informed as to the condition of trade. Such information is obtainable by a consul not only from printed statistics, but more particularly by mixing freely with the leading merchants and inhabitants of his district, and becoming thereby imbued with the local current of commercial thought. But the following quotation from Mr. Washburn will give an idea of the extent to which the national revenue may suffer:

"The aggregate amount lost to the government in this way is almost incalculable; but some idea of it may be gathered when it is remembered that an increase of only 2½ per cent. in invoice valuations at the little industrial centre of Crefeld alone would result in an annual accession to the customs receipts of $150,000. It is beyond mere conjecture that an addition of at least 5 per cent. could be brought about and maintained at many posts by competent and trained officers."

A consul cannot attain a thorough familiarity with the value of every article exported from his district, nor be able to detect frauds in invoice valuations, nor acquire a thorough knowledge of the people among whom he lives and of their methods of business, unless he be able to speak the language of the country and live there a number of years. Nevertheless, in Mexico, Central and South America, where we are supposed, and certainly ought, to exercise a greater influnece than any other power, we require of our consuls neither a prolonged residence nor a knowledge of the Spanish language.

The following incidents will help to show what is possible and has occurred under the present system.

Shortly before President Harrison went out of office a communication was made by a leading European power to the United States legation at its capital, requesting that the new administration be asked not to appoint as consul in an important dependency of that power an American citizen who had made himself objectionable to the local authorities by alleged attempts to cheat the customs, boasts of "getting a rise out of the government," and otherwise, and who had announced that upon the assumption of the Presidency by Mr. Cleveland he would receive the appointment in question. This communication was promptly transmitted to the Department of State, and under any other system but ours the matter would have ended there.

Shortly afterwards, however, the name of the individual in question appeared in a list of new appointments as consul at the very place at which we had been given to understand that he could not be received. Telegraphic inquiries were at once made, and elicited the fact that owing to the pressure of applications for office with which the State Department was just then overwhelmed, this important request of a friendly power had been overlooked. The appointment had, of course, to be withdrawn; but I need scarcely point out the difference from an international point of view between not making it and being compelled to withdraw one actually made.

The other incident to which I refer occurred in Spain. In 1890, the consular agent at Seville—sent there, be it remembered, not as a missionary, but to represent the civilization of the United States and to further our commerce—thought it his duty to bombard with Protestant tracts the procession of the Corpus Christi as it passed through the streets. The excitement caused by this singular proceeding was great, and the official in question was arrested, being thereby protected from personal violence on the part of those who witnessed and were outraged by his conduct, which was promptly brought by the Spanish government to the attention of our minister at Madrid, who had him removed. This was bad enough, but it is not all. The same individual has actually been sent back to Seville in a consular capacity.

The efficiency of a consul cannot be otherwise than seriously impaired when there exists a strong local animosity or prejudice against him. For this reason it is a great mistake, as has been pointed out by others, to send, as we often do, naturalized citizens as consuls to countries from which they originally emanated, our native citizens being much less likely to excite such local feeling. It is even more objectionable, however, to appoint members of the Jewish religion to consular posts in countries in which public opinion is strongly anti-Semitic, as the latter involves social, and to a considerable extent political, ostracism. The same man sent elsewhere might prove a very useful consul; but under the above conditions it is impossible.

Great Britain, France, Germany, and other European countries take a very different view of the importance of their consular services, which are organized with the utmost care.

The British service was established in its present form by act of Parliament in 1825 (6 Geo. IV., cap. 87). Up to that time its members had been appointed, on no regular system, by the King, and were paid from his civil list. This act placed the service under the Foreign Office, and provided for its payment out of funds to be voted by Parliament. Since then it has been the subject of periodical investigation by royal commissions and parliamentary committees, with a view to the improvement of its efficiency. The evidence taken on these occasions is published in voluminous blue books, the perusal of which I recommend to those interested in the reform in our service.

Appointments are made by the secretary of state for foreign affairs. Candidates must be recommended by some one known to him, and their names and qualifications are thereupon entered on a list, from which he selects a name when a vacancy occurs. The candidate selected, whose age must be between twenty-five and fifty, is then required to pass an examination before the civil-service commissioners in the following subjects: (1) English language. (2) French language, which the candidate must be able to write and speak "correctly and fluently." (3) Language of the place at which the consular official is to reside. It must be known sufficiently to enable him to communicate directly with the authorities and natives of the place. (4) British mercantile law. (5) Arithmetic to a sufficient extent to enable the consul to draw up commercial tables and reports.

Men usually enter the service as vice-consuls, and are promoted or not according to their merits, but there is no regularity or certainty about promotion, owing to the fact that a man may be very suitable for one place and not at all for another. There is a strong feeling against removing a consul from a post in which he is doing well. To such an extent is this the case that a man is sometimes promoted to be consul-general without a change of post. The majority of British consuls will, consequently, be found to have occupied very few posts. The entire career of the late consul-general at New York, which covered a period of over forty years, was spent at San Francisco (1851–1883) and New York (1883–1894); and the late British consul at Paris held that post from 1865 until his death recently.

There are two **important** branches of the service for which candidates are specially trained, and admission to which is by means of a competitive examination open to the public, and whereof due notice is given beforehand in the newspapers —namely, The Levant (Turkey, Egypt, Persia), and the China, Japan, and Siam services.

Those who are successful in these examinations are appointed "student interpreters." They must be unmarried and between the ages of eighteen and twenty-four. These student interpreters must study Oriental languages either at Oxford or at a British legation or consulate in the country to which they are to be accredited. They are called on to pass further examinations at intervals, and, if successful, they become eligible for employment, first as assistants and afterwards as interpreters, vice-consuls and consuls, as vacancies occur.

The salaries of British consular officers are fixed, under the act of Parliament of July 21, 1891 (54 and 55 Vict., cap. 36), by the secretary of state, with the approval of the treasury, and no increase can be made in any salary without the approval of the latter. They average about £600 ($3,000) a year, but, of course, some of the important posts are much more highly paid; the salary of the consul-general at New York being £2,000 (nearly $10,000), with an office allowance besides of £1,660, and a staff consisting of a consul at £600, and two vice-consuls at £400 and £250, respectively; that of the consul at San Francisco, £1,200 (nearly $6,000), with an office allowance of £600 besides.

British consular officials are retired at the age of seventy with a pension.

There is also an unpaid branch of the service, consisting chiefly of vice-consuls, appointed at places which are not of sufficient importance to merit a paid official. They are usually British merchants, but may be foreigners. They are not subjected to an examination, and are rarely promoted to a paid appointment.

Consular clerks are required to pass an examination in handwriting and orthography, arithmetic, and one foreign language (speaking, translating, and copying).

In France, the consular service has for years past been an object of the most careful solicitude to successive governments, and the subject of frequent decrees tending to improve its efficiency on the part of the chief of state.

Many of these decrees, and of the recommendations by ministers of foreign affairs on which they were based, are interesting, and they show how the French have realized, under all recent forms of government, and particularly under the present republic, the absolute necessity of keeping "politics" out of their consular service, and devoting its energies exclusively to the interests of French trade.

The French service consists of consuls-generals, first and second class consuls, vice-consuls, and pupil consuls (*élève consuls*). From the latter, vacancies are chiefly filled. A competitive examination takes place once a year for vacancies in the list of attaché of embassy and pupil consul. In order to compete therein, a man must have previously obtained admission to the "stage"—a probationary period of not less than one nor more than three years—during which his fitness for the career contemplated (foreign office, diplomatic, or consular) is tested. The foreign minister nominates these probationers (*stagiaires*), who must be under twenty-seven years of age, and possessors of a collegiate degree in law, science, or letters, or who must have passed certain other examinations or be holders of a commission in the army or navy.

This examination for pupil consuls is in international law, and English or German, political economy, or political and commercial geography. Those whose papers are sufficiently creditable in the opinion of the examiners to warrant their going any further are then subjected to a public oral examination in geography, maritime and customs law, in addition to the subjects already mentioned. The successful competitors become eligible for appointment as pupil consuls, and before being assigned to a consulate they are obliged to spend at least one year at one of the principal chambers of commerce, whence they must send the minister periodical reports on the trade of the district. After three years' service as pupil consuls they are eligible for promotion to a vice-consulship. No official in the French consular service can be promoted until he has served at least three years in a grade.

There are, furthermore, chancellors also whose chief functions are to keep the accounts; interpreters and dragomen for the Levant and Asiatic services, who attain those posts by means of special examinations, and may eventually become vice-consuls, with hope of subsequent promotion.

In addition to the foregoing safeguards, a committee of consultation on consulates (*Comité Consultative de Consulats*) was created by Presidential decree in 1891. It consists of twenty-five members, of whom three are senators, five members of the Chamber of Deputies, and nine presidents of leading chambers of commerce.

Its functions are to advise the minister on matters pertaining to the consular service, particularly in connection with the development of trade.

Many more details might be given of the elaborate precautions taken by the French, but this sketch will suffice to give a general idea on the subject.

Want of space prevents me from giving similar details as to the German and other services, whose efficiency is well known.

It is not unreasonable to suppose that if consular services recruited in the manner I have described are productive of satisfactory results, we should, under a system somewhat similar, have one quite as good.

There is but one way, however, to obtain such a service—namely, a determination on the part of the American people to eliminate from it politics and "the spoils system," and to establish it on the same permanent footing as our naval and military services.

I would suggest that our service should consist of consuls-general, consuls (of two or three classes), and vice-consuls, the number of officials in each grade to be determined by Congress, and the unmeaning designation of vice or deputy consul-*general* abolished; consular agents and consuls permitted to engage in business to be only retained (not as a portion of the regular service) where absolutely necessary, and with a view to their abolition at as early a date as may be practicable.

Those seeking admission to the service after a certain date (to be fixed by Congress) should be compelled to pass an examination in (1) the English language, (2) arithmetic, (3) commercial law, and (4) one or two foreign languages, either French, German, or Spanish (with a view to our interests in South America), to be compulsory, and the examination therein rigid. Successful candidates should be appointed vice-consuls.

Each original appointment as vice-consul and each subsequent promotion must be made by the President and confirmed by the Senate, as provided by the

Constitution; but the assignment to posts of those appointed should, so long as no increase of rank takes place, be left to the Secretary of State. I can see nothing in the Constitution to compel the President to assign consuls to particular posts at the moment of their appointment, and there is no more sense in his doing so than there would be in his giving a captain in the navy the command of a ship or an admiral that of a squadron at the moment of his promotion.

The only foundation upon which a reorganization such as I have suggested can be based with any hope of success, is the consular service as existing at the time the same goes into effect; all vacancies after a certain date to be filled under the new system, and no removals to take place after the same date, save for causes to be determined by a board of officials, and which should, in each case, be communicated to Congress.

"Equalizing" the appointments between both political parties as a preliminary to consular reform is, to my mind, impossible, as it would admit of the continuation of the present system of removals.

Nor would the proposal to raise the consular salaries be of any avail, under the present system, in improving the service. Many of our consuls are insufficiently paid, and under a reformed system many salaries should undoubtedly be increased and a number of unnecessary posts should at the same time be abolished; but to increase the salaries before the organization of a permanent service would merely augment the competition for, and consequent acquisition of, places on the part of those unfitted to fill them.

It has been said that it will be difficult for us thus to reorganize our service owing to the fact that no congressional legislation can modify the power given to the President by the Constitution to appoint whomsoever he pleases as consul, provided the Senate assent. But surely, if Congress was able to prescribe, as it did by the act of 1855, and has often done since, where consular representatives should be appointed and what should be their rank and salary, the people can insist, through their Senators and Representatives, upon the appointment to posts thus created of such persons only as are duly qualified to fill them, and to prescribe the manner in which such qualifications shall be proved.

Even if this cannot be done by an act of Congress, a resolution can be passed by that body requesting the President in future only to appoint those who have demonstrated their fitness by means of an examination; and, if popular feeling were sufficiently strong on the subject, it is not to be supposed that any President would venture to disregard it in his consular appointments, or, if he did, that the Senate would confirm the appointees, or that the House of Representatives would vote their salaries.

It is presumable, moreover, that the President would welcome relief from any portion of the importunity on the part of office-seekers, with which he is overwhelmed.

The whole matter is, therefore, absolutely in the hands of the people of the United States, who have only to bring pressure to bear upon Congress, without which no great reform was ever accomplished.

The chief obstacle to the creation of a service such as I have suggested appears to me to lie in the sacrifice likely to be entailed upon the political party which, being in possession of the executive branch of the government when the proposed reform goes into effect, is compelled to leave a considerable number of the opposite party's appointees in office. It is scarcely to be doubted, however, that such party will gain far more in the way of popular approval than it will lose through inability to give away a certain number of offices to its retainers; and there need be no fear that those retaining the consular offices would become "offensive partisans." They will, on the contrary, become what most of our diplomatic and consular officials long to be—servants of their country and not of a political party.

II.

WILLIAM F. WHARTON, EX-ASSISTANT SECRETARY OF STATE.

Ordinarily the constitution and condition of the consular service of the United States are subjects of entire indifference to the citizens of the United States. In times marked by less energy of executive action in regard to it no particular notice is taken of the peculiar characteristics of the service, and nobody turns his attention to it unless he is desirous of occupying some post within its circle himself, of procuring such a position for some one of his friends, or of obtaining some assistance from a member of it when in need or alone in a foreign country. The consular reports are little known and little read except by those who are interested in certain business enterprises in the countries whence they proceed, or by those at whose instigation the consuls have been instructed by the Department of State to render them. The consular despatches to the Department of State are mostly of a confidential and private nature, and the public has ordinarily little knowledge of their existence, much less any idea of the value of their contents. It seems to be the common opinion that anybody can fill a consular office, and it is curious to note how the character of the applicants for these offices has reflected the popular sentiment. With some exceptions, of course, they have been largely made up of politicians in the narrowest meaning of the term, of broken-down and unsuccessful professional or business men, of invalids, of men of moderate means who desired to stay abroad to educate their children and at the same time wanted some occupation for themselves as a pastime, and sometimes of men whose sole claim to an appointment was that they had worn out the patience and endurance of their friends in this country by their worthlessness, and were to be sent away to free their friends from the burden of caring for them. It very rarely happens that a man offers himself for appointment to the service because he is attracted by its character or hopes to make it his profession. As a rule the service is entered into as a makeshift to tide over a difficult season, or as furnishing an opportunity to study for a time in a foreign country, or to recuperate from the hard work and cares of a professional or business career. The reason for this is of course very apparent. No right-minded young man, with his life before him and with all the hopes and ambitions that that implies, will voluntarily take up with a service which offers no stability of tenure in office, and in a large majority of its posts presents no reasonable expectation of furnishing more than a bare subsistence at the best for his old age, nor will a man of riper age, if he has any prospects whatever in the world, sacrifice what he has and enter, as a profession, a service which presents to him so poor an outlook.

It is not intended by the foregoing to convey the impression that the consular service of the United States is wholly bad. There are good men in the service, and their work is valuable, and their influence and example are admirable. But this is not enough to those who have the welfare and the improvement of the service at heart. They desire to place the consular service on a securer and broader foundation, either because they have had experience in it and desire to see remedied the evils which that experience has taught them to recognize as existing, or because they are interested in it as a branch of that government to which they are wholly devoted. They realize that with the growth in power and wealth of this country its position in the great family of nations is growing daily of greater importance, and that its commercial interests are of more vital interest. They know that its influence commercially depends in a marked degree upon the character and bearing of its commercial representatives abroad, which its consuls are; and as the commerce of the country increases so the necessity arises of insuring a more perfect representation of its commercial interests in foreign countries, and a fuller and more competent assistance in the development of its commercial relations. They are always looking earnestly for an improvement of the service. Now there are at least three directions by which the consular service can be approached with a view to improvement—namely, the manner of appointment, the tenure of office, and the compensation. The limits of this paper will allow only a cursory glance at a few suggestions which are believed to be pertinent to these subjects.

The Constitution provides, in Article II., Section 2, that the President shall appoint consuls by and with the advice and consent of the Senate, and one of the first duties of the incoming President, under the present practice, is to see to the filling of these offices. The persons to be appointed are generally agreed upon by the President and his Secretary of State, the latter being the officer under whose instructions the future consul is to do his work. The President naturally has little time in the first months of his administration to attend, himself, to these appointments, and the Secretary of State has largely within his sole control the selection of the persons to be recommended for favorable action by the President. The Secretary of State is, in the ordinary course of events, entirely new to the duties of his office. It very seldom occurs in present times that he has had any diplomatic or consular experience whatever, and he can know but little, if anything, about the duties of a consular officer, and his is ignorant of the kind of men who should be sent respectively to the different posts. In the exercise of the best judgment he can form, he cannot know, except from a vague confidence in a man's ability, that he is in any way suited for the position for which he is named; and yet he is expected, under the present practice, to select the persons to be appointed to the greater number of consular offices within the first six months of his incumbency. The applicants, moreover, themselves, for the most part, are strangers to the service. They have no knowledge of its requirements, nor can they judge of their own fitness for the positions to which they lay claim. Naturalized citizens seek to be accredited to the country whence they originally came, and persons living in the United States on the borders of Canada petition to be appointed to a post just over the boundary-line from their home; the former because they desire to revisit their native land, and the latter in order that they may live and carry on their business at home, slipping across the border when it is convenient to attend to consular matters, thus evading the spirit, at least, of the rule which forbids consular officers receiving salaries in excess of $1,000 from transacting business within their districts. No examination is made into their qualifications. Some few may have been in the consular service before. but usually it is their political or social influence, and not their experience, which eventually secures a new place for them. Political backing brings better results than the claims of previous experience and of good service. The most the appointing power can do is to make the sponsors vouch for the character and the ability of the applicant, and hold them responsible if their representations eventually are proved to have been false.

There can be no question that the present method of selection as applied to the existing consular system is bad. If there is to be no change in that system, some different method from that which now exists should be devised whereby the wheat could be separated from the chaff, and only men who have been proved to be fit in character and ability and attainments presented to the President for his selection, free as far as possible from political pressure. But how to determine the fitness is the stumbling-block. This might be done by examination conducted under the direction of the civil service commission, only persons who are certified by them to be eligible for appointment; but among other objections to this method it is not at all clear that it would be a satisfactory manner of selecting the fittest person, because, as can be easily understood, there are elements which go to make up a good consular officer which could hardly be ascertained or determined by such an examination. There is no advantage in making a change for change's sake only, and it seems that the method of selection might with safety be left as it is at present, if only the system of the service were so changed that the tenure of office in the service itself were securely fixed to last during good behavior. By this is meant that the service should be so organized that if a man were once appointed to any consular office he should thereby become a member of the consular service during good behavior and be removable only for cause, not necessarily to remain always at the port to which he was originally appointed, but subject from time to time to be transferred by the President from one port to another, as it might be deemed best for the interests of the service. If the elements of permanency of tenure and of adequate compensation were assured, there would, in the nature of things, be few vacancies at any one time, and at the time of a change of administration there would be no more than at any other. The pressure upon an incoming administration would be avoided, there would be time in which to make a proper selection, and the knowledge that the appointment was to be made for good behavior would place a greater responsibility upon the appointing power and upon the persons recommending the applicant, while correspondingly greater care would be exercised both in the selection and in the recommendation. Moreover, it seems inevitable that with fixity of tenure joined to proper compensation would come a better class of persons seeking appointment.

The tenure of office of consular officers now is dependent solely upon the will of the appointing power, and has long been governed by the exigencies of political expediency. It would not be worth the while for Congress to change this and fix a period of time by statute unless at the same time they increased the pay for the different offices. The fixity or certainty of tenure must go *pari passu* with an increase in pay. What is wanting is to tempt able and stirring men to enter the service for what it can offer them as a life career, and it cannot be expected that such men would find any inducement in the assurance of a permanency of service at an inadequate compensation. With the exception of a comparatively few posts the compensation at present allowed is totally inadequate to the proper or, in many instances, decent maintenance of the dignity of the officer or of the office. A man of humble means must be satisfied with a humble position in the community in which he lives, and many persons are perfectly content to occupy such a position so far as they individually are concerned, and their being so is a subject of reproach to them. But if the representative of a great nation, in a foreign country, is unable, for lack of means, to maintain himself in a manner similar to the like representative of other nations, it is a reproach to all men of the nation which he is sent to represent. Of course it is always possible to send somebody of private means to the places where the compensation is too small for a man to live properly without such means, but assuredly nothing could be more undemocratic and contrary to the true spirit of all of the institutions of this country than to have a branch of the public service in which the compensation of most of the offices is so small that for the sake of the dignity of the country abroad they can only be filled by persons of independent fortune.

There are in all about 777 consular offices, of which about 330 are principal offices, so called, the remaining 447 being designated as consular agencies. A consular agency is subordinate to the principal office within whose jurisdiction it comes. It is created ordinarily at the suggestion of the principal consular officer, or of the people of the place itself, with the consent of the Department of State, and in almost every instance the agent is nominated by the principal officer and approved by the Department of State. The agent is paid solely from the fees received, and is almost invariably a citizen of a foreign country engaged in business in the place where he is agent, often hardly able to speak a word of English, who accepts the place simply for the honor and position which come to him from being the representative of the United States in the locality to which he belongs. As has been intimated, he is paid no salary, but obtains what emoluments he can from that amount of the fees or receipts coming to his office which he is allowed to retain by his superior officer, which amount is usually fixed by agreement between himself and such officer. It should be remembered in this connection that the superior officer has named him for the agency, and is entitled, under the regulations, to pocket his share of the fees coming from his agencies as unofficial fees up to $1,000 in amount. Ordinarily the purpose of creating these agencies is to accommodate merchants who desire near them a consular office for the authentication of invoices of goods exported to the United States, and seek very naturally to avoid the delay and expense which may be caused if they are obliged to apply to the principal office, which may be at some distance from them. The business of the shipper of goods to the United States has been the governing reason for the creation of the consular office, and the impossibility of finding a citizen of the United States to take the office for the compensation has obliged the government to resort to the device of a consular agency.

Besides the manifest impropriety of having a foreigner to represent in his native place the commercial interests of the citizens of this country, it can readily be seen that, inasmuch as the principal officer shares in the fees collected by his agent, the temptation to the former to lend his influence in favor of the creation of agencies within his district, and thus help out his meagre and inadequate salary, is often great. Fees which naturally, in the absence of an agency, would be collected for services rendered at the principal office, and which would be turned in that case into the treasury of the United States, are in this manner diverted, and, being collected for services rendered at the agency, are divided between the principal officer and his agent. It would be most advantageous that all consular agencies should be abolished, and that the official fees which now go to their support should go to the principal office, which ought, in every case, to be a salaried one, and be turned into the treasury, with the other official fees which come to that office. If these agencies were abolished there would then remain 330 principal offices, of which 237 are now salaried, and ninety-three receive no salaries. These last are compensated entirely by the official and unofficial fees which they may from time to time collect.

The highest salary paid is $7,500, and that amount is paid only at Seoul, Korea, where the consul-general is also minister resident, and consequently occupies a diplomatic position with all the expenses incident thereto. The consul-general at Athens, Bucharest, and Belgrade is paid $6,500. He is also envoy extraordinary and minister plenipotentiary to Greece, Rumania, and Servia, and serves in all the above offices for one and the same salary. The consul-general at Havana receives $6,000, and the consul-general at Melbourne $4,500. There are twelve offices where $5,000 are paid, viz.: Rio de Janeiro, Shanghai, Paris, Calcutta, Hong-Kong, Liverpool, London, Port au Prince, Boma, Teheran, Cairo, and Bangkok (where the consul is also minister resident); seven offices where $4,000 are paid, viz.: Panama, Berlin, Montreal, Honolulu, Kanagawa, Monrovia, and Mexico; seven where $3,500 are paid, viz.: Vienna, Amoy, Canton, Tientsin, Havre, Halifax, and Callao; thirty-one where $3,000 are paid; thirty where $2,500 are paid; and fifty-one where $2,000 are paid. The remaining ninety-five of the salaried officers receive salaries of only $1,500 or $1,000 per annum.

Consular officers are not allowed their travelling expenses to and from their posts, no matter how distant the latter may be. They are simply entitled to their salaries during the transit, provided they do not consume more than a certain number of days *in transitu*, which number is fixed by the Secretary of State, nor are they allowed to transact any business in the place to which they are accredited where their salary exceeds $1,000. They are allowed a certain sum of money for rent of consular offices, which has been fixed at 20 per cent. of the salary, but this sum is spent under the direction of the Department of State, and can be used only for the renting of offices, strictly so speaking, and cannot be applied to the rental of their own house or lodgings. A clerk is allowed in some cases, and sometimes also a messenger where there seems to be an absolute need of such; but the appropriations made by Congress for clerk hire and for contingent expenses of consuls for many years past have been so grossly inadequate to the needs of the service that in most posts the offices are miserably equipped both as to clerks and messengers.

There are certain emoluments coming to consuls at certain posts of an unofficial nature, such as fees for taking depositions, oaths, etc., which are not considered official in their nature, and which a consular officer is therefore allowed to retain as his private property. All official fees—and these are prescribed by the President—every consular officer receiving a salary is bound to account for and to turn over to the treasury of the United States. The unofficial fees in some places amount to large sums, and in London, Liverpool, Paris, and a few others of the important business centres, render the office of unusual value. In London, for instance, the unofficial fees amount to five or six times the prescribed salary. But the places where such large fees are to be secured are very few indeed, and might almost be said to be covered by the three places above named. By an odd perversion of justice, the receipts from unofficial fees are largest in the places where the largest salaries are paid.

It is not difficult to picture the plight of the man who finds himself, for example, in Ceylon, Auckland, or Cape Town, or, not quite so bad, but bad enough, in Malta, or Santos, or Para, all of which are places where the salaries are fixed at $1,500, with no financial resources except his salary. What must be the desperate financial embarrassment of the consul to either of these places who starts off for his post with the month's pay allowed him for what is called his instruction period and with no opportunity even to draw in advance that portion of his pay allowed him for his transit period, which can only be paid after he has rendered his accounts upon his arrival at the post, and with the remainder of his $1,500 to keep him for the rest of the year? It is not to be wondered at that some of our consular officers get into financial difficulties and leave their offices at the expiration of their terms, with debts unpaid. It is rather a matter of surprise that they manage as well as they appear to do. It may not, to be sure, cost a great deal for a man to live at Ceylon or Cape Town, when once he manages to reach those places; but even if that be a fact, he must live away from his family and in a most meagre manner to eke out existence upon the present allowance. So, too, in Europe, in such places as Liege, and Copenhagen, and Nice, and many others where the salary is $1,500 and the unofficial work yields hardly any return.

These are only a few of the most glaring cases, but the position of a man without property of his own sufficient to make him practically independent of his salary so far as subsistence is concerned, who goes, for instance, to Trieste, Cologne, Dublin, or Leeds, or to Sydney, New South Wales, or to Guatemala, or Managua, or to Tamatave, Madagascar, or to Odessa, or Manila, or Beirut, or Jerusalem, on a salary of $2,000 is relatively little better off. Nor is the position of a consul at Buenos Ayres, or at Brussels, or at Marseilles, Hamburg, Sheffield, Nuevo Laredo, Athens, Ningpo, or Victoria, B. C., with a salary of $2,500 to be envied, with the necessary demands which he is obliged to meet.

It is of course notorious that there are many more applicants for even the worst of these offices than there are offices, and that numberless men will be readily found to sacrifice themselves for the good of their country and go to Tamatave or Sydney on $2,000, or to Tahiti or Sierra Leone on $1,000. But the interest of the citizens of the United States is presumably centred more upon the welfare of the public service than on furnishing places for self-sacrificing individuals. They take no satisfaction in the creation of a consular office unless its existence is for the efficiency of the service as organized for their benefit. If such conditions are annexed to its creation as to militate against its effectiveness to accomplish the purpose for which it is created, the reason for its creation ceases to exist. That reason is primarily that the consular officer may encourage the increase of trade between his country and the country to which he is accredited by giving assistance in the way of information and protection to his fellow-citizens. In order to do this effectively he must be a man whose character inspires respect among the people with whom he associates and who has influence through his character, abilities, and position, not only as an officer, but also as a man among the people with whom he is to transact the business of his office. If the pecuniary allowance given him by his government is such as to render it impossible for him to live on an equality with his colleagues, or to maintain a social position in the community such as they are able to maintain, his government is the loser. It is far better to have no consular office in any given place than to cripple its efficiency by the conditions of its creation.

CONSULAR SERVICE

Unless Congress can see its way to make more generous appropriations for the consular service with a view principally to creating larger salaries, it would be far wiser to reduce the number of salaried officers and to distribute the sum of money now appropriated for the pay of 237 officers among one-half that number, with salaries proportionately greater. In any case there should be no unsalaried officers whatever and no salary below $2,500. There are now, as we have seen, besides the subordinate agencies which we have suggested should be abolished, about ninety-three unsalaried principal officers who receive their compensation in fees. These offices should either be abolished or be made salaried offices and the fees received by them turned into the treasury.

In several countries the United States maintains a far greater number of consular offices than is required by the demands of commerce, and one which seems, moreover, disproportionate to the number maintained by these countries respectively in this country. For instance, in Germany we have fifty-one consular offices, while Germany has twenty-two in this country. In France the United States has thirty-seven, and France has twenty-five in this country. In the islands of Great Britain alone the United States has fifty-seven, in British North America about 130, besides others scattered over the world in other possessions of the British Empire. Great Britain has, in all, forty-two consular offices in this country. A great reduction in the number of United States consular offices could most advantageously be made in Canada, especially in the provinces of Quebec and Ontario. It is not going too far to state that two-thirds of the offices in these provinces could be discontinued with the best results for the interests of the service.

If the prizes are larger, the competitors will be of superior quality. The best men will not compete for an inferior prize, and in order to induce such men as should be in the consular service to enter it as a life career there should be assured to them as long as they remain in it at least a livelihood approximate to that which they would have secured if they had remained in the ordinary walks of life.

Duties of Consular Officers.—Consular officers are expected to endeavor to maintain and promote all the rightful interests of American citizens, and to protect them in all privileges provided for by treaty or conceded by usage; to visé and, when so authorized, to issue passports; when permitted by treaty, law, or usage, to take charge of and settle the personal estates of Americans who may die abroad without legal or other representatives and remit the proceeds to the Treasury in case they are not called for by a legal representative within one year; to ship, discharge, and, under certain conditions, maintain and send American seamen to the United States; to settle disputes between masters and seamen of American vessels; to investigate charges of mutiny or insubordination on the high seas and send mutineers to the United States for trial; to render assistance in the case of wrecked or stranded American vessels, and in the absence of the master or other qualified person take charge of the wrecks and cargoes if permitted to do so by the laws of the country; to receive the papers of American vessels arriving at foreign ports and deliver them after the discharge of the obligations of the vessels towards the members of their crews, and upon the production of clearances from the proper foreign port officials to certify to the correctness of the valuation of merchandise exported to the United States where the shipment amounts to more than $100; to act as official witnesses to marriages of American citizens abroad; to aid in the enforcement of the immigration laws and to certify to the correctness of the certificates issued by Chinese and other officials to Chinese persons coming to the United States; to protect the health of our seaports by reporting weekly the sanitary conditions of the ports at which they reside, and by issuing to vessels clearing for the United States bills of health describing the condition of the ports, the vessels, crews, passengers, and cargoes; and to take depositions and perform other acts which notaries public in the United States are authorized or required to perform. A duty of prime importance is the promotion of American commerce by reporting available opportunities for the introduction of our products, aiding in the establishment of relations between American and foreign commercial houses, and lending assistance wherever practicable to the marketing of American merchandise abroad.

In addition to the foregoing duties consular officers in China, Turkey, Siam, Korea, Maskat, Morocco, and a few other so-called un-Christian countries are invested with judicial powers over American citizens in those countries. These powers are usually defined by treaty, but generally include the trial of civil cases to which Americans are parties, and in some instances extend to the trial of criminal cases.

Examinations for the Consular Service.—In pursuance of the Executive order of June 27, 1906, whereby the President promulgated regulations governing appointments and promotions in the consular service, the following rules were adopted by the board of examiners, who, under that order, were designated to formulate rules for and hold examinations of applicants for admission to the consular service whom the President shall have designated for examination to determine their eligibility for appointment therein.

1. The examinations will be the same for all grades, and will be to determine a candidate's eligibility for appointment to the consular service, irrespective of the grade to which he may have been designated for examination, and without regard to any particular office for which he may be selected.

2. The examination will consist of an oral and a written one, the two counting equally. The object of the oral examination will be to determine the candidate's business ability, alertness, general contemporary information, and natural fitness for the service, including moral, mental, and physical qualifications, character, address, and general education and good command of English. In this part of the examination the applications previously filed will be given due weight by the board of examiners, especially as evidence of the applicant's business experience and ability. The written examination will include those subjects mentioned in the Executive order, to wit: French, German, or Spanish, or at least one modern language other than English; the natural, industrial, and commercial resources and the commerce of the United States, especially with reference to possibilities of increasing and extending the foreign trade of the United States; political economy, and the elements of international, commercial, and maritime law. It will likewise include American history, government, and institutions; political and commercial geography; arithmetic (as used in commercial statistics, tariff calculations, exchange, accounts, etc.); the modern history, since 1850, of Europe, Latin America, and the Far East, with particular attention to political, commercial, and economic tendencies. In the written examination, composition, grammar, punctuation, spelling, and writing will be given attention.

3. To become eligible for appointment, except as student interpreter, in a country where the United States exercises extraterritorial jurisdiction, the applicant must pass the examination outlined above, but supplemented by questions to determine his knowledge of the fundamental principles of common law, the rules of evidence, and the trial of civil and criminal cases.

4. The examinations to be given candidates for appointment as student interpreters will follow the same course as in the case of other consular officers, provided, however, that no one will be examined for admission to the consular service as a student interpreter who is not between the ages of nineteen and twenty-six, inclusive, and unmarried; and provided further, that upon appointment each student interpreter shall sign an agreement to continue in the service so long as his services may be required within a period of five years.

5. Upon the conclusion of the examinations the names of the candidates who shall have attained upon the whole examination an average mark of at least eighty, as required by the Executive order, will be certified by the board to the Secretary of State as eligible for appointment in the consular service, and the successful candidates will be informed that this has been done.

6. The names of candidates will remain

on the eligible list for two years, except in the case of such candidates as shall within that period be appointed or shall withdraw their names. Names which have been on the eligible list for two years will be dropped therefrom. See CIVIL SERVICE, COLONIAL; DIPLOMATIC SERVICE.

Continental Army. See ARMY.

Continental Currency. See CURRENCY, CONTINENTAL.

Continental System. See EMBARGO.

Contraband of War, a term said to have been first employed in the treaty of Southampton between England and Spain in 1625. During the war between Spain and Holland both powers acted with rigor towards the ships of neutrals conveying goods to belligerents. This provoked England. A milder policy was adopted by the treaty of Pyrenees, 1650, and by the declaration of Paris, April 26, 1856.

While it is generally conceded that any article that will enable one party to maintain hostilities against another is contraband of war, just what articles constitute contraband has never been authoritatively determined. In some instances a nation about to engage in war has announced that it would regard certain specified articles as contraband. The other party in the conflict might not adopt the list and might put forward one of its own. The interest in these declarations would be keenest among neutral nations, because they could not risk the seizure of their commercial vessels by permitting them to carry anything of a contraband character. Whatever articles may be regarded by belligerents as contraband, a formal declaration of war is necessary to justify their seizure. In general, it may be said that war vessels, ammunition, implements of war either complete or capable of being assembled after delivery, explosives and their components, torpedoes, submarine electric and contact mines, and, conditionally, food and fuel, are among the articles that are justly contraband of war. Every war develops new articles of this character.

In the early part of the war with Spain the United States forbade the shipment to Cuba of a large number of mules for use by the Spanish troops there, thus virtually declaring a mule contraband in that particular instance. It also laid an embargo against the shipment of coal on Spanish account. General Butler, in 1861, added a novel article to the list when he refused to surrender to their masters a number of fugitive slaves, on the ground that they were contraband of war. A free or a captive balloon, to be used for military observation and signalling; one of the modern scientific kites, by which photographs of the earth may be taken at high altitudes above it; and a homing pigeon trained to carry messages long distances may become contraband of war when about to be used by one belligerent to the disadvantage of the other. Coal and liquid fuel, as well as food, are contraband under some circumstances, and free articles under other. See DECLARATION OF LONDON; NEUTRALITY.

Contrabands. On the day after his arrival at Fort Monroe, General Butler sent out Colonel Phelps, of the Vermont troops, to reconnoitre the vicinity of Hampton. The citizens had just fired the bridge. The flames were extinguished by the troops, who crossed the stream, drove armed Confederates out of Hampton, and found the inhabitants in sullen mood; but the negroes were jubilant, regarding the Union troops as their expected deliverers. In the confusion caused by this dash into Hampton three negroes held as slaves by Colonel Mallory of that village escaped into the Union lines, and declared that many of their race, who were employed in building fortifications for the insurgents, desired to follow. They were taken before General Butler. He needed laborers in field-works which he was about to construct. Regarding these slaves, according to the *laws of Virginia*, as much the property of Colonel Mallory as his horses or his pistols, and as properly seizable as they, as aids in warfare, and which might be used against the national troops, "These men are contraband of war," said Butler; "set them at work." This order was scarcely announced before Major Carey, as agent of Colonel Mallory and "in charge of his property," appeared, wishing to know what the General intended to do with his runaways. "I shall detain them as contraband of war," said the general; and they were held as such. Other slaves speedily came in. General Butler wrote to the Secretary of War, telling him what he had done, on the assumption that they were the property of an enemy of the republic used in warfare, and asking instructions. His course was approved by his government; and thenceforward all fugitive slaves were considered "contraband of war," and treated as such from May 27, 1861.

Contracts, INVIOLABILITY OF. See *Dartmouth College Decision* in article on DARTMOUTH COLLEGE.

Contrecoeur, military officer; born in France about 1730; came to America as an officer in the French army; and in 1754 went up the Alleghany River to prevent the British from making settlements in the Ohio Valley, which France claimed. The British fort on the site of Pittsburg was taken by Contrecœur, and renamed Fort Duquesne. When Braddock advanced against it, Captain Beaujeu, who had arrived to relieve the place, routed the army of Braddock, July 9, 1755. Although Contrecœur remained in the fort, he was wrongly given the credit of the victory, and, as Beaujeu had fallen, he continued in command. To him were due the subsequent Indian atrocities.

Contreras, BATTLE OF. General Scott resumed his march from Puebla for the city of Mexico, Aug. 7, 1847. General Twiggs, with his division, led the way; and on Aug. 11 encamped at St. Augustine, with the strong fortress of San Antonio before him. Close upon his right were the heights of Churubusco, and not far off was the strongly fortified camp of Contreras. In the rear of it was Santa Ana with 12,000 men as a reserve. In the afternoon of Aug. 19, Generals Twiggs and Pillow, assisted by Generals Persifer F. Smith and Cadwallader, attacked the camp of Contreras, and a sharp conflict ensued, with almost continual skirmishing around. This indecisive conflict continued about six hours. At the moment when some Mexican cavalry were preparing for a charge, General Scott arrived at the scene of conflict, and ordered up General Shields with reinforcements. When night fell, the wearied Americans lay down and slept, expecting to renew the contest in the morning. Generals Scott and Worth started early the next morning (Aug. 20) from St. Augustine for Contreras, and were met on the way by a courier with the news that the enemy's camp was captured. The battle had been begun at sunrise by Smith's division. While Generals Shields and Pierce had kept Santa Ana's reserve at bay, Smith's troops had marched towards the works in the darkness and gained a position, unobserved, behind the crest of a hill near the Mexican works. Springing up suddenly from their hiding-place, they dashed pell-mell into the intrenchments; captured the batteries at the point of the bayonet; drove out the army of Valencia; and pursued its flying remnants towards the city of Mexico. The contest, which had lasted only seventeen minutes, was fought by 4,500 Americans, against 7,000 Mexicans. The trophies of victory were eighty officers and 3,000 Mexican troops made prisoners, and thirty-three pieces of artillery. See MEXICO, WAR WITH.

Controller Bay, an indentation on the s. e. coast of the main portion of Alaska; near the Chugach National Forest and the vast Bering River coal-fields. The harbor is protected by a natural double breakwater, and is the only available protected deep-water harbor within reasonable access to the coal-fields; hence, control of transportation and access to the coal-fields is equivalent to control of the coal itself. On Feb. 26, 1909, the national government withdrew from public entry that portion of the shore lines of the bay which was essential in the use of its harbor and navigable channel; but on Oct. 28, 1910, this shore line was restored to public entry by an Executive order, and immediately thereafter James J. Ryan, and others connected with the railroad and navigation company, made application to enter certain portions of the shore of the bay, which would give the company the monopoly of the use of the bay as a harbor and of the only available deep-water access to the great coal-fields. On June 26, 1911, the Secretary of the Interior ordered the cancellation of the notorious Cunningham coal claims in Alaska, on charges of fraudulent entries, and the next day resolutions were introduced in Congress for a thorough inquiry into the attempt to secure a monopoly of the Controller Bay advantages, which seemed to be a part of a carefully prepared scheme to gain control of the great coal-fields and of the most convenient means of exploiting them. See ALASKA.

Convention, CONSTITUTIONAL. Original statute law is the result of action by the legislature jointly with the Executive. The Constitutional Convention acts jointly with the electors or citizens, who have a veto upon its action. A constitutional convention is not bound by any pre-existing constitution or form of government. The new constitutions formed by the colonies during the Revolutionary period were made by conventions which the people called for that purpose. The Articles of Confederation, under which the United States existed from 1781 to 1789, proved too weak, and these articles could be amended only by " alterations agreed to in a Congress of the United States, and afterwards confirmed by the legislatures of every State." The Constitutional Convention of 1787 simply ignored the Articles of Confederation and proceeded to form and adopt the Constitution of the United States, under which we are living at present. See NOMINATING CONVENTIONS; CONSTITUTION OF THE UNITED STATES.

Convention of 1787. See CONSTITUTION OF THE UNITED STATES.

Conventions, assemblies of delegates, or representatives acting independently of the ordinary legislatures. Thus, the English convention parliament of 1660 voted the restoration of Charles II., and that of 1689 offered the crown of England to William and Mary. The word was applied in America to irregular meetings of the colonial legislatures, after they had been legally dissolved by the governors. During the Revolution the conventions exercised sovereign power until a State constitution was adopted. The constitutional convention of 1787 was called to remedy the defects of the confederacy (see CONFEDERATION, ARTICLES OF); the Hartford convention of 1814–15 was a Federalist movement inspired chiefly to protest against the war with England; the South Carolina convention of 1832 claimed power to nullify a law of the United States (see NULLIFICATION: CALHOUN, JOHN C.); the conventions of 1861 in the Southern States adopted ordinances of secession; and the Montgomery convention of 1861 framed the constitution of the Confederate States. See NOMINATING CONVENTIONS; CONSTITUTION OF THE UNITED STATES.

Convention Troops. When Burgoyne's army surrendered to General Gates, these generals agreed that the prisoners (over 5,000) should be marched to Cambridge, near Boston, to embark for England, on their parole not to serve again against the Americans. Suspecting that the parole would be violated, Congress, after ratifying, revoked it. As the British government did not recognize the authority of Congress, these troops remained near Boston until Congress ordered them to Virginia, where they remained until October, 1780, when the British were removed to Fort Frederick, in Maryland, and the Germans to Winchester. In the course of 1782 they were dispersed by exchange or desertion. See BURGOYNE, SIR JOHN.

Convicts. Transportation to America by British government previous to Revolution. See REDEMPTIONERS.

Conway, THOMAS, military officer; born in Ireland, Feb. 27, 1733; taken to France when he was six years old; attained the rank of colonel, came to America in 1777, and entered the Continental army as brigadier-general. He was engaged in the conspiracy with Gates and others to supplant Washington as commander-in-chief, and, when discovered, he left the service and returned to France. He died about 1800. See CONWAY CABAL, THE.

Conway, WILLIAM, sailor; born in Camden, Me., in 1802; was on duty as quartermaster at the Pensacola navy-yard when that place was seized by the Confederates, Jan. 12, 1861. When commanded to lower the United States flag, he exclaimed: "I have served under that flag for forty years, and I won't do it." He died in Brooklyn, N. Y., Nov. 30, 1865.

Conway Cabal, THE. In 1777 Generals Gates, Mifflin, and Conway plotted to deprive Washington of the supreme command. They were aided by a strong faction in the Continental Congress which secured the appointment of a new board of war. Without consulting Washington as commander-in-chief, an invasion of Canada was suggested by the board and approved by Congress. Lafayette was chosen to the command, with Conway as his second, but he refused to accept unless DeKalb was made second and Conway third in command. After waiting in Albany three months for the promised men and munitions, Lafayette returned to Valley Forge, under instructions from Congress to suspend the Canadian expedition. This ended the attempts of the conspirators. Gates and Mifflin disclaimed any other than a patriotic design to advance the true interests of the country, and denied the charge of a desire to displace Washington.

Conyngham, JOHN BUTLER; military officer; born in 1827; graduated at Yale College in 1846; practised law in Wilkesbarre, Pa., and St. Louis, Mo.; and served throughout the Civil War. At Charleston he was one of the prisoners chosen to be shot as hostages in case the National forces should bombard that city. He received the brevet of lieutenant-colonel, U. S. A., in 1871. He died in Wilkesbarre, Pa., May 27, 1871.

Coodies, THE, the name of a small party of Federalists in New York City in 1812, who attacked De Witt Clinton and approved the war with Great Britain.

Cook, FREDERICK ALBERT, physician and explorer; born in Callicoon Depot, Sullivan county, N. Y., June 10, 1865; was graduated in medicine at the University of New York in 1890; surgeon of the Peary arctic expedition of 1891–92; surgeon of Belgian antarctic expedition, 1897–99; claimed to have climbed Mt. McKinley, Alaska, 1906; and started on another arctic expedition, 1907. On Sept. 1, 1909, he telegraphed from Shetland Islands that he had discovered the North Pole, April 21, 1908. He had been landed by John R. Bradley's yacht at Annootok, nearly 800 miles from the Pole, in August, 1907. Cook's assertion was that on Feb. 19, 1908, with eleven men and 103 dogs, he left Annootok, crossed Smith Sound, traversed Ellesmere Land to Nansen Sound, which he followed to Land's End. On March 19, with two Esquimos and 26 dogs, he left Cape Thomas Hubbard for the Pole, 460 miles distant, which he claims to have reached on April 21. On Feb. 18 he started for Annootok, where he arrived on April 15, and thence at Upernavik, May 21, 1909.

Five days after Cook's announcement was received came word from Indian Harbor that Commander Robert E. Peary had reached the Pole, April 6, 1909. And a few hours later the assertion followed that Cook had not been within 450 miles of the North Pole. Commander Peary's records were examined by an expert commission of the National Geographic Society, and his claim of having reached the Pole was sustained. Dr. Cook's records were examined by the University of Copenhagen, which, in December, 1909, announced the following decision:

"The documents handed the university for examination do not contain observations and information which can be regarded as proof that Dr. Cook reached the North Pole on his recent expedition."

Cook, JOSEPH, lecturer; born in Ticonderoga, N. Y., Jan. 26, 1838; graduated at Harvard College in 1865; became a lecturer of national repute. His lectures include *Ultimate America; England and America as Competitors and Allies; Political Signs of the Times; Labor; Socialism*, etc. He died in Ticonderoga, N. Y., June 24, 1901.

Cooke, EDWIN FRANCIS, military officer; born in Brooklyn, Pa., Sept. 11, 1835; joined the Union army at the beginning of the Civil War. In 1863 he was captured, and was confined in different prisons till March 13, 1864. In 1865 he was brevetted a brigadier-general of volunteers. He died in Santiago, Chili, Aug. 6, 1867.

Cooke, JAY, financier; born in Sandusky, O., Aug. 10, 1821; established in Philadelphia the banking firm of Jay Cooke & Co., in 1861. He was the agent of the government in negotiating loans during the Civil War to the extent of $2,000,000,000. His firm became agents for the Northern Pacific Railroad, and their suspension in 1873 led to the great panic of that year. He died in Ogontz, Penn., Feb. 16, 1905.

Cooke, JOHN ESTEN, author; born in Winchester, Va., Nov. 3, 1830; served in the Confederate army throughout the Civil War. Among his publications are *Life of Gen. Robert E. Lee; Life of Stonewall Jackson; Surrey of Eagle's Nest; Wearing of the Gray; Stories of the Old Dominion; Virginia; The Youth of Jefferson,* and many novels depicting life in the South. He died near Boyce, Va., Sept. 27, 1886.

Cooke, PHILIP ST. GEORGE, military officer; born near Leesburg, Va., June 13, 1809; graduated at West Point in 1827. He served in the war against Mexico, and late in 1861 was made brigadier-general of volunteers. He had seen much service in wars with the Indians, commanded in Kansas during the troubles there, and took part in the Utah expedition in 1858. He commanded all the regular cavalry of the Army of the Potomac, and was distinguished in the campaign on the Peninsula in 1862. He was retired with the rank of brevet major-general in 1873, and died in Detroit, Mich., March 20, 1895.

Cooley, THOMAS McINTYRE, jurist; born near Attica, N. Y., Jan. 6, 1824; admitted to the bar in Michigan in 1846; became professor of law in the University of Michigan in 1859; was a justice of the Supreme Court of that State in 1864-85, and during part of that time chief-justice; professor of American history and lecturer on constitutional law in the University of Michigan in 1885–88; and chairman of the interstate commerce commission for four years under President Cleveland. Judge Cooley was a recognized authority on constitutional law, and besides a large number of contributions to periodical literature, was author of *The Constitutional Limitations which Rest upon the Legislative Power of the States of the American Union; A Treatise on the Law of Taxation; the General Principles of Constitutional Law in the United States; Michigan: a History of Government;* and *The Acquisition of Indiana.* He died in Ann Arbor, Mich., Sept. 12, 1898.

Coolidge, THOMAS JEFFERSON, diplomatist; born in Boston, Mass., Aug. 26, 1831; educated at Harvard College; engaged in the East India trade, and later was president of the Chicago, Burlington, and Quincy Railroad Company. He was United States minister to France in 1892–96, and a member of the Anglo-American commission to settle the differences between the United States and Canada in 1898-99. He presented the Jefferson Research Laboratory to Harvard University, and a library building to Manchester, Mass.

Coombs, LESLIE. See COMBS, LESLIE.

Cooper, EDWARD, son of Peter Cooper; born in New York City, Oct. 26, 1824; educated in the public schools and in Columbia University; anti-Tweed-ring leader; mayor of New York, 1879–81. He died in New York, Feb. 25, 1905.

Cooper, JAMES FENIMORE, author; born in Burlington, N. J., Sept. 15, 1789; studied at Yale College, but did not graduate. He was ten years in the United States naval service. Choosing literature as a profession, he took the path of romance and wrote and published in the course of his life thirty-two volumes of fiction, the most famous of which were his *Leather-stocking Tales.* His first book, *Precaution,* was published anonymously in 1820; *The Spy* (1821) was his first success. *The Last of the Mohicans* insured his immortality. He wrote *History of the United States Navy,* in two volumes; *Lives of American Naval Officers; Battle of Lake Erie; Gleanings in Europe; Sketches of Switzerland,* and a comedy. He died in Cooperstown, N. Y., Sept. 14, 1851.

JAMES FENIMORE COOPER.

Cooper, MILES, clergyman; born in England in 1735; graduated at Oxford University in 1761, and came to America the next year, sent by Archbishop Secker as an assistant to Dr. Samuel Johnson, president of King's College. He succeeded Johnson as president in 1763. He was an active Tory when the Revolution broke out, and was reputed one of the authors, if not the author, of a tract entitled *A Friendly Address to all*

Reasonable Americans. Alexander Hamilton was then a pupil in the college, and he answered the pamphlet with ability. Cooper became very obnoxious to the Whigs, and a public letter, signed "Three Millions," warned him and his friends that their lives were in danger. On the night of May 10 a mob, led by Sons of Liberty, after destroying or carrying guns on the Battery, proceeded to drive him from the college. He succeeded in escaping to a British vessel, and sailed for England. He commemorated this stirring event by a poem printed in the *Gentleman's Magazine* in 1776. He died in Edinburgh, May 1, 1785.

Cooper, PETER, philanthropist; born in New York City, Feb. 12, 1791. His life was one of remarkable activity and enterprise. First, after leaving his father, who was a hatter, he engaged in learning coach-making, then cabinet-making, then entered the grocery business, and finally, about 1828, became a manufacturer of glue and isinglass. In 1830 he engaged quite extensively in iron-works at Canton, near Baltimore, and there he manufactured the first locomotive engine ever made in America, which worked successfully on the Baltimore and Ohio Railroad. Then he erected a rolling-mill and iron-mill in the city of New York, in which he first successfully used anthracite coal in puddling iron. In 1845 he removed the machinery to Trenton, N. J., where he erected the largest rolling-mill then in the United States for manufacturing railroad iron. There were rolled the first wrought-iron beams for fire-proof buildings. He became an alderman in the city of New York about 1840. Prospering greatly in business, Mr. Cooper conceived the idea of establishing in New York a free institute, something after the Polytechnic Institute in Paris. He erected a building, and endowed art schools and other means for fitting young men and young women of the working-classes for business, at a cost of between $600,000 and $700,000, and presented the Cooper Institute to the city in 1858. In the spring of 1854 he was one of the five gentlemen who met in the house of Cyrus W. Field and formed the New York, Newfoundland, and London Telegraph Company (see ATLANTIC TELEGRAPH), and the first cable was laid partly under Mr. Cooper's supervision. He did everything in his power to aid the Union cause in the Civil War. An outspoken advocate of paper currency to be issued by the national government, he was urged in 1876 to become a candidate for the Presidency by friends of that financial system. He refused at first, but finally consented, though without any idea of being elected. In the campaign that followed he expended more than $25,000 in aid of the cause. He died April 4, 1883.

PETER COOPER.

Cooper, SAMUEL, military officer; born in Hackensack, N. J., June 12, 1798; graduated at the United States Military Academy in 1815; brevetted colonel for services in the Mexican War; and became adjutant-general of the army. In March, 1861, he resigned and entered the Confederate army, becoming adjutant-general and inspector-general. He published *A Concise System of Instructions and Regulations for the Militia and Volunteers of the United States.* He died in Cameron, Va., Dec. 3, 1876.

Copley, JOHN SINGLETON, artist; born in Boston, Mass., July 3, 1737; in 1774 he went to Rome, and in 1775 to London. He became so famous as an historical painter that he was admitted to the Royal Academy in 1783. His *Death of the Earl of Chatham* gave him great fame in England. It was followed by others which increased his reputation; and he left unfinished a picture on the subject of Nelson's death at Trafalgar. His wife was daughter of Richard Clarke, a loyalist of Boston, and one of the consignees of the tea that was destroyed there. He died in London, Sept. 9, 1813.

Copper. There are evidences that copper-mines were worked in the United States by the MOUND-BUILDERS (*q. v.*). The first mines worked systematically were chiefly in New Jersey and Connecticut. From 1709 until the middle of the eighteenth century a mine at Simsbury, Conn., yielded much ore when, for about sixty years, the mine was a State prison. The Lake Superior copper mines (the most considerable in the world) were first worked, in modern times, in 1845, when traces of ancient mining were found near the Ontonagon River. The Jesuit missionaries had noticed copper ore in that region as early as the middle of the seventeenth century. In making excavations in 1848 a mass of copper supported upon blocks of wood, with charred wood under it, was found 20 feet below the surface. When taken out it weighed 8 tons. The record for production in the United States was made in 1909, when the total output was 1,092,951,624 pounds, valued at $142,083,711; and the record for production value in 1906, when an output of 917,805,682 pounds had a value of $177,595,888. Since 1845, when the total output was 224,000 pounds, the copper industry has shown a steady growth, and in recent years the growth has been very rapid.

Copperheads. A nickname given to a political faction in the Northern and Eastern States during the Civil War, which was generally considered to be in secret sympathy with the Southern Confederacy, and gave them aid and comfort by trying to thwart the measures of the national government. The name is derived from a poisonous serpent, the copperhead, whose bite is as deadly as that of the rattlesnake, but, unlike the latter, it gives no warning of its intended attack, and is, therefore, typical of a concealed foe. See KNIGHTS OF THE GOLDEN CIRCLE; KU-KLUX KLAN.

Coppinger, JOHN JOSEPH, military officer; born in Ireland, Oct. 11, 1834; entered the national army at the beginning of the Civil War, and was made captain of the 14th United States Infantry; served with distinction throughout the war; promoted brigadier-general, U. S. A., April 25, 1895; appointed a major-general of volunteers, May 4, 1898; and retired Oct. 11, 1898. He married Alice, daughter of James G. Blaine, in 1870; died in Washington, D. C., Nov. 4, 1909.

Copway, GEORGE, Indian chief and author; born on the Ojibway reservation in Michigan, in August, 1820. His Indian name was Koligegwagebow. He wrote for the press of New York City for many years, and made lecturing tours in the United States and Europe. His publications include *Recollections of a Forest Life; The Ojibway Conquest* (a poem); *Traditional History and Characteristic Sketches of the Ojibway Nation; Organization of a New Indian Territory*, etc.

Copyright Law. On April 5, 1789, Dr. David Ramsay, of South Carolina, sent a petition to Congress setting forth that he was the author of two books—a *History of South Carolina* and a *History of the American Revolution*—and praying that body to pass a law giving him and his legal successors the exclusive right to vend and dispose of those works in the United States for a term of years. A general bill to that effect was passed in 1790; and afterwards other bills were passed incorporating with the copyright bill another for securing patents for mechanical inventions. The term of a copyright was then fixed at fourteen years for books already published, and the same term for unpublished books, with the privilege of a renewal for fourteen years longer. In 1831 a general copyright law was passed granting copyright for twenty-eight years, and providing for a renewal for fourteen years. In 1856 a law was passed giving to the authors of dramatic compositions the exclusive right of publicly representing them or causing them to be represented. In 1870 all copyright statutes were repealed by a general copyright law (to which some amendments were added in 1874) permitting any citizen of the United States who shall be the "author, inventor, designer, or proprietor of any book, map, chart, dramatic or musical composition, engraving, cut, print, or photograph or negative thereof, or a painting, drawing, chromo, statue or statuary, and of models and designs intended to be perfected as works of the fine arts, to secure a copyright thereof for twenty-eight years, with the privilege of a renewal for himself, his widow, or children, for fourteen years more." Copyright certificates are issued solely by the Librarian of Congress. A copy of the title of a book, or description of a picture, must be deposited with him before the publication thereof; and two copies of a book or picture (the latter by photograph) must be sent to such librarian within ten days after publication. A copy of every new edition must be sent to the librarian. A failure to comply with these conditions is punishable by a fine of $25.

Although the first copyright law in this country was passed in 1790, it was not until a little more than 100 years later that the principle of protection was extended to others than citizens of the United States. The injustice done to foreigners by excluding them from the privileges of copyright was early apparent, and the only excuse to be offered therefor was that the laws of Great Britain permitted a similar injustice to be practised upon Americans. Literary "piracy," as it was called, became common in both countries. Books by British authors were freely republished in America without compensation to their authors, and American books were likewise reproduced in England. And yet the English law was more just than the American, for it allowed a foreigner to secure British copyright, provided the work was first published within the United Kingdom, and the author was at the time of publication anywhere within the British dominions. A movement to secure the passage of some kind of international copyright law was begun in Cong ss as early as 1837, when Henry Clay presented a petition of British authors asking for the protection of their works. This petition was favorably reported upon by the select committee to which it was referred, but no further action was taken. In 1843, George P. Putnam presented to Congress a memorial signed by many leading publishers which declared that the absence of international copyright was "alike injurious to the business of publishing and to the best interests of the public." After this frequent efforts were made to secure a change in the law, and several bills were introduced into Congress from time to time with that object in view.

In 1883 an association called The American Copyright League was founded for the purpose of securing the co-operation of authors and publishers in advancing the cause of international justice, and through its persistent efforts the copyright bill of 1891 was finally passed. When first voted upon in the House of Representatives this bill was defeated by a very small majority. Early in the next session of Congress it was again brought up and passed by a vote of 139 to 95. In the Senate action was delayed until almost the last day of the session. It was at length passed with several objectionable amendments attached, but through the conference committee, to which it was referred, it was adopted substantially as reported from the House. It was signed by President Harrison, March 4, 1891, and went into effect on July 1, following. The law thus secured, after so long a struggle, provides that foreigners may take American copyright on the same basis as American citizens, in case (1) that the nation of the foreigner permits copyright to American citizens on substantially the same basis as its own citizens, or (2) that the nation of the foreigner is a party to an international agreement providing for reciprocity in copyright, by the terms of which agreement the United States may become a party thereto. The existence of these conditions shall be determined by the President of the United States. It required, however, that foreign books, etc., so copyrighted in the United States must be printed from type set in the United States, or from plates made therefrom, or from negatives or drawings on stone which have been made in the United States. The revised act, taking effect July 1, 1909, made many changes, the most important being the extension from fourteen to twenty-eight years on renewals.

Corbin, Henry Clark, military officer; born in Clermont county, O., Sept. 15,

1842; received an academic education, and studied law. In 1862 he joined the National army as a second lieutenant in the 79th Ohio Volunteers; served through the remainder of the war; and was then appointed to the regular army. In 1880 he was promoted major; in 1898, brigadier-general and adjutant-general; in June, 1900, major-general; and in 1906, lieutenant-general, and retired. He planned and was umpire at the army manœuvres on the old Bull Run battle-field in September, 1904. He died in New York City, Sept 8, 1909.

Corcoran, MICHAEL, military officer; born in Carrowkeel, Sligo, Ireland, Sept. 21, 1827; came to the United States in 1849, and first came into notice as colonel of the 69th New York Regiment, when the President called for troops, in 1861. He hastened with his regiment to Washington, and was distinguished for gallantry in the battle of Bull Run, where he was wounded and made prisoner, suffering confinement in Richmond, Charleston, Columbia, and Salisbury, while kept for execution, in case the national government put to death the crews of Confederate privateers as pirates. He was exchanged in 1862, and made a brigadier-general. He raised an "Irish Legion," served in lower Virginia and upper North Carolina, and checked the advance of the Confederates on Norfolk. He died of injuries received from a fall from his horse, near Fairfax Court-house, Dec. 22, 1863.

Corcoran, WILLIAM WILSON, philanthropist; born in Georgetown, D. C., Dec. 27, 1798; educated at Georgetown College; became a banker in Washington in 1837, and retired in 1854. He was the founder of the Corcoran Art Gallery, in Washington, D. C., to which he gave a large endowment. His contributions to public and private charities are said to have aggregated more than $5,000,000. He died in Washington, D. C., Feb. 24, 1888.

Cordova, FRANCISCO FERNANDEZ DE, discoverer of Mexico. In February, 1517, he sailed from Havana, Cuba, accompanied by 100 men, and landed on the coast of Yucatan. In a battle with the natives, forty-seven of his men were killed, and he was wounded in twelve places. Hastening back to Cuba, he died of his wounds in 1518.

Corea, see KOREA.

Coree Indians, a small tribe in North Carolina. They were allies of the Tuscaroras in an attack upon the English in 1711.

Corey, GILES. See TORTURE.

Corinth, city and capital of Alcorn county, Miss., 93 miles southeast of Memphis, Tenn.; is chiefly engaged in agriculture and manufacturing; has Civil War military defenses in fair state of preservation. Pop. (1910), 5,020.

Battle of 1862.—General Halleck arrived on the battle-ground of SHILOH (*q. v.*) from his headquarters at St. Louis on April 12, 1862, and, being Grant's superior in rank, took command of the National troops. Grant was preparing to pursue and strike Beauregard while his shattered army was weak; but Halleck restrained Grant, and twenty days after the victory he began a march against Beauregard at Corinth. On May 3 his advance, under General Sherman, was within six or seven miles of Beauregard's lines. His forces had been reorganized under the name of the Grand Army of the Tennessee, and Grant was made his second in command. His whole force, approaching Corinth with great caution, numbered, with the accession of Buell's army, about 108,000 men. Beauregard had been reinforced by Van Dorn and Price, with Missouri and Arkansas troops, and by the command of Gen. Mansfield Lovell, who had come up from New Orleans. For twenty-seven days the National troops were busy piling up fortifications in the approaches to Corinth, interrupted by frequent sorties from that town. Then the Confederates were driven from their advanced works (May 29), and Halleck prepared for a conflict the next day. Although much strengthened, Beauregard was unwilling to risk a battle with the Grand Army of the Tennessee. All the night of May 29 the National sentinels had heard the incessant roar of moving railway-cars at Corinth; and at daybreak, just as Halleck sent out skirmishers to "feel the enemy," the earth was shaken with a series of explosions, and dense columns of smoke arose above the town. There was no enemy to "feel"; Beauregard had evacuated Corinth during the night, burned and blown up whatever of stores he could not carry away, and fled in haste to Tupelo, many miles southward, where he left General Bragg in command of the Confederate forces (now called the Army of the Mississippi), and repaired to Mineral Springs, in Alabama, for the restoration of his impaired health. Halleck took possession of Corinth, and was soon afterwards called to Washington to perform the duties of general-in-chief of all the armies of the republic. He left General Thomas in command at Corinth, and General Grant of his old army, with enlarged powers.

At Ripley, Miss., the troops of Price and Van Dorn were concentrated, 40,000 strong, after the battle at IUKA (*q. v.*), and at the close of September, 1862, they moved on Corinth. They bivouacked within 10 miles of Corinth on the night of Oct. 2. On the morning of the 3d Rosecrans was prepared to meet an attack. Hamilton's division formed his right, Davies's his centre, and McKean's his left, on the front of Corinth. A brigade, under Colonel Oliver, with a section of artillery, was then formed, while the cavalry watched every approach. Early in the morning the Confederate advance, under Colonel Lovell, encountered Oliver. The latter being hard pressed, General McArthur was sent to his support, but both were pushed back. To these both McKean and Davies sent help. Very soon afterwards the Confederates made a desperate charge, drove the Nationals, and captured two guns. The Confederates had resolved to capture Corinth, with its immense stores. They now pressed heavily on the National centre. Davies was pushed back, when Stanley sent Colonel Mower with a brigade to his assistance; and Hamilton was pressing through a thick mire on Lovell's left, when darkness fell, and the struggle ceased. The Confederates enveloped Rosecrans's front, and rested on their arms. Van Dorn believed he would have possession of Corinth before sunrise. He had sent a shout of triumph to Richmond by telegraph. The battle was resumed before the dawn. Both parties had prepared for it. The National batteries around Corinth were well manned, and a new one, mounting five guns, had been constructed during the night. After a considerable cannonading, the Confederates, in heavy force, came out at a little past nine o'clock, advanced rapidly, and fell violently, in wedge-form, upon Davies, intending to break his line and rush into Corinth. The struggle was very severe. Grape and canister shot made fearful lanes through the Confederate ranks, yet they pressed on. Davies's forces gave way, but soon rallied. The Confederates captured Fort Powell on Davies's right, and fully twenty men penetrated Corinth to the headquarters of Rosecrans, on the public square, which they captured. But the victorious Confederate column was soon pushed back, and Fort Powell was retaken by the 56th Illinois Regiment. At the

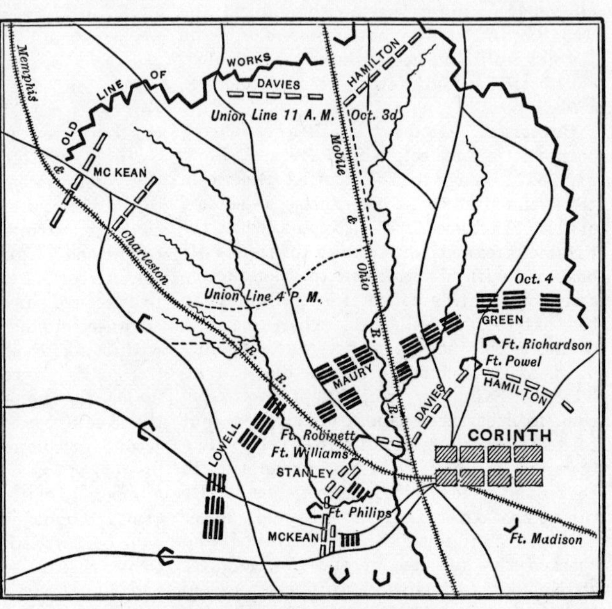

PLAN OF BATTLE AT CORINTH.

same time Hamilton's guns were making fearful havoc in the Confederate ranks. The latter soon fled to the woods. Meanwhile Lovell had fallen upon Fort Robinett and the adjacent lines, and a terrible battle ensued. The fort was stormed by a strong Confederate force, led by Colonel Rogers, of Texas. Within lay prone Colonel Fuller's Ohio brigade, who, aroused, delivered such a murderous fire that the assailants recoiled. In a moment they rallied, and again charged. The 11th Missouri and 27th Ohio poured a terrific storm of bullets upon them, and at the command "Charge!" the Nationals swarmed over the parapet, and sent the assailants flying in confusion to the forest. By noon the battle at Corinth was ended, and the whole Confederate force was retreating southward, vigorously pursued. The National loss in the battle at Corinth and in the pursuit was 2,363, of whom 315 were killed. Of the Confederate loss there is no positive record. One of their historians (Pollard) admits a loss of 4,500, and Rosecrans estimated it at 9,363, of whom 1,423 were killed and 2,248 made prisoners. The Confederates had 38,000 men in the battle; the Nationals less than 20,000.

Corliss, GEORGE HENRY, inventor; born in Easton, N. Y., June 2, 1817; was educated in Castleton, Vt.; settled in Providence, R. I., in 1844. After several minor inventions he became famous by perfecting the great engine which bears his name, and is now known the world over. At the Centennial Exposition at Philadelphia, in 1876, a single Corliss engine, of 1,400 horse-power, ran all the machinery in Machinery Hall. Eminent engineers predicted that the great engine, which weighed over 700 tons, would cause much noise and trouble, but it proved a smooth-running and complete success. He died in Providence, R. I., Feb. 21, 1888.

Corn. See INDIAN CORN.

Cornbury, EDWARD HYDE, LORD, colonial governor; was sent to the province of New York as governor in 1702, when he was Sir Edward Hyde, grandson of the first Earl of Clarendon, and nephew, by marriage, of James II. He was one of the officers of that monarch's household, and was the first to desert him and go over to the Prince of Orange, who became William III. of England. Grateful for this act, William made him governor of the united provinces of New York and New Jersey. He was cordially and generously received. The Assembly, which was largely "Leislerian" in its political composition, and claimed Hyde as a friend, voted him a double salary, a disbursement of the expenses of his voyage, and a reversion of seven years. A public dinner was given him, and the freedom of the city in a gold box. His suite, the soldiers of the garrison, and all citizens unable to purchase their freedom, were made freemen, with rights of suffrage, trade, and of holding office. This generous reception was ill requited. In debt when he came, and rapacious and bigoted, he plundered the public treasury, involved himself in private debts, and opposed every effort on the part of the representatives of the people for the security of their rights and the growth of free institutions. When the yellow fever appeared in New York, in 1703, he retired to Jamaica, L. I., and the best house in the place happening to belong to the Presbyterian minister, he requested to have it vacated for his accommodation. Instead of returning it to the owner, he made it over to the Episcopal party. His conduct as ruler of New Jersey was equally reprehensible, where there were four religious parties—Quakers, Episcopalians, Presbyterians, and Congregationalists—to any of which the governor seemed willing to sell himself. The Assembly adopted a pungent address, which was read to Cornbury by the speaker, in which he was directly accused, among other things, of being an extortioner and "the merchandise of faction." Finally, such representations went from both provinces to the board of trade that Queen Anne removed him (1708), though he was her cousin. Then his creditors threw him into prison, from which he was released by accession to the peerage on the death of his father, when he returned to England and became Earl of Clarendon. He died in London, April 1, 1723.

Cornell, EZEKIEL, military officer; born in Scituate, R. I.; was self-educated. When the Revolutionary War began he entered the army as lieutenant-colonel of Hitchcock's regiment, and was present at the siege of Boston; later was promoted brigadier-general, and commanded a brigade of State troops, which were of much service during the occupation of Massachusetts by the British. In 1780–83 he was a member of the Continental Congress.

Cornell, Alonzo Barton, statesman; born in Ithaca, N. Y., Jan. 22, 1832; appointed surveyor of the port of New York in 1869; sub-naval officer of the port of New York, 1877–78; elected governor of the State in 1879; retired to private life in 1882. He died in Ithaca, N. Y., Oct. 15, 1904.

Cornell, Ezra, philanthropist; born at Westchester Landing, N. Y., Jan. 11, 1807, of Quaker parents; settled in Ithaca in 1828, and accumulated a large fortune in the development of the electric telegraph. In 1865 he founded Cornell University, with an original endowment of $500,000, subsequently increased by $400,000, and by his profits (more than $3,000,000) in purchasing and locating public lands for the benefit of the university. He died in Ithaca, Dec. 9, 1874.

Cornell University, a co-educational institution at Ithaca, N. Y. It is under the supervision of the State regents; and, in addition to the usual university studies, has departments of agriculture and mechanics, and, in New York City, a medical college. It has 638 professors and instructors, 5,190 students, twenty-three fellowships; 15 scholarships; 385,000 volumes in the library; grounds and buildings valued at $4,300,000; endowment funds, about $9,000,000; and income about $1,500,000. **Jacob G. Schurman,** LL. D., president.

Cornplanter, or Garyan-Wah-Gah, a Seneca Indian chief; born in Conewaugo, on the Genesee River, N. Y., in 1732; was a half-breed, the son of an Indian trader named John O'Bail. He led Indian allies with the French against the English; was in the sharp battle of Monongahela in 1755; and, joining the British in the war of the Revolution, led destroyers of the settlements in New York and Pennsylvania. An inveterate foe of the Americans during the war, he was their firm friend afterwards. He died at the Seneca reservation, Pennsylvania, Feb. 17, 1836.

Cornstalk. Indian chief. See Dunmore, John M.

Cornwaleys, or **Cormwaleys,** Thomas, pioneer; born about 1600; was one of the leaders in the establishment of the colony at St. Mary's. In 1635 he led a force against Claiborne, and in 1638, when Lord Baltimore sent out a code to be adopted by the General Assembly, he opposed it, alleging that the charter of the freemen gave them the right to enact their own laws. During 1638 he was made deputy governor; in 1642 was commissioned commander of an expedition against the Indians; in 1652 became a member of the General Court; and in 1657 assistant governor to Lord Baltimore. He returned to England in 1659, and died there in 1676.

Cornwallis, Lord Charles, military officer; born in London, Dec. 31, 1738; was educated at Eton and Cambridge, and entered the army as captain when twenty years of age. In the House of Lords he opposed the measures that caused the war with the Americans; yet he accepted the commission of major-general and the command of an expedition against the Carolinas under Sir Peter Parker in 1776. He commanded the reserves of the British in the battle on Long Island in August; was outgeneralled by Washington at Princeton; was with Howe on the Brandywine and in the capture of Philadelphia; he returned to England, but soon came back; was at the capture of Charleston in May, 1780; was commander of the British troops in the Carolinas that year; defeated Gates near Camden in August; fought Greene at Guilford Court-house early in 1781; invaded Virginia, and finally took post at and fortified Yorktown, on the York River, and there surrendered his army to the American and French forces in October, 1781. He was appointed governor-general and commander-in-chief in India in 1786; and was victorious in war there in 1791–92, compelling Tippoo Sahib to cede, as the price of peace, half his dominions to the British crown. He returned to England in 1793, was created a marquis, and appointed lord-lieutenant of Ireland in 1798. He negotiated the treaty of Amiens in 1802, and received the appointment of governor-general of India in 1805. He died at Ghazipur, India, Oct. 5, 1805.

In 1776 Sir Henry Clinton waited long

on the Cape Fear River for the arrival of Sir Peter Parker's fleet with Cornwallis and a reinforcement of troops. They came early in May and soon prepared to make an attack on Charleston. Clinton received, by the fleet, instructions from his King to issue a proclamation of pardon to "all but principal instigators and abettors of the rebellion, to dissolve the provincial congresses and committees of safety, to restore the administration of justice, and to arrest the persons and destroy the property of all who should refuse to give satisfactory tests of their obedience." He was expressly ordered to "seize the persons and destroy the property of persistent rebels whenever it could be done with effect." When the British forces were about to leave the North Carolina coast, Clinton sent Lord Cornwallis, at the instigation of Governor Martin, to burn the house of Hooper, a delegate in the Continental Congress, and to burn and ravage the plantation of Gen. Robert Howe. Cornwallis landed in Brunswick county with about 900 men,

LORD CORNWALLIS (From an English print).

and proceeded to his assigned work. In this ignoble expedition—his first in America—he lost two men killed and one taken prisoner. Clinton, in a proclamation (May 5), invited the people to "appease the vengeance of an incensed nation" by submission, and offered pardon to all, excepting General Howe and Cornelius Harnett.

Howe sent Cornwallis in November, 1777, with a strong body of troops, by way of Chester, to Billingsport to clear the New Jersey banks of the Delaware. Washington immediately sent General Greene with a division across the river to oppose the movement. Cornwallis was reinforced by five British battalions from New York, while expected reinforcements from the northern army were still delayed through the bad conduct of General Gates. The consequence was the forced abandonment of Fort Mercer, at Red Bank, and the levelling of its ramparts by the British troops. The leaders of both armies recrossed the Delaware, Cornwallis to Philadelphia and Greene to the camp of Washington.

Lord Cornwallis was left in chief command of about 4,000 troops when, in the summer of 1780, Sir Henry Clinton departed for New York. The earl, for the purpose of rooting out all signs of rebellion, sought, by cruel acts, to completely subdue the people through fear. He issued proclamations and instructions which encouraged hostility towards every patriot; and under these instructions his agents and the Tories committed many crimes. Tarleton and his legion spread terror in many districts. A quartermaster of his command entered the house of Samuel Wyley, near Camden, and cut him in pieces with his sword, because he had served as a volunteer in defence of Charleston. Because the Presbyterians generally supported the American cause, they were specially singled out for persecution. Huck, a captain of the British militia, burned the library and dwelling of a Presbyterian clergyman in the upper part of South Carolina; and also burned every Bible in which the Scottish translation of the Psalms was found. Prisoners who had been paroled at Charleston were subjects of perpetual persecution under the immediate observation of Cornwallis, unless they would exchange their paroles for oaths of allegiance. An active officer was deputed to visit every district in the State, and procure, on the spot, lists of its militia. Any Carolinian thereafter taken in arms might be sentenced to death for desertion and "bearing arms against his country." Cornwallis never regarded a deserter, or any whom a court-martial sentenced to death, as an object

CORNWALLIS'S CAVE.

of mercy. His lieutenant, Lord Rawdon, was particularly hard on deserters from his Irish regiment. "I will give the inhabitants," he proclaimed, "10 guineas for the head of any deserter belonging to the volunteers of Ireland, and 5 guineas only if they bring him in alive." To punish Sumter, who had commanded a Continental regiment, a British detachment turned his wife out-of-doors and burned his dwelling-house. These proceedings, and others equally atrocious, were approved by Cornwallis, who tried to crush out every vestige of independence in the State by requiring every able-bodied man to join the British army and take an active part in the re-establishment of royal rule. All who refused were treated as "rebels." Then, under instructions from Minister Germaine, he determined to establish a system of terrorism that should wipe out every semblance of revolt in that State. He put military despotism in the place of civil law. He ordered all militia-men who had served in loyalist corps and were afterwards found in arms against the King to be hanged without mercy; and in this way many perished. He gave Tory leaders full license to execute these orders, and instantly murders and plunderings and the scourge of the torch everywhere prevailed. Property was wantonly destroyed by fire and violence; the chastity of women was set at naught; and Whigs, both men and women, cultivated and tenderly reared, were treated by the ravenous Tory wolves as legitimate prey to their worst passions. These measures created revolt and a thirst for vengeance, and when the partisan leaders appeared they instantly found hundreds of followers. Cornwallis soon found South Carolina too hot for him, and he was driven through North Carolina into Virginia.

After the battle at GUILFORD COURT-HOUSE (*q. v.*) Cornwallis marched towards the seaboard, satisfied that he could no longer hold the Carolinas. He arrived at Wilmington April 7, 1781, then garrisoned by a small force under Major Craig, where he remained long enough to rest and recruit his shattered army. Apprised of Greene's march on Camden, and hoping to draw him away from Lord Rawdon, the earl marched into Virginia and joined the forces of Phillips and Arnold at Petersburg. So ended British rule in the Carolinas forever. He left Wilmington April 25, crossed the Roanoke at Halifax, and reached Petersburg May 20. Four days afterwards he entered upon his destructive career in Virginia.

A few days after he reached Williamsburg, Cornwallis received an order from Sir Henry Clinton to send 3,000 of his troops to New York, then menaced by the allied (Americans and French) armies. Clinton also directed the earl to take a defensive position in Virginia. Satisfied that after he should send away so large a part of his army he could not cope with Lafayette and his associates, Cornwallis determined to cross the James River and make his way to Portsmouth. This movement was hastened by the boldness of the American troops, who were pressing close upon him, showing much strength and great activity. On July 6 a detachment sent out by Wayne to capture a British field-piece boldly resisted a large portion of Cornwallis's army, as the former fell back to Lafayette's main army near the Green Spring Plantation, where a sharp skirmish occurred, in which the marquis had a horse shot under him and each party lost about 100 men. Cornwallis then hastened across the James (July 9) and marched to Portsmouth. Disliking that situation, the earl proceeded to Yorktown, on the York River, and on a high and healthful plain he established a fortified camp. At Gloucester Point, on the opposite side of the river, he cast up strong military works, and while Lafayette took up a strong position on Malvern Hill and awaited further developments, Cornwallis spent many anxious days in expectation of reinforcements by sea. In August, however, the Count de Grasse arrived off the coast of Virginia with a powerful French fleet, and Washington took advantage of this good fortune, and suddenly moved his army from the Hudson to the James, and invested Yorktown with an overwhelming force.

Finding escape impossible, and further resistance futile, Cornwallis sent a flag to

MRS. MOORE'S HOUSE.

Washington, with a request that hostilities should be suspended for twenty-four hours, and that commissioners should be appointed on both sides to meet at Mrs. Moore's house, on the right of the American lines, to arrange terms for the surrender of the post and the British army. Commissioners were accordingly appointed, the Americans being Col. John Laurens and Viscount de Noailles (a kinsman of Lafayette), and the British Lieutenant-Colonel Dundas and Major Ross. The terms agreed upon were honorable to both parties, and were signed on Oct. 19, 1781. They provided for the surrender of Cornwallis as a prisoner of war, with all his troops, and all public property as spoils of victory. All slaves and plunder found in possession of the British might be reclaimed by their owners; otherwise private property was to be respected. The loyalists were abandoned to the mercy or resentment of their countrymen. Such were the general terms; but Cornwallis was allowed to send away persons most obnoxious to the Whigs in the vessel that carried despatches to Clinton.

Late in the afternoon of Oct. 19, the surrender of the British troops took place. Washington and Rochambeau were at the head of their respective troops, on horseback. The field of surrender was about half a mile from the British lines. A vast multitude of people, equal in numbers to the troops to be humiliated, was present at the impressive ceremony. Cornwallis, it was said, feigned sickness, and did not appear, but sent his sword by General O'Hara to act as his representative. That officer led the vanquished troops out of their intrenchments, with their colors cased, and marched them between the two columns of the allied forces. When he arrived at their head he approached Washington to hand him the earl's sword, when the commander-in-chief directed him to General Lincoln as his representative. It was a proud moment for Lincoln, who, the previous year, had been compelled to make a humiliating surrender to the royal troops at Charleston. He led the vanquished army to the place chosen for the surrender of their arms, and then received from O'Hara the sword of Cornwallis, which was politely returned to him to be restored to the earl. The surrender of the colors of the vanquished army, twenty-eight in number, now took place. Twenty-eight British captains, each bearing a flag in a case, were drawn up in line. Opposite to them, at a distance of six paces, twenty-eight American sergeants were placed in line to receive the colors. The interesting ceremony was conducted by an ensign (Robert Wilson), then only eighteen years of age. The troops then laid down their arms. The whole number surrendered was about 7,000. To these must be added 2,000 sailors, 1,800 negroes, and 1,500 Tories, making the total number of prisoners 12,300. The British lost, in killed, wounded, and

Article 14th

No Article of the Capitulation to be infringed on pretext of Reprisal, & if there be
any doubtfull Expressions
in it, they are to be interpreted according to the common Meaning & Acceptation
of the Words.

Done at York in Virginia
this 9th day October 1781

Cornwallis
Thos: Symonds:

ONE OF THE ARTICLES OF CAPITULATION, WITH CORNWALLIS'S SIGNATURE.

missing, during the siege 550 men. The Americans lost about 300. The spoils were nearly 8,000 muskets, seventy-five brass and 160 iron cannon, and a large quantity of munitions of war and military stores. The French furnished for gaining this victory thirty-seven ships of the line and 7,000 men. The Americans furnished 9,000 troops, of which number 5,500 were regulars. On the day after the surrender Washington, in general orders, expressed full approbation of the conduct of the allied armies; and, that every soldier might participate in the general joy and thanksgiving, he ordered every one under arrest or in confinement to be set at liberty; and, as the following day would be the Sabbath, he closed his orders by directing divine service to be performed in the several brigades on the morrow. See YORKTOWN.

News of the surrender, which reached England, by way of France, Nov. 25, 1781, gave a stunning blow to the British ministry and the Tory party in Great Britain. It was clearly perceived that final disseverance of the colonies from the mother-country was inevitable; that war could no longer serve a useful purpose, and that humanity and sound policy counselled peace. The King and his ministers were astounded. "Lord North received the intelligence," said Lord George Germaine, "as he would have taken a cannon-ball in his breast; for he opened his arms, exclaiming wildly as he paced up and down the apartment a few minutes, 'O God! it is all over.'" In deepest consternation he repeated these words many times. The stubborn King was amazed and struck dumb for a few minutes: then. recovering his equanimity, he wrote, in view of a proposition in the Parliament to give up the contest and allow the independence of the colonies, "No difficulties can get me to consent to the getting of peace at the expense of a separation from America."

The city of London petitioned the King to "put an end to the unnatural and unfortunate war"; and in Parliament a great change in sentiment was immediately visible. Late in February, General Conway moved an address to the King in favor of peace. A warm debate ensued. Lord North defended the royal policy, because it maintained British rights and was just. "Good God!" exclaimed Burke, "are we yet to be told of the rights for which we went to war? O excellent rights! O valuable rights! Valuable you should be, for we have paid dear in parting with you. O valuable rights! that have cost Britain thirteen provinces, four islands, 100,000 men, and more than £70,000,000 ($350,000,000) of money." At the beginning of March Conway's proposition was adopted. Lord North, who, under the inspiration of the King, had misled the nation for twelve years, was relieved from office, and he and his fellow-ministers were succeeded by friends of peace. The King stormed, but was compelled to yield. Parliament resolved to end the war, and the King acquiesced with reluctance. Early in May (1782) Sir Guy Carleton arrived in New York, bearing propositions to Congress for reconciliation, and Richard Oswald, a London merchant, was sent to Paris as a diplomatic agent to confer with Franklin on the subject of a treaty of peace.

CORONADO, FRANCISCO VASQUEZ DE

Coronado, FRANCISCO VASQUEZ DE, explorer; born in Salamanca, Spain, about 1510; set out in 1540, by command of Mendoza, viceroy of Mexico, from Culiacan, on the southeast coast of the Gulf of California, with 350 Spaniards and 800 Indians, to explore the country northward. He followed the coast nearly to the head of the gulf, and then penetrated to the Gila, in the present Arizona Territory. Following that stream to its head-waters, he crossed the great hills eastward, to the upper waters of the Rio Grande del Norte, which he followed to their sources. Then, crossing the Rocky Mountains, he traversed the great desert northeastwardly to the present States of Colorado or Kansas, under lat. 40° N. In all that vast region he found little to tempt or reward a conquest—rugged mountains and plains and a few Indian villages in some of the valleys. He made quite an elaborate report, accompanying it with drawings of the cities and houses built by the Indians (see below). He died in March, 1542, insane, it is believed.

Coronado's Relation to Mendoza.—On Aug. 3, 1540, Coronado addressed the following report to the Mexican viceroy, concerning his journey into what is now a considerable part of the United States:

THE RELATION OF FRANCIS VAZQUEZ DE CORONADO, CAPTAINE GENERALL OF THE PEOPLE WHICH WERE SENT IN THE NAME OF THE EMPEROURS MAIESTIE TO THE COUNTREY OF CIBOLA NEWLY DISCOUERED, WHICH HE SENT TO DON ANTONIO DE MENDOCA VICEROY OF MEXICO, OF SUCH THINGS AS HAPPENED IN HIS VOYAGE FROM THE 22. OF APRILL IN THE YEERE 1540. WHICH DEPARTED FROM CULIACAN FORWARD, AND OF SUCH THINGS AS HEE FOUND IN THE COUNTREY WHICH HE PASSED.

CHAP. 1.

Francis Vazquez departeth with his armie from Culiacan, and after diuers troubles in his voyage, arriueth at the valley of the people called Los Caracones, which he findeth barren of Maiz: for obtaining whereof hee sendeth to the valley called The valley of the Lord: he is informed of the greatnesse of the valley of the people called Caracones, and of the nature of those people, and of certaine Islands lying along that coast.

THe 22. of the moneth of Aprill last past I departed from the prouince of Culiacan with part of the army, and in such order as I mentioned vnto your Lordship, and according to the successe I assured my selfe, by all likelihood that I shall not bring all mine armie together in this enterprise: because the troubles haue bene so great and the want of victuals, that I thinke all this yeere wil not be sufficient to performe this enterprise, & if it should bee performed in so short a time, it would be to the great losse of our people. For as I wrote vnto your Lordship, I was fourescore dayes in trauailing to Culiacan, in all which time I and those Gentlemen my companions which were horsemen, carried on our backs, and on our horses, a little victuall, so that from henceforward wee carried none other needefull apparell with vs, that was aboue a pound weight: and all this notwithstanding, and though wee put our selues to such a small proportion of victuals which wee carried, for all the order that possibly wee could take, wee were driuen to our ships. And no maruayle, because the way is rough and long: and with the carriage of our Harquebuses downe the mountaines and hilles, and in the passage of Riuers, the greater part of our corne was spoyled. And because I send your Lordship our voyage drawen in a Mappe, I will speake no more thereof in this my letter.

Thirtie leagues before wee arriued at the place which the father prouinciall told vs so well of in his relation, I sent Melchior Diaz before with fifteene horses, giuing him order to make but one dayes iourney of two, because hee might examine all things, against mine arriuall: who trauailed foure dayes iourney through exceeding rough Mountaines where hee found neither victuals, nor people, nor information of any things, sauing that hee found two or three poore little villages containing 20. or 30. cottages a piece, and by the inhabitants thereof hee vnderstoode that from thence forward there were nothing but exceeding rough mountaines which ran very farre, vtterly disinhabited and voyd of people. And because it was labour lost, I would not write vnto your Lordship thereof.

It grieued the whole company, that a thing so highly commended, and whereof the father had made so great bragges, should be found so contrary, and it made them suspect that all the rest would fall out in like sort. Which when I perceiued I sought to encourage them the best I coulde, telling them that your Lordshippe alwayes was of opinion, that this voyage was a thing cast away, and that wee should fixe our cogitation vpon those seuen Cities, and other prouinces, whereof wee had knowledge; that there should bee the ende of our enterprise; and with this resolution and purpose wee all marched cheerefully through a very badde way which was not passable but one by one, or else wee must force out with Pioners the path which wee founde, wherewith the Souldiours were not a little offended, finding all that the Frier had sayde to bee quite contrary; for among other things which the father sayde and affirmed, this was one, that the way was plaine and good, and that there was but one small hill of halfe a league in length. And yet in trueth there are mountaines which although the way were well mended could not bee passed without great danger of breaking the horses neckes; and the way was such that of the cattell which your Lordship sent vs for the prouision of our armie wee lost a great part in the voyage through the roughnesse of the rockes. The lambes and sheepe lost their hoofes in the way; and of those which I brought from Culiacan, I left the greater part at the Riuer of Lachimi, because they could not keepe company with vs, and because they might come softly after vs, foure men on horsebacke remained with them which are nowe come vnto vs, and haue brought vs not past foure and twentie lambes, and foure sheepe, for all the rest were dead with trauailing through that rough passage, although they trauailed but two leagues a day, and rested themselues euery day.

At length I arriued at the valley of the people called Caracones, the 26. day of the moneth of May; and from Culiacan vntill I came thither, I could not helpe my selfe, saue onely with a great quantitie of bread of Maiz; for seeing the Maiz in the fieldes were not yet ripe, I was constrained to leaue them all behind me. In this valley of the Caracones wee found more store of people than in any other part of the Countrey which wee had passed, and great store of tillage. But I vnderstood that there was store thereof in another valley called The Lords valley, which I woulde not disturbe with force, but sent thither Melchior Diaz with wares of exchange to procure some, and to giue the sayde Maiz to the Indians our friendes which wee brought with vs, and to some others that had lost their cattell in the way, and were not able to carry their victuals so farre which they brought from Culiacan. It pleased God that wee gate some small quantitie of Maiz with this traffique, whereby certaine Indians were relieued and some Spanyards.

And by that time that wee were come to this valley of the Caracones, some tenne or twelue of our horses were dead through wearinesse; for being ouercharged with great burdens, and hauing but little meate, they could not endure the trauaile. Likewise some of our Negros and some of our Indians dyed here; which was no small want vnto vs for the performance of our enterprise. They tolde me that this valley of the Coracones is fiue dayes iourney from the Westerne Sea. I sent for the Indians of the Sea coast to vnderstand their estate, and while I stayed for them the horses rested; and I stayed there foure dayes, in which space the Indians of the Sea coast came vnto mee; which told mee, that two dayes sayling from their coast of the Sea, there were seuen or eight Islands right ouer against them, well inhabited with people, but badly furnished with victuals, and were a rude people: And they told mee, that they had seene a Shippe passe by not farre from the shore: which I wote not what to think whither it were one of those that went to discouer the Countrey, or else a Ship of the Portugals.

CHAP. 2.

They come to Chichilticale: after they had rested themselues two dayes there, they enter into a Countrey very barren of victuals, and hard to trauaile for thirtie leagues, beyond which they found a Countrey very pleasant, and a riuer called Rio del Lino, they fight with the Indians being assaulted by them, and with victorie vanquishing their citie, they relieued themselues of their pinching hunger.

I Departed from the Caracones, and alwayes kept by the Sea coast as neere as I could iudge, and in very deed I still found my selfe the farther off: in such sort that when I arriued at Chichilticale I found myselfe tenne dayes iourney from the Sea: and the father prouinciall sayd that it was onely but fiue leagues distance, and that hee had seene the same. Wee all conceiued great griefe and were not a little confounded, when we saw that wee found euery thing contrary to the information which he had giuen your Lordship.

The Indians of Chichilticale say, that if at any time they goe to the Sea for fish, and other things that they carry, they goe trauersing, and are tenne dayes iourney in going thither. And I am of opinion that the information which the Indians giue me should be true. The sea returneth toward the West right ouer against the Coracones the space of tenne or twelue leagues. Where I found that your Lordships ships were seene, which went to discouer the hauen of Chichilticale, which father Marcus of Niça sayd to bee in fiue and thirtie degrees. God knoweth what griefe of mind I haue sustained: because I am in doubt that some mishappe is fallen vnto them: and if they follow the coast, as they sayde they would, as long as their victuals last which they carry with them, whereof I left them store in Culiacan, and if they be not fallen into some misfortune, I hope well in God that by this they haue made some good discouerie, and that in this respect their long staying out may be pardoned.

I rested myselfe two dayes in Chichilticale, and to haue done well I should haue stayed longer, in respect that here wee found our horses so tyred: but because wee wanted victuals, wee had no leasure to rest any longer: I entred the confines of the desert Countrey on St. Iohns eue, and to refresh our former trauailes, the first dayes we founde no grasse, but worser way of mountaines and badde passages, then wee had passed alreadie: and the horses being tired, were greatly molested therewith: so that in this last desert wee lost more horses then wee had lost before: and some of my Indians which were our friendes dyed, and one Spanyard whose name was Spinosa; and two Negroes, which dyed with eating certaine herbes for lacke of victuals. From this place I sent before mee one dayes iourney the master of the fielde Don Garcia Lopez de Cardenas with fifteene horses to discouer the Countrey, and prepare our way: wherein hee did like himselfe, and according to the confidence which your Lordship reposed in him. And well I wote he fayled not to do his part: for as I haue enformed your Lordship, it is most wicked way, at least thirtie leagues and more, because they are inaccessible mountaines.

But after wee had passed these thirtie leagues, wee found fresh riuers, and grasse like that of Castile, and specially of that sort which we call Scaramoio, many Nutte trees and Mulberie trees, but the Nutte trees differ from those of Spayne in the leafe: and there was Flaxe, but chiefly neere the bankes of a certayne riuer which therefore wee called El Rio del Lino, that is say, the riuer of Flaxe: wee found no Indians at all for a dayes trauaile, but afterward foure Indians came out vnto vs in peaceable maner, saying that they were sent euen to that desert place to signifie vnto vs that wee were welcome, and that the next day all the people would come out to meete vs on the way with victuals: and the master of the fielde gaue them a crosse, willing them to signifie to those of their citie that they should not feare, and they should rather let the people stay in their houses, because I came onely in the name of his Maiestie to defend and ayd them.

And this done, Fernando Aluarado returned to aduertise mee that certaine Indians were come vnto them in peaceable maner, and that two of them stayed for my comming with the master of the fielde. Whereupon I went vnto them and gaue them beades and certaine short clokes, willing them to returne vnto their citie, and bid them to stay quiet in their houses, and feare nothing. And this done I sent the master of the field to search whether there were any bad passage which the Indians might keepe against vs, and that hee should take and defend it vntill the next day that I shoulde come thither. So hee went, and found in the way a very bad passage, where wee might haue sustayned very great harme: wherefore there hee seated himselfe with his company that were with him: and that very night the Indians came to take that passage to defend it, and finding it taken, they assaulted our men there, and as they tell mee, they assaulted them like valiant men; although in the ende they retired and fledde away; for the master of the fielde was watchfull, and was in order with his company: the Indians in token of retreate sounded on a certaine small trumpet, and did no hurt among the Spanyards. The very same night the master of the fielde certified mee hereof. Whereupon the next day in the best order that I could I departed in so great want of victuall, that I thought that if wee should stay one day longer without foode, wee should all perish for hunger, especially the Indians, for among vs all we had not two bushels of corne: wherefore it behooued mee to pricke forward without delay. The Indians here and their made fires, and were answered againe afarre off as orderly as wee for our liues could haue done, to giue their fellowes vnderstanding, how wee marched and where we arriued.

As soone as I came within sight of this citie of Granada, I sent Dôn Garcias Lopez Campemaster, frier Daniel, and frier Luys, and Fernando Vermizzo somewhat before with certaine horsemen, to seeke the Indians and to aduertise them that our comming was not to hurt them, but to defend them in the name of the Emperour our Lord, according as his maiestie had giuen vs in charge: which message was deliuered to the inhabitants of that countrey by an interpreter. But they like arrogant people made small account thereof; because we seemed very few in their eyes, and that they might destroy vs without any difficultie; and they strooke frier Luys with an arrow on the gowne, which by the grace of God did him no harme.

In the meane space I arriued with all the rest of the horsemen, and footemen, and found in the fieldes a great sort of the Indians which beganne to shoote at vs with their arrowes: and because I would obey your will and the commaund of the Marques, I woulde not let my people charge them, forbidding my company, which intreated mee that they might set vpon them, in any wise to prouoke them, saying that that which the enemies did was nothing, and that it was not meete to set vpon so fewe people. On the other side the Indians perceiuing that wee stirred not, tooke great stomacke and courage vnto them: insomuch that they came hard to our horses heeles to shoote at vs with their arrowes. Whereupon seeing that it was now time to stay no longer, and that the friers also were of the same opinion, I set vpon them without any danger: for suddenly they fled part to the citie which was neere and well fortified, and other into the field, which way they could shift: and some of the Indians were slaine, and more had beene if I would haue suffered them to haue bene pursued.

But considering that hereof wee might reape but small profite, because the Indians that were without, were fewe, and those which were retired into the citie, with them which stayed within at the first were many, where the victuals were whereof wee had so great neede, I assembled my people, and deuided them as I thought best to assault the citie, and I compassed it about: and because the famine which wee sustained suffered no delay, my selfe with certaine of these gentlemen and souldiers put our selues on foote, and commaunded that the crossebowes and harquebusiers shoulde giue the assault, and shoulde beate the enemies from the walles, that they might not hurt vs, and I assaulted the walles on one side, where they tolde me there was a scaling ladder set vp, and that there was one gate: but the crossebowmen suddenly brake the strings of their bowes, and the harquebusiers did nothing at all: for they came thither so weake and feeble, that scarcely they coulde stand on their feete: and by this meanes the people that were aloft on the wals to defend the towne were no way hindered from doing vs all the mischiefe they could: so that twise they stroke mee to the ground with infinite number of great stones, which they cast downe: and if I had not beene defended with an excellent good headpiece which I ware, I thinke it had gone hardly with mee: neuerthelesse my companie tooke mee vp with two small wounds in the face, and an arrowe sticking in my foote, and many blowes with stones on my arms and legges, and thus I went out of the battell very weake. I thinke that if Don Garcias Lopez de Cardenas the second time that they strooke mee to the ground had not succoured mee with striding ouer mee like a good knight, I had beene in farre greater danger then I was. But it pleased God that the Indians yeelded themselues vnto vs, and that this citie was taken: and such store of Maiz was found therein, as our necessitie required. The Master of the fielde, and Don Pedro de Touar, and Fernando de Aluarado, and Paul de Melgosa Captaines of the footemen escaped with certaine knocks with stones: though none of them were wounded with arrowes, yet Agoniez Quarez was wounded in one arme with the shot of an arrowe, and one Torres a townesman of Panuco was shot into the face with another, and two footemen more had two small woundes with arrowes. And because my armour was gilded and glittering, they all layd load on mee, and therefore I was more wounded than the rest, not that I did more than they, or put my selfe forwarder than the rest, for all these Gentlemen and souldiers carried themselues as manfully as was looked for at their hands. I am nowe well recouered I thanke God, although somewhat bruised with stones. Likewise in the skirmish which wee had in the fieldes, two or three other souldiers were hurt, and three horses slaine, one of Don Lopez, the other of Viliega and the third of Don Alonzo Manrique, and seuen or eight other horses were wounded; but both the men and horses are whole and sound.

CHAP. 3.

Of the situation and state of the seuen cities called the kingdome of Cibola, and of the customes and qualities of those people, and of the beasts which are found there.

IT remaineth now to certifie your Honour of the seuen cities, and of the kingdomes and prouinces whereof the Father prouinciall made report vnto your Lordship. And to bee briefe, I can assure your honour, he sayd the trueth in nothing that he reported, but all was quite contrary, sauing onely the names of the cities, and great houses of stone: for although they bee not wrought with Turqueses, nor with lyme, nor brickes, yet are they very excellent good houses of three or foure or fiue lofts high, wherein are good lodgings and faire chambers with lathers instead of staires, and certaine cellars vnder the ground very good and paued, which are made for winter, they are in maner like stooues: and the lathers which they haue for their houses are all in a maner mooueable and portable, which are taken away and set downe when they please, and they are made of two pieces of wood with their steppes, as ours be. The seuen cities are seuen small townes, all made with these kinde of houses that I speake of: and they stand all within foure leagues together, and they are all called the kingdome of Cibola, and euery one of them haue their particular name: and none of them is called Cibola, but altogether they are called Cibola. And this towne which I call a citie, I haue named Granada, as well because it is somewhat like vnto it, as also in remembrance of your lordship. In this towne where I nowe remaine, there may be some two hundred houses, all compassed with walles, and I thinke that with the rest of the houses which are not so walled, they may be together fiue hundred. There is another towne neere this, which is one of the seuen, & it is somwhat bigger than this, and another of the same bignesse that this is of, and the other foure are somewhat lesse: and I send them all painted vnto your lordship with the voyage. And the parchment wherein the picture is, was found here with other parchments. The people of this towne seeme vnto me of a reasonable stature, and wittie, yet they seeme not to bee such as they should bee, of that judgment and wit to builde these houses in such sort as they are. For the most part they goe all naked, except their priuie partes which are couered: and they haue painted mantles like those which I send vnto your lordship. They haue no cotton wooll growing, because the countrey is colde, yet they weare mantels thereof as your honour may see by the shewe thereof: and true it is that there was found in their houses certaine yarne made of cotton wooll. They weare their haire on their heads like those of Mexico, and they are well nurtured and condicioned: And they haue Turqueses I thinke good quantitie, which with the rest of the goods which they had, except their corne, they had conueyed away before I came thither: for I found no women there, nor no youth vnder fifteene yeeres olde, nor no olde folkes aboue sixtie, sauing two or three olde folkes, who stayed behinde to gouerne all the rest of the youth and men of warre. There were found in a certaine paper two poynts of Emralds, and certaine small stones broken which are in colour somewhat like Granates very bad, and other stones of Christall, which I gaue one of my seruaunts to lay vp to send them to your lordship, and hee hath lost them as hee telleth me. Wee found heere Guinie cockes, but fewe. The Indians tell mee in all these seuen cities, that they eate them not, but that they keepe them onely for their feathers. I beleeue them not, for they are excellent good, and greater then those of Mexico. The season which is in this countrey, and the temperature of the ayre is like that of Mexico: for sometime it is hotte, and sometime it raineth: but hitherto I neuer sawe it raine, but once there fell a little showre with winde, as they are woont to fall in Spaine.

The snow and cold are woont to be great, for so say the inhabitants of the Countrey: and it is very likely so to bee, both in respect to the maner of the Countrey, and by the fashion of their houses, and their furres and other things which this people haue to defend them from colde. There is no kind of fruit nor trees of fruite. The Countrey is all plaine, and is on no side mountainous: albeit there are some hillie and bad passages. There are small store of Foules: the cause whereof is the colde, and because the mountaines are not neere. Here is no great store of wood, because they haue wood for their fuell sufficient foure leagues off from a wood of small Cedars. There is most excellent grasse within a quarter of a league hence, for our horses as well to feede them in pasture, as to mowe and make hay, whereof wee stoode in great neede, because our horses came hither so weake and feeble. The victuals which the people of this countrey haue, is Maiz, whereof they haue great store, and also small white Pease: and Venison, which by all likelyhood they feede vpon, (though they say no) for wee found many skinnes of Deere, of Hares, and Conies. They eate the best cakes that euer I sawe, and euery body generally eateth of them. They haue the finest order and way to grinde that wee euer sawe in any place. And one Indian woman of this countrey will grinde as much as foure women of Mexico. They haue most excellent salte in kernell, which they fetch from a certaine lake a dayes iourney from hence. They haue no knowledge among them of the North Sea, nor of the Westerne Sea, neither can I tell your lordship to which wee bee neerest: But in reason they should seeme to bee neerest to the Westerne Sea: and at the least I thinke I am an hundred and fiftie leagues from thence: and the Northerne Sea should bee much further off. Your lordship may see howe broad the land is here. Here are many sorts of beasts, as Beares, Tigers, Lions, Porkespicks, and certaine Sheep as bigge as an horse, with very great hornes and little tailes, I haue seene their hornes so bigge, that it is a wonder to behold their greatnesse. Here are also wilde goates whose heads likewise I haue seene, and the pawes of Beares, and the skins of wilde Bores. There is game of Deere, Ounces, and very great Stagges: and all men are of opinion that there are some bigger than that beast which your lordship bestowed vpon me, which once belonged to Iohn Melaz. They trauell eight dayes iourney vnto certaine plaines lying toward the North Sea. In this countrey there are certaine skinnes well dressed, and they dresse them and paint them where they kill their Oxen, for so they say themselues.

CHAP. 4.

Of the state and qualities of the kingdomes of Totonteac, Marata, and Acus, quite contrary to the relation of Frier Marcus. The conference which they haue with the Indians of the citie of Granada which they had taken, which had fiftie yeres past foreseene the comming of the Christians into their countrey. The relation which they haue of other seuen cities, whereof Tucano is the principall, and how he sent to discouer them. A present of diuers things had in these countreys sent vnto the Viceroy Mendoça by Vasques de Coronado.

THe kingdome of Totonteac so much extolled by the Father prouinciall, which sayde that there were such wonderfull things there, and such great matters, and that they made cloth there, the Indians say is an hotte lake, about which are fiue or sixe houses; and that there were certaine other, but that they are ruinated by warre. The kingdome of Marata is not to be found, neither haue the Indians any knowledge thereof. The kingdome of Acus is one onely small citie, where they gather cotton which is called Acucu. And I say that this is a towne. For Acus with an aspiration nor without is no word of the countrey. And because I gesse that they would deriue Acucu of Acus, I say that it is this towne whereinto the kingdom of Acus is conuerted. Beyond this towne they say there are other small townes which are neere to a riuer which I haue seene and haue had report of by the relation of the Indians. I would to God I had better newes to write vnto your lordship: neuerthelesse I must say the trueth: And as I wrote to your lordship from Culiacan, I am nowe to aduertise your honour as wel of the good as of the bad. Yet this I would haue you bee assured, that if all the riches and the treasures of the world were heere, I could haue done no more in the seruice of his Maiestie and of your lordshippe, than I haue done in comming hither whither you haue sent mee, my selfe and my companions carrying our victuals vpon our shoulders and vpon our horses three hundred leagues; and many dayes going on foote trauailing ouer hilles and rough mountaines, with other troubles which I cease to mention, neither purpose I to depart vnto the death, if it please his Maiestie and your lordship that it shall be so.

Three dayes after this citie was taken, certaine Indians of these people came to offer mee peace, and brought mee certaine Turqueses, and badde mantles, and I receiued them in his Maiesties name with all the good speaches that I could deuise, certifying them of the purpose of my comming into this countrey, which is in the name of his Maiestie, and by the commaundement of your Lordship, that they and all the rest of the people of this prouince should become Christians, and should knowe the true God for their Lorde, and receiue his Maiestie for their King and earthly Soueraigne: and herewithall they returned to their houses, and suddenly the next day set in order all their goods and substance, their women and children, and fled to the hilles, leauing their townes as it were abandoned, wherein remained very fewe of them. When I sawe this, within eight or tenne dayes after being recouered of my woundes, I went to the citie, which I sayed to bee greater than this where I am, and found there some fewe of them, to whom I sayde that they should not be afrayd, and that they should call their gouernour vnto me: Howbeit forasmuch as I can learne or gather, none of them hath any gouernour: for I saw not there any chiefe house, whereby any preeminence of one ouer another might bee gathered. After this an olde man came, which sayd that hee was their lord, with a piece of a mantel made of many pieces, with whom I reasoned that small while that hee stayed with mee, and hee sayd that within three dayes after, hee and the rest of the chiefe of that towne would come and visite mee, and giue order what course should bee taken with them. Which they did: for they brought mee certaine mantles and some Turqueses. I aduised them to come downe from their holdes, and to returne with their wiues and children to their houses, and to become Christians, and that they would acknowledge the Emperours maiestie for their King and lorde. And euen to this present they keepe in those strong holdes their women and children, and all the goods which they haue. I commaunded them that they should paint mee out a cloth of all the beastes which they knowe in their countrey: And such badde painters as they are foorthwith they painted mee two clothes, one of their beastes, another of their birdes and fishes. They say that they will bring their children, that our religious men may instruct them, and that they desire to knowe our lawe; and they assure vs, that aboue fiftie yeeres past it was prophecied among them, that a certaine people like vs should come, and from that part that wee came from, and that they should subdue all that countrey.

That which these Indians worship as farre as hitherto wee can learne, is the water: for they say it causeth their corne to growe, and maintaineth their life; and that they know none other reason, but that their ancestors did so. I haue sought by all meanes possible to learne of the inhabitants of these townes, whether they haue any knowledge of other people, countreys and cities: And they tell mee of seuen cities which are farre distant from this place, which are like vnto these, though they haue not houses like vnto these, but they are of earth, and small: and that among them much cotton is gathered. The chiefe of these townes whereof they haue knowledge, they say is called Tucano: and they gaue mee no perfect knowledge of the rest. And I thinke they doe not tell me the trueth, imagining that of necessitie I must speedily depart from them, and returne home. But herein they shall soone finde themselues deceiued. I sent Don Pedro de Touar with his companie of footemen and with certaine other horsemen to see this towne: And I would not haue dispatched this packet vnto your lordship, vntill I had knowen what this towne was, if I had thought that within twelue or fifteene dayes I might haue had newes from him: for hee will stay in this iourney thirtie dayes at least. And hauing examined that the knowledge hereof is of small importance, and that the colde and the waters approch: I thought it mẏ duety to doe according as your lordship gaue mee charge in your instructions, which is, that immediately vpon mine arriuall here, I should signifie so much vnto your lordship, and so I doe, sending withall the bare relation of that which I haue seene. I haue determined to send round about the countrey from hence to haue knowledge of all things, and rather to suffer all extremitie, then to leaue this enterprise to serue his maiestie, if I may finde any thing wherein I may performe it, and not to omit any diligence therein, vntill your lordship send mee order what I shall doe. Wee haue great want of pasture: and your lordship also shal vnderstand, that among all those which are here, there is not one pound of raisins, nor sugar, nor oyle, nor any wine, saue only one pinte which is saued to say Masse: for all is spent & spilt by the way. Now your lordship may prouide vs what you thinke needefull. And if your honour meane to send vs cattell, your lordship must vnderstand that they will bee a sommer in comming vnto vs: for they will not be able to come vnto vs any sooner. I would haue sent your lordshippe with this dispatch many musters of things which are in this countrey: but the way is so long and rough, that it is hard for me to doe so; neuerthelesse I send you twelue small mantles, such as the people of the countrey are woont to weare, and a certaine garment also, which seemeth vnto me to bee well made: I kept the same, because it seemed to mee to bee excellent well wrought, because I beleeue that no man euer saw any needle worke in these Indies, except it were since the Spaniards inhabited the same. I send your Lordshippe also two clothes painted with the beasts of this countrey, although as I haue sayde, the picture bee very rudely done, because the painter spent but one day in drawing of the same. I haue seene other pictures on the walles of the houses of this citie with farre better proportion, and better made. I send your honour one Oxe-hide, certaine Turqueses, and two earerings of the same, and fifteene combes of the Indians, and certain tablets set with these Turqueses, and two small baskets made of wicker, whereof the Indians haue great store. I send your lordship also two rolles which the women in these parts are woont to weare on their heads when they fetch water from their welles, as wee vse to doe in Spaine. And one of these Indian women with one of these rolles on her head, will carie a pitcher of water without touching the same with her hande vp a lather. I send you also a muster of the weapons wherewith these people are woont to fight, a buckler, a mace, a bowe, and certaine arrowes, among which are two with points of bones, the like whereof, as these conquerours say, haue neuer beene seene. I can say nothing vnto your lordshippe touching the apparell of their women. For the Indians keepe them so carefully from vs, that hitherto I haue not seene any of them, sauing onely two olde women, and these had two long robes downe to the foote open before, and girded to them, and they are buttoned with certaine cordons of cotton. I requested the Indians to giue me one of these robes, which they ware, to send your honour the same, seeing they would not shewe mee their women. And they brought mee two mantles which are these, which I send you as it were painted: they haue two pendents like the women of Spaine, which hang somewhat ouer their shoulders. The death of the Negro is most certaine: for here are many of the things found which hee carried with him: And the Indians tell me that they killed him here, because the Indians of Chichilticale tolde them that hee was a wicked villaine, and not like vnto the Christians: because the Christians kill no women: and hee killed women: and also he touched their women, which the Indians loue more then themselues; therefore they determined to kill him: But they did it not after such sort as was reported, for they killed none of the rest of those that came with him: neither slewe they the young lad which was with him of the prouince of Petatlan, but they tooke him and kept him in safe custodie vntill nowe. And when I sought to haue him, they excused themselues two or three dayes to giue him mee, telling mee that hee was dead, and sometimes that the Indians of Acucu had carried him away. But in conclusion, when I tolde them that I should be very angry if they did not giue him mee, they gave him vnto mee. Hee is an interpreter, for though hee cannot well speake their language, yet he vnderstandeth the same very well. In this place there is found some quantitie of golde and siluer, which those which are skillfull in minerall matters esteeme to be very good. To this houre I could neuer learne of these people from whence they haue it: And I see they refuse to tell mee the trueth in all things, imagining, as I haue sayde, that in short time I would depart hence, but I hope in God they shall no longer excuse themselues. I beeseech your lordship to certifie his Maiestie of the successes of this voyage. For seeing we haue no more then that which is aforesayd, and vntill such time as it please God that wee finde that which wee desire, I meane not to write my selfe. Our Lorde God keepe and preserue your Excellencie.

From the Prouince of Cibola, and from this citie of Granada the third of August 1540. Francis Vasques de Coronado kisseth the hands of your Excellencie.

Corporation Tax. The Payne-Aldrich tariff act of 1909 contained a provision imposing a tax of 1 per cent. upon the net income, in excess of $5,000, of every corporation, joint stock company or association organized for profit and having a capital stock represented by shares, and every insurance company now or hereafter reorganized. The first tax was levied in July, 1910. Corporations were expected to have their reports in by March 1. It required that the net income shall be ascertained by deducting from the gross income the ordinary expenses actually paid out of the income in the maintenance and operation of the business. The companies are required to make reports of their business and the government shall have the right to examine the same, and also to examine the books and papers of any company when, in its judgment, it is necessary. For the ascertainment of what is actually the net income, provision is made for the jurisdiction of the Circuit and District Courts of the United States, through which persons, books, and papers may be summoned. This tax does not apply to labor, agricultural, or horticultural organizations, or to fraternal beneficiary societies, operating under the lodge system, and providing for the payment of life, sick, accident, and other benefits to the members of such societies, nor to domestic building and loan associations organized and operated exclusively for the mutual benefit of their members, nor to any religious, charitable, or educational organization, no part of the net income of which inures to the benefit of any private stockholder or individual. This tax is made payable to the Commissioner of Internal Revenue. In case any return is falsely made, 100 per cent. of the amount is added. In case of refusal or neglect to pay the tax 50 per cent. of the tax is added. When the assessments shall have been made by the commissioner they shall constitute a public record and be open for inspection. In the first year of this tax the receipts therefrom aggregated $20,959,783.

Corps, Army, in the Civil war. See ARMY.

Corregidor, a small island commanding the entrance to Manila Bay, P. I. It is three miles long by one mile wide, rising abruptly from the sea to a height of 635 feet. There is a light-house at the summit. The island was strongly fortified by the Spaniards in the 18th century, but the defenses were not kept up. When Admiral Dewey made his dash into Manila Bay, May 1, 1898, he steamed past this island, which was supposed to be very strongly fortified, and the base of operations for the mines and torpedoes with which the bay was declared to be thickly strewn. The forts have been strengthened by the United States government, which established an arsenal here in 1900. Pop. (1903), 707.

Corrigan, MICHAEL AUGUSTINE, clergyman; born in Newark, N. J., Aug. 13, 1839; graduated at Mount St. Mary's

College, Emmitsburg, Md., in 1859; professor of dogmatic theology and sacred Scripture in Seton Hall College, Orange, N. J., in 1864–68; president of the same in 1868–73; administrator of the diocese of Newark, 1870–73; became bishop of Newark in 1873; coadjutor to Cardinal McCloskey in 1880, with the right of succession under the title of Archbishop of Petra (*in partibus infidelium*); archbishop of New York in 1885. He died in New York City, May 5, 1902.

Corruption in Politics. Montesquieu, in his *Spirit of the Laws*, characterizes three forms of government, and attributes to each form the principle which he believes to be its supreme essence. These are: Virtue, to the Republic; Honor, to the Monarchy; Fear, to the Despotism. He ascribes corruption in every form of government as beginning with the corruption of its principle, and adds that the principle of democracy is corrupted not only by the loss of the spirit of equality, but also by the assumption of too extreme a spirit of equality, whereby each one wishes to be equal to those whom he has chosen to represent or command him, resulting in the desire on the part of the people to do everything for themselves; to deliberate and make laws in place of the legislature; to enforce the laws in place of the executive; and to deprive the judges of their power.

Corse, JOHN MURRAY, military officer; born in Pittsburg, Pa., April 27, 1835; graduated at the United States Military Academy in 1857; then studied law; and enlisted in the Union army at the beginning of the Civil War. In 1864, with about 1,000 troops, he was ordered to Allatoona, Ga., where were stored large commissary supplies. The place was soon attacked by about 4,000 Confederates, but Corse refused to surrender, and bravely repulsed every onslaught of the enemy till reinforcements arrived from Sherman. Sherman had signalled Corse, "Hold the fort, for I am coming," and this phrase was afterwards made the subject of an inspiring hymn by Ira D. Sankey. For this heroic defence Corse was brevetted a brigadier-general. He died in Winchester, Mass., April 27, 1893.

Corson, JULIET, cooking reformer; born in Roxbury, Mass., Feb. 14, 1842; established the New York School of Cookery in 1876, and soon achieved celebrity by her writings on cookery and domestic science. Her works include: *Fifteen-Cent Dinners*, a manual for the poor; *Cooking Manual; Meals for the Million; Family Living on Five Hundred a Year*, etc. She died in New York City, June 18, 1897.

Cortelyou, GEORGE BRUCE, executive officer; born in New York, July 26, 1862; was graduated at the Hempstead (Long Island) Institute in 1879, and at the State Normal School, Westfield, Mass., in 1889; engaged in general law-reporting in New York in 1883–85; was principal of preparatory schools in that city in 1885–89; and entered public service in the latter year. After serving several officials as private secretary he was appointed stenographer to President Cleveland, Nov. 1, 1895; executive clerk to the President three months afterwards; assistant secretary to President McKinley, July 1, 1898; and was secretary to Presidents McKinley and Roosevelt from May 1, 1900, till Feb. 16, 1903, when he was appointed Secretary of the newly created Department of Commerce and Labor. In 1904 as chairman of the Republican National Committee, he managed the Republican Presidential campaign of that year. He was Postmaster-General in 1905–07; Secretary of the Treasury in 1907–09; then became president of a gas company in New York City.

Cortereal, GASPER, Portuguese navigator; born in Lisbon; was in the service of the King of Portugal when, in 1500, he left the mouth of the Tagus with two ships to make discoveries in the Northwest. He first touched, it is believed, the northern shores of Newfoundland, discovered the Gulf of St. Lawrence, and sailed along the coast of the American continent to lat. 60°, and named the neighboring coast Labrador. The natives appearing to him rugged and strong and capital material for slaves, he seized fifty of them, and, carrying them to Portugal, made a profitable sale of his captives. Cortereal went on a second voyage in 1501, but was supposed to have been lost at sea. The King declared that Cortereal was the first discoverer of the American continent.

Cortez, HERNANDO, military officer; born in Medellin, Estremadura, Spain, in 1485, of a good family; studied law two years at Salamanca, and in 1504 sailed from San Lucar for Santo Domingo in a merchant vessel. The governor received him kindly, and he was soon employed, under Diego Velasquez, in quelling a revolt. In 1511 DIEGO COLUMBUS (*q. v.*), governor of Santo Domingo, sent Velasquez to conquer and colonize Cuba. Cortez accompanied him. Santiago was founded, and Cortez was made alcalde, or mayor. He married a Spanish lady and employed the natives in mining gold, treating them most cruelly. Velasquez placed him at the head of an expedition to conquer and colonize Mexico, portions of which Cordova and Grijalva had just discovered. Before he sailed Velasquez countermanded the order, but the ambitious Cortez, disobedient, sailed for Mexico, in 1519, with ten vessels, bearing 550 Spaniards, over 200 Indians, a few negroes and horses, and some brass cannon. He landed at Tabasco, where he fought the natives and heard of Montezuma, emperor of a vast domain, possessor of great treasures, and living in a city called Mexico. After founding Vera Cruz, Cortez set out for Montezuma's capital. Fighting his way, he made the conquered natives own their vassalage to Spain and become his followers, and in November, 1519, he entered the city of Mexico with a handful of Spaniards who had survived the battles, and 6,000 native followers. Montezuma received him kindly. Cortez took a strong position in the city and put on the airs of a conqueror instead of a guest. Some of the irritated Mexicans attacked the invaders, when Cortez, making that a pretext, seized the monarch in his palace, conveyed him to the headquarters of the troops, and threatened him with instant death if he did not quietly submit.

Placing the Emperor in irons, Cortez caused seventeen of the men who had made the attack to be burned to death in front of the palace. Then Montezuma was compelled to acknowledge himself and his subjects vassals of Charles V., and Cortez forced the fallen monarch to give him gold to the value of $10,000. Suddenly startled by the news that Narvaez, whom Velasquez had sent to displace him, had landed on the shores of Mexico with 900 men, 80 horses, and a dozen cannon, Cortez, leaving 200 men in Mexico, hastened to confront his rival with a few followers. In a battle Narvaez was defeated. The vanquished troops joined the standard of Cortez, who hastened back to Mexico. The people had revolted against the Spaniards. The captive Montezuma tried to pacify them, but, endeavoring to address them, he was assailed by a mob and mortally wounded. The Spaniards were driven out of the city; their rear-guard was cut in pieces, and they were terribly harassed in a flight for six days before the exasperated Mexicans. On the plain of Otompan a sharp battle was fought (July 7, 1520), and Cortez was victor. Marching to Tlascala, he collected reinforcements of natives, marched upon Mexico, and captured the city after a gallant defence of seventy-seven days, Aug. 13, 1521. His exploits wiped out the stain of his disobedience, and he was made civil and military ruler of Mexico, and a marquis, with a handsome revenue. The natives, however, were terribly embittered by his cruelties and his zeal in destroying their idols, for he resolved to force the pagans to become Christians. Cortez went to Spain, where he was cordially received by the monarch. Returning to Mexico, he explored the country northward and discovered the Gulf and Peninsula of California. He died near Seville, Spain, Dec. 2, 1547.

The City of Mexico.—The following, being his second letter to the Emperor Charles V., contains the account of the conqueror of Montezuma's capital. It is to be observed that Cortez spells the Emperor's name Muteczuma and applies the name of Temixtitan to the capital while speaking of the province of Mexico:

In order, most potent Sire, to convey to your Majesty a just conception of the great extent of this noble city of Temixtitan, and of the many rare and wonderful objects it contains: of the government and dominions of Muteczuma, the sovereign; of the religious rites and customs that prevail, and the order that exists in this as well as other cities appertaining to his realm: it would require the

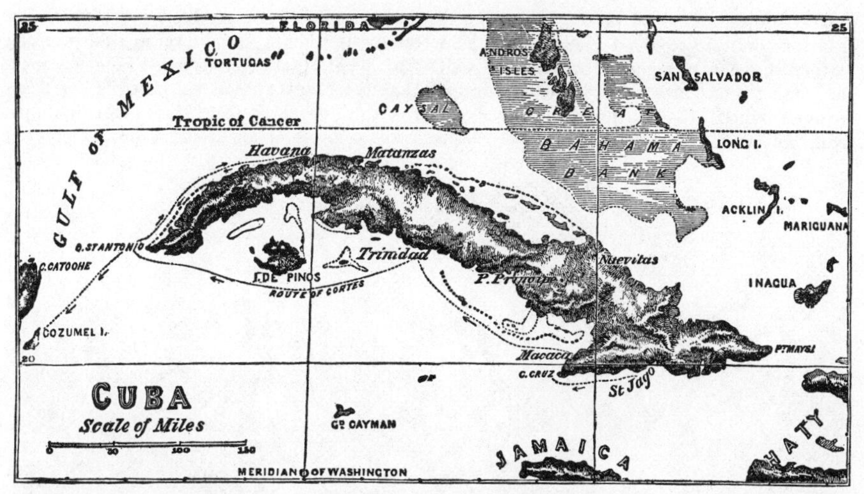

CORTEZ'S ROUTE TO MEXICO.

labor of many accomplished writers, and much time for the completion of the task. I shall not be able to relate an hundredth part of what could be told respecting these matters; but I will endeavor to describe, in the best manner in my power, what I have myself seen; and imperfectly as I may succeed in the attempt, I am fully aware that the account will appear so wonderful as to be deemed scarcely worthy of credit; since even we who have seen these things with our own eyes, are yet so amazed as to be unable to comprehend their reality. But your Majesty may be assured that if there is any fault in my relation, either in regard to the present subject, or to any other matters of which I shall give your Majesty an account, it will arise from too great brevity rather than extravagance or prolixity in the details; and it seems to me but just to my Prince and Sovereign to declare the truth in the clearest manner, without saying anything that would detract from it, or add to it.

Before I begin to describe this great city and the others already mentioned, it may be as well for the better understanding of the subject to say something of the configuration of Mexico, in which they are situated, it being the principal seat of Muteczuma's power. This province is in the form of a circle, surrounded on all sides by lofty and rugged mountains; its level surface comprises an area of about 70 leagues in circumference, including two lakes, that overspread nearly the whole valley, being navigated by boats more than 50 leagues round. One of these lakes contains fresh and the other, which is the larger of the two, salt water. On one side of the lakes, in the middle of the valley, a range of highlands divides them from one another, with the exception of a narrow strait which lies between the highlands and the lofty sierras. This strait is a bow-shot wide, and connects the two lakes; and by this means a trade is carried on between the cities and other settlements on the lakes in canoes without the necessity of travelling by land. As the salt lake rises and falls with its tides like the sea, during the time of high water it pours into the other lake with the rapidity of a powerful stream; and on the other hand, when the tide has ebbed, the water runs from the fresh into the salt lake.

This great city of Temixtitan is situated in this salt lake, and from the mainland to the denser parts of it, by whichever route one chooses to enter, the distance is 2 leagues. There are four avenues or entrances to the city, all of which are formed by artificial causeways, 2 spears' length in width. The city is as large as Seville or Cordova; its streets—I speak of the principal ones—are very wide and straight; some of these, and all the inferior ones, are half land and half water, and are navigated by canoes. All the streets at intervals have openings, through which the water flows, crossing from one street to another; and at these where are daily assembled more than 60,000 souls, engaged in buying and selling; and where are found all kinds of merchandise that the world affords, embracing the necessaries of life, as for instance articles of food, as well as jewels of gold

CORTEZ AND THE AMBASSADORS OF MONTEZUMA.

openings, some of which are very wide, there are also very wide bridges, composed of large pieces of timber, of great strength and well put together; on many of these bridges ten horses can go abreast. Foreseeing that if the inhabitants of this city should prove treacherous, they would possess great advantages from the manner in which the city is constructed, since by removing the bridges at the entrances, and abandoning the place, they could leave us to perish by famine without our being able to reach the main-land—as soon as I had entered it, I made great haste to build four brigantines, which were soon finished, and were large enough to take ashore 300 men and the horses, whenever it should become necessary.

The city has many public squares, in which are situated the markets and other places for buying and selling. There is one square twice as large as that of the city of Salamanca, surrounded by porticos, and silver, lead, brass, copper, tin, precious stones, bones, shells, snails, and feathers. There are also exposed for sale wrought and unwrought stone, bricks burned and unburned, timber hewn and unhewn, of different sorts. There is a street for game, where every variety of birds found in the country are sold, as fowls, partridges, quails, wild ducks, fly-catchers, widgeons, turtle-doves, pigeons, reed-birds, parrots, sparrows, eagles, hawks, owls, and kestrels; they sell likewise the skins of some birds of prey, with their feathers, head, beak, and claws. There are also sold rabbits, hares, deer, and little dogs, which are raised for eating. There is also an herb street, where may be obtained all sorts of roots and medicinal herbs that the country affords. There are apothecaries' shops, where prepared medicines, liquids, ointments, and plasters are sold; barbers' shops, where they wash and shave the head; and restaurateurs, that furnish food and drink at a certain price. There is also a class of men like those called in Castile porters, for carrying burdens. Wood and coal are seen in abundance, and brasiers of earthenware for burning coals; mats of various kinds for beds, others of a lighter sort for seats, and for halls and bedrooms. There are all kinds of green vegetables, especially onions, leeks, garlic, watercresses, nasturtium, borage, sorrel, artichokes, and golden thistle; fruits also of numerous descriptions, among which are cherries and plums, similar to those in Spain; honey and wax from bees and from the stalks of maize, which are as sweet as the sugar-cane; honey is also extracted from the plant called maguey, which is superior to sweet or new wine; from the same plant they extract sugar and wine, which they also sell. Different kinds of cotton thread of all colors in skeins are exposed for sale in one quarter of the market, which has the appearance of the silk-market at Granada, although the former is supplied more abundantly. Painters' colors as numerous as can be found in Spain, and as fine shades; deerskins dressed and undressed, dyed different colors; earthenware of a large size and excellent quality; large and small jars, jugs, pots, bricks, and an endless variety of vessels, all made of fine clay, and all or most of them glazed and painted; maize, or Indian corn, in the grain and in the form of bread, preferred in the grain for its flavor to that of the other islands and *terra firma;* patés of birds and fish; great quantities of fish, fresh, salt, cooked and uncooked; the eggs of hens, geese, and of all the other birds I have mentioned, in great abundance, and cakes made of eggs; finally, everything that can be found throughout the whole country is sold in the markets, comprising articles so numerous that to avoid prolixity, and because their names are not retained in my memory, or are unknown to me, I shall not attempt to enumerate them. Every kind of merchandise is sold in a particular street or quarter assigned to it exclusively, and thus the best order is preserved. They sell everything by number or measure; at least so far we have not observed them to sell anything by weight. There is a building in the great square that is used as an audience house, where ten or twelve persons, who are magistrates, sit and decide all controversies that arise in the market, and order delinquents to be punished. In the same square there are other persons who go constantly about among the people observing what is sold, and the measures used in selling; and they have been seen to break measures that were not true.

This great city contains a large number of temples, or houses for their idols, very handsome edifices, which are situated in the different districts and the suburbs; in the principal ones religious persons of each particular sect are constantly residing, for whose use beside the houses containing the idols there are other convenient habitations. All these persons dress in black, and never cut or comb their hair from the time they enter the priesthood until they leave it; and all the sons of the principal inhabitants, both nobles and respectable citizens, are placed in the temples and wear the same dress from the age of seven or eight years until they are taken out to be married; which occurs more frequently with the first-born who inherit estates than with the others. The priests are debarred from female society, nor is any woman permitted to enter the religious houses. They also abstain from eating certain kinds of food, more at some seasons of the year than others. Among these temples there is one which far surpasses all the rest, whose grandeur of architectural detail no human tongue is able to describe; for within its precincts, surrounded by a lofty wall, there is room enough for a town of 500 families. Around the interior of this enclosure there are handsome edifices, containing large halls and corridors, in which the religious persons attached to the temple reside. There are full forty towers, which are lofty and well built, the largest of which has fifty steps leading to its main body, and is higher than the tower of the principal church at Seville. The stone and wood of which they are constructed are so well wrought in every part that nothing could be better done, for the interior of the chapels containing the idols consists of curious imagery, wrought in stone, with plaster ceilings, and wood-work carved in relief, and painted with figures of monsters and other objects. All these towers are the burial-places of the nobles, and every chapel in them is dedicated to a particular idol, to which they pay their devotions.

There are three halls in this grand temple, which contain the principal idols; these are of wonderful extent and height, and admirable workmanship, adorned with figures sculptured in stone and wood; leading from the halls are chapels with very small doors, to which the light is not admitted, nor are any persons except the priests, and not all of them. In these chapels are the images of idols, although, as I have before said, many of them are also found on the outside; the principal ones, in which the people have greatest faith and confidence, I precipitated from their pedestals, and cast them down the steps of the temple, purifying the chapels in which they had stood, as they were all polluted with human blood, shed in the sacrifices. In the place of these I put images of Our Lady and the saints, which excited not a little feeling in Muteczuma and the inhabitants, who at first remonstrated, declaring that if my proceedings were known throughout the country the people would rise against me; for they believed that their idols bestowed on them all temporal good, and if they permitted them to be ill-treated, they would be angry and withhold their gifts, and by this means the people would be deprived of the fruits of the earth and perish with famine. I answered, through the interpreters, that they were deceived in expecting any favors from idols, the work of their own hands, formed of unclean things; and that they must learn there was but one God, the universal Lord of all, who had created the heavens and earth, and all things else, and had made them and us; that He was without beginning and immortal, and they were bound to adore and believe Him, and no other creature or thing. I said everything to them I could to divert them from their idolatries and draw them to a knowledge of God our Lord. Muteczuma replied, the others assenting to what he said, that they had already informed me they were not the aborigines of the country, but that their ancestors had emigrated to it many years ago; and they fully believed that after so long an absence from their native land they might have fallen into some errors; that I having more recently arrived must know better than themselves what they ought to believe; and that if I would instruct them in these matters, and make them understand the true faith, they would follow my directions, as being for the best. Afterwards, Muteczuma and many of the principal citizens remained with me until I had removed the idols, purified the chapels, and placed the images in them, manifesting apparent pleasure; and I forbade them sacrificing human beings to their idols, as they had been accustomed to do; because, besides being abhorrent in the sight of God, your sacred Majesty had prohibited it by law, and commanded to put to death whoever should take the life of another. Thus, from that time, they refrained from the practice, and during the whole period of my abode in that city they were never seen to kill or sacrifice a human being.

The figures of the idols in which these people believe surpass in stature a person of more than the ordinary size; some of them are composed of a mass of seeds and leguminous plants, such as are used for food, ground and mixed together, and kneaded with the blood of human hearts taken from the breasts of living persons, from which a paste is formed in a sufficient quantity to form large statues. When these are completed they make them offerings of the hearts of other victims, which they sacrifice to them, and besmear their faces with the blood. For everything they have an idol, consecrated by the use of the nations that in ancient times honored the same gods. Thus they have an idol that they petition for victory in war; another for success in their labors; and so for everything in which they seek or desire prosperity they have their idols, which they honor and serve.

This noble city contains many fine and magnificent houses; which may be accounted for from the fact that all the nobility of the country, who are the vassals of Muteczuma, have houses in the city, in which they reside a certain part of the year; and besides, there are numerous wealthy citizens who also possess fine houses. All these persons, in addition to the large and spacious apartments for ordinary purposes, have others, both upper and lower, that contain conservatories of flowers. Along one of these causeways that lead into the city are laid two pipes, constructed of masonry, each of which is 2 paces in width and about 5 feet in height. An abundant supply of excellent water, forming a volume equal in bulk to the human body, is conveyed by one of these pipes, and distributed about the city, where it is used by the inhabitants for drinking and other purposes. The other pipe, in the mean time, is kept empty until the former requires to be cleansed, when the water is let into it and continues to be used till the cleansing is finished. As the water is necessarily carried over bridges on account of the salt water crossing its route, reservoirs resembling canals are constructed on the bridges, through which the fresh water is conveyed. These reservoirs are of the breadth of the body of an ox, and of the same length as the bridges. The whole city is thus served with water, which they carry in canoes through all the streets for sale, taking it from the aqueduct in the following manner: the canoes pass under the bridges on which the reservoirs are placed, when men stationed above fill them with water, for which service they are paid. At all the entrances of the city, and in those parts where the canoes are discharged—that is, where the greatest quantity of provisions is brought in—huts are erected, and persons stationed as guards, who receive a *certum quid* of everything that enters. I know not whether the sovereign receives this duty or the city, as I have not yet been informed; but I believe that it appertains to the sovereign, as in the markets of other provinces a tax is collected for the benefit of their cacique. In all the markets and public places of this city are seen daily many laborers and persons of various employments waiting for some one to hire them. The inhabitants of this city pay a greater regard to style in their mode of living, and are more attentive to elegance of dress and politeness of manners than those of the other provinces and cities; since, as the Cacique Muteczuma has his residence in the capital, and all the nobility, his vassals, are in constant habit of meeting there, a general courtesy of demeanor necessarily prevails. But not to be prolix in describing what relates to the affairs of this great city, although it is with difficulty I refrain from proceeding, I will say no more than that the manners of the people, as shown in their intercourse with one another, are marked by as great an attention to the proprieties of life as in Spain, and good order is equally well observed; and considering that they are a barbarous people, without the knowledge of God, having no intercourse with civilized nations, these traits of character are worthy of admiration.

In regard to the domestic appointments of Muteczuma, and the wonderful grandeur and state that he maintains, there is so much to be told, that I assure your Highness I know not where to begin my relation, so as to be able to finish any part of it. For, as I have already stated, what can be more wonderful than that a barbarous monarch, as he is, should have every object found in his dominions imitated in gold, silver, precious stones, and feathers; the gold and silver being wrought so naturally as not to be surpassed by any smith in the world; the stone work executed with such perfection that it is difficult to conceive what instruments could have been used; and the feather work superior to the finest productions in wax or embroidery. The extent of Muteczuma's dominions has not been ascertained, since to whatever point he despatched his messengers, even 200 leagues from his capital, his commands were obeyed, although some of his provinces were in the midst of countries with which he was at war. But as nearly as I have been able to learn, his territories are equal in extent to Spain itself, for he sent messengers to the inhabitants of a city called Cumatan (requiring them to become subjects of your Majesty), which is 60 leagues beyond that part of Putunchán watered by the river Grijalva, and 230 leagues distant from the great city; and I sent some of our people a distance of 150 leagues in the same direction. All the principal chiefs of these provinces, especially those in the vicinity of the capital, reside, as I have already stated, the greater part of the year in that great city, and all or most of them have their oldest sons in the service of Muteczuma. There are fortified places in all the provinces, garrisoned with his own men, where are also stationed his governors and collectors of the rents and tribute rendered him by every province; and an account is kept of what each is obliged to pay, as they have characters and figures made on paper that are used for this purpose. Each province renders a tribute of its own peculiar productions, so that the sovereign receives a great variety of articles from different quarters. No prince was ever more feared by his subjects, both in his presence and absence. He possessed out of the city as well as within numerous villas, each of which had its peculiar sources of amusement, and all were constructed in the best possible manner for the use of a great prince and lord. Within the city his palaces were so wonderful that it is hardly possible to describe their beauty and extent; I can only say that in Spain there is nothing equal to them.

There was one palace somewhat inferior to the rest, attached to which was a beautiful garden with balconies extending over it, supported by marble columns, and having a floor formed of jasper elegantly inlaid. There were apartments in this palace sufficient to lodge two princes of the highest rank with their retinues. There were likewise belonging to it ten pools of water, in which were kept the different species of water-birds found in this country, of which there is a great variety, all of which are domesticated; for the sea-birds there were pools of salt water. and for the river-birds, of fresh water. The water is let off at certain times to keep it pure, and is replenished by means of pipes. Each species of bird is supplied with the food natural to it, which it feeds upon when wild. Thus fish is given to the birds that usually eat it; worms, maize, and the finer seeds to such as prefer them. And I assure your Highness, that to the birds accustomed to eat fish there is given the enormous quantity of ten arrobas every day, taken in the salt lake. The Emperor has 300 men whose sole employment is to take care of these birds; and there are others whose only business is to attend to the birds that are in bad health.

Over the pools for the birds there are corridors and galleries, to which Muteczuma resorts, and from which he can look out and amuse himself with the sight of them. There is an apartment in the same palace in which are men, women, and children whose faces, bodies, hair, eyebrows, and eyelashes are white from their birth. The Emperor has another very beautiful palace, with a large court-yard, paved with handsome flags, in the style of a chess-board. There are also cages, about 9 feet in height and 6 paces square, each of which was half covered with a roof of tiles, and the other half had over it a wooden grate, skilfully made. Every cage contained a bird of prey of all the species found in Spain, from the kestrel to the eagle, and many unknown there. There was a great number of each kind; and in the covered part of the cages there was a perch, and another on the outside of the grating, the former of which the birds used in the nighttime, and when it rained; and the other enabled them to enjoy the sun and air. To all these birds fowls were daily given for food, and nothing else. There were in the same palace several large halls on the ground floor, filled with immense cages built of heavy pieces of timber, well put together, in all or most of which were kept lions, tigers, wolves, foxes, and a variety of animals of the cat kind, in great numbers, which were also fed on fowls. The care of these animals and birds was assigned to 300 men. There was another palace that contained a number of men and women of monstrous size, and also dwarfs, and crooked and ill-formed persons, each of which had their separate apartments. These also had their respective keepers. As to the other remarkable things that the Emperor had in his city for his amusement, I can only say that they were numerous and of various kinds.

He was served in the following manner. Every day, as soon as it was light, 600 nobles and men of rank were in attendance at the palace, who either sat, or walked about the halls and galleries, and passed their time in conversation, but without entering the apartment where his person was. The servants and attendants of these nobles remained in the court-yards, of which there were two or three of great extent, and in the adjoining street, which was also very spacious. They all remained in attendance from morning till night; and when his meals were served, the nobles were likewise served with equal profusion, and their servants and secretaries also had their allowance. Daily his larder and wine-cellar were open to all who wished to eat and drink. The meals were served by 300 or 400 youths, who brought on an infinite variety of dishes; indeed, whenever he dined or supped, the table was loaded with every kind of flesh, fish, fruits, and vegetables that the country produced. As the climate is cold, they put a chafing-dish with live coals under every plate and dish to keep them warm. The meals were served in a large hall, in which Muteczuma was accustomed to eat, and the dishes quite filled the room, which was covered with mats and kept very clean. He sat on a small cushion curiously wrought of leather. During the meals there were present, at a little distance from him, five or six elderly caciques, to whom he presented some of the food. And there was constantly in attendance one of the servants, who arranged and handed the dishes, and who received from others whatever was wanted for the supply of the table. Both at the beginning and end of every meal they furnished water for the hands; and the napkins used on these occasions were never used a second time; this was the case also with the plates and dishes, which were not brought again, but new ones in place of them; it was the same also with the chafing-dishes. He is also dressed every day in four different suits, entirely new, which he never wears a second time. None of the caciques who enter his palace have their feet covered, and when those for whom he sends enter his presence they incline their heads and look down, bending their bodies; and when they address him they do not look him in the face; this arises from excessive modesty and reverence. I am satisfied that it proceeds from respect, since certain caciques reproved the Spaniards for their boldness in addressing me, saying that it showed a want of becoming deference. Whenever Muteczuma appeared in public, which was seldom the case, all those who accompanied him, or whom he accidentally met in the streets, turned away without looking towards him, and others prostrated themselves until he had passed. One of the nobles always preceded him on these occasions, carrying three slender rods erect, which I suppose was to give notice of the approach of his person. And when they descended from the litters he took one of them in his hand, and held it until he reached the place where he was going. So many and various were the ceremonies and customs observed by those in the service of Muteczuma, that more space than I can spare would be required for the details, as well as a better memory than I have to recollect them; since no sultan or other infidel lord, of whom any knowledge now exists, ever had so much ceremonial in their courts.

Corwin, Thomas, statesman; born in Bourbon county, Ky., July 29, 1794; reared to manhood on a farm, attending a common school in winter; began the study of law in 1815; admitted to the bar in 1818; became a member of the Ohio legislature in 1822, and was elected to Congress in 1830. He remained in the

THOMAS CORWIN.

House until elected governor of Ohio in 1840. In 1845 he was chosen United States Senator, and was called to the cabinet of President Fillmore in 1850, as Secretary of the Treasury. He was again elected to Congress in 1859. In 1861 President Lincoln sent him as minister to Mexico. Mr. Corwin was an eloquent, witty, and effective speaker. He died in Washington, D. C., Dec. 18, 1865.

The War with Mexico.—The action of Congress upon the subject of the Mexican War, in the winter of 1846–47, gave rise to a question in which an important principle was involved. Is it the duty of the legislature to provide the means of prosecuting a war made unconstitutionally? Disconnected from the declaration that war existed by the act of Mexico, bills to furnish money had received an almost unanimous vote. The Whig members, generally, while protesting that the war not only was unjust, but had been made by the executive without constitutional authority, yet voted for the means to help the executive carry his purposes into effect, justifying their votes on the general principle that, in what manner, or for what purpose soever, a war is begun, it is the duty of Congress to furnish the aid to prosecute it, and hold its projector and author responsible. The question here arose, Can the legislature, while it furnishes the aid, avoid the responsibility?

Senator Corwin who stood almost alone in the Senate on this question, vindicated his position in a speech of acknowledged ability. He said:

"While the American President can command the army, thank God I can command the purse. While the President, under the penalty of death, can command your officers to proceed, I can tell them to come back for supplies, as he may. He shall have no funds from me in the prosecution of such a war. That I conceive to be the duty of a Senator. I am not mistaken in that. If it is my duty to grant whatever the President demands, for what am I here? Have I no will upon the subject? Is it not placed at my discretion, understanding, and judgment? Have an American Senate and House of Representatives nothing to do but to obey the bidding of the President, as the mercenary army he commands is compelled to obey under penalty of death? No! your Senate and House of Representatives were never elected for such purpose as that. They have been modelled on the good old plan of English liberty, and are intended to represent the English House of Commons, who curbed the proud power of the King in olden time, by withholding supplies if they did not approve the war. . . . While Charles could command the army, he might control the Parliament; and because he would not give up that command, our Puritan ancestors laid his head upon the block. How did it fare with others?

"It was on this very proposition of controlling the executive power of England by withholding the money supplies that the House of Orange came in; and by their accession to the throne commenced a new epoch in the history of England, distinguishing it from the old reign of the Tudors and Plantagenets and those who preceded it. Then it was that Parliament specified the purpose of appropriation; and since 1688, is has been impossible for a king of England to involve the people of England in a war, which your President, under your republican institution, and with your republican Constitution, has yet managed to do. Here you stand powerless. He commands this army, and you must not withhold their supplies. He involves your country in wasteful and exterminating war against a nation with whom we have no cause of complaint; but Congress may say nothing!"

In a letter to a friend he subsequently wrote: "I differed from all the leading Whigs of the Senate, and saw plainly that they all were, to some extent, bound to turn, if they could, the current of public opinion against me. They all agreed with me that the war was unjust on our part; that, if properly begun (which none of them admitted), we had already sufficiently chastised Mexico, and that the further prosecution of it was wanton waste of both blood and treasure; yet they would not undertake to stop it. They said the President alone was responsible. I thought we who aided him, or furnished him means, must be in the judgment of reason and conscience, equally responsible, equally guilty with him."

On Feb. 11, 1847, he delivered a speech concerning the territory which it was proposed to wrest from Mexico, of which the following is an abstract:

"What is the territory, Mr. President, which you propose to wrest from Mexico? It is consecrated to the heart of the Mexican by many a well-fought battle with his old Castilian master. His Bunker Hills, and Saratogas, and Yorktowns are there. The Mexican can say, 'There I bled for liberty! and shall I surrender that consecrated home of my affections to the Anglo-Saxon invaders? What do they want with it? They have Texas already. They have possessed themselves of the territory between the Nueces and the Rio Grande. What else do they want? To what shall I point my children as memorials of that independence which I bequeath to them, when those battle-fields shall have passed from my possession?'

"Sir, had one come and demanded Bunker Hill of the people of Massachusetts, had England's lion ever showed himself there, is there a man over thirteen and under ninety who would not have been ready to meet him—is there a river on this continent that would not have run red with blood — is there a field but would have been piled high with the unburied bones of slaughtered Americans before these consecrated battle-fields of liberty should have been wrested from us? But this same American goes into a sister republic, and says to poor, weak Mexico, 'Give up your territory—you are unworthy to possess it —I have got one-half already—all I ask you is to give up the other!' England might as well, in the circumstances I have described, have come and demanded of us, 'Give up the Atlantic slope—give up this trifling territory from the Alleghany Mountains to the sea; it is only from Maine to St. Mary's—only about one-third your republic, and the least interesting portion of it.' What would be the response? They would say, 'We must give this up to John Bull. Why?' 'He wants room.' The Senator from Michigan says he must have this. Why, my worthy Christian brother, on what principle of justice? 'I want room!'

"Sir, look at this pretence of want of room. With 20,000,000 people you have about 1,000,000,000 acres of land, inviting settlement by every conceivable argument—bringing them down to a quarter of a dollar an acre, and allowing every man to squat where he pleases. But the Senator from Michigan says we will be 200,000,000 in a few years, and we want room. If I were a Mexican, I would tell you, 'Have you not room in your own country to bury your dead men? If you come into mine we will greet you with bloody hands, and welcome you to hospitable graves.'

"'Why,' says the chairman of this committee of foreign relations, 'it is the most reasonable thing in the world! We ought to have the Bay of San Francisco.' Why? Because it is the best harbor on the Pacific! It has been my fortune, Mr. President, to have practised a good deal in criminal courts in the course of my life, but I never yet heard a thief, arraigned for stealing a horse, plead that it was the best horse that he could find in the country! We want California. What for? 'Why,' says the Senator from Michigan, 'we will have it;' and the Senator from South Carolina, with a very mistaken view, I think, of policy, says, 'You can't keep our people from going there.' I don't desire to prevent them. Let them go and seek their happiness in whatever country or clime it pleases them.

"All I ask of them is, not to require this government to protect them with that banner consecrated to war waged for principles—eternal, enduring truth. Sir, it is not meet that our flag should throw its protecting folds over expeditions for lucre or for land. But you still say you want room for your people. This has been the plea of every robber-chief from Nimrod to the present hour. I dare say, when Tamerlane descended from his throne, built of 70,000 human skulls, and marched his ferocious battalions to further slaughter, I dare say he said, 'I want room.' Bajazet was another gentleman of kindred taste and wants with us Anglo-Saxons—he 'wanted room.' Alexander, too, the mighty 'Macedonian madman,' when he wandered with his Greeks to the plains of India, and fought a bloody battle on the very ground where recently England and the Sikhs engaged in strife for 'room,' was, no doubt, in quest of some California there. Many a Monterey had he to storm to get 'room.' Sir, he made quite as much of that sort of history as you ever will. Mr. President, do you remember the last chapter in that history? It is soon read. Oh!

I wish we could but understand its moral. Ammon's son (so was Alexander named), after all his victories, died drunk in Babylon! The vast empire he conquered to get room became the prey of the generals he had trained; it was disparted, torn to pieces, and so ended. Sir, there is a very significant appendix; it is this: the descendants of the Greeks—of Alexander's Greeks—are now governed by the descendants of Attila! Mr. President, while we are fighting for room, let us ponder deeply this appendix. I was somewhat amazed, the other day, to hear the Senator from Michigan declare that Europe had quite forgotten us till these battles waked them up. I suppose the Senator feels grateful to the President for 'waking up' Europe. Does the President, who is, I hope, read in civic as well as military lore, remember the saying of one who had pondered upon history long—long, too, upon man, his nature and true destiny? Montesquieu did not think highly of this way of 'waking up.' 'Happy,' says he, 'is the nation whose annals are tiresome.'

"The Senator from Michigan has a different view of this. He thinks that a nation is not distinguished until it is distinguished in war; he fears that the slumbering faculties of Europe have not been able to ascertain that there are 20,000,000 Anglo-Saxons here, making railroads and canals, and speeding all the arts of peace to the utmost accomplishment of the most refined civilization. They do not know it! And what is the wonderful expedient which the democratic method of making history would adopt in order to make us known? Storming cities, desolating peaceful, happy homes, shooting men—ay, sir, such is war—and shooting women, too!

"Sir, I have read, in some account of your battle of Monterey, of a lovely Mexican girl, who, with the benevolence of an angel in her bosom, and the robust courage of a hero in her heart, was busily engaged during the bloody conflict, amid the crash of falling houses, the groans of the dying, and the wild shriek of battle, in carrying water to slake the burning thirst of the wounded of either host. While bending over a wounded American soldier, a cannon ball struck her and blew her to atoms. Sir, I do not charge my brave, generous-hearted countrymen who fought that fight with this. No, no! We who send them—we who know that scenes like this, which might send tears of sorrow 'down Pluto's iron cheek,' are the invariable, inevitable attendants on war—we are accountable for this. And this—this is the way we are to be made known to Europe. This—this is to be the undying renown of free, republican America! 'She has stormed a city—killed many of its inhabitants of both sexes—she has room!' *So* it will read. Sir, if this were our only history, then may God of his mercy grant that its volume may speedily come to a close.

"Why is it, sir, that we of the United States, a people of yesterday compared with the older nations of the world, should be waging war for territory—for 'room'? Look at your country, extending from the Alleghany Mountains to the Pacific Ocean, capable itself of sustaining in comfort a larger population than will be in the whole Union for 100 years to come. Over this vast expanse of territory your population is now so sparse that I believe we provided, at the last session, a regiment of mounted men to guard the mail from the frontier of Missouri to the mouth of the Columbia; and yet you persist in the ridiculous assertion, 'I want room.' One would imagine, from the frequent reiteration of the complaint, that you had a bursting, teeming population, whose energy was paralyzed, whose enterprise was crushed, for want of space. Why should we be so weak or wicked as to offer this idle apology for ravaging a neighboring republic? It will impose on no one at home or abroad.

"Do we not know, Mr. President, that it is a law never to be repealed, that falsehood shall be short-lived? Was it not ordained of old that truth only shall abide forever? Whatever we may say to-day, or whatever we may write in our books, the stern tribunal of history will review it all, detect falsehood, and bring us to judgment before that posterity which shall bless or curse us, as we may act *now*, wisely or otherwise. We may hide in the grave (which awaits us all) in vain; we may hope there, like the foolish bird that hides its head in the sand, in the vain belief that its body is not seen, yet even there this preposterous excuse of want of 'room' shall be laid bare, and the quick-coming future will decide that it was a hypocritical pretence, under which we sought to conceal the avarice which prompted us to covet and to seize by force that which was not ours.

"Mr. President, this uneasy desire to augment our territory has depraved the moral sense and blunted the otherwise keen sagacity of our people. What has been the fate of all nations who have acted upon the idea that they must advance? Our young orators cherish this notion with a fervid but fatally mistaken zeal. They call it by the mysterious name of 'destiny.' 'Our destiny,' they say, is 'onward,' and hence they argue, with ready sophistry, the propriety of seizing upon any territory and any people that may lie in the way of our 'fated' advance. Recently these progressives have grown classical; some assiduous student of antiquities has helped them to a patron saint. They have wandered back into the desolated Pantheon, and there, among the Polytheistic relics of that 'pale mother of dead empires,' they have found a god whom these Romans, centuries gone by, baptized 'Terminus.'"

Cosby, WILLIAM, governor; born about 1695; became a colonel in the British army; served as governor of Minorca, and of the Leeward Islands; and from 1731 till his death in New York City, March 10, 1736, was governor of New York. He was an exceedingly unpopular governor, largely through his contempt for the elective franchise, and continued one Assembly in office during the entire administration by refusing assent to its dissolution at the usual time.

Cottineau, DENIS NICHOLAS, naval officer; born in Nantes, France, in 1746; became a lieutenant in the French navy; and in the battle between the American squadron under Paul Jones and the British fleet under Sir Richard Pearson, Sept. 23, 1779, commanded the American ship *Pallas.* Cottineau is mentioned in high terms by James Fenimore Cooper in his *History of the Navy of the United States.* He died in Savannah, Ga., Nov. 29, 1798.

COTTON, JOHN

Cotton, JOHN, clergyman; born in Derby, England, Dec. 4, 1585; became minister of St. Botolph's Church, Boston, Lincolnshire, about 1612, and remained there, a noted preacher and controversialist, for twenty years, constantly leaning towards Puritanism. For his non-conformity he was cited to appear before Archbishop Laud, when he fled to America, arriving in Boston in September, 1633. He was soon afterwards ordained a colleague with Mr. Wilson in the Boston Church. His ministry there for nineteen years was so influential that he has been called "The Patriarch of New England." He was a firm opponent of Roger Williams, and defended the authority of ministers and magistrates. He and Davenport were invited to assist in the assembly of divines at Westminster, but were dissuaded from going by Hooker. He died in Boston, Dec. 23, 1652.

God's Promise to His Plantations.—The following sermon, to which a large historical importance has been given, was preached in England, as a farewell address to Winthrop's Massachusetts Company (see WINTHROP, JOHN), and the first London edition of it was published in 1630:

---

2 Sam. 7. 10. *Moreover I will appoint a place for my people Israell, and I will plant them, that they may dwell in a place of their owne, and move no more.*

In the beginning of this chapter we reade of *Davids* purpose to build God an house, who thereupon consulted with *Nathan* about it, one Prophet standing in neede of anothers help in such waightie matters. *Nathan* incourageth the King unto this worke, verse 3. God the same night meetes *Nathan* and tells him a contrary purpose of his: Wherein God refuseth *Davids* offer, with some kind of earnest and vehement dislike, *verse* 4, 5: Secondly, he refuseth the reason of *Davids* offer, from his long silence. For foure hundred yeares together he spake of no such thing, unto any of the Tribes of *Israel* saying, *Why build you not me an house?* in 6. 7. verses.

Now lest *David* should be discouraged with this answer, the Lord bids *Nathan* to shut up his speech with words of encouragement, and so he remoues his discouragement two wayes.

First, by recounting his former favours dispensed unto *David.* Secondly, by promising the continuance of the like or greater: and the rather, because of this purpose of his. And five blessings God promiseth unto *David,* and his, for his sake.

The first is in the 10. verse: *I will appoint a place for my people Israell.*

Secondly, seeing it was in his heart to build him an house, God would therefore, *build him an house renowned forever,* verse 11.

Thirdly, that he would accept of an house from *Solomon*, verse 12.

Fourthly, hee will be a Father to his sonne, vers. 14. 15.

Fifthly, that he will *establish the throne of his house for ever.*

In this 10 verse is a double blessing promised:

First, the designment of a place for his people.

Secondly, a plantation of them in that place, from whence is promised a threefold blessing.

First, they shall dwell there like Freeholders in a place of their owne.

Secondly, hee promiseth them firme and durable possession, they shall move no more.

Thirdly, they shall have peaceable and quiet resting there. The Sonnes of wickedness shall afflict them no more: which is amplified by their former troubles, as before time.

From the appointment of a place for them, which is the first blessing, you may observe this note.

The placing of a people in this or that Countrey is from the appointment of the Lord.

This is evident in the Text, and the Apostle speakes of it as grounded in nature, *Acts* 17. 26. *God hath determined the times before appointed, and the bounds of our habitation. Dut. 2 chap.* 5. 9. God would not have the *Israelites* meddle with the *Edomites,* or the *Moabites,* because he had given tnem their land for a possession. God assigned out such a land for such a posterity, and for such a time.

Quest. Wherein doth this worke of God stand in appointing a place for a people?

Answ. First, when God espies or discovers a land for a people, as in *Ezek.* 20. 6. he brought them into a land that he had espied for them: And that is, when either he gives them to discover it themselves, or heare of it discovered by others. and fitting them.

Secondly, after he hath espied it, when he carrieth them along to it, so that they plainly see a providence of God leading them from one Country to another: As in *Exod.* 19. 4. *You have seene how I have borne you as on Eagles wings, and brought you unto my selfe.* So that though they met with many difficulties. yet hee carried them high above them all, like an eagle, flying over seas and rockes. and all hindrances.

Thirdly, when he makes roome for a people who dwell there, as in *Psal.* 80. 9. *Thou preparedst roome for them.* When *Isaac* sojourned among the *Philistines,* he digged one well, and the *Philistines* strove for it, and he called it *Esek,* and he digged another well, and for that they strove also, therefore he called it *Sitnah:* and he removed thence, and digged an other well, and for that they strove not, and he called it *Rohoboth,* and said, *For now the Lord hath made roomee for us, and we shall be fruitfull in the Land.* Now no *Esek* no *Sitnah,* no quarrel or contention, but now he sits downe in *Rohoboth* in a peace able roome.

Now God makes room for a people 3 wayes:

First, when he casts out the enemies of a people before them by lawfull warre with the inhabitants, which God cals them unto: as in *Ps.* 44. 2. *Thou didst driue out the heathen before them.* But this course of warring against others, & driving them out without provocation, depends upon speciall Commission from God, or else it is not imitable.

Secondly, when he gives a forreigne people favour in the eyes of any native people to come and sit downe with them either by way of purchase, as *Abraham* did obtaine the field of *Machpelah;* or else when they give it in courtesie, as *Pharaoh* did the land of *Goshen* unto the sons of *Jacob*.

Thirdly, when hee makes a Countrey though not altogether void of inhabitants, yet voyd in that place where they reside. Where there is a vacant place, there is liberty for the sonne of *Adam* or *Noah* to come and inhabite, though they neither buy it, nor aske their leaves. *Abraham* and *Isaac*, when they sojourned amongst the Philistines, they did not buy that land to feede their cattle, because they said There is roome enough. And so did *Jacob* pitch his Tent by *Sechem*, *Gen.* 34. 21. There was *roome enough* as *Hamor* said, *Let them sit down amongst us.* And in this case if the people who were former inhabitants did disturbe them in their possessions, they complained to the King, as of wrong done unto them: As *Abraham* did because they took away his well, in *Gen.* 21. 25. For his right whereto he pleaded not his immediate calling from God, (for that would have seemed frivolous amongst the Heathen) but his owne industry and culture in digging the well, verse 30. Nor doth the King reject his plea, with what had he to doe to digge wells in their soyle? but admitteth it as a Principle in Nature. That in a vacant soyle, hee that taketh possession of it, and bestoweth culture and husbandry upon it, his Right it is. And the ground of this is from the grand Charter given to *Adam* and his posterity in Paradise, *Gen.* 1. 28. *Multiply and replenish the earth, and subdue it.* If therefore any sonne of *Adam* come and finde a place empty, he hath liberty to come, and fill, and subdue the earth there. This Charter was renewed to *Noah*, *Gen.* 9. 1. *Fulfill the earth and multiply:* So that it is free from that comon Grant for any to take possession of vacant Countries. Indeed no Nation is to drive out another without speciall Commission from heaven, such as the Israelites had, unless the Natives do unjustly wrong them, and will not recompence the wrongs done in peaceable fort, & then they may right themselves by lawfull war, and subdue the Countrey unto themselves.

This placeing of people in this or that Countrey, is from Gods soveraignty over all the earth, and the inhabitants thereof: as in *Psal.* 24. 1. *The earth is the Lords, and the fulnesse thereof.* And in *Ier.* 10. 7. God is there called, *The King of Nations:* and in *Deut.* 10. 14. Therefore it is meete he should provide a place for all Nations to inhabite, and haue all the earth replenished. Onely in the Text here is meant some more speciall appointment, because God tells them it by his owne mouth; he doth not so with other people, he doth not tell the children of *Sier*, that hee hath appointed a place for them: that is, He gives them the land by promise; others take the land by his providence, but Gods people take the land by promise: And therefore the land of *Canaan* is called a land of promise. Which they discerne, first, by discerning themselves to be in Christ, in whom all the promises are yea, and amen.

Secondly, by finding his holy presence with them, to wit, when he plants them in the holy Mountaine of his Inheritance: *Exodus.* 15. 17. And that is when he giveth them the liberty and purity of his Ordinances. It is a land of promise, where they have provision for soule as well as for body. *Ruth* dwelt well for outward respects while shee dwelt in *Moab*, but when shee cometh to dwell in *Israel*, shee is said to come under the wings of God: *Ruth* 2. 12. When God wrappes us in with his Ordinances, and warmes us with the life and power of them as with wings, there is a land of promise.

This may teach us all where we doe now dwell, or where after wee may dwell, be sure you looke at every place appointed to you, from the hand of God: wee may not rush into any place, and never say to God, By your leave; but we must discerne how God appoints us this place. There is poore comfort in sitting down in any place, that you cannot say, This place is appointed me of God. Canst thou say that God spied out this place for thee, and there hath setled thee above all hinderances? didst thou finde that God made roome for thee either by lawfull descent, or purchase, or gift, or other warrantable right? Why then this is the place God hath appointed thee; here hee hath made roome for thee, he hath placed thee in *Rehoboth*, in a peaceable place: This we must discerne, or els we are but intruders upon God. And when wee doe withall discerne, that God giveth us these outward blessings from his love in Christ, and maketh comfortable provision as well for our soule as for our bodies, by the meanes of grace, then doe we enjoy our present possession as well by gracious promise, as by the common, and just, and bountifull providence of the Lord. Or if a man doe remove, he must see that God hath espied out such a Countrey for him.

Secondly, though there be many difficulties yet he hath given us hearts to overlook them all, as if we were carried upon eagles wings.

And thirdly, see God making roome for us by some lawfull means.

Quest. But how shall I know whether God hath appointed me such a place, if I be well where I am, what may warrant my removeall?

Answ. There be foure or five good things, for procurement of any of which I may remove. Secondly, there be some evill things, for avoiding of any of which wee may transplant our selves. Thirdly, if withall we find some speciall providence of God concurring in either of both concerning our selves, and applying general grounds of removall to our personall estate.

First, wee may remove for the gaining of knowledge. Our Saviour commends it in the Queene of the south, that she came from the utmost parts of the earth to heare the wisdom of *Solomon: Matth.* 12. 42. And surely with him she might have continued for the same end, if her personall calling had not recalled her home.

Secondly, some remove and travaile for merchandize and gaine-sake; *Daily bread may be sought from farre, Prov.* 31. 14. Yea our Saviour approveth travaile for Merchants, *Matth.* 13. 45, 46. when hee compareth a Christian to a Merchantman seeking pearles: For he never fetcheth a comparison from any unlawfull thing to illustrate a thing lawfull. The comparison from the unjust Steward, and from the Theefe in the night, is not taken from the injustice of the one, or the theft of the other; but from the wisdome of the one, and the sodainnesse of the other; which in themselves are not unlawfull.

Thirdly, to plant a Colony, that is, a company that agree together to remove out of their owne Country, and settle a Citty or commonwealth elsewhere. Of such a Colony wee reade in *Acts* 16. 12. which God blessed and prospered exceedingly, and made it a glorious Church. Nature teacheth Bees to doe so, when as the hive is too full, they seeke abroad for new dwellings: So when the hive of the Common wealth is so full, that Tradesmen cannot live one by another, but eate up one another, in this case it is lawfull to remove.

Fourthly, God alloweth a man to remove, when he may employ his Talents and gift better elsewhere, especially when where he is, he is not bound by any speciall engagement. Thus God sent *Ioseph* before to preserve the Church: *Iosephs* wisedome and spirit was not fit for a shepheard, but for a Counsellour of State, and therefore God sent him into *Egypt. To whom much is given of him God will require the more: Luk* 12. 48.

Fifthly, for the liberty of the Ordinances. 2 *Chron.* 11. 13, 14, 15. When *Ieroboam* made a desertion from *Iudah,* and set up golden Calves to worship, all that were well affected, both Priests and people, sold their possessions, and came to *Ierusalem* for the Ordinances sake. This case was of seasonable use to our fathers in the dayes of Queene *Mary;* who removed to *France* and *Germany* in the beginning of her Reign, upon Proclamation of alteration of religion, before any persecution began.

Secondly, there be evills to be avoyded that may warrant removeall. First, when some grievous sinnes overspread a Country that threaten desolation. *Mic.* 2. 6 to 11 verse: When the people say to them that prophecie, *Prophecie not;* then verse 10. *Arise then, this is not your rest.* Which words though they be a threatning, not a commandement; yet as in a threatning a wise man foreseeth the plague, so in the threatning he seeth a commandement, to hide himselfe from it. This case might have been of seasonable use unto them of the *Palatinate,* when they saw their Orthodox Ministers banished, although themselues might for a while enjoy libertie of conscience.

Secondly, if men be overburdened with debts and miseries, as *Davids* followers were; they may then retire out of the way (as they retired to *David* for safety) not to defraud their creditors (for *God is an avenger of such things,* 1 *Thess.,* 4. 6.) but to gaine further opportunity to discharge their debts, and to satisfie their Creditors. 1 *Sam.* 22. 1, 2.

Thirdly, in case of persecution, so did the Apostle in *Acts* 13. 46, 47.

Thirdly, as these generall cases, where any of them doe fall out, doe warrant removeall in generall: so there be some speciall providences or particular cases which may give warrant unto such or such a person to transplant himselfe, and which apply the former generall grounds to particular persons.

First, if soveraigne Authority command and encourage such Plantations by giving way to subjects to transplant themselves, and set up a new Commonwealth. This is a lawfull and expedient case for such particular persons as he designed and sent; *Matth.* 8. 9. and for such as they who are sent, have power to command.

Secondly, when some special providence of God leades a man unto such a course. This may also single out particulars. *Psal.* 32. 8. *I will instruct, and guide thee with mine eye.* As the childe knowes the pleasure of his father in his eye, so doth the child of God see Gods pleasure in the eye of his heavenly Fathers providence. And this is done three wayes.

First, if God give a man an inclination to this or that course for that is the spirit of man; and *God is the father of spirits; Rom.* 1. 11, 12. 1 Cor. 16. 12. *Paul* discerned his calling to goe to *Rom.* by his τὸ πρόθυμον, his ready inclination to that voyage; and *Apollos* his loathing to goe to *Corinth, Paul* accepted as a just reason of his refusall of a calling to go thither. And this holdeth, when in a mans inclination to travaile, his heart is set on no by-respects, as to see fashions, to deceive his Creditours, to fight Duels, or to live idly, these are vaine inclinations; but if his heart be inclined upon right judgment to advance the Gospell, to maintaine his family, to use his Talents fruitfully, or the like good end, this inclination is from God. As the beames of the Moone darting into the Sea leades it to and fro, so doth a secret inclination darted by God into our hearts leade and bowe (as a byas) our whole course.

Secondly, when God gives other men hearts to call us as the men of *Mecedon* did *Paul, Come to us into Macedonia, and help us.* When wee are invited by others who have a good calling to reside there, we my goe with them, unlesse we be detained by waightier occasions. One member hath interest in another, to call to it for helpe, when it is not diuerted by great employment.

Thirdly, there is another providence of God concurring in both these, that is, when a mans calling and person is free, and not tyed by parents, or Magistrates, or other people that have interest in him. Or when abroad hee may doe himselfe and others more good than he can doe at home. Here is then an eye of God that opens a doore there, and sets him loose here, inclines his heart that way, and outlookes all difficulties. When God makes roome for us, no binding here, and an open way there, in such a case God tells them, he will appoint a place for them.

Vse 2. Secondly, this may teach us in every place where God appoints us to sit downe, to acknowledge him as our Landlord. The earth is the Lords and the fulnesse thereof; his are our Country, our Townes, our houses; and therefore let us acknowledge him in them all. The Apostle makes this use of it amongst the *Athenians, Acts* 17. 26, 27. *He hath appointed the times and places of our habitation; that we might seeke and grope after the Lord.* There is a threefold use thaat we are to make of it, as it appeareth there; Let us seek after the Lord, why? Because if thou commest into an house thou wilt aske for the owner of it: And so if thou commest into a forreigne land, and there findest an house and land provided for thee, wilt thou not enquire, where is the Landlord? where is that God that gave me this house and land? He is missing, and therefore seek after him.

Secondly, thou must feele after him, grope after him by such sensible things, strive to attaine the favour of your Landlord, and labour to be obedient to him that hath given you such a place.

Thirdly, you must labour to finde him

in his Ordinances, in prayer and in Christian communion. These things I owe him as my Landlord, and by these I find and enjoy him. This use the very Pagans were to make of their severall Plantations: And if you knew him before, seeke him yet more, and feele after him till you find him in his Ordinances, and in your consciences.

Vse 3. Thirdly, when you have found God making way and roome for you, and carrying you by his providence into any place, learne to walke thankfully before him, defraud him not of his rent, but offer yourselves unto his service: Serve that God, and teach your children to serve him, that hath appointed you and them the place of your habitation.

2 Observation. *A people of Gods plantation shall enjoy their owne place with safety and peace.*

This is manifest in the Text: I will plant them and what followes from thence? They shall dwell in their owne place; But how? Peaceably, they shall not be moved any more. Then they shall dwell safely, then they shall live in peace. The like promise you reade of in *Psal.* 89. 21, 22. *The enemie shall not exact upon them any more. And in Psal.* 92. 13. *Those that be planted in the house of the Lord, shall flourish in the Courts of our God. Gods plantation is a florishing plantation, Amos* 9. 15.

Quest. What is it for God to plant a people?

Answr. It is a Metaphor taken from young Impes; I will plant them, that is, I will make them to take roote there; and that is, where they and their soyle agree well together, when they are well and sufficiently provided for, as a plant suckes nourishment from the soyle that fitteth it.

Secondly, When hee causeth them to grow as plants doe, in *Psal.* 80. 8, 9, 10, 11. When a man growes like a tree in tallnesse and strength, to more firmnesse and eminency, then hee may be said to be planted.

Thirdly, When God causeth them to *fructifie. Psal.* 1. 5.

Fourthly, When he establisheth them there, then he plants, and rootes not up.

But here is something more especiall in this planting; for they were planted before in this land, and yet he promiseth here againe, that he will plant them in their owne land; which doth imply, first, That whatever former good estate they had already, he would prosper it, and increase it.

Secondly, God is said to plant a people more especially, when they become *Trees of righteousnesse, Isay* 61. 3: That they may be called trees of righteousnesse, the planting of the Lord. So that there is implyed not onely a continuance of their former good estate, but that hee would make them a good people, a choice generation: which he did, first, by planting the Ordinances of God amongst them in a more glorious manner, as he did in *Salomons* time.

2. He would give his people *a naile,* and *a place in his Tabernacle, Isay* 56. 5. And that is to give us part in Christ; for so the Temple typified. So then hee plants us when hee gives us roote in Christ.

Thirdly, When he giveth us to *grow up in him as Calves in the stall. Mal.* 4. 2, 3.

Fourthly, & to *bring forth much fruit,* Joh. 15. 1, 2.

Fifthly, and to continue and abide in the state of grace. This is to plant us in his holy Sanctuary, he not rooting us up.

Reasons. This is taken from the kinde acceptance of *Davids* purpose to build God an house, because he saw it was done in the honesty of his heart, therefore he promiseth to give his people a place wherein they should abide forever as in a house of rest.

Secondly, it is taken from the office God takes upon him, when he is our planter, hee becomes our husbandman; and *if he plant us, who shall plucke us up? Isay.* 27. 1, 2. *Job.* 34. 29. When he giveth quiet, who can make trouble? If God be the Gardiner, who shall plucke up what he sets down? Every plantation that he hath not planted shall be plucked up, and what he hath planted shall surely be established.

Thirdly, from the nature of the blessing hee conferres upon us: When he promiseth to plant a people, their dayes shall be as the dayes of a Tree, *Isay* 65. 22: As the Oake is said to be an hundred yeares in growing, and an hundred yeares in full strength, and an hundred yeares in decaying.

Quest: But it may be demanded, how was this promise fulfilled by the people, seeing after this time they met with many persecutions, at home, and abroad, many sources of wickednesse afflicted them; *Ieroboam* was a sonne of wickedness, and so was *Ahab*, and *Ahaz*, and divers others.

Answ. Because after *Davids* time they had more setlednesse than before.

Secondly, to the godly these promises were fulfilled in Christ.

Thirdly, though this promise was made that others should not wrong them, yet it followes not but that they might wrong themselves by trespassing against God, and so expose themselves to affliction. Whilst they continued Gods plantation, they were a noble Vine, a right seede, but if *Israel* will destroy themselves, the fault is in themselves. And yet even in their captivity the good amongst them God graciously provided for: The *Basket of good figges* God sent into the land of *Caldea* for their good: *Jer.* 24. 5. But if you rebell against God, the same God that planted you will also roote you out againe, for all the evill which you shall doe against your selves: *Jer.* 11. 17. When the Israelites liked not the soile, grew weary of the Ordinances, and forsooke the worship of God, and said, *What part have we in David?* after this they never got so good a King, nor any settled rest in the good land wherein God had planted them. As they waxed weary of God, so hee waxed wearie of them, and cast them out of his sight.

Vse 1. To exhort all that are planted at home, or intend to plant abroad, to looke well to your plantation, as you desire that the sonnes of wickedness may not afflict you at home, nor enemies abroad, looke that you be right planted, and then you need not to feare, you are safe enough: God hath spoken it, I will plant them, and they shall not be moved, neither shall the sonnes of wickedness afflict them any more.

Quest. What course would you have us take?

Answ. Have speciall care that you ever have the Ordinances planted amongst you, or else never looke for security. As soone as Gods Ordinances cease, your security ceaseth likewise; but if God plant his Ordinances among you, feare not, he will mainetaine them. *Isay* 4. 5, 6. *Vpon all their glory there shall be a defence;* that is, upon all Gods Ordinances: for so was the Arke called *the Glory of Israel,* 1 *Sam.* 4. 22.

Secondly, have a care to be implanted into the Ordinances, that the word may be ingrafted into you, and you into it: If you take rooting in the ordinances, grow up thereby, bring forth much fruite, continue and abide therein, then you are vineyard of red wine, and the Lord will keepe you, *Isay* 27. 2. 3. that no sonnes of violence shall destroy you. Looke into all the stories whether divine or humane, and you shall never finde that God ever rooted out a people that had the Ordinances planted amongst them, and themselves planted into the Ordinances: never did God suffer such plants to be plucked up; on all their glory shall be a defence.

Thirdly, be not unmindfull of our *Ierusalem* at home, whether you leave us, or stay at home with us. *Oh pray for the peace of Ierusalem, they shall prosper that love her. Psal.* 122. 6. *They shall all be confounded and turned backe that hate Sion, Psal.* 129. 5. As God continueth his presence with us, (blessed be his name) so be ye present in spirit with us, though absent in body: Forget not the wombe that bare you and the brest that gave you sucke. Even ducklings hatched under an henne, though they take the water, yet will still have recourse to the wing that hatched them: how much more should chickens of the same feather, and yolke? In the amity and unity of brethren, the Lord hath not onely promised, but commanded a blessing, even life forevermore: *Psal.* 133. 1, 2.

Fourthly, goe forth, every man that goeth, with a publick spirit, looking not on your owne things onely, but also on the things of others: *Phil.* 2. 4. This care of universall helpfullnesse was the prosperity of the first Plantation of the Primitive Church, *Acts* 4. 32.

Fifthly, have a tender care that you looke well to the plants that spring from you, that is, to your children, that they doe not degenerate as the Israelites did;

after which they were vexed with afflictions on every hand. How came this to passe? *Ier.* 2. 21. *I planted them a noble Vine, holy, a right seede, how then art thou degenerate into a strange Vine before mee?* Your Ancestours were of a noble divine spirit, but if they suffer their children to degenerate, to take loose courses, then God will surely plucke you up: Otherwise if men have a care to propagate the Ordinances and Religion to their children after them, God will plant them and not roote them up. For want of this, the seede of the repenting *Ninivites* was rooted out.

Sixthly, and lastly, offend not the poore Natives, but as you partake in their land, so make them partakers of your precious faith: as you reape their temporalls, so feede them with your spiritualls: winne them to the love of Christ, for whom Christ died. They never yet refused the Gospell, and therefore more hope they will now receive it. Who knoweth whether God have reared this whole Plantation for such an end:

Vse 2. Secondly, for consolation to them that are planted by God in any place, that finde rooting and establishing from God, this is a cause of much encouragement unto you, that what hee hath planted he will maintaine, every plantation his right hand hath not planted shalbe rooted up, but his owne plantation shall prosper, & flourish. When he promiseth peace and safety, what enemies shalstbe able to make the promise of God of none effect? Neglect not walls, and bulwarkes, and fortifications for your owne defence; but

ever let the name of the Lord be your
strong Tower; and the word of his
Promise the Rocke of your refuge.
His word that made heaven
and earth will not faile, till
heaven and earth
be no more
Amen.

Cotton. Mention is made of cotton "planted as an experiment" in the region of the Carolinas so early as 1621, and its limited growth there is noted in 1666. In 1736 it was cultivated in gardens as far north as latitude 36°, on the eastern shore of Maryland. Forty years later it was cultivated on Cape May, N. J.; but it was almost unknown, except as a garden plant, until after the Revolutionary War. At the beginning of that conflict General Delagall had thirty acres under cultivation near Savannah, Ga. In 1748 seven bags of cotton-wool were exported to England from Charleston, S. C., valued at £3 11*s.* 5*d.* a bag. There were two or three other small shipments afterwards, before the war. At Liverpool eight bags shipped from the United States in 1784 were seized, on the ground that so much cotton could not be produced in the United States. In 1786 the first sea-island cotton was raised, off the coast of Georgia, and its exportation began in 1788 by Alexander Bissell, of St. Simon's Island. The seeds were obtained from the Bahama Islands. The first successful crop of this variety was raised by William Elliott on Hilton Head Island, in 1790. It has always commanded a higher price on account of its being more staple than any other variety. In 1791 the cotton crop in the United States was 2,000,000 lbs. The invention and introduction of the cotton-gin (see WHITNEY, ELI) caused a sudden and enormous increase in the production of cotton. In 1801 the cotton crop in the United States was 48,000,000 lbs., of which 20,000,000 lbs. were exported. The increase in its production was greatly accelerated, and the product of the year ending in June, 1860, on a surface of little less than 11,000 square miles, was over 5,387,000 bales, or over 2,500,000,000 lbs. The value of the cotton crop in 1791 was about $30,000; of that of 1859–60 over $220,000,000. The annual production of cotton in the United States was less for several years after 1860. The Civil War interfered with it; but in 1871 it was nearly 4,000,000 bales, or about 1,800,000,000 lbs. In 1890 the total crop amounted to 7,313,726 bales, or 3,218,000,000 lbs. The commercial cotton crop of the year ending Aug. 31, 1900, was up to that time one of the most remarkable in the history of this industry. There never had been a time when so many American spindles were in operation, and rarely, if ever, when they were so severely taxed to meet the demand for cotton goods. The United States consumed more raw cotton than any other country in the world, leading Great Britain, which, for more than a century, had held supremacy in this industry, by over 500,000 bales. Another feature of this crop was its total value as compared with that of the preceding year, which was then the largest on record; for, although over 2,000,000 bales less, its value was over $29,000,000 greater. The crop aggregated 9,142,838 commercial bales, valued at $334,847,868, and there was a total of 18,100,000 spindles in operation—14,150,000 in the Northern States and 3,950,000 in the Southern.

In 1911, the United States Department of Agriculture reported a total of 14.885,000 bales, Texas (4,280.000), Georgia (2,560,000), Alabama (1,600,000), South Carolina (1,480,000), and Mississippi (1,195,000) leading; total acreage planted, 35,004,000. By 1910 the number of spindles in operation had increased to 29,188,945. Massachusetts exceeded every other State in number, having 9,835,610. South Carolina ranked second, with 3,793,387, and North Carolina third, with 3,124,456. Rhode Island was fourth, Georgia fifth, New Hampshire sixth, Connecticut seventh, New York eigthth, and Maine ninth—all other States reporting less than 1,000,000. The largest consumption on record was in 1909, when the cotton-growing States used 2,553,797 bales, the New England States 2,144,448, and all other States 542,474—a total of 5,240,719. In the fiscal year ended June 30, 1911, cotton became king again in the exports of products of agriculture, the value exported during the year being $585,000,000, by far the largest total ever shown in the cotton export trade, against $481,000,000 in 1907, the former high record year. One peculiar feature of the cotton export trade is found in the fact that although the value exceeded by more than $100,000,000 that of any earlier year, the quantity exported was less than in several years, being about 4,029,000,000 pounds.

Manufacturing Development.—A bulletin of the federal Bureau of the Census gives the following résumé of the development of the cotton manufacturing industry in the United States since 1640:

The rapid development of the cotton manufacturing industry in the United States is one of the most remarkable events in the history of the country. As early as 1640 the General Court of Massachusetts made an order for the encouragement by bounties of the manufacture of linen, woollen, and cotton cloth. In this it was followed about nine months later by the Assembly of Connecticut, which took measures to encourage the importation of cotton wool from the Barbados. About the same time a company of Yorkshire men who settled at Rowley, Mass., in 1638, engaged in spinning and weaving cotton, flax, and wool, later, in 1643 erecting at that place the first fulling mill in America.

As in Great Britain, however, the manufacture in this country properly dates from the introduction of the Arkwright machinery, which took place in 1790, although as early as 1775 a spinning jenny of 24 threads was put in operation by a joint stock company at Philadelphia. Here in 1782 Samuel Wetherell, Jr., one of the company, advertised for sale what were probably the first factory-made "jeans, fustians, everlastings, etc.," in this country; but up to 1790 no sheetings, shirtings, checks, or ginghams had been made here. The warp for the first goods manufactured wholly of cotton was supplied by a water-frame cotton mill at Pawtucket, the equipment of which consisted of three carding machines, one drawing and roving machine, and two Arkwright spinning frames of 72 spindles, the latter being the first machine of the kind successfully operated in the United States. The product of this mill, small as it was during the first twenty months, far exceeded the demand of the hand weavers and buyers.

In 1794 the first cotton sewing-thread ever made is said to have been spun from sea-island cotton, the cultivation of which was just beginning in the South. The introduction of stocking yarn in America was made about this time by Samuel Slater. The prices of yarn in Rhode Island at this time are recorded as being 88 cents per pound for No. 12, $1.04 for No. 16, and $1.21 for No. 20. About 1804 cotton machinery, clandestinely obtained from England, was introduced into a large factory previously run as a woollen mill at Byfield, Mass., and for a time was employed upon warp yarn and wicking for household manufactures. A few years later the manufacture of tickings, coarse ginghams, sheetings, and similar heavy materials was commenced at this factory, the first, it is said, of that class of goods made in this country. These were all woven on hand looms, as power weaving was not in use at that date. The price of ginghams at that time was 75 cents, and of sheetings 50 cents a yard. It was during this year (1804) that the first consignment for sale of American cotton manufactures was made by Almy & Brown, of Providence, to Elijah Warren, of Philadelphia, who became their agent for selling American yarns and threads in great variety, to which were added as business improved stripes, plaids, checks, denims, tickings, etc. In 1808 a company with a capital of $1,000,000 was incorporated in Maryland to manufacture coarse cotton goods on a large scale, beginning operations at Ellicott's Mills, on the Patapsco River, in 1810.

In an official report made by the Secretary of the Treasury to Congress in 1810, the number of cotton mills erected up to the close of the previous year, including 25 then building, was given as 87. Of these 62 were in operation and worked 31,000 spindles, requiring a capital of about $100 per spindle, of which $60 was actively employed. The average annual consumption of cotton per spindle was 45 pounds, worth 20 cents per pound, and the product 36 pounds of yarn per spindle worth on an average $1.125 per pound. These mills employed on an average 5 men and 35 women to every 800 spindles. The mills were distributed as follows: Rhode Island, 25, including 7 under construction; Massachusetts, 15, including 5 under construction; Connecticut, 6; Pennsylvania, 4; New York, 6; Maryland, 5; New Hampshire, 6; Kentucky, 6; Vermont, 4; New Jersey, 2; Delaware, 2; and in Maine, Virginia, South Carolina, Georgia, Tennessee, and Ohio, 1 each. Of these 87 mills, all those in Kentucky, South Carolina, Georgia, Tennessee, and Ohio, 2 in Pennsylvania, and 1 each in Delaware and Maryland, were operated by animal power.

The first census of manufactures taken by the government was in 1810, when 269 cotton manufacturing establishments, scattered throughout 18 States and Territories and operating about 87,000 spindles, were reported. These factories were small, producing chiefly yarn and from 1,000 to 8,000 yards of cloth each per annum. The greater part of the domestic cotton then consumed was spun and woven in the homes of the people, and the aggregate quantity returned as so made was 16,581,299 yards, an amount estimated to exceed in measurement all the cloth made that year from flax, hemp, wool, and silk combined. Cotton duck, which of late years has been so extensively made and consumed in this country, and which has entered so largely into our exports of domestic cotton fabrics, was then a new article, having just been introduced by Seth Bemis, a manufacturer of Watertown, Mass. During the year 1809 a small quantity of this material, made in Boston from sea-island cotton, was sold at 65 cents per yard for No. 1 and 58 cents for No. 2.

It was in 1819 that cotton goods were first printed in this country upon copper rollers. This took place at a bleachery and print works established near Philadelphia, where calico printing from wooden blocks had been carried on since the year 1788, or even earlier. The first cylinder machine, enabling one man and two boys to print daily 10,000 yards of cloth, was imported from England in 1809 and put in operation by water power near Philadelphia. In 1822 the engraving of metallic rollers for calico printers was commenced in Philadelphia, and this led to the building of a number of plants about this time in Massachusetts, New Hampshire, New York, New Jersey, and Maryland. For the successful introduction of the power loom we are indebted to a Boston manufacturing company chartered in February, 1813. This company built a factory of about 1,700 spindles at Waltham, Mass.; for the manufacture of cotton products by the aid of the power loom, which was constructed with several improvements upon the basis of the English loom then in use.

In 1840 there were 1,240 mills in the United States with 2,284,631 spindles, in 1880 there were 756 mills with 10,653,435 spindles, while in 1908 there were 1,941 mills with 27,964,387 spindles. The decrease in the number of mills between 1840 and 1880 was due to the concentration of the industry in larger establishments. For instance, in 1840 the average number of spindles per mill was 1,842, in 1880 the number was 14,092, while in 1908 it was 14,407. The number of mills in 1840 and in 1880 includes weaving mills, while in 1908 only mills operating cotton spindles are considered.

Cotton-Seed Industry.—The total value of the crude products of the cotton-seed crushing industries of the United States increased 154 per cent. during the decade of 1899–1909, aggregating $107,538,000 in 1909 in contrast with $42,412,000 in 1899. Cotton-seed to the extent of 3,827,300 tons, costing $78,112,000 in 1909, and 2,479,400 tons, costing $28,633,000 in 1899, was needed for the manufacture of these crude products.

The output of cotton-seed oil amounted to 158,328,500 gallons, worth $55,328,000 in 1909, and to 93,325,700 gallons, worth $21,391,000 in 1899. The meal and cake totalled 1,674,500 tons, valued at $40,493,000 in 1909, and 884,400 tons, valued at $16,031,000 in 1899. Hulls weighing 1,269,200 tons, and worth $7,711, 000 in 1909, compared with 1,169,200 tons, worth $3,189,000 in 1899, were also included among the products of the crushing mills; likewise 175,512,100 pounds of linters in 1909 and 57,272,000 pounds in 1899, having a value of $4,006,000 and $1,801,000 in these years, respectively.

The number of establishments increased from 357 in 1899 to 809 in 1909, or 127 per cent. This increase was general throughout the several cotton States. The quantity of cotton-seed crushed during the decade rose only 54 per cent., but the increase in the cost of the seed to the manufacturer was 173 per cent., and the gain in the production of oil was 70 per cent, the latter indicating the employment of better methods and greater economy in the use of machinery. The increase in the quantity of cake and meal was 89 per cent., which can probably be accounted for in part by the opening of a number of mills operated under the cold-process system, by which the hulls and meats are pressed together and disposed of as cake and meal.

With the improvement in refining methods new uses for cotton-seed oil have been developed, among the most important of which is the manufacture of lard compound. So large a percentage of the home consumption of cotton-seed oil is used in the lard compound that the value of the oil varies with the supply of animal lard.

While much of the cotton-seed meal consumed in the United States is used either directly as a fertilizer or as an ammonia base in the manufacture of commercial fertilizers, its use as an American feed stuff is rapidly increasing.

During the calendar year 1909 the exports of American cotton-seed oil aggregated 45,514,435 gallons, valued at $19,567,067, and of cotton-seed cake and meal, 407,212 tons, valued at $10,660,760—total value, $30,227,827.

Old King Cotton.—" King Cotton " was a popular personification of the cotton-plant. Its supremacy in commerce and politics was strongly asserted by the politicians of the cotton-growing States when civil war was ripening. " You dare not make war upon cotton; no power on earth dare make war upon it. Cotton is *King!* " said Senator James Hammond, of South Carolina. " Cotton is King! " shouted back the submissive spindles of the North. A Northern poet sang:

" Old Cotton will pleasantly reign
When other kings painfully fall,
And ever and ever remain
The mightiest monarch of all."

A Senator from Texas exclaimed, on the floor of Congress, " I say, Cotton is King, and he waves his sceptre not only over these thirty-three States, but over the island of Great Britain and over Continental Europe; and there is no crowned head there that does not bend the knee in fealty, and acknowledge allegiance to the monarch." This boasting was caused by the erroneous estimate by the politicians of the money value of the cotton crop compared with the other agricultural products of the United States. It was asserted that it was greater than all the latter combined. The census of 1860 showed that the wheat crop alone exceeded in value the cotton crop by $57,000,000; and the value of the combined crops of hay and cereals exceeded that of cotton over $900,000,000. The sovereignty of cotton was tested by the Civil War. At its close a poet wrote:

"*Cotton* and *Corn* were mighty kings,
Who differed, at times, on certain things,
To the country's dire confusion;
Corn was peaceable, mild, and just,
But *Cotton* was fond of saying, 'You must!'
So after he'd boasted, bullied, and cussed,
He got up a revolution.
But in course of time the bubble is bursted,
And *Corn* is King and *Cotton*—is worsted."

Cotton Famine, a period of distress in Lancashire and other seats of cotton manufacture in England, caused by the cutting off of the importation of raw material from the United States by the blockade of Southern ports during the Civil War. The English market was overstocked with American cotton at the beginning of the Civil War, and the actual distress did not begin till nearly a year thereafter. In December, 1863, it was found necessary to organize systems of relief, and at the end of that month 496,816 persons in the cotton-manufacturing cities were dependent on charitable or parochial funds for sustenance. In February, 1863, three American vessels, the *George Griswold*, the *Achilles*, and the *Hope*, loaded with relief supplies contributed by the citizens of the United States, reached Liverpool, and by the end of June the distress began to diminish. At that time the sum of $9,871,015 had been contributed to the various relief funds. In connection with this, see BEECHER, HENRY WARD, *System of Slavery*.

Cotton-Gin. See WHITNEY, ELI.

Cotton Loans, eight per cent. bonds, negotiated in Europe by the Confederate government. Proved a total loss to the investors, who were mainly English sympathizers with the Confederacy.

Cotton-Seed Industry. See COTTON.

Cotton Whigs, an epithet applied to those Whigs in the North who were willing to make little or no opposition to the extension of slavery in the Territories.

Couch, DARIUS NASH, military officer; born in South East, Putnam county, N. Y., July 23, 1822; graduated at West Point in 1846; served in the war with Mexico; aided in suppressing the last outbreak of the Seminoles, and resigned in 1855. In January, 1861, while residing in Taunton, Mass., he was commissioned colonel of a Massachusetts regiment, and made a brigadier-general of volunteers in August. He commanded a division in General Keyes's corps in the BATTLE OF FAIR OAKS, or SEVEN PINES (*q. v.*) He also distinguished himself at Williamsburg and at Malvern Hills, and on July 4, 1862, was promoted to major-general. Soon after his service at Antietam he was put in command of Sumner's corps, and took a prominent part in battles under Burnside and Hooker; also under Thomas, in the defeat of Hood at NASHVILLE (*q. v.*), and in North Carolina early in 1865. He was the unsuccessful Democratic candidate for governor of Massachusetts in 1865; was collector of the port of Boston in 1866–67; adjutant-general of Connecticut in 1883-84. He died in Norwalk, Conn., Feb. 12, 1897.

Coudert, FREDERICK RENÉ, lawyer; born in New York City, of French parentage, in 1832; graduated at Columbia College in 1850; and admitted to the Bar in 1853. For many years he represented France in its legal interests in the United States, and was widely known as an expert in international law. He was a member of the Venezuela boundary commission in 1896; government receiver of the Union Pacific Railroad in 1892-98; and one of the counsel of the United States before the Bering Sea Tribunal of Arbitration in Paris in 1893–95. Mr. Coudert several times declined appointment to the Supreme Court of the United States. He died in Washington, D. C., Dec. 20, 1903.

Council Bluffs, city and capital of Pottawattamie county, Ia.; on the Missouri River, opposite Omaha, Neb., with which it is connected by several bridges, and at the foot of high bluffs, overlooking a wide plain commanding a fine view of the city and river. The city has exceptional railroad facilities, is the farming trade centre of southern Iowa, and has large stockyard, grain, and manufacturing interests. Council Bluffs derives its name from a council held on the bluffs between the Indians and the explorers Lewis and Clarke. It was a Mormon settlement in

1846, and received a city charter in 1853. Pop. (1900) 25,802; (1910) 29,292.

Councils. A body partaking of the nature and powers of a branch of the legislature, and also of a privy council. South Carolina retained the name for the Upper House of the legislature until 1790; Delaware until 1792; Georgia until 1798; and Vermont until 1836.

Counties. The several United States are divided into districts, called counties (in Louisiana, parishes). Several hundred years ago there were large districts of country in England and on the Continent governed by earls, who were, however, subject to the crown. These districts were called *counties*, and the name is still retained even in the United States, and indicates certain judicial and other jurisdiction. The Saxon equivalent for county was *shire*, which simply means division, and was not applied to such counties as were originally distinct sovereignties, such as Kent, Norfolk, etc. Thus we have Lancashire and Yorkshire. New Netherland (New York) was constituted a county of Holland, having all the individual privileges appertaining to an earldom, or separate government. On its seal appears as a crest to the arms a kind of cap called a coronet, which is the armorial distinction of a count or earl.

Country Life, COMMISSION ON. On Aug. 10, 1908, President Theodore Roosevelt appointed the following commissioners to report on the means now available for supplying the deficiencies which exist in the country life of the United States and upon the best methods of organized permanent effort in investigation and actual work along the lines of betterment of rural conditions:

Prof. L. H. Bailey, New York State College of Agriculture, Ithaca, N. Y., chairman; Henry Wallace, *Wallace's Farmer*, Des Moines, Iowa; President Kenyon L. Butterfield, Massachusetts Agricultural College, Amherst, Mass.; Gifford Pinchot, United States Forest Service; William H. Page, editor *The World's Work*, New York, N. Y.; Charles S. Barrett, Georgia; William A. Beard, California.

The commission made its report to the President Jan. 23, 1909, and the document was transmitted by him to Congress, with a message calling attention to the importance of the subject under consideration. The report is thus summarized by the commission:

The commission finds that agriculture in the United States, taken altogether, is prosperous commercially, when measured by the conditions that have obtained in previous years, although there are regions in which this is only partially true. The country people are producing vast quantities of supplies for foods, shelter, clothing, and for use in the arts. The country homes are improving in comfort, attractiveness, and healthfulness. Not only in the material wealth that they produce, but in the supply of independent and strong citizenship, the agricultural people constitute the very foundation of our national efficiency. As agriculture is the immediate basis of country life, so it follows that the general affairs of the open country, speaking broadly, are in a condition of improvement.

Many institutions, organizations, and movements are actively contributing to the increasing welfare of the open country. The most important of these are the United States Department of Agriculture, the colleges of agriculture and the experiment stations in the States, and the national farmers' organizations. With these agencies must be mentioned State departments of agriculture, agricultural societies and organizations of very many kinds, teachers in schools, workers in church and other religious associations, travelling libraries and many other groups, all working with commendable zeal to further the welfare of the people of the open country.

Prominent Deficiencies.—Yet it is true that agriculture is not commercially as profitable as it is entitled to be, for the labor and energy that the farmer expends and the risks that he assumes, and that the social conditions in the open country are far short of their possibilities. We must measure our agricultural efficiency by its possibilities rather than by comparison with previous conditions. The farmer is almost necessarily handicapped in the development of his business, because his capital is small and the volume of his transactions limited, and he usually stands practically alone against organized interests. The reasons for the lack of a highly organized rural society are very many. The leading specific causes are:

A lack of knowledge on the part of farmers of the exact agricultural conditions and possibilities of their regions. Lack of good training for country life in the schools. The disadvantage or handicap of the farmer as against the established business systems and interests, preventing him from securing adequate returns for his products, depriving him of the benefits that would result from unmonopolized rivers and the conservation of forests, and depriving the community, in many cases, of the good that would come from the use of great tracts of agricultural land that are now held for speculative purposes. Lack of good highway facilities. The widespread continuing depletion of soils, with the injurious effect on rural life. A general need of new and active leadership. Other causes contributing to the general result are: Lack of any adequate system of agricultural credit, whereby the farmer may readily secure loans on fair terms; the shortage of labor, a condition that is often complicated by intemperance among workmen; lack of institutions and incentives that tie the laboring man to the soil; the burdens and narrow life of farm women; lack of adequate supervision of public health.

Nature of Remedies.—Some of the remedies lie with the national government, some of them with the States and communities in their corporate capacities, some with voluntary organizations, and some with individuals acting alone. From the great number of suggestions that have been made, covering every phase of country life, the commission now enumerates those that seem to be most fundamental or most needed at the present time.

Congress can remove some of the handicaps of the farmer, and it can also set some kinds of work in motion, such as:

The encouragement of a system of thorough-going surveys of all agricultural regions in order to take stock and to collect local facts, with the idea of providing a basis on which to develop a scientifically and economically sound country life.

The encouragement of a system of extension work of rural communities through all the land-grant colleges with the people at their homes and on their farms.

A thorough-going investigation by experts of the middleman system of handling farm products, coupled with a general inquiry into the farmer's disadvantages in respect to taxation, transportation rates, co-operative organizations and credit, and the general business system.

An inquiry into the control and use of the streams of the United States, with the object of protecting the people in their ownership and of saving to agricultural uses such benefits as should be reserved for these purposes.

The establishing of a highway engineering service or equivalent organization, to be at the call of the States in working out effective and economical highway systems.

The establishing of a system of parcels posts and postal savings banks.

And providing some means or agency for the guidance of public opinion towards the development of a real rural society that shall rest directly on the land.

Other remedies recommended for consideration by Congress are:

The enlargement of the United States Bureau of Education, to enable it to stimulate and co-ordinate the educational work of the nation.

Careful attention to the farmers' interests in legislation on the tariff, on regulation of railroads, control or regulation of corporations and of speculation, legislation in respect to rivers, forests, and the utilization of swamp lands.

Increasing the powers of the Federal government in respect to the supervision and control of the public health.

Providing such regulations as will enable the States that do not permit the sale of liquors to protect themselves from traffic from adjoining States.

In setting all these forces in motion the co-operation of the States will be necessary, and in many cases definite State laws may greatly aid the work.

Remedies of a more general nature are: A broad campaign of publicity that must be undertaken until all the people are informed on the whole subject of rural life, and until there is an awakened appreciation of the necessity of giving this phase of our national development as much attention as has been given to other phases or interests; a quickened sense of responsibility in all country people to the community and to the State in the conserving of soil fertility and in the necessity for diversifying farming in order to conserve this fertility and to develop a better rural society, and also in the better safeguarding of the strength and happiness of the farm women; a more widespread conviction of the necessity for organization, not only for economic but social purposes, this organization to be more or less co-operative, so that all the people may share equally in the benefits and have voice in the essential affairs of the community; a realization on the part of the farmer that he has a direct natural responsibility towards the laborer in providing him with good living facilities and in helping in every way to be a man among men, and a realization on the part of all the people of the obligation to protect and develop the natural scenery and attractiveness of the open country.

Certain remedies lie with voluntary organizations and institutions. All organized forces, both in town and country, should understand that there are country phases as well as city phases of our civilization, and that one phase needs help as much as the other. All these agencies should recognize their responsibility to society. Many existing organizations and institutions might become practically co-operative or mutual in spirit, as, for example, all agricultural societies, libraries, Young Men's Christian Associations, and churches. All other organizations standing for rural progress should be federated in States and nation.

Forces to be Utilized.—The commission has pointed out a number of remedies that are extremely important, but running through all these remedies are several great forces or principles which must be utilized in the endeavor to solve the problems of country life. All the people should recognize what those fundamental forces and agencies are.

Knowledge.—To improve any situation the underlying facts must be understood. The farmer must have exact knowledge of his business and of the particular conditions under which he works. The United States Department of Agriculture and the experiment stations and colleges are rapidly acquiring and distributing this knowledge, but the farmer may not be able to apply it to the best advantage because of lack of knowledge of his own soils, climate, animal and plant diseases, markets and other local facts. The farmer is entitled to know what are the advantages and disadvantages of his conditions and environment. A thorough-going system of surveys in detail of the exact conditions underlying farming in every locality is now an indispensable need to complete and apply the work of the great agricultural institutions. As an occupation agriculture is a means of developing our internal resources; we cannot develop these resources until we know exactly what they are.

Education.—There must be not only a fuller scheme of public education, but a new kind of education adapted to the real needs of the farming people. The country schools are to be so re-directed that they shall educate their pupils in terms of the daily life. Opportunities for training towards agricultural callings are to be multiplied and made broadly effective. Every person on the land, old or young, in school or out of school, educated or illiterate, must have a chance to receive the information necessary to successful business and for a healthful, comfortable, resourceful life, both in home and neighborhood. This means redoubled efforts for better country schools and a vastly increased interest in the welfare of country boys and girls on the part of those who pay the school taxes. Education by means of agriculture is to be a part of our regular public-school work. Special agricultural schools are to be organized. There is to be a well-developed plan of extension teaching conducted by the agricultural colleges, by means of the printed page, face-to-face talks and demonstration or object lessons, designed to reach every farmer and his family, at or near their homes, with knowledge and stimulus in every department of country life.

Organization.—There must be a vast enlargement of voluntary organized effort among the farmers themselves. It is indispensable that farmers shall work together for their common interests and for the national welfare. If they do not do this no governmental activity, no legislation, not even better schools, will greatly avail. There is a multitude of clubs and associations for social, educational, and business purposes, and great national organizations are effective. But the farmers are nevertheless relatively unorganized. We have only begun to develop business co-operation in America. Farmers do not influence legislation as they should. They need a more fully organized social and recreative life.

Spiritual Forces.—The forces and institutions that make for morality and spiritual ideals among rural people must be energized. We miss the heart of the problem if we neglect to foster personal character and neighborhood righteousness. The best way to preserve ideals for private conduct and public life is to build up the institution of religion. The Church has great power of leadership. The whole people should understand that it is vitally important to stand behind the rural church and to help it to become a great power in developing concrete country life ideals. It is especially important that the country church recognize that it has a social responsibility to the entire community as well as a religious responsibility to its own group of people.

Recommendations.—There are, in the opinion of the commission, two or three great movements of the utmost consequence that should be set under way at the earliest possible time, because they are fundamental to the whole problem of ultimate permanent reconstruction; these call for special explanation.

1. Taking stock of country life. There should be organized under government leadership a comprehensive plan for an exhaustive study or survey of all the conditions that surround the business of farming and the people who live in the country in order to take stock of our resources and to supply the farmer with local knowledge. Federal and State governments, agricultural colleges and other educational agencies, organizations of various types, and individual students of the problem should be brought into co-operation for this great work of investigating with minute care all agricultural and country life conditions.

2. Nationalized extension work. Each State college of agriculture should be empowered to organize as soon as practicable a complete department of college extension, so managed as to reach every person on the land in its State, with both information and inspiration. The work should include such forms of extension teaching as lectures, bulletins, reading courses, correspondence courses, demonstration and other means of reaching the people at home and on their farms. It should be designed to forward not only the business of agriculture, but sanitation, education, homemaking, and all interests of country life.

3. A campaign for rural progress. We urge the holding of local, State, and even national conferences on rural progress, designed to unite the interests of education, organization, and religion into one forward movement for the rebuilding of country life. Rural teachers, librarians, clergymen, editors, physicians, and others may well unite with farmers in studying and discussing the rural question in all its aspects. We must in some way unite all institutions, all organizations, all individuals having any interest in country life into one great campaign for rural progress.

County Democracy, NEW YORK. For many years it was the chief opponent of Tammany Hall in local Democratic politics. It joined Tammany Hall in nominating Abram S. Hewitt for mayor in 1886, after which time it had little influence.

Courcel, ALPHONSE CHODRON, BARON DE, diplomatist; born in Paris, France, July 30, 1835; entered the diplomatic service in 1859; became minister to Germany in 1881, and ambassador to Great Britain in 1895; was several years a member of the French Senate; was the French arbitrator in the BERING SEA ARBITRATION (*q. v.*), and president of that tribunal, 1893.

Courcelles, DANIEL DE REMI, SEIGNEUR DE, French governor of Canada; arrived there in 1665 with a regiment of soldiers. To prevent the irruptions of the Five Nations by way of Lake Champlain he projected a series of forts between that lake and the mouth of the Richelieu, or Sorel, its outlet. Forced to return to France in 1672, his plans were carried out by his successor, Frontenac.

Court Leet. This court in England consisted of the tenants of the manor, presided over by the steward of the proprietor. It had jurisdiction over petty criminal cases, and in addition also had

Painting by Howard Pyle

A MIDNIGHT COURT-MARTIAL

some administrative powers. Court leets were held in Maryland by the lords of the manors during the seventeenth century, and their records have been preserved. See MANOR, LORDS OF THE.

Court of Appeals in Cases of Capture. From 1776 to 1780 these appeals were heard by committees of Congress. A permanent Court of Appeals in cases of capture was instituted in 1780 and lasted until 1787. It was the predecessor of the United States Supreme Court.

Court-Martials. Courts consisting of army or navy officers to try persons accused of offending military or naval laws. The members are both judge and jury. The members are sworn in by the judge advocate, and usually take their seats in the order of the official order designating the court. No sentence of a court-martial can be carried into effect until it has been approved by the officer convening the court, but the President of the United States, as commander-in-chief of the army and the navy, can modify or cancel any sentence, or can pardon any offender. Summary and informal courts held in the field are usually called "drumhead court-martials."

Court of Commerce. See COMMERCE COURT.

Court of Customs Appeals. See CUSTOMS, COURT OF.

Court of Domestic Relations. See DOMESTIC RELATIONS, COURT OF.

Courts of Admiralty. The colonies had such courts to deal with evasion of the trade laws, before the English navigation acts were passed. Rhode Island erected an admiralty court in 1653, at the time of the Dutch war; Virginia passed an act in 1660 authorizing the governor and council to be a court of admiralty; Massachusetts, in 1673, and Connecticut, in 1684, authorized their respective courts of assistants to act in that capacity; Plymouth placed this power with the governor and assistants in 1684; and in 1684 Pennsylvania gave the power to the president and members of the council. New York declared in 1678 that in her colony admiralty cases had been tried by a special commission or by a court composed of the mayor and aldermen. From the point of view of admiralty jurisdiction, all these courts were irregular, and it is noteworthy that nowhere, except in Maryland (1639), was a regular admiralty court established till 1697, when a general system was provided.

Courts of Equity, FEDERAL. In his message of Dec. 7, 1909, President Taft called the attention of Congress to "the deplorable delays in the administration of civil and criminal law"; stated his belief that "a change in judicial procedure, with a view to reducing its expense to private litigants in civil cases and facilitating the dispatch of business and final decision in both civil and criminal cases, constitutes the greatest need in our American institutions"; and recommended legislation for the appointment of a commission to undertake a revision of the rules of procedure in the Federal Courts of Equity "simplifying and expediting the procedure as far as possible and making it as inexpensive as may be to the litigant of little means."

Congress authorized the appointment of a committee of the United States Supreme Court to revise the rules, which date back to the organization of that court in 1789, and have not been revised or amended since 1842, and on June 3, 1911, Chief-Justice White announced the committee, consisting of himself and Associate Justices Lurton and Van Deventer.

Courts of the United States. See FEDERAL GOVERNMENT; JUDICIARY OF THE UNITED STATES; SUPREME COURT OF THE UNITED STATES.

Covenhoven, ROBERT, military officer; born in Monmouth county, N. J., Dec. 17, 1755. He joined the Continental army under Washington in 1776, participated in the battles of Trenton and Princeton. An incident in his life furnishes a glimpse of the state of society at that time. In February, 1778, Covenhoven was married to Mercy Kelsey in New Jersey. While the nuptial ceremony was in progress it was interrupted by the sudden arrival of a troop of Hessian soldiers. The groom escaped through a window, but, returning at night, he carried away his bride. He participated as watcher, guide, and soldier in opposing the forays of the English; and was in the desperate engagement of Wyalusing. He ranks in tradition among the genuine heroes of America. In 1796–97 he superintended the construction of a wagon-road from Lycoming to Painted

Post, Steuben co., N. Y. He died in Northumberland, Pa., Oct. 29, 1846.

Covington, LEONARD, military officer; born in Aquasco, Prince George co., Md., Oct. 30, 1768; was commissioned lieutenant of dragoons March 14, 1792; joined the army under General Wayne, and behaved so gallantly in the war with the Indians in 1794 that his general made honorable mention of his services. He was promoted to captain, and soon afterwards retired from the military service. After occupying a seat in the legislature of Maryland, he was a member of Congress from 1805 to 1807. In the latter year he was appointed lieutenant-colonel of cavalry, and was made a brigadier in 1813, and ordered to the northern frontier. In the battle at Chrysler's Field (Nov. 11, 1813) he was mortally wounded, and died three days afterwards, Nov. 14, 1813.

Covode, JOHN, statesman; born in Westmoreland county, Pa., March 17, 1808; member of Congress, 1855–63, 1869–71; chairman of the committee to investigate charges against President Buchanan in 1860; commissioner to aid in reconstructing the Southern States in 1865, but was recalled by President Johnson; died in Harrisburg, Pa., Jan. 11, 1871.

Cowan's Ford, on the Catawba River, N. C. Lord Cornwallis, in rapid pursuit of the Americans under General Morgan, moved down a few miles towards Cowan's Ford, where Morgan had stationed 300 militia under General Davidson to oppose his crossing. The British forced a crossing, Feb. 1, 1781, and the militia were dispersed, General Davidson being killed.

Cowboys. During the Revolution a band of marauders, consisting mostly of Tory refugees who adhered to the British interests, infested the neutral ground in Westchester county, N. Y., between the American and British lines. In recent years the phrase has been applied to the men employed on the great cattle-ranches of the West and Southwest. Many modern "cowboys" were mustered into the two volunteer cavalry regiments for service in the war with Spain (1898), popularly known as the "Rough Riders."

"Cow Chace," THE. In the summer of 1780 Washington sent General Wayne, with a considerable force, to storm a British block-house at Bull's Ferry, on the Hudson, near Fort Lee, and to drive into the American camp a large number of cattle on Bergen Neck exposed to British foragers, who might go out from Paulus's Hook (now Jersey City). Wayne was repulsed at the block-house, with a loss of sixty-four men, but returned to camp with a large number of cattle driven by his dragoons. This event inspired Major André, Sir Henry Clinton's adjutant-general, to write a satirical poem, which he called *The Cow Chace,* in which Wayne and his fellow-"rebels" were severely ridiculed. It was written in the style of the English ballad of *Chevy Chace,* in three cantos. The following is a copy of the poem; we also give fac-similes of its title from André's autograph, and of the concluding verse of the original:

ELIZABETHTOWN, *Aug.* 1, 1780.

CANTO I.

To drive the kine one summer's morn,
  The tanner took his way,
The calf shall rue that is unborn
  The jumbling of that day.

And Wayne descending steers shall know,
  And tauntingly deride,
And call to mind, in ev'ry low,
  The tanning of his hide.

Yet Bergen cows still ruminate
  Unconscious in the stall,

What mighty means were used to get,
  And lose them after all.

For many heroes bold and brave
  From New Bridge and Tapaan.
And those that drink Passaic's wave,
  And those that eat soupaan.

And sons of distant Delaware,
  And still remoter Shannon,
And Major Lee with horses rare,
  And Proctor with his cannon.

All wondrous proud in arms they came—
  What hero could refuse,
To tread the rugged path to fame,
  Who had a pair of shoes?

At six the host, with sweating buff,
  Arrived at Freedom's Pole,
When Wayne, who thought he'd time enough,
  Thus speechified the whole:

"O ye whom glory doth unite,
  Who Freedom's cause espouse,
Whether the wing that's doom'd to fight,
  Or that to drive the cows;

"Ere yet you tempt your further way,
  Or into action come,
Hear, soldiers, what I have to say,
  And take a pint of rum.

"Intemp'rate valor then will string
  Each nervous arm the better,
So all the land shall IO! sing,
  And read the gen'ral's letter.

"Know that some paltry refugees,
  Whom I've a mind to fight,
Are playing h—l among the trees
  That grow on yonder height.

"Their fort and block-house we will level,
  And deal a horrid slaughter;
We'll drive the scoundrels to the devil,
  And ravish wife and daughter.

"I under cover of th' attack,
  While you are all at blows,
From English Neighb'rhood and Tinack
  Will drive away the cows.

"For well you know the latter is
  The serious operation,
And fighting with the refugees
  Is only demonstration."

His daring words from all the crowd
  Such great applause did gain,
That every man declared aloud
  For serious work with Wayne.

Then from the cask of rum once more
  They took a heady gill,
When one and all they loudly swore
  They'd fight upon the hill.

But here—the Muse has not a strain
  Befitting such great deeds,
Hurra, they cried, hurra for Wayne!
  And, shouting, did their needs.

Canto II.

Near his meridian pomp, the sun
  Had journeyed from the horizon,
When fierce the dusky tribe moved on,
  Of heroes drunk as poison.

The sounds confused of boasting oaths
  Re-echoed through the wood,
Some vow'd to sleep in dead men's clothes,
  And some to swim in blood.

At Irvine's nod, 'twas fine to see
  The left prepared to fight,
The while the drovers, Wayne and Lee,
  Drew off upon the right.

Which Irvine 'twas Fame don't relate,
  Nor can the Muse assist her,
Whether 'twas he that cocks a hat,
  Or he that gives a glister.

For greatly one was signalized
  That fought at Chestnut Hill,
And Canada immortalized
  The vender of the pill.

Yet the attendance upon Proctor
  They both might have to boast of,
For there was business for the doctor,
  And hats to be disposed of.

Let none uncandidly infer
  That Stirling wanted spunk;
The self-made peer had sure been there,
  But that the peer was drunk.

But turn we to the Hudson's banks,
  Where stood the modest train,
With purpose firm, though slender ranks,
  Nor cared a pin for Wayne.

For then the unrelenting hand
  Of rebel fury drove,
And tore from ev'ry genial band
  Of friendship and of love.

And some within a dungeon's gloom,
  By mock tribunals laid,
Had waited long a cruel doom,
  Impending o'er their heads.

Here one bewails a brother's fate,
  There one a sire demands,
Cut off, alas! before their date,
  By ignominious hands.

And silvered grandsires here appeared
  In deep distress serene,
Of reverend manners that declared
  The better days they'd seen.

Oh! cursed rebellion, these are thine,
  Thine are these tales of woe;
Shall at thy dire insatiate shrine
  Blood never cease to flow?

And now the foe began to lead
  His forces to th' attack;
Balls whistling unto balls succeed,
  And make the block-house crack.

No shot could pass, if you will take
  The gen'ral's word for true;
But 'tis a d—ble mistake,
  For ev'ry shot went through.

The firmer as the rebels pressed,
  The loyal heroes stand;
Virtue had nerved each honest breast,
  And Industry each hand.

In* valor's frenzy, Hamilton
  Rode like a soldier big,
And secretary Harrison,
  With pen stuck in his wig.

But, lest chieftain Washington
  Should mourn them in the mumps,**
The fate of Withrington to shun,
  They fought behind the stumps.

But ah! Thaddeus Posset, why
  Should thy poor soul elope?
And why should Titus Hooper die,
  Ah! die—without a rope?

Apostate Murphy, thou to whom
  Fair Shela ne'er was cruel;
In death shalt hear her mourn thy doom,
  Och! would ye die, my jewel?

Thee, Nathan Pumpkin, I lament,
  Of melancholy fate,
The gray goose, stolen as he went,
  In his heart's blood was wet.

Now as the fight was further fought
  And balls began to thicken,
The fray assumed, the gen'rals thought,
  The color of a licking.

Yet undismayed the chiefs command,
  And, to redeem the day,
Cry, "Soldiers, charge!" they hear, they stand,
  They turn and run away.

CANTO III.

Not all delights the bloody spear,
  Or horrid din of battle,
There are, I'm sure, who'd like to hear
  A word about the rattle.

The chief whom we beheld of late,
  Near Schralenberg haranguing,
At Yan Van Poop's unconscious sat
  Of Irvine's hearty banging.

While valiant Lee, with courage wild,
  Most bravely did oppose
The tears of women and of child,
  Who begged he'd leave the cows.

But Wayne, of sympathizing heart,
  Required a relief,
Not all the blessings could impart,
  Of battle or of beef.

For now a prey to female charms,
  His soul took more delight in
A lovely Hamadryad's* arms
  Than cow driving or fighting.

A nymph, the refugees had drove
  Far from her native tree,
Just happen'd to be on the move,
  When up came Wayne and Lee.

She in mad Anthony's fierce eye
  The hero saw portrayed,
And, all in tears, she took him by
  — the bridle of his jade.

Hear, said the nymph, O great commander,
  No human lamentations,
The trees you see them cutting yonder
  Are all my near relations.

And I, forlorn, implore thine aid
  To free the sacred grove:
So shall thy prowess be repaid
  With an immortal's love.

Now some, to prove she was a goddess!
  Said this enchanting fair
Had late retired from the *Bodies,***
  In all the pomp of war.

That drums and merry fifes had played
  To honor her retreat,
And Cunningham himself conveyed
  The lady through the street.

Great Wayne, by soft compassion swayed,
  To no inquiry stoops,
But takes the fair, afflicted maid
  Right into Yan Van Poop's.

So Roman Antony, they say,
  Disgraced th' imperial banner,
And for a gypsy lost a day,
  Like Anthony the tanner.

The Hamadryad had but half
  Received redress from Wayne,
When drums and colors, cow and calf,
  Came down the road amain.

All in a cloud of dust were seen,
  The sheep, the horse, the goat,
The gentle heifer, ass obscene
  The yearling and the shoat.

And pack-horses with fowls came by,
  Befeathered on each side,
Like Pegasus, the horse that I
  And other poets ride.

Sublime upon the stirrups rose
  The mighty Lee behind,
And drove the terror-smitten cows,
  Like chaff before the wind.

But sudden see the woods above
  Pour down another corps,
All helter-skelter in a drove,
  Like that I sung before.

* See Lee's trial.

** A disorder prevalent in the rebel lines.

* A deity of the woods.

** A cant appellation given among the soldiery to the corps that has the honor to guard his majesty's person.

Irvine and terror in the van
  Came flying all abroad,
And cannon, colors, horse, and man
  Ran tumbling to the road.

Still as he fled, 'twas Irvine's cry,
  And his example too,
"Run on, my merry men all—for why?"
  The shot will not go through.*

As when two kennels in the street,
  Swell'd with a recent rain,
In gushing streams together meet,
  And seek the neighboring drain,

So meet these dung-born tribes in one,
  As swift in their career,
And so to New Bridge they ran on—
  But all the cows got clear.

Poor Parson Caldwell, all in wonder,
  Saw the returning train,
And mourned to Wayne the lack of plunder,
  For them to steal again.

For 'twas his right to seize the spoil, and
  To share with each commander,
As he had done at Staten Island
  With frost-bit Alexander.

In his dismay, the frantic priest
  Began to grow prophetic,
You had swore, to see his lab'ring breast,
  He'd taken an emetic.

"I view a future day," said he,
  "Brighter than this day dark is,
And you shall see, what you shall see,
  Ha! ha! one pretty marquis;

"And he shall come to Paulus' Hook,
  And great achievements think on,
And make a bow and take a look,
  Like Satan over Lincoln.

"And all the land around shall glory
  To see the Frenchman caper,
And pretty Susan tell the story,
  In the next Chatham paper."

This solemn prophecy, of course,
  Gave all much consolation,
Except to Wayne, who lost his horse
  Upon the great occasion.

His horse that carried all his prog,
  His military speeches,
His corn-stalk whiskey for his grog—
  Blue stockings and brown breeches.

And now I've clos'd my epic strain,
  I tremble as I show it,
Lest this same warrio-drover, Wayne,
  Should ever catch the poet.

And now I've clos'd my Epic Strain,
I tremble as I shew it,
Lest this same warrio-drover Wayne
Should ever catch the Poet.

Finis

The last canto was published on the day when André was captured at Tarrytown. At the end of the autograph copy was written the following stanza, in a neat hand:

"When the epic strain was sung,
The poet by the neck was hung;
And to his cost he finds too late,
The *dung-born tribe* decides his fate."

Wayne was in command of the troops from whom the guard was drawn that attended André's execution.

Cowdery, JONATHAN, surgeon; born in Sandisfield, Mass., April 22, 1767; appointed an assistant surgeon in the navy, Jan. 1, 1800; was on the frigate *Philadelphia*, which was stranded on the coast of Tripoli, Oct. 31, 1803; and held a prisoner by the Turks for nearly two years. After his return to the United States he published a history of his imprisonment. He died in Norfolk, Va., Nov. 20, 1852.

Cowdrey, ROBERT H., pharmacist; born in Lafayette, Ind., Oct. 1, 1852; grad-

* Five refugees ('tis true) were found
  Stiff on the block-house floor,
But then 'tis thought the shot went round,
  And in at the back-door.

uated at the Pharmaceutical College in Chicago; and for several years was editor of the *Pharmacist and Chemist*. He withdrew from the Republican party in 1876, and was the candidate of the United Labor party for the Presidency of the United States in 1888, receiving 2,808 popular votes.

GOLD MEDAL AWARDED TO MORGAN.

Cowell, Benjamin, historian; born in Wrentham, Mass., in 1781; graduated at Brown University in 1803; settled in Providence, R. I., became chief-justice of the Court of Common Pleas; and was author of *The Spirit of '76*. He died in Providence, R. I., May 6, 1860.

Cowpens, The. This name was derived from the circumstance that, some years before the Revolution, before that section of South Carolina was settled, some persons in Camden (then called Pine-Tree) employed two men to go up to the Thicketty Mountain, and in the grassy intervals among the hills raise cattle. As a compensation, they were allowed the entire use of the cows during the summer, for making butter and cheese, and the steers in tillage. In the fall large numbers of the fatted cattle would be driven down to Camden to be slaughtered for beef on account of the owners. This region, on account of its grass and fine springs, was peculiarly favorable for the rearing and use of cows, and consequently was called "The Cowpens." Subsequently the name of Cowpens was given to a village in Spartanburg county, which became the scene of a spirited battle in the Revolutionary War (1781).

From his camp, eastward of the Pedee, Greene sent Morgan, with the Maryland regiment and Washington's dragoons of Lee's corps, across the Broad River, to operate on the British left and rear. Observing this, Cornwallis left his camp at Winnsborough, and pushed northward between the Broad River and the Catawba, for the purpose of interposing his force between Greene and Morgan. Against the latter he had detached Tarleton with about 1,000 light troops. Aware of Tarleton's approach, Morgan retired behind the Pacolet, intending to defend the ford; but Tarleton crossed 6 miles above, when Morgan made a precipitate retreat. If he could cross the Broad River, he would be safe. On his right was a hilly district, which might afford him protection; but, rather than be overtaken in his flight, he prepared to fight on the ground of his own selection. He chose for that purpose the place known as "The Cowpens," about 30 miles west of King's Mountain. He arranged about 400 of his best men in battle order on a little rising ground. There were the Maryland light infantry, under Lieut.-Col. John Eager Howard, composing the centre, and Virginia riflemen forming the wings. Lieut.-Col. William Washington, with eighty dragoons, were placed out of sight, as a reserve, and about 400 Carolinians and Georgians, under Col. Andrew Pickens, were in the advance, to defend the approaches to the camp. North Carolina and Georgia sharp-shooters acted as skirmishers on each flank. At eight o'clock on the morning of Jan. 17, Tarleton, with 1,100 troops, foot and horse, with two pieces of cannon, rushed upon the republicans with loud shouts. A furious battle ensued. In a skilful movement, in the form of a feigned retreat, Morgan turned so suddenly upon his pursuers, who believed the victory was secured to them, that they wavered. Seeing this, Howard charged the British lines with bayonets, broke their ranks, and sent them flying in confusion. At that moment Washington's cavalry broke from their concealment, and made a successful charge upon Tarleton's horsemen. The British were completely routed, and were pursued about 20 miles. The Americans lost seventy-two killed and wounded. The British lost over 300 killed and wounded, and nearly 500 made prisoners. The spoils were two cannon, 800 muskets, horses, and two standards. The cannon had been taken from the British at Saratoga, and retaken from Gates at Camden. The Congress gave Morgan the thanks of the nation and a gold medal, and to Howard and Washington each a silver medal.

Cox, JACOB DOLSON, military officer; born in Montreal, Canada, Oct. 27, 1828. His mother was a lineal descendant of Elder William Brewster, of the *Mayflower*. He was admitted to the bar in 1852, and practised in Warren, O., until elected State Senator, in 1859. He was appointed brigadier-general of State militia, and commanded a camp of instruction, in April, 1861, and in May was made brigadier-general of volunteers, doing good service in western Virginia. In August, 1862, he was assigned to the Army of Virginia, under General Pope, and in the fall was ordered to the district of the Kanawha. After the death of Reno, at South Mountain, he commanded the 9th Army Corps. He was in command of the district of Ohio in 1863; served in the Atlanta campaign in 1864; and was promoted to major-general in December of that year. He served in Sherman's army early in 1865; was governor of Ohio in 1866–68; Secretary of the Interior under President Grant, in 1869–70; and Representative in Congress in 1877–79. He published *Atlanta; The March to the Sea; Franklin and Nashville; The Second Battle of Bull Run*, etc. He died in Magnolia, Mass., Aug. 4, 1900.

Cox, SAMUEL SULLIVAN, statesman; born in Zanesville, O., Sept. 30, 1824; graduated at Brown University in 1846; became editor of the *Statesman* of Columbus, O., in 1853; was a Democratic Representative in Congress from Ohio in 1857–65; and from New York in 1868–82. During his service in Congress he secured an increase of salary for the letter-carriers throughout the country, and also an annual vacation without loss of pay. In 1885–86 he was United States minister to Turkey, and on his return was again elected to Congress. He was a pleasing speaker, writer, and lecturer. Chief among his many publications are *Puritanism in Politics; Eight Years in Congress; Free Land and Free Trade; Three Decades of Federal Legislation;* and *The Diplomat in Turkey.* He died in New York City, Sept. 10, 1889.

Coxe, TENCH, political economist; born in Philadelphia, May 22, 1755. He was a grandson of Dr. Daniel Coxe, Queen Anne's physician; was an industrious writer on political economy, and especially upon the subjects of the manufacturing interests of the United States. From 1787 until his death, July 17, 1824, there never was an important movement in favor of the introduction and promotion of manufactures in which his name did not appear prominent. In 1794 he published a large volume on the subject of cotton culture and cognate topics. At that time he was commissioner of the revenue at Philadelphia. In 1806 he published an essay on the naval power and the encouragement of manufactures; and the following year he issued a memoir on the cultivation and manufacture of cotton.

Coxey, JACOB J., political agitator; born in Snyder county, Pa., April 16, 1854. The spring of 1894 was marked by one of the most unique popular uprisings ever witnessed in any country. Coxey, then living in Massillon, O., organized what he called "The Army of the Commonwealth," to be composed of men out of work, for a march to Washington in order to influence Congress to take some action for the benefit of trade in the country. Coxey appointed March 10 as the day the army would start from Massillon, and early in the year a great number of small companies started from the South and West to join him. For a time it seemed as if the movement would be an impressive one. Fully 1,500 men, composing the Western detachment, under Colonel Fry, reached the Mississippi. This detachment was constantly growing in numbers, and was well received by the people through the States as it progressed towards Massillon to join Coxey. But at this time three weeks of constant rain interfered, the army was unable to progress, and soon scattered, as did many smaller detachments. Thus it was that Coxey was obliged to make his start with but 400 men, and about the same number, despite another rainy spell, arrived in Washington on May 2. Coxey attempted to make a speech from the steps of the Capitol, was arrested for violating a local ordinance, and obliged to spend a month in jail. The movement ended in a perfect farce, although at one time it was estimated that 20,000 men were marching to join the army. Coxey had hoped to make Congress pass a law allowing each State to issue legal-tender certificates to citizens, whenever the citizens could give personal or real property as security. In 1895, Coxey was the unsuccessful Populist candidate for governor of Ohio, and received 52,675 votes.

Cozzens, FREDERICK SWARTWOUT, author; born in New York City, March 5, 1818; entered mercantile life; and contributed to the *Knickerbocker Magazine* a series of humorous articles called the *Sparrowgrass Papers*. His other publications include *Acadia: a Sojourn among the Blue-noses; True History of New Plymouth; Memorial of Col. Peter A. Porter;* and *Memorial of Fitz-Greene Halleck*. He died in Brooklyn, N. Y., Dec. 23, 1869.

"Cradle of American Liberty," a name given to Faneuil Hall, in Boston, because it was the usual meeting-place of the patriots during the long contest with royal power, before the kindling of the Revolutionary War. It was erected in 1742, at the sole expense of Peter Faneuil,

FANEUIL HALL (From an old English print).

of Boston, who generously gave it to the town. The lower story was used for a market, and in the upper story was an elegant and spacious hall, with convenient rooms for public use. It was burned in 1761, when the town immediately rebuilt it. The engraving shows it as it was during the Revolution. The hall is about 80 feet square, and contains some fine paintings of distinguished men. The original vane, in the form of a grasshopper, was copied from that of the Royal Exchange of London. In 1805 another story was added to the original building.

THE APOLLO ROOM IN THE RALEIGH TAVERN.

The name "Cradle of Liberty" was also given to the "Apollo Room," a large apartment in the Raleigh Tavern at Williamsburg, Va., where the members of the House of Burgesses met after its dissolution by Governor Lord Dunmore in 1774. There they adopted non-importation resolutions, appointed a fast-day, and chose delegates to the First Continental Congress, which assembled at Philadelphia in September.

Cradock, MATTHEW, English merchant; chosen the first governor of the Massachusetts Company, who founded the Massachusetts Bay colony. He never came to America, but was a munificent supporter of the colony during its early struggles. He was a member of the celebrated Long Parliament, and died in London, May 27, 1641.

Craig, HENRY KNOX, military officer; born in Pittsburg, Pa., March 7, 1791; entered the army as a lieutenant of artillery in 1812; took part in the occupation of Fort George, and the assault at Stony Creek, Canada; was chief of ordnance of the Army of Occupation in Mexico in 1847, and distinguished himself in the battles of Palo Alto, Resaca de la Palma, and Monterey; was chief of the ordnance bureau at Washington in 1851–61; and was retired in 1863. He died in Washington, D. C., Dec. 7, 1868.

Craig, SIR JAMES HENRY, military officer; born in Gibraltar in 1749; entered the British army as ensign in 1763, was aide-de-camp to General Boyd at Gibraltar in 1770, and came to America in 1774. He remained in service here from the battle of Bunker Hill until the evacuation of Charleston, in 1781, when he held the rank of lieutenant-colonel. He was made a major-general in 1794, lieutenant-general in 1801, and governor-general and commander-in-chief of Canada in 1807. Totally unfit for civil rule, he was a petty oppressor as governor; his administration was short, and he returned to England in 1811, where he died Jan. 12, 1812.

Craig, LEWIS S., military officer; born in Virginia; entered the army as a lieutenant of dragoons in 1837; became assistant commissary of subsistence in 1840; and won the brevets of major and lieutenant-colonel by bravery at Monterey, Contreras, and Churubusco, being wounded in the latter battle. He was killed by some deserters while on duty near New River, Cal., June 6, 1852.

Craighill, WILLIAM PRICE, military engineer; born in Charlestown, Va., July 1, 1833; graduated at the United States Military Academy in 1853; superintended the building of Fort Sumter in 1854–55, and of Fort Delaware in 1858; planned and erected the defences of Pittsburg, Pa., in 1863; and subsequently was engaged on the defences of New York and Baltimore, and on the improvement of several rivers. He was promoted brigadier-general and chief of engineers May 10, 1895; retired Feb. 1, 1897. He published *Army Officers' Pocket Companion;* translated Dufour's *Cours de Tactiques.* He died in Charlestown, W. Va., Jan. 18, 1909.

Craik, JAMES, physician; born in Scotland, in 1731; came to America in early life, and practised his profession in Fairfax county, Va. He was the intimate friend and family physician of Washington; was with him in his expedition against the French in 1754, and in Braddock's campaign in 1755. In 1775 he was placed in the medical department of the Continental army, and rose to the first rank. He unearthed many of tne secrets of the Conway cabal and did much to defeat the conspiracy. He was director of the army hospital at Yorktown in the siege of that place, in 1781, and after the Revolution settled near Mount Vernon, where he was the principal attendant of Washington in his last illness. He died in Fairfax county, Va., Feb. 6, 1814.

Cramp, CHARLES HENRY, ship-builder; born in Philadelphia, Pa., May 9, 1828; son of William Cramp; received a public school education; learned the ship-building trade with his father; became a partner in the firm of William Cramp & Son, and subsequently president of William Cramp & Son Ship and Engine Building Company, the largest ship-building concern in the United States. From the Cramp yards have been turned out many of the best-known ships of the American naval and mercantile services. He died in Philadelphia, June 6, 1913.

Crampton's Gap, BATTLE AT. See SOUTH MOUNTAIN, BATTLES OF.

Cranch, WILLIAM, jurist; born in Weymouth, Mass., July 17, 1769; graduated at Harvard in 1789; admitted to the bar in 1790; appointed judge of the circuit court of the District of Columbia in 1801; chief-justice of the same court in 1805, which office he held until his death, Sept. 1, 1855.

Crane, STEPHEN, author; born in Newark, N. J., Nov. 1, 1871; studied at Lafayette College. In 1897 was the correspondent for the New York *Journal* in the Græco-Turkish War. He died June 5, 1900.

Crane, WINTHROP MURRAY, legislator; born in Dalton, Mass., April 23, 1853; acquired a public school and academic education; became a paper manufacturer; was lieutenant-governor of Massachusetts in 1897–99, and governor in 1900–02; and was appointed United States Senator to succeed the late George F. Hoar, Oct. 12, 1904.

Craney Island, OPERATIONS AT. On June 1, 1813, Admiral Sir J. Borlase Warren entered the Chesapeake with a considerable reinforcement for the marauding squadron of SIR GEORGE COCKBURN (*q. v.*), bearing a large number of land troops and marines. There were twenty ships of the line and frigates and several smaller British war-vessels within the capes of Virginia. The cities of Baltimore, Annapolis, and Norfolk were equally menaced. Norfolk was the first point of attack. For its defence on the waters were the frigate *Constellation*, thirty-eight guns, and a flotilla of gunboats; on the land were Forts Norfolk and Nelson (one on each side of the Elizabeth River), and Forts Tar and Barbour, and the fortifications on Craney Island, 5 miles below the city. Towards midnight of June 19 Captain Tarbell, by order of Commodore Cassin, commanding the station, went down the Elizabeth River with fifteen gunboats, to attempt the capture of the frigate *Junon*, thirty-eight guns, Captain Sanders, which lay about 3 miles from the rest of the British fleet. Fifteen sharp-shooters from Craney Island were added to the crews of the boats. At half-past three in the morning the flotilla approached the *Junon*, and, under cover of the darkness and a thick

THE BLOCK-HOUSE ON CRANEY ISLAND, 1813.

fog, the American vessels approached her to within easy range without being discovered. She was taken by surprise. After a conflict of half an hour, and when victory seemed within the grasp of the Americans, a wind sprung up from the northeast, and two vessels lying becalmed below came to the *Junon's* assistance, and by a severe cannonade repulsed them. In this affair the Americans lost one man killed and two slightly wounded.

This attack brought matters to a crisis. The firing had been distinctly heard by the fleet, and with the next tide, on a warm Sunday morning in June, fourteen of the British vessels entered Hampton Roads, and took position at the mouth of the Nansemond River. They bore land troops, under General Sir Sidney Beckwith. The whole British force, including the sailors, was about 5,000 men. Governor Barbour, of Virginia, had assembled several thousand militia, in anticipation of invasion. Craney Island, then in shape like a painter's palette, was separated from the main by a shallow strait, fordable at low tide, and contained about 30 acres of land. On the side commanding the ship-channel were intrenchments armed with 18 and 24 pounder cannon. A successful defence of this island would save Norfolk and the navy-yard there, and to that end efforts were made. Gen. Robert B. Taylor was the commanding officer of the district. The whole available force of the island, when the British entered Hampton Roads were two companies of artillery, under the general command of Maj. James Faulkner; Captain Robertson's company of riflemen; and 416 militia infantry of the line, commanded by Lieut.-Col. Henry Beatty. If attacked and overpowered, these troops had no means of escape. These were reinforced by thirty regulars under Capt. Richard Pollard, and thirty volunteers under Lieutenant-Colonel Johnson, and were joined by about 150 seamen under Lieuts. B. J. Neale, W. B. Shubrick, and J. Sanders, and fifty marines under Lieutenant Breckinridge. The whole force on Craney Island on June 2 numbered 737 men.

At midnight the camp was alarmed by the crack of a sentinel's rifle. It was a false alarm; but before it was fairly daylight a trooper came dashing across the fordable strait with the startling information that the British were landing in force on the main, only about 2 miles distant. The drum beat the long-roll, and Major Faulkner ordered his guns to be transferred so as to command the strait. At the same time, fifty large barges, filled with 1,500 sailors and marines, were seen approaching from the British ships. They were led by Admiral Warren's beautiful barge *Centipede* (so called because of her numerous oars), and made for the narrow strait between Craney Island and the main. Faulkner had his artillery in position, and when the invaders were within proper distance his great guns were opened upon them with terrible effect. The British were repulsed, and hastened back to their ships. Warren's barge, which had a 3-pounder swivel-gun at the bow, with four others, was sunk in the shallow water, when some American seamen, under the direction of Lieutenant Tattnall, waded out, secured the vessels, and dragged them ashore, securing many prisoners. The British loss, in killed, wounded, and missing, was 144; the Americans lost none. The invaders now abandoned all hope of seizing Norfolk, the *Constellation*, and the navy-yard, and never attempted it afterwards.

Cranfill, JAMES BRITTON, Prohibitionist; born in Parker county, Tex., in 1857; was brought up on a farm; became a physician; and subsequently publisher of the *Advance* in Gatesville, Tex., a paper that became widely noted as a Prohibition organ. In 1886 he called the first Prohibition convention of Texas; afterwards became chairman of the State Prohibition Committee and a member of the National Prohibition Committee. In 1892 he was the candidate of his party for the Vice-Presidency.

Craven, JOHN JOSEPH, physician; born in Newark, N. J., in September, 1822; superintended the erection of the first telegraph line between New York and Philadelphia, using many original devices, in 1846; was the first to insulate telegraph wires with gutta-percha, to perfect a submarine cable, and to use glass on telegraph poles to prevent the grounding of the wires. In 1861 he was appointed surgeon of the 1st New Jersey Volunteers; soon afterwards became brigade surgeon;

was appointed medical director of the Department of the South, and in January, 1865, was assigned to duty at Fort Monroe, where he had full charge of Jefferson Davis during his imprisonment. After the war he published *The Prison Life of Jefferson Davis*. He died on Long Island, N. Y., Feb. 14, 1893.

Craven, THOMAS TINGLEY, naval officer; born in Washington, D. C., Dec. 30, 1808; entered the United States navy as midshipman in 1822, and was made captain June 7, 1861. A year later he became commodore. He materially assisted in the reduction of the forts on the Mississippi below New Orleans (May, 1862) and the destruction of the Confederate flotilla there. He had been lieutenant-commander of the flag-ship *Vincennes* in Wilkes's exploring expedition in 1838–42, and was instructor of the United States Naval Academy at Annapolis in 1851–55. In 1866 (Oct. 10) he was made a rear-admiral; in 1868–69 was in command of the North Pacific squadron; and in 1869 was retired. He died in Boston, Aug. 23, 1887.

Craven, TUNIS AUGUSTUS MACDONOUGH, naval officer; born in Portsmouth, N. H., Jan. 11, 1813; entered the United States navy as midshipman in February, 1829. He was commissioned lieutenant in 1841, and made commander in 1861. In command of the iron-clad *Tecumseh*, he perished when she was blown up by a torpedo in Mobile Bay, Aug. 5, 1864, he then holding the rank of commodore.

Crawford, GEORGE WASHINGTON, statesman; born in Columbia county, Ga., Dec. 22, 1798; graduated at Princeton in 1820; appointed attorney-general of Georgia in 1827; elected to the State legislature in 1837, and to Congress in 1843. The same year he was elected governor of Georgia, and re-elected in 1845. President Taylor appointed him Secretary of War in 1849. He died June 22, 1872.

Crawford, SAMUEL WYLIE, military officer; born in Franklin county, Pa., Nov. 8, 1829; graduated at the University of Pennsylvania in 1847; studied medicine, and in 1851 was made assistant surgeon in the United States army. He was in Texas and New Mexico on duty, and in 1856 went to Mexico, where he pursued scientific researches. Dr. Crawford was surgeon of the garrison of Fort Sumter during its siege in 1861, and performed valuable military service there.

SAMUEL WYLIE CRAWFORD.

In May he was made major of infantry and inspector-general in eastern Virginia. With Banks, he bore a conspicuous part in the Shenandoah Valley and in the battle of Cedar Mountain as brigadier-general. At the battle of Antietam he commanded the division of Mansfield after that general's death. He was brevetted colonel in the Unites States army for his conduct at Gettysburg. In Grant's campaign (1864–65) against Richmond, General Crawford bore a conspicuous part from the Wilderness to Appomattox Court-house. He was retired in 1873 with the rank of brigadier-general. He died in Philadelphia, Nov. 3, 1892.

Crawford, THOMAS, sculptor, born in New York, March 22, 1814. Manifesting at an early age a talent and taste for art, he went to Italy and profited by the instruction of Thorwaldsen at Rome. There he established a studio, soon rose to eminence, and had abundant employment. His works, of superior character, are quite numerous. Those widest known are the bronze equestrian statue of Washington for the monument at Richmond, ordered by the State of Virginia; the colossal bronze statue of the *Genius of America* that surmounts the dome of the Capitol at Washington; and the historical designs for the bronze doors in the new Capitol. He was exceedingly industrious, and worked with great facility. During less than twenty-five years of artistic labor he finished more than sixty works, some of them colossal, and left about fifty sketches in plaster, besides designs of various kinds. Two of the finest of his works in marble are *The Last of His Race* (colossal), and *The Peri*, both in the New York Historical Society. He died in London, Oct. 10, 1857.

Crawford, William, military officer; born in Berkeley county, Va., in 1732; was early engaged in surveying with Washington, and served with him in Braddock's expedition against Fort Duquesne. He also served during the Pontiac Indian war, and after the opening of the Revolutionary War he became colonel of the 5th Virginia Regiment. Throughout the war he was intimately associated with Washington. In May, 1782, although he had resigned from the army, he accepted at the request of Washington the command of the expedition against the Wyandotte and Delaware Indians on the banks of the Muskingum River. His force became surrounded by Indians, and after it had cut its way out his men became separated. Colonel Crawford was captured and, after being horribly tortured, was burned to death by the Indians, June 11, 1782.

Crawford, William Harris, statesman; born in Amherst county, Va., Feb. 24, 1772; taught school several years and became a lawyer, beginning practice in Lexington, Ga., in 1799. He compiled the first digest of the laws of Georgia, published in 1802; was a member of his State legislature from 1803 to 1807; was United States Senator from 1807 to 1813, in which body he was regarded as its ablest member. In 1813 he was sent as United States minister to France, and on his return (1815) was appointed Secretary of War; but in October, 1816, he was transferred to the Treasury Department, which post he held until 1825, when he was defeated as Democratic candidate for the Presidency, having been nominated the previous year by a congressional caucus. He had four other candidates to oppose—Adams, Calhoun, Jackson, and Clay. At about that time his health failed, and he never fully recovered it. He became a circuit judge in Georgia, and warmly opposed nullification. He died near Elberton, Ga., Sept. 18, 1834. See A. B. Plot.

Crazy Horse, chief of the Ogallalla Sioux and brother-in-law of Red Cloud; born about 1842. He was a leader of a large band of hostile Indians that for several years made much trouble for the national government in the Northwest Territories. The murder of a brother in 1865 induced him to leave Fort Laramie, Wyo., and gather a force to war upon the whites. In 1876, he united this force with that of Sitting Bull, and these two chiefs surprised the command under General Custer on the Little Big Horn River, June 25, 1876, and massacred almost every member of it. As soon as the fate of Custer and his comrades became known General Terry started in pursuit of the Indians, and followed them into the Black Hills region, but the wily leader escaped capture. In the spring of 1877 a larger expedition was organized under command of General Crook, which surprised Crazy Horse's force at the Red Cloud Agency, and forced him to surrender with about 900 of his men.

Credit, Bills of. See Bills of Credit.

Crĕdit Mobilier, "credit on movable personal property," a name given to a great joint-stock company in France in 1852, with a capital of $12,000,000, which was sanctioned by the government. Its object was to carry on a general loan and contract business. In 1859 a corporation for this purpose was chartered in Pennsylvania. It was organized in 1863, with a capital of $2,500,000. In 1867 its charter was purchased by a company formed for the construction of the Union Pacific Railroad. The stock was increased to $3,750,000, and soon rose in value to a very great extent, paying enormous dividends. In 1872 it was charged that a number of members of both Houses of Congress were privately owners of the stock. As legislation concerning the matter might be required, and as grants of land had been made to the railroad company, Congress ordered an investigation. The Senate committee reported the innocence of several who had been accused. The expulsion of one member was recommended, but no further action was taken. In the House a resolution censuring two members was adopted. On the whole, the charges, though not without some basis, had been applied so promiscuously as to involve some men who were absolutely free from offence. See AMES, OAKES.

Creedmoor, a former famous rifle-range belonging to the State of New York, located at Queen's Station, on the Long Island Railroad, where the militia of the State were required to practise. The range covered about eighty-five acres and had thirty targets which could be used at any distance from fifty to 1,200 yards. On its abandonment the militia were given the privileges of the New Jersey State Range at Sea Girt, where they still practise when the New Jersey militiamen are not using it.

Creek Indians, members of a noted confederacy whose domain extended from the Atlantic westward to the highlands, including a greater portion of the States of Alabama and Georgia and the whole of Florida. It was with the people of this confederacy that Oglethorpe held his first interview before building on the site of Savannah. Those remaining in Florida became the Seminoles of a later period. De Soto penetrated their country as early as 1540, and twenty years later De Luna formed an alliance with the tribe of the Coosas. When the Carolinas and Louisiana began to be settled by the English, Spaniards, and French, they all courted the Creek nation. The English won the Lower Creeks, the French the Upper Creeks, while the Spaniards, through their presents, gained an influence over a portion of them. In 1710 some of these (the Cowetas) made war on the Carolinas, and were petted by the Spaniards at St. Augustine, but in 1718 they joined the French, who built a fort at Mobile. In 1732 eight Creek tribes made a treaty with Oglethorpe at Savannah; and in 1739 he made a treaty with the Cowetas, and they joined him in his expedition against St. Augustine.

When the French power in North America was overthrown, the entire Creek nation became subject to English influence. At that time they had fifty towns, and numbered nearly 6,000 warriors. They were the allies of the British during the American Revolution. Many Tories fled to the Creek towns from the Carolinas and Georgia at the close of the war, and excited the Indians to ravage the frontiers of those States. A peace was concluded with the Creeks by Washington in 1790; yet some of them joined the Cherokees in incursions into Tennessee in 1792. Another treaty was made in 1796, and in 1802 they began to cede lands in the United States. But when the War of 1812 broke out they joined their old friends, the English; and by an awful massacre at Fort Mims, in August, 1813, they aroused the Western people to vengeance. Troops led by General Jackson and others entered the Creek country; and in 1813 they ravaged the finest portion of it, destroyed the towns, slew or captured 2,000 Creek warriors, thoroughly subdued them, and, in fact, destroyed the nation. Their last stand against the United States troops was made at Horseshoe Bend in March, 1814. Some of them had already settled in Louisiana, and finally in Texas, where they remained until 1872, when

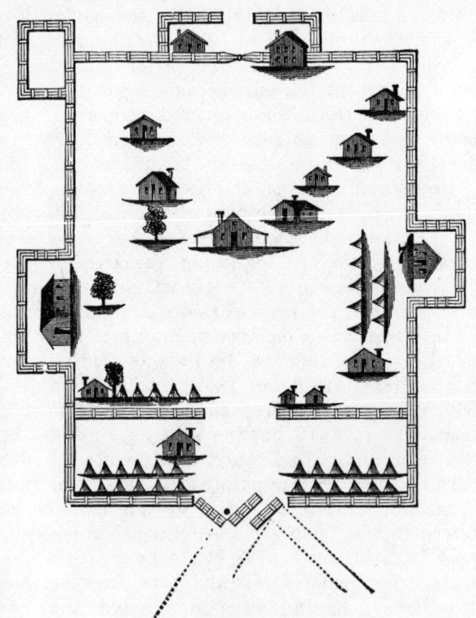

FORT MIMS (From an old print).

the government took steps to reunite the nation in the Indian Territory. They had ceded all their lands east of the Mississippi. With those who had removed there was trouble at times. Some favored removal west of the Mississippi; others opposed it. In 1825 they put one of their chiefs (William McIntosh) to death for signing a treaty for the cession of lands. In 1836 some of the Creeks joined their kindred, the Seminoles, in Florida in attacks upon the white people, and others joined the United States troops against them (see SEMINOLE WAR). They were finally nearly all removed beyond the Mississippi, where they numbered about 25,000 in 1876. Unsuccessful attempts to Christianize them were made. They refused missions and schools for a long time. Their nation declined, and in 1857 numbered less than 15,000. During the Civil War the tribe was divided in sentiment, 6,000 of them joining the Confederates. Their alliance with the Confederates was disastrous to their nation. In 1866 they ceded 3,000,000 acres of their domain in the Indian Territory to the United States for 30 cents an acre. They are now peaceable and order-loving. In 1904 the Creeks by blood, living in the Creek Nation, then in Indian Territory, numbered 9,905, and Creek freedmen, 5,473.

A CHIEF ADDRESSING THE CREEK INDIANS.

The men of the Creek Confederacy were well-proportioned, active, and graceful; the women were smaller, exquisitely formed, and some of them were very beautiful. In summer both sexes went without clothing, excepting a drapery of Spanish moss that was fastened at the waist and fell to the thighs. The principal people painted their faces and bodies in fanciful colors, and fops sometimes appeared in beautiful mantles of feathers or deer-skins, and on their heads were lofty plumes of the eagle and the flamingo. The houses of the chiefs stood upon mounds, sometimes in the form of a great pavilion, and the inside of their winter dwellings were daubed with clay. Hunting, fishing, and cultivating their fertile lands were their employment, for they seldom made aggressive war. They were skilful artisans in making arms, houses, barges, canoes, and various ornaments. They made pottery for kitchen service, and some of it was very ornamental. Fortifications were constructed with moats, and walled towns and grand and beautiful temples abounded. They made mats of split cane, with which they covered their houses and upon which they sat. These resembled the rush carpeting of the Moors. In their temples, dedicated to the worship of the sun, were votive offerings of pearls and rich furs. They regarded the sun as the superior deity, and in all their invocations they appealed to it as to God. To it they made sacrifices of grain and animals. The chief, while he was alive, was held in the greatest veneration as priest and king. As a symbol of devotion to him of the entire strength of the nation, the sacrifice of the first-born male child was required, while the young mother was compelled to witness the slaughter of her child. Their marriages were attended with great displays of ornaments and flowers, and at the setting of the sun the bride and groom and their friends prostrated themselves before that luminary and implored his blessing. Like the Iroquois, the civil power in their government was widely distributed; and, like the Iroquois, the Creeks were an exception, in their approach to civilization, to all the Indian tribes of North America. Such were the Creek (or Muscogee) Indians when first seen by Europeans.

Creek War. See CREEK INDIANS.

Creighton, JOHNSTON BLAKELEY, naval officer; born in Rhode Island, Nov. 12, 1822; entered the navy in 1838; and during the Civil War served on the *Ottawa*, the *Mahaska*, and the *Mingo*, all of the South Atlantic blockading squadron; and took part in the bombardment of Forts Wagner and Gregg. He was retired as rear-admiral in 1883, and died in Morristown, N. J., Nov. 13, of that year.

Creighton, JOHN ORDE, naval officer; born in New York City about 1785; entered the navy in 1800; served with Preble in the expedition to Tripoli; was on the *Chesapeake* when she was attacked by the *Leopard* in 1807; was first lieutenant on the *President* during her fight with the *Little Belt* in 1811; and commanded the *Rattlesnake* in 1813. He was promoted captain in 1816; commanded the Brazilian squadron in 1829–30; and died in Sing Sing, N. Y., Oct. 13, 1838.

Crele, JOSEPH, centenarian; born in Detroit, Mich., in 1725. It is said that the date of his birth is established by the record of baptisms in the French Roman Catholic Church at Detroit. In 1755 he married his first wife, and was twice married afterwards. He bore arms against Braddock at the time of his defeat, and was a letter-carrier on the frontier several years before the Revolution. At the time of his death at Caledonia, Wis., Jan. 27, 1866, he lived with a daughter by his third wife, born when he was sixty-nine years of age. Towards the close of his life he would sometimes say, despondingly, "I fear Death has forgotten me."

Cremation, the disposition of the dead by burning. The practice has come down from great antiquity, having prevailed in eastern Asia and western Europe, and also among many North and South American Indian tribes. Among the Romans it was practised during the last years of the republic, and under the empire till near the end of the fourth century, when it was abandoned. It was also at one time the custom of the Chinese. Marco Polo, who travelled in China during the latter part of the thirteenth century, saw a crematory in every town he visited. The custom has long been abolished in China, although it is universal in Japan, where it was introduced by the Buddhists. Even in northern Europe cremation prevailed, according to the statement of Cæsar, who relates that the Gauls burned their dead, and placed the ashes in urns which were then buried in mounds. The ancient method was to cremate the corpse upon a funeral pyre, upon which oil, spices, and incense, and, frequently, food and clothing were placed. The practice was never allowed among the early Christians, who followed the old Hebrew method of entombing the dead, a method which was hallowed by the burial of their Lord. The more Christianity spread, the more was cremation condemned, chiefly because it seemed inconsistent with the belief of the resurrection of the dead. At present the custom prevails in India,

Japan, and other eastern countries. The practice is of comparatively recent origin in England, Germany, Italy and the United States. In the United States crematories are in operation in Washington, Lancaster, Philadelphia, Buffalo, Fresh Pond (L. I.), Detroit, St. Louis, Los Angeles, and other cities.

Creole, CASE OF THE. See GIDDINGS, JOSHUA REED.

Creole State, a name sometimes given to Louisiana, in which a large portion of the inhabitants are descendants of the French and Spanish settlers.

Crerar, JOHN, philanthropist; born in New York City about 1828; entered mercantile life and accumulated a fortune; removed to Chicago in 1862; bestowed large sums upon charitable undertakings, and bequeathed $2,500,000 to found the John Crerar Public Library, from which sensational novels and skeptical works should be excluded. He died in Chicago, Oct. 19, 1889.

Cresap, MICHAEL, trader; born in Allegheny county, Md., June 29, 1742; removed to Ohio in 1774; organized a company of pioneers for protection against the Indians, and on April 26 declared war and defeated a band of Indians on the river. About the same time another party of whites massacred the family of the famous chief Logan. Cresap was accused by Logan with having led the party which killed his family, but it was subsequently proved that Cresap was in Maryland at the time of the occurrence. He joined the army under Washington, but ill-health forced him soon afterwards to retire from active service. He died in New York City, Oct. 18, 1775. See LOGAN.

Crescent City, a name given to New Orleans. Its older portion was built around a bend of the Mississippi of crescent form.

Cresson, ELLIOTT, philanthropist; born in Philadelphia, Pa., March 2, 1796; was a member of the Society of Friends; was actively engaged in establishing the first colony of liberated slaves at Bassa Cove. Subsequently he was president of the AMERICAN COLONIZATION SOCIETY (*q. v.*). He died in Philadelphia, Pa., Feb. 20, 1854, and bequeathed property valued at over $150,000 to charitable purposes.

Creswell, JOHN ANGELL JAMES, legislator; born in Port Deposit, Md., Nov. 18, 1828; graduated at Dickinson College in 1848; admitted to the bar in 1850; elected to Congress, 1863; and to the United States Senate to fill a vacancy in 1864. He was a delegate to the Baltimore Convention in 1864; the Loyalists' Convention in Philadelphia in 1866; the Border States Convention in Baltimore in 1867; and the National Republican Convention in 1868. In 1869-74 he was Postmaster-General of the United States, and was one of the counsel for the United States before the Court of Alabama Claims Commissioners. He died in Elkton, Md., Dec. 23, 1891.

Crèvecoeur, HECTOR ST. JOHN DE; born in France in 1731; emigrated to America in 1754; arrested as a spy in New York City in 1780 as he was about to sail for England; French consul to New York in 1783. He wrote *Letters of an American Farmer; Travels in Pennsylvania and New York,* etc. He died near Paris in 1813.

Crime against Kansas, THE. See KANSAS.

Crime of 1873. See BRYAN, WILLIAM JENNINGS.

Crisis, COMMERCIAL AND MONETARY, a critical moment when a great number of merchants and traders either have, or think they shall have, difficulty in meeting their engagements. The great crises in the United States occurred in 1816, 1825, 1837, 1857, 1873, 1893 and 1907. See PANICS. Several seem to have been largely due to unwise financial legislation.

"**Crisis,** THE," a series of fourteen patriotic papers by THOMAS PAINE (*q. v.*) during the Revolution, extending from 1775 to 1783. The second paper, written just after Congress left Philadelphia, fearing its capture by the British, to meet at Baltimore, is dated Dec. 19, 1776. It begins with the well-known words, "These are the times that try men's souls." Most, if not all, were published in Philadelphia.

Crisp, CHARLES FREDERICK, jurist; born in Sheffield, England, Jan. 9, 1845, of American parents travelling abroad; was brought to the United States when a few months old, the family settling in Georgia. He served in the Confederate army, and, settling to the practice of law, became a judge of the Superior Court of Georgia. In 1883 he entered the national House of Representatives as a Democrat, and there gained a high reputation as an able, judicial, and conservative leader on his side of the House. In 1891, and again in 1893, he was elected speaker of the House, succeeding Thomas B. Reed, and being succeeded by him. He died in Atlanta, Ga., Oct. 23, 1896.

Crittenden, George Bibb, military officer; born in Russellville, Ky., March 20, 1812; graduated at West Point in 1832. He resigned the next year, served in the war against Mexico (1846–48) under General Scott, joined the Confederates, and became a major-general and, with Zollicoffer, was defeated in the battle at Mill Spring, in January, 1862. He was a son of John J. Crittenden. He died in Danville, Ky., Nov. 27, 1880.

Crittenden, John Jordan, statesman; born in Woodford county, Ky., Sept. 10, 1787; was aide-de-camp to Governor Shelby at the battle of the Thames; became a lawyer; entered the Kentucky legislature in 1816, and was speaker several years, and was first a member of the United States Senate in 1817–19. From 1835 to 1841 he was again in the Senate, when President Harrison called him to his cabinet as Attorney-General. He was again in the Senate from 1842 to 1848, when he was elected governor of his State, which post he held when President Fillmore appointed him Attorney-General in 1850. Mr. Crittenden was one of the most useful and trustworthy of the members of the national legislature, and was regarded as the "patriarch of the Senate."

In the session of 1860–61 he introduced the "Crittenden Compromise," which substantially proposed: 1. To re-establish the line fixed in the Missouri Compromise (*q. v.*) as the boundary-line between free and slave territory; that Congress should by statute law protect slave property from interference by all the departments of the Territorial governments during their continuance as such; that such Territories should be admitted as States with or without slavery, as the State constitutions should determine. 2. That Congress should not abolish slavery at any place within the limits of any slave State, or wherein slavery might thereafter be established. 3. That Congress should not abolish slavery in the District of Columbia so long as it should exist in the adjoining States of Maryland and Virginia, without the consent of the inhabitants thereof, nor without just compensation made to the owners of slaves who should not consent to the abolishment; that Congress should not prevent government officers sojourning in the District on business bringing their slaves with them, and taking them with them when they should depart. 4. That Congress should have no power to prohibit or hinder the transportation of slaves from one State to another, or into Territories where slavery should be allowed. 5. That the national government should pay to the owner of a fugitive slave, who might be rescued from the officers of the law, upon attempting to take him back to bondage, the full value of such "property" so lost; and that the amount should be refunded by the county in which the rescue might occur, that municipality having the power to sue for and recover the amount from the individual actors in the offence. 6. That no future amendments to the Constitution should be made that might have an effect on the previous amendments, or on any sections of the Constitution on the subject already existing; nor should any amendment be made that should give to the Congress the right to

JOHN JORDAN CRITTENDEN.

abolish or interfere with slavery in any of the States where it existed by law, or might hereafter be allowed.

In addition to these amendments Senator Crittenden offered four joint resolutions, declaring substantially as follows: 1. That the Fugitive Slave act was constitutional and must be enforced, and that laws ought to be made for the punishment of those who should interfere with its due execution. 2. That all State laws which impeded the execution of the Fugitive Slave act were null and void; that such laws had been mischievous in producing discord and commotion, and therefore the Congress should respectfully and earnestly recommend the repeal of them, or by legislation make them harmless. 3. This resolution referred to the fees of commissioners acting under the Fugitive Slave Law, and the modification of the section which required all citizens, when called upon, to aid the owner in capturing his runaway property. 4. This resolution declared that strong measures ought to be adopted for the suppression of the African slave-trade.

On March 2, two days before the close of the session, Mason, of Virginia, the author of the Fugitive Slave Law, called up the Crittenden propositions and resolutions. After a long debate, continued into the small hours of Sunday, March 3, 1861, the Crittenden Compromise was rejected by a vote of twenty against nineteen. A resolution of the House of Representatives was then adopted to amend the Constitution so as to prohibit forever any amendment to that instrument interfering with slavery in any State. Senator Crittenden's term in the Senate expiring March, 1861, he entered the Lower House as a representative in July following, in which he was a very ardent but conservative Union man, but was opposed to the emancipation of slaves. He died near Frankfort, Ky., July 26, 1863.

Crittenden, THOMAS LEONIDAS, military officer; second son of John J. Crittenden; born in Russelville, Ky., May 15, 1815; studied law with his father, and became commonwealth's attorney in 1842. He served under General Taylor in the war against Mexico. In September, 1861, was made a brigadier-general and assigned a command under General Buell. For gallantry in the battle of Shiloh he was promoted to major-general of volunteers and assigned a division in the Army of the Tennessee. He afterwards commanded the left wing of the Army of the Ohio under General Buell. Then he served under Rosecrans, taking part in the battles at Stone River and Chickamauga. He commanded a division of the 9th Corps in the campaign against Richmond in 1864. In March, 1865, he was brevetted major-general, United States Army; and in 1881 he was retired. He died on Staten Island, N. Y., Oct. 23, 1893.

Crittenden Compromise. See CRITTENDEN, JOHN JORDAN.

Crocker, CHARLES, capitalist; born in Troy, N. Y., Sept. 16, 1822; went to California in 1849; with Leland Stanford, Mark Hopkins, and Collis P. Huntington he projected and completed the Union Pacific Railway system. He died in Monterey, Cal., Aug. 14, 1888.

Crockett, DAVID, pioneer; born in Limestone, Greene county, Tenn., Aug. 17, 1786. With little education, he became a noted hunter in his early life; served under Jackson in the Creek War; was a member of Congress from 1828 to 1834, and removed to Texas in the latter year, where he became zealously engaged in the war for Texan independence. While fighting for the defence of the ALAMO (*q. v.*) he was captured and put to death by order of Santa Ana, March 6, 1836.

Croffut, WILLIAM AUGUSTUS, author; born in Redding, Conn., Jan. 29, 1835; enlisted in the National army in 1861; served throughout the war; organized the Anti-Imperialist League in 1899. Among his publications are a *War History of Connecticut; The Vanderbilts; Fifty Years in Camp and Field,* etc. He was also author of the opening ode for the World's Columbian Exposition.

Croghan, GEORGE, Indian agent; born in Ireland; was educated in Dublin; emigrated to Pennsylvania; and in 1746 was engaged in trade with the Indians. Pennsylvania made him Indian agent. Captain in Braddock's expedition in 1755, he showed such excellence in military matters that in 1756 he was intrusted with the defence of the western frontier of Pennsylvania, and was made by Sir William Johnson his deputy, who, in 1763, sent him to England to confer with the ministry about an Indian boundary-line. On that voyage he was wrecked on the coast of France. In May, 1776, Croghan founded a settlement 4 miles above Fort Pitt (now Pittsburg). He was active in securing the attachment of the Indians to the British interest until 1776, but took no active part in the events of the Revolution. He died in Passayunk, Pa., in August, 1782.

Croghan, GEORGE, military officer; born near Louisville, Ky., Nov. 15, 1791; educated at the College of William and Mary, which he left in 1810; was aide to Colonel Boyd in the battle of TIPPECANOE (*q. v.*) in 1811, and made captain of infantry in March, 1812. In March, 1813, he became an aide of General Harrison, and in August of the same year sustained the siege of FORT STEPHENSON (*q. v.*) against a force of British and Indians, for which he was brevetted a captain and awarded a gold medal by Congress. He was made lieutenant-colonel early in 1814, and resigned in 1817. Colonel Croghan was postmaster at New Orleans in 1824, and late in the next year was appointed inspector-general of the army, with the rank of colonel. He served under Taylor at the beginning of the war with Mexico. He died in New Orleans, Jan. 8, 1849.

Croker, RICHARD, politician; born in Black Rock, Ireland, Nov. 24, 1843; received a public-school education in New York; was alderman in 1868–70 and 1883; coroner in 1873–76; fire commissioner in 1883; and city chamberlain in 1889–90. He took a prominent part in opposing the Tweed Ring, and after the death of John Kelly was for many years the recognized leader of Tammany Hall. For several years Mr. Croker has resided at Glencairne, Ireland.

Cromwell, BARTLETT JEFFERSON, naval officer; born in Spring Place, Ga., Feb. 9, 1840; entered the navy in 1857, and during the Civil War served on the *St. Lawrence*, *Quaker City*, *Conemaugh*, and *Proteus*, with the South Atlantic and East Gulf blockading squadrons; took part in the attacks on Morris Island and Battery Gregg. He was promoted captain in 1889; commodore in 1898; and rear-admiral in 1899; appointed commandant of the Portsmouth navy-yard in 1900; retired in 1902.

CROMWELL, OLIVER

Cromwell, OLIVER, Lord Protector of England; born in Huntingdon, April 25, 1599. His social position was thus described by himself: "I was by birth a gentleman, neither living in any considerable height nor yet in obscurity." His family was connected with the St. Johns, Hampdens, and other English historical families. It is a curious fact that when he was five years of age he had a fight with Prince Charles, who, as king, was beheaded and succeeded by Cromwell as the ruler of England. He flogged the young prince, who was then with his family visiting Cromwell's uncle. As a boy he was much given to robbing orchards and playing unpleasant pranks. He lived a wild life at Sidney-Sussex College, Cambridge, whither he was sent in 1616. He left college after his father's death next year, and in 1620 married a daughter of Sir James Bourchier, when his manner of life changed, and he became an earnest Christian worker for good, praying, preaching, and exhorting among the Puritans. He became a member of Parliament in 1628, and always exercised much influence in that body. He was a radical in opposition to royalty in the famous Long Parliament.

When the civil war began he became one of the most active of the men in the field, and was made a colonel in 1643 under the Earl of Essex, the parliamentary lord-general. He raised a cavalry regiment, and excited in them and other troops which he afterwards led the religious zeal of the Puritans, and directed it with force against royalty. That regiment became the most famous in the revolutionary army. After the death of the King he resolved to become sole ruler of England. He had effected the prostration of the monarchy, not from ambitious, but from patriotic motives; but in his efforts

OLIVER CROMWELL.

for power after the execution he was a bold operator. When the Scotch partisans of the son of the King (afterwards Charles II.) invaded England and penetrated to Worcester, Cromwell, with 30,000 English troops, gained a decisive victory over them. Grateful to the victor, the government gave him an estate worth $20,000 a year and assigned him Hampton Court as his abode.

He now sought supreme rule. On April 20, 1653, he boldly drove the remnant of the Long Parliament, which ruled England, out of the House of Commons by military force. The same day the council of state was broken up, and for weeks anarchy prevailed in England. Cromwell issued a summons for 156 persons named to meet at Westminster as a Parliament. They met (all but two) in July. This was the famous "Barebones's Parliament," so called after one of its Puritan members named Praise God Barebones. It was a weak body, and in December, 1653, Cromwell was declared Lord Protector of Great Britain, and the executive and legislative power were vested in him and a Parliament. In his administration of affairs he exerted considerable influence in the English-American colonies. His administration was a stormy one, for plots for his assassination were frequently discovered, and he was constantly harassed by the opposition of men who had acted with him but were honest republicans, which he was not. With shattered body and distracted mind, he sank into the grave from the effects of a tertian fever. He died on the anniversary of the battle of Worcester, Sept. 3, 1658.

First Protectorate Parliament.—The following is Cromwell's speech at the opening session of this body, Sept. 4, 1654:

Gentlemen,—You are met here on the greatest occasion that, I believe, England ever saw; having upon your shoulders the Interests of Three great Nations with the territories belonging to them;—and truly, I believe I may say it without any hyperbole, you have upon your shoulders the Interest of all the Christian People in the world. And the expectation is, that I should let you know, as far as I have cognizance of it, the occasion of your assembling together at this time.

It hath been very well hinted to you this day, that you come hither to settle the Interests above mentioned: for your work here, in the issue and consequences of it, *will* extend so far, even to all Christian people. In the way and manner of my speaking to you, I shall study plainness; and to speak to you what is truth, and what is upon my heart, and what will in some measure reach to these great concernments.

After so many changes and turnings, which this Nation hath labored under,—to have such a day of hope as this is, and such a door of hope opened by God to us, truly I believe, some months since, would have been beyond all our thoughts! —I confess it would have been worthy of such a meeting as this is, To have remembered that which was the rise of, and gave the first beginning to, all these Troubles which have been upon this Nation: and to have given you a series of the Transactions,—not of men, but of the Providence of God, all along unto our late changes: as also the ground of our first undertaking to oppose that usurpation and tyranny which was upon us, both in civils and spirituals; and the several grounds particularly applicable to the several changes that have been. But I have two or three reasons which divert me from such a way of proceeding at this time.

If I should have gone in that way, then that which lies upon my heart as to these things,—which is so written there that if I would blot it out I could not,—would itself have spent this day: the providences and dispensations of God have been so stupendous. As David said in the like case, *Psalm* xl. 5, "Many, O Lord my God, are thy wonderful works which thou hast done, and thy thoughts which are to-usward: they cannot be reckoned up in order unto thee: if I would declare and speak of them, they are more than can be numbered."—Truly, another reason, unexpected by me, you had to-day in the Sermon: you had much recapitulation of Providence; much allusion to a state and dispensation in respect of discipline and correction, of mercies and deliverances, to a state and dispensation similar to ours, —to, in truth, the only parallel of God's dealing with us that I know in the world, which was largely and wisely held forth to you this day: To Israel's bringing-out of Egypt through a wilderness by many signs and wonders, towards a Place of Rest,—I say *towards* it. And that having been so well remonstrated to you this day, is another argument why I shall not trouble you with a recapitulation of those things;—though they are things which I hope will never be forgotten, because written in better Books than those of paper; —written, I am persuaded, in the heart of every good man!

But a third reason was this: What I judge to be the end of your meeting, the great end, which was likewise remembered to you this day; to wit, Healing and Settling. The remembering of Transactions too particularly, perhaps instead of healing,—at least in the hearts of many of you,—might set the wound fresh a-bleeding. And I must profess this unto you, whatever thoughts pass upon me: That if this day, if this meeting, prove *not* healing, what shall we do! But, as I said before, I trust it is in the minds of you all, and much more in the mind of God, to cause healing. It must be first in His mind:—and He being pleased to put it into yours, this will be a Day indeed, and such a Day as generations to come will bless you for!—I say, for this and the other reasons, I have foreborne to make a particular remembrance and enumeration of things, and of the manner of the Lord's bringing us through so many changes and turnings as have passed upon us.

Howbeit, I think it will be more than necessary to let you know, at least so well as I may, in what condition this Nation, or rather these Nations were, when the present Government was undertaken. And for order's sake: It's very natural to consider what our condition was, in Civils; and then also in Spirituals.

What was our condition! Every man's hand almost was against his brother;—at least his heart was; little regarding anything that should cement, and might have a tendency in it to cause us to grow into one. All the dispensations of God; His terrible ones, when He met us in the way of His judgment in a Ten-years Civil War; and His merciful ones: they did not, they did not work upon us! No. But we had our humors and interests;—and indeed I fear our humors went for more with us than even our interests. Certainly, as it falls out in such cases, our passions were more than our judgments.—Was not everything almost grown arbitrary? Who of us knew where or how to have right done him, without some obstruction or other intervening? Indeed we were almost grown arbitrary in everything.

What was the face that was upon our affairs as to the Interest of the nation! As to the Authority in the Nation; to the Magistracy; to the Ranks and Orders of men,—whereby England hath been known for hundreds of years? A nobleman, a gentleman, a yeoman; the distinction of these: that is a good interest of the Nation, and a great one! The natural Magistracy of the Nation, was it not almost trampled under foot, under despite and contempt, by men of Levelling principles? I beseech you, For the orders of men and ranks of men, did not that Levelling principle tend to the reducing of all to an equality? Did it consciously think to do so; or did it only unconsciously practise towards that for property and interest? At all events, what was the purport of it but to make the Tenant as liberal a fortune as the Landlord? Which, I think, if obtained, would not have lasted long! The men of that principle, after they had served their own turns, would *then* have cried-up property and interest fast enough!—This instance is instead of many. And that the thing did and might well extend far, is manifest; because it was a pleasing voice to all Poor Men, and truly not unwelcome to all Bad Men. To my thinking, this is a consideration which, in your endeavors after settlement, you will be so well minded of, that I might have spared it here: but let that pass.—

Now as to Spirituals. Indeed in Spiritual things the case was more sad and deplorable still;—and that was told to you this day eminently. The prodigious blasphemies; contempt of God and Christ, denying of Him, contempt of Him and His ordinances, and of the Scriptures: a spirit visibly acting those things foretold by Peter and Jude; yea, those things spoken of by Paul to Timothy! Paul declaring some things to be worse than the Antichristian state (of which he had spoken in the *First to Timothy*, Chapter fourth, verses first and second, under the title of the Latter times), tells us what should be the lot and portion of the *Last* Times. He says (*Second to Timothy*, Chapter third, verses second, third, fourth), "In the Last Days perilous times shall come; men shall be lovers of their own selves, covetous, boasters, proud, blasphemers, disobedient to parents, unthankful," and so on. But in speaking of the Antichristian state, he told us (*First to Timothy*, Chapter fourth, verses first and second), that "in the *latter* days" that state shall come in; not the *last* days, but the latter,—wherein "there shall be a departing from the faith, and a giving heed to seducing spirits and doctrines of devils, speaking lies in hypocrisy," and so on. This is only his description of the *latter* times, or those of Antichrist; and we are given to understand that there are *last* times coming, which will be worse!—And surely it may be feared, these are *our* times. For when men forget all rules of Law and Nature, and break all the bonds that fallen man hath on him; obscuring the remainder of the image of God in their nature, which they cannot blot out, and yet shall endeavor to blot out, "having a form of godliness without the power,"—surely these are sad tokens of the last times!

And indeed the character wherewith this spirit and principle is described in that place of Scripture, is so legible and visible, that he who runs may read it to be amongst us. For by such "the grace of God is turned into wantonness," and Christ and the Spirit of God made a cloak for all villany and spurious apprehensions. And though nobody will own these things publicly as to practice, the things being so abominable and odious; yet the consideration how this principle extends itself, and whence it had its rise, makes me to think of a Second sort of Men, tending in the same direction; who, it's true, as I said, will not practise nor own these things, yet can tell the Magistrate "That he hath nothing to do with men holding such notions: These, forsooth, are matters of conscience and opinion: they are matters of Religion; what hath the Magistrate to do with these things? He is to look to the outward man, not to the inward,"—and so forth. And truly it so happens that though these things do break out visibly to all, yet the principle wherewith these things are carried on so forbids the Magistrate to meddle with them, that it hath hitherto kept the offenders from punishment.

Such considerations, and pretensions to "liberty of conscience," what are they leading us towards? Liberty of Conscience, and Liberty of the Subject,—two as glorious things to be contended for as any that God hath given us; yet both these abused for the patronizing of villanies! Insomuch that it hath been an ordinary thing to say, and in dispute to affirm, "That the restraining of such pernicious notions was not in the Magistrate's power; he had nothing to do with it. Not so much as the printing of a Bible in the Nation for the use of the People was competent to the Magistrate, lest it should be imposed upon the consciences of men,"—for "they would receive the same traditionally and implicitly from the Magistrate, if it were thus received!" The afore-mentioned abominations did thus swell to this height among us.

So likewise the axe was laid to the root of the Ministry. It was Antichristian, it was Babylonish, said they. It suffered under such a judgment that the truth is, as the extremity was great according to the former system, I wish it prove not as great according to this. The former extremity we suffered under was, That no man, though he had never so good a testimony, though he had received gifts from Christ, might preach, unless ordained. So now I think we are at the other extremity, when many affirm, That he who is ordained hath a nullity, or Antichristianism, stamped thereby upon his calling; so that he ought not to preach, or not be heard.—I wish it may not be too justly said, That there were severity and sharpness in our old system! Yea, too much of an imposing spirit in matters of conscience; a spirit unchristian enough in any times, most unfit for these times;—denying liberty of conscience to men who have earned it with their blood; who have earned civil liberty, and religious also, for those who would thus impose upon them!—

We may reckon among these our Spiritual evils, an evil that hath more refinedness in it, more color for it, and hath deceived more people of integrity than the rest have done;—for few have been catched by the former mistakes except such as have apostatized from their holy profession, such as, being corrupt in their consciences, have been forsaken by God, and left to such noisome opinions. But, I say, there is another error of more refined sort; which many honest people whose hearts are sincere, many of them belonging to God, have fallen into: and that is the mistaken notion of the Fifth Monarchy. A thing pretending more spirituality than anything else. A notion I hope we all honor, and wait, and hope for the fulfilment of: That Jesus Christ *will* have a time to set up His Reign in our hearts; by subduing those corruptions and lusts and evils that are there; which now reign more in the world than, I hope, in due time they shall do. And when more fulness of the Spirit is poured forth to subdue iniquity and bring-in everlasting righteousness, then will the approach of that glory be. The carnal divisions and contentions among Christians, so common, are not the symptoms of that Kingdom!—But for men, on this principle, to betitle themselves, that they are the only men to rule kingdoms, govern nations, and give laws to people, and determine of property and liberty and everything else,—upon such a pretension as this is:—truly they had need to give clear manifestations of God's presence with them, before wise men will receive or submit to their conclusions! Nevertheless, as many of these men have good meanings, which I hope in my soul they have, it will be the wisdom of all knowing and experienced Christians to do as Jude saith. Jude, when he reckoned-up those horrible things, done upon pretences, and haply by some upon mistakes: "Of some," says he, "have compassion, making a difference"; others save "with fear, pulling them out of the fire." I fear they will give too often opportunity for this exercise! But I hope the same will be for their good. If men do but so much as pretend for justice and righteousness, and be of peaceable spirits, and will manifest this, let them be the subjects of the Magistrate's encouragement. And if the magistrate, by punishing visible miscarriages, save them by that discipline, God having ordained him for that end.—I hope it will evidence *love* and not hatred, so to punish where there is cause.

Indeed this is that which doth most declare the danger of that spirit. For if these were but notions,—I mean these instances I have given you of dangerous doctrines both in Civil things and Spiritual; if, I say, they were but notions, they were best let alone. Notions will hurt none but those that have them. But when they come to such practices as telling us, for instance, That Liberty and Property are not the badges of the Kingdom of Christ; when they tell us, not that we are to regulate Law, but that Law is to be abrogated, indeed subverted; and perhaps wish to bring in the Judaical Law; instead of our known laws settled among us: this is worthy of every Magistrate's consideration. Especially where every stone is turned to bring in confusion. I think, I say, this will be worthy of the Magistrate's consideration.

Whilst these things were in the midst of us; and whilst the Nation was rent and torn in spirit and principle from one end to the other, after this sort and manner I have now told you; family against family, husband against wife, parents against children; and nothing in the hearts and minds of men but "Overturn, overturn, overturn!" (a Scripture phrase very much abused, and applied to justify unpeaceable practices by all men of discontented spirits),—the common Enemy sleeps not: our adversaries in civil and religious respects did take advantage of these distractions and divisions, and did practise accordingly in the three Nations of England, Scotland and Ireland. We know very well that Emissaries of the Jesuits never came in such swarms as they have done since those things were set on foot. And I tell you that divers Gentlemen here can bear witness with me How that they, the Jesuits, have had a Consistory abroad which rules all the affairs of things in England, from an Archbishop down to the other dependents upon him. And they had fixed in England,—of which we are able to produce the particular Instruments in most of the limits of their Cathedrals or pretended Dioceses,—an Episcopal Power with Archdeacons, &c. And had persons authorized to exercise and distribute those things; who pervert and deceive the people. And all this, while we were in that sad, and as I said deplorable condition.

And in the mean time all endeavors possible were used to hinder the work of God in Ireland, and the progress of the work of God in Scotland; by continual intelligences and correspondences, both at home and abroad, from hence into Ireland, and from hence into Scotland. Persons were stirred up, from our divisions and discomposure of affairs, to do all they could to ferment the War in both these places. To add yet to our misery, whilst we were in this condition, we were in a foreign War. Deeply engaged in War with the Portuguese; whereby our Trade ceased: the evil consequences by that War were manifest and very considerable. And not only this, but we had a War with Holland; consuming our treasure; occasioning a vast burden upon the people. A War that cost this nation full as much as the whole Taxes came unto; the Navy being a Hundred-and-sixty Ships, which cost this Nation above 100,000*l*. a-month; besides the contingencies, which would make it 120,000*l*. That very one War did engage us to so great a charge.—At the same time also we were in a War with France. The advantages that were taken of the discontents and divisions among ourselves did also ferment that War, and at least hinder us of an honorable peace; every man being confident we could not hold out long. And surely they did not calculate amiss, if the Lord had not been exceedingly gracious to us! I say, at the same time we had a War with France. And besides the sufferings in respect to the Trade of the Nation, it's most evident that the Purse of the Nation could not have been able much longer to bear it,—by reason of the advantages taken by other States to improve their own, and spoil our Manufacture of Cloth, and hinder the vent thereof; which is the great staple commodity of this Nation. Such was our condition: spoiled in our Trade, and we at this vast expense; thus dissettled at home, and having these engagements abroad.

Things being so,—and I am persuaded it is not hard to convince every person here they were so,—what a heap of confusions were upon these poor Nations! And either things must have been left to sink into the miseries these premises would suppose, or else a remedy must be applied. A remedy hath been applied: that hath been this Government; a thing I shall say little unto. The thing is open and visible to be seen and read by all men; and therefore let it speak for itself. Only let me say this,—because I can speak it with comfort and confidence before a Greater than you all: That in the intention of it, as to the approving of our hearts to God, let men judge as they please, it was calculated with our best wisdom for the interest of the People. For the interest of the people alone, and for their good, without respect had to any other interest. And if that be not true I shall be bold to say again, Let it speak for itself. Truly I may,—I hope, humbly before God, and modestly before you,—say somewhat on the behalf of the Government. Not that I would discourse of the particular heads of it, but acquaint you a little with the effects it has had: and this not for ostentation's sake, but to the end I may at this time deal faithfully with you, and acquaint you with the state of things, and what proceedings have been entered into by this Government, and what the state of our affairs is. This is the main end of my putting you to this trouble.

The Government hath had some things in desire; and it hath done some things actually. It hath desired to reform the Laws. I say to reform them:—and for that end it hath called together Persons, without offence be it spoken, of as great ability and as great interest as are in these Nations, to consider how the Laws might be made plain and short, and less chargeable to the People; how to lessen expense, for the good of the Nation. And those things are in preparation, and Bills prepared; which in due time, I make no question, will be tendered to you. In the mean while there hath been care taken to put the administration of the Laws into the hands of just men; men of the most known integrity and ability. The Chancery hath been reformed; I hope, to the satisfaction of all good men: and as for the things, or causes, depending there, which made the burden and work of the honorable Persons intrusted in those services too heavy for their ability, it hath referred many of them to those places where Englishmen love to have their rights tried, the Courts of Law at Westminster.

This Government hath, further, endeavored to put a stop to that heady way (likewise touched of in our Sermon this day) of every man making himself a Minister and Preacher. It hath endeavored to settle a method for the approving and sanctioning of men of piety and ability to discharge that work. And I think I may say it hath committed the business to the trust of Persons, both of the Presbyterian and Independent judgments, of as known ability, piety and integrity, as any, I believe, this Nation hath. And I believe also that, in that care they have taken, they have labored to approve themselves to Christ, to the Nation and to their own consciences. And indeed I think, if there be anything of quarrel against them,—though I am not here to justify the proceedings of any,—it is that they, in fact, go upon such a character as the Scripture warrants: To put men into that great Employment, and to approve men for it, who are men that have "received gifts from Him that ascended up on high, and gave gifts" for the work of the Ministry, and for the edifying of the Body of Christ. The Government hath also taken care, we hope, for the expulsion of all those who may be judged any way unfit for this work; who are scandalous, and the common scorn and contempt of that function.

One thing more this Government hath done: it hath been instrumental to call a free Parliament;—which, blessed be God, we see here this day! I say, a free Parliament. And that it may continue so, I hope is in the heart and spirit of every good man in England,—save such discontented persons as I have formerly mentioned. It's that which as I have desired above my life, so I shall desire to keep it above my life.

I did before mention to you the plunges we were in with respect to Foreign States; by the War with Portugal, France, the Dutch, the Danes, and the little assurance we had from any of our neighbors round about. I perhaps forgot, but indeed it was a caution upon my mind, and I desire now it may be so understood, That if any good hath been done, it was the Lord, not we His poor instruments. —I did instance the Wars; which did exhaust your treasure; and put you into such a condition that you must have sunk therein, if it had continued but a few months longer: this I can affirm, if strong probability may be a fit ground. And now you have, though it be not the first in time,—Peace with Swedeland; an honorable peace; through the endeavors of an honorable Person here present as the instrument. I say you have an honorable peace with a Kingdom which, not many years since, was much a friend to France, and lately perhaps inclinable enough to the Spaniard. And I believe you expect not much good from any of your Catholic neighbors; nor yet that they would be very willing you should have a good understanding with your Protestant friends. Yet, thanks be to God, that Peace is concluded; and as I said before, it is an honorable Peace.

You have a Peace with the Danes,—a State that lay contiguous to that part of this Island which hath given us the most trouble. And certainly if your enemies abroad be able to annoy you, it is likely they will take their advantage (where it best lies) to give you trouble from that country. But you have a Peace there, and an honorable one. Satisfaction to your Merchants' ships; not only to their content, but to their rejoicing. I believe you will easily know it is so,—an honorable peace. You have the Sound open; which used to be obstructed. That which was and is the strength of this Nation, the Shipping, will now be supplied thence. And whereas you were glad to have anything of that kind at secondhand, you have now all manner of commerce there, and at as much freedom as the Dutch themselves, who used to be the carriers and venders of it to us; and at the same rates and tolls;—and I think, by that Peace, the said rates now fixed-upon cannot be raised to you in future.

You have a Peace with the Dutch: a Peace unto which I shall say little, seeing it is so well known in the benefit and consequences thereof. And I think it was as desirable, and as acceptable to the spirit of this Nation, as any one thing that lay before us. And, as I believe nothing so much gratified our enemies as to see us at odds with that Commonwealth; so I persuade myself nothing is of more terror or trouble to them than to see us thus reconciled. Truly as a Peace with the Protestant States hath much security in it, so it hath as much of honor and of assurance to the Protestant Interest abroad; without which no assistance can be given thereunto. I wish it may be written upon our hearts to be zealous for that Interest! For if ever it were like to come under a condition of suffering, it is now. In all the Emperor's Patrimonial Territories, the endeavor is to drive the Protestant part of the people out, as fast as is possible; and they are necessitated to run to Protestant States to seek their bread. And by this conjunction of Interests, I hope you will be in a more fit capacity to help them. And it begets some reviving of their spirits, that you will help them as opportunity shall serve.

You have a Peace likewise with the Crown of Portugal; which Peace, though it hung long in hand, yet is lately concluded. It is a Peace which, your Merchants make us believe, is of good concernment to their trade; the rate of insurance to that Country having been higher, and so the profit which could bear such rate, than to other places. And one thing hath been obtained in this treaty, which never before was, since the Inquisition was set up there: That our people which trade thither have Liberty of Conscience,—liberty to worship in Chapels of their own.

Indeed, Peace is, as you were well told to-day, desirable with all men, as far as it may be had with conscience and honor! We are upon a Treaty with France. And we may say this, That if God give us honor in the eyes of the Nations about us, we have reason to bless Him for it, and so to own it. And I dare say that there is not a Nation in Europe but is very willing to ask a good understanding with you.

I am sorry I am thus tedious: but I did judge that it was somewhat necessary to acquaint you with these things. And things being so,—I hope you will not be unwilling to hear a little again of the Sharp as well as of the Sweet! And I should not be faithful to you, nor to the interest of these Nations which you and I serve, if I did not let you know *all*.

As I said before, when this Government was undertaken, we were in the midst of those domestic divisions and animosities and scatterings; engaged also with those foreign enemies round about us, at such a vast charge,—120,000*l*. a-month for the very Fleet. Which sum was the very utmost penny of your Assessments. Ay; and then all your treasure was exhausted and spent when this Government was undertaken: all *accidental* ways of bringing-in treasure were, to a very inconsiderable sum, consumed;—the forfeited Lands sold, the sums on hand spent; Rents, Fee-farms, Delinquents' Lands, King's, Queen's, Bishops', Dean-and-Chapters' Lands, sold. These were *spent* when this Government was undertaken. I think it's my duty to let you know so much. And that's the reason why the Taxes do yet lie so heavy upon the People;—of which we have abated 30,000*l*. a-month for the next three months. Truly I thought it my duty to let you know, That though God hath dealt thus bountifully with you, yet these are but entrances and doors of hope. Whereby, through the blessing of God, you *may* enter into rest and peace. But you are not yet entered!

You were told to-day of a People brought out of Egypt towards the Land of Canaan; but through unbelief, murmuring, repining, and other temptations and sins wherewith God was provoked, they were fain to come back again, and linger many years in the Wilderness before they came to the Place of Rest. *We* are thus far, through the mercy of God. We have cause to take notice of it, That we are not brought into misery, not totally wrecked; but have, as I said before, a door of hope open. And I may say this to you: If the Lord's blessing and His presence go along with the management of affairs at this Meeting, you will be enabled to put the topstone to the work, and make the Nation happy. But this must be by knowing the true state of affairs! You are yet, like the People under Circumcision, but raw. Your Peaces are but newly made. And it's a maxim not to be despised, "Though peace be made, yet it's interest that keeps peace;"—and I hope you will not trust such peace except so far as you see interest upon it. But all settlement grows stronger by mere continuance. And therefore I wish that you may go forward, and not backward; and in brief that you may have the blessing of God upon your endeavors! It's one of the great ends of calling this Parliament, that the Ship of the Commonwealth may be brought into a safe harbor; which, I assure you, it will not be, without your counsel and advice.

You have great works upon your hands. You have Ireland to look unto. There is not much done to the Planting thereof, though some things leading and preparing for it are. It is a great business to settle the Government of that Nation upon fit terms, such as will bear that work through.—You have had laid before you some considerations, intimating your peace with several foreign States. But yet you have not made peace with *all.* And if they should see we do not manage our affairs with that wisdom which becomes us,—truly we may sink under disadvantages, for all that's done. And our enemies will have their eyes open, and be revived, if they see animosities amongst us; which indeed will be their great advantage.

I do therefore persuade you to a sweet, gracious and holy understanding of one another, and of your business. Concerning which you had so good counsel this day; which as it rejoiced my heart to hear, so I hope the Lord will imprint it upon your spirits,—wherein you shall have my Prayers.

Having said this, and perhaps omitted many other material things through the frailty of my memory, I shall exercise plainness and freeness with you; and say, That I have not spoken these things as one who assumes to himself dominion over you; but as one who doth resolve to be a fellow-servant with you to the interest of these great affairs, and of the People of these Nations. I shall trouble you no longer; but desire you to repair to your House, and to exercise your own liberty in the choice of a Speaker, that so you may lose no time in carrying on your work.

[" At this speech," say the old newspapers, " all generally seemed abundantly to rejoice, by extraordinary expressions and hums at the conclusion. His Highness withdrew into the old House of Lords, and the Members of Parliament into the Parliament House. His Highness, so soon as the Parliament were gone to their House, went back to Whitehall, privately in his barge, by water."]

Cromwell the Buccaneer. One of the earliest of the famous buccaneers was Captain Cromwell, who had been a common sailor in New England. In 1646 he was in command of three fast-sailing brigantines, filled with armed men, and was driven into the harbor of New Plymouth by a storm. Cromwell, under the authority of a sort of second-hand commission from High-Admiral (Earl of) Warwick, had captured in the West Indies several richly laden Spanish vessels. These freebooters spent money freely at Plymouth. Cromwell and his men soon afterwards went to Boston, where he lodged with a poor man who had helped him when he was poor, and gave him generous compensation. Winthrop, who had lately been re-elected governor, received from this freebooter an elegant sedan-chair captured in one of his prizes, designed as a gift by the viceroy of Mexico to his sister.

Crook, GEORGE, military officer; born near Dayton, O., Sept. 8, 1828; graduated at West Point in 1852. In May, 1861, he was promoted to captain. He did good service in western Virginia, and in September was made brigadier-general and took command of the Kanawha district. In command of a division of cavalry in the Army of the Cumberland, he was at CHICKAMAUGA (*q. v.*) and drove Wheeler across the Tennessee. Brevetted major-general of volunteers (July, 1864), he was put in command of the Army of West Virginia, and took part in Sheridan's operations in the Shenandoah Valley. He was made major-general of volunteers in October, and late in February, 1865, was captured by guerillas, but exchanged the next month. He was brevetted brigadier-general and major-general in the regular army March 13, 1865, and afterwards distinguished himself in several campaigns against the Indians, and particularly in the battles of Powder River, Tongue River, and the Rosebud. He died in Chicago, Ill., March 21, 1890.

Crooks, GEORGE RICHARD, clergyman; born in Philadelphia, Pa., Feb. 3, 1822; graduated at Dickinson College in 1840; ordained a minister of the Methodist Episcopal Church in 1841; professor in Dickinson College in 1842–48, when he returned to the pastorate until his election in 1860 as editor of *The Methodist,* the organ of the supporters of lay representation. The paper was discontinued when their efforts were successful in 1872, and Dr. Crooks again returned to the pastorate. He died in Madison, N. J., Feb. 20, 1897.

Crosby, PEIRCE, naval officer; born near Chester, Pa., Jan. 16, 1823; entered the navy as midshipman in 1844; was engaged in the war with Mexico; and was very active as commander on the coast of North Carolina during portions of the Civil War. He was specially brave and skilful in the capture of the forts at Cape Hatteras, at the passage of the forts on the lower Mississippi in the spring of 1862, and at Vicksburg in June and July the same year. He was in command of the *Metacomet* during the operations which led to the capture of Mobile in 1865. In 1882 he was promoted to rear-admiral, and in the following year was retired. He died near Washington, D. C., June 15, 1899.

Cross Keys, ACTION AT. When Banks was expelled from the Shenandoah Valley in 1862 the city of Washington could only be relieved from peril by the defeat of the Confederates. For this purpose McDowell sent a force over the Blue Ridge to intercept them if they should retreat, and Frémont pressed on from the west towards Strasburg with the same object in view. Perceiving the threatened danger, Jackson fled up the valley with his whole force, hotly pursued by the Nationals, and at Cross Keys, beyond Harrisonburg, Frémont overtook Ewell, when a sharp but indecisive battle occurred. Ewell had about 5,000 men, strongly posted. There he was attacked on Sunday morning, June 7, by Frémont, with the force with which he had moved out of Harrisonburg. General Schenck led the right, General Milroy the centre, and General Stahl the left. Between the extreme was a force under Colonel Cluseret. At eleven o'clock the conflict was general and severe, and continued several hours, Milroy and Schenck all the while gaining ground, the former with heavy loss. At four o'clock the whole National line was ordered to fall back at the moment when Milroy had pierced Ewell's centre and was almost up to his guns. Milroy obeyed the order, but with great reluctance, for he felt sure of victory. The Confederates occupied the battle-field that night, and the Nationals rested within their first line until morning, when Ewell was called to aid Jackson beyond the Shenandoah River. The National loss in the battle was 664, of which two-thirds fell in Stahl's brigade.

Croswell, EDWIN, editor; a member of the ALBANY REGENCY (*q. v.*). From 1824 to 1854 he was the editor of the Albany *Argus*, the official organ of the Democratic party, and the interpreter of its policy. He was born in Catskill, N. Y., May 29, 1797, and died in Princeton, N. J., June 13, 1871.

Croton Aqueduct, which supplies New York City with water from the Croton River, was begun in 1837, and finished in 1842 at a cost of $12,500,000. Its capacity is about 98,000,000 gallons in 24 hours. A new aqueduct was approved by the legislature in 1883; the work was begun in January, 1884, and the aqueduct opened for use July 15, 1890. Total cost, $24,767,477. Its discharging capacity is 318,000,000 gallons in 24 hours. In connection with the aqueduct the dam at Quaker Bridge was built, 1887–91, at a cost of $3,000,000. It is 1,350 feet long, 277 feet high, and 216 feet wide at the bottom. The capacity of this dam is nearly 70,000,000,000 gallons. The new water-works now building (1912) are on a gigantic scale.

Crow Indians, a Siouan tribe, forming part of the Hidatsa group; were a wandering tribe of hunters; called the "proudest of Indians"; at one time divided into numerous bands; now officially classified as Mountain Crows and River Crows; dwelt at various times along the Big Horn, Missouri, Yellowstone, Platte and Powder rivers and the Rocky Mountains; numbered in 1904 about 1,825.

Crown, COLONIAL POLICY OF, was the policy of its official advisers. Matters of importance were determined by the privy council, composed, for practical purposes, of the King's ministers of state. Details were managed by individual ministers, by subordinate officials, or by administrative committees or boards. Government by homogeneous party ministries was not yet established, and the ministries were usually composite, including both Whigs and Tories, so that one of the secretaries of state might be a Tory and the other a Whig. Generally one party or the other had a preponderance, but sometimes the attempt was made to keep an even balance. In the minds of party politicians colonial politics took a subordinate place, and it could rarely be said that any particular ministry had its own distinctive colonial policy. The most important work in colonial administration was done by executive boards, some of which were restricted to specific departments of colonial administration; thus the commissioners of customs were specially charged with the enforcement of the navigation acts; and the commissioners of admiralty transacted a considerable amount of colonial business, especially in time of war. Much the most important executive boards, however, were the committee of the privy council on trade and plantations, and its successor, the board of commissioners for trade and plantations; or, more briefly, the board of trade. In royal governments the right of the crown to disallow provincial laws had been recognized from the outset; but fifty years elapsed after the revocation of the Virginia charter before another royal province was fully organized on the continent. In the mean time a large number of charters had been issued to proprietary and self-governing colonies without any provision for a royal veto.

During the reign of James II., imperial control of legislation was carried to a violent extreme by the abolition of assemblies in the new royal provinces, and it was not until after the English revolution of 1688 that the royal veto became a normal factor in the colonial system. By 1692 the right of disallowance existed in the five royal provinces of Massachusetts, New Hampshire, New York, Maryland, and Virginia, and in the proprietary province of Pennsylvania. In 1702 New Jersey became a royal government and was subjected to the same restriction. Attempts were made to apply the principle in other colonies also: Rhode Island laws were sent over for examination; in 1705 a Connecticut law banishing Quakers was disallowed; and in 1706 a royal order in council annulled two South Carolina statutes. The legality of the royal orders in all these cases was doubtful.

Crowninshield, Arrant Schuyler, naval officer; born at Seneca Falls, N. Y., March 14, 1843; graduated at the United States Naval Academy in 1863; was commended for his gallantry in both attacks on Fort Fisher; promoted captain July 21, 1894; became chief of the Bureau of Navigation in 1897; rear-admiral in 1902; during the American-Spanish War was a member of the Board of Naval Strategy; retired in 1903. He died in Philadelphia, Pa., May 27, 1908.

Crowninshield, Benjamin William; born in Boston, Mass., Dec. 27, 1772; elected to the State Senate in 1811, and appointed Secretary of the Navy by President Madison in 1814. President Monroe also appointed him Secretary of the Navy. He resigned in November, 1818. In 1823 he was elected to Congress, and served until March 3, 1831. He died in Boston, Feb. 3, 1851.

Crowninshield, Jacob, statesman; born in Salem, Mass., March 31, 1770; served in the State legislature until his election to Congress in 1803. Jefferson appointed him Secretary of the Navy in 1805. He died in Washington, April 14, 1808.

Crown Lands. Great Britain in 1763 proclaimed all lands west of the colonies as *Crown Lands*, to be under exclusive jurisdiction of the home government, and to be reserved for the use of the Indians. Colonists were forbidden to purchase or to settle in any portion of this reserved territory without the consent of the Crown. After the Revolution the various States claimed these lands.

Crown Point, a town in Essex county, N. Y., 90 miles north of Albany, which was quite an important trading-station between the English and the Indians until 1731, when the French took possession of the cape projecting into Lake Champlain on its western side and built Fort Frederick. The plan of the campaign for 1755 in the French and Indian War contemplated an expedition against the French at Crown Point, to be commanded by William Johnson. He accomplished more than Braddock or Shirley, yet failed to achieve the main object of the expedition. The Assembly of New York had voted £8,000 towards the enlistment in Connecticut of 2.000 men for the Niagara and Crown Point expedition; and after hearing of Braddock's defeat they raised 400 men of their own, in addition to 800 which they had already in the field. The troops destined for the northern expedition, about 6,000 in number, were drawn from New England, New Jersey, and New York. They were led by Gen. Phineas Lyman, of Connecticut, to the head of boat navigation on the Hudson where they built Fort Lyman, afterwards called Fort Edward. There Johnson joined them (August) with stores, took the chief command, and advanced to Lake George. The Baron Dieskau had, meanwhile, ascended Lake Champlain with 2,000 men, whom he brought from Montreal. Landing at South Bay, at the southern extremity of Lake Champlain, Dieskau marched against Fort Lyman, but suddenly changed his route, and led his troops against Johnson, at the head of Lake George, where his camp was protected on two sides by an impassable swamp. Informed of this movement of the French and Indian allies (Sept. 7), Johnson sent forward (Sept. 8) 1,000 Massachusetts troops, under the command of Col. Ephraim Williams, and 200 Mohawk Indians, under King Hendrick, to intercept the enemy.

The English fell into an ambuscade. Williams and Hendrick were both killed, and their followers fell back in great confusion to Johnson's camp, hotly pursued. The latter had heard of the disaster before the fugitives appeared, cast up breastworks of logs and limbs, and placed two cannon upon them, and was prepared to receive the pursuers of the English. Dieskau and his victorious troops came rushing on, without suspicion of being confronted with artillery. They came, a motley host, with swords, pikes, muskets, and tomahawks, and made a spirited attack, but at the discharge of cannon the Indians fled in terror to the forests. So, also, did the Canadian militia. Johnson had been wounded early in the fight, and it was carried through victoriously by General Lyman, who, hearing the din of battle, had come from Fort Lyman with troops. The battle continued several hours, when, Dieskau being severely wounded and made a prisoner, the French withdrew, and hastened to Crown Point. Their baggage was captured by some New Hampshire troops. The French loss was estimated at 1,000 men; that of the English at 300. Johnson did not follow the discomfited enemy, but built a strong military work on the site of his camp, which he called Fort William Henry. He also changed the name of Fort Lyman to Fort Edward, in compliment to the royal family; and he was rewarded for the success achieved by Lyman with a baronetcy and $20,000 to support the new title. The French strengthened their works at Crown Point, and fortified Ticonderoga.

CROWN POINT IN 1857.

The conduct of the second campaign against Crown Point was intrusted to Gen. John Winslow (a great-grandson of Edward Winslow, governor of Plymouth), who led the expedition against the Acadians in 1755. The Earl of Loudoun was commander-in-chief of the British forces in America, and GEN. JAMES ABERCROMBIE (*q. v.*) was his lieutenant. General Winslow had collected 7,000 men at Albany before Abercrombie's arrival, with several British regiments, in June. Difficulties immediately occurred respecting military rank. These, unadjusted when Loudoun arrived, were made worse by his arrogant assumption of supreme rank for the royal officers, and the troops were not ready to move until August. Vigorous measures were meanwhile taken to supply and reinforce the forts at Oswego. John Bradstreet, appointed commissary-general, employed for this purpose forty companies of boatmen, of fifty men each. Before this could be accomplished, the French, under Montcalm, captured the post at Oswego, which event so alarmed the inefficient Loudoun that he abandoned all other plans of the campaign for the year. A regiment of British regulars, under Colonel Webb, on their march to reinforce Oswego, on hearing of the disaster, fell back to Albany with terror and precipitation; and other troops, moving towards Ticonderoga, were ordered to halt, and devote their efforts towards strengthening Forts Edward and William Henry.

The post remained in possession of the French until 1759, when the approach of a large English force, under General Amherst, caused the garrison there to join that at Ticonderoga, in their flight down the lake to its outlet. Amherst remained at Crown Point long enough to construct a sufficient number of rude boats to convey his troops, artillery, and baggage, and then started to drive the enemy before him across the St. Lawrence. The delay prevented his joining Wolfe at Quebec. When ready to move, it was mid-autumn (Oct. 11), and heavy storms compelled him to return to Crown Point, after going a short distance down the lake. There he placed his troops in winter quarters, where they constructed a fortress, whose picturesque ruins, after the lapse of more than a century, attested its original strength. The whole circuit, measuring along the ramparts, was a trifle less than half a mile; and it was surrounded by a broad ditch, cut out of the solid limestone, with the fragments taken out of which massive stone barracks were constructed. In it was a well 90 feet deep, cut out of the limestone. The fortress was never entirely finished, although the British government spent nearly $10,000,000 upon it. Crown Point was an important place during the Revolutionary War. See CHAMPLAIN, LAKE, OPERATIONS ON.

Cruger, HENRY, JR., merchant; born in New York City, in 1739. His father became a merchant in Bristol, England, where he died in 1780. Henry was associated with him in trade, and succeeded him as mayor of Bristol in 1781. He had been elected to Parliament as the colleague of Edmund Burke in 1774, and was re-elected in 1784, and on all occasions advocated conciliatory measures towards his countrymen. After the war he became a merchant in New York, and, while yet a member of the British Parliament, was elected to the Senate of the State of New York. He died in New York, April 24, 1827.

Cruger, JOHN, legislator; born in New York City, July 18, 1710; elected alderman in 1754; mayor in 1756, which office he filled ten years; member of the General Assembly of New York colony in 1759, 1761, and 1769, of which last he was speaker until 1775. He died in New York City, Dec. 27, 1792.

Cruger, JOHN HARRIS, military officer; born in New York City in 1738; brother of Henry Cruger, Jr., and succeeded his father as member of the governor's council. He married a daughter of Col. Oliver De Lancey, and commanded a battalion of his loyalist corps. He served under Cornwallis in South Carolina, and was in command of Fort Ninety-six when besieged by Greene in May, 1781, and was praised for his successful defence of the post until relieved by Lord Rawdon. In the battle of Eutaw Springs, in September, he commanded the British centre. At the close of the war he went to England, and his property was confiscated. He died in London, Jan. 3, 1807.

Cruisers. See NAVY.

Crusades, TEMPERANCE. In the movement for the promotion of temperance in the United States there have been two instances in which exceptionally vigorous crusades, led by women, attracted much more than local interest. The first of these crusades was originated and carried on by Mrs. Eliza D. Stewart, of Springfield, O., who, prior to her personal attacks on liquor saloons in 1887–88, had become widely known as "Mother" Stewart for her philanthropic labors in behalf of temperance reform, of the soldiers in the Civil War, and of the freedmen of the South. "Mother" Stewart led what scoffers called "praying bands," which attempted to alleviate the curse of intemperance by prayer and moral suasion. In her visits to various saloons she was accompanied by both men and women, and in a majority of places was subjected to much ridicule, but no personal violence.

The second of these crusades was led by Mrs. Carrie Nation, of Medicine Lodge, Kan. She made her first raid on a saloon about 1890 in Medicine Lodge. Subsequently she wrecked several saloons in Kiowa, and in 1900–1 she carried her work into Wichita. After wrecking several saloons with her hatchet, she was arested on the complaint of a saloon-keeper and imprisoned, refusing for several weeks release on bail which was freely extended to her.

Crystal Palace, an exhibition building in New York City; was opened July 14, 1853, by President Pierce, for a universal industrial exhibition. Its main buildings and galleries covered 173,000 square feet. After the exhibition the American Institute fairs and other meetings were held there. On Oct. 5, 1858, it was destroyed by fire, with many articles for exhibition at the Institute.

CUBA

Cuba, the largest of the West India Islands. Early in the sixteenth century it was a conspicuous point of departure for discoverers, explorers, and conquerors of the American continent. The island was discovered by Columbus on Oct. 28, 1492, when, it is believed, he entered a bay near Nuevitas, on the north coast. He gave it the name of Juana, in honor of Prince Juan, or John, son of Isabella. Other names were afterwards given to it, but that of the natives—Cuba—is retained. It was very thickly populated by a docile and loving copper-colored race, who were rightfully called by themselves The Good. When, in the winter of 1509–10, Ojeda was sailing from Central America to Santo Domingo with some of his followers, his vessel was stranded on the southern shores of Cuba. He and his crew suffered dreadfully in the morasses, and more than half of them perished. They feared the natives, to whose protection persecuted ones in Santo Domingo had fled, but hunger compelled the Spaniards to seek for food among them.

These suffering Christians were treated most kindly by the pagans, and through their good offices Ojeda was enabled to reach Jamaica, then settled by his countrymen. He had built a chapel in Cuba, and over its altar-piece he placed a small Flemish painting of the Virgin, and taught the natives to worship her as the "Mother of God." Then Ojeda, on reaching Santo Domingo, told his countrymen of the abundance of precious metals in Cuba, when Diego Velasquez, appointed governor of Cuba by Diego Columbus, went with 300 men and made an easy conquest of it. The natives had kept Ojeda's chapel swept clean, made votive offerings to the Virgin, composed couplets to her, and sung them with accompaniments of instrumental music as they danced in the surrounding groves, and tried to convince their pious conquerors that they were fellow-Christians, but in vain. The conquerors made slaves of them, and so cruelly worked and treated them, men and women, in the fields and mines, that in less than fifty years only a few natives were left, and their places were partially supplied by negro slaves. Cruelty was the rule with the conquerors. Velasquez found there a rich and potent cacique, who had fled from Hispaniola to avoid slavery or death, and he condemned the fugitive to the flames. When he was fastened to the stake, a Franciscan friar, laboring to convert him, promised him immediate admittance to the joys of heaven if he would embrace the Christian faith, and threatened him with eternal torment if he should continue in his unbelief. The cacique asked whether there were any Spaniards in that region of bliss, and being answered in the affirmative, replied, "I will not go to a place where I may meet one of that accursed race."

De Soto was made captain-general of Cuba in 1537, and from that island he sailed to make a conquest of Florida. From it Cordova also sailed, and Grijalva, when they went and discovered Mexico; and from it Velasquez sent Cortez to make a conquest of the empire of Montezuma. From the advent of the Spaniards in 1511 the natives began to suffer, and they were persecuted steadily till 1898. During its early history the island changed hands several times, the Dutch once owning it for a short time and England conquering it in 1762, but restoring it to Spain in return for Florida. In 1829 occurred the Black Eagle rebellion, which was directed from the United States, and only put down by Spain after three years' fighting. In 1844 occurred the insurrection of the blacks. At the end of this rebellion 700 Cubans were put to death by torture, and the people of America became so aroused that President Polk offered Spain $100,000,000 for the island. President Buchanan also tried to buy Cuba (see SOULÉ, P.). In 1868 a rebellion broke out on the island and lasted ten years. The revolutionists proclaimed a republic, and Spain, after spending $200,000,000 and sending over 50,000 troops, finding that she could not conquer the patriots, sent over Gen. Martinez Campos, who, by promises, induced the patriots to lay down their arms. Spain's promises were never fulfilled.

MURDER AND MUTILATION OF THE NATIVES OF CUBA BY THE SPANIARDS (From an old print).

In December, 1894, a bill presented in the Spanish Cortes, for the purpose of giving Cuba a larger measure of control in its own affairs, was greatly opposed. The government attempted to make a compromise by offering to appoint a council to consist of twelve members, including the highest church officials and the president of the high court, and permitting Cuba to elect fifteen other members by popular vote. It was proposed that this council should meet in Havana, arrange the local budget, administer local and financial affairs, and direct a general supervision over the municipal government. Before this compromise was arranged, however, there was so much local dissatisfaction, that Spain proclaimed martial law over the island Feb. 24, 1895. This action precipitated another revolution in the eastern and western provinces, although José Marti, its promoter, had been busy for several years previous secretly shipping arms to the island. As soon as the rebellion began the republic was again proclaimed, and the old flag of 1868, a triangular blue union with a single star and five stripes, three red and two white, was adopted. On Aug. 7, Gen. Bartolomo Masco was made President of the provisional government. On Sept. 23

the revolutionists proclaimed the independence of Cuba, established a permanent republican government, and adopted a constitution. Salvadore Cisneros Betancourt

CAPTAIN-GENERAL'S PALACE, HAVANA.

was proclaimed President, Gen. Maximo Gomez was made commander-in-chief, and Gen. Antonio Maceo was made lieutenant-general. The patriots were uniformly successful in the early engagements. During 1895 Spain sent 50,000 troops to the island.

On Feb. 5, 1896, a resolution recommending that the Cubans be recognized as belligerents was introduced in the United States Senate, and on Feb. 27, a similar one was presented to the House. On Feb. 28, the Senate resolution was adopted by a vote of 64 to 6. This action aroused great indignation in Spain, and led to riots throughout the country. The resolution presented to the House was adopted on March 2, by a vote of 263 to 17; but on March 4 the Senate refused to agree with the House resolution, and sent it to a conference committee, whose report became the subject of an animated debate till it was returned to the conference by a unanimous vote on March 23. The House accepted the Senate resolutions on March 26. From the beginning of the rebellion the Cubans carried on a guerilla warfare, burning many small towns, and destroying much plantation property. On March 14, 1896, the strength of the Cuban army was estimated in Havana at about 43,000 men, but the revolutionists themselves claimed 60,000, two-thirds of whom were well mounted, and about half well armed. During 1896 Spain sent 80,000 more troops to the island. In spite of this great force, however, only one province, that of Pinar del Rio, remained in the hands of the Spanish, the other five being either wholly or partly given up to the patriots. General Campos was again sent to put down the rebellion, but as he failed to do so, Gen. Valeriano Weyler, of Nicolau, was sent to supersede him in February, 1896. Weyler's course was one of extreme cruelty, and aroused the people of the United States.

During the progress of the revolution that year relations between the United States and Spain became daily more strained. Many vessels left ports in the United States loaded with arms for the Cubans. One of the leading incidents of the war thus far was the death of the Cuban General Maceo. He was found dead Dec. 17, 1896. The truth regarding his death may never be known, but the belief of the Cubans was that he was betrayed by his physician, who was afterwards loaded with honors by General Weyler and sent to Spain. Several Americans were imprisoned by the Spanish during January, 1897. Their release, or at least a speedy civil trial, was demanded by this country. Spain at first refused to grant this, and it seemed for a time as if war was inevitable, but Spain finally agreed to grant the men a trial, after which they were set free.

In February, 1897, a number of reforms for the island were proposed by the Spanish government, and their general features were made public, but they did not meet with favor. In October, 1897, General Weyler was succeeded as governor-general by Marshal BLANCO Y ARENAS (*q. v.*), who immediately began a more humane régime, granted many pardons, and undertook relief measures for the thousands of Weyler's reconcen-

Rep. Cannon Sen. Elkins Sec. Wilson Ass. Sec. Adee Postmaster-Gen. Chas. Emory Smith Sec. Porter Ass. Sec. Day Sec. Bliss Ass. Sec. Pruden

Sec. Alger Lieut.-Col. Montgomery Fresident McKinley Att.-Gen. Griggs Ass. Sec. Cortelyou

THE SPANISH-AMERICAN WAR—PRESIDENT McKINLEY SIGNING THE ULTIMATUM

trados who were starving in the interior. So great did the distress become during that year that President McKinley appointed a central Cuban relief committee to raise funds for the sufferers. Later Clara Barton, president of the American Red Cross Association, went to the island, with the consent of the Spanish government, and supervised the distribution of needed supplies. When Señor Sagasta became prime minister for Spain, a new policy of dealing with the trouble in Cuba was attempted. He declared that autonomy under the suzerainty of Spain would be given to the island. Accordingly, when Marshal Blanco arrived in Havana, he issued a proclamation to the inhabitants announcing that he had been sent by the home government to begin reforms and to establish self-government.

The full text of the decree granting autonomy to both Cuba and Porto Rico was published in the *Official Gazette* of Madrid, on Nov. 27, of which the following is a synopsis:

Article I. explains the principles of the future government of the two islands.

Article II. decrees that the government of each island shall be composed of an insular parliament, divided into two chambers, while a governor-general, representing the home government, will exercise in its name the supreme authority.

Article III. declares that the faculty of many laws on colonial affairs rests with the insular chambers and the governor-general.

Article IV. directs that the insular representation shall be composed of two corporations, with equal powers, a Chamber of Representatives and a Council of Administration.

Article V. provides that the Council of Administration shall consist of thirty-five members, of whom eighteen shall be elected and seventeen nominated by the home government.

Article VI. provides that the members of the Council of Administration must be Spaniards, thirty-five years of age, who were born in the island or who have resided there continuously for four years. It specifies numerous officials, such as senators, presidents of courts and of chambers of commerce and other bodies, as eligible to election to the Council.

Articles VII. to XIV., inclusive, deal with nominations and the conditions of election to councils.

Article XV. empowers the throne or the governor-general to convoke, suspend, or dissolve the Chambers, with an obligation to reassemble them within three months.

Article XVI. and the following articles deal with the procedure of the Chambers, and grant immunity to members.

Article XXIX. empowers the insular parliament to receive the governor's oath and make effective the responsibility of

HAVANA HARBOR.

the secretaries forming the governor's council. When the secretaries are impeached by the Chambers they are to be judged by the Council of Administration. Negotiations for treaties of commerce are to be made by the home government, with the assistance of the secretaries of the island.

Article XXXIX. confers upon parliament the imposing of customs duties.

Article XL. deals with the commercial relations of the islands with the peninsula, and provides that no import or export tax may differentiate to the prejudice of the productions of either island or the peninsula. A list will be formed of articles coming from Spain direct, which will be granted favorable treatment in regard to similar articles coming from abroad, and the same will be done for productions of the islands entering Spain, the differential duty in no case to exceed 35 per cent.

The remaining features of the decree explained the powers of the governor-general. He was to have supreme command, be responsible for the preservation of order, have the power to nominate officials, was to publish and execute the laws and decrees, conventions, international treaties, etc., and the power of pardoning, suspending constitutional guarantees, and ordering a state of siege, should circumstances require it.

In accordance with these provisions Marshal Blanco, on Dec. 29, issued a decree announcing the plans on which autonomy was to be established. In this decree was also included a synopsis of the duties of the several officers of the proposed cabinet pending the assemblage of the Cuban legislature and the establishment by it of permanent duties. The members of this first cabinet were sworn into office on Jan. 1, 1898, and immediately assumed charge of their offices with a view of getting the new system well under way by the time the legislature met. In the following month this new colonial government undertook to bring the insurrection to an end by offering the following proposition to the insurgents:

1. The volunteers will be dissolved and a Cuban militia formed.

2. The insurgent colonels and generals will be recognized.

3. Cuba will be called upon to pay only $100,000,000 out of the $600,000,000 indebtedness due for both wars.

4. Cuba will pay $2,000,000 a year for the crown list.

5. Cuba will make her own treaties without interference by the Madrid government.

6. Spanish products will have only a 10 per cent. margin of protection over similar products from other countries.

7. No exiles or deportations will be made, even in war time, to Spain, Africa, or to penal settlements elsewhere.

8. Death sentences for rebellion shall be abolished.

9. Martial law cannot be ordered by the captain-general without the assent of both the House and the Senate, if those bodies are in session, or without the assent of a majority of the cabinet if they are not in session.

10. The Archbishop of Santiago de Cuba shall always be a native Cuban.

11. The actual insurgent party shall have three seats in the first cabinet.

12. An armistice of fifteen days will be granted for the discussion of the terms of peace.

All efforts failed to open negotiations with the insurgents, and the scheme of autonomy never materialized.

On Jan. 9, 1898, the first distribution of relief stores from the United States for the starving Cubans took place in Havana. During the same week riots occurred in that city which required the presence of regular troops. On Jan. 25 the United States battle-ship *Maine* entered the harbor on a friendly visit. Her officers made the customary formal calls on the Spanish authorities, who, in turn, were received with the prescribed honors aboard ship. On Feb. 11, Captain Sigsbee, of the *Maine*, and Consul-General Lee called officially on General Blanco, who was absent from Havana when the *Maine* arrived, and on Feb. 12 a visit of courtesy was paid to President Galvez, of the new Cuban cabinet, who soon returned it. All of these courtesies were marked by the warmest cordiality by both parties On the night of Feb. 15, the *Maine* was suddenly blown up at the anchorage designated for her by the Spanish authorities on her arrival, with the result that two officers and 264 men perished. Great excitement immediately ensued, and every effort was made to save the survivors. In this work of relief the Spaniards bore a prompt and large share.

UNITED STATES BATTLE-SHIP MAINE.

The officers, crews, and boats of the Spanish cruiser *Alfonso XII.*, and of the *City of Washington*, the mail steamship plying between New York and Cuba, both lying near; the Havana officials, police, military, firemen, clergy, and citizens generally, were indefatigably engaged in the work of succor. The remains of all the victims recovered up to the 18th were laid in state in the city hall, and later were buried with marks of deepest feeling by the Spanish authorities, who bore the expense. The home and local Spanish governments sent condolences to the United States, all assigning the great catastrophe to an accident.

A naval court of inquiry was at once appointed, which held its first session in Havana, and subsequent ones there and in Key West. For the expenses of this inquiry Congress voted $200,000, and professional wreckers were put to work on the ship's hull. After a few days rumors gained currency that the disaster had been deliberately planned, instead of having been an accident.

On Feb. 20, the Spanish cruiser *Vizcaya* steamed into New York Harbor to return the visit of the *Maine* to Havana, her commander being in ignorance of the disaster. As soon as the captain learned of the fate of the *Maine* he lowered his flags to half-mast, and expressed his sympathy. During her brief stay in New York the *Vizcaya* was under close protection by both the city and federal authorities, a step never taken before towards a war-vessel of a friendly country. The usual official visits were made, and when Captain Eulate left for Havana he expressed himself as highly gratified with his treatment.

On account of the great need of food, clothing, and medical supplies in Cuba, President McKinley ordered two naval vessels to carry to the island the articles collected in the United States. The government of Spain suggested that merchant vessels would be more desirable for this work, and that it would be pleased if Consul-General Lee were recalled; but neither of these intimations were heeded by the President. On March 8, a bill appropriating $50,000,000 for national defence was passed in the House, and on March 9 in the Senate, neither house raising a dissenting vote.

The court of inquiry completed its investigation on March 21, and on the 28th President McKinley transmitted the findings and evidence to Congress, accompanying them with a special message. The following is the text of the report:

UNITED STATES SHIP *Iowa*—FIRST RATE.
KEY WEST, FLA., Monday, *March* 21, 1898.

After full and mature consideration of all the testimony before it, the court finds as follows:

1. That the United States battle-ship *Maine* arrived in the harbor of Havana, Cuba, on the 25th of January, 1898, and was taken to Buoy No. 4, in from 5½ to 6 fathoms of water, by the regular government pilot.

The United States consul-general at Havana had notified the authorities at that place, the previous evening, of the intended arrival of the *Maine*.

2. The state of discipline on board the *Maine* was excellent, and all orders and regulations in regard to the care and safety of the ship were strictly carried out.

All ammunition was stowed in accordance with prescribed instructions, and proper care was taken whenever ammunition was handled.

Nothing was stowed in any of the magazines or shell-rooms which was not permitted to be stowed there.

The magazines and shell-rooms were always locked after having been opened, and after the destruction of the *Maine* the keys were found in their proper place, in the captain's cabin, everything having been reported secure that evening at 8 P.M.

The temperature of the magazine and shell-rooms was taken daily and reported. The only magazine which had an undue amount of heat was the after 10-inch magazine, and that did not explode at the time the *Maine* was destroyed.

The dry gun-cotton primers and detonators were stowed in the cabin aft, and remote from the scene of the explosion. Waste was carefully looked after on the *Maine* to obviate danger. Special orders in regard to this had been given by the commanding officer.

Varnishes, driers, alcohol, and other combustibles of this nature were stowed on or above the main deck, and could not have had anything to do with the destruction of the *Maine*.

The medical stores were stored aft under the ward-room and remote from the scene of the explosion.

No dangerous stores of any kind were stowed below in any of the other store-rooms.

The coal bunkers were inspected daily. Of those bunkers adjacent to the forward magazine and shell-rooms, four were empty—namely, B 3, B 4, B 5, B 6. A 15 had been in use that day, and A 16 was full of New River coal. This coal had been carefully inspected before receiving it on board. The bunker in which it was stowed was accessible on three sides at all times and the fourth side at this time, on account of bunkers B 4 and B 6 being empty. This bunker, A 16, had been inspected that day by the engineer officer on duty.

The fire-alarms in the bunkers were in working-order, and there had never been a case of spontaneous combustion of coal on board the *Maine*.

The two after-boilers of the ship were in use at the time of the disaster, but for auxiliary purposes only, with a comparatively low pressure of steam, and being tended by a reliable watch. These boilers could not have caused the explosion of the ship. The four forward boilers have since been found by the divers and are in a fair condition.

WRECK OF THE MAINE IN HAVANA HARBOR.

The torpedo warheads were all stowed in the after part of the ship under the ward-room, and neither caused nor participated in the destruction of the *Maine*.

On the night of the destruction of the *Maine* everything had been reported secure for the night at 8 P.M. by reliable persons through the proper authorities to the commanding officer. At the time the *Maine* was destroyed the ship was quiet and therefore least liable to accident, caused by movements from those on board.

5. At Frame 17 the outer shell of the warship from a point 11½ feet from the middle line of the ship and 6 feet above the keel when in its normal position has been braced up so as to be now about 4 feet above the surface of the water; therefore, about 34 feet

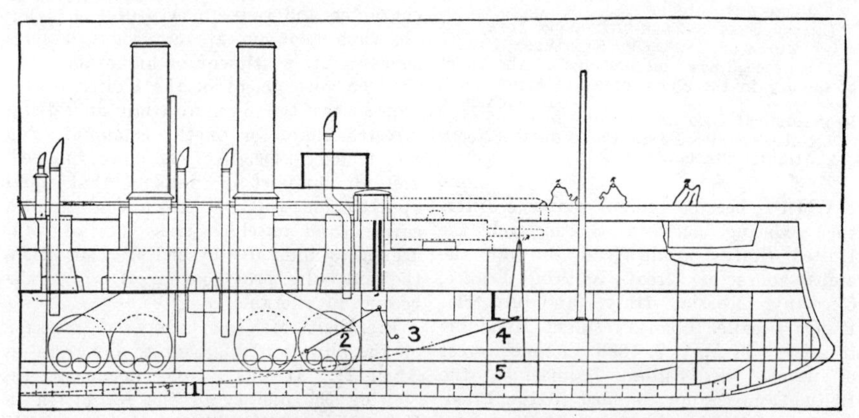

PROJECTION SHOWING POSITION OF BOW AND KEEL OF THE MAINE.

1. Dotted line shows part of keel not accessible for direct measurement. 2. Line of break in bottom plating. 3. Bilge keel. 4. Line of keel. 5. Stem enters mud here, where a hole in the mud was found 7 feet deep and 15 feet in diameter.

3. The destruction of the *Maine* occurred at 9.40 P.M., on the 15th day of February, 1898, in the harbor of Havana, Cuba, she being at the time moored to the same buoy to which she had been taken upon her arrival.

There were two explosions of a distinctly different character, with a very short but distinct interval between them, and the forward part of the ship was lifted to a marked degree at the time of the first explosion. The first explosion was more in the nature of a report, like that of a gun, while the second explosion was more open, prolonged and of greater volume. This second explosion was, in the opinion of the court, caused by a partial explosion of two or more of the forward magazines of the *Maine*. The evidence bearing upon this, being principally obtained from divers, did not enable the court to form a definite conclusion as to the condition of the wreck, although it was established that the after part of the ship was practically intact and sank in that condition a very few minutes after the destruction of the forward part.

4. The following facts in regard to the forward part of the ship are, however, established by the testimony: That portion of the port side of the protective deck which extends from about Frame 50 to about Frame 41 was blown up aft and over to port. The main deck from about Frame 41 was blown up aft and slightly over to starboard, folding the forward part of the middle structure over and on top of the after part.

This was, in the opinion of the court, caused by the partial explosion of two or more of the forward magazines of the *Maine*.

above where it would be had the ship sunk uninjured. The outside bottom plating is bent into a reversed V-shape, the other wing of which, about 15 feet broad and 30 feet in length (from Frame 17 to Frame 25), is doubled back upon itself against the continuation of the same plating extending forward.

At Frame 18 the vertical keel is broken in two, and the flat keel bent into an angle similar to the angle formed by the outside bottom plating. This break is now about 6 feet below the surface of the water and about 30 feet above its normal position.

In the opinion of the court, this effect could have been produced only by the explosion of a mine situated under the bottom of the ship at about Frame 18 and somewhere on the port side of the ship.

6. The court finds that the loss of the *Maine* on the occasion named was not in any respect due to fault or negligence on the part of any of the officers or members of the crew of said vessel.

7. In the opinion of the court, the *Maine* was destroyed by the explosion of a submarine mine, which caused the partial explosion of two or more of her forward magazines.

8. The court has been unable to obtain evidence fixing the responsibility for the destruction of the *Maine* upon any person or persons.

W. T. SAMPSON,
Captain, United States Navy, President.
A. MARIX,
Lieutenant-Commander, United States Navy, Judge-Advocate.

The court having finished the inquiry it was ordered to make, adjourned at 11 A.M., to await the action of the convening authority.

W. T. SAMPSON,
Captain, United States Navy, President.
A. MARIX,
Lieutenant-Commander, United States Navy, Judge-Advocate.

UNITED STATES FLAG-SHIP *New York*,
March 22, 1898, OFF KEY WEST, FLA.

The proceedings and findings of the court of inquiry in the above case are approved.

M. SICARD,
Rear-Admiral, Commander-in-Chief of the United States Naval Force on the North Atlantic Station.

When it became evident that the difference existing between Spain and the United States would lead to war the ambassadors of Great Britain, France, Germany, Russia, Italy, and Austria-Hungary called upon President McKinley in a body on April 7, 1898, in the interest of peace. Sir Julian Pauncefote, the British ambassador, handed to the President the following joint note:

"The undersigned representatives of Germany, Austria-Hungary, France, Great Britain, Italy, and Russia, duly authorized in that behalf, address, in the name of their respective governments, a pressing appeal to the feelings of humanity and moderation of the President and of the American people in their existing differences with Spain.

"They earnestly hope that further negotiations will lead to an agreement which, while securing the maintenance of peace, will afford all necessary guarantees for the re-establishment of order in Cuba.

"The powers do not doubt that the humanitarian and purely disinterested character of this representation will be fully recognized and appreciated by the American nation."

President McKinley's reply to the powers was:

"The government of the United States recognizes the good will which has prompted the friendly communication of the representatives of Germany, Austria-Hungary, France, Great Britain, Italy, and Russia, as set forth in the address of your excellencies, and shares the hope therein expressed that the outcome of the situation in Cuba may be the maintenance of peace between the United States and Spain by affording the necessary guarantee for the re-establishment of order in the island, so terminating the chronic condition of disturbance there which so deeply injures the interests and menaces the tranquillity of the American nation by the character and consequences of the struggle thus kept up at our doors, besides shocking its sentiment of humanity.

"The government of the United States appreciates the humanitarian and disinterested character of the communication now made, on behalf of the powers named, and for its part is confident that equal appreciation will be shown for its own earnest and unselfish endeavors to fulfil a duty to humanity by ending a situation, the indefinite prolongation of which has become insufferable."

President McKinley's special message on the situation was sent to Congress on April 11. It was a long document, reviewing the history of the revolution in Cuba from 1895, giving many precedents bearing on the questions of recognition, intervention, and independence; and citing the reasons which he claimed justified the intervention of the United States. The message concluded as follows:

"In view of these facts and of these considerations, I ask Congress to authorize and empower the President to take measures to secure a full and final termination of hostilities between the government of Spain and the people of Cuba, and to secure in the island the establishment of a stable government, capable of maintaining order and observing its international obligations, insuring peace and tranquillity and the security of its citizens, as well as our own, and to use the military and naval forces of the United States as may be necessary."

On April 13 the House passed the following resolution by a vote of 322 to 19:

"Whereas, the government of Spain for three years past has been waging war on the island of Cuba against a revolution by the inhabitants thereof, without making any substantial progress towards the suppression of said revolution, and has conducted the warfare in a manner contrary to the laws of nations, by methods inhuman and uncivilized, causing the death by starvation of more than 200,000 innocent non-combatants, the victims being for the most part helpless women and children, inflicting intolerable injury to the commercial interests of the United States, involving the destruction of the lives and property of many of our citizens, entailing the expenditure of millions of money in patrolling our coasts and policing the high seas in order to maintain our neutrality; and,

"Whereas, this long series of losses, injuries, and murders for which Spain is responsible has culminated in the destruction of the United States battle-ship *Maine* in the harbor of Havana and in the death of 266 of our seamen;

"Resolved, by the Senate and House of Representatives of the United States of America in Congress assembled, that the President is hereby authorized and directed to intervene at once to stop the war in Cuba, to the end and with the purpose of securing permanent peace and order there, establishing by the free action of the people thereof a stable and independent government of their own in the island of Cuba; and the President is hereby authorized and empowered to use the land and naval forces of the United States to execute the purpose of this resolution."

The Senate on the 16th passed the following resolutions by a vote of 67 to 21, the recognition amendment being adopted by a vote of 51 to 37:

"Joint resolutions for the recognition of the independence of the people and republic of Cuba, demanding that the government of Spain relinquish its authority and government in the island of Cuba, and withdraw its land and naval forces from Cuba and Cuban waters, and directing the President of the United States to use the land and naval forces of the United States to carry these resolutions into effect.

"Whereas, the abhorrent conditions which have existed for more than three years in the island of Cuba, so near our own borders, have shocked the moral sense of the people of the United States, have been a disgrace to Christian civilization, culminating, as they have, in the destruction of a United States battle-ship, with 266 of its officers and crew, while on a friendly visit in the harbor of Havana, and cannot longer be endured, as has been set forth by the President of the United States in his message to Congress of April 11, 1898, upon which the action of Congress was invited; therefore,

"Resolved, by the Senate and House of Representatives of the United States of America, in Congress assembled,

"1. That the people of the island of Cuba are, and of a right ought to be, free and independent, and that the government of the United States hereby recognizes the republic of Cuba as the true and lawful government of the island.

"2. That it is the duty of the United States to demand, and the government of the United States does hereby demand, that the government of Spain at once relinquish its authority and government in the island of Cuba and withdraw its land and naval forces from Cuba and Cuban waters.

"3. That the President of the United States be and he hereby is directed and empowered to use the entire land and naval forces of the United States, and to call into the actual service of the United States the militia of the several States to such extent as may be necessary to carry these resolutions into effect.

"4. That the United States hereby disclaims any disposition or intention to exercise sovereignty, jurisdiction, or control over said island except for the pacification thereof; and asserts its determination, when that is accomplished, to leave the government and control of the island to its people."

In the resolutions of the House the President was directed to intervene, which was the power he desired; but the resolutions of the Senate not only gave directions for intervention but for recognition. The latter act was contrary to the President's policy. Thereupon both Houses of Congress held an all-night session; their resolutions were sent to a conference committee; mutual concessions were made, and early on the morning of the 19th, the resolutions of the Senate, with the recognition clause stricken out, were adopted by a vote of 42 to 35 in the Senate and 310 to 6 in the House.

The President sent the following message to Congress on the 25th:

"To the Senate and House of Representatives of the United States of America:

"I transmit to the Congress for its consideration and appropriate action copies of correspondence recently had with the representative of Spain in the United States, with the United States minister at Madrid, and, through the latter, with the government of Spain, showing the action taken under the joint resolution approved April 20, 1898, 'for the recognition of the independence of the people of Cuba, demanding that the government of Spain relinquish its authority and government in the island of Cuba and withdraw its land and naval forces from Cuba and Cuban waters, and directing the President of the United States to use the land and naval forces of the United States to carry these resolutions into effect.'

"Upon communicating to the Spanish minister in Washington the demand which it became the duty of the executive to address to the government of Spain in obedience to said resolution, the minister asked for his passports and withdrew. The United States minister at Madrid was in turn notified by the Spanish minister for foreign affairs that the withdrawal of the Spanish representative from the United States had terminated diplomatic relations between the two countries, and that all official communications between their respective representatives ceased therewith.

"I commend to your special attention the note addressed to the United States minister at Madrid by the Spanish minister for foreign affairs on the 21st inst., whereby the foregoing notification was conveyed. It will be perceived therefrom that the government of Spain, having cognizance of the joint resolution of the United States Congress, and in view of the things which the President is thereby required and authorized to do, responds by treating the reasonable demands of this government as measures of hostility, following with that instant and complete severance of relations by its action, which by the usage of nations accompanies an existent state of war between sovereign powers.

"The position of Spain being thus made known, and the demands of the United States being denied, with a complete rupture of intercourse by the act of Spain, I have been constrained in exercise of the power and authority conferred upon me by the joint resolution aforesaid, to proclaim under date of April 22, 1898, a blockade of certain ports of the north coast of Cuba lying between Cardenas and Bahia Honda, and of the port of Cienfuegos, on the south coast of Cuba, and, further, in exercise of my constitutional powers, and using the authority conferred upon me by the act of Congress, approved April 22, 1898, to issue my proclamation, dated April 23, 1898, calling for volunteers in order to carry into effect the said resolutions of April 20, 1898. Copies of these proclamations are hereto appended.

"In view of the measures so taken, and with a view to the adoption of such other measures as may be necessary to enable me to carry out the expressed will of the Congress of the United States in the premises, I now recommend to your honorable body the adoption of a joint resolution declaring that a state of war exists between the United States of America and the kingdom of Spain, and I urge speedy action thereon to the end that the definition of the international status of the United States as a belligerent power may be made known, and the assertion of all its rights and the maintenance of all its duties in the conduct of a public war may be assured."

In response to this, Congress immediately made a formal declaration of war in the following terms:

"1. That war be, and the same is, hereby declared to exist, and that war has existed since the 21st day of April, A.D. 1898, including said day, between the United States of America and the kingdom of Spain.

"2. That the President of the United States be and he is hereby directed and empowered to use the entire land and naval forces of the United States, and to call into the actual service of the United States the militia of the several States to such extent as may be necessary to carry this act into effect."

This was succeeded on the following day by the executive proclamation:

"By the President of the United States of America.

"Whereas, by an act of Congress, ap-

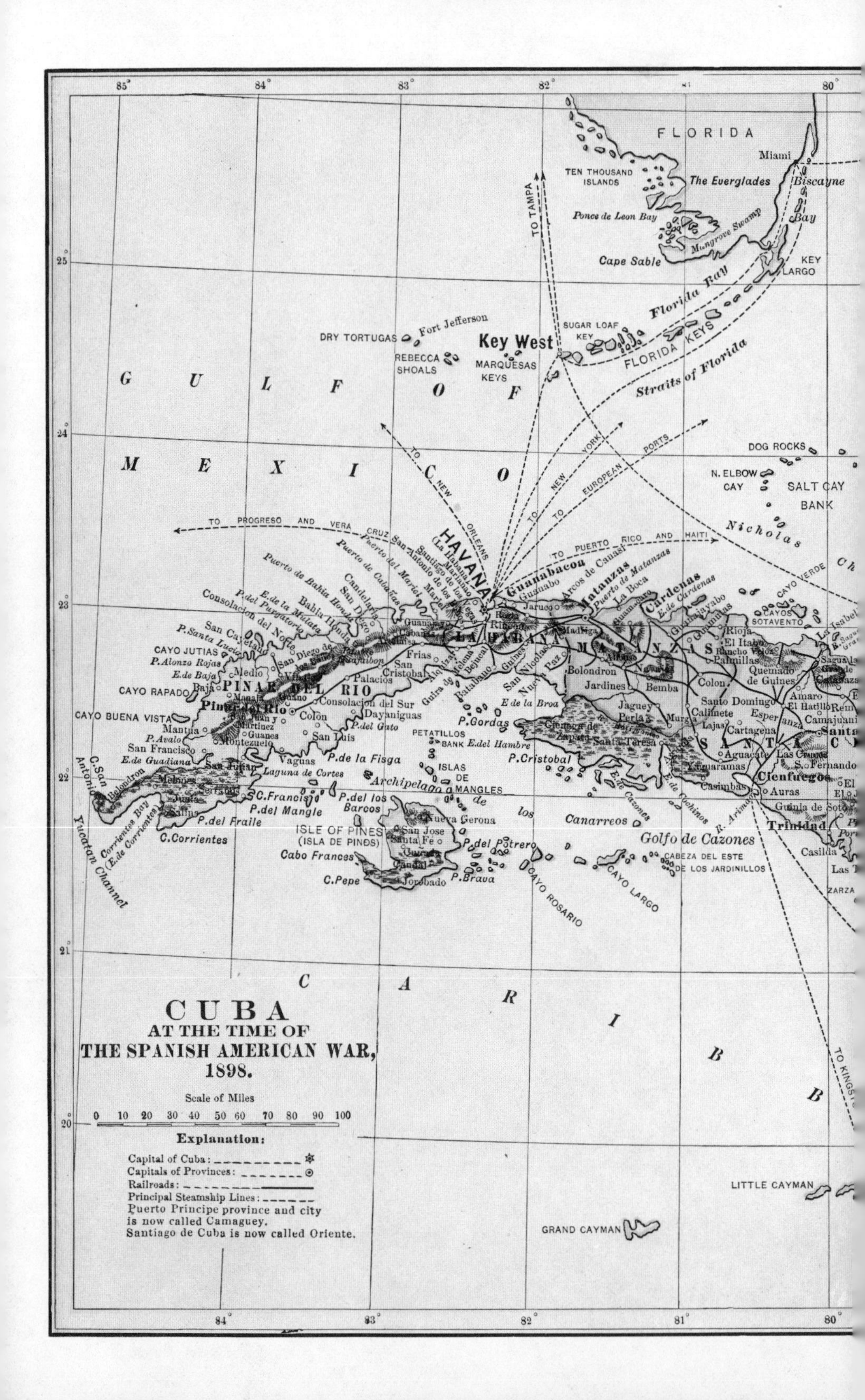

CUBA
AT THE TIME OF
THE SPANISH AMERICAN WAR,
1898.
Scale of Miles
0 10 20 30 40 50 60 70 80 90 100
Explanation:
Capital of Cuba:
Capitals of Provinces:
Railroads:
Principal Steamship Lines:
Puerto Principe province and city
is now called Camaguey.
Santiago de Cuba is now called Oriente.
FLORIDA
Miami
TEN THOUSAND ISLANDS
The Everglades
Biscayne Bay
Ponce de Leon Bay
Mangrove Swamp
Cape Sable
KEY LARGO
Florida Bay
FLORIDA KEYS
SUGAR LOAF KEY
Key West
DRY TORTUGAS
Fort Jefferson
REBECCA SHOALS
MARQUESAS KEYS
Straits of Florida
TO TAMPA
GULF OF MEXICO
TO NEW ORLEANS
TO NEW YORK
TO EUROPEAN PORTS
TO PROGRESO AND VERA CRUZ
TO PUERTO RICO AND HAITI
DOG ROCKS
N. ELBOW CAY
SALT CAY BANK
Nicholas
CAYO VERDE
CAYOS SOTAVENTO
HAVANA
LA HABANA
Guanabacoa
Matanzas
MATANZAS
Cardenas
PINAR DEL RIO
Pinar del Rio
CAYO JUTIAS
CAYO RAPADO
CAYO BUENA VISTA
C. San Antonio
Yucatan Channel
Corrientes Bay
C. Corrientes
P. del Fraile
C. Francis
P. del Mangle
ISLE OF PINES
(ISLA DE PINOS)
Nueva Gerona
Cabo Frances
C. Pepe
P. Brava
P. del Potrero
Archipelago de los Canarreos
ISLAS DE MANGLES
PETATILLOS BANK
P. Gordas
P. Cristobal
Cienaga de Zapata
Golfo de Cazones
CAYO ROSARIO
CAYO LARGO
CABEZA DEL ESTE DE LOS JARDINILLOS
Cienfuegos
Trinidad
SANTA CLARA
Santo Domingo
Colon
Jaguey
Bolondron
Jardines
Bemba
CARIBBEAN
TO KINGSTON
LITTLE CAYMAN
GRAND CAYMAN
85° 84° 83° 82° 81° 80°
25° 24° 23° 22° 21° 20°

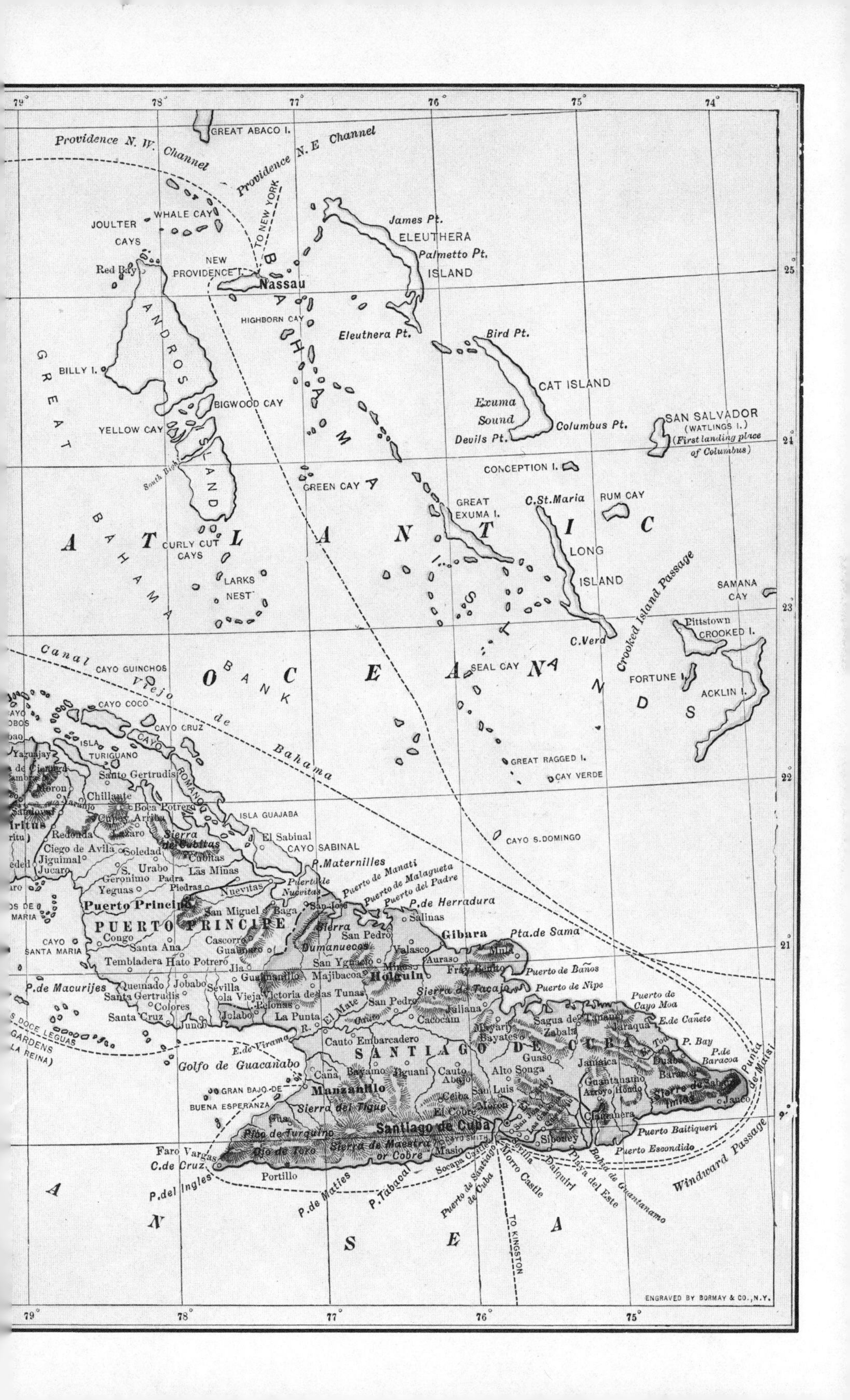

GREAT ABACO I.
Providence N. W. Channel
Providence N. E Channel
TO NEW YORK
JOULTER CAYS
WHALE CAY
Red Bay
NEW PROVIDENCE I.
Nassau
James Pt.
ELEUTHERA
Palmetto Pt.
ISLAND
HIGHBORN CAY
Eleuthera Pt.
Bird Pt.
ANDROS
ISLAND
GREAT BAHAMA BANK
BILLY I.
BIGWOOD CAY
YELLOW CAY
CAT ISLAND
Exuma Sound
Columbus Pt.
Devils Pt.
SAN SALVADOR
(WATLINGS I.)
(First landing place of Columbus)
CONCEPTION I.
South Bight
GREEN CAY
GREAT EXUMA I.
C.St.Maria
RUM CAY
BAHAMA ISLANDS
ATLANTIC OCEAN
CURLY CUT CAYS
LONG ISLAND
LARKS NEST
Crooked Island Passage
SAMANA CAY
Pittstown
CROOKED I.
C.Verd
Canal Viejo de Bahama
CAYO GUINCHOS
SEAL CAY
FORTUNE I.
ACKLIN I.
CAYO COCO
CAYO CRUZ
ISLA TURIGUANO
CAYO ROMANO
GREAT RAGGED I.
CAY VERDE
Santo Gertrudis
Chillate
Moron
Boca Potrero
ISLA GUAJABA
Redonda
Lazaro
Sierra de Cubitas
El Sabinal
CAYO SABINAL
CAYO S.DOMINGO
Ciego de Avila
Soledad
Cubitas
Jiguimal
Jucaro
S. Urabo
Las Minas
P.Maternilles
Puerto de Manati
Puerto de Malagueta
Puerto del Padre
Geronimo
Padra
Yeguas
Piedras
Nuevitas
Puerto de Nuevitas
Puerto Principe
PUERTO PRINCIPE
San Miguel
Baga
San Jose
P.de Herradura
Salinas
Congo
Santa Ana
Cascorro
Guaimaro
Sierra Dumanuecos
San Pedro
Gibara
Pta.de Sama
CAYO SANTA MARIA
Tembladera
Hato Potrero
Valasco
Auraso
Mula
San Ygnacio
Minas
Fray Benito
Puerto de Baños
P.de Macurijes
Quemado
Jobabo
Sevilla
Majibacoa
Holguin
Puerto de Nipe
Santa Gertrudis
ola Vieja
Victoria de las Tunas
Sierra de Tacajo
Colores
Pelonas
San Pedro
Juliana
Puerto de Cayo Moa
Santa Cruz
Jucaro
Jolabo
La Punta
El Mate
Cauto
Cacocum
Sagua de Tanamo
Zabala
Jaraqua
E.de Cañete
JARDINES DOCE LEGUAS GARDENS (LA REINA)
E.de Virama
R.
Cauto Embarcadero
SANTIAGO DE CUBA
Mayari
Bayates
Toa
P. Bay
P.de Baracoa
Punta de Maisi
Golfo de Guacanabo
Caña
Bayamo
Jiguani
Cauto Abajo
Guaso
Alto Songa
Jamaica
Duaba
Baracoa
GRAN BAJO DE BUENA ESPERANZA
Manzanillo
Ceiba
San Luis
Guantanamo
Arroyo Hondo
Sierra de Sabana Imias
Sierra del Tigue
El Cobre
Jauco
Gua
Santiago de Cuba
Sibonev
Caimanera
Pico de Turquino
Ojo de Toro
Sierra de Maestra or Cobre
Puerto Baitiqueri
Faro Vargas
C.de Cruz
Masio
Puerto Escondido
Portillo
P.del Ingles
P.de Maties
P.Tabacal
Socapa Castle
Puerto de Santiago de Cuba
Morro Castle
Sevilla
Daiquiri
Playa del Este
Bahia de Guantanamo
Windward Passage
CARIBBEAN SEA
TO KINGSTON
ENGRAVED BY BORMAY & CO., N.Y.

proved April 25, 1898, it is declared that war exists, and that war has existed since the 21st day of April, A.D. 1898, including said day, between the United States of America and the kingdom of Spain; and,

"Whereas, it being desirable that such war should be conducted upon principles in harmony with the present views of nations and sanctioned by recent practice, it has already been announced that the policy of this government will be not to resort to privateering, but to adhere to the rules of the declaration of Paris.

"Now, therefore, I, William McKinley, President of the United States of America, by virtue of the power invested in me by the Constitution and the laws, do hereby declare and proclaim:

"1. The neutral flag covers enemy's goods excepting contraband of war.

"2. Neutral goods not contraband of war are not liable to confiscation under the enemy's flag.

"3. Blockades, in order to be binding, must be effective.

"4. Spanish merchant vessels in any port or places within the United States shall be allowed until May 21, 1898, inclusive, for loading their cargoes and departing from such ports or places, and such Spanish merchant vessels, if met at sea by any United States ship, shall be permitted to continue their voyage if on examination of their papers it shall appear that their cargoes were taken on board before the expiration of the above terms, provided that nothing herein contained shall apply to Spanish vessels having on board any officers in the military or naval service of the enemy, or any coal (except such as may be necessary for their voyage), or any other article prohibited or contraband of war, or any despatch of or to the Spanish government.

"5. Any Spanish merchant vessel, which, prior to April 21, 1898, shall have sailed from any foreign port bound for any port or place in the United States shall be permitted to enter such port or place, and to discharge her cargo and afterwards forthwith to depart without molestation, and any such vessel, if met at sea by any United States ship, shall be permitted to continue her voyage to any port not blockaded.

"6. The right of search is to be exercised with strict regard for the right of neutrals, and the voyages of mail steamers are not to be interfered with except on the clearest ground of suspicion of a violation of law in respect to contraband or blockade."

On April 22 Congress adopted a conference report on the volunteer army bill, under the authority of which the President, on April 23, issued a call for 125,000 volunteers to serve for two years unless mustered out sooner. On April 26 a similar report on a bill to reorganize the regular army, and increase its strength to 61,919 officers and men, was passed. For a list of the principal operations in and around Cuba during the war, see BATTLES.

On Aug. 9, 1898, proposals for peace, at the initiative of Spain, were submitted to the President by M. JULES MARTIN-CAMBON (*q. v.*), the ambassador of France at Washington. On the 10th an agreement was negotiated between M. Cambon and Secretary Day, was accepted by the Spanish government on the 11th, and proclaimed by the President on the 12th. The following articles in the agreement show the terms under which the United States was willing to make peace:

"Article I. Spain will relinquish all claim of sovereignty over and title to Cuba.

"Art. II. Spain will cede to the United States the island of Porto Rico and other islands now under Spanish sovereignty in the West Indies, and also an island in the Ladrones, to be selected by the United States.

"Art. III. The United States will occupy and hold the city, bay, and harbor of Manila, pending the conclusion of a treaty of peace, which shall determine the control, disposition, and government of the Philippines.

"Art. IV. Spain will immediately evacuate Cuba, Porto Rico, and other islands now under Spanish sovereignty in the West Indies, and to this end each government will, within ten days after the signing of this protocol, appoint commissioners, and the commissioners so appointed shall, within thirty days after the signing of this protocol, meet at Havana for the purpose of arranging and carrying out the details of the aforesaid evacuation of Cuba and the adjacent islands. . . .

"Art. V. The United States and Spain will each appoint not more than five commissioners to treat of peace, and the commissioners so appointed shall meet at Paris not later than Oct. 1, 1898, and proceed to the negotiation and conclusion of a treaty of peace, which treaty shall be subject to ratification according to the respective constitutional forms of the two countries.

"Art. VI. Upon the conclusion and signing of this protocol hostilities between the two countries shall be suspended, and notice to that effect shall be given as soon as possible by each government to the commanders of its military and naval forces."

Under Article IV., the following military commission was appointed for Cuba: American, Maj.-Gen. James F. Wade, Rear-Admiral William T. Sampson, Maj.-Gen. Matthew C. Butler; Spanish, Maj-Gen. Gonzales Parrado, Rear-Admiral Pastor y Landero, Marquis Montero. Under the direction of these commissioners Cuba was formally evacuated Jan. 1, 1899. After the American occupation MAJ.-GEN. JOHN R. BROOKE (*q. v.*) was appointed the first American military governor. He served as such till early in 1900, when he was succeeded by Maj.-Gen. Leonard Wood, who had been in command of the district and city of Santiago. A constitutional convention was held in November following. For text of treaty with Spain, see SPAIN, TREATY WITH.

Cuban Constitution.—The following is the text of the proposed constitution, as submitted by the central committee to the constitutional convention sitting in Havana, in January, 1901:

We, the delegates of the Cuban people, having met in assembly for the purpose of agreeing upon the adoption of a fundamental law, which, at the same time that it provides for the constitution into a sovereign and independent nation of the people of Cuba, establishes a solid and permanent form of government, capable of complying with its international obligations, insuring domestic tranquillity, establishing justice, promoting the general welfare, and securing the blessings of liberty to the inhabitants, we do agree upon and adopt the following Constitution, in pursuance of the said purpose, invoking the protection of the Almighty, and prompted by the dictates of our conscience:

FIRST SECTION.

FORM OF GOVERNMENT—THE FORM OF GOVERNMENT AND NATIONAL TERRITORY.

1. The people of Cuba shall be constituted into a sovereign and independent state, under a republican form of government.

2. The territory of the republic comprises the island of Cuba and the islands and keys adjacent thereto, which were under the jurisdiction and control of the general government of the island of Cuba while it was a Spanish possession.

3. The territory of the republic shall be divided into six provinces, the boundaries and names of which shall be those of the present provinces, as long as not modified by the laws.

SECOND SECTION.

REQUIREMENTS FOR CITIZENSHIP—METHODS OF LOSING AND REGAINING IT—DUTIES OF CITIZENS.

The following are Cuban citizens:

1. All persons born within or outside Cuban territory of Cuban parents.

2. The children of foreign parents born in the territory of the republic who, after arriving at their majority, inscribe themselves as Cubans in the proper register.

3. Those persons who were born outside of Cuban territory of Cuban parents who had lost Cuban citizenship, provided that on attaining their majority they inscribe in the proper register.

4. Those foreigners who have belonged to the liberating army and who, residing in Cuba, claim Cuban citizenship within six months following the promulgation of the constitution.

5. Those Africans who may have been slaves in Cuba, and also those who were emancipated and referred to in Article XIII. of the treaty between Spain and England, June 28, 1835.

6. The Spaniards residing in Cuban territory on April 11, 1899, who shall not have inscribed themselves as Spaniards up to April 11, 1900.

7. Foreigners who have been domiciled in Cuba since Jan. 1, 1899, provided they demand Cuban citizenship within six months following the promulgation of the constitution, or in case of minors within six months after attaining majority.

8. Foreigners after five years' residence in the territory of the republic who obtain naturalization papers, in accordance with the laws.

GROUNDS FOR FORFEITING CUBAN CITIZENSHIP.

1. By securing naturalization papers in a foreign country.

2. By accepting a position under another government without the consent of Congress.

3. By entering into the military or naval service of any foreign power without the aforesaid consent.

Cuban citizenship may be regained in accordance with the provisions which the law may establish.

DUTIES OF ALL CUBAN CITIZENS.

1. To serve in arms according to the requirements of the law.

2. To contribute to public expenses, in the manner established by the laws.

THIRD SECTION.

RIGHTS GUARANTEED BY THE CONSTITUTION.

1. All Cubans shall have equal rights under the law.

2. No law can have a retroactive effect, except in penal matters, when the new law is favorable to the delinquent.

3. Obligations of a civil character which spring from contracts or from the acts or omissions which produce them cannot be altered or annulled by any posterior act, neither by the legislature nor the executive.

4. No person shall be arrested, except in the cases and manner prescribed by law.

5. All persons arrested shall be either placed at liberty or delivered to the judicial authorities within twenty-four hours after their arrest.

6. All persons arrested shall either be placed at liberty or committed to prison within seventy-two hours after having been delivered to the competent judge or court. The party interested shall be notified of the order for discharge or commitment within the same period.

7. No person shall be arrested, except by virtue of a warrant from a competent judge; the writ directing the issuance of the warrant of arrest shall be ratified or amended after the accused shall have been given a hearing, within seventy-two hours following his imprisonment.

8. All persons arrested or in prison without due legal formalities, or in cases not provided for in the constitution and the laws, shall be placed at liberty at their own request or at that of any citizen. The law shall determine the method of prompt action in such cases.

9. No person shall be tried or sentenced, except by a competent judge or tribunal, in consequence of laws existing prior to the commission of the crime, and in the manner that the latter prescribe.

10. No person shall be required to testify against a wife or husband, or against relatives within the fourth degree of consanguinity or second degree of affinity.

11. The privacy of correspondence and of other private documents shall not be violated, and the same shall not be seized, except by order of a competent authority, and with the formalities prescribed by the laws, and in this case all points therein not relating to the matter under investigation shall be kept secret.

12. The expression of thought shall be free, be it either by word of mouth, by writing, by means of the public press, or by any other method whatsoever, without being subject to any prior censorship, and under the responsibility determined or specified by the laws.

13. No person shall be molested by reason of his religious opinion, nor for engaging in his special method of worship. The church and state shall be separate.

14. Every individual or association will have the right of petition.

15. The inhabitants of the republic shall have the right to meet and combine peacefully without arms for all licit purposes.

16. All persons shall have the right to enter and leave the republic, travel throughout its territory, and change their residence, without requiring a safe-guard,

passport, or any other like equivalent, except what may be required in the laws governing immigration and by the rights of the administrative or judicial authorities in cases of criminal responsibility.

17. The penalty of confiscation of properties shall not be inflicted, and no person shall be deprived of his property except by the competent authority for the justified reason of public benefit, and after being paid the proper indemnity therefor. Should this latter requirement not have been complied with, the judges shall give due protection, and, should the case so demand, they shall restore possession of the property to the person who may have been deprived thereof.

18. Private dwellings shall be held inviolate, and no person may enter therein at night without the consent of the occupants, excepting for the purpose of taking aid to victims of crime or disaster, nor in the daytime excepting in the cases and manner prescribed by law.

19. No person shall be obliged to change his place of dwelling except by orders of competent authority.

20. No person shall be obliged to pay any tax or contribution of any kind whatsoever the collection of which has not previously been legally decided upon.

21. Every author or inventor shall possess the ownership of his work or invention for the time and in the manner as may be determined by the laws.

22. Every man shall be free to learn or teach whatever science, profession, industry, or work he may deem fit. The law will determine what professions need proper decrees or qualifications, and how such decrees and qualifications shall be granted.

23. The guarantees mentioned in paragraphs 5, 6, 7, 8, 9, 11, 12, 15, 18, 19, of this section cannot be suspended in any part of the republic, except when the safety of the state requires this suspension, in case of the invasion of the state's territory, or grave perturbations of order so as to threaten the public peace.

24. The territory in which the said guarantees may be suspended will be ruled, during the suspension, by the laws relating to public order, dictated in former times. But neither in the law relating to public order, nor in any other law can other guarantees but those mentioned be suspended. Only those acts characterized as crimes by the formerly existing penal laws can be considered crimes during said suspension, neither can new punishments be inflicted save those provided by said laws, nor can the executive power be authorized to banish or transport citizens, nor to remove them more than 20 kilometres from their place of dwelling, nor to arrest citizens except for the purpose of delivering them to the judicial authority; but no citizen can remain so arrested for more than fifteen days, nor can they be so arrested more than once during the suspension of the said guarantees, nor shall citizens be confined elsewhere than in special departments of public establishments designed for the detention of those accused of common misdemeanors.

25. The suspension of said guarantees can only be ordered by means of a law, or by means of a decree of the President of the republic if Congress be not sitting. The President cannot decree such suspension for more than thirty days, or for an indefinite space of time without convoking Congress in the same decree, and in every case he must give an account to Congress of the suspension ordered, in order that Congress may resolve what it thinks fit.

Fourth Section.

FOREIGNERS.

Foreigners residing in the territory of the new republic have equal rights with Cubans in regard to the following matters: Protection of their persons and property; enjoyment of all rights mentioned in the preceding section, with exception of those referring exclusively to native Cubans; exercise of civil rights; observance of laws and decrees; being bound by decisions of the courts and other authorities; obligations contributing to public expenses.

Fifth Section.

NATIONAL SOVEREIGNTY AND PUBLIC POWERS.

The national sovereignty shall be vested in the people of Cuba, from whom shall emanate the public powers.

Sixth Section.

THE LEGISLATIVE POWER.

The legislative power shall be exercised by two elective bodies to be named "House of Representatives" and "Senate," and conjointly known as "Congress."

Seventh Section.

THE SENATE, ITS MEMBERS AND INHERENT POWERS.

1. The Senate shall be composed of six senators from each one of the six departments of the republic, elected for a period of six years by electors whom the ayuntamientos shall name in the manner prescribed by law.

2. One-third of the senators shall be elected every two years.

3. To become a senator the following qualifications are necessary: To be a native-born or naturalized Cuban citizen, the naturalized citizen to have been such for a period of at least ten years, to have attained the age of thirty years, and to be in full enjoyment of civil and political rights.

4. The inherent powers of the Senate shall be as follows:

First. To try, after they have been accused by the House of Representatives, the President of the republic, and the governors of the departments, for which purpose it shall constitute itself into a court of law to be presided over by the president of the Supreme Court, without the right in this case of imposing any other penalty than that of removal from or disqualification to hold office. After the charges have been filed with the Senate, the latter shall order forthwith the suspension of the President from office. Should the President be proved criminally responsible, he shall at once be placed at the disposal of the Supreme Court. In any case whatsoever, except infraction of the Constitution, to impeach him the consent of the Senate shall be necessary.

Second. To confirm or not the appointments that the President of the republic may make, of associate justices of the Supreme Court, of diplomatic representatives, and consular agents, and of such other functionaries required by law.

Third. To authorize Cubans to accept employment or honors from another government.

Fourth. To judge the governors of the provinces, when accused by the provincial assemblies or by the President of the republic. When the accusation is made before the Senate, the Senate can order the suspension of the governor, but cannot impose any other penalty but dismissal from office.

Eighth Section.

THE HOUSE OF REPRESENTATIVES AND ITS INHERENT POWERS.

1. The House of Representatives shall be composed of one representative for every 25,000 inhabitants or fraction of more than 12,000, elected for a period of four years, by direct vote, and in the manner prescribed by law.

2. One-half of the House of Representatives shall be elected every two years.

3. To be a representative, the following qualifications are required: To be a native-born or a naturalized Cuban citizen, the naturalized citizen to have been such for a period of not less than eight years, to have attained the age of twenty-five years, and to be in the full enjoyment of all civil and political rights.

4. The inherent powers of the House of Representatives shall be as follows:

First. To file an accusation before the Senate against the President of the republic for violation of the Constitution or of the laws, committed in the exercise of his duties, provided that two-thirds of the representatives should so resolve in secret session.

Ninth Section.

REGULATIONS COMMON TO BOTH LEGISLATIVE BODIES.

1. The positions of representatives and senators shall be incompatible with the holding of any paid position and of appointment of the government.

2. The representatives and senators shall receive from the nation a pecuniary remuneration, alike for all, which shall not be increased nor diminished during the period of their representation.

3. The representatives and senators shall not be held responsible for the opinions that they may express in the exercise of their duties.

4. Representatives and senators shall not be arrested nor tried without the consent of the body to which they belong, except in the case of being discovered in the act of committing some crime, in which case and in that of their being arrested or tried when Congress is not in session, report thereof shall be made as quickly as possible to the body to which they belong for its information and proper action.

5. Congress shall meet and organize at their own option; both Houses shall open and close their sessions on the same day; they shall be established at the same place, and neither of them shall move to any other place nor suspend its sessions for more than three days without the consent of the other, neither shall they commence their sessions without two-thirds of the total number of their members being present, nor shall they be allowed to continue their sessions without an absolute majority of the members being present.

6. Congress shall decide as to the validity of elections and as to the resignation of its members, and none of the latter shall be expelled except by vote of two-thirds of the members at least of the respective legislative bodies, in which case it shall be decided in a like manner whether the expulsion is temporary or final, and if therefore the position should be declared vacant or not.

7. The Houses of Congress shall adopt their respective rules and regulations and elect their presidents. But the Senate president will only occupy the position in the absence of the Vice-President of the republic or when the latter is discharging the duties of President of the same.

Tenth Section.

CONGRESS AND ITS POWERS.

1. Congress shall meet in regular session every year on the first Monday in November, and shall remain in session for at least ninety consecutive days, excepting holidays and Sundays. And it shall meet in special session whenever the President may issue a call therefor in accordance with this Constitution, in which case it shall solely treat of the express object or objects of the call.

2. Congress shall meet in joint session to proclaim, after rectifying and counting the electoral vote, the President and Vice-President of the republic, at which act the president and vice-president of Congress respectively shall be the president of the Senate and the president of the House of Representatives.

3. The powers of Congress shall be as follows:

First. To examine into and approve annually of the general budget of the nation. Should a vote not be able to be taken prior to the first day of the fiscal year, the preceding budget shall continue in force.

Second. Decide as to the issue of loans, at the same time voting the necessary permanent incomes for the payment of interest thereon, and for its redemption.

Third. To regulate domestic and foreign commerce, postal and telegraphic services, and of railroads.

Fourth. To declare war and to make treaties of peace.

Fifth. To coin money, specifying the weight, value, and denomination of the same, and to regulate the system of weights and measures.

Sixth. To establish rules of procedure for naturalization of citizens.

Seventh. To grant amnesties.

Eighth. To organize naval and military forces.

Ninth. To establish taxes, duties, and contributions of national character.

Tenth. To regulate the establishment and service of roads, canals, and ports.

Eleventh. To decide who shall be President in case the President and Vice-President should be removed, dead, resigned, or incapacitated.

Twelfth. To prepare the national codes, to establish the electoral for the election of Congress, governors, governors of provinces, and the provincial and municipal corporations; to dictate laws for the guidance of the general administration.

Eleventh Section.

THE PREPARATION, THE SANCTION AND PROMULGATION OF THE LAW.

1. The initiative action of all laws pertains to either of the two co-legislative bodies, except in the cases specified in the Constitution.

2. Every project of law that may have received the approval of the Senate and

the House of Representatives shall be, before it becomes a law, presented to the President of the republic. Should the latter approve the same, he will sign it; if not, he shall return it, with his objections, to the legislative body that recommended it, which body shall in turn spread the same objections in full upon the minutes, and will again discuss the project. If, after this second discussion, two-thirds of the members of the co-legislative body should vote in favor of the project, it shall be sent, together with the objections of the President, to the other body, which shall discuss it in a like manner, and if the latter should approve it by a like majority it shall become a law. In every case the vote shall be taken by recording the names of members. If within ten days (excluding holidays) the President shall not have returned the project of the law presented to him, the same shall become a law, in a like manner as if the President had signed it. Whenever Congress shall take a vote upon any law within the last ten days of its sessions, and the President should have objections to sanction the same, he shall be under obligations to immediately notify Congress thereof, in order that the latter may remain in session until the aforesaid period has expired, and should he not do so the law shall be considered as sanctioned.

3. No project of law, after being wholly rejected by one of the co-legislative bodies, may be again presented at the sessions of that year.

4. Every law shall be promulgated within five days immediately following its approval.

Twelfth Section.

THE EXECUTIVE POWER—THE PRESIDENT OF THE REPUBLIC—HIS POWERS AND DUTIES.

1. The executive power shall be exercised by the President of the republic.

2. To become President of the republic the following qualifications are required: To be a Cuban citizen by birth or naturalization, and, in this latter case, to have served with the Cuban army in its wars for independence ten years at least; to have attained the age of forty years, and to be in the full enjoyment of all civil and political rights.

3. The President shall be elected to serve a term of four years. No one can be elected President for three consecutive terms.

4. The President shall be elected by direct votes, and an absolute majority thereof, cast on one single day, in accordance with the provisions of the law.

5. The President, on taking possession of office, shall swear or affirm before the Supreme Court to faithfully discharge the duties thereof, complying with and causing to be enforced the Constitution and laws.

6. The President shall receive from the public a pecuniary remuneration which shall be fixed by law, and which shall not be increased or diminished during the Presidential term.

7. The powers and duties of the President shall be as follows:

First. To promulgate the laws and execute the same.

Second. To issue calls for special sessions of Congress.

Third. To suspend the sessions of Congress when, in the matter relating to their suspension, no agreement is possible between the co-legislative bodies.

Fourth. To present to Congress at the commencement of each session, and as often as he may deem proper, a message referring to the acts of the administration and to the general state of the republic, recommending the adoption of measures that he may deem necessary and useful for the country.

Fifth. To send to Congress all the necessary data of all kinds for the preparation of the budgets, and furnish the information that said Congress might ask for concerning matters or business that do not require secrecy.

Sixth. To direct diplomatic negotiations and make treaties with foreign powers, submitting them for confirmation to the approval of Congress.

Seventh. To appoint, with the approval of the Senate, the associate justices of the supreme court of justice, diplomatic representatives and consular agents of the republic, he having the right to make provisional appointments of said representatives and agents when the Senate is not in session, and when vacancies occur.

Eighth. To freely appoint and remove his consulting secretaries that the law may provide him with, reporting actions in the premises to Congress.

Ninth. To appoint to positions established by law all other functionaries whose appointment does not specially pertain to other functionaries and corporations.

Tenth. To command and direct, as commander-in-chief, the naval and military forces of the republic, being under obligations, in case of invasion of the territory or sudden attack thereon, to forthwith adopt the necessary means of defence, and call Congress to session without delay to inform it of the facts.

Eleventh. To receive diplomatic representatives and admit consular agents.

Twelfth. To pardon convicts in accordance with the laws.

Thirteenth. To suspend the action of departmental assemblies and ayuntamientos, in the cases specified by the Constitution.

8. The President shall not be allowed to leave the territory of the republic without the express consent of Congress.

Thirteenth Section.

VICE-PRESIDENT OF THE REPUBLIC.

1. There shall be one Vice-President of the republic, who shall be elected in the same manner as the President, conjointly with the latter and for a like term.

2. To become Vice-President the same qualifications as those established by the Constitution for President are necessary.

3. The Vice-President shall be president of the Senate, but shall not vote except in cases of a tie.

4. Through accidental absence of the President of the republic, the executive power shall be exercised by the Vice-President. In case of an absolute vacancy in the office of the President the Vice-President shall assume charge thereof until the termination of the current term.

5. The Vice-President shall receive from the republic a pecuniary remuneration which shall be decided by law, and which shall not be increased nor diminished during the period of his administration.

Fourteenth Section.

JUDICIAL POWER.

The judicial power shall be exercised by the supreme court of justice and such other courts as may be established by law, which shall regulate their respective organization, their rights, methods of exercising the same, and qualifications that the individuals composing them shall possess.

Fifteenth Section.

THE SUPREME COURT OF JUSTICE.

1. To become an associate supreme justice the following qualifications are necessary:

First. To be a Cuban citizen by birth or naturalization, in the latter case for a period of not less than ten years.

Second. To have attained the age of forty years.

Third. To be in full possession of all civil and political rights.

Fourth. To possess some of the following qualifications: To have practised the profession of law for ten years within the territory of the republic or have performed for a like period judicial duties or taught for the same time a class of fundamental law in a public establishment.

2. Besides those established in the preceding bases and those specified by the laws it shall be the inherent right of the supreme court of justice:

First. To have cognizance of appeals in conformity with the law.

Second. To decide questions that may arise between the courts of law immediately inferior to it as to their relative rights and jurisdiction.

Third. To have cognizance of inter-administrative suits concerning the nation or which are litigations between the departments or the municipalities.

Fourth. To decide as to the constitutionality of legislative acts that may have been objected to as unconstitutional.

Fifth. To decide as to the validity or nullity of decisions of departmental assemblies or of ayuntamientos that may have been suspended by the government or complained of by private individuals in such cases as the Constitution and laws establish.

Sixteenth Section.

GENERAL DISPOSITIONS CONCERNING THE ADMINISTRATION OF JUSTICE.

1. Justice shall be administered gratuitously.

2. The courts shall have cognizance of all civil and criminal and interadministrative suits. They shall also have cognizance, in cases specified by the laws, of the questions relating to the exercise and possession of political rights.

3. No judicial commissions nor extraordinary courts of justice of whatever kind shall be created.

4. All hearings shall be public, unless in the opinion of the court and for special reasons they should be private.

5. No judicial functionary shall be suspended from nor deprived of his position except for crime or other serious cause, duly proved after his defence shall have been heard.

6. Judicial functionaries shall be personally responsible for all violations of the law that they may commit.

7. The remuneration of judicial functionaries shall not be changed within a period of less than five years, a general law being necessary for the purpose.

8. Courts having cognizance of maritime and land matters shall be governed by their special organic law.

Seventeenth Section.

DEPARTMENT RÉGIME.

1. Each department shall be formed by the municipal terminos that are comprised within the boundaries thereof.

2. At the head of each department there will be a governor, elected by direct vote for a period of three years, in the manner specified by law.

3. There will also be a departmental assembly, to consist of not less than eight or more than twenty, elected by direct vote for a like period of three years, which election shall be held in the form specified by law.

Eighteenth Section.

DEPARTMENTAL ASSEMBLIES AND THEIR POWERS.

1. The departmental assemblies shall have the right of independent action in all things not antagonistic to the Constitution, to the general laws, nor to international treaties, nor to that which pertains to the inherent rights of the municipalities, which may concern the department, such as the establishment and maintenance of institutions of public education, public charities, public departmental roads, means of communication by water or sea, the preparation of their budgets, and the appointment and removal of their employés.

They may also agree as to the placing of a loan for public works of interest to the department, voting at the same time the permanent income necessary for the payment of interest thereon and its redemption. In order that loans may be realized the approval of two-thirds of the ayuntamientos of the department must be secured.

2. The departmental assemblies shall freely provide the income necessary to meet their budgets, without any other limitation than that of making it compatible with the general tributary system of the republic.

3. The provincial assembly cannot suppress or reduce taxes of a permanent nature without establishing others to take their place, except when the suppression or reduction precedes the suppression or reduction of permanent, equivalent expenses.

4. The decision of the departmental assemblies shall be presented, in order that they may have executive character, to the governor of the department. Should the latter approve them, he will attach his signature thereto; otherwise he will return them, together with his objections, to the assembly, and if, after being reconsidered, the said decisions should be sustained by two-thirds of the members of the assembly, they shall become effective. If within ten days (excepting Sundays and holidays) the governor should not return any decision that had been presented to him, the said decision shall be effective in character the same as if the governor had approved the same.

Nineteenth Section.

THE GOVERNORS OF DEPARTMENTS, THEIR POWERS AND DUTIES.

1. The powers of the governors shall be as follows:

First. To appoint the employés of their offices that the law may specify or which the departmental assembly may designate.

Second. To execute and cause to be executed in the department the general laws of the nation.

Third. To publish the acts of the departmental assembly having an executive character, complying therewith, and causing them to be enforced.

Fourth. To issue orders, instructions, and regulations for the enforcement of the rulings of the departmental assembly when the latter has omitted to do so.

Fifth. To call the departmental assembly to a special session whenever there may be cause, therefor, which cause shall be stated in the call.

Sixth. To suspend the decision of the departmental assembly and those of the ayuntamiento in such cases as may be established by the Constitution.

2. The governor shall receive from the departmental treasury a pecuniary remuneration, which shall not be changed during the period for which he was elected.

3. The governor shall be substituted in office by the president of the provincial assembly, the said substitution to be, in case of vacancy, for the whole term for which the governor was elected.

4. The governor shall be responsible to the Senate for all infractions of the Constitution. For any other fault he shall be responsible to the court in the form demanded by law.

Twentieth Section.

THE MUNICIPAL RÉGIME.

1. The municipal terminos shall be governed by ayuntamientos composed of councilmen elected by a direct vote in the manner prescribed by law.

2. In each municipal termino there shall be a mayor elected by direct vote in the form prescribed by law.

3. The organization of municipal terminos will be the object of the general law.

Twenty-first Section.

THE AYUNTAMIENTOS AND THEIR POWERS.

1. The ayuntamientos shall be self-governing and shall take action on all matters that solely and exclusively concern their municipal termino, such as appointment and removal of employés, preparation of their budgets, freely establishing the means of income to meet them without any other limitation than that of making them compatible with the general system of taxation of the republic.

2. The ayuntamientos can issue loans, at the same time fixing what taxes are to be devoted to the payment of interest and the forming of a sinking-fund. The voters of the terminos must approve by direct vote the issue of a loan.

3. The ayuntamientos cannot suppress or reduce taxes of a permanent nature without establishing others in their places, except when the suppression or reduction corresponds to an equivalent reduction in permanent expense.

4. The resolutions adopted by the ayuntamientos shall be presented, in order that they may have executive character, to the mayor. Should the latter approve them, he will attach his signature thereto; otherwise he shall return them with his objections to the ayuntamiento, and if, after being reconsidered, two-thirds of the members of the ayuntamiento should sustain them, they shall become effective. If within ten days (excepting Sundays and holidays) the mayor should not return any decision that had been presented to him, the latter shall become effective the same as if the mayor had approved it.

5. The acts of the ayuntamientos may be suspended by the mayor or by the governor of the department, or by the President of the republic whenever said acts are antagonistic to the Constitution, to the general laws, to international treaties, or to action taken by the departmental assembly, within its inherent attributes, by submitting the matter to the decision of the Supreme Court.

6. Councilmen shall be responsible for their acts before the courts in the manner prescribed by law.

Twenty-second Section.

MAYORS, THEIR DUTIES AND POWERS.

1. The mayors shall publish, as soon as the same have been approved, the acts of the ayuntamientos, complying therewith and causing the same to be enforced; and they shall exercise without any limita-

tion whatsoever the active functions of municipal administration as executors of the acts of the ayuntamientos and representatives thereof.

2. The municipal mayors shall receive from the municipal treasuries a pecuniary remuneration that shall not be changed during the period of their administration.

3. The municipal mayors shall be responsible for their acts before the courts, in the manner prescribed by law.

4. The municipal mayors shall be substituted in office by the presidents of the ayuntamientos, and in cases of vacancy the substitution shall be for the unexpired term for which the mayor was elected.

TWENTY-THIRD SECTION.

THE NATIONAL TREASURY, ITS PROPERTIES AND DUTIES.

The republic of Cuba does not recognize, nor will not recognize, any debts or compromises contracted prior to the promulgation of the Constitution. From the said prohibition are excepted the debts and compromises legitimately contracted for in behalf of the revolution, from and after Feb. 24, 1895, by corps commanders of the liberating army, until the day upon which the constitution of Jimaguayi was promulgated; and those which the revolutionary governments contracted, either by themselves or by their legitimate representatives in foreign countries, which debts and compromises shall be classified by Congress, and which body shall decide as to the payment of those which, in its judgment, are legitimate.

TWENTY-FOURTH SECTION.

CONSTITUTIONAL AMENDMENTS.

The Constitution cannot be changed, in whole or in part, except by a two-thirds vote of both legislative bodies. Six months after deciding on the reform, a constitutional assembly shall be elected, which shall confine itself to the approval or disapproval of the reform voted by the legislative bodies. These will continue in their functions independently of the constitutional assembly. The members in this assembly shall be equal to the number of the members in the two legislative bodies together.

TWENTY-FIFTH SECTION.

CONCERNING TRANSITORY DISPOSITIONS.

1. The Senate being organized for the first time, the senators shall be divided into three classes; the seats of the senators of the first class shall be vacated at the expiration of the second year, of the second class at the expiration of the fourth year, and of the third class at the expiration of the sixth year. Lots shall decide which senator shall belong to each class for each one of the departments.

2. Ninety days after the promulgation of the electoral law that may be prepared and adopted by the convention, the election of the functionaries provided for in the Constitution shall be proceeded with for the transfer of the government of Cuba to those who may be elected, in conformity with order No. 301 from the headquarters of the Division of Cuba of July 25, 1900.

3. All laws, regulations, orders, and decrees which may be in force at the time of the promulgation of the Constitution shall continue to be observed until they are replaced by others.

The Platt Amendment.—The following resolution was reported to the United States Senate by the committee on the relations with Cuba on Feb. 25. It was passed by the Senate Feb. 27, and by the House on March 1:

That in fulfilment of the declaration contained in the joint resolution approved April 20, 1898, entitled "For the Recognition of the Independence of the People of Cuba," demanding that the government of Spain relinquish its authority and government in the island of Cuba, and withdraw its land and naval forces from Cuba and Cuban waters, and directing the President of the United States to use the land and naval forces of the United States to carry these resolutions into effect, the President is hereby authorized to leave the government and control of the island of Cuba to its people as soon as a government shall have been established in said island under a constitution which, either as a part thereof or in any ordinance appended thereto, shall define the future relations of the United States with Cuba, substantially as follows:

1. That the government of Cuba shall never enter into any treaty or other compact with any foreign power or powers which will impair or tend to impair the independence of Cuba, nor in any manner authorize or permit any foreign power or powers to obtain, by colonization, or for military or naval purposes, or otherwise, lodging in or control over any portion of said island.

2. That said government shall not assume or contract any public debt to pay the interest upon which and to make reasonable sinking-fund provision for the ultimate discharge of which the ordinary revenues of the island, after defraying the current expenses of government, shall be inadequate.

3. That the government of Cuba consents that the United States may exercise the right to intervene for the preservation of Cuban independence, the maintenance of a government adequate for the protection of life, property, and individual liberty, and for discharging the obligations with respect to Cuba imposed by the treaty of Paris on the United States, now to be assumed and undertaken by the government of Cuba.

4. That all acts of the United States in Cuba during its military occupancy thereof are ratified and validated, and all lawful rights acquired thereunder shall be maintained and protected.

5. That the government of Cuba will execute, and as far as necessary extend, the plans already devised, or other plans to be mutually agreed upon, for the sanitation of the cities of the island, to the end that a recurrence of epidemic and infectious diseases may be prevented, thereby assuring protection to the people and commerce of Cuba, as well as to the commerce of the Southern ports of the United States and the people residing therein.

6. That the Isle of Pines shall be omitted from the proposed constitutional boundaries of Cuba and the title thereto left to future adjustment by treaty.

7. That to enable the United States to maintain the independence of Cuba and to protect the people thereof, as well as for its own defence, the government of Cuba will sell or lease to the United States lands necessary for coaling or naval stations at certain specified points to be agreed upon with the President of the United States.

8. That by way of further assurance, the government of Cuba will embody the foregoing provisions in a permanent treaty with the United States.

On Feb. 27 the constitutional convention adopted a declaration of relations between Cuba and the United States.

The preamble cited that the convention received from the military government a letter telling the convention what were the wishes of the administrative branch of the American government regarding future relations. The convention understood that the object of the administration in wishing these relations to exist was to preserve the independence of Cuba, the United States wishing coaling-stations for this purpose. This, however, would in itself militate against that independence which it was the desire of both parties to preserve. With regard to the other conditions which the executive branch of the United States government suggested, the object of those which tended to protect the independence of Cuba, such as stipulating the conditions under which Cuba might raise loans, were fully covered by the Constitution, which, in the opinion of the convention, fully protected the independence of Cuba. Regarding hygiene, the preamble stated that the future government of Cuba should make laws and arrange with the United States how best to preserve a good state of hygiene in the island. The preamble concluded by stating that the convention considers that the following relations might exist between Cuba and the United States, provided the future government of Cuba thinks them advisable:

First. The government of the republic of Cuba will make no treaty arrangements with any foreign power which limits or compromises the independence of Cuba, or which in any way permits or authorizes any foreign power to obtain, by means of colonization or for military or naval aims, or in any other manner, a hold upon the authority or a right over any portion of Cuba.

Second. The government of the republic

of Cuba will not permit its territory to serve as the base of operations in a war against the United States nor against any other country.

Third. The government of the republic of Cuba accepts in its entirety the treaty of Paris of Dec. 10, 1898, both wherein it affirms the rights of Cuba and with regard to the obligations specifically mentioned as belonging to Cuba, especially with regard to those which international law imposes for the protection of lives and property. Cuba will take the place of the United States which the latter acquired in this sense in conformity with Articles I. and XVI. of the Treaty of Paris.

Fourth. The government of the republic of Cuba will recognize as legally valid the acts of the American military government done in representation of the government of the United States during the period of its occupation for the good government of Cuba, as well as the rights that spring from them, in conformity with the joint resolution and amendment to the Army bill known as the Foraker law, or with the laws in force in the country.

Fifth. The government of the republic of Cuba should regulate its commercial relations by means of an arrangement based on reciprocity, and which, with the tendencies to a free exchange of their natural and manufactured products, would mutually assure the two countries ample special advantages in their respective markets.

The Cuban constitutional convention accepted the Platt amendment June 12, 1901; general elections, resulting in the choice of the Nationalist candidates, were held Dec. 31; Thomas Estrada Palma was elected the first president of the republic and Señor Estevez vice-president, Feb. 24, 1902; the president and vice-president were inaugurated, the Cuban flag replaced the American over Morro Castle, Havana, and Governor-General Wood formally delivered the island to President Palma, May 20; President Roosevelt signed an agreement with Cuba for a United States naval station on Guantanamo Bay, and a coaling station at Bahia Honda, Feb. 24, 1903; the United States Senate passed a bill providing for commercial reciprocity with Cuba, Dec. 16; and a Cuban loan of $35,000,000 was placed by the New York banking house of Speyer & Co., Feb. 15, 1904.

In the four years of President Palma's administration the republic prospered to an extent that surprised the Cubans, and on May 20, 1906, he was inaugurated for a second term. Not long after this, however, a smouldering revolutionary spirit broke out. On Sept. 8 President Palma sought the intervention of the United States; on the 11th he suspended the constitutional guaranties in several provinces. United States marines were landed at Havana to protect American lives and property; President Roosevelt sent Secretary of War Taft to investigate conditions and endeavor to reconcile the opposing factions; President Palma resigned Sept. 28, and Secretary Taft proclaimed United States intervention and announced himself as provisional governor on the following day. Additional war-ships and several thousand American troops were sent to the island; the insurgents were disarmed; a proclamation of general amnesty was issued Oct. 10; Charles E. Magoon succeeded Secretary Taft as provisional governor Oct. 13, and announcement was made that when order was fully restored a new census would be taken and elections would be held under a new electoral law for a native government. The presidential election was held Nov. 14, 1908, and resulted in the choice of Gen. José Miguel Gomez for president and Señor Alfredo Zayas for vice-president, who were inaugurated Jan. 28, 1909, for a term of four years. In the meantime a census had been taken (1907) by American census experts, which showed a total population of 2,048,980. With the inauguration of the new president and vice-president the American provisional government terminated, and on March 31, 1909, the second American occupation came to an end by the withdrawal of the United States troops and war-ships. The question of the ownership of the Isle of Pines was settled by the United States Supreme Court in favor of Cuba, April 8, 1907.

Raising of the "Maine."—On May 9, 1910, President Taft approved the following act of Congress: "The Secretary of War and the Chief of Engineers are authorized to provide with all convenient speed for the raising or the removal of the wreck of the United States battleship *Maine* from the harbor of Havana, Cuba, and for the proper interment of the bodies therein in Arlington Cemetery, and the Secretary of War is directed to remove the mast of the *Maine* and place the same on a proper foundation in Arlington National Cemetery at or near the spot where the bodies of those who died through the wreck are interred: provided, however, that the consent in proper form of the republic of Cuba shall be first obtained. The sum of $100,000 is appropriated for the work."

In November, 1911, the following board of experts was appointed to make an examination of the wreck as laid bare by the army engineers: Rear-Admiral Charles E. Vreeland, aid for inspections of the Navy Department; R. M. Watt, chief constructor of the navy; Colonel William M. Black, president of the army board charged with the raising of the wreck; Commander Joseph Straus, powder expert of the navy, who was formerly in charge of the naval proving ground at Indian Head and later assistant to the aid for material, and Commander Charles Hughes of the Naval Board of Inspection.

On Dec. 14 following, the President transmitted to Congress the full text of the report of the board of experts, of which the following is a summary, by the Secretary of the Navy:

"The board finds that the injuries to the bottom of the *Maine* were caused by the explosion of a charge of a low form of explosive exterior to the ship between frames 28 and 31, strake B, port side.

This resulted in igniting and exploding the contents of the six-inch reserve magazine, A-14-M, said contents including a large quantity of black powder.

The more or less complete explosion of the contents of the remaining forward magazine followed. The magazine explosion resulted in the destruction of the vessel."

This conclusion, it should be noted, confirms the report of the Sampson board of inquiry, which made its investigation immediately after the destruction of the vessel, Feb. 15, 1898.

Except a portion of the wreck of the *Maine* given to the Naval Academy and other public institutions, the hulk was towed out to deep sea and sunk with naval honors, March 16, 1912.

Cullom, Shelby Moore, statesman; born in Monticello, Ky., Nov. 22, 1829; taken to Illinois in 1830; member of Congress, 1865–71; governor of Illinois, 1877–83; United States Senator from 1883. In 1898 he was appointed one of the commissioners to establish American civil government in Hawaii. He died Jan. 28, 1914.

Cullum, George Washington, military officer; born in New York City, Feb. 25, 1809; graduated at West Point in 1833, entering the engineering corps, and becoming captain in July, 1838. He was made major in August, 1861; lieutenant-colonel in March, 1863, and colonel, March, 1867, and was retired in 1874. In the volunteer service he reached the rank of brigadier-general and brevet major-general during the Civil War. From 1845 to 1848 he was instructor of practical engineering in the West Point Military Academy, and from 1864 to 1866 superintendent, during which time he spent two years in Europe. General Cullum published several books on military affairs, and a *Biographical Register of the Officers and Graduates of West Point.* He bequeathed $250,000 for the erection of a military memorial hall at West Point, and a fund for the continuation of the *Biographical Register.* He died in New York City, Feb. 28, 1892.

Culpeper, John, surveyor-general in the Carolinas; born in England; in 1678 headed an insurrection in the Albemarle or North Colony in favor of popular liberty. He was indicted for high treason, but was acquitted. He laid the foundations of the city of Charleston in 1680.

Culpeper, Thomas, Lord, colonial governor; born in England. In 1673 King Charles gave to Lord Culpeper and the Earl of Arlington "all the domain of land and water called Virginia" for thirty years. A commission was given to Culpeper as governor for life. He did not go to Virginia until 1680. His rapacity disgusted the people and led to an insurrection. By the king's order the governor caused several of the insurgents, who were men of influence, to be hanged. A reign of terror, miscalled tranquillity, followed. At length the King himself became incensed against Culpeper, revoked his grant in 1684, and deprived him of office. He died in England in 1719.

Cumberland. See MONITOR AND MERRIMAC.

Cumberland, ARMY OF THE, one of the principal armies of the United States during the Civil War. On Oct. 24, 1862, the troops under GEN. WILLIAM S. ROSECRANS (*q. v.*), commanding the Department of the Cumberland, were ordered to constitute the 14th Army Corps, and the same day the former Army of the Ohio, commanded by Gen. Don Carlos Buell, was renamed the Army of the Cumberland. In January, 1863, the Army of the Cumberland was divided into the 14th, 20th, and 21st Army Corps, and in September of the same year the 20th and 21st Corps were consolidated into the 4th Corps. In the following month the 11th and 12th Corps were added to the Army of the Cumberland, and GEN. GEORGE H. THOMAS (*q. v.*) was placed in command, and at the beginning of 1864 the 11th and 12th Corps were consolidated into the 20th Corps.

Cumberland, FORT, ACTION AT. At the head of the Bay of Fundy the British had maintained Fort Cumberland from 1755. In 1776 only a small garrison was there to take care of the public property. Capt. Jonathan Eddy, a native of Massachusetts. who had lived many years in the vicinity of the fort, believing it might be easily captured, applied to the Provincial Congress of Massachusetts for men and supplies for that purpose. These were not furnished, and Eddy returned to Nova Scotia, where he raised a few men, and on the night of Nov. 20, 1776, attacked the fort. Apprised of the movement, the little garrison, prepared, repulsed the assailants. A British reinforcement soon arrived, and the assailants fled in haste. The inhabitants, who had joined the standard of Eddy, soon saw their houses in flames, and then, fearing British vengeance, made their way to New England in a famishing condition.

Cumberland Gap, ACTIONS AT. Cumberland Gap is a passage through the Cumberland Mountains, on the line between Kentucky and Tennessee and the western extremity of Virginia. It is a place about which clusters many a Civil War incident. It was occupied by Zollicoffer in his retreat, Nov. 13, 1861. On March 22, 1862, a reconnoissance in force was made from Cumberland Fort to this place. The Confederate pickets were driven in, and firing began early in the morning, which continued all day, without any definite results. The Gap was occupied by the National forces under General Morgan, June 18. Skirmishing was of almost daily occurrence. In an engagement, Aug. 7, the Confederates lost, in killed and wounded, 125 men; National loss, 3 killed, 15 wounded, and 50 prisoners, large quantities of forage, tobacco, stores, horses and mules. General Morgan destroyed everything of value as war material, and evacuated the place Sept. 17, and, though surrounded by the enemy, he succeeded in saving his command, which reached Greenupsburg on Oct. 3. The Gap was occupied by General Bragg, Oct. 22. On Sept. 8, 1863, the place, with 2,000 men and fourteen pieces of artillery, under the Confederate General Frazer, surrendered, without firing a gun, to General Shackleford; forty wagons, 200 mules, and a large quantity of commissary stores were captured. A three hours' skirmish occurred Jan. 29, 1864, on the Virginia road, 13 miles distant. Colonel Love, with 1,600 cavalry, 400 only of whom were mounted, and with no artillery, held his position till dark, and then fell back 3 miles to camp. On April 28, 1865, 900 Confederates surrendered and were paroled here.

Cumberland Presbyterian Church, a religious denomination which originated from the efforts of the Rev. James McCready, who settled in Kentucky in 1796 over two congregations in Logan county, and another at Red River, just across the line in Tennessee. Being a man of great zeal and feeling the need of a revival in religion, he began an effective work. In July, 1800, he held what is believed to have been the first camp-meeting. His plan met with rapid success and resulted in numerous camp-meetings, which spread over that part of Kentucky which was then called Cumberland country, now middle Tennessee. Great numbers professed religion in these meetings, and many new congregations were organized, creating a necessity for more ministers. These the regular Presbyterian Church could not supply upon immediate demand. Consequently young men from the district who were adjudged most competent to do ministerial work were selected to carry on the work. These, however, did not meet with the approval of the Presbytery. This resulted in dissension and was the main cause of the formation of the Cumberland Presbytery, which was established in Dickson county, Tenn., on Feb. 4, 1810. It is established principally in the States of Tennessee, Missouri, Texas and Kentucky.

According to a special census report on *Religious Bodies* (1910), the Cumberland Presbyterian Church had 2,850 organizations, 17 synods and 114 presbyteries in 24 States; 195,770 communicants or members; 2,474 church edifices; 108 halls used for religious purposes; 1,514 ministers; church property (2,325 organizations) valued at $5,803,960; and 1,846 Sunday-schools (reported by 1,817 organizations), with 15,596 officers and teachers and 120,311 scholars.

Cumberland Road, a famous thoroughfare authorized by act of Congress March 29, 1806, which directed the President to appoint three commissioners to lay out a public road from Cumberland, Md., on the Potomac River, to the Ohio River. The act also appropriated $30,000 for the work. This road was continued from time to time until 1838, when it reached Illinois, and lost its importance by the development of the railroads. Up to that time the cost of the road for construction and maintenance was $6,821,246. In all, Congress passed sixty acts relating to this road.

Cummings, Amos Jay, journalist; born in Conkling, N. Y., May 15, 1841; enlisted in the National army at the beginning of the Civil War, and participated in the battles of Fredericksburg and Chancellorsville. After the war he was connected with the New York *Tribune* and the New York *Sun,* and was a representative in Congress from 1886 till his death at Baltimore, Md., May 2, 1902.

Cummings, Andrew Boyd, naval officer; born in Philadelphia, Pa., June 22, 1830; appointed midshipman in the United States navy in 1847; was executive officer of the *Richmond* when Farragut attacked Forts Jackson and St Philip; mortally wounded during the battle, and died four days later, March 18, 1863.

Cunard, Sir Samuel, capitalist; born in Halifax, N. S., Nov. 15, 1787; established the Cunard Steamship Company in 1838. He died in England, April 28, 1865.

Cunningham, William, provost-marshal; born in Dublin, Ireland; landed in New York in 1774; became provost-marshal there; and in 1778 had charge of the prisoners there and in Philadelphia. Of the prisoners under his care nearly 2,000 were starved to death (whose rations he sold), and more than 250 were privately hanged without trial to gratify his brutal appetite. He was executed in England for forgery, Aug. 10, 1791.

Curfew Bell, the name applied to a bell signal introduced in England in 1068. It was rung at 8 P.M., and all fires and candles were to be immediately extinguished. The curfew was abolished in 1100, so far as its original purpose was concerned. In the United States there has been quite an agitation within the last few years for the enactment of laws providing for the ringing of bells at 9 P.M., as a signal for all youth of a specified age playing or wandering in the streets to return immediately to their homes. In several States laws for this purpose have already been enacted, and the name of curfew bell has been popularly given to the signal rung out on a church or fire bell.

Currency, Continental. The issue of paper money or bills of credit, not only by the several colonies, but by the Continental Congress, became a necessity when the Revolutionary War began in 1775. The second Congress met in Philadelphia May 10, 1775, and on that day, in secret session, the measure was agreed upon, but the resolution was not formed and adopted until June 22, the day on which news of the battle on Breed's Hill was received by the Congress. Then it was resolved "that a sum not exceeding 2,000,000 Spanish milled dollars be emitted by the Congress in bills of credit for the defence of America," and that "the twelve confederate colonies [Georgia was not then represented] be pledged for the redemption of the bills of credit now directed to be emitted." Each colony was required to pay its proportion, in

FAC-SIMILE OF CONTINENTAL BILLS.

four annual payments, the first by the last of November, 1779, and the fourth by the last of November, 1782. A committee appointed for the occasion reported the following day the annexed resolution:

"Resolved, that the number and denominations of the bills be as follows:

49,000 bills of 8 dollars each	$392,000
49,000 bills of 7 dollars each	343,000
49,000 bills of 6 dollars each	294,000
49,000 bills of 5 dollars each	245,000
49,000 bills of 4 dollars each	196,000
49,000 bills of 3 dollars each	147,000
49,000 bills of 2 dollars each	98,000
49,000 bills of 1 dollar each	49,000
11,800 bills of 20 dollars each	236,000
Total, 403,800	$2,000,000

"Resolved, that the form of the bill be as follows:

CONTINENTAL CURRENCY.

No.——— ———*Dollars.*

This Bill entitles the Bearer to receive ———Spanish milled Dollars, *or the value thereof in* Gold or Silver, *according to the resolutions of the* CONGRESS, *held at* Philadelphia *the 10th* of May, A.D. 1775."

A committee was appointed to procure the plates and superintend the printing of the bills. The plates were engraved by Paul Revere, of Boston. The paper was so thick that the British called it "the pasteboard currency of the rebels." The size of the bills averaged about 3½ by 2¾ inches, having a border composed partly of repetitions of the words "Continental Currency." On the face of each bill was a device (a separate one for each denomination) significant in design and legend; for example, within a circle a design representing a hand planting a tree, and the legend "*Posteritate*"—for posterity. Twenty-eight gentlemen were appointed to sign these bills. New issues were made at various times until the close of 1779, when the aggregate amount was $242,000,000. Then the bills had so much depreciated that $100 in specie would purchase $2,600 in paper currency. Laws, penalties, entreaties, could not sustain its credit. It had performed a great work in enabling the colonists, without taxes the first three years of the war, to fight and baffle one of the most powerful nations in Europe. And the total loss to the people, by depreciation and failure of redemption, of $200,000,000, operated as a tax, for that depreciation was gradual. Continental bills of credit are now very rare—only in the collections of antiquaries. Counterfeits of the bills were sent out of New York by the British by the cart-load, and put into circulation. The following appeared in *Rivington's Gazette:*

"Advertisement.—Persons going into other colonies may be supplied with any number of counterfeit Congress notes for the price of the paper per ream. They are so neatly and exactly executed that there is no risk in getting them off, it being almost impossible to discover that they are not genuine. This has been proven by bills to a very large amount which have already been successfully circulated. Inquire of Q. E. D., at the Coffee-house, from 11 A.M. to 4 P.M., during the present month."

An ill-advised expedition against the Spaniards at St. Augustine, by land and sea, undertaken by Governor Moore, of South Carolina, in September, 1702, was unsuccessful, and involved the colony in a debt of more than $26,000, for the payment of which bills of credit were issued, the first emission of paper money in that colony.

In 1723 Pennsylvania made its first issue of paper currency. It issued, in March, paper bills of credit to the amount of $60,000, made them a legal tender in all payments on pain of confiscating the debt or forfeiting the commodity, imposed sufficient penalties on all persons who presumed to make any bargain or sale on cheaper terms in case of being paid in gold or silver, and provided for the gradual reduction of the bills by enacting that one-eighth of the principal, as well as the whole interest, should be paid annually. It made no loans but on land security or plate deposited in the loan office, and obliged borrowers to pay 5 per cent. for the sums they took up. The scheme worked so well that, in the latter end of the year, the government emitted bills to the amount of $150,000 on the same terms. In 1729 there was a new emission of $150,000 to be reduced one-sixteenth a year. Pennsylvania was one of the last—if not the very last—provinces that emitted a paper currency.

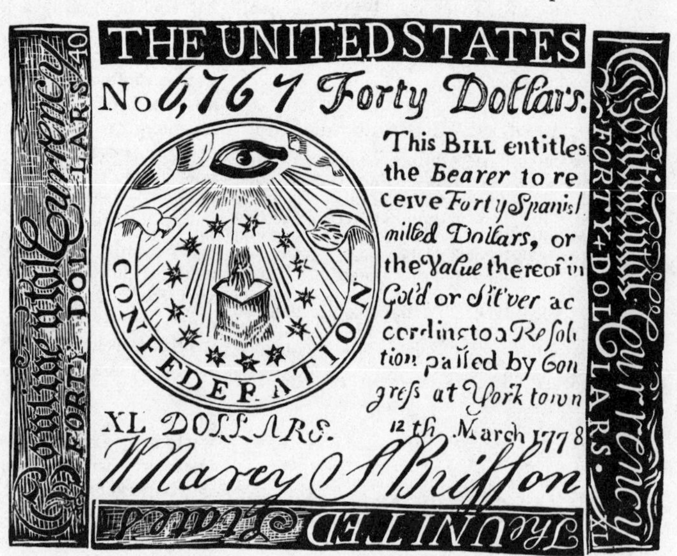

FAC-SIMILE OF COUNTERFEIT CONTINENTAL BILL.

In the course of the French and Indian War, the French officers in Canada, civil and military, had been guilty of immense peculations. At the close of hostilities there was outstanding, in unpaid bills on France and in card or paper money, more than $20,000,000, a large portion of which the French government declared, had been fraudulently issued. The holders of this currency, payment of which had been suspended immediately after the fall of Quebec (1759), received but a small indemnity for it.

Very little money had been in circulation in the Massachusetts colony during its earlier years, for what coin the settlers brought with them soon went back to England to pay for imported articles. Taxes were paid in grain and cattle, at rates fixed by the General Court. Every new set of emigrants brought some money with them, and the lively demand for corn and cattle on the part of the new-comers raised the prices to a high pitch. When the political changes in England stopped emigration, prices fell, and a corresponding difficulty was felt in paying debts. In 1640 the legislature of Massachusetts enacted that grain, at different prices for different sorts, should be a legal tender for the payment of all debts. To prevent sacrifices of property in cases of inability to pay, corn, cattle, and other personal goods, or, in default of such goods, the home and lands of the debtor, when taken in execution, were to be delivered to the creditor in full satisfaction, at such value as they might be appraised at by "three intelligent and indifferent men"—one to be chosen by the creditor, another by the debtor, and a third by the marshal. Beaver skins were also paid and received as money, and held a place next to coin in the public estimation. At one time musket-balls, at one farthing each, were made legal tender. A more available currency was found in WAMPUM (*q. v*), the money of the Indians.

In 1645 the legislature of Virginia prohibited dealing by barter, and abolished tobacco as currency. They established the Spanish dollar, or "piece of eight," at six shillings, as the standard of currency for that colony. In 1655 the "piece of eight" was changed from six shillings to five shillings sterling as the standard of currency.

Currency, NATIONAL. On June 3, 1864, Congress provided for a separate bureau in the Treasury Department, the chief officer of which is called the comptroller of the currency, whose office is under the general direction of the Secretary of the Treasury. It provided that associations for carrying on the business of banking might be formed, consisting of not less than five persons; that no association should be organized under the act with a less capital than $100,000, nor, in a city the population of which exceeded 50,000, with a less capital than $200,000; but that banks with a capital of not less than $50,000 might, with the approval of the Secretary of the Treasury, be established in any place the population of which did not exceed 6,000. It also provided that such associations should have existence for twenty years, and might exercise the general powers of banking companies; that the capital should be divided into shares of $100 each; that stockholders should be liable to the extent of the stock for the debts and contracts of the bank; that every association, preliminary to the commencement of banking business, should transfer bonds of the United States to an amount not less than $30,000, and not less than one-third of the capital stock paid in; that upon the proper examination being made into the affairs of the proposed institution, it should be entitled to receive from the comptroller of the currency circulating notes equal in amount to 20 per cent. of the current market value of the bonds transferred, but not exceeding 90 per cent. of the par value of such bonds. It was also provided that notes to an amount not exceeding in value $300,000,000 should be issued; that these notes should be received at par in all parts of the United States in payment of taxes, excises, public lands, and all other dues to the United States, except for duties on imports, and also for all salaries and other debts and demands owing by the United States to individuals, corporations, and associations within the United States, except interest on the public debt, and in redemption of the national currency; that the rate of interest to be charged should be that allowed by the State or Territory where the bank should be located, and that any State bank might become a national bank under the act. By an act passed in March, 1867, it was provided that temporary loan-certificates, bearing 3 per cent. interest, might be issued to an amount not exceeding $50,000,000, and that such certificates might constitute for any national bank a part of the reserve provided for by law, provided that not less than three-fifths of the reserve of each bank should consist of lawful money of the United States. In January, 1868, an additional amount of $25,000,000 of temporary loan-certificates was authorized, and in July, 1870, provision made for issuing $54,000,000 additional currency to national banks. By a law which taxed all banks chartered by States 10 per cent. on all circulation paid out by them, Congress effectually drove their notes from circulation. This national paper currency is at par in every part of the United States, and affords the soundest paper currency ever contrived. In 1875 Congress passed an act making banking free under the national system, without any restrictions as to the amount of circulating notes that may be issued to any part of the country. See BANKS, NATIONAL; CIRCULATION.

Currency Reform. See MONETARY REFORM; NATIONAL MONETARY COMMISSION.

Curry, DANIEL, clergyman; born near Peekskill, N. Y., Nov. 26, 1809; graduated at Wesleyan College in 1837; accepted a professorship at the female college of Macon, Ga., in 1839; was ordained in the Methodist Episcopal Church in 1841. When the denomination was divided he settled in New York State, where he filled a number of important appointments. He was editor of the *Christian Advocate* in 1864–76; the *National Repository* in 1876–80; and the *Methodist Review* in 1884–87. His publications include *New York: A Historical Sketch,* etc. He died in New York City, Aug. 17, 1887.

Curry, JABEZ LAMAR MONROE, educator; born in Lincoln county, Ga., June 5, 1825; graduated at the University of Georgia in 1843; served with the Texas Rangers in the Mexican War in 1846; member of the United States Congress in 1857–61, and of the Confederate Congress in 1861–63; was lieutenant-colonel of cavalry in the Confederate army in 1863–65; president of Howard College, Alabama, 1866–68; professor of constitutional and international law in Richmond College, Virginia, in 1868–81; United States minister to Spain in 1885–88; and general agent of the Slater and Peabody Education Funds till his death in Asheville, N. C., Feb. 12, 1903. His publications include *The Southern States of the American Union in their Relation to the Constitution and the Resulting Union; Establishment and Disestablishment in the United States; History of the Peabody Education Fund;* and *Civil History of the Confederate States.*

Curtin, ANDREW GREGG, war governor; born in Bellefonte, Pa., April 22, 1817; was an active lawyer and politician, and governor of his native State when the Civil War broke out. He had been secretary of state from 1855 to 1858, and superintendent of common schools in 1860.

ANDREW GREGG CURTIN.

He was re-elected governor in 1863; was minister to Russia in 1869–72, and Democratic Congressman in 1880–86. He died in Bellefonte, Oct. 7, 1894.

Curtis, BENJAMIN ROBBINS, jurist; born in Watertown, Mass., Nov. 4, 1809; graduated at Harvard in 1829; admitted to the bar in 1832; appointed to the United States Supreme Court in 1851; resigned in 1857; was one of the two dissenting judges in the Dred Scott case; was one of the counsel for President Johnson during the impeachment trial. He died in Newport, R. I., Sept. 15, 1874.

Curtis, GEORGE TICKNOR, lawyer; born in Watertown, Mass., Nov. 28, 1812; graduated at Harvard in 1832; admitted to the bar in 1836; removed to New York City in 1862. Among his publications are *History of the Origin, Formation, and Adoption of the Constitution of the United States; Life of Daniel Webster; Life of James Buchanan,* etc. He died in New York, March 28, 1894.

CURTIS, GEORGE WILLIAM

Curtis, GEORGE WILLIAM, editor; born in Providence, R. I., Feb. 24, 1824; became a member of the BROOK FARM ASSOCIATION (*q. v.*) in 1842. In 1846 he went abroad, and, after spending a year in Italy, entered the University of Berlin, where he saw the revolutionary movements of 1848. He spent two years in travelling in

GEORGE WILLIAM CURTIS.

Europe, Egypt, and Syria, returning to the United States in 1850, in which year he published *Nile Notes of a Howadji.* He joined the editorial staff of the New York *Tribune*, and was one of the original editors of *Putnam's Monthly.* He was for many years an eloquent and successful lyceum lecturer, and was generally regarded as one of the most accomplished orators in the United States. In 1867 he became editor of *Harper's Weekly*, and was extremely influential. In his writings and speeches he was a very efficient supporter of the Republican party for nearly a generation. He contributed a vast number of very able short essays through *Harper's Monthly*, in the department of "The Easy Chair." In 1871 President Grant appointed Mr. Curtis one of a commission to draw up rules for the regulation of the civil service. He was a member of the constitutional convention of the State of New York in 1868, in which he was chairman of the committee on education. In 1864 he was appointed one of the regents of the University of the State of New York. He died Aug. 31, 1892.

The Spoils System.—The following is an abridgment of his celebrated speech on the evils of the spoils system in politics, delivered before the American Social Science Association, in Saratoga, N. Y., Sept. 8, 1881:

The spoils spirit struggled desperately to obtain possession of the national administration from the day of Jefferson's inauguration to that of Jackson's, when it succeeded. Its first great but undesigned triumph was the decision of the first Congress, in 1789, vesting the sole power of removal in the President, a decision which placed almost every position in the civil service unconditionally at his pleasure. This decision was determined by the weight of Madison's authority. But Webster, nearly fifty years afterwards, opposing his authority to that of Madison, while admitting the decision to have been final, declared it to have been wrong. The year 1820, which saw the great victory of slavery in the Missouri Compromise, was also the year in which the second great triumph of the spoils system was gained, by the passage of the law which, under the plea of securing greater responsibility in certain financial offices, limited such offices to a term of four years. The decision of 1789, which gave the sole power of removal to the President, required positive executive action to effect removal; but this law of 1820 vacated all the chief financial offices, with all the places dependent upon them, during the term of every President, who, without an order of removal, could fill them all at his pleasure.

A little later a change in the method of nominating the President from a congressional caucus to a national convention still further developed the power of patronage as a party resource, and in the session of 1825–26, when John Quincy Adams was President, Mr. Benton introduced his report upon Mr. Macon's resolution declaring the necessity of reducing and regulating executive patronage; although Mr. Adams, the last of the Revolutionary line of Presidents, so scorned to misuse patronage that he leaned backward in standing erect. The pressure for the overthrow of the constitutional system had grown steadily more angry and peremptory with the progress of the country, the development of party spirit, the increase of patronage, the unanticipated consequences of the sole executive power of removal, and the immense opportunity offered by the four-years' law. It was a pressure against which Jefferson held the gates by main force, which was relaxed by the war under Madison and the fusion of parties under Monroe, but which swelled again into a furious torrent as the later parties took form. John Quincy Adams adhered, with the tough tenacity of his father's son, to the best principles of all his predecessors. He followed Washington, and observed the spirit of the Constitution in refusing to remove for any reason but official misconduct or incapacity. But he knew well what was coming, and with characteristically stinging sarcasm he called General Jackson's inaugural address "a threat of reform." With Jackson's administration in 1830 the deluge of the spoils system burst over our national politics. Sixteen years later, Mr. Buchanan said, in a public speech, that General Taylor would be faithless to the Whig party if he did not proscribe Democrats. So high the deluge had risen which has ravaged and wasted our politics ever since, and the danger will be stayed only when every President, leaning upon the law, shall stand fast where John Quincy Adams stood.

But the debate continued during the whole Jackson administration. In the Senate and on the stump, in elaborate reports and popular speeches, Webster, Calhoun, and Clay, the great political chiefs of their time, sought to alarm the country with the dangers of patronage. Sargent S. Prentiss, in the House of Representatives, caught up and echoed the cry under the administration of Van Buren. But the country refused to be alarmed. . . .

It heard the uproar like the old lady upon her first railroad journey, who sat serene amid the wreck of a collision, and, when asked if she was very much hurt, looked over her spectacles and answered blandly, "Hurt? Why, I supposed they always stopped so in this kind of travelling." The feeling that the denunciation was only a part of the game of politics, and no more to be accepted as a true statement than Snug the joiner as a true lion, was confirmed by the fact that when the Whig opposition came into power with President Harrison, it adopted the very policy which, under Democratic administration, it had strenuously denounced as fatal. The pressure for place was even greater than it had been ten years before, and although Mr. Webster, as Secretary of State, maintained his consistency by putting his name to an executive order asserting sound principles, the order was swept away like a lamb by a locomotive. "Nothing but a miracle," said General Harrison's Attorney-General, "can feed the swarm of hungry office-seekers."

Adopted by both parties, Mr. Marcy's doctrine that the places in the public service are the proper spoils of a victorious party was accepted as a necessary condition of popular government. One of the highest officers of the government expounded this doctrine to me long afterwards. "I believe," said he, "that when the people vote to change a party administration they vote to change every person of the opposite party who holds a place, from the President of the United States to the messenger at my door." It is this extraordinary but sincere misconception of the function of a party in a free government that leads to the serious defence of the spoils system. Now, a party is merely a voluntary association of citizens to secure the enforcement of a certain policy of administration upon which they are agreed. In a free government this is done by the election of legislators and of certain executive officers who are friendly to that policy. But the duty of a great body of persons employed in the minor administrative places is in no sense political. It is wholly ministerial, and the political opinions of such persons affect the discharge of their duties no more than their religious view or their literary preferences. All that can be justly required of such persons, in the interest of the public business, is honesty, intelligence, capacity, industry, and due subordination; and to say that when the policy of the government is changed by the result of an election from protection to free-trade every bookkeeper and letter-carrier and messenger and porter in the public offices ought to be a free-trader is as wise as to say that if a merchant is a Baptist every clerk in his office ought to be a believer in total immersion. But the officer of whom I spoke undoubtedly expressed the general feeling. The necessarily evil consequences of the practice which he justified seemed to be still speculative and inferential, and to the national indifference which followed the war the demand of Mr. Jenckes for reform appeared to be a mere whimsical vagary most inopportunely introduced.

It was, however, soon evident that the war had made the necessity of reform imperative, and chiefly for two reasons: First, the enormous increase of patronage, and, second, the fact that circumstances had largely identified a party name with patriotism. The great and radical evil of the spoils system was carefully fostered by the apparent absolute necessity to the public welfare of making political opinion and sympathy a condition of appointment to the smallest place. It is since the war, therefore, that the evil has run riot and that its consequences have been fully revealed. Those consequences are now familiar, and I shall not describe them. It is enough that the most patriotic and intelligent Americans and the most competent foreign observers agree that the direct and logical results of that system are the dangerous confusion of the executive and legislative powers of the government; the conversion of politics into mere place-hunting; the extension of the mischief to State and county and city administration, and the consequent degradation of the national character; the practical disfranchisement of the people wherever the system is most powerful; and the perversion of a republic of equal citizens into a despotism of venal politicians. . . .

The whole system of appointments in the civil service proceeds from the President, and in regard to his action the intention of the Constitution is indisputable. It is that the President shall appoint solely upon public consideration, and that the officer appointed shall serve as long as he discharges his duty faithfully. This is shown in Mr. Jefferson's familiar phrase in his reply to the remonstrance of the merchants of New Haven against the removal of the collector of that port. Mr. Jefferson asserted that Mr. Adams had purposely appointed in the last moments of his administration officers whose designation he should have left to his successor. Alluding to these appointments, he says: "I shall correct the procedure, and that done, return with joy to that state of things when the only question concerning a candidate shall be, Is he honest? Is he capable? Is he faithful to the Constitution?" Mr. Jefferson here recognizes that these had been the considerations which had usually determined appointments; and Mr. Madison, in the debate upon the President's sole power of removal, declared that if the President should remove an officer for any reason not connected with efficient service, he would be impeached. Reform, therefore, is merely a return to the principle and purpose of the Constitution and to the practice of the early administrations.

What more is necessary, then, for reform than that the President should return to that practice? As all places in the civil service are filled either by his direct nomination or by officers whom he appoints, why had not any President ample constitutional authority to effect at any moment a complete and thorough reform? The answer is simple. He has the power. He has always had it. A President has only to do as Washington did, and all his successors have only to do likewise, and reform would be complete. Every President has but to refuse to remove non-political officers for political or personal reasons; to appoint only those whom he knows to be competent; to renominate, as Monroe and John Quincy Adams did, every faithful officer whose commission expires, and to require the heads of departments and all inferior appointing officers to conform to this practice, and the work would be done. This is apparently a short and easy constitutional method of reform, requiring no further legislation or scheme of procedure. But why has no President adopted it? For the same reason that the best of Popes does not reform the abuses of his Church. For the same reason that a leaf goes over Niagara. It is because the opposing forces are overpowering. The same high officer of the government to whom I have alluded said to me as we drove upon the Heights of Washington, "Do you mean that I ought not to appoint my subordinates for whom I am responsible?" I answered: "I mean that you do not appoint them now; I mean that if, when we return to the capital, you hear that your chief subordinate is dead, you will not appoint his successor. You will have to choose among the men urged upon you by certain powerful politicians. Undoubtedly you ought to appoint the man whom you believe to be the most fit. But you do not and cannot. If you could or did appoint such men only, and that were the rule of your department and of the service, there would be no need of reform." And he could not deny it. . . .

A President who should alone undertake thoroughly to reform the evil must feel it to be the vital and paramount issue, and must be willing to hazard everything for its success. He must have the absolute faith and the indomitable will of Luther. How can we expect a President whom this system elects to devote himself to its destruction? General Grant, elected by a spontaneous patriotic impulse, fresh from the regulated order of military life, and new to politics and politicians, saw the reason and the necessity of reform. The hero of a victorious war, at the height of his popularity, his party in undisputed and seemingly indisputable supremacy, made the attempt. Congress, good-naturedly tolerating what it considered his whim of inexperience, granted money to try an experiment. The adverse pressure was tremendous. "I am used to pressure," said the soldier. So he was, but not to this pressure. He was driven by unknown and incalculable currents. He was enveloped in whirlwinds of sophistry, scorn, and incredulity. He who upon his own line had fought it out all summer to victory, upon a line absolutely new and unknown was naturally bewildered and dismayed. . . .

When at last President Grant said, "If Congress adjourns without positive legislation on civil service reform, I shall regard such action as a disapproval of the system and shall abandon it," it was, indeed, a surrender, but it was the surrender of a champion who had honestly mistaken both the nature and the strength of the adversary and his own power of endurance.

It is not, then, reasonable, under the conditions of our government and in the actual situation, to expect a President to go much faster or much further than public opinion. But executive action can aid most effectively the development and movement of that opinion, and the most decisive reform measures that the present administration might take would be undoubtedly supported by a powerful public sentiment. The educative results of resolute executive action, however limited and incomplete in scope, have been shown in the two great public offices of which I have spoken, the New York custom-house and the New York post-office. . . .

The root of the complex evil, then, is personal favoritism. This produces congressional dictation, senatorial usurpation, arbitrary removals, interference in elections, political assessments, and all the consequent corruption, degradation, and danger that experience has disclosed. The method of reform, therefore, must be a plan of selection for appointment which makes favoritism impossible. The general feeling undoubtedly is that this can be accomplished by a fixed limited term. But the terms of most of the offices to which the President and the Senate appoint, and upon which the myriad minor places in the service depend, have been fixed and limited for sixty years, yet it is during that very period that the chief evils of personal patronage have appeared. The law of 1820, which limited the term of important revenue offices to four years, and which was afterwards extended to other offices, was intended, as John Quincy Adams tells us, to promote the election to the Presidency of Mr. Crawford, who was then Secretary of the Treasury. The law was drawn by Mr. Crawford himself, and it was introduced into the Senate by one of his devoted partisans. It placed the whole body of executive financial officers at the mercy of the Secretary of the Treasury and of a majority of the Senate, and its design, as Mr. Adams says, "was to secure for Mr. Crawford the influence of all the incumbents in office, at the peril of displacement, and of five or ten times an equal number of ravenous office-seekers, eager to supplant them." This is the very substance of the spoils system, intentionally introduced by a fixed limitation of term in place of the constitutional tenure of efficient service;

and it was so far successful that it made the custom-house officers, district attorneys, marshals, registers of the land office, receivers of public money, and even paymasters in the army, notoriously active partisans of Mr. Crawford. . . .

To fix by law the terms of places dependent upon such officers would be like an attempt to cure hydrophobia by the bite of a mad dog. The incumbent would be always busy keeping his influence in repair to secure reappointment, and the applicant would be equally busy in seeking such influence to procure the place, and, as the fixed terms would be constantly expiring, the eager and angry intrigue and contest of influence would be as endless as it is now. This certainly would not be reform.

But would not reform be secured by adding to a fixed limited term the safeguard of removal for cause only? Removal for cause alone means, of course, removal for legitimate cause, such as dishonesty, negligence, or incapacity. But who shall decide that such cause exists? This must be determined either by the responsible superior officer or by some other authority. But if left to some other authority the right of counsel and the forms of a court would be invoked; the whole legal machinery of mandamuses, injunctions, certioraris, and the rules of evidence would be put in play to keep an incompetent clerk at his desk or a sleepy watchman on his beat. Cause for the removal of a letter-carrier in the post-office or of an accountant in the custom-house would be presented with all the pomp of impeachment and established like a high crime and misdemeanor. Thus every clerk in every office would have a kind of vested interest in his place because, however careless, slovenly, or troublesome he might be, he could be displaced only by an elaborate and doubtful legal process. Moreover, if the head of a bureau or a collector or a postmaster were obliged to prove negligence or insolence or incompetency against a clerk as he would prove theft, there would be no removals from the public service except for crimes of which the penal law takes cognizance. Consequently, removal would be always and justly regarded as a stigma upon character, and a man removed from a position in a public office would be virtually branded as a convicted criminal. Removal for cause, therefore, if the cause were to be decided by any authority but that of the responsible superior officer, instead of improving, would swiftly and enormously enhance the cost and ruin the efficiency of the public service by destroying subordination and making every lazy and worthless member of it twice as careless and incompetent as he is now.

If, then, the legitimate cause for removal ought to be determined in public as in private business by the responsible appointing power, it is of the highest public necessity that the exercise of that power should be made as absolutely honest and independent as possible. But how can it be made honest and independent if it is not protected so far as practicable from the constant bribery of selfish interest and the illicit solicitation of personal influence? The experience of our large patronage offices proves conclusively that the cause of the larger number of removals is not dishonesty or incompetency; it is the desire to make vacancies to fill. This is the actual cause, whatever cause may be assigned. The removals would not be made except for the pressure of politicians. But these politicians would not press for removals if they could not secure the appointment of their favorites. Make it impossible for them to secure appointment, and the pressure would instantly disappear and arbitrary removal cease.

So long, therefore, as we permit minor appointments to be made by mere personal influence and favor, a fixed limited term and removal during that term for cause only would not remedy the evil, because the incumbents would still be seeking influence to secure reappointment, and the aspirants doing the same to replace them. Removal under plea of good cause would be as wanton and arbitrary as it is now, unless the power to remove were intrusted to some other discretion than that of the superior officer, and in that case the struggle for reappointment and the knowledge that removal for the term was practically impossible would totally demoralize the service. To make sure, then, that removals shall be made for legitimate cause only, we must provide that appointment shall be made only for legitimate cause.

All roads lead to Rome. Personal influence in appointments can be annulled only by free and open competition. By that bridge we can return to the practice of Washington and to the intention of the Constitution. That is the shoe of swiftness and the magic sword by which the President can pierce and outrun the protean enemy of sophistry and tradition which prevents him from asserting his power. If you can say that success in a competitive literary examination does not prove fitness to adjust customs duties or to distribute letters or to appraise linen or to measure molasses, I answer that the reform does not propose that fitness shall be proved by a competitive literary examination. It proposes to annul personal influence and political favoritism by making appointments depend upon proved capacity. To determine this it proposes first to test the comparative general intelligence of all applicants and their special knowledge of the particular official duties required, and then to prove the practical faculty of the most intelligent applicants by actual trial in the performance of the duties before they are appointed. If it be still said that success in such a competition may not prove fitness, it is enough to reply that success in obtaining the favor of some kind of boss, which is the present system, presumptively proves unfitness.

Nor is it any objection to the reformed system that many efficient officers in the service could not have entered it had it been necessary to pass an examination; it is no objection, because their efficiency is a mere chance. They were not appointed because of efficiency, but either because they were diligent politicians or because they were recommended by diligent politicians. The chance of getting efficient men in any business is certainly not diminished by inquiry and investigation. . . .

Mr. President, in the old Arabian story, from the little box upon the sea-shore carelessly opened by the fisherman arose the towering and haughty demon, evermore monstrous and more threatening, who would not crouch again. So from the smallest patronage of the earlier day, from a civil service dealing with a national revenue of only $2,000,000, and regulated upon sound business principles, has sprung the un-American, un-Democratic, un-Republican system which destroys political independence, honor, and morality, and corrodes the national character itself. In the solemn anxiety of this hour the warning words of the austere Calhoun, uttered nearly half a century ago, echo enstartled recollection like words of doom: "If you do not put this thing down, it will put you down." Happily it is the historic faith of the race from which we are chiefly sprung that eternal vigilance is the price of liberty. It is the faith which has made our mother England the great parent of free States. The same faith has made America the political hope of the world. Fortunately removed by our position from the entanglements of European politics, and more united and peaceful at home than at any time within the memory of living men, the moment is most auspicious for remedying that abuse in our political system whose nature, proportions, and perils the whole country begins clearly to discern. The will and the power to apply the remedy will be a test of the sagacity and the energy of the people. The reform of which I have spoken is essentially the people's reform. With the instinct of robbers who run with the crowd and lustily cry "Stop thief!" those who would make the public service the monopoly of a few favorites denounce the determination to open that service to the whole people as a plan to establish an aristocracy. The huge ogre of patronage, gnawing at the character, the honor, and the life of the country, grimly sneers that the people cannot help themselves and that nothing can be done. But much greater things have been done. Slavery was the Giant Despair of many good men of the last generation, but slavery was overthrown. If the spoils system, a monster only less threatening than slavery, be unconquerable, it is because the country has lost its convictions, its courage, and its common-sense. "I expect," said the Yankee, as he surveyed a stout antagonist—"I expect that you're pretty ugly, but I cal'late I'm a darned sight uglier." I know that patronage is strong, but I believe that the American people are very much stronger.

Curtis, James Langdon, politician; born in Stratford, Conn., about 1820; engaged in business in New York City; was the candidate of the American party for President in 1888; and received 1,591 popular votes. He died at Stratford, Conn., Nov. 12, 1903.

Curtis, Samuel Ryan, military officer; born near Champlain, N. Y., Feb. 3, 1805; graduated at West Point in 1831, and the following year left the army and studied law; served under General Taylor in the war with Mexico, and was General Wool's assistant adjutant-general in that war. He was for a while governor of Saltillo. He became a member of Congress in 1857, retaining that post until 1861, and was a member of the Peace Congress. In May, 1861, he was appointed brigadier-general of volunteers, and in March, 1862, major-general. Commanding the army in Missouri, he gained the Battle of Pea Ridge (*q. v.*). After the war he was appointed United States commissioner to treat with Indian tribes—Sioux, Cheyennes, and others. He died in Council Bluffs, Ia., Dec. 26, 1866.

SAMUEL RYAN CURTIS.

Curtis, William Baker, military officer; born in Sharpsburg, Md., April 18, 1821; was a member of the Wheeling convention to organize a State government for West Virginia in 1861; entered the Union army as captain in the 12th West Virginia Infantry in 1862; and was promoted colonel and given command of a brigade in 1864. Subsequently he was appointed commander of the 2d Brigade, 24th Army Corps, in the Army of the James, with which he took part in the siege of Richmond and captured Fort Gregg, near Petersburg, on April 2, 1865; for which he was promoted brigadier-general. He died in West Liberty, W. Va., Aug. 25, 1891.

Curtis, William Eleroy, author; born in Akron, O., Nov. 5, 1850; graduated at Western Reserve College in 1871; was special commissioner from the United States to the Central and South American republics; executive officer of the International American Conference in 1889–90; director of the Bureau of American Republics in 1890–93; and special envoy to the Queen Regent of Spain and to Pope Leo XIII., in 1892. His publications include *The Life of Zachariah Chandler; Trade and Transportation; Relics of Columbus; Recent Discoveries Concerning the Early Settlement of America in the Archives of the Vatican; The True Thomas Jefferson; The True Abraham Lincoln;* and *Handbooks on the American Republics.* He died in Philadelphia, Pa., Oct. 5, 1911.

Curwen, Samuel, jurist; born in Salem, Mass., Dec. 28, 1715; graduated at Harvard in 1735; took part in the Louisburg expedition; was appointed judge of the Admiralty Court in 1775. Being a loyalist, he was obliged to leave Salem, and did not return until 1784. His journal which he kept during his exile, and his letters, were published in 1842. He died in Salem, Mass., April 9, 1802.

Cushing, Caleb, jurist; born in Salisbury, Mass., Jan. 17, 1800; graduated at Harvard University in 1817; became a distinguished lawyer, in which profession he began practice at Newburyport, Mass. He served in the State legislature, and was in Congress from 1835 to 1843, as a Whig representative, when, with Mr. Tyler, he became an active member of the Democratic party. President Tyler sent him as commissioner to China, where, in 1844, he negotiated an important treaty. He advocated the policy of war with Mexico, and led a regiment to the field. In 1853 President Pierce called Mr. Cushing to his cabinet as Attorney-General. In 1860 he was president of the Democratic convention at Charleston. President Buchanan appointed him in 1860 confidential commissioner to South Carolina to work against secession. During the Civil War he supported the administration of President Lincoln and was given several confidential missions. In 1866 he was one of three commissioners appointed to codify the laws of the United States; in 1871 was one of the counsel on the part of the United States before the Geneva Arbitration Tribunal; and in 1873–77 was minister to Spain. He died in Newburyport, Mass., Jan. 2, 1879.

CALEB CUSHING.

Cushing, FRANK HAMILTON, ethnologist; born in Northeast, Pa., July 22, 1857; became interested early in life in collecting Indian relics. In 1875 he was commissioned to make surveys and collections for the National Museum; in 1879 was with Maj. J. W. Powell in the expedition to New Mexico; and at his own request was left with the Zuni Indians, where he lived for three years, and later for three additional years; acquired their language and traditions; was initiated into their priesthood. In 1881 he discovered the ruins of the Seven Cities of Cibola, and conducted excavations among them and the great buried cities in southern Arizona. In 1895 he discovered the extensive remains of a sea-dwelling people along the Gulf coast of Florida, and in 1896 led there the Pepper-Hearst expedition. He died in Washington, D. C., April 10, 1900.

Cushing, HARRY ALONZO, educator; born in Lynn, Mass., in 1870; graduated at Amherst in 1891; was lecturer on history in 1895–1900; on constitutional law in 1901–03; professor of law from 1907, at Columbia University. He is the author of *King's College in the American Revolution; The Transition from Provincial to Commonwealth Government in Massachusetts;* editor of *The Writings of Samuel Adams,* etc.

Cushing, LUTHER STEARNS, jurist; born in Lunenburg, Mass., June 22, 1803; graduated at Harvard in 1826; editor of the *Jurist* and *Law Magazine.* He wrote many books on legal subjects, but is most generally known as the author of *Cushing's Manual of Parliamentary Practice.* He died in Boston, June 22, 1856.

Cushing, THOMAS, statesman; born in Boston, March 24, 1725; graduated at Harvard in 1744, and for many years represented his native city in the General Court, of which body he became speaker in 1763, and held that post until 1774. His signature was affixed, during all that time, to all public documents of the province, which made his name so conspicuous that, in his pamphlet *Taxation no Tyranny,* Dr. Johnson said, "One object of the Americans is said to be to adorn the brows of Cushing with a diadem." He was a member of the first and second Continental Congresses; was commissary-general in 1775; judge of Court of Common Pleas, 1776–77; and in 1779 was elected lieutenant-governor of Massachusetts, which office he held until his death, in Boston, Feb. 28, 1788.

Cushing, WILLIAM, jurist; born in Scituate, Mass., March 1, 1732; graduated at Harvard University in 1751; studied law; became eminent in his profession; was attorney-general of Massachusetts; a judge of probate in 1768; judge of the Superior Court in 1772; and in 1777 succeeded his father as chief-justice of that court. Under the Massachusetts constitution of 1788 he was made chief-justice of the State; and in 1789 President Washington appointed him a justice of the Supreme Court of the United States. He offered him the chief-justiceship in 1796, as the successor of Jay, but he declined it. He administered the oath of office to Washington in his second inauguration. He died in Scituate, Sept. 13, 1810.

Cushing, WILLIAM BARKER, naval officer; born in Delafield, Wis., Nov. 4, 1843; entered the navy in 1857; resigned, and was reappointed in 1861. He performed exploits remarkable for coolness and courage during the war, the most notable of which was the destruction of the Confederate ram *Albemarle* (*q. v.*) at Plymouth, N. C. For this he received a vote of thanks from Congress. In 1868–69 he commanded (as lieutenant-commander) the steamer *Maumee* in the Asiatic squadron. He died in Washington, D. C., Dec. 17, 1874.

Destruction of the "Albemarle."—The following handsome tribute to Cushing and detailed narrative of his famous ex-

WILLIAM BARKER CUSHING.

ploit were penned by Admiral David D. Porter, in a private letter under date of Nov. 21, 1888:

I like to talk and write about Cushing. He was one of those brave spirits developed by the Civil War who always rose to the occasion. He was always ready to undertake any duty, no matter how desperate, and he generally succeeded in his enterprises, from the fact that the enemy supposed that no man would be foolhardy enough to embark in such hazardous affairs where there seemed so little chance of success. A very interesting volume could be written on the adventures of Cushing from the time he entered the navy until his death, during which period he performed some remarkable deeds and left a reputation unparalleled for so young an officer.

One of the most gallant and successful affairs accomplished during the Civil War was the destruction of a Confederate ironclad ram by Lieutenant Cushing at Plymouth, N. C., on the night of Oct. 27, 1864. It may be remembered that the ram *Albemarle* had suddenly appeared at Plymouth, causing the destruction of the United States steamer *Southfield,* the death of the brave Lieutenant Flusser, and the retreat of the double-ender *Miami,* and had subsequently attacked a flotilla under Capt. Melancton Smith, inflicting much damage, but was obliged finally to retire before the Union vessels under the guns of Plymouth, which had fallen into the hands of the Confederates owing to the advent of the *Albemarle.*

As soon as Lieutenant Cushing heard of this affair he offered his services to the Navy Department to blow up the *Albemarle,* provided the department would furnish proper torpedo-boats with which to operate. His services were accepted, and he was ordered to the New York navy-yard to superintend the fitting-out of three torpedo-launches on a plan deemed at that time a very perfect one.

Cushing, though a dashing "free-lance," was not so well adapted to the command of a "flotilla" (as he called his three steam-launches). When completed, he started with his boats from New York, *via* the Delaware and Raritan Canal, as proud as a peacock. One of them sank in the canal soon after he started; another was run on shore by the officer in charge, on the coast of Virginia, in Chesapeake Bay, where she was surrendered to the Confederates; while Cushing, with that singular good luck which never deserted him, steamed down the bay through the most stormy weather, and arrived safely at Hampton Roads, where he reported to me on board the flag-ship *Malvern.*

This was my first acquaintance with Cushing, and, after inquiring into all the circumstances of the loss of the other two torpedo-boats, I did not form the most favorable opinion of Cushing's abilities as a flotilla commander. Cushing's condition when he reported on board the flag-ship was most deplorable. He had been subjected to the severest exposure for over a week, without shelter, had lost all his clothes except what little he had on, and his attenuated face and sunken eyes bore witness to the privations he had suffered. Officers and crew had subsisted on spoiled ship's biscuit and water and an occasional potato roasted before the boiler fire.

I at once ordered Cushing and his men to stow themselves away for rest, and directed them not to appear till sent for. In the mean time the launch, which had been very much disarranged and shattered, was being put in complete order. After the officers and crew had obtained forty-eight hours' rest, I sent for Cushing and gave him his instructions, which were to proceed through the Dismal Swamp Canal and the sounds of North Carolina, and blow up the *Albemarle*, then lying at Plymouth preparing for another raid on the Union fleet. Commander W. H. Macomb, commanding in the sound, was ordered to give Cushing all the assistance in his power with men and boats.

When rested and dressed, Cushing was a different-looking man from the pitiable object who had presented himself to me two days before. Scanning him closely, I asked him many questions, all of which were answered satisfactorily, and, after looking steadily into his cold gray eye and finding that he did not wink an eyelid, I said: "You will do. I am satisfied that you will perform this job. If you do, you will be made a lieutenant-commander."

On the very morning appointed for Cushing to sail on his perilous expedition an order came from the Navy Department to try him by court-martial for some infraction of international law towards an English vessel, which, according to Mr. Seward, had endangered the *entente cordiale* between England and the United States. I showed Cushing the order, but he was not disconcerted. "Admiral," he said, "let me go and blow up the *Albemarle*, and try me afterwards."

"Well done for you," I said; "I will do it. Now get off at once, and do not fail, or you will rue it."

So Cushing, who dreaded a court-martial more than he did the ram, went on his way rejoicing, passed through the canal, and on Oct. 27 reported to Commander Macomb.

Cushing was near coming to grief on his first setting-out. Like all "free-lances," he liked a frolic, and could not resist champagne and terrapin; so on the evening of his arrival at Norfolk he gave a supper to his numerous friends, "and then—the deluge!" I heard of the supper, of course—it was my business to hear of such things—and I despatched Fleet-Captain Breese in a swift steam-launch to arrest the delinquent and have him tried for intruding on the *entente cordiale* between the United States and Great Britain; but Captain Breese returned with the report that Cushing was on his way, and that "it was all right." "No," I said, "it is not 'all right'; and if the expedition fails, you—" But never mind what I said.

By eight o'clock on Oct. 27 Cushing had picked out his volunteers from Macomb's flotilla. They consisted of thirteen officers and men, one of whom was the faithful William L. Howarth, who had accompanied him in most of his daring adventures, and these two together felt that they were a match for any iron-clad in the Confederacy. That night Cushing started off on the expedition, towing the *Otsego's* cutter with an armed crew, who were to be employed in seizing the Confederate lookouts on board of the late United States steamer *Southfield*, which lay below Plymouth with her decks just above water.

The ram lay about 8 miles from the mouth of the river, which was 200 or 300 yards in width and supposed to be lined with Confederate pickets. The wreck of the *Southfield* was surrounded by schooners, and it was understood that a gun had been mounted here to command the bend of the river. When the steam-launch and her tow reached the *Southfield*, the hearts of the adventurers began to beat with anxiety. Every moment they expected a load of grape and canister, which would have been the signal for *qui vive* all along the river-bank.

The expedition was looked upon as a kind of forlorn hope by all who saw it start, and Cushing himself was not certain of success until after he passed the *Southfield* and the schooners. His keen gray eye looked into the darkness ahead, intent only on the *Albemarle*. The boat astern of the launch cast off at the right time and secured the pickets on board the schooners without firing a shot, and Cushing and his party passed unobserved by the pickets on the river-banks, who depended on the lookouts on board the *Southfield* and were making themselves comfortable under cover. This was a fortunate circumstance for Cushing, for otherwise the expedition might have failed. As it was, the torpedo-launch was enabled to approach unobserved to within a few yards of the *Albemarle*.

DESTRUCTION OF THE ALBEMARLE.

The ram had been well prepared for defence, and a good lookout was kept up on board. She was secured to a wharf with heavy logs all around her—in fact, she was in a pen. Half of her crew were on deck with two field-pieces and a company of artillery, and another company of artillery was stationed on the wharf with several field-pieces, while a bright fire of pine logs burned in front of them.

Cushing immediately comprehended the situation, and while he was making his plans the lookout on board the *Albemarle* discovered the launch and hailed, when there succeeded great excitement and confusion among the enemy. Cushing dashed at the logs on which the light was reflected, and by putting on all steam he pushed them aside and struck the *Albemarle* bows on. In the mean time the enemy had become thoroughly aroused, and the men on board the ram rushed to quarters and opened on the torpedo-boat, but the Confederates were swept away by the discharge of a 12-pound howitzer in the bow of the launch. A gun loaded with grape and canister was fired by the enemy, but the fire of the boat howitzer disconcerted the aim of the Confederate gunner, and the charge passed harmlessly over.

While all this firing was going on the torpedo boom was deliberately lowered until it was under the *Albemarle's* bottom, or overhang, and by a quick pull of the firing-rope the torpedo was exploded. There was a tremendous crash and a great upward rush of water which instantly filled the torpedo-boat, and she went drifting off with the current, but she left the *Albemarle* rapidly sinking. The Confederate commander, Lieut. A. W. Warley, encouraged his crew and endeavored to keep his vessel afloat as soon as he discovered the damage done, but the water gained so rapidly through the aperture made by the explosion that the *Albemarle* was soon on the bottom, her smoke-stack only remaining above water. As the Confederates had no appliances for raising the iron-clad, they did all they could to damage her further, knowing that the

Federal flotilla would not be long in appearing to claim the prize.

The *Albemarle* had been fully prepared for this attack, and had her crew at their posts; which makes the successful raid the more to be appreciated. A good watch was kept on board the ram, as was shown by the alertness with which the crew got to quarters and fired their guns; but they escaped to the shore with equal alertness, for the *Albemarle* sank with great rapidity. It was fortunate for Cushing that he succeeded in passing the pickets along the river undisturbed, for otherwise he would have had a warm reception all along the line; but he seemed to be the child of fortune, and his good luck followed him to the close of the war.

When the fire was opened on the torpedo-boat, Assistant-Paymaster Frank H. Swan was wounded at Cushing's side. How many others had been injured was not known. It seemed as if a shower of grapeshot had hit the boat, and that a rifle shell had passed through her fore and aft; but this was not so. The boat had sunk from the rush of water caused by the torpedo; and when Cushing saw that she would probably fall into the hands of the enemy he jumped overboard with some of the crew and swam down the river under a heavy fire of musketry, which, however, did no harm.

When some of the crew of the torpedo-boat who had jumped overboard saw that she had only filled with water and did not sink, they swam back to her and climbed on board, hoping that the boat would float away with the current from the scene of danger; but in this they were mistaken; for as soon as the Confederates recovered from their panic and saw the torpedo-boat drifting away, they manned the boats of the *Albemarle* which were still intact and followed the author of the mischief. Surrounding the steam-launch, with oaths and imprecations they demanded the surrender of the Union party. Nothing else was left for the latter to do. Their arms were all wet in the bottom of the boat and the enemy was lining the banks with sharp-shooters, so that "discretion was the better part of valor."

"Blast you," said one of the Confederates, "if you sunk us with your cowardly torpedo-boat, we licked your whole squadron last week, and we will make you fellows smell thunder with a ball and chain to your leg."

This was the first the torpedo-boat's crew had heard of the sinking of the *Albemarle*. In fact, they were under the impression that the attack was a failure, and that the boat had been filled by a rifle shell striking her, and not by the water thrown up by the explosion. They all gave three cheers, though they knew that the Confederates were exasperated and their carbines were pointed at the captives' heads.

In the mean time Cushing was quietly swimming down the river, keeping in the middle of the stream, when, hearing a noise near him, he looked around and found that two other persons were in company with him. One of them whispered: "I am getting exhausted; for God's sake help me to the shore."

"Who are you?" said Cushing.

"I am Woodman. I can go no farther; save me if you can."

At the same moment a gurgling sound was heard a little to the rear, and the third man sank to rise no more.

Cushing himself was much exhausted. He had managed to rid himself of his heaviest clothing and his boots, and was just letting himself drift with the current, but he could not resist this appeal from Woodman, who had risked his life to assist him in his perilous undertaking. He put an arm around him and tried to reach the bank, only sixty yards away, but all his efforts were futile. Woodman was too much exhausted. He could not help himself, and, cramps coming on, he was drawn all up, got away from Cushing, and sank.

Thus the only two survivors known to Cushing from the steam-launch had sunk before his eyes, and he did not know how soon his own time would come, for he was now so much exhausted that he could scarcely use his arms for swimming. At the same time he heard the shouts of the Confederates as they captured the launch, and, supposing that the enemy would send their boats down the river in search of fugitives, he determined to swim to the shore. He could barely crawl out of the water when he reached the bank at a point about a mile below Plymouth.

Cushing dragged himself into an adjacent swamp, and, while lying concealed a few feet from a path along the river, heard two of the *Albemarle's* officers and a picket-guard pass by, and learned from their conversation that the iron-clad was at the bottom of the river. He did not care now what became of him; that was glory enough for one day, and he would take no heed for the morrow.

As soon as his strength would allow, Cushing plunged into the dense swamp, where he was not likely to be followed, and, after incredible difficulties in forcing his way through the mud, slime, and brambles, reached a point well below the town, where he felt safe. Here he fell in with a negro who, for a consideration (being a Union man), volunteered to go to Plymouth to find out exactly how matters stood. The negro soon returned with the cheering news that the *Albemarle* was actually sunk, and that the Confederates were in great consternation. Thus cheered, Cushing pursued his tedious journey through the swamps till, coming suddenly to a creek, he found one of the enemy's picket-boats, of which he took possession. He pulled away with all his remaining strength, not knowing at what moment he might get a bullet through his head from the guard to whom the boat belonged, who was, no doubt, not far off in some shanty playing cards with a fellow-picket.

By eleven o'clock the following night Cushing reached the gunboat *Valley City*, out in the sound, and was taken on board more dead than alive, after one of the most remarkable and perilous adventures on record. Certain it was that Cushing had made himself famous by performing an achievement the dangers of which were almost insurmountable, for the enemy had taken every precaution against just such an attempt as had been made.

The success of Cushing shows that a man who makes up his mind to a certain thing and goes direct to the point, undeterred by obstacles, is almost sure to win, not only in blowing up ships, but in every-day affairs of life where great stakes are at risk. Here was a chance, and Cushing "seized the bull by the horns," *voilà tout*. No doubt he would have made the attempt if he had been obliged to run the gantlet of all the pickets from the mouth of the river to Plymouth.

This gallant affair led to the recapture of Plymouth from the Confederates, for Commander Macomb had been ordered by me to attack the town (in case the *Albemarle* was destroyed) with the Federal gunboats, which he did most successfully, and Plymouth remained in possession of the Federal forces to the end of the war. Cushing was promoted a little later, and received some $60,000 or $70,000 in prize-money; and suffice it to say that I never tried Cushing by court-martial on Secretary Seward's charges of endangering the *entente cordiale* between England and the United States.

Cushman, Robert, a founder of the Plymouth colony; born in Kent, England about 1580; joined the Society of the "Pilgrims" in Holland, and became very active. He and John Carver were appointed agents to make arrangements for the emigration of the church to America, and he was one of the number who sailed in the *Speedwell*, and were compelled to return on account of her unseaworthiness. Mr. Cushman remained with those who did not go in the *Mayflower*. He went to New Plymouth in the autumn of 1621, taking with him thirty-five other persons, and there delivered the charter to the colonists. He preached the first sermon by an ordained minister in New England on Dec. 12. On the following day he sailed for England. The vessel and cargo were captured by the French, and plundered of everything, and Cushman was detained two weeks on the French coast. On his return to London he published his sermon in New England *On the Sin and Danger of Self-love*, and also an eloquent vindication of the colonial enterprise. He made a strong appeal for missions to be sent to the American Indians. He continued the agent of the Plymouth colony in London until his death, in 1625.

Custer, Elizabeth Bacon, author; born in Michigan, about 1844; married to General Custer in 1864; and shared army life with him till his death. She has published *Boots and Saddles; Tenting on the Plains; Following the Guidon*, etc.

Custer, George Armstrong, military officer; born in New Rumley, O., Dec. 5, 1839; graduated at West Point in 1861, and was an active and daring cavalry officer during the Civil War, distinguishing himself on many occasions. He never lost a gun nor a color. In June, 1863, he was made brigadier-general of volunteers, and was brevetted major-general in 1864. He was particularly distinguished in the battles immediately preceding the surrender of Lee at Appomattox Court-house. He was exceptionally fortunate in his military career during the Civil War, and was made lieutenant-colonel of the 7th Cavalry in 1866, receiving the brevet of major-general, U. S. A., for services ending in Lee's surrender. He afterwards commanded expeditions against the Indians in the West, and on June 25, 1876,

GEORGE ARMSTRONG CUSTER.

he and his entire command were killed by hostile Sioux Indians on the Little Big Horn River, Montana. In 1879 a statue of General Custer was erected at West Point.

Custis, George Washington Parke, adopted son of George Washington; born in Mount Airy, Md., April 30, 1871; was a grandson of Mrs. Washington. His father was John Parke Custis, and his mother was Eleanor Calvert, of Maryland. At the siege of Yorktown his father was aide-de-camp to Washington; was seized with camp-fever; retired to Eltham, and there died before Washington (who hastened thither immediately after the surrender) could reach his bedside. Washington afterwards adopted his two children—Eleanor Parke and George Washington Parke Custis—as his own. Their early home was at Mount Vernon. George was educated partly at Princeton, and was eighteen years of age at the time of Washington's death, who made him an executor of his will and left him a handsome estate, on which he lived until his death, Oct. 10, 1857, in literary, artistic, and agricultural pursuits. In his early days Mr. Custis was an eloquent speaker; and in his later years he produced a series of historical pictures, valuable, not as works of art, but for the truthfulness of the costume and equipment of the soldiers delineated in them. His *Personal Recollections of Washington* were arranged and fully annotated by Benson J. Lossing and published in 1859, with a memoir by his daughter, Mrs. Robert E. Lee.

Custom-house, the place where commercial shipping is reported on its arrival from a foreign port, and receives its clearance papers on departure; also where foreign goods liable to duty are inspected on their arrival.

Customs Appeals, Court of, a federal tribunal authorized by the Payne-Aldrich tariff law of 1909 and constituted by President Taft March 9, 1910, by the appointment of the following members: Chief-Justice Robert M. Montgomery, of the Supreme Court of Michigan, to be presiding judge. Associate judges: William H. Hunt, of Montana; James F. Smith, of California; Orton M. Barber, of Vermont, and Marion Devries, of California. It is the business of these judges to hear and decide questions as to the classification of dutiable goods and the rates imposed on them. Cases may be appealed from the Collector of Customs to the Board of Appraisers and then to the new court, whereas before cases had to pass from the board through several intermediate appellate tribunals to the Supreme Court.

Customs Duties. See Tariff Legislation.

Cutler, Ephraim, surveyor; born in Edgarton, Mass., in 1767; appointed agent of the Ohio Company in 1788; removed to Ohio in 1794; appointed Judge of Common Pleas in 1795. He was the author of

History of the First Settlement of Amestown, Ohio, etc. He died in Amestown, O., in 1853.

Cutler, MANASSEH, clergyman; born in Killingly, Conn., May 3, 1742; graduated at Yale College in 1765; studied theology; was ordained in 1771; was a chaplain of a regiment in the army in 1776; became an excellent botanist; and gave the first scientific description of the plants of New England. As agent for the Ohio Company in 1787, he bought 1,500,000 acres of land northwest of the Ohio, and started the first company of emigrants to that region, who founded the town of Marietta in April, 1787. He travelled thither in a "sulky" (a two-wheeled, one-seated carriage), 750 miles in twenty-nine days. He was a member of Congress in 1800–04. He died in Hamilton, Mass., July 28, 1823.

Cutter, CHARLES AMMI, librarian; born in Boston, March 14, 1837; graduated at Harvard in 1855; was connected with the Harvard College, the Boston Athenæum and the Forbes (Northampton, Mass.) libraries, and probably contributed more than any other individual to the establishment of the science of library economy. He published *Rules for a Dictionary Catalogue, The Expansive Classification,* etc. He died in Walpole, N. H., Sept. 6, 1903.

Cutter, WILLIAM PARKER, librarian; born in Washington, D. C., Dec. 19, 1867; graduated at Cornell in 1888; librarian of the Department of Agriculture in Washington, D. C., in 1893–1900; chief of order department, Library of Congress, in 1901–04; then became librarian of the Forbes Library, Northampton, Mass.

Cuttyhunk, Mass., a settlement made by BARTHOLOMEW GOSNOLD (*q. v.*) in 1602.

Cuyler, THEODORE LEDYARD, clergyman; born in Aurora, N. Y., Jan. 10, 1822; graduated at Princeton in 1841; ordained in 1848; pastor of Presbyterian churches in Burlington and Trenton, N. J., and of the Market Street Reformed Dutch Church in New York City; called to the Lafayette Avenue Presbyterian Church in Brooklyn in June, 1860; became pastor emeritus in 1890. He was a prolific contributor to the religious press during the last fifty years of his life. He died in Brooklyn, N. Y., Feb. 26, 1909.

Cyane (ship). See CONSTITUTION.

Cynthiana, a city and county-seat of Harrison county, Ky.; on the Louisville & Nashville Railroad, 33 miles northeast of Lexington; has large grain, tobacco, hay, distillery and live-stock interests, and is widely noted for its thoroughbred horse farms. It was destroyed by the Confederates, under Gen. John Morgan, June 10, 1864. Two days later Morgan was defeated at Cynthiana by General Burbridge.

Czolgosz, LEON, assassin; born about 1874, of Polish-German ancestry; worked at various trades in the United States and became affiliated with anarchists. On Sept. 6, 1901, while President McKinley was holding a public reception at the Pan-American Exposition in Buffalo, N. Y., Czolgosz shot him twice. On Sept. 14 the President died; on Sept. 23 Czolgosz was brought to trial; on the 26th was sentenced to death, and was electrocuted at Auburn, N. Y., Oct. 29, 1901.